# Attention and Performance XV

 **Attention and Performance**

*Attention and Performance XIV: Synergies in Experimental Psychology, Artificial Intelligence, and Cognitive Neuroscience*, edited by David E. Meyer and Sylvan Kornblum, 1992

*Attention and Performance XV: Conscious and Nonconscious Information Processing*, edited by Carlo Umiltà and Morris Moscovitch, 1994

# Attention and Performance XV

Conscious and Nonconscious Information Processing

edited by Carlo Umiltà and Morris Moscovitch

*This book is based on the papers that were presented at the Fifteenth International Symposium on Attention and Performance held at the Ettore Majorana Centre for Scientific Culture, Erice, Sicily, Italy, July 26–31, 1992.*

A Bradford Book
The MIT Press
Cambridge, Massachusetts
London, England

© 1994 The International Association for the Study of Attention and Performance

All rights reserved. No part of this book may be reproduced in any form by any electronic or mechanical means (including photocopying, recording, or information storage and retrieval) without permission in writing from the publisher.

This book was set in Palatino by Asco Trade Typesetting Ltd., Hong Kong and was printed and bound in the United States of America.

ISSN: 1047-0387
ISBN: 0-262-21012-6

*To our teachers with gratitude and affection*
*Renzo Canestrari, Gaetano Kanizsa, Ray Hyman*—CU
*Peter Milner, Paul Rozin, Brenda Milner*—MM

# Contents

Preface ix
Participants xvii
Group Photo xx

## I  Association Lecture 1

1. Hypermnesia, Incubation, and Mind Popping:
On Remembering without Really Trying 3
*George Mandler*

## II  Visual Processes 35

2. Visual Perception and Visual Awareness after Brain Damage:
A Tutorial Overview 37
*Martha J. Farah*

3. The Organization of Sensory Motor Representations in the
Neocortex: A Hypothesis Based on Temporal Coding 77
*Wolf Singer*

4. The Role of Parallel Pathways in Visible Persistence 109
*C. A. Marzi, M. Girelli, G. Tassinari, L. Cristofori, A. Talacchi,
M. Gentilin, and G. Marchini*

5. Motor Responses to Nonreportable, Masked Stimuli: Where Is the
Limit of Direct Parameter Specification? 123
*Odmar Neumann and Werner Klotz*

## III  Face Recognition 151

6. Conscious and Nonconscious Recognition of Familiar Faces 153
*Andrew W. Young*

7. Repetition Priming of Face Recognition 179
*Vicki Bruce, Mike Burton, Derek Carson, Elias Hanna, and Oli Mason*

8. Structural and Functional Organization of Knowledge about Faces and Proper Names: A Positron Emission Tomography Study   203
*Justine Sergent, Brennan MacDonald, and Eric Zuck*

## IV  Spatial Attention   229

9. Space and Selective Attention   231
*Giacomo Rizzolatti, Lucia Riggio, and Boris M. Sheliga*

10. Multiple Sources of Spatial Information for Aimed Limb Movements   267
*Richard A. Abrams, Linda Van Dillen, and Vicki Stemmons*

11. Visual Attention and the Control of Eye Movements in Early Infancy   291
*Mark H. Johnson*

12. Spatial Synergies between Auditory and Visual Attention   311
*Jon Driver and Charles J. Spence*

13. Does Oculomotor Readiness Mediate Cognitive Control of Visual Attention? Revisited!   333
*Raymond M. Klein and Amanda Pontefract*

14. Object-Based Attentional Mechanisms: Evidence from Patients with Unilateral Neglect   351
*Marlene Behrmann and Steven P. Tipper*

15. Awareness of Contralesional Information in Unilateral Neglect: Effects of Verbal Cueing, Tracing, and Vestibular Stimulation   377
*Giuseppe Vallar, Maria Luisa Rusconi, and Edoardo Bisiach*

## V  Control Processes   393

16. Multiple Levels of Control Processes   395
*Tim Shallice*

17. Shifting Intentional Set: Exploring the Dynamic Control of Tasks   421
*Alan Allport, Elizabeth A. Styles, and Shulan Hsieh*

18. Progress in the Use of Interactive Models for Understanding Attention and Performance   453
*Jonathan D. Cohen and Therese A. Huston*

19. Interhemispheric Control in the Normal Brain: Evidence from Redundant Bilateral Presentations   477
*Eran Zaidel and Janice Rayman*

## VI  Semantic Memory — 505

20. Of Cabbages and Things: Semantic Memory from a Neuropsychological Perspective: A Tutorial Review — 507
*Eleanor M. Saffran and Myrna F. Schwartz*

21. Category Specificity and Informational Specificity in Neuropsychological Impairment of Semantic Memory — 537
*Giuseppe Sartori, Max Coltheart, Michele Miozzo, and Remo Job*

22. Semantic Processing of Ignored Stimuli: The Role of Attention in Memory — 551
*Shlomo Bentin*

23. The Effect of Orthographic-Semantic Systematicity on the Acquisition of New Words — 571
*Jay G. Rueckl and Itiel E. Dror*

24. Semantic Effects on Syntactic Ambiguity Resolution: Evidence for a Constraint-Based Resolution Process — 589
*Patrizia Tabossi, Michael J. Spivey-Knowlton, Ken McRae, and Michael K. Tanenhaus*

## VII  Explicit and Implicit Memory — 617

25. Memory without Conscious Recollection: A Tutorial Review from a Neuropsychological Perspective — 619
*Morris Moscovitch, Yonatan Goshen-Gottstein, and Ellen Vriezen*

26. Measuring Recollection: Strategic versus Automatic Influences of Associative Context — 661
*Larry L. Jacoby*

27. Explicit and Implicit Memory: A Decade of Research — 681
*Peter Graf*

28. Acquiring General Knowledge from Specific Episodes of Experience — 697
*Thomas H. Carr, Dale Dagenbach, Debra VanWieren, Laura A. Carlson Radvansky, Ann Janette R. Alejano, and Joseph S. Brown*

29. A Connectionist View on Dissociations — 725
*R. Hans Phaf, Nico M. Mul, and Gezinus Wolters*

## VIII  Explicit and Implicit Learning — 753

30. Implicit Learning: Twenty-Five Years On. A Tutorial — 755
*Dianne C. Berry*

31. The Representation of Structure in Sequence Prediction Tasks  783
*Axel Cleeremans*

32. Learning from Complex Rule-Governed Environments: On the Proper Functions of Nonconscious and Conscious Processes  811
*Pierre Perruchet*

33. A Critical Examination of the Evidence for Unconscious (Implicit) Learning  837
*David R. Shanks, Robin E. A. Green, and Jonathan A. Kolodny*

34. Implicit Learning in Neural Networks: The Importance of Starting Small  861
*Jeffrey L. Elman*

35. Recognition, Categorization, and Perceptual Learning (or, How Learning to Classify Things Together Helps One to Tell Them Apart)  889
*I. P. L. McLaren, H. J. Leevers, and N. J. Mackintosh*

Author Index  911
Subject Index  933

# Preface

Consciousness, and its relation to psychological processes, has been a topic of discussion and often of investigation since psychology emerged as a science in the late nineteenth century. The scientific investigation of consciousness has had a checkered history. In the beginning, it was considered a worthy enterprise and occupied a privileged position in experimental psychology. With the rise, and eventually dominant position, of behaviorism in the early part of the twentieth century, however, consciousness and other mentalistic concepts were effectively banned for over fifty years as legitimate topics of discussion or investigation.

As with all heresies, however, consciousness continued to attract its adherents, so that the line of research on consciousness did not entirely disappear. Occasionally, it even flared into the open and captured a new following, as was the case in the 1950s when "the new look" tackled head-on the issue of conscious awareness in perception and learning.

The movement foundered on serious theoretical and methodological problems that it was unable to overcome (Eriksen 1960). Nevertheless, it left a legacy that is detectable in the work of the early proponents of cognitive psychology (Bruner 1957; Miller, Galanter, and Pribram 1960). The increased interest in consciousness coincided with the emergence of cognitive psychology and neuropsychology in the 1960s. Once mental concepts such as attention and memory were readmitted into psychology, it was only a matter of time before consciousness followed.

By the 1970s, a number of papers on consciousness were published by respected investigators (e.g., Mandler 1975; Posner 1978; Shallice 1972). Some papers even found their way into earlier volumes of *Attention and Performance* (e.g., Marcel 1980; Posner and Snyder 1975; Shallice and McGill 1978). These papers, which were primarily concerned with consciousness and its relation to voluntary and automatic control, were influential in making consciousness a legitimate topic of investigation. Nevertheless, severe problems of definition and theory, as well as methodological problems, continued to plague the experimental study of consciousness. These difficulties, quite rightly, dissuaded many from jumping on board what at that time was more of a cart than a bandwagon.

The turning point, we think, came with the discovery of a number of striking neuropsychological syndromes that were often seen in single individuals, and made a compelling case for the existence of consciousness, or the need of consciousness as an explanatory construct (but see Velmans 1991 for a contrary view). These phenomena captured the interest of psychologists in a way that theoretical papers on the topic, or even the experimental investigation of normal people, could not.

Among such phenomena were "blindsight," in which patients with damage to the occipital cortex professed not to see (they lacked the conscious experience of sight) but could nonetheless respond to visual stimuli (Weiskrantz 1986); memory without awareness in patients who were profoundly amnesic in daily life and in experimental tests of memory that required conscious recollection (Milner 1966; Cohen and Squire 1980); and perception without awareness in prosopagnosic patients who could not recognize faces at a conscious level but could do so in so-called implicit, nonconscious tests of knowledge (Bauer 1984; Tranel and Damasio 1985). Following closely on the heels of these discoveries were demonstrations that similar phenomena could be evoked and investigated in normal people (see, e.g., Reber 1992 and Velmans 1991 for reviews). It is significant, we think, that some of those pioneering studies were conducted by investigators with active research programs and an interest in neuropsychology (e.g., Marcel 1983; Rozin 1976).

Methodological and theoretical problems, even problems of definition, abound. However, the attitude in the field has changed. These difficulties are now seen as problems to be confronted and solved rather than as fatal flaws that would bring the very legitimacy of research on consciousness into question.

What we have said so far of course applies to mainstream experimental psychology. The study of the so-called cognitive unconscious—the term was coined by Rozin (1976) and then adopted by, among others, Kihlstrom (1987) and Reber (1992)—had survived in other areas of psychology. Psychodynamic therapies are based on the possibility that material lost to consciousness may be recovered (e.g., Erdelyi 1985). The relation between conscious and unconscious cognition lies at the very core of the study of dreaming (e.g., Foulkes 1990) and hypnosis (e.g., Kihlstrom 1985). Also in social psychology, research continued to some extent to be concerned with consciousness (e.g., the various contributions in Uleman and Bargh 1989). From this research it emerged that there are important cognitive gaps between the knowledge that we think we use in making decisions and choices, and the knowledge we actually use. These areas were deliberately left out from the collection of papers in this volume because they are meant to reflect the state of the art in the scientific investigation of consciousness in the areas of cognitive psychology and cognitive neuropsychology.

The topic of consciousness has become so pervasive that it is difficult to ignore—even by as new a field as connectionism. Thus, together, cognitive psychology, cognitive neuropsychology, and connectionism have taken up the challenge of trying to provide an account of consciousness. This development seems remarkable when one considers that as recently as a decade ago consciousness was often relegated to the realm of epiphenomena that did not merit serious scientific attention.

It was most fitting that George Mandler should have given the Association Lecture. His scientific career spans the period of revival of interest in consciousness and, in many ways, parallels the developments that have occured in experimental psychology since the late 1950s. This is not mere coincidence since it is fair to say that his research and other professional contributions have helped shape the direction that the field eventually took. He was unusual in one other regard: unlike many other psychologists who may have thought deeply about consciousness and related matters but remained silent, George Mandler wrote openly about them from the inception of his career. His ideas on consciousness also informed his elegant and important theoretical and empirical work on memory, which continues to exert a strong influence on the field. His association lecture on "mind popping" typified his approach to theory and experimentation.

The rest of the book is divided into seven sections: visual processes, face recognition, spatial attention, control processes, semantic memory, explicit and implicit memory, and learning. Together, these topics encompass the most interesting and productive areas of current research on consciousness. Each section is introduced by a tutorial overview and followed by experimental papers.

Although consciousness is now viewed as a respectable topic for scientific investigation, the readers of this volume will still note a certain lingering wariness and caution on the part of many contributors in confronting the topic openly. This behavior is not unlike that of a closely knit, well-established group's reluctance fully to accept a newcomer into their midst, especially if that newcomer comes with a somewhat questionable reputation.

The subtitle of the book clearly indicates that this volume is concerned with conscious and nonconscious processes in cognition, as did our letters of invitation to the participants. Yet many of the contributors address this topic obliquely, while others, who deal with the topic directly, often revert quickly to more neutral, less committed terms, such as *implicit* and *explicit* processes, or *controlled* and *automatic* ones, rather than deploy the term *consciousness*. We had thought of exposing closet consciousness theorists and researchers but decided that the best, and fairest, course of action was to let each contributor appear in whatever theoretical or empirical guise he or she chose and trust the alert and sensitive (and now sensitized) reader to determine the underlying identity.

## ACKNOWLEDGMENTS

This volume is based on the papers that were presented at the Fifteenth International Symposium on Attention and Performance, held in Erice (Sicily, Italy) from July 26–31, 1992. We thank the Ettore Majorana Centre for Scientific Culture for the use of their splendid facilities and for their extremely friendly and effective cooperation. We are particularly indebted to Professor Antonino Zichichi, Director of the Centre, and Professor Danilo Mainardi, Director of the School of Ethology.

From the International Association for the Study of Attention and Performance (IASAP), we would like to thank the members of the Executive Committee and the Advisory Council for their very helpful suggestions concerning possible topics and contributors. We are especially grateful to the secretary, Sylvan Kornblum, for his continued guidance.

Needless to say, special thanks should go to the sixty-five participants of the symposium. Without their enthusiastic involvement before, during, and after the meeting, neither the symposium nor the book would have been possible. The production staff of our publisher, The MIT Press, and most notably Teri Mendelsohn, Sandra Minkkinen, and Kathleen Caruso, greatly aided our editorial efforts.

Funding for *Attention and Performance XV* was obtained in Italy from the National Council for Research (contract 92000194-PF41), Ministry of Education, Ministry of University and Scientific Research, Sicilian Regional Government, and in the United States (grant N00014-92-J1603) from the Office of Naval Research, the Air Force Office of Scientific Research, and the Army Research Institute.

Both editors consider the meeting and book to have been a joint venture. It should be pointed out that the Executive Committee of IASAP invited Carlo Umiltà to be the organizer of the meeting and the editor of the volume. He accepted with the understanding that Morris Moscovitch would be his co-organizer and co-editor. This is the only reason why Carlo Umiltà appears as principal editor.

Although the invitation to organize this meeting came in 1988, unbeknownst to the Executive Committee of the IASAP, preparation for it had already begun in 1986, when we spent a sabbatical period at the Institute for Advanced Studies of the Hebrew University in Jerusalem. During that time, we discussed topics in cognitive neuropsychology and modularity with each other and with other members of our group (see Moscovitch and Umiltà 1990, 1991). In the course of these discussions, we came to realize how important it is to deal directly with issues concerning consciousness and became aware of a growing literature on the topic. We thank the institute, and our colleagues, for providing an ideal environment in which to pursue these studies. This preface was written at the institute where our group reconvened for a seventh anniversary workshop.

All sixty-five participants at the conference acted as reviewers. In addition to contibuting their chapters and reviews, the participants provided thoughtful comments and stimulating discussion during the sessions and breaks. They also often provided lively entertainment outside the formal venue of the conference. To our delight, this extracurricular activity was highlighted by a recitation of poems that were composed and delivered with great panache at the closing banquet by various participants from the United Kingdom. We would be pleased to make copies of these poems available to anyone on request.

# REFERENCES

Bauer, R. M. (1984). Automatic recognition of names and faces in prosopagnosia: A neuropsychological application of guilty knowledge test. *Neuropsychologia, 22*, 457–469.

Bruner, J. S. (1957). On perceptual readiness. *Psychological Review, 64*, 123–152.

Cohen, N. J., and Squire, L. R. (1980). Preserved learning and retention of pattern-analyzing skills in amnesia: Dissociation of "knowing how" and "knowing that." *Science, 20*, 207–209.

Erdelyi, M. H. (1985). *Psychoanalysis: Freud's cognitive psychology*. New York: W. H. Freeman.

Eriksen, C. W. (1960). Discrimination and learning without awareness: A methodological survey and evaluation. *Pychological Review, 67*, 279–300.

Foulkes, D. (1990). Dreaming and consciousness. *European Journal of Cognitive Psychology, 2*, 39–55.

Kihlstrom, J. F. (1985). Hypnosis. *Annual Review of Psychology, 36*, 385–418.

Kihlstrom, J. F. (1987). The cognitive unconscious. *Science, 237*, 1445–1452.

Mandler, G. (1975). *Mind and emotion*. New York: Wiley.

Marcel, A. J. (1980). Conscious and preconscious recognition of polysemous words: Locating the selective effects of prior verbal context. In R. S. Nickerson (Ed.), *Attention and performance VIII*. Hillsdale, NJ: Erlbaum.

Marcel, A. J. (1983). Conscious and unconscious perception: Experiments on visual masking and word recognition. *Cognitive Psychology, 15*, 197–237.

Miller, G. A., Galanter, E., and Pribram, K. (1960). *Plans and the structure of behavior*. New York: Holt, Rinehart, and Winston.

Milner, B. (1966). Amnesia following operation on the temporal lobe. In C. W. M. Whitty and O. L. Zangwill (Eds.), *Amnesia*. London: Butterworth.

Moscovitch, M., and Umiltà, C. (1990). Modularity and neuropsychology: Modules and central processes in attention and memory. In M. F. Schwartz (Ed.), *Modular deficits in Alzheimer-type dementia*. Cambridge, MA: The MIT Press.

Moscovitch, M., and Umiltà, C. (1991). Conscious and nonconscious aspects of memory: A neuropsychological framework of modules and central systems. In R. G. Lister and H. J. Weingartner (Eds.), *Perspectives on cognitive neuroscience*. Oxford: Oxford University Press.

Posner, M. I. (1978). *Chronometric explorations of mind*. Hillsdale, NJ: Erlbaum.

Posner, M. I., and Snyder, C. R. R. (1975). Facilitation and inhibition in the processing of signals. In P. M. A. Rabbitt and S. Dornic (Eds.), *Attention and performance V*. New York: Academic Press.

Reber, A. S. (1992). The cognitive unconscious: An evolutionary perspective. *Consciousness and Cognition, 1*, 93–133.

Rozin, P. (1976). The evolution of intelligence and access to the cognitive unconscious. In J. M. Sprague and A. N. Epstein (Eds.), *Progress in physiological psychology*, vol. 6. New York: Academic Press.

Shallice, T. (1972). Dual functions of consciousness. *Psychological Review, 79*, 383–393.

Shallice, T., and McGill, J. (1978). The origins of mixed errors. In J. Requin (Ed.), *Attention and performance VII*. Hillsdale, NJ: Erlbaum.

Tranel, E., and Damasio, A. R. (1985). Knowledge without awareness: An automatic index of facial recognition by prosopagnosics. *Science, 228,* 1453–1454.

Uleman, J. S., and Bargh, J. A. (1989). *Unintended thought.* New York: Guilford.

Velmans, M. (1991). Is human information processing conscious? *Behavioral and Brain Sciences, 14,* 651–726.

Weiskrantz, L. (1986). *Blindsight.* Oxford: Clarendon Press.

# Participants

*No asterisks: participant who gave a paper*
*One asterisk: coauthor*
*Two asterisks: nonpresenting participant*

Richard A. Abrams
Department of Psychology,
Washington University

**Terry Allard
Office of Naval Research

D. Alan Allport
Department of Experimental
Psychology, University of Oxford

**Sebastiano Bagnara
Dipartimento di Filosofia e Scienze
Sociali, Università di Siena

Marlene Behrmann
Department of Psychology,
Carnegie-Mellon University

Shlomo Bentin
Department of Psychology,
The Hebrew University

Dianne C. Berry
Department of Psychology,
University of Reading

**Anna Berti
Istituto di Fisiologia Umana,
Università di Parma

*Edoardo Bisiach
Dipartimento di Psicologia Generale,
Università di Padova

Vicki Bruce
Department of Psychology,
University of Stirling

Thomas H. Carr
Department of Psychology,
Michigan State University

Axel Cleeremans
Industrial Psychology Laboratory,
Université Libre de Bruxelles

Jonathan D. Cohen
Department of Psychology,
Carnegie-Mellon University

*Max Coltheart
Department of Psychology,
Maquaire University

**Michael C. Corballis
Department of Psychology,
University of Auckland

*Dale Dagenbach
Department of Psychology,
Wake Forest University

Jonathan Driver
Department of Psychology,
University of Cambridge

Jeffrey L. Elman
Institute of Cognitive Science,
University of California, San Diego

Martha J. Farah
Department of Psychology,
University of Pennsylvania

**Daniel Gopher
Department of Psychology,
Technion—Israel Institute of Technology

Peter Graf
Department of Psychology,
University of British Columbia

**Toshio Inui
Department of Psychology,
Kyoto University

Larry L. Jacoby
Department of Psychology,
McMaster University

**Marc Jeannerod
Laboratoire de Neuropsychologie Expèrimentale,
I.N.S.E.R.M.

Mark H. Johnson
Department of Psychology,
Carnegie-Mellon University

**Annette Karmiloff-Smith
MCR Cognitive Development Unit

**Steven W. Keele
Department of Psychology,
University of Oregon

**Kim Kirsner
Department of Psychology,
University of Western Australia

Ray Klein
Department of Psychology,
Dalhousie University

**Asher Koriat
Institute of Information Processing and Decision Making,
University of Haifa

**Sylvan Kornblum
Mental Health Research Institute,
University of Michigan

**James L. McClelland
Department of Psychology,
Carnegie-Mellon University

Nicholas J. Mackintosh
Department of Experimental Psychology, University of Cambridge

George Mandler
Center of Human Information Processing, University of California, San Diego
and
Department of Psychology,
University College

**Jean Mandler
Department of Cognitive Science,
University of California, San Diego

Anthony J. Marcel
MRC Applied Psychology Unit

Carlo A. Marzi
Istituto di Fisiologia Umana,
Università di Verona

**David E. Meyer
Department of Psychology,
University of Michigan

**A. David Milner
Psychological Laboratory,
University of St. Andrews

**Stephen Monsell
Department of Experimental Psychology, University of Cambridge

Morris Moscovitch
Department of Psychology,
University of Toronto,
and
Baycrest Centre

Odmar Neumann
Abteilung für Psychologie,
Universität Bielefeld

**Roberto Nicoletti
Istituto di Fisiologia Umana,
Università di Modena

**Karalyn E. Patterson
MRC Applied Psychology Unit

**Roy D. Patterson
MRC Applied Psychology Unit

Pierre Perruchet
Faculté des Sciences,
Université de Bourgogne

R. Hans Phaf
Faculty of Psychology,
University of Amsterdam

**Wolfgang Prinz
Max-Planck Institut für
Psychologische Forschung

Giacomo Rizzolatti
Istituto di Fisiologia Umana,
Università di Parma

Jay G. Rueckl
Department of Psychology,
University of Connecticut

Eleanor M. Saffran
Department of Neurology,
Temple University School of
Medicine

Giuseppe Sartori
Dipartimento di Psicologia Generale,
Università di Padova

**Anima Sen
Department of Psychology,
University of Delhi

Justine Sergent
Montreal Neurological Institute and
Hospital

Tim Shallice
Department of Psychology,
University College

David R. Shanks
Department of Psychology,
University College

**Francesca Simion
Dipartimento di Psicologia dello
Sviluppo e della Socializzazione,
Università di Padova

Wolf Singer
Max-Planck Institute for Brain
Research

*Elisabeth A. Styles
Department of Experimental
Psychology, University of Oxford

Patrizia Tabossi
Istituto di Filosofia,
Università di Ferrara

**Carlo Umiltà
Dipartimento di Psicologia Generale,
Università di Padova

Giuseppe Vallar
Dipartimento di Psicologia,
Università di Roma

**Paolo Viviani
Department of Psychology and
Educational Sciences,
University of Geneva

Andrew W. Young
MRC Applied Psychology Unit

Eran Zaidel
Department of Psychology,
University of California, Los
Angeles

Starting with the front row, from left to right:

J. Elman, T. Allard, A. Marcel, D. Gopher, M. Coltheart, A. Koriat, L. Jacoby, P. Viviani, G. Rizzolatti, F. Simion, C. Umiltà, M. Moscovitch, G. Mandler, D. Meyer, S. Kornblum, S. Monsell, A. Karmiloff-Smith, C. Marzi, A. Sen, D. Dagenbach, A. Allport, T. Shallice, J. Driver, M. Johnson, E. Styles, D. Berry, G. Sartori, S. Bagnara, R. Nicoletti, R. Patterson, D. Shanks, T. Inui, J. Rueckl, P. Perruchet, M. Jeannerod, M. Farah, A. Berti, P. Tabossi, E. Zaidel, N. Mackintosh, O. Neumann, M. Behrmann, A. Cleeremans, J. Cohen, S. Bentin, J. McClelland, E. Saffran, R. Klein, A. Young, J. Sergent, D. Milner, S. Keele, M. Corballis, G. Vallar, W. Singer, K. Patterson, H. Phaf, W. Prinz, E. Bisiach, R. Abrams, T. Carr, P. Graf, K. Kirsner, V. Bruce.

# I Association Lecture

# 1 Hypermnesia, Incubation, and Mind Popping: On Remembering without Really Trying

## George Mandler

ABSTRACT  Anecdotes abound about inaccessible thoughts and memories coming to mind with repeated attempts, after periods of delay or rest, or unintentionally when engaged in an unrelated activity. The first two of these phenomena have been explored in studies of hypermnesia/reminiscence and incubation. The third (here called mind popping) has received relatively little attention. The literature on hypermnesia and incubation is briefly reviewed, and the phenomena are placed in the context of activation/integration and elaboration processes. It is concluded that hypermnesia and incubation can be understood in terms of currently available theoretical mechanisms of direct and spreading activation, elaboration and organization, "forgetting," and extrasituational priming. Particular emphasis is placed on the effect of organizational processes on activation, and on revisions in the time course and extent of spreading activation. In mind popping, in addition to the mechanisms active in incubation, apparently inaccessible mental contents are more easily brought to consciousness when one is preoccupied with other irrelevant tasks or thoughts. Mind popping is shown to be similar to the activations observed in dreams and is related to the restricting effects of awareness.

## 1.1 INTRODUCTION

*La mémoire a ses raisons que la raison ne connait pas.*
(with apologies to B. Pascal)

You try to remember a name, and being unsuccessful you abandon the search, only to have the name pop into your mind unbidden some time later. I work on a crossword puzzle and find myself stuck halfway through. I leave the puzzle, and when I return to it an hour later, I easily finish it. One tries to remember a shopping list and brings only a few items to mind, but on another try, more items appear. Anecdotes such as these are well known to all of us, but the plural of "anecdote" is not "data." In recent years, however, the experimental literature has produced evidence that these phenomena are reproducible in the laboratory.

The two areas of research that have addressed these issues are generally subsumed under the labels of hypermnesia (which includes reminiscence) and incubation. I shall add a third set of evidence that suggests that deliberate search for the target perception or memory may inhibit successful performance, whereas nonintentional attitudes favor such performance. In all of these cases, access to some mental content is increased with little deliberate effort, such as a delay or the mere request for another recall; the individual is not actually trying to improve on the performance. Much of this work is of current interest because it implies at various points contrasts between explicit and implicit processes.

I start with an overview and a critical analysis of these three areas.[1] I do not intend this to be a complete or exhaustive review; rather it is intended to summarize the state of the art and to cite some of the relevant literature. Following this overview, I move to a theoretical analysis of the phenomena involved. The general thrust of these analyses will be informed by a framework that stresses activation and elaboration processes. The result of my excursion will be the conclusion that hypermnesia and incubation can be understood in terms of currently accepted notions about human information processing but that new and interesting theoretical issues arise when we try to understand the facilitation of things coming to mind unexpectedly and unintentionally.

**1.2 HYPERMNESIA**

The tale of hypermnesia starts with the phenomenon of reminiscence (Ballard 1913)—the discovery that items that had been forgotten (could not be recalled) could be retrieved later without any intervening opportunities for learning. Against the background of the then-recent results from Ebbinghaus and his followers, this seemed peculiar since learning materials should be at their maximum strength immediately following acquisition, not on subsequent trials. The phenomenon was doubly intriguing since reminiscence apparently increased under some circumstances, with increasing intervals following acquisition.[2] The effect had a rather rocky history, leading Buxton in 1943 to question whether it was a real effect at all. One of the major problems was that introducing proper controls for test-retest effects and for covert review "controlled [reminiscence] out of existence" (Payne 1987). A temporary solution came with an experiment by Ammons and Irion (1954), who directly addressed the test-retest question by using both within- and between-subjects designs and found no reminiscence in the between-subjects design, which excluded any rehearsal or reactivation effects due to repeated testing. The within-subject groups showed the reminiscence effect, and Ammons and Irion concluded that reminiscence is an artifact of design. One other problem was that definitional issues clouded the phenomenon; some investigators were looking at increases in net recall—the increase in the total number of items recalled—rather than just the recall of previously nonrecalled items. Improvement in net recall, including previously recalled items as well as nonremembered items that are recalled on a subsequent trial, is what eventually came to be called hypermnesia. Since relatively few studies have addressed reminiscence directly in the past three decades, I shall deal primarily with hypermnesia (Payne 1987).[3]

The renewed interest in the basic phenomenon of hypermnesia started in earnest with the work by Erdelyi and his associates (e.g., Erdelyi and Becker 1974). Generally, hypermnesia is demonstrated over increasing retention intervals by an increase in the net recall on the delayed test over the net recall on the original test. Hypermnesia, when present, will always include the reminiscence effect, that is, items recalled on the delayed test that were not recalled originally.[4]

Payne (1987) discusses and investigates extensively the two major hypotheses that have been advanced for the occurrence of hypermnesia: the imagery hypothesis of Erdelyi (e.g., Erdelyi and Becker 1974) and the cumulative recall hypothesis of Roediger (see Roediger and Challis 1989 for a review and summary). The imagery hypothesis postulates that hypermnesia is due to the use of imagery in the processing of the target material and is, therefore, found preferentially when pictures are used or whenever imaginal processing is invoked. The theoretical argument presented by Erdelyi and his co-workers (Erdelyi and Becker 1974; Erdelyi and Stein 1981) for the superiority of picture stimuli and imaginal encoding over words and other encoding operations is based on the generate/recognize model of recall (Kintsch 1970). Erdelyi argues that the recognition of pictures is well known to be much superior to that of words and that it can be assumed that all items are potentially available in long-term memory. It follows that the superior recognition of pictures will produce better recall and that with more items having been successfully recalled in one trial, more time and effort is available for retrieving other items on subsequent trials. Conversely, words are less successfully and often incorrectly recognized, resulting in fewer recalls on subsequent trials. Apart from begging the question of why pictures are better recognized in the first place, the generate/recognition model does not stand up to scrutiny. It is at best a useful ancillary strategy in immediate recall and is essentially dysfunctional after long delays (Rabinowitz, Mandler, and Barsalou 1979; Rabinowitz, Mandler, and Patterson 1977). Nevertheless, the empirical finding that picture stimuli are more likely than words to produce hypermnesia is not contested.

The cumulative recall hypothesis (Roediger et al. 1982; Roediger and Thorpe 1978) starts with the finding that the rate of approach to the asymptotic cumulative level of recall is negatively correlated with the level of the asymptote. As a consequence, after an initial test, the potential improvement for materials with a higher asymptote (higher recall levels) will be greater than that for materials with lower asymptotes. The level of recall hypothesis was refined by Madigan and O'Hara (1992), who showed conclusively that the percentage of items newly recalled on a second test is a linear function of percentage of items recalled on a first test. Together with the recall time hypothesis (Roediger and Thorpe 1978), which states that hypermnesia is more likely to be found the more total time is available for recall, the level of recall hypothesis accounts for many of the data on hypermnesia. In particular, it deals with the occurrence of hypermnesia with pictorial and imaginal materials, which usually produce higher levels of initial as well as asymptotic recall. These explanations do not, and do not claim to, explain why hypermnesia occurs at all—given more time and more room for improvement. What produces the recall of previously forgotten material? How is the extra time used?

Both Erdelyi (1982) and Roediger (1982) have entertained, but not endorsed, the notion that depth of processing is the controlling variable in hypermnesia. Erdelyi, in particular, notes that it is difficult, if not impossible, to disentangle an imagery and a depth-of-processing hypothesis. I argue here that the depth-of-processing explanation, interpreted as differences in elaboration (see Craik and Tulving 1975), is close to the most reasonable interpretation of the results (see also Bower and Bryant 1991 for a discussion of the relation between elaboration and organization). Another possible explanation in terms of autonomous changes over time, in the form of consolidation, was eliminated by Roediger and Payne (1982).

Payne's conclusions are that hypermnesia is a reliable phenomenon, that it is readily demonstrable with pictorial material but may also be obtained with verbal material, that it is not affected by changes in response criteria, that it is critically dependent on repeated attempts to retrieve the target material, and that it is dependent on both recall time and recall level but that imaginal encoding affects hypermnesia over and above raised recall levels (Payne 1987, pp. 24–25). These conclusions are based on Payne's review of 172 cases in the literature that have appeared since 1965 and in which hypermnesia/reminiscence was investigated. Of these, 129 provided statistical tests, 83 showed the unequivocal presence of hypermnesia, and 46 failed to find any significant effects. I shall argue that organization/elaborative processing is at the heart of the hypermnesia effect. and I present first the appropriate breakdown of Payne's cases. The argument is that the cases that provide the material and encoding conditions appropriate for elaboration and organization are most likely to produce organizational processes. If one divides the 129 cases into those that required or encouraged elaborative (deep) processing and those that were unlikely to do so or that require shallow processing, the cases divide as shown in table 1.1. Although it made use of Payne's assuredly reliable descriptions, the classification was necessarily noisy. In cases involving elaboration, the stimuli were pictures or high-imagery words, imagery instructions were given, semantic processing was required (comparisons, differences, etc.), and categorical organizations were invoked. For the nonelaboration tasks I included "standard" word presentation, graphemic and phonemic judgments, and the use of low-imagery words. The inclusion of the "standard picture" cases in the elaboration category is based on the argument that the superior acquisition of picture lists is probably due to some kind of enriched encoding of the pictures. For example, Paivio's dual-code theory (e.g., 1976)

**Table 1.1** The Effect of Elaboration on the Appearance of Hypermnesia: All Cases

|  | Orienting task | |
|---|---|---|
|  | Elaboration | Nonelaboration |
| Present | 71 | 12 |
| *Hypermnesia* | | |
| Absent | 4 | 42 |

Note: Chi-square (1 df) = 71.82, $p < .001$, phi-coefficient = .746.

assumes that pictures are encoded in both a visual/imagery and a verbal/propositional mode, which would provide two possible ways of organizing these items. However, if one wishes to question this reasoning and to exclude the standard picture cases from the elaboration category, one arrives at table 1.2. The relationship between elaboration and hypermnesia remains strong. Finally, I included the standard word cases under the nonelaboration category under the assumption that being presented lists of words with minimal instructions may lead to only minimal elaboration/categorization. Even removing these cases (as well as the "picture" cases), a strong, though reduced relationship still remains (table 1.3). It is important to note, too, that the reduction for the crucial "elaboration" category in the percentage of cases showing positive hypermnesia is only from 95 to 93 percent after the picture and word studies have been removed. Thus, elaboration is strongly related to hypermnesia; the nonelaboration cases are more questionable since subjects may actually organize the study material.

## 1.3 INCUBATION

Most definitions of incubation invoke the nondeliberate, usually sudden occurrence of an idea or solution to a problem, following a previous unsuccessful search for the solution (Posner 1973; Wallas 1926). Such a definition is the hallmark of the description by Henri Poincaré of his solution to a mathematical problem that has become the obligatory prolegomenon for any discussion of incubation in the literature. Unfortunately, it is practically impossible to monitor the sudden appearance of a solution when a subject is not thinking

Table 1.2  The Effect of Elaboration on the Appearance of Hypermnesia: Without "Standard Picture" Cases

|  | Orienting task | |
|---|---|---|
|  | Elaboration | Nonelaboration |
| Present | 41 | 12 |
| *Hypermnesia* | | |
| Absent | 3 | 42 |

Note: Chi-square (1 df) = 49.16, $p < .001$, phi-coefficient = .708.

Table 1.3  The Effect of Elaboration on the Appearance of Hypermnesia: Without "Standard Picture" and "Standard Word" Cases

|  | Orienting task | |
|---|---|---|
|  | Elaboration | Nonelaboration |
| Present | 41 | 7 |
| *Hypermnesia* | | |
| Absent | 3 | 9 |

Note: Chi-square (1 df) = 17.92, $p < .001$, phi-coefficient = .546.

about the problem. As far as I can tell, all the experimental work on incubation has involved deliberate attempts at solution. This does not mean that subjects may not report that the solution comes to them suddenly; the question is whether they are working on the problem at the time. Most recent work has followed something like the bare bones definition used by Kaplan, who defined incubation as "any positive effect of [a delay] on problem solving performance" (Kaplan 1989, p. 8)."[5] Nearly all definitions have in common a reference to problem solving; when recovery of specific memories is involved, the phenomenon of positive effects is usually called reminiscence or hypermnesia. However, in some instances when a significant delay is used in hypermnesia studies, the phenomenon is described as incubation. Given the rather spotty nature of the incubation literature, I will concentrate on some specific instances that show the "pause that refreshes."[6] Kaplan (1989) reviewed eighteen studies of incubation that varied over a large variety of nonroutine tasks, from composing poems to solving anagrams. Difficult as comparisons among these studies are, Kaplan's review concludes that knowledge that one will return to the task does not produce or inhibit incubation, that some minimum initial (preparation) time is needed for incubation (but the ratio of delay time to preparation time is generally high for studies that report incubation effects), and that the target task and an interpolated task are not simply related to the occurrence of incubation, although related activities do tend to produce incubation in shorter delay periods.

Probably the best-established and -replicated demonstration of incubation is found in Fulgosi and Guilford's (1968, 1972) studies. They used the Consequences task in which subjects are presented for 2 min with problems such as, "What would happen if everybody lost their ability to read and write?" followed by a delay of 10 to 60 min filled with difficult number-series problems, after which the subjects are given another 2 min on the task. Compared with a group that worked continuously for 4 min, delays of 20 to 30 min were most beneficial in producing responses. Kaplan (1989) replicated the general effect using different versions of the Consequences task and different delay activities but failed to find significant effects (although in the right direction) when the intervening activity was related to the task. Kaplan also presents a "field study" in which subjects, going about their daily business, were exposed to priming events for puzzles given to them earlier. Priming clearly improved performance, although the subjects were not generally aware of the occurrence of the primes.

Kaplan (1989) noted, and presented some evidence, that incubation involves some significant degree of "forgetting" during the delay interval, such that irrelevant ideas and responses lose activation and permit other competing, and possibly "better," responses to become activated and dominant. Direct evidence that incorrect information is forgotten or removed during an incubation period is provided by Smith and Blankenship (1989, 1991). Using rebus problems (Smith and Blankenship 1989) and later the Remote Associates Test (Smith and Blankenship 1991), they presented misleading cues or information on specific problems prior to the incubation delay. Both studies supported the prediction that an incubation period improves performance and also reduces memory for the misleading cues, with the degree of forgetting of the "fixated" incorrect responses related to the amount of incubation observed. Type of task in the delay period did not appear to affect incubation effects.

In summary, acceptable incubation experiments have shown that a delay may improve problem solving and that such a delay may be subject to a variety of different variables. No more than anecdotal evidence has been obtained of solutions' coming suddenly to mind when one is not trying to solve the problem.

I now move to a more novel, and possibly more controversial, area, with a series of observations that suggest that a variety of different productions or perceptions can occur under conditions when no deliberate effort is made to generate them. In fact, these are cases in which access is more likely to occur when no deliberate effort is made at all.

## 1.4 MIND POPPING

One of the hallmarks of contemporary cognitive psychology has been the exploration of the effects of unconscious mental events on conscious (intentional) perceptions and memories. Apart from the fact that cognitive theories usually invoke "unconscious" representations as the underlying mental contents for observable thought and action, the main thrust of these recent investigations has been twofold: to show the operation of networks—mental, neural, semantic, distributed, schematic—in perception and memory and to demonstrate that representations can be activated, primed, or otherwise energized by operations of which the subject is generally unaware. The former are usually exhibited in suprathreshold studies; the latter represent the realm of sub- and near-threshold phenomena.[7] However, the demonstration of either sub- or suprathreshold priming always involves an intentional (conscious) effort. Specifically, subjects are required to decide whether they have seen a word, can remember an item, can decide whether a string is a word, can identify a degraded stimulus, can complete an incomplete letter string, or some other similar task. In short they are instructed to produce a response that will illustrate the putative priming operation. In all of these cases, subjects are required to make intentional judgments about the target stimulus; such judgments are then examined for influences of the prior prime. The requirement of an intentional judgment is the case for both sub- and suprathreshold studies.

This section examines instances in which prior experiences have an effect on subsequent judgments or responses that are not intentional in the usual sense of the term; they have an effect when there is no deliberate attempt to recover the material. Mind popping is also shown in cases in which solutions to persisting problems, often very creative solutions, come to mind unintentionally and quite unexpectedly.[8] I shall illustrate the mind-popping phenomenon with cases in which there is a discrepancy in performance between intentional attempts to make a particular choice and nonintentional performance, where the individual may often be not aware of or instructed what the target of the performance is.

I omit from my discussion several areas of investigation that are only indirectly relevant to the mind-popping topic. The impressive collation of data and theory on unintended thought presented by Uleman and Bargh (1989), for example, primarily addresses the case in which the initiation of some activation or priming process is unintended (not deliberate or conscious). However, the target task for the individual is usually clear-cut and intended. Neither will I address the presence or absence of awareness of the required task. It involves free-flowing, ruminative thought (Martin and Tesser 1989), where it is not possible to make a distinction between task-relevant and task-irrelevant intentions. Nor shall I discuss the problem of the implicit, nonconscious acquisition of rules, strategies, and so forth (Berry and Broadbent 1988; Reber, Kassin, Lewis, and Cantor 1980; but see Perruchet and Pacteau 1990 and subsequent interchanges).

Mind popping occurs when there is no conscious intention to retrieve or access the target material. "Intention" in the wider sense invokes notions of intentionality, and the equation of intentionality with consciousness appears frequently in the psychological literature (Dagenbach, Carr, and Wilhelmsen, 1989) and, particularly, philosophical disquisitions (Searle 1983). It is intuitively appropriate that a person needs to be conscious of an intention, as it is usually interpreted. The cases I discuss are occasions when the individual is instructed to perceive, recall, or judge some event different from the actual target event or to try to be nonintentional—that is, not to try to perceive or remember anything in particular, reporting "whatever comes to mind." The cases come from a variety of different areas of investigation. The purpose of this collection is not to claim that the same mechanisms are necessarily operating in all these cases but rather to demonstrate that the mind-popping effect exists. The evidence will come from both anecdotal and experimental sources.

In the area of *perception*, Nelson (1974) was apparently the first to report a phenomenon sometimes called the "anthill effect." He noted that his awareness of what he thought were bits of gravel on an anthill was suddenly replaced by awareness of moving ants over a very wide area. He was aware of single ants, various orientations, and patterns of the moving elements. Awareness of these movements and patterns was not possible when the gravel texture was perceptually dominant. The two kinds of percepts (awareness) alternated, and the perception of motion was aided by stationary gaze and boredom. Any intentional tracking of the moving ants, however, terminated the motion percept. He concluded that the focal percept required task-oriented attention. His observations also imply that task-oriented attention eliminates the peripheral percept. A similar conclusion about the importance of a passive state for marginal perceptions emerged from the subliminal perception activity during the 1950s and 1960s, which produced several reports of the importance of subjects being in a relaxed state in order to demonstrate such perception (Fisher and Paul 1959; Fiss, Goldberg, and Klein 1963; Dixon 1981, pp. 93–94).

The most pervasive anecdotal evidence for the nonintentional effect in memory is found in the psychoanalytic literature. Brenner (1976, p. 191), among many others, has put it concisely: "To the extent that anyone renounces conscious control over his thoughts, to the degree that he ignores his customary conscious interests, unconscious stimuli take over and control his thoughts." Pine (1964) made the bridge between such psychoanalytic observations and the subliminal perception literature when he noted that the reduction of adaptive demands and of additional stimulus inputs makes it more likely that preconscious and unconscious material will emerge into awareness (see also Koriat and Feuerstein 1976).

In the area of *priming and identification*, there are a number of demonstrations. Marcel (1983a, Experiment 1) had subjects make judgments of graphic and semantic similarity for words that presumably could not be detected. His major finding was that semantic judgments were superior to graphic judgments, which in turn were more probable than correct "presence or absence" judgments at the lowest exposure rates. However, two kinds of subjects were discarded from his analysis: those who refused to make judgments about stimuli that they could not see and those who "felt the task to be nonsensical once they could not be sure of whether a stimulus was present" but continued with the judgments by adopting idiosyncratic strategies. The remainder of the subjects, who showed he predicted effect, adopted a passive attitude and chose the words that felt right. The phenomenon falls into the group of nonintentional processes Marcel (1983b) discussed.

In Graf and Mandler (1984, Experiment 3) we reported a case in which intentional search produced large interference effects as compared with a passive task requirement. Subjects were given a list of words with instructions for nonsemantic processing; they were required to count T-junctions and enclosures in the letters of the presented words. Following this presentation, the subjects were shown the initial three letters—the stems of the words—together with an equal number of stems unrelated to the presentation list. Half of the subjects were asked to complete the stems with the first word that came to mind, and the other half were told to complete the stems with words from the list they had just seen. The intentional ("cued") group completed 7.8 percent of the target stems with words from the presentation list, whereas the nonintentional ("passive") group completed 20.0 percent of the target stems with list words. The deleterious effect in the intentional group carried over to an intentional ("cued") test on the identical words immediately following the nonintentional test, which yielded a hit rate of only 5.6 percent.[9]

A similar phenomenon was reported in Overson and Mandler (1987). Subjects were presented with connected passages followed by a stem completion test for some of the words in the passages. When subjects were instructed that some of the stems could be completed with words from the passages, the response times for correct responses were seven times greater than for subjects who were asked to give the first word that came to mind. Thus, just as in Graf and Mandler, the positive effect was obtained when subjects did not try to retrieve the specific target items, but in contrast to the Graf and Mandler data, these subjects had processed the input items semantically; their ability to recall the items had not been impaired.

In another study in our laboratory, Nakamura (1989) found the Marcel (1983a) effect of access to categorical information only under conditions in which subjects did not intentionally attempt to make categorical or perceptual decisions. Nakamura used word triplets, such as *corn, horn,* and *peas*. One of the words (such as *corn*) was presented, followed by instructions to choose between the other two words (*horn* and *peas*), thus either making a categorical choice (*peas*) or a choice based on perceptual/phonological information (*horn*). Presentation times ranged from 7 to 20 ms followed by a pattern mask. In one condition (intentional choices), the subjects were instructed to choose the word that they believed on the basis of immediate impression to have been presented. In a second condition (nonintentional choices), the same words were presented, but the subjects were instructed that no words were presented and that they were part of a control group to determine whether people preferentially chose any particular words and that they should pick one of the two words as quickly as possible. In fact, the same masked words were presented as in the first group. A third condition was an actual control for the second condition (nonintentional control), and a white blank field was always presented prior to the mask and the two-word choice task. The instructions were the same as for the second condition. In the range of 7 to 17 ms, the subjects in the second nonintentional "control" condition chose the categorically related words significantly more frequently than chance; subjects in the third (nonintentional) control group were at chance levels between the two kinds of words, and subjects in the first (intentional) condition were either at chance or chose the perceptual alternative. The results are consistent with Marcel's "passive" subjects. In this case, the absence of any attempt to decide which word had actually been presented produced evidence for categorical priming. When subjects intentionally tried to decide between the two words, they either were at chance or relied (at exposures of 20 ms or more) on the available perceptual information.

There are occasional observations of a *neuropsychological* nature that imply interference due to goal-directed activity and the advantage of passivity. Coslett and Saffran (1989; see also Coslett et al. 1993) have presented data on patients with "pure alexia" who are unable to identify briefly presented words but perform above chance on lexical decision and forced-choice categorization tasks. The latter "implicit" access is in apparent contradiction to these patients' usual letter-by-letter technique for reading words. The implicit access improved when subjects were encouraged to develop a "feel" or intuition for the word and to inhibit the letter-by-letter approach. Weiskrantz (1986, e.g., p. 151) reported that some blindsight subjects have refused to "play the guessing game," and that "if the subject is pressed ... to be a 'conscientious' subject, he may fail." Marcel reports an observation of a blindsighted patient who was tested for spatial frequency resolution. Frequency sensitivity in the blindfield was better when the patient was distracted by conversation than when not so distracted. It approached and even exceeded sensitivity in the sighted field when the patient was not paying full attention (A. J. Marcel, personal communication).

In the area of *problem solving* I have already noted suggestions that irrelevant activity in the delay period might improve incubation. Schooler, Ohlsson, and Brooks (1993) interrupted work on insight problems and required subjects to report their current strategies or asked for concurrent "thinking aloud" protocols during problem solving. In both cases, such verbalization interfered with the eventual solution. However, linear, incremental, noninsight problems were not affected by such interruptions. Schooler, Ohlsson, and Brooks relate this phenomenon to verbal overshadowing shown in decision processes (Wilson and Schooler 1991) and face recognition (Schooler and Engstler-Schooler 1990).

To add a more speculative example, it may be the case that arguments for the utility of irrationality—that is, unconsidered judgments and decisions—are related to letting unconscious activations take charge of one's actions. For example, a contemporary prophet of "irrationality," Jon Elster, noted in illustration of his argument that some human dysfunctions (such as insomnia, impotence, and stuttering) are more easily repaired when one does not think about them and that they get worse if one deliberately tries to repair them (Elster 1989).

Finally, I want to mention the peculiar characteristics of dreams, because they provide important clues to the occurrence of nonintentional thought. Dreams are conscious constructions that are independent of conscious intentions, just as the examples I have given of unintended consciousness in the awake state. Dreams come to consciousness without any intent on the part of the dreamer. I am primarily concerned here with the objects and actors of the dream, not with its meaning; I address the manifest content. The manifest content of dreams has long been known to be a reflection of our most recent experiences—material of which we have been conscious shortly before. Both ancient and modern sources are best summarized by Maury (1878): *"Nous rêvons de ce que nous avons vu, dit, désiré ou fait."* The residues tend to include actions that have not been brought to a conclusion, unsolved problems, rejected or suppressed thoughts, and often mundane occurrences that have not been further attended to in the pressure of everyday life (Freud [1900] 1975). At the same time, manifest dream content frequently exhibits subsidiary and unnoticed "memories," as well as hypermnesic content—material that seems long forgotten.[10] Thus, dreams contain to a large extent recent activations but not necessarily the most activated events of one's recent life. One of the apparent similarities between the manifest content of dreams and the instances of nonintentional thought is that in both, what becomes conscious or is dreamed is not necessarily, or even usually, the dominant preoccupation of the dreamer, perceiver, or rememberer but may be initially a rather peripheral event or object.

## 1.5 PHENOMENA, EXPLANATIONS, AND A FRAMEWORK

I have described three phenomena superficially related by their apparent violation of traditional views of memory and thought. Common thought and the inheritance of nineteenth-century views of human rationality both argue against the acceptance of improved memory with no intervening learning, of solving problems by simply stopping to think about them, of problem solutions coming to mind by deliberately thinking about something else. Since these phenomena are only superficially related, the explanations that will make them comprehensible will invoke more than a single theoretical process.

In approaching a theoretical analysis of these phenomena, I start with a framework that has guided my work over the past years. The two processes that are emphasized are activation and elaboration of underlying representations. These theoretical notions were first presented in detail in Mandler (1979); they originated with my concern to find a reasonable explanation of recognition memory (Mandler, Pearlstone, and Koopmans 1969). Dual process theory is reviewed extensively in Mandler (1991), where it is related to a number of psychological and neuropsychological observations.

The dual process approach postulates two processes that operate on mental representations: activation/integration and elaboration.[11] Figure 1.1 uses a graphic metaphor for the distinction. The vertical dimension shows increasing activation/integration; the horizontal one shows increasing elaboration. Integration affects the relations among the features of an object or event, and interevent elaboration reflects relations between the event representation and other mental contents. Activation/integration is an automatic process that occurs whenever the representation of an event is processed. The presentation of information (objects, events, actions) activates relevant existing knowledge units (schemas) and boosts the level of activation of all the constituent features of the event. Integration occurs automatically as the previously established connections or relations among the features lead to further activation of the "connected" features of the item and thus "integrate" the specific event that is

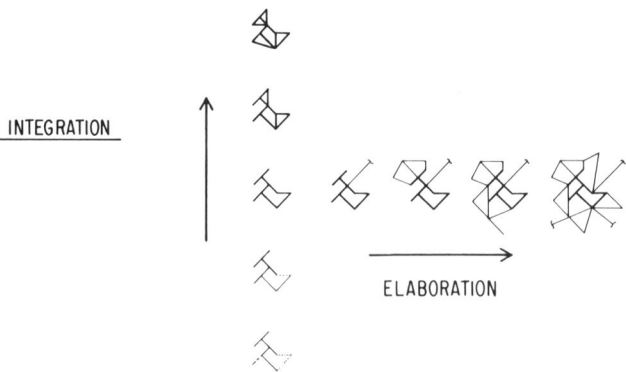

**Figure 1.1** Graphic presentation of the distinction between activation/integration and elaboration.

activated. Activation/integration increases with extended or repeated access of the representation. In the absence of such additional activation, the steady-state activation of the representation is reduced to a low but nonzero level. The more integrated a structure is, the more easily it is retrieved as a unit, the more distinct it is from other (similar) schemas, and the more likely it is that parts of the schema will activate the whole. Some of the consequences of such activation are the phenomenal experience of increased familiarity (Mandler 1980) and the perceptual fluency described by Jacoby and his associates (e.g., Jacoby and Dallas 1981).

In contrast, elaboration is the process whereby mental contents are related to one another. It is most evident in the establishment of new organizations that make possible subsequent retrieval and successful search processes. The concept has been variously used in the past, and it is generally relevant to many of the phenomena we find in deliberate memory, such as recall, partially in recognition, and in any kind of organization of target material. Elaboration is presumably a conscious process that activates previously established relationships among mental structures and allows new relations to be formed, enhancing both activation and retrievability at the same time. That is, activation can occur without elaboration or consciousness, but any elaboration accesses the representation of the event and necessarily produces activation. In the extreme cases, activation involves only the features or attributes of the target representation, but elaboration recruits other items and features. In general, however, activation/integration can occur at any level of elaboration; the two-dimensional space of figure 1.1 can produce instances for all values of activation and elaboration (Mandler 1979, 1982).

The class of phenomena usually called implicit is a function of activation, whereas explicit processes require elaborated structures (Mandler 1989). It is therefore also the case that the availability of interitem organization will improve performance on explicit tasks but should not affect perceptual implicit tasks (Rappold and Hashtroudi 1991).

I have noted that activation is primarily a perceptual phenomenon. Atkinson, Herrmann, and Wescourt (1974) specifically made the perceptual/conceptual distinction for the dual-process model. What is activated in the first instance at a presentation in a particular modality are the features for that modality. However, some other features are also activated by indirect verbalization, spread of activation, and so forth. The total schema of a concept has potentially a large number of features, some of them perception specific. Thus, there should be specific modality effects, but other modalities would be expected to show some activation.

One set of activations is especially important as we move about our environment, engage in social interactions, and negotiate our habitual world: state-of-the-world (SOW) activations, constituted of all those features, attributes, and schemas that define who we are, where we are, what we are doing, an so on. These representations are presumably activated throughout the day, with varying intervals, but with some high frequency. Such activations arise because, for example, one refers to oneself, observes oneself (Bem 1967) and one's environment, refers to immediate or just-past actions and events. In the absence of pathological states, we are never in doubt about those objects and events, and although most of them are not conscious most of the time, they come to mind (consciousness) continuously and easily. These underlying representations make it seem ridiculous, or at least banal, to ask others whether they know who or where they are. When hypermnesia is demonstrated in a multiple recall paradigm, frequently recalled items (and presumably the focal organizing items) will have a similar status to the SOW knowledge; they are highly activated and immediately accessible. These items represent nonconscious short-term memory—recently activated but not currently conscious items, in contrast to conscious primary memory (cf. Mandler 1985, chap. 4).

With these theoretical tools at hand, we turn to specific discussions of the mechanisms assumed to be operating in hypermnesia, incubation, and mind popping.

## 1.6 THEORETICAL RESOLUTIONS OF HYPERMNESIA, AND INCUBATION

### Hypermnesia

If we are going to ask what produces improved recall/performance some time after initial "learning" has taken place, we need some guidance as to what makes it possible for recall to occur in the first place. In the 1960s, many thought that problem had been laid to rest. A number of experiments had shown that organization is a necessary precursor to recall and that repeated trials primarily serve as opportunities for organization to occur (see, for example, Bower et al. 1969; Mandler 1967; Tulving 1962; and Crowder 1976 for an early summary).[12] It is somewhat puzzling that the memory of contemporary cognitive psychologists is so short. Discussions of hypermnesia have raised the question of the organizational determinants of recall at best only tangentially. Roediger and Challis (1989) note that "internal retrieval cues" may be responsible for increased recall across time, citing the finding by Payne (1986) that with categorized lists (where organization can be directly observed) additional recall across tests was due to increases in the number of categories recalled rather than increases in the number of items (Tulving and Pearlstone 1966).[13] However no attempt has been made to generalize this to noncategorized (random) lists, which show exactly the same phenomenon (Mandler 1967, 1977; Sawyers 1975), as do even free emissions of items from natural categories (Graesser and Mandler 1978).

Of the few experiments that have examined organizational factors in hypermnesia, those of Klein et al. (1989) are of special interest. They compared item-specific elaboration of items (pleasantness ratings) that related the item to general mental contents with categorical elaboration (sorting), which organizes items in relation to other list items for lists of weakly or strongly categorized items. Significant hypermnesia effects were shown for all conditions. In addition, they found that item-specific elaborations were more effective in the recall of new items on a second trial, whereas categorical organization was more effective in preventing the loss of items recalled on the first trial. The effect of categorical organization depends in part on the recall of all the categories, but no such intermediate step is necessary when individual items are elaborated. On the other hand, once an item has been recalled, it is likely that it (and its category) will be recalled on a subsequent trial. Belmore (1981) concluded from a series of experiments that hypermnesia is accompanied by "meaningful processing, regardless of whether verbal or imagery encoding is emphasized" (p. 191). The explanation that I propose is consistent with her statement that "increased reminiscence and decreased forgetting overtime may be associated with any factor that facilitates learning" (p. 202). Finally, hypermnesia and incubation are combined in a recent study by Smith and Vela (1991) in which organization was encouraged by presenting lists of pictures in groups of five. They found generally increasing reminiscence (recovery of previously forgotten items) with longer intervals (up to 10 min). The state of the art is summarized by the position taken in a recent text that "subjects seem to rely spontaneously on an organizational strategy, and the better they can organize, the better they can remember" (Schwartz and Reisberg 1991). If one takes a strong view of organizational factors—that any facilitation of learning implies at least some organizational activity—then the findings of Madigan and O'Hara (1992) support the view that organization facilitates reminiscence and hypermnesia.

How are lists of unrelated words organized? In 1974, we showed that there exist focal items that are more frequently recalled in multiple trial–multiple recall tests. Other list items are organized by these focal items that occur on each of three successive recalls. If focal items are removed from the list, performance declines to the level of a group receiving a new list on every trial (Mandler, Worden, and Graesser 1974; see also Mandler and Graesser 1976, where these focal items where shown to organize temporal clusters of output). In addition, the more frequently an item is recalled, the higher is its probability of later recall, but this effect is independent of prior number of presentations of the item, and number of prior presentations does not affect final recall (Mandler, Worden, and Graesser 1974, figs. 3, 8).

An experiment from our laboratory by Borges (1972) approaches another aspect of list learning relevant to hypermnesia. Subjects were given categorized lists for two successive recalls. A control group was given just two successive trials; the second group was told prior to the second recall that they should not be concerned about repeating words and to "keep going over the list words [that they knew] while searching for new words" (p. 67). The second group showed a 10 percent hypermnesia effect; the control group showed none. More important, the second group showed 40 percent fewer words forgotten between recalls 1 and 2 and a reminiscence effect that was 56 percent greater than the values for the control group. I assume that the instructions that encouraged repetitions made available items from the first recall that were organizational foci for other words, thus reducing forgetting and increasing reminiscence.

A direct reference to organizational processes in hypermnesia is found in the protocol of subject J. K. in Erdelyi and Kleinbard (1978). J. K. was given repeated recalls over 7 days. He reports: "During the early trials, I began to organize the words into small clusters of two or three items each" (p. 279). He also noted priming by events encountered during intertrial intervals and metacognitive visual experiences ("tip-of-the eye").

As far as the superior recall of pictures and of high-imagery material is concerned, it is probably due to a variety of factors: (1) Paivio's (1976) dual-encoding hypothesis envisages both imaginal and verbal encoding, thus providing multiple organization and easier access to the items: (2) pictures are probably more easily organized into thematic structures, and the latter produce better recall than categorical organization, which is the preferred form for organizing word lists (Rabinowitz and Mandler 1983); (3) whatever the organization, pictures provide a more specific and concrete memory code than do words (compare memory for a picture of a cocker spaniel with that for an unspecified generic dog); and (4) imagery is likely to encourage meaningful, elaborated representations (Belmore 1981).

Categorical and focal organization establishes access routes both among members of a category or clusters and between a representation of the category or cluster and its members. Elaboration (as in semantic judgments) relates the target item to other similar items and also activates judgment-related mental representations (e.g., what makes for pleasantness, meaningfulness). Both kinds of organization/elaboration make subsequent recalls as well as spreading activation more likely by providing activated pathways that facilitate retrieval and extend and amplify the spread of activation. The process is, of course, not perfect, producing imperfect recall on early trials and retrieval of new items on later trials through their organization and the intervening spreading activation.

The problem of how organized clusters are accessed in the first instance is central to an organizational view of recall. There are essentially three possibilities: (1) some cluster/category information is available at time of recall because it is still held in primary memory (consciousness) or in immediate memory (highly activated and directly accessible); (2) given that subjects expect a recall, implicit recovery of category information occurs at time of recall; and (3) some contextual/experimental cues produce cluster/category information. Once any one cluster/category is accessed, cross-category organization and multidimensional organization will provide access to the other clusters or to some higher-level organizing principle that subsumes two or more of the clusters established during encoding. In addition, we know that previously recalled items are easily accessed (have very high activation), and, to the extent that they are focal organizing items, they will provide access to other organized material.

In summary, amount of hypermnesia (and reminiscence) will be a function of the degree of elaboration/organization of the target material. It will also be a function of adequate cues for retrieval of the organized material, of the activity during the delay that encourages spreading activation of the organized structures and that primes the organized material, and of adequate time to recall the remaining items to be accessed.

## Incubation

All explanations of incubation have in common some subset of a list of variables mentioned by Woodworth in 1938, including periodic conscious work on the problem, unconscious work, some version of advertent or inadvertent priming of the correct solution, diminution over time of interference from incorrect solutions, and reduction in fatigue (Posner 1973; Woodworth 1938).

Important evidence for the processes operative in incubation comes from a series of studies by Yaniv and Meyer (1987). Using a definitions test that required the recall of rare words given a series of definitions, subjects were also asked for "feeling of knowing" (FOK) judgments for words they could not retrieve, followed by a lexical decision task for these target words and control words. In one of their studies, subjects were also given a yes-no recognition test for words tested in the lexical, decision task. Lexical decision times were faster for target words, especially for targets that had elicited strong feelings of knowing.[14] A similar effect occurred in recognition. Yaniv and Meyer conclude that spreading activation (Meyer and Schvaneveldt 1971, 1976) following unsuccessful retrieval attempts primes later access to the target words. Because the effect lasted as long as 1 hour, and considering activation effects produced by subconscious stimuli (Marcel 1983a), they suggest that revisions of traditional views of spreading activation (that invoke short decay times and suprathreshold activation) are called for.

In a related demonstration, Dorfman (1990) used a task adapted from Bowers et al. (1990) in which subjects were given sets of words with the instruction to find the common associative connection (e.g., *high* for *school, chair, jump, noon, heels, wire*). In addition subjects made metacognitive "coherence" judgments of the sets, which were presented either in their entirety or incrementally, as well as for sets of unrelated words. Problems that would eventually be correctly solved were given higher coherence judgments than were judgments given for problems that were not solved or for unrelated sets of words. In an investigation of the incubation of previously unsolved sets, metacognitive judgments again were higher for sets that would be eventually solved, and maximal incubation was obtained for a filled delay of 13 min, compared with 0, 3-min, and 8-min delays. Dorfman interprets the data in terms of spread of activation during problem solving and during incubation.

It is fairly obvious that priming for specific responses and solutions must work in incubation. Second, the longer the initial work period is, the more activated are the solution attempts used during that period, and the longer the period is needed to reduce the activation of these unsuccessful responses. Loss of activation of inappropriate thoughts and responses reduces interference after the delay. Related pause activity may, under some circumstances, prevent such a reduction in activation or prime new solutions.

To the extent that incubation studies have been concerned with problem solving, the initial task and instructions develop the appropriate organizations. These will differ from task to task. For example, in the Consequences task, a large number of candidate responses are activated, which in turn spread activation to other related possible responses. In the Common Associates task, there is probably an organization of the stimulus words, both as a group and in subsets (e.g., "What does the set have in common?" "What do any two/three/four words have in common?"). These processes will activate related items in the organized memory structures, and spreading activation will provide further candidate responses.

In contrast to the hypermnesia studies, where we have a large number of reliable tests of specific hypotheses and a reasonable explanation of the effect, the incubation effect is due to a number of different processes operating at different times or in concert, but no single theoretical explanation—such as unconscious work—applies to the phenomenon. Whereas hypermnesia calls —within the dual process framework—for primarily elaborative processes, incubation depends apparently primarily on activation processes. There is no direct evidence that complex unconscious "work" (new elaborations and creations of mental contents) contributes to the incubation effects. However, neither is there any evidence that processes such as blind variation and selective retention (Campbell 1960) may not contribute to the incubation effect. Campbell's proposal can be interpreted in the present framework as the undifferentiated spreading of activation leading to a fit with a preliminary structure of the problem.

## 1.7 THEORETICAL APPROACHES TO THE MIND-POPPING PHENOMENON

I start with a view of constructive consciousness that argues for current conscious content's being responsive to the immediate history of the individual, as well as to current needs and demands (Mandler 1985, chap. 3; 1992). Following a brief description of the manner in which the usual, daily conscious contents may be constructed, I relate that view to some differences exhibited in the conscious content of dreams. I then discuss how processes similar to those occurring in dreams, coupled with extensive spreading activation, may account for mind popping.

### The Construction of Consciousness in Daily Life and in Dreams

Current consciousness is constructed from activated representations—the preconscious in Freud's terms. A conscious content is a construction that best assimilates the available evidence. Evidence (occurrences) from both extra- and intrapsychic sources activates the relevant schemas. Specific and concrete schemas will be activated that represent objects and events together with relevant memories (themselves constructed). Eventually more abstract and generic schemas receive activation and represent hypotheses about external events and appropriate action schemas. Any set of sensory evidence may, and usually will, activate more than one schema or generic hypothesis. All of these activated schemas are available for a conscious construction, and the selection (conscious representation) of a schema will depend on current as well as prior activation. I will experience (be conscious of) whatever is consistent with my immediate preceding history as well as with currently impinging events. The most important schemas that determine current conscious contents are those that represent the demands and requirements of the current situation. Thus, sitting in a lecture room activates possible schemas (hypotheses) of university actions, scenes, and occurrences. Absent surviving personal preoccupations, I will not be conscious of the roof at home that needs fixing but rather of the themes developed by the lecturer. In that way, current consciousness makes sense of as much evidence as possible that is available and relevant to current expectations and requirements (see also Marcel 1983b). Given that the objects and events of our surrounds are the dominant instigators of currently activated schemas, it is highly likely that in most, if not all, instances, what we are conscious of is constrained by the evidence from the external world that activates specific "world-related" schemas.[15]

In dreams there is no constraint on the possible constructions by the reality and lawfulness of the external world. But dreams are highly structured; they are not random events. They present a structured mixture of real-world events, current events (sensory events in the environment of the dreamer), contemporary preoccupations, and ancient themes. They may be weird and novel, but they are meaningful. What they are not is dependent on the imperatives and continuity of the real world, inhabited by physically and socially possible problems and situations. In the waking world, our conscious experience is historically bound, dependent on context and possible historical sequences. In contrast, dreams do not depend to a great extent on current sensory activations: they are constructed out of the activation of the previous hours and days (for a previous discussion, see Mandler 1984).[16] These leftovers of our daily lives are both abstract themes—our preoccupations and our generic view of the world—and concrete and specific activated schemas of events and objects encountered. These active schemas are initially not organized with respect to each other; they are, in that sense, random detritus of our daily experiences and thoughts. Without the structure of the real world, they are free floating. They are free to find accommodating higher-order structures. These may combine quite separate, unrelated thoughts about events, about happy or unhappy occurrences, but since there are no real-world constraints, they may be combined into sequences and categories by activating higher-order schemas to which they are relevant (of which they are features). It is in this fashion that abstract (and unconscious) preoccupations and complexes may find their expression in the consciousness of dreams. It is what Freud has called the residue of daily life that produces some of the actors and events, whereas the scenario is free to be constructed by otherwise quiescent higher-order schemas. The higher-order schemas—the themes of dreams—may be activated by events of the preceding days, or they may be activated simply because a reasonable number of their features have been left over as residues from the days before. Dream theories that concentrate only on the residues in dreams fail to account for the obviously organized nature of dream sequences, however bizarre these might be. On the other hand, Hobson's (1988) activation-synthesis hypothesis of dreaming supposes that, apart from aminergic neurons, "the rest of the system is buzzing phrenetically, especially during REM sleep" (p. 291). Such additional activations provide ample material to construct dreams and, as Hobson suggests, to be creative and generate solutions to old and new problems.

This view is not discrepant with some modern as well as more ancient views about the biological function of dreams (in modern times, specifically rapid eye movement dreams), which are seen as cleaning up unnecessary, unwanted, and irrelevant leftovers from daily experiences. The argument is that these experiential leftovers would seriously impair functioning, unless regularly removed or "unlearned." Robert (1886), for example, in illustrating the "excretive" function of dreams, noted that one deprived of dreaming "would in course of time become mentally deranged, because a great mass of uncompleted, unworked-out thoughts and superficial impressions would accumulate" (p. 10). Crick and Mitchison (1983) similarly note that the failure to remove (unlearn) undesirable modes of excitation might lead to "a state of almost perpetual obsession or spurious, hallucinatory associations" (p. 114). It is frequently this mental detritus that is used in constructing dreams.

In short, dreams are unintentional, they are constructed out of a large variety of activated mental contents, or of mental contents activated by a rather wide-ranging process of spreading activation, and they are organized by existing mental structures.

**Mind Popping, Dreams, and Unconscious Activity**

In the exploration of possible bases for mind popping, I turn first to a phenomenon that has received relatively little attention in recent psychological research: the apparent facilitating role of preconscious mental content and, conversely, the restricting role of conscious material. As an example, consider an experiment by Spence and Holland (1962; see also Paul and Fisher 1959; Eagle 1959). They presented the word *cheese* subliminally (five separate projections on a screen at approximately 7 ms without a mask in a lighted room) or supraliminally for 2 sec. They then presented a list of ten associates of *cheese* and ten control words, followed by recall. Subjects in the subliminal condition recalled significantly more associated than control words and more associates than the supraliminal group, which showed no difference in the recall of the two kinds of words. A replication by Barber and Rushton (1975) found the same pattern of results but only marginal ($p < .10$) statistical significance. Spence and Holland interpret the data as supporting Freud's ([1900] 1975) notion that preconscious material fans out over an associative network to a greater degree than conscious material, which shows the "restricting effects of awareness." In other words, activated representations of which we are not aware produce a wider spreading than does "aware" material.

The general processes at work in mind popping are presumably similar to those outlined for both hypermnesia and incubation. At the time that the problem is established (prior to the mind-popping event), target structures and candidate responses (initially incorrect) continue to activate other structures and representations. In the case of mind popping, however, it appears that such activation occurs more easily and fans out more widely than under conditions when active conscious searches are in place. I have argued previously (Mandler 1985) that conscious problem solving results in way stations that represent the current progress toward the goal (usually demonstrated in talk-aloud protocols). However, current conscious contents activate in turn their relevant unconscious representations, and this preferential activation of current conscious contents narrows the unconscious material available for further attempts.

The phenomenon of verbalization interfering with insight tasks (Schooler, Ohlsson, and Brooks 1993) is consistent with these general arguments. The tasks Schooler et al. use require unique insight solutions, and they will, prior to solution, most frequently yield reports of incorrect guesses and strategies. Such reports will activate continuing pursuit of erroneous solutions, and spreading activation will interfere with the activation of relevant appropriate structures and retrievals (Schooler, Ohlsson, and Brooks 1993). On the other hand, in incremental, serial tasks, verbal reports indicate way stations in the solution process and preferential, privileged activation of access routes that frequently lead to the correct solutions.

I have previously noted that "consciousness ... serves to restrict and focus subsequent pathways by selectively activating those that are currently within the conscious construction" (Mandler 1985, p. 77). That is the usual process during serial problem solving; incubation and mind popping illustrate another process by not restricting possible solutions and permitting extensive (unconscious) activations that may lead to a solution.

The interesting implication of this approach is that with respect to the phenomena addressed here, it is not crucial whether the individual is conscious or aware of the "subliminally" presented material (Cheesman and Merikle 1986). The important aspect is whether there is a conscious or deliberate attempt to retrieve the subliminally presented material. It is that process that seems to interfere with access. If the individual believes or asserts that he or she saw "nothing," then there is no deliberate search, and there will be minimal interference with the underlying activation process.

If dreams and dreamlike states (daydreaming, hypnagogic states) indeed make it possible for us to engage in thoughts that would otherwise be constrained by the reality of the impinging world, then the restricting functions of consciousness play an important role in our daily lives. They prevent us from going too far beyond the bounds of the givens; they prevent—in normal states and normal individuals—fantasy from taking over our transactions with the world. Conversely, poets, artists, creative scientists, and others are able to engage this less restricted world in producing poems, art, and theories.

In the other examples of mind popping, a similar state of affairs occurs. The target is not intentionally sought out; it is preconscious and thus has the characteristic of fanning out, of engaging wider spreading of activation and more extensive elaboration and activation. Thus, "thinking" about something else makes it possible for the actual targets to become available for conscious construction. Interestingly, Taoism's *wu-wei* (possibly "nonacting") incorporates the notion of effective thought and decisions' being dependent on a passive, nonactive attitude (Watts 1957).

"Thinking about something else" is, of course, the defining characteristic of what I have called mind popping. However, there should be similar effects for deliberate retrievals (e.g., following delays in studies of hypermnesia and incubation) if the period preceding the retrieval is filled with material not relevant to the target task. And there is some indication that incubation is more effective when the delay is filled with activities unrelated to the target material (Dorfman 1990; Payne 1987; Smith and Vela 1991).

Why does awareness restrict the utilization of unconscious material? One possible explanation is a relatively simple interference notion. Consider a search process for somebody's name. The immediately obvious conscious contents are replete with the bringing to mind of possible names, of contexts in which one has seen the person, and so forth. All of these incorrect "thoughts" will provide activation to their underlying representations, which in turn will be the dominant preconscious material available for conscious constructions. The result is the well-known but little researched looping effect, in which the incorrect solutions repeatedly come to mind.[17] In the context of tip-of-the-tongue experiences, these incorrect intrusions have been called blockers or interlopers that block access to the target words (see Brown 1991, p. 216, for a review; Reason and Lucas 1984 for relevant data). If, however, material totally irrelevant to the task is the primary occupation of conscious constructions, there will be little interference with the mental structure initiated by the relevant task, such as, "What is that person's name?" or "What is the right word for that definition?" Repeated search processes and spreading activation can eventually produce the appropriate integration of the correct target item. But note that mind popping in response to difficult problems is not a frequent phenomenon; unfortunately, we do not solve all or most unsolved problems. Another aspect of interference is the restricting character of the surrounding real world. Just as in dreams, the time and space requirements of the waking environment restrict what can be constructed in response to conscious demands. The unconscious activation process, on the other hand, is presumably continuing without such constraints.

Second, there might be inhibitory processes at work when more than one possible solution is being consciously considered (Rumelhart and McClelland 1982). If an incorrect solution is dominant at any one time or becomes dominant because of conscious preoccupation, the correct solution may well be inhibited, and a reduction in activation may ensue. Again, irrelevant preoccupations will not interfere with the underlying process.

A third possibility is a genuine autonomous restriction of awareness. One should not dismiss the possibility that some states of passive thought approach the sleeping state described by Hobson (1988), where quasi-random neuronal activity significantly increases. If that can happen in some awake states of passivity, then new elaborations (novel solutions) are more likely to be generated. Such a state of affairs would be close to the "blind variation and selective retention" approach to problem solving advocated by Campbell (1960). All of these processes may, of course, be operating at different times or at the same time, or some might be specific to certain instances of mind popping. Given the multidimensional and overdetermined nature of human thought, that is the most likely conclusion.

I cannot leave this topic without considering the question of why and how ideas come to mind at unprepared, nondeliberate times in the continuing thought process. Given that the increased activation and elaboration produce a fairly well-activated and integrated "solution," why does it come to mind at a particular time? Two possibilities exist: one is that the demand for the solution, the question posed, is itself in a continuing high state of activation, and autonomous processes combine this "demand" with the newly integrated solution; the other possibility is that fortuitous and haphazard events (both extra- and intrapsychic) become cues or primes for the solution that is now readily accessible.

There are two conclusions I wish to draw from the examples of mind popping and their possible theoretical basis. First, we need to revise our notions of the time course and the extensiveness of spreading activation, a point previously made by Yaniv and Meyer (1987). There may well be conditions in which such spreading or fanning out reaches recesses of the unconscious that dynamic psychology has considered, but experimental psychology has not. The second conclusion, not unrelated to the first, is that conscious intention is not a necessary condition for transforming an "unconscious" representation into a conscious one. In previous discussions of consciousness I have stressed that conscious contents are constructed out of unconscious ones in response to the requirements and demands of the immediately current situation (Mandler 1985, 1992). These latter requirements are often intentions, in the sense that the perceiver or rememberer "intends," for example, to see or hear an event or to recall a specific previously experienced event. However, many, indeed most, of our perceptions and memories come to mind unbidden and not intended in the usual sense. Thus, requirements or demands need not be conscious intentions.

## 1.8 PHENOMENA AND EXPLANATIONS REVISITED

Hypermnesia, incubation, and mind popping were, at least as recently as eighty years ago, counterintuitive. During the ensuing years, they became first the property of anecdotal dispersion and then the object of theoretical and empirical dispute. During the past decade or so, enough evidence and theory accumulated to make them amenable to detailed theoretical analyses.

We can understand these phenomena at least in part within the framework of activation and elaboration processes. Moreover, we can use notions about the functions and structure of conscious processes to understand some of the issues at hand.

With respect to activation and elaboration, the analyses presented make it fairly obvious that hypermnesia is to a large degree dependent on elaborative processes, whereas incubation and mind popping draw primarily on activation and spread of activation. Of course, both kinds of processes will be invoked to some extent whenever underlying representation are accessed, but the primary contributors to the phenomena seem evident. Some of the mind-popping effects suggest that elaboration might be more effective than previous analyses of unconscious processing have suggested. The possibility needs to be explored that some elaboration might occur nonconsciously.

As far as consciousness is concerned, two apparently opposing processes may be operating. On the one hand, the construction of a conscious content (being conscious of something) activates the underlying un- and preconscious representation, while on the other hand, awareness may restrict conscious contents and their activation. The contradiction is resolved if we note that the restricting effect of consciousness restricts only the further spread of activation from the currently activated material and not the activation of what is currently in consciousness.

Much of our daily action and thought is occasioned without deliberation or intent, and the study of memory in particular has started to move away from the study of deliberate searches and retrievals. I have tried to contribute to this move by showing that many of our thoughts and memories may be without reasons but still useful and creative.

## NOTES

I am grateful to Jennifer Dorfman, Matthew Erdelyi, Craig Kaplan, Asher Koriat, Jean Mandler, David Payne, Roddy Roediger, and Steve Smith for comments on and critiques of earlier drafts of this chapter. All the remaining errors and inconsistencies are mine. Correspondence to: George Mandler, Center for Human Information Processing, University of California, San Diego, La Jolla, CA 92093-0109.

1. For complementary processes, see Bjork and Bjork (1992) for a discussion of how memorial materials become less accessible.

2. For an extensive and reasoned history of the phenomenon, see the review by Payne (1987), to whom I am indebted for much of the information presented here. See also Erdelyi (1984).

3. I shall not deal with the possibility of hypermnesia in recognition, since recognition performance depends complexly on the interaction of several variables (Mandler 1980).

4. For a detailed discussion of the definitional issues, see Erdelyi (1984, p. 108n).

5. Kaplan says "interruption" rather than "delay."

6. I am indebted to two recent doctoral dissertations, by Craig Kaplan (1989) and by Jennifer Dorfman (1990), for providing both data and new insights for this discussion.

7. I do not intend to review here either the extensive literature on near-threshold phenomena or the relevant theoretical discussions. However, the phenomena that do concern me obviously address issues of nonconscious access.

8. Wallas (1926) called the phenomenon "illumination."

9. I leave out of this discussion the phenomenon of word priming with amnesic patients. As is well known, these patients show unimpaired performance on implicit memory of previously primed words (Warrington and Weiskrantz 1970, 1974; Graf, Squire, and Mandler 1984). One could argue that since these patients cannot remember the priming list, they are accessing the material "unintentionally."

10. See Freud ([1900] 1975, chaps. 1, 5) for extensive discussions and illustrations of these observations by him and others.

11. Similar arguments have been made in the connectionist literature (Hinton 1981) and recently elaborated by Hinton as a distinction between "simple" (intuitive) and "complex" (rational) inferences, where only the latter require a change in the way the world is mapped into the network (Hinton 1990).

12. I use the concept of organization in the broadest sense, the establishment of relations (which can be of many different kinds) among the items to be recalled.

13. Roediger et al. (1982) suggest that modifications of a stimulus sampling model (Raaijmakers and Shiffrin 1980) might permit that model to account for hypermnesia effects.

14. But see Connor, Balota, and Neely (1992) for an alternative interpretation of the FOK judgments.

15. I shall not enter into a discussion of any differences between attention and consciousness. The distinction can and has been made (Kahneman and Treisman 1984; Mandler 1985), and for the present purposes, it will suffice to agree that attentional processes (under some definitions) will produce conscious contents but that a conscious content does not presuppose prior attention.

16. Similar arguments have been made in contemporary biological approaches to the function of dreaming. Thus, "in REM sleep the brain is isolated from its normal input and output channels" (Crick and Mitchison 1983, p. 112). And Hobson et al. (1987) note that the brain/mind is focused in the waking state on the linear unfolding of plot and time. In REM dreaming, the brain/mind cannot maintain its orientational focus.

17. See Brown (1988) for an example of rare empirical work in which induced spelling errors keep recurring.

## REFERENCES

Ammons, H., and Irion, A. I. (1954). A note on the Ballard reminiscence phenomenon. *Journal of Experimental Psychology, 48*, 184–186.

Atkinson, R. C., Herrmann, D. J., and Wescourt, K. T. (1974). Search processes in recognition memory. In R. L. Solso (Ed.), *Theories in cognitive psychology: The Loyola Symposium*. Hillsdale, NJ: Erlbaum.

Ballard, P. B. (1913). Oblivescence and reminiscence. *British Journal of Psychology Monograph Supplements, 1*, 1–82.

Barber, P. J., and Rushton, J. P. (1975). Experimenter bias and subliminal perception. *British Journal of Psychology, 66*, 357–372.

Belmore, S. M. (1981). Imagery and semantic elaboration in hypermnesia for words. *Journal of Experimental Psychology: Human Learning and Memory, 7*, 191–203.

Bem, D. J. (1967). Self-perception: An alternative interpretation of cognitive dissonance phenomena. *Psychological Review, 74*, 183–200.

Berry, D. C., and Broadbent, D. E. (1988). Interactive tasks and the implicit-explicit distinction. *British Journal of Psychology, 79*, 251–272.

Bjork, R. A., and Bjork, E. L. (1992). A new theory of disuse and an old theory of stimulus fluctuation. In A. F. Healy, S. M. Kosslyn, and R. M. Shiffrin (Eds.), *From learning processes to cognitive processes: Essays in honor of William K. Estes*, vol. 2, 35–67. Hillsdale, NJ: Erlbaum.

Borges, M. A. (1972). Increasing item accessibility in free recall. *Journal of Experimental Psychology, 95*, 66–71.

Bower, G. H., and Bryant, D. J. (1991). On relating the organizational theory of memory to levels of processing. In W. Kessen, A. Ortony, and F. Craik (Eds.), *Memories, thoughts, and emotions: Essays in honor of George Mandler*, 149–168. Hillsdale, NJ: Erlbaum.

Bower, G. H., Clark, M. C., Lesgold, A. M., and Winzenz, D. (1969). Hierarchical retrieval schemes in recall of categorized word lists. *Journal of Verbal Learning and Verbal Behavior, 8*, 323–343.

Bowers, K. S., Regehr, G., Balthazard, C., and Parker, K. (1990). Intuition in the context of discovery. *Cognitive Psychology, 22*, 72–110.

Brenner, C. (1976). *Psychoanalytic technique and psychic conflict*. New York: International Universities Press.

Brown, A. S. (1988). Encountering misspellings and spelling performance: What's wrong isn't right. *Journal of Educational Psychology, 80*, 488–494.

Brown, A. S. (1991). A review of the tip-of-the-tongue experience. *Psychological Bulletin, 109*, 204–223.

Buxton, C. E. (1943). The status of research in reminiscence. *Psychological Bulletin, 40*, 313–340.

Campbell, D. T. (1960). Blind variation and selective retention in creative thought as in other knowledge processes. *Psychological Review, 67*, 380–400.

Cheesman, J., and Merikle, P. (1986). Distinguishing conscious from unconscious perceptual processes. *Canadian Journal of Psychology, 40*, 343–367.

Connor, L. T., Balota, D. A., and Neely, J. H. (1992). On the relation between feeling of knowing and lexical decision: Persistent subthreshold activation or topic familiarity? *Journal of Experimental Psychology: Learning, Memory, and Cognition, 18*, 544–554.

Coslett, H. B., and Saffran, E. M. (1989). Evidence for preserved reading in "pure alexia." *Brain, 112*, 327–359.

Coslett, H. B., Saffran, E. M., Greenbaum, S., and Schwartz, H. (1993). Reading in pure alexia: The effect of strategy. *Brain, 116*, 21–37.

Craik, F. I. M., and Tulving, E. (1975). Depth of processing and the retention of words in episodic memory. *Journal of Experimental Psychology: General, 104*, 268–294.

Crick, F., and Mitchison, G. (1983). The function of dream sleep. *Nature, 304*, 111–114.

Crowder, R. G. (1976). *Principles of learning and memory*. Hillsdale, NJ: Erlbaum.

Dagenbach, D., Carr, T. H., and Wilhelmsen, A. (1989). Task-induced strategies and near-threshold priming: Conscious influences on unconscious perception. *Journal of Memory and Language, 28*, 412–443.

Dixon, N. F. (1981). *Preconscious processing*. Chichester: J. Wiley.

Dorfman, J. (1990). *Metacognitions and incubation effects in insight problem solving*. Unpublished doctoral dissertation, University of California, San Diego.

Eagle, M. (1959). The effects of subliminal stimuli of aggressive content upon conscious cognition. *Journal of Personality, 27*, 578–600.

Elster, J. (1989). *Nuts and bolts for the social sciences*. New York: Cambridge University Press.

Erdelyi, M. (1982). A note on the level of recall, level of processing, and imagery hypotheses of hypermnesia. *Journal of Verbal Learning and Verbal Behavior, 21*, 656–661.

Erdelyi, M. (1984). The recovery of unconscious (inaccessible) memories: Laboratory studies of hypermnesia. In G. H. Bower (Ed.), *The psychology of learning and motivation*, vol. 18. San Diego: Academic Press.

Erdelyi, M. H., and Becker, J. (1974). Hypermnesia for pictures: Incremental memory for pictures but not words in multiple recall trials. *Cognitive Psychology, 6*, 159–171.

Erdelyi, M. H., and Kleinbard, J. (1978). Has Ebbinghaus decayed with time? The growth of recall (hypermnesia) over days. *Journal of Experimental Psychology: Human Learning and Memory, 4*, 275–289.

Erdelyi, M. H., and Stein, J. B. (1981). Recognition hypermnesia: The growth of recognition memory ($d'$) over time with repeated testing. *Cognition, 9*, 23–33.

Fisher, C., and Paul, I. H. (1959). The effect of subliminal visual stimulation on imagery and dreams: A validation study. *Journal of the American Psychoanalytic Association, 7*, 35–83.

Fiss, H., Goldberg, F., and Klein, G. S. (1963). Effects of subliminal stimulation on imagery and discrimination. *Perceptual and Motor Skills, 17*, 31–44.

Freud, S. [1900] (1975). The interpretation of dreams. In *The standard edition of the complete psychological works of Sigmund Freud*, vols. 4, 5. London: Hogarth Press.

Fulgosi, A., and Guilford, J. P. (1968). Short term incubation in divergent production. *American Journal of Psychology, 81*, 241–248.

Fulgosi, A., and Guilford, J. P. (1972). A further investigation of short-term incubation. *Acti Instituti Psychologici*, 67–70.

Graesser, A. C., and Mandler, G. (1978). Limited processing capacity constrains the storage of unrelated sets of words and retrieval from natural categories. *Journal of Experimental Psychology: Human Learning and Memory, 4*, 86–100.

Graf, P., and Mandler, G. (1984). Activation makes words more accessible, but not necessarily more retrievable. *Journal of Verbal Learning and Verbal Behavior, 23*, 553–568.

Graf, P., Squire, L. R., and Mandler, G. (1984). The information that amnesic patients do not forget. *Journal of Experimental Psychology: Learning, Memory, and Cognition, 10*, 164–178.

Hinton, G. E. (1981). Implementing semantic networks in parallel hardware. In G. E. Hinton and J. A. Anderson (Eds.), *Parallel models of associative memory*, 161–187. Hillsdale, NJ: Erlbaum.

Hinton, G. E. (1990). Mapping part-whole hierarchies into connectionist networks. *Artificial Intelligence, 46*, 47–75.

Hobson, J. A. (1988). *The dreaming brain*. New York: Basic Books.

Hobson, J. A., Hoffman, S. A., Helfand, R., and Kostner, D. (1987). Dream bizarreness and the activation-synthesis hypothesis. *Human Neurobiology, 6*, 157–164.

Jacoby, L. L., and Dallas, M. (1981). On the relationship between autobiographical memory and perceptual learning. *Journal of Experimental Psychology: General, 110*, 306–340.

Kahneman, D., and Treisman, A. (1984). Changing views of attention and automaticity. In R. Parasuraman and D. R. Davies (Eds.), *Varieties of attention*, 29–61. New York: Academic Press.

Kaplan, C. A. (1989). *Hatching a theory of incubation: Does putting a problem aside really help? If so, why?* Unpublished doctoral dissertation, Carnegie-Mellon University.

Kintsch, W. (1970). Models for free recall and recognition. In D. A. Norman (Ed.), *Models of human memory*, 331–373. New York: Academic Press.

Klein, S. B., Loftus, J., Kihlstrom, J. F., and Aseron, R. (1989). Effects of item-specific and relational information on hypermnesic recall. *Journal of Experimental Psychology: Learning, Memory, and Cognition, 15,* 1192–1197.

Koriat, A., and Feuerstein, N. (1976). The recovery of incidentally acquired information. *Acta Psychologica, 40,* 463–474.

Madigan, S., and O'Hara, R. (1992). Initial recall, reminiscence, and hypermnesia. *Journal of Experimental Psychology: Learning, Memory, and Cognition, 18,* 421–425.

Mandler, G. (1967). Organization and memory. In K. W. Spence and J. T. Spence (Eds.), *The psychology of learning and motivation: Advances in research and theory*, vol. 1, 328–372. New York: Academic Press.

Mandler, G. (1977). Commentary on "Organization and memory." In G. H. Bower (Ed.), *Human memory: Basic processes*, 297–308. New York: Academic Press.

Mandler, G. (1979). Organization and repetition: Organizational principles with special reference to rote learning. In L.-G. Nilsson (Ed.), *Perspectives on memory research*, 293–327. Hillsdale, NJ: Erlbaum.

Mandler, G. (1980). Recognizing: The judgment of previous occurrence. *Psychological Review, 87,* 252–271.

Mandler, G. (1982). The integration and elaboration of memory structures. In F. Klix, J. Hoffmann, and E. van der Meer (Eds.), *Cognitive research in psychology*. Amsterdam: North-Holland.

Mandler, G. (1984). *Mind and body: Psychology of emotion and stress*. New York: Norton.

Mandler, G. (1985). *Cognitive psychology: An essay in cognitive science*. Hillsdale, NJ: Erlbaum.

Mandler, G. (1989). Memory: Conscious and unconscious. In P. R. Solomon, G. R. Goethals, C. M. Kelley, and B. R. Stephens (Eds.), *Memory: Interdisciplinary approaches*, 84–106. New York: Springer-Verlag.

Mandler, G. (1991). Your face looks familiar but I can't remember your name: A review of dual process theory. In W. E. Hockley and S. Lewandowsky (Eds.), *Relating theory and data: Essays on human memory in honor of Bennet B. Murdock*, 207–225. Hillsdale, NJ: Erlbaum.

Mandler, G. (1992). Toward a theory of consciousness. In H.-G. Geissler, S. W. Link, and J. T. Townsend (Eds.), *Cognition, information processing, and psychophysics: Basic issues*, 43–65. Hillsdale, NJ: Erlbaum.

Mandler, G., and Graesser, A. (1976). Analyse dimensionelle et le "locus" de l'organisation. In S. Ehrlich and E. Tulving (Eds.), *La mémoire sémantique*, 198–205. Paris: Bulletin de Psychologie.

Mandler, G., Pearlstone, Z., and Koopmans, H. J. (1969). Effects of organization and semantic similarity on recall and recognition. *Journal of Verbal Learning and Verbal Behavior, 8,* 410–423.

Mandler, G., Worden, P. E., and Graesser, A. C. II. (1974). Subjective disorganization: Search for the locus of list organization. *Journal of Verbal Learning and Verbal Behavior, 13,* 220–235.

Marcel, A. J. (1983a). Conscious and unconscious perception: Experiments on visual masking and word recognition. *Cognitive Psychology, 15,* 197–237.

Marcel, A. J. (1983b). Conscious and unconscious perception: An approach to the relations between phenomenal experience and perceptual processes. *Cognitive Psychology, 15,* 238–300.

Martin, L. L., and Tesser, A. (1989). Toward a motivational and structural theory of ruminative thought. In J. S. Uleman and J. A. Bargh (Eds.), *Unintended thought.* New York: Guilford Press.

Maury, L.-F.-A. (1878). *Le sommeil et les rêves.* 4th ed. Paris: Didier.

Meyer, D. E., and Schvaneveldt, R. W. (1971). Facilitation in recognizing pairs of words: Evidence of a dependence between retrieval operations. *Journal of Experimental Psychology, 90,* 227–234.

Meyer, D. E., and Schvaneveldt, R. W. (1976). Meaning, memory structure, and mental process. In C. N. Cofer (Ed.), *The structure of human memory.* San Francisco: Freeman.

Nakamura, Y. (1989). *Explorations in implicit perceptual processing: Studies of preconscious information processing.* Unpublished doctoral dissertation, University of California, San Diego.

Nelson, J. I. (1974). Motion sensitivity in peripheral vision. *Perception, 3,* 151–152.

Overson, C., and Mandler, G. (1987). Indirect word priming in connected semantic and phonological contexts. *Bulletin of the Psychonomic Society, 25,* 229–232.

Paivio, A. (1976). Imagery in recall and recognition. In J. Brown (Ed.), *Recall and recognition,* 103–129. New York: Wiley.

Paul, I. H., and Fisher, C. (1959). Subliminal visual stimulation: A study of its influence on subsequent images and dreams. *Journal of Nervous and Mental Diseases, 129,* 315–340.

Payne, D. G. (1986). Hypermnesia for pictures and words: Testing the recall level hypothesis. *Journal of Experimental Psychology: Learning, Memory, and Cognition, 12,* 16–29.

Payne, D. G. (1987). Hypermnesia and reminiscence in recall: A historical and empirical review. *Psychological Bulletin, 101,* 5–27.

Perruchet, P., and Pacteau, C. (1990). Synthetic grammar learning: Implicit rule abstraction or explicit fragmentary knowledge? *Journal of Experimental Psychology: General, 119,* 264–275.

Pine, F. (1964). The bearing of psychoanalytic theory on selected issues in research on marginal stimuli. *Journal of Nervous and Mental Diseases, 138,* 68–75.

Posner, M. I. (1973). *Cognition: An introduction.* Glenview, IL: Scott, Foresman.

Raaijmakers, J. G. W., and Shiffrin, R. M. (1980). SAM: A theory of probabilistic search of associative memory. In G. H. Bower (Ed.), *The psychology of learning and motivation: Advances in research and theory,* vol. 14. New York: Academic Press.

Rabinowitz, J. C., Mandler, G., and Barsalou, L. W. (1979). Generation-recognition as an auxiliary retrieval strategy. *Journal of Verbal Learning and Verbal Behavior, 18,* 57–72.

Rabinowitz, J. C., Mandler, G., and Patterson, K. E. (1977). Determinants of recognition and recall: Accessibility and generation. *Journal of Experimental Psychology: General, 106,* 302–329.

Rabinowitz, M., and Mandler, J. M. (1983). Organization and information retrieval. *Journal of Experimental Psychology: Learning, Memory, and Cognition, 9,* 430–439.

Rappold, V. A., and Hashtroudi. S. (1991). Does organization improve priming? *Journal of Experimental Psychology: Learning, Memory, and Cognition, 17,* 103–114.

Reason, J. T., and Lucas, D. (1984). Using cognitive diaries to investigate naturally occurring memory blocks. In J. E. Harris and P. E. Morris (Eds.), *Every memory, actions and absentimindedness,* 53–69. San Diego, CA: Academic Press.

Reber, A. S., Kassin, S. M., Lewis, S., and Cantor, G. (1980). On the relationship between implicit and explicit modes in the learning of a complex rule structure. *Journal of Experimental Psychology: Human Learning and Memory, 6,* 492–502.

Robert, W. (1886). *Der Traum als Naturnotwendigkeit erklärt*. Hamburg: H. Seippel.

Roediger, H. L. III. (1982). Hypermnesia: The importance of recall time and asymptotic level of recall. *Journal of Verbal Learning and Verbal Behavior, 21*, 662–665.

Roediger, H. L. III, and Challis, B. H. (1989). Hypermnesia: Improvements in recall with repeated testing. In C. Izawa (Ed.), *Current issues in cognitive processes: The Tulane Floweree Symposium on cognition*, 175–199. Hillsdale, NJ: Erlbaum.

Roediger, H. L. III, and Payne, D. G. (1982). Hypermnesia: The role of repeated testing. *Journal of Experimental Psychology: Learning, Memory, and Cognition, 8*, 66–72.

Roediger, H. L. III, Payne, D. G., Gillespie, G. L., and Lean, D. S. (1982). Hypermnesia as determined by level of recall. *Journal of Verbal Learning and Verbal Behavior, 21*, 635–655.

Roediger, H. L. III, and Thorpe, L. A. (1978). The role of recall time in producing hypermnesia *Memory and Cognition, 6*, 296–305.

Rumelhart, D. E., and McClelland, J. L. (1982). An interactive activation model of context effects in letter perception: Part 2. The contextual enhancement effect and some tests and extensions of the model. *Psychological Review, 89*, 60–94.

Sawyers, B. K. (1975). *Category and item retrieval from memory*. Unpublished doctoral dissertation, University of California, San Diego.

Schooler, J. W., and Engstler-Schooler, T. Y. (1990). Verbal overshadowing of visual memories: Some things are better left unsaid. *Cognitive Psychology, 22*, 36–71.

Schooler, J. W., Ohlsson, S., and Brooks, K. (1993). Thoughts beyond words: When language overshadows insight. *Journal of Experimental Psychology: General, 122*, 166–183.

Schwartz, B., and Reisberg, D. (1991). *Learning and memory*. New York: W. W. Norton.

Searle, J. R. (1983). *Intentionality*. New York: Cambridge University Press.

Smith, S. M., and Blankenship, S. E. (1989). Incubation effects. *Bulletin of the Psychonomic Society, 27*, 311–314.

Smith, S. M., and Blankenship, S. E. (1991). Incubation and the persistence of fixation in problem solving. *American Journal of Psychology, 104*, 61–87.

Smith, S. M., and Vela, E. (1991). Incubated reminiscence effects. *Memory and Cognition, 19*, 168–176.

Spence, D. P., and Holland, B. (1962). The restricting effects of awareness: A paradox and an explanation. *Journal of Abnormal and Social Psychology, 64*, 163–174.

Tulving, E. (1962). Subjective organization in free recall of "unrelated" words. *Psychological Review, 69*, 344–354.

Tulving, E., and Pearlstone, Z. (1966). Availability versus accessibility of information in memory for words. *Journal of Verbal Learning and Verbal Behavior, 5*, 381–391.

Uleman, J. S., and Bargh, J. A. (1989). *Unintended thought*. New York: Guilford Press.

Wallas, G. (1926). *The art of thought*. New York: Harcourt, Brace.

Warrington, E. K., and Weiskrantz, L. (1970). Amnesia: Consolidation or retrieval? *Nature, 228*, 628–630.

Warrington, E. K., and Weiskrantz, L. (1974). The effect of prior learning on subsequent retention in amnesic patients. *Neuropsychologia, 12*, 419–428.

Watts, A. W. (1957). *The way of Zen*. New York: Pantheon Books.

Weiskrantz, L. (1986). *Blindsight: A case study and implications*. Oxford: Clarendon Press.

Wilson, T. D., and Schooler, J. W. (1991). Thinking too much: Introspection can reduce the quality of preferences and decisions. *Journal of Personality and Social Psychology, 60,* 181–192.

Woodworth, R. S. (1938). *Experimental psychology.* New York: Holt.

Yaniv, I., and Meyer, D. E. (1987). Activation and metacognition of inaccessible stored information: Potential bases for incubation effects in problem solving. *Journal of Experimental Psychology: Learning, Memory, and Cognition, 13,* 187–205.

# II Visual Processes

# 2   Visual Perception and Visual Awareness after Brain Damage: A Tutorial Overview

Martha J. Farah

ABSTRACT   In recent years, neuropsychologists have documented several syndromes in which visual perception and awareness of perception appear to be dissociated. These include blindsight, covert recognition of faces in prosopagnosia, unconscious perception of extinguished or neglected stimuli, and implicit reading in pure alexia. The general goal of this tutorial is to elucidate the implications of these syndromes for the neural correlates of visual awareness. In the first section, a general scheme is presented for classifying the different explanations that have been proposed for perception/awareness dissociations. The three general types of explanation are privileged role accounts, in which only certain privileged brain systems play a role in mediating conscious awareness; integration accounts, in which conscious awareness requires the integration of activity across different brain systems; and quality of representation accounts, in which conscious awareness requires a relatively higher quality of perceptual representation than do many types of perceptual performance. In the next four sections, I focus on each of the syndromes in turn, reviewing representative findings, laying out the different proposed accounts of the findings, and weighing these accounts against the available evidence. In the final section, I discuss the broader implications of these syndromes. I conclude that they are probably a heterogeneous set of phenomena, and unlikely to be explainable by a single common type of account. The existence of brain systems whose primary role is to mediate conscious awareness is discussed, and found lacking in empirical support. Finally, I emphasize the need for more empirical investigation, aimed at distinguishing among the currently viable explanations of the four syndromes.

## 2.1   INTRODUCTION AND GOALS

Perception and awareness of perception are normally inextricably related. Most people would say that one has not perceived something if one is not consciously aware of that thing. Yet recent findings in neuropsychology are forcing us to revise this notion of the relation between perception and conscious awareness. Brain-damaged people may manifest considerable knowledge of stimuli, or of particular properties of stimuli, of which they deny any conscious perceptual experience. Although these findings challenge the intuitive idea that part and parcel of perceiving something is being aware of it, they also offer an empirical means of understanding the relations between the neural systems underlying perception and conscious awareness.

Four neuropsychological syndromes involving apparent dissociations between vision and awareness of vision have been documented in some detail: blindsight, covert recognition of faces in prosopagnosia, unconscious perception of extinguished or neglected stimuli, and implicit reading in pure alexia. Although any one of these syndromes could, on its own, be the topic of a whole chapter or even a whole book, I will consider each one in much less detail here. Rather than provide exhaustive reviews, my goals for this tutorial are to review representative findings about each syndrome, to lay out the different possible mechanistic explanations of each of the dissociations in patient performance, to consider the implications of each of the mechanistic accounts for the relation between conscious awareness and neural information processing, to weigh the different accounts against the available evidence, to examine the relations among the different syndromes, and to consider the broader implications of these findings for the functional and neural systems underlying conscious awareness.

## 2.2 BRAIN MECHANISMS AND CONSCIOUS AWARENESS: WHAT KIND OF RELATION?

Before proceeding towards these goals, I will offer a general framework for discussing the different ways in which conscious awareness has been related to brain states in neuropsychology. I will distinguish between three broad types of accounts.

### Consciousness as the Privileged Role of Particular Brain Systems

The most straightforward account of the relation between consciousness and the brain is to conceive of particular brain systems as mediating conscious awareness. The great-grandfather of this type of account is Descartes' theory of mind-body interaction through the pineal gland. Patterns of brain activity impinging on the pineal gland, unlike patterns of activity in other parts of the brain, were consciously experienced. The most direct and influential descendant of this tradition is the DICE (dissociated interactions and conscious experience) model of Schacter, McAndrews, and Moscovitch (1988) (fig. 2.1). Although they do not propose a localization for the conscious awareness system (CAS), their account does suppose that there is some brain system or systems, the CAS, separate from the brain systems concerned with perception, cognition, and action, whose activity is necessary only for conscious experience. Within this framework, unconscious perception can be explained very simply in terms of a disconnection between perceptual systems and the CAS.

The brain systems that play a privileged role in mediating conscious awareness could also carry out other functions as well. For example, Gazzaniga (1988) attributes many of the differences between what one would call conscious and unconscious behavior to the involvement of left hemisphere interpretive mechanisms, closely related to speech. Thus, unconscious perception could be explained as the failure of a perceptual representation to access critical areas of the left hemisphere. For brevity, this first class of accounts will be referred to as *privileged role* accounts, because only certain systems play a role in mediating conscious awareness.

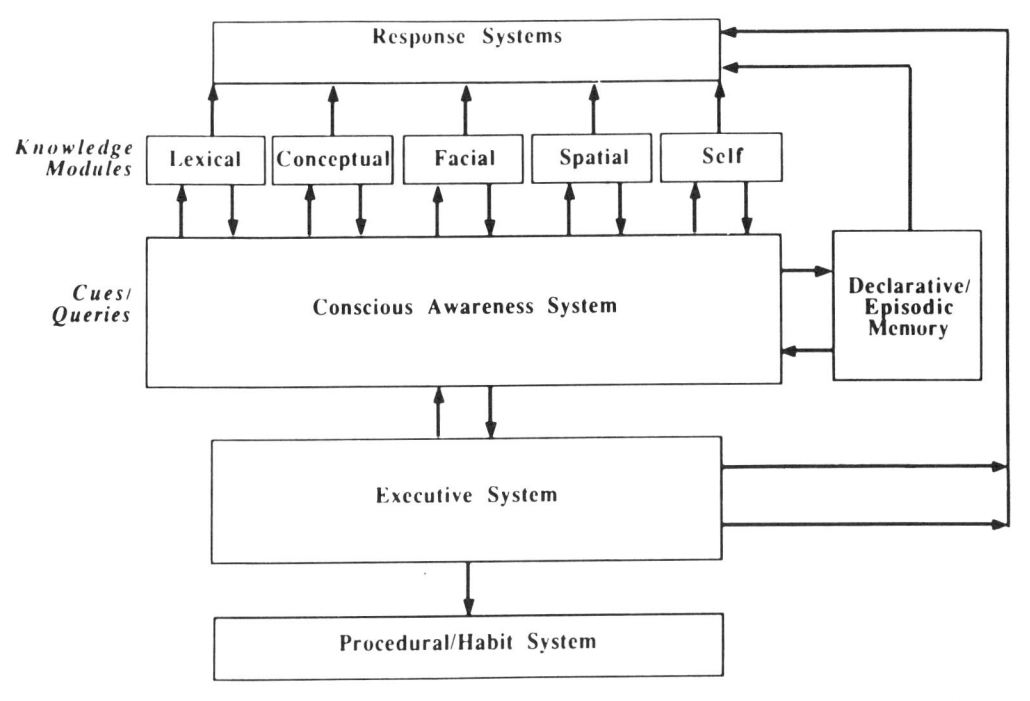

**Figure 2.1** The DICE (dissociated interactions and conscious experience) model of Schacter, McAndrews, and Moscovitch (1988).

## Consciousness as a State of Integration among Distinct Brain Systems

In contrast, the next two types of approach attempt to explain the relations between conscious and unconscious information processing in terms of the dynamic states of brain systems rather than in terms of the enduring roles of particular brain systems themselves. Kinsbourne's (1988) integrated field theory will be taken as the index case of the approach that emphasizes integration as the underlying basis of conscious awareness. According to Kinsbourne, conscious awareness is a brain state in which the various modality-specific perceptions, recollections, current actions, and action plans are mutually consistent. Normally, the interactions among these disparate brain systems automatically bring the ensemble into an integrated state, continually updated to reflect the current information available in all parts of the brain. However, anatomical disconnection can prevent integration, as in split-brain patients who may have two separate awarenesses, or damage to one system may weaken its influence on the global brain state, thus preventing it from updating the contents of awareness, as in neglect patients who remain unaware of stimuli in their neglected hemifield. Thus, unconscious perception could be explained by either disconnection of or damage to the perceptual system, preventing it from participating in the integrated patterns of activity over the rest of the brain.

Related accounts have been proposed by Crick and Koch (1990) and by Damasio (1990). Crick and Koch limit themselves to the issue of visual awareness and equate this phenomenon with the binding together of the different, separately represented visual properties of a stimulus (e.g., color, shape, depth, motion) into a single integrated percept. They call upon the work of Singer and colleagues (Gray and Singer 1989; Singer, chap. 3, this volume), who found synchronization of the oscillations of neuronal activity within visual cortex for different parts of the same representation of a stimulus. Such synchrony provides an attractive solution to the so-called binding problem, which arises when multiple objects are present and the features of different objects must be distinguished. For example, if color and orientation were separately represented features, then without some way to "bind" the features of an object, a red vertical bar and a green horizontal bar would be indistinguishable from a red horizontal and a green vertical bar. Crick and Koch suggest that synchronization across visual areas could enable both binding and conscious awareness of stimuli. Damasio has proposed a similar identification of binding with conscious awareness. The type of binding he discusses operates across different modality-specific representations of an object rather than within the visual system, as in Crick and Koch's account. In the remainder of the chapter, accounts of this second type will be referred to as *integration* accounts.

**Consciousness as a Graded Property of Neural Information Processing**

Information representation in neural networks is not all or none, such that a stimulus must either be represented within the visual system or not. Rather, it may be partially represented, as a result of either impoverished input or damage to the network itself. The third view of the relation between brain mechanisms and conscious awareness is based on the observation that, in normal and in brain-damaged subjects, there is a correlation between the "quality" of the perceptual representation and the likelihood of conscious awareness. Experiments on subliminal perception in normal subjects invariably dissociate perception and awareness by using very brief, masked stimulus presentations, by dividing attention, or by embedding the stimulus to be perceived in a high level of noise. In other words, to reduce the likelihood of conscious awareness in normal subjects, one must use experimental manipulations known to degrade the quality of the perceptual representation. Similarly, one could argue that in many, if not all, of the neuropsychological syndromes in which visual perception has been dissociated from conscious awareness, patients' visual performance reflects a degree of impairment in visual perception per se, not merely the stripping away of conscious experience from a normal percept (Farah, Monheit, and Wallace 1991; Farah, O'Reilly, and Vecera 1993; Wallace and Farah 1992). Consciousness may be associated only with the higher-quality end of the continuum of degrees of representation. This type of account will be referred to as a *quality of representation* account.

These different types of explanation are not necessarily mutually exclusive. For example, if a particular part of the brain were needed to enable the activity of widespread regions to become integrated, there would be a sense in which both the first type of explanation and the second were correct. Alternatively, if a representation in one part of the brain were degraded, it might be less able to participate in an integrated state with other parts of the brain, in which case both the second and third types of explanation would be correct. Nevertheless, many of the explanations to be considered in this chapter exemplify just one of these categories, and the proposed three-category framework helps make clear the relations among the different explanations to be considered, even in the hybrid cases.

Finally, it should be noted explicitly what these three types of approach cannot explain and are not intended to explain. None of these accounts offers any insight into the question of what consciousness is, above and beyond its hypothesized dependence on a certain brain system, or state of integration, or quality of representation. Nor do they tell us why a certain brain system, state of integration, or quality of representation should be necessary for consciousness. Nevertheless, they are not vacuous or question begging. Although they do not answer metaphysical questions about consciousness, they are substantive claims about the neural correlates of conscious experience.

## 2.3  BLINDSIGHT

Blindsight refers to the preserved visual abilities of patients with damage to primary visual cortex, for stimuli presented in regions of the visual field formerly represented by the damaged cortex. The first documentation of this phenomenon was made by Poppel, Held, and Frost (1973), who found that patients with large scotomata could move their eyes to the location of a light flash presented in the scotomatous region of their visual field. Although the eye movements were not highly accurate, they were better than would be expected by chance and were not accompanied by any conscious visual experience according to patients' reports.

**Representative Findings**

Shortly after this initial report, Weiskrantz and his colleagues undertook extensive and rigorous investigations of what they termed "blindsight" (Weiskrantz, Sanders, and Marshall 1974; Weiskrantz 1986). They were able to demonstrate a much greater degree of preserved visual function in some of their subjects than in the initial series. Case D.B., in particular, was the subject of many investigations in which the abilities to point to stimulus locations, to detect movement, to discriminate the orientation of lines and gratings, and to discriminate shapes such as X's and O's were found to be remarkably preserved. Figure 2.2 shows the results of an early study of localization by pointing in this patient. Over subsequent years, a number of different patients with blindsight have been studied in different laboratories (Weiskrantz 1990). The pattern of preserved and impaired abilities has been found to vary considerably from case to case. Detection and localization of light and detection of

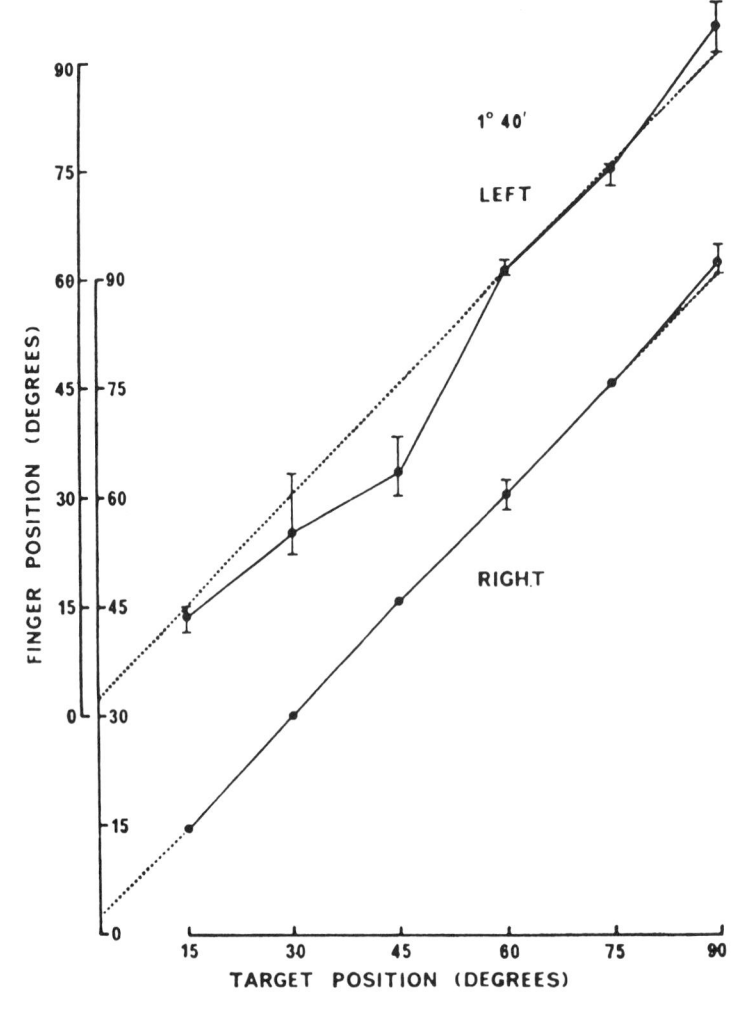

**Figure 2.2** Average finger-reaching responses to targets at different positions in left (blind) and right visual field for case D.B. Bars show range of responses. From Weiskrantz et al. (1974).

motion are invariably preserved to some degree. In addition, many patients can discriminate orientation, shape, direction of movement, and flicker. Color vision mechanisms appear to be preserved in some cases, as indicated by Stoerig and Cowey's (1990) findings (fig. 2.3). Normal subjects show a characteristic profile of spectral sensitivity, that is, different intensity thresholds for detection of light of different wavelengths. Although subjects with blindsight showed overall higher thresholds for above-chance detection, their spectral sensitivity functions had the same shape, indicating preserved functioning of opponent-process color mechanisms, despite no conscious awareness of color (or even light) perception.

An interesting new source of data on blindsight comes from the use of indirect measures of the subject's visual information processing capabilities in the blind field. Marzi et al. (1986) showed that subjects with blindsight, like

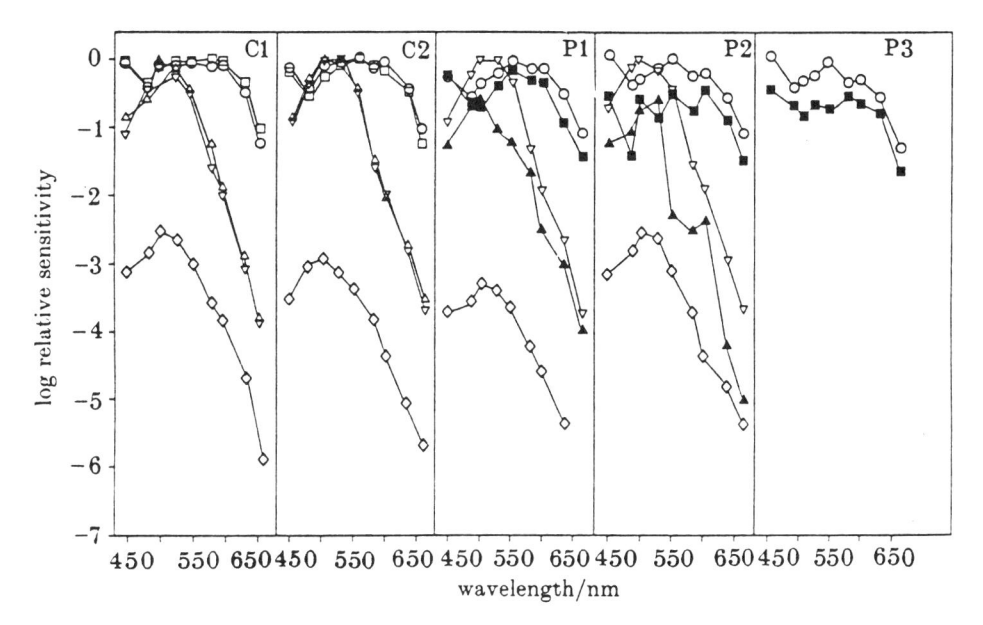

**Figure 2.3** Relative spectral sensitivity of normal subjects (C) and patients with blindsight (P). From Stoerig and Cowey (1990).

normal subjects, respond more quickly in a simple reaction time task when there are two stimuli instead of one and that this is true even when the second stimulus falls in the blind field. Rafal et al. (1990) studied the effects of a second stimulus in the blind field on the speed with which hemianopic subjects could make a saccade to a stimulus in their normal field. With their task, a second stimulus was found to inhibit the saccade. Like the facilitation of manual reaction time found by Marzi et al., this inhibition shows that the stimulus was perceived, in that it influenced performance. Significantly, Rafal et al. found this effect only when the second stimulus was presented to the temporal half of the retina, that is, to the half of the retina that projects to the superior colliculus. The projections from the retina to the cortical visual system are symmetrical, with equal connectivity between each hemiretina and the lateral geniculate nucleus (LGN).

**Awareness of Perception**

Just as the particular set of visual abilities and level of performance vary from patient to patient, so does the nature of patients' subjective report. Some subjects claim to be guessing on the basis of no subjective sense whatsoever. These include the subjects whose highly systematic data are shown in figures 2.2 and 2.3. In other studies, patients report some "feeling" that guides their responses, but the feeling is not described as specifically visual in nature. For example, patients will state that they felt the onset of a stimulus or felt it to be in a certain location. Shape discriminations between circles and crosses are made on the basis of "jagged" versus "smooth" feelings, which are nevertheless not subjectively visual. Some subjects may occasionally report specifically visual sensations, such as "dark shadows," particularly for very intense or salient stimuli. In his 1986 book, Weiskrantz includes descriptions of the subjective reports of his subjects, as well as the objective data collected from them in a variety of studies.

**Explanations of Blindsight**

The mechanism of blindsight has been a controversial topic. Some researchers have argued that the phenomenon is mediated, directly or indirectly, by residual functioning of primary visual cortex and should therefore be considered an artifact. Even for researchers who reject the artifact explanation, the mechanism of blindsight has not been settled decisively, and there remain at least two different types of account.

Campion, Latto, and Smith (1983) presented the most comprehensive and influential critique of blindsight, alleging that it is no different from normal vision in being mediated by primary visual cortex, either indirectly, by light from the scotomatous region of the visual field reflecting off other surfaces into regions of the visual field represented by intact primary visual cortex, or directly, by residual functioning of lesioned areas of primary visual cortex. The latter idea is an example of a quality of representation account. They supported their arguments with experiments involving both hemianopic subjects, whose blindsight performance was correlated with conscious awareness, and normal subjects, presenting stimuli to the natural blind spot and assessing the degree to which scattered light was sufficient for various visual judgments. More recently, Fendrich, Wessinger, and Gazzaniga (1992) showed that what appeared to be a small island of functional primary visual cortex in one subject could support above-chance detection and even shape discrimination, despite the subject's belief that he was guessing in these tasks. The hypothesis of primary visual cortex mediation of blindsight meets several difficulties in accounting for the totality of the empirical data now available on blindsight. For example, it is difficult to see how scattered light would enable case D.B. to perceive black figures on a bright background or how this account could explain the qualitative differences in his performance within his natural blind spot and his aquired blind region. Unlike Fendrich et al.'s subject, the blindsight performance of most subjects is not sharply limited to a small patch of the blind field. Residual functioning of spared cortex is clearly not a possibility for hemidecorticate subjects, and yet they too show a wide range of blindsight abilities. Finally, recall the results of Rafal et al. (1990) on inhibition of saccades by stimuli presented to the blind field. This result has the important property of demonstrating subcortical mediation of blindsight by a positive finding, nasal-temporal asymmetries, rather than by the negation of possibilities for primary visual cortex involvement. Although it is possible that some of the abilities classified in some patients as blindsight do derive from spared striate cortex, the available data seem to suggest that additional mechanisms play an important role too.

Other than spared primary visual cortex, what other neural systems might mediate the preserved abilities in blindsight? Initially, the answer was thought to be the so-called subcortical visual system, which consists of projections from the retina to the superior colliculus, and on to the pulvinar and cortical visual areas. This is an instance of a privileged role account, in that both cortical and subcortical visual systems are hypothesized to mediate various types of visual information processing but the mediation of visual awareness is taken to be the privileged role of the cortical visual system. Although it might at first seem puzzling that both visual systems mediate vision but only one mediates awareness thereof, the puzzle may be more apparent than real. There is, after all, much neural information processing that operates outside the realm of conscious awareness—for example, body temperature regulation. According to the hypothesis of subcortical mediation of blindsight, at least some of the neural information processing of visual representations also operates without conscious awareness. Perhaps the reason this seems strange at first, and in fact engendered such extreme skepticism in some quarters, is that we use the phrase "visual perception" in two ways: to process representations of visual stimuli within our nervous systems and to become aware of visually transduced stimuli. According to the subcortical mediation hypothesis, both visual systems mediate visual perception in the first sense, whereas only the cortical visual system mediates visual perception in the second sense.

There is evidence in favor of the subcortical mediation hypothesis for at least some blindsight abilities. The close functional similarities between the known specializations of the subcortical visual system and many of the preserved abilities in blindsight, such as detection and localization of onsets and moving stimuli (Schiller and Koerner 1971), constitute one source of evidence. In addition, the nasal-temporal asymmetries found in Rafal et al.'s (1990) study are indicative of collicular mediation.

Recently, however, Cowey and Stoerig (1989) have suggested that the so-called cortical visual system, which projects from the retina to cortex by way of the LGN, may also contribute to blindsight. They marshaled evidence, from their own experiments and other research, of a population of cells in the LGN that project directly to extrastriate visual cortex and could therefore bring stimulus information into such areas as V4 and MT in the absence of primary visual cortex. This type of mechanism fits most naturally with the quality of representation hypotheses. According to this account, many of the same visual association areas are engaged in blindsight as in normal vision. What distinguishes normal vision and visual performance without awareness is that in the latter, only a subset of the normal inputs arrives in extrastriate visual cortex. The remaining inputs are both fewer in number and lacking whatever type of processing is normally accomplished in primary visual cortex. Consciousness of the functioning of extrastriate visual areas may occur only when these areas are operating on more complete and more fully processed visual representations. Evidence for this hypothesis is still preliminary. Although the anatomical connections between the LGN and the extrastriate visual areas have been shown to exist, their functional significance in blindsight has not been fully established. A systematic comparison between the blindsight abilities of patients with circumscribed striate lesions and with hemidecortication (which removes extrastriate visual areas as well) should reveal the functional role of the LGN-to-extrastriate projections in blindsight.

In sum, although some dissociations between visual performance and subjective awareness may be mediated by spared primary visual cortex, it seems fairly clear that the range of abilities documented in blindsight does not result from degraded normal vision (where "normal" means relying on primary visual cortex). It is also clearly not a single homogeneous phenomenon. At the level of preserved visual abilities, subjective experience, and neural mechanisms, there is apparently much variation from subject to subject. An important research goal in this area would be to establish correspondences among these three levels of individual difference as a means of characterizing the functional and experiential roles of different components of the visual system. In the meantime, we can discern two main types of mechanism that may account for the dissociations between visual abilities and conscious awareness in blindsight: subcortical visual mechanisms and direct projections from the LGN to extrastriate areas.

## 2.4 COVERT RECOGNITION OF FACES IN PROSOPAGNOSIA

Prosopagnosia is an impairment of face recognition following brain damage, which can occur relatively independently of impairments in object recognition and is not caused by impairments in lower-level vision or memory. In some cases of prosopagnosia, there is a dramatic dissociation between the loss of face recognition ability as measured by standard tests of face recognition, as well as patients' own introspections, and the apparent preservation of face recognition when tested by certain indirect tests.

### Representative Findings

Covert recognition in prosopagnosia has been demonstrated using psychophysiological measures such as skin conductance response (SCR) and indirect behavioral measures. In the first clear demonstration of covert recognition, Bauer (1984) presented a prosopagnosic patient with a series of photographs of familiar faces. While viewing each face, the patient heard a list of names read aloud, one of them the name of the person in the photograph. For normal subjects, the SCR is greatest to the name belonging to the pictured person. Bauer found that although the prosopagnosic patient's SCRs to names were not as strongly correlated with the names as a normal subject's would be, they were nevertheless significantly correlated. In contrast, the patient performed at chance levels when asked to select the correct name for each face. In a different use of the SCR measure, Tranel and Damasio (1985) and Tranel, Damasio, and Damasio (1988) showed that prosopagnosic patients had larger SCRs to familiar faces than to unfamiliar faces, although their overt ratings of familiarity versus unfamiliarity did not reliably discriminate between the two.

Bruyer et al. (1983) pioneered the use of a paired-associate face-name relearning task as a way of demonstrating covert recognition in prosopagnosia. Their patient was asked to learn to associate the facial photographs of famous people with the names of famous people. When the pairing of names and faces was correct, the patient required fewer learning trials than when it was incorrect, suggesting that the patient did possess some knowledge of the people's facial appearance. Unfortunately, this demonstration of covert recognition is not as meaningful as it could be, because the subject was only mildly prosopagnosic. However, several more severe prosopagnosic patients have recently been tested in the face-name relearning task, and some have shown the same pattern of faster learning of correct than incorrect face-name associations, despite little or no success at the overt recognition of the same faces. For example, De Haan, Young, and Newcombe (1987b) documented consistently faster learning of face-name and face-occupation pairings in their prosopagnosic subject, even when the stimulus faces were selected from among those that the patient had been unable to identify in a preexperiment stimulus screening test.

Evidence of covert recognition has also come from reaction time tasks in which the familiarity or identity of faces is found to influence processing time. In a visual identity match task with simultaneously presented pairs of faces, de Haan, Young, and Newcombe (1987b) found that a prosopagnosic patient was faster at matching pairs of previously familiar faces than unfamiliar faces, as is true of normal subjects. In contrast, he was unable to name any of the previously familiar faces.

In another reaction time (RT) study, De Haan, Young, and Newcombe (1987b; also see 1987a) found evidence that photographs of faces could evoke covert semantic knowledge of the depicted person, despite the inability of the prosopagnosic patient to report such information about the person when tested overtly. Their task was to categorize a printed name as belonging to an actor or a politician as quickly as possible. On some trials an irrelevant (i.e., to be ignored) photograph of an actor's or politician's face was simultaneously presented (fig. 2.4). Normal subjects are slower to categorize the names when the faces come from a different occupation category relative to a no-photograph baseline. Although their prosopagnosic patient was severely impaired at categorizing the faces overtly as belonging to actors or politicians, he showed the same pattern of interference from different-category faces.

A related finding was reported by Young, Hellawell, and De Haan (1988) in a task involving the categorization of names as famous or nonfamous. Both normal subjects and a prosopagnosic patient showed faster RTs to the famous names when the name was preceded by a picture of a semantically related face (e.g., the name "Diana Spencer" preceded by a picture of Prince Charles) than by an unfamiliar or an unrelated face. Furthermore, the same experiment was carried out with printed names as the priming stimulus, so that the size of the priming effect with faces and names could be compared. The prosopagnosic patient's priming effect from faces was not significantly different from the priming effect from names. However, the patient was able to name only two of the twenty face prime stimuli used.

**Figure 2.4** Examples of stimuli from De Haan, Young, and Newcombe's (1987a) study. The name of the politician is presented with his own face (top), with the face of another politician, Peter Walker (middle), or with the face of a nonpolitician, Michael Aspel (bottom).

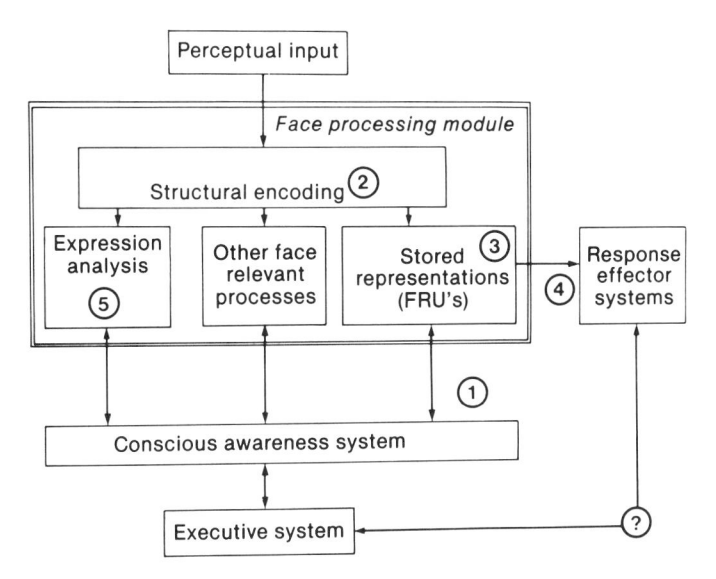

**Figure 2.5** Functional architecture of face recognition and awareness. Covert face recognition is attributed to a lesion at location 1. From De Haan, Bauer, and Greve (1992).

### Awareness of Perception

Prosopagnosic patients who manifest covert recognition appear to lack the subjective experience of recognition, at least for many of the faces for which they show covert recognition. These patients may occasionally recognize a face overtly, that is, assign it the correct name and express a degree of confidence that they know who the person is. However, this happens rarely, and the dissociation between covert recognition and awareness of recognition holds for many faces that they fail to identify and for which they report no sense of familiarity.

### Explanations of Covert Face Recognition

Several competing explanations have been offered for the dissociation between overt and covert recognition of faces in prosopagnosia. The oldest, and still predominant, explanation is that the face recognition system is intact in these patients but has been prevented from conveying information to other brain mechanisms necessary for conscious awareness. In one of the earliest reports of the dissociation, De Haan, Young, and Newcombe (1987a) described their subject's prosopagnosia as involving a "loss of awareness of the products of the recognition system rather than ... a breakdown in the recognition system per se." Perhaps the most explicit and general statement of this view was made recently by De Haan, Bauer, and Greve (1992), who proposed the model shown in figure 2.5. According to their model, the face-specific visual and mnemonic processing of a face (carried out within the "face processing module") proceeds normally in covert recognition, but the results of

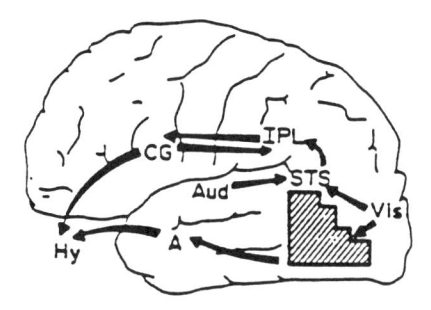

Figure 2.6  Diagram of the two hypothesized face recognition pathways. From Bauer (1984).

this process cannot access the "conscious awareness system" because of a lesion at location 1. This account clearly falls into the privileged role category; it entails a specific brain system needed for conscious awareness, separate from the brain systems needed to carry out perception and cognition. Indeed these authors cite the DICE model as an important source of inspiration for their model.

A second type of explanation was put forth by Bauer (1984), who suggested that there may be two neural systems capable of face recognition, only one of which is associated with conscious awareness. According to Bauer, the ventral cortical visual areas, which are damaged in prosopagnosic patients, are the location of normal conscious face recognition. The dorsal visual areas are hypothesized to be capable of face recognition as well, although they do not mediate conscious recognition but, instead, affective responses to faces. Covert recognition is explained as the isolated functioning of the dorsal face system, as diagrammed in figure 2.6. Like the account depicted in figure 2.5, this account also fits into the general category of consciousness as a privileged property of particular brain systems. However, this account does not feature a neural system whose primary function is to enable conscious awareness, like the "conscious awareness system" of DICE and figure 2.3. Rather, this account is more analogous to theorizing about the subcortical visual system in blindsight, in that two systems are postulated, each carrying out related but distinct functions, and only one of which is endowed with conscious awareness.

Tranel, Damasio, and Damasio (1988) interpret covert recognition as the normal activation of visual face representations, which is prevented by the patients' lesions from activating representations in other areas of the brain, such as representations of the people's voices in auditory areas, affective valences in limbic areas, and names in language areas. This interpretation is therefore of the second type described in section 2.2, in that it requires an integration of active representations across different brain areas in order for conscious awareness to occur; we cannot be consciously aware of an isolated, modality-specific representation. A similar idea was recently embodied in a computer simulation of semantic priming effects, in which covert recognition was modeled as a partial disconnection separating intact visual recognition units from the rest of the system (Burton et al. 1991) (fig. 2.7).

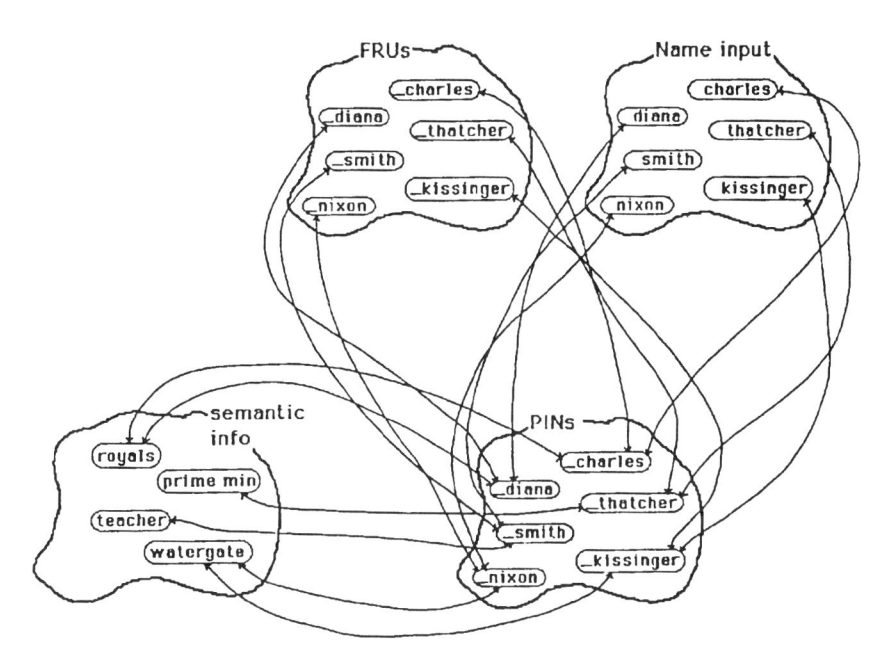

**Figure 2.7** Model of face recognition proposed by Burton et al. (1991), in which covert recognition is simulated by attenuating connections between FRUs (face recognition units) and PINs (personal identity units).

The last account of the mechanism by which overt and covert recognition are dissociated is that covert recognition reflects the residual processing capabilities of a damaged but not obliterated visual face recognition system. My colleagues and I have argued that lower-quality visual information processing is needed to support performance in tests of covert recognition (e.g., to show savings in relearning, and the various RT facilitation and interference effects) relative to the quality of information processing needed to support normal overt recognition performance (e.g., naming a face, sorting faces into those of actors and politicians). This account falls into the third category reviewed, in that the difference between face recognition with and without conscious awareness is the quality of representations activated by the face.

What evidence is available to distinguish among these hypotheses? In general, prosopagnosics are impaired in their perception of faces, although this impairment may be subtle enough to require chronometric measures to detect (Farah 1990). To take an example from the body of research under discussion, the prosopagnosic studied by De Haan, Young, and Newcombe (1987b) was both slower and considerably less accurate than normal subjects in the face matching task. This is not what one would expect assuming that the underlying impairment in prosopagnosia occurs downstream from visual face recognition processes. However, this assumption is central to all of the explanations reviewed so far, with the exception of the dual-route account of Bauer (1984) and our degraded systems hypothesis. Of course, brain-damaged patients often have deficits in more than one functional system, so in principle it is possible that problems with face matching are distinct from prosopagnosia.

If covert recognition reflects the normal functioning of a preserved face recognition system, then, in addition to normal face perception, we should also find normal levels of covert recognition, as opposed to merely partial preservation of recognition. The issue here is analogous to that in amnesia research of whether nondeclarative memory measures such as priming are truly normal in amnesic patients. Much research has been devoted to answering this question, and the finding that such patients are normal in at least some measures of nondeclarative memory has played an important role in theorizing about the functional organization of memory (e.g., see Squire 1992). Unfortunately, the data needed to test the analogous prediction for prosopagnosics are not available. In some cases, data from normal subjects would be impossible to obtain, as when famous faces and names are retaught with either the correct or incorrect pairings. In other cases, the problem of comparing effect sizes on different absolute measures arises. In both the SCR and RT paradigms, covert recognition is measured by differences between the dependent measures in two conditions (e.g., familiar and unfamiliar faces). Unfortunately, patients' SCRs are invariably weaker than those of normal subjects (Bauer 1986), and their RTs are longer (De Haan, Young, and Newcombe 1987b). It is difficult to know how to assess the relative sizes of differences when the base measures are different. For example, is an effect corresponding to a 200-ms difference between RTs on the order of 2 sec bigger than, comparable to, or smaller than an effect corresponding to a 100-ms difference between RTs of less than a second?

The study that comes closest to allowing a direct comparison of covert recognition in patients and normal subjects is the priming experiment of Young, Hellawell, and de Haan (1988). Recall that they found equivalent effects of priming name classification for their prosopagnosic patient with either photographs or names of semantically related people. Of course, this fact alone does not imply that the face-mediated priming was normal, because the priming in this task might normally be larger than name-mediated priming. They devised an ingenious way to address this problem. They refer back to an earlier experiment, reported in the same article, in which normal subjects were tested with both face primes and name primes. The normal subjects also showed equivalent amounts of priming in the two conditions. Unfortunately, the earlier experiment differed in several ways from the latter, which could conceivably shift the relative sizes of the face-mediated and name-mediated priming effects: normal subjects in the earlier experiment performed only 30 trials each, whereas the prosopagnosic patient performed 240 trials; items were never repeated in the earlier experiment, whereas they were in the later one; the type of prime was varied among subjects in the earlier experiment, whereas the patient received both types; different faces and names were used in the two experiments; and the primes were presented for about half as long in the earlier experiment as in the later one. Ideally, to answer the question of whether this prosopagnosic patient shows normal priming from faces, a group of normal control subjects should be run through the same experiment as the patient. Finally, as if empirical progress in this area is not difficult enough, there is an inherent ambiguity in one of the possible outcomes to such an experiment. Just as the finding of normal perception would disconfirm a quality of representation account but the finding of impaired perception is not decisive against the privileged role and integration accounts, so a finding of subnormal levels of covert recognition would disconfirm the privileged role and integration accounts, but the finding of normal covert recognition would not be decisive against the quality of representation account. This is because the covert measures might have lower ceilings than overt measures of recognition, that is, they might work equally well with intact or partly degraded representations. Parametric study of the relations between covert and overt performance in normal subjects would determine whether this is true.

In sum, most of the current explanations of covert recognition assume both normal face perception and normal covert recognition in prosopagnosics, but neither assumption is empirically supported at present. When tested rigorously, face perception is not normal. However, this result should not be taken as decisive evidence against this class of hypotheses, because the perceptual impairments could be due to functionally distinct lesions from those causing the prosopagnosia. As to the question of whether covert recognition is truly normal, appropriate tests have not yet been carried out. When and if they are, a finding of impaired covert recognition would be immediately interpretable, but a finding of normal covert recognition would require further scaling studies with normal subjects to determine whether the normalcy is due to a ceiling effect.

Bauer's (1984) dual-route version of a privileged role explanation has not been subject to any direct tests. Its most distinctive prediction concerns the difference between face recognition for enabling appropriate affective responses and face recognition for other purposes. Consistent with this prediction is Greve and Bauer's (1990) finding that a prosopagnosic patient rated previously seen faces as more likeable, just as normal subjects tend to do. However, most findings of covert recognition have little to do with affective responses, instead engaging implicit knowledge of names or occupations, and this seems inconsistent with the dual-route hypothesis.

Turning to the quality of representation account of covert recognition, is there any independent evidence that a degraded, but not obliterated, face recognition system would lead to a dissociation between overt and covert recognition? In one study, Wallace and Farah (1992) showed that savings in face-name relearning can be obtained with normal subjects who are trained on a set of face-name associations and then allowed for forget these associations over a 6-month interval. Presumably normal forgetting does not involve the diverting of intact information from conscious awareness but rather the degradation of representations (albeit in a different way from prosopagnosia).

Probably the strongest evidence for this view, however, is computational. Farah, O'Reilly, and Vecera (1993) trained a neural network to associate "face" patterns with "semantic" patterns and to associate these, in turn, with "name" patterns (fig. 2.8). We found that at levels of damage to the face representations that led to poor or even chance performance in overt tasks, the network

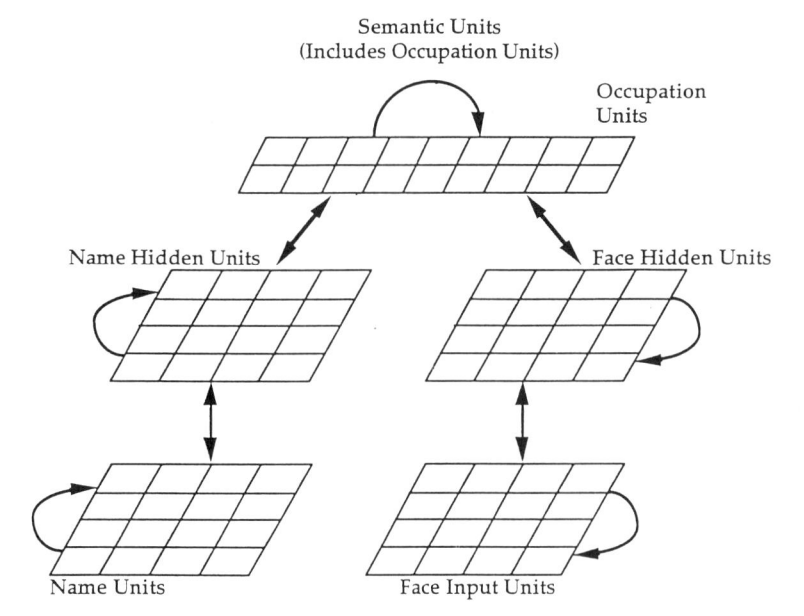

**Figure 2.8** Model of face recognition proposed by Farah, O'Reilly, and Vecera (1993), in which covert recognition is simulated by damaging either face-input units or face hidden units.

showed all of the behavioral covert recognition effects reviewed above: it relearned correct associations faster than novel ones, it completed the visual analysis of familiar faces faster than unfamiliar, and it showed priming and interference from the faces on judgments about names (fig. 2.9).

Why should this be? To answer this question requires a brief digression into neural network models. In these models, representations consist of a pattern of activation over a set of highly interconnected neuronlike units. The extent to which the activation of one unit causes an increase or decrease in the activation of a neighboring unit depends on the weight of the connection between them. For the network to learn that a certain face representation goes with a certain name representation, the weights among units in the network are adjusted so that presentation of either the face pattern in the face units or the name pattern in the name units causes the corresponding other pattern to become activated. Upon presentation of the input pattern, all of the units connected with the input units will begin to change their activation in accordance with the activation value of the units to which they are connected and the weights on the connections. As activation propagates though the network, a stable pattern of activation eventually results, determined jointly by the input activation and the pattern of weights among the units of the network.

Our account of covert face recognition is based on the following key idea: the set of the weights in a network that cannot correctly associate patterns because it has never been trained (or has been trained on a different set of patterns) is different in an important way from the set of weights in a network that cannot correctly associate patterns because it has been trained on those patterns and then damaged. The first set of weights is random with respect to the associations in question, whereas the second is a subset of the necessary weights. Even if it is an inadequate subset for performing the association, it is not random; it has embedded in it some degree of knowledge of the associations. Hinton and colleagues (Hinton and Sejnowski 1986; Hinton and Plaut 1987) have shown that such embedded knowledge can be demonstrated when the network relearns, suggesting the findings of savings in relearning face-name associations may be explained in this way. In general, consideration of the kinds of tests used to measure covert recognition suggests that the covert measures would be sensitive to this embedded knowledge. The most obvious example is that a damaged network would be expected to relearn associations that it originally knew faster than novel associations because of the nonrandom starting weights. Less obvious, but confirmed by our simulations, the network would settle faster when given previously learned inputs than novel inputs, although the pattern into which it settles is not correct, because the residual weights come from a set designed to create a stable pattern from that input. Finally, to the extent that the weights continue to activate partial and subthreshold patterns over the nondamaged units in association with the input, these resultant patterns could prime (contribute activation toward) the activation of patterns by intact routes.

The general implication of these ideas is that as a neural network is increasingly damaged, there might be a window of damage in which overt associations between patterns (e.g., faces and names) would be extremely poor, while the kinds of performance measures tapped by the covert tasks might remain at high levels.

In conclusion, the mechanism by which overt and covert face recognition are dissociated has not been established. All three types of explanation outlined in section 2.2 have been advanced to account for covert recognition in prosopagnosia. Many of the explanations would appear to run aground on evidence of perceptual impairment in prosopagnosia because they maintain that the locus of impairment is postperceptual. However, the perceptual impairments could conceivably be distinct but associated impairments. The quality of representation explanation has the advantage of accounting for these perceptual impairments, and of accounting for performance in three types of covert recognition task, and is therefore favored here. However, a decisive resolution to the issue of mechanism will require much more careful, quantitative analyses of covert recognition, analogous to the work that established the normalcy of nondeclarative learning in amnesics. Further computational work would also be helpful to account for more fine-grained features of the empirical data and to generate new predictions that could be tested with patients.

## 2.5 UNCONSCIOUS PERCEPTION IN NEGLECT AND EXTINCTION

Neglect is a disorder of spatial attention that generally follows posterior parietal damage and results in patients' failure to report or even orient to stimuli occurring on the side of space contralateral to the lesion. Patients with

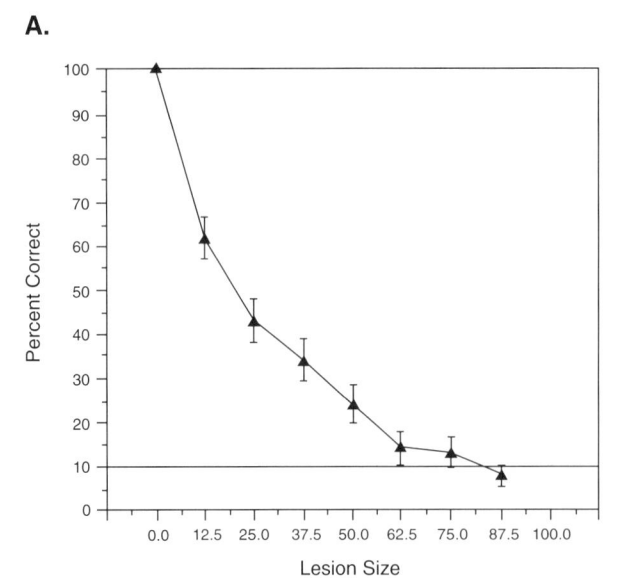

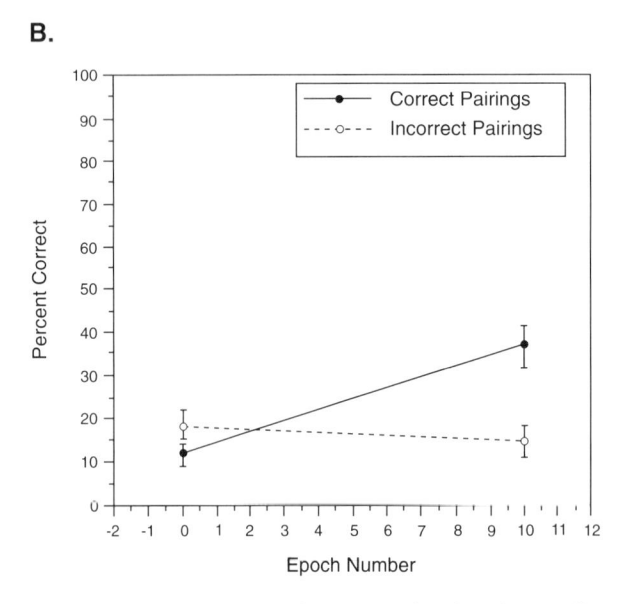

**Figure 2.9** Selected results from the model of Farah, O'Reilly, and Vecera (1993). *A*. Performance of model in 10-alternative forced-choice naming task after different amounts of damage to face hidden units. *B*. Relearning correct and incorrect face-name associations after removal of 75 percent of face-hidden units. *C*. Speed of perception of familiar and unfamiliar faces after different amounts of damage to face-hidden units. *D*. Effect of faces with same or different occupation on time to categorize a name according to occupation, after different amounts of face-hidden unit damage.

**C.**

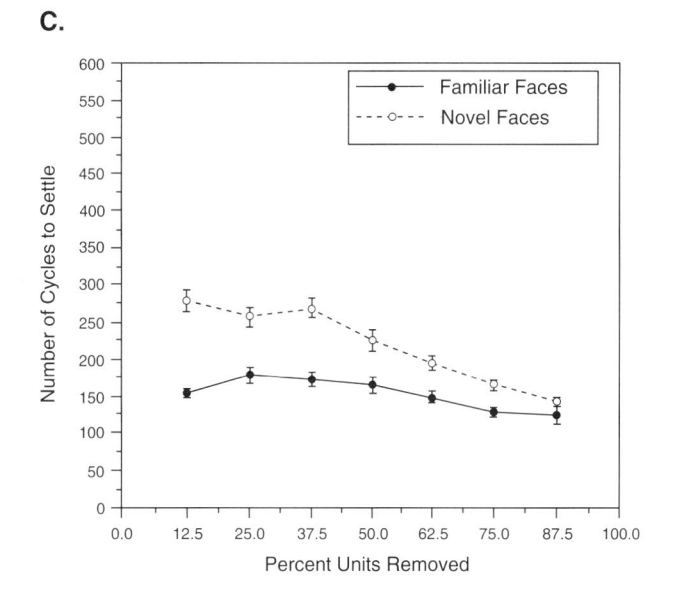

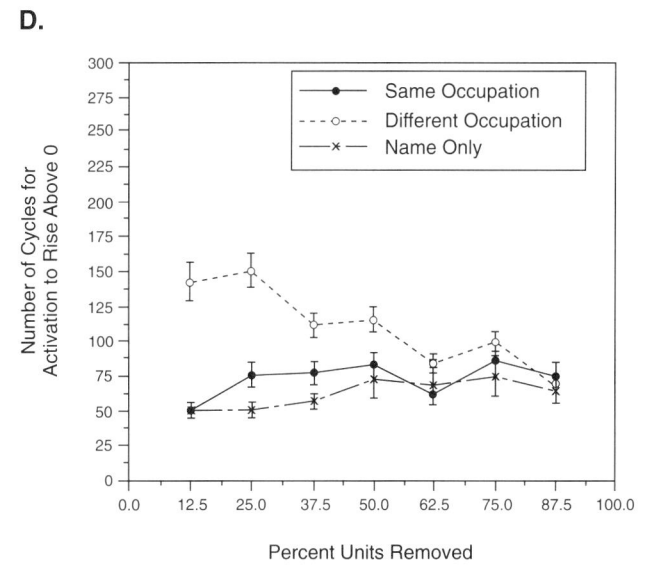

**D.**

**Figure 2.9** (cont.)

neglect need not be hemianopic (blind in the affected side of space), although they may behave as if they are. Simple hemianopia is distinguishable from neglect in that a hemianopic patient will search, with eye and head movements, for contralateral stimuli, whereas a patient with neglect, hemianopic or not, will fail to do so. Extinction is often viewed as a mild form of neglect. It also occurs predominantly in parietal-damaged patients but results in difficulty with contralateral stimuli only when an ipsilateral stimulus is presented at the same time.

The behavior of patients with neglect and extinction suggests that they do not perceive neglected and extinguished stimuli. However, evidence is beginning to accumulate showing that, in at least some cases, considerable information about neglected and extinguished stimuli is extracted by patients. As with covert recognition in prosopagnosia, this information is generally detectable only using indirect tests.

**Representative Findings**

Evidence for unconscious perception comes from two general types of experimental paradigms: those employing brief, bilateral stimulus presentations, to produce extinction in patients with full visual fields and either extinction alone or extinction and neglect; and those employing single stimuli in central vision, with no limitation on viewing time, in patients with neglect. (A relatively complete review of research in this area can be found in Wallace 1994).

The first suggestion that patients with extinction may see more of the extinguished stimulus than is apparent from their conscious verbal report came from Volpe, LeDoux, and Gazzaniga (1979). They presented four right-parietal-damaged extinction patients with pairs of visual stimuli, including drawings of common objects and three-letter words, one in each hemifield. On each trial, subjects were required to perform two types of task: to state whether the two stimuli shown were the same or different and to name the stimuli. Figure 2.10 shows the stimuli and results from a typical trial. As would be expected, the subjects did poorly at overtly identifying the stimuli on the left. Two subjects failed to name any of the left stimuli correctly, and the other two named fewer than half. In view of this, their performance on the same/different matching task was surprising. Although this task also requires perception of the left stimulus, subjects achieved between 88 percent and 100 percent correct. More recently, the same dissociation between identification of the left stimulus and cross-field same/different matching was obtained with parietal-damaged neglect patients whose attentional impairment is so severe that contralesional stimuli may fail to be identified even in the absence of a simultaneously occurring ipsilesional stimulus (Karnath and Hartje 1987; Karnath 1988).

Farah, Monheit, and Wallace (1991) noted that the dissociation between naming and same/different matching could, in principle, be explained by the differing demands these tasks make on the quality of the representation of the left stimulus. Consider the example of the comb and apple, shown in figure

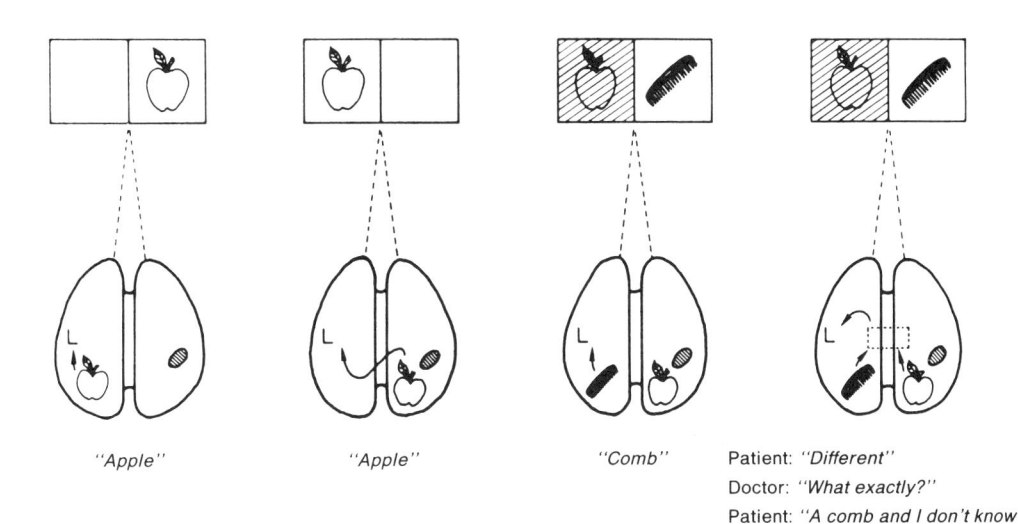

"Apple"    "Apple"    "Comb"    Patient: *"Different"*
Doctor: *"What exactly?"*
Patient: *"A comb and I don't know what the other was."*

**Figure 2.10** Typical trials from the experiment of Volpe, LeDoux, and Gazzaniga (1979), showing extinction of the left stimulus with preserved same/different matching.

2.10. If only partial stimulus information were picked up on the left—for example, the perception that there is something roundish and light-colored—this would be sufficient to enable fairly accurate same/different judgments. However, there are so many roundish, light-colored objects in the world that this partial perception would be of no help in naming the stimulus on the left. We performed two experiments to test the hypothesis that the differential amounts of stimulus information required for same/different matching and overt identification is what causes the dissociation between them. First, we degraded the left side of the display with a translucent mask and repeated Volpe, LeDoux, and Gazzaniga's experiment with normal subjects. This manipulation was not intended as a simulation of extinction but rather as test of our hypothesis concerning the quality of visual information needed in the two kinds of task. Merely depriving normal subjects of some information from the left stimulus produced the same dissociation in normal subjects that by Volpe, LeDoux, and Gazzaniga observed in patients with extinction. Second, we repeated the paradigm with extinction patients in its original form, and replicated the original finding, and also in an altered form, in which the overt identification task was administered in a forced-choice format. The purpose of this alteration was to enable us to equate the same/different trials and identification trials for the amount of information needed from the left stimulus. We did this by yoking trials from the two conditions, such that if there was a same/different trial with a triangle and a square, there was an identification trial in which one of these stimuli was presented on the left and the subject was asked, "Did you see a triangle or a square?" When same/different matching and identification were equated for their demands on the quality of the subjects' representations of the left stimuli, the dissociation vanished. We concluded that the task of same/different matching and identification differ significantly in their demands on the quality of visual representation. This implies that the results of Volpe, LeDoux, and Gazzaniga are consistent with extinction's affecting perception per se and do not require us to conclude that perception is normal and only postperceptual access to conscious awareness is impaired by extinction. Specifically, our results suggest that extinction results in partial, low-quality perceptual representations of stimuli.

Berti et al. (1992) extended these findings in a different direction, with a study of one patient who showed extinction following a temporal lobectomy. The goal of their study was to determine the level of processing to which extinguished stimuli were encoded. In Volpe, LeDoux, and Gazzaniga's (1979) study, stimuli were either physically identical or entirely different, and subjects could therefore make accurate responses on the basis of relatively early perceptual representations, be they of high or low quality. Berti et al. included pairs of pictures that were physically different but depicted either the same object from a different view or different-looking exemplars of the same type of object, such as two different cameras, and they instructed their subject to say "same" if the two stimuli had the same name. If extinguished stimuli are encoded to early levels of visual perception prior to object constancy but do not make any contact with stored object representations or meaning, then the subject should perform well only when the two stimuli are physically identical. In contrast, if extinguished stimuli are encoded to the level of meaning, then the subject should be able to say, for example, that two different cameras are the same. In fact, this is what was found, implying that extinguished stimuli are not only registered at some early level of visual processing but that they receive perceptual and even conceptual processing, despite subjects' inability to report specifically what they saw.

A recent study by McGlinchey-Berroth et al. (1993) showed semantic priming by neglected pictures in a lexical decision task. On each trial of this experiment, subjects with left neglect viewed a picture in one hemifield, followed by a letter string in central vision to which they made a "word"/"nonword" response (fig. 2.11). When the picture was semantically related to the word, "word" responses were faster, even when the picture had been presented on the left side of the display. Perhaps most striking about this result is that the amount of priming did not differ significantly between left- and right-field stimuli. Although this might appear to imply that the amount

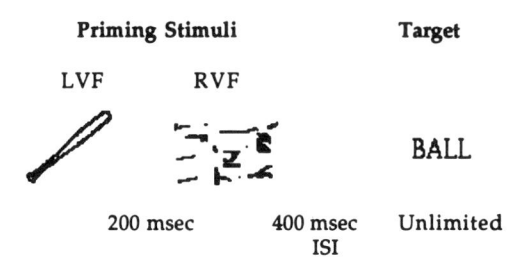

**Figure 2.11** Sequence of stimuli from a typical trial in the experiment of McGlinchy-Berroth et al. (1993).

of semantic priming from neglected stimuli is quantitatively normal, such a conclusion is not warranted because normal subjects show greater left- than right-field semantic priming (Chiarello 1988). In fact, this asymmetry was visible in the control subjects in McGlinchy-Berroth et al.'s experiment.

The finding of preserved semantic priming by left-field stimuli must also be interpreted in the context of the degree of neglect for left-field stimuli. McGlinchy-Berroth et al. conducted a second experiment in which the degree of neglect for left stimuli was assessed in a delayed matching task. Patients were indeed poor at matching a left stimulus picture with a central one presented shortly after, achieving on average only 56 percent correct. However, they were also surprisingly poor at performing the same task with stimuli presented on the right, achieving on average only 74 percent correct, raising the worry that performance in this matching task was limited by difficulties other than neglect and that not all left stimuli would therefore necessarily have been neglected in the priming task.

Unconscious perception of neglected stimuli has also been investigated under conditions of nontachistoscopic viewing in central vision. Sieroff, Pollatsek, and Posner (1988) analyzed the reading capabilities of patients with neglect and found that letters falling in the neglected regions of the visual field (as assessed by poor naming of letters in nonword letter strings) could nevertheless be used to identify familiar words. For example, patients might read *table* correctly, but read *taspi* as "f-o-s-p-i" or "s-p-i," misperceiving or omitting the letters on the left. Sieroff, Posner and Pollatsek argue against the possibility that patients were simply guessing the letters on the left sides of words by pointing out that words and nonwords were intermixed in their experiments, and patients did not often guess words when shown the nonword letter strings. Although these authors were not specifically concerned with the issue of conscious awareness in neglect, their findings seem to imply that the leftmost letters were unconsciously perceived and therefore available to the word recognition system, despite patients' inability to report the letters.

Marshall and Halligan (1988) described a patient with neglect who evinced a consistent preference for a picture of a normal house over a picture of the same house with flames coming from the left side, despite her inability to say how (or even whether) the two stimuli differed. This pattern of performance is consistent with the hypothesis that neglected stimuli are perceived and understood, at least to the degree that they can evoke an affective response, without being accessible to the mechanisms of conscious verbal report.

In further research, by Bisiach and Rusconi (1990), who tested four patients with four pairs of drawings, the striking finding of Marshall and Halligan (1988) was not replicated. Often patients displayed no consistent preference. Perhaps more revealing, when patients did have a preference, it was not necessarily in the normal, rational direction. For example, the only patients who showed a preference with the house stimuli preferred the burning house! Bisiach and Rusconi queried their subjects as to the reasons for their preferences and found that the reasons fell into two categories: real but minor differences on the right sides of the stimulus materials, and confabulated differences, such as alleged differences in the layouts of the houses or the numbers of rooms. These confabulations are not uninteresting; they suggest that patients with neglect may detect differences on the left that they cannot describe verbally, instead evoking confabulations. However, the results of Bisiach and Rusconi do suggest that Marshall and Halligan's case was probably responding to some minor difference on the right side of the stimulus pair or to some dimly perceived difference on the left, rather than to the unconscious realization that one of the houses was on fire and would therefore be a dangerous place to live.

**Awareness of Perception**

Patients with neglect and extinction generally report no awareness of having seen stimuli that they fail to detect or of having recognized stimuli that they fail to identify. One measure of the extent to which the subjects were not aware of their own perceptions in the studies reviewed here is their tendency to remark on the silliness or absurdity of answering questions about stimuli on the left, or choosing between a pair of stimuli identical except for a feature on the left (Marshall and Halligan 1988; Volpe, LeDoux, and Gazzaniga 1979). Such tasks would indeed seem silly if one were not aware of a stimulus on the left or of the difference between the paired stimuli. It should be noted, however, that the ways in which awareness of perception was formally operationalized in these studies was not to ask the subjects whether they detected a stimulus. Rather, the most common means was verbal identification of the stimulus. This was used in the studies of same/different matching ability and in the studies of letter perception within word and nonword letter strings. Although Volpe, LeDoux, and Gazzaniga stated that their subjects sometimes denied seeing any stimulus at all on the left, no systematic data are reported on detection; they contrasted same/different matching performance only with naming. Other tasks intended to assess conscious awareness of stimulus identity included the delayed matching task of McGlinchy-Berroth et al. and the same/different judgment of Marshall and Halligan. In contrast to the research on covert recognition in prosopagnosia, research on unconscious perception in neglect and extinction has not drawn a clear and principled line between tasks that require overt conscious awareness of perception and tasks considered to be indirect tests of unconscious perception. The fact that same/different matching was considered an indirect test of unconscious perception by Volpe, LeDoux, and Gazzaniga and a test of overt conscious perception by Marshall and Halligan is symptomatic of this problem.

**Explanations of Perceptual Dissociations in Patients with Neglect and Extinction**

The earliest and most straightforward interpretation of the dissociation between perception and awareness in patients with neglect and/or extinction was offered by Volpe, LeDoux, and Gazzaniga. They suggested that extinction in their subjects consisted of "a breakdown in the flow of information between conscious and nonconscious mental systems. The stimulus comparison task in our study appears to have been carried out at a postperceptual, preverbal level, with only the resultant comparison entering consciousness." This account clearly falls into the privileged rote category, because consciousness is being attributed to certain systems and not others. Although the authors are not very explicit on the point, it appears from the quotation just cited and another reference to "some level of neuronal processing which allows for verbal description, if not conscious awareness" that the system required for consciousness is closely related to the language system (Gazzaniga 1988).

An alternative interpretation of the kinds of dissociations reviewed here has been offered by Kinsbourne (1988). Rather than viewing consciousness as a property of some neural systems and not others, he considers it a state of integration among different neural systems. According to this view, neglect does not divert percepts from conscious awareness by somehow preventing their transmission to another system that is required for consciousness. Rather, it weakens or degrades the representation of the stimulus, such that the representation does not have sufficient influence over the other, concurrent, patterns of activity in the brain to create a new global brain state into which the stimulus representation is integrated. This contrasts with the integration account of covert face recognition by Damasio (1990), according to which the percept is normal but disconnected from other systems. A related interpretation seems to be advocated by Bisiach (1992). He rejects the notion of a single central locus of consciousness, which he identifies with Cartesianism and the homunculus, and calls our attention to the possibility of numerous parallel mechanisms linking stimuli and responses.

The dissociations reviewed earlier can also be explained by a quality of representation account. According to this type of account, extinction and neglect result in poor-quality perceptual representations, which supply input, albeit degraded input, to higher levels of conceptual and linguistic processing. This type of account is similar to Kinsbourne's integration account; both emphasize the degradation of perception and consequent weakening of the influence of neglected and extinguished percepts on other parts of the system. The accounts differ in emphasis in that the integration account stresses the lessening of influence on the rest of the system, whereas the quality of representation account stresses the existence of the residual influence.

The available data provide some constraints on possible mechanisms but do not discriminate decisively among them. The privileged role account of Volpe, LeDoux, and Gazzaniga can be distinguished from the others in that it hypothesizes normal perception, with the impairment occurring downstream, whereas the other accounts hinge on an impairment in perception per se. The finding of Farah, Monheit, and Wallace (1991) that same/different matching was dissociated from identification only by virtue of the demands on visual perception is more consistent with the integration and quality of representation accounts than with the privileged role account.

It might appear that several of the other findings described earlier are inconsistent with the hypothesis that perception is impaired. For example, McGinchy-Berroth et al.'s subjects showed semantic priming from left field stimuli; Sieroff, Pollatsek, and Posner's subjects could use letters from neglected regions of the field to read words; and Berti et al.'s subject could match extinguished stimuli on the basis of conceptual rather than structural equivalence. However, as noted earlier, neural representation is not all or none, and it is probably not necessary for the visual system to have completed its processing of a stimulus and to have derived a high-quality representation in order for it to pass some information on to subsequent levels of processing. A degraded or incomplete visual representation will therefore presumably activate, to some degree, conceptual and semantic representations.

The possibility of semantic priming by words that are poorly perceived is well established in the cognitive psychology literature. Marcel (1983) and others have shown that subliminal tachistoscopic presentations of words can prime judgments about subsequent supraliminal words. The most natural and direct interpretation of the effect of limiting the exposure duration of a word and following it with a mask is that the perceptual processing of the word is impaired.[1] Therefore, we should not infer that if a word or picture can semantically prime subsequent stimulus processing, that it must have been perceived normally.

A mechanistic explanation of how poor-quality perceptual representations could produce priming at semantic levels is suggested by the covert face recognition model of Farah, O'Reilly, and Vecera (1993). In our model the locus of damage was visual, and the quality of the visual representations was such that multiple-choice naming was poor or at chance. However, the model showed semantic priming. This was because the patterns of activation reaching semantic levels of representation contained partial, noisy, and subthreshold information about the semantic identity of the stimulus. The resultant pattern in semantics would, on average, be more consistent with the semantics of that stimulus, or a semantically related stimulus, than with an unrelated stimulus, and hence tended to have a net facilatory effect on the semantic representation of identical or related stimuli, relative to unrelated stimuli. However, because much of this priming effect was caused by subthresold activation in the semantics units, the semantic representations engendered by the poor-quality visual input were not, themselves, able to activate response representations such as names. This suggests a reason why indirect tests may be more sensitive to the residual capabilities of damaged systems: such tests generally require that residual knowledge affect the processing of a probe stimulus within the perceptual and semantic layers, as opposed to requiring that knowledge to be propagated through additional levels of representation for an overt response. The model of Farah, O'Reilly, and Vecera is sufficiently simple and generic that it is equally relevant to priming in neglect as in prosopagnosia.

The ability of neglect patients to use letters on the left sides of words to read, despite their inability to identify letters in equivalent spatial positions in nonword letter strings, is another phenomenon that might at first seem to imply that perception has been spared. However, like semantic priming, it has been explained in terms of impaired perception and interactions among graded representations. Mozer and Behrmann (1990) present a computer simulation in which an impairment of spatial attention results in impoverished stimulus information reaching stored word knowledge. By a completion-like process characteristic of distributed neural networks, the good-quality information from the right side of the word and the stored word structure combine with the poor-quality information from the left side of the word to "complete" or "clean up" the perceptual representation of the left side. Behrmann et al. (1990) present additional data from patients that support this account. Brunn and Farah (1991) demonstrated that the top-down effects of stored word representations on perception include an attenuation of the neglect during word reading. For example, patients named more colors, of different colored letters, when the letters made words than when they made nonwords. This implies that the preserved letter perception of Sieroff, Pollatsek, and Posner's neglect patients with words may not have been a case of preserved perception despite neglect but of a lessening of the neglect.

There are no independent demonstrations that conceptual matching of the kind documented by Berti et al. (1992) could be accomplished on the basis of impaired visual percepts. However, the same general principles invoked by Farah, O'Reilly, and Vecera (1992) and Mozer and Behrmann (1990) suggest that this finding, too, can be explained without hypothesizing normal visual perception and semantic representation, deprived of access to other brain systems necessary for conscious awareness. With the relatively light demands on representational quality made by the same/different matching task (Farah, Monheit and Wallace 1991) and the additional constraints provided by a limited stimulus set, it seems at least possible that a poor-quality visual representation could be used to make reasonably accurate judgments of the kind made by Berti et al.'s subject. In addition, Berti et al. point out that perception of the extinguished stimulus on "same" trials may have been semantically primed by the ipsilesional stimulus.

In sum, we find ourselves in roughly the same position with respect to explanations of unconscious perception in neglect and extinction as we did with explanations of covert face recognition. The current body of empirical knowledge is of great interest and utility in establishing certain important qualitative conclusions: that patients can be unable to report the identity of a neglected or extinguished stimulus but still manifest a fair degree of perceptual and even semantic knowledge about it. Yet these results are ambiguous with respect to the mechanisms by which neglect and extinction have these effects. The hypothesis that neglect and extinction spare perceptual and semantic processing, and affect only subsequent processing by some other system that plays a privileged role in mediating conscious awareness, seems inconsistent with the finding that perception is not normal in neglect and extinction (Farah, Monheit, and Wallace 1991). Demonstrations of semantic processing in neglect and extinction have not provided the kind of careful quantitation of effect sizes needed to determine whether semantic processing is normal or merely partially preserved. Thus, there is no decisive evidence in favor of the privileged role account and a small amount of evidence against it.

The available data appear compatible with the view of Kinsbourne (1988), Bisiach (1992), and Farah, Monheit, and Wallace (1991), that the effect of neglect and extinction is to degrade perceptual representation and thus attenuate its influence on the integrated state of the cognitive system as a whole. This conclusion could be strengthened, or disconfirmed, by further quantitative empirical studies of the degree of preservation of implicit processing and by computational simulations of a fuller range of the experimental paradigms used to demonstrate unconscious perception in neglect and extinction.

## 2.6 IMPLICIT READING IN PURE ALEXIA

Patients with pure alexia are impaired at reading, despite being able to write normally and understand spoken words. To the extent that they can read at all, they appear to do so in a letter-by-letter fashion, spelling the word to themselves before they can recognize it. There are three main hypotheses about the cause of pure alexia and letter-by-letter reading:

1. Disconnection account: Visual input from the occipital cortices is unable to access left hemisphere language representations because of some combination of visual cortical damage and disconnection, and at most one letter at a time can be transmitted by alternate routes (e.g., Geschwind, 1965).

2. Word form hypothesis: Reading-specific knowledge of visual word structure has been destroyed, or is partly disconnected from earlier levels of visual representation such as letter representations, so that word recognition must proceed letter by letter, without the benefit of larger-scale word structure (e.g., Warrington and Shallice 1980).

3. Visual impairment hypothesis: The ability to encode multiple visual shapes of any sort rapidly and accurately, including but not limited to letters in words, is impaired, so that the most reliable strategy is to read letter by letter (e.g., Farah and Wallace 1991).

What the three hypotheses have in common is that there is some capacity essential for reading—linguistic knowledge in general, word forms in particular, or the ability to encode multiple visual shapes—that incoming visual information cannot gain access to because of either the loss of that capacity or disconnection from it. These analyses suggest that patients' oral reading abilities reflect their comprehension abilities, and indeed the everyday behavior and clinical test performance of pure alexics suggest that they cannot understand words that they fail to decipher by letter-by-letter reading.

This belief was first called into question by Landis, Regard, and Serrat (1980) in a case study of a patient recovering from surgery for a left occipital tumor. The patient was a pure alexic, and when tested with a week of the surgery, was unable to read words that were flashed for only 30 ms in a tachistoscope. However, he was able to point to objects in the room whose names had been presented in this manner. Unfortunately, he was tested with relatively few words on that day, and when retested a week later, he had lost his ability to point to the words' referents, even though his explicit reading performance had improved.

**Representative Findings**

Subsequent studies have examined the implicit reading of pure alexics more thoroughly. Patterson and Kay (1982) reported several unsuccessful attempts to elicit evidence of comprehension of briefly presented unread words in their pure alexic subjects. Shortly after, Grossi et al. (1984) presented evidence of disproportionately preserved picture-word matching in one case of pure alexia, and Shallice and Saffran (1986) described a comprehensive investigation of implicit word recognition and comprehension in another pure alexic. Shallice and Saffran's subject was able to perform lexical decision with relatively high accuracy on letter strings that were presented for 2 sec, which was too quickly for him reliably to identify the words explicitly. The subject was best at recognizing high-frequency words, and the closer the resemblance was between nonwords and words, the harder it was for him to reject the nonwords. For high-frequency words, he was able to classify 90 percent as words, and false-alarmed to only 38 percent of the pseudowords derived from the high-frequency words by changing one or two letters. An interesting exception to his generally good lexical decision ability was that he was unable to discriminate appropriately and inappropriately affixed words, for example, calling *applaudly* a word. Shallice and Saffran also demonstrated that their subject was able to make reasonably accurate semantic categorizations of words presented too briefly to be read. For example, he correctly classified 94 percent of unread place names as in or out of Europe, 93 percent of unread people's names as authors or politicians, and 87 percent of unread concrete nouns as living or nonliving.

Coslett and Saffran (1989) replicated and extended these findings with four new cases of pure alexia. Like Shallice and Saffran (1986), they found effects of word frequency on lexical decision and an insensitivity to affixes. They also found better lexical decison performance for concrete and imageable words and for content words, in general, relative to functors. In a subsequent study, Coslett and Saffran (1994) report that they tested one of their subjects on rhyme/nonrhyme judgments with written words and found that he performed at chance. Perhaps their most striking finding is that their subjects performed the implicit reading tasks more accurately with extremely brief exposures of the words, such as 250 ms, than with exposures of 2 sec. They interpret this in terms of the different strategies needed for implicit and explicit reading. Explicit letter-by-letter reading is incompatible with the strategy needed for implicit reading. Coslett and Saffran were able to foil subjects' attempts at letter-by-letter reading by using extremely short exposure durations and thereby enabled the alternative strategy to be expressed. This is consistent with Landis, Regard, and Serrat's original case study, in which implicit reading was lost as explicit reading improved. It also suggests a reason that Patterson and Kay may not have detected any preserved implicit reading in their subjects: in attempting to maximize the chances of eliciting implicit reading in their subjects, they used words that were most likely to be recognized explicitly—that is, very short words and words that had been successfully read explicitly.

**Awareness of Perception**

Although patients' reports of their subjective experiences are not reported in great detail in most cases, there is a suggestion of some variability among cases. Whereas Landis, Regard, and Serrat and Coslett and Saffran's subjects generally complained of not even being able to see the stimuli clearly when they were manifesting implicit reading, Shallice and Saffran's subject was able to give rather detailed descriptions of how he performed the lexical decision and semantic categorization tasks. For lexical decision, he described "a process of looking at the whole length of the word and finding a combination of letters that can't be right, or looking at the whole word and seeing that it looked sensible." For semantic categorization, he reported getting a "first impression" of each word and, with a particular category in mind, deciding whether he "feels the first flash is right." Karen Klein and I have studied a similar patient, R.H., and with the help of Coslett and Saffran replicated all of their findings with him. In terms of his implicit reading performance, he seems to differ from their subjects only in that he is able to perform implicit reading at any exposure duration and never needs prompting to abandon the letter-by-letter reading strategy (at which he is extremely poor). Like Shallice and Saffran's subject, R.H. seems quite aware of the information he gleans during implicit reading and is reasonably confident of his responses.

From this very small and sketchy empirical base, I would tentatively suggest that for pure alexics who are able to abandon the letter-by-letter strategy and manifest implicit reading at relatively long exposure durations, there is no dissociation between the information that has been processed in implicit reading and awareness of having processed that information. The striking dissociation in these cases is between knowing the specific word presented and knowing its lexical status and semantic category. However, this dissociation does not have any direct implications for the relation between word perception and awareness thereof. Only when exposure durations must be extremely short, for subjects who would otherwise persist in letter-by-letter reading, do subjects manifest knowledge in their implicit reading performance that they themselves are not aware of possessing. Under these circumstances, however, the dissociation between performance and awareness may be attributable to the same mechanisms as subthreshold perception in normal subjects, with thresholds being higher for brain-damaged subjects.

## Explanations of Implicit Reading

Because it is not clear whether implicit reading necessarily involves a dissociation between subjects' experience of reading and their performance, it is equally unclear whether explanations of making reference to the neural mechanisms of conscious awareness will have any relevance to the phenomena of implicit reading. Nevertheless, some of the proposed explanations can be applied either to performance/awareness dissociations or simply to accounting for the surprising pattern of performance in these patients.

Recall that several accounts of pure alexia exist and that they have in common some hypothesized capacity that is necessary for reading and is either damaged or disconnected from early visual representations of words. The capacity in question has been hypothesized to be language in general, word form knowledge in particular, or the ability to encode multiple visual shapes rapidly, and in all cases is assumed to be localized to the left hemisphere. The different accounts of implicit reading can be differentiated from one another with respect to the role played by these left hemisphere mechanisms.

The DICE model has been applied to implicit reading and suggests that implicit reading is simply normal reading, drawing as usual on the critical left hemisphere—mediated processing, deprived of access to other systems necessary for conscious awareness (Schacter, McAndrews, and Moscovitch 1988). This is an example of a privileged role account.

Implicit reading has also been explained by a quality of representation account. Shallice and Saffran (1986) suggested that "lexical decision above chance but well below normal levels; recognition of morphemes but insensitivity to the appropriateness of their combination; limited access to semantic information [and] the failure to identify the stimulus explicitly, could conceivably be explained in terms of decreased levels of activation within the system that normally subserves explicit identification."

Finally, Shallice and Saffran also discuss the possibility that implicit reading reflects the operation of right hemisphere reading mechanisms, a view that Coslett and Saffran (1989) later endorsed. This constitutes a different type of privileged role account, according to which the normal left-hemisphere component of the reading system is uniquely endowed with the ability to mediate conscious awareness of reading (if the account is to be applied to awareness) and with the more fine-grained semantic distinctions and syntactic and morphological capabilities found to be lacking in implicit reading.

How does the available evidence adjudicate among these alternatives? The DICE model does not provide an explanation of the peculiarities of implicit reading with regard to part of speech, morphology, and concreteness, and so on, and is therefore not a very satisfactory account of the phenomenon. In contrast, the right-hemisphere hypothesis seems particularly well-suited to explaining these findings. On the basis of independent evidence with split-brain patients and with normal subjects, the right hemisphere appears to be better at reading high-frequency and concrete words, and to be ignorant of morphology (see, e.g., Baynes 1990 for a review). The right hemisphere is also believed to be deficient at deriving phonology from print, consistent with the inability of one of Coslett and Saffran's subjects to make rhyme judgments on pairs of printed words, which Klein and I also observed with our implicit reader.

It is not clear exactly how well the hypothesis of a degraded reading system accounts for these phenomena. On the basis of general properties of neural network models, one might well expect higher-frequency words to be better preserved, on the basis of more initial learning. One might also predict greater preservation of concrete and imageable words, especially with the assumption that such words have more associated semantic attributes (Plaut and Shallice 1993). On these points, the quality of representation approach does well in accounting for some of the features of implicit reading. In contrast, the more regular mapping between orthography and phonology, relative to the mapping between orthography and semantics, would seem to predict the relative preservation of phonological judgments relative to semantic ones, just the opposite of what is observed, on grounds similar to the prediction concerning frequency effects: to the extent that sets of similar-looking words have similar-sounding pronunciations, the learning accomplished for each one will also generalize toward the others. Finally, the finding that shorter exposure durations lead to better implicit reading in at least some patients is awkward for a quality of representation account.

In sum, there is a good deal of relatively fine-grained information about implicit reading concerning the effects of different stimulus properties, instructions, and tasks, and these enable us to evaluate the different explanations of the phenomena that have been put forward. Pending some counterintuitive results concerning the modes of failure in damaged reading networks, the available evidence seems most consistent with right hemisphere mediation of implicit reading. However, dissociated awareness is not an essential aspect of implicit reading, and the mechanism of implicit reading is therefore not necessarily relevant to the neural bases of visual awareness.

## 2.7 GENERAL CONCLUSIONS

The goal of this final section is to review and compare the different syndromes in terms of the ways in which conscious awareness has been operationalized and the mechanisms that seem most likely to account for dissociated awareness, and to consider what general conclusions might follow about the relations between perception and conscious awareness.

### Awareness and the Likely Mechanisms of Its Dissociation from Perceptual Performance in the Four Syndromes

There is a range of ways that the absence of patients' conscious awareness has been demonstrated in the four different syndromes reviewed here. Within the literature on blindsight, there are two common types of introspective report. Subjects often claim that they are guessing on the basis of no subjective experience, with resulting very low confidence. In other instances, subjects say that they are answering based on an experience but not one that they would classify as visual. Occasionally a specifically visual experience is reported. Prosopagnosic subjects are, of course, aware of when they are viewing a face. But they typically report no sense of familiarity when they view a face, perform poorly when trying to identify faces, and have low confidence in their identifications. In neglect and extinction, subjects may fail even to report detecting a stimulus. However, the only systematically collected data on awareness in the experiments demonstrating unconscious perception measure the ability to make various explicit judgments of such stimuli. Nevertheless, these data suggest a dissociation between awareness and performance, as explicit performance is poor, and confidence is generally low. Finally, in implicit reading, the dissociation that holds for all patients is between the ability to report a specific word and the ability to make judgments about the lexicality and semantic category of the word, not the dissociation between word perception and awareness of that perception. For two cases, at least, subjects are aware of the information they are using to make these judgments, and they have confidence in their answers. In sum, the four syndromes comprise a heterogeneous group from the point of view of awareness.

The four syndromes also appear to be heterogeneous from the point of view of mechanism. I will tentatively suggest that the groupings of the syndromes according to the status of awareness in each syndrome correspond with the groupings one might impose on the basis of the currently most likely mechanisms. For example, in blindsight, there appear to be two main types of subjective report, depending on the patient and task. There are also two main types of mechanism that have been proposed, without any intended mutual exclusivity. There is evidence consistent with both subcortical mediation of some blindsight abilities, and extrastriate cortical mediation of others, interpretable with privileged role and quality of representation accounts, respectively. Whether these two mechanisms can, in fact, be placed in correspondence with the two types of subjective experience is an empirical question for which I know of no direct evidence.

Covert face recognition in prosopagnosia and unconscious perception of stimuli in neglect and extinction are similar in that subjects are generally unaware of those aspects of the stimulus for which they manifest unconscious knowledge. The mechanisms responsible for the dissociations observed in these two syndromes are not well established because of a dearth of evidence capable of discriminating among them. However, both syndromes currently seem explainable in terms of a quality of representation account or, equivalently, in terms of the version of Kinsbourne's (1988) integration account that postulates a failure of integration due to low quality representation. In prosopagnosia the poor quality of the representations is due to a loss of stored perceptual knowledge of faces, whereas in neglect and extinction it is due to a more dynamic processing failure of the attention system.

Implicit reading seems distinct from all of the foregoing dissociations, both in terms of subjects' conscious awareness of the information they are able to extract from stimuli and in terms of mechanism. Unless word presentations are so brief that subjects report not seeing the words, implicit reading is accompanied by awareness of the information gleaned from the words. Although the issue of mechanism is far from settled, currently the right hemisphere reading hypothesis, a type of privileged role hypothesis, appears more plausible than a quality of representation hypothesis.

**General Implications**

One general conclusion that should be abundantly clear is that the four different syndromes reviewed here are unlikely to share a common explanation. Although there is a family resemblance among them, a close inspection reveals that the kinds of perceptual abilities and forms of experience that are preserved and impaired are not uniform. If we are still inclined to characterize them as demonstrating perception in the absence of conscious awareness (which seems reasonable to me, at least for the first three), then we may need to consider the possibility that the relation between conscious awareness and neural systems is itself not explicable by just one type of account. For example, we might conclude that enabling conscious awareness is a privileged role of certain cortical regions and that within these regions, a certain quality of representation is also necessary (thus denying consciousness to both the normal-quality functioning of the superior colliculus and the impaired functioning of cortical face representations).

Among all of the syndromes, there is none for which visual perception, in its totality, has been convincingly demonstrated to be normal or near normal. Therefore, there is no reason to view these syndromes as consisting of normal perception with conscious awareness merely stripped away. This, in turn, should deprive theories like DICE of their basic motivation: to explain a straightforward dissociation between perception and awareness of perception. Although the results of future research could reverse this situation, at present we lack evidence of such a straightforward dissociation. There is currently no evidence for a dedicated conscious awareness system, distinct from the systems that perform specific perceptual or cognitive functions.

The study of perception and awareness in brain-damaged patients is fairly new, particularly for syndromes other than blindsight, and our empirical knowledge of them is still rudimentary. Alan Allport urged in his 1988 article, "*What* concept of consciousness?" that researchers in this area do more conceptual analysis of their subject matter. This is certainly a highly desirable goal, especially with a subject matter that so tempts us to cross and confuse explanatory domains, such as the personal and subpersonal and the empirical and metaphysical. To this wise advice I would like to add a plea for more humble old empirical analysis as well. Are levels of performance on implicit perceptual tasks in these various syndromes normal? Is performance on explicit tasks poor but above chance, or truly at chance by a reasonably powerful test? How do these measures relate to the likelihood of reporting some awareness of the visual information being tested? What additionally can we discover about the more fine-grained charateristics of unconscious visual performance that might provide further constraints on mechanistic explanations (e.g., the part-of-speech effects in implicit reading, the relative sizes of interference and facilitation in priming by faces in prosopagnosia and neglected stimuli in parietal-damaged patients, or the nasal/temporal asymmetries in blindsight)? These questions must be answered if we are to distinguish among the different accounts of the syndromes reviewed here and thereby distinguish their associated views of the neural correlates of conscious awareness.

## NOTES

The writing of this chapter was supported by ONR grant N00014-93-I0621, NIMH grant R01 MH48274, NIH career development award K04-NS01405, and a grant from the McDonnell-Pew Program in Cognitive Neuroscience. I thank several colleagues who read an early draft of this chapter and made many helpful suggestions: Tom Carr, Max Coltheart, David Finkelstein, Morris Moscovitch, and Larry Weiskrantz.

1. This interpretation has been questioned by Marcel, among others, because of the preservation of semantic processing. This reasoning appears to be based on the assumption that impairment in visual processing is inconsistent with evidence of semantic processing. The simulation results described in the next paragraph demonstrate that this assumption need not be true.

## REFERENCES

Allport, A. (1988). What concept of consciousness? In A. J. Marcel and E. Bisiach (Eds.), *Consciousness in contemporary science*. Oxford: Clarendon Press.

Bauer, R. M. (1984). Autonomic recognition of names and faces in prosopagnosia: A neuropsychological application of the guilty knowledge test. *Neuropsychologia, 22*, 457–469.

Bauer, R. M. (1986). The cognitive psychophysiology of prosopagnosia. In H. D. Ellis, M. A. Jeeves, F. Newcombe, and A. Young (Eds.), *Aspects of face processing*. Dordrecht: Martinus Nijhoff.

Bauer, R. M., and Trobe, J. D. (1984). Visual memory and perceptual impairments in prosopagnosia. *Journal of Clinical Neuro-ophthalmology, 4*, 39–46.

Baynes, K. (1990). Language and reading in the right hemisphere: Highways or byways of the brain? *Journal of Cognitive Neuroscience, 2*, 159–179.

Behrmann, M., Moscovitch, M., Black, S. E., and Mozer, M. (1990). Perceptual and conceptual mechanisms in neglect dyslexia. *Brain, 113*, 1163–1183.

Berti, A., Allport, A., Driver, J., Dienes, Z., Oxbury, J., and Oxbury, S. (1992). Levels of processing for visual stimuli in an "extinguished" field. *Neuropsychologia, 30*, 403–415.

Bisiach, E. (1992). Understanding consciousness: Clues from unilateral neglect and related disorders. In A. D. Milner and M. D. Rugg (Eds.), *The neuropsychology of consciousness*. San Diego: Academic Press.

Bisiach, E., and Rusconi, L. L. (1990). Break-down of perceptual awareness in unilateral neglect. *Cortex, 26*, 643–649.

Brunn, J. L., and Farah, M. J. (1991). The relation between spatial attention and reading: Evidence from the neglect syndrome. *Cognitive Neuropsychology, 8*, 59–75.

Bruyer, R., Laterre, C., Seron, X., Feyereisne, P., Strypstein, E., Pierrard, E., and Rectem, D. (1983). A case of prosopagnosia with some preserved covert remembrance of familiar faces. *Brain and Cognition, 2*, 257–284.

Burton, A. M., Young, A. W., Bruce, V., Johnston, R. A., and Ellis, A. W. (1991). Understanding covert recognition. *Cognition, 39,* 129–166.

Campion, J., Latto, R., and Smith, Y. M. (1983). Is blindsight an effect of scattered light, spared cortex, and near-threshold vision? *Behavioral and Brain Sciences, 3,* 423–447.

Chiarello, C. (1988). *Right hemisphere contributions to lexical semantics.* Berlin: Springer-Verlag.

Coslett, H. B., and Saffran, E. M. (1989). Evidence for preserved reading in "pure alexia." *Brain, 112,* 327–359.

Coslett, H. B., and Saffran, E. M. (1994). Mechanisms of implicit reading in alexia. In M. J. Farah and G. Ratcliff (Eds.), *The neuropsychology of high-level vision: collected tutorial essay.* Hillsdale, NJ: Erlbaum Associates.

Cowey, A., and Stoerig, P. (1989). Projection patterns of surviving neurons in the dorsal lateral geniculate nucleus following discrete lesions of striate cortex: Implications for residual vision. *Experimental Brain Research, 75,* 631–638.

Crick, F., and Koch, C. (1990). Function of the thalamic reticular complex: The searchlight hypothesis. *Seminars in the Neurosciences, 2,* 263–275.

Damasio, A. R. (1990). Synchronous activation in multiple cortical regions: A mechanism for recall. *Seminars in the Neurosciences, 2,* 287–296.

De Haan, E. H. F., Bauer, R. M., and Greve, K. W. (1992). Behavioral and physiological evidence for covert recognition in a prosopagnosic patient. *Cortex, 28,* 77–95.

De Haan, E. H. F., Young, A., and Newcombe, F. (1987a). Faces interfere with name classification in a prosopagnosic patient. *Cortex, 23,* 309–316.

De Haan, E. H. F., Young, A. W., and Newcombe, F. (1987b). Face recognition without awareness. *Cognitive Neuropsychology, 4,* 385–415.

Farah, M. J. (1990). *Visual agnosia: Disorders of object recognition and what they tell us about normal vision.* Cambridge, MA: MIT Press/Bradford Books.

Farah, M. J., Monheit, M. A., and Wallace, M. A. (1991). Unconscious perception of "extinguished" visual stimuli: Reassessing the evidence. *Neuropsychologia, 29,* 949–958.

Farah, M. J., O'Reilly, R. C., and Vecera, S. P. (1993). Dissociated overt and covert recognition as on emergent property of lesioned attractor networks. *Pychological Review, 100,* 571–588.

Farah, M. J., and Wallace, M. A. (1991). Pure alexia as a visual impairment: A reconsideration. *Cognitive Neuropsychology, 8,* 313–334.

Fendrich, R., Wessinger, C. M., and Gazzaniga, M. S. (1992). Residual vision in a scotoma: Implications for blindsight. *Science, 258,* 1489–1491.

Gazzaniga, M. S. (1988). Brain modularity: Towards a philosphy of conscious experience. In A. J. Marcel and E. Bisiach (Eds.), *Consciousness in contemporary science.* Oxford: Clarendon Press.

Geschwind, N. (1965). Disconnexion syndromes in animals and man. Part II. *Brain, 88,* 585–645.

Gray, C. M., and Singer, W. (1989). Stimulus specific neuronal oscillations in the orientation columns of cat visual cortex. *Proceedings of the National Academy of Science, 86,* 1698–1702.

Greve, K. W., and Bauer, R. M. (1990). Implicit learning of new faces in prosopagnosia: An application of the mere exposure paradigm. *Neuropsychologia, 28,* 1035–1041.

Grossi, D., Fragassi, N. A., Orsini, A., De Falco, F. A., and Sepe, O. (1984). Residual reading capacity in a patient with alexia without agraphia. *Brain and Language, 23,* 337–348.

Hinton, G., and Plaut, D. C. (1987). Using fast weights to beblur old memories. *Proceedings of the Ninth Annual Meeting of the Cognitive Science Society.* Hillsdale, NJ: Erlbaum Associates.

Hinton, G. E., and Sejnowski, T. J. (1986). Learning and relearning in Boltzmann machines. In D. E. Rumelhart and J. L. McClelland (Eds.), *Parallel distributed processing: explorations in the microstructure of cognition*. Cambridge, MA: MIT Press.

Karnath, H. O. (1988). Deficits of attention in acute and recovered visual hemineglect. *Neuropsychologia, 26*, 27–43.

Karanath, H.-O., and Hartje, W. (1987). Residual information processing in the neglected visual half-field. *Journal of Neurology, 234*, 180–184.

Kinsbourne, M. (1988). Integrated field theory of consciousness. In A. J. Marcel and E. Bisiach (Eds.), *Consciousness in contemporary science*. Oxford: Clarendon Press.

Landis, T., Regard, M., and Serrat, A. (1980). Iconic reading in a case of alexia without agraphia caused by brain tumor: A tachistoscopic study. *Brain and Language, 11*, 45–53.

Marcel, A. J. (1983). Conscious and unconscious perception: Experiments on visual masking and word recognition. *Cognitive Psychology, 15*, 197–237.

Marshall, J. C., and Halligan, P. W. (1988). Blindsight and insight in visuospatial neglect. *Nature, 336*, 766–767.

Marzi, C. A., Tassinari, C., Aglioti, S., and Lutzemberger, L. (1986). Spatial summation across the vertical meridian in hemianopics: A test of blindsight. *Neuropsychologia, 24*, 749–758.

McGlinchey-Berroth, R., Milberg, W. P., Verfaellie, M., Alexander, M., and Kilduff, P. T. (1993). Semantic processing in the neglected visual field: Evidence from a lexical decision task. *Cognitive Neuropsychology, 10*, 79–108.

Mozer, M. C., and Behrmann, M. (1990). On the interaction of selective attention and lexical knowledge: A connectionist account of neglect dyslexia. *Journal of Cognitive Neuroscience, 2*, 96–123.

Patterson, K. E., and Kay, J. (1982). Letter-by-letter reading: Psychological descriptions of a neurological syndrome. *Quarterly Journal of Experimental Psychology, 34A*, 411–441.

Plaut, D. C., and Shallice, T. (1993). Deep dyslexia: A case study of connectionist neuropsychology. *Cognitive Neuropsychology, 10*, 377–500.

Poppel, E., Held, R., and Frost, D. (1973). Residual visual functions after brain wounds involving the central visual pathways in man. *Nature, 243*, 2295–2296.

Rafal, R., Smith, J., Krantz, J., Cohen, A., and Brennan, C. (1990). Extrageniculate vision in hemianopic humans: Saccade inhibition by signals in the blind field. *Science, 250*, 118–121.

Schacter, D. L., McAndrews, M. P., and Moscovitch, M. (1988). Access to consciousness: Dissociations between implicit and explicit knowledge in neuropsychological syndromes. In L. Weiskrantz (Ed.), *Thought without language*. Oxford: Oxford University Press.

Schiller, P. H., and Koerner, F. (1971). Discharge characteristics of single units in superior colliculus of the alert rhesus monkey. *Journal of Neurophysiology, 36*, 920–936.

Shallice, T., and Saffran, E. (1986). Lexical processing in the absence of explicit word identification: Evidence from a letter-by-letter reader. *Cognitive Neuropsychology, 3*, 429–458.

Sieroff, E., Pollatsek, A., and Posner, M. I. (1988). Recognition of visual letter strings following injury to the posterior visual spatial attention system. *Cognitive Neuropsychology, 5*, 427–449.

Squire, L. (1992). Memory and the hippocampus: A synthesis of findings from rats, monkeys and humans. *Psychological Review, 99*, 195–231.

Stoerig, P., and Cowey, A. (1990). Wavelength sensitivity in blindsight. *Nature, 342*, 916–918.

Tranel, D., and Damasio, A. (1985). Knowledge without awareness: An autonomic index of facial recognition by prosopagnosics. *Science, 228*, 1453–1454.

Tranel, D., Damasio, A. R., and Damasio, H. (1988). Intact recognition of facial expression, gender, and age in patients with impaired recognition of face identity. *Neurology, 38,* 690–696.

Volpe, B. T., LeDoux, J. E., and Gazzaniga, M. S. (1979). Information processing of visual stimuli in an "extinguished" field. *Nature, 282,* 722–724.

Wallace, M. A. (1994). Unconscious perception in neglect and extinction. In M. J. Farah and G. Ratcliff (Eds.), *The neuropsychology of high-level vision: Collected tutorial essays.* Hillsdale, NJ: Erlbaum Associates.

Wallace, M. A., and Farah, M. J. (1992). Savings in relearning face-name associations as evidence for "covert recognition" in prosopagnosia. *Journal of Cognitive Neuroscience, 4,* 150–154.

Warrington, E. K., and Shallice, T. (1980). Word-form dyslexia. *Brain, 103,* 99–112.

Weiskrantz, L. (1986). *Blindsight: A case study and implications.* Oxford: Oxford University Press.

Weiskrantz, L. (1990). Outlooks for blindsight: Explicit methodologies for implicit processes. *Proceedings of the Royal Society of London,* B239, 247–278.

Weiskrantz, L., Sanders, M. D., and Marshall, J. (1974). Visual capacity in the hemianopic visual field following a restricted occipital ablation. *Brain, 97,* 709–728.

Young, A. W., Hellawell, D., and De Haan, E. H. F. (1988). Cross-domain semantic priming in normal subjects and a prosopagnosic patient. *Quarterly Journal of Experimental Psychology, 38A,* 297–318.

# 3 The Organization of Sensory Motor Representations in the Neocortex: A Hypothesis Based on Temporal Coding

Wolf Singer

## 3.1 INTRODUCTION

A major, and by and large unresolved issue in contemporary brain research is the question of how brains develop representations of perceptual objects and of the environment in which these are embedded. A related and equally unresolved problem is how representations of motor acts are established. Accordingly, numerous proposals have been offered at different times, and supportive experimental evidence has been provided for all of them. It is thus likely that there is no unique and general solution for the organization of representations in neuronal systems. Rather, it appears that different species with differently organized nervous systems have developed different strategies, that even the same species employs different strategies in different sensory modalities, and that even within the same modality, different solutions are implemented for the representation of different contents.

Evidence from animals with simple nervous systems, such as insects or molluscs, indicates that individual neurons or small groups of neurons with fixed connectivity are used to represent complex constellations of sensory features and particular action patterns. Neurons have been identified in the brain of flying insects that encode selectively the complex constellation of motion vectors that emerges from flow field motion during flight maneuvers. These neurons achieve their selectivity by convergence of selected inputs from large sets of motion- and direction-specific neurons at more peripheral stages of processing. Their responses, in turn, are fed rather directly to the motor system. Thus, in these comparatively simple structured brains, sensory activity appears to converge onto a relatively small set of higher-order sensory cells, commonly called grandmother cells, which, through their selective responses, represent complex feature constellations and, through diverging efferent connections, activate the appropriate set of effector neurons. A similar strategy appears to be employed in the motor system of lower animals. Here, comand neurons have been identified whose activation gives rise to complex coordinated motor programs such as swallowing, swimming left turns, or running sideways. Command cells with similar properties have also been found in the nervous system of vertebrates. The famous Mauthner cells that coordinate escape behaviour in fish are an example.

At higher levels of processing, and especially in neocortical areas of the mammalian brain, neurons that could be considered as sensory grandmother cells or motor command neurons seem to be infrequent. Complex feature constellations or coordinated motor sequences no longer appear to be represented by the responses of individual neurons. Apart from neurons in the temporal lobe of primates which are activated preferentially by faces (Gross, Rocha-Miranda, and Bender 1972; Rolls 1991; Desimone et al 1984; Desimone et al. 1985; Perret, Mistlin, and Chitty 1987), no neurons have been found until now that respond selectively to other objects with which the animal is familiarized, such as particular food containers, various kinds of fruit, and cleaning equipment. This suggests that the representation of complex feature constellations by responses of individual neurons is used only as a coding strategy for certain classes of patterns. These could be patterns that are of particular behavioral relevance, need to be recognized very rapidly, require fast responses, and have distinctive features that facilitate their classification. For primates, faces may be such patterns because it is of utmost importance for these social animals to find out rapidly about the orientation of the face of a conspecies and about its facial expression. As newborn babies show a spontaneous preference for feature constellations characteristic of faces, templates for face recognition may even be genetically determined and hence may have been acquired during phylogeny through selection of connection patterns that favor preferential responses of neurons to various distinct aspects of faces. The same can be assumed to be the case for the representation of other stereotyped and behaviorally relevant patterns, such as the characteristic features of natural enemies or of prey (for review of the literature on inborn, phylogenetically acquired representations of complex feature constellations, see Coss 1991). However, even in the case of face-specific cells, it has to be assumed that many thousand cells respond if a particular face is seen. This makes it unlikely that an individual face is represented by the responses of a few cells that are tuned to that particular face.

As far as the representations of complex motor programs are concerned, evidence for the existence of command neurons is missing altogether. There are no individual cells in the motor cortex that could encode complicated motor acts involving the coordinated activation of a large number of different muscle groups. Rather, the trajectories of movements appear to be encoded by cooperative interactions between a large number of distributed neurons whereby a particular cell appears to participate in the programming of many different movement patterns (Georgopoulos 1990). Even for the complex flight programs in birds, which to a large extent are innate and can be expressed without much practice, there is, to my knowledge, no evidence for a representation of these movement patterns by individual command neurons.

In conclusion, then, available evidence from the relatively well-explored brains of higher vertebrates and mammals provides only scant support for the notion that representations of sensory patterns and motor programs consist of individual cells or small groups of cells with highly selective response properties. In the few cases where neurons with selectivity for highly specific and unique constellations of features have been encountered, these seem to be part of recognition systems with devoted functions. This raises the question of whether there are alternative concepts to single cell representations and, if so, whether there is any experimental support for them.

## 3.2 REPRESENTATIONS AND THE BINDING PROBLEM

Sensory and motor patterns are always composed of components. In the case of sensory patterns, the components are the various features that in their unique constellation characterize a particular perceptual object. In the case of motor patterns, the components are the individual muscle contractions or, at a higher programming level, the motion trajectories produced by the contraction of muscle groups that in their unique constellation and succession characterize a particular motor pattern. Hence, for the representation of sensory patterns and motor programs, mechanisms are required that allow the binding of those components together while preserving the specificity of their relations. The simplest way to achieve this binding and to establish an unambiguous code for the specific relations of features characterizing a particular pattern is, first, to represent the component features of the particular pattern by a set of neurons that respond selectively to the component features of the pattern and, second, to have this set of feature-selective neurons converge onto a single higher-order neuron. If the thresholds of this higher neuron are adjusted so that it responds only if a nearly complete set of feature detectors sensitive to the component features of the pattern is active simultaneously, the responses of this higher-order neuron would provide an unambiguous description of the relations between the component features and hence would be equivalent to the representation of the pattern. In this scheme, the features of the object are bound together by convergence of rigid connections that link neurons representing component features with neurons representing the whole pattern, and the relations between features are encoded by the specific architecture of these convergent connections. In essence, this is the coding strategy employed in the original perceptron architectures and in the subsequently developed multilayered feedforward neuronal networks.

Concerning early steps of processing, the predictions derived from this coding strategy are supported by experimental evidence from both simple and highly developed brains. The firing rate of neurons at peripheral levels of sensory systems signals the intensity of sensory stimuli, and in motor systems, the speed and force of muscle contractions and the location of the neuron within the cortical sheet reflect the location of stimuli and effector muscles. These observations led to the notion of rate and place coding. Moreover, individual neurons respond selectively only to particular features of sensory patterns or, in motor systems, trigger selectively the contraction of only particular muscle groups. Again, there is a close relation between the position of a neuron in the cortical sheet and its feature or effector selectivity. Thus, at peripheral levels of sensory and motor processing, individual neurons actually do seem to represent the component features of complex sensory and motor patterns, and rate and place codes appear sufficient to define the location and nature of these component features. This evidence encouraged systematic search for pattern-specific cardinal cells (Barlow 1972) at higher levels of processing. The subsequent discovery of face-specific cells appeared as strong support for binding by convergence and single neuron representations.

At about the same time, experimental evidence became available that indicated that both sensory and motor processes in the neocortex are organized in a rather distributed manner. This has been demonstrated particularly clearly for the mammalian visual system. There are more than twenty cortical areas, distinguished by either cytoarchitectonic features or their connectivity to which specific visual functions have been assigned. Many of these numerous processing stages are organized in parallel and are heavily interconnected. Nevertheless, there is a serial progression of signal transformation from occipital to more frontal cortical territories, and there appear to be two major processing streams: a ventral occipitotemporal and a dorsal occipitoparietal route (Mishkin, Ungerleider, and Macko 1983; Desimone et al. 1985; Newsome and Pare 1988; Felleman and van Essen 1991). Neurons of the ventral stream are sensitive to features such as color, contrast, and orientation and, at higher levels, also to rather complex geometrical shapes, including the stereotypes of faces. Neurons along the dorsal stream respond preferentially to moving contours and are selective for the speed and the direction of motion and at higher levels also for the compositions of motion vectors such as occur for movements in three dimensions. This has led to the proposal of a functional dichotomy of the visual system, with the ventral pathway dealing preferentially with the analysis and representation of visual objects and the dorsal pathway processing preferentially spatial information required for the programming of targeting movements (for review, see Rizzolatti, Riggio, and Sheliga, chap. 9, this volume). Thus, any visual object, in particular when it moves, evokes a highly fragmented and widely distributed pattern of activity. Depending on the features constituting the object, neurons become activated in different, often noncontiguous cortical areas, and it can be predicted that even simple visual patterns will give rise to simultaneous responses in a vast number of neurons distributed throughout the occipital, parietal, and temporal parts of the cortical sheath.

In the framework of the binding by convergence hypothesis, these distributed activities would still have to be considered as rather low level in the processing hierarchy, the assumption being that these distributed responses are reintegrated by convergence onto cardinal cells at higher levels of processing. However, not all of the predictions following from this assumption are supported by experimental evidence. First, cells occupying higher levels in the processing hierarchy are often less selective for particular features than those at earlier stages. Second, apart from cells responding preferentially to features of faces and hands (Baylis, Rolls, and Leonard 1985; Desimone et al. 1984; Gross, Rocha-Miranda, and Bender 1972; Perrett, Mistlin, and Chitty 1987; Rolls 1991), no other object-specific cells have been found so far. Third, it has been argued that there would probably not be enough cells in the brain if all distinguishable objects, including their many different views, each had to be represented by a specialized neuron or by small groups of neurons. Fourth, no single area in the visual processing stream has been identified so far that could serve as the ultimate site of convergence and would be large enough to accommodate the exceedingly large number of required neurons. Finally, it has been argued that binding by convergence may not be flexible enough to account for the rapid formation of representations of new patterns. In order to allow for the representation of new, hitherto-unknown objects, one would have to postulate a large reservoir of uncommitted cells. These neurons would have to maintain latent input connections from all feature-selective neurons at lower processing stages, and subsets of these connections would have to be selected and consolidated instantaneously when a new representation is to be established.

Similar binding problems arise in the case of motor control, but they have received less theoretical consideration. Here, the solution equivalent to binding by convergence is that there are individual command neurons at the top of the hierarchically organized motor systems whose activity is distributed through divergent and highly selective connections to specific subsets of effector neurons, each of which, in turn, activates a particular muscle group. Thus, the activation of a particular command neuron would trigger selectively a particular motor pattern. This coding concept encounters the same problem as its homologous on the sensory side. First, no such command neurons were found in areas that could perhaps be regarded as being on the top of the processing hierarchy, such as the supplementary motor field or prefrontal motor areas. Second, it is hard to see how activation of only a few neurons could give rise to the mass action required for the execution of a movement. Third, one would have to postulate a large reservoir of uncommitted cells in order to allow for the representation of newly learned motor patterns. These uncommitted command cells would have to maintain latent connections to virtually all effector muscles, and the appropriate subsets of these connections would have to become functional only, but then would have to be recruited permanently, when the particular motor skill is established for which these connections are required. Finally, another problem in the motor system becomes obvious, one related to temporal patterning. For the execution of a motor act, it is not sufficient to activate neurons simultaneously that innervate particular muscle groups, but it is necessary to generate complex and precisely coordinated temporal patterns according to which the distributed muscle groups are activated. This would necessitate sets of delay lines that distribute the activity of the command neuron in the appropriate temporal order to the effector neurons at more peripheral levels. This would further increase the number of command neurons because motions executed at different speeds would each require a command cell connected to a different set of delay lines.

In studies on sensory processing and pattern recognition, time has received much less attention as a coding dimension than in studies of motor control. It is clear, however, that binding has to occur in sensory processes not only across spatially segregated features but also across temporally disparate events. Sensory patterns are often spread out in time, and hence there must be mechanisms to establish relations between temporally disparate events and to represent these relations with an unambiguous code. According to the binding by convergence hypothesis, the solution would again consist in reserving individual neurons for the representation of different temporal patterns and, hence, to translate temporal patterns into position codes. To some extent this does indeed appear to be the case. In the visual system, motion trajectories, speed of motion, and direction of motion are represented by individual neurons (Newsome et al. 1990), and in the acoustic system, temporal patterns, such as frequency, frequency modulation, crescendo, and decrescendo, are also encoded by individual neurons whose response properties are specialized to these features (Scheich 1991). Again, one might consider representing more complex dynamic patterns by devoted cardinal cells that receive highly selective convergent input from cells responding selectively to features of dynamic patterns. Apart from raising exactly the same problems as the representation of static patterns by individual neurons, this introduces the complication of temporal integration. It is hard to see how temporally disparate events could be funneled through a simple feedforward net in a way that would ensure effective convergence, implying simultaneity at the level of the integrating cardinal cells.

Because of these numerous difficulties, which are characteristic for all perceptronlike architectures with predominant feedforward connections and convergence points in the form of cardinal and command cells, alternative proposals have been developed.

## 3.3 ASSEMBLIES AND TEMPORAL CODES

The alternative solutions to the binding problem all depart from the assumption that representations consist of assemblies of a large number of simultaneously active neurons that are distributed over many cortical areas (Abeles 1991; Braitenberg 1978; Crick 1984; Edelman 1989; Edelman and Mountcastle 1978; Grossberg 1980; Hebb 1949; Palm 1982, 1990; Singer 1985, 1990a; von der Malsburg 1985). The essential advantage of assembly coding is that individual cells can participate at different times in the representation of different objects. The assumption is that just as a particular feature can be shared by many different patterns, a particular neuron can be shared by many different representations in that it participates at different times in different "assemblies" of coactive neurons. The code is thus relational; the significance of an individual response depends entirely on the context set by the other members of the assembly. There are no further convergence centers beyond the assemblies.

There are three basic requirements for representing objects by such assemblies: (1) the responses of the many simultaneously active cells need to be examined for possible meaningful relations, (2) cells coding for features that can be related have to become organized in an assembly, and (3) neuronal elements that have joined a particular assembly must be identifiable as members of this very assembly and remain distinguishable from members of other assemblies. Their responses have to be labeled so that they can be recognized as being related; that is, the distributed responses of the assembly must be recognizable as representing a whole. It is commonly assumed that all three functions—the probing of relations, the subsequent organization of an assembly, and the labeling of responses—are achieved by selective reciprocal connections among the distributed neuronal elements. Several proposals have been made concerning the mechanisms by which these connections could serve to label the responses of neurons joined into the same assembly. Most of them assume that the assembly-generating connections are excitatory and reciprocal, thus enhancing and prolonging the responses of neurons that got organized in an assembly (Hebb 1949; Palm 1982; Grossberg 1980; Singer 1979, 1985). Neurons having joined an assembly would be distinguished by their strengthened and sustained responses.

The probabilities with which certain neurons tend to organize into particular assemblies are thus determined by the respective constellation of features and the functional architecture of coupling connections between the potential elements of an assembly. It follows that the assembly-generating connections must be endowed with adaptive synapses, the efficiency of which can be modified in a use-dependent way according to some kind of associative learning algorithm. Such adaptivity is required in order to allow for the generation of assemblies representing new objects and patterns. This notion establishes close relations between concepts of assembly coding and associative memory networks (Palm 1990).

A recent variant of the assembly hypothesis departs from the assumption that the functional units embodying features and constituting the elements of assemblies should be local groups of reciprocally coupled neurons rather than individual cells (Edelman 1987, 1989; Edelman and Mountcastle 1978). This postulate follows from the concept that analogous to clonal selection in the immune system, representations are created by selection from a vast repertoire of preexisting constellations. Introducing groups that differ from one another by variations of within-group interactions was considered as a possibility to create a sufficiently large and diversified repertoire. In this concept, assemblies would then be constituted by sets of spatially distributed and interconnected groups rather than by distributed individual neurons.

The implication of the concept of assembly coding is that a given set of neurons can be used for the formation of as many different representations as there are possible combinations of active and inactive cells in this set. This economizes on cell numbers but puts high demands on the specificity and diversity of ensemble-forming coupling connections. The following constraints must be met by such networks:

1. There must be selectively tuned reciprocal connections between neurons within the same cortical area and between neurons located in many different areas. Such connections are required for the selection and dynamic stabilization of specific assemblies.

2. These connections must be exceedingly numerous because their number, together with the number of cells, limits the number of possible constellations.

3. The network must exhibit dynamic properties because a particular cell must be able to link at different times with different partners.

4. The linking connections must have adaptive synapses in order to allow for the formation and stabilization of new representations.

Implementation of some of these coding principles in artificial neuronal networks allowed the realization of a number of attractive functions that in many respects resemble those of natural systems. But there was a serious limitation. As assemblies were distinguished solely by the strengthened responses of their constituents, assemblies representing different objects could not be represented simultaneously in the same matrix because they became confounded. It was impossible to know which of the numerous active and spatially intermingled cells would actually belong to a particular assembly. This superposition problem can be alleviated to some extent by place coding. In principle, overlap can be avoided by spatial segregation, and at higher levels one can create several matrices (cortical areas) in parallel and use a spatial code to segregate simultaneously active assemblies from one another. But this solution is a compromise. It reduces ambiguity, but it is expensive in terms of neuron numbers and, most important, it sacrifices flexibility. Position coding greatly constrains the degrees of freedom for partner selection. In order to maintain the position code, interactions between assemblies in different areas are forbidden because they would reintroduce the ambiguity that one wants to overcome.

It has been proposed, therefore, that assemblies should be distinguished by a temporal code rather than by a rate code (von der Malsburg 1985; von der Malsburg and Schneider 1986). A related proposal, although formulated less explicitly, had been made previously by Milner (1974). The suggestion was that the selective connections should establish temporal coherence on a millisecond time scale between the responses of the coupled cells, thereby making these responses distinguishable as coming from the same assembly. Thus, neurons joining into an assembly should synchronize their discharges. Expressing relations between members of an assembly by such a temporal code allows the superposition problem to be overcome because several assemblies can be active simultaneously in the same cortical area without becoming confounded. Assemblies that code for different figures in a scene could each engage in their own rhythm. Consequently, even if responses of neurons overlap on a coarse time scale, they remain distinguishable as members of a particular assembly because their responses are correlated at a millisecond time scale with the responses of other cells of the same assembly but not with cells of other assemblies. This concept of binding by synchrony has been developed further and generalized to intermodal integration (Damasio 1990) and even to integrative processes underlying phenomena such as attention (Crick 1984) and consciousness (Crick and Koch 1990).

## 3.4 SEARCH FOR ASSEMBLIES

Since assemblies are defined by relations between the responses of the constituting elements, one way to identify them is to record simultaneously from spatially distributed neurons in the brain and to search for covariance of responses (Abeles 1991; Aertsen and Gerstein 1985; Aiple and Krüger 1988). Another possibility is to look for stereotyped temporal response patterns of individual neurons. The idea behind this latter approach is that the specific architecture of the reciprocal connections between the elements of an assembly should lead to specific temporal patterning of the activity circulating within the assembly. This pattern should recur whenever the assembly is organized and, hence, its occurrence should show some correlation with stimulation or response conditions (Abeles 1991).

Both experimental strategies have been applied. For closely spaced cells within single functional columns, interactions were rather frequent, and cross-correlation analysis proved capable of distinguishing constellations where cells receive either common excitatory or inhibitory input or one cell excites or inhibits the other (Abeles and Gerstein 1988; Gochin et al. 1991; Michalski et al. 1983; Toyama, Kimura, and Tanaka 1981a, 1981b). However, for cells located farther apart, correlations were difficult to detect and, if present, were interpreted as indicative of common excitatory input (Gochin et al. 1991; Krüger and Aiple 1988; Ts'o Gilbert, and Wiesel 1986) or of global modulation of excitability (Aiple and Krüger 1988; Krüger and Aiple 1988). Thus, it appeared as if there were no indications of reciprocal cooperative interactions between the analyzed pairs of neurons or of dynamic changes in the relations among the respective discharge patterns. The observed relations could be accounted for by assuming bifurcating feedforward connections and lateral inhibition. It turned out also that recurring temporal patterns in neuronal responses were rare and showed only a loose correlation with particular stimulus or response conditions (Abeles 1991).

A new motivation to reinvestigate the hypothesis of temporally coded assemblies came from the recent observation that spatially adjacent neurons in the cat visual cortex have a strong tendency to engage in highly synchronous discharges when presented with their preferred stimulus (Gray and Singer 1987, 1989). The phenomenon of local response synchronization has since been observed at the multiunit level in several areas of the visual cortex of anesthetized (Eckhorn et al. 1988; Engel et al. 1991a) and awake cats (Raether, Gray, and Singer 1989), in the optic tectum of awake pigeons (Neuenschwander and Varela 1993), and recently also in the visual cortex of anesthetized (Livingstone 1991) and awake behaving monkeys (Kreiter and Singer 1992). This supports the proposal (Edelman 1987) that local clusters of neurons with similar response properties behave as a group consisting of tightly coupled elements. Typically, the synchronously occurring discharges follow each other at intervals of 15 to 30 ms and hence appear as oscillations in the $\beta$- and $\gamma$-frequency band. In the cat visual cortex, each of these synchronous events is associated with a large negativity in the field potential that is recordable from the same electrode (Gray et al. 1990; Gray and Singer 1989). Hence, the local field potential (LFP) exhibits pronounced oscillations in the range of 30 to 60 Hz. The frequency of these oscillations usually fluctuates over a range of 5 to 10 Hz even within a single oscillatory episode. Such episodes of synchronous activity are usually of short duration (100–300 ms) and often reoccur several times throughout the response to a continuously moving stimulus (Gray et al. 1990, 1992; Kreiter and Singer 1992). Neither the time of occurrence of these synchronized response episodes nor the phase of the oscillations is related to the position of the stimulus within the neuron's receptive field. When cross-correlation functions are computed between responses to subsequently presented identical stimuli, these "shift predictors" reveal no relation between the respective time series (Gray et al. 1990; Gray and Singer 1989). It has further been shown in anesthetized and awake cats (Engel et al. 1990; Gray and Singer 1989; Kreiter and Singer 1992; Kreiter, Engel, and Singer 1992; Raether, Gray, and Singer 1989) and anesthetized and awake monkeys (Kreiter and Singer 1992; Kreiter, Engel, and Singer 1992) that similar response synchronization can occur also between spatially segregated cell groups recorded with different electrodes within the same visual area. These episodes of long-distance synchronization usually occur at times when the local groups of neurons engage in synchronous, repetitive bursting. Hence, the cross-correlograms typically show a broad peak centered around zero delay, flanked on either side by troughs reflecting the synchronous bursts and the pauses between the bursts. When the duration of these pauses is sufficiently constant throughout the episode of synchronization, the cross-correlograms show, in addition, a modulation with multiple peaks and troughs. However, it needs to be emphasized that it is not a requirement for the synchronization of the responses of spatially distributed responses that these neurons engage in regular oscillatory activity. The synchronized burst-and-pause sequence may be quite aperiodic, not giving rise to regularly spaced multiple peaks in the cross-correlogram.

## 3.5 THE FEATURE DEPENDENCE OF RESPONSE SYNCHRONIZATION

Two central requirements of the assembly coding hypothesis are that the probability for distributed cells to join an assembly must in some way reflect the *Gestaltcriteria* according to which features tend to be grouped together and that individual cells can join different assemblies at different times, with these shifts depending on the configuration of the patterns used to activate the cells. Experimental evidence is compatible with these important and central predictions of the assembly concept.

Detailed studies in anesthetized cats and, recently, anesthetized and awake monkeys have revealed that synchronization probability for remote groups of cells depends on the spatial segregation and the feature preference of the respective cell groups, as well as on the configuration of the stimuli (Engel et al. 1990, 1991a, 1991b; Engel, König, and Singer 1991; Gray et al. 1989; Kreiter, Engel, and Singer 1992). Stimuli that according to common *Gestaltcriteria*, appear as single figures lead to synchronization among the responding groups, while stimuli appearing as independent figures or as parts of different figures fail to establish synchrony among the groups they excite (Engel, König, and Singer 1991; Gray et al. 1989).

In the primary visual cortex of cats, neurons with overlapping receptive fields usually synchronize their responses, provided that they are activated with a single stimulus and that their orientation and direction preferences are sufficiently similar to allow for their simultaneous activation by a single moving light bar (Gray et al. 1989; Engel et al. 1990). For more widely spaced cell groups with nonoverlapping receptive fields, synchronization probability decreases with increasing separation and becomes more and more dependent on the neurons' feature preferences, synchronization probability being higher for neurons preferring the same stimulus orientation and the same direction of motion. Thus, over the largest intra-areal distances investigated so far (7 mm), synchronization has been observed only between cell groups with similar orientation preferences when these were activated with bar stimuli that had the same orientation and moved with the same speed in the same direction. In these cases synchronization was strongest when the receptive fields were aligned colinearly and the cell groups activated by a single long light bar moving across both receptive fields at the same time. Synchronization decreased when this light bar was broken up into two coherently moving segments, and it disappeared altogether when the two light bars were moved in opposite directions across the two receptive fields and thus were no longer coherent with regard to the direction of motion (Gray et al. 1989). These results indicate clearly that synchronization probability depends critically on the feature preferences of the neurons and, hence, on their position within the columnar architecture of the cortex, on their spatial segregation, and, most important, on the configuration of the stimuli, especially on their coherence. Thus, synchronization probability reflects well some of the *Gestaltcriteria* for perceptual grouping. The high synchronization probability of nearby cells corresponds to the binding criterion of "vicinity," the dependence on receptive field similarities agrees with the criterion of "similarity," the strong synchronization observed in response to continuous stimuli obeys the criterion of "continuity," and the lack of synchrony in responses to stimuli moving in opposite directions relates to the criterion of "common fate."

In agreement with the second central prediction of the assembly concept is the recent demonstration that two different, spatially overlapping stimuli can be represented by two independently synchronized assemblies of cells and that individual groups can switch among different assemblies depending on stimulus configuration (Engel, König, and Singer 1991; Kreiter, Engel, and Singer 1992). If groups of cells with overlapping receptive fields but different orientation preferences are activated with a single moving light bar, they synchronize their responses even if some of these groups are suboptimally activated (Engel, König, and Singer 1991). If such a set of groups is stimulated with two independent stimuli moving in different directions, they no longer form one coherently active assembly but split into two independently synchronized assemblies, those groups joining the same synchronously active assembly that have a preference for the same stimulus. Thus, the two stimuli become represented by two spatially interleaved but temporally segregated assemblies. Groups representing the same stimulus synchronize their responses, and no consistent correlations exist among the activities of assemblies representing different stimuli. Local response parameters of the individual groups, such as the amplitude or the oscillatory patterning of the responses, are unaffected by changes in the global configuration of the stimuli. Thus, it is not possible to tell from the responses of individual groups whether they were activated by one coherent stimulus or by two different stimuli. The only cue for this distinction is provided by the evaluation of synchronicity of the responses of the activated groups. These results indicate that response synchronization between simultaneously activated groups depends not only on the feature preference of the respective groups but also, and to a crucial extent, on stimulus configuration. One methodological caveat is that cross-correlation analysis does not reliably reflect anatomical connectivity (see also Aertsen and Gerstein 1985). The conclusion is that the coupling between distributed cell groups is dynamic and can change in a stimulus-dependent way.

## 3.6 SYNCHRONIZATION BETWEEN AREAS

The hypothesis of assembly coding implies further that assemblies should be distributed entities extending across different cortical areas. In agreement with this prediction, response synchronization has also been found among groups located in different cortical areas. In the cat, interareal synchronization has been observed between cells in areas 17 and 18 (Eckhorn et al. 1988; Nelson et al. 1992), between cells in area 17 and area PLMS, an area specialized for motion processing (Engel et al. 1991a), and even between neurons in A17 of the two hemispheres (Engel et al. 1991b). In all of these cases, synchronization depended on receptive field constellations and stimulus configurations, similar to the intra-areal synchronization (Engel et al. 1991a, 1991b). Assemblies of neurons with temporally coherent responses can thus be very distributed and comprise cell groups located in different cortical areas.

## 3.7 THE SUBSTRATE FOR RESPONSE SYNCHRONIZATION

It is commonly assumed in cross-correlation studies that synchronization of neuronal responses with zero-phase lag is indicative of common input (Gerstein and Perkel 1972). It has been proposed, therefore, that the observed synchronization phenomena in the visual cortex are due to common oscillatory input from subcortical centers. This notion has received support by the discovery of oscillatory activity in the 40-Hz range in thalamic neurons

(Ghose and Freeman 1990, 1992; Steriade et al. 1991). However, synchronization by common subcortical input alone would be incompatible with the postulated role of synchronization in binding because it would allow for neither the required combinatorial flexibility nor for the dependency on feature constellations. The concept of assembly coding requires that the binding together of elements constituting an assembly is achieved through reciprocal connections between the elements representing particular features and not only by common input, which does not yet represent different features by different neurons. Synchronization by reciprocal connections was thought to be unlikely because of the conduction delays of nerve fibers. It seemed difficult to establish synchronization with zero-phase lag by reciprocal interactions between spatially distributed neurons given the rather long conduction delays in the coupling connections. Recent evidence shows, however, that response synchronization with zero-phase lag can indeed be achieved by cortico-cortical connections despite considerable conduction delays. It has been demonstrated that response synchronization between cell groups in area 17 of the two hemispheres is mediated by the corpus callosum (Engel et al. 1991b) and, hence, by a reciprocal cortico-cortical projection that shares many features with the tangential fiber systems interconnecting cell groups within the same visual area and across different cortical areas.

In higher mammals, signals coming from either side of the fixation point are projected to different hemispheres because of the partial decussation of the optic nerves. Neurons responding to figures extending across the vertical meridian are therefore located in different hemispheres. The responses of these cells have to be bound together in the same way as those of cells located within the same hemisphere. Consequently, the hypothesis that binding is achieved by response synchronization predicts that response synchronization between cells in area 17 of different hemispheres should follow the same rules as synchronization between cells in area 17 of the same hemisphere. The data show that this is indeed the case, that is, synchrony is established preferentially by stimuli that, according to *Gestaltcriteria*, appear as components of a single object. The demonstration that interhemispheric response synchronization reflects the coherence of stimuli and is mediated by callosal connections has two implications: it emphasizes the putative significance of response synchronization for perceptual grouping and proves that cortico-cortical connections can synchronize responses with zero-phase lag.

In the meantime, simulation studies are available confirming that it is possible to establish synchrony without phase lag in the absence of common input and despite variable conduction delays in the synchronizing connections (König and Schillen 1991; Schillen and König 1990; Schuster and Wagner 1990a, 1990b). Moreover, it is conceivable that during development, synchronizing connections are selected not only as a function of the feature selectivity of interconnected cells but also as a function of their conduction velocity. This would facilitate the establishment of synchrony because it would allow the selective consolidation of those connections that can effectively contribute to synchronization. However, the possibility of achieving synchrony through reciprocal connections does not exclude a contribution of common input to the establishment of cortical synchronization. Especially if temporal patterns of responses need to be coordinated across distant cortical areas, bifurcating cortico-cortical projections or divergent cortico-petal projections from subcortical structures such as the "nonspecific" thalamic nuclei, the basal ganglia, and the nuclei of the basal forebrain could play an important role. By modulating in synchrony the excitability of selected cortical areas, they could influence very effectively the probability with which neurons distributed across these selected areas engage in synchronous firing. This could be a way by which attentional mechanisms could bias binding between responses that are distributed across cortical areas and represent different feature domains or even modalities.

## 3.8 THE SELECTIVITY OF SYNCHRONIZING CONNECTIONS

The theory of assembly coding implies that assemblies are bound together by the coupling connections among the constituting elements. Therefore, the criteria according to which particular features are grouped together reside in the functional architecture of the connections. Thus, knowledge about the factors determining this architecture will help to answer the question whether *Gestaltcriteria* are inborn or acquired by experience. If this architecture is specified entirely by genetic instructions, perceptual grouping criteria will have to be regarded as genetically determined. If the architecture is modifiable by activity and hence experience, criteria for the segmentation of the visual scene into distinct figures could be acquired by learning. The numerous interindividual similarities in the layout of cortico-cortical connections indicate that basic principles of organization, such as laminar termination patterns, maximal spatial extent, and area specificity, are determined genetically. But there is also evidence for extensive epigenetic modifications and several reasons suggest that such additional epigenetic shaping may not only be advantageous but also indispensable. First, the topographical arrangement of cell groups preferring particular features is not solely determined by genetic instructions but is, in addition, influenced by experience (Blakemore and Cooper 1970; Singer, Freeman, and Rauschecker 1981). Therefore, it would seem that the architecture of the coupling connections cannot be fully predetermined by genetic instructions either. Second, it would be advantageous if the grouping criteria could be adapted to frequently occurring feature constellations in natural scenes—particularly to constellations that are behaviorally relevant. Third, use-dependent selection would make it possible to consolidate connections as a function of their conduction velocities. This could facilitate generation of architectures that support the establishment of synchrony.

Evidence compatible with such a use-dependent selection of cortico-cortical connections is available. In mammals, these connections develop mainly postnatally (Callaway and Katz 1990; Innocenti 1981; Luhmann, Martinez-Millan, and Singer 1986; Price and Blakemore 1985a) and attain their final specificity through an activity-dependent selection process (Callaway and Katz 1991; Innocenti and Frost 1979; Luhmann, Singer, and Martinez-Millan 1990; Price and Blakemore 1985b).

Direct evidence that this selection is based on a correlation analysis and leads to disruption of connections between cells that exhibit mainly decorrelated activity comes from experiments with strabismic kittens (Löwel and Singer 1992). Raising kittens with artificially induced strabismus leads to changes in the connections between the two eyes and cortical neurons so that individual cortical neurons become connected to only one eye (Hubel and Wiesel 1965). Thus, the population of cortical neurons splits into two subpopulations of about equal size, each responding rather selectively to stimulation of one eye only. This reorganization goes along with a modification of perceptual abilities. Strabismic subjects usually develop normal monocular vision in both eyes, but they become unable to bind signals conveyed by different eyes into coherent percepts even if these signals are made retinotopically contiguous by optical compensation of the squint angle (von Noorden 1990). This indicates that in strabismics, binding mechanisms are abnormal or missing between cells driven from different eyes.

Recently, it was found that in strabismics, response synchronization no longer occurs between cell groups connected to different eyes but is normal between cell groups connected to the same eye (König et al. 1990, 1993). Moreover, it was found that cortico-cortical connections had reorganized and, unlike in normal animals, no longer connected neurons receiving input from different eyes (Löwel and Singer 1992).

These results have several important implications. First, they corroborate the notion that tangential intracortical connections are the substrate for response synchronization. Second, they support the view that response synchronization serves perceptual binding. Third, they prove that the architecture of tangential connections is shaped by experience. And fourth, they suggest that this selection occurs according to a correlation rule in similar ways as experience-dependent circuit selection at other levels of the visual system (for reviews see Singer 1990b; Stryker 1990).

The last conclusion is based on the plausible assumption that in strabismics, once cortical cells have become monocular, responses of cells connected to the same eye will on the average show a much higher degree of correlation than responses of cells connected to different eyes. The close correlation between the loss of the ability to bind signals conveyed by the two eyes, the loss of response synchronization between cells driven by the two eyes, and the loss of connections between the cortical territories of the two eyes is thus in very good agreement with the hypothesis that the architecture of cortico-cortical connections, by determining the probability of response synchronization, determines the criteria for feature binding. Since this architecture is shaped by experience, it follows that at least some of the binding and segmentation criteria are acquired by experience; in other words, they are learned during early life.

## 3.9 MODIFICATION OF GROUPING CRITERIA IN THE ADULT

Everyday experience tells us that grouping criteria can be modified by learning and that new representations can be generated throughout life. This implies that the cortico-cortical connections need to preserve some plasticity in the adult. Recent evidence from in vitro studies on tissue slices of the visual cortex indicates that this is indeed the case. It was found that excitatory connections to cells in supragranular layers are still susceptible to use-dependent long-term modifications of their coupling strength (Artola and Singer 1987, 1990). The gain of a given set of connections can both increase and decrease in a reversible way; the control parameters are the coincidence of pre- and postsynaptic activation and the degree of postsynaptic depolarization (Artola, Bröcher, and Singer 1990). Thus, the modifications occur according to an associative algorithm, but the correlation rule is more complicated than that initially proposed by Hebb. It resembles in some respects the biphasic modification rule that has been proposed by Bienenstock, Cooper, and Munroe (1982) for the self-organization of thalamocortical connections, but it differs in that it also allows for weakening of inactive presynaptic afferents. Simulation studies indicate that such a biphasic modification rule is very effective when applied in associative memory networks (Hancock, Smith, and Phillips 1991). Available evidence indicates that intracortical connections are endowed with such adaptive synapses, but there is still no direct proof that the connections in question participate also in response synchronization. If they did—and there is no evidence against this possibility—it would imply that binding and segmentation criteria can still be acquired or at least modified in adults. Because such modifications would be addressed as learning, we might actually be looking at the substrate of learning new associations when we look at use-dependent synaptic modifications of cortico-cortical connections. The only difference between the developmental modifications of cortico-cortical connections and the synaptic changes in adults would be the extent and the reversibility of the modifications. The developmental process leads to actual modifications of the wiring scheme that are irreversible once growth of these pathways has come to an end, while the malleability that persists in the adult is confined to modifications of synaptic gain of existing connections.

This new view that experience-dependent synaptic modifications and, hence, learning might occur at processing levels as peripheral as the primary visual cortex is supported by recent psychophysical studies. These demonstrate that certain forms of visual learning remain restricted to a particular area in the visual field, are confined to a narrow range of stimulus orientations, and show little or no interocular generalization (Karni and Sagi 1991; Poggio, Fahle, and Edelman 1992). This indicates that synaptic modifications occur at processing stages as early as the primary visual cortex. The notion that synaptic plasticity persists into adulthood even in a primary sensory area agrees well with predictions derived from the hypothesis of assembly coding. This hypothesis emphasizes the need for cooperative and modifiable interactions between distributed neurons at levels where rather elementary features are extracted and represented. The cardinal cell hypothesis, by contrast, requires modifiable synapses only at processing levels where signals from elementary feature detectors converge onto the cells or cell groups that represent entire visual objects.

## 3.10  EVIDENCE FOR SYNCHRONY IN NONVISUAL STRUCTURES

The preceding sections have mainly dealt with possible functions of response synchronization as revealed by multielectrode recordings from visual cortical areas. The data indicate that response synchronization occurs often in conjunction with oscillatory burst-and-pause discharge patterns of local cell groups. The following paragraphs deal with whether similar oscillatory response patterns occur in nonvisual cortical structures, whether there is evidence for long-range response synchronization in nonvisual areas, and whether there is a relation between oscillatory discharge patterns and response synchronization.

Oscillatory activity in the $\beta$- and $\gamma$-range has been reported to occur spontaneously in both humans and higher mammals in a variety of nonvisual cortical and subcortical structures when the subjects are in a state of focused attention (Bouyer, Montaron, and Rougeul 1981; Montaron et al. 1982; Ribary et al. 1991; Rougeul et al. 1979; Sheer 1984, 1989; Spydell, Ford, and Sheer 1979) or when they are performing new and complicated motor acts (Murthy and Fetz 1992). Oscillatory components in the $\gamma$-frequency range are also contained in field-potential responses evoked by sensory stimuli outside visual cortex. This has been shown to be the case for the cortical responses following acoustic stimulation (Basar 1988; Basar et al. 1987; Basar-Eroglu and Basar 1991; Galambos and Hillyard 1981; Galambos, Makeig, and Talmachoff 1981; Galambos and Makeig 1988; Madler and Pöppel 1987; Pantev et al. 1991), for visual responses in the optic tectum of pigeons (Neuenschwander and Varela 1993), and for the event-related P300-wave, which is thought to reflect high-level cognitive processes related to selective attention (Basar-Eroglu and Basar 1991). Particularly regular and prominent field-potential oscillations in the range of 40 Hz occur also in the olfactory bulb during the inspiration phase of the respiratory cycle (Adrian 1941; Freeman 1975; Freeman and Skarda 1985).

There is ample evidence also from brain structures other than the visual cortex that groups of cells engage in rhythmic activity in the $\gamma$-frequency range. The fact that such periodic fluctuations of field potentials can be recorded with macroelectrodes from the scalp or the dura or from within the brain indicates further that a large number of neurons must be engaged in synchronized rhythmic discharges at the respective oscillation frequency. Otherwise, the weak currents associated with synaptic activity and action potentials of individual neurons would not sum up to recordable macropotentials. With the exception of the olfactory bulb, however, the amplitudes of these high-frequency oscillations are usually small. This could indicate that the groups of neurons engaged in such synchronous activity are small or dissipated, but it could also reflect phase jitter. At such high frequencies, even a small jitter in the range of a few milliseconds would produce a substantial smearing of field-potential responses and a reduction of their amplitude.

In contrast to the numerous field-potential studies that have disclosed the presence of $\gamma$-oscillations in many different cortical and subcortical areas, single-unit analyses designed specifically for the search of $\gamma$-oscillations have often failed to confirm their presence or have led to controversial results. So far, all investigators agree that oscillating unit activity in the $\gamma$-range occurs in the primary visual cortex of cats and monkeys, whether anesthetized or awake (Eckhorn et al. 1988; Ghose and Freeman 1990, 1992; Gray and Singer 1987, 1989; Jagadeesh, Ferster, and Gray 1991; Raether, Gray, and Singer 1989), in cat area 18 (Eckhorn et al. 1988; Gray and Singer 1989), and in area PMLS of cat visual cortex (Engel et al. 1991a). For area MT(V5) of the monkey visual cortex, there is one positive (Kreiter and Singer 1992) and one negative report (Young, Kanaka, and Yamara 1992). No evidence was found in temporal visual areas of the monkey (Tovee and Rolls 1992), but Nakamura, Mikami, and Kubota (1992) observed both low- and high-frequency oscillations associated with a recognition task in the temporal pole of macaca mulatta. High-frequency oscillations in single cell activity have also been observed in somatosensory cortex, where they were suppressed during sensory stimulation (Ahissar and Vaadia 1990), and in the frontal cortex, where they occurred in relation with particular behavioral sequences (Aertsen et al. 1991). Finally, oscillatory multiunit responses similar to those occurring in the cat visual cortex have been observed in the optic tectum of awake pigeons (Neuenschwander and Varela 1993). Thus, single unit data agree with the evidence from field-potential and electroencephalographic recordings that oscillatory activity in the $\gamma$-range is a robust phenomenon in certain brain structures, but there are also several negative findings.

No conclusions can be drawn from the presence or absence of oscillatory signs in autocorrelograms as to whether the cells' activity is or is not synchronized with other units. Such evidence can be obtained only with simultaneous recordings from several units or with field-potential analyses. Thus, analyses of autocorrelation functions are not appropriate for testing the hypothesis of binding by synchrony. What is required are multielectrode recordings and cross-correlation analyses.

So far only a few investigations have addressed the question of stimulation or context-dependent synchronization across spatially segregated groups of neurons in structures other than the visual cortex. Data are available only for the somatosensory and motor cortex (Murthy and Fetz 1992), the acoustic and the frontal cortex (Aertsen et al. 1992; Vaadia et al. 1991), and the pigeon optic tectum (Neuenschwander and Varela 1993). In every case, evidence has been obtained for transient interactions among simultaneously recorded neurons. As in the visual cortex, these episodes of manifest interactions were usually of short duration. In the acoustic and frontal cortex, the type of interaction was variable. In the optic tectum and the somatomotor cortex, the interactions resembled those in the visual cortex; the cells synchronized their responses with zero-phase lag. Some indications are available that these episodes of coupled discharges and synchrony are correlated with behavior. Synchronization among units in the somatosensory and motor cortex is particularly pronounced while the monkey tries to solve a difficult reaching task but vanishes once the task is learned, and reaching is executed without difficulty (Murthy and Fetz 1992). Synchronization among units in the frontal cortex has been reported to occur in contiguity with certain behavioral sequences in a complex delayed matching to sample task (Aertsen et al. 1992).

## 3.11 THE RELATION BETWEEN OSCILLATORY ACTIVITY AND RESPONSE SYNCHRONIZATION

The evidence that phases of response synchronization are often associated with episodes of oscillatory activity raises the question as to whether the two phenomena are causally related. One possibility is that oscillatory activity favors the occurrence of synchrony and hence is instrumental for response synchronization. In oscillatory responses, the occurrence of a burst predicts with some probability the occurrence of the next. It has been argued that this predictability is a necessary prerequisite to synchronize remote cell groups with zero-phase lag, despite considerable conduction delays in the coupling connections (for a review see Engel et al. 1992).

Another question is why the stimulus-induced synchronization events tend to occur on the basis of oscillations in the $\beta$- and $\gamma$-range and not on the basis of the more prominent low-frequency oscillations. The following considerations suggest that there may be good reasons that mechanisms subserving perceptual grouping at low levels of visual processing should operate at such a rapid time scale.

Psychophysical studies show that segmentation of natural scenes can be accomplished within 100 to 200 ms (Biedermann 1990; Burr 1981). If several simultaneously active assemblies have to be distinguished, a few successive synchronous bursts will have to be evaluated before such distinctions become possible. Thus, oscillations in the $\alpha$- and $\beta$-frequency range would be too slow to serve as carrier signal for binding at this level of processing. Much higher frequencies than those observed experimentally would not be tolerable because the conduction times of coupling connections do not permit synchrony to be established at much higher frequencies. Simulation studies indicate that reciprocally coupled groups of neurons can be synchronized only if the coupling delays do not exceed about one-third of the average period time. For much larger delays, temporal correlation with zero-phase lag cannot be established (König and Schillen 1991; Schillen and König 1990; Schuster and Wagner 1990a, 1990b). Transcallosal synchronization, for example, which has to cope with delays of at least 5 to 6 ms (Innocenti 1986), requires a minimum period time of roughly 15 ms. Thus, oscillatory activity in the $\beta$- and $\gamma$-range appears as a good compromise between the opposing constraints to establish synchrony rapidly and with high temporal resolution on the one hand and over long distances on the other. The first requires rapid succession of short bursts; the latter sets an upper limit to the frequency of reverberation.

These considerations do not exclude functionally relevant synchronization phenomena at lower oscillation frequencies. It is conceivable that binding across modalities or between widely distributed assemblies is achieved by synchronization at much slower rhythms. Limbic structures have been identified as essential for the formation of associations between different sensory representations, such as are required for storage and recall of episodic memory, for example (Mishkin 1978). Thus, the prominent low-frequency oscillations in the theta band that characterize the activity of limbic structures—in particular of the septo-hippocampal complex—could serve as a carrier frequency for the binding of widely distributed assemblies of cells. Each of these local assemblies could maintain its internal synchrony in the $\gamma$-frequency range while simultaneously participating in the slower rhythms of such a larger meta-assembly. In this case, one should see in addition to the high-frequency oscillation of the individual assemblies a more slowly oscillating modulation of their activity. These slower "envelope" oscillations of distributed assemblies rather than the synchronous $\gamma$-oscillations of the individual subassemblies could then again become synchronized.

## 3.12 THE ROLE OF OSCILLATIONS IN SYNAPTIC PLASTICITY

The fact that the temporal correlation between converging inputs to a cell is a critical variable in use-dependent plasticity adds another aspect to the putative functional significance of an oscillatory time structure in neuronal discharge patterns. The responses of neurons are usually rather long, extending over several hundred milliseconds. Thus, most of the responses evoked by a visual scene in the visual cortex are overlapping in time. According to the established synaptic modification rules, this would in the long run increase the gain of most of the coupling connections in the visual cortex and, hence, lead to unselective and meaningless association of neurons. This superposition problem can be avoided if the responses of the connected neurons have an oscillatory time structure. During the response, the envelope of the membrane potential should show a sustained depolarization; in addition, there should be a superimposed oscillatory modulation, as shown recently by Jagadeesh, Ferster, and Gray (1991). In this case, only the simultaneously active inputs, which oscillate in precise synchrony with the target cell, will have a chance to improve synaptic gain. Only then will the active synapses be able to activate voltage and ligand gated $Ca^{++}$ conductances (Mayer, Westbrook, and Guthrie 1984; Nowack et al. 1984), identified as necessary for homosynaptic potentiation of synaptic transmission in the hippocampus (Collingridge, Kehl, and McLennan 1983) and neocortex (Artola and Singer 1987, 1990). For oscillations in the $\gamma$-frequency range, this implies that the temporal window for cooperative interactions among converging inputs narrows to 10 ms or less. Thus, imposing an oscillatory burst-and-pause modulation on neuronal responses improves by an order of magnitude the temporal precision with which mechanisms can operate that rely on coincidence detection and cooperativity. In a sense, the functional role of temporally structured responses in synaptic plasticity is the same as that proposed for assembly coding. It serves to resolve superposition problems by providing a finely grained temporal code to express relations.

In conclusion, several independent lines of argumentation concerning the nature of neuronal representations, the constraints for signal transmission, and conditions of use-dependent synaptic plasticity lead to the postulate of a temporal code. All emphasize the significance of synchrony at a millisecond time scale. This, in turn, requires a temporal structure in neuronal responses that allows first for the distinction of synchronous from asynchronous states with high temporal resolution and then for the establishment of synchrony over large distances. Both requirements appear to be met best by oscillatory discharge patterns in which bursts and pauses follow one another with a certain degree of regularity, which should be neither too high nor too low. The fact that such rhythmic, synchronous activities are ubiquitous in the brain suggests that temporal codes may indeed be of similar importance as position and amplitude codes. The evidence that the average frequency of these rhythms changes in a state-dependent way and differs in different brain structures would indicate that different states and different functions require integration at different temporal and spatial scales. As the rhythm slows, the temporal window during which events can be distinguished as synchronous or asynchronous broadens and temporal discrimination becomes less precise, but binding by synchrony can be achieved over larger distances and among more cells. The consistent observation that the amplitude of field-potential oscillations increases as oscillation frequency decreases underlines this inverse relation between oscillation frequency and size of synchronously active cell assemblies.

## 3.13 THE DURATION OF COHERENT STATES

Assemblies defined by synchronous discharges need not oscillate at a constant frequency over prolonged periods of time. It is conceivable that neuronal networks that have been shaped extensively by prior learning processes can settle rapidly into a coherent state when the sensory patterns match perfectly with the architecture of the weighted connections in the network. Such a good match can be expected to occur for familiar patterns that during previous learning processes had the opportunity to mold the architecture of connections and to optimize the fit. If what matters for the nervous system is the simultaneity of discharges in large arrays of neurons, a single synchronous burst in thousands of distributed neurons may be sufficient for recognition. Obviously the nervous system can evaluate and attribute significance to coherent activity even if synchrony is confined to a single burst because its parallel organization allows for simultaneous assessment of highly distributed activity.

Especially if no further ambiguities have to be resolved or if no further modifications of synaptic connectivity are required, it would be advantageous if the system would not enter into prolonged cycles of reverberation after having converged toward such a highly organized state of synchrony. Rather, the activity in the assembly should be terminated as soon as possible in order to allow for the buildup of new representations. When processing highly familiar patterns or executing well-trained motor acts that raise no combinatorial problem, the system would thus function nearly as fast as a simple feed-forward network. Activity would be routed selectively through the network of tuned connections, and a pattern of simultaneous discharges could emerge in the corresponding assembly of distributed cells with latencies that are only little longer than the sum of the conduction and integration delays along the path of excitation. The differential and flexible routing of activity that is required in order to solicit the appropriate assembly could be achieved by the weighted association fibers within only a few reentrant cycles if there are no ambiguities. The duration of such cycles would be of about the same order of magnitude as the delays for simple feedforward processing as the parallel organization of the system allows for simultaneous exchange of signals between distributed processes. This possibility of rapid convergence toward coherent states and the option to maintain such states for only short durations is fully compatible with the hypothesis that representations consist of large assemblies of coherently active neurons. But it may become very difficult for the experimenter to identify the coherent states of assemblies if these last for only very short periods of time and if only a few neurons can be recorded simultaneously. As long as experimenters can assess the activity of only a few neurons at the same time, coherence will be detectable only if it is maintained over a sufficiently long period of time. Such is likely to be the case when ambiguities have to be resolved and novel patterns have to be learned. Murthy and Fetz (1992) have observed prolonged episodes of coherent activity over the sensory-motor cortex when the animal had to solve a new and difficult reaching task. Once the animal had learned how to perform it and the actions became skillful and rapid, it was no longer possible to record prolonged sequences of coherent activity.

Why, then, do episodes of prolonged coherence also occur in anesthetized preparations and in response to rather simple stimulus configurations? In this case, there are no ambiguities to be resolved, and there is no learning. We can only speculate. It is conceivable that because of anesthesia, the efficiency of feedback loops and associative connections is reduced, preventing the system from settling into nonambiguous states. In that case, what we observe could be the attempt of a frustrated system to converge toward a nonambiguous state. Due to missing feedback, neurons at peripheral processing levels would attempt to organize their responses solely according to the criteria set by the architecture of synchronizing connections at these levels, and the failure to organize corresponding assemblies at higher levels would result in rather stereotyped repetitions of these attempts to organize. This interpretation would agree with the consistent observation that episodes of response synchronization are shorter and less stereotyped in awake behaving animals, especially if these are challenged with very simple detection tasks (Kreiter and Singer 1992).

Further investigation of the validity of the hypothesis presented in this chapter will have to proceed along two lines. First, techniques will have to be developed that allow one to record simultaneously from much larger numbers of neurons in order to detect the expectedly very brief synchronous events that should occur during processing of familiar patterns and execution of well-trained motor acts. Second, as long as analysis has to be confined to only a few neurons, behavioral tasks will have to be designed that lead to a prolongation of coherent states. Such is to be expected if tasks are fraught with combinatorial problems requiring the solution of binding ambiguities or if new representations have to be learned.

## 3.14 RESPONSE SYNCHRONIZATION, ATTENTION, AND PERFORMANCE

The data and concepts reviewed here suggest that the activity of distributed neurons has to be organized in the temporal domain in order to become influential. The reason is that only coherent activity has a chance of being relayed over successive processing stages. Even more organization is likely to be required for the induction of synaptic modifications such as are thought to underlie processes of memory and learning. The reason is that thresholds for synaptic modifications are higher than for signal transmission and reached only if presynaptic input is sufficiently synchronized and coincident with postsynaptic depolarization (Artola and Singer 1987; Artola, Bröcher, and Singer 1990). My proposal is that the organization required for transmission and for synaptic modifications consists of the synchronization on a millisecond time scale of the responses of numerous distributed neurons.

This notion is likely to have some bearing also on the organization of attentional mechanisms. It is commonly assumed that stimulus-induced shifts of selective attention are caused in a bottom-up process by neuronal responses that are particularly salient. Because of neuronal adaptation, novel stimuli evoke particularly vigorous responses. It is assumed also that inhomogeneities in textures that lead to pop-out effects in visual search attract attention because the responses to the odd elements are enhanced due to inhibitory interactions in the matrix of feature-encoding neurons. The assumption is that neurons responsive to the same features inhibit each other, leading to a relative enhancement of responses to the uncommon features of the odd texture elements (Crick and Koch 1992). If the same arguments are applied to the concept of assembly coding, it follows that those assemblies should be particularly effective in attracting attention that make their discharges coherent with shorter latency and higher temporal precision than others. Conversely, responses of neurons reacting to features that cannot be grouped or bound successfully and, hence, cannot be synchronized with the responses of other neurons would have only a low chance of being relayed further and influencing shifts of selective attention. It is thus conceivable that out of the many responses that occur at peripheral stages of visual processing, only a few are actually passed on toward higher levels. These would be responses to particularly salient stimuli causing strong and simultaneous discharges in a sufficient number of neurons or responses of cells that succeeded in getting organized in sufficiently coherent assemblies. Thus, responses to changes in stimulus configuration or to moving targets would have a good chance to be passed on even without getting organized internally because they would be synchronized by the external event. But responses to stationary pattern elements would have to become organized through internal synchronization mechanisms in order to be propagated. This interpretation implies that neuronal responses that attract attention and gain control over behavior should differ from nonattended responses, not so much because they are stronger but because they are synchronized among each other. In order to test this prediction, one would have to record from arrays of cells and measure the coherence of the respective responses as a function of shifts in selective attention. The coherence rather than the amplitude of individual responses should increase when the animal directs its attention to the feature constellation encoded by the array of recorded neurons. This experimental strategy should also be suited to analyze top-down effects of changes in selective attention, in particular, at levels of processing more peripheral than those at which attention-dependent changes in response amplitude have been observed. The assumption here is that feedback connections from higher to lower levels bias the synchronization probability of neurons at lower levels. Thereby they could favor the emergence of coherent states in certain subpopulations of neurons as a function of activation patterns generated at higher levels. In a similar way, shifts of attention across different modalities could be achieved by enhancing selectively synchronization probability in particular sensory areas and not in others. This could be achieved, for example, by modulatory input from the basal forebrain or nonspecific thalamic nuclei. Preliminary data indicate that activation of these central core projection systems actually does enhance synchronization probability at the cortical level (Gray et al. 1992a; Singer 1990c). It is even conceivable that such subcortical modulation could bias selective association of assemblies across different cortical areas. If these projection systems were able to modulate in synchrony the excitability of cortical neurons distributed in different areas, this would greatly increase the probability that these neurons link selectively with each other and join into coherent activity. Such linking would be equivalent with the binding of the features represented in the respective cortical areas. Again, one would not be able to detect such coordinating influences with conventional single-unit recordings because these modulatory systems do not by themselves produce responses in cortical neurons. Rather, they modulate the integrative capacities of these neurons and the efficacy of excitatory and inhibitory influences exerted by the specific processing circuits (Singer 1990c). Thus, these systems would have to provide a temporal frame within which distributed responses can self-organize toward coherent states through the network of selective cortico-cortical connections. It is conceivable that the field-potential oscillations that are recordable from the scalp in humans (Sheer 1984) or from somatosensory (Rougeul et al. 1979; Murthy and Fetz 1992) and motor cortex (Murthy and Fetz 1992) in cats and monkeys reflect such modulatory input. In the monkey sensory motor cortex, these field-potential oscillations are related to the discharge probability of individual neurons, but this relation is loose, which would be compatible with a modulatory biasing function. In agreement with the temporal frame hypothesis is that these large-amplitude oscillations are coherent across different cortical areas and are particularly pronounced when the subjects are in states of focused attention and busy with tasks requiring integration of activity across different cortical areas.

Following the same line of reasoning, it is possible that access to the level of processing where representations reach consciousness is gated by coherence. It may be that the only activation patterns (assemblies) that reach the threshold of conscious awareness are those that are sufficiently organized or coherent (Crick and Koch 1990).

## REFERENCES

Abeles, M., ed. (1991). *Corticonics*. Cambridge: Cambridge University.

Abeles, M., and Gerstein, G. L. (1988). Detecting spatiotemporal firing patterns among simultaneously recorded single neurons. *J. Neurophysiol., 60*, 909–924.

Adrian, E. D. (1941). Afferent discharges to the cerebral cortex from peripheral sense organs. *J. Physiol. (Lond.), 100*, 159–191.

Aertsen, A. M. H. J., and Gerstein, G. L. (1985). Evaluation of neuronal connectivity: Sensitivity of cross-correlation. *Brain Res., 340*, 341–354.

Aertsen, A., Vaadia, E., Abeles, M., Ahissar, E., and Bergmann I. I. (1991). Neural interactions in the frontal cortex of a behaving monkey: Signs of dependence on stimulus context and behavioral states. *J. f. Hirnforschung., 32*, 735–743.

Ahissar, E., and Vaadia, E. (1990). Oscillatory activity of single units in the somatosensory cortex of an awake monkey and their possible role in texture analysis. *Proc. Natl. Acad. Sci. USA, 87*, 8935–8939.

Aiple, F., and Krüger, J. (1988). Neuronal synchrony in monkey striate cortex: Interocular signal flow and dependency on spike rates. *Exp. Brain Res., 72*, 141–149.

Artola, A. Bröcher, S., and Singer, W. (1990). Different voltage-dependent thresholds for the induction of long-term depression and long-term potentiation in slices of the rat visual cortex. *Nature, 347*, 69–72

Artola, A., and Singer, W. (1987). Long-term potentiation and NMDA receptors in rat visual cortex. *Nature, 330*, 649–652.

Artola, A., and Singer, W. (1990). The involvement of N-methyl-D-aspartate rat visual cortex. *Eur. J. Neurosci., 2*, 254–269.

Barlow, H. B. (1972). Single units and cognition: A neuron doctrine for perceptual psychology. *Perception, 1*, 371–394.

Basar, E. (1988). EEG-dynamics and evoked potentials in sensory and cognitive processing by the brain. In E. Basar (Ed.), *Dynamics of sensory and cognitive processing by the brain*, 30–55. Springer Series in Brain Dynamics, vol. 1. New York: Springer.

Basar-Eroglu, C., and Basar, E. (1991). A compound P300-40 Hz response of the cat hippocampus. *Intern. J. Neurosci., 60*, 227–237.

Basar, E., Rosen, B., Basar-Eroglu, C., and Greitschus, F. (1987). The association between 40 Hz-EEG and the middle latency response of the auditory evoked potential. *Intern. J. Neurosci.,* 33, 103–117.

Baylis, G. C., Rolls, E. T., and Leonard, C. M. (1985). Selectivity between faces in the responses of a population of neurons in the cortex in the superior temporal sulcus of the monkey. *Brain Res.,* 342, 91–102.

Biedermann, J. (1990). Higher-level vision. In D. N. Osherson, S. M. Kosslyn, and J. M. Hollerbach (Eds.), *Visual cognition and action,* 41–72. Cambridge, MA: MIT Press.

Bienenstock, E., Cooper, L. N., and Munroe, P. (1982). Theory for the development of neuron selectivity: Orientation specificity and binocular interaction in visual cortex. *J. Neuroscience,* 2, 32–48.

Blakemore, C., and Cooper G. F. (1970). Development of the brain depends on the visual environment. *Nature,* 228, 477–478.

Bouyer, J. J., Montaron, M. F., and Rougeul, A. (1981). Fast fronto-parietal rhythms during combined focused attentive behaviour and immobility in cat: Cortical and thalamic localizations. *Electroencephalogr. Clin. Neurophysiol.,* 51, 244–252.

Braitenberg, V. (1978). Cell assemblies in the cerebral cortex. In R. Heim and G. Palm (Eds.), *Lecture Notes in Biomathematics 21, Theoretical Approaches in Complex Systems,* 171–188. Berlin: Springer.

Burr, D. C. (1981). Temporal summation of moving images by the human visual system. *Proc. R. Soc. London B,* 211, 321–339.

Callaway, E. M., and Katz, L. C. (1990). Emergence and refinement of clustered horizontal connections in cat striate cortex. *J. Neurosci.,* 10, 1134–1153.

Callaway, E. M., and Katz, L. C. (1991). Effects of binocular deprivation on the development of clustered horizontal connections in cat striate cortex. *Proc. Natl. Acad. Sci. USA,* 88, 745–749.

Collingridge, G. L., Kehl, S. J., and McLennan, H. (1983). Excitatory amino acids in synaptic transmission in the Schaffer collateral commissural pathway of the rat hippocampus. *J. Physiol.,* 334, 33–46.

Coss, R. G. (1991). Evolutionary persistence of memory-like processes. *Concepts in Neuroscience,* 2, 129–168.

Crick, F. (1984). Function of the thalamic reticular complex: The searchlight hypothesis. *Proc. Natl. Acad. Sci. USA,* 81, 4586–4590.

Crick, F., and Koch, C. (1990). Towards a neurobiological theory of consciousness. *Sem. Neurosci.,* 2, 263–275.

Crick, F., and Koch, C. (1992). The problem of consciousness. *Scientific American,* 9, 111–117.

Damasio, A. R. (1990). Synchronous activation in multiple cortical regions: A mechanism for recall. *Sem. Neurosci.,* 2, 287–296.

Desimone, R., Albright, T. D., Gross, C. G., and Bruce, C. (1984). Stimulus-selective properties of inferior temporal neurons in the macaque. *J. Neurosci.,* 4, 2051–2062

Desimone, R., Schein, S. J., Moran, J., and Ungerleider, L. G. (1985). Contour, color and shape analysis beyond the striate cortex. *Vision Res.,* 24, 441–452.

Eckhorn, R., Bauer, R., Jordan, W., Brosch, M., Kruse, W., Munk, M., and Reitboeck, H. J. (1988). Coherent oscillations: A mechanism for feature linking in the visual cortex? *Biol. Cybern.,* 60, 121–130.

Edelmann, G. M. (1987). *Neural Darwinism: The theory of neuronal group selection.* New York: Basic Books.

Edelman, G. M. (1989). *The remembered present.* New York: Basic Books.

Edelman, G. M., and Mountcastle, V. B. (1978). *The mindful brain.* Cambridge, MA: MIT Press.

Engel, A. K., König, P., Gray, C. M., and Singer, W. (1990). Stimulus-dependent neuronal oscillations in cat visual cortex: Inter-columnar interaction as determined by cross-correlation analysis. *Eur. J. Neurosci.,* 2, 588–606.

Engel, A. K., König, P., Kreiter, A. K., and Singer, W. (1991b). Interhemispheric synchronization of oscillatory neuronal responses in cat visual cortex. *Science,* 252, 1177–1179.

Engel, A. K., König, P., Kreiter, A. K., Schillen, T. B., and Singer, W. (1992). Temporal coding in the visual cortex: New vistas on integration in the nervous system. *Trends in Neuroscience,* 15, 218–226.

Engel, A. K., König, P., and Singer, W. (1991). Direct physiological evidence for scene segmentation by temporal coding. *Proc. Natl. Acad. Sci. USA,* 88, 9136–9140.

Engel, A. K., Kreiter, A. K., König, P., and Singer, W. (1991a). Synchronization of oscillatory neuronal responses between striate and extrastriate visual cortical areas of the cat. *Proc. Natl. Acad. Sci. USA,* 88, 6048–6052.

Felleman, D. J., and van Essen, D. C. (1991). Distributed hierarchical processing in the primate cerebral cortex. *Cerebral Cortex,* 1, 1–47.

Freeman, W. J. (Ed.) (1975). *Mass action in the nervous system.* New York: Academic Press.

Freeman, W. J., and Skarda, C. A. (1985). Spatial EEG-patterns, non-linear dynamics and perception: The neo-Sherringtonian view. *Brain Research Review,* 10, 147–175.

Galambos, R., and Hillyard, S. A. (1981). Electrophysiological approaches to human cognitive processing. *Neurosci. Res. Progr. Bull.,* 20 (2).

Galambos, R., and Makeig, S. (1988). In E. Basar and T. Bullock (Eds.), *Dynamics of sensory and cognitive processing by the brain,* 103–122. Berlin: Springer.

Galambos, R., Makeig, S., and Talmachoff, P. J. (1981). A 40-Hz auditory potential recorded from the human scalp. *Proc. Nat. Acad. Sci. USA,* 78, 2643–2647.

Georgopoulos, A. P. (1990). Neural coding of the direction of reaching and a comparison with saccadic eye movements. In *Cold Spring Harbor Symposium on Quantitative Biology,* vol. 55, 849–859. Cold Spring Harbor, NY: Laboratory Press.

Gerstein, G. L., and Perkel, D. H. (1972). Mutual temporal relationship among neuronal spike trains. Statistical techniques for display and analysis. *Biophys. J.,* 12, 453–473.

Ghose, G. M., and Freeman, R. D. (1990). Origins of oscillatory activity in the cortex. *Soc. Neurosci. Abstr.,* 16, 523.4.

Ghose, G. M., and Freeman, R. D. (1992). Oscillatory discharge in the visual system: Does it have a functional role? *J. Neurophys.,* 68, 1558–1574.

Gochin, P. M., Miller, E. K., Gross, C. G., and Gerstein, G. L. (1991). Functional interactions among neurons in inferior temporal cortex of the awake macaque. *Exp. Brain Res.,* 84, 505–516.

Gray, C. M, Engel, A. K., König, P., and Singer, W. (1990). Stimulus-dependent neuronal oscillations in cat visual cortex: Receptive field properties and feature dependence. *Eur. J. Neurosci.,* 2, 607–619.

Gray, C. M., Engel, A. K., König, P., and Singer, W. (1992a). Mechanisms underlying the generation of neuronal oscillations in cat visual cortex. In E. Basar and T. H. Bullock (Eds.), *Induced rhythms in the brain,* 29–45. Brain Dynamic Series. Boston: Birkhäuser.

Gray, C. M., Engel, A. K., König, P., and Singer, W. (1992b). Synchronization of oscillatory neuronal responses in cat striate cortex: Temporal properties. *Vis. Neurosci., 8,* 337–347.

Gray, C. M., König, P., Engel, A. K., and Singer, W. (1989). Oscillatory responses in cat visual cortex exhibit inter-columnar synchronization which reflects global stimulus properties. *Nature, 338,* 334–337.

Gray, C. M., and Singer, W. (1987). Stimulus-specific neuronal oscillations in the cat visual cortex: A cortical functional unit. *Soc. Neurosci. Abstr., 13,* 404.3.

Gray, C. M., and Singer, W. (1989). Stimulus-specific neuronal oscillations in orientation columns of cat visual cortex. *Proc. Natl. Acad. Sci. USA, 86,* 1698–1702.

Gross, C. G., Rocha-Miranda, E. C., and Bender, D. B. (1972). Visual properties of neurons in inferotemporal cortex of the macaque. *J. Neurophysiol., 35,* 96–111.

Grossberg, S. (1980). How does the brain build a cognitive code? *Psychol. Rev., 87,* 1–51.

Hancock, P. J. B., Smith, L. S., and Phillips, W. A. (1991). A biologically supported error correcting learning rule. *Neural Comput., 3,* 201–212.

Hebb, D. O. (1949). *The organization of behavior.* New York: Wiley.

Hubel, D. H., and Wiesel, T. N. (1965). Binocular interaction in striate cortex of kittens reared with artificial squint. *J. Neurophysiol., 28,* 1041–1059.

Innocenti, G. M. (1981). Growth and reshaping of axons in the establishment of visual callosal connections. *Science, 212,* 824–827.

Innocenti, G. M. (1986). General organization of callosal connections in the cerebral cortex. In E. G. Jones and A. Peters (Eds.), *Cerebral cortex,* 291–353. New York: Plenum Press.

Innocenti, G. M., and Frost, D. O. (1979). Effects of visual experience on the maturation of the efferent system to the corpus callosum. *Nature, 280,* 231–234.

Jagadeesh, B., Ferster, D., and Gray, C. M. (1991). Visually evoked oscillations of membrane potential in neurons of cat area 17. *Soc. Neurosci. Abstr., 17,* 73.2.

Karni, A., and Sagi, D. (1991). Where practice makes perfect in texture discriminations: Evidence for primary visual cortex plasticity. *Proc. Natl. Acad. Sci. USA, 88,* 4966–4970.

König, P., Engel, A. K., Löwel, S., and Singer, W. (1990). Squint affects occurrence and synchronization of oscillatory responses in cat visual cortex. *Soc. Neurosci. Abstr., 16,* 523.2.

König, P., Engel, A. K., Löwel, S., and Singer, W. (1993). Squint affects synchronization of oscillatory responses in cat visual cortex. *Eur. J. Neurosci., 5,* 501–508.

König, P., and Schillen, T. B. (1991). Stimulus-dependent assembly formation of oscillatory responses: I. synchronization. *Neural Computation, 3,* 155–166.

Kreiter, A. K., Engel, A. K., and Singer, W. (1992). Stimulus-dependent synchronization of oscillatory neuronal activity in the superior temporal sulcus of the macaque monkey. *Eur. Neurosci. Ass. Abstract., 15,* 1076.

Kreiter, A. K., and Singer, W. (1992). Oscillatory neuronal responses in the visual cortex of the awake macaque monkey. *Eur. J. Neurosci., 4,* 369–375.

Krüger, J., and Aiple, F. (1988). Multimicroelectrode investigation of monkey striate cortex: Spike train correlations in the infragranular layers. *J. Neurophysiol., 60,* 798–828.

Livingstone, M. S. (1991). Visually evoked oscillations in monkey striate cortex. *Soc. Neurosci. Abstr., 17,* 73.3.

Löwel, S., and Singer, W. (1992). Selection of intrinsic horizontal connections in the visual cortex by correlated neuronal activity. *Science, 255,* 209–212.

Luhmann, H. J., Martinez-Millan, L., and Singer, W. (1986). Development of horizontal intrinsic connections in cat striate cortex. *Exp. Brain Res., 63*, 443–448.

Luhmann, H. J., Singer, W., and Martinez-Millan, L. (1990). Horizontal interactions in cat striate cortex: I. Anatomical substrate and postnatal development. *Eur. J. Neurosci., 2*, 344–357.

Madler, C., and Pöppel, E. (1987). Auditory evoked potentials indicate the loss of neuronal oscillations during general anaesthesia. *Naturwissenschaften, 74*, 42–43.

Mayer, M. L., Westbrook, G. L., and Guthrie, P. B. (1984). Voltage-dependent block by $Mg^{2+}$ of NMDA responses in spinal cord neurons. *Nature, 309*, 261–263.

Michalski, A., Gerstein, G. L., Czarkowska, J., and Tarnecki, R. (1983). Interactions between cat striate cortex neurons. *Exp. Brain Res., 51*, 97–107.

Milner, P. M. (1974). A model for visual shape recognition. *Psychological Review, 81*, 521–535.

Mishkin, M. (1978). Memory in monkeys severely impaired by combined but not by separate removal of amygdala and hippocampus. *Nature, 273*, 278–297.

Mishkim, M., Ungerleider, L. G., and Macko, K. A. (1983). Object vision and spatial vision: Two cortical pathways, *Trends in Neuroscience, 6*, 414–418.

Montaron, M. P., Bouyer, J. J., Rougeul, A., and Buser, P. (1982). Ventral mesencephalic tegmentum (VMT) controls electrocortical beta rhythms and associated attentive behavior in cat. *Behav. Brain Res., 6*, 129–145.

Murthy, V. N., and Fetz, E. E. (1992). Coherent 25- to 35-Hz oscillations in the sensorimotor cortex of awake behaving monkeys. *Proc. Natl. Acad. Sci. USA, 89*, 5670–5674.

Nakamura, K., Mikami, A., and Kubota, K. (1992). Oscillatory neuronal activity related to visual short-term memory in monkey temporal pole. *NeuroReport, 3*, 117–120.

Nelson, J. I., Salin, P. A., Munk, M. H. J., Arzi, M., and Bullier, J. (1992). Spatial and temporal coherence in cortico-cortical connections: A cross-correlation study in areas 17 and 18 in the cat. *Visual Neurosci., 9*, 21–38.

Neuenschwander, S., and Varela, F. J. (1990). Sensory-triggered oscillatory activity in the avian optic tectum. *Soc. Neurosci. Abstr., 16*, 47.6.

Neuenschwander, S., and Varela, F. J. (1993). Visually-triggered neuronal oscillations in birds: An autocorrelation study of tectal activity. *Eur. J. Neurosci., 5*, 870–881.

Newsome, W. T., and Pare, E. B. (1988). A selective impairment of motion perception following lesions of the middle temporal visual area (MT). *J. Neurosci., 8*, 2201–2211.

Newsome, W. T., Britten, K. H., Salzman, C. O., and Moushon, M. A. (1990). Neuronal mechanisms of motion perception. *Cold Spring Harbor Symposium on Quantitative Biology, 55*, 697–705.

Nowak, L., Bregestovski, P., Ascher, P., Herbet, A., and Prochiantz, A. (1984). Magnesium gates glutamate-activated channels in mouse central neurons. *Nature, 307*, 462–465.

Palm, G. (1982). *Neural Assemblies*. Heidelberg: Springer.

Palm, G. (1990). Cell assemblies as a guideline for brain research. *Concepts in Neuroscience, 1*, 133–137.

Pantev, C., Makeig, S., Hoke, M., Galambos, R., Hampson, S., and Gallen, C. (1991). Human auditory evoked gamma-band magnetic fields. *Proc. Natl. Acad. Sci. USA, 88*, 8996–9000.

Perrett, D. I., Mistlin, A. J., and Chitty, A. J. (1987). Visual neurons responsive to faces. *Trends in Neuroscience, 10*, 358–364.

Poggio, T., Fahle, M., and Edelman, S. (1992). Fast perceptual learning in visual hyperacuity. *Science, 256,* 1018–1021.

Price, D. J., and Blakemore, C. (1985a). The postnatal development of the association projection from visual cortical area 17 to area 18 in the cat. *J. Neurosci., 5,* 2443–2452.

Price, D. J., and Blakemore, C. (1985b). Regressive events in the postnatal development of association projections in the visual cortex. *Nature, 316,* 721–724.

Raether, A., Gray, C. M., and Singer, W. (1989). Intercolumnar interactions of oscillatory neuronal responses in the visual cortex of alert cats. *Eur. Neurosci. Ass., 12,* 72.5.

Ribary, U., Joannides, A. A., Singh, K. D., Hasson, R., Bolton, J. P. R., Lado, F., Mogilner, A., and Llinas, R. (1991). Magnetic field tomography of coherent thalamocortical 40 Hz oscillations in humans. *Proc. Natl. Acad. Sci. USA, 88,* 11037–11041.

Rolls, E. T. (1991). Neural organization of higher visual functions. *Curr. Opin. Neurobiol., 1,* 274–278.

Rougeul, A., Bouyer, J. J., Dedet, L., and Debray, O. (1979). Fast somato-parietal rhythms during combined focal attention and immobility in baboon and squirrel monkey. *Electroenceph. Clin. Neurophysiol., 46,* 310–319.

Scheich, H. (1991). Auditory Cortex: Comparative aspects of maps and plasticity. *Current Opinion in Neurobiology, 1,* 236–247.

Schillen, T. B., and König, P. (1990). Coherency detection by coupled oscillatory responses—Synchronization connections in neural oscillator layers. In R. Eckmiller (Ed.), *Parallel processing in neural systems and computers,* 139–142. Amsterdam: Elsevier.

Schuster, H. G., and Wagner, P. (1990a). A model for neuronal oscillations in the visual cortex. 1. Mean-field theory and derivation of the phase equations. *Biol. Cybern., 64,* 77–82.

Schuster, H. G., and Wagner, P. (1990b). A model for neuronal oscillations in the visual cortex. 2. Phase description of the feature dependent synchronization. *Biol. Cybern., 64,* 83–85.

Sheer, D. E. (1984). Focused arousal, 40 Hz EEG, and dysfunction. In T. Elbert, B. Rockstroh, W. Lutzenberger, and N. Birbaumer (Eds.), *Self-regulation of the brain and behavior,* 66–84. New York: Springer.

Sheer, D. E. (1989). Sensory and cognitive 40-Hz event-related potentials. In E. Basar and T. H. Bullock (Eds.), *Brain dynamics,* 338–374. Berlin: Springer.

Singer, W. (1979). Central-core control of visual cortex functions. In F. O. Schmitt and F. G. Worden (Eds.), *The neurosciences: Fourth study program,* 1093–1110. Cambridge, MA: MIT Press.

Singer, W. (1985). Activity-dependent self-organization of the mammalian visual cortex. In D. Rose and V. G. Dobson (Eds.), *Models of the visual cortex,* 123–136. Chichester: Wiley.

Singer, W. (1990a). Search for coherence: A basic principle of cortical self-organization. *Concepts in Neuroscience, 1,* 1–26.

Singer, W. (1990b). The formation of cooperative cell assemblies in the visual cortex. *J. Exp. Biol., 153,* 177–197.

Singer, W. (1990c). The role of acetylcholine in use-dependent plasticity of the visual cortex. In M. Steriade and D. Biesold (Eds.), *Brain cholinergic systems,* 314–336. New York: Oxford University Press.

Singer, W., Freeman, B., and Rauschecker J. (1981). Restriction of visual experience to a single orientation affects the organization of orientation columns in cat visual cortex. A study with deoxyglucose. *Exp. Brain Res., 41,* 199–215.

Spydell, J. D., Ford, M. R., and Sheer, D. E. (1979). Task dependent cerebral lateralization of the 40 Hertz EEG rhythm. *Psychophysiology*, 16, 347–350.

Steriade, M., Curro-Dossi, R., Paré, D., and Oakson, G. (1991). Fast oscillations (20–40 Hz) in thalamocortical systems and their potentiation by mesopontine cholinergic nuclei in the cat. *Proc. Natl. Acad. Sci. USA*, 88, 4396–4400.

Stryker, M. P. (1990). Activity-dependent reorganization of afferents in the developing mammalian visual system. In D. M. K. Lam and C. J. Shatz (Eds.), *Development of the visual system*, 267. Cambridge, MA: MIT Press.

Tovee, M. J., and Rolls, E. T. (1992). Oscillatory activity is not evident in the primate temporal visual cortex with static stimuli. *NeuroReport*, 3, 369–372.

Toyama, K., Kimura, M., and Tanaka, K. (1981a). Cross-correlation analysis of interneuronal connectivity in cat visual cortex. *J. Neurophysiol.*, 46, 191–201.

Toyama, K., Kimura, M., and Tanaka, K. (1981b). Organization of cat visual cortex as investigated by cross-correlation techniques. *J. Neurophysiol.*, 46, 202–214.

Ts'o, D., Gilbert, C., and Wiesel, T. N. (1986). Relationship between horizontal interactions and functional architecture in cat striate cortex as revealed by cross-correlation analysis. *J. Neurosci.*, 6, 1160–1170.

Vaadia, E., Ahissar, E., Bergman, H., and Lavner, Y. (1991). Correlated activity of neurons: A neural code for higher brain functions? In J. Krüger (Ed.), *Neuronal cooperativity*, 249–279. Springer Series in Synergistics. Berlin: Springer-Verlag.

von der Malsburg, C. (1985). Nervous structures with dynamical links. *Ber. Bunsenges. Phys. Chem.*, 89, 703–710.

von der Malsburg, C., and Schneider, W. (1986). A neural cocktail-party processor. *Biol. Cybern.*, 54, 29–40.

von Noorden, G. K. (1990). *Binocular vision and ocular motility: Theory and management of strabismus*. St. Louis, MO: C. V. Mosby.

Young, M. P., Kanaka, K., and Yamane, S. (1992). On oscillating neuronal responses in the visual cortex of the monkey. *J. Neurophysiol.*, 67, 1464–1474.

# 4 The Role of Parallel Pathways in Visible Persistence

C. A. Marzi, M. Girelli, G. Tassinari,
L. Cristofori, A. Talacchi, M. Gentilin, and
G. Marchini

ABSTRACT  Patients with compression of the visual pathways at the optic chiasma by a pituitary adenoma have been tested for temporal integration of visual form. The task requires that a stimulus, consisting of parts of a digit, persist in the visual system until it can be integrated with a complementary successive stimulus to give a unitary percept of the digit. Four interstimulus intervals (ISIs) were tested (15, 30, 45, 60 ms) by means of tachistoscopic presentations lateralized to either visual hemifield of either eye. Patients did not differ significantly from control subjects in overall accuracy or speed of recognition of the digits. However, they were impaired in accuracy of recognition in the temporal hemifields (nasal hemiretinae) at ISIs of 15 and 30 ms but not at longer ISIs (45 and 60 ms). These results suggest that visual persistence can be dissociated into two components: one lasting less than 45 ms that is markedly impaired by compression of the visual pathways, and another one lasting up to 60 ms (and probably longer) that shows no impairment. The former type of persistence might be analogous to "visible" persistence described by Coltheart (1980) and be mediated by neurones with transient response properties typical of the magnocellular system. The latter might instead be analogous to a longer-lasting form of persistence subserved by the sustained responses of the parvocellular system.

## 4.1 INTRODUCTION

Converging evidence from structural, physiological, and psychophysical studies indicates that the mammalian visual system can be subdivided into at least two functional channels (Stone 1983; Sherman 1985; DeYoe and Van Essen 1988; Livingstone and Hubel 1988; Lennie et al. 1990; Schiller, Logothetis, and Charles 1990; Shapley 1990; Zeki 1990; Merigan and Maunsell 1993). Such a dichotomy should not be confused with the classic two-visual-systems hypothesis, which advocates a system for "what," which is subserved by the retino-geniculo-striate pathway, and a system for "where," which is subserved by the retinotectal pathway (see Johnson, chap. 11 this volume). The two parallel pathways explored in this chapter belong largely to the retino-geniculo-striate pathway. In primates, it has become increasingly clear that the two channels originate from, respectively, beta or alpha retinal ganglion cells and their thalamic targets: the parvocellular (P) and the magnocellular (M) laminae of the lateral geniculate nucleus (Leventhal, Rodieck, and Dreher 1981; Perry, Oehler, and Cowey 1984). Single-cell recordings have documented that cells in the P stream show different response properties from those in the M stream. This is paralleled by corresponding behavioral impairments when one or the other system is selectively lesioned (Merigan and Maunsell 1990; Schiller, Logothetis, and Charles 1990; Merigan, Katz, and Maunsell 1991; Merigan, Byrne, and Maunsell 1991). Briefly, the P pathway is thought to be involved mainly in processing stimuli of high spatial and low temporal frequency, as well as isoluminant color stimuli, and the M pathway is considered to be more sensitive to stimuli of low spatial frequency and high temporal frequencies and is not differentially sensitive to isoluminant chromatic stimuli. These properties are in keeping with an important role of the P system in high-acuity and chromatic vision and with an important role of the M system for motion perception (but see recent contrary evidence; Merigan, Byrne, and Maunsell 1991) and temporal resolution.

In contrast with the relative wealth of data on parallel pathways in monkeys, direct evidence in humans is still lacking. Our general approach in trying to provide this evidence consists in testing patients with a behaviorally and radiologically documented compression of the visual pathways at an anatomical site where such damage is likely to affect the two visual channels differentially. In principle, the most suitable candidate is the optic tract, where, in nonhuman primates, the two channels are anatomically segregated (Reese and Guillery 1987; Reese and Cowey 1988). However, selective lesions of the optic tract are an uncommon clinical occurrence; moreover, the neurophthalmologic symptoms resulting from them (Bender and Bodis-Wollner 1978; Savino et al. 1978; Newman and Miller 1983) do not suggest a selective impairment of the functional channels. Recently, Reese and Cowey (1989) found in one monkey that a subchiasmal tumor of meningeal origin compressing dorsally the optic tract, the optic chiasma (OC), and the optic nerves resulted in a retrograde as well as an anterograde degeneration affecting mainly (but by no means, exclusively) the P pathway. Given the lack of a clear-cut fiber size segregation in the OC, the structure most severely affected by the tumor, these findings can be tentatively related to a greater susceptibility of the P axons to compression independent of their anatomical course.

In the light of this evidence, we thought it worthwhile to study a possible selective visual impairment in patients suffering from pituitary adenomas, a relatively common clinical condition. These benign tumors produce typical visual impairments affecting predominantly the crossed optic fibers, hence the temporal hemifields and the nasal hemiretinas, although some degree of impairment is occasionally seen in the nasal hemifields (temporal hemiretinas) as well (O'Connell 1973).

We have focused attention on the putative differences between the two channels in temporal response properties on the base of the following rationale. There is good agreement that the P system originates from "tonic" ganglion cells and that it is largely coincident with the "sustained" channel advocated by psychophysical studies. By the same token, the M system is closely related to "phasic" or "transient" channels (for a recent review see Lennie et al. 1990). The duration of visible persistence—a short-lasting representation of a brief display that remains visually available after stimulus offset —should depend on activity in the sustained rather than in the transient system. This possibility has been confirmed by several psychophysical studies in normal human subjects (Coltheart 1980; Breitmeyer 1984). One can hypothesize that a selective damage of the P system should impair visual persistence at long durations, while damage of the M system should, if anything, impair visual persistence at short durations, although both systems presumably are working together in such conditions.

We have tested normal subjects and patients with OC compression in a task requiring temporal integration of form (Eriksen and Collins 1968) using a procedure similar to that used recently by Christman (1987, 1989). Temporal integration of form is one of several methods for estimating the duration of visible persistence (Coltheart 1980; Breitmeyer 1984). The rationale of the task rests on the observer's ability to integrate temporally and spatially separate stimuli at different interstimulus intervals (ISIs). Each of the stimuli is meaningless on its own but when temporally integrated with the next stimulus produces a meaningful percept (a digit, for example). It is assumed that the ability to fuse the two complementary stimuli depends on postexposure visible persistence of the first stimulus and its integration with the second one. The largest ISI at which subjects can still correctly identify the digit at an above-chance level is taken as an estimate of duration of visible persistence (Coltheart 1980; Breitmeyer 1984).

## 4.2 METHOD

### Subjects

A group of normal subjects and a group of inpatients of the Department of Neurosurgery of the University of Verona gave their informed consent to be tested.

**Normals** Twelve subjects (five males and seven females) of a mean age similar to that of patients (39 years; range, 20–57) were employed.

**Patients** Ten patients (four males and six females—mean age, 43 years; range, 19–64)—were tested. The criteria for selection were: clinical diagnosis of pituitary adenoma; computed tomography scan or magnetic resonance imaging evidence of compression exerted by the tumor on the optic chiasma; visual field perimetry showing either a lack of or an incomplete bitemporal hemianopia sparing the area of visual stimulus presentation (5 degrees on the horizontal meridian in either the nasal or in the temporal visual field); and good physical and mental general conditions. All patients were tested before neurosurgical intervention; five were tested following postoperative recovery as well. Postoperative data were not included in the statistical analyses described in the results and were analyzed separately. Table 4.1 shows a brief clinical history of the patients.

**Table 4.1** Summary of Ten Patients with Pituitary Adenoma

| Patient, Age, Sex | Visual Acuity | Visual Fields[a] | Optic Discs |
|---|---|---|---|
| B.S., 19, F | 20/50 OD<br>20/67 OS | BTH | Normal |
| C.C., 52, F | 20/33<br>20/25 | BTH | — |
| M.G., 64, F | 20/33<br>20/25 | BTH | Normal |
| M.L., 57, F | 20/33<br>20/33 | BTH | Normal |
| P.A., 22, F | 20/20<br>20/20 | Normal | Normal |
| P.F., 43, F | 20/20<br>20/20 | Normal | Normal |
| M.F., 28, M | 20/20<br>20/20 | Normal | Pallor OD |
| S.O., 57, M | 20/200[b]<br>20/50 | Normal | Pallor OD |
| S.A., 44, M | 20/20<br>20/33 | BTH | Pallor OS |
| Z.R., 43, M | 20/20<br>20/20 | Normal | Normal |

a. BTH = bitemporal hemianopia. In all patients BTH was relative rather than absolute and typically affected only portions of the upper visual hemifields. Only in three patients (B.S., M.G., M.L.) was the visual field area of stimulus presentation not entirely spared and showing signs of diminished light sensitivity as assessed by computerized campimetry (Humphrey).
b. The poor acuity in this patient was related to a nuclear cataract.

Examination of the visual field was performed by means of a manual perimeter and a computerized apparatus that allowed the study of light sensitivity thresholds (Allergan Humphrey).

**Stimuli and Apparatus**

The stimulus consisted of a digit formed from a standard seven-element light-emitting diode (LED) array 3.0 cm high (3.0 degrees of visual angle) and 1.1 cm wide (1.1 degree) positioned with its center at 5 degrees right or left to the fixation point (a white spot of 0.7 degree diameter). Lateralized rather than central presentations were used so as to be able to compare performances in each hemiretina/hemifield. Mean luminance of overall display was about 14 cd/m$^2$, and the background illumination (unlit display) was 0.04 cd/m$^2$. Lighting of the display was automatically performed by means of an interface driven by an Apple IIe computer, which also stored the subject's vocal reaction times (RT).

The subjects sat in a partially soundproof room and viewed the display and the fixation point at a distance of 57 cm. The subject's head was restrained by a chin and forehead rest and was aligned with the fixation point. Eye fixation was monitored by a closed-circuit television system; the occurrence of an eye movement during stimulus presentation was checked on each trial. If eye movements occurred, the trial was repeated; such an occurrence was extremely rare after preliminary training. Subjects wore an eye occluder on one eye; the eye alternation order was balanced within and across subjects, taking into account the hemifield (right or left) of stimulus presentation in order to have an equal and balanced number of presentations to the right and left nasal and temporal hemiretinas.

## Procedure

At the beginning of each trial, an acoustic warning signal delivered over headphones preceded display onset by 1 sec. Subsequently, a pseudorandom subset of two or three elements of the LED display was lit for 4 ms followed by a blank ISI of 15, 30, 45, or 60 ms. Afterward, a second subset of two to three elements was lit for another 4 ms. Displayed simultaneously, the two sets of elements formed one of four digits—2, 5, 6, or 9—and the subjects were informed of these digits. Such selection was dictated by the purpose of avoiding digits requiring an unequal overall number of lit LED elements and by the need to avoid unique configurations of elements that in either the first or the second half of stimulus presentation might allow the subjects to recognize the stimulus with no need of temporal integration. The subjects' task was to name the correct digit as fast as possible. The ISI durations were chosen on the basis of pilot experiments showing that the performance of subjects declined considerably after an ISI of 60 ms and even more so after an ISI of 100 ms. Such values were also justified by the physiological evidence on the duration of ganglion cell discharge following presentation of brief light stimuli (Lehmkuhle, Baro, and Hughes 1990). At the shortest ISI (15 ms), complete visual temporal integration usually enabled the subjects to see a single digit with great accuracy. Performance was much less accurate at the longer ISIs. We did not include an ISI of 0 since it was immediately obvious from a brief assessment in a normal subject that a digit presented at that ISI was indistinguishable from one presented at ISI 15. In both cases, the vivid perceptual impression was that of seeing a whole digit. By the same token, other normal subjects judged a digit presented at ISI 15 as perfectly fused whereas 80 to 90 percent of the digits presented at ISI 30 and all those presented at ISI 45 and 60 were judged as partially fused or not fused at all.

There were two dependent variables in the design of the experiment: number of errors and speed of vocal RT. The voice of the subject was fed into the computer by means of a microphone positioned in front of the mouth in order to measure vocal RTs to the nearest ms starting from onset of the second half of stimulus presentation. The number of errors (including erroneous responses, omissions, and responses faster than 250 ms and slower than 1500 ms) was recorded together with RT. Subjects were instructed to report aloud the number as fast as possible, refraining from producing noises that could stop the electronic clock and give an artifactual estimate of vocal RT.

Subjects were tested in one experimental session consisting of four blocks of eighty trials each. Prior to formal testing, a series of stimuli were presented binocularly and foveally to allow subjects to learn how to master the temporal integration task. During formal testing, on each block the four digits were presented five times at each ISI in a pseudorandom order. Within a given block, the stimuli were presented to only one of the four possible hemiretina/hemifield locations. After each block, the subjects were allowed a brief rest. The order of blocks was counterbalanced across subjects.

### 4.3 RESULTS

**Accuracy of Performance**

A mixed-design analysis of variance (ANOVA) was carried out on the percentage of correct responses with one between-subject (Group: normals versus patients) and three within-subject (ISI, Eye, Visual Hemifield) factors. Since preliminary analyses did not show reliable differences among the stimuli, accuracy scores were averaged across the four digits.

Among the main effects, only ISI was significant, $F(3,60) = 44.50; p < .0001$, with percentage of errors showing a progressive increase at increasing ISIs (ISI 15 = 5.6 percent; ISI 30 = 8.8 percent; ISI 45 = 16.5 percent; ISI 60 = 29.3 percent).

Only one interaction reached significance; Group × Eye × Field × ISI: $F(3,60) = 3.49; p < .021$ (figure 4.1). Given the relationship between Eye and Hemifield (=Hemiretina), this interaction can be interpreted as related to the presence of a hemiretinal difference at ISIs 15 and 30 only in the patients' group (fig. 4.1).

Figure 4.1 shows data analyzed as a function of the two hemiretinas (averaged across the four combinations Eye × Field: Right Eye/Right Field and

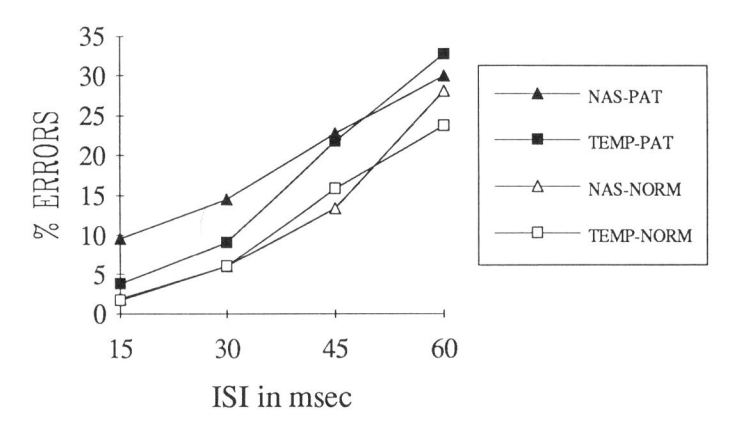

**Figure 4.1** Mean percentage of errors at the various ISIs for the nasal and temporal hemiretinas of normals ($N = 12$) and patients ($N = 10$).

Left Eye/Left Field = Nasal Hemiretinas; Right Eye/Left Field and Left Eye/Right Field = Temporal Hemiretinas) of stimulus presentation at the various ISIs in the two groups. The presence of an ISI- and Group-dependent hemiretinal difference was statistically confirmed by preplanned t-tests showing a significant hemiretinal difference at ISI 30, $t(9) = 2.66$; $p < .026$, with patients being less accurate in the nasal (errors = 14.5 percent) than in the temporal (9.0 percent) hemiretinas. The nasotemporal difference at ISI 15, although large (see fig. 4.1) did not reach statistical significance because of a marked variability in the patient group.

Two considerations are in order at this stage. First, the significant effect of ISI shows clearly that the task taps the effects of visible persistence on recognition performance, since as the ISI increases, performance undergoes a progressive decrease in accuracy. However, even at the longest ISI, performance is still well above the theoretical chance level of 75 percent errors (four alternatives). Second, the significant interaction and the results of post hoc tests showing nasotemporal differences only at ISI 30 are in keeping with an effect of tumoral compression only on the nasal hemiretinas and only for short durations of visible persistence.

**Speed of Response**

A mixed-design ANOVA similar to that used for accuracy scores was carried out on vocal RTs. RTs were averaged across the four digits to be recognized. Only the main effect of ISI was significant, $F(3,60) = 56.19$, $p < .0001$, with speed of response decreasing at progressively higher ISIs (ISI 15 = 567 ms; ISI 30 = 582 ms; ISI 45 = 613 ms; ISI 60 = 650 ms). Several interactions were significant: Field × ISI, $F(3,60) = 3.18$, $p < .03$; Field × Eye × ISI, $F(3,60) = 3.69$, $p = .01$; and finally, Group × Field × Eye × ISI, $F(3,60) = 2.74$, $p = .051$. The meaning of the highest-order interaction can be grasped by inspection of figure 4.2, showing speed of response at various ISI for the two hemiretinas in the two groups. Although there are no reliable nasotem-

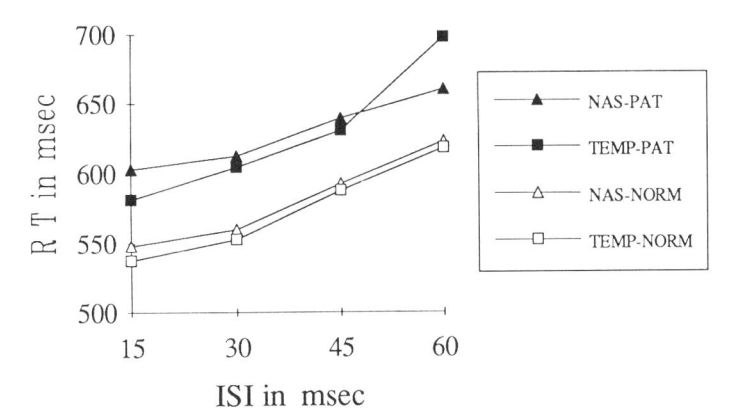

**Figure 4.2** Mean vocal RT at various ISIs for the nasal and temporal hemiretinas of normals ($N = 12$) and patients ($N = 10$).

poral differences in the normal group at any ISI, in patients there is a marked slowing of responses in the temporal hemiretina as one goes from ISI 45 to ISI 60. This impression is statistically validated by an intergroup comparison between hemiretinal differences showing a large and significant advantage of the nasal hemiretina in patients at ISI 60 and a minuscule opposite advantage of the temporal hemiretina in normals at the same ISI, $t(20) = 2.21, p = .039$. A final analysis was motivated by the presence of a first-order interaction involving Field that might be suggestive of a laterality effect independent of, or in addition to, that of Hemiretina. It was clear from this analysis (fig. 4.3) that the slowing down of the temporal hemiretina at ISI 60 can be ascribed mainly to the left temporal hemiretina (hence, to the right visual hemifield). A series of post hoc t-tests showed that the only reliable comparison was between left temporal retina at ISI 60 and right nasal retina at the same ISI. We are inclined to think that the impairment of the patients' left temporal hemiretina (projecting to the left cerebral hemisphere) at the longest ISI might be related to hemispheric asymmetries (superiority of the right hemisphere due to the crucial visuospatial component of the recognition task at long ISIs) emerging only at long durations of visual persistence.

For both accuracy and speed of response in patients, there is an advantage of temporal hemiretina at ISIs 15, 30, and 45 and an advantage of nasal hemiretina at ISI 60 (figs. 4.1 and 4.2). Thus, a justifiable conclusion is that the results of speed and accuracy of response are in broad agreement, although only accuracy scores showed a reliable hemiretinal difference (at ISI 30). Undoubtedly, accuracy of performance turned out to be a more effective measure in revealing an impairment, while RT disclosed a potentially interesting laterality effect confined to the temporal hemiretinas that requires further study to be substantiated.

**Postoperative Recovery**

In five patients (C.C., M.G., S.O., S.A., and Z.R.; see table 4.1), it was possible to study postoperative performance in the same temporal form integration

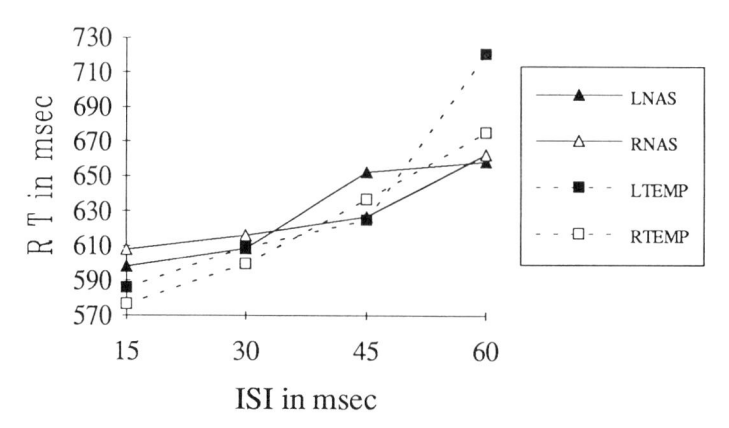

**Figure 4.3** Mean vocal RT at various ISIs for the left and right nasal and temporal hemiretinas of the patients' group ($N = 10$).

task as that tested preoperatively. On average, the patients were tested 69 days after preoperative testing (range, 57–84), which usually was carried out a few days before surgical intervention.

Figure 4.4 shows mean pre- and postoperative performance of the five patients as a function of ISI and Hemiretina. Clearly, there is a greater improvement of performance for the nasal over the temporal hemiretina, which tends to be larger at shorter ISI. The differential rate of recovery for the two hemiretinas rules out the possibility of a mere practice effect.

The pre-post comparison of speed of response data is shown in figure 4.5 as mean RTs at each ISI. Overall improvement of performance is very clear, as is the disappearance of the slowing of temporal hemiretina present at ISI 60 in preoperative testing.

A straightforward conclusion from the pre-postoperative comparisons is that the task we employed is a more sensitive measure of visual performance than perimetry since it can detect an impairment and its postoperative recovery, even when computerized perimetry does not show substantial defects.

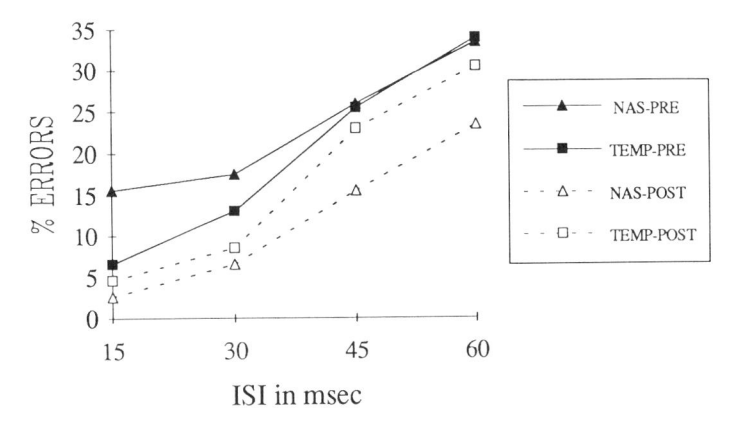

**Figure 4.4** Mean percentage of errors at the various ISIs for the nasal and temporal hemiretinas of patients ($N = 5$) before and after surgery.

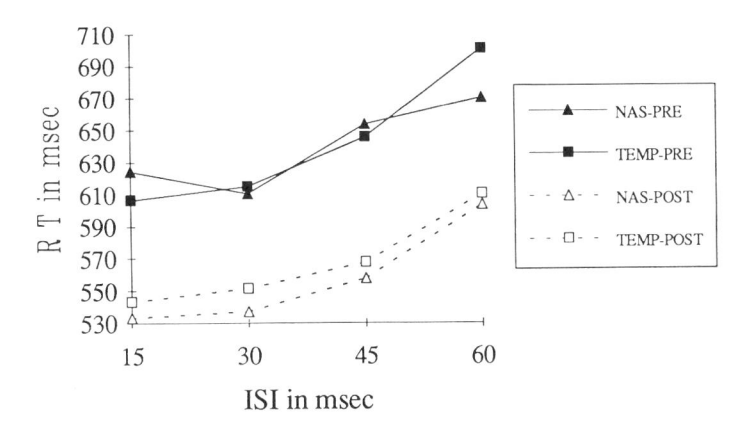

**Figure 4.5** Mean vocal RT at the various ISIs for the nasal and temporal hemiretinas of patients ($N = 5$) before and after surgery.

## 4.4 GENERAL DISCUSSION

We sought to ascertain whether a tumoral compression of the OC induces a selective change in visible persistence that might be related to a malfunctioning of a component of the visual pathway. The finding of an impairment of visible persistence at short but not long ISIs is compatible with this possibility. In agreement with the well-known neurophthalmologic consequences of pituitary adenomas, only the nasal hemiretina was affected in accuracy of recognition, while the RT slowing observed for the left temporal hemiretina at the longest ISI tested is a somewhat puzzling effect that needs further scrutiny. The finding of an ISI-dependent effect on visible persistence with an impairment at short but not at long ISIs rules out an unselective effect of damage to the visual pathways.

A possible explanation of the results is that the tumoral compression of the OC exerts its ill effects on a neural channel operating at short durations of visible persistence. When a longer persistence is required, visual integration of form presumably is subserved by another channel that is less affected (or spared) by the disease. Such a channel is probably operating also at durations greater than those tested in our study, since in our own pilot experiments in normals, we found a progressively deteriorating but still above-chance performance even at an ISI as great as 125 ms (ISI 50 = 20.2 percent; ISI 75 = 34.0 percent; ISI 100 = 43.5 percent; ISI 125 = 44.3 percent). In our experiments, performance reached the asymptote at about 45 percent; this is a long way from the theoretical chance level of 75 percent errors. Despite our efforts, there still may be some partial cues available to the subject. Notwithstanding this, the progressive deterioration of performance at increasing ISIs (roughly a doubling of the error rate between ISI 50 and ISI 125) argues convincingly that a form of persistence, probably identifiable with the iconic memory of Coltheart (1980), is operating at such ISIs. From a neurophysiological viewpoint, such a long persistence is in keeping with the response of sustained cat retinal ganglion cells (corresponding to the P system of monkeys; see Leventhal, Rodieck, and Dreher 1981), which have been found by Cleland, Levick, and Sanderson (1973) to respond to a 2-ms light flash with a discharge longer than 100 ms. On the contrary, it was found in the same study that the response of transient ganglion cells (M system) fades away after less than 50 ms.

In the light of these considerations, it is tempting to attribute the impairment of performance of our patients at short ISIs to a selective effect of the OC compression on the M system. If one is justified in extrapolating from transient ganglion cells in the cat to M system in monkeys (for a positive answer to this question, see Leventhal, Rodieck, and Dreher 1981) and to a putative homologous M system in humans, then the impairment seen in our patients is well in keeping with a loss of M neurons. The discharge duration of transient ganglion cells (about 40–50 ms) in response to a brief flash of light (Cleland, Levick, and Sanderson 1973; Lehmkuhle, Baro, and Hughes 1990) seems to be a likely neural correlate of the type of visible persistence impaired in our patients. If a proportion of M axons are injured by compression, an impairment might show up even though a presumably less affected P system is simultaneously contributing to visible persistence. However, once, at longer ISIs, performance becomes increasingly more dependent on the P system, the impairment progressively disappears or decreases considerably. We think that our results bring weight to the hypothesis of the existence of two types of visual persistence: one operating only for brief durations, which is subserved mainly (but not exclusively) by the M system, and another that is subserved by the P system and is operating at longer durations (probably up to 100–150 ms). These two forms of persistence not only are subserved by different visual channels but also differ in the types of cognitive operations that characterize them. The former requires a perceptual fusion of the stimulus halves to yield a vivid and unitary percept. The latter requires a mental reconstruction of the digit based on unfused successive arrays of lines, and this entails a qualitatively different, complex visuospatial operation. In other words, these two stages of persistence represent different operations that are not necessarily sequential and can be dissociated by damage to the subcortical visual pathways. On the basis of these considerations, it is neither surprising nor illogical to find an impairment in accuracy of recognition at short but not at long durations of visual persistence. On the other hand, the presence of a laterality effect in speed of response at a long ISI (60 ms) only is in broad agreement with the hypothesis that hemispheric asymmetries arise only at the level of more complex cognitive visual operations (Marzi et al. 1979), such as those that characterize temporal integration at long ISIs.

Our findings are at odds with the evidence provided by Reese and Cowey (1989) in the monkey with a suprasellar meningioma. They found massive degenerative changes of optic axons that "are best considered relatively advanced in, rather than selective for, the beta cell pathway" and argued that the coarse optic axons arising from alpha retinal cells presumably would have undergone degeneration also. It is difficult to speculate on why our patients are likely to suffer from a greater impairment of M axons than Reese and Cowey's monkey, but possibly part of the discrepancy may be found in the different type of tumor. Given their good recovery following surgery, there could not have been such massive degeneration of axons in our patients as in the monkey of Reese and Cowey. Obviously, one also has to bear in mind that a behavioral correlate of the neuropathological findings is lacking for the monkey described by Reese and Cowey. On the other hand, our results are in keeping with the evidence on experimental glaucoma in monkeys (Glovinski, Quigley, and Dunkelberger 1991; Quigley et al. 1987) and on clinical glaucoma in humans (Holopigian et al. 1990). All of these studies point to a selective impairment of the M system following an increase in intraocular pressure. By the same token, our findings are in broad agreement with the results of Burke and co-workers in cats with pressure block of the optic nerve (Burke, Burke, and Martin 1985; Burke et al. 1986; Burke et al. 1987) where both neurophysiological and behavioral data show a higher susceptibility of the transient channel to pressure block. Clearly, further work is needed to assess which other functions presumably mediated by one or the other channel are impaired in patients with damage of the pregeniculate visual pathways in addition to the early stages of visible persistence.

**NOTE**

This study was supported by Contratto CNR: 89.01703.04. We thank V. Di Lollo, M. Goodale, and G. Berlucchi for their helpful comments on a preliminary draft of this chapter.

**REFERENCES**

Bender, M. B. and Bodis-Wollner, I (1978). Visual dysfunction in optic tract lesions. *Annals of Neurology, 3*, 187–193.

Breitmeyer, B. G (1984). *Visual masking: An integrative approach*. Oxford: Clarendon Press.

Burke, W., Burke, J. A., and Martin, P. R. (1985). Selective block of optic nerve fibres in the cat and the occurrence of inhibition in the lateral geniculate nucleus. *Journal of Physiology, 364*, 81–92.

Burke, W., Cottee, L. J., Garvey, J., Kumarasinghe, R., and Kyriacou, C. (1986). Selective degeneration of optic nerve fibres in the cat produced by a pressure block. *Journal of Physiology, 376*, 461–476.

Burke, W., Cottee, L. J., Hamilton, K., Kerr, L., Kyriacou, C., and Milosavljevic, M. (1987). Function of the Y optic nerve fibres in the cat: Do they contribute to acuity and ability to discriminate fast motion? *Journal of Physiology, 392*, 35–50.

Christman, S. (1987). Effects of perceptual quality on hemispheric asymmetries in visible persistence. *Perception and Psychophysics, 41*, 367–374.

Christman, S. (1989). Temporal integration of form as a function of subject handedness and retinal locus of presentation. *Neuropsychologia, 27*, 1373–1382.

Cleland, B. G., Levick, W. R., and Sanderson, K. J. (1973). Properties of sustained and transient ganglion cells in the cat's retina. *Journal of Physiology, 228*, 649–680.

Coltheart, M. (1980). Iconic memory and visible persistence. *Perception and Psychophysics, 27*, 183–228.

DeYoe, E. A., and Van Essen, D. C. (1988). Concurrent processing streams in monkey visual cortex. *Trends in Neurosciences, 11*, 219–226.

Eriksen, C., and Collins, J. (1968). Sensory traces versus the psychological moment in the temporal organization of form. *Journal of Experimental Psychology, 77*, 754–769.

Glovinski, Y., Quigley, H. A., and Dunkelberger, G. R. (1991). Retinal ganglion cell loss is size dependent in experimental glaucoma. *Investigative Ophthalmology and Visual Science, 32*, 484–491.

Holopigian, K., Seiple, W., Mayron, C., Kory, R., and Lorenzo, M. (1990). Electrophysiological and psychophysical flicker sensitivity in patients with primary open-angle glaucoma and ocular hypertension. *Investigative Ophthalmology and Visual Science, 31*, 1863–1868.

Lehmkuhle, S., Baro, J. H., and Hughes, H. C. (1990). Response properties of X and Y retinal ganglion cells in cat. *Investigative Ophthalmology and Visual Science, 31*(4), 210.

Lennie, P., Trevarten, C., Van Essen, D., and Waessle, H. (1990). Parallel processing of visual information. In L. Spillman and J. S. Werner (Eds.), *Visual perception: The neurophysiological foundations*, 103–128. San Diego: Academic Press.

Leventhal, A. G., Rodieck, R. W., and Dreher, B. (1981). Retinal ganglion cell classes in the Old-World monkey: Morphology and central projections. *Science, 213,* 1139–1142.

Livingstone, M. S., and Hubel, D. H. (1988). Segregation of form, color, movement, and depth: Anatomy, physiology, and perception. *Science, 240,* 740–749.

Marzi, C. A., Di Stefano, M., Tassinari, G., and Crea F. (1979). Iconic storage in the two hemispheres. *Journal of Experimental Psychology: Human Perception and Performance, 5,* 31–41.

Merigan, W. H., Byrne, C. E., and Maunsell, J. H. R. (1991). Does primate motion perception depend on the magnocellular pathway? *Journal of Neuroscience, 11,* 3422–3429.

Merigan, W. H., Katz, L. M., and Maunsell, J. H. R. (1991). The effects of parvocellular lateral geniculate lesions on the acuity and contrast sensitivity of macaque monkeys. *Journal of Neuroscience, 11,* 994–1001.

Merigan, W. H., and Maunsell, J. H. R. (1990). Macaque vision after magnocellular lateral geniculate vision. *Visual Neuroscience, 5,* 347–352.

Merigan, W. H., and Maunsell, J. H. R. (1993). How parallel are the primate visual pathways? *Annual Review of Neuroscience, 16,* 369–402.

Newman, S. A., and Miller, N. R. (1983). Optic tract syndrome. Neurophthalmologic considerations. *Archives of Ophthalmology, 101,* 1241–1250.

O'Connell, J. E. A. (1973). The anatomy of the optic chiasma and heteronymous hemianopia. *Journal of Neurology, Neurosurgery, and Psychiatry, 36,* 710–723.

Perry, V. H., Oehler R., and Cowey A. (1984). Retinal ganglion cells that project to the dorsal lateral geniculate nucleus in the macaque monkey. *Neuroscience, 12,* 1101–1123.

Quigley, H. A., Sanchez, R. M., Dunkelberger, G. R., L'Hernault, N. L., and Baginski, T. A. (1987). Chronic glaucoma selectively damages large optic nerve fibers. *Investigative Ophthalmology and Visual Science, 28,* 913–920.

Reese, B. E., and Cowey, A. (1988). Segregation of functionally distinct axons in the monkey's optic tract. *Nature, 331,* 350–351.

Reese, B. E., and Cowey, A. (1989). The neurologic consequences of a sub-chiasmal tumour on the retino-geniculo-striate pathway of a macaque monkey. *Clinical Vision Sciences, 4,* 341–356.

Reese, B. E., and Guillery, R. W. (1987). Distribution of axons according to diameter in the monkey's optic tract. *Journal of Comparative Neurology, 260,* 453–460.

Savino, P. J., Paris, M., Schatz, N. J., Orr, L. S., and Corbett, J. J. (1978). Optic tract syndrome. A review of 21 patients. *Archives of Ophthalmology, 96,* 656–663.

Schiller, P. H., Logothetis, N. K., and Charles, E. R. (1990). Functions of the colour-opponent and broad-band channels of the visual system. *Nature, 343,* 68–70.

Shapley, R. (1990). Visual sensitivity and parallel retinocortical channels. *Annual Review of Psychology, 41,* 635–658.

Sherman, S. M. (1985). Functional organization of the W-, X-, and Y-cell pathways in the cat: A review and hypothesis. In J. M. Sprague and A. N. Epstein. (Eds.), *Progress in psychobiology and physiological psychology,* vol. 11, 233–314. Orlando, FL: Academic Press.

Stone, J. (1983). *Parallel processing in the visual system: The classification of retinal ganglion cells and its impact on the neurobiology of vision.* New York: Plenum.

Zeki, S. (1990). Colour vision and functional specialisation in the visual cortex. *Discussions in Neuroscience, 6*(2). Amsterdam: Elsevier.

# 5 Motor Responses to Nonreportable, Masked Stimuli: Where Is the Limit of Direct Parameter Specification?

## Odmar Neumann and Werner Klotz

ABSTRACT  The concept of direct parameter specification (Neumann 1989a, 1990a) refers to the case that a stimulus specifies parameters of a motor response without mediation by a conscious representation of the stimulus. We report five experiments that explored direct parameter specification, using a variant of the Fehrer-Raab metacontrast paradigm (Fehrer and Raab 1962). Experiments 1 and 2 established that masked primes that could not be detected (i.e., primes for which a signal detection part of the experiments yielded $d'$ values of zero) nevertheless had strong and reliable effects on RT in a compatible choice RT task. Experiments 3 and 4 extended this finding to incompatible S-R mappings and to a condition in which the S-R mapping rule was redefined from trial to trial by means of a cue signal that preceded the stimulus sequence. However, the strength of priming was diminished when the cue SOA was reduced to 250 ms, suggesting that direct parameter specification may approach its limits if action planning has not yet been completed when the stimulus is presented. Experiment 5 demonstrated that at least part of the priming is located at the response stage. These findings indicate that sensory stimuli that are not consciously perceived can affect motor responses in a flexible, task-dependent manner. We discuss implications for the concepts of automatic processing, of discrimination without awareness, and of continuous processing.

### 5.1  INTRODUCTION

The experiments that we report in this chapter may be viewed from two perspectives. They represent an attempt to establish the existence of an alleged empirical phenomenon, and to explore its limits, and they validate a theoretical concept. The empirical phenomenon that we examine is the Fehrer-Raab effect, first reported by Fehrer and Raab (1962). The theoretical concept is direct parameter specification (Neumann 1989a, 1990a; Neumann et al. 1992; Neumann and Müsseler 1990; Neumann and Prinz 1987).

We begin at the empirical level and first describe the experimental context of our study. We next report five experiments. Finally, we discuss the concept of direct parameter specification, elaborate it in the light of our results, and relate it to similar other concepts, such as automatic processing and discrimination without awareness.

## 5.2 EMPIRICAL BACKGROUND

**Metacontrast**

Metacontrast is a particular form of visual backward masking that was first described by Stigler (1910). Stigler presented the two hemifields of a circular photometer field in close temporal succession and found that the first hemifield was masked by the second. Since he regarded this phenomenon as a special case of lateral brightness contrast, which operates on the "metaphotic image" of the stimulus (its visual trace), he called it "metaphotic contrast," or metacontrast.

Metacontrast was rediscovered several times within quite different experimental and theoretical contexts. For example, Werner (1935), who had his theoretical roots in the Leipzig school of *Ganzheitspsychologie* (a close kin of Gestalt psychology), was interested in the microgenesis of contour formation. To study it, he introduced the classical variant of metacontrast in which the test stimulus is a filled circle and the mask a surrounding ring. This produces strong masking. Under optimal conditions, the disk becomes invisible. Werner's interpretation was that the disk triggers a contour formation process that is "absorbed" by the ring. A quarter of a century later, Averbach and Coriell (1961) rediscovered metacontrast in experiments on short-term visual information storage. To indicate the letter that the subject was to report selectively from a multiletter array, they used either a bar marker or a ring. The bar marker was an efficient selection cue, but the ring produced a large drop in performance. Averbach and Corriel termed this kind of masking "erasure," because they assumed that the ring erased the letter in visual short-term memory.

Thus, these three discoverers and rediscoverers of metacontrast located its mechanism at three different levels of visual processing: brightness coding, contour formation, and short-term visual storage. Other theories have added even more divergent hypotheses. For example, metacontrast has been assumed to be based on photochemical processes on the retina (Alpern 1953), as well as on inhibition in neuronal networks for brightness coding (Weisstein 1968), lateral inhibition in networks for contour coding (Mayzner, Tresselt, and Helfer 1967), and interchannel inhibition between transient and sustained channels (Breitmeyer 1984; Breitmeyer and Ganz 1976). It has been related to apparent motion (Kahneman 1967) and to saccadic suppression (Grüsser 1972), and some theoreticians have even assumed that it is not perceptual at all but rather a cognitive misjudgment (Schiller 1969). In short, a survey of theories of metacontrast resembles a journey through the visual system, from the retina all the way to attentional and higher cognitive processes. This does not necessarily mean that most theories of metacontrast are wrong; rather, metacontrast may result from the interplay of mechanisms at different levels of processing (Neumann and Müsseler 1990).

Besides the wide array of underlying mechanisms that have been proposed, a second aspect of metacontrast renders it theoretically interesting. It encompasses several seemingly paradoxical empirical aspects. First, metacontrast shares with all variants of backward masking the apparent paradox that a later stimulus (the mask) influences the perception of an earlier stimulus (the test stimulus), seemingly exerting its effect backward in time. Second, the masking function is nonmonotonic. Masking is normally slight at short SOAs (stimulus onset asynchronies) and attains its maximum only at SOAs in the order of 40 to 80 ms (Kahneman 1968; Breitmeyer 1984). This is a kind of temporal distance paradox. Third, several studies in the 1960s suggested that even when the test stimulus is strongly masked, it is still processed by the system. It can, for example, cause apparent motion (Schiller 1969), its sensory evoked potential is similar to that of an unmasked stimulus (Schiller and Chorover 1966), and reaction time (RT) to the phenomenally masked stimulus seems to be largely unaffected by masking (Fehrer and Raab 1962; Taylor and McCloskey 1990). This last finding is the one that we explore here.

**The Fehrer-Raab Effect**

In Fehrer and Raab's (1962) original experiment, the masked test stimulus was a lighted square, and the mask consisted of two flanking squares that followed it with an SOA of between 0 and 75 ms. The amount of masking was not systematically measured, but the authors report that the test stimulus was barely visible at an SOA of 75 ms with foveal presentation and was phenomenally absent at the same SOA when presentation was peripheral. Yet when subjects were presented with these test stimulus–mask sequences and asked to press a button as soon as a stimulus appeared, simple RT was completely unaffected by masking. In all conditions, RT under masking was either equal to, or even shorter than, RT to the unmasked test stimulus. These data are shown in figure 5.1, together with those from three replication studies.

We have reanalyzed the data from these studies in order to make them directly comparable. RT, as measured from the beginning of test stimulus presentation, is plotted against the SOA. The thin, straight lines show the RTs that are predicted if the response is elicited by the test stimulus alone (T) or by the mask alone (M). (These estimates are based on data from control conditions in which either the test stimulus or the mask was presented in isolation.) Since RT is measured from the beginning of the test stimulus, the prediction for the case that the response is triggered by the test stimulus alone is a straight line that runs parallel to the abscissa at the level of the test-stimulus-alone control condition. If the mask alone triggers the response, the prediction is a line with the slope 1, whose intercept is given by RT in the mask-alone control condition.

The data show that RT under masking is never longer than in the test-stimulus-alone condition and is shorter at small SOAs if RT to mask alone is shorter than RT to test stimulus alone. (This is usually found when the mask has a higher energy than the target.) Thus, RT does not show any sign of masking. Rather, the form of the curves suggests a kind of race between the two stimuli, with the winner triggering the response. In the temporal regions

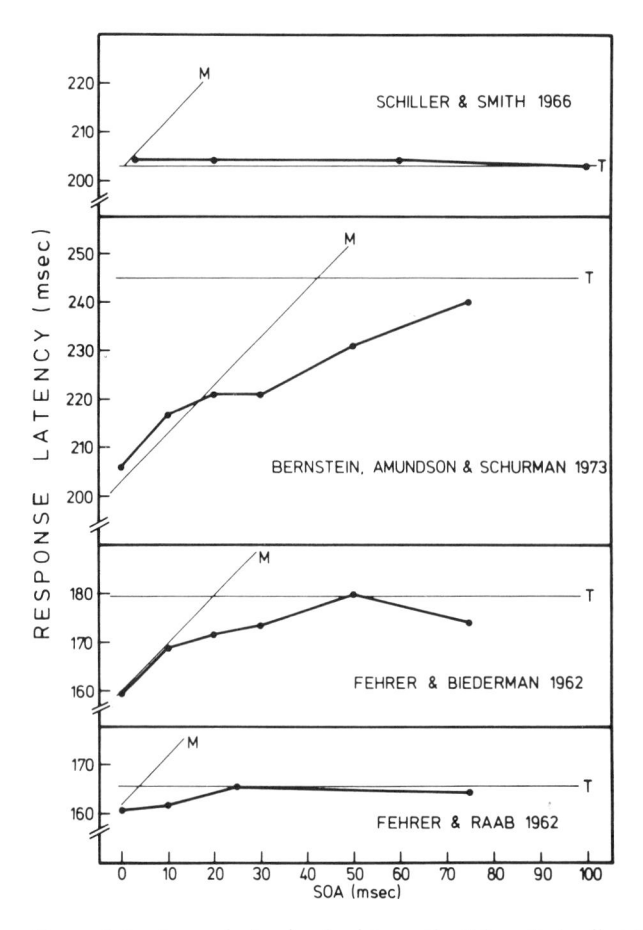

**Figure 5.1** A reanalysis of early data on the Fehrer-Raab effect (after Neumann and Prinz 1987).

where only one stimulus is the exclusive winner, it will alone determine RT, and hence the empirical RTs will fall on the predicted line. In the transition region, both stimuli will have a chance of winning, and due to statistical facilitation, the mean empirical RT will tend to lie below both predicted values.

It appears, then, that metacontrast affects the conscious perception of the test stimulus, yet its ability to trigger a motor response remains largely intact. There seems to be a dissociation between conscious perception and the specification of response parameters. However, this conclusion is both tentative, because there are methodological problems with the data, and incomplete, because it leaves a decisive question unanswered: under the assumption that the effect is genuine, where are its limits? The data in figure 5.1 come from simple RT experiments (Donders's a-reactions). The Fehrer-Raab effect could be restricted to this particular situation, or it could be a general phenomenon that only happened to be discovered with this specific experimental paradigm.

An assessment of the limits of the Fehrer-Raab effect is not only desirable in order to get a better empirical understanding of this effect. It has also potentially important theoretical implications. The Fehrer-Raab effect may be subsumed under a class of phenomena that we have explained in terms of direct parameter specification (Neumann 1989a, 1990a; Neumann et al. 1992). Direct parameter specification is defined as the case that sensory information determines response parameters by means of a direct linkage, without mediation by processes that are accompanied by a conscious representation. If we succeed in finding out under which conditions this assumed mode of sensorimotor control is possible, and under which conditions it fails and has to be superseded by conscious mediation, this could offer insights into the functions of "consciousness" (those brain processes that have an equivalent in subjective experience).

The series of experiments that we report thus had the dual purpose of confirming the existence of direct parameter specification with a new, methodologically improved version of the Fehrer-Raab paradigm and of finding conditions under which direct parameter specification breaks down. Our strategy with respect to the latter question was to render the task more and more complex, until a level of complexity would be reached that, we expected, could no longer be coped with via direct parameter specification. In experiments 1 and 2, we went one step beyond the classic paradigm by using choice RT instead of simple RT. In experiment 3, we added an incompatible stimulus-response (S-R) mapping. In experiment 4, additional complexity was introduced by redefining the S-R mapping rule from trial to trial. The purpose of experiment 5 was to ascertain that the priming effects in the previous experiments could not be explained by purely sensory facilitation.

## 5.3 EXPERIMENT 1

The major methodological problem with the data that we have so far considered relates to the fact that RT on one hand, and verbal reports of masking on the other hand, are not only different but also differentially sensitive measures (cf. Weintraub and Fidell 1979). This problem has long been recognized by Eriksen (1956, 1960). Verbal reports usually employ only a few categories, whereas RT is a continuous variable. Further, subjects' reports that they did not "see" or "detect" a test stimulus may be based on a criterion quite different from the criterion that the processing system uses for triggering the motor response. Hence, at least some of the observed dissociations between RT and verbal report could be due simply to the fact that RT is a finely grained measure, based on a low response criterion, whereas verbal responses use a high criterion and are only coarsely grained.

Experiment 1 represents an attempt to overcome this difficulty by creating a masking situation in which subjects were definitely unable to detect the masked stimulus consciously. Our criterion for not detecting was very strict: a $d'$ of zero in a signal detection part of the experiment. If it is ascertained that there is no conscious discrimination whatsoever, we can measure RT and test whether the completely masked stimulus still has an effect on RT.

This approach reverses the logic of the Fehrer-Raab experiment and the subsequent replications. These earlier studies were intended to demonstrate that masking leaves RT completely unaffected, although it affects phenomenal experience (that is, a verbal report). The logic of this paradigm, by contrast, consists of creating a situation where there is complete masking at the level of conscious experience and then looking for effects of the masked stimulus on RT. In other words, the classical Fehrer-Raab paradigm was intended to show that there is no effect of the mask on RT despite its (more or less pronounced) effect on phenomenal perception, while our paradigm has been designed to demonstrate no phenomenal perception of the masked stimulus despite its (more or less pronounced) effect on RT. If no phenomenal perception is defined as a $d'$ of zero, then such a dissociation, if it is obtained, cannot be attributed to criterion setting or to an insufficient grain of resolution for verbal report.[1]

Second, we wanted to go beyond most of the previous experiments by using choice RT rather than simple RT. This was intended as a first step toward exploring the limits of the expected dissociation between verbal report and RT. One study with a similar intention was that of Proctor, Nunn, and Pallos (1983). However, whereas their subjects responded to the spatial position of a single stimulus, the subjects in experiment 1 were presented with two stimuli and had to discriminate the target's shape in order to respond to its position.

**Method**

The experiment consisted of two parts: RT measurement and detection. We first describe the RT task, for which the stimuli and the sequence of events are shown in figure 5.2.

Each trial began with a warning signal that consisted of the appearance of four points arranged in a squarelike manner that moved toward the center of the screen, where they met after 1,000 ms. After a delay of 100, 200, or 300 ms, chosen randomly, the sequence of events began as shown in figure 5.2.

The imperative stimulus display contained a horizontal stimulus pair, a square and a diamond (with internal contours, as shown in fig. 5.2), that appeared, unpredictably, either above or below fixation. The stimuli were about 1.5 degrees high, and the distance between their near edge and the fixation point was also 1.5 degrees of visual angle. In half of the trials, the square was on the left, and in the other half, it was on the right. Half of the subjects had to respond to the square as their target by pressing the corresponding button—the right button if the target was on the right, the left button if it was on the left. The other half had to respond in the same way to the diamond's position. Thus, one of the stimuli was task relevant, and the other was task irrelevant.

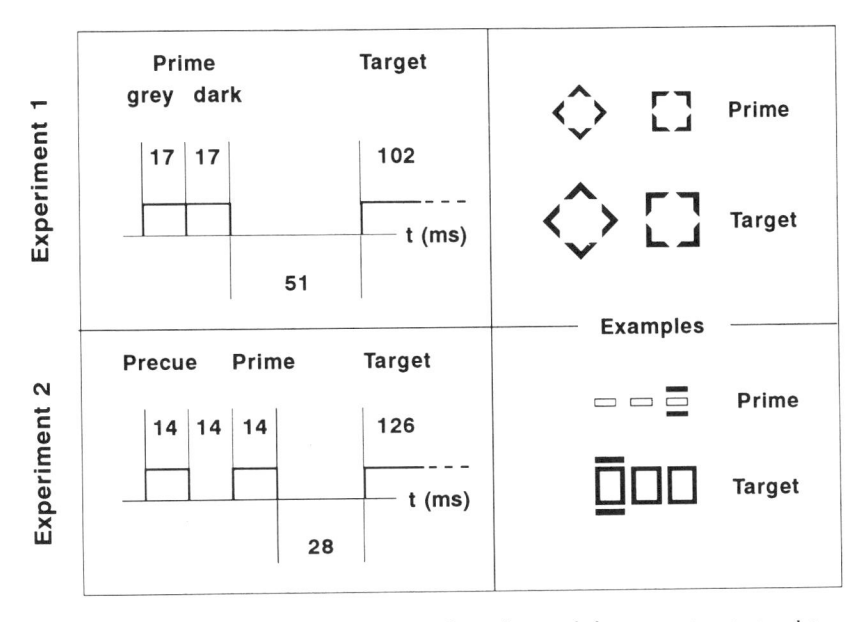

**Figure 5.2** Sequences of stimulus events and sample stimuli from experiments 1 and 2.

The imperative stimulus display was shown for 102 ms. It was preceded by a prime that was neutral, congruent, or incongruent, and that was masked by the imperative stimulus display. The neutral prime consisted of two smaller replicas of the irrelevant stimulus. The congruent and the incongruent prime contained one replica of the relevant stimulus and one replica of the irrelevant stimulus. In the congruent case, the replica of the relevant stimulus was on the correct side—that is, on the same side as the relevant stimulus. In the incongruent case, it was on the opposite side. The replicas fitted exactly into the stimuli in the imperative display and were well masked by their (partially virtual) internal contours. Since these internal contours contained both a square and a diamond, we expected equally good masking with congruent as with incongruent prime target pairs. This was confirmed by pilot research, and the experiment provided an additional check on it.

The prime was presented for 34 ms—first for 17 ms in faint gray and for the remaining 17 ms in full black. (The 17-ms "preexposure" of a faint stimulus was supposed to draw visual attention to the prime's location without reducing its maskability.) The SOA (from the onset of the prime to the onset of the imperative stimulus display) was 85 ms.

After the RT part of experiment was completed (240 trials, 50 percent neutral and 25 percent each congruent and incongruent in a random order, different for each subject), the signal detection part followed. Subjects were informed that the imperative stimuli had been preceded by primes, and examples of the primes were shown. They were then told that the experiment would be repeated but that their task now was to decide whether the prime contained a replica of their target. After each stimulus presentation, a five-point scale appeared on the screen, with 5 meaning "I am pretty sure that the

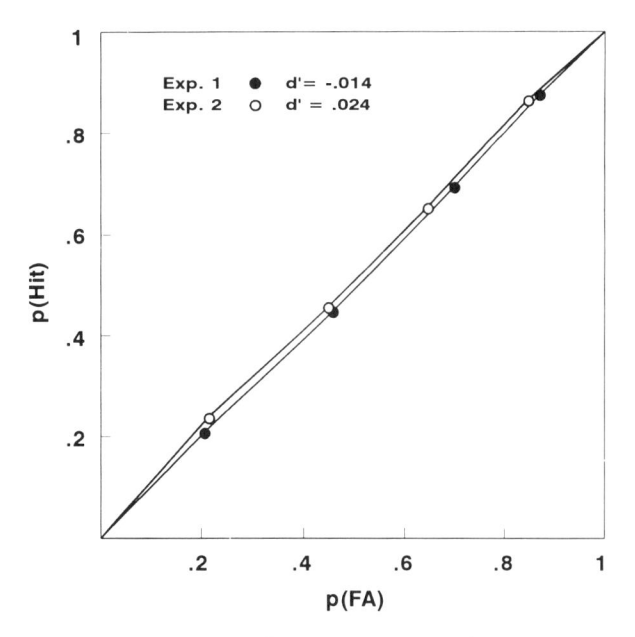

**Figure 5.3** ROC curves from experiments 1 and 2.

prime contained a target," and 1 meaning "I am pretty unsure whether the prime contained a target." They were to put the cursor on the appropriate scale position, using a mouse. In half of the trials the 5 pole of the scale was on the right; in the other half, it was on the left. These two display conditions varied randomly from trial to trial. Subjects were instructed to pay attention to these changes and to be careful to choose the correct position. Apart from the task, the second part of the experiment was identical to the first.

**Subjects**

Fourteen undergraduate subjects took part in the experiment. They were naive as to the purpose of the experiment and were paid 10 deutsche marks for participating.

**Results**

Figure 5.3 shows the ROC curve, averaged across subjects. The mean of the individual estimates of $d'$ was $-.014$, which is not different from zero ($p > .25$). The subjects were obviously unable to detect the prime. To find out if congruent and incongruent targets masked the primes equally well, separate estimates of $d'$ were computed for these two cases; $d'$ was $-.009$ for congruent and $-.010$ for incongruent prime-target pairs, clearly indicating that there was no difference.

The results from the RT part of the experiment are displayed in figure 5.4. RTs are the arithmetic means from correct responses. RTs of more than

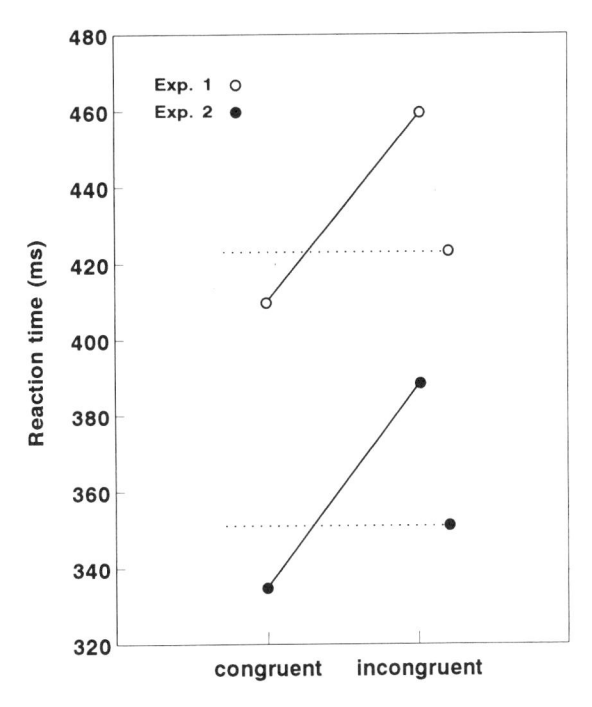

**Figure 5.4** Mean RTs from experiments 1 and 2. The dotted lines show RTs in the neutral condition.

1000 ms were omitted from the analysis. (This was also done in the other experiments and will not be noted when discussing those experiments. The proportion of discarded data was well below 1%).

Although the primes were not detectable, they had a strong effect on RT. RTs were 424, 410, and 460 ms for the neutral, congruent, and incongruent conditions, respectively. A one-way ANOVA yielded a highly significant effect of priming conditions ($F(2,26) = 47.42; p < .001$), with all three conditions differing from each other ($p < .01$ for all comparisons; Tukey test).

The error rates are shown in table 5.1. Errors were rare in the congruent and neutral conditions but unusually high (7.0 percent) in the incongruent condition. For statistical analysis, error rates were arcsine transformed. (This was also done in all subsequent error analyses.) A one-way ANOVA yielded a highly significant effect ($F(2,26) = 22.93; p < .001$), which was entirely due to the high error rate in the incongruent condition. It differed reliably ($p < .01$; Tukey test) from the other two conditions, which did not differ among themselves.

### Discussion

The findings from experiment 1 are clear. We were successful in completely eliminating any conscious awareness of the prime, as indicated by $d'$'s of factually zero for both congruent and incongruent prime-target pairs. Yet the

**Table 5.1** Percentage Errors in Experiments 1–3

|  | Experiment 1 | Experiment 2 | Experiment 3 Compatible | Incompatible |
|---|---|---|---|---|
| Congruent | 1.4 | 0.1 | 1.6 | 2.0 |
| Incongruent | 7.0 | 6.7 | 9.6 | 10.1 |
| Neutral | 1.1 | 1.5 | 2.3 | 3.2 |

prime had a powerful effect on both RT and the error rate. A congruent prime reduced RT as compared to a neutral prime. An incongruent prime did not only delay the response; in addition, it produced more than five times as many errors as occurred in the other two conditions—strong evidence that the masked prime triggered the response in a considerable number of trials. The general implication of these findings is that a stimulus can have access to the motor system and activate or even start an intended, planned response without being represented in consciousness.

Further, we obtained this effect in a two-choice situation that required not only detecting a stimulus but also integrating form information with position information. If the processing of the target is to be called "preattentive," then these data suggest that preattentive processing can include the binding of position and form information.

It seems, then, that processing considerably beyond the mere detection of the presence of a stimulus can occur without that stimulus being represented in consciousness. Experiment 1 has demonstrated direct parameter specification.

In the following experiments we tried to determine the limits of direct parameter specification by rendering the task more complex. This required a slight change in method. One shortcoming of the method of experiment 1 is that it did not permit varying spatial compatibility. (Subjects would, in all probability, translate the instruction, "Press the right button when the square appears on the left," into its compatible equivalent, "Press the right button when the diamond appears on the right"). Therefore, different stimuli were used in the subsequent experiments. Experiment 2 was designed to test whether the results from experiment 1 could be replicated with these new stimuli.

## 5.4 EXPERIMENT 2

### Method and Subjects

Experiment 2 was an exact replication of experiment 1, with the exception that new stimuli were used and that the time parameters were slightly different. The lower panel of figure 5.2 illustrates these changes. The imperative stimulus consisted of three boxes, one marked by two horizontal bars. The marked box (the target) was always on the left or on the right. (The center box was added because we intended to use it in a later experiment.) The prime consisted of three smaller, flat boxes. In half of the trials (neutral condition), they were unmarked. In 25 percent, the prime box on the side of the target was marked (congruent trials), and in 25 percent the marked prime box was on the opposite side (incongruent trials). A further change was a precue (intended to draw visual attention to the location where the prime would appear—above or below fixation) that appeared for 14 ms at an SOA of 28 ms before the prime; it consisted of a faint rectangle, equal in size to one of the target boxes. As in experiment 1, the stimulus sequence was preceded by the zooming of four points. The precue was presented immediately after the end of the 1000-ms zooming phase.

The subjects' task in the RT part of the experiment was to press the button on the side on which the marked box had appeared. In the signal detection part, they had to indicate their confidence that the prime contained a marked box. Fourteen undergraduates who had not participated in the first experiment served as subjects.

**Results and Discussion**

The results were very similar to those from the first experiment. The ROC curve is shown in figure 5.3. $d'$ was .024, again not different from zero ($p > .25$). RTs were 351, 335, and 388 ms for, respectively, the neutral, congruent, and incongruent conditions (fig. 5.4). A one-way ANOVA yielded a significant effect of priming conditions ($F(2,26) = 68.06; p < .001$), with all three conditions differing reliably ($p < .01$; Tukey test). The pattern of errors was also similar to that in the first experiment (table 5.1). The effect of priming conditions was again significant ($F(2,26) = 38.17; p < .001$). A Tukey test showed all conditions to differ reliably ($p < .01$).

The differences between the priming conditions were almost identical in the two experiments (fig. 5.4), although overall response speed was faster in experiment 2 than in experiment 1, probably due to better stimulus discriminability. (As an additional statistical check, a joint ANOVA was computed for experiments 1 and 2. There was no hint of an interaction between experiments and conditions; $F = .21$; n.s.) The fact that the priming effects were virtually identical in the two experiments permits an additional data analysis in answer to one possible objection against our interpretation of the data. One might argue that not only positive but also negative individual values of $d'$ reflect some discriminative power. There could have been some subjects who were able to discriminate between displays with and without a prime but who interpreted the cues incorrectly, tending to report "prime present" when there was actually no prime, and vice versa. This would result in a negative $d'$. Together with positive $d'$s from other subjects who also displayed some discrimination, this could have summed up to an overall $d'$ of zero, incorrectly suggesting that none of the subjects displayed any conscious discrimination. In reality, according to this objection, the priming effects that we observed in the RT data were due to these cases of residual conscious discrimination.

This possibility can be tested by correlating the individual subjects' absolute $d'$ values with the individual strengths of priming (defined as RT in the incongruent condition minus RT in the congruent condition). The combined data from experiments 1 and 2 offer a sufficient basis for such a correlational analysis. If the objection were valid, there should be a positive correlation between absolute $d'$ and strength of priming. This was definitely not the case (Pearson's $R = .027$). Thus, this objection can be discarded.

There is, then, little reason to doubt that experiments 1 and 2 have demonstrated direct parameter specification in the sense that a prime that could not be detected in the signal detection task had a strong influence on both the speed and the error rate of motor responses. These data provide a basis for exploring the limiting conditions of direct parameter specification. In the next experiment, we introduce a higher level of complexity by including an incompatible S-R mapping.

## 5.5 EXPERIMENT 3

### Method and Subjects

Experiment 3 replicated experiment 2 with the sole change that there were two RT blocks: one with a compatible and the other with an incompatible S-R mapping. The instruction in the compatible block was identical to that in experiment 2. In the incompatible block, subjects had to press the left button when the marker appeared in the right box, and vice versa. Seven subjects got the compatible block first; the other seven started with the incompatible block. Since stimulus conditions were identical to those in experiment 2, the signal detection part of the experiment was omitted in this and the following experiments.

### Results and Discussion

The reaction time data are shown in figure 5.5.

A two-way ANOVA for RTs yielded highly significant effects of priming conditions ($F(2,26) = 53.64; p < .001$) and of compatibility ($F(1,13) = 28.87; p < .001$) but no interaction ($p > .10$). The priming effect has thus survived the shift from a compatible to an incompatible S-R mapping—strong evidence that the processing of the prime, although it does not result in a conscious representation, is sensitive to the instruction. In the incompatible condition, an undetectable prime apparently activated the response of the contralateral hand, despite any presumably natural tendency to react with the spatially corresponding effector. This effect was even numerically similar to the amount of priming with compatible S-R mapping.

The error results (table 5.1) corroborate these findings. A two-way ANOVA with the factors priming conditions and compatibility yielded a highly significant effect of priming conditions ($F(2,26) = 16.16; p < .001$),

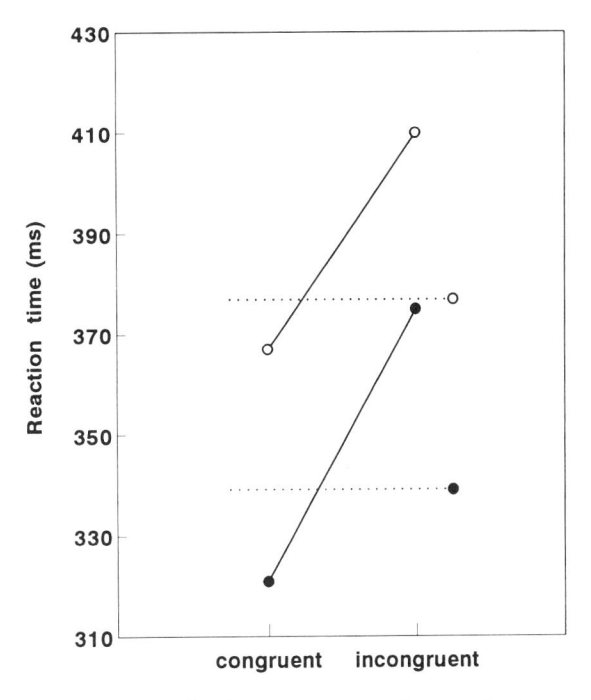

**Figure 5.5** RT data from experiment 3. Open circles: Incompatible. Filled circles: Compatible. Dotted lines snow RT in the neutral conditions.

while neither the main effect of compatibility nor the interaction approached significance ($p > .20$ in both cases). While the incongruent condition differed reliably from the other two ($p < .01$; Tukey test), the difference between the latter conditions failed to reach significance. The most important aspect of this pattern of results is that the combination incongruent/incompatible, in which the prime appeared on the side of the correct response, nevertheless produced a high error rate (10.1 percent), while the combination congruent/incompatible, in which the prime was on the opposite side, did not yield an elevated error rate (2.0 percent). This is in full accord with the RT data and confirms the conclusion that the prime's effect depended on the task instruction.

This result implies that direct parameter specification is not limited to "wired-in" S-R connections, which might have been a sufficient explanation of the data from the first two experiments. One alternative possibility, which would explain the findings from experiment 3, is that direct parameter specification is mediated by means of S-R links that need not be structurally based (wired in or formed as a result of extended training) but that have to be temporarily established, in a setlike manner, through a moderate amount of experience with a constant S-R mapping rule. According to this possibility, direct parameter specification survived the shift to an incompatible S-R mapping in experiment 3 because the mapping was kept constant within a block of trials. To test this possibility, the instruction was varied from trial to trial in experiment 4.

## 5.6 EXPERIMENT 4

### Method and Subjects

The main new feature of experiment 4 was the introduction of an additional cue in the form of a square that was either open or filled. "Filled" indicated "compatible," and "open" indicated "incompatible." The square appeared in the center of the screen during the zooming of the warning signal (which lasted for 1250 ms in this experiment), with SOAs of 250, 750, or 1250 ms prior to the onset of the prime. The experiment was preceded by a block of trials that replicated experiment 2. Fourteen new undergraduate subjects participated under the same conditions as in the preceding experiments.

### Results and Discussion

The RT data are shown in figure 5.6.

A three-way ANOVA of the RT data with the factors priming conditions, compatibility, and cue SOA yielded highly significant effects of priming conditions ($F(2,22) = 28.75; p < .001$; all differences between means $p < .01$; Tukey test) and compatibility ($F(1,11) = 47.47; p < .001$), while the effect of cue SOA failed to reach significance. The only significant interaction was that between priming conditions and cue SOA ($F(4.44) = 3.82; p < .01$). Priming was reduced in the 250-ms condition as compared to the other two SOAs (fig. 5.6). Separate Tukey tests for each cue SOA yielded significant ($p < .01$) differences between congruent and incongruent conditions for SOAs 1250 and 750 ms, while the corresponding difference at the 250-ms SOA (26 ms)

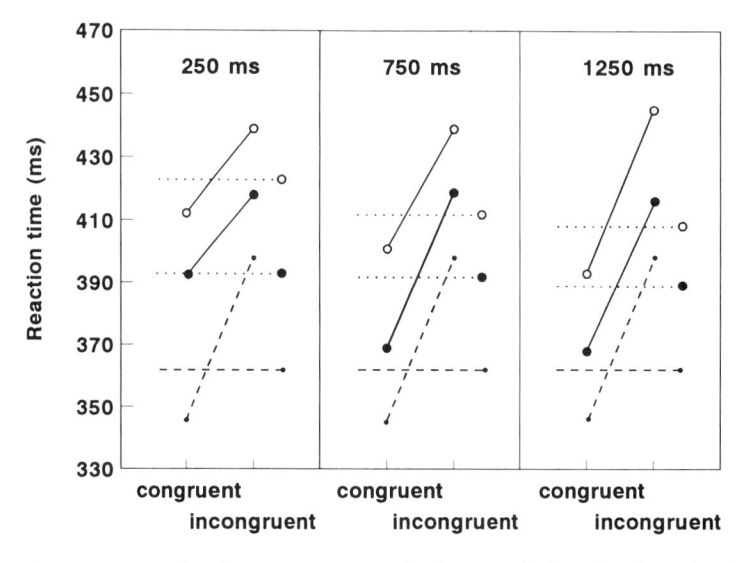

**Figure 5.6** RT data from experiment 4. The three panels show data from the three cue SOAs. Dashed lines: Control trials in which compatible and incompatible trials were blocked. Symbols as in figure 5.5.

just failed to reach the critical value of 27 ms for significance at the 5 percent level. This confirms that the interaction between priming conditions and cue SOA was essentially due to reduced priming at the 250-ms cue SOA.

As in the preceding experiments, the error data support the RT findings (table 5.2). There were significant main effects of priming conditions ($F(2,22) = 11.90; p < .001$), compatibility ($F(1,11) = 22.32; p < .001$), and cue SOA ($F(2,22) = 4.26; p < .05$). The only difference between the RT and error data concerns the effect of cue SOA. Although there was an insignificant trend for RT to increase when cue SOA was reduced, the error rate shows an opposite effect, indicating a possible speed-accuracy trade-off.

This pattern of results suggests two conclusions. First, the effect of priming conditions has clearly been preserved, despite the fact that the S-R mapping was redefined from trial to trial. This implies that direct parameter specification is not only task dependent but that it can also adapt rapidly to changes in the task instruction.

The second conclusion relates to the interaction between priming conditions and cue SOA. For the 1250- and 750-ms cue SOAs, the priming effect was similar in size to the standard effect that we obtained in the preliminary block of trials that replicated experiment 2 (dashed curves in fig. 5.6). By contrast, priming was reduced with the 250-ms cue SOA. This suggests that direct parameter specification may approach its limit when the interval between the cue and the imperative stimulus becomes very short. One possible interpretation is that direct parameter specification becomes impossible if action planning (the implementation of the S-R mapping) is still under way when the prime is presented. We will return to this possibility in the general discussion.

The first of these two conclusions presents a problem for theories that conceive of nonconscious processing as automatic or preattentive, implying that it is inflexible and stimulus driven. One might argue, however, that there is a way to avoid this conclusion. It could be that the effect of the prime is purely sensory. Possibly, a congruent prime does not activate a response but simply speeds up stimulus identification. Similarly, an incongruent prime might hamper target identification. In this case, we would expect the priming effect to be immune against all changes at the level of S-R mapping, and the assumption that it is a purely bottom-up effect could be maintained.

Such an explanation can handle the RT data from experiments 1–3 but cannot easily explain why the prime's effect was reduced in the 250-ms cue SOA condition in experiment 4. Further, it has serious difficulties with the

Table 5.2  Percentage Errors in Experiment 4

|  | Control | 250 ms | 750 ms | 1250 ms |
| --- | --- | --- | --- | --- |
| Congruent | 1.4 | 1.7 | 3.5 | 3.9 |
| Incongruent | 7.1 | 5.3 | 6.2 | 9.2 |
| Neutral | 1.4 | 3.5 | 3.3 | 3.8 |

unusually high error rates that incongruent primes produce. To interpret them as sensory based, one would have to assume that they were due to misperceptions of the target's position. This is strongly against the subjects' introspective reports, which indicated that they were clearly aware of the errors and were surprised that they could not prevent them ("The target was on the left, but somehow my hand hit the right button"). Yet our assumption that priming is not simply a sensory effect requires a formal test. Experiment 5 was designed to provide this test.

## 5.7 EXPERIMENT 5

The basic logic of experiment 5 was to use the center box of the stimulus array as an additional possible position of the target stimulus, besides the left and right boxes, in order to generate two-to-one S-R mappings. The prime could appear in all three positions. This change allowed us to vary response congruence while keeping sensory stimulus conditions (and hence opportunities for sensory priming) constant. If response congruence continues to affect RT under these conditions, then this effect must be located at the response selection or response activation level (for short, we call this a motor effect). More specifically, the hypothesis of a motor locus of priming makes two predictions:

Hypothesis 1: Responses to a central target, with the prime in one of the lateral positions, should be shorter if the prime and target positions map on the same hand (are response congruent) than if they map on different hands (are response incongruent).

Hypothesis 2: Responses to a lateral target, with the prime in the central position, should be shorter if the target and prime are response congruent than if they are response incongruent.

Confirmation of these hypotheses would demonstrate differential priming under identical sensory conditions and, hence, support the notion that there is priming at the motor level. This does not imply that priming acts exclusively at that level. There might be other priming effects in addition.

**Method and Subjects**

Since the central box was included as a potential position of both the target and the prime, there were twelve stimulus combinations: three possible positions of the target, each combined with three possible positions of the prime plus the neutral condition. The three target positions were mapped onto the two responses in the following way. The two lateral positions were always mapped onto the corresponding compatible responses; the right button had to be pressed in response to the right target and the left button in response to the left target. The central target was mapped onto the left button for half of the subjects and onto the right button for the other half. Thus, each subject had one response with a one-to-one mapping and one response with a two-to-one mapping.

Further, we used twenty-eight instead of fourteen subjects, half of whom were assigned to each of two different frequency conditions. In condition "Equal Stimulus Frequency," all three targets appeared equally often, with the consequence that the two-to-one response had to be given twice as often as the one-to-one response. In condition "Equal Response Frequency," the one-to-one stimulus appeared twice as often as each of the other two targets. Hence, response frequency was constant for the two hands, but stimulus frequency was unequal for the three targets. In this way, we expected to detect possible disturbing effects of unequal frequencies of either kind. In all other respects, the experiment was identical to the preceding experiments. Subjects were recruited from the same group as in the preceding experiments, had not participated in any of these experiments, and served under the same conditions.

**Results and Discussion**

A mixed ANOVA with the between-groups factor frequencies (equal response versus equal stimulus frequencies) and the within-groups factors target position and prime position yielded no significant effect of the between-groups factor or any interaction with one of the other two factors. The data were therefore collapsed over groups. The results from all conditions are shown in table 5.3.

**RT Analyses** The comparisons that are critical for the two hypotheses under test are illustrated in figure 5.7. The left panel shows the data that are relevant to hypothesis 1. These are the conditions in which the target was at the central position and there was no prime at this position. The remaining three conditions are no prime (neutral), lateral prime that maps on the same hand as the target (response congruent), and lateral prime that maps on the

Table 5.3  Reaction Times in Experiment 5 (percentage errors)

|  | 2 : 1 Mapping | | 1 : 1 Mapping |
|---|---|---|---|
|  | Lateral | Central | Lateral |
| Congruent[a] | *338 (0.2)*[b] | *403 (4.2)*[b] | *362 (1.4)* |
|  | 353 (1.0)[c] | 396 (4.2)[c] |  |
| Incongruent[a] | 379 (4.1) | 424 (8.6) | 409 (10.3)[b] |
|  |  |  | 393 (4.1)[c] |
| Neutral | 355 (0.5) | 403 (4.4) | 383 (2.9) |

Note: Italicized entries are data from conditions that were perceptually as well as response congruent.
a. The reference is to response congruence.
b. Lateral prime.
c. Central prime.

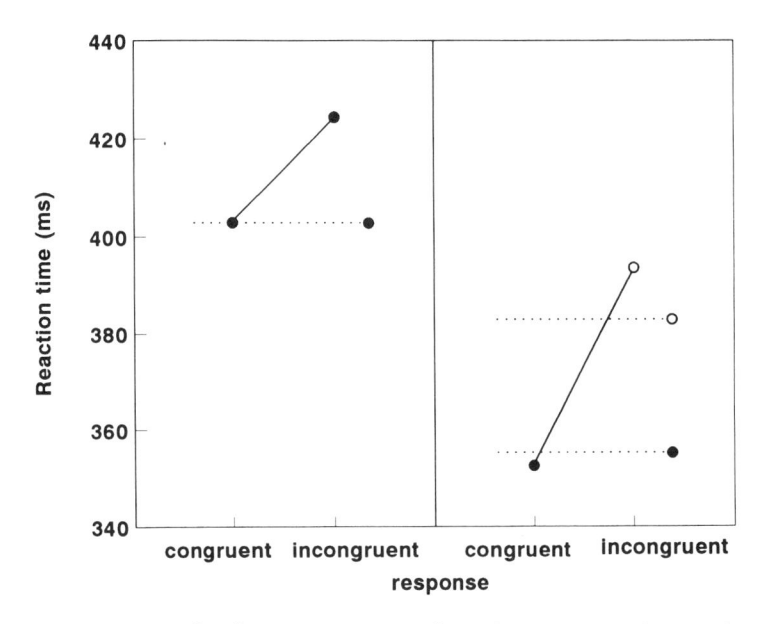

**Figure 5.7** RT data from experiment 5. Left panel: Responses to the central target with the prime in a lateral position that maps on the same (congruent) or on the opposite (incongruent) hand. Right panel: Responses to a lateral target with a central prime that maps on the same (congruent) or the opposite (incongruent) hand. Dotted lines: Neutral condition with no prime. Note that congruent (filled circles) and incongruent (open circles) prime conditions have different neutral conditions as their baselines.

other hand (response incongruent). A one-way ANOVA yielded a significant effect ($F(2,54) = 7.20; p < .01$). There was a difference between response incongruent and the other two conditions ($p < .01$; Tukey test), which did not differ among themselves. Since the difference between response congruent and response incongruent went into the predicted direction, this confirms hypothesis 1.

The right panel of figure 5.7 displays the data relevant to hypothesis 2. They comprise the conditions in which the target was in one of the lateral positions and the prime was either absent or in the central position. When there was a central prime, it could either map on the same hand as the lateral target (response congruent) or on the other hand (response incongruent). This had the necessary implication that the lateral target in the response congruent condition was a two-to-one target (one of two targets converging on the same response), while the target in the response incongruent condition was a one-to-one target. This turned out to make a difference even in the neutral condition, in which two-to-one lateral targets produced consistently shorter RTs than one-to-one targets (dotted lines in fig. 5.7, right panel).

Because of these different baselines, hypothesis 2 had to be reformulated: responses to a lateral target, with the prime in the central position, should be shorter, relative to a neutral condition with no prime, if the target and prime are response congruent than if they are response incongruent. This predicts an interaction between response congruence (confounded with two-to-one versus one-to-one mapping) and priming (central prime versus no prime). This interaction was significant ($F(1,27) = 13.33; p < .01$), as was the main effect of response congruence ($F(1,27) = 38.04; p < .001$). Priming had no significant effect; the presence or absence of the prime as such, independent of S-R mapping, did not systematically affect RT. The important finding is the interaction, which confirms hypothesis 2. A Tukey test revealed that it was due to the response-incongruent condition ($p < .01$ for the difference between central prime and neutral), while the corresponding difference in the response congruent condition was small (3 ms) and insignificant.

**Error Analyses** The same analyses were performed for the error data. The analysis for the central target mirrored the RT results. There was a significant effect of conditions ($F(2,54) = 8.41; p < .001$), which was entirely due to errors being more numerous in the response incongruent than in the other two conditions ($p < .01$; Tukey test). By contrast, while the ANOVA for hypothesis 2 yielded a significant ($F(1,27) = 30.35, p < .001$) effect of response congruence (confounded with two-to-one versus one-to-one mapping), the critical interaction with priming was not significant. However, the differences went into the same direction as in the RT data (table 5.3).

Taken together, these data provide strong and unequivocal evidence that the priming effects observed in the preceding experiments cannot be simply attributed to sensory facilitation and inhibition, that is, to the prime's accelerating or slowing the sensory analysis of the target. Whether and how a prime influences RT to a target clearly depends on whether they converge on the same response. In this sense, priming is a motor effect.

On the other hand, demonstrating motor priming does not necessarily disconfirm the existence of sensory priming. Indeed, some aspects of our data may be interpreted as resulting from sensory priming. Although the data in figure 5.7 show the usual incongruence effects (longer RTs in the incongruent than in the neutral condition), the congruence effects (shorter RTs in the congruent than in the neutral conditions) observed in all previous experiments are absent. As the data in table 5.3 suggest, the usual facilitation by a congruent prime may have reappeared, however, when prime and target were not only response congruent but also perceptually congruent, that is, when they shared the same spatial position. One possible interpretation is that inhibition by an incongruent prime is mainly a motor effect and facilitation by a congruent prime is predominantly sensory. On the assumption that errors are chiefly due to motor priming, this may also explain why the error data do not show consistent differences between the neutral and congruent conditions.

This interpretation assumes that the data in figure 5.7 fail to show a congruence effect because its specific cause (purportedly sensory priming) is absent if the prime and the target do not share the same spatial position. An alternative possibility is that different spatial positions create an additional source of interference (e.g., because the prime acts as a distractor that draws visual attention away from the target's position). Furthermore, there could be some kind of mutual inhibition between two S-R connections that couple the same response to different stimuli. Such effects could have counteracted the facilitation by response congruent primes that were not also perceptually congruent, producing a net effect close to zero.

These are, however, speculations, based on aspects of the data that the experiment was not designed to test. Further experiments are required to confirm or disconfirm them. The important finding from experiment 5 is that motor priming does exist. Given the earlier evidence that the effect of the prime is preserved with incompatible and even with variable S-R mappings, the conclusion seems inevitable that the prime may exert its effect on motor output in a highly flexible and malleable manner, despite the fact that it does not reach a representation at the level of conscious perception.

## 5.8 GENERAL DISCUSSION

Direct parameter specification seems to be a far more general phenomenon than could be surmised on the basis of the earlier work on the Fehrer-Raab effect. Experiments 1 and 2 demonstrated that the ability of a completely masked prime to influence RT strongly is not restricted to simple reactions but occurs also with choice reactions. Experiment 3 showed that it is not restricted to compatible choice reactions but occurs also with an incompatible S-R mapping. Experiment 4 added the finding that it is not limited to experiments in which the S-R mapping remains unchanged during a block of trials but is present when the mapping rule is redefined from trial to trial. With cue SOAs of 1,250 and 750 ms, priming with variable mapping was as strong as it had been when the mapping rule was held constant over a block of trials. When the cue SOA was 250 ms, there was a reduction in the amount of priming, indicating that direct parameter specification might have approached its limit in this condition.

These findings have implications for several theoretical issues. We will first discuss them with respect to the concept of direct parameter specification and then relate them to three other theoretical concepts: automaticity, discrimination without awareness, and continuous-flow processing.

### Direct Parameter Specification

A sensory stimulus may be consciously perceived, and it may elicit a voluntary motor response (that is, a response that would not have occurred without an explicit intention, or, in operational terms without a corresponding instruction). How are these two types of effects functionally related?

Traditionally, there have been three types of answers. One is in accordance with folk psychology and states that the stimulus first has to be consciously perceived before it can trigger a voluntary response. The second answer dates back to Wilhelm Wundt, who distinguished between "complete" and "foreshortened" reactions (Wundt 1903; see also Lange 1888). In complete reactions, a conscious perception ("apperception") intervenes between stimulus and response. In foreshortened reactions, there is a direct linking between perception and response, with apperception occurring only after the response has already been executed. According to Lange's (1888) experiments, foreshortened reactions can be obtained with simple, well-practiced S-R mappings if the subject adopts a particular set, called "muscular set," in which attention is directed to the response rather than to the stimulus.

A third and much more radical answer was proposed by Wundt's student Hugo Münsterberg: "When we apperceive the stimulus, we have usually already started responding to it; our motor apparatus does not wait for consciousness, but does restlessly its duty, and our consciousness watches it and is not entitled to order it about" (Münsterberg [1889] 1990, p. 173; translation ours). Thus, Münsterberg believed that there are two largely independent effects of a stimulus: it determines the motor response, and it may have a later effect in consciousness ("apperception") that is, however, not causally related to its motor effects. This is, according to Münsterberg, the "usual" functional architecture, not restricted to special S-R connections, as Wundt had assumed with his concept of foreshortened reactions.

Until recently, little systematic empirical work had been done on the issue. However, various observations from different research areas indicate that motor performance may become dissociated from conscious experience, as assessed by explicit verbal reports. Among the best-known phenomena are implicit learning (Berry, chap. 30, this volume; Shanks, Green, and Kolodny, chap. 33, this volume) and implicit memory (Graf, chap. 27, this volume; Jacoby, chap. 26, this volume) and diverse dissociations that can be observed in neuropsychological patients (Farah, chap. 2, this volume). In addition, findings from standard laboratory experiments with normal subjects have demonstrated dissociations between the conscious experience of a stimulus and the effect that it has on motor behavior (Neumann 1989a). Besides the Fehrer-Raab effect, they include spatial dissociations (e.g., induced motion is almost not reflected in motor pointing behavior; Bridgeman, Kirch, and Sperling 1981) and temporal dissociations (e.g., RT to an auditory stimulus is faster than RT to a visual stimulus, yet the visual stimulus is reported as being perceived first; Neumann et al. 1992; Neumann et al., n.d.).

These examples suggest that the Fehrer-Raab effect is not an isolated curiosity. There are probably many ways in which behavior can become dissociated from the contents of awareness. They have in common that a stimulus affects behavior in a way that is not congruent with the manner in which it is consciously represented, suggesting that the coupling between stimulus and response is not cognitively mediated. The special characteristic of the Fehrer-Raab effect, in the version of our paradigm, is that the stimulus is not at all consciously represented, which renders this particular demonstration of direct parameter specification perhaps a bit more spectacular than it appears in some of the other cases.

Given the short modern research history in this area, it is not surprising that we are still far away from an adequate theoretical understanding of these phenomena. Our strategy has been to try to determine the limits of direct parameter specification. The results suggest that with respect to this question,

Münsterberg may have been closer to truth than Wundt. Direct parameter specification was clearly not restricted to simple, well-practiced S-R connections. Experiment 4 suggested that the way in which the masked prime affects the response can be rapidly modified through an instruction cue, although the effect of the prime is weakened if the cue SOA is reduced to 250 ms. Although this finding needs further investigation, it is interesting that an analogous experiment exploring the limits of a temporal dissociation (sensory modality has opposite effects on RT and on sensory order judgment) yielded very similar results (Neumann, Niepel, and Tappe, n.d.). These findings are in accord with the suggestion (Neumann 1989a, 1990a) that direct parameter specification breaks down, and there is a need for cognitive mediation, if action planning has not yet been completed when the stimulus is presented. To put it positively, direct parameter specification is possible if all parameters of the to-be-executed action have already been specified when the stimulus appears, except for those that will be specified by the stimulus itself.

**Automaticity**

According to early theorizing about automaticity (LaBerge 1981; Neumann 1989b; Schneider, Dumais, and Shiffrin 1984), automatic processing was thought to be essentially bottom-up processing, based on either wired-in connections or extensive training and unrelated to current intentions. Voluntary, intentional ("controlled") processes were believed to be accompanied by conscious awareness. It is clear that the contrast between direct parameter specification and cognitive mediation cuts across these distinctions. The effect of the prime in our experiments was controlled in the sense that it depended on the subject's intention and could be rapidly changed. Further, as far as we can tell from our data, direct parameter specification by the prime required no previous training. However, the prime was not represented in conscious awareness, which would, according to most definitions, suggest that its effects were automatic.

One implication of this study then is, that the conventional criteria of automaticity do not necessarily converge. This agrees with the results of a survey that summarized and evaluated the literature on automaticity about a decade ago (Neumann 1984). Instead of supporting a monolithic concept of automaticity, the data seem to call for more specific and restricted distinctions. The contrast between direct parameter specification and cognitive mediation is based on the awareness criterion. Other offsprings of the original automatic-controlled distinction focus on one of the other criteria, such as unavoidability (Jacoby, chap. 26, this volume), or changes as a result of training (Logan 1988). Perhaps all of these distinctions will turn out to be functionally related in some complex manner, but it does not seem that they are simply convergent operations that define a common, homogeneous concept of automaticity. In this respect, the concept of automaticity may share the fate of the concept of attention, which also seems to be dissolving in favor of more specific constructs (Neumann 1987, 1990b).

## Discrimination without Awareness

Since the beginnings of the "New Look" research on discrimination without awareness (McGinnies 1949; Lazarus and McCleary 1951), research in this area has been beset by the kind of methodological problems noted in the introduction to experiment 1. The most sophisticated and most influential theoretical contributions to the field have often been those of skeptics who argued that subjects in these experiments were not really (not all, not completely, not always, etc.) unaware of the stimuli (Eriksen 1960; Neisser 1967; Holender 1986). Indeed, researchers have usually been faced with the following methodological dilemma (Cheesman and Merikle 1985, 1986; Greenwald 1992; Reingold and Merikle 1990): If one chooses a very conservative criterion of awareness, such as chance performance in a forced-choice task, then the dissociation can no longer be established; that is, performance with respect to this criterion is not different from performance as assessed by the indirect measure supposed to indicate discrimination without awareness. To produce a performance difference, one needs a less strict criterion (most often, subjective reports of no awareness), which will, alas, not convince the skeptic.

Our series of experiments comprises several aspects that shed some light on this dilemma. First, we used a very strict, objective measure (a $d'$ value of zero in a signal detection task) to assess no awareness. Still we obtained a strong and reliable dissociation. In our opinion, this leaves no room for the skeptic's suspicion that there was still some awareness of the prime left that could account for the RT data.

Second, why is our paradigm apparently more successful in this respect than many others? In our opinion, there are several reasons. One is that discrimination without awareness is measured by RT—that is, in a very fast, direct manner. Other measures, such as semantic or associative priming, may involve intermediate steps and take more time. If the processes that underlie discrimination without awareness are based on a transient, fast-decaying trace of the stimulus, this could be a critical feature. Further, the metacontrast paradigm requires that the prime and the target/mask are similar in shape. This brings about optimal metacontrast masking and has the effect that the system can easily confound prime and target, responding to the former with a response that is required to the latter. Thus, the high prime-mask similarity favors the prime's effect on RT while hampering its conscious perception. These are optimal conditions for a dissociation.

Finally, the notion of direct parameter specification offers a clue as to why forced-choice criteria of subjective awareness tend to destroy the dissociation. If a stimulus of which the subject is unaware can directly specify a voluntary manual response, it can possibly also specify a verbal response directly. At least there is no guarantee whatsoever that forced-choice verbal behavior measures exclusively subjective awareness and does not also result from direct parameter specification. This is similar to the problem, discussed by Jacoby (chap. 26, this volume), that measures of explicit recollection in memory experiments may be contaminated by informed guessing.

Our results indicate that the signal detection method is not strongly affected by this problem, perhaps because this method—or at least the scaling variant that we used—requires a judgment (How sure am I that a signal was present?) rather than a response (Neumann and Müsseler 1990). This may indeed be the critical difference between what Cheesman and Merikle (1985, 1986) have called objective and subjective thresholds. The particular advantage of the signal detection method (in its scaling variant) is that it requires a subjective (that is, "introspective") judgment and yet produces an objective (that is, criterion-free) estimate of sensitivity. Therefore, in our opinion, it is an adequate method of operationalizing subjective awareness in this kind of experiment.

**Continuous Flow**

Our paradigm is a variant of a type of experiment in which a context stimulus ("distractor" or "prime"), which is presented either simultaneously with a target or briefly before or after it, is found either to interfere with or facilitate target processing, depending (among other factors) on whether it is response congruent. Other variants include the classical Stroop color-word experiment (Stroop 1935), a picture-word variant (Underwood 1976), and a word-word variant (Van der Heijden 1981) of the Stroop task, and the letter flanker experiment introduced by Eriksen and Eriksen (1974) (LaHeij 1988 for a comprehensive review). Our paradigm is similar to these types of experiments, except that our primes were completely masked. Nevertheless, the standard pattern of results—response incongruent primes cause inhibition, while congruent primes produce facilitation—was replicated.

This demonstrates that a stimulus need not be processed fully, up to its conscious identification, in order to be an effective prime or distractor. This result is in accord with a growing body of evidence that suggests that primes start activating responses while they are still being perceptually analyzed ("continuous flow of information"; Coles et al. 1985; Eriksen et al. 1985; Smid, Mulder, and Mulder 1990; Smid et al. 1991). However, the notions of direct parameter specification and continuous flow are not identical. Although they share the assumption that full perceptual processing of a stimulus is not a necessary prerequisite for its affecting response processes, they differ with respect to what they mean by full perceptual processing. In the case of direct parameter specification, this denotes processing that leads to a representation in conscious awareness. In the context of the notion of continuous flow, full processing means that stimulus recognition has been completed. These two meanings of full processing need not coincide. A stimulus may be partially recognized at the level of conscious awareness and completely recognized in a functional sense without being represented in conscious awareness. Electrophysiological evidence suggests that stimulus information can influence response processes before it has been completely analyzed. Our demonstration of direct parameter specification indicates that it can do so without being represented in conscious awareness.

## NOTES

Correspondence should be addressed to Odmar Neumann, Abteilung für Psychologie, Universität Bielefeld, D-3350 Bielefeld, Germany. The work that this chapter is based on was supported by grant Ne 366/1-2 from the Deutsche Forschungsgemeinschaft. We thank Marcus Ludewig and Elena Carbone for programming and/or running the experiments and helping to analyze the data and Michael Niepel for his untiring support in many phases of the work. Thanks are also due to Günther Gediga and Reinhard Suck for statistical advice and Wolfgang Prinz, Thomas Tappe, and Dirk Vorberg for helpful comments on an earlier version of this chapter. We are deeply indebted to Peter Wolff, who has had a strong influence on our thinking and whose own contributions to our subject, soon to be published, will provide major breakthroughs on many questions that are discussed in this chapter.

1. These different experimental logics are also reflected in our terminology. In the description of the early studies, we used the terms "test stimulus" and "mask" for the first and the second stimuli, respectively. When describing our experiments, we shall call the first, masked stimulus the "prime" and the second stimulus, to which the subject has to react, and that also masks the prime, the "target."

## REFERENCES

Alpern, M. (1953). Metacontrast. *Journal of the Optical Society of America, 43,* 648–657.

Averbach, E., and Coriell, S. (1961). Short-term memory in vision. *Bell System Technical Journal, 40,* 309–328.

Bernstein, I. H., Amundson, V. E., and Schurman, D. L. (1973). Metacontrast inferred from reaction time and verbal report: Replication and comment on the Fehrer-Biederman experiment. *Journal of Experimental Psychology, 100,* 195–201.

Breitmeyer, B. G. (1984). *Visual masking: An integrative approach.* Oxford: Oxford University Press.

Breitmeyer, B. G., and Ganz, L. (1976). Implications of sustained and transient channels for theories of visual pattern masking, saccadic suppression, and information processing. *Psychological Review, 83,* 1–36.

Bridgeman, B., Kirch, M., and Sperling, A. (1981) Segregation of cognitive and motor aspects of visual function using induced motion. *Perception and Psychophysics, 29,* 336–342.

Cheesman, J., and Merikle, P. M. (1985). Word recognition and consciousness. In D. Besner, T. G. Waller, and G. E. MacKinnon (Eds.), *Reading research: Advances in theory and practice,* 311–352. New York: Academic Press.

Cheesman, J., and Merikle, P. M. (1986). Distinguishing conscious from unconscious perceptual processes. *Canadian Journal of Psychology, 40,* 3443–367.

Coles, M. G. H., Gratton, G., Bashore, T. R., Eriksen, C. W., and Donchin, E. (1985). A psychophysiological investigation of the continuous flow model of human information processing. *Journal of Experimental Psychology: Human Perception and Performance, 11,* 529–553.

Eriksen, B. A., & Eriksen, C. W. (1974). Effects of noise letters upon the identification of a target letter in a nonsearch task. *Perception and Psychophysics, 16,* 143–149.

Eriksen, C. W. (1956). An experimental analysis of subception. *American Journal of Psychology, 69,* 625–634.

Eriksen, C. W. (1960). Discrimination and learning without awareness: A methodological survey and an evaluation. *Psychological Review, 67,* 279–300.

Eriksen, C. W., Coles, M. G. H., Morris, L. R., and O'Hara, W. P. (1985). An electromyographic examination of response competition. *Bulletin of the Psychonomic Society, 23,* 165–168.

Fehrer, E., and Biederman, I. (1962). A comparison of reaction time and verbal report in the detection of masked stimuli. *Journal of Experimental Psychology, 64,* 126–130.

Fehrer, E., and Raab, E. (1962). Reaction time to stimuli masked by metacontrast. *Journal of Experimental Psychology, 63,* 143–147.

Greenwald, A. G. (1992). New Look 3: Unconscious cognition reclaimed. *American Psychologist, 47,* 766–779.

Grüsser, O.-J. (1972). Metacontrast and the perception of the visual world. *Pflüger's Archiv für die gesamte Physiologie, 223,* R 98.

Holender, D. (1986). Semantic activation without conscious identification in dichotic listening, parafoveal vision, and visual masking: A survey and appraisal. *Behavioral and Brain Sciences, 9,* 1–66.

Jacoby, L. L. (1991). A process dissociation framework: Separating automatic from intentional uses of memory. *Journal of Memory and Language, 30,* 513–541.

Kahneman, D. (1967). An onset-onset law for one case of apparent motion and metacontrast. *Perception and Psychophysics, 2,* 577–584.

Kahneman, D. (1968). Method, findings, and theory in studies of visual masking. *Psychological Bulletin, 70,* 404–425.

LaBerge, D. (1981). Automatic information processing: A review. In J. Long and A. Baddeley (Eds.), *Attention and performance IX.* Hillsdale, NJ: Erlbaum.

LaHeij, W. (1988). *Lexical context effects in reading and naming.* Unpublished doctoral dissertation, University of Leiden.

Lange, L. (1888). Neue Experimente über den Vorgang der einfachen Reaction auf Sinneseindrücke (New experiments on the process of the simple reaction to sensory impressions). *Philosophische Studien, 4,* 479–510.

Lazarus, R. S., and McCleary, R. A. (1951). Autonomic discrimination without awareness: A study of subception. *Psychological Review, 58,* 113–122.

Logan, G. D. (1988). Towards an instance theory of automatization. *Psychological Review, 95,* 492–527.

Mayzner, M. S., Tresselt, M. E., and Helfer, M. S. A. (1967). A provisional model of visual information processing with sequential inputs. *Psychonomic Monograph Supplements, 2,* 91–108.

McGinnies, E. (1949). Emotionality and perceptual defense. *Psychological Review, 56,* 244–251.

Münsterberg, H. [1889] (1990). *Beiträge zur experimentellen Psychologie, Heft 1: Über willkürliche und unwillkürliche Vorstellungsverbindungen.* (Contributions to experimental psychology. Fascicle 1: On voluntary and involuntary associations of ideas). Reprinted in H. Hildebrandt and E. Scheerer (Eds.), *Hugo Münsterberg. Frühe Schriften* (Hugo Münsterberg: Early writings). Berlin: Deutscher Verlag der Wissenschaften.

Neisser, U. (1967). *Cognitive Psychology.* New York: Appleton-Century-Crofts.

Neumann, O. (1984). Automatic processing: A review of recent findings and a plea for an old theory. In W. Prinz and A. F. Sanders (Eds.), *Cognition and motor processes,* 255–293. Berlin: Springer.

Neumann, O. (1987). Beyond Capacity: A functional view of attention. In H. Heuer and A. F. Sanders (Eds.), *Perspectives on perception and action,* 361–394. Hillsdale, NJ: Erlbaum.

Neumann, O. (1989a). Kognitive Vermittlung und direkte Parameterspezifikation. Zum Problem mentaler Repräsentation in der Wahrnehmung (Cognitive mediation and direct parameter specification: On the problem of mental representation in perception). *Sprache und Kognition, 8*, 32–49.

Neumann, O. (1989b). On the origins and status of the concept of automatic processing. *Zeitschrift für Psychologie, 197*, 411–428.

Neumann, O. (1990a). Direct parameter specification and the concept of perception. *Psychological Research, 52*, 207–215.

Neumann, O. (1990b). Visual attention and action. In O. Neumann and W. Prinz (Eds.), *Relationships between perception and action: Current approaches*, 227–267. Berlin: Springer.

Neumann, O., Koch, R., Niepel, M., and Tappe, Th. (1992). Reaktionszeit und zeitliches Reihenfolgeurteil: Übereinstimmung oder Dissoziation? (Reaction time and temporal order judgment: Correspondence or dissociation?). *Zeitschrift für experimentelle und angewandte Psychologie, 39*, 621–645.

Neumann, O., and Müsseler, J. (1990). "Judgment" vs. "response": A general problem and some experimental illustrations. In H.-G. Geissler, M. Müller, and W. Prinz (Eds.), *Psychophysical explorations of mental structures*, 445–455. Göttingen: Hogrefe.

Neumann, O., Niepel, M., and Tappe, Th. (n.d.). Stimulus modality effects on RT and the limits of direct parameter specification.

Neumann, O., Niepel, M., Tappe, Th., and Koch, R. (n.d.). Temporal order judgment and reaction time to visual and auditory stimuli of different intensities: Further evidence for dissociations. *Perception and Psychophysics*. Under revision.

Neumann, O., and Prinz, W. (1987). Kognitive Antezedenzien von Willkürhandlungen (Cognitive antecedents of voluntary actions). In H. Heckhausen, P. M. Gollwitzer, and F. E. Weinert (Eds.), *Jenseits des Rubikon: Der Wille in den Humanwissenschaften*, 195–215. Berlin: Springer.

Proctor, R. W., Nunn, M. B., and Pallos, I. (1983). The influence of metacontrast masking on detection and spatial-choice judgments: An apparent distinction between automatic and attentive response mechanisms. *Journal of Experimental Psychology: Human Perception and Performance, 9*, 278–287.

Reingold, E. M., Merikle, P. M. (1990). On the inter-relatedness of theory and measurement in the study of unconscious processes. *Mind and Language, 5*, 9–28.

Schiller, P. H. (1969). Behavioral and electrophysiological studies of visual masking. In K. N. Leibovic (Ed.), *Information processing in the nervous system*, 141–165. Berlin: Springer.

Schiller, P. H., and Chorover, S. L. (1966). Metacontrast: Its relation to evoked potentials. *Science, 153*, 1398–1400.

Schiller, P. H., and Smith, M. C. (1966). Detection in metacontrast. *Journal of Experimental Psychology, 71*, 32–39.

Schneider, W., Dumais, S. T., and Shiffrin, R. M. (1984). Automatic and control processing and attention. In R. Parasuraman and R. D. Davies (Eds.), *Varieties of attention*. New York: Academic Press.

Smid, H. G. O. M., Lamain, W., Hogeboom, M. M., Mulder, G., and Mulder, L. J. M. (1991). Psychophysiological evidence for continuous information transmission between visual search and response processes. *Journal of Experimental Psychology: Human Perception and Performance, 17*, 696–714.

Smid, H. G. O. M., Mulder, G., and Mulder, L. J. M. (1990). Selective response activation can begin before stimulus recognition is complete: A psychophysiological and error analysis of continuous flow. *Acta Psychological, 74*, 169–201.

Stigler, R. (1910). Chronophotische Studien über den Umgebungskontrast. (Chronophotic studies on surround contrast). *Pflügers Archiv für die gesamte Physiologie, 134*, 365–435.

Stroop, J. R. (1935). Studies of interference in serial verbal reactions. *Journal of Experimental Psychology, 18*, 643–662.

Taylor, T. L., and McCloskey, D. (1990). Triggering of preprogrammed movements as reactions to masked stimuli. *Journal of Neurophysiology, 63*, 439–446.

Underwood, G. (1976). Semantic interference from unattended printed words. *British Journal of Psychology, 67*, 327–338.

Van der Heijden, A. H. C. (1981). *Short-term visual information forgetting*. London: Routledge & Kegan Paul.

Weintraub, D. J., and Fidell, L. S. (1979). A signal-detection approach to subception: Concomitant verbal and finger latency responses in metacontrast. *Perception and Psychophysics, 26*, 143–153.

Weisstein, N. (1968). A Rashevsky-Landahl neural net: Simulation of metacontrast. *Psychological Review, 75*, 494–521.

Werner, H. (1935). Studies on contour: I. Qualitative analysis. *American Journal of Psychology, 47*, 40–64.

Wundt, W. (1903). *Grundzüge der physiologischen Psychologie* (Outlines of physiological psychology). Leipzig: Engelmann.

# III Face Recognition

# 6  Conscious and Nonconscious Recognition of Familiar Faces

## Andrew W. Young

ABSTRACT   There has been a considerable increase in interest in how familiar faces are recognized. Studies in neuropsychology and experimental psychology have shown the value of theoretical models proposing that recognition of the face's identity is achieved independently from the determination of other types of socially important information. Recognition itself is best considered a multistage process, and computer simulation has led to a model that can account for priming effects in face recognition and some of the different consequences of brain injury. This represents good progress.

An unexpected consequence of many of these studies, however, has been to highlight issues concerning conscious and nonconscious recognition. These issues arise in work on priming effects for normal people, but they are most pressing in neuropsychological studies. Relevant neurological conditions include prosopagnosia, unilateral neglect, and anosognosia, but there are also important points to be gleaned from examination of conditions more usually considered to fall within the province of psychiatry. Investigations of face recognition may thus throw light on fundamental problems of consciousness and related mental phenomena.

## 6.1   INTRODUCTION

Until the 1980s research on face recognition concentrated on the recognition of faces of unfamiliar people who had been seen once before in a photograph or in a simulated incident (Ellis 1975). The focus of interest was often directed to applied questions about eyewitness testimony or issues concerning recognition memory for nonverbal material, but it was widely assumed that such studies would reveal general principles that would account for the recognition of faces of highly familiar as well as less familiar people. During the past decade, there has been a notable change of emphasis; it is now accepted that to find out how familiar faces are recognized, it is essential to use these faces as materials. This shift can be traced to the seminal work of Bruce (1979) in experimental psychology and Benton (1980) in neuropsychology.

Bruce (1979) asked people to decide whether faces were those of former British prime ministers; she chose distractor faces so that they were visually related (similar in appearance) or semantically related (another politician) to the targets. The result was that both visual similarity and semantic similarity slowed rejection latencies for the distractors but that these factors had additive (rather than interactive) effects, indicating that visual and semantic analyses can proceed in parallel.

From his review of neuropsychological studies, Benton (1980) reached a similar conclusion, arguing that identification of familiar faces and discrimination of unfamiliar faces involve different cerebral mechanisms. Initially, it had been thought that tests that involved deciding whether photographs showed faces of the same or different people could be used to detect mild forms of face recognition impairment. However, Warrington and James (1967) demonstrated that impairments affecting the processing of familiar or unfamiliar faces were associated with different brain lesion sites, and there were several reports that prosopagnosic patients (whose recognition of familiar faces is severely impaired) were successfully able to perform face matching tasks, though it was noted that they may use idiosyncratic strategies (Newcombe 1979). Benton's position has been supported by later studies that have also reported contrasting patterns of impairment of ability to recognize familiar faces or match views of unfamiliar faces (Malone et al. 1982; Parry et al. 1991).

Other studies in neuropsychology and experimental psychology have followed these promising leads and shown the value of theoretical models proposing that recognition of the face's identity is achieved independent of the determination of other types of socially important information (Bruce and Young 1986). Recognition itself is best considered a multistage process, and computer simulations of different types of potential organization have led to a model that provides a neat account of priming effects in face recognition and some of the different consequences of brain injury (Bruce, Burton, and Craw 1992; Burton, Bruce, and Johnston 1990; Burton et al. 1991). Although other central questions concerning the nature of the representations used to effect recognition remain less tractable, some promising pointers have emerged (Bruce 1990; Valentine 1991; Young and Bruce 1991).

There has also been useful progress in understanding the underlying neurobiology of face recognition resulting from positron emission tomography (PET) studies (Sergent, Ohta, and MacDonald 1992; Sergent and Signoret 1992), single-cell and lesion studies in primates (Desimone 1991; Gross and Sergent 1992; Heywood and Cowey 1992; Perrett et al. 1992), and investigations of innate face-processing abilities in infants (Johnson et al. 1991; Johnson and Morton 1991).

An unintended and unexpected consequence of many of these studies has been to highlight issues concerning conscious and nonconscious recognition, raising the possibility that investigations of face recognition may help in understanding fundamental problems of consciousness and related mental phenomena.

## 6.2 HIERARCHIC AND HETERARCHIC ORGANIZATION OF FACE PROCESSING

In an attempt to systematize existing findings and provide a theoretical focus for further work, Hay and Young (1982) introduced a simple schematic representation in the form of a functional model, which was further developed by Bruce and Young (1986). The Bruce and Young model claims that recognition proceeds in parallel with other types of face processing ability, including expression analysis, lipreading, and directed visual processing. Recognition itself involves sequential stages of perceptual classification (by domain-specific face recognition units), semantic classification (involving domain-independent person identity nodes that can access previously learned semantic information from the person's face, voice, or name), and name retrieval. This is meant as an idealized sequence and would be compatible with a cascade mode of operation.

Bruce and Young's (1986) claim of a heterarchic relation between face recognition and the processing of other types of information carried by the face (such as expression) is supported by reports indicating that face recognition impairments caused by brain injury can dissociate from impairments affecting the matching of unfamiliar faces, lipreading, and processing of facial expressions (Benton 1980; Campbell, Landis, and Regard 1986; Malone et al. 1982; Parry et al. 1991; Young and Bruce 1991). In addition, studies of normal subjects have identified factors that can differentially affect the ability to make decisions about a face's identity, expression, or sex (Bruce 1986a; Bruce et al. 1987; Roberts and Bruce 1988; Young et al. 1986). These findings are also consistent with the heterarchic conception.

Hierarchic organization within the recognition system itself is supported by studies of everyday errors (Young, Hay, and Ellis 1985), laboratory errors (Hanley and Cowell 1988; Hay, Young, and Ellis 1991), effects of brain injury (Young 1992), and experiments with normal subjects (Bruce 1988; Bruce and Young 1986; Young and Ellis 1989b). Studies of everyday and laboratory errors show that breakdown can occur at different levels of recognition: we may completely fail to recognize a face as belonging to a familiar person, we may recognize the face as familiar but be unable to bring to mind any other details about the person, or we may recognize the face as familiar and remember appropriate semantic information but fail to remember the person's name. Each of these types of error can also arise as a distinct symptom after neuropsychological impairment (de Haan, Young, and Newcombe 1991b; Flude, Ellis, and Kay 1989; Lucchelli and De Renzi 1992; Semenza and Zettin 1988, 1989; Young 1992).

These findings suggest that the face recognition system itself uses some form of sequential access to different types of information, in the order familiarity, then semantics, then name retrieval. Experiments with normal subjects support this idea (Bruce 1988; Young and Bruce 1991; Young and Ellis 1989b).

Some of the most compelling findings come from studies of the types of cue needed to resolve errors made under laboratory conditions (Brennen et al. 1990; Hanley and Cowell 1988; Hay, Young, and Ellis 1991). These eliminate the reporting biases that can cause problems in naturalistic studies yet still find the types of error predicted by the sequential access view.

Table 6.1 shows data from Hanley and Cowell's (1988) study. Subjects who found a famous face to be unfamiliar, familiar only, or knew who the person was but could not remember the name were cued by being given semantic

**Table 6.1** Percentages of Names Successfully Retrieved after Cueing by Semantic Information or Initials in Hanley and Cowell's (1988) Study

|  | Initial Knowledge State | | |
| --- | --- | --- | --- |
|  | Face Unfamiliar | Face Familiar Only | Face Familiar and Occupation Known |
| Semantic cue | 41 | 52 | 35 |
| Initials cue | 12 | 22 | 47 |

information (e.g., "Brilliant cavalier Spanish golfer whose raw ability and adventurous play have carried him to the top of the sport") or a card containing the initials of four famous people (one being the person in question), with blank spaces for the remaining letters. The semantic cue was most effective at promoting correct naming when subjects found the face familiar only, whereas cueing with the initials was more effective when the occupation was already known. This is exactly as would be expected from a sequential access model, since people who find the face familiar only would be blocked at the stage where semantic information would normally be retrieved (and hence will be assisted by a semantic cue more than an initials cue), whereas people who can already access the occupation but are still searching for the name should derive more benefit from an initials cue than a semantic cue (they have the semantic information already).

An interesting extension of this technique was made by Brennen et al. (1990), who induced tip-of-the-tongue states by asking subjects to name famous people from snippets of semantic information (e.g., "The nervous man with the knife in the shower scene in Hitchcock's *Psycho*"). When subjects felt sure that they knew the name but could not recall it (the tip-of-the-tongue state, or TOT), they were cued by giving the target person's initials, by showing the person's face, or by repeating the question (to control for the possibility that more time or a second attempt is all that is required). Whereas cueing from the person's initials was beneficial, cueing from seeing the person's face had no effect, since no more TOTs were resolved by this than by simply repeating the question. This is as a sequential access model would predict (the face can access only the same pool of semantic information as the original question, but the block occurs later).

We thus have converging evidence from studies of everyday errors, laboratory errors, experiments, and neuropsychological case studies indicating that the recognition of a familiar face involves sequential access to different types of information. An interesting point with respect to themes that will emerge later is that the blocks we have examined occur in conscious, overt recognition.

## 6.3 MODELING PRIMING EFFECTS

Repetition priming and semantic priming effects have been used to examine more closely the organization of mechanisms involved in the recognition of

**Table 6.2** Reaction Times for Familiarity Decisions to Face Targets (in milliseconds)

|  | Related Prime | Neutral Prime | Unrelated Prime |
|---|---|---|---|
| Stimulus onset asynchrony |  |  |  |
| 250 ms | 782 | 848 | 855 |
| 500 ms | 705 | 804 | 816 |
| 1000 ms | 662 | 828 | 805 |

Source: Bruce and Valentine (1986).

familiar faces. (There is nothing particular to face or person recognition about these patterns of repetition and semantic priming effects; faces are simply convenient stimuli for showing what seem to be quite general properties of visual recognition mechanisms [Dannenbring and Briand 1982].)

Repetition priming involves the facilitation of later recognition of a previously seen stimulus; for example, recognition of Prince Charles's face is faster if his face has appeared previously in the experiment than if it has not come up before (Bruce 1986b; Bruce and Valentine 1985; Brunas et al. 1990; Ellis, Young, and Flude 1990; Ellis et al. 1987; Young et al. 1986b). The effects of repetition on face recognition seem to be located in the face recognition system itself, since decisions about the face's expression or sex, which can be made without needing to recognize the person, do not show repetition priming (Ellis et al. 1990).

Semantic priming tasks investigate the effect of having previously recognized a related stimulus, such as the effect of having recently recognized Princess Diana's face on recognition of Prince Charles's face (Bruce 1983; Bruce 1986b; Bruce and Valentine 1986; Young, Hellawell, and de Haan 1988). Table 6.2 shows data from a study in which Bruce and Valentine (1986) examined reaction times in a face familiarity decision task (this involves deciding whether faces are those of familiar people). Each of the familiar target faces could be preceded by a Related face prime (e.g., Ronnie Barker's face preceding the target face of Ronnie Corbett; both are British comedians who often appeared together), a Neutral prime (an unfamiliar face), or an Unrelated face prime (e.g., Sebastian Coe's face preceding the target face of Ronnie Corbett; Coe was an athlete). These primes were presented with stimulus onset asynchronies (SOAs) of 250 ms, 500 ms, or 1000 ms before each target. Recognition was facilitated by Related primes at all SOAs.

There are marked contrasts between the properties of repetition priming and semantic priming effects. Repetition priming effects are comparatively long-lasting (being found across intervals of several minutes in existing published studies and as long as 3 months in as yet unpublished work of our own) and domain specific (for example, recognition of Prince Charles's face is not facilitated by previously having recognized the name "Prince Charles"), whereas the facilitation produced by semantic priming is short-lived (generally dissipating within seconds) yet can cross stimulus domains (for example, from recognition of Princess Diana's face to recognition of Prince Charles's name).

Although these differences between repetition priming and semantic priming have been taken to indicate that these sources of facilitation arise from different loci (Bruce 1986b; Young 1988; Young and Ellis 1989b), more precise specification of the underlying reasons for the differences has proved difficult. However, a considerable advance has been made with the computer implementation of a variant of the Bruce and Young (1986) model of face recognition by Burton, Bruce, and Johnston (1990). The basic structure of this model is shown in figure 6.1. As in other interactive activation models, pools of functional units are interconnected by bidirectional excitatory links, and within each pool the rival units compete by inhibiting each other. There are pools of face recognition units (FRUs) and name input units (NIUs), to allow input from processes responsible for the visual analysis of faces and names. These FRUs and NIUs are connected to person identity nodes (PINs), which provide a means of maintaining further links to semantic information units (SIUs) independent of input domain (that is, regardless of whether the input is a face or a name). There is one PIN for each known person, and this is connected to the FRU for that person's face, the NIU for the person's name, and whichever SIUs are appropriate (though this is only sketched in fig. 6.1).

Although the Burton, Bruce, and Johnston model can be considered to implement part of Bruce and Young's (1986) model, it also involves certain differences. The most important of these concern the PINs. Burton, Bruce, and Johnston see these as providing an interface to semantic information (the SIUs) rather than holding semantic information themselves. In addition, the PINs are held to form the level at which an input can be classified as familiar,

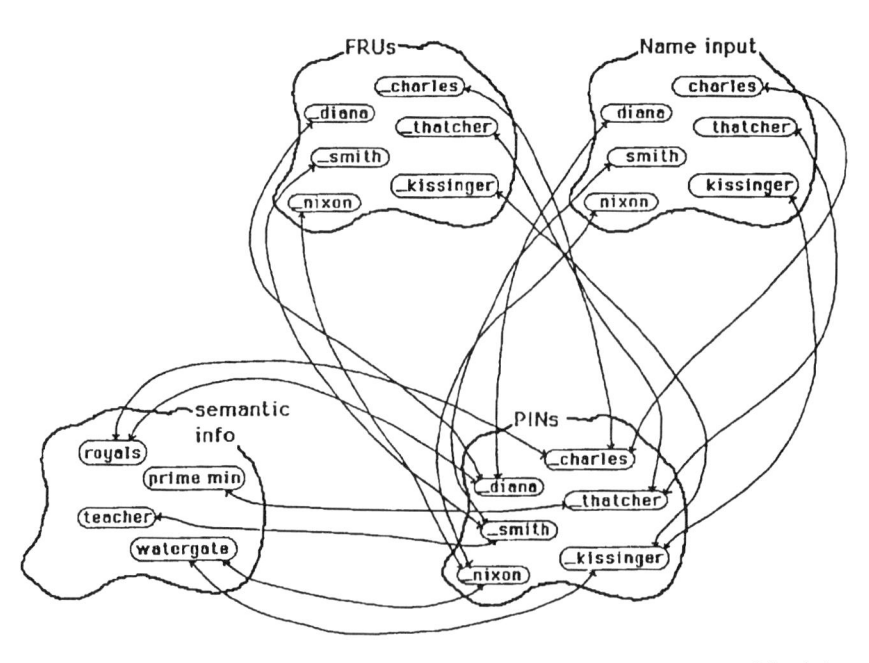

**Figure 6.1** Burton, Bruce, and Johnston's (1990) interactive activation model of face recognition.

instead of the FRUs or NIUs, as Bruce and Young (1986) had envisaged. A further difference is that there is no separate store for name output codes; problems in name retrieval are accounted for by proposing that they reflect the status of names as relatively unique items of semantic information (Burton and Bruce 1992).

The mechanism for repetition priming in the Burton, Bruce, and Johnston model lies in changes in the strengths of the excitatory connections between FRUs and PINs for seen faces or between NIUs and PINs for seen names. Hence, repetition priming is domain specific because it arises in the part of the system dedicated to analyzing input from a particular domain. In contrast, semantic priming is due to the interaction between PINs and SIUs. When itself activated, an SIU will pass back activation to all the PINs with which it is associated. This activation remains below threshold level in the PINs that are receiving no other input, but it allows them to respond more quickly if there is any input from the appropriate FRU or NIU. Thus, semantic priming will cross stimulus domains because it originates beyond the level at which there are domain-specific representations.

These different underlying mechanisms also allow repetition and semantic priming to have quite different time courses. In fact, the Burton, Bruce, and Johnston model makes clear that semantic priming must have a short time course under most conditions, because the effect of any given input at the PIN level is quickly abolished by a subsequent input if this is unrelated to the original.

This simulation of the effects of repetition and semantic priming is an important step, because it brings greater precision to our understanding (Bruce, Burton, and Craw 1992). Such a simulation demands that we specify the exact functions and interrelations of the components proposed, and Burton, Bruce, and Johnston tried and discarded a number of other architectures before this successful simulation was achieved. This does not mean that this particular simulation is exactly correct, and it certainly should not be mistaken for a full solution to the problem of face recognition; for example, the front end is left unspecified. But we now have a detailed account of how priming and other effects can arise; to be seriously considered, any rival model will need to be able to account for these phenomena and something else besides.

## 6.4 PRIMING AND CONSCIOUS RECOGNITION

Visual recognition usually proceeds automatically. We cannot look at a familiar face and decide not to recognize it; the processes involved are not open to introspection or conscious intervention. We are aware of only the outcome of the recognition process.

Priming techniques can probe these automatic aspects of recognition. Consider the implications of the fact that repetition priming effects do not cross stimulus domains. The decision that a particular face is familiar can be made more quickly if that face has been previously seen but is unaffected by having seen the person's name or even her or his (clothed) body (Bruce and Valentine

1985; Ellis et al. 1987). It follows that repetition priming is not due to subjects' deliberately remembering which people have been encountered in the experiment. Explicit memory would be little different across faces, names, or bodies, yet it is only seeing faces that affects subsequent reaction times for face recognition. Thus, there is an independence between repetition priming and explicit memory for the items that have been seen, which is consistent with the idea that the priming effects have a relatively automatic origin. This claim is borne out by findings of preserved face repetition effects in amnesic patients (Paller et al. 1992).

The same point is also seen in findings that repetition priming occurs only if the face was recognized spontaneously on its initial presentation. Table 6.3 shows data from experiments in which reaction times for familiarity decisions were compared across familiar faces that had been recognized spontaneously or after cueing in an initial session (Brunas-Wagstaff, Young, and Ellis 1992). To reduce spontaneous recognition rates, some of the faces had been initially presented as internal features (eyes, nose, mouth) or external features (hair, face outline) only. In one experiment (the top row of table 6.3), subjects were told the person's name if they did not recognize him or her in the initial session. This produced no repetition priming; the faces were recognized as familiar in the subsequent test, but reaction times were no faster than for unprimed faces that had not been shown in the initial session. Even in another experiment in which subjects had to work out the person's identity from the unrecognized face and a vague semantic cue that would not in itself have been sufficient for recognition (e.g., "politician"), there was still no repetition priming from cued recognition (data shown in the bottom row of table 6.3). Only uncued, spontaneous recognition leads to repetition priming.

Semantic priming also involves automatic effects. In Bruce and Valentine's (1986) data, semantic priming was found even when the prime preceded the target by only 250 ms (table 6.2), so it is unlikely to be based on subjects' deliberately predicting which target might follow each prime. As Bruce and Valentine pointed out, this SOA is too short to support an intentional use of the prime, since latencies for overt recognition are much longer (Young et al.

**Table 6.3** Mean Correct Reaction times for Familiarity Decisions to Familiar Faces (in milliseconds)

| Previously Recognized Spontaneously | | | Previously Recognized after Cueing | | | Unprimed |
|---|---|---|---|---|---|---|
| From Internal Features | From External Features | From Whole Face | From Internal Features | From External Features | From Whole Face | |
| Name prompt | | | | | | |
| 642 | 653 | 674 | 892 | 847 | 941 | 846 |
| Semantic cue | | | | | | |
| 730 | 762 | 638 | 861 | 877 | 1019 | 936 |

Source: Brunas-Wagstaff, Young, and Ellis (1992).

1986b). In addition, Posner and Snyder (1975) noted that priming might be mediated intentionally, by subjects' trying to predict to themselves which target would follow the prime, or automatically, without conscious anticipation. If the intentional effect applied, we would expect some cost in the form of slowed responses when the target was not as had been predicted from the prime (in the Unrelated condition). Purely automatic priming will produce facilitation even at short SOAs, whereas conscious anticipation of possible targets would be more effective at longer SOAs and would also lead to inhibition (slower responses) for unrelated prime-target pairs. There is no evidence of this conscious strategy in the data shown in table 6.2, since facilitation was found at all SOAs, and reaction times did not differ between the Neutral and Unrelated conditions.

Again, then, it would seem that automatic aspects of the recognition system are implicated. Further support for this conclusion comes from findings that semantic priming effects can occur even with prime presentation times that are too brief for overt recognition (Carr et al. 1982; McCauley et al. 1980), though this has yet to be demonstrated for face recognition.

## 6.5 COVERT RECOGNITION IN PROSOPAGNOSIA

We have seen that priming effects can be used to examine automatic aspects of recognition. A dramatic illustration of the fact that recognition mechanisms can operate automatically and nonconsciously has come from studies of prosopagnosia.

Prosopagnosic patients usually fail all tests of overt recognition of familiar faces (Hécaen and Angelergues 1962; Meadows 1974). They cannot name the face, give the person's occupation or other biographical details, or even state whether a face belongs to a familiar person. Even the most well-known faces may not be recognized, including famous people, friends, family, and the patient's own face when looking in a mirror. In contrast, recognition from nonfacial cues (such as voice, name, and sometimes even clothing or gait) is usually successful.

Although prosopagnosic patients no longer overtly recognize familiar faces, there is substantial evidence of covert recognition from physiological and behavioral measures (Bruyer 1991; Young and de Haan 1992).

Bauer (1984) measured skin conductance while a prosopagnosic patient, L.F., viewed a familiar face and listened to a list of names. When the name belonged to the face L.F. was looking at, there was a greater skin conductance change than when someone else's name was read out. Yet if L.F. was asked to choose which name in the list was correct for the face, his performance was at chance level. Comparable findings have been reported with a different technique in which the patients simply looked at a series of familiar and unfamiliar faces (Tranel and Damasio 1985, 1988).

Behavioral indexes of covert recognition complement these electrophysiological measures. Eye movement scan paths differ to familiar and unfamiliar faces, despite the absence of overt recognition (Rizzo, Hurtig, and Damasio

1987). The patients are better at matching photographs of familiar faces than photographs of unfamiliar faces across transformations of orientation or age (de Haan, Young, and Newcombe 1987a; Sergent and Poncet 1990). In name classification tasks, they show interference from simultaneously presented face distractors (de Haan, Bauer, and Greve, 1992; de Haan, Young, and Newcombe 1987a, 1987b). When looking at a face, they are better at learning correct information than incorrect information about that person (Bruyer et al. 1983; de Haan, Young, and Newcombe 1987a, 1991a; McNeil and Warrington 1991; Sergent and Poncet 1990; Young and de Haan 1988). This superior learning of correct over incorrect information is found even for faces of people who have been known only since the patient's illness (de Haan, Young, and Newcombe 1987a).

Some of the most intriguing data come from priming techniques. Table 6.4 shows the results of priming experiments using printed names as targets with patients L.F. (de Haan, Bauer, and Greve 1992) and P.H. (Young, Hellawell, and de Haan 1988). For P.H., the task was a standard semantic priming experiment in which the recognition of target names was primed by an immediately preceding Related, Neutral, or Unrelated face or name, whereas for L.F. the Related condition was replaced by one in which the prime was the Same person as the target. Using a Same person condition makes the experiment easier to set up; however, in terms of the Burton, Bruce, and Johnston (1990) model, one would still expect a short-lived form of cross-domain priming from the face of the Same person onto the next target name, which would be mediated by the PIN-SIU links that also support semantic priming. For both L.F. and P.H., the results fit Posner and Snyder's (1975) characterization of an automatic effect, since there was facilitation of responses from Same person or Related primes, without inhibition of responses to Unrelated targets.

Even more interesting, it is possible to compare the size of the priming effect across face primes (which the patients mostly do not recognize overtly) and name primes (which they can recognize). These are exactly equivalent; the possibility of overt recognition of the name primes has made no additional contribution to the priming effects observed (the faster overall responses in the name prime than face prime conditions for L.F. are probably an artifact of task order).

Table 6.4 Reaction Times for Correct Responses to Target Names of Familiar People (in milliseconds)

| Subject | | Same Person | Related | Neutral | Unrelated |
| --- | --- | --- | --- | --- | --- |
| L.F. | Face primes | 962 | | 1074 | 1086 |
| | Name primes | 674 | | 826 | 886 |
| P.H. | Face primes | | 1016 | 1080 | 1117 |
| | Name primes | | 945 | 1032 | 1048 |
| M.S. | Face primes | | 1260 | 1276 | 1264 |
| | Name primes | | 1178 | 1370 | 1439 |

Sources: de Haan, Bauer, and Greve (1992); Young, Hellawell, and de Haan (1988); Newcombe, Young, and de Haan (1989).

A question that naturally arises concerns whether such findings will hold for all patients with severely impaired overt face recognition ability. Covert recognition has been demonstrated for L.F. and P.H. with a number of other techniques (Bauer 1984; de Haan, Bauer, and Greve 1992; de Haan, Young, and Newcombe 1987a, 1987b, 1991a; Greve and Bauer 1990; Young and de Haan 1988), but several patients who failed to show covert recognition have also been reported in the literature (Bauer 1986; Etcoff, Freeman, and Cave 1991; Humphreys et al. 1992; McNeil and Warrington 1991; Newcombe, Young, and de Haan 1989; Sergent and Villemure 1989; Young and Ellis 1989a).

Table 6.4 shows data for one such patient, M.S., who showed no priming from faces (Newcombe, Young, and de Haan 1989). As clinicians have long suspected, there is more than one form of prosopagnosia (De Renzi 1986; De Renzi et al. 1991; Meadows 1974); the presence or absence of covert recognition may thus provide an important pointer to the nature of the functional impairment in each case.

For cases like L.F. or P.H., what seem to be preserved are those aspects of recognition whose operation is relatively automatic and does not require conscious initiation; there is a clear parallel between the findings for normal subjects and prosopagnosic patients (Young 1988). Another good example of this parallel comes from a study by Greve and Bauer (1990). They showed faces to L.F. for 500 ms each and then paired each of these faces with a completely novel face. L.F. tended to choose the faces shown to him previously as being "more likeable" than the faces he had not seen before, whereas when he was told that he had seen one of the faces before and asked which it was, he performed at chance level. An equivalent phenomenon of preference for briefly presented stimuli without overt recognition can be demonstrated in normal subjects (Bornstein 1989; Kunst-Wilson and Zajonc 1980; Zajonc 1980).

Preserved priming effects without explicit classification of face inputs can be simulated quite simply with the Burton, Bruce, and Johnston (1990) model by halving the connection strengths between FRUs and PINs (Burton et al. 1991). This makes the finding of this pattern in some cases of prosopagnosia much less mysterious. The problem of understanding how covert responses can be preserved when there is no overt discrimination may thus be less intractable than it at first appears, but this type of simulation does not provide any solution to the more philosophical problems concerning awareness; we do not claim that the computer is aware just because it passes an arbitrary threshold.

This leads to the issue of damage and disconnection accounts of covert effects. A distinction is often made in neurology between effects that are due to damage to a functional system and effects due to disconnection of one system from another (Geschwind 1965a, 1965b). The same distinction has been applied to work on covert processing after brain injury, where patterns of preserved abilities have been taken to reflect the disconnection of intact processing systems from mechanisms that can sustain awareness, rather than damage to processing systems per se (de Haan, Young, and Newcombe 1987a; Schacter, McAndrews, and Moscovitch 1988; Young and de Haan 1988, 1990). Our simulation (Burton, Bruce, and Johnston 1991) shows that this contrast needs to be treated cautiously. The same simulation can be taken to model disconnection (it is connection strengths that are changed to impair the model's functions) or damage (changing one set of connection strengths affects all components because of their interconnectivity and therefore damages the functioning of the system considered as a whole); it is simply a question of the level at which one prefers to describe it.

A further implication of Burton, Bruce, and Johnston's (1991) simulation of covert recognition is that the deficit of overt recognition need not be absolute. This has been confirmed by recent work. Sergent and Poncet (1990) observed that their patient, P.V. could achieve overt recognition of some faces if several members of the same semantic category were presented together. This happened only when P.V. could determine the category herself. For the categories P.V. could not determine, she continued to fail to recognize the faces overtly even when the occupational category was pointed out to her. This phenomenon of overt recognition provoked by multiple exemplars of a semantic category has been replicated with P.H. (de Haan, Young, and Newcombe 1991a). Both P.V. and P.H. were very surprised at being able to recognize faces overtly.

Sergent and Poncet (1990) suggested that their demonstration shows that "neither the facial representations nor the semantic information were critically disturbed in P.V., and her prosopagnosia may thus reflect faulty connections between faces and their memories." They thought that the simultaneous presentation of several members of the same category may have temporarily raised the activation level above the appropriate threshold.

Such findings in prosopagnosia show that the boundary between awareness and lack of awareness is not as completely impassable as it seems to the patients' everyday experience. The fact that certain types of stimulation can trigger the experience of overt recognition that they no longer enjoy routinely fits readily with a model in which activation must cross some form of threshold before it can result in awareness (Burton, Bruce, and Johnston 1991; Sergent and Poncet 1990). However, the circumstances under which this has been found to happen are very limited.

## 6.6 OTHER IMPAIRMENTS OF AWARENESS

The evidence we have reviewed shows that although cases of prosopagnosia show very severe impairments of overt recognition, automatic aspects of recognition can be relatively preserved in some cases. The effects of brain injury thus provide an important insight into the organization of recognition mechanisms. Prosopagnosia, however, is not the only such impairment; other neuropsychological conditions also have implications for understanding conscious and nonconscious recognition.

Unilateral neglect is an interesting example, though in some ways it is more a distortion than a loss of awareness (Bisiach 1992; Bisiach and Rusconi 1990). Patients with unilateral neglect fail to respond to stimuli located contralaterally to the side of their brain lesion. The condition is more common after lesions of the right cerebral hemisphere, when left-sided stimuli are neglected.

Neglect can severely compromise visual recognition (Gainotti et al. 1986), including recognition of familiar faces. Examples come from our study of B.Q., who had a severe and longstanding left-sided neglect (Young, Hellawell, and Welch 1992). When asked to recognize crudely constructed chimeric face stimuli, B.Q. was very poor at identifying the left half of each chimeric (the half falling to her left), yet she could recognize these same left sides if they were presented in isolation.

Figure 6.2 and table 6.5 show examples of stimuli used with B.Q. and her error rates for each type of stimulus. The presence of a central gap led to a marked improvement in her ability to recognize the left sides of chimeric faces (table 6.5, comparison A), she was much better able to recognize the left sides

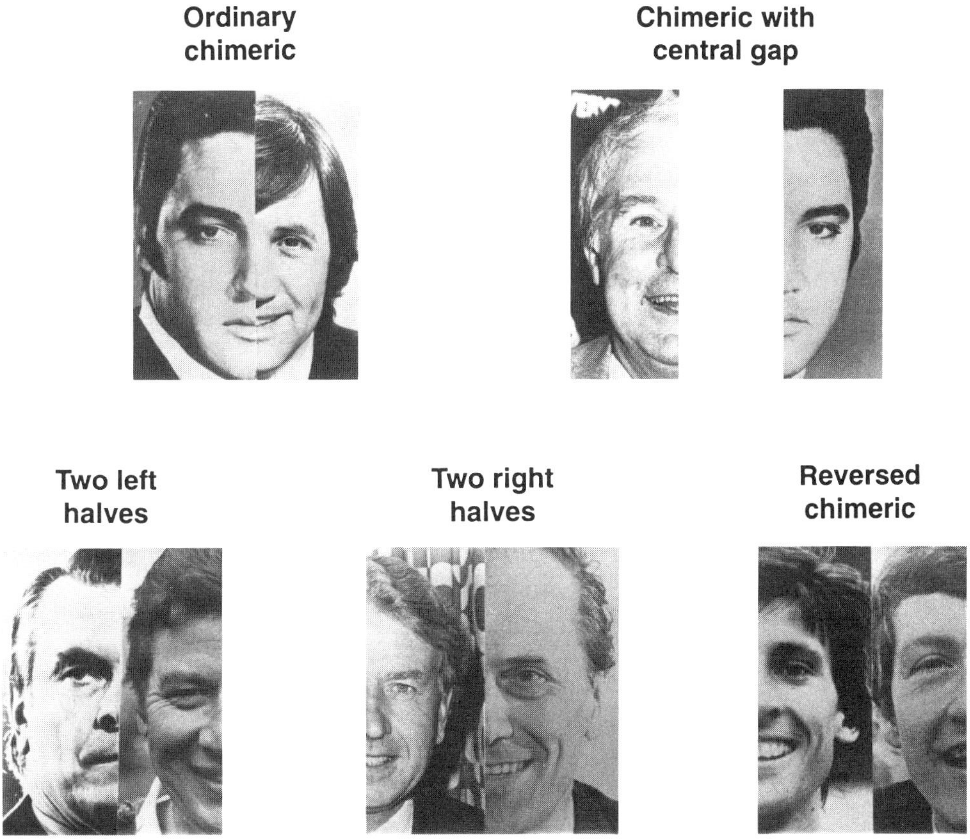

**Figure 6.2** Examples of ordinary chimeric face, chimeric with central gap, chimeric of two left half-faces, chimeric of two right half-faces, and reversed chimeric used with B.Q. (Young, Hellawell, and Welch 1992.)

**Table 6.5** B.Q.'s Error Rates for Recognizing Left and Right Sides of Face Chimerics

|  | Left Side | Right Side |
|---|---|---|
| Comparison A | | |
|   Ordinary chimeric | 20/20 | 0/20 |
|   Chimeric with central gap | 4/20 | 0/20 |
| Comparison B | | |
|   Chimeric of two left half-faces | 3/20 | 1/20 |
|   Chimeric of two right half-faces | 5/20 | 1/20 |
| Comparison C | | |
|   Ordinary chimeric | 14/20 | 1/20 |
|   Reversed chimeric | 1/20 | 1/20 |

of chimerics made from two left half-faces or two right half-faces than ordinary chimerics (table 6.5, comparison B), and recognition of left and right sides was equally good for reversed chimerics (table 6.5, comparison C).

These findings show that the key factor in whether B.Q. failed to identify the left side of a chimeric was the extent to which it approximated something the visual system would treat as a single object. When highly salient differences were introduced that would break up the chimera's resemblance to a single face, the problem was considerably ameliorated.

B.Q.'s problem in recognizing the left sides of chimeric faces was very marked. Even when shown how the chimerics were constructed and told to report both sides, she would often deny that she was looking at anything other than a single face and identify only the right side. However, if we pointed to parts of the chimeric on the left, B.Q. could describe them accurately, yet she nearly always identified only the right half-face. With a chimeric in which the left half came from Mick Jagger's face and the right half from Roger Moore, she described accurately the shape of the left eye, the long hair over the left ear, the full lips on the left, and the stubble on the left chin when we pointed to these features; yet even after describing all of these features of Mick Jagger's face successfully, B.Q. identified the chimeric as Roger Moore and did not accept that part of another person's face was present. On another occasion, she showed partial insight. When made to describe parts of a face chimeric with the left half of Michael Parkinson and the right half of Terry Wogan, she commented, "It's Terry Wogan ... but there's a touch of a Picasso about him." There was only occasional full insight. For example, with a face chimeric of the left half of Elvis Presley and the right half of Steve Davis, B.Q. commented that it was "Elvis Presley ... but there's a bit of Steve Davis somewhere," and then she noticed there were "two faces stuck together."

B.Q.'s problems affected all classes of visual object; they were not face specific. However, cases in which face-specific disturbances affect the left side of seen faces have also been described (Brust and Behrens, 1977; Ebata et al. 1991; Young et al. 1990). Figure 6.3 shows examples, in the form of

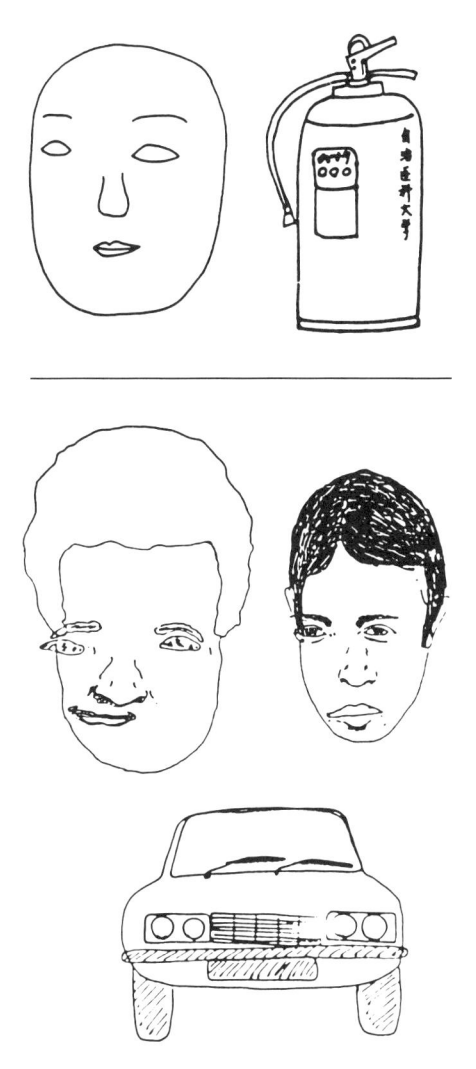

**Figure 6.3** *Top,* drawings of a face and a fire extinguisher by the patient described by Ebata et al. (1991); *bottom,* constructions made by arranging fragments of pictures into the correct order by K.L. (Young et al. 1990.)

drawings made by a patient described by Ebata et al. (1991) and constructions made by arranging fragments of a picture into the correct order by K.L. (Young et al. 1990). For both patients, there is no problem with nonfaces, but the faces are distorted on the side falling to the viewer's left.

Further investigations of K.L. showed that he had difficulty recognizing the left sides of seen faces when they formed part of a chimeric and when only a left half-face was shown (Young et al. 1990). The problem was clearly central in origin, because defective recognition of left half-faces was found even when they were presented in K.L.'s perimetrically intact right visual field. Young et al. (1990b) suggested that this might be considered a domain-specific form of unilateral neglect. K.L.'s problems with isolated left half-faces as well as chimerics could then be accounted for by suggesting that the left-right gradient of the underlying deficit (Behrmann et al. 1990) was particularly steep (Young, Hellawell, and Welch 1992).

Work on impairments of face recognition in unilateral neglect is still at an early stage, but our observations show that in such cases, it is not at all easy to distinguish what is seen from what is not seen; even stimuli that have been accurately described in one task (and of which the patients are therefore presumably aware) do not get reported or seem directly to influence performance in another task.

A different function of consciousness is in monitoring one's performance. For visual recognition, we need to do this to correct errors and also because different types of information must sometimes be intentionally combined and evaluated. For instance, if you see what looks to be your daughter going into a restaurant when you thought she was at school, you must weigh up the degree of resemblance to your daughter against the probability that the person could be her given your other knowledge. Studies of recognition errors made by normal people have found several examples of problems of this type (Young, Hay, and Ellis 1985). The point was neatly illustrated by Thomson (1986), who asked the daughter of an Australian couple to stand outside a London hotel when her parents thought she was in Australia. They recognized their daughter, but when she (deliberately) did not respond, her father apologized; "I am terribly sorry. I thought you were someone else."

Young, de Haan, and Newcombe (1990) argued that monitoring mechanisms are implicated in neuropsychological impairment in which patients fail to comprehend their problems or even actively deny them (anosognosia). Unawareness of face recognition impairments has been noted in several reports (Landis et al. 1986; Sergent and Villemure 1989; Young, de Haan, and Newcombe 1990). A case we investigated, S.P., showed a severe and stable face processing impairment yet had complete lack of insight into her face recognition difficulties (Young, de Haan, and Newcombe 1990). S.P. was not distressed by her inability and maintained that she recognized familiar faces "as well as before." When confronted with her failure to recognize a photograph, she would say that it was a "poor likeness" or that she had "no recollection of having seen that person before." S.P. had been a talented painter, but after her illness, she could recognize her portraits only by careful deduction from the sitter's age, sex, and other details and did not seem to think that there was anything unusual about this laborious method. As Anton (1899) noted, anosognosic patients seem to lose their knowledge of what it was like to have the relevant ability; this is consistent with the problem's being due to impaired monitoring.

In contrast to her lack of insight into her face recognition impairment, S.P. showed adequate insight into other physical and cognitive impairments produced by her illness; her unawareness of her face recognition impairment involved a deficit-specific anosognosia. This bears out Bisiach et al.'s (1986) claim that "monitoring of the internal working is not secured in the nervous system by a general, superordinate organ, but is decentralized and apportioned to the different functional blocks to which it refers."

## 6.7 COGNITIVE NEUROPSYCHIATRY

Studies of face recognition force us to consider issues involving conscious and nonconscious recognition. So far, I have concentrated on cognitive aspects of recognition, but it has marked emotional components too. Bauer (1984) argued that there are separate corticolimbic pathways involved in overt recognition and in orienting responses to emotionally salient stimuli: the ventral route, damaged in prosopagnosia, provides overt recognition, whereas the dorsal route, spared in prosopagnosia, gives the face its emotional significance. This proposal may provide a pointer to understanding how brain injuries can sometimes lead to bizarre delusions.

Two examples are the Capgras delusion, in which patients claim that people (usually close relatives) have been replaced by identical or near-identical impostors (Capgras and Reboul-Lachaux 1923), and the Cotard delusion, in which patients are convinced that they are dead (Cotard 1882). These delusional beliefs can follow brain injury (Alexander, Stuss, and Benson 1979; Cutting 1991; Lewis 1987; Young et al. 1992); the associated brain lesions vary but often include damage to temporoparietal areas of the right hemisphere and bilateral frontal regions. We think that the Capgras and Cotard delusions reflect an interaction of impairments at two levels. One set of contributory factors involves anomalous perceptual experience; the other factors lead to an incorrect interpretation of this.

Ellis and Young (1990) developed Bauer's (1984) suggestion that separable neurological pathways mediate overt recognition of familiar faces and reactions to their emotional significance. The basis of the Capgras delusion may thus lie in damage to neuroanatomical mechanisms responsible for appropriate emotional reactions to familiar visual stimuli (Anderson 1988; Lewis 1987). On this account, the Capgras delusion typically involves close relatives because these would normally produce the strongest reactions and, hence, suffer the greatest discrepancy. Since substantial parts of these pathways are in close proximity to those involved in visual recognition (Bauer 1984), one would expect that few brain lesions will compromise emotional reactions to visual stimuli without also affecting other visual functions involved in recognition to some extent. Hence, most Capgras patients will show co-occurrent defective face processing abilities (Ellis and Young 1990; Young et al. 1993).

A patient who had suffered the Cotard delusion after brain injury, whom we were able to investigate in detail, also showed defective face processing abilities (Young et al. 1992). In fact, people suffering the Cotard delusion commonly report that they must be dead because they "feel nothing inside," and they describe feelings of derealization, which have also been noted in Capgras cases. We therefore think that although these delusions are phenomenally distinct, they may represent patients' attempts to make sense of fundamentally similar experiences. This suggestion is strengthened by occasional reports of patients who suffer both the Capgras and Cotard delusions (Joseph 1986; Wright, Young, and Hellawell 1993).

A clue as to how this could happen comes from studies that have shown that people with persecutory delusions tend to attribute negative events to external rather than internal causes, whereas depressed people tend to attribute them to internal causes (Candido and Romney 1990; Kaney and Bentall 1989). The relevance of these findings is that it is quite common for the Cotard delusion to arise in the setting of a depressive illness and for the Capgras delusion to be accompanied by persecutory delusions and suspiciousness (Enoch and Trethowan 1991). Hence, the persecutory delusions and suspiciousness that are often noted in Capgras cases could contribute to the patients' mistaking a change in themselves for a change in others ("they are impostors"), whereas people who are depressed might exaggerate the negative effects of a similar change while correctly attributing it to themselves ("I am dead").

These delusions show that studies of the processes involved in conscious and nonconscious recognition may be of quite general importance in furthering our understanding of cognition and emotion and the neural mechanisms involved in feeling that things are as they should be, even that they are "real."

## 6.8 SUMMARY AND CONCLUSIONS

Work on the recognition of familiar faces has drawn on an eclectic range of sources of evidence and addressed these to a relatively widely shared theoretical perspective. This has produced good progress on a number of questions.

I have summarized examples in which investigations of familiar face recognition force us to consider issues concerning conscious and nonconscious recognition. We have seen that studies of repetition priming and semantic priming effects in normal subjects have noted that these are often automatic in origin and that this is confirmed by striking observations of preserved priming effects for prosopagnosic patients. Findings of covert recognition in prosopagnosia show responses based on the unique identities of familiar faces, even though overt recognition of these faces is not achieved. Prosopagnosia can thus be considered a selective deficit of awareness, in which there is no global change in consciousness, but awareness of recognition of familiar faces is lost.

In general, these findings fit the commonsense conception that nonconscious mechanisms have relatively automatic functions, whereas conscious recognition supports intentional action. Despite the extensive range of covert effects demonstrated in the laboratory, prosopagnosic patients do not act as if they recognize faces in everyday life. This is not a trivial point; one could imagine that a prosopagnosic patient with covert recognition might find himself or herself greeting people in the street without knowing why. This has not been found.

Why should we have recognition mechanisms that can operate without conscious intervention? Part of the answer lies in the delicate balance between speed of response and flexibility of response. The purpose of perceptual systems is to create representations of external events that can permit effective action in the world that an organism inhabits. But flexibility of response requires more sophisticated representations of events, which take longer to compute. Automatic components of the recognition system can help to reduce some of this loss of speed—for example, by predicting what is likely to follow. The point has been made by Fodor (1983), who argued for associative connections in the word recognition system on the grounds that they would help a stupid system to behave as if it were smart.

This argument has been extended to face recognition by Ellis, Young, and Hay (1987) and Young and Ellis (1989b). It may be useful to build up associative connections that can allow us to recognize Norma Major's face more quickly after we have seen John Major's face or read his name in a newspaper. These associative connections would serve the purpose of making the recognition system prepared for what it might encounter next. On this account, semantic priming is probably based on associative connections rather than semantic category membership per se. The simulation developed by Burton, Bruce, and their colleagues has this property and provides a neat account of priming effects and a simple explanation as to how they could be preserved after brain injury (Bruce, Burton, and Craw 1992; Burton, Bruce, and Johnston 1990; Burton et al. 1991).

Studies of other neurological conditions, such as neglect and anosognosia, show that consciousness has multiple functions that can break down in different ways after brain injury. Here, I have mostly concentrated on cognitive aspects of recognition, but it also has marked emotional components, which may be particularly important in understanding the role of face processing impairments in the production of delusional beliefs.

A persistent theme of this review has been that investigations of face recognition can throw light on fundamental problems of consciousness and related mental phenomena, but it is also true that addressing these issues shows areas in which our models of face recognition need refinement. One of these is the notion of familiarity. A striking form of everyday recognition error is to know that a face is familiar but have no idea who it is (Young, Hay, and Ellis 1985), and such observations have led us to treat familiarity as if it was a relatively basic piece of cognitive information. This has been a useful tactic, but studies of the Capgras delusion and related conditions show that familiarity is more complex; a commonly reported claim of Capgras patients is that people and things seem somehow unfamiliar, and this is also found in other psychiatric and neurological conditions (Critchley 1989; Sno and Linszen 1990). We will need to pay more attention to distinguishing different kinds of familiarity (Mandler 1980), especially those aspects that involve emotional and orienting reactions to people, things, and events with personal relevance (Van Lancker 1991).

It is clear that we are a long way from any detailed understanding of conscious and nonconscious recognition. It is even too early to know whether this renewed interest in consciousness should be considered a sign of increased confidence and maturity, or mere recklessness. But now that we have begun to pose the questions, perhaps we will find out.

## NOTE

Much of my work in this area has been funded by ESRC grant R 00023 1922. I am grateful to Dr. A. M. Burton and the British Psychological Society for permission to reproduce figure 6.1 (from Burton, Bruce, and Johnston 1990), and to Professor Y. Mizuno and the British Medical Association for permission to reproduce material that forms part of figure 6.3 (from Ebata et al. 1991).

## REFERENCES

Alexander, M. P., Stuss, D. T., and Benson, D. F. (1979). Capgras syndrome: A reduplicative phenomenon. *Neurology, 29,* 334–339.

Anderson, D. N. (1988). The delusion of inanimate doubles. *British Journal of Psychiatry, 153,* 694–699.

Anton, G. (1899). Ueber die Selbstwahrnemung der Herderkrankungen des Gehirns durch den Kranken bei Rindenblindheit und Rindentaubheit. *Archiv für Psychiatrie und Nervenkrankheiten, 32,* 86–127.

Bauer, R. M. (1984). Autonomic recognition of names and faces in prosopagnosia: A neuropsychological application of the guilty knowledge test. *Neuropsychologia, 22,* 457–469.

Bauer, R. M. (1986). The cognitive psychophysiology of prosopagnosia. In H. D. Ellis, M. A. Jeeves, F. Newcombe, and A. Young (Eds.), *Aspects of face processing,* 253–267. Dordrecht: Martinus Nijhoff.

Behrmann, M., Moscovitch, M., Black, S. E., and Mozer, M. (1990). Perceptual and conceptual mechanisms in neglect dyslexia. *Brain, 113,* 1163–1183.

Benton, A. L. (1980). The neuropsychology of facial recognition. *American Psychologist, 35,* 176–186.

Bisiach, E. (1992). Understanding consciousness: Clues from unilateral neglect and related disorders. In A. D. Milner and M. D. Rugg (Eds.), *The neuropsychology of consciousness,* 113–137. London: Academic Press.

Bisiach, E., and Rusconi, M. L. (1990). Break-down of perceptual awareness in unilateral neglect. *Cortex, 26,* 643–649.

Bisiach, E., Vallar, G., Perani, D., Papagno, C., and Berti, A. (1986). Unawareness of disease following lesions of the right hemisphere: Anosognosia for hemiplegia and anosognosia for hemianopia. *Neuropsychologia, 24,* 471–482.

Bornstein, R. F. (1989). Exposure and affect: Overview and meta-analysis of research, 1968–1987. *Psychological Bulletin, 106,* 265–289.

Brennen, T., Baguley, T., Bright, J., and Bruce, V. (1990). Resolving semantically induced tip-of-the-tongue states for proper nouns. *Memory and Cognition, 18,* 339–347.

Bruce, V. (1979). Searching for politicians: An information-processing approach to face recognition. *Quarterly Journal of Experimental Psychology, 31,* 373–395.

Bruce, V. (1983). Recognizing faces. *Philosophical Transactions of the Royal Society, London, B302,* 423–436.

Bruce, V. (1986a). Influences of familiarity on the processing of faces. *Perception, 15,* 387–397.

Bruce, V. (1986b). Recognising familiar faces. In H. D. Ellis, M. A. Jeeves, F. Newcombe, and A. Young (Eds.), *Aspects of face processing,* 107–117. Dordrecht: Martinus Nijhoff.

Bruce, V. (1988). *Recognising faces.* London: Erlbaum.

Bruce, V. (1990). Perceiving and recognising faces. *Mind and Language*, 5, 342–364.

Bruce, V., Burton, A. M., and Craw, I. (1992). Modelling face recognition. *Philosophical Transactions of the Royal Society, London, B335*, 121–128.

Bruce, V., Ellis, H. D., Gibling, F., and Young, A. W. (1987). Parallel processing of the sex and familiarity of faces. *Canadian Journal of Psychology*, 41, 510–520.

Bruce, V., and Valentine, T. (1985). Identity priming in the recognition of familiar faces. *British Journal of Psychology*, 76, 363–383.

Bruce, V., and Valentine, T. (1986). Semantic priming of familiar faces. *Quarterly Journal of Experimental Psychology*, 38A, 125–150.

Bruce, V., and Young, A. (1986). Understanding face recognition. *British Journal of Psychology*, 77, 305–327.

Brunas, J., Young, A. W., and Ellis, A. W. (1990). Repetition priming from incomplete faces: Evidence for part to whole completion. *British Journal of Psychology*, 81, 43–56.

Brunas-Wagstaff, J., Young, A. W., and Ellis, A. W. (1992). Repetition priming follows spontaneous but not prompted recognition of familiar faces. *Quarterly Journal of Experimental Psychology*, 44A, 423–454.

Brust, J. C. M., and Behrens, M. M. (1977). "Release hallucinations" as the major symptom of posterior cerebral artery occlusion: A report of 2 cases. *Annals of Neurology*, 2, 432–436.

Bruyer, R. (1991). Covert face recognition in prosopagnosia: A review. *Brain and Cognition*, 15, 223–235.

Bruyer, R., Laterre, C., Seron, X., Feyereisen, P., Strypstein, E., Pierrard, E., and Rectem, D. (1983). A case of prosopagnosia with some preserved covert remembrance of familiar faces. *Brain and Cognition*, 2, 257–284.

Burton, A. M., and Bruce, V. (1992). I recognise your face but I can't remember your name: A simple explanation? *British Journal of Psychology*, 83, 45–60.

Burton, A. M., Bruce, V., and Johnston, R. A. (1990). Understanding face recognition with an interactive activation model. *British Journal of Psychology*, 81, 361–380.

Burton, A. M., Young, A. W., Bruce, V., Johnston, R., and Ellis, A. W. (1991). Understanding covert recognition. *Cognition*, 39, 129–166.

Campbell, R., Landis, T., and Regard, M. (1986). Face recognition and lipreading: A neurological dissociation. *Brain*, 109, 509–521.

Candido, C. L., and Romney, D. M. (1990). Attributional style in paranoid vs. depressed patients. *British Journal of Medical Psychology*, 63, 355–363.

Capgras, J., and Reboul-Lachaux, J. (1923). L'illusion des "sosies" dans un délire systématisé chronique. *Bulletin de la Société Clinique de Médicine Mentale*, 11, 6–16.

Carr, T. H., McCauley, C., Sperber, R. D., and Parmelee, C. M. (1982). Words, pictures, and priming: On semantic activation, conscious identification, and the automaticity of information processing. *Journal of Experimental Psychology: Human Perception and Performance*, 8, 757–777.

Cotard, J. (1882). Du délire des négations. *Archives de Neurologie*, 4, 150–170, 282–295.

Critchley, E. M. R. (1989). The neurology of familiarity. *Behavioural Neurology*, 2, 195–200.

Cutting, J. (1991). Delusional misidentification and the role of the right hemisphere in the appreciation of identity. *British Journal of Psychiatry*, 159, 70–75.

Dannenbring, G. L., and Briand, K. (1982). Semantic priming and the word repetition effect in a lexical decision task. *Canadian Journal of Psychology*, 36, 435–444.

de Haan, E. H. F., Bauer, R. M., and Greve, K. W. (1992). Behavioural and physiological evidence for covert face recognition in a prosopagnosic patient. *Cortex, 28,* 77–95.

de Haan, E. H. F., Young, A., and Newcombe, F. (1987a). Face recognition without awareness. *Cognitive Neuropsychology, 4,* 385–415.

de Haan, E. H. F., Young, A., and Newcombe, F. (1987b). Faces interfere with name classification in a prosopagnosic patient. *Cortex, 23,* 309–316.

de Haan, E. H. F., Young, A. W., and Newcombe, F. (1991a). Covert and overt recognition in prosopagnosia. *Brain, 114,* 2575–2591.

de Haan, E. H. F., Young, A. W., and Newcombe, F. (1991b). A dissociation between the sense of familiarity and access to semantic information concerning familiar people. *European Journal of Cognitive Psychology, 3,* 51–67.

De Renzi, E. (1986). Current issues in prosopagnosia. In H. D. Ellis, M. A. Jeeves, F. Newcombe, and A. Young (Eds.), *Aspects of face processing,* 243–252. Dordrecht: Martinus Nijhoff.

De Renzi, E., Faglioni, P., Grossi, D., and Nichelli, P. (1991). Apperceptive and associative forms of prosopagnosia. *Cortex, 27,* 213–221.

Desimone, R. (1991). Face-selective cells in the temporal cortex of monkeys. *Journal of Cognitive Neuroscience, 3,* 1–8.

Ebata, S., Ogawa, M., Tanaka, Y., Mizuno, Y., and Yoshida, M. (1991). Apparent reduction in the size of one side of the face associated with a small retrosplenial haemorrhage. *Journal of Neurology, Neurosurgery, and Psychiatry, 54,* 68–70.

Ellis, A. W., Young, A. W., and Flude, B. M. (1990). Repetition priming and face processing: Priming occurs within the system that responds to the identity of a face. *Quarterly Journal of Experimental Psychology, 42A,* 495–512.

Ellis, A. W., Young, A. W., Flude, B. M., and Hay, D. C. (1987). Repetition priming of face recognition. *Quarterly Journal of Experimental Psychology, 39A,* 193–210.

Ellis, A. W., Young, A. W., and Hay, D. C. (1987). Modelling the recognition of faces and words. In P. E. Morris (Ed.), *Modelling cognition,* 269–297. Chichester: Wiley.

Ellis, H. D. (1975). Recognizing faces. *British Journal of Psychology, 66,* 409–426.

Ellis, H. D., and Young, A. W. (1990). Accounting for delusional misidentifications. *British Journal of Psychiatry, 157,* 239–248.

Enoch, M. D., and Trethowan, W. H. (1991). *Uncommon psychiatric syndromes,* 3d ed. Oxford: Butterworth-Heinemann.

Etcoff, N. L., Freeman, R., and Cave, K. R. (1991). Can we lose memories of faces? Content specificity and awareness in a prosopagnosic. *Journal of Cognitive Neuroscience, 3,* 25–41.

Flude, B. M., Ellis, A. W., and Kay, J. (1989). Face processing and name retrieval in an anomic aphasic: Names are stored separately from semantic information about familiar people. *Brain and Cognition, 11,* 60–72.

Fodor, J. (1983). *The modularity of mind.* Cambridge, MA: MIT Press.

Gainotti, G., D'Erme, P., Monteleone, D., and Silveri, M. C. (1986). Mechanisms of unilateral spatial neglect in relation to laterality of cerebral lesions. *Brain, 109,* 599–612.

Geschwind, N. (1965a). Disconnexion syndromes in animals and man. Part I. *Brain, 88,* 237–294.

Geschwind, N. (1965b). Disconnexion syndromes in animals and man. Part II. *Brain, 88,* 585–644.

Greve, K. W., and Bauer, R. M. (1990). Implicit learning of new faces in prosopagnosia: An application of the mere-exposure paradigm. *Neuropsychologia, 28,* 1035–1041.

Gross, C. G., and Sergent, J. (1992). Face recognition. *Current Opinion in Neurobiology, 2,* 156–161.

Hanley, J. R., and Cowell, E. S. (1988). The effects of different types of retrieval cues on the recall of names of famous faces. *Memory and Cognition, 16,* 545–555.

Hay, D. C., and Young, A. W. (1982). The human face. In A. W. Ellis (Ed.), *Normality and pathology in cognitive functions,* 173–202. London: Academic Press.

Hay, D. C., Young, A. W., and Ellis, A. W. (1991). Routes through the face recognition system. *Quarterly Journal of Experimental Psychology, 43A,* 761–791.

Hécaen, H., and Angelergues, R. (1962). Agnosia for faces (prosopagnosia). *Archives of Neurology, 7,* 92–100.

Heywood, C. A., and Cowey, A. (1992). The role of the "face-cell" area in the discrimination and recognition of faces by monkeys. *Philosophical Transactions of the Royal Society, London, B335,* 31–38.

Humphreys, G. W., Troscianko, T., Riddoch, M. J., Boucart, M., Donnelly, N., and Harding, G. F. A. (1992). Covert processing in different visual recognition systems. In A. D. Milner and M. D. Rugg (Eds.), *The neuropsychology of consciousness,* 39–68. London: Academic Press.

Johnson, M. H., Dziurawiec, S., Ellis, H., and Morton, J. (1991). Newborns' preferential tracking of face-like stimuli and its subsequent decline. *Cognition, 40,* 1–19.

Johnson, M. H., and Morton, J. (1991). *Biology and cognitive development: The case of face recognition.* Oxford: Blackwell.

Joseph, A. B. (1986). Cotard's syndrome with coexistent Capgras' syndrome, syndrome of subjective doubles, and palinopsia. *Journal of Clinical Psychiatry, 47,* 605–606.

Kaney, S., and Bentall, R. P. (1989). Persecutory delusions and attributional style. *British Journal of Medical Psychology, 62,* 191–198.

Kunst-Wilson, W. R., and Zajonc, R. B. (1980). Affective discrimination of stimuli that cannot be recognized. *Science, 207,* 557–558.

Landis, T., Cummings, J. L., Christen, L., Bogen, J. E., and Imhof, H.-G. (1986). Are unilateral right posterior cerebral lesions sufficient to cause prosopagnosia? Clinical and radiological findings in six additional patients. *Cortex, 22,* 243–252.

Lewis, S. W. (1987). Brain imaging in a case of Capgras' syndrome. *British Journal of Psychiatry, 150,* 117–121.

Lucchelli, F., and De Renzi, E. (1992). Proper name anomia. *Cortex, 28,* 221–230.

Malone, D. R., Morris, H. H., Kay, M. C., and Levin, H. S. (1982). Prosopagnosia: A double dissociation between the recognition of familiar and unfamiliar faces. *Journal of Neurology, Neurosurgery, and Psychiatry, 45,* 820–822.

Mandler, G. (1980). Recognizing: The judgment of previous occurrence. *Psychological Review, 87,* 252–271.

McCauley, C., Parmelee, C., Sperber, R., and Carr, T. (1980). Early extraction of meaning from pictures and its relation to conscious identification. *Journal of Experimental Psychology: Human Perception and Performance, 6,* 265–276.

McNeil, J. E., and Warrington, E. K. (1991). Prosopagnosia: A reclassification. *Quarterly Journal of Experimental Psychology, 43A,* 267–287.

Meadows, J. C. (1974). The anatomical basis of prosopagnosia. *Journal of Neurology, Neurosurgery, and Psychiatry, 37,* 489–501.

Newcombe, F. (1979). The processing of visual information in prosopagnosia and acquired dyslexia: Functional versus physiological interpretation. In D. J. Oborne, M. M. Gruneberg, and J. R. Eiser (Eds.), *Research in psychology and medicine,* vol. 1, pp. 315–322. London: Academic Press.

Newcombe, F., Young, A. W., and de Haan, E. H. F. (1989). Prosopagnosia and object agnosia without covert recognition. *Neuropsychologia, 27,* 179–191.

Paller, K. A., Mayes, A. R., Thompson, K. M., Young, A. W., Roberts, J., and Meudell, P. R. (1992). Priming of face matching in amnesia. *Brain and Cognition, 18,* 46–59.

Parry, F. M., Young, A. W., Saul, J. S. M., and Moss, A. (1991). Dissociable face processing impairments after brain injury. *Journal of Clinical and Experimental Neuropsychology, 13,* 545–558.

Perrett, D. I., Hietanen, J. K., Oram, M. W., and Benson, P. J. (1992). Organization and functions of cells responsive to faces in the temporal cortex. *Philosophical Transactions of the Royal Society. London, B335,* 23–30.

Posner, M. I., and Snyder, C. R. R. (1975). Facilitation and inhibition in the processing of signals. In P. M. A. Rabbitt and S. Dornic (Eds.), *Attention and performance V,* 669–682. London: Academic Press.

Rizzo, M., Hurtig, R., and Damasio, A. R. (1987). The role of scanpaths in facial recognition and learning. *Annals of Neurology, 22,* 41–45.

Roberts, T., and Bruce, V. (1988). Feature saliency in judging the sex and familiarity of faces. *Perception, 17,* 475–481.

Schacter, D. L., McAndrews, M. P., and Moscovitch, M. (1988). Access to consciousness: Dissociations between implicit and explicit knowledge in neuropsychological syndromes. In L. Weiskrantz (Ed.), *Thought without language,* 242–278. Oxford: Oxford University Press.

Semenza, C., and Zettin, M. (1988). Generating proper names: A case of selective inability. *Cognitive Neuropsychology, 5,* 711–721.

Semenza, C., and Zettin, M. (1989). Evidence from aphasia for the role of proper names as pure referring expressions. *Nature, 342,* 678–679.

Sergent, J., Ohta, S., and MacDonald, B. (1992). Functional neuroanatomy of face and object processing. A positron emission tomography study. *Brain, 115,* 15–36.

Sergent, J., and Poncet, M. (1990). From covert to overt recognition of faces in a prosopagnosic patient. *Brain, 113,* 989–1004.

Sergent, J., and Signoret, J.-L. (1992). Functional and anatomical decomposition of face processing: Evidence from prosopagnosia and PET study of normal subjects. *Philosophical Transactions of the Royal Society, London, B335,* 55–62.

Sergent, J., and Villemure, J.-G. (1989). Prosopagnosia in a right hemispherectomized patient. *Brain, 112,* 975–995.

Sno, H. N., and Linszen, D. H. (1990). The déjà vu experience: Remembrance of things past? *American Journal of Psychiatry, 147,* 1587–1595.

Thomson, D. M. (1986). Face recognition: More than a feeling of familiarity? In H. D. Ellis, M. A. Jeeves, F. Newcombe, and A. Young (Eds.), *Aspects of face processing,* 118–122. Dordrecht: Martinus Nijhoff.

Tranel, D., and Damasio, A. R. (1985). Knowledge without awareness: An autonomic index of facial recognition by prosopagnosics. *Science, 228,* 1453–1454.

Tranel, D., and Damasio, A. R. (1988). Non-conscious face recognition in patients with face agnosia. *Behavioural Brain Research, 30,* 235–249.

Valentine, T. (1991). Representation and process in face recognition. In R. J. Watt (Ed.), *Pattern recognition by man and machine,* 107–124. Basingstoke: Macmillan.

Van Lancker, D. (1991). Personal relevance and the human right hemisphere. *Brain and Cognition, 17,* 64–92.

Warrington, E. K., and James, M. (1967). An experimental investigation of facial recognition in patients with unilateral cerebral lesions. *Cortex, 3,* 317–326.

Wright, S., Young, A. W., and Hellawell, D. J. (1993). Sequential Cotard and Capgras delusions. *British Journal of Clinical Psychology, 32,* 345–349.

Young, A. W. (1988). Functional organization of visual recognition. In L. Weiskrantz (Ed.), *Thought without language,* 78–107. Oxford: Oxford University Press.

Young, A. W. (1992). Face recognition impairments. *Philosophical Transactions of the Royal Society, London, B335,* 47–54.

Young, A. W., and Bruce, V. (1991). Perceptual categories and the computation of "grandmother." *European Journal of Cognitive Psychology, 3,* 5–49.

Young, A. W., and de Haan, E. H. F. (1988). Boundaries of covert recognition in prosopagnosia. *Cognitive Neuropsychology, 5,* 317–336.

Young, A. W., and de Haan, E. H. F. (1990). Impairments of visual awareness. *Mind and Language, 5,* 29–48.

Young, A. W., and de Haan, E. H. F. (1992). Face recognition and awareness after brain injury. In A. D. Milner and M. D. Rugg (Eds.), *The neuropsychology of consciousness,* 69–90. London: Academic Press.

Young, A. W., de Haan, E. H. F., and Newcombe, F. (1990). Unawareness of impaired face recognition. *Brain and Cognition, 14,* 1–18.

Young, A. W., de Haan, E. H. F., Newcombe, F., and Hay, D. C. (1990). Facial neglect. *Neuropsychologia, 28,* 391–415.

Young, A. W., and Ellis, H. D. (1989a). Childhood prosopagnosia. *Brain and Cognition, 9,* 16–47.

Young, A. W., and Ellis, H. D. (1989b). Semantic processing. In A. W. Young and H. D. Ellis (Eds.), *Handbook of research on face processing,* 235–262. Amsterdam: North-Holland.

Young, A. W., Hay, D. C., and Ellis, A. W. (1985). The faces that launched a thousand slips: Everyday difficulties and errors in recognizing people. *British Journal of Psychology, 76,* 495–523.

Young, A. W., Hellawell, D., and de Haan, E. H. F. (1988). Cross-domain semantic priming in normal subjects and a prosopagnosic patient. *Quarterly Journal of Experimental Psychology, 40A,* 561–580.

Young, A. W., Hellawell, D. J., and Welch, J. (1992). Neglect and visual recognition. *Brain, 115,* 51–71.

Young, A. W., McWeeny, K. H., Hay, D. C., and Ellis, A. W. (1986a). Matching familiar and unfamiliar faces on identity and expression. *Psychological Research, 48,* 63–68.

Young, A. W., McWeeny, K. H., Hay, D. C., and Ellis, A. W. (1986b). Access to identity-specific semantic codes from familiar faces. *Quarterly Journal of Experimental Psychology, 38A,* 271–295.

Young, A. W., Reid, I., Wright, S., and Hellawell, D. (1993). Face processing impairments and the Capgras delusion. *British Journal of Psychiatry, 162,* 695–698.

Young, A. W., Robertson, I. H., Hellawell, D. J., de Pauw, K. W., and Pentland, B. (1992). Cotard delusion after brain injury. *Psychological Medicine, 22,* 799–804.

Zajonc, R. B. (1980). Feeling and thinking: Preferences need no inferences. *American Psychologist, 35,* 151–175.

# 7 Repetition Priming of Face Recognition

Vicki Bruce, Mike Burton, Derek Carson,
Elias Hanna, and Oli Mason

ABSTRACT  Repetition priming has recently been used by Schacter, Biederman, and others as a means to explore the nature and access of structural representations of objects. Indeed, it has been claimed that repetition priming provides a more appropriate tool for probing the representation of objects than do matching or memory tasks that may tap properties of a distinct, episodic memory system. After reviewing this literature, in this chapter we consider what has been learned about the representations used to identify familiar faces from studies of repetition priming. This background motivates the new experiments reported here.

In face familiarity decision tasks, priming is reduced if the view of a face is changed between the prime phase and the test phase. Here we show that repetition priming of familiarity decisions is similarly reduced if prime and target faces merely differ in "format"—that is, if primes are shown as computer-drawn "cartoons" and targets as photographs, or vice versa. The cartoons preserve the details of pose and expression of the original picture, and are almost as well recognized as photographic images (Bruce et al. 1992). Nevertheless, in experiment 1 we showed that priming is substantially reduced if there is a change in format from prime to test phase, compared with that obtained when format is maintained. In experiment 2 we found that the priming obtained from bi-level quantized ("thresholded") images to photographs was the same as that obtained from four-level quantised images (containing light and dark grey as well as black and white regions), and in each case less than that obtained from full photographs. In experiment 3 we showed that the "format" effect was unaffected when the prime-test interval was increased to a week. These effects imply that facial representations preserve very low-level information indeed, but alternative interpretations are also discussed.

## 7.1 INTRODUCTION

Repetition priming (sometimes called identity priming) is the facilitation that is observed on the identification of an item due to earlier exposure to that item. It has been frequently used as a tool to probe lexical representations of words (Scarborough, Cortese, and Scarborough 1977; Monsell, 1985) but has been used more recently as a means to explore the nature and access of structural representations of objects (Biederman and Cooper 1991; Cooper et al. 1992; Schacter, Cooper, and Delaney 1990; Schacter et al. 1991). Indeed in recent research, it has been claimed that repetition priming provides a more appropriate tool for probing the representation of objects than matching or memory tasks (Biederman and Cooper 1992). This chapter to examines critically what can be learned about the representations mediating facial identification by using repetition priming as a tool.

## 7.2 REPETITION PRIMING OF OBJECT RECOGNITION

An early demonstration of repetition priming of object identification was provided by Warren and Morton (1982), who showed reduced tachistoscopic exposure thresholds for the identification of objects that previously had been named, compared with objects not previously shown. Facilitation of object identification was greatest if the same picture was shown at test, was lower if a different exemplar of the same object category was shown, and was not shown at all if subjects had merely read the name of the object category in the first phase. Thus, repetition priming of objects seems to operate at a level of the system that involves visual representations of object shape, and not at the level of access of an object's name or (probably) verbal semantics. Warren and Morton used these findings to suggest that objects were recognized through object recognition units called "pictogens," somewhat analogous to "logogens." They suggested that two different exemplars of the same object category activated the same pictogen, and repetition lowered the threshold on this pictogen, thus allowing the pictogen to be reactivated on the basis of less stimulus information. The advantage shown by repetition of the same view of the object was attributed to an additional, visual memory component, which can retain information about particular pictorial instances. This interpretation was supported by a post hoc analysis that showed that, for different exemplars, degree of priming between the first and second phase was not affected by rated degree of similarity between the two different exemplars. According to Warren and Morton, the priming between different views arises from the abstractive pictogen level. Biederman and colleagues (e.g., Biederman and Cooper 1991, 1992) have more recently used repetition priming as a tool to explore Biederman's (1987) theory of object recognition by components. Following computational approaches to object recognition such as that of Marr and Nishihara (1978), Biederman suggested that the primitive elements that mediate recognition of (most) objects are volumetric components called "geons" and their spatial arrangement. In explorations of this theory using repetition priming, priming was demonstrated by a reduction in the naming latencies from the first to the second phase of an object-naming experiment. An object named in the second phase might previously have been seen as a different exemplar (e.g., a grand piano followed by an upright piano) or as the same exemplar. Like Warren and Morton, more priming was shown from the same exemplar than the different exemplar, but Biederman and colleagues used this difference as an index of *visual* priming. Their argument was that because two different exemplars access the same conceptual and verbal information about the object, it is only the difference between "same" and "different" exemplars that taps visual priming, thereby implicitly assuming (in contrast to Warren and Morton) that two different exemplars of the same category do not access a common visual representational level. Biederman and Cooper (1991) then went on to show that two different images of the same object produced the same amount of priming as two identical images of that object provided that the two different images showed the same set of elementary components ("geons"). Thus, two images that showed the same geons through complementary sets of edges gave as much priming as two images showing identical edges. However, two different images that showed complementary sets of geons gave no more priming than two different exemplars of the same object type. From these data, the authors concluded that priming operates at the level of the object recognition "primitives"—the geons.

In subsequent work, Biederman and Cooper (1992) showed that priming was unaffected by a change in size or in position between the first and second naming task, whereas episodic recognition was impaired by such a change. They argued that the episodic memory task is likely to tap memory for any aspects of the visual scene that are encoded. Size, orientation, and so forth are likely to be encoded in the representational system subserving action and may therefore be remembered via that system. However, size and orientation are irrelevant for an object's identity, and the priming results suggested that the identification system operates on representations that are invariant across such variations.

Similar conclusions about the relationships between priming and episodic memory were reached by Schacter and colleagues, who used a priming task to explore the perception and recognition of unfamiliar (novel) object shapes. In the priming test phase of such tasks, subjects were required to decide whether the pictured object was possible (i.e., could exist as a three-dimensional structure). Decisions to possible objects were made more quickly if they were processed in a pretest in a manner likely to encourage the encoding of the three-dimensional shape (e.g., if the first phase involved a decision about which way the object was pointing), but no priming was observed if the first phase encouraged encoding the object at a purely pictorial or semantic level. Priming was unaffected by a change in image size from first to second phase, but this did impair recognition memory (Cooper et al. 1992). In contrast, memory for which objects were shown in the first phase was facilitated by instructions that should have encouraged a distinctive encoding of the item in memory, a manipulation that did not affect priming (Schacter, Cooper, and Delaney 1990; Schacter et al. 1991).

Both Biederman's and Schacter's research programs demonstrate that repetition priming is insensitive to variations of retinal size or position that object recognition should also ignore, since the goal of object identification is to recognize the same item wherever it appears. In contrast, memory and matching tasks are affected by such changes. These observations suggest that repetition priming can be used as a sensitive tool to probe the nature of the structural description system that subserves object identification, without contamination from influences of object attributes that are irrelevant for their identification. The identification of faces, like that of objects, involves accessing an identity across variations of image size, position, viewpoint, and so forth. Moreover, the organization of the major stages of face and object identification appears to be very similar (Bruce and Young 1986). However, the demands of basic level object identification are clearly slightly different from those of face identification, where discrimination within a category of objects that share the same overall shape must be achieved. These different demands may result in different representational primitives and processes being used for faces (Young and Bruce 1991). Nevertheless, although the representational primitives mediating face and object identification may differ, repetition priming might nevertheless provide the right kind of tool to test hypotheses about what these primitives are for face recognition.

## 7.3 REPETITION PRIMING OF FACE RECOGNITION

Considerable progress has been made at understanding the cognitive processes involved in person identification (Hay and Young 1982; Bruce and Young 1986; Burton, Bruce, and Johnston 1990; Young, chap. 6, this volume). However, the nature of the perceptual processes that form the first stage of person identification remains elusive (Young and Bruce 1991). Perhaps the repetition priming procedure can be used to probe the structural descriptions derived from and stored for faces.

Bruce and Valentine (1985) reported an initial examination of repetition priming of face recognition. In their first experiment, they used a design like Warren and Morton's, where the dependent variable was the tachistoscopic exposure duration needed to name a face correctly in the second phase of the experiment. Faces shown at test were unprimed (seen for the first time in the second phase), primed by earlier presentation of the name, primed by earlier presentation of a different picture of the same person, or primed by an identical picture. Repetition of an identical picture reduced exposure thresholds the most, but significant priming was also obtained from repeating a different view of the same person and from earlier exposure to the name of the person. The demonstrated facilitation from exposure to the name differed from effects shown by Warren and Morton. However, Bruce and Valentine argued that since the test phase involved naming and since face names are notoriously difficult to retrieve (Yarmey 1973; Young, Hay, and Ellis 1985; Hay and Young 1982; Burton and Bruce 1992), the facilitation observed in this condition may have been to do with name retrieval.

In their second experiment, Bruce and Valentine moved to a task that did not require naming in the test phase. The task of face familiarity decision (Bruce 1983) is analogous to lexical decision. Subjects must respond positively to faces that are familiar to them (whether as celebrities or as personal acquaintances) and negatively to those that are unfamiliar. Using latency of positive decisions to the famous faces in the test phase as dependent variable, Bruce and Valentine found no priming from earlier exposure to the name of the face but significant priming from earlier exposure to the face, with same views giving more priming than different views. In a post hoc analysis, Bruce and Valentine found no correlation between the amount of facilitation gained from different views and the rated similarity between these two views. Like Warren and Morton, they suggested that there were two components to priming: one arising from a level of face recognition units at which all views of a face accessed a common representation and the other arising from a separate memory for pictorial detail.

Ellis et al. (1987) replicated and extended Bruce and Valentine's study. In addition to confirming that face familiarity decisions were not speeded by earlier exposure to the person's name, they showed no facilitation from earlier exposure to the headless body of the person. Moreover, they explored the effect of changing view more systematically than had Bruce and Valentine. They examined priming from faces shown in identical views, similar views, and dissimilar views of the person, where allocation to the similar or dissimilar condition was made on the basis of preexperimental ratings. In this case, they found graded effects of resemblance. Most priming was found from identical views and least from dissimilar views. They explained these results as demonstrating that representations mediating face recognition are based on the superposition of discrete instances rather than the abstractive recognition unit account favored by Bruce and Valentine (1985). Subsequent work by Brunas, Young, and Ellis (1990), however, has shown that priming transfers completely between one part of an image of the face and the whole image of that face (thus, the internal or external features of a familiar face prime recognition of the full image of that face as much as the whole image of that face does). They argued that this supports a PDP interpretation of the representations underlying face recognition, since part-whole completion is a property of such representations (Kohonen, Oja, and Lehtio 1981). However, we should also note that part-whole completion is a property of abstractive recognition units. Thus, the strongest evidence for instance-based representations for recognition comes from the Ellis et al. (1987) result of graded resemblance. Such a result would also be expected to arise from any component of priming that arose from episodic memory, since the pictorial or associative components in memory would also show sensitivity to changes in view (Bruce 1982 showed that episodic recognition memory decisions to familiar faces were made more slowly if view and expression had changed from study, even though accuracy for changed as well as unchanged views of these faces was at ceiling).

The repetition priming effects found with faces either require an episodic component to priming in addition to effects at recognition unit level (Warren and Morton 1982), or they seem to force us to think in terms of nonabstractive recognition units. A further possibility is that repetition priming of faces is a purely episodic phenomenon, which arises as a result of repeating interpretative acts of perception across successive occasions. However, research by Ellis, Young, and Flude (1990) appears to demonstrate conclusively that repetition priming of faces does not arise merely as a function of the repetition of encoding processes or previous decisions, as might be expected if episodic memory processes were solely responsible. They showed that priming occurred only when the test phase involved a face familiarity decision, irrespective of the prime phase task. Thus, priming was found when subjects judged the familiarity of the faces in the first phase, when they judged the sex of the faces in the first phase, or when they judged the expression in the first phase, provided the test phase was familiarity decision. Priming was not found if the test phase involved sex judgments or expression judgments even if this repeated the operations required of the prime phase. A control experiment suggested that this was not just a result of the relative speeds of sex judgment and familiarity judgment, since the latter showed priming even when subjects performed as quickly as in sex judgment. Roberts (1991) has confirmed the differential susceptibility of familiarity and sex judgment tasks to priming. Only short-term facilitation was observed for repeating sex judgments to the same faces that recurred within an item of two in the trial sequence. Facilitation of a familiarity judgment to the same faces, however, remained strong across all the lags tested in the experiment.

Furthermore, later work by Brunas-Wagstaff, Young, and Ellis (1992) showed that priming of familiarity judgments occurs only from faces that were recognized spontaneously in the first phase. Even if subjects recognize the first face following a general semantic prompt, such as, "If you tell me it's a politician, then it must be Ronald Reagan," this does not yield priming in the second phase. This is further evidence against a simple episodic account of repetition priming, and indeed Brunas-Wagstaff, Young, and Ellis provided some evidence for dissociation between priming and episodic performance since subjects were accurate at remembering faces that they had earlier failed to recognize spontaneously, yet these faces did not yield priming.

## 7.4 EXPLAINING REPETITION PRIMING OF FACE RECOGNITION WITHIN THE INTERACTIVE ACTIVATION MODEL

We have so far proposed that the observed repetition priming effects suggest that representations mediating face recognition are either instance based, (perhaps superimposed in the ways suggested in some PDP models) or that priming reflects the operation of a separate episodic memory component in addition to reactivation of structural representations that access identity. Neither of these suggestions is very well integrated within our overall model of face recognition, however, where we must explain repetition priming alongside other experimental and neuropsychological observations. Here we explore how well the theoretical model for face identification that has developed over the past decade within our own and colleagues' laboratories can handle repetition priming alongside other phenomena.

One of the challenges posed by repetition priming has been to account for the different patterns of effect shown by repetition and semantic (associative) priming within the same theoretical framework. In face recognition (Bruce 1986) and word recognition (Dannenbring and Briand 1982) repetition priming is very long-lived (Flude 1991), while associative priming does not survive for more than a few seconds and/or one intervening item between prime and target. Models that attribute both effects to altered thresholds of recognition units have problems accounting for this. Thus, the Bruce and Young (1986) model of face identification, which suggested familiarity, was mediated by activation of face recognition units but did not spell out mechanisms very clearly, could not offer a satisfactory account of this. Nor could this account explain why repetition priming does not cross domains (e.g., names do not prime faces), but associative priming does (e.g., Young, Hellawell, and de Haan 1988 showed that a familiar face can prime recognition of a related name).

Recently, Burton, Bruce, and Johnston (1990) demonstrated how an interactive activation and competition (IAC) implementation of aspects of the Bruce and Young (1986) model of face recognition could produce such differential patterns of performance. (Young, chap. 6, this volume, provides more detail of this model.) On this account, repetition priming arises from Hebb-type modification of the connection strengths between face recognition units (FRUs) and the person identity nodes (PINs), the level at which familiarity decisions are presumed to be taken. In contrast, associative priming arises as a result of activation levels in PINs rising by means of semantic information units that are shared by members of associated pairs. This account can accommodate several of the extant phenomena. It explains why repetition priming does not cross domains while associative priming does; it explains the differential time course, with repetition priming diminishing as a function of the decay on the weight changes, and associative priming abolished by anything that affects activation levels in the PINS (intervening items, as well as time, will affect these). It explains why repetition priming should transfer completely from part of a face to the whole face (provided the part face produces above-threshold activation at the PIN, the link from FRU to PIN will be strengthened); why repetition priming arises only from spontaneous recognition of a familiar face (both FRU and PIN must be active for that link to be strengthened; prompted recognition will activate the PIN partly by a different route); and why repetition priming is found only when the test phase involves judgment of familiarity (other judgments may automatically activate PINs, and hence prime familiarity judgments, but will not themselves benefit from the strengthened FRU-PIN link).

Moreover, Bruce, Dench, and Burton (1993) have shown that repetition facilitates distinctive faces as much as more typical ones, although the former are recognized reliably more quickly than the latter (Valentine and Bruce 1986a, 1986b). This suggests that repetition priming influences a stage subsequent to that where distinctive faces have an advantage over more typical ones. Burton, Bruce, and Johnston (1990) suggest that the FRUs are themselves activated by links from more primitive "feature" units (where the nature of the "features" is deliberately unspecified). According to the Burton, Bruce, and Johnston account, distinctiveness effects can arise as a result of the relative rate of activation at the FRUs due to the different distributions of more primitive features driving these. On this account, additive effects of distinctiveness and repetition could be explained.

In the published IAC account, only the link between FRUs and PINs was strengthened as a result of face recognition. However, the Hebb-type modification of link weights is a very general and powerful way to include learning within a system initially set up to model a static snapshot of adult cognitive processes. Recently, Burton (1992) has demonstrated how this same procedure can provide a simple way of learning "new" faces from novel combinations of feature units. If link strengthening from features to FRUs underlies our acquisition of new facial identities, then this could also play a role, in addition to strengthening of links between FRUs and PINs, in repetition priming of well-known faces. If links between FRUs and the feature units that feed them were strengthened following any successful recognition, then this would provide a mechanism whereby our representations of the faces of familiar people would be continuously updated over time. Moreover, graded priming effects as a function of resemblance could arise because the further the test exemplar is from the priming exemplar, the less likely it is that the same set of feature units would become active the second time.

Although this discussion suggests that an extended IAC model has considerable potential as a theory that could unify accounts of priming and learning, several problems remain due to the lack of specification of the features that form the input to FRUs. If the IAC model were extended so that links between features and FRUs were strengthened as well as between FRUs and PINs, why is there full priming when part of a face is recognized successfully (as opposed to a different view of the same face)? We could suggest that either the same feature units are activated by a part as by the whole face (plausible if features are construed as very global rather than local properties) or that the subset of features corresponding to the part face becomes more activated than when embedded within the whole (also plausible, given the release from certain inhibitory influences of the missing features). We would also have to consider whether such an account could allow us to preserve the (observed) additive effects of repetition priming and distinctiveness (Bruce, Dench, and Burton 1993). The problem here is that any precise predictions about how and why priming should be affected by a change in viewpoint, or by substitution of one part of an image with another part, or by "distinctiveness," depends critically on what the facial features are and that understanding of front-end processing is what we currently lack and therefore cannot implement within our model (Bruce 1988; Young and Bruce 1991; Bruce, Burton, and Craw 1992).

Although the IAC model provides a promising framework for understanding repetition priming of faces and although it seems to have the potential to accommodate effects of changing view and picture part, there are some phenomena that seem more difficult in principle. Flude (1991), for example, found that priming survived a twelve-week interval between exposure to the prime face and test. Moreover, priming across this interval was shown even for faces that are frequently encountered in the media and whose single exposure in the laboratory should be swamped by occurrences in the newspapers and television over this interval. Ellis (1992) suggests that this may demonstrate that repetition priming is not just strengthening the connections within the identification route but is a strengthened connection between an individual face and a particular place or context of occurrence. Flude (1991) produced some evidence that changing the context of the test phase from that prevailing at priming did reduce priming, consistent with this interpretation. Such an account seems to reintroduce an episodic component into the repetition priming account; we will return to consider this possibility later.

For now we conclude that the IAC model has the potential to offer a unifying account of repetition priming as well as face learning within a framework that has comfortably accounted for a range of phenomena in the face recognition literature (e.g., see Burton et al. 1991 for an account of covert recognition in prosopagnosia using IAC; Burton and Bruce 1992 for an account of difficulty with name retrieval; Young, chap. 6, this volume). The difficulty is that we cannot progress until we understand more about the initial representational stage—the features, which mediate face recognition. If we accept the arguments of Biederman and his associates that priming provides a means of exploring the nature of structural descriptions that mediate object recognition, then perhaps we can use priming to probe these representations rather than worrying ahead of time what the features may be. From this angle, we have so far learned rather little about the structural representations of faces from repetition priming to date. From the research of Ellis et al. (1987), it might seem that these descriptions are view sensitive rather than viewpoint invariant, since priming is reduced systematically as the difference between prime and target views increases. Such viewpoint sensitivity would be consistent with the properties of single cells responding to faces in monkey cortex, which generally show selectivity to viewpoint (Perrett et al 1992). However, the view sensitivity that affects repetition priming has not been explored systematically. We do not know whether the "very dissimilar" views used by Ellis et al. (1987) differed more in terms of viewpoints, expressions, ages, sizes of image, or superficial pictorial quality than did the "slightly dissimilar" views. The part-to-whole priming experiments of Brunas, Young, and Ellis provide good control of the images, but the distinction between "internal" (eyes, nose, and mouth) and "external" (hair and chin) features is arbitrary with respect to visual processes.

## 7.5 INTRODUCTION TO THE EXPERIMENTS: COMPUTER-DRAWN CARTOONS

The aim of the experiments reported here was to use repetition priming to probe in more detail the nature of the primitive descriptive elements that mediate facial recognition. The specific question examined is whether priming will transfer completely between two different pictures of faces, when these show identical views, expressions, hair style, and so forth, but differ in the way that these are depicted. We achieve this by comparing priming obtained from accurate line drawings ("cartoons") of faces, to photographs of faces, or vice versa, with priming obtained when format (cartoon or photograph) is maintained between repetitions. In Biederman's research, the emphasis is on part-based representations, which are usually accessed through information from the contours. We know that faces are not well recognized from contours alone (Davies, Ellis, and Shepherd 1978; Rhodes, Brennan, and Carey 1987;

Bruce et al. 1992). However, Bruce et al. (1992) have shown that a computer algorithm for producing line drawings of faces automatically provided very good likenesses of familiar faces provided that, in addition to contours, some elements of mass were preserved.

Bruce et al.'s research was aimed at assessing objectively the performance of the cartoon-drawing algorithm of Pearson and Robinson (1985). That algorithm was produced in order to compress video images to 1-bit for economical transmission down telephone lines and forms the basis of a successful videophone used by deaf people over the British public telephone network since 1989 (Pearson 1992). The cartoon algorithm comprises two components. The first is a "valledge" detector, a filter sensitive to luminance valleys, which arise in front or top lighting from places where the surface shifts sharply away from the viewer's line of sight. This filter is also responsive to contrast edges (e.g., the border between hair and skin). The valledge detector therefore marks contours. The second component is a threshold operator, which fills in with black any region whose gray is darker than a certain level. This has the result of filling in regions of mass arising from dark hair, or shadow, with black. Figure 7.1 shows examples of full cartoons produced from famous faces with the filter and thresholds of each set by eye to produce the most satisfactory image of the person. Bruce et al. (1992) showed that full cartoons with both contour and mass components were recognized almost as accurately as original images of these faces, but cartoons with only one of these components (valledges or thresholds alone) were recognized much less well.

The high performance shown on full cartoons suggests that these preserve the key representational primitives needed for recognizing faces. These seem to involve the spatial layout of parts and some information about pigmentation or shading that is conveyed by the mass information. Since a computer-

**Figure 7.1** Examples of full cartoons of famous faces produced using Pearson and Robinson's (1985) algorithm.

generated cartoon of a particular portrait of a familiar face preserves all other information about viewpoint, expression, and so forth from the original, the computer-drawn cartoons present a rather interesting example of a different view from the original photograph. If the cartoon preserves the majority of the structural primitives needed to recognize a face and if priming arises at the level of these structural primitives, then priming should transfer as readily from cartoon to photograph as from photograph to photograph (particularly given the part-whole completion effects reviewed earlier). Our experiments investigated whether such transfer was found.

## 7.6 EXPERIMENTS

### Materials and General Methods

Twenty famous faces were used in these experiments, including politicians, television celebrities, and film stars. Eighteen of these were used as targets in each experiment, and the other two (which varied between experiments) were used as fillers. Twenty unfamiliar faces were selected from a variety of media sources so that they portrayed similar poses and expressions to the celebrities' faces. All faces were digitized, and full cartoons of each face were produced by applying the Pearson and Robinson (1985) algorithm with parameters set to produce the most acceptable full cartoon (as judged by eye). Previous research (Bruce et al. 1992) has established that these specific cartoons are recognized almost as accurately as the full image versions from which they were derived. It is only when large numbers of subjects are tested that a statistically significant advantage can be observed for the full image compared with the cartoon format.

In pilot research preceding this series of experiments, the average naming latency obtained to the cartoons was found not to differ from the average naming latency obtained to the full images of the same people (cartoons 2,000 ms; images 2,052 ms on average, from the eight subjects naming each type of image). Thus, there is no evidence that naming cartoons correctly takes longer than naming photographs correctly, which is the task required in the prime phases of the current experiments.

In all experiments, subjects made speeded familiarity decisions in the test phase of eighteen famous faces, plus twenty unfamiliar faces, with two additional famous faces serving as filler items occurring in the first four trials that served as practice (though subjects were not informed of this). The experimental items were ordered randomly in the test series, with the constraint that there should be no more than three familiar or unfamiliar items in succession. Depending on experiment, the test phase items might be all photographs or all cartoons, but format was never mixed at test.

Only subjects who recognized at least four of the six faces in each cell of each phase of the experiment were retained in the experiments. A minority of subjects (approximately 10 percent in each experiment) who failed to meet these criteria were replaced by new subjects. Because of this accuracy criterion, the results sections focus on the analysis of the correct response latencies. Remaining errors were infrequent, with the vast majority of subjects making only no or one error per cell. Unless otherwise mentioned, naming accuracies in the first phase were above 90 percent correct for both cartoons and images, and familiarity decisions in the test phase were over 95 percent accurate for both familiar and unfamiliar items. Only reaction times (RTs) from correctly identified primes (where shown) and correct responses at test were used for calculating the mean RT for each priming condition. Mean RTs were used for comparability with other published work on repetition priming of face recognition. (Where in previous research projects using the face familiarity decision task we have compared analysis of means with analysis of median RTs we have not found any difference in the pattern of effects).

## Experiment 1a

The aim of this first experiment was to investigate whether changing the format from cartoon to photograph, or vice versa, reduced repetition priming. The test phase involved one group of subjects making familiarity decisions to photographs of faces and the other group making decisions to cartoons of faces. In the preceding, prime phase, subjects had viewed photographs, cartoons, or no pictures (unprimed condition) of each of the familiar faces they responded to at test.

**Method** These were twenty-four subjects recruited from the undergraduate and postgraduate population in Nottingham. This was a 2 (format at test) × 3 (type of prime) mixed design, with subjects allocated to one of two groups making familiarity decisions to either photographs of faces or to cartoons of faces at test. The within-subjects factor was the type of prime. Of the eighteen familiar faces seen at test, six were primed with photographs, six were primed with cartoons, and six were unprimed. Which items appeared in which conditions was counterbalanced across subsets of the subjects in each group.

In the first phase, subjects were asked, without time pressure, to name or otherwise describe (unambiguously) each of the twelve priming slides. Each slide remained in view until it was named in order to maximize the opportunity for correct naming (only named items were subsequently analysed). An unrelated filler task was then performed for 10 min. For the test phase, subjects were instructed to make a familiarity decision to each of the forty faces by pressing the appropriate response button as quickly and accurately as possible. After a warning tone 500 ms before exposure of the slide, each face was shown for 2 sec, with a 1-sec interval between the subject's response and the beginning of the next trial. In both phases of the experiment, slides were displayed using Kodak Carousel slide projectors controlled by a microcomputer, which recorded response latencies. Faces subtended visual angles of about 6 degrees at the subject's seat.

**Results** The mean reaction times in each condition of the experiment are shown in table 7.1. A 2 (test format) × 3 (prime type—"unprimed"/"same format"/"different format") design revealed only a significant main effect of prime type ($F(2,36) = 45.58, p < 0.001$) but no interaction with test format ($F < 1$). Subsequent pairwise comparisons showed that all three mean reaction times differed significantly from each other. Thus, a change in format reduces priming whether the test phase involves photograph or cartoon recognition. There was no significant effect of format of test phase per se, though this was significant on an items analysis where the manipulation is within items rather than between subjects ($F(1,17) = 47.1, p < 0.001$)) showing that familiarity decisions to photographs are made more quickly than to cartoons. The items analysis also showed a significant main effect of prime type ($F(2,34) = 16.86$, $p < 0.001$). However, pairwise comparisons did not yield a significant difference between same and different prime format ($t = 1.32, p > 0.05$). We note, however, that the design by items is relatively insensitive (only four subjects saw each item subset in each condition of priming), and the rotation of items around these subsets of items was itself intended to reduce the possibility that results reflected item differences. Subsequent experiments allow more powerful items analyses to be conducted.

In this experiment, the naming accuracies were 85 percent to cartoons and 97 percent to photographs in the first phase. This led us to adjust the set of items used in subsequent experiments to reduce this difference.

**Experiment 1b: Replication**

In experiment 1a and the others in this chapter, subjects named the faces presented as primes in their own time, and no control was exerted over the time that they spent viewing each face in the prime phase. Jacoby and Dallas (1981) report that repetition priming of word identification is not affected by an increase in exposure duration, and our own pilot work indicated that, on average, face naming and cartoon naming took the same time. It is possible, however, that the cartoons might have been studied for longer, on average, than the photographs, and this might have distorted the pattern of the format effect. Experiment 1b was therefore a control experiment in which all items

**Table 7.1** Subject Mean Correct Familiarity Decision Latencies to Familiar Faces, Experiment 1a

| Prime Condition | Test Format | Latencies (ms) |
| --- | --- | --- |
| Unprimed | Photographs | 735 |
| Photo | Photographs | 573 |
| Cartoon | Photographs | 639 |
| Unprimed | Cartoons | 831 |
| Photo | Cartoons | 753 |
| Cartoon | Cartoons | 699 |

were studied for an identical period in phase 1. In other respects, it was a replication of experiment 1a.

**Method** This was the same as experiment 1a, except that slide presentation and response timing was via a modified Bell and Howell back projector. In the prime phase, each face was shown for 5 sec, followed by a 5-sec blank interval. Subjects were told to stare at each face for the full 5 sec and then to give the name of the person in the blank interval that followed. In the test phase, a new slide appeared every 5 sec, and subjects were requested to make a familiarity decision as quickly as possible after the onset of each slide. Responses and latencies were recorded manually from a millisecond timer that picked up the latency between the onset of the slide and the subject's manual response. The majority of the items used overlapped with experiment 1a, but two of the less well-recognized faces were taken out of the critical set of eighteen and replaced with different ones.

**Results** The mean response times are shown in table 7.2. The pattern is virtually identical to that shown in experiment 1, with a change in format reducing priming to both faces and cartoons. This was confirmed in an ANOVA on the subjects' mean correct reaction times to familiar faces, which showed a significant effect of prime type (same format, changed format or unprimed $F(2,44) = 16.8$, $p < 0.001$) but no interaction with format at test ($F < 1$). Planned comparisons showed a significant difference between priming by "same" and "different" format ($t = 2.2, p < 0.05$). The effect of the test format itself (cartoon versus photo) was not significant on the subjects analysis ($p > 0.2$) but was on an items analysis, where it became a within-items factor ($F(1,17) = 8.98, p < 0.01$). The items analysis also confirmed the main effect of prime type ($F(2,34) = 13.8, p < 0.001$) and no interaction ($F < 1$). The planned comparison between the same and different format condition in the items analysis was significant with a one-tailed comparison ($t = 1.8$), but again we note the relatively low power of the design from the perspective of individual items.

**Discussion of Experiment 1**

Both replications of this experiment reveal (on the subjects analysis, which is designed with more power) significantly less priming when the format of the faces is switched between presentation and test than when format remains constant. The replication used different equipment, different subjects, and a slightly different set of items. The format effects observed in experiment 1a do not seem to be an artifact of differential viewing times of either kind of item in the prime phase, which experiment 1b was designed to eliminate.

Thus, repetition priming, and by implication the representations subserving face recognition, appears to be sensitive to changes of view that do not include a change of viewing angle, or expression, but merely the manner in

**Table 7.2** Subject Mean Familiarity Decision Latencies to Familiar Faces, Experiment 1b

| Prime Condition | Test Format | Latencies (ms) |
|---|---|---|
| Unprimed | Photographs | 628 |
| Photo | Photographs | 553 |
| Cartoon | Photographs | 588 |
| Unprimed | Cartoons | 710 |
| Photo | Cartoons | 635 |
| Cartoon | Cartoons | 599 |

which the same picture is depicted by a pattern of light and dark elements. Experiment 2 explores this by examining whether the format effect is affected by the range of grey levels visible.

**Experiment 2**

In this experiment we examined the amount of priming onto photographs of faces obtained from cartoons which showed either two levels of gray (black and white) or four levels of gray (black, dark gray, light gray, and white). We achieved this by using thresholded versions of the cartoons (with no valledge component) and adjusting the way in which thresholding was applied.

**Method** This was the same as experiment 1a, except for the following details. All subjects were tested on photographs in the second phase. Two groups of fifteen subjects per group were tested. Subject groups differed in the format of the faces in the first phase. For one group, faces were unprimed, primed by images thresholded to two levels of gray, (black or white), or primed by full photographs. In the other group, faces were unprimed, primed by images thresholded to four levels of gray (black, dark gray, light gray, or white), or primed by full photographs (see the examples in fig. 7.2).

**Results** The mean response times in each of the conditions of interest are shown in table 7.3. Both subject groups appear to show less priming from thresholded than from photographed faces, and there seems no difference in the pattern of the RT between the groups. Consistent with these observations, a 2 (number of gray levels) × 3 (prime type) mixed design ANOVA revealed only a main effect of prime type ($F(2,56) = 45.97, p < 0.001$) and no interaction with subject group ($F < 1$). Pairwise comparisons showed all three means to be significantly different. Thus, the effect of changing format from a thresholded image to a photograph at test is unaffected by an increase in the range of grays shown. (Due to an administrative error we have been unable to conduct an items analysis for this experiment.)

**Discussion** This experiment suggests that the format effect does not arise merely as a result of a switch from monochrome to varied gray images,

**Figure 7.2** Examples of two-level and four-level thresholded images used in experiment 2.

**Table 7.3** Subject Mean Correct Familiarity Decision Latencies, Experiment 2

| Prime Condition | Group | Latencies (ms) |
| --- | --- | --- |
| Unprimed | Two levels | 684 |
| Photo | Two levels | 585 |
| Thresholds | Two levels | 628 |
| Unprimed | Four levels | 729 |
| Photo | Four levels | 627 |
| Thresholds | Four levels | 664 |

Note: The two groups of subjects differed only in the threshold condition, with one group primed by two-level and the other by four-level thresholded images.

though more subtle effects of changes in the spatial frequency spectrum have not, of course, been ruled out. The results of experiments 1 and 2 together suggest that the representations mediating facial identification preserve very low-level information about the pattern of intensities by which a face is depicted. However, both experiments have made use of a relatively short delay (10 min or so) between prime and test phase, which may encourage use of explicit memory for the faces shown, and their format, in responses made in the test phase. In experiment 3 we investigated whether the format effect survived a week's delay between prime and test phase. The experiment also used a larger group of subjects in order to increase power for the items analysis.

**Experiment 3**

**Method** This was the same as the photograph test phase conditions of experiment 1b, but one group of eighteen subjects was tested 1 week after exposure to the primes, while the other was tested 10 min later (as in earlier

**Table 7.4** Subject Mean Correct Familiarity Decision Latencies, Experiment 3.

| Prime Condition | Delay | Latencies (ms) |
|---|---|---|
| Unprimed | 10 minutes | 739 |
| Photo | 10 minutes | 612 |
| Cartoon | 10 minutes | 660 |
| Unprimed | 1 week | 712 |
| Photo | 1 week | 590 |
| Cartoon | 1 week | 670 |

experiments). The 10-min group therefore provides a further replication of half of experiments 1a and 1b. All subjects saw photographs in the test phase, following exposure to no prime, cartoon primes, or photographic primes.

**Results and Discussion** Overall accuracy in the test phase was 94 percent in this experiment (7 percent errors to familiar and 5 percent errors to unfamiliar faces for each of the immediate and delayed testing groups). A 2 (delay condition) × 3 (prime type) mixed design ANOVA was performed on the mean correct RTs, which are shown in table 7.4. This showed a main effect of prime type ($F(2,68) = 16.75, p < 0.001$) but no effects of delay condition or any interaction ($F$s $< 1$). Paired comparisons showed that mean RTs to faces primed by photographs were significantly quicker than to faces primed by cartoon ($t = 2.97, df = 68, p < 0.01$), which were in turn faster than RTs to unprimed faces ($t = 2.82, df = 68, p < 0.01$). The same pattern of significance was found in an items analysis, where six subjects contribute to the means for each item in each condition of the experiment. The items' ANOVA showed only a main effect of prime type ($F(2,34) = 11.75, p < 0.001$) and no interaction with delay ($F < 1$). Planned comparisons showed all three prime types to differ significantly from each other (photo versus cartoon primes, $t = 2.39$, $p < 0.02$).

The format effect is therefore not affected by a week's delay between prime and test. Indeed, the means in table 7.3 show that if anything, the trend is for the effect to increase rather than to decrease over time. The experiment also shows that the standard priming effect (same photograph versus unprimed condition) appears unaffected by an interval of 7 days between exposure and test. Previous work by Flude (1991) showed that priming over 12 weeks, while still highly significant, was slightly reduced compared with that seen at 5 min (unprimed-primed difference of 165 ms at 5 min compared with 81 ms at 12 weeks). Our experiment shows no decline over a 1-week period (122 ms versus 127 ms difference between photo-primed and unprimed conditions at 1 week and 10 min, respectively).

## 7.7 GENERAL DISCUSSION

If we accept that repetition priming is a sensitive tool with which to probe structural descriptions mediating recognition, then these experiments lead us to the conclusion that the features that mediate facial representations preserve very low-level properties of the images. Cartoons and the photographs from which they were derived share the same viewpoint and expression but differ in the way that these are depicted by a pattern of light and dark elements. Our results suggest that the fine details of this pattern of image intensities are preserved and must be reproduced for full priming.

If low-level image features are preserved, how low level are these? A problem with the materials that we used in the experiments reported here was that the slides of photographs were taken directly from the original photographs, while the slides of the cartoons were made from the prints that resulted from image processing. There was inevitably some difference in size of image between photographs and cartoons as a result. Did size changes between changed-format pairs contribute to the reduction in priming? To investigate, post hoc analysis of the data from experiment 3 compared priming in faces where the cartoon and photograph slides showed a clear size difference with priming where the slides were about the same size and found identical priming in each case. Moreover, in a new control experiment, we deliberately manipulated size, comparing photographs primed by same-sized images with those primed by images of half the size. There was no effect of varying size on priming (primed same size, 596 ms; primed different size, 599 ms; unprimed, 748 ms for familiarity decisions at test). This result is consistent with the findings of Biederman and Cooper (1992) and Cooper et al. (1992) reviewed in the introduction to this chapter.

The low-level features that are preserved must then arise at a level after size invariance has been achieved. Clearly our results are not consistent with the mediation of face recognition by structural primitives of the "geon" type, which might be specified by the spatial layout of "edge" features, suggesting that faces and objects may be represented rather differently for recognition (Biederman 1987). Moreover, our results show that repetition priming of face recognition is affected by a change in image features, and this clearly differs from results obtained with objects by Biederman and Cooper (1991). If this reflects a genuine difference in the nature of the representations used for face and (basic level) object recognition, we must predict that we should not get an effect of format change using pictures of objects, since both photographs and cartoons of objects will portray the same set of edge features, and hence "geons," to mediate recognition. This prediction is being investigated in our laboratory.

Our results with faces suggest that representational descriptions must preserve information about the gray levels of the images in a size-invariant format. What are the implications of this result for the IAC model? Clearly, the original IAC account of repetition priming (Burton, Bruce, and Johnston 1990), in terms of strengthening of connections between FRUs and PINs, alone cannot accommodate these data. In our introduction, we suggested a modification, to accommodate among other things the graded effects of view change on priming. In the suggested modification, links between feature units and FRUs are also strengthened as a result of face identification. However, this modification is also insufficient as an explanation of the format effect unless we can articulate in what way the features differ between photographs and cartoons of the type used in these experiments.

One promising approach to face encoding that could be consistent with these data involves principal components analysis (PCA) of facial images (Turk and Pentland 1991). Here the individual pixels of different face images are regarded as correlated measurements, and PCA is used to extract a set of significant axes to describe the space of facial variation. O'Toole et al. (1991) have demonstrated that such an account might provide a natural way to explain why faces of a different race are difficult to recognize, and in ongoing work they are investigating whether PCA can produce an account of distinctiveness effects in recognition memory. Since PCA (or some functionally equivalent implementation in the brain) operates on gray levels rather than abstracted features, the PCA description could differ between a cartoon and a photograph of the same face. The approach thus seems to have some potential as a psychologically plausible front end to the IAC model of face identification, which could provide an account of the current data.

However, because such a statistically based analysis is meaningless if face images have different scales or orientations (since the different pixels in different faces then bear no sensible relationship with each other), such systems require that the images are carefully normalized prior to their analysis. It is this prior standardization of the images that has allowed the problem of size and position invariance to be avoided in published work on automatic face recognition. The challenge for a model of human facial image processing is to specify how this can be achieved (Bruce, Burton, and Craw 1992). At present, it is not clear whether part-whole priming effects (Brunas, Young, and Ellis 1990; Brunas-Wagstaff, Young, and Ellis 1992) and the additive effects of distinctiveness and repetition could also arise naturally with a PCA front end to an IAC model of person identification.

Our suggestion is that the format effect reported here, along with other recent results we have obtained in studies of line drawings (Bruce et al. 1992), photographic negation (Bruce and Langton 1993), and lighting (Hill and Bruce 1993), motivate the development of an account of facial features as the principal components of variation in low-level image properties. Identification of a person from his or her face results in the strengthening of all links on the path to that identification, to include links between feature units and FRUs as well as between FRUs and PINs. The suggested mechanism for effects of change in view, or format, on repetition priming does not create any inconsistency with the observation that repetition priming is not found when tasks such as sex or expression judgment are repeated, since it is only familiarity decisions, taken at PIN level, that will be speeded by the strengthening of links earlier on in this route within the identification system.

Although we believe this may be a fruitful direction for further development of the IAC model, we are left with some unsolved problems about repetition priming. Why does it survive for 3 months if it arises from simple strengthening of connections between the analyzed patterns and more abstract identity nodes? It seems difficult to avoid the necessity of an additional episodic or contextual component contributing to the weight-adjustment process. The problem is that the effect of format change could itself operate at this level. People know when they are looking at faces or cartoons, and a further experiment in our laboratory has shown that they are at ceiling if tested on their explicit memory for whether the faces were earlier shown in the same or a different format. But if we must postulate a contextual component and if aspects of the depicted view yield associations that form part of context, how can we use the priming paradigm to explore structural representations of faces? In current work, we are adapting the paradigm of Schacter and colleagues in order to study whether we can observe clear dissociations between factors that affect repetition priming and those affecting episodic memory for faces, in an attempt to clarify the contributions of pattern identification and contextual association processes in repetition priming of faces.

This issue brings us back to the theme of this book: that of conscious versus nonconscious information processing. It has been assumed by many, and supported by considerable work, much of it reviewed elsewhere in this book, that repetition priming results from learning or memory processes that are implicit or automatic in nature. The contrast is with episodic memory processes that are explicit or intentional in nature. Certainly, repetition priming effects do not appear to reflect any deliberate, explicit, or conscious attempts to remember information, since the effects are not influenced by certain factors (e.g., presentation time) that should influence explicit episodic memory. Nevertheless, the nature of the effects observed in the literature on face identification make it difficult to rule out contributions from episodic or contextual influences on repetition priming, and therefore it is not clear to us that priming is a straightforward tool to probe structural representations uncontaminated by such influences. In our own work we will continue to use priming alongside other methods to investigate how faces are represented for recognition.

## NOTE

The experimental work described in this chapter has been supported by grants from the Science and Engineering Research Council (SERC) (Image Interpretation Initiative: GR/F 33698) and Economic and Social Research Council (ESRC) (R000 23 2898). Ian Craw has made invaluable contributions to our thinking by pointing out the potential, and limitations, of principal components analysis for facial image processing. Andy Young, Andy Ellis, and Brenda Flude have all contributed to our thinking about repetition priming.

## REFERENCES

Biederman, I. (1987). Recognition by components: A theory of human image understanding. *Psychological Review, 94*, 115–145.

Biederman, I., and Cooper, E. E. (1991). Priming contour-deleted images: Evidence for intermediate representations in visual object recognition. *Cognitive Psychology, 23*, 393–419.

Biederman, I., and Cooper, E. E. (1992). Size invariance in visual object priming. *JEP: Human Perception and Performance, 18*, 121–133.

Bruce, V. (1982). Changing faces: Visual and nonvisual coding processes in face recognition. *British Journal of Psychology, 73,* 105–116.

Bruce, V. (1983). Recognising faces. *Philosophical Transactions of the Royal Society of London, B302,* 423–436.

Bruce, V. (1986). Recognising familiar faces. In H. D. Ellis, M. A. Jeeves, F. Newcombe, and A. Young (Eds.), *Aspects of face processing,* 107–117. Dordrecht: Martinus Nijhoff.

Bruce, V. (1988). *Recognising faces.* London: Erlbaum.

Bruce, V., Burton, A. M., and Craw, I. (1992). Modelling face recognition. *Philosophical Transactions of the Royal Society, B335,* 121–128.

Bruce, V., Dench, N., and Burton, A. M. (1993). Effects of distinctiveness, semantic priming and repetition on the recognition of face familiarity. *Canadian Journal of Experimental Psychology, 47,* 38–60.

Bruce, V., and Langton, S. (1993). The use of pigmentation and shading information in recognizing the sex and identities of faces. Submitted.

Bruce, V., Hanna, E., Dench, N., Healey, P., and Burton, M. (1992). The importance of "mass" in line-drawings of faces. *Applied Cognitive Psychology, 6,* 619–628.

Bruce, V., and Valentine, T. (1985). Identity priming in the recognition of familiar faces. British *Journal of Psychology, 76,* 363–383.

Bruce, V., and Valentine, T. (1986). Semantic priming of familiar faces. *Quarterly Journal of Experimental Psychology, 38A,* 125–150.

Bruce, V., and Young, A. (1986). Understanding face recognition. *British Journal of Psychology, 77,* 305–327.

Brunas, J., Young, A. W., and Ellis, A. W. (1990). Repetition priming from incomplete faces: Evidence for part to whole completion. *British Journal of Psychology, 81,* 43–56.

Brunas-Wagstaff, J., Young, A. W., and Ellis, A. W. (1992). Repetition priming follows spontaneous but not prompted recognition of familiar faces. *Quarterly Journal of Experimental Psychology, 44A,* 423–454.

Burton, A. M. (1992). Learning in an IAC model of face recognition: How to live without distributed representations. Paper presented to the Experimental Psychology Society, July.

Burton, A. M., and Bruce, V. (1992). I recognise your face but I can't remember your name: A simple explanation? *British Journal of Psychology, 83,* 45–60.

Burton, A. M., Bruce, V., and Johnston, R.A. (1990). Understanding face recognition with an interactive activation model. *British Journal of Psychology, 81,* 361–380.

Burton, A. M., Young, A. W., Bruce, V., Johnston, R. A. and Ellis, A. W. (1991). Understanding covert recognition. *Cognition, 39,* 129–166.

Cooper, L. A., Schacter, D. L, Ballesteros, S., and Moore, C. (1992). Priming and recognition of transformed three-dimensional objects: Effects of size and reflection. *Journal of Experimental Psychology: Learning, Memory and Cognition, 18,* 43–57.

Dannenbring, G. L., and Briand, K. (1982). Semantic priming and the word repetition effect in a lexical decision task. *Canadian Journal of Psychology, 36,* 435–444.

Davies, G. M., Ellis, H. D., and Shepherd, J. W. (1978). Face recognition accuracy as a function of mode of representation. *Journal of Applied Psychology, 63,* 180–187.

Ellis, A. W. (1992). Cognitive mechanisms of face processing. *Philosophical Transactions of the Royal Society, B335,* 113–119.

Ellis, A. W., Young, A. W., and Flude, B. M. (1990). Repetition priming and face processing: Priming occurs within the system that responds to the identity of a face. *Quarterly Journal of Experimental Psychology, 42A*, 495–512.

Ellis, A. W., Young, A. W., Flude, B. M., and Hay, D. C. (1987). Repetition priming of face recognition. *Quarterly Journal of Experimental Psychology, 39A*, 193–210.

Flude, B. (1991). Long-term repetition priming of faces. Paper presented at the International Conference on Memory, University of Lancaster, July.

Hay, D. C., and Young, A. W. (1982). The human face. In A. W. Ellis (Ed.), *Normality and pathology in cognitive functions*, 173–202. London: Academic Press.

Hill, H., and Bruce, V. (1993). An investigation into the effects of lighting and viewpoint on face processing with the use of a simultaneous matching task. *Perception, 22* (Supp), 22–23.

Kohonen, T., Oja, E., and Lehtio, P. (1981). Storage and processing of information in distributed associative memory systems. In G. Hinton and J. A. Anderson (Eds.), *Parallel models of associative memory*. Hillsdale, NJ: Erlbaum.

Marr, D., and Nishihara, H. K. (1978). Representation and recognition of the spatial organisation of three-dimensional shapes. *Proceedings of the Royal Society of London, Series B200*, 269–294.

McClelland, J. L., and Rumelhart, D. E. (1985). Distributed memory and the representation of general and specific information. *Journal of Experimental Psychology: General, 114*, 159–188.

Monsell, S. (1985). Repetition and the lexicon. In A. W. Ellis (Ed.), *Progress in the psychology of language*, vol 2, London: Erlbaum.

O'Toole, A. J., Deffenbacher, K., Abdi, H., and Bartlett, J. C. (1991). Simulating the "other-race effect" as a problem in perceptual learning. *Connection Science, 3*, 163–178.

Pearson, D. E. (1992). The extraction and use of facial features in low bit-rate visual communication. *Philosophical Transactions of the Royal Society of London, B335*, 79–85.

Pearson, D. E., and Robinson, J. A. (1985). Visual communication at very low data rates. *Proceedings of the IEEE, 73*, 795–811.

Perrett, D. I. P., Hietanen, J. K., Oram, M. W., and Benson, P. J. (1992). Organization and functions of cells responsive to faces in the temporal cortex. *Philosophical Transactions of the Royal Society of London, B335*, 23–30.

Rhodes, G., Brennan, S., and Carey, S. (1987). Recognition and ratings of caricatures: Implications for mental representations of faces. *Cognitive Psychology, 19*, 473–497.

Roberts, A. D. (1991). *Investigating the early stages of face perception with speeded classification tasks.* Unpublished doctoral dissertation, University of Nottingham.

Scarborough, D. L., Cortese, C., and Scarborough, H. L. (1977). Frequency and repetition effects in lexical memory. *Journal of Experimental Psychology: Human Perception and Performance, 3*, 1–17.

Schacter, D. L., Cooper, L. A., and Delaney, S. M. (1990). Implicit memory for unfamiliar objects depends on access to structural descriptions. *Journal of Experimental Psychology: General, 119*, 5–24.

Schacter, D. L., Cooper, L. A., Delaney, S. M., Peterson, M. A., and Tharan, M. (1991). Implicit memory for possible and impossible objects: Constraints on the construction of structural descriptions. *Journal of Experimental Psychology: Learning, Memory and Cognition, 17*, 3–19.

Turk, M., and Pentland, A. (1991). Eigenfaces for recognition. *Journal of Cognitive Neuroscience, 3*, 71–86.

Valentine, T., and Bruce, V. (1986a). Recognising familiar faces: The role of distinctiveness and familiarity. *Canadian Journal of Psychology, 40*, 300–305.

Valentine, T., and Bruce, V. (1986b). The effects of distinctiveness in recognising and classifying faces. *Perception, 15,* 525–536.

Warren, C., and Morton, J. (1982). The effects of priming on picture recognition. *British Journal of Psychology, 73,* 117–129.

Yarmey, A. D. (1973). I recognise your face but I can't remember your name: Further evidence on the tip-of-the-tongue phenomenon. *Memory and Cognition, 1,* 287–290.

Young, A. W., and Bruce, V. (1991). Perceptual categories and the computation of grandmother. *European Journal of Cognitive Psychology, 3,* 5–49.

Young, A. W., Hay, D. C., and Ellis, A. W. (1985). The faces that launched a thousand slips: Everyday difficulties and errors in recognising people. *British Journal of Psychology, 76,* 495–523.

Young, A. W., Hellawell, D., and de Haan, E. H. F. (1988). Cross-domain semantic priming in normal subjects and a prosopagnosic patient. *Quarterly Journal of Experimental Psychology, 40A,* 561–580.

# 8 Structural and Functional Organization of Knowledge about Faces and Proper Names: A Positron Emission Tomography Study

Justine Sergent, Brennan MacDonald, and Eric Zuck

ABSTRACT   The idea that the brain is organized into distinct areas of relative functional autonomy is a fundamental principle of cognitive neuroscience. It implies that the brain realizes its functions by the conjoint activation of several of its component structures, each performing specific operations. Although one may a posteriori uncover part of the rules that govern this principle in particular instances, the actual logic of the functional organization of the brain still eludes us. For instance, if one were to ask whether the same cognitive task, performed on different stimuli but involving the same mental operations with the same underlying processes leading to the same information, engages the same structures of the brain, the answer would, a priori, be affirmative. More specifically, this study used positron emission tomography (PET) measurement of rCBF to examine the participation of cerebral structures in three types of tasks, each carried out both on faces and on names of individuals. The purpose was to uncover whether the processing of faces and of proper names unfolds in a similar, or parallel, manner in the brain or whether distinct cerebral structures, and asymmetric pathways, are recruited in these identical tasks. The processing of faces essentially engaged the ventro-medial cortex of the right hemisphere, unfolding in a postero-anterior progression from the gender categorization to the familiarity decision to the semantic categorization. On the other hand, the processing of proper names resulted essentially in the activation of the lateral cortex of the left hemisphere. As expected, different hemispheres were engaged in the processing of faces and of names. Less expected was the asymmetric organization of the cerebral structures sustaining similar functions with respect to the processing of information about individuals. Still less expected was the absence of overlap in the cerebral activation associated with the name and the face semantic tasks, as it suggests that the same information must be stored in different formats and distinct regions of the brain. Comparison with an earlier PET study on face processing also indicated that the rate of stimulus presentation during an activation condition significantly influences the pattern of cerebral blood flow and, therefore, the validity of the inferences one makes about the neurofunctional organization of a given cognitive function.

## 8.1   INTRODUCTION

Evidence from cognitive psychology and neuropsychology suggests that the recognition of faces involves a series of operations that must necessarily be performed for recognition to be successful (Ellis 1992). The most explicit description of this series of operations was proposed by Bruce and Young (1986), and it comprises four main stages: (1) a structural encoding of the face's appearance that highlights the physical information that makes a face unique and conveys cues about properties of the bearer of the face (e.g., gender, age, emotion); (2) the activation of a long-standing visual representation of the face, whereby it can be seen as familiar or not depending on whether a match occurs between the perceived face and one of the stored visual representations; (3) access to semantic information associated with the person and stored in long-term memory, without which a face would remain that of a stranger; and (4) retrieval of the person's name. Support for such a model comes from laboratory studies of normal subjects (Brennen et al. 1990; Ellis, Young, and Critchley 1987; Young et al. 1986), from naturally occurring failures of face recognition by normal subjects (Young, Hay, and Ellis 1985), and from the patterns of deficits displayed by prosopagnosic and other brain-damaged patients with difficulties in face recognition (Damasio, Tranel, and Damasio 1990; De Haan, Young, and Newcombe 1987; Sergent and Poncet 1990; Sergent and Signoret 1992b; Young 1992).

The validity of this model has received further confirmation from anatomo-functional studies of prosopagnosic patients (Sergent and Signoret 1992a) and of normal subjects performing a variety of face processing tasks during positron emission tomography (PET) measurement of regional cerebral blood flow (rCBF) (Sergent, Ohta, and MacDonald 1992). Thus, the examination of prosopagnosic patients has revealed that the disturbance of one of the operations underlying the recognition of faces is sufficient to disable the entire face recognition system and that the qualitative nature of the deficit varies as a function of the location of the cerebral damage responsible for prosopagnosia. Such findings concur with the view that the different mental operations that comprise the face recognition system are realized by distinct cerebral structures, and they are consistent with an essentially hierarchical unfolding of the processes involved in the recognition of faces. Similarly, the patterns of cerebral activation identified in PET studies of normal subjects performing face recognition tasks suggest a caudo-rostral recruitment of cortical structures participating in the recognition of faces. Together, these findings offer converging evidence in support of the framework devised by Bruce and Young (1986) and provide their functional model with relevant neurobiological foundations.

There is some evidence regarding the neural substrates of two of the main categories of operations involved in face recognition. One concerns the structural encoding of facial representations, and there are reasons to believe that the lingual and fusiform gyri of the right hemisphere play an essential role in these operations. Destruction of these areas are sufficient to produce prosopagnosia, and the deficits displayed by patients with damage in this ventral part of the posterior cortex are characterized by a failure to perform perceptual operations on facial representations. That is, the impairment is not merely one of face recognition but one of face processing; even information that may normally be visually derived (e.g., gender, age, emotion), irrespective of identity, can no longer be accessed (Sergent and Signoret 1992b). It is noteworthy that such a severe perceptual deficit at the structural encoding level does not necessarily extend to other visually complex stimuli and can be selective to faces. For instance, a patient (R. M.; Sergent and Signoret 1992b) who was unable to tell whether two simultaneously presented identical views of a face

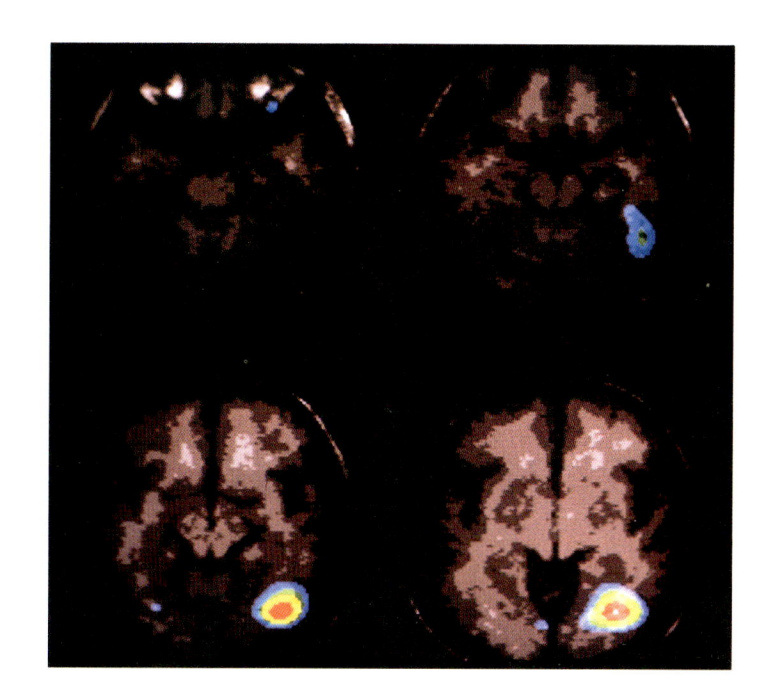

A

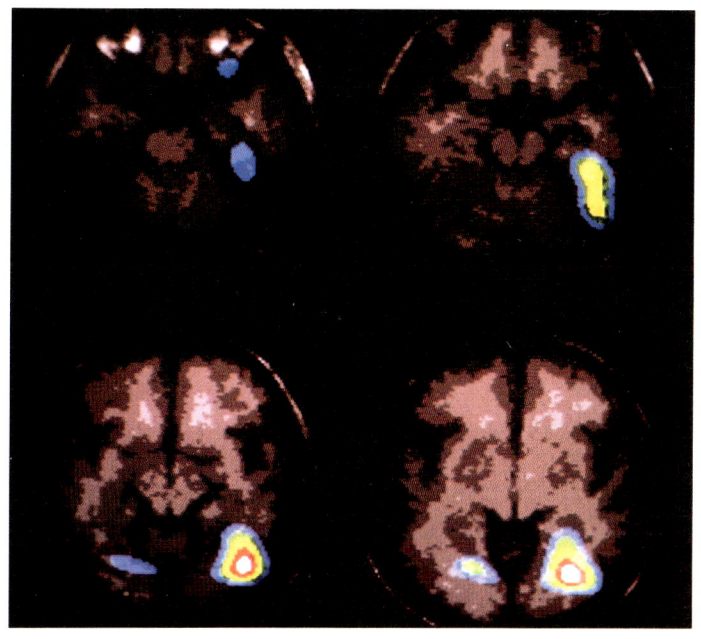

B

C

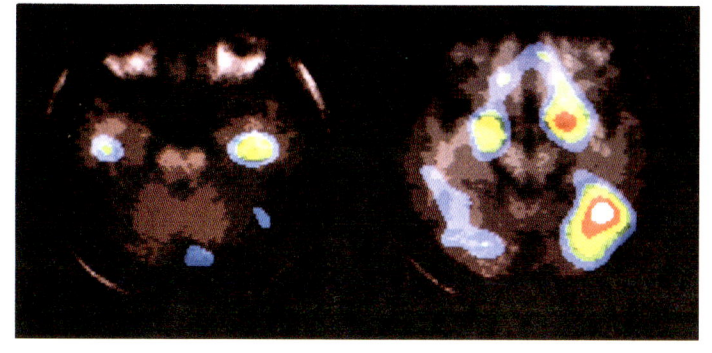

*(caption overleaf)*

**Figure 8.1** Foci of activation in the face conditions, superimposed on structural images of the brain in the horizontal plane. These foci were obtained by subtracting from each of the face conditions the activation associated with the name gender categorization condition. (a) Activation in the face-gender categorization task: The top left slice represents the more ventral part of the brain, and the next slices are 6 mm up; the two bottom slices indicate activation in the right lingual gyrus and the posterior part of the fusiform gyrus but not more anteriorly. (b) Activation in the familiarity decision task: The same slices as in (a) are shown, and the activation is more intense in the right fusiform gyrus and extends into the posterior part of the parahippocampal gyrus. (c) Activation in the professional categorization task: The two slices correspond to the two top slices of (a) and (b). They illustrate a strong activation of the right fusiform gyrus and of the right parahippocampal gyrus.

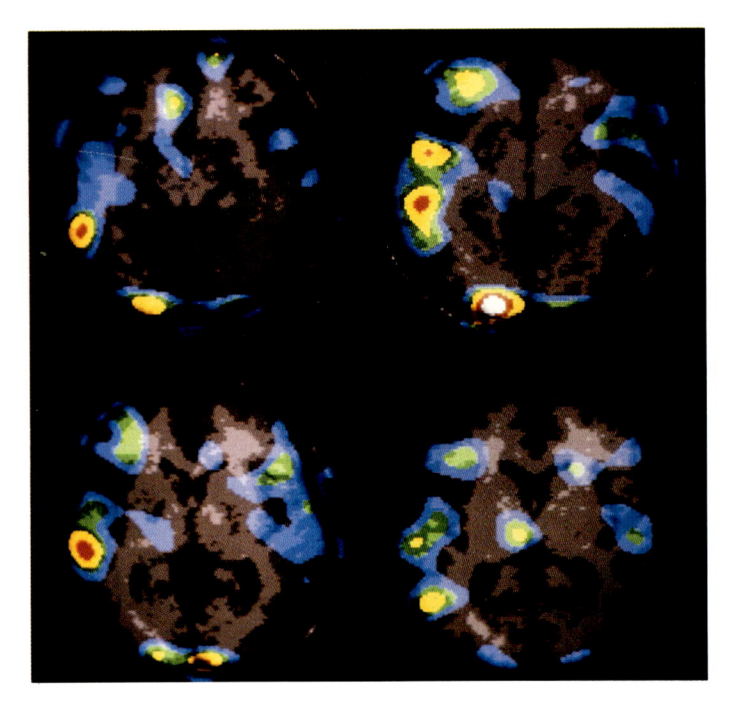

**Figure 8.2** Foci of activation in the name-professional categorization, superimposed on structural images of the brain, after subtracting the face-professional categorization task The images correspond to slices at −10 mm to +8 mm on the ventrodorsal axis, the top right slice illustrates the engagement of the left occipital, temporal, and frontal lobes; the activation in the left posterior part of the bottom right slice shows corresponds to the angular gyrus.

were the same or different could identify more cars by name, make, and year of fabrication than any normal subjects so far tested on such a task involving the presentation of 210 cars. There is, therefore, some support to the idea that the structural encoding stage leading to face recognition may be specific to faces and may be selectively disrupted after damage to the lingual and fusiform gyri of the right hemisphere.

Data from normal subjects concur with this localization of the structural encoding stage. Any task that calls for the processing of specific properties of faces (gender, professional category, identity) produces activation of the lingual gyrus and at least the posterior part of the fusiform gyrus of the right hemisphere (Sergent, Ohta, and MacDonald 1992). By contrast, a face discrimination task, similar to that involved in Benton's test (Benton et al. 1983), does not engage these areas and instead recruits the lateral occipital cortex of both hemispheres (Haxby et al. 1991), suggesting that face discrimination and face recognition rely on different cerebral structures and are dissociable. Indeed, some prosopagnosic patients perform Benton's Face Recognition Test as well as matched controls do (Benton and Van Allen 1972; Sergent and Poncet 1990).

The second category of operations involved in face recognition whose neural substrates have been localized with some certainty concerns the access to semantic information related to a perceived face and without which a face cannot be identified. Such access to semantic information appears to require the engagement of the parahippocampal gyrus of the right hemisphere. This is an area that is either destroyed or disconnected in prosopagnosic patients who display little, if any, perceptual impairment and whose lingual and fusiform gyri are intact (McCarthy and Warrington 1990; Sergent and Signoret 1992a). Support for such a localization comes from PET findings (Sergent, Ohta, and MacDonald 1992) that show intense activation of this area only when the task cannot be performed without accessing some biographical information related to the individual whose face is presented. Further activation of the more anterior region of the temporal lobe has been detected in face identification tasks in both the right and the left hemispheres, but the actual function of this cerebral region cannot yet be unequivocally determined on the sole basis of PET data. One may assume that the anterior regions of the temporal lobe are part of a system that serves as a depository of biographical information, some of which must be reactivated in order to access specific semantic properties related to a perceived known face (Damasio, Tranel, and Damasio 1990).

Although our understanding of the neurobiological substrates of face recognition has progressed significantly, much remains to be done to specify better the neural network underlying this function. This study is an attempt to contribute to such an understanding. One purpose is to replicate the earlier PET findings about the structural encoding and the access to semantic information in order to obtain assurance of their validity and robustness. A second purpose is to gather new data regarding other stages of face recognition not yet examined in normal subjects: the reactivation of the long-standing visual representations of faces, by which a perceived face is seen as familiar or unfamiliar, and access to semantic knowledge from an individual's name and, therefore, the storage of the person's name.

How new faces are learned, under what format such known faces are stored, what processes underlie a familiarity decision at the view of a known face, and what cerebral structures sustain such processes are questions whose answers are essential to the understanding of the cognitive and neural architecture of face recognition, but several problems have made it hard to address such questions effectively. One main reason is probably that there is no dissociation between the failure to make a familiarity decision and the inability to identify faces in prosopagnosic patients. These two deficits constitute the very core of the prosopagnosic disturbance, and, despite the diversity of lesion sites responsible for prosopagnosia and the variety of cognitive breakdowns across patients, familiarity decision and identification are always conjointly disrupted. However, there are at least two patients who have been described in the literature as being able to discriminate between familiar and unfamiliar persons but unable to identify these persons (de Haan, Young, and Newcombe 1991; Warrington and McCarthy 1988), suggesting that familiarity decision and identification are dissociable. However, the face recognition deficit of these patients was only one of their impairments (they were not strictly prosopagnosics, and their deficit in recognizing faces was part of large memory impairment), and it resulted from diffuse brain damage that made it impossible to establish precise correlations between structural injury and functional deficit.

One paradox associated with the study of the visual representations of faces and the familiarity decision in prosopagnosic patients is that much of what is known about these issues comes from studies of implicit memory. For instance, patient P.H. (de Haan, Young, and Newcombe 1987) was able to match familiar faces faster than unfamiliar ones, although he was unable to tell which faces were familiar and which were not. Similarly, patient P.V. (Sergent and Poncet 1990) and patient P.C. (Sergent and Signoret 1992c) were more accurate at matching two faces shown at different ages when the faces were familiar than when they were unfamiliar, yet they too were unable to tell which were familiar to them. In none of these patients did the cerebral lesion invade the lingual and fusiform gyri of the right hemisphere, but it affected the parahippocampal gyrus. In contrast, the performance of two other patients (P.M. and R.M.; Sergent and Signoret 1992c), whose lesion destroyed the lingual and fusiform gyri, was not influenced by the familiarity of the faces (that is, no covert access to the representations of known faces could be demonstrated). These patterns of results thus indicate that the stored representations of known faces were not destroyed in the first three patients; performance was facilitated by the presentation of known faces in the same way as it was in normal subjects. Yet these preserved representations were of no use to the subjects in their daily activity because even the faces of their close relatives looked like those of strangers to them. Thus, it is not sufficient that a stored representation of a known face be reactivated for that face to be perceived as being familiar, and there must be other information, normally connected to these representations, that too must be activated for a sense of familiarity to be experienced. The nature of such information may not be easily identified, however. It may be any type of specific information (episodic, semantic, emotional) that would signal that the perceived face has already been encountered, or no specific information as such may have to be reactivated; it might be sufficient that connections exist between the ensemble of neurons coding the representation of a particular face and other parts of the brain. The latter explanation, however, may be purely academic; there may be no circumstances under which one would have only to make a familiarity decision without recalling any information about the individual.

On the basis of anatomical data and cognitive deficits of prosopagnosics, one may suggest that the lingual or fusiform gyri, or both, are essential not only for the structural encoding but also for representing and storing descriptions of known faces. Such descriptions would be purely visual; they would not carry with them any information about earlier occurrence as such, let alone identity, but would covertly facilitate perceptual processing by virtue of previous firing of the ensemble of neurons conjointly activated by the particular configuration unique to specific faces. A familiarity decision, therefore, would require the integrity of these longstanding facial representations but would not take place at this level as such and would depend on the activation of a minimum of biographical information from signals received from these representations. Under such a scheme, then, a familiarity decision would require the engagement of the parahippocampal gyrus and would result from the reactivation of any pertinent memory associated with this face.

A second main issue addressed in this study concerns the processing of proper names in an attempt to identify the differences in the neurofunctional organization of the cerebral structures underlying face and name processing. For this purpose, identical tasks were designed for the two categories of stimuli: gender categorization, familiarity decision, and professional categorization. There is ample evidence that the processing of names and of faces engages distinct cerebral structures, can be impaired independently (Hécaen and Albert 1978; McCarthy and Warrington 1990), and calls for the dominant participation of the left and the right hemisphere, respectively. Two main questions related to name processing are examined in this study. One concerns the extent to which the same processes, applied to different categories of stimuli engaging different hemispheres, unfold in a similar way. For instance, is the left ventral posterior cortex involved in the initial perceptual analysis of words in the same way as the homotopic region of the right hemisphere is in the perceptual analysis of faces? Does the left parahippocampal gyrus play the same pivotal role in reactivating semantic information associated with names as the right parahippocampal gyrus does with faces? The second question bears on whether the same biographic information is accessed after prompting by a name or a face. For instance, is the semantic information required to perform a professional categorization task activated in the same cerebral regions after stimulation by names or by faces, or is such information stored in distinct cerebral areas?

These questions are examined through PET measurement of rCBF in normal subjects, using six activation conditions and one control fixation condition. In addition to the recording of rCBF, the subjects' reaction time and accuracy of responses were recorded so as to obtain relevant information ensuring that each subject was actually performing the required task without too many errors. Two of the activation conditions were identical to those already examined in an earlier PET study (Sergent, Ohta, and Macdonald 1992). There is evidence that the rate of stimulus presentation is a critical variable in the level and pattern of rCBF during activation studies. This has been reported by Fox and Raichle (1985), who examined rCBF in visual sensory areas and found significant differences in amplitude and pattern of activation as a result of changes in the rate of stimulus presentation.

This raises important questions regarding the reliability of PET activation studies. One may expect that the effects of such changes in presentation rates are not restricted to sensory aspects of processing but extend to higher-order cognitive operations. Indeed, whereas initial sensory processing is relatively constrained in terms of cortical structures likely to be activated, cognitive processing requirements can engage a much larger variety of cerebral structures. The possibility that presentation rate could be an important variable to take into account is supported by findings from lateral tachistoscopic studies showing variations in patterns of hemisphere functional asymmetry as a result of changes in exposure duration (Sergent and Hellige 1986). That is, apparently trivial factors were found to have a significant influence on the respective involvement or contribution of the cerebral hemispheres in cognitive tasks, and there is no reason to believe that PET activation studies would be immune to such an influence. Thus, in this study, a presentation rate of one stimulus every 2 seconds (instead of every 3 seconds, resulting in the presentation of thirty instead of twenty stimuli during a scanning session) was used. One additional potential problem with a shorter presentation rate is its implications for the actual processing of the stimuli because less time is devoted to the required operations.

Another methodological issue will come up during the interpretation of the results. As argued and demonstrated by Sergent et al. (1992), the processing of familiar stimuli is usually automatic and unstoppable, and it unfolds in an obligatory manner without necessarily terminating at the requested stage. For instance, when subjects are asked to perform a face familiarity decision, they may not terminate processing at such a stage and may, in fact, automatically proceed to the recognition of the face. This is not a major problem in a reaction time study in which responses are measured at each trial. A decision can then be made at the familiarity stage, which precedes the recognition stage, resulting in latencies being shorter for the familiarity than for the recognition decision. In a PET activation study, however, the cerebral blood flow is being continuously recorded on line, and the counts of emitted positrons accumulate over a period of time (e.g., 60 sec), such that every mental operation performed by the subject during scanning (those inherent in the task but also those not requested in the particular task) will contribute to the final count of the radioactive tracer in each of the scanned cerebral regions of interest. It is impossible to determine from such information which part of the activation was due to the familiarity decision as such and which part can be attributed to the recognition of the face.

## 8.2 METHODS

**Subjects**

Eight students, half of each gender between 21 and 26 years of age, participated in the experiment. They were in good health, under no medication, and had no neurological or psychiatric disorders. They were right-handed, as assessed with Bryden's (1982) questionnaire, with no left-handers among their close relatives, and they had normal visual acuity and contrast sensitivity. They were fully informed of the risks associated with exposure to radioactive material, in accordance with the regulations of the Medical Research Council of Canada and the Control Board of Atomic Energy of Canada, and they read and signed consent forms for their participation. Each was remunerated $100.

**Procedures and Equipment**

The experiment comprised four phases, described in the order they took place.

**Preparatory Phase**  This phase consisted of introducing the subjects to the experiment, explaining the risks, obtaining their formal consent, testing their handedness and vision, and preparing them to the experimental tasks in order to lessen potential anxiety and to reduce hesitations during the experiment proper. Each experimental task was explained and run, in conditions identical to those prevailing in the PET study, except that different stimuli were used. The subjects were also requested to fill in a questionnaire containing a list of 250 names of famous persons and to indicate whether the name was familiar, and, if so, whether they could image a representation of the corresponding face and how clear this representation was. The faces used in the familiarity and professional categorization conditions of the PET study were selected from this list for each subject, using names that were familiar and whose corresponding faces the subjects were able to "image" mentally.

**PET Experiment**  The second phase was the PET study, which took place the day following the preparatory phase and consisted of measuring rCBF in seven different conditions run at fifteen-min intervals, with a different order of conditions for each subject. The stimuli were presented on a high-resolution Mitsubishi monitor, driven by a PS/2 IBM computer, in total darkness. The computer also controlled the duration of stimulus presentation (1 sec) and the interstimulus interval (2 sec) and recorded the speed and accuracy of the subject's responses. The monitor was located above the subject's abdomen, at 85 cm from the eyes, and was oriented obliquely so that the screen was perpendicular to the subject's line of gaze. The stimuli appeared in the center of the screen, and their size (8 degrees in height and 6 degrees in width for the faces, and an average of 1 degree in height and width for each letter of the words) and luminance were constant across conditions within each stimulus category. In each condition, forty stimuli were presented (ten more than required for the 60-sec scanning), except for a fixation condition.

The subjects were in a supine position, the head firmly held in a customized frame containing rapidly hardening self-inflating foamlike material, and located in the center of the tomograph scanner. Ears were occluded with wax, and an intravenous catheter was placed into the left brachial vein for injection of $H_2^{15}O$ (34 mCi per injection), which served as cerebral blood flow tracer. In each experimental condition, stimulus presentation started conjointly with the injection of the radioactive solution, and the recording of the emission of positrons began 15 sec later and lasted for 60 sec. In six conditions, the subjects responded by pressing, with the index or middle finger of the right hand, one of two buttons of the computer mouse, which was placed on their abdomen.

The study comprised three control conditions and four experimental conditions.

1. Fixation: The subject looked at a fixation point located in the center of the screen and was required to concentrate on this point. The illuminated area of the screen was of the same size and average luminance as the faces and objects presented in the other conditions.

2. Face gender discrimination: The stimuli were black-and-white faces of individuals unfamiliar to the subjects, half of each gender. They appeared one at a time, and the subjects had to categorize each one as male or female by pressing one of the two buttons.

3. Name gender discrimination: The stimuli were first names, half masculine and half feminine. On each trial, each name was presented above and below the fixation point simultaneously. This was done for consistency across conditions because the other two name conditions involved the presentation of first and last names. The subjects had to categorize the name by pressing one of the two buttons.

4. Face familiarity decision: The stimuli were black-and-white faces of both genders, half of which represented well-known persons and the other half persons unknown to the subjects. The task consisted of categorizing the faces as familiar or unfamiliar and of responding by pressing one of the two buttons.

5. Name familiarity decision: The stimuli were first and last names of actual individuals, half of whom were well known to subjects (celebrities) and the other half were unknown. The first name appeared above the fixation point and the last name appeared below the fixation point.

6. Face professional categorization: The stimuli were black-and-white faces of famous persons, drawn from the list presented to the subject the day before, and they were therefore all known by the subjects. Half the faces were of actors, and half were of other professional categories (politicians, sportsmen, news personalities, singers), and the subjects' task was to decide whether a face was that of an actor and to press one of the two buttons accordingly.

7. Name professional categorization: The stimuli were first and last names of famous persons known to the subjects as established the day before (the selected names were different from those whose faces were presented in the preceding conditions). Half the names were of actors, and the other half were of persons from other professional categories (politicians, sports, figures, news personalities, singers). The subjects' task was to decide whether the name was that of an actor and to press one of the two buttons to indicate the response.

The face categorization does not require identification of the individual; however, such a categorization cannot be performed unless the face is actually recognized (Sergent 1985), and, as such, it can be considered as involving the same processes as those inherent in face identification, except for the retrieval of the name. In all conditions, and particularly in conditions 4–7, the subject was specifically instructed not to name the faces, to vocalize the names, explicitly or implicitly, or attempt to retrieve their names in the case of face presentation. In addition, as already done in an earlier study (Sergent et al. 1992), the subjects had to place their tongue between their teeth during each of the 1-min duration of the scanning to prevent them from uttering the names. However, after the preparatory phase, the PET experiment, and the subsequent divided visual-field study, all the subjects commented that they had been unable to refrain from thinking of the names of the famous faces, but they indicated that they had not attempted to vocalize the names.

**Divided Visual Field Study**  The third phase took place 2 to 4 weeks after the PET study. It consisted of a divided visual field experiment using the same conditions and stimuli as in the PET study, without PET scanning and with two main differences: only conditions 2–7 were tested (the three face and the three name conditions), and the stimuli were presented twice—once in each visual field at an eccentricity of 5 degrees of visual angle, resulting in the presentation of eighty stimuli in each condition.

To ensure as much similarity of stimulus presentation in this and the PET experiments, the same monitor, computer, stimulus duration, and interstimulus interval were used in the two studies. Because of the lateral presentation, the size of the stimuli was reduced by half; however, to keep the actual visual angle of the stimuli the same in the two studies, the subjects viewed the stimuli from half the distance used in the PET experiment (43 cm). In addition, the stimuli were presented for 1 sec as in the PET study. This made it necessary to control for eye fixation in the center of the screen in order to ensure that the laterally presented stimuli would effectively be projected to the contralateral hemisphere. This was achieved on line with an Applied Science Laboratories (Model 1994B) Eye-View-Monitor system using corneal reflection to determine the locus of fixation. Before the experiment, central fixation was established for each subject, and the digital coordinates of central eye position were entered in the computer. During the experiment, eye position was sampled every 16.7 ms. Stimulus presentation required five consecutive samples of accurate eye position before being triggered, and any departure from central fixation by more than 0.5 degree would delay stimulus presentation. In addition, during the 1 sec of exposure, deviation of the eyes by more than 0.5 degree would interrupt the presentation of the stimulus, in which case that trial was discarded. This procedure guaranteed that initial stimulation was projected to the contralateral hemisphere. Subjects were accurate in maintaining central fixation, and less than 1 percent of the trials had to be discarded because of eye deviation from the center.

**MRI Study**  The final phase took place directly after the laterality study. It consisted of a magnetic resonance imaging (MRI) scan of each subject's brain, with a Philips Gyroscan (1.5 Tesla), using the same head holder and the same orientation of the head as for the PET scan.

**Scanning and Analyses**

PET scanning was performed by measuring rCBF using the intravenous oxygen-15 water bolus technique (Raichle, Martin, Herscovitch, Minturn, and Markham 1983) and a Scanditronix PC-2048 PET scanner with in-plane and spatial resolutions of 5- to 6-mm full width at half maximum. Fifteen slices with a center-to-center distance of 6.8 mm were simultaneously imaged, which could be further divided by bilinear interpolation to produce eighty transaxial slices. A rotating germanium-68 source was used to correct the images for attenuation of the gamma rays in the skull and brain tissue. The image planes were chosen parallel to the subject's glabella-inion line, which was aligned with the tomograph's laser reference line and transcribed onto the head holder as a marker for the correlation of PET and MRI. The MR images were obtained at the same fifteen planes as in the PET study. Slice registration was ensured using a thin $CuSO_4$-filled (5-mm) catheter attached to the side of the customized head holder, and visible in an MR image, coincident with the reference line identifying the PET scan reference plane (Evans et al. 1989).

The PET activation functional images were mapped onto the MR structural images using a PIXAR three-dimensional (3-D) computer and landmark-matching software (Evans et al. 1989). Interactive 3-D image software was used to establish an orthogonal coordinate frame based on the anterior commissure-posterior commissure (AC-PC) line as identified in the MR image volume. These coordinates were used to apply a linear resampling of each matched pair of MRI and PET data sets into a standardized stereotactic coordinate system (Talairach and Tournoux 1988). This mapping of PET data on MR images was performed for each subject and each condition separately before averaging group data, and anatomical landmarks were used to resample each data set into a standardized 3-D coordinate system of the brain. This procedure made it possible to correct for large individual differences in the brain's morphology and to allow the subsequent averaging to be performed on standardized data.

The next step in the analysis consisted of normalizing the PET images for global CBF and determining the difference between control and experimental conditions for each subject. The mean state-dependent change image volume was obtained by averaging across subjects (Fox, Perlmutter, and Raichle 1985) and then converted to a $t$-statistic by dividing the mean state-dependent change by the mean standard deviation in normalized CBF for all intracerebral voxels and by multiplying this quotient by the square root of $N$ (number of subjects). Anatomical and functional images were merged to allow direct localization on the MR images of $t$-statistic peaks identified by an automatic peak-detection algorithm (Mintun, Fox, and Raichle 1989) and for the anatomical correlation of extended zones of activation not expressible in terms of isolated peaks. The peak distribution was then searched for significant signals using change distribution analysis (Fox et al. 1988; Fox 1991) and $z$-score thresholding. Because this two-tiered statistical approach is fairly conservative, no Bonferroni correction was used in the analyses. Nonetheless the level of significance was set at $p < .01$.

Although separate analysis of single subject's data is an alternative procedure for deriving the pattern of activation associated with the realization of a given task in PET studies (Lueck et al. 1989), it was not used in this experiment for several reasons. When comparing an activation condition to a control condition with the subtraction method, responses appear as discrete foci of activity over a background of spatially random noise. This activity is typically less intense in cortical areas underlying cognitive operations than in those sustaining primary sensory or motor functions. With the $^{15}O$ water bolus technique, it is necessary, to improve the signal-to-noise ratio, to include data from more than one set of observation, either by repeating an activation condition within the same subject or by testing several subjects on the same activation condition. Because of limits in the quantity of radioactive material that can be injected into a subject, the repetition of the same activation conditions within a subject by necessity restricts the number of different tasks that can be carried out on each subject. Consequently, for the purpose of examining the neurofunctional anatomy of diverse aspects of face and name processing and to perform comparisons between them, the group study approach was deemed preferable to the single-subject data analysis.

## 8.3 RESULTS AND DISCUSSION

Three main sets of data were collected in this investigation: two during the PET study and one during the divided visual field study.

## PET Behavioral Data

Reaction times (RTs) and accuracy were recorded during the six activation conditions. The data, presented in table 8.1, are based on the thirty trials (the first seven and last three trials were eliminated because they occurred outside scanning) during which rCBF was measured in each condition, averaged across subjects, and only correct reaction times were considered in the analyses. The RTs were subjected to a repeated-measure analysis of variance, with stimulus (name, face) and task (gender categorization, familiarity decision, professional categorization) as independent variables. The main effect of stimulus was significant ($F(1,7) = 14.76, p < .01$), with words being responded to faster than faces (688 ms and 706 ms, respectively). The main effect of task was also significant ($F(1,7) = 36.20, p < .01$); the categorization of gender, familiarity, and profession resulted in increasing latency, respectively in that order. Planned comparisons indicated that the three tasks yielded RTs that were significantly different from one another ($p < .01$). The interaction between task and stimulus did not approach significance ($F < 1$), and the same pattern of increasing latency—from gender categorization, to familiarity decision, to professional categorization—prevailed for both the names and the faces.

A similar analysis of variance (ANOVA) on errors produced essentially the same findings: a significant main effect of stimulus and a significant main effect of task but no significant interaction between stimulus and task. However, whereas the gender categorization was made more accurately than the other two tasks with both names and faces, there was no significant difference in accuracy between the familiarity decision and the professional categorization.

Together, the findings of the face conditions are consistent with a sequential unfolding of the three main categories of operations leading to the recognition of faces: the structural encoding, the activation of the stored visual representations of known faces, and the access to semantic information. In addition, the results provide guarantee that the subjects effectively performed the requested tasks and did so without making too many errors that could have invalidated the PET findings. The fact that the same pattern of results prevailed in the name conditions could suggest a similar sequential organization of the respective operations underlying the performance of the three

**Table 8.1** Reaction Times (in ms) and Percentage of Errors in the Six Conditions Performed during the PET Scanning

|  | Gender | | Familiarity | | Profession | |
| --- | --- | --- | --- | --- | --- | --- |
|  | Male | Female | Yes | No | Actor | Nonactor |
| *Words* | | | | | | |
| Reaction time | 601 | 626 | 678 | 734 | 715 | 775 |
| Error | 1.87 | 2.42 | 6.56 | 5.31 | 3.75 | 6.06 |
| *Faces* | | | | | | |
| Reaction time | 631 | 652 | 695 | 752 | 735 | 769 |
| Error | 2.81 | 3.98 | 8.74 | 9.19 | 8.50 | 8.97 |

tasks. There is, however, little independent evidence that could support such an interpretation. The same type of perceptual analysis is required in the three name conditions but not in the three face conditions. For instance, a gender categorization does not call for the extraction of the physiognomical invariants without which a face cannot be recognized, and it can be performed on the basis of less physical information than is required to recognize a face as that of a unique individual. In addition, each of the three name conditions requires access to semantic information, and the gender categorization of first names is not made on the basis of the visual characteristics of the stimuli as it is with faces. The differences in reaction times among these three name conditions, therefore, may not so much reflect a sequential organization of their respective operations as a different degree of accessibility of the pertinent semantic information necessary to perform each of the name tasks. Thus, despite a pattern of results consistent with a sequential unfolding of operations in both the face and the name conditions, such a sequential organization is not demonstrated by these results and may not be an appropriate account of the latencies obtained in the name tasks.

**PET Activation Data**

Significant increases in CBF in the activation conditions were derived through the subtraction method (Posner et al. 1988), first by subtracting the control fixation condition from each of the gender categorization tasks and then by subtracting the activation associated with the gender categorization (now considered as control) from the other two experimental conditions for each stimulus category. The results of these subtractions are shown in table 8.2, presenting the significant foci of activation in terms of Talairach and Tournoux's stereotactic coordinates, the common name of the cerebral region corresponding to these coordinates, and the Brodmann area. The coordinates correspond to the three Euclidean axes: X is the lateral (left-right) axis, 0 corresponding to the midline separating the two hemispheres and negative values corresponding to the left side of the brain; Y is the antero-posterior axis, 0 corresponding to the posterior edge of the anterior commissure, and negative values corresponding to the posterior part of the brain; Z is the dorso-ventral axis, 0 corresponding to the virtual line joining the anterior and the posterior commissure, and negative values corresponding to the ventral region of the brain.

**Face Conditions** When compared to the fixation condition, the face-gender categorization resulted in activation restricted to the occipital lobe, essentially in the striate, lingual, and cuneus of both hemispheres, and in the posterior part of the right fusiform gyrus. Although the activation was more intense in the right than in the left hemisphere, the left hemisphere did participate in the operations underlying this categorization. These findings differ slightly from those reported in the earlier study (Sergent, Ohta, and MacDonald 1992), mainly because the subtracted condition was a grating discrimination in the

**Table 8.2** Significant ($p < .01$) Foci of Activation Derived by Subtraction Expressed in Stereotaxic Coordinates and Their Corresponding Brodmann Areas

| X | Y | Z | | |
|---|---|---|---|---|
| *Face Gender–Fixation* | | | | |
| 1 | −85 | 8 | Striate Cortex | Central area 17 |
| 23 | −73 | −2 | Lingual gyrus | Right area 18 |
| 8 | −78 | 13 | Cuneus | Right area 18 |
| −17 | −68 | −5 | Lingual | Left area 18 |
| 35 | −68 | −6 | Fusiform gyrus | Right area 19 |
| −5 | −95 | 24 | Cuneus | Left area 19 |
| 26 | −92 | 15 | Cuneus | Right area 19 |
| *Face Familiarity–Face Gender* | | | | |
| 55 | −45 | −18 | Fusiform gyrus | Right area 37 |
| 32 | −20 | −13 | Parahippocampal gyrus | Right area 36 |
| 23 | −58 | −8 | Fusiform gyrus | Right area 19 |
| *Face Profession–Face Gender* | | | | |
| 39 | −61 | −12 | Fusiform gyrus | Right area 37 |
| 38 | −42 | −17 | Fusiform gyrus | Right area 37 |
| −29 | −71 | −9 | Fusiform gyrus | Left area 19 |
| 19 | −49 | 3 | Parahippocampal gyrus | Right area 36 |
| 20 | −22 | −16 | Parahippocampal gyrus | Right area 36 |
| 23 | −9 | −13 | Parahippocampal gyrus | Right area 28 |
| *Name Gender–Fixation* | | | | |
| −20 | −99 | −6 | Inferior occipital gyrus | Left area 18 |
| 19 | −93 | 9 | Middle occipital gyrus | Right area 18 |
| −34 | −45 | −15 | Fusiform gyrus | Left area 37 |
| −50 | −59 | 13 | Angular gyrus | Left area 39 |
| −56 | −33 | −2 | Middle temporal gyrus | Left area 21 |
| −56 | −47 | 26 | Supramarginal gyrus | Left area 40 |
| 52 | −38 | 47 | Supramarginal gyrus | Right area 40 |
| *Name Familiarity–Name Gender* | | | | |
| −50 | −7 | −21 | Middle temporal gyrus | Left area 21 |
| −58 | −26 | 5 | Superior temporal gyrus | Left area 22 |
| −44 | 13 | −5 | Superior temporal gyrus | Left area 38 |
| −43 | 24 | 12 | Inferior frontal gyrus | Left area 45 |
| *Name Profession–Name Gender* | | | | |
| −28 | 5 | −31 | Temporal pole | Left area 38 |
| −56 | −42 | 5 | Superior temporal gyrus | Left area 22 |
| −16 | 5 | −22 | Medial temporal gyrus | Left area 28 |
| −44 | 24 | 15 | Inferior frontal gyrus | Left area 45 |
| −44 | 15 | −2 | Inferior frontal gyrus | Left area 47 |

earlier study instead of a passive fixation condition in the present analysis. These results show a crucial contribution of the ventral occipital cortex (lingual and fusiform gyri) to this categorization, but they do not allow a more detailed specification of the respective contribution of each of these areas to the component operations inherent in the task. In particular, it cannot be determined whether the participation of the left lingual gyrus is essential to the gender categorization. Whatever the role played by the left lingual gyrus in this task, however, it cannot be sufficient since prosopagnosic patients with damage restricted to the right hemisphere can be defective in categorizing male and female faces (Sergent and Signoret 1992b).

Cerebral activation associated with the familiarity decision task was derived by subtracting the activation associated with the gender categorization task. As indicated in table 8.2, the cerebral areas significantly involved in judging whether a face is familiar are all located in regions anterior to those engaged during the gender categorization task, in the ventral part of the brain, and the highest levels of activation were obtained in the right hemisphere (see fig. 8.1.). This was particularly the case of the fusiform gyrus and the parahippocampal gyrus. Less intense activation was detected in the middle temporal cortex of the left hemisphere, but it did not reach a reliable level of significance ($p = .05$).

Essentially the same regions of the brain were activated during the familiarity decision and the professional categorization, as the significant changes in rCBF were detected in the right fusiform gyrus and parahippocampal gyrus. These results replicate earlier findings and confirm the critical contribution of these areas of the right ventral medial cortex to operations underlying the recognition of faces. However, the rCBF change observed in the anterior temporal cortex in the earlier study did not reach a reliable level of significance in this study ($p < .10$). One likely reason for the difference is the faster rate of presentation in this than in the earlier study, suggesting that faster rates may result in lower activation, even in cerebral areas, which, according to neurological evidence, play a crucial role in the realization of a given task.

Overall, the results of the face conditions are essentially in accordance with earlier PET findings and with neurological data from prosopagnosic patients. Divergence with earlier findings reflects less intense activation of the anterior temporal lobes in the professional categorization task, presumably due to the faster rate of stimulus presentation used in this study.

**Name Conditions** The same series of subtractions as for the face conditions were performed for the name conditions, and the significant foci of activation are shown in table 8.2. Three main cerebral regions were found to underlie the name gender categorization task. One consisted of the visual cortex, with intense activation ($p < .0001$) in the left inferior occipital gyrus (area 18), as well as in the right-middle occipital gyrus and in the left fusiform gyrus (area 37). These findings are consistent with earlier PET results (Posner et al. 1988) in showing the contribution of the medial occipital cortex of the left hemisphere in word processing. The activation of the inferior occipital gyrus was not detected in Posner's (1988) studies, however, yet it was intense in the this study and was present in the three name conditions when compared to fixation or to the three face conditions, and it was more intense than the activation observed in the left fusiform gyrus (see fig. 8.2, top right slice of image *a*). Destruction of this area has in fact been associated with posterior alexia (Benson 1985), and this region seems to perform perceptual analysis of written words in a way that may not be compensated for by other areas in the left or the right hemisphere. The second cerebral region with a significant rCBF increase consisted of the inferior parietal lobule of the left hemisphere, including the angular gyrus (area 39) and the supramarginal gyrus (area 40), as well as the superior region of the supramarginal gyrus of the right hemisphere. The contribution of these areas to reading is well established (Hécaen and Albert 1978), and damage to this region results in central alexia (Benson 1985). The third region involved in the name-gender categorization task was the middle temporal gyrus (area 21) of the left hemisphere. Although the role of this area cannot be unequivocally determined, there is some evidence that it may be involved in the storage of names (Damasio, Tranel, and Damasio 1990).

The same cerebral areas that were recruited during the name-gender categorization task were also activated in the name-familiarity and the name-profession conditions (fig. 8.2), as evidenced by comparisons with the fixation condition, but additional cerebral regions were also engaged in the realization of each of the latter two tasks. Thus, activation of the posterior superior temporal gyrus (area 22) was observed in both the familiarity and professional categorization tasks, as well as of the inferior frontal gyrus (area 45). Whether the participation of these areas reflects a necessary involvement in accessing knowledge about individuals from their names or reflects some subvocalization of the names cannot be determined, although the absence of activation of these areas in the gender categorization task would favor an interpretation suggesting an involvement specific to the familiarity decision and the professional categorization tasks and related to access to semantic information. There was also activation of the middle temporal gyrus (area 21) in the familiarity decision task, in a region anterior to that activated in the gender categorization task. On the other hand, the name-profession task resulted in activation of the left temporal pole (area 38), consistent with neurological data showing a role of this region in the storage and evocation of proper names (Damasio et al. 1991).

To compare professional categorization in the name and the face conditions, subtractions were reciprocally conducted in an attempt to determine whether the access to semantic information from the presentation of either a face or a name activates the same cerebral structures. The results of these two subtractions showed very little overlap in significant rCBF changes in the face and name-professional categorization conditions. Except for the activation in the left fusiform gyrus, which was common to both conditions and was therefore cancelled out in the two reciprocal subtractions, all other foci activation that were significant in the main analyses within stimulus category were also significant when the comparison was made between name and face.

**Divided Visual Field Study** In this study, the subjects performed the same tasks as they did during the PET study, except that the stimuli were presented in the lateral periphery. Reaction times and percentage of errors in the six tasks are presented in table 8.3, averaged across subjects, as a function of task (gender, familiarity, profession), stimulus (name, face), and visual field (left visual field [LVF], right visual field [RVF]). A repeated-measure analysis of variance was conducted on the reaction times, and the three main effects were significant. Words were responded to faster than faces (700 ms and 719 ms, respectively, $F(1,7) = 7.23, p < .05$), reaction times were faster to RVF (701 ms) than to LVF (718 ms) presentations ($F(1,7) = 6.42, p < .05$), and the three tasks were performed at different speed ($F(1,7) = 23.65, p < .01$), gender: 652 ms, familiarity: 715 ms; profession: 762 ms). The only interaction to reach a reliable level of significance was that between stimulus and visual field ($F(1,7) = 9.31, p < .05$), and it indicated a larger difference between the two visual fields in favor of the RVF with words than with faces. An analysis of the simple effects of this interaction, using the Tukey test, indicated that the RVF advantage was significant in each of the three name conditions ($p < .01$) but in none of the face conditions ($p > .20$).

Given the results of the PET study with these subjects and the clear illustration in figure 8.1 of an involvement of the right hemisphere in the processing of faces, the patterns of results in the face conditions of the divided visual field study were not as expected. A similar discrepancy had already obtained in an earlier experiment (Sergent and Signoret 1992a). Because the pattern of visual field asymmetry was then found to depend on the order of stimulus presentation, this discrepancy was attributed to the repetition of the stimuli during the divided visual field study, whereby once the subjects knew in advance which face they would be seeing, the initial right hemisphere superiority disappeared and even reversed to a left hemisphere advantage. To examine whether a similar pattern prevailed in this study, the RTs were analyzed further, adding the factor of order of face presentation (first or second) (table 8.4). As found in the earlier study, the results of this analysis showed a main effect of order of presentation, indicating faster response to a face on its second presentation. More important, they also indicated a significant interaction of visual field,

**Table 8.3** Reaction Times (in ms) and Percentage of Errors in the Divided Visual Field Study

|  | Gender | | Familiarity | | Profession | |
| --- | --- | --- | --- | --- | --- | --- |
|  | LVF | RVF | LVF | RVF | LVF | RVF |
| *Words* | | | | | | |
| Reaction time | 651 | 632 | 718 | 687 | 777 | 736 |
| Error | 2.38 | 2.01 | 5.93 | 5.21 | 6.72 | 5.41 |
| *Faces* | | | | | | |
| Reaction time | 663 | 661 | 732 | 722 | 749 | 746 |
| Error | 3.12 | 3.04 | 8.30 | 8.14 | 9.82 | 9.14 |

**Table 8.4** Reaction Times (in ms) in the First and Second Presentations of Stimuli in the Divided Visual Field Study

|  | Gender | | Familiarity | | Profession | |
| --- | --- | --- | --- | --- | --- | --- |
|  | LVF | RVF | LVF | RVF | LVF | RVF |
| *Words* | | | | | | |
| First presentation | 687 | 660 | 769 | 745 | 824 | 776 |
| Second presentation | 615 | 604 | 667 | 629 | 730 | 696 |
| *Faces* | | | | | | |
| First presentation | 696 | 702 | 793 | 808 | 811 | 825 |
| Second presentation | 630 | 620 | 671 | 636 | 687 | 667 |

order of presentation, and stimulus category, suggesting that whereas an RVF superiority prevailed at first and second presentations in each of the name tasks, an LVF advantage obtained in each of the first presentations of the face tasks that shifted to an RVF advantage in the second presentation. This finding suggests a contribution of the left hemisphere to face processing that becomes apparent only after the subjects have already been familiarized with the faces. On the other hand, the pattern of visual field asymmetry in the name conditions conformed with expectations and concurred with the PET activation data that clearly showed the participation of the left hemisphere, with little involvement of the right hemisphere.

Overall, the findings of the divided visual field study conform with the pattern of results in similar earlier studies (Hellige 1993) in showing robust evidence of left hemisphere involvement in name reading and processing but fluctuating patterns of visual field asymmetry in face processing tasks. These fluctuations have no clear explanation, especially in view of the accumulating evidence, from the study of prosopagnosic patients and normal subjects in PET experiments, that the right hemisphere is both necessary and sufficient to achieve face processing and recognition. That the left hemisphere has the ability to process faces has been documented by Sergent and Signoret (1992b), who had severe prosopagnosics with unilateral right cerebral injury learn the association between twelve faces and names. The patients were able to remember these associations nearly perfectly the following day, suggesting that they successfully discriminated and recognized the twelve faces, but they performed at chance 5 min later when new versions of the faces of the same individuals were presented instead. Presumably, the left hemisphere does not possess the perceptual capacity to extract the physiognomical invariants but can nonetheless achieve a faithful representation of well-learned faces appearing in a fixed format. The activation of the left fusiform gyrus obtained in this PET study may thus reflect a participation of the left hemisphere in the perceptual analysis of faces, but the actual contribution of this area remains to be uncovered. In addition, the fact that projecting faces directly to the left hemisphere may result in faster processing in the right hemisphere once the faces have become familiar is equally unaccounted for.

## 8.4 GENERAL DISCUSSION

This study was designed to identify, in normal subjects, the neurofunctional organization of face and proper name processing. The results replicate earlier findings and provide new information about the participation of cortical areas in the operations underlying the realization of these functions. Although specific patterns of cerebral activation were found in the experimental conditions, the interpretation of these findings cannot be straightforward and raises several problems of a methodological and theoretical nature.

### Neurofunctional Organization of Face Processing

With respect to the processing of gender and identity of faces, the results replicate earlier findings obtained in a study that used the same stimuli, experimental design, and subtraction method (Sergent, Ohta, and MacDonald 1992). Determining whether a face is that of a man or a woman, which requires a structural encoding of the relevant facial information, activates the lingual gyrus and posterior fusiform gyrus, predominantly in the right hemisphere but with a significant participation of the left hemisphere as well. The issue of cerebral dominance as such cannot be resolved on the sole basis of the PET findings, since we still do not know how greater functional competence of one cortical area over its symmetric counterpart in the other hemisphere manifests itself in terms of CBF. It may very well be that the more competent structure needs less energy (Sergent 1990), and it would be simplistic to assume that a larger activation in an area of one hemisphere than in the homotopic area of the other hemisphere necessarily entails a greater competence or specialization of the former compared to the latter. On the other hand, despite the observed activation of the left hemisphere during the face-gender categorization task of the PET study, the left lingual gyrus appears to be of little use on its own in discriminating the gender of faces, since prosopagnosics whose right lingual and fusiform gyri are destroyed can be quite defective at telling men from women on the basis of their faces. This suggests that the effective engagement of the left hemisphere in this gender categorization task is conditional on a functional right hemisphere.

The results from the face-professional categorization task also revealed the crucial role of the right fusiform gyrus and parahippocampal gyrus, and our PET findings provide a useful replication of earlier findings (Sergent, Ohta, and MacDonald 1992) showing activation of the parahippocampal gyrus, which was not then thought to play such a crucial role in the processes leading to face recognition. By contrast, the involvement of the anterior temporal cortex, which proved significant in the earlier study, did not replicate in this experiment; there was an increase in rCBF in this area but not of sufficient magnitude to be significantly different from the control conditions. The only difference between the two studies was the stimulus presentation rate, which was faster in this than in the earlier studies, suggesting that such an apparently trivial factor may have important implications for uncovering the functional anatomy of a given function. One can only speculate as to the reasons that may underlie the absence of significant stimulation of the anterior temporal cortex when faces are presented every 2 sec rather than 3 sec, and one such reason may be that the subjects had time to reactivate only a few pieces of relevant information before preparing for the next trial, which may not have been sufficient to raise the blood flow significantly. (It is worth noting that this difference of 1 sec in stimulus presentation rate amounts to a total of 20 sec out of 60 sec of scanning, during which the subjects are not performing any specifically required task and may thus keep processing the just presented stimulus.) Whatever the reasons, this failure to replicate should serve as a warning that what we obtain in a PET study cannot be the whole story and that the pattern of activation derived by subtraction is relative, not only because it depends on the particularities of the condition that is subtracted but because it is influenced by factors such as stimulus presentation rate, response accuracy rate, and anxiety that have a nontrivial influence on rCBF.

The new face task introduced in this study was a familiarity decision, and caution must be exercised in interpreting the results. There can be no guarantee that the subjects terminated processing at the familiarity decision stage and did not attempt to identify the familiar face. As a result, the pattern of activation may reflect both familiarity decision and recognition. Indeed, the same cortical areas (right fusiform and parahippocampal gyri) were found to be activated in both tasks, although at somewhat different places within each area, and this could suggest that our findings from the familiarity decision task are confounded with a recognition process and have little validity regarding the neural substrates of a familiarity decision. However, one could present arguments supporting the validity of the present results with respect to their relevance to the familiarity decision.

Failure to perform a familiarity decision and to recognize a face is always associated in prosopagnosics, so there must be some common underlying processes and substrates to the two functions. This association occurs whether the lesion affects the fusiform gyrus and spares the parahippocampal gyrus or spares the fusiform gyrus and affects the parahippocampal gyrus (Sergent and Signoret 1992b). Therefore, each of these structures must be involved to achieve a successful perception of a face as being familiar. On the basis of anatomoclinical data from prosopagnosic patients, one would thus predict that the integrity of both the fusiform and the parahippocampal gyri of the right hemisphere is necessary for a face familiarity decision and for a face recognition. Our PET findings therefore concur with such a prediction and confirm that a familiarity decision requires the reactivation of stored representations of known faces, presumably in the right fusiform gyrus, and the reactivation of pertinent memories associated with the face, presumably triggered at the level of the right parahippocampal gyrus.

The fact that these two structures are required for a familiarity decision may explain why prosopagnosic patients with damage that invades the lingual and fusiform gyri of the right hemisphere fail to show evidence of covert recognition because their performance does not differ whether they are shown familiar or unfamiliar faces (Sergent and Signoret 1992c). This same fact also explains why prosopagnosic patients whose lingual and fusiform gyri are spared, who are capable of a normal structural encoding (as evidenced by normal performance at matching different views of faces), and who still possess stored representations of known faces (as evidenced by signs of covert recognition) perceive familiar faces as those of strangers. As suggested by Young and Bruce (1991), these stored representations do not contain information about identity, and, as illustrated here, this information must be accessed through biographical data by activation of the parahippocampal gyrus. More surprising, the combined clinical and PET findings suggest that the reactivation of stored facial representations cannot by itself signal the familiarity of a face if it does not conjointly activate some form of semantic, episodic, or emotional information indicating that an earlier encounter with that face has taken place. In this sense, it is through a process of retroactivation (Damasio, Tranel, and Damasio 1990; Sergent and Poncet 1990) that a perceived face acquires its meaning. The difference, in terms of speed of processing, between a familiarity decision and a recognition may then lie in the fact that any piece of information is sufficient to make a face look familiar, whereas more specific, and presumably longer-to-access, information is needed for recognition.

One further argument suggests that our results on the familiarity task are relevant. Pilot study on this task had been conducted with a presentation rate of one stimulus every 3 sec. Under such conditions, when the face-gender condition was subtracted from the familiarity condition, no rCBF change was significant, as if there was no different cerebral involvement in the two tasks. In addition, when the familiarity and the recognition tasks were compared, the right anterior fusiform and the parahippocampal gyri were activated only in the recognition task. One likely reason for this, it was reasoned, is the fact that whereas in the recognition task all the faces have to be recognized and have semantic information stored in some cerebral structures, only half the faces are familiar in a familiarity decision task. At a presentation rate of one face every 3 sec, this amounted to only ten familiar faces during an activation condition, and this may not have been a large enough number of stimuli to produce the amount of activation that would lead to a significant rCBF increase. This was the reason that motivated the choice of a presentation rate of one face every 2 sec. This faster rate, however, resulted in the loss of significant activation in the anterior temporal cortex during the professional categorization condition, illustrating how difficult it is to find the appropriate value for each of the procedural variables.

**Structural Organization of Proper Name Processing**

Single word processing has already been the object of much PET research (Posner et al. 1988), and our results replicated part of the findings obtained in earlier studies. In particular, the processing of proper names engaged the same ventromedial region of the left hemisphere found to be involved in the representation of the visual form of words. There was, however, a very distinct area of activation in the posterolateral region of the occipital cortex (see fig. 8.2), which was present in each of the three name conditions and had not been identified in earlier studies. Our experiment was not designed to tell apart the actual role played by each of the activated areas of the occipital cortex; more research is required to determine the actual contribution of this area to the process of reading. Nonetheless, the role played by the left posterolateral occipital cortex in the process of reading must be crucial because its destruction results in alexia (Benson 1985), whereas lesion of the left ventromedial occipital cortex does not necessarily disturb reading. Also activated in the three name conditions were the left angular and supramarginal gyri, the two areas that form the inferior parietal lobule and whose contribution to the process of reading is well established (Benson 1985).

Of more direct relevance were the differences among the three name conditions. Each activated different parts of the left temporal lobe, a region whose destruction is frequently associated with name finding difficulties (Flude, Ellis, and Kay 1989; McCarthy and Warrington 1990), and the different locations of activation within this lobe in the three name tasks may be related to the different semantic information that had to be accessed in each of them. Activation of the temporal lobe (area 21) was more posterior in the gender categorization than in the other two tasks. What differentiates the former from the latter two tasks is the absence of a unique entity associated with a first name, whereas the other two tasks involved the presentation of real names, each corresponding to a unique individual. These two tasks resulted in activation of the most anterior region of the left temporal lobe (area 38, as well as area 28 in the professional categorization task). Whether one should attribute any significance to the fact that proper names are stored in the most rostral region of the temporal lobe is uncertain, but it nonetheless fits well with the fact that proper names are no more than arbitrary labels and by themselves do not carry any pertinent information.

The finding of activation in the left temporal pole concurs with preliminary evidence from brain-damaged patients; as Damasio et al. (1991) report, "damage to the anteriormost sector of the temporal region (area 38) on the left is accompanied by a defect in the retrieval of proper names."

**Faces and Names**

Although similar tasks were carried out in the face and the name conditions, quite different cerebral structures were recruited for the performance of the tasks in these conditions. On the one hand, different hemispheres performed most of the relevant processes; on the other, the neural network underlying the performance of the tasks with faces and names is not symmetrically organized, since processing unfolds along quite different routes within the right and the left hemispheres in the face and the name conditions, respectively. As figures 8.1 and 8.2 illustrate by presenting foci of activation after subtracting from the face tasks the corresponding name tasks, and vice versa, there was little overlap in the cortical areas recruited for the two types of stimuli. This should be expected from research on brain-damaged patients, since, for instance, prosopagnosics have little difficulty in performing the type of name tasks used in our study (Sergent and Signoret 1992c) and global aphasics do not lose the ability to recognize faces.

Our results, nonetheless, allow a more precise specification of the actual functional organization of the neural network underlying face and name processing. Thus, the processing of faces unfolds essentially through a ventromedial route in the right hemisphere, with at least two crucial structures whose integrity is essential for effective processing and recognition: the lingual-fusiform gyri and the parahippocampal gyrus. In contrast, the processing of words seems to follow a more lateral course, although the medial region of the occipital cortex does participate in the realization of this function. The activation of the left parahippocampal gyrus is not necessary for access to semantic information from a verbal cue, and this suggests a different organization of the neural networks underlying access to knowledge about individuals in the case of names and faces. In addition, the absence of overlap in cerebral activation between the face and name professional categorization tasks suggests that semantic information bearing on the same properties of the same individuals can be stored in distinct cerebral structures. Different areas of the left temporal cortex are involved in the semantic processing of words depending on the generality or uniqueness of the words, and proper names referring to unique individuals appear to engage structures in the more anterior region of the temporal lobe.

## 8.5 CONCLUSIONS

There is necessarily a logic in the functional organization of the brain, but this logic must be overdetermined by a multitude of factors, only some of which we begin to uncover and understand. One may, obviously, formulate some aspects of this logic a posteriori, to make sense of our findings, by taking into account the particular properties of the information that the brain has to process, the specific processing demands made by each task, the order in which these demands have to be accommodated, the purpose for which these processes are performed, and the consequences for the adaptation of the organism to its environment. These aspects can be specified in cognitive models of mental functions, and they constitute the sine qua non of any investigation into the neurobiological substrates of cognition. Whether the fractionation of a cognitive function into component suboperations corresponds to the structural organization of processing in cerebral structures is a matter for empirical investigation, but our results, and many others before, clearly suggest that the correspondence between the functional and anatomical organization of a given function is far from perfect. For instance, what is conceived as two distinct operations from a cognitive standpoint (e.g., a face familiarity decision and a face identification) does not result in significantly distinct patterns of cerebral involvement. Nonetheless, the progress achieved during the past few years, especially as a result of the development of functional models of mental functions that have better delineated the right questions to be asked, may raise the hope of achieving a better understanding of the functional organization of cerebral structures.

## NOTE

This research was supported by the National Institute of Mental Health, the Medical Research Council of Canada, and the EJLB Foundation. We gratefully acknowledge the helpful comments and suggestions of two anonymous reviewers and the help and assistance of our colleagues at the McConnell Brain Imaging Center and the Neurochemistry Unit of the Montreal Neurological Institute, without whom this research would not have been carried out.

## REFERENCES

Benson, D. F. (1985). Alexia. In P. J. Vinken, G. W. Bruyn, and H. L. Klawans (Eds.), *Handbook of clinical neurology*, vol. 45, *Clinical neuropsychology*, 433–455. Amsterdam: Elsevier.

Benton, A. R., Hamsher, K. D. S., Varney, N., and Spreen, O. (1983). *Contributions to neuropsychological assessment: A clinical manual*. New York: Oxford University Press.

Benton, A. L., and Van Allen, M. W. (1972). Prosopagnosia and facial discrimination. *Journal of the Neurological Sciences, 15*, 167–172.

Brennen, T., Baguley, T., Bright, J., and Bruce V. (1990). Resolving semantically induced tip-of-the-tongue states for proper nouns. *Memory and Cognition, 18*, 339–347.

Bruce, V., and, Young, A. W. (1986). Understanding face recognition. *British Journal of Psychology, 77*, 305–327.

Bryden, M. P. (1982). *Laterality*. New York: Academic Press.

Burton, A. M., Bruce, V., and Johnston, R. A. (1990). Understanding face recognition with an interactive interaction model. *British Journal of Psychology, 81*, 361–380.

Burton, A. M., Young, A. W., Bruce, V., Johnston, R. A., and Ellis, A. W. (1991). Understanding covert recognition. *Cognition, 39*, 129–166.

Damasio, A. R., Damasio, H., Tranel, D., and Brandt, J. P. (1991). The neural regionalization of knowledge access: Preliminary evidence. *Cold Spring Harbor Symposium of Quantitative Biology, 55*, 1039–1047.

Damasio, A. R., Tranel, D., and Damasio H. (1990). Face agnosia and the neural substrates of memory. *Annual Review of Neuroscience, 13*, 89–109.

de Haan, E. H. F., Young, A. W., and Newcombe, F. (1987). Face recognition without awareness. *Cognitive Neuropsychology, 4*, 385–415.

de Haan, E. H. F., Young, A. W., and Newcombe, F. (1991). A dissociation between the sense of familiarity and access to semantic information concerning familiar people. *European Journal of Cognitive Psychology, 3*, 51–67.

Ellis, A. W. (1987). Repetition priming of face recognition. *Quarterly Journal of Experimental Psychology, 39A*, 193–210.

Ellis, A. W. (1992). Cognitive mechanisms of face processing. *Philosophical Transactions of the Royal Society, London, Series B, 335*, 113–119.

Ellis, A. W., Young, A. W., and Critchley, E. M. R. (1989). Loss of memory for people following temporal lobe damage. *Brain, 112,* 1469–1483.

Evans, A., Marrett, S., Collins, L., and Peters, T. M. (1989). Anatomical-functional correlative analysis of the human brain using three-dimensional imaging systems. *Proceedings of the Society of Photographic and Optical Instrumentation and Engineering, 1092,* 264–274.

Flude, B. M., Ellis, A. W., and Kay, J. (1989). Face processing and name retrieval in an aphasic anomic: Names are stored separately from semantic information about familiar people. *Brain and Cognition, 11,* 60–72.

Fox, P. T. (1991). Physiological ROI definition by image subtraction. *Journal of Cerebral Blood Flow and Metabolism, 11,* A79–A82.

Fox, P. T., Mintun, M. A., Reinman, E. M., and Raichle, M. E. (1988). Enhanced detection of focal brain responses using intersubject averaging and change-distribution analysis of subtracted PET images. *Journal of Cerebral Blood Flow and Metabolism, 8,* 642–653.

Fox, P. T., Perlmutter, J. S., and Raichle, M. E. (1985). A stereotactic method of anatomical localization for positron emission tomography. *Journal of Computer Assisted Tomography, 9,* 141–153.

Fox, P. T., and Raichle, M. E. (1985). Stimulus rate determines regional blood flow in striate cortex. *Annals of Neurology, 17,* 303–305.

Haxby, J. V., Grady, C. L., Horwitz, B., Ungerleider, L. G., Mishkin, M., Carson, R. E., Herscovitch, P., Schapiro, M. B., and Rapoport, S. I. (1991). Dissociation of object and spatial visual processing pathways in human extrastriate cortex. *Proceedings of the National Academy of Sciences, U.S.A., 88,* 1621–1625.

Hécaen, H., and Albert, M. (1978). *Human neuropsychology.* New York: Wiley.

Hellige, J. B. (1993). *Hemispheric asymmetry. What is left and what is right.* Cambridge: Harvard University Press.

Lueck, C. J., Zeki, S., Friston, K. J., Deiber, M.-P., Cope, P., Cunningham, V. J., Lammertsma, A. A., Kennard, C., and Frackowiak, R. S. J. (1989). The colour center in the cerebral cortex of man. *Nature, 340,* 386–389.

McCarthy, R. A., and Warrington, E. K. (1990). *Cognitive Neuropsychology. A clinical introduction.* London: Academic Press.

Mintun, M., Fox, P. T., and Raichle, M. E. (1989). A highly accurate method of localizing neuronal activity in the human brain with positron emission tomography. *Journal of Cerebral Blood Flow and Metabolism, 9,* 96–103.

Posner, M. I., Petersen, S. E., Fox, P. T., and Raichle, M. E. (1988). Localization of cognitive operations in the human brain. *Science, 240,* 1627–1631.

Raichle, M. E., Martin, W. R. W., Herscovitch, P., Mintun, M. A., and Marham, J. (1983). Brain blood flow measured with intravenous $H_2^{15}O$. II. Implementation and validation. *Journal of Nuclear Medicine, 24,* 790–798.

Sergent, J. (1985). Influence of task and input factors on hemispheric involvement in face processing. *Journal of Experimental Psychology: Human Perception and Performance, 11,* 846–861.

Sergent, J., and Hellige, J. B. (1986). Role of input factors in visual field asymmetry. *Brain and Cognition, 5,* 174–200.

Sergent, J., and Poncet, M. (1990). From covert to overt recognition of faces in a prosopagnosic patient. *Brain, 113,* 989–1004.

Sergent, J. and Signoret, J.-L. (1992a). Functional and anatomical decomposition of face processing: Evidence from prosopagnosia and PET study of normal subjects. *Philosophical Transactions of the Royal Society, London, Series B, 335*, 55–62.

Sergent, J., and Signoret, J.-L. (1992b). Varieties of functional deficits in prosopagnosia. *Cerebral Cortex, 2*, 375–388.

Sergent, J., and Signoret, J.-L. (1992c). Implicit access to knowledge derived from unrecognized faces in prosopagnosia. *Cerebral Cortex, 2*, 389–400.

Sergent, J., Ohta, S., and MacDonald, B. (1992). Functional neuroanatomy of face and object processing: A PET study. *Brain, 115*, 15–29.

Sergent, J., Zuck, E., Lévesque, M., and MacDonald, B. (1992). Positron emission tomography study of letter and object processing: Empirical findings and methodological considerations. *Cerebral Cortex, 2*, 68–80.

Talairach, J., and Tournoux, P. (1988). *Co-planar stereotaxic atlas of the human brain. Three-dimensional proportional system: An approach to cerebral imaging.* Stuggart: Thieme.

Warrington, E. K., and McCarthy, R. A. (1988). The fractionation of retrograde amnesia. *Brain and Cognition, 7*, 184–200.

Young, A. W. (1992). Face recognition impairments. *Philosophical Transactions of the Royal Society, London, Series B, 335*, 47–54.

Young, A. W., and Bruce, V. (1991). Perceptual categories and the computation of "grandmother." *European Journal of Cognitive Psychology, 3*, 5–49.

Young, A. W., Hay, D. C., and Ellis, A. W. (1985). The faces that launched a thousand slips. *British Journal of Psychology, 76*, 495–523.

Young, A. W., Ellis, A. W., Flude, B. M., McWeeny, H. H., and Hay, D. C. (1986). Face-name interference. *Journal of Experimental Psychology: Human Perception and Performance, 12*, 466–475.

*Editors' note: We mourn the untimely death of Justine Sergent.*

# IV  Spatial Attention

# 9 Space and Selective Attention

Giacomo Rizzolatti, Lucia Riggio, and
Boris M. Sheliga

ABSTRACT  This chapter is divided into three parts. In the first part we discuss the issue of how space is represented in the brain. After reviewing a series of recent anatomical and physiological data we reach the following conclusions: (1) space representation derives from the activity of several independent brain circuits, (2) those cortical areas that code space are also involved in programming motor actions (spatial pragmatic maps), and (3) neuron mechanisms for coding space are different in the oculomotor and in the somatomotor pragmatic maps.

The second part deals with spatial attention. After dismissing the possibility that there is something like a unitary superordinate system for selective attention, we argue that there is no need to postulate for spatial attention a system anatomically separated from the systems processing data. In contrast to this theoretical position, we propose a theory of attention (*premotor theory*) whose main tenets are the following: (1) Spatial selective attention is a consequence of an activation of neurons located in the spatial pragmatic maps. (2) The activation of these neurons starts in concomitance with the preparation to perform goal-directed spatially coded movements and depends upon this preparation. (3) Different spatial pragmatic maps become active according to the task requirements. Spatial attention can originate therefore from any map that codes space. (4) In primates and in man, as a consequence of the strong development of the foveal vision and the neural apparatus for foveation, a central role in selective spatial attention is played by the oculomotor pragmatic maps.

In the last part of the chapter we present a series of new data that strongly support the premotor theory. We show that the trajectory of vertical saccades in response to an imperative (visual or acoustic) stimulus deviates according to the location of subject's attention on different positions along a horizontal line. We argue that if spatial attention were independent of motor programming, there would be no reason why a vertical saccade should be influenced by where the subject's attention was allocated.

## 9.1  INTRODUCTION

In psychology, as in other sciences, the scientific concepts derive from a prescientific description of the observed phenomena and an initial, often naive attempt to interpret them. It is easy to understand why an object may fall when it is pushed. It is hard, however, even to imagine that an object may fall when nobody touches it. In spite of this, force, as a scientific concept, does not imply the physical proximity between what is acting and what is acted upon. The two concepts we will deal with in this chapter—selective attention and space—belong to the category of concepts in which the subjective intuition does not coincide with and is, in fact, contradicted by experimental evidence.

The broadest possible definition of selective attention is one that links, without any further assumption, attention with selection. To attend is to select for further processing. Our subjective perception of attention is of something unitary—an internal device that we can use when the circumstances require it. Our intuition is therefore that in the brain there must be a center or a circuit devoted to attention. It has to be a single entity, and it has to possess all those properties that selective attention subjectively has.

The same is true for space. We live in space. Although the definition of space is not easy (Can there be a space without objects? Granted that extension is a property of the objects, can it be attributed also to space that is not an object?), the idea of space as something real, fixed, and unitary is compelling. We live in a kind of large box in which objects are located. Some are close to us and some are far, but they are all contained in the same box. Our intuition is therefore that in order to perceive space, the brain should have an area or a circuit that is able to reconstruct the box. This area (responsible for space perception) is used for judging distances, for describing a scene, for reaching an object, or for walking. It is so obvious that it must be so.

Recent neurophysiological and neuropsychological data appear, however, to contradict these intuitive notions of space and attention. In this chapter we review these data and attempt to provide a theoretical framework to explain them. The main theses of this theoretical attempt are the following:

1. Conscious space perception results from the activity of several cortical and subcortical areas, each with its own neural space representation. By neural space representation, we mean the coding of the external world in a system of nonretinal coordinates.

2. The cortical areas, in which space is represented, are also involved in programming motor actions related to specific sets of effectors.

3. Spatially selective attentional processes are embedded within these areas. They depend on the motor programming carried out in the same areas rather than on an anatomically separate, superordinate control system.

4. In primates, the development of foveal vision and mechanisms necessary for foveation gives a particular prominence for spatial attention to areas that code space for programming oculomotion.

## 9.2 SPACE REPRESENTATION

### Visual Cortical Areas and Space Representation

The visual cortical system of primates is formed by a mosaic of heavily interconnected areas in which two broad streams of visual centers, arising from the primary visual cortex, can be recognized: a ventral stream largely projecting to the inferior temporal lobe and a dorsal stream that terminates in the inferior parietal lobule (Ungerleider and Mishkin 1982; Felleman and Van-Essen 1991).

The ventral stream is responsible for the analysis of the qualities of an object. It enables the visual system to categorize visual inputs as visual objects, regardless of the visual conditions in which the objects are presented. The dorsal stream is responsible for space computation. It transforms retinal representations into spatial descriptions and transmits these descriptions to the frontal lobe for immediate and delayed action.

Two issues concerning the functional organization of the dorsal stream are crucial for understanding space perception. The first issue concerns the notion of a unitary, multipurpose brain structure (area or circuit) that mediates space perception. Is this notion consistent with the organization of the dorsal stream and, in particular, of the inferior parietal lobule? The second issue is whether the dorsal stream codes primarily space. The alternative possibility is that the dorsal stream codes action. Space is represented inasmuch as it must be computed in order to act.

## Space Representation in the Parietal and Frontal Lobes

The inferior parietal lobule is constituted of several distinct anatomical (Brodmann 1925; Von Bonin and Bailey 1947; Pandya and Seltzer 1982) and functional areas (Hyvarinen 1982; Goldman-Rakic 1988; Andersen et al. 1990). Recent studies, carried out on monkeys, showed that each of these areas has specific connections with premotor, oculomotor, and prefrontal areas (Pandya and Kuypers 1969; Petrides and Pandya 1984; Godschalk et al. 1984; Matelli et al. 1986; Cavada and Goldman-Rakic 1989; Andersen et al. 1990). Among the various frontoparietal circuits, three circuits have been extensively studied: lateral intraparietal area (LIP)–area 8, PF (area 7b)–premotor F4, and "manipulation" anterior intraparietal (AIP) area–premotor F5.

The LIP–area 8 circuit contains three main classes of neurons: neurons responding to visual stimuli (visual neurons), neurons firing in association with eye movements (movement neurons), and neurons with both visual- and movement-related activity (visuomovement cells) (Bruce and Goldberg 1985; Bruce 1988; Andersen and Gnadt 1989; Goldberg and Segraves 1989; Barash et al. 1991a, 1991b). Visual neurons respond vigorously to stationary light stimuli. Their receptive fields are large, varying from a few degrees to an entire quadrant of the visual field. Movement neurons fire in relation to ocular saccades, most of them discharging before the saccade onset. Of these, the vast majority become active only during goal-directed movements. Visuomovement neurons have both visual and saccade-related activity. Visual receptive field and "motor" fields are in register.

The neural machinery of the PF-F4 circuit reveals a functional organization analogous to that of the saccade circuit. As in the LIP–area 8 circuit, neurons in areas PF-F4 can be subdivided into three main classes: sensory neurons, movement neurons, and sensory-movement neurons. The majority of the cells belong to the last category (Leinonen et al. 1979; Gentilucci et al. 1983; Gentilucci et al. 1988). Sensory and sensory-movement neurons respond to tactile stimuli or to tactile and visual stimuli (Leinonen et al. 1979; Gentilucci et al. 1983, 1988; Graziano and Gross 1992; Graziano and Gross, n.d.). Their visual properties, however, are markedly different from those of neurons in the LIP–area 8 circuit. In contrast to the latter neurons, they typically do not respond to stimuli located far from the animal. Their receptive fields are restricted to the space around the animal's face or body (peripersonal space). The extension in depth of individual receptive fields is not fixed. In many neurons, the fields expand when the stimulus velocity increases (Fadiga et al. 1992). Movement cells become active during proximal arm movements (especially reaching), as well as during oro-facial and axial movements. Sensory-movement neurons exhibit both sensory and movement-related activity. The primary function of this circuit appears to be that of transforming visual information into signal for reaching and other arm and body movements.

It is clear from this description that the parietofrontal circuits code space not per se but in function of the motor requirements. Thus, in the arm reaching circuit, the peripersonal space is essentially coded. Peripersonal space coincides with the motor space of the arms. Far space, important for exploration and for motor activities such as walking but not for reaching, is not represented. It is important to note also that sensory-movement neurons in both the oculomotor and arm reaching circuits code position of the stimulus and a specific motor command. This command is a command for either an eye movement or an arm movement. Therefore, the neurophysiological evidence does not appear to support the idea that the same spatial information is used for programming both saccade and arm movements. The spatial information necessary for these acts appears to be segregated.

**Space Coding at the Single Neuron Level**

Recent data on the neural mechanisms responsible for space coding provide further evidence against the idea that space perception is mediated by a single multipurpose area. The neurons located in the LIP–area 8 circuit show retinotopic receptive fields (Andersen and Gnadt 1989; Goldberg and Segraves 1989). Space coding results here indirectly from a computation performed by these neurons. There are two competing theories on how this may occur. According to one of them, space representation is achieved by retinotopic neurons whose response intensity is modulated (in contrast to that of neurons in the earlier visual stations) by the eye position in the orbita (Andersen, Essick, and Siegel 1985). These neurons would integrate retinal signals about the visual target with extraretinal signals about eye position. By using this double information, the LIP–area 8 circuit would be able to compute the position of the targets in space and direct the gaze toward them.

Another way in which the oculomotor system can achieve a spatial frame of reference is suggested by Goldberg and Bruce (1990): when there is a dissonance between the retinal vector of a stimulus and the movement vector of the saccade necessary to acquire it, a change occurs in the topographical location of the retinal receptive field. This remapping, possibly based on a vector subtraction, should be responsible for the correct acquisition of a target (Duhamel, Colby, and Goldberg 1992).

In contrast to the indirect space coding of the oculomotor circuit, the PF-F4 area circuit codes space explicitly at the single neuron level. The large majority of neurons in F4 have receptive fields anchored to the body. When the monkey moves the gaze and fixates a new target, the receptive field does not change position, as it should if the field were coded in retinal coordinates (Gentilucci et al. 1983; Fogassi et al. 1992). This way of coding space fits well the motor requirements of the PF-F4 circuit. It would be a computational burden to update the eye position continuously for a circuit whose goal is to organize arm and other body part movements, regardless of eye location. In contrast, such an updating should not give particular trouble to a circuit specifically devoted to eye movements. Regardless of the reasons for the different coding, what interests us more here is that not only the space circuits for eye and arm movement are anatomically segregated, but they also use different mechanisms for space coding.

From this brief review of the neuronal properties of the frontoparietal circuits the following conclusions emerge: (1) computation of space is performed in different cortical circuits, in parallel; (2) space representation is linked to movement organization; and (3) mechanisms for representing space are different in different circuits and most likely are related to and depend on the motor requirements of the effectors controlled by a given circuit. The question left is whether the inferior parietal lobe, which appears to have a nodal position between the posterior visual retinotopic areas and the frontal motor centers, should be considered spatial, the traditional view (Critchley 1953; Hyvarinen 1982; Ungerleider and Mishkin 1982; Grüsser and Landis 1991), or whether a more appropriate description of its function is in terms of visual information coding for action.

**Space versus Action**

The study of arm movements during prehension showed that this action consists of two main components, reaching and grasping. In order to generate these movements effectively, the nervous system has to solve a series of computational problems, which differ for reaching and grasping. Reaching requires the localization of objects in space with respect to the body. This implies the formation of a stable frame of reference independent of eye position and the encoding of visual information in body-centered coordinates. By contrast, grasping deals with intrinsic qualities of the objects. The coordinate system in which grasping movements are generated relates to the object and the hand. The knowledge of the position of the object in the external space is irrelevant (Arbib 1981; Jeannerod 1988).

The properties of neurons forming the PF-F4 circuit fit well the computational requirements for reaching movements. Those neurons compute the extrinsic spatial relations between the target object and the body and transform it into a pattern of proximal movements (Gentilucci and Rizzolatti 1990).

The properties of PF-F4 neurons are therefore consistent with both the idea that the parietal lobe is for space representation and the idea that this lobe is related to action.

Recent data show that the visuomotor integration of grasping is also carried out in the parietal lobe, and precisely in a circuit that involves the parietal AIP (Sakata and Musunoki 1992) and the premotor area F5 (Rizzolatti et al. 1988). Parietal neurons specifically related to grasping ("manipulation neurons"; Mountcastle et al. 1975) fall into three classes:

1. Motor dominant neurons, which are similarly activated during grasping movement executed in light and darkness. A large number of neurons of this class fire exclusively during particular types of grasping movements.

2. Visual dominant neurons, which are not active when grasping is made in the dark.

3. Visual-and-motor neurons, which are less active in the dark than in the light.

Many neurons of the last two classes respond to the sight of objects in the absence of hand movements (Taira et al. 1991).

Neurons of area F5 are also selective for different types of grip. Some of them fire at the object presentation in the absence of any movement. The visual discharge is evoked only if the object size is congruent with the coded grip (Rizzolatti et al. 1988). Areas AIP and F5 appear, therefore, to code the intrinsic visual characteristics of the objects and to transform them into the appropriate distal movements.

The interest of these findings for the understanding of the parietal lobe functions lies in the fact that manipulation neurons do not compute space. The stimulus processing they perform is for many aspects similar to that performed by the neurons in the visual ventral stream and in the temporal lobe in particular. As those neurons, they describe objects. The description, they carry on, however, is not for object recognition but for the organization of the appropriate object-related hand movements. This pragmatic function is shared with the adjacent circuits that organize reaching and oculomotion. It appears therefore that the notion that the dorsal stream—inferior parietal lobe is the brain region related to space representation is only partially true. A more comprehensive interpretation is that this region codes the visual information for the organization of actions. The areas of this region provide a series of pragmatic representations of the visual world as opposed to the semantic representations of the temporal lobe.

A similar interpretation of the functional organization of parietal lobe has been recently advanced by Goodale and Milner and their co-workers (Goodale et al. 1991; Milner et al. 1991) on the basis of their neuropsychological findings. They analyzed in great detail the visual behavior of a patient with a severe visual agnosia following carbon monoxide poisoning. The patient was unable to perceive the size, shape, and orientation of visual objects, yet she showed accurate reaching and grasping of those same objects whose qualities she was unable to perceive. When she was presented, for example, with a pair of rectangular blocks of the same or different dimensions, she was unable to indicate whether they were the same or different. Yet when she was asked to reach and grasp the block, the aperture between her index finger and thumb was systematically related to size of the object in a manner not dissimilar from that of normal subjects. The authors concluded that the distinction between object vision and spatial vision cannot account for the described dissociation and convincingly argued that the main role of the inferior parietal lobule is to provide visual information required for acting on objects (Goodale and Milner 1992).

## Conclusions

In summary, the neurophysiological and neuropsychological studies of the parietofrontal circuits indicate that the scenario of space perception is radically different from that of a simple spatial box. There is no evidence of a spatial map on which the "light" of attention could act. Furthermore, even the idea of a brain region specifically devoted to space is under dispute. The inferior parietal lobe, rather than being a spatial lobe, appears to be the cortical region where visual information is coded for different types of actions, some of them requiring spatial information.

One may argue that if the organization of the cortical parietofrontal circuits appears to contradict the notion of a multipurpose space map, nevertheless, such a map could exist elsewhere—for example, in the subcortical structures. The hippocampus, the basal ganglia, and the cerebellum are all centers that use spatial information and one (or more) of them could code space using rules different from those of spatial cortical maps. Even if this were so, however, the principle on the basis of space representation should not change radically. Evidence from a large number of clinical and experimental studies shows that damage to the parietal lobe and the related frontal areas produces severe space perception deficits (Critchley 1953; De Renzi 1982; Ungerleider and Mishkin 1982). Among them, particularly dramatic is the neglect syndrome, a syndrome in which part of space representation (Bisiach and Vallar 1988; Rizzolatti and Berti 1990, 1993) is "truncated" (De Renzi 1982). Thus, the existence of a hypothetical subcortical multipurpose center would not contradict our conclusions.

It is important to note that lesions of the parietofrontal circuits coding space produce perceptual deficits that are much more severe and diffuse than those one may expect from the physiological properties of the damaged circuits. Stimuli in the affected space sector are ignored and not responded to, not only when the required responses depend on the activity of the damaged circuits but also when they depend on circuits that are spared by the lesion. For example, following a unilateral lesion of the frontal eye fields, monkeys are unable to detect and respond manually to visual stimuli presented to the space contralateral to the lesion, in spite of the fact that the circuits responsible for the visual control of arm movements are intact (Latto and Cowey 1971).

Similarly, monkeys with restricted lesions to the premotor areas do not react emotionally to threatening stimuli, although there are plenty of intact circuits that may convey visual information to the emotional centers (Rizzolatti, Matelli, and Pavesi 1983). These findings indicate that conscious space representation depends on the concomitant activity of a multiplicity of cortical (and subcortical) centers. Although it is by no means clear how this multiple system is coordinated, there is little doubt that the unity of space perception is not due to the activity of a unitary space map but results from the coordinated activity of several highly specialized sensorimotor circuits. An interesting consequence of this type of organization is that it predicts implicit processing of information coming from the space sector contralateral to the lesion in neglect patients. Recent experiments confirmed this prediction (Volpe, Ledoux, and Gazzaniga 1979; Marshall and Halligan 1988; Berti et al. 1992; Berti and Rizzolatti 1992). Visual information, although not consciously perceived, can be processed in the spared circuits and its effect revealed with specific tests. For a discussion of this issue see chapter 2 of this book.

We now turn to how the activity of these spatial centers is related to selective spatial attention. Selective attention in the semantic maps is outside the scope of this chapter and will be not dealt with here.[1]

## 9.3 SPATIAL ATTENTION

**Selective Attention: One superordinate system, many superordinate systems, or intrinsic mechanisms within the pragmatic and semantic representations?**

Although attention can be conceptualized as an outcome that characterizes the behavioral state of the organism, the term, as used by most current theories of attention, indicates some hypothetical agency that can be directed or focused on an entity (Johnston and Dark 1986; Allport 1993). Introspectively, this mechanism is unitary, and this unity has been implicitly accepted by most attention theorists.

Evidence accumulated in the past ten years shows that this idea is untenable. The literature on this issue has been reviewed elsewhere (Rizzolatti, Gentilucci, and Matelli 1985; Rizzolatti and Gallese 1988; Posner and Petersen 1990; Allport 1989, 1993) and will be not dealt with here in details. We will summarize only the results of two studies that have been particularly influential in disproving the notion of a central attentional system. Both used positron emission tomography (PET) to identify the neural systems involved in selective attention. In the first study (Posner et al. 1988), changes in cerebral blood flow were examined during a series of visuo-verbal tasks (fixation of a target, passive looking at foveally presented nouns, repetition of concrete nouns, and generation of words describing the use for concrete nouns). The results showed that, besides the occipital cortical areas, which were active when the material was presented visually, the areas that were selectively activated during the attentionally highly demanding generation task were a lateral frontal region and the anterior cingulate gyrus. These researchers concluded, "There is no evidence of activation of any parts of the posterior visual spatial attention system (for example, parietal lobe) in any of our PET language studies" (p. 1629). The parietal lobe was traditionally the favorite cortical region for localizing the attention center in the human brain.

The task of the second PET study (Corbetta et al. 1990, 1991) was to discriminate a stimulus change of shape, color, or velocity. In one condition (Selective Attention), the subjects were instructed to focus on one stimulus attribute and disregard possible changes in the other attributes. In a second condition (Divided Attention) the subjects had to detect changes in any stimulus attribute, dividing attention across stimulus attributes. The results showed that Selective Attention for a given attribute increased the metabolism of different sectors of extrastriate cortex specialized for processing the selected feature. Outside the visual areas, Divided Attention activated the frontal lobe and the cingulate cortex, while Selective Attention activated essentially subcortical centers. "The only region commonly activated across conditions was the left globus pallidus" (Corbetta et al. 1991, p. 2392).

These results are obviously devastating for any theory that maintains that there is an attentional unitary central system. So how can attention be conceived following these findings? Two alternatives appear to be logically possible. The first, more linked to the old unitary conception, is to postulate a few distinct attention systems related to different cognitive functions—for example, attention for space, for object attributes, or for language. This idea has in common with the previous unitary conception the tenet that the attention systems are anatomically separated from the data processing systems (semantic, pragmatic, language representations) (Posner and Petersen 1990). The other alternative is that attention mechanisms are intrinsic to pragmatic and semantic maps. Attention derives from the activity of these representations without any intervention of other hypothetical anatomical structures. As far as the spatial attention is concerned, attention is the consequence of the activity of pragmatic maps and is strictly related to motor preparation. The theory that maintains this point of view was first formulated by Rizzolatti (1983; see also Rizzolatti and Camarda 1987) on the basis of a series of neurophysiological data. This theory, usually referred to as the premotor theory of attention, was subsequently expanded by Rizzolatti, Umiltà, and Riggio (see below) and used to explain some intriguing psychological findings.

**Selective Attention as an Intrinsic Mechanism**

The premotor theory of attention has three main claims:

1. The mechanisms responsible for spatial attention are localized in the spatial pragmatic maps. There are no such things as selective attention circuits defined as anatomical entities separated from the spatial maps.

2. Spatial attention is a consequence of a facilitation of neurons in the spatial pragmatic maps. This facilitation depends on the preparation to perform goal-directed, spatially coded movements.

3. Different spatial pragmatic maps become active according to the task requirements. Spatial attention can be produced by any map that codes space. In humans and primates, as a consequence of the strong development of the foveal vision and the neural mechanisms for foveation, a central role in selective attention is played by those maps that code space for programming oculomotion.

In this section, we will discuss to which psychological experiments the premotor theory can apply and its limitations. In the next sections, we will present evidence for the validity of the theory in cases in which spatial attention appears to be related to oculomotion or to other types of movements.

In very general terms, the psychological studies of selective attention fall into two main broad classes: studies based on the filtering paradigm and studies based on the selective-set paradigm (Kahneman and Treisman 1984). The filter paradigm experiments are characterized by the following features: (1) the subjects are presented simultaneously with relevant and irrelevant stimuli; (2) the relevant stimuli control a relatively complex process of response selection and execution; and (3) most frequently a physical feature distinguishes relevant from irrelevant stimuli and determines the correct response. Examples of filtering paradigm can be found in the work of Broadbent (1952, 1958), Cherry (1953), and Treisman (1964), among others. The selective-set paradigm experiments are based on the expectation by the subject of a particular stimulus. As soon as the expected stimulus is detected or recognized, a speeded response has to be emitted. There are two main variants of selective-set paradigm: studies of search (Schneider and Shiffrin 1977) and studies of cost and benefits of expectations (Posner 1978). In both variants, attention is set to detect one or more potential targets.

The premotor theory of attention is strictly related to the experimental paradigm described by Posner and his co-workers (1978, 1980). In this paradigm the task is essentially spatial. Usually, it demands only a detection of an unstructured visual stimulus. The required manual response is arbitrary. It does not depend on the solution of a spatial problem. The "austerity" of the experimental conditions renders the Posner paradigm particularly suitable for an analysis in terms of psychological and physiological mechanisms and, as will be discussed later, the data obtained by employing this paradigm are well explained by the premotor theory of attention.

Can the premotor theory explain also the findings obtained using other paradigms, such as, for example, the filtering paradigm? The main claim of the premotor theory is that movement preparation facilitates the input side of the pragmatic maps involved in the task, thus improving the stimulus detection. The theory is therefore a selective-set one. The machinery involved in spatial attention, however, is not exclusively facilitatory. In several visuo-oculomotor centers (see below), the abrupt presentation of a new stimulus concomitantly to a facilitation of the neurons related to its visual field location produces an inhibition of the remaining unstimulated neurons. This inhibition, by reducing or even blocking the information coming from visual field locations different from that where the new stimulus is presented, gives subjective relevance to this stimulus and facilitates the disengagement of the gaze (and attention) from the spatial locus that is processed at the moment of the new stimulus presentation. The mechanism acting in the case of filtering paradigm experiments could be similar in its essence to this disengagement mechanism but oriented in the reverse direction. In a visual experiment based on a filtering paradigm, fundamental for the task is the maintenance of the fixation on a certain part of a spatial scene in spite of the simultaneous occurrence of competing distracting stimuli. In such a task, the presence of oculomotor commands that impose fixation and simultaneously inhibit those sectors of the involved pragmatic maps that are related to the visual periphery should be critical. Such an oculomotor mechanism would decrease the relevance of the simultaneously incoming stimuli competing with the attended one and would allow the information contained in it to be adequately processed.

We are not aware of experiments that have formally tested these predictions. The findings of Moran and Desimone (1985), however, are indicative of the existence of a filtering mechanism similar to that postulated above. These authors recorded single neurons from two areas of the visual ventral stream, area V4 and the inferotemporal cortex, in behaving monkeys. The monkeys were trained to attend to stimuli at one location and to ignore them at another. The results showed that the responses to the unattended stimuli were dramatically reduced. One cannot infer from these data the mechanisms that subserve the filtering of the irrelevant information and where they originate. However, although other explanations of the phenomenon are possible, our proposal is that the filtering process originates in the pragmatic maps and that it is related to commands for fixation maintenance.

In contrast to Posner's paradigm, where the expectancy concerns exclusively the locus of stimulus appearance, search paradigm requires that specific stimuli be detected and identified. It is usually assumed that the detection and identification process requires the activation of units (single neurons, assembly of neurons, nodes in long-term memory) that are tuned for specific stimuli. When these units are fully activated, we perceive familiar objects, their properties, or events (Schneider and Shiffrin 1977; Johnston and Dark 1982). Stimulus expectancy, although unable to activate these units fully, renders their activation more likely (LaBerge 1975; Schneider and Shiffrin 1977). Regardless of what exactly the detection and identification units could be, according to our subdivision of the cortical areas, they should belong to the semantic areas. The issue of attentional mechanisms of these area is outside the limits of this chapter and will be not dealt here.

**Premotor Theory of Spatial Attention**

**Active (Endogenous) Orienting of Attention**   Attention can be oriented actively or passively. Passive orienting describes cases in which a stimulus attracts the individual's attention for its intrinsic properties or for the way in which it is presented. Active orienting arises from the subject and is characterized by an effort to increase the clearness of a given external stimulus (James 1890; Titchener 1966). This distinction between active and passive attention has been developed by, among others, Posner (1980), Jonides (1981), and Muller and Rabbitt (1989). Using criteria such as capacity demands, resistance to suppression, and sensitivity to expectancy, they showed that external, abruptly presented stimuli ("peripheral cues") cause "automatic" (passive) shifts of attention, whereas cues presented centrally and that have to be interpreted in order to orient attention ("central" or "cognitive" cues) cause "voluntary" (active) shifts of attention. These and other results showing differential time courses of orienting in response to peripheral and central cues (Yantis and Jonides 1984; Muller and Findlay 1988; Spencer, Lambert, and Hockey 1988; Muller and Rabbitt 1989) suggest that different mechanisms are involved in the two phenomena.

**Psychological Experiments**  Figure 9.1 shows the visual display used in most of our experiments (Rizzolatti et al. 1987; Umiltà et al. 1991). The subject's task was to direct attention to the cued box while maintaining fixation on a central point and to press a response key as fast as possible at the occurrence of the imperative stimulus. Trials on which the imperative stimulus was shown in the cued box are referred to as valid; trials on which the stimulus was shown in a box different from the cued one are referred to as invalid; and trials on which all boxes were cued are referred to as neutral (see Posner, Snyder, and Davidson 1980). Table 9.1 illustrates the results typically obtained in these experiments.

**Table 9.1**

| Arrangement of stimulus boxes | Type of trial | | | | |
|---|---|---|---|---|---|
| | Valid | Invalid | | | |
| | | $4°s$ | $4°o$ | $8°o$ | $12°o$ |
| Horizontal | 212 | 234 | 255 | 261 | 265 |
| Vertical | 208 | 222 | 242 | 253 | 266 |
| | 210 | 228 | 249 | 257 | 266 |

Abbreviations: s, same hemifield; o, opposite hemifield (with regard to the attended location).

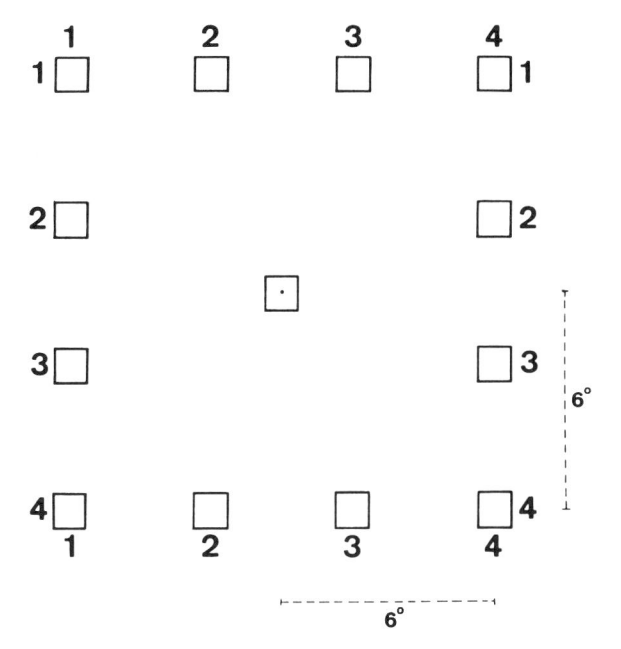

**Figure 9.1** Stimulus display in the experiment by Rizzolatti et al. (1987). Four possible configurations of boxes (two horizontal and two vertical) were used. Only one configuration was shown in each experimental condition. Each configuration consisted of a central fixation box with the fixation spot inside, and four boxes, marked by an adjacent digit (1–4), for stimulus presentation.

The main findings can be summarized as follows:

1. Valid trials are faster than neutral trials and neutral trials are faster than invalid trials.

2. Invalid trials are longer than valid trials also when the imperative stimulus that triggers them is presented in the cued hemifield.

3. When the imperative stimulus is presented at the same distance from the cued location in the cued and noncued hemifield, reaction times are slower in the noncued hemifield. This effect is called the meridian effect.

4. Within the noncued hemifield, reaction times increase as a function of the distance from the cued location. This effect is referred to as the distance effect.

The premotor theory offers a satisfactory explanation of most of these findings and suggests some neurophysiological mechanisms that may underlie them. Its first assumption is that, in the described, impoverished, experimental situation, attention is linked to the oculomotor circuits. There is no need for activation of other pragmatic areas.[2] The second assumption is that both covert orienting of attention and motor programming (in this case programming of ocular saccades) are controlled by the same pragmatic maps. Covert orienting occurs when a behavioral situation or a verbal command prevents eye movements but leaves unchanged the oculomotor program. This programming of saccades is responsible for the endogenous attention movement, whereas inhibition of the saccade that in natural conditions, outside the laboratory, would be the response to a peripheral cue determines the complex pattern of facilitation-inhibition typical of this condition (Posner and Cohen 1984; Maylor 1985; Maylor and Hockey 1985; Possamai 1986; Berlucchi et al. 1989; Rafal et al. 1989).

Given these premises, the sequence of the events consequent to the presentation of a cognitive cue is the following. As soon as the location of the imperative stimulus can be predicted, a motor program for a saccade toward the expected location is prepared. This program specifies the direction and the amplitude of the saccade. When the two parameters are set, two events occur. First, the location of the expected stimulus becomes salient with respect to all other locations (Bashinski and Bacharach 1980; Downing 1988; Muller and Humphreys 1991; Hawkins et al. 1990; Riggio and Kirsner, n.d.). Then the stimuli appearing in that location are responded to faster (Posner 1980). This is true both when the required response is an ocular saccade toward the target or a manual pressing of a switch.

The situation is obviously different when the imperative stimulus occurs in an unexpected position. In this case, in agreement with the original proposal by Posner (1980), the premotor theory postulates that the manual response (and other not hard-wired, arbitrary responses) can be emitted only when attention is allocated to the new point. Thus, the invalid response is delayed both because the expected location is not facilitated and because a time-consuming change in the saccade program should take place before the manual response is emitted.[3]

Once it is accepted that attention is subserved by the same mechanisms that program eye movements, several puzzling experimental findings become easier to explain. One of them is the intriguing meridian effect, a robust effect that is constantly observed when attention is directed by cognitive cues (Downing and Pinker 1985; Hughes and Zimba 1985; Rizzolatti et al. 1987; Shepherd and Muller 1989; Umiltà et al. 1991; Gawryszewski et al. 1992; Reuter-Lorenz and Fendrich 1992). Typically, its value is in the order of 20 to 25 ms. If one conceives of the attentional system as independent of any physiological and anatomical constraint, this result is hard to explain. Why should attention movement be delayed when attention crosses something like the horizontal meridian, of whose presence we are not aware and whose existence is known only to those acquainted with the anatomy of the eyes and the nervous system? The situation becomes different if one considers the organization of the oculomotor system.

There is good agreement that goal-directed saccades are prepared in two steps. First, a decision concerning the direction is taken (Wheeless, Boynton, and Cohen 1966; Komoda et al. 1973; Becker and Jurgens 1979; Findlay 1982). As Becker and Jurgens stated, "The decision to elicit a saccade is identical with the decision about the direction of the saccades." Second, when the direction is established, the amplitude is calculated. There are two main consequences of this formulation: changes in saccade direction require a radical modification in oculomotor program, and changes in saccade amplitude imply only a readjustment of a preexisting program. According to the premotor theory, the meridian effect results from identical causes. When the amplitude of the attention movement has to be modified without changing direction, what is needed is only an adjustment in the parameters of a set of eye movements whose general programming has already been made. In contrast, when the imperative stimulus appears in the hemifield opposite the one containing the cued location, then it is the direction of the attention that has to be modified. In this case, the process is more time-consuming because a new program, involving (if executed) a radically different set of muscles, has to be constructed. This complete program change would be the origin of the meridian effect.

Less straightforward is the prediction of what should occur when both the direction and the amplitude of the oculomotor program have to be changed. Granted that changing direction determines a large cost, the issue is whether (once direction is set) programming a large-amplitude eye movement costs more than programming a small one or whether the cost is the same regardless of the amplitude to be programmed. If the first hypothesis is correct, the distance effect would be, analogous to the meridian effect, a pure consequence of the time necessary for programming eye movements. However, the facilitation of a given sector in an oculomotor map is frequently accompanied by inhibition of other sectors. One cannot exclude, therefore, that even if the first hypothesis is correct, some inihibitory factors can intervene in the origin of the distance effect. These factors, by decreasing the responsiveness of the oculomotor maps, would impair the detection of stimuli located far from the attended location. Inhibition might be the major factor responsible for the distance effect if, as postulated by the second hypothesis, the same amount of time is required to program small and large movements (Remington and Pierce 1984).

**Neurophysiological Experiments** Let us see now how the premotor interpretation of the psychological findings fits with the neurophysiological evidence. A situation of stimulus expectancy similar to that determined by cognitive cues in the Posner paradigm has been studied by Wurtz, Goldberg, Hikosaka, and their associates in conditioned monkeys (for a detailed review, see Robinson and McClurkin 1989; Hikosaka and Wurtz 1989). The animals were taught two basic tasks: a fixation task, consisting of the detection of a brief dimming of a spot of light presented in front of the animal, and an eye response task, which started as a fixation task, but, after a brief time interval, the fixation point was turned off and a second spot presented peripherally. The monkey had to make a saccade to the second stimulus and detect its dimming. The stimuli were presented in blocks, in the same spatial position within a block. Thus, after the first trials, the monkey could predict the stimulus location.

Once the animals mastered the tasks, single neurons were recorded from the superior colliculus (SC) and other visual and oculomotor centers. Taking advantage of the temporary immobility of the gaze during the fixation task, the authors could map the neuron receptive fields and establish the intensity of the neuronal response to light stimuli. Subsequently, the neurons were tested during the eye response task. The same visual stimulus as in the first task was used, but now, unlike in that task, the animal expected the occurrence of the stimulus (target of the required saccadic eye movements) and could predict its location (Goldberg and Wurtz 1972; Mohler and Wurtz 1976; Wurtz and Mohler 1976).

We will review here only the results concerning the SC, which are very detailed and the easiest to interpret. The SC has a peculiar anatomical and functional position in the visual system. It receives direct projections from the retina, its neurons located in the superficial layers have clear sensory properties, it is connected, although indirectly, with motor centers controlling eye and head movements, and the neurons of the layers below the stratum opticum (intermediate and deep layers) have essentially premotor properties (Sprague, Berlucchi, and Rizzolatti 1973; Goldberg and Robinson 1978).

The experiments showed that a large proportion of SC neurons responded stronger to light stimuli during the eye response task than during the fixation task. Note that the stimuli were identical in both conditions. This response increase due to internally generated stimulus relevance was named an enhancement effect (Goldberg and Wurtz 1972). A particularly important finding was that the enhancement effect concerned the purely visual neurons of the superficial layers. This indicates that the preparation to make a saccade toward a certain space position not only facilitates the motor response toward that point but also increases the responsiveness of visual neurons related to that position.

Another finding of great interest is the temporal course of the enhancement effect. The stimuli were presented in blocks. Thus, during the first trials of the eye response task, the monkey could not predict the stimulus location, while subsequently she could. It is likely, therefore, that in the first trials, the monkey responded passively to the stimulus without preparing the ocular motor program toward the stimulus, while later she prepared it. The enhancement effect was absent in the first trials (Mohler and Wurtz 1976).

Two other results of these experiments are also relevant for the premotor theory of attention. The first is that when the saccades occurred soon after stimulus presentation, the early part of the visual response was facilitated. In contrast, when the saccades occurred late, the late part of the response was enhanced (Wurtz and Mohler 1976). The second result concerns the activity of the neurons located in the intermediate and deep SC layers. These premotor neurons become active in concomitance with saccadic eye movements, and their discharge typically precedes the saccades of about 100 ms (Schiller and Koerner 1971; Wurtz and Goldberg 1972). However, when the monkey expected a stimulus, these neurons started to discharge well in advance of the saccade bringing the eye to the target (Mohler and Wurtz 1976). The premotor activity, therefore, prepares the eye movement toward the cued location and simultaneously activates the neurons of the superficial layers corresponding to the expected location.

The modifications in the SC excitability are modulated by a circuit formed by the cortical oculomotor areas, the caudate and the pars reticulata of the substantia nigra (SNr). The essence of this control mechanism is the following. At rest, the SNr neurons are tonically active and inhibit the SC (Hikosaka and Wurtz 1983a, 1983b). The inhibition is topographically organized. In turn, the SNr is under inhibitory control from the caudate. When a saccade has to be generated, the cortical activity excites the caudate neurons, which, in turn, inhibit the topographically related neurons in the SNr (Hikosaka, Sakamoto, and Usui 1989a, 1989b). The SC neurons are therefore disinhibited and ready to generate the appropriate saccade (Hikosaka and Wurtz 1989).

This disinhibitory mechanism may explain the excitability changes that occur in the SC during expectancy. The cortical motor program (prepared, but not implemented) disinhibits, by means of the caudate nucleus and SNr, the SC premotor neurons related to the cued space position. The increase in firing of these neurons facilitates the collicular superficial neurons, allowing a better detection of the stimuli. In addition, the readiness to respond when the expected stimulus occurs is increased.

**Passive (Exogenous) Orienting of Attention** In the section on active orienting of attention we started with a review of psychological data and finished with the physiological mechanisms that may underlie them. In this section we use the reverse strategy. We examine first the physiological changes determined by the presentation of stimuli endowed with attentional properties (Titchener 1966; Berlyne 1960, 1970), and we end by comparing the physiological processes with the psychological findings. As for active attention, our review of physiological data will concern essentially the SC.

The most detailed study on the modification induced by visual attentional stimuli on neuron activity was carried out by Rizzolatti and his co-workers on the SC of the cat (Rizzolatti et al. 1973, 1974). They plotted the receptive fields of SC neurons and determined for each neuron the best stimulus parameters. The neuron was then stimulated at regular intervals with the most effective stimulus (called S1). When it was clear that the response was stable, a second stimulus (S2) was abruptly presented simultaneously with S1 and moved outside the neuron's receptive field. The main finding of the experiments was that neuron responses were strongly inhibited every time the extra field stimulus was presented to the animal. This inhibitory effect was present in the great majority of collicular neurons, including those located in the superficial layers. Large S2s (e.g., 10 degrees in diameter) were typically more effective than small S2s. Black, high-contrast stimuli were more effective than low-contrast light stimuli. A similar inhibition due to an abrupt presentation of visual stimuli is present also in the cat extrastriate visual areas but not in the primary visual cortex (Rizzolatti et al. 1973).

An important variable for the inhibitory effect was the location of S2 in respect to S1. In virtually all neurons, the inhibitory effect was found to be stronger when S2 was presented in the same hemifield as S1. In contrast, the distance between S1 and S2 within the same hemifield did not appear to influence the neuron responses. The direction of movement of S2 toward, away from, or parallel to direction of S1 was immaterial for the occurrence of the inhibitory effect.

Typically Rizzolatti et al. (1973, 1974) presented S2 for a short time. In one set of experiments, however, they examined whether S2 would continue to exert an inhibitory influence over the responses to S1 after prolonged presentation (Rizzolatti et al. 1973). This point is fundamental for maintaining that the inhibitory effect is related to attention. If it is related, one should anticipate that a prolonged presentation of the stimulus would determine a progressive decrease of its effectiveness, by analogy, with what occurs in behavioral experiments, when the same stimulus is repetitively presented to the animal. In contrast, if the inhibitory effect is due to visual receptive field properties of SC neurons, one should expect no changes in the inhibitory effect intensity even after a prolonged S2 presentation. The inhibitory flanks adjacent to the excitatory part of the receptive field that some visual neurons have do not disappear with repetitive visual stimulation.

The results clearly showed that when S2 is kept in motion and S1 is periodically swept across the neuron's discharge area, the inhibitory effect disappears. The time length between the presentation of S2 and that of S1, which completely nullifies the S2 inhibitory action, ranges between 1 and 2 sec. Delays of 250 ms between the two stimuli produce a marked decrease in the inhibition strength.

The inhibitory effect is present in the monkey as well. Wurtz, Richmond, and Judge (1980) recorded single neurons from SC in conditioned monkeys and examined the effect of restricted light stimuli flashed in different parts of the visual field on the neuron's responses. They found that, as in cats, the presentation of an extra field stimulus produces a marked decrease of collicular responses. The effect of the stimulus is present when it is flashed simultaneously with S1 or precedes S1 by small intervals (about 100 ms). In good agreement with the findings in cats, stimuli presented in the hemifield opposite to that where the receptive fields is located give an inhibition much weaker than stimuli located on the same side of the vertical meridian as the receptive field.

From these data, it is clear that peripheral attentional stimuli determine a series of modifications in the SC which are absent in the case of voluntary attention. These peripheral cue effects can be summarized as follows:

1. A recruitment of premotor neurons topographically related to the stimulus location.[4]

2. A short-lasting facilitation of the superficial neurons topographically related to the stimulus location. (This facilitation should result from the activation of the premotor neurons).

3. A short-lasting inhibition of the visual responses outside the stimulated area ("inhibitory effect").

4. An inhibition of the natural orienting reaction. There is no physiological evidence for this point, but, as suggested by Tassinari et al. (1987), because of instructions, the subjects "have to generate a central command that counteracts the natural orienting reaction and vetoes the eye movement."

**Psychological Experiments** If the premotor theory of attention is correct, the changes in the excitability of oculomotor centers produced by the presentation of peripheral stimuli should have a counterpart in the findings of psychological experiments in which attention is summoned by these stimuli. In the case of valid trials, if the cue is not informative (that is, it does not predict the location of the imperative stimulus), the attention should remain only briefly on the cued location, since the premotor activation, due to local collicular circuits, is short-lasting. In contrast, if the cue is informative, the facilitation should be long-lasting because the local premotor activation is subsequently substituted by the cognitive facilitation determined by the central oculomotor program. In the case of invalid trials, the presence of an early inhibition ("inhibitory effect"), which is strong for stimuli ipsilateral to the cue and weak for stimuli contralateral to the cue, should favor the contralateral invalid trials. Finally, the suppression of the orienting toward the peripheral cue should produce a long-lasting bias in favor of the contralateral field (Tassinari et al. 1987).

Recently Umiltà et al. (1991) examined the effects of peripheral cues on spatial attention and compared the relationships between the cued location and the target location following presentation of cognitive and peripheral cues. The visual display was the same as in the experiment of Rizzolatti et al. (1987; see fig. 9.1). The manipulated variables were type of cue (cognitive or peripheral) and time interval between cue and imperative stimulus onset (SOA). The results obtained with peripheral cues clearly differed from those obtained with central cues. There were two main differences: (1) with peripheral cues, the meridian effect was absent with both long and short SOAs, and (2) the distance effect was present but did not show the regular increase in cost observed with central cues. Identical results were recently obtained by Reuter-Lorenz and Fendrich (1992).

These results appear to fit well with the data one would have predicted to obtain on the basis of the SC (and other oculomotor centers) modifications following presentation of passive cues. Let us start with the absence of meridian effect with long SOAs. According to the premotor theory, a peripheral cue automatically activates a collicular local motor program for a saccade in the direction of the stimulated visual field. This local program, however, must be counteracted by a central program in the opposite direction (a kind of antisaccade program) because of the previous instructions to keep the eyes still at the occurrence of the peripheral cue. The central program should cause a bias against eye movements (and attentional shifts) that share direction with the local program and, possibly, a bias in favor of movements (and attentional shifts) in the opposite direction (Tassinari et al. 1989). As a consequence, the meridian effect should disappear, or at least decrease, because orienting within the cued hemifield is hindered, whereas orienting to the opposite hemifield is not affected or even facilitated.

The explanation of the absence of the meridian effect with short SOAs is even more straightforward. The responses of neurons in the SC (and related cortical areas) are inhibited by presentation of stimuli outside the receptive fields that capture the animal's attention. This inhibition is maximal at the time of stimulus presentation and is particularly evident on the side where the attentional stimulus is presented. This early, fast-acting inhibitory process, which increases the salience of the stimulated location, should have as a behavioral counterpart the slowing of reaction times to stimuli located in the same hemifield where the cue was presented. This is exactly what was found by Umiltà et al. (1991). With SOAs of 100 ms, the responses to invalid trials across the vertical meridian were faster than those on the same side of the vertical meridian. The difference exceeded 10 ms.

**Criticisms of the Premotor Theory of Attention**  The link between oculomotion and attention is phenomenologically so obvious that the idea that there should be a close relation between the "movements of the body's eye" and the "movements of the mind's eye" has been advanced in the past by several authors (Crovitz and Daves 1962; Jonides 1976; Rayner, McConkie, and Ehrlich 1978; Klein 1980; Shepherd, Findlay, and Hockey 1986). The disputed point is whether (as the premotor theory states) the two phenomena are causally related. Particularly influential in refusing a causal relationship between oculomotion and attention has been an article by Klein (1980), whose purpose was to test the oculomotor hypothesis directly. In a first experiment, he examined whether a preprogrammed eye saccade facilitates the manual response to visual stimuli presented in the close proximity of the saccade target. In a second experiment, he studied whether the latency of an ocular saccade decreases after cuing a location. Although the results of the second experiment are difficult to interpret, those of the first, which are very clear, have been considered to be strong evidence against the oculomotor hypothesis.

Klein's subjects were presented with three dots, horizontally arranged, and were instructed to fixate the central one. After an interval, three types of events could occur: (1) the left or the right dot brightened, (2) an asterisk could appear over the left or the right dot, or (3) there was no change in the display. The subjects were instructed to respond manually if one of the dots brightened or to make a saccade in a prespecified direction if an asterisk appeared. According to Klein, since the subjects were told to move the eyes toward a fixed point, the detection of stimuli in that point should be facilitated, if the oculomotor hypothesis were true. The facilitation was not found and the premotor hypothesis rejected. The experiment, however, had a logical flaw.

The stimuli appeared randomly to the right or left of fixation. If in order to detect and discriminate these stimuli the subjects had to direct attention toward them, the best strategy for solving the task was to wait until the stimuli appeared and then orient attention in the direction specified by the instructions. It would have been uneconomical to prepare a motor program that in at least half of the cases should be subsequently cancelled. Subjects quite rightly waited for the stimuli, directed accordingly their attention (prepared the relevant oculomotor program, according to the premotor theory), and finally made the saccade. The experiment therefore neither proves nor disproves the premotor hypothesis.[5]

Another "disproof" of the premotor theory was recently reported by Crawford and Muller (1992). They used an experimental procedure and a display similar to that of Rizzolatti et al. (1987), the main differences being that there were six boxes instead of four. Three were on the right of the fixation point and three on the left. In one experiment, the response to the imperative stimulus was a saccade toward the illuminated box; in another, it was a simple speeded manual response. The vertical meridian effect was absent in the case of eye responses and present in the case of manual responses. Because of this incongruence between ocular and manual responses, the authors concluded that spatial attention and oculomotor preparation are mediated by different mechanisms.

The cue that Crawford and Muller (1992) used was a flash of light, that is, a peripheral cue. The meridian effect is not observed (also in the case of manual responses) with this type of cue (Shepherd and Muller 1989; Umiltà et al. 1991; Reuter-Lorenz and Fendrich 1992). Thus, the surprising finding in those experiments was the appearance of the meridian effect in a situation in which it usually does not occur. If the data are carefully analyzed, however, it is clear that in spite of the authors' claim, no meridian effect was present. The so-called meridian effect of their manual response experiment results from a mistake. In order to calculate the meridian effect, they erroneously pooled together all the invalid trials of the cued field and compared the resulting value with that obtained by pooling all the invalid trials of the uncued hemifield. However, when three boxes are placed in each hemifield, the distance between cue and imperative stimulus locations is, by necessity, greater in the uncued than in the cued hemifield. Thus, the so-called meridian effect was less surprisingly a distance effect. The meridian effect, if properly calculated, was absent (Crawford and Muller 1992, fig. 6).

The assumption that cognitive and peripheral cues determine identical attentional effects is at the basis of the criticism of premotor theory made by Egly and Bouma (1991). In their experiment, they calculated the time attention takes to cross the principal visual meridians following presentation of peripheral cues. The results showed that the distance between cue and the imperative stimulus, plus some quadrant effects, most likely related to inhibition of return, were the factors controlling the rapidity of attentional shifts. The meridian effect was not found, and, consequently, the premotor theory rejected. An experiment conceptually similar to that of Egly and Bouma was recently carried out by Gawryszewski et al. (1992). Cognitive cues instead of peripheral cues were used. The data confirmed the previous data by Rizzolatti et al. (1987). In addition, the results showed that the cost for reorienting attention across both the vertical and horizontal meridians is greater than the cost for crossing one meridian only.

**Evidence Supporting Directly the Premotor Theory of Spatial Attention**
The psychological evidence thus far discussed supporting the premotor theory of spatial attention is only indirect. It is based on analogies between attention orienting and eye movement programming. In this section, we report two new experiments that yielded direct evidence in favor of the premotor theory.

The basic experimental situation for many aspects was similar to that employed by Rizzolatti et al. (1987). There was a visual display of four boxes arranged in a horizontal row and a fixation point. In addition there was a fifth box located 6 degrees below the fixation point (fig. 9.2). Digit cues indicated in which of the four boxes the imperative stimulus (a small cross) was most likely to appear. Seventy percent of the trials were valid and thirty percent invalid. The subject's task was to look at the fixation point, to direct attention to the cued box, and to perform a saccadic eye movement toward the fifth (lower) box as fast as possible at the appearance of the imperative stimulus. The eye movements were recorded using an infrared oculometer. The head was fixed.

The response required from the subjects was very simple. If attention is independent of motor programming, there is no reason that a vertical saccade should be influenced by the fact that the subject allocates attention to one box or to another. In contrast, if directing attention implies an oculomotor program, the trajectory of the saccade should be influenced by the direction of attention because the local oculomotor program evoked by the imperative stimulus and the central oculomotor program necessary for directing spatial attention will interfere with that necessary for executing the ocular saccade. Evaluation of the deviation of saccadic trajectory was carried out in two ways:

1. Average saccade deviation (AD). The value of the X-component of the saccades was calculated from the moment of saccade initiation until the saccade reached its vectorial peak velocity, with sampling rate of 1 ms. The value of the X-component at the moment of saccade initiation was used as the reference value. The differences between the current values of the X-component and the reference value were summed and the sum of differences divided by the number of the performed summations.

2. Average velocity (AV). The average velocity of the X-component was calculated by measuring the velocity of this component from the saccade onset to the peak of vectorial velocity. Reaction time was also measured.

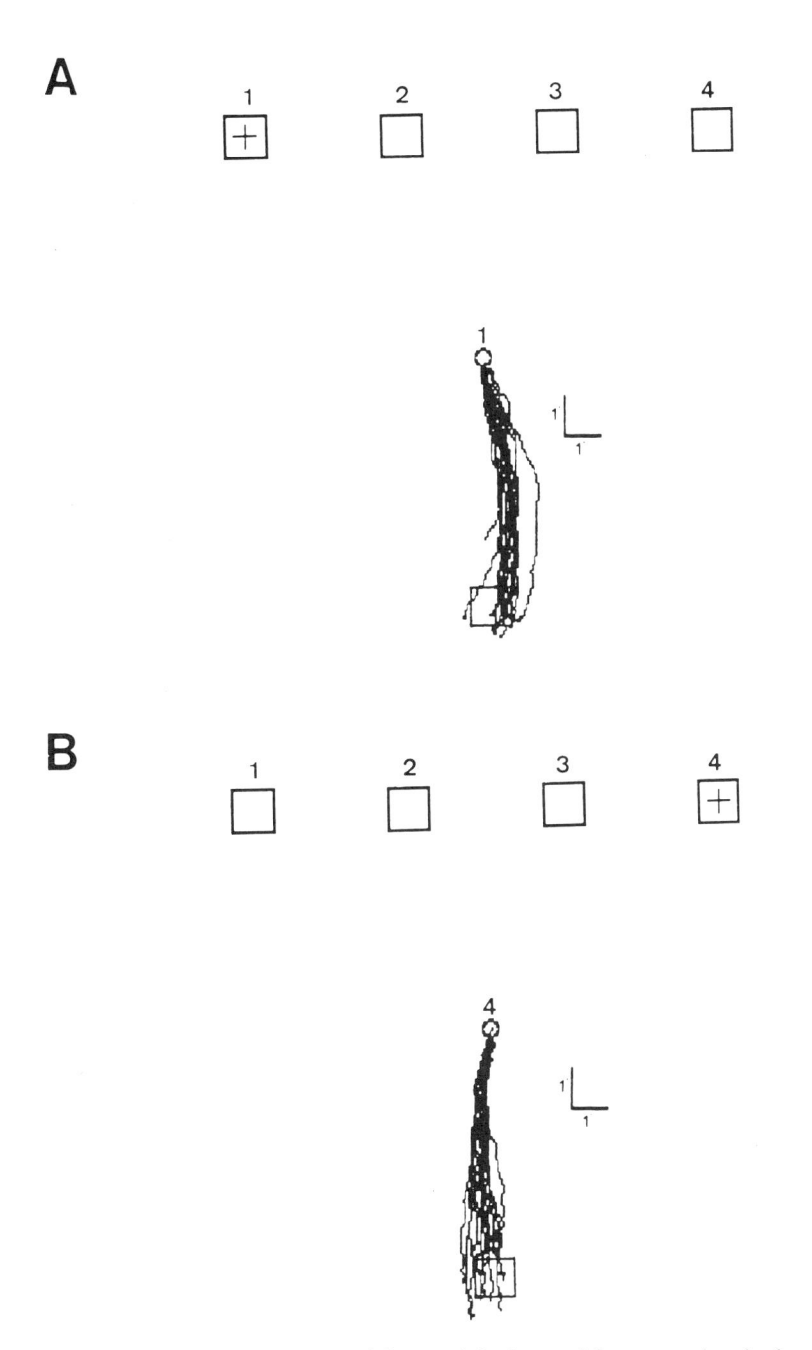

**Figure 9.2** Schematic drawing of the visual display used for testing directly the premotor theory of attention together with a series of individual saccadic trajectories. *A*. Valid condition with imperative stimulus presented in box 1. *B*. Valid condition with imperative stimulus presented in box 4. Notice the horizontal deviation of the saccadic trajectories contralateral to the side of the imperative stimulus presentation. For condition *A*, the first twenty trials are presented; for condition *B*, those with the clearest deviation.

The results showed that the valid trials were faster than invalid trials (248 ms versus 268 ms). The analysis of saccade deviation and velocity was carried out using two separate ANOVAs. In both of them, the main factors were Stimulated Field (left or right), Within Field Location of Imperative Stimuli (near to or far from the vertical meridian), and Cued Field (cued or not cued). For both AD and AV, Stimulated Field was significant: AD, $F(1,8) = 14.18, p < 0.005$; AV, $F(1,8) = 7.02, p < 0.05$. Figure 9.2 clarifies this finding. When the imperative stimulus is presented to the left hemifield, the saccades deviate to the right, and, conversely, when the stimulus is presented to the right hemifield, the saccades deviate to the left. Among the two-way interactions, the only significant was Stimulated Field × Cued Field: AD, $F(1,8) = 15.79, p < 0.005$; AV, $F(1,8) = 29.4, p < 0.001$. The reason for this interaction is as follows. Deviations away from a straight trajectory were larger when the imperative stimulus was presented to the cued field than when it was presented to the uncued field. Thus, when the imperative stimulus was presented to the left hemifield, AD and AV were more deviated to the right if the left hemifield had been previously cued than if the right hemifield had been previously cued. The opposite was true for presentations of the imperative stimulus to the right hemifield. In this case, both AD and AV were more deviated to the left if the right hemifield had been previously cued than if the left hemifield had been previously cued.

These results strongly support the premotor theory of attention. The first finding indicates that the presentation of the imperative stimulus triggers a strong tendency to orient toward it. This stimulus-driven orientation is responsible for passive spatial attention. Given the instruction to keep the eyes still, the subject has to suppress the overt orienting. This suppression command is reflected in the trajectory of the vertical saccade, which deviates to the side opposite to the stimulus presentation. The second finding indicates that when active (endogenous) spatial attention is allocated to a given hemifield, its effect is additive to that of passive attention. This is shown by the vertical saccade deviation, which is larger when the imperative stimulus is presented to the cued hemifield than when it is presented to the uncued hemifield. This increase in deviation suggests that endogenous attention activates oculomotor mechanisms as it occurs in the case of passive attention and that the activation of both mechanisms has to be suppressed for the execution of the vertical saccade.

In the experiment, the imperative stimulus was a visual signal. Thus, active and passive attentional phenomena were partially intermixed. To avoid this, a second experiment was carried out. Here, the visual display consisted of five boxes that formed a cross, with the two arms orthogonal one to another. The central box served as the fixation point. A small line, attached to the central box and pointing in different directions, indicated where the imperative stimulus would appear. In fifty percent of the trials, the imperative stimulus was a thin line, which could appear in one of the two lateral boxes or in the central box. In fifty percent of the trials, a sound was given while the subject waited for the line appearance. Half of the subjects were instructed to make a saccade to the upper box when the line was presented and a saccade to the lower box when the sound was presented. Half of the subjects had the opposite instructions. There were no invalid trials.

The results confirmed the deviation of the vertical saccades contralateral to the cue. In the case of visual imperative stimuli, the deviation was markedly larger than in the previous experiment. This deviation increase is very likely due to the fact that the detection of the imperative stimulus was more difficult than in the former experiment. This implies that the more strongly attention is engaged, the greater is the suppressing oculomotor signal. Most important, the deviation of the vertical saccades was present with the auditory imperative stimuli. This finding provides direct evidence in favor of the premotor theory. When subjects attend to a given location, their oculomotor system is also engaged in the attended direction, in spite of eye immobility.

**Attention and Arm-Related Pragmatic Maps**

We began this chapter by showing that space is represented in several pragmatic maps. Some of them control oculomotion, others control movements of the arms and other body parts. Is spatial attention related always to oculomotion, as in the case of Posner paradigm, or can it result from the activity of other nonoculomotor pragmatic maps? Logically, there is nothing unique in the oculomotor system that should grant it a special status. The basic neurophysiological organization of nonoculomotor spatial maps is similar to those controlling eye movements. Thus, the preparation to reach an object (or, possibly, to walk toward a target) should improve the capacity to select a location in the same way as the preparation to make a saccade does it. The experimental evidence for this claim, however, is not particularly rich.

A finding that suggests that attention is controlled, in addition to oculomotor centers, by maps related to body movements is the symptomatology exhibited by monkeys with damage to inferior area 6 (Rizzolatti, Matelli, and Pavesi 1983). Following such a lesion, the monkeys show a contralateral neglect, which is limited to the body and the space immediately around it (personal and peripersonal neglect). They tend to ignore their contralateral arm and are unable to grasp food with the mouth when it is presented contralateral to the lesion. Eye movements are normal. When two stimuli are simultaneously presented in the peripersonal space ipsilateral to the lesion (in the normal field), in contrast to normal animals that constantly prefer the stimulus near the fixation point, the animals with neglect choose the one located most peripherally in the normal field (Rizzolatti, Gentilucci, and Matelli 1985). An attraction toward the ipsilesional stimuli is observed commonly in patients with extrapersonal neglect (Kinsbourne 1987; De Renzi et al. 1989; Ladavas, Petronio, and Umiltà 1990), and there is a general consensus that this attraction reflects a perturbation of attentional mechanisms. The fact that a similar disturbance occurs following damage to a pragmatic map for arm and head movements suggests that circuits other than those for oculomotion also subserve attention.

The importance of arm movement for spatial attention was recently documented by Tipper, Lortie, and Baylis (1992), who instructed normal subjects to depress one button of a series of nine located on a board and arranged in horizontal rows. The subject's hand was located at either the bottom or the top of the board. The arm movements toward a button were triggered by turning on a red light adjacent to the selected button. In most cases, a yellow light, also located near the buttons, was turned on simultaneously to the red light, and the interference effect produced by it was studied. The results showed that the interference depended on the arm's starting position. When the arm movement started from the board bottom, the most interfering stimuli were those located in the board's lower row, whereas when the arm was located at the top of the board, the most interfering stimuli were those of the upper row. It appears, therefore, that arm location produces an attentional field extending from the hand to the target location. A second, and extremely important finding of the experiment, was that the arm-related attentional field changed location according to which hand was used. When the subject used the right hand, the stimuli presented in the right part of the board produced a greater interference than those in the left part. In contrast, when the left hand was used, the left stimuli were more interfering. These data are in good agreement with previous observations that each arm acts better in its ipsilateral field (Prablanc et al. 1979; Fisk and Goodale 1985). Together, these data demonstrate that programming arm movements produces a spatial attentional field and that this field does not depend on oculomotion.

In summary, although the evidence that programming body movements can produce attentional shifts is not rich, the available data suggest that this may occur. The poverty of data on this issue is most likely due to fact that experimental paradigms in which spatial attention is required for successive arm or other body movements were very rarely used in both psychological and physiological experiments.

## 9.4 CONCLUSIONS

The aim of this chapter was to give a unitary account of spatial attention using psychological and neurophysiological data. We are aware of the difficulty of the task and that many important issues have been dealt with superficially or not at all. We hope, however, to have demonstrated that there is no need to postulate two control systems in the brain—one for spatial attention and one for action. The system that controls action is the same that controls what we call spatial attention.

### NOTES

The authors wish to thank G. Berlucchi, L. Fadiga, G. Luppino, and M. Matelli, and J. M. Sprague for a critical reading of the manuscript. Research was funded by the Human Frontier Science Program.

1. The attentional searchlight hypothesis of Crick (1984) represents an attempt to explain the brain capacity to give a unitary description of a visual stimulus simultaneously processed by a large number of visual maps. It deals, therefore, with object- rather than space-related attention. The notion, however, of a synchronous activity between maps might be of interest also for space perception. Unfortunately, the Crick theory, as originally formulated, has no neurophysiological basis. There is no evidence that the inhibitory action of the reticular thalamic complex can provide a positive feedback to the dorsal thalamus. Furthermore, the reticular neuron rapid bursts of firing, which, according to Crick, should facilitate the dorsal thalamic nuclei, occur in artificial unphysiological conditions (Jahnsen and Llinas 1984) and during synchronized sleep but not during wakefulness (Mukhametov, Rizzolatti, and Tradardi 1970). The theory, albeit interesting, is devoid of any empirical support and will not discussed further.

2. It is possible that areas controlling head orienting movements become active when the task requires attention allocation to visual stimuli distant from the fixation point. This possibility, although interesting, will be not considered here.

3. One may argue that there is no need to shift attention in order to detect a light stimuli. Evidence from neglect studies, however, indicates that damage to one of many pragmatic cortical representations is sufficient to render an individual unaware of the stimuli. When there is no full agreement in the pragmatic representations about the presence of a stimulus, the stimulus is ignored in spite of its being processed in several cortical and subcortical centers (Rizzolatti and Berti 1990). This requirement of a "unanimous consensus" before a response could be emitted lends support to Posner's idea that arbitrary (not hard-wired) responses occur only when the stimulus is within the focus of attention.

4. The evidence for a recruitment of premotor neurons after attentional stimulus presentation is as follows. First, the most effective stimuli in eliciting the inhibitory effect are dark, relatively large stimuli. Stimuli with these characteristics do not activate the neurons of the SC superficial layers better than white stimuli. However, they are much more effective than the latter in driving the premotor neurons of the deep layers (Gordon 1973). Second, there is evidence that the deep SC neurons, unlike the superficial ones, are often multimodal. They can be triggered by tactile, nociceptive, and auditory stimuli, as well as by visual stimuli (Stein 1984). These nonvisual stimuli may also produce the inhibitory effect. Third, a repetitive presentation of a visual stimulus determines a strong habituation of the deep collicular neurons, as well as marked decay in the intensity of the inhibitory effect. Habituation is weak or absent altogether in the superficial collicular neurons.

5. Recently, Klein, Kingstone, and Pontefract (1992) readdressed the issue of the relations between eye movements and orienting of attention in two experiments conceptually similar to the previous ones. In the first experiment, the auditorily presented words *left* and *right* served as cues to orient covertly toward the indicated direction. The imperative stimuli could be either the same two words or light probes occasionally presented to the right or left of fixation. The verbal imperative stimuli required a saccade in the indicated direction; the light imperative stimuli required a manual response. The results showed a large cue effect (84.5 ms) for eye responses and a small cue effect (13.5 ms) for manual responses. However, whereas the cueing effect for rightward and leftward eye movements was approximately the same, the cueing effect for the manual responses was significant only when rightward ocular movements were prepared (24 ms versus 3 ms). Of these results, the first—that is, the presence of a cue effect for manual responses—supports the premotor theory, while the last one, the asymmetry of the effects, appears to contradict it. In the second experiment, central visual cues indicated the location likely to contain the visual signal requiring a manual response. Occasionally, the verbal command "right" or "left" was presented. The subjects were required to respond with a saccade in the corresponding direction. The results showed a significant cueing effect for the manual responses but no evidence of cueing for the verbally elicited saccades.

Both experiments are rather complex and not easy to interpret. Unlike in the usual Posner's paradigm, in which the (manual) responses are identical in valid and invalid trials, in the first experiment here, the valid saccades differed from the invalid ones for their direction. Furthermore, the detection of the verbal imperative stimulus did not require allocation of spatial attention. Thus, when the verbal imperative stimulus was invalid, the subjects had to change both their central and peripheral motor sets in order to respond correctly; this was not the case for the manual responses, which remained the same regardless of the imperative command. The huge cost of the invalid eye responses as compared with the invalid manual responses is not surprising. The two response situations are not comparable. An interesting result is the asymmetry in the advantage of cued manual responses. This result obviously needs confirmation. It is important to note, however, that when subjects engage in mental processes that are largely based on the activity of one hemisphere, they "emit a selective orienting response observable behaviorally in terms of submotor attentional (Kinsbourne 1970) and overt gaze (Kinsbourne 1972) shifts towards contralateral space" (Kinsbourne 1987). Thus, in Klein's experiments, the activation of the left hemisphere due to the expectancy of verbal command should have increased the effectiveness of the command "right" and thus produced a marked advantage in manual responses to right stimuli. In contrast, the same left hemisphere activation should have decreased the effectiveness of the command "left" and the advantage of cued manual responses to left stimuli. This is exactly what was found. The first experiment is therefore more in favor of than against the premotor theory. Considering the interpretation difficulties, however, its relevance as a test of the premotor theory is rather dubious. The same is true for the second experiment. It is hard to know a priori the effectiveness of the verbal command "right" or "left" in producing an orienting reaction. It might well be that the effectiveness is so high that it overrides any motor preparation.

## REFERENCES

Allport, A. (1989). Visual attention. In M. I. Posner (Ed.), *Foundations of cognitive science*. Cambridge, MA: MIT Press.

Allport, A. (1993). Attention and control. In D. E. Meyer and S. Kornblum (Eds.), *Attention and Performance XIV*. Hillsdale, NJ: Erlbaum.

Andersen, R. A., Asanuma, C., Essick, G., and Siegel, R. M. (1990). Corticocortical connections of anatomically and physiologically defined subdivisions within the inferior parietal lobule. *Journal of Comparative Neurology, 296*, 65–113.

Andersen, R. A., Essick, G. K., and Siegel, R. M. (1985). The encoding of spatial location by posterior parietal neurons. *Science, 230*, 456–458.

Andersen, R. A., and Gnadt, J. W. (1989). Role of posterior parietal cortex in saccadic eye movements. In R. Wurts and M. Goldberg (Eds.), *The neurobiology of saccadic eye movements*. Reviews of Oculomotor Research series, vol. 3. Amsterdam: Elsevier.

Arbib, M. A. (1981). Perceptual structures and distributed motor control. In V. B. Brooks (Ed.), *Handbook of physiology: The nervous system*, Vol. 2: *Motor control*. Bethesda, MD: American Physiological Society.

Barash, S., Bracewell, R. M., Fogassi, L., Gnadt, J. W., and Andersen, R. A. (1991a). Saccade-related activity in the lateral intraparietal area I. Temporal properties; comparison with area 7a. *Journal of Neurophysiology, 66*, 1095–1108.

Barash, S., Bracewell, R. M., Fogassi, L., Gnadt, J. W., and Andersen, R. A. (1991b). Saccade-related activity in the lateral intraparietal area II. Spatial properties. *Journal of Neurophysiology, 66*, 1109–1124.

Bashinski, H. S., and Bacharach, V. R. (1980). Enhancement of perceptual sensitivity as the result of selectively attending to spatial locations. *Perception and Psychophysics, 28*, 241–248.

Becker, W., and Jurgens, R. (1979). An analysis of the saccadic system by means of double step stimuli. *Vision Research, 19,* 967–983.

Berlucchi, G., Tassinari, G., Marzi, C. A., and Di Stefano, M. (1989). Spatial distribution of the inhibitory effect of peripheral non-informative cues on simple reaction-time to non-foveal visual targets. *Neuropsychologia, 27,* 201–221.

Berlyne, D. E. (1960). *Conflict, arousal and curiosity.* New York: McGraw-Hill.

Berlyne, D. E. (1970). Attention as a problem in behavior theory. In D. I. Mostofsky (Ed.), *Attention: Contemporary theory and analysis.* New York: Appleton-Century-Crofts.

Berti, A., Allport, A., Driver, J., Denies, Z., Oxbury, J., and Oxbury, S. (1992). Levels of processing in an "extinguished" field. *Neuropsychologia, 30,* 403–415.

Berti, A., and Rizzolatti, G. (1992). Visual processing without awareness: Evidence from unilateral neglect. *Journal of Cognitive Neuroscience, 4,* 345–351.

Bisiach, E., and Vallar, G. (1988). Hemineglect in humans. In F. Boller and J. Grafman (Eds.), *Handbook of neuropsychology,* vol. 1. Amsterdam: Elsevier.

Broadbent, D. E. (1952). Speaking and listening simultaneously. *Journal of Experimental Psychology, 43,* 267–273.

Broadbent, D. E. (1958). *Perception and communication.* London: Pergamon.

Brodmann, K. (1925). *Vergleichende Lokalisationslehre der Grosshirnrinde.* Leipzig: Barth.

Bruce, C. J. (1988). Single neuron activity in the monkey's prefrontal cortex. In P. Rakic and W. Singer (Eds.), *Neurobiology of neocortex.* Chichester: Wiley.

Bruce, C. J., and Goldberg, M. E. (1985). Primate frontal eye fields. I. Single neurons discharging before saccades. *Journal of Neurophysiology, 53,* 603–635.

Cavada, C., and Goldman-Rakic, P. (1989). Posterior parietal cortex in rhesus monkey. II. Evidence for segregated corticocortical networks linking sensory and limbic areas with the frontal lobe. *Journal of Comparative Neurology, 287,* 422–445.

Cherry, E. C. (1953). Some experiments on the recognition of speech with one and with two ears. *Journal of the Acoustical Society of America, 25,* 975–979.

Corbetta, M., Miezin, F. M., Dobmeyer, S., Shulman, G. L., and Petersen, S. E. (1990). Attentional modulation of neural processing of shape, color and velocity in humans. *Science, 248,* 1556–1559.

Corbetta, M., Miezin, F. M., Dobmeyer, S., Shulman, G. L., and Petersen, S. E. (1991). Selective and divided attention during visual discriminations of shape, color, and speed: Functional anatomy by positron emission tomography. *Journal of Neuroscience, 11,* 2383–2402.

Crawford, T. J., and Muller, H. J. (1992). Spatial and temporal effects of spatial attention on human saccadic eye movements. *Vision Research, 32,* 293–304.

Crick, F. (1984). Function of the thalamic reticular complex: The searchlight hypothesis. *Proceedings of National Academy of Science, USA, 81,* 4586–4590.

Critchley, M. (1953). *The parietal lobes.* London: Edward Arnold.

Crovitz, H. F., and Daves, W. (1962). Tendencies to eye movement and perceptual accuracy. *Journal of Experimental Psychology, 63,* 495–498.

De Renzi, E. (1982). *Disorders of space exploration and cognition.* Chichester: Wiley.

De Renzi, E., Gentilini, M., Faglioni, P., and Barbieri, C. (1989). Attentional shift towards the rightmost stimuli in patients with left visual neglect. *Cortex, 25,* 231–237.

Downing, C. J. (1988). Expectancy and visual-spatial attention: Effects on perceptual quality. *Journal of Experimental Psychology: Human Perception and Performance, 14,* 188–202.

Downing, C. J. and Pinker, S. (1985). The spatial structure of visual attention. In M. I. Posner and O. S. M. Marin (Eds.), *Attention and performance XI.* Hillsdale, NJ: Erlbaum.

Duhamel, J., Colby, C. L., and Goldberg, M. E. (1992). The updating of the representation of visual space in parietal cortex by intended eye movements. *Science, 255,* 90–92.

Egly, R., and Bouma, D. (1991). Reallocation of visual attention. *Journal of Experimental Psychology: Human Perception and Performance, 17,* 142–159.

Fadiga, L., Toni, I., di Pellegrino, G., Gallese, V., and Fogassi, L. (1992). Velocity coding by inferior premotor cortex (area F4) of macaque monkey. *Neuroscience Letters, 43,* S43.

Felleman, D. J., and Van Essen, D. C. (1991). Distributed hierarchical processing in the primate cerebral cortex. *Cerebral Cortex, 1,* 1–47.

Findlay, J. M. (1982). Global visual processing for saccadic eye movements. *Vision Research, 22,* 1033–1045.

Fisk, J. D., and Goodale, M. A. (1985). The organization of eye and limb movements during unrestricted reaching to targets in contralateral and ipsilateral visual space. *Experimental Brain Research, 60,* 159–178.

Fogassi, L., Gallese, V., di Pellegrino, G., Fadiga, L., Gentilucci, M., Luppino, G., Matelli, M., Pedotti, A., and Rizzolatti, G. (1992). Space coding by premotor cortex. *Experimental Brain Research, 89,* 686–690.

Gawryszewski, L., Faria, R. B., Thomaz, T. G., Pinheiro, W. M., Rizzolatti, G., and Umiltà, C. (1992). Reorienting visual spatial attention: Is it based on cartesian coordinates? In R. Lent (Ed.), *The visual system from genesis to maturity.* Boston, MA.: Birkhauser.

Gentilucci, M., Fogassi, L., Luppino, G., Matelli, M., Camarda, R., and Rizzolatti, G. (1988). Functional organization of inferior area 6 in the macaque monkey. I. Somatotopy and the control of proximal movements. *Experimental Brain Research, 71,* 475–490.

Gentilucci, M., and Rizzolatti, G. (1990). Cortical motor control of arm and hand movements. In M. A. Goodale (Ed.), *Vision and action: The control of grasping.* Norwood, NJ: Ablex.

Gentilucci, M., Scandolara, C., Pigarev, I. N., and Rizzolatti, G. (1983). Visual responses in the postarcuate cortex (area 6) of the monkey that are independent of eye position. *Experimental Brain Research, 50,* 464–468.

Godschalk, M., Lemon, R. N., Kuypers, H. G. J. M., and Ronday, H. K. (1984). Cortical afferents and efferents of monkey postarcuate area: An anatomical and electrophysiological study. *Experimental Brain Research, 56,* 410–424.

Goldberg, M. E., and Bruce, C. J. (1990). Primate frontal eye fields. III. Maintenance of a spatially accurate saccade signal. *Journal of Neurophysiology, 64,* 489–508.

Goldberg, M. E., and Robinson, D. L. (1978). The superior colliculus. In R. B. Masterton (Ed.), *Handbook of behavioral neurobiology,* Vol. 1: Sensory integration. New York: Plenum.

Goldberg, M. E., and Segraves, M. A. (1989). The visual and frontal cortices. In R. H. Wurtz and M. E. Goldberg (Eds.), *The neurobiology of saccadic eye movements.* Reviews of Oculomotor Research series, vol. 3. Amsterdam: Elsevier.

Goldberg, M. E., and Wurtz, R. H. (1972). Activity of superior colliculus in behaving monkey: II. The effect of attention on neuronal responses. *Journal of Neurophysiology, 35,* 560–574.

Goldman-Rakic, P. S. (1988). Topography of cognition: Parallel distributed networks in primate association cortex. *Annual Review of Neuroscience, 11,* 137–156.

Goodale, M. A., and Milner, A. D. (1992). Separate visual pathways for perception and action. *Trends in Neurosciences, 15*, 20–25.

Goodale, M. A., Milner, A. D., Jakobson, L. S., and Carey, D. P. (1991). Perceiving the world and grasping it. A neurological dissociation. *Nature, 349*, 154–156.

Gordon, B. (1973). Receptive fields in deep layers of act superior colliculus. *Journal of Neurophysiology, 36*, 157–178.

Graziano, M. S. A., and Gross, C. G. (1992). Coding of extrapersonal visual space in body-part centered coordinates. *Society for Neuroscience Abstracts, 18*, 256.9.

Graziano, M. S. A., and Gross, C. G. (n.d.). The representation of extrapersonal space: A possible role for bimodal visual-tactile neurons. In press.

Grüsser, O.-J., and Landis, T. (1991). *Visual agnosia and other disturbances of visual perception and cognition*. London: Macmillan.

Hawkins, H. L., Hillyard, S. A., Luck, S. J., Mouloua, M., Downing, C. J., and Woodward, D. P. (1990). Visual attention modulates signal detectability. *Journal of Experimental Psychology: Human Perception and Performance, 16*, 802–811.

Hikosaka, O., Sakamoto, M., and Usui, S. (1989a). Functional properties of monkey caudate neurons. I. Activities related to saccadic eye movements. *Journal of Neurophysiology, 61*, 780–798.

Hikosaka, O., Sakamoto, M., and Usui, S. (1989b). Functional properties of monkey caudate neurons. III. Activities related to expectation of target and reward. *Journal of Neurophysiology, 61*, 814–832.

Hikosaka, O., and Wurtz, R. (1983a). Visual and oculomotor functions of monkey substantia nigra pars reticulata. I. Relation of visual and auditory responses to saccades. *Journal of Neurophysiology, 49*, 1230–1253.

Hikosaka, O., and Wurtz, R. (1983b). Visual and oculomotor functions of monkey substantia nigra pars reticulata. IV. Relation of substantia nigra to superior colliculus. *Journal of Neurophysiology, 49*, 1285–1301.

Hikosaka, O., and Wurtz, R. H. (1989). The basal ganglia. In R. H. Wurtz and M. E. Goldberg (Eds.), *The neurobiology of saccadic eye movements*. Reviews of Oculomotor Research, vol. 3. Amsterdam: Elsevier.

Hughes, H. C., and Zimba, L. D. (1985). Spatial maps of directed visual attention. *Journal of Experimental Psychology: Human Perception and Performance, 11*, 409–430.

Hyvarinen, J. (1982). Parietal association cortex: Posterior parietal lobe of the primate brain. *Physiological Reviews, 62*(3), 1060–1129.

Jahnsen, H., and Llinas, R. (1984). Electrophysiological properties of guinea-pig thalamic neurones: An in vitro study. *Journal of Physiology, 349*, 205–226.

James, W. (1890). *Principles of psychology*. New York: Holt.

Jeannerod, M. (1988). *The neural and behavioural organization of goal-directed movements*. Oxford: Oxford University Press.

Johnston, W. A., and Dark, V. J. (1982). In defense of intraperceptual theories of attention. *Journal of Experimental Psychology: Human Perception and Performance, 8*, 407–421.

Johnston, W. A., and Dark, V. J. (1986). Selective attention. *Annual Review of Psychology, 37*, 43–75.

Jonides, J. (1976). Voluntary vs reflexive control of the mind's eye movement. Presented at Psychonomic Society, St. Louis, November.

Jonides, J. (1981). Voluntary versus automatic control over the mind's eye's movement. In J. B. Long and A. D. Baddeley (Eds.), *Attention and performance IX*. Hillsdale, NJ: Erlbaum.

Kahneman, D., and Treisman, A. (1984). Changing views of attention and automaticity. In R. Parasuraman and D. R. Davies (Eds.), *Varieties of attention*. London: Academic Press.

Kinsbourne, M. (1970). The cerebral basis of lateral asymmetries in attention. *Acta Psychologica, 33*, 193–201.

Kinsbourne, M. (1972). Eye and head turning indicates cerebral lateralization. *Science, 176*, 539–541.

Kinsbourne, M. (1987). Mechanisms of unilateral neglect. In M. Jeannerod (Ed.), *Neurophysiological and neuropsychological aspects of spatial neglect*. Amsterdam: North-Holland.

Klein, R. (1980). Does oculomotor readiness mediate cognitive control of visual attention? In R. S. Nickerson (Ed.), *Attention and performance VIII*. Hillsdale, NJ: Erlbaum.

Klein, R. M., Kingstone, A., and Pontefract, A. (1992). Orienting of visual attention. In K. Rayner (Ed.), *Eye movements and visual cognition: Scene perception and reading*. New York: Springer-Verlag.

Komoda, M. K., Festinger, L., Phillips, L. J., Duckman, R. H., and Young, R. A. (1973). Some observations concerning saccadic eye movements. *Vision Research, 12*, 1009–1020.

LaBerge, D. (1975). Acquisition of automatic processing in perceptual and associative learning. In P. M. A. Rabbitt and S. Dornic (Eds.), *Attention and performance V*. New York: Academic Press.

Ladavas, E., Petronio, A., and Umiltà, C. (1990). The deployment of attention in the intact field of hemineglect patients. *Cortex, 26*, 307–317.

Latto, R., and Cowey, A. (1971). Visual field defects after frontal eye-field lesions in monkeys. *Brain Research, 30*, 1–24.

Leinonen, L., Hyvarinen, J., Nyman, G., and Linnankoski, I. (1979). Functional properties of neurons in lateral part of associative area 7 in awake monkeys. *Experimental Brain Research, 34*, 299–320.

Marshall, J. C., and Halligan, P. W. (1988). Blindsight and insight in visuospatial neglect. *Nature, 336*, 766–767.

Matelli, M., Camarda, R., Glickstein, M., and Rizzolatti, G. (1986). Afferent and efferent projections of the inferior area 6 in the macaque monkey. *Journal of Comparative Neurology, 251*, 281–298.

Maylor, E. A. (1985). Facilitatory and inhibitory components of orienting in visual space. In M. I. Posner and O. S. M. Marin (Eds.), *Mechanisms of attention: Attention and performance XI*. Hillsdale, NJ: Erlbaum.

Maylor, E. A., and Hockey, R. (1985). Inhibitory component of externally-controlled covert orienting in visual space. *Journal of Experimental Psychology: Human Perception and Performance, 11*, 777–787.

Milner, A. D., Perrett, D. I., Johnston, R. S., Benson, P. J., Jordan, T. R., Heeley, D. W., Bettucci, D., Mortara, F., Mutani, R., Terazzi, E., and Davidson, D. L. W. (1991). Perception and action in "visual form agnosia." *Brain, 114*, 405–428.

Mohler, C. W., and Wurtz, R. H. (1976). Organization of monkey superior colliculus: Intermediate layer cells discharging before eye movements. *Journal of Neurophysiology, 39*, 722–744.

Moran, J., and Desimone, R. (1985). Selective attention gates visual processing in the extrastriate cortex. *Science, 229*, 782–784.

Mountcastle, V. B., Lynch, J. C., Georgopoulos, A., Sakata, H., and Acuna, C. (1975). Posterior parietal association cortex of the monkey: Command function for operations within extrapersonal space. *Journal of Neurophysiology, 38,* 871–908.

Mukhametov, L. M., Rizzolatti, G., and Tradardi, V. (1970). Spontaneous activity of neurons of nucleus reticularis thalami in freely moving cats. *Journal of Physiology, 210,* 651–667.

Muller, H. J., and Findlay, J. M. (1988). The effect of visual attention on peripheral discrimination thresholds in single and multiple element displays. *Acta Psychologica, 69,* 129–155.

Muller, H. J., and Humphreys, G. W. (1991). Luminance-increment detection: Capacity limited or not? *Journal of Experimental Psychology: Human Perception and Performance, 17,* 107–124.

Muller, H. J., and Rabbitt, P. M. A. (1989). Reflexive and voluntary orienting of visual attention: Time course of activation and resistance to interruption. *Journal of Experimental Psychology: Human Perception and Performance, 15,* 315–330.

Pandya, D. N., and Kuypers, H. G. J. (1969). Cortico-cortical connections in the rhesus monkey. *Brain Research, 13,* 13–36.

Pandya, D. N., and Seltzer, B. (1982). Intrinsic connections and architectonics of posterior parietal cortex in the rhesus monkey. *Journal of Comparative Neurology, 204,* 196–210.

Petrides, M., and Pandya, D. N. (1984). Projections to the frontal cortex from the posterior parietal region in the rhesus monkey. *Journal of Comparative Neurology, 228,* 105–116.

Posner, M. I. (1978). *Chronometric explorations of mind.* Hillsdale, NJ: Erlbaum.

Posner, M. I. (1980). Orienting of attention. *Quarterly Journal of Experimental Psychology, 32,* 3–25.

Posner, M. I., and Cohen, Y. (1984). Components of visual orienting. In H. Bouma and D. G. Bouwhuis (Eds.), *Attention and performance X.* Hillsdale, NJ: Erlbaum.

Posner, M. I., and Petersen, S. E. (1990). The attention system of the human brain. *Annual Review of Neuroscience, 13,* 25–42.

Posner, M. I., Petersen, S. E., Fox, P. T., and Reichle, M. E. (1988). Localization of cognitive operations in the human brain. *Science, 240,* 1627–1631.

Posner, M. I., Snyder, C. R. F., and Davidson, B. J. (1980). Attention and the detection of signals. *Journal of Experimental Psychology: General, 109,* 160–174.

Possamai, C. A. (1986). Relationship between inhibition and facilitation following a visual cue. *Acta Psychologica, 61,* 243–258.

Prablanc, C., Echallier, J. F., Komilis, E., and Jeannerod, M. (1979). Optimal response of eye and hand motor systems in pointing at a visual target: I. Spatiotemporal characteristics of eye and hand movements and their relationships when varying the amount of visual information. *Biological Cybernetics, 35,* 113–124.

Rafal, R. D., Calabresi, P. A., Brennan, C. W., and Sciolto, T. K. (1989). Saccade preparation inhibits reorienting to recently attended locations. *Journal of Experimental Psychology: Human Perception and Performance, 15,* 673–685.

Rayner, K., McConkie, G. W., and Ehrlich, S. (1978). Eye movements and integrating information across fixations. *Journal of Experimental Psychology: Human Perception and Performance, 4,* 529–544.

Remington, R., and Pierce, L. (1984). Moving attention: Evidence for time-invariant shifts of visual selective attention. *Perception and Psychophysics, 35,* 393–399.

Reuter-Lorenz, P. A., and Fendrich, R. (1992). Oculomotor readiness and covert orienting: Differences between central and peripheral precues. *Perception and Psychophysics, 52,* 336–344.

Riggio, L., and Kirsner, K. (n.d.). The relationship between central cues and peripheral cues in covert visual orientation. In preparation.

Rizzolatti, G. (1983). Mechanisms of selective attention in mammals. In J. P. Ewert, R. R. Capranica, and D. J. Ingle (Eds.), *Advances in vertebrate neuroethology*. New York: Plenum Press.

Rizzolatti, G., and Berti, A. (1990). Neglect as a neural representation deficit. *Revue Neurologique, 146*, 626–634.

Rizzolatti, G., and Berti, A. (1993). Neural mechanisms of spatial neglect. In J. Marshall and I. Robertson (Eds.), *Unilateral neglect: Clinical and experimental studies*. London: Taylor & Francis Ltd.

Rizzolatti, G., and Camarda, R. (1987). Neural circuits for spatial attention and unilateral neglect. In M. Jeannerod (Ed.), *Neurophysiological and neuropsychological aspects of spatial neglect*. Amsterdam: North-Holland.

Rizzolatti, G., Camarda, R., Fogassi, M., Gentilucci, M., Luppino, G., and Matelli, M. (1988). Functional organization of inferior area 6 in the macaque monkey. II. Area F5 and the control of distal movements. *Experimental Brain Research, 71*, 491–507.

Rizzolatti, G., Camarda, R., Grupp, L. A., and Pisa, M. (1973). Inhibition of visual responses of single units in the cat superior colliculius by the introduction of a second visual stimulus. *Brain Research, 61*, 390–394.

Rizzolatti, G., Camarda, R., Grupp, L. A., and Pisa, M. (1974). Inhibitory effect of remote visual stimuli on the visual responses of the cat superior colliculus: Spatial and temporal factors. *Journal of Neurophysiology, 37*, 1262–1275.

Rizzolatti, G., and Gallese, V. (1988). Mechanisms and theories of spatial neglect. In F. Boller and J. Grafman (Eds.), *Handbook of neuropsychology*, vol. 1. Amsterdam: Elsevier.

Rizzolatti, G., Gentilucci, M., and Matelli, M. (1985). Selective spatial attention: One center, one circuit or many circuits? In M. I. Posner and O. Marin (Eds.), *Attention and performance XI*. Hillsdale, NJ: Erlbaum.

Rizzolatti, G., Matelli, M., and Pavesi, G. (1983). Deficit in attention and movement following the removal of postarcuate (area 6) and prearcuate (area 8) cortex in monkey. *Brain, 106*, 655–673.

Rizzolatti, G., Riggio, L., Dascola, I., and Umiltà, C. (1987). Reorienting attention across the horizontal and vertical meridians: Evidence in favor of a premotor theory of attention. *Neuropsychologia, 25*, 31–40.

Robinson, D. L., and McClurkin, J. W. (1989). The visual superior colliculus and pulvinar. In R. H. Wurts and M. E. Goldberg (Eds.), *The neurobiology of saccadic eye movements*. Reviews of Oculomotor Research series, vol. 3. Amsterdam: Elsevier.

Sakata, H., and Musunoki, M. (1992). Organization of space perception: Neural representation of three-dimensional space in the posterior parietal-cortex. *Current Opinion in Neurobiology, 2*, 170–174.

Schiller, P. H., and Koerner, F. (1971). Discharge characteristics of single units in superior colliculus of the alert rhesus monkey. *Journal of Neurophysiology, 34*, 920–936.

Schneider, W., and Shiffrin, R. M. (1977). Controlled and automatic human information processing: I. Detection, search and attention. *Psychological Review, 84*, 1–66.

Shepherd, M., and Muller, H. J. (1989). Movement versus focusing of visual attention. *Perception and Psychophysics, 46*, 146–154.

Shepherd, M., Findlay, J. M., and Hockey, R. J. (1986). The relationship between eye movements and spatial attention. *Quarterly Journal of Experimental Psychology, 38A*, 475–491.

Spencer, M. B. H., Lambert, A. J., and Hockey, R. (1988). The inhibitory component of orienting, alertness and sustained attention. *Acta Psychologica, 69*, 165–184.

Sprague, J. M., Berlucchi, G., and Rizzolatti, G. (1973). The role of the superior colliculus and pretectum in vision and visually guided behavior. In R. Jung (Ed.), *Handbook of sensory physiology*, vol. VII/3 B. New York: Springer.

Stein, B. E. (1984). Multimodal representation in the superior colliculus and optic tectum. In H. Vanegas (Ed.), *Comparative neurology of the optic tectum*. New York: Plenum.

Taira, M., Mine, S., Georgopoulos, A. P., Murata, A., and Sakata, H. (1991). Parietal cortex neurons of the monkey related to the visual guidance of hand movements. *Experimental Brain Research, 83*, 29–36.

Tassinari, G., Aglioti, S., Chelazzi, L., Marzi, C. A., and Berlucchi, G. (1987). Distribution in the visual field of the costs of voluntarily allocated attention and the inhibitory after-effects of covert orienting. *Neuropsychologia, 25*, 55–71.

Tassinari, G., Biscaldi, M., Marzi, C. A., and Berlucchi, G. (1989). Ipsilateral inhibition and contralateral facilitation of simple reaction time to nonfoveal visual targets from non-informative visual cues. *Acta Psychologica, 70*, 267–291.

Tipper, S. P., Lortie, C., and Baylis, G. C. (1992). Selective reaching: Evidence for action-centered attention. *Journal of Experimental Psychology: Human Perception and Performance, 18*, 891–905.

Titchener, E. B. (1966). Attention as sensory clearness. In P. Bakan (Ed.), *Attention: An enduring problem in psychology*. Princeton, NJ: Van Nostrand.

Treisman, A. M. (1964). Selective attention in man. *British Medical Bulletin, 20*, 12–16.

Umiltà, C., Riggio, L., Dascola, I., and Rizzolatti, G. (1991). Differential effects of central and peripheral cues on the reorienting of spatial attention. *European Journal of Cognitive Psychology, 3*, 247–267.

Ungerleider, L. G., and Mishkin, M. (1982). Two cortical visual systems. In D. J. Ingle, M. A. Goodale, and R. J. W. Mansfield (Eds.), *Analysis of visual behavior*. Cambridge, MA: MIT Press.

Volpe, B. T., Ledoux, J. E., and Gazzaniga, M. S. (1979). Information processing of visual stimuli in an "extinguished" field. *Nature, 282*, 722–724.

Von Bonin, G., and Bailey, P. (1947). *The neocortex of macaca mulatta*. Urbana: University of Illinois Press.

Wheeless, L. Jr., Boynton, R. E., and Cohen, G. H. (1966). Eye movement responses to step and pulse-step stimuli. *Journal of the Optic Society of America, 56*, 956–960.

Wurtz, R. H., and Goldberg, M. E. (1972). Activity of superior colliculus in behaving monkey III: Cells discharging before eye movements. *Journal of Neurophysiology, 35*, 575–586.

Wurtz, R. H., and Mohler, C. W. (1976). Organization of monkey superior colliculus: Enhanced visual response of superficial layer cells. *Journal of Neurophysiology, 39*, 745–765.

Wurtz, R. H., Richmond, B. J., and Judge, S. J. (1980). Vision during saccadic eye movements III: Visual interactions in monkey superior colliculus. *Journal of Neurophysiology, 43*, 1168–1181.

Yantis, S., and Jonides, J. (1984). Abrupt visual onsets and selective attention: Evidence from visual search. *Journal of Experimental Psychology: Human Perception and Performance, 10*, 601–621.

# 10 Multiple Sources of Spatial Information for Aimed Limb Movements

Richard A. Abrams, Linda Van Dillen, and Vicki Stemmons

ABSTRACT  The present research addresses details of the mental mechanisms that underlie the control of human-aimed limb movements. In particular, we focus on the nature of the visual-spatial information that is available about objects in the environment, and the manner in which that information is used to guide movements directed toward such objects. Previous research has shown that at least two distinct types of information exist about objects in the environment: information about the *distance* between the target and some reference position, and information about the spatial *location* of the target. To examine the role of these types of information in aimed movements, experiments were conducted in which subjects pointed to targets whose perceived spatial attributes (i.e., distance and location) were manipulated by the presence of extraneous objects, by motion of a visual background, and by the number of eye movements used to fixate the target. These manipulations were chosen because they appear to separately affect perceived distance and location. The limb-pointing movements were then analyzed using a parsing algorithm that partitions them into two components: an initial primary submovement that propels the limb most of the way to the target, and a final secondary submovement during which the limb homes in and lands near the target. Analysis of the movements showed that the experimental manipulations affected the primary and secondary submovements in different ways. The primary submovement appears to be programmed to travel a specific distance, whereas the secondary submovement is programmed to arrive at a specific final location. The results show that people separately encode and use distinct types of visual-spatial information for the control of limb movements.

## 10.1  INTRODUCTION

In order to interact effectively with the world, people must be able to reach for and manipulate objects in their immediate environment. Although people are quite good at this, the mental and physical mechanisms underlying reaching and pointing are quite complex, and much remains to be learned about them. This chapter is concerned with the nature of the visual-spatial information that people acquire about objects in the world and the manner in which that information is used to guide movements directed toward those objects.

In order to produce movement of a limb to a visually presented target, an actor must transform visual-spatial information about the target into an appropriate set of commands for the muscles needed to reach for or point to the object.[1] This sensorimotor transformation has been the focus of considerable research scrutiny, and a number of theoretical formulations have been proposed to describe details of the transformation (Bizzi, Mussa- Ivaldi, and Giszter

1991; Flanders and Soechting 1990; Kalaska and Crammond 1992; Kuperstein 1988; Massone and Bizzi 1989; Soechting and Flanders 1989). Such approaches to understanding motor behavior assume, implicitly or explicitly, that a person first encodes the location of a target based on retinal information (and nonretinal eye position information). That information is then used for whatever computations are necessary to produce the target-directed movement. The various models differ in terms of the specific transformations that are presumed to be necessary to produce movements.

We have taken an approach that diverges from these earlier ones. Our concern is not with the nature of the sensorimotor transformation per se; instead, we focus on identifying the information that is involved in the transformation and the way in which that information is used to control movement. Thus, while prior research has addressed what happens to information about the movement target after it is sensed, we are concerned with learning more about precisely what is sensed. Our inquiry is limited to two specific types of spatial information: distance and location information.

**Distance and Location Information for Movement Planning**

It is generally assumed that a person encodes the location of a movement target on the basis of some kind of perceptual information (e.g., retinal information about the target combined with information about eye position relative to the body). The details of precisely what information is encoded, however, have not received much attention. Although a number of types of spatial information may be available for planning movements, two types in particular have been identified as being especially relevant: distance information, which refers to the perceived distance between the target and some other reference object, such as the hand, and location information, which refers to the absolute location of the target in space.[2] These two types of spatial information appear to be perceived, encoded, and used for guiding some movements at least partially independently (Mack et al. 1985; Abrams and Landgraf 1990; Abrams, Meyer, and Kornblum 1990).

There are also two distinct classes of models that have arisen from earlier work on motor control. The two classes differ in terms of the type of information that is presumed to be necessary to produce a limb movement and the manner in which the motor system is presumed to use that information to produce movements.

**Location Specification**  According to one class of models, movements are produced by specifying information about the final desired state—the location in space—of the limb or joints on the limb. Details of the movement itself supposedly would not require explicit planning, and no information need be available about the location of the limb prior to movement. Such a view is consistent with traditional mass-spring or equilibrium-point models of movement control (Feldman 1986; Polit and Bizzi 1979; Sakitt 1980). Those models regard a limb-muscle system as a mass (the limb) supported by opposing springs (the agonist and antagonist muscles). The limb is at rest only when the forces exerted on it by the opposing sets of muscles are exactly equal. Resetting the resting lengths or tensions in opposing muscle pairs establishes a new equilibrium point for the limb, and a movement will be generated any time the limb is not at equilibrium. Specification of only the desired end location is also characteristic of some more recent attempts to model motor learning and control using neural networks (Kuperstein 1988). According to Kuperstein's analysis, a person may learn to associate a particular position of the hand in space with the joint angles that would maintain the hand at that position. If the commands to the muscles specified joint angles, then limb movements could be produced without explicitly considering the starting position of the limb. Either of these schemes could produce accurate movements based only on information about the location of the target in space; a person would not need to know the initial position of the limb in order to move accurately. An additional advantage of producing movements in this way is that unexpected perturbations to the limb during the movement should not affect the ability to achieve the correct final position accurately.

Evidence does exist that is consistent with these views. For example, deafferented monkeys are able to produce accurate movements despite unexpected and undetected perturbations of the moving limb during or prior to the movement (Bizzi, Polit, and Morasso 1976; Polit and Bizzi 1979; also Mays and Sparks 1980 for eye movements). Specification of the desired state apparently is sufficient to yield an accurate movement even though unforeseen changes in the movement itself may be necessary. Additional support comes from work on the mechanisms that produce saccadic eye movements: Saccades are produced in part by a step change in the tonic level of eye muscle innervation—essentially a change in the position at which the eye is at equilibrium (Sparks and Mays 1990). Finally, neural network models that make no assumptions about details of the movement path can successfully model aiming behavior (Kuperstein 1988).

**Distance Specification**  A second class of models proposes that limb movements result from a very different set of processes. According to these models, movement production involves specifying information about the difference between the desired state of a limb and its current state. In particular, several models of movement control assume that people produce movements by specifying the direction and amount of force that the muscles must apply over time to the moving limb (Schmidt et al. 1979; Meyer, Smith, and Wright 1982). According to these and other models (e.g., Soechting and Flanders 1989), the specification of a movement involves some computation of the distance between the current and desired locations of the limb.

A considerable amount of evidence also exists in support of this possibility. For example, Georgopoulos, Schwartz, and Kettner (1986) have shown that neurons in the motor cortex encode the direction of an upcoming movement, not merely its final location. Thus, neural activity prior to a variety of movements to a fixed target will differ depending on the starting location of the movement (Kettner, Schwartz, and Georgopoulos 1988). Such a result implies that some aspect of the movement itself other than the final position is computed as part of the preparation to move. Furthermore, it seems that the initial position of the limb is involved in that computation. Additionally, quantitative models of the forces involved in producing movements make assumptions that depend on knowledge of movement distance (Meyer et al. 1982, 1988). Such models accurately account for many aspects of movement behavior.[3]

**Hybrid Models** The considerable support that exists for both distance specification and location specification suggests that movement planning may involve more than one type of control mechanism and more than one type of movement specification. For example, some movements involve a graded application of force that develops over a period of several hundred milliseconds (Bizzi and Mussa-Ivaldi 1989). Such a result is inconsistent with a simple equilibrium-point model in which a movement is produced by a single change in resting lengths and tensions of opposing muscle pairs. Instead, it may be that a series of new equilibrium points are specified (Bizzi and Mussa-Ivaldi 1989; Hogan 1984). In this way, each segment of a movement can be prepared in terms of its desired final location only (without knowledge of the initial limb position; consistent with location specification), yet a person could still have considerable control over detailed aspects of the movement trajectory (consistent with distance specification).

Electromyographic and neurophysiological evidence also suggests that a combination of distance and location mechanisms may be involved in movement planning and control. Many limb and eye movements consist of both a phasic and a tonic component (a "pulse" and a "step"; Ghez 1979; Sparks and Mays 1990). The phasic component consists of a brief application of high force that can propel the limb or eye rapidly toward its destination. This component must rely on information about the difference between the current and desired locations (such as the direction and distance of the movement) much like the distance specification processes. The tonic component consists of a step change in the resting lengths of opposing muscle pairs, much like a simple location specification mechanism. This component ensures that the limb (or eye) will ultimately be held steadily at the correct final location. Although the pulse and step are usually prepared together, some evidence suggests that they can be specified at least somewhat independently (Easter 1973).

**Independent Submovements**

The preceding analysis suggests that some aspects of movements might be planned in terms of the distance to move and other aspects in terms of the final desired location. One way that this could happen would be if different parts of a movement were programmed in different ways (Keele 1981). For example, consider rapid aimed limb movements. Several researchers have shown that such movements often consist of two or more distinct submovements (Abrams, Meyer, and Kornblum 1990; Carlton 1981; Meyer et al. 1988; Woodworth 1899): an initial primary submovement in which the limb is rapidly propelled most of the way to the target, and a final, secondary submovement in which the limb homes in on the target and eventually comes to rest. It is possible that the different submovements involve different types of movement specification. For example, the primary submovement might be programmed on the basis of distance information. This would be reasonable because some knowledge of the distance and direction between the current and desired locations would be needed to produce the large forces needed to move a limb rapidly. The secondary submovement, on the other hand, could be planned based on a specification of the desired end location. This might ensure accurate attainment of the movement goal despite some variability in the primary submovement.

The proposal that different submovements might be planned in different ways has been made by Abrams, Meyer, and Kornblum (1990), who reported evidence in support of that possibility. In particular, they showed that primary submovements were affected by the type of eye movement (saccadic or smooth-pursuit) that subjects used to fixate a movement target, but secondary submovements (i.e., the end of the overall movements) were not. They concluded that the two submovements were programmed on the basis of distinct types of information. Some additional support also exists for the possibility that individual submovements are planned on the basis of distinct types of visual-spatial information. For example, Flanders and Soechting (1990) have shown that movements are partitioned into two independent spatial dimensions that are controlled at least partially independently. And Velay, Roll, and Paillard (1989) have shown the presence of multiple spatial codes for arm movements.

## Overview of Experiments

In this chapter we provide additional support for the possibility that two different types of movement specification may be operating during rapid aimed limb movements, each at different times during a movement. Our approach involves first presenting the movement target in a manner that is likely to distort one type of visual-spatial information. We then examine the effects of such a distortion on the component submovements of subsequent aimed limb movements. In particular, in experiment 1, we show that a manipulation that is known to affect perceived distance more than perceived location also affects primary submovements more than secondary submovements. In experiments 2 and 3 we explore perceptual manipulations that have less certain effects on distance and location information.

## 10.2 EXPERIMENT 1

In our first experiment, we sought to determine whether the spatial information used for programming the primary submovement differs from that used to guide the secondary submovement. There are some good reasons to believe that such a difference exists. If true, such a finding would have important implications for models of motor control processes. To examine this, we manipulated the quality of the available spatial information by using an induced motion illusion. Induced motion has been previously shown to affect perceived distance and location differentially (Abrams and Landgraf 1990). In particular, when subjects judge the distance moved by a target that has undergone induced motion, the illusion has a much greater effect on their responses than when the subjects are asked to judge the starting and ending locations of the target. Similar results have also been reported by Bridgeman, Kirch, and Sperling (1981).

Subjects first produced rapid arm-pointing movements to a visible target that had recently undergone a combination of real and illusory (induced) motion. The pointing movements were then partitioned into their component submovements to determine the extent to which the illusion affected either the primary or the secondary submovement. If primary submovements are planned mainly on the basis of distance information (as opposed to location information), the illusion would be expected to have a greater effect on the primary submovement than it does on the secondary submovement because induced motion has been shown to affect perceived distance more than perceived location (Abrams and Landgraf 1990).

### Method

**Subjects** Nine right-handed university students each served in one 1-hour session. The subjects had no known perceptual or motor deficits. They were paid $4 per session plus bonuses based on performance.

**Apparatus and Procedure** Subjects were seated at a table in a light-tight, sound-attenuated booth. Visual stimuli were presented on a cathode ray tube monitor that was 38 cm from the subjects. Below and in front of the monitor was a handle that could be used for pointing to objects on the display. The handle, which subjects grasped with their right hand, was mounted on a track and could be easily moved from side to side. Movement of the handle produced corresponding movement of a small vertical line (the cursor) on the monitor. At the beginning of each trial, a plus sign appeared directly in front of the subject. The subjects next aligned the cursor with the plus sign, at which point the plus sign was replaced by a dot and the cursor disappeared. One second later, a rectangular frame appeared around the dot. The frame was 18 degrees (of visual angle) wide and 10 degrees high. Subjects were instructed to fixate upon the dot, which was initially located .5 degree from the left edge of the frame. After a 1,000-ms delay, the dot moved smoothly (the velocity had a sinusoidal time course) to the right through a distance of 11 degrees. The frame also moved on each trial, in synchrony with the dot, either 6 degrees to the right (*frame-right condition*) or to the left (*frame-left condition*). Subjects were instructed to follow the dot by eye, leaving their gaze at its final location. No mention was made of the motion of the frame. Subjects only occasionally perceived it to have moved.

One-half second after the target and frame stopped moving, the frame was removed, the cursor reappeared, and subjects received an auditory prompt to produce their response.[4] They were then required to produce a rapid pointing movement that began from the home location and ended as close as possible to the target location. The movement was to be as brief as possible subject to the constraint that it land close to the target. After the pointing movement, the screen blanked. The cursor then reappeared to indicate the location at which the computer determined the movement to have ended.

**Movement Analysis**  In order to identify the beginning and end of the overall movement and to locate the primary and secondary submovements, we used an algorithm similar to that we described previously (Abrams, Meyer, and Kornblum 1990; Meyer et al. 1988). Briefly, the movement trajectories were filtered and differentiated several times in order to obtain smoothed records of velocity and acceleration as a function of time. The beginning of movement was defined as the first moment in time when the velocity of the handle exceeded 2.7 cm/sec and remained above that value for at least 50 ms. The primary submovement was considered to be over at the first moment after the point of maximum velocity when either a reversal in movement direction was detected, velocity increased after a period of deceleration had occurred, or an increase in braking force was detected during a period of deceleration. After identifying the end of the primary submovement, we identified the tentative end of the overall movement as the first moment in time at which the velocity of the handle fell below 2.7 cm/sec and remained below that value for 180 ms. The interval between the end of the primary submovement and the end of the overall movement was then tentatively defined as the secondary submovement. The tentative secondary submovement was examined to be sure that it contained at least 0.6 cm of movement and had a duration of at least 60 ms. Otherwise, the movement was considered to have ended at the end of the primary submovement. Examples of movements parsed into their components are shown in figure 10.1.

**Design**  Each session began with a practice block of twelve trials: six in which the subjects could practice making pointing movements to the target and six that included the induced motion stimulus. The remainder of the session included ten blocks of trials, which consisted of two types of blocks that alternated: (1) a block of ten trials in which no frame was presented and subjects could practice producing rapid aiming movements, and (2) a

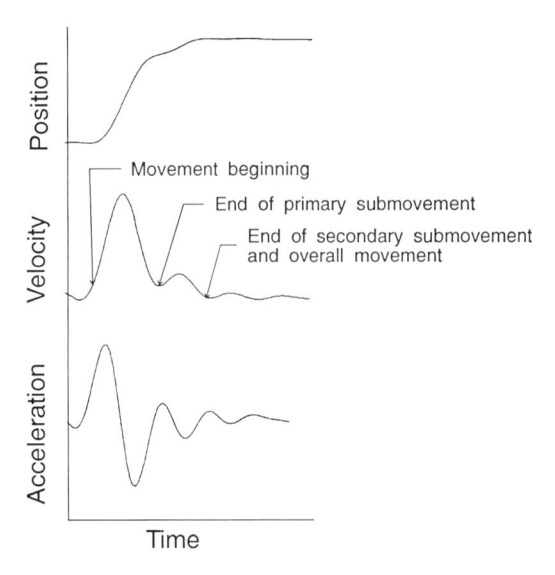

**Figure 10.1** Typical movement trajectory, with velocity and acceleration traces, partitioned into its component submovements. (Adapted from Meyer et al. 1988.)

block consisting of four initial target practice trials, followed by fourteen induced-motion trials. The fourteen experimental trials included seven frame-left trials and seven frame-right trials presented in random order.

## Results

Figure 10.2 shows the position of the hand at the end of the primary submovement and at the end of the secondary submovement plotted against the time elapsed from movement onset, separately for frame-left and frame-right trials. There was a strong effect of the illusion: pointing responses in the frame-left condition were farther to the right than in the frame-right condition ($F(1,8) = 13.7, p < .01$). The direction of the effect is what would be expected: motion of the frame in one direction is partially attributed to movement of the target object in the opposite direction. Data in the figure are also revealing with respect to the component submovements. First, most of the movement distance was traveled during the primary submovement. (All movements began at time zero and position zero.) Nevertheless, a considerable amount of movement also occurred after the end of the primary submovement, yielding a difference between the positions at the end of the primary and secondary submovements ($F(1,8) = 7.6, p < .05$).

Most important, the illusion affected the primary submovement more than the overall movement ($F(1,8) = 5.6, p < .05$). Primary submovements were 1.98 degrees longer after frame-left movements relative to after frame-right movements. But the direction of frame movement had only a 0.5 degree effect on the overall movement endpoints.

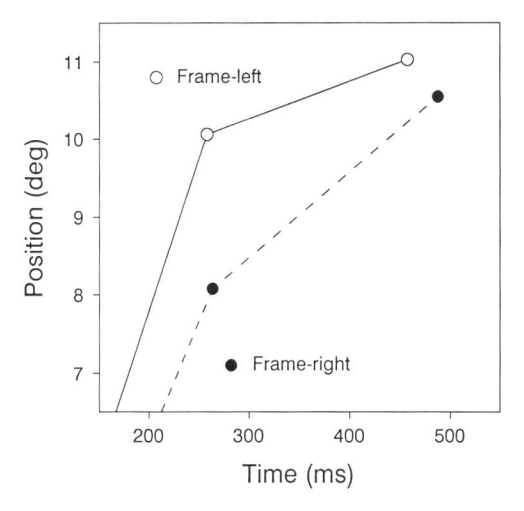

**Figure 10.2** Mean time and hand position at the end of the primary submovement (leftmost two points) and at the end of the secondary submovement (the overall movement) separately for the two directions of frame movement, from experiment 1.

We also analyzed the durations of the two submovements for the different frame movement conditions. The illusion had no effect on durations overall ($F(1,8) < 1$), nor did the two submovements differ in their mean duration ($F(1,8) < 1$).

## Discussion

The results of the experiment show that an illusory distortion in spatial attributes of the target for an aiming movement can differentially affect the component submovements of the movement. Our interpretation is that the component submovements are programmed on the basis of distinct types of spatial information, and the distortion affects the different types of information to varying degrees. In particular, induced motion illusions affect the perceived distance moved by a target more than the perceived final target location (Abrams and Landgraf 1990). Thus, the results suggest that the primary submovement is more dependent on distance information than the secondary submovement is because the former was more affected by distorted information about distance. This conclusion is consistent with that of Abrams, Meyer, and Kornblum (1990), who found that primary submovements were affected more than secondary submovements by a manipulation believed to affect perceived distance more than perceived location.[5]

These conclusions suggest that the programming of a movement may not be a unitary process; rather, different types of spatial information may be used to control different aspects of a movement. In other words, the production of a movement toward a visible target may require more than a single sensorimotor transformation. Instead, several types of sensory information may eventually need to be transformed to yield an accurate movement.

In our next experiment, we sought to extend the general pattern reported here to another perceptual manipulation.

## 10.3 EXPERIMENT 2

One limitation of the previous experiment is that the method used to distort spatial attributes of the target (induced motion illusion) involves the perception of smooth movement.[6] Several researchers have shown, however, that the perception of moving stimuli may involve mechanisms that are very different from those involved in the perception of static stimuli (Livingstone and Hubel 1988). Thus, it is possible that our results reflect phenomena that are limited to moving stimuli and are not a general property of the motor system.

To investigate this possibility, we used in this experiment a perceptual manipulation that did not require the perception of smooth movement. Instead, we varied the number of eye movements that the subject was required to make as he or she shifted gaze from the initial fixation point to the final target location. Saccade numerosity has been shown to affect subjects' attempts to point their hands to the object fixated upon at the end of the sequence of eye movements. People tend to underestimate the eccentricity of a target as the number of saccades to the target increases (Honda 1984). If the underestimation caused by increased numerosity is similar to the underestimation caused by smooth-pursuit eye movements (relative to a single saccade), then increased numerosity would be expected to influence the primary submovement more than the secondary submovement because the type of eye movement (saccade or smooth-pursuit) had a greater effect on the primary submovement in earlier work (Abrams, Meyer, and Kornblum 1990). Additionally, other findings suggest that manipulations that affect the oculomotor system may also affect hand movements (Abrams, Meyer, and Kornblum 1990; Honda 1985, 1990; Nemire and Bridgeman 1987), further suggesting that this investigation might be a productive one.

### Method

**Subjects**  Eight right-handed students each served in one 1-hour session. None had served previously. Subjects were paid $5 for participation.

**Apparatus and Procedure**  The apparatus and procedure were very similar to those used in experiment 1, with the primary exception being the nature of the visual stimuli presented prior to the target-directed hand movement. After the subject aligned the handle, the target dot was the only object visible on the screen. The target then moved to a final location 11 degrees to the right in either a single step (*one-saccade condition*), or three equal (3.67-degree) steps (*three-saccade condition*) separated by 750 ms. Subjects were instructed to follow the dot as it stepped because that presumably would facilitate their pointing movements.[7] After the last step, a delay of 750 ms ensued, after which subjects received an auditory prompt to produce their response. The subjects' task was to move the handle rapidly in order to point to the final location of the target. Subjects were not pressured to reduce response latency, but they were encouraged to minimize the duration of the pointing movements while still maintaining a high degree of spatial accuracy.

**Movement Analysis**  The pointing movements were analyzed using the same method as used for experiment 1.

**Design**  Each session began with a practice block of six trials in which the subjects could practice making pointing movements to the target. After each such movement, they were shown a marker on the monitor indicating the position at which the computer determined the movement to have ended. They then received three practice trials in each of the two conditions (one-saccade and three-saccade). The remainder of the session consisted of ten blocks of trials in which two types of blocks alternated: (1) a block of ten trials in which eye movement behavior was unconstrained and subjects could practice producing rapid aiming movements, and (2) a block consisting of four initial target-practice trials, followed by sixteen experimental trials. The sixteen experimental trials included eight one-saccade trials and eight three-saccade trials presented in random order.

### Results

Figure 10.3 shows the mean position of the hand at the end of the primary submovement and at the end of the overall movement plotted against the time elapsed from movement onset. As in experiment 1, much more distance

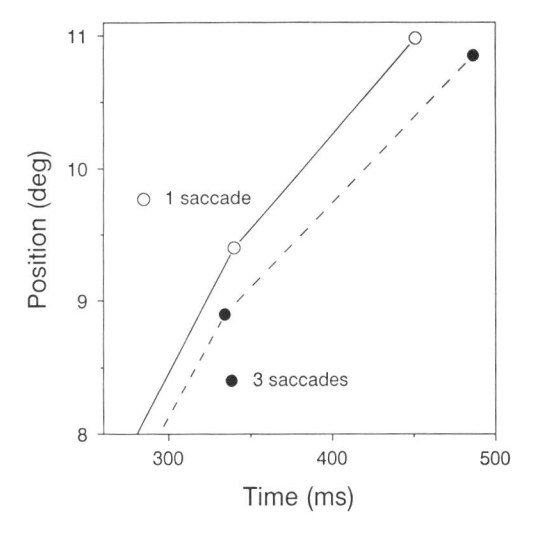

**Figure 10.3**  Mean time and hand position at the end of the primary submovement (leftmost two points), and at the end of the secondary submovement (the overall movement) separately for the two eye-movement conditions, from experiment 2.

was traversed during the primary submovement than during the secondary submovement. Nevertheless, the position at the end of the overall movement was significantly greater than that after the primary submovement, indicating that substantial movement did take place after the primary submovement $(F(1,7) = 24.8, p < .005)$. There was also a main effect of saccade numerosity: mean positions at the end of the primary submovement and overall movement were greater in the one-saccade condition as compared to the three-saccade condition $(F(1,7) = 5.6, p < .05)$. This finding is in the direction reported previously by others (Honda 1984). Finally, effects of saccade numerosity interacted with those of submovement. Numerosity had a greater effect on the position at the end of the primary submovement than it did on the position at the end of the overall movement $(F(1,7) = 5.8, p < .05)$. In fact, there was no difference in the overall end location in the one-saccade and three-saccade conditions $(T(7) = 1.93; p > .05)$.

We also analyzed the durations of the primary submovement and the overall movement in each condition. Primary submovements were longer in duration than secondary submovements $(F(1,7) = 16.9, p < .01)$. Saccade numerosity had no overall effect on the primary and secondary submovement durations $(F(1,7) < 1)$. However, numerosity and submovement were involved in a marginally significant interaction $(F(1,7) = 4.5, p = .07)$. Durations of primary submovements were not at all affected by numerosity, but secondary submovements were slightly longer in duration in the three-saccade condition than in the one-saccade condition.

## Discussion

The results of this experiment show that saccade numerosity distorts the spatial information used for the control of the primary submovement more than that involved in controlling the secondary submovement. The perceived eccentricity of a target decreases with increases in the number of saccades used to fixate that target (Honda 1984). According to Honda (1984), this occurs because the perceived target eccentricity is strongly influenced by the size of the largest component saccade executed. Since the size of the largest saccade decreases with increasing numerosity, the eccentricity of the target is underestimated. Interestingly, the underestimation had a greater effect on the primary submovement than it did on the secondary submovement. Such a finding is consistent with the assumption that primary submovements are more dependent on distance than are secondary submovements. If true, that would imply that saccade numerosity distorts perceived distance more than perceived location. That is a prediction that has yet to be confirmed.[8]

The results also serve to extend the findings of experiment 1 to a different perceptual manipulation and to a situation in which perception of smooth movement was not involved. This rules out the possibility that the results from the earlier experiment were unique to the perception of smooth movement.

## 10.4 EXPERIMENT 3

Experiments 1 and 2 employed two very different kinds of perceptual manipulations, yet each manipulation had a greater effect on the primary submovement than it did on the secondary submovement. Our interpretation was that both manipulations affected the perceived distance to the target more than the perceived final location of the target, and the primary submovement was more dependent on the (distorted) distance information. However, although only experiment 1 involved smooth movement, both experiments used stimuli that moved. In each experiment, subjects needed to follow the target as it moved from the initial fixation location to its final destination. Thus, their subsequent attempts to point to the target may have been dominated by perception of the target's movement. As a result, the manipulations we used may have been biased toward affecting the primary submovements—that component of the movement that relies most heavily on the perceived distance to the target. In this experiment, we sought to eliminate that possibility by manipulating spatial information using stimuli that remained fixed in space.

The manipulation that we selected is called the global effect (Findlay 1982) or the center-of-gravity illusion (Coren 1986). This effect occurs when the proximity of an extraneous (to be ignored) object influences hand movements (Coren 1986) or eye movements (Findlay 1982) directed toward a nearby target object. The movements tend to land toward the center of gravity of the two objects, although subjects can clearly distinguish between the target and distractor. Thus, the global effect involves distorted spatial information about a target object, but the effect is due entirely to the proximity of the distractor, not to movement of any kind. In this experiment, we had subjects make rapid, aimed, limb movements to targets in the presence of nearby distractors, and examined the component submovements. If the earlier results are limited to perceptual distortions that involve movement, no such effects should be observed here. However, if the results from experiments 1 and 2 reflect general principles of motor control mechanisms, then the distortion here should differentially affect the submovements.

There is already some reason to believe that the global effect is similar to the other manipulations and might be expected to affect the primary submovement more than the secondary submovement. Mack et al. (1985) have shown that the Muller-Lyer illusion[9] is more an illusion of the length of the central shaft than of the locations of the shaft end points. It has been suggested that the global effect is responsible for at least part of the Muller-Lyer illusion (Coren 1986). If true, then the global effect might be more likely to affect the perceived distance to the target (and hence the primary submovement) than the perceived final location of the target (the secondary submovement). This possibility was examined in experiment 3 in a manner similar to that used in experiments 1 and 2, except that wrist-rotation movements were employed here. Wrist rotations have been shown to be sensitive to subtle changes in features of the movement task and are believed to be a good movement for study due to their biomechanical simplicity (Abrams, Meyer, and Kornblum 1990; Meyer et al. 1988).

**Method**

**Subjects**   Eight right-handed students each served in one 1-hour session. None had served previously. Subjects were paid $5 for participation.

**Apparatus and Procedure**   The apparatus and procedure were similar to those used in experiments 1 and 2. The primary differences were that different stimuli were presented here, and a different type of movement was used. Subjects grasped a handle comfortably in their right hand. Rotation of the handle produced movement of the cursor on the display in much the same way that pointing movements did in experiments 1 and 2. At the beginning of each trial, subjects fixated upon a plus sign that was located directly in front of them. The letter X was presented 11 degrees to the right and served as the target for the upcoming movement. Also on the screen was a small, to-be-ignored distractor dot, presented 2.5 degrees to the left or right of the target. Subjects first turned the handle in order to align the cursor with the plus sign. One second after alignment, the plus sign was replaced by a dot. One-half second later, the target blinked off and on twice over a period of 600 ms to remind the subject that the X was the target. The target then remained on, and the blinking was followed by an auditory response signal.

As in experiments 1 and 2, subjects were instructed to move the handle rapidly in order to point to the target. They were not pressured to reduce response latency, but they were encouraged to minimize the duration of the pointing movements while still maintaining a high degree of spatial accuracy. In experiment 3, the handle was covered by a cardboard shield, and no cursor was visible during the pointing movements. Thus, subjects would not have been able to use visual feedback information to help guide the pointing movements.

**Movement Analysis**   The pointing movements were analyzed using the same method as in the previous experiments, except that the various parameters used to define movement onsets and offsets and to locate submovements were converted to values more appropriate for wrist rotations.

**Design**   The design was the same as that used in experiment 2, with the exception of the experimental manipulation.

**Results**

Figure 10.4 shows the mean hand position (in degrees of wrist arc) at the end of the primary and secondary submovements, for each condition. There was a highly reliable global effect: when the distractor was on the right, subjects pointed farther than when it was on the left ($F(1,7) = 29.5, p < .005$). Subjects

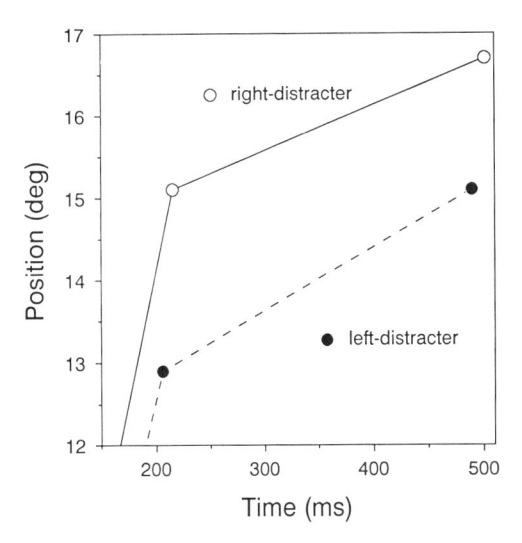

**Figure 10.4** Mean time and hand position at the end of the primary submovement (leftmost two points), and at the end of the secondary submovement (the overall movement) separately for the two distracter conditions, from experiment 3.

also had traveled farther at the end of the overall movement than they had at the end of the primary submovement ($F(1,7) = 4.2, p < .10$). One subject had unusually long primary submovements; when he was removed, the results were clearer: $F(1,6) = 6.2, p < .05$). Most important, the effects of distractor location and submovement interacted: the distractor location had a larger effect on the primary submovement than it did on the secondary submovement ($F(1,7) = 17.7, p < .005$).

**Discussion**

As in experiments 1 and 2, a manipulation of visual-spatial information had a larger effect on the primary submovement than it did on the secondary submovement. If the global effect does indeed influence perceived distance more than perceived location, as we had speculated, then the experiment results support the possibility that the primary submovement is more dependent on perceived distance than the secondary submovement is. This finding extends our earlier results to a situation in which the distorted spatial information is produced by static, nonmoving stimuli.

## 10.5 General Discussion

We have presented evidence that the planning and preparation of rapid aimed limb movements involves at least two distinct types of visual-spatial information. The two types of information are each primarily involved in the planning of two separate phases of movement.

Perceived distance appears to play an important role in the planning of the initial, "ballistic," primary submovement that propels the limb rapidly toward the target. Such an impulse would require advance information about the direction and distance of movement in order to produce the appropriate forces. The existence of such processes is supported by the finding that neurons in the motor cortex encode the direction of movement (Georgopoulos, Schwartz, and Kettner 1986). It is this phase of movement that is addressed by models of force impulse variability (Meyer, Smith, and Wright 1982; Schmidt et al. 1979).

Perceived final location, on the other hand, appears to be involved in the preparation of the final, secondary submovement in which the limb homes in and lands on the target. Such a position-seeking mechanism would ideally be immune to minor perturbations in the limb during the movement or to variability in the position at the end of the primary submovement (and at the beginning of the secondary submovement). The existence of such processes is supported by the finding that accurate movements can be produced in the presence of undetected perturbations to the limb (Bizzi, Polit, and Morasso 1976). It is this phase of movement that is addressed by traditional mass-spring or equilibrium-point models of motor control (Feldman 1986; Sakitt 1980).[10]

Our results support a hybrid view of movement planning and control in which two different mechanisms are involved in planning different aspects of a movement. In this way, movements can exhibit properties that are often associated with one class of motor control models (e.g., equilibrium-point models) yet not be inconsistent with another class (e.g., impulse-variability models). The two-process view is also consistent with neurophysiological evidence that shows that both kinematic and dynamic features of movements are encoded within the central nervous system (Kalaska and Crammond 1992). Movement kinematics (changes in position over time) correspond loosely to desired locations of a limb, whereas dynamics (changes in forces) seem more closely aligned with perceived distances.

**Complementary Analyses**

Our conclusions are supported by additional research from our laboratory. In particular, Abrams, Meyer, and Kornblum (1990) had subjects make rapid wrist-rotation movements to a target that subjects had fixated using either saccadic or smooth-pursuit eye movements. Previous work by others had suggested that people underestimate the distance to a target fixated by smooth-pursuit movements, compared to one reached by a saccade (Honda 1985, 1990; Mack and Herman 1972). Indeed, the primary submovements of the target-directed wrist rotations were shorter after smooth-pursuit eye movements than after saccades to the target. However, the end locations of the wrist-rotations were unaffected by the type of eye movement. Abrams, Meyer, and Kornblum (1990) proposed a hybrid model to explain the results: perceived distance is involved in the preparation of the primary submovement, and perceived location is used for preparing the secondary submovement. Furthermore, the type of eye movement made to the target affected perceived distance but not the perceived location of the target. Hence, pointing movements could end accurately after smooth-pursuit eye movements to the target, even though the primary submovements were distorted (compared to after a saccade to the target).

Additional support comes from a study by Abrams and Landgraf (1990). They had subjects point an unseen hand to stimuli that had undergone real and illusory movement, as in our experiment 1. In one experiment, subjects pointed beginning with their hand at either the position that the target had begun its movement from or some other position. They reasoned that in the first situation, subjects might be able to use the perceived distance of target movement in order to produce the pointing movement. In the latter condition, however, distance would be a less reliable cue because the starting location of the hand did not correspond to the starting location of the target. Because illusory motion distorts perceived distance, pointing movements that began from the initial location of the target were expected to be more affected by the induced motion illusion than pointing that began elsewhere, and that is what was observed. These results further support the proposal that there are two distinct spatial codes involved in the guidance of aiming movements.

**Role of Feedback**

Our results are not likely due to the subjects' use of feedback information to correct a perceived error in the primary submovement. First, there was no visual information available at all about the position of the subject's hand in experiment 3. Thus, corrections there could not have been made on the basis of visual feedback information. (There was also no opportunity for subjects to use visual feedback information in the Abrams, Meyer, and Kornblum [1990] experiments discussed earlier.) Additionally, although it is possible that subjects could have made corrections on the basis of kinesthetic feedback, several sources argue against that possibility. For example, Schmidt and McGown (1980) have shown that people do not typically use kinesthetic feedback to correct rapid limb movements to compensate for unexpected changes in the load on the arm, despite the fact that such changes can cause the movements to be inaccurate. Also, the mere existence of a change in limb position after the end of the primary submovement does not imply that feedback information was used. Deafferented monkeys also produce what look like corrective secondary submovements, yet those could not possibly be based on feedback (Polit and Bizzi 1979).

**Relation to Eye Movement Mechanisms**

Our findings are analogous in many ways to a phenomenon observed with eye movements. Saccades are produced by a phasic pulse of force followed by a step change in the tonic level of eye muscle innervation (Sparks and Mays 1990). Usually the pulse and step are appropriately matched in amplitude, but occasionally the magnitude of the pulse and step are inappropriately matched, and a slow gliding movement known as a glissade is appended to the end of the saccade. When that happens, it may take an additional 100 ms or more for the eye to reach its final destination. Such a result demonstrates that phasic and tonic components of eye movements that are usually linked to each other can be dissociated. Similarly, we have shown that factors that affect the magnitude of the pulse (primary submovement) need not affect the magnitude of the step (secondary submovement) of limb movements. In either case, it appears that the eye and limb do eventually arrive at the location specified by the step change (the secondary submovement), despite some delays along the way. These and other similarities between the eye and limb movements suggest that common mechanisms may underlie their control (Abrams, Meyer and Kornblum 1989).

**Perceptual versus Motor systems**

Our results may also help to explain a distinction that has been made between the quality of the spatial information available to the perceptual system, and that available to the motor system. Several researchers have shown that people can point accurately to objects even though illusions may affect verbal reports of the objects' positions or other judgments about the objects (Bridgeman et al. 1979; Bridgeman, Kirch, and Sperling 1981; Honda 1985, 1990). Such findings have been used to argue that the spatial information available to the motor system somehow differs from (and is superior to) that available to the cognitive or perceptual system. Such a conclusion may be unwarranted. Consider the study by Honda (1985). Honda had subjects follow by eye a visual target that moved either smoothly or abruptly from a central fixation point to a peripheral target location (such stimuli required subjects to make either smooth-pursuit or saccadic eye movements, respectively). Subjects then (1) pointed their hand to the target, with the hand beginning from the same location that the target began its movement from; (2) pointed to the target with the hand beginning from some location other than the initial target location; or (3) adjusted the distance between two lights to match the perceived distance of target movement. Honda found that the judgments of distance were reduced after smooth-pursuit eye movements, compared to saccades of the same size. This finding presumably reflects an underestimation of smooth-pursuit eye movements by the perceptual system (Mack and Herman 1972). Hand-pointing movements also were shorter after smooth-pursuit eye movements relative to saccades, but that was true for only the pointing movements that began from the same location from which the target began its movement. Pointing that began with the hand somewhere other than the initial location of the target was unaffected by the type of eye movement. Honda's interpretation of these results was that pointing that began from the same location that the target began its movement from was dominated by the perceptual system. Hence, such pointing was affected by the type of eye movement (as the explicit perceptual judgments had been). Pointing that began from elsewhere reflected the operation of the motor system. Thus, because pointing in the latter condition was not distorted by the type of eye movement, the motor system presumably has access to higher-quality spatial information about the tracked target than that available to the perceptual system.

Our results suggest a different interpretation of the Honda (1985) results. Specifically, the tasks presumed to reflect the perceptual or the motor system may have depended differentially on distance and location information. In particular, Honda's perceptual task was one in which subjects were explicitly asked to judge the perceived distance of target movement. Pointing from the initial position of the target would also be dependent on the perceived distance that the target moved (see the previous discussion about Abrams and Landgraf's 1990 study.) The task that was presumed to reflect the motor system, on the other hand, required subjects to point to the location of the target. Thus, the differences between conditions may simply have reflected differences in the quality of distance and location information after saccadic and smooth-pursuit eye movements and not differences in the quality of the information available to perceptual and motor systems. Such differences between distance and location information are very similar to those reported in this chapter (and also in Abrams, Meyer, and Kornblum 1990).

A similar distinction between perceptual and motor systems has been suggested by Goodale, Pelisson, and Prablanc (1986). They showed that people could accurately point their unseen hands to targets that were displaced during the initial part of the hand movement toward the target. Adjustments were made in the hand movements even though subjects were unaware of the change in the position of the target (the displacements occurred during the subjects' eye movements toward the target). Presumably these results show that "the neural mechanisms mediating the perception of target position can be dissociated from those mediating visually guided reaching movements directed at that target" (p. 749). Similar results and conclusions have also been reported by Bridgeman et al. (1979). However, our conclusions suggest an alternative interpretation. It may be that the type of spatial information needed to terminate a hand movement accurately differs from the spatial information needed to judge that a target has moved. If such a difference exists, then the differences between motor pointing and perceptual judgment reported by Goodale, Pelisson, and Prablanc (1986) may not reflect differences between motor and perceptual systems, as those researchers suggest. Instead, the results may demonstrate that the experimental manipulation used (displacement of a target during an eye movement) affects one type of spatial information more than another. That is precisely what we have suggested in this chapter. In particular, the information involved in assessing target location (used for terminating the hand-pointing movement) may be different from that involved in detecting target movement (used to make judgments about the target's displacement). Such a possibility is supported by reports of paradoxical motion: a perception of target movement that is inconsistent with perceived changes in target position (Shebilske and Proffitt 1983).

Our results may also bear on some neuropsychological data regarding a condition known as optic ataxia. Perenin and Vighetto (1983, 1988) have reported a number of cases in which patients with parietal lesions have impaired hand movements toward visual targets but unimpaired performance on simple motor and perceptual tasks. The implication is that the lesion disrupts the integration of visual and proprioceptive information, while leaving basic motor and perceptual functions intact. An alternate interpretation is possible; it is possible that the perceptual tasks, which were performed normally, relied on a different type of spatial information than the motor (pointing) task. In particular, the perceptual tasks that showed an intact visual and perceptual system required subjects to provide a "verbal estimate of the distance or the relative position of objects within each hemifield" (Perenin and Vighetto 1988, p. 648). Such a task may be one that relies heavily on the perceived distance to the target object. Accurate termination of a hand-pointing movement, however, may rely more on an accurate assessment of the location of the target, as we have suggested. If true, then it may be that the perceptual and motor tasks Perenin and Vighetto (1983, 1988) used differentially required subjects to use either distance or location information, respectively. Thus, lesions that result in optic ataxia may not disrupt particular processes; rather, they may distort specific types of spatial information.

**Directions for the Future**

One interesting feature of our results is the relative insensitivity of the secondary submovement to our perceptual manipulations (this was also true in Abrams, Meyer, and Kornblum 1990). All of the manipulations that we studied affected the primary submovement more than the end of the overall movement (the secondary submovement). It is possible that we have simply not found a manipulation that affects perceived location.[11] One way to do this might be to have subjects produce movements while viewing the world through wedge prisms. Such prisms displace all visual stimuli a constant amount in one direction and thus distort the locations of visual objects, but they leave distances intact. Thus, the distance traversed by a moving object would be perceived accurately, although the final location of the object might be misperceived. Unexpected introduction or removal of the displacing prisms would alter perceived locations but would not affect perceived distances. It remains to be seen whether movements under such conditions would reflect accurate distances (normal primary submovements) and distorted locations (inaccurate movement termination).[12] Alternatively, it may be that the secondary submovement is truly more robust than the primary submovement. We hope that answers to these and other questions will provide some insight into the mechanisms involved in the control of movement.

**NOTES**

Preparation of this chapter, and the research described in it, was supported by Grant R29-MH45145 from the National Institutes of Health. The authors thank Steve Keele, Morris

Moscovitch, and Paolo Viviani for helpful comments on an earlier draft. Address correspondence to Richard A. Abrams, Department of Psychology, Campus Box 1125, Washington University, St. Louis, MO 63130. E-mail: rabrams@artsci.wustl.edu

1. We are considering only visually defined targets (as opposed to felt or remembered target locations).

2. Of course, the location information would have to be encoded in some meaningful coordinate system, such as relative to the head or body. In the remainder of this chapter, we will simply use "location" to refer to such information.

3. The distinction between distance and location specification is similar in many ways to another distinction that has been made regarding details of movement planning: To what extent are movements planned in terms of kinematic attributes, such as changes in the position of a limb over time, as opposed to dynamic attributes, such as the forces and torques that need to act on the limb to accomplish the desired movement? Although planning in terms of kinematics may be simpler (because the goal of a movement is often formulated in kinematic terms—e.g., "Move the hand to where the object is"), the dynamics must ultimately be worked out. Similarly, although achieving the correct final location may be all that really matters from the perspective of one who wants to grasp an object, details of the distance that needs to be traversed and other aspects of the trajectory must eventually be reckoned with, at least at some level.

Another related issue involves the extent to which a kinematic representation of a forthcoming movement is one that encodes the desired changes in limb position, as opposed to the changes needed in joint angles to produce the limb movements (Hollerbach and Atkeson 1985; Morasso 1981). Although limb position units seem more directly relevant, the motor system eventually must change the joint angles in order to produce movement.

4. The presence of a visible cursor may have allowed subjects to use visual feedback to correct some of their responses. This potential limitation is overcome in experiment 3.

5. This study is discussed more fully in the general discussion.

6. The Abrams, Meyer, and Kornblum (1990) study also used smoothly moving stimuli.

7. In this experiment, we did not monitor the subjects' eye movements. In similar situations when we have monitored eye position, subjects complied with the request to follow the target.

8. Recall that the earlier assumption that induced motion illusions distort perceived distance more than perceived location was based on empirical evidence (Abrams and Landgraf 1990).

9. The Muller-Lyer illusion is a classic illusion with a number of variations. Typically, two shafts (lines) of equal length are perceived to differ in length due to the direction of extraneous lines (or "wings") added to the ends of the shafts.

10. We are not making any assumptions about when the two submovements are prepared. Possibly the secondary submovement is not finalized until after some movement has taken place. However, it is also possible that both submovements are planned and implemented simultaneously, before movement ever begins. The point is simply that the setting of the equilibrium point (presumably on the basis of location information) determines the ultimate final position of the limb, whereas the force impulse during the primary submovement (presumably computed on the basis of distance information) plays a role in determining the shape of the movement trajectory prior to the end of the movement.

11. If such a manipulation was identified, it might be difficult to interpret the results, because a factor that influenced both submovements might be expected to have cumulative effects—affecting the secondary submovement more. The same pattern would be expected if a factor affected only the secondary submovement.

12. We thank Steve Keele for suggesting these possibilities.

# REFERENCES

Abrams, R. A., and Landgraf, J. Z. (1990). Differential use of distance and location information for spatial localization. *Perception and Psychophysics, 47*, 349–359.

Abrams, R. A. Meyer, D. E., and Kornblum, S. (1989). Speed and accuracy of saccadic eye movements: Characteristics of impulse variability in the oculomotor system. *Journal of Experimental Psychology: Human Perception and Performance, 15*, 529–543.

Abrams, R. A., Meyer, D. E., and Kornblum, S. (1990). Eye-hand coordination: Oculomotor control in rapid aimed limb movements. *Journal of Experimental Psychology: Human Perception and Performance, 16*, 248–267.

Bizzi, E., and Mussa-Ivaldi, F. A. (1989). Geometrical and mechanical issues in movement planning and control. In M. I. Posner (Ed.), *Foundations of cognitive science*, 769–792. Cambridge, MA: MIT Press.

Bizzi, E., Mussa-Ivaldi, F. A., and Giszter, S. (1991). Computations underlying the execution of movement: A biological perspective. *Science, 253*, 287–291.

Bizzi, E., Polit, A., and Morasso, P. (1976). Mechanisms underlying achievement of final head position. *Journal of Neurophysiology, 39*, 435–444.

Bridgeman, B., Kirch, M., and Sperling, A. (1981). Segregation of cognitive and motor aspects of visual function using induced motion. *Perception and Psychophysics, 29*, 336–342.

Bridgeman, B., Lewis, S., Heit, G., and Nagle, M. (1979). Relation between cognitive and motor-oriented systems of visual position perception. *Journal of Experimental Psychology: Human Perception and Performance, 5*, 692–700.

Carlton, L. G. (1981). Processing visual feedback information for movement control. *Journal of Experimental Psychology: Human Perception and Performance, 7*, 1019–1030.

Coren, S. (1986). An efferent component in the visual perception of direction and extent. *Psychological Review, 93*, 391–410.

Easter, S. S. (1973). A comment on the "glissade." *Vision Research, 13*, 881–882.

Feldman, A. (1986). Once more on the equilibrium-point hypothesis (Lambda model) for motor control. *Journal of Motor Behavior, 18*, 17–54.

Findlay J. M. (1982). Global visual processing for saccadic eye movements. *Vision Research, 22*, 1044–1045.

Flanders, M., and Soechting, J. F. (1990). Parcellation of sensorimotor transformations of arm movements. *Journal of Neuroscience, 10*, 2420–2427.

Georgopoulos, A. P., Schwartz, A. B., and Kettner, R. E. (1986). Neuronal population coding of movement direction. *Science, 233*, 1416–1419.

Ghez, C. (1979). Contribution of central programs to rapid limb movement in the cat. In H. Asanuma and V. J. Wilson (Eds.), *Integration in the nervous system*. Tokyo: IGAKU-SHOIN.

Goodale, M. A., Pelisson, D., and Prablanc, C. (1986). Large adjustments in visually guided reaching do not depend on vision of the hand or perception of target displacement. *Nature, 320*, 748–750.

Hogan, N. (1984). An organizing principle for a class of voluntary movements. *Journal of Neuroscience, 4*, 2745–2754.

Hollerbach, J. M., and Atkeson, C. G. (1985). Deducing planning variables from experimental arm trajectories: Pitfalls and possibilities. *Biological Cybernetics, 56*, 279–292.

Honda, H. (1984). Eye-position signals in successive saccades. *Perception and Psychophysics, 36,* 15–20.

Honda, H. (1985). Spatial localization in saccade and pursuit-eye-movement conditions: A comparison of perceptual and motor measures. *Perception and Psychophysics, 38,* 41–46.

Honda, H. (1990). The extraretinal signal from the pursuit-eye-movement system: Its role in the perceptual and the egocentric localization systems. *Perception and Psychophysics, 48,* 509–515.

Kalaska, J. F., and Crammond, D. J. (1992). Cerebral cortical mechanisms of reaching movements. *Science, 255,* 1517–1523.

Keele, S. W. (1981). Behavioral analysis of movement. In V. Brooks (Ed.), *Handbook of physiology: The nervous system,* Vol. 2: *Motor control.* Baltimore, MD: American Physiological Society.

Kettner, R. E., Schwartz, A. B., and Georgopoulos, A. P. (1988). Primate motor cortex and free arm movements to visual targets in three-dimensional space. III. Positional gradients and population coding of movement direction from various movement origins. *Journal of Neuroscience, 8,* 2938–2947.

Kuperstein, M. (1988). Neural model of adaptive hand-eye coordination for single postures. *Science, 239,* 1308–1311.

Livingstone, M., and Hubel, D. (1988). Segregation of form, color, movement, and depth: Anatomy, physiology, and perception. *Science, 240,* 740–749.

Mack, A., and Herman, E. (1972). A new illusion: The underestimation of distance during pursuit eye movements. *Perception and Psychophysics, 12,* 471–473.

Mack, A., Heuer, F., Villardi, K., and Chambers, D. (1985). The dissociation of position and extent in Muller-Lyer figures. *Perception and Psychophysics, 37,* 335–344.

Massone, L., and Bizzi, E. (1989). A neural network model for limb trajectoy formation. *Biological Cybernetics, 61,* 417–425.

Mays, L. E., and Sparks, D. L. (1980). Saccades are spatially, not retinotopically coded. *Science, 208,* 1163–1164.

Meyer, D. E., Abrams, R. A., Kornblum, S., Wright, C. E., and Smith, J. E. K. (1988). Optimality in human motor performance: Ideal control of rapid aimed movements. *Psychological Review, 95,* 340–370.

Meyer, D. E., Smith, J. E. K., and Wright, C. E. (1982). Models for the speed and accuracy of aimed movements. *Psychological Review, 89,* 449–482.

Morasso, P. (1981). Spatial control of arm movements. *Experimental Brain Research, 42,* 223–227.

Nemire, K., and Bridgeman, B. (1987). Oculomotor and skeletal motor systems share one map of visual space. *Vision Research, 27,* 393–400.

Perenin, M.-T., and Vighetto, A. (1983). Optic ataxia: A specific disorder in visuomotor coordination. In A. Hein and M. Jeannerod (Eds.), *Spatially oriented behavior,* 305–326. New York: Springer.

Perenin, M.-T., and Vighetto, A. (1988). Optic ataxia: A specific disruption in visuomotor mechanisms. *Brain, 111,* 643–674.

Polit, A., and Bizzi, E. (1979). Characteristics of motor programs underlying arm movements in monkeys. *Journal of Neurophysiology, 42,* 183–194.

Sakitt, B. (1980). A spring model and equivalent neural network for arm posture control. *Biological Cybernetics, 37,* 227–234.

Schmidt, R. A., and McGown, C. M. (1980). Terminal accuracy of unexpectedly loaded rapid movements: Evidence for a mass-spring mechanism in programming. *Journal of Motor Behavior, 12*, 149–161.

Schmidt, R. A., Zelaznik, H., Hawkins, B., Frank, J. S., and Quinn, J.T., Jr. (1979). Motor-output variability: A theory for the accuracy of rapid motor acts. *Psychological Review, 86*, 415–451.

Shebilske, W. L., and Proffitt, D. R. (1983). Paradoxical retinal motions during head movements: Apparent motion without equivalent apparent displacement. *Perception and Psychophysics, 34*, 476–481.

Soechting, J. F., and Flanders, M. (1989). Errors in pointing are due to approximations in sensorimotor transformations. *Journal of Neurophysiology, 62*, 595–608.

Sparks, D. L., and Mays, L. E. (1990). Signal transformations required for the generation of saccadic eye movements. *Annual Review of Neuroscience, 13*, 309–336.

Velay, J.-L., Roll, R., and Paillard, J. (1989). Elbow position sense in man: Contrasting results in matching and pointing. *Human Movement Science, 8*, 177–193.

Woodworth, R. S. (1899). The accuracy of voluntary movement. *Psychological Review, 3* (2, Whole No. 13).

# 11 Visual Attention and the Control of Eye Movements in Early Infancy

Mark H. Johnson

ABSTRACT  Experiments concerned with the development of volitional (endogenous) control of eye movements (overt orienting) in infants are described. This evidence indicates that infants are capable of the voluntary control of eye movements by around 4 months of age. Next, experiments that attempt to measure covert shifts of visual attention in early infancy are reviewed, and the results of a study involving the exogenous cueing of covert attention reported. These results indicate that 4-month-old infants, like adults, show both facilitation and subsequent inhibition of responding to a cued spatial location. In contrast, a group of 2-month-old infants did not show these effects within the temporal parameters studied. Finally, I speculate on the underlying neural basis of these developments, and on their implication for the relation between covert shifts of attention and eye movements.

## 11.1  INTRODUCTION

It has become evident in recent years that there are multiple brain pathways involved in the control of eye movements and visual attention in adults (Schiller 1985; Posner and Peterson 1990). Investigating the sequential development of these pathways, and the construction of the visual attention system during ontogeny, may be informative given the obvious difficulty in analyzing the complex combinations of hierarchical and parallel systems found in adults (see Johnson 1990, 1994). In this chapter I review studies and present new evidence on the ontogeny of both overt and covert aspects of visual orienting, focusing in particular on the transition from exogenous to endogenous control. I conclude by assessing the implications of these experiments on development for the debate in adult literature about the role of covert shifts of attention in saccade execution and planning.

While our understanding of visual attention and orienting in adults is far from complete, a number of distinctions have been proposed that will be helpful in our analysis of the ontogeny of attention (see fig. 11.1). Eye movements that shift gaze from one location to another may be referred to as overt orienting. In contrast, shifts of visual attention between spatial locations or objects that occur independently of eye and head movements are referred to as covert (Posner 1980). Only in the past few years has work on covert shifts of attention in infancy been performed, and much of that work is reviewed in this chapter. Although shifts of covert visual attention are, by definition, dissociable from eye and head movements, they may be clearly related to

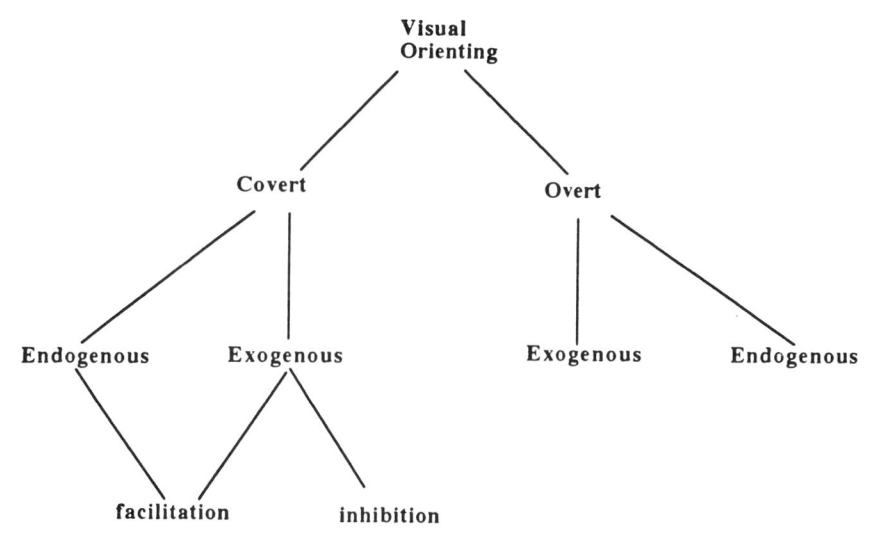

**Figure 11.1** An illustration of some dissociations used in the literature on visual attention.

overt orienting in some respects. The exact relation between covert attention and overt orienting will be discussed in more detail later.

A further distinction in the adult literature is that between *endogenous* and *exogenous* control. This distinction refers to whether, for example, responses to a particular spatial location were cued by a briefly presented stimulus that appeared at that location (exogenous), or whether that spatial location was cued by a more indirect form of instruction to the subject, such as a centrally presented arrow pointing to the right or left, or a verbal instruction to look in a certain direction (endogenous). This distinction is of interest in development since the onset of endogenous control over eye movements may be indicative of the transition from a primarily input-driven, automatic form of orienting to a system under the influence of volitional (and possibly conscious) control.

## 11.2 OVERT VISUAL ORIENTING IN EARLY INFANCY

Bronson (1974, 1982) reviewed evidence in support of the contention that the newborn human infant sees primarily through the subcortical retinotectal visual pathway and that it is only by around 2 or 3 months of age that the primary visual pathway becomes functional to the extent that it influences the visually guided behavior of the young infant. This putative shift of visually guided behavior from subcortical to cortical processing, he argued, was accompanied by a shift from exogenous (input-driven) orienting to endogenous (volitional) orienting. Atkinson (1984) and Johnson (1990) have updated and extended Bronson's original account in the light of more recent knowledge about the independent streams of visual processing in the cortex (de Yoe and Van Essen 1988; Van Essen 1985). Both Atkinson and Johnson proposed models based on the sequential development of particular cortical streams, resulting in phases of partial cortical functioning.

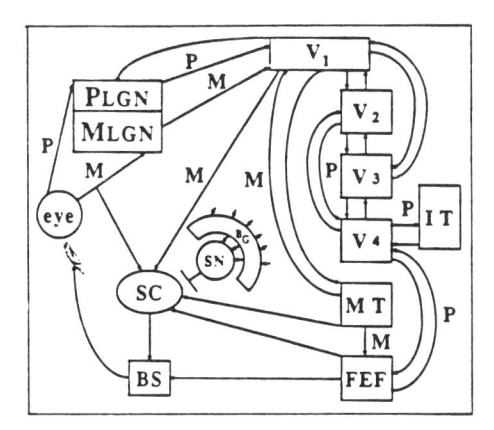

**Figure 11.2** A schematic representation of the model proposed by Schiller (1985) for the neuroanatomical pathways thought to underlie oculomotor control in primates. LGN = lateral geniculate nucleus; SC = superior colliculus; SN = substantia nigra; BG = basal ganglia; BS = brainstem; FEF = frontal eye fields; M = Broad band (magnocelullar) stream; P = color opponent (parvocellular) stream. (Adapted from Schiller 1985.)

Figure 11.2 illustrates a number of pathways thought to underlie oculomotor control in the primate brain (Schiller 1985). In brief, these pathways are (1) a subcortical pathway involving the superior colliculus and thought to be involved in rapid, input-driven (exogenous) saccades; (2) a diffuse cortical projection to the superior colliculus via the basal ganglia and substantia nigra, apparently involved in the regulation of the colliculus; (3) a cortical pathway that passes through area MT and that is probably involved in motion detection and the smooth tracking of moving stimuli; and (4) a cortical pathway through the frontal eye fields that is important for more complex forms of scanning patterns.

Johnson (1990) used evidence from human postnatal developmental neuroanatomy to argue for the following developmental sequence of onset: (1) before (2), then (3), then (4). This developmental sequence was then traced to the onset of components of visual orienting. For example, the development of the frontal eye field pathway (4) at around 3 to 4 months of age coincides with the onset of "anticipatory" saccades, the predictive tracking of moving stimuli, and the ability to use prior information to guide subsequent saccades. The onset of this endogenous eye movement control raises the issue of its interaction with exogenously driven saccades, such as those that are the product of the subcortical pathway (1). In adult subjects, the interaction between endogenous and exogenous eye movement systems can be studied in so-called antisaccade tasks. In an antisaccade task subjects are instructed not to make a saccade toward a cue stimulus but rather to saccade in the opposite direction where a target stimulus is subsequently presented (Hallett 1978). One component of this task is that subjects have to inhibit a spontaneous, automatic (exogenous) eye movement toward a stimulus and direct their saccade in the opposite direction. Thus, it is of interest to apply this task to infants.

Fixation Stimulus

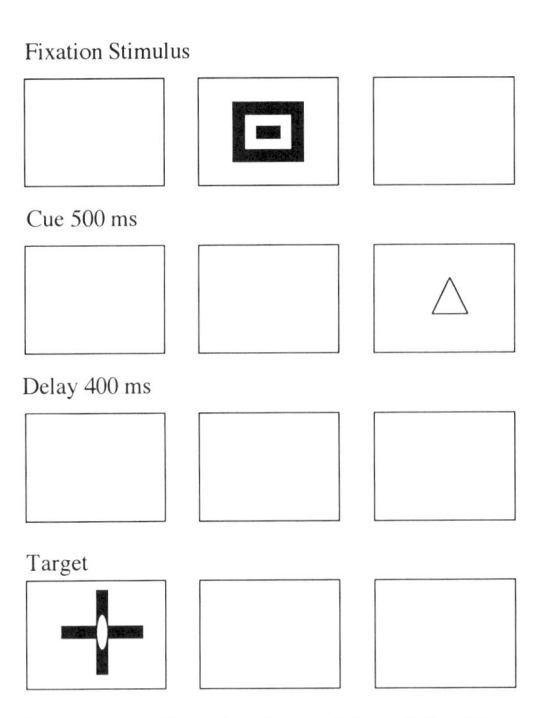

Cue 500 ms

Delay 400 ms

Target

**Figure 11.3**  The order of presentation of stimuli in experiment 1.

## Experiment 1

Clearly, one cannot give verbal instructions to a young infant to look to the side opposite from where the first stimulus appears. Instead, we have to motivate the infant to want to look at a second (target) stimulus more than at the first (cue) stimulus. This can be done by making the second stimulus more dynamic and colorful than the first. Thus, over a series of trials an infant may learn to withold a saccade to the first stimulus in order to anticipate the appearance of the second (more attractive) stimulus. The first stimulus also becomes a cue to predict the appearance of the second stimulus on the opposite side (see fig. 11.3 for details of the stimulus presentation sequence).

In a pilot experiment to determine the feasibility of this approach, I have collected data from five 4-month-old infants (range, 122 to 128 days), with no known birth or other complications.[1] Using general procedures and stimuli described in detail for experiment 2, and a presentation schedule as shown in figure 11.3, a steady decrease in the extent of orienting toward the first (cue) stimulus was observed over a number of training trials from an initial level of over 80 percent to a level of under 50 percent (see table 11.1). Clearly this preliminary finding needs to be replicated and extended with a larger sample. Furthermore, control conditions in which the first stimulus (cue) is not predictive of the second (target) need to be run, in order to be sure that the infants are not merely habituating faster to the cue stimulus than to the target during the course of the experiment. While bearing these caveats in mind, the large number of trials in which infants made a saccade straight from the fixation

**Table 11.1** Frequency of Making a Saccade toward the First Stimulus within Each Block of Training Trials (mean and standard error)

| Trial Numbers | 1–4 | 5–8 | 9–12 | 13–16 |
|---|---|---|---|---|
| Mean % | 86.8 | 68.4 | 75.0 | 46.6 |
| Standard error | 8.1 | 9.3 | 12.4 | 14.1 |

point to the second (target) stimulus in the later stages of the experiment is consistent with the ability to inhibit input-driven saccades and may indicate volitional control over saccades. Further, the evidence that adults with lesions around the frontal eye fields cannot readily withhold input-driven saccades in a similar task (Guitton, Buchtel, and Douglas 1985) supports the contention that the development of this cortical structure is a necessary prerequisite for endogenous eye movement control in infants.

## 11.3 COVERT VISUAL ORIENTING IN EARLY INFANCY

At present we can study covert shifts of attention only in indirect ways. For example, in adults, covert attention may be directed to a spatial location by a very briefly presented visual stimulus. Although subjects do not make a saccade to this stimulus, they are faster to report (often by means of a button press) the appearance of a target stimulus in the cued location than in another location. With infants we are also limited to indirect methods of studying covert shifts of attention. Further, we have the problem that infants do not accept verbal instruction and are poor at motor responses readily used with adults such as a button press. One motor response that can be readily elicited even from very young infants is eye movement (overt orienting). Thus, in the experiments that follow, we attempt to use measures of overt orienting to study covert shifts of attention. We can do this by examining the influence of a cue stimulus, to which infants do not make an eye movement, on their subsequent saccades toward target stimuli. This approach has also been taken in some adult studies purporting to measure shifts of covert attention (e.g., Maylor 1985). Experiments in which infants do make a saccade toward a cue stimulus I will regard as not being informative with regard to covert shifts of visual attention.[2]

### Exogenously Cued Covert Orienting

One way in which evidence for covert shifts of attention has been provided in adults is by studying the effect on detection of cueing saccades to a particular spatial location. A briefly presented cue serves to draw covert attention to the location, resulting in the subsequent facilitation of responses toward that location (Posner and Cohen 1980; Maylor 1985). This facilitatory effect lasts for about 100–200 ms in the adult. While facilitation of detection and saccades toward a covertly attended location occurs if the target stimulus appears very shortly after the cue offset, with longer latencies between cue and target, inhibition of saccades toward that location occurs. This latter phenomenon, referred to as "inhibition of return" (Posner et al. 1985), may reflect an evolutionarily important mechanism for preventing attention returning to a spatial location that has been very recently processed. In adults facilitation is reliably observed when targets appeared at the cued location within about 100 ms of the cue, whereas targets that appear between 300 and 1,300 ms after a peripheral (exogenous) cue result in longer latency responses (e.g., Posner and Cohen 1980, 1984; Maylor 1985). It is worth noting that inhibition of return has been reported only in studies that involve exogenous, rather than endogenous, cueing.

One of the first studies pertinent to exogenous orienting in human infants was concerned with inhibition of return following overt orienting. Clohessy et al. (1991) report an experiment in which infants sat in front of three monitor screens on which colorful dynamic stimuli were presented. At the start of each trial an attractive fixation stimulus appeared on the central screen. Once the infant had fixated on this stimulus, a cue stimulus was presented on one of the two side monitor screens. When the infant had made a saccade toward the cue, it was turned off. Following this, infants returned their gaze to the center screen before an identical stimulus was presented bilaterally on both side screens. While infants of 3 months of age showed no significant preferential orienting toward the bilateral targets as a result of the cue, infants of 6 months of age oriented more toward the side opposite from that where the cue stimulus had appeared. The authors argued that this preferential orienting toward the opposite side from the cue is indicative of inhibition of return and its development between 3 and 6 months of age.

This result was replicated and extended by Hood and Atkinson (1991) also with 3- and 6-month-old infants. This study had two important differences from that reported by Clohessy et al. (1991). First, by using a shorter cue stimulus duration, Hood and Atkinson ensured that the infants did not make a saccade toward this stimulus. Thus, any effects of the cue presentation on subsequent saccades to the target could be attributed to a covert shift of attention during the cue presentation. The second difference was that Hood and Atkinson used unilateral target presentations, as opposed to the bilateral targets used by Clohessy and colleagues.

In their experiment Hood and Atkinson (1991) used a 100 ms cue that was followed by a target presented either ipsilateral or contralateral to the the location where the cue had appeared. The target appeared either immediately after the cue or with an interstimulus interval (ISI) of 500 ms. The authors predicted that if the target appeared immediately after the cue, then they should see facilitation of reaction times to make a saccade toward the target when it appears on the ipsilateral side. In contrast, in trials where there was a 500 ms ISI between the stimuli they ought to see inhibition (slowed reaction times, RTs) for making a saccade toward the same location as that in which the cue had appeared.

The group of 6-month-old infants showed the predicted effects: a faster mean RT to make a saccade when the target appeared in the cued location on the no ISI trials and a slower mean RT to make a saccade toward the cued location on the long ISI trials. However, the facilitation toward the cued location in the no ISI trials was a small (and nonsignificant) effect. Three-month-olds showed no significant effects of the cue in both the ISI and no ISI conditions, providing preliminary evidence that the mechanisms underlying the facilitation and inhibition following exogenous cueing develop between 3 and 6 months of age.

Hood (1993) reports an experiment similar to that of Hood and Atkinson (1991), but with an improved method allowing, among other things, more accurate assessment of RTs to make a saccade toward the target. In this experiment a group of 6-month-olds was exposed to a longer duration cue (180 ms) before immediately being presented with a single target on either the ipsilateral or the contralateral side. Infants did not make a saccade toward the cue since the attractive fixation stimulus was still being presented. This procedure resulted in a clear difference in mean RT to orient toward the target depending on whether it appeared in the same spatial location as the cue.[3]

The observations to date indicate that inhibition of return has developed by at least 6 months of age.[4] The issue of whether facilitatory effects are present by the same age remains unresolved, however, especially since inhibitory and facilitatory aspects of covert attention may have different neural substrates. Inhibition of return has been associated with midbrain oculomotor pathways (Posner et al. 1985; Rafal et al. 1989), while facilitatory effects have been attributed to cortical structures such as the parietal lobe (Posner et al. 1984).

The above review indicates that the state of our knowledge with regard to covert shifts of attention in infants is still somewhat patchy and provisional. For example, it is unclear whether facilitatory and inhibitory effects develop at the same age. Answering this question is of importance for understanding the extent to which they share a common neural substrate. Another factor is that while some studies have used RT as the dependent measure, others have used the direction of looking following bilateral target presentation. Further, the evidence for facilitatory effects is rather weak at present. Since all of the studies concerned with facilitatory effects so far have used unitary target presentations, an experiment involving bilateral target presentations might provide clearer evidence for this ability. In experiment 2, I report initial results from an exogenous cueing experiment on infants from 2 to 4 months of age.[5]

## Experiment 2

The procedure employed was a combination of those used in earlier studies. A single cue was presented for 100 ms on one of two side screens before bilateral targets were presented either 100 ms or 600 ms later. The 100 ms ISI should be short enough to produce facilitation, while the longer ISI should be long enough to produce inhibition. This procedure has the advantage that inhibition and facilitation can be studied in the same experiment, and two measures can be recorded: RT to make a saccade toward the target and direction of saccade.

**Subjects**  Subjects were fifteen 2-month-olds (mean, 64.5 days; range, 57 to 71 days) and fifteen 4-month-old infants (mean, 127.3 days; range, 115 to 149 days), all with no known birth or other complications. The data from another three infants were discarded due to excessive fussing or drowsiness. Judging by the frequency of spontaneous smiles, infants appeared to enjoy the procedure.

**Procedure**  The babies sat in a baby chair 55 cm from the center of three color monitors. Displays on these monitors were controlled by a Macintosh IIci microcomputer. Each trial began with the presentation of an attractor/fixation display on the central screen. The display was multicolored and dynamic, was accompanied by an auditory stimulus, and served to ensure that the infant was looking at the central screen at the start of each trial. The stimulus was composed of looming squares expanding and contracting to a regular bleeping sound and subtended 5 degrees of visual angle.

The experimenter could see the infant by means of a video camera mounted above the display screens. When the infant was judged to be looking at the attractor pattern, the experimenter pressed a key. The first thirty-two trials of the experiment consisted of short ISI and long ISI trials presented according to a pseudorandom schedule balanced within each block of four trials. Following this, if the infant was still in an attentive state, twenty-four baseline trials were run.

*Short ISI trials*: In these trials, when the experimenter was sure that the infant was looking toward the fixation stimulus he or she would press a key that initiated presentation of the cue stimulus on one of the two side screens (29 degrees to the right or left of the fixation stimulus). Whether the cue stimulus appeared to the right or to the left of the fixation stimulus was determined by a pseudorandom schedule. The cue stimulus was identical on both sides: a green diamond (3 degrees in width) that was presented for 100 ms. Following the offset of both the central stimulus and the cue, there was a 100-ms ISI before bilateral presentation of the target stimulus, both in the same location as that in which the cue had appeared and on the opposite side (fig. 11.4). The stimulus onset asynchrony[6] (SOA) was thus 200 ms. The target stimulus was composed of a dynamic, multicolored, rotating cogwheel shape. When the infant shifted gaze toward one or another of the targets, the trial was terminated and the next one begun by presentation of the central attractor stimulus.

*Long ISI trials*: These trials were identical to those previously described except that the ISI between the cue and the target was of a length likely to produce inhibition, 600 ms (an SOA of 700 ms).

*Baseline trials*: After infants had completed thirty-two trials as described above, most of the subjects were presented with twenty-four baseline trials in which no cue stimulus was presented. That is, after the offset of the fixation stimulus, bilateral targets appeared after an ISI of 600 ms.

Videotapes of infants' eye movements during the experiment were subsequently coded by persons, some of whom were not directly involved in the

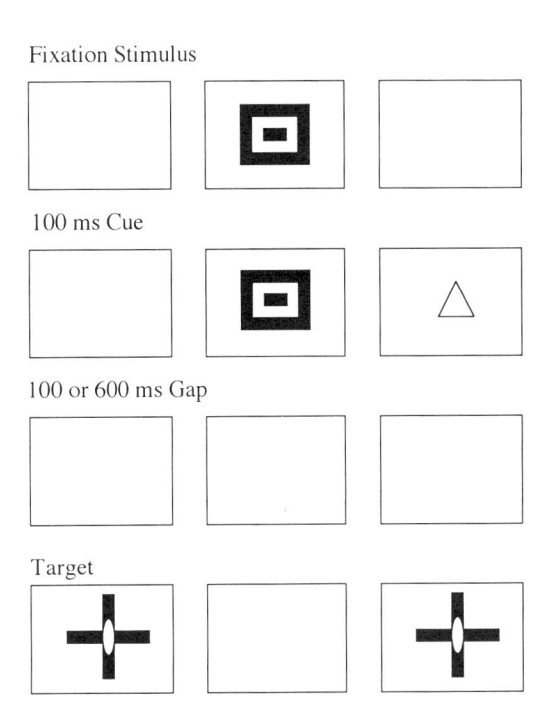

**Figure 11.4** The order of presentation of stimuli in experiment 2.

testing. Those trials in which the infant shifted gaze directly[7] from the fixation stimulus to one or another of the targets were analyzed with both the direction of the saccade (toward the cued or opposite side) and the RT to make a saccade being recorded. For most infants, at least twenty-four of the thirty-two experimental trials (75 percent) were scorable in this way. Trials were most commonly rejected because the infant was not looking at the fixation stimulus at the start of the trial, or because they looked up (to the camera) or down (to their feet) during the ISI. In the baseline trials, the median RT to make a saccade toward the target from the first six scorable trials was calculated. Reliability between coders was excellent (mean correlation of 0.92 between coders for RT and 1.0 for direction of looking).

**Results** Figure 11.5 illustrates the mean direction of orienting following presentation of the cue for the two age groups. A two-way ANOVA of mixed design (one between subjects factor—Age, and one within subjects factor—ISI length) was performed on the direction of orienting measures for the two age groups. There was a significant main effect of trial type (short or long ISI) on orienting ($F(1,27) = 12.76, p = 0.0014$), and a borderline significant interaction between age group and trial type ($F(1,27) = 4.00, p = 0.056$). This interaction indicated a different pattern of responding in the two age groups. Planned comparisons (paired t-tests) revealed no significant difference between the percentage of saccades toward the cued side between the short and long ISIs for the 2-month-old group ($t = 1.23, df = 14$, n.s.) In contrast, the 4-month-old group showed a significantly greater tendency to orient to the

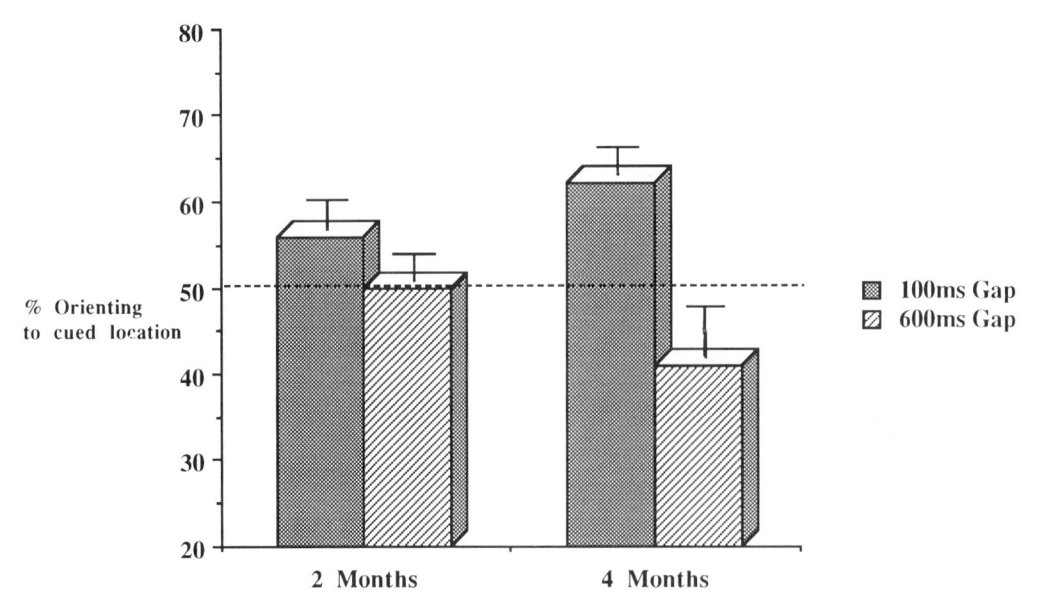

**Figure 11.5** The direction of orienting toward target bilateral target stimuli at short and long ISIs for the two age groups.

cued side in trials with the short ISI than they did in trials with the long ISI ($t = 3.77, df = 13, p = 0.0023$). This effect was due to both increased orienting to the cued side in short ISI trials and decreased orienting to this side in the long ISI trials.

Figure 11.6 and table 11.2 show the RT data. A two-way ANOVA of mixed design was performed on the median reaction times to the four types of trials (cued and opposite sides at short and long ISIs, within subjects factor) for the two age groups (between subjects factor). There was a significant effect of Age (2 or 4 months) on RT ($F(1,26) = 8.64, p = 0.0068$). Not surprisingly, 4-month-olds showed faster RTs. Although there was no significant overall effect of trial type ($F(3,78) = 1.19$, n.s.), there was a highly significant interaction between age and trial type ($F(3,78) = 5.30, p = 0.022$). This interaction indicated a different pattern of responding in the two age groups. Planned comparisons (paired t-tests) between cued and opposite trials for each SOA and age group revealed only one significant difference: that which exists between cued and opposite conditions with the short ISI in 4-month-olds ($t = 2.90, df = 13, p = 0.0125$). The mean of median RT for the baseline trials are shown in table 11.2. The fact that the 2-month-olds readily oriented toward the target in the baseline condition is evidence that they had no difficulty in seeing the stimuli.

**Discussion** On the basis of the adult literature, we would expect that in short ISI trials subjects should respond more rapidly to stimuli appearing in the cued (valid) location (facilitation). If infants show this effect, then they should also orient more frequently to the cued side in the presence of bilateral targets.

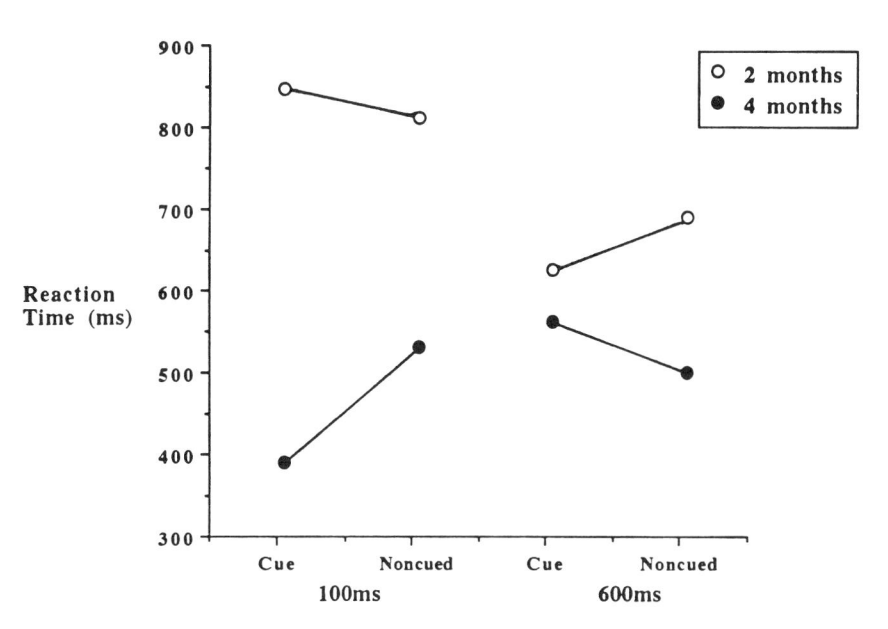

**Figure 11.6** The mean reaction time to orient toward the cued and uncued sides at the two ISIs lengths and ages.

**Table 11.2** Mean of Median RT to Respond to the Target Stimulus for the Various Trial Types (in ms)

| Age group | Baseline RT | 100 Cued | 100 Opposite | 600 Cued | 600 Opposite |
|---|---|---|---|---|---|
| 2 months old | 760 | 840 | 803 | 617 | 683 |
| 4 months old | 447 | 400 | 523 | 553 | 490 |

In contrast, in the long ISI trials subjects may orient preferentially to the opposite (invalid) location (inhibition). From figure 11.5 it can be seen that there was no significant difference in the extent of orienting to the cued target between the long and the short ISI trials for the 2-month-old infants. The 4-month-olds, however, showed a significant difference in the extent to which they directed their orienting toward the cued target: at the short ISI they oriented more toward the cued target, while at the long ISI they oriented more toward the opposite target. Clearly, the difference between the 2- and 4-month-old groups is one of degree, suggesting that at least some 2-month-olds showed a tendency in the same direction as the older infants.

The RT data also show no significant effects in the 2-month-old infants (see fig. 11.6). At neither the short nor the long ISI trials was there a significant difference in their RT to orient toward the cued and opposite target. In contrast, 4-month-olds showed a clear facilitatory effect in the short ISI trials; their RT to orient toward the cued target was significantly shorter than their RT to orient toward the opposite target. Further, and consistent with inhibition of return, in the long ISI trials they were slower to make a saccade to the cued location. The RT evidence is therefore consistent with both facilitation and inhibition to a cued location being present in the human infant by 4-months of age. There are, however, a number of reasons that we cannot yet conclude with any certainty that covert shifts of attention develop between 2 and 4 months of age.

The first of these reasons is that the pattern of "baseline" RT data obtained in this experiment is difficult to interpret. In order to provide strong evidence for facilitatory effects, baseline RT should ideally be significantly slower than cued trials at the short ISI. Similarly, for inhibition, the baseline RT should be significantly faster than the cued trial RT. In the 4-month-old group, the baseline RT was between the cued and uncued RTs for the short ISI, but faster than both of the means at the long ISI. Establishing the most appropriate baseline RT measure in infancy experiments such as this one has proved difficult, with baseline RTs commonly lying outside the range of experimental RTs (Hood and Atkinson 1991). It should also be noted that similar difficulties have been noted in experiments of this kind with adult subjects. Possibly future experiments of this type should involve "double-cue" baseline RT data, rather than the "no-cue" baseline used here.

A second note of caution with regard to the interpretation of the results obtained in this experiment concerns the possibility that the facilitatory effect obtained at the short ISI in the 4-month-old group may be partly attributable to saccades in response to the cue. While studies from other laboratories (e.g. Hood and Atkinson 1991) and pilot studies in our own laboratory had indicated that 4-, and 6-month-olds do not make saccades in response to a 100-ms cue stimulus in the presence of a central fixation stimulus, a post hoc analysis of the data from the present experiment revealed that some 4-month-olds do indeed show evidence of saccades in response to the cue in the 600-ms ISI trials. Specifically in, on average, 26.5 percent of 600-ms ISI trials, 4-month-old infants made an anticipatory saccade (prior to target appearance) toward the cued location. The question arises whether these saccades could have contributed to the facilitatory effect found in the short ISI trials. That is, the infants are faster to respond to the cued target simply because they began their saccade in response to the earlier presented cue. In order to investigate this issue, we defined "cue-triggered" saccades as being those occurring to the cued location during the ISI and within 200-ms of target onset in the 600-ms ISI trials.[8] Note that since any long ISI trial condition with infants leads to a number of trial losses due to looks away from the central fixation point, our criterion for "cue-triggered" saccades is likely to overestimate their frequency by including a few spontaneous looks away from the central screen that happen to be directed to the cued location. Thus, several infants in our sample showed one or more saccades toward the opposite side during the 600-ms ISI.

The first reason it is believed that cue-triggered saccades do not contribute substantially to the facilitatory effect observed is that they tend to be of very long latency. While the mean RTs to make a saccade in the 4-month-old group in this experiment varied between 400 and 550 ms, the mean for cue-driven saccades was 650 ms (standard error 33 ms). One possibility is that this long RT is a reflection of the fact that the cue stimulus only just exceeds the threshold for eliciting a saccade in these cases. If we subtract the SOA (100-ms cue plus 100-ms ISI), then these cue-triggered saccades would have a mean RT from target onset of 450 ms in the short ISI trials. This mean RT lies between the mean RTs to the cued (400 ms) and uncued (523 ms) targets. Thus, it is apparent that while cue-triggered saccades could contribute to the facilitatory effect, they cannot account for it entirely.

A second approach to assessing the contribution of cue-triggered saccades to the facilitatory effect observed is to take advantage of the fact that some infants in our sample of 4-month-olds showed very few or no such saccades. The results from the 6-infants who showed one or less cue-driven saccade under 700 ms (500 ms after target onset in the short ISI trials) are presented in table 11.3. While these infants showed very few cue-driven saccades (and even these were of such long latency that they would only weaken any facilitation effect), their mean RTs to the cued and opposite targets are virtually identical to those of the whole sample. Further, they show an even stronger preference to orient to the cued side. This post hoc analysis indicates that while the cue does occasionally drive saccades in the long ISI trials, these saccades are not a major contributor to the facilitatory effects observed in the short ISI trials.

The above observations about the relation between cue-driven saccades in the long ISI trials and the facilitation effect at the short ISI trials may be accounted for in the following way. Covert shifts of attention occur in response to the cue. When the target stimuli are presented in the short ISI trials, the earlier covert shift results in facilitation of saccades to that location. In the long ISI trials, however, not only is the ISI longer but so is the time between the central fixation stimulus going off (at the same time as the cue) and the target onset. In some of these long ISI trials, infants spontaneously looked away from the central location prior to target onset, presumably due to the absence of the central fixation stimulus. If covert attention is still directed to the cued location, however, they will tend to look more frequently to that location. By this view then, the cue-driven saccades are not directly driven by the cue but rather are spontaneous saccades that follow the earlier covert shift of attention.

Turning to the inhibitory effects observed in this experiment, it appears that the age when inhibition of return (IOR) can first be demonstrated may be

**Table 11.3** Facilitation Effect in the Short ISI Trials of Infants with Few Cue-Driven Saccades

| Mean RT to | Cued Target | Opposite Target | % Preference for Cued Side |
|---|---|---|---|
| Whole sample ($N = 15$) | 400 ms (S.E. 30) | 523 ms (S.E. 40) | 64.7 (S.E. 4.0)[a] |
| Criterion sample ($N = 6$) | 400 ms (S.E. 43) | 537 ms (S.E. 77) | 68.0 (S.E. 4.1)[a] |

a. Significance at $p = 0.01$ or greater.

dependent on the size of the visual angle between the central fixation point and the cue/target. There is reason to believe that this may be the case since Rafal et al. (1989) showed that IOR is dependent upon the (adult) subjects planning a saccade and infants under 4 months of age commonly show hypometric saccades toward a target (Aslin 1981). Thus, if young infants are not accurately planning a saccade, they may not show IOR.

Harman, Posner, and Rothbart (1992) reasoned that if infants have to make several saccades to a target at 30 degrees' eccentricity, then they will not show IOR at the target destination. This should not be the case for a target at only 10 degrees' eccentricity since this shift of gaze can easily be achieved by one saccade in the very young infant. In accordance with their prediction, Harman, Posner, and Rothbart (1992) found evidence of IOR in 3-month-old infants at 10 degrees but not at 30 degrees. While it is possible that IOR could be found at still younger ages (Valenza et al. 1992), Harman and colleagues argue that its developmental onset is probably linked to the maturation of cortical structures involved in the development of programmed eye movements, namely, the frontal eye fields. Although a visual angle of 29 degrees was used in the present study, the evidence obtained was consistent with the idea that IOR develops at around the same age as facilitatory aspects of covert attention. This may be because both facilitation and inhibition are dependent upon maturation of the frontal eye fields. Later I will argue that the apparent discrepancy between the IOR results reported in this chapter, and the work of Harman, Posner, and Rothbart (1992) and Valenza et al. (1992) may also be accounted for by the fact that covert shifts of attention are used to elicit IOR in the present experiment, whereas infants were allowed to make a saccade to the cue in the other studies.

A final caveat to the conclusion that exogenously cued covert shifts of visual attention develop between 2 and 4 months of age concerns the possibility that the temporal dynamics of facilitation and inhibition vary during infancy. In the present experiment only two ISIs were investigated, 100 and 600 ms. If it had been possible to sample a several other ISI times, the group of 2-month-olds may have shown facilitatory effects between somewhere between 100 and 600 ms, and inhibitory effects at longer gaps. That is, the ISI lengths that produce facilitation of RTs and orienting may become shorter with increasing age. Such a result could reflect slower shifts of covert attention in younger infants. A longitudinal study with multiple ISI lengths is underway in order to resolve this issue.

**Endogenous Covert Orienting**

While most of the attention studies in infants have been concerned with exogenous (peripheral) cueing, Johnson, Posner, and Rothbart (1991) attempted to train infants to use a stimulus presented in a central location as a cue to predict the peripheral location (right or left of center) at which a target stimulus would subsequently appear. The sequences of stimulus presentation within trials are illustrated in figure 11.7. This experiment is analogous in some

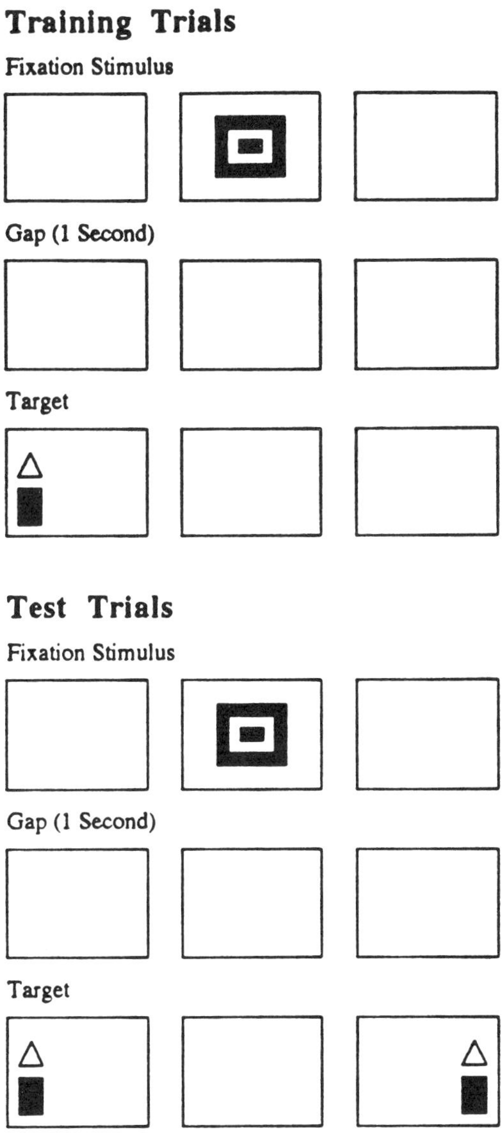

**Training Trials**

Fixation Stimulus

Gap (1 Second)

Target

**Test Trials**

Fixation Stimulus

Gap (1 Second)

Target

Figure 11.7  The order of stimulus presentation in the experiment of Johnson et al. (1991).

respects to studies in adults in which attention is cued to a peripheral location by means of a central (endogenous) cue such as an arrow. Groups of 2-, 3-, and 4-month-old infants were exposed to a number of training trials in which there was a contingent relation between which of two dynamic stimuli were presented on the central monitor, and the location (right or left of center) where an attractive target stimulus was subsequently presented. After a number of such training trials, we occasionally presented "test" trials in which the target subsequently appeared on both of the side monitors, regardless of which central stimulus preceded it. In these test trials we measured whether the infants looked more toward the cued location than toward the uncued location. While 2- and 3-month-old infants looked equally frequently to the cued and opposite sides, 4-month-olds looked significantly more often toward the cued location. This result, taken together with a similar finding in an earlier study (de Schonen and Bry 1987), is at least consistent with endogenously cued shifts of attention being present in 4-month-old infants.

## 11.4 THE VOLITIONAL CONTROL OF ORIENTING IN EARLY INFANCY

In the section on overt orienting, evidence was reviewed indicating that saccadic control in the infant goes from being mainly driven by exogenous factors to being primarily under endogenous control.[9] This transition from exogenous to endogenous was not observed in studies designed to measure covert orienting in infants. Rather, results obtained so far are consistent with both exogenous and endogenous cueing of covert attention becoming effective between 2 and 4 months of age. A plausible explanation of this apparent difference between overt and covert orienting is simply that the ability to shift attention covertly is the limiting critical factor in development. That is, under 4 months of age infants show exogenously cued overt orienting but not exogenously cued covert orienting simply because they are unable to shift their attention covertly.[10] Support for this view comes from IOR studies. IOR is associated with exogenously cued shifts of attention. It can also be obtained with infants in experiments in which the cue is presented long enough for infants to make a saccade toward it consistently (overt orienting) (Clohessy et al. 1991). Recent studies that involve overt orienting toward the cue have found evidence for IOR in infants under 4 months of age (Harman et al. 1992), and possibly even in newborns (Valenza et al. 1992). Thus, IOR may be elicited in infants under 4 months but only following overt orienting to a cue.

In the earlier section on overt orienting, I also argued that the onset of endogenous control of eye movements coincided with the development of the frontal eye fields (FEF). In the subsequent section on covert orienting, evidence was presented that infants have the ability to perform covert shifts of visual attention by around the same age, 4 months. What underlying neural events might give rise to this latter development? Both neuroanatomical (Conel 1939–1967) and neuroimaging evidence relating to the postnatal growth of the human cortex suggests that the posterior parietal lobe, a cortical region associated with shifts of covert attention (e.g., Posner et al. 1984), is undergoing rapid maturation around 3 to 4 months of age. For example, results of a positron emission tomography study led Chugani, Phelps, and Mazziotta (1987) to conclude that parietal regions undergo their most rapid period of development between 3 and 6 months of age in the human infant. Thus, while sufficient development of the FEF may be crucial for the endogenous control of eye movements, adequate development of the parietal lobe may be necessary for the ability to shift attention covertly.

Clearly, it would be simpleminded to believe that the functions of the FEF and the parietal cortex are completely independent of each other. Further, it would also be misleading to describe the onset of functioning in these structures are being an all-or-none phenomenon. It is much more likely that functioning develops in a more graded and coordinated manner. With these considerations in mind, it is interesting to note that there are a number of closed loop circuits that project down from the cortex to the basal ganglia before returning to one of the cortical regions from which they originated (for review, see Alexander, Delong, and Strick 1986). One of these pathways is commonly referred to as the oculomotor circuit, due to evidence from neurophysiological studies of its involvement in eye movements. It has been proposed that this circuit is crucial for voluntary saccades (Alexander, DeLong, and Strick 1986). The circuit receives projections from both the frontal eye fields and the parietal cortex (as well as from the dorsolateral prefrontal cortex). After passing through a number of subcortical structures such as the caudate and portions of the substantia nigra, it returns to the frontal eye fields. I suggest that the graded development of the cortical components of this circuit is the critical underlying neural event that gives rise to the transitions observed in both overt and covert orienting between 2 and 4 months of age.

What are the implications of these experiments on development for the debate in the adult literature regarding the role of covert shifts of attention in eye movements? The relation between covert shifts of visual attention and the control of eye movements is somewhat complex and controversial in the adult literature (e.g., Klein, Kingstone, and Pontefract 1992; Klein and Pontefract, chap. 13, this volume; Rizzolatti, Riggio, and Sheliga, chap. 9, this volume). While covert shifts of attention and overt orienting (saccades) may be dissociated under some circumstances, several authors have proposed that covert shifts of attention are necessary for, or equivalent to, the planning or execution of saccades (e.g., Rizzolatti et al. 1987). Klein (1980) and Klein and Pontefract (chap. 13, this volume) have presented evidence from endogenous cueing studies in adults against a particular type of relation between overt and covert orienting known as the oculomotor readiness hypothesis: planning an eye movement to a spatial location does not necessitate a shift of covert attention to the same spot. Despite this observation, in many situations covert shifts of attention appear to precede eye movements (Henderson, Pollatsek, and Rayner 1989; Shephard, Findlay, and Hockey 1986; Posner 1980), suggesting that these covert shifts contribute to saccade planning. Following this latter view, we would expect that the ability to shift attention covertly may be a necessary prerequisite for the volitional control of saccades. In development therefore, the endogenous control of saccades should follow, or develop simultaneously with, the ability to shift visual attention covertly. In contrast, note that if we found that the endogenous control of saccades developed significantly before the ability to shift attention covertly, this would support the view that overt and covert orienting are entirely independent. The experiments reported in this chapter indicate that covert shifts of attention (at least as measured by facilitatory effects) and the volitional control of saccades develop around the same age, 4 months, consistent with their being some dependence relation between the two processes.

In conclusion, studying how various components of the visual attention system develop provides a useful supplement to information gained from both normal and brain-damaged adult subjects. In particular, predictions about the sequence of development of components of overt orienting have been put forward on the basis of evidence from developmental neuroanatomy, and some of these predictions have been confirmed. Further, while the investigation of covert shifts of attention in early infancy is at an early stage, the results obtained so far indicate that these processes are present in infants as young as 4 months of age.

## NOTES

I wish to thank Annette Karmiloff-Smith, Raymond Klein, Jean Mandler, Morris Moscovitch, and Francesca Simion for constructive comments on an earlier version of this chapter. Thanks are also due to Mike Posner and Mary Rothbart for nurturing and guiding my initial forays into visual attention during my extended visits to Eugene in fall 1989 and 1990. The experiments reported in this chapter would not have been possible without the capable assistance of Leslie Tucker and Kathy Sutton. Leslie was not only instrumental in running the experiments but also in setting up my laboratory at Carnegie Mellon. I acknowledge financial assistance from Carnegie Mellon University, the CMU faculty development fund, and the National Science Foundation (grant DBS-9120433).

1. The data from infants who fussed, or who failed to look toward the cue for 50 percent or more of the first block of trial, were discarded.

2. Of course, this does not mean that covert shifts of attention are not involved in tasks in which the infant makes a saccade toward the cue, merely that we have no way of establishing that this is the case.

3. However, it is difficult to say whether this effect is due to facilitation or inhibition, or both, for the following reason. Hood demonstrated that in the absence of the central fixation stimulus, the 6-month-olds readily oriented toward cue stimulus. Since the cue had similar visual characteristics to the target stimulus and there was no temporal gap between their presentations, this is functionally the same as keeping the cue stimulus on while removing the central fixation point. In other words, we would expect no difference between the "baseline" RT to orient toward the target in the absence of the cue and the ipsilateral cue trials: the result that was indeed observed (Hood 1993). In short, the lack of a transition between cue and target means that there is little scope for demonstrating facilitatory effects.

4. Recent evidence obtained by Harman, Posner, and Rothbart (1992) and Valenza et al. (1992) that shows evidence of inhibition of return in younger infants will be discussed later.

5. Data from 6-month-olds using the same procedure are currently being collected.

6. The stimulus onset asynchrony refers to the time between the onset of the cue stimulus and the onset of the target.

7. We defined direct saccades as those in which the eyes moved straight from the stimulus to one or other of the targets. Sometimes the younger infants stopped momentarily while on the way to the target. These trials were included as long as the infant reached the target without saccading elsewhere beforehand.

8. Saccades occuring within 200 ms of target onset in infants are commonly classified as "anticipatory" (Haith, Hazan, and Goodman 1988; Johnson, Posner, and Rothbart 1991).

9. Of course, even in the adult, there remain many situations where exogenous saccades can be elicited.

10. This statement is subject to the caveats about the evidence for covert orienting mentioned earlier.

## REFERENCES

Alexander, G. E., DeLong, M. R., and Strick, P. L. (1986). Parallel organization of functionally segregated circuits linking basal ganglia and cortex. *Annual Review of Neuroscience, 9,* 357–382.

Aslin, R. N. (1981). Development of smooth pursuit in human infants. In D. F. Fisher, R. A. Monty, J. W. Senders (Eds.), *Eye movements: Cognition and visual perception,* 31–51. Hillsdale, NJ: Erlbaum.

Atkinson, J. (1984). Human visual development over the first six months of life: A review and a hypothesis. *Human Neurobiology, 3,* 61–74.

Bronson, G. W. (1974). The postnatal growth of visual capacity. *Child Development, 45,* 873–890.

Bronson, G. W. (1982). Structure, status and characteristics of the nervous system at birth. In P. Stratton (Ed.), *Psychobiology of the human newborn.* Chichester: Wiley.

Chugani, H. T., Phelps, M. E., and Mazziotta, J. C. (1987). Positron emission tomography study of human brain functional development. *Annals of Neurology, 22,* 487–497.

Clohessy, A. B., Posner, M. I., Rothbart, M. K., and Vecera, S. (1991). The development of inhibition of return in early infancy. *Journal of Cognitive Neuroscience, 3,* 346–357.

Conel, J. L. (1939–1967). *The postnatal development of the human cerebral cortex.* Vols. 1–8. Cambridge, MA: Harvard University Press.

de Schonen, S., and Bry, I. (1987). Interhemispheric communication of visual learning: A developmental study in 3–6 month old infants. *Neuropsychologia, 25,* 73–83.

de Yoe, E. A., and Van Essen, D. C. (1988). Concurrent processing streams in monkey visual cortex. *TINS, 11,* 219–226.

Guitton, H. A., Buchtel, H. A., and Douglas, R. M. (1985). Frontal lobe lesions in man cause difficulties in suppressing reflexive glances and in generating goal-directed saccades. *Experimental Brain Research, 58,* 455–472.

Haith, M. M., Hazan, C., and Goodman, G. S. (1988). Expectation and anticipation of dynamic visual events by 3.5-month-old babies. *Child Development, 59,* 467–479.

Hallett, P. E. (1978). Primary and secondary saccades to goals defined by instructions. *Vision Research, 18,* 1279–1296.

Harman, C., Posner, M. I., and Rothbart, M. K. (1992). Spatial attention in 3-month-olds: Inhibition of return at 10° and 30° target eccentricities. *Infant Behavior and Development, 15* (Special ICIS issue), 449.

Henderson, J. M., Pollatsek, A., and Rayner, K. (1989). Covert visual attention and extrafoveal information use during object identification. *Perception and Psychphysics, 45,* 196–208.

Hood, B. (1993). Inhibition of return produced by covert shifts of visual attention in 6-month-old infants. *Infant Behavior and Development, 16,* 245–254.

Hood, B., and Atkinson, J. (1991). Shifting covert attention in infants. Paper presented at SRCD, Seattle.

Johnson, M. H. (1990). Cortical maturation and the development of visual attention in early infancy. *Journal of Cognitive Neuroscience, 2*, 81–95.

Johnson, M. H. (1994). Dissociating components of visual attention: A neurodevelopmental approach. In M. J. Farah and G. Radcliffe (Eds.), *The neural basis of high-level vision*. Hillsdale, NJ: Erlbaum.

Johnson, M. H., Posner, M. I., and Rothbart, M. K. (1991). Components of visual orienting in early infancy: Contingency learning, anticipatory looking, and disengaging. *Journal of Cognitive Neuroscience, 3*, 335–344.

Klein, R. M. (1980). Does oculomotor readiness mediate cognitive control of visual attention? In R. Nickerson (Ed.), *Attention and performance VIII*. Hillsdale, NJ: Erlbaum.

Klein, R. M., Kingstone, A., and Pontefract, A. (1992). Orienting of visual attention. In K. Rayner (Ed.), *Eye movements and visual cognition: Scene perception and reading*.

Maylor, E. A. (1985) Facilitatory and inhibitory components of orienting in visual space. In M. I. Posner and O. M. Marin (Eds.), *Attention and performance XI*. Hillsdale, NJ: Erlbaum.

Posner, M. I., (1980). Orienting of attention. *Quarterly Journal of Experimental Psychology, 32*, 3–25.

Posner, M. I., and Cohen, Y. (1980). Attention and the control of movements. In G. E. Stelmach, and J. Requin (Eds.), *Tutorials in motor behavior*, 243–258. Amsterdam: North-Holland.

Posner, M. I., and Cohen, Y. (1984). Components of visual orienting. In H. Bouma and D. Bouwhuis (Eds.), *Attention and performance X*, 531–556. Hillsdale, NJ: Lawrence Erlbaum.

Posner, M. I., and Peterson, S. E. (1990). The attention system of the human brain. *Annual Review of Neuroscience, 13*, 25–42.

Posner, M. I., Rafal, R. D., Choate, L. S., and Vaughan, J. (1985). Inhibition of return: Neural basis and function. *Cognitive Neuropsychology, 2*, 211–228.

Posner, M. I., Walker, J. A., Freidrich, F. J., and Rafal, R. D. (1984). Effects of parietal lobe injury on covert orienting of visual attention. *Journal of Neuroscience, 4*, 1863–1874.

Rafal, R. D., Calabresi, P. A., Brennan, C. W., and Sciolto, T. K. (1989). Saccade preparation inhibits reorienting to recently attended locations. *Journal of Experimental Psychology: Human Perception and Performance, 15*, 673–685.

Rizzolatti, G., Riggio, L., Dascolo, I., and Umiltà, C. (1987). Reorienting attention across the horizontal and vertical meridians: Evidence in favor of a premotor theory of attention. *Neuropsychologia, 25*, 31–40.

Schiller, P. H. (1985). A model for the generation of visually guided saccadic eye movements. In D. Rose and V. G. Dobson (Eds.), *Models of the visual cortex*, 62–70. Chicester: Wiley.

Shephard, M., Findlay, J. M. and Hockey, R. J. (1986). The relationship between eye movements and spatial attention. *Quarterly Journal of Experimental Psychology, 38A*, 475–491.

Valenza, E., Simion, F., Umilta, C., and Paiusco, E. (1992). *Inhibition of return in newborn infants*. Unpublished manuscript, University of Padua.

Van Essen, D. C. (1985) Functional organisation of primate visual cortex. In A. Peters and E. G. Jones (Eds.), *Cerebral cortex*, vol. 3. New York: Plenum.

# 12 Spatial Synergies between Auditory and Visual Attention

## Jon Driver and Charles J. Spence

ABSTRACT  Three experiments examined spatial links between endogenous attention in vision and audition. In experiment 1 subjects were presented auditorily with two verbal messages, one from either side of their midline. They had to repeat one message, for which they were also given lip-read information in some conditions. The lip-read information produced a larger improvement in performance when presented on the same side as the target sounds rather than the opposite side, suggesting a difficulty in attending to different locations in the two modalities. This difficulty cannot be attributed to the direction of gaze, since passively fixating meaningless lip movements on the same versus opposite side as the target sounds had no effect. A similar (albeit reduced) difficulty in attending to different locations in the two modalities was observed in experiment 2, where the auditory and visual tasks were unrelated. The auditory task was shadowing as before, while the visual task was monitoring for a specified target in a stream of visual characters appearing successively at a single location. A decrement in shadowing was observed when the monitored visual events were in a different location than that of the target sounds. Again, the direction of passive fixation had no effect. A final experiment found that the cost of attending to different locations in the two modalities can be observed in the conventional dual-task situation—namely, with no distractor stimuli. These results demonstrate synergetic links between endogenous spatial attention in vision and audition.

## 12.1 INTRODUCTION

A substantial research effort has gone into examining the mechanisms of selective attention in audition and vision. The classic work of the 1950s concentrated on auditory attention, using the selective shadowing paradigm (Cherry 1953; Broadbent 1958). Many such studies found that subjects could select one of two verbal messages for report quite readily, provided that there was a physical distinction between them, with differences in location leading to particularly efficient selection. In subsequent years, research has shifted toward investigations of the mechanisms of visual attention (Kahneman and Treisman 1984; Neumann, van der Heijden, and Allport 1986), and many authors have proposed that space has special status in the control of visual attention, as well as for auditory attention (Posner 1980; Treisman and Gelade 1980; Tsal and Lavie 1988).

Previous research has tended to focus on selection within a single modality at a time. However, in the real world, we are typically faced with multimodal stimulation and thus require selective mechanisms to operate simultaneously in several modalities. To take the textbook example of selective attention (listening to one conversation at a noisy cocktail party), the relevant information can be selected both auditorily and visually, by lip-read information. Indeed, shadowing performance is improved when the actors speaking the relevant and irrelevant messages can be seen by the subject (Reisberg 1978). Assuming that the purpose of selective attention is primarily to select relevant objects from cluttered and noisy scenes for the selective control of action (Allport 1987; Driver and Baylis 1989; Duncan 1984; Tipper, Driver, and Weaver 1991), these cross-modal considerations lead to an immediate computational problem. Selection has to be coordinated across the modalities, so that attention is directed to sights and sounds emanating from the same distal object. However, this is potentially problematic, given the existence of modality-specific sensory systems that do not have corresponding spatiotopic organizations at input. For instance, there is no auditory equivalent to the inherent retinotopic organization in vision and therefore no direct spatial correspondence at input between sights and sounds coming from the same object.

Two fundamental questions arise: to what extent can attentional mechanisms operate independently in distinct unimodal systems, and how is attention coordinated across modalities despite their different input organizations? We approach these questions by examining whether there are spatial links between auditory and visual attention, such that it is relatively difficult to attend to one location visually while attending to another auditorily.

Existing research on cross-modal links in attention has primarily examined overt orienting responses, involving shifts in the direction of peripheral receptors. The primate visual system tends to foveate rapidly the spatial location of unexpected or salient auditory events (Thompson and Masterton 1978; Whittington, Hepp-Reymond, and Flood 1981), suggesting that overt orienting mechanisms have strong audiovisual links. Does this also apply for covert orienting—that is, shifts in attention without corresponding shifts in peripheral receptors? Covert orienting has been widely studied in the now-familiar cueing paradigm (Posner 1980). Although most of this work has examined vision, the distinction between overt and covert orienting applies to audition as well (Spence and Driver 1994) since auditory attention can be shifted with or without corresponding shifts of the head or pinna. In the case of vision, it is well established that visual detection can be facilitated if the location of a target is precued even if no eye movement is made toward the cued location (Muller and Humphreys 1991). This benefit is attributed to covert orienting and can be found following cues such as uninformative peripheral flashes at the target location that do not predict the likely target locus or following informative cues such as an arrow at fixation pointing in the direction of the likely target locus (Posner 1980). Uninformative peripheral cues are thought to engage different covert orienting systems to informative symbolic cues. The former produce exogenous orienting (bottom-up control of attention by salient peripheral events), whereas informative cues produce endogeneous orienting (strategic, voluntary shifts as a result of the subject's expectancies). Several qualitative differences between these forms of covert orienting have now been demonstrated (Jonides 1981; Muller and Rabbitt 1989; Rafal, Henik, and Smith 1992), suggesting the involvement of distinct mechanisms.

Such findings imply that the nature of cross-modal links in covert orienting should be examined separately for exogeneous and endogenous mechanisms. Previous work using the cueing paradigm has demonstrated clear cross-modal links in the exogenous case. Cueing effects are found when uninformative peripheral auditory events are presented prior to visual targets (Klein 1987; Farah, Wong, Monheit, and Morrow 1989), suggesting either that exogenous orienting systems are polymodal or that when auditory attention is exogenously drawn to a location, a visual orienting system also shifts toward that locus.

Current evidence is less clear on the nature of cross-modal links in endogenous orienting. Cross-modal cueing effects for targets in one modality following informative peripheral cues in another modality have been demonstrated (Buchtel and Butter 1988, between auditory and visual stimuli; Butter, Buchtel, and Santucci 1989, between tactile and visual stimuli), but these findings are difficult to interpret. Since the cues were informative, endogenous orienting mechanisms should have been involved. However, the critical issue is whether endogenous orienting in one modality has effects on another modality, and unfortunately cross-modal effects from informative cues do not establish that this is the case. They simply show that a signal in one modality (e.g., a tone) can instruct subjects about the likely locus of a target in another modality (e.g., a flash), in a manner analogous to the interpretation of a central visual arrow prior to a visual target. After such an interpretation, the endogenous orienting may take place entirely within the target modality (vision in the example with an informative tone as the cue). For this reason, the cueing paradigm is unsatisfactory for examining cross-modal links in endogenous attention, when the direction of attention is strategic rather than the automatic outcome of salient peripheral events.

Accordingly, we devised a novel technique for examining cross-modal links in endogenous attention. In essence, we presented subjects with visual events on either side of their midline and also with auditory events on either side of their midline. We required them to attend to one side while ignoring the other side in each modality. The attended side could be the same or different for the two modalities. If there are cross-modal links in the endogenous direction of attention, it may be difficult to attend to different sides in the two modalities. The specified target and distractor sides were quite arbitrary; the target stimuli were no more salient in bottom-up terms than the distractor stimuli. This ensured that endogenous, strategic mechanisms of selection were required to fulfill the task requirements rather than exogenous, stimulus-driven mechanisms.

## 12.2 EXPERIMENT 1

Our subjects heard two verbal messages simultaneously: one presented from a loudspeaker to their left and the other to their right. One message had to be shadowed, the other ignored. The side of the target message was arbitrarily specified by the experimenter, so that endogenous selection mechanisms were involved. Each message was composed of a series of triplets of unrelated words spoken in rapid succession. Both messages were spoken by the same person. The task was to repeat each triplet from the target auditory location in the interval between successive triplets. Subjects were also presented with visual information. In the active visual tasks, this comprised synchronous lip-read information for the target verbal message, which had to be fixated. In the passive visual tasks, meaningless lip movements (chewing) were presented for fixation. The main manipulation was whether the visual information was presented on the same side as the target sounds or on the side of the distractor sounds. If there is a difficulty in attending to different locations in vision and audition simultaneously, shadowing performance should be worse when the lip-read information was presented on the opposite side to the target sounds. If any such difficulty simply reflects the direction of fixation, it should also be found when subjects fixated meaningless lip movements on the opposite side to the target sounds.

### Subjects

The subjects were sixteen unpaid volunteers; thirteen were undergraduates, and three were research staff in the psychology department. All were naive as to the purpose of the experiment. The mean age was 22 years, and the range 19 to 35 years. All reported normal hearing and normal or corrected vision. Each participated for around 75 min.

### Apparatus and Materials

Two monitors were placed 170 cm apart (center-to-center), symmetrically to the right or left in front of the subject. Each was 155 cm from the subject, who was seated at a table. Thus, the angle between the monitors was 57 degrees. One monitor was a Sony PVM201OQM, the other a Panasonic BTD2000PSN. Immediately below each monitor was a KEF SP1146 loudspeaker, and at the midpoint between these two loudspeakers (directly in front of the subject) was a third loudspeaker, which produced continuous white noise. There were four videoplayers.

The first six subjects used a chin rest and were verbally reminded several times during the experiment not to turn their heads toward either monitor or loudspeaker. Although they appeared to comply with this request, the remaining subjects used a chin rest that also clamped their temples, precluding any headmovements. Omitting the initial six subjects does not affect the pattern of results. Subjects' eyes were level with the loudspeaker cones. The direction of fixation was monitored by the experimenter in the first fourteen subjects; for the final two subjects, eye movements were also recorded by video cameras, one above each monitor.

The materials were video recordings of the second author reading two-syllable words presented to him off-camera. A full frontal view of his head was shown continuously. During the recording, he attempted to pronounce the words at a regular rate by means of computerized clicks played to him over headphones. The 774 different words were all two-syllable nouns, with stress on the initial syllable. Two tapes of the second author reading 387 words were recorded, with no repetitions within or between tapes. On each tape, the words were grouped into lists, which themselves consisted of several triplets of words. The triplets were read aloud at the rate of approximately 1.3 sec per triplet. There were eight experimental lists on each tape, each consisting of fourteen triplets, with 4-sec intervals between successive triplets. The interval between each list was 60 sec, with a longer interval of 240 sec after four experimental lists. Each video began with two practice lists—the first containing nine triplets and the second eight triplets.

These two tapes were played back simultaneously to provide concurrent pairs of different audiovisual words. Each tape had a visual frame counter at the top left. Synchrony of the tapes was achieved by starting the tapes simultaneously with an editor at predetermined frames that were judged to maximize phenomenal simultaneity when used as starting positions. Thus, while the synchrony of concurrent word pairs was approximate and fluctuated with the second author's skill in maintaining a regular reading rate during the video recording, it was the same for each subject. Concurrent pairs of words were matched as far as possible on Brown (1984) spoken frequency and on number of letters. In addition there were two different 25-min video recordings, both showing a full frontal view of the second author vigorously chewing gum without opening his mouth. These tapes had no soundtrack. Their use may seem somewhat bizarre, but they were intended to provide transient visual information within the same face as for the word tapes but without yielding any phonological information via lipreading.

Each of the four videotapes remained in one videoplayer throughout the experiment. The four players were connected to the two monitors such that the four tapes could be run continuously and simultaneously, with switches determining which of the four visual channels appeared on any monitor. Each of the two spoken soundtracks went separately to a different lateralized loudspeaker and was presented from this loudspeaker throughout the session. The spoken words were presented through either lateralized loudspeaker at approximately 60 dB(A) on average, with a peak of around 64 dB, as measured from the subject's position. White noise was presented at about 56 dB centrally. The same level was used for all subjects. It was intended to bring performance in naming the target words below ceiling, so that any benefit from the additional presence of relevant lip-read information was likely to be observed. The talking and chewing heads subtended about 11.1 degrees of visual angle vertically and about 6.6 degrees horizontally on the monitors. The lips appeared about 8.1 degrees above the center of the loudspeaker positioned below the monitor.

## Design

There were three within-subject factors. The first was whether the auditory target words appeared on the left or right. The second was whether meaningful lip-read information was provided or not (Speaking-Lips versus Chewing-Lips). In the Speaking-Lips conditions, the visual channels from both tapes of the spoken words were shown on different monitors. In the Chewing-Lips conditions, the two tapes of chewing were presented visually. The third within-subjects factor was whether the visual information that subjects had to fixate was presented on the Same side as the auditory words they had to repeat or on the Opposite side. The Speaking/Chewing and Same/Opposite factors were crossed to yield the four conditions described below, which were then duplicated for auditory target words appearing on the left versus right:

Same Speaking-Lips; subjects had to name the words coming from one loudspeaker while fixating the monitor on the same side that showed lip-read information for the target words. The visual and auditory channels for the distractor words were both presented on the opposite side.

Opposite Speaking-Lips: Subjects had to name the words coming from one loudspeaker. However, the lip-read information for these words now appeared on the monitor at the opposite side, which subjects fixated. The audio channel for the distractor words came from this opposite side, while the visual channel for the distractor words came from the same side as the target sounds.

Same Chewing-Lips: Subjects had to name the words coming from one loudspeaker. Distractor words were presented from the other loudspeaker, and the two monitors showed different videos of chewing. Subjects had to fixate the chewing lips on the side of the target sounds.

Opposite Chewing-Lips: The same conditions prevailed as for Same Chewing-Lips, except that subjects had to fixate the chewing lips on the side of the distractor sounds.

If there is any difficulty in attending to different locations in vision and audition, shadowing performance should be worse in the Opposite conditions. This could arise either because of a difficulty in selecting information from different locations in distinct modalities or because of a difficulty in rejecting distractor information in one modality from a location that is relevant for another modality, (or as a result of both difficulties). Any effect due to the direction of fixation alone should be found equally for the Speaking-Lips and Chewing-Lips conditions, provided subjects adhere to fixation instructions.

The contrast between Speaking-Lips and Chewing-Lips conditions also provides a measure of any benefit provided by having visual lip-read information in addition to auditory information for the target words.

## Procedure

The experiment was conducted under dim illumination to preclude reflections on the monitors. The experimenter started the two chewing tapes and then initiated the two word tapes simultaneously from their predetermined starting frames. The four tapes ran continuously (except where stated) so that words were presented at the rates already noted. The subject had to name as many words as possible from each triplet on the specified channel in the interval between successive triplets. A session began with practice, comprising 102 pairs of concurrent words. The practice materials were the first seventeen triplets of words from each tape, run through twice. The first triplet was used for demonstration, and then each subject had blocked practice giving equal experience in the four conditions. The remaining eight lists of fourteen triplets were then run through twice to provide the experimental data. The condition was changed after every fourteen triplets. The order of conditions was different for each of the first eight subjects, with every condition appearing equally often in each serial position overall. Whether the target sounds were on the left or right alternated every fourteen triplets. Across subjects, each word was equally likely to appear as a target or distractor in each condition overall. On the second run through the experimental materials, each subject had to repeat the words that had previously been irrelevant for him or her.

The last eight subjects were run as for the first eight, except that all equipment on the left or right—monitors, loudspeakers, and videoplayers—was swapped. The videotapes stayed in the exchanged videoplayers so that their soundtracks changed side of presentation.

Between each list of fourteen triplets, the experimenter explained the task for the next list. For example, in the Opposite Speaking-Lips condition, he might explain that the subject had to name the words from the left loudspeaker but would see the lip movements for these words on the right monitor and had to fixate those lips.

The experimenter recorded subjects' responses, which were scored as correct, incorrect, or intrusions (reports of the distractor words) without regard to the order of report for words within each triplet. Close approximations (e.g., derivational errors) were scored as incorrect.

**Results and Discussion**

Monitoring by the experimenter (and by means of video in the case of the final two subjects) suggested that the fixation instructions were followed. No differences in this respect were detected between the Speaking- and Chewing-Lips conditions. While the eye movement monitoring was admittedly somewhat crude, it should certainly be sufficient to detect whether subjects were fixating toward the appropriate monitor, given the substantial distances involved.

The percentages of correctly repeated target words for each subject in each condition were subjected to a three-way within-subject analysis of variance (ANOVA) with these factors: Left or Right auditory targets, Speaking- or Chewing-Lips, and fixation at the Same or Opposite side as the target sounds. The ANOVA found a main effect of Left versus Right target sounds ($F(1,15) = 14.8, p < .002$), with more accurate performance when auditory targets came from the subject's left (mean of 52.2 percent) than right (mean of 44.6 percent). This result is the opposite of the right-sided advantage normally found in selective listening for words (Kimura 1961; Morais and Bertelson 1975). Since this effect may simply reflect the acoustics of the testing room and there is no hint of any interaction with the other factors, we shall not consider the Left/Right factor further (neither in the subsequent analyses, nor in our subsequent experiments, where no main effects or interactions involving side of the auditory targets were observed).

Pooling across the side of the auditory targets, the mean percentages of words named correctly for the remaining conditions are shown in figure 12.1 (out of 168 words per subject for each condition). This figure suggests that Speaking-Lips led to better word recognition and that they produced a greater benefit when on the same side as the target sounds. This was confirmed by a two-way within-subject ANOVA, with Speaking-versus Chewing-Lips as one factor, and the relation of fixation to the auditory target words as the other (Same versus Opposite side). There was a powerful effect of Speaking-versus Chewing-Lips ($F(1,15) = 321.2, p < .0001$) and an effect of Same versus Opposite side ($F(1,15) = 49.2, p < .0001$). These factors interacted ($F(1,15) = 58.5, p < .0001$). Wilcoxon matched-pairs signed-rank tests confirmed that while Same performance exceeded Opposite performance with Speaking-Lips ($T = 0, p < .001$), there was no effect of the direction of fixation with Chewing-Lips ($T = 37.5$, n.s.), producing the observed interaction.

The substantial drop in performance for the Opposite Speaking-Lips condition relative to the Same Speaking-Lips condition suggests a difficulty in actively attending to visual lip-read information on one side while selecting auditory information from the other side. Note, however, that performance benefited from the presence of visual lip-read information relative to the corresponding Chewing-Lips condition in both the Same and Opposite cases ($T = 0, p < .001$ for each comparison). This suggests that while it was difficult to select one side visually and the other auditorily, it was nevertheless possible to some extent; otherwise no benefit from relevant lip-read information should be observed for the Opposite conditions.

Assuming that fixation patterns were indeed the same in the Chewing-Lips and Speaking-Lips conditions, the results suggest that the difficulty in attending to one location visually and another auditorily applies only for active endogenous visual attention—that is, when the fixated visual events contribute to task performance. There was no detectable difficulty in passively fixating meaningless events on one side while attending auditorily to the other side in the Chewing-Lips Conditions.

Accurate reports of words from the irrelevant channel were occasionally observed, although these intrusion-error data were lost for one subject due to experimenter error. Pooling over the remaining fifteen subjects, there were twenty-seven such errors in total for Same Chewing-Lips, thirty-one for Opposite Chewing-Lips, eleven for Same Speaking-Lips, and forty-five for Opposite Speaking-Lips. These data are consistent with the suggestion that it was difficult to ignore distractor auditory words when attending to visual

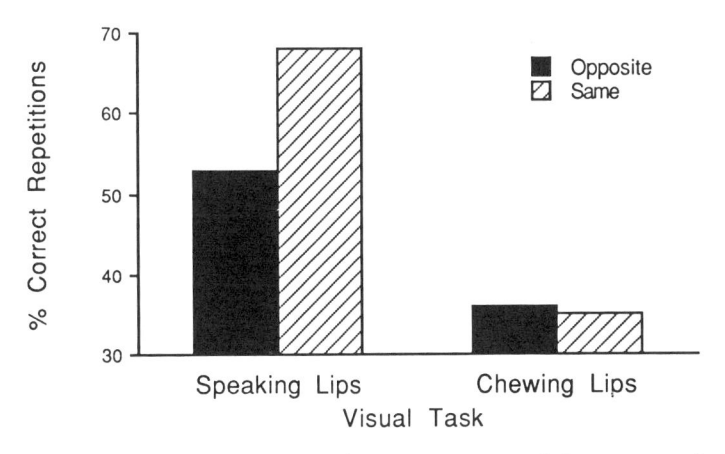

**Figure 12.1** Mean percentage of correct repetitions of the target words in experiment 1, averaged over subjects for each condition. The same-side conditions are indicated with hatched columns, the opposite-side conditions with solid columns.

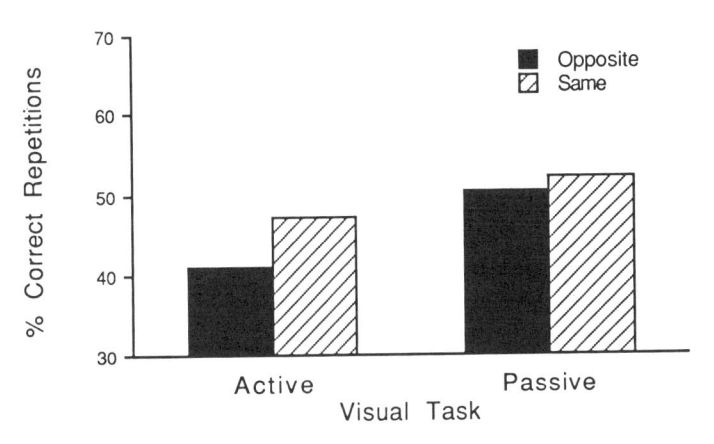

**Figure 12.2** Mean percentage of correct repetitions of the auditory target words in experiment 2, averaged over subjects for each condition. The same-side conditions are indicated with hatched columns, the opposite-side conditions with solid columns.

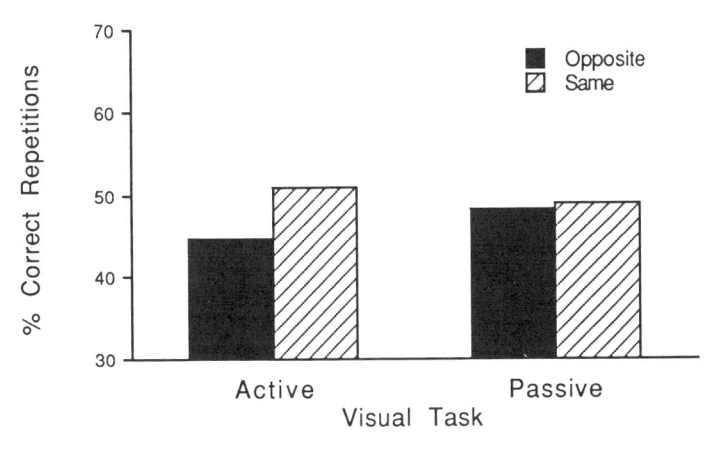

**Figure 12.3** Mean percentage of correct repetitions of the auditory target words in experiment 3, averaged over subjects for each condition. The same-side conditions are indicated with hatched columns, the opposite-side conditions with solid columns.

lip-read information on their side in the Opposite Speaking-Lips condition. Despite the small number of intrusions overall, a two-way ANOVA on the intrusion-error data showed an interaction between Same versus Opposite side and Chewing-versus Speaking-Lips ($F(1,14) = 8.3, p = .01$). There were more intrusion errors in the Opposite than the Same condition for Speaking-Lips ($T = 0, p < .01$), but not for Chewing-Lips ($T = 58.5$, n.s.), producing the interaction.

In summary, performance was poorer when the relevant lip-read information was on the opposite side to the target auditory information rather than on the same side. Intrusions from auditory distractors on the same side as the relevant lip-read information contributed to this decrement but were not frequent enough to account for the whole effect. Despite the observed difficulty in attending to different locations in vision and audition, there was some benefit from lip-read information even in the Opposite side conditions. Shadowing performance was unaffected by the direction of passive fixation, suggesting that the observed links between vision and audition apply only when the fixated visual events are relevant to the ongoing task.

It is possible that these findings reflect not attentional mechanisms but rather spatial limitations on the mechanisms that integrate visual and auditory information in lipreading (Jack and Thurlow 1973). In other words, the cost in the Opposite Speaking-Lips may simply arise because the target auditory and visual speech events that must be integrated are farther apart and integration falls off with increasing distance. There are at least two counters to this suggestion. First, the intrusion data suggest an attentional effect, whereby it is difficult to ignore auditory distractors at the current locus of visual attention. Second, it may be that spatial limitations on cross-modal integration result from difficulties in attending to distinct locations simultaneously rather than vice versa. Nevertheless, we ran a further experiment to examine whether we had simply rediscovered a spatial restriction on cross-modal integration. In this follow-up, the subjects performed unrelated auditory and visual tasks on stimuli presented in the same or different locations, with no requirement for cross-modal integration. Thus, they had to divide their attention among unrelated streams of auditory and visual events rather than selectively attending to related audiovisual events that had to be perceptually integrated. If the results of experiment 1 depend on the requirement for integration, they should not obtain in the follow-up study. On they other hand, if they reflect a general difficulty in endogenously attending to different locations in distinct modalities, they should still be observed.

Another rationale for this follow-up study was that lipreading may be a special (albeit interesting) case. In the real world, speech originates from the lips of the person making the utterance. Through experience of this contingency, auditory and visual locations might come to have an especially powerful synergy in the case of lipreading. On the other hand, from the armchair, one could equally argue that it may be particularly easy to attend to different locations in two modalities while lipreading since the target visual and auditory information will be linked by temporal and phonemic correspondences that subjects may employ to circumvent the mismatch in locations. This might explain our observation in experiment 1 that while it was relatively difficult to select lip-read information from one side and corresponding auditory information from the other side, it must have been possible to some extent (since a lip-read benefit was observed even in this Opposite-side case). Given the equivocality of these speculations about the possible special status of cross-modal integration for lipreading, we examined whether it is difficult to attend endogenously to different locations when performing completely independent auditory and visual tasks.

## 12.3  EXPERIMENT 2

The auditory stimuli were as for experiment 1, and subjects again had to repeat triplets of rapidly presented words from one side while ignoring concurrent auditory words presented on the opposite side. However, the visual tasks were now unrelated to the auditory materials in every case. A series of visual characters were presented in front of one or the other loudspeaker, all the characters appearing in the same location in rapid serial visual presentation (RSVP). They were presented at the loudspeaker that produced the target words or at the loudspeaker that produced the distractor words. In the passive visual tasks, subjects simply fixated the stream of characters, which were otherwise irrelevant to the ongoing task, analogously to the Chewing-Lips conditions from experiment 1. In the active visual tasks (intended to be analogous to the previous Speaking-Lips conditions), subjects continually monitored the RSVP stream for a prespecified character, which occasionally appeared. If the visual target appeared, they had to stop shadowing and verbally report that they had detected it.

The question was whether the pattern of results observed in experiment 1 would be replicated when the auditory and visual tasks were unrelated, with no requirement for cross-modal integration. If so, performance should be worse when the RSVP stream appears on the opposite side to the target words. However, if the spatial synergy between active visual and auditory attention observed in experiment 1 is specific to lipreading or to tasks requiring cross-modal integration, it should not be found with the unrelated active visual task. Given the results of experiment 1, we would expect that passively fixating one side versus the other would have no effect in the passive visual tasks.

### Subjects

The twenty-four new subjects were unpaid volunteers, all undergraduates. The mean age was 21 years and the range 18 to 23 years. All were naive as to the purpose of the study, which took about 65 min.

## Apparatus and Materials

The apparatus and spatial layout were as for experiment 1, except that the two auditory messages were transferred from video onto audiotape, which was played back on a Revox machine, and an IBM microcomputer was used to generate the visual stimuli on one of the monitors used previously. These visual stimuli were presented to the subject immediately in front of one of the loudspeaker cones on a small mirror via another mirror from the monitor. The stimuli were visible to the subject only on the mirror in front of either loudspeaker, where they subtended a visual angle of 1.6 degrees in width and 3.3 degrees in height on average. The background stimuli for the visual monitoring task were characters from the set <, >, !, (, ), *, {, }, [, ], —, =, /, :, &, ^, |, and + was the visual target. The visual stimuli for the passive fixation task were the characters Z and O. The sequence of characters was random in the monitoring task, except for the insertion of visual targets. The characters alternated in the passive fixation task. The auditory stimuli were as in experiment 1.

## Design

There were again two within-subjects factors of interest. One factor was as before: fixation was on the Same side as the target auditory information or on the Opposite side. The other factor was analogous to the previous Speaking- versus Chewing-Lips comparison; the visual task was either active monitoring or passive fixation. These two factors were crossed to yield four conditions: Same Active, Opposite Active, Same Passive, and Opposite Passive.

## Procedure

This was identical to experiment 1, except for the change in visual tasks. Passive conditions were substituted for Chewing-Lips and Active conditions for Speaking-Lips in the sequences used previously.

The RSVP stimuli were presented at a rate of one character every 56 ms and ran continuously during each auditory list. The visual target appeared as the next item in the RSVP sequence if the experimenter pressed a remote button during the monitoring conditions. Button pushes were neither visible nor audible to the subject. Visual targets occurred equally often in the three positions within spoken triplets. The targets appeared pseudorandomly with the constraint that they were equally likely to appear during two, three, four, or five triplets from each list of fourteen triplets. They appeared fourteen times during each of the two Active conditions. Subjects were not informed about the probabilities of visual target occurrence but were told that they would occur only during auditory words in the Active conditions.

The accuracy of naming for the target auditory words was recorded as before and also each hit, miss, or false alarm for visual targets. Naming was not scored for triplets when a target was presented. Thus, performance on 126 words was scored for each condition rather than the full 168 as in experiment 1. Fixation was again monitored by the experimenter and additionally by video recording for the final two subjects. No fixation differences were detected between the Active and Passive conditions.

**Results**

The mean percentage of words named correctly (out of 126 words per subject in each condition) is shown in figure 12.2, which indicates that the requirement to perform concurrent visual monitoring disrupted shadowing performance less when the visual events were on the same side as the target sounds. A two-way within-subject ANOVA was conducted, with visual task as one factor and side of fixation as the other. There was an effect of visual task ($F(1,23) = 29.7, p < .0001$) with slightly poorer shadowing during the active visual task; in other words, a conventional dual-task cost was observed. There was also a main effect of Same versus Opposite side of fixation ($F(1,23) = 16.8, p < .0001$). The interaction was significant ($F(1,23) = 6.2, p = .02$). Wilcoxon tests confirmed that while Same performance exceeded Opposite performance in the Active tasks ($T = 25.5, p < .01$), there was no effect of the direction of fixation in the passive tasks ($T = 92$ with two ties, n.s.), producing the observed interaction. Thus, as for experiment 1, a cost in shadowing performance was observed when subjects had to attend actively to one side visually and another auditorily, but there was no effect of the direction of passive fixation.

Pooling over the twenty-four subjects, there were twenty-four intrusion errors in total for the Same Passive condition, eighteen for Opposite Passive, thirty-two for Same Active, and forty-five for Opposite Active. A two-way ANOVA on these relatively scarce errors found a main effect of Active versus Passive visual task ($F(1,23) = 7.4, p < .01$), but the effect of Same versus Opposite side did not reach significance ($F(1,23) = .6$) and similarly for the interaction ($F(1,23) = 2.24$), although the trend is toward the pattern found in the accuracy data (i.e., more of an Opposite versus Same cost in the Active tasks). The mean number of correct visual target detections out of a possible 14 was 11.2 for the Same Active task and 10.8 for the Opposite Active task, with no reliable difference ($F(1,23) = 1.6$).

Thus, a decrement in shadowing performance was found when subjects had to attend endogenously to one location visually and another auditorily. As in experiment 1, there was no effect of the direction of passive endogenous fixation. Since the shadowing and visual monitoring tasks were unrelated, these results confirm a spatial synergy between active visual and auditory attention that is specific neither to lipreading nor to a difficulty in cross-modal integration across space, as might have been proposed to account for experiment 1.

At least two possible explanations for the cost of endogenously attending to distinct locations remain, because our Same- versus Opposite-side manipulation confounded two factors. When the target visual information was presented on the Opposite side to the target sounds, it was both farther from the target sounds and closer to the distractor sounds. Either factor might be responsible for the performance decrement. It might be difficult to select information from different locations in distinct modalities or difficult to reject distractor information in one modality from a location that is relevant for another modality (or both difficulties may apply). Intrusion errors presumably reflect a difficulty in rejection, and these errors were only partly responsible for our effects, suggesting that both difficulties may be involved.

To examine the issue further, we conducted a final study that was like experiment 2 except with no distracting information—in other words, a conventional dual-task situation. Any different-location cost in this situation could be attributed only to a difficulty in selecting from different locations rather than a difficulty in selecting one modality at a particular location while rejecting another at the same location.

## 12.4 EXPERIMENT 3

### Subjects

The eight new subjects were again unpaid volunteers. All were undergraduates reporting normal hearing and normal or corrected vision. They were naive as to the purpose of the study, which took about 65 min.

### Method

The method was as for experiment 2 except that only one auditory message was presented at any time. Its volume was reduced to bring shadowing performance down to a level comparable with the earlier studies. No fixation differences were detected between the Active and Passive conditions.

### Results and Discussion

The mean percentage of words named correctly out of 126 words per subject are shown in figure 12.3. A two-way within-subject ANOVA was conducted as before, with visual task as one factor and Same versus Opposite side of fixation as the other. There was no effect of visual task on this occasion ($F(1,7) = .02$). If this null effect can be relied upon, one might speculate that the dual-task decrement found in experiment 2 with the active visual task is eliminated when the auditory task is data limited by a low signal-to-noise ratio rather than resource limited as a result of competition from distracting auditory messages. There was a main effect of Same versus Opposite side of fixation ($F(1,7) = 9.0, p = .02$) and a significant interaction ($F(1,7) = 8.6, p = .02$). Wilcoxon tests confirmed that while Same performance exceeded Opposite performance in the Active tasks ($T = 0, p < .01$), there was no effect of the direction of fixation in the passive tasks ($T = 10.5$ with one tie, n.s.), producing the observed interaction. Thus, as for experiments 1 and 2, a cost in shadowing performance was observed when subjects had to attend actively and endogenously to one side visually and another auditorily, but there was no effect of passively fixating the same or opposite side. The mean number of correct visual target detections out of a possible 14 was 10.3 for the Same Active task and 9.1 for the Opposite Active task, with no reliable difference ($F(1,7) = 1.3$).

Thus, the Active Opposite-side decrement found in experiment 2 was replicated when no distracting stimuli were presented, suggesting that the previous results did not solely reflect a difficulty in rejecting information from one modality at a position that is attended in another modality. Instead, we appear to have identified a difficulty in combining auditory and visual tasks when the stimuli come from different locations. As in the previous experiments, this difficulty cannot be attributed to the direction of gaze, since it was not found in the Passive conditions.

The null effect of the direction of passive fixation in all three of our studies is somewhat surprising since Reisberg, Scheiber, and Potemken (1981) reported that selective listening is enhanced when subjects are allowed to fixate the loudspeaker source for the target auditory message, extending the earlier work of Gopher (1973). Similarly, Larmande et al. (1983) found that the ear advantage in dichotic listening to nonverbal sounds can be reversed by directing gaze in the opposite direction. Honoré, Bordeaud'hui, and Sparrow (1989) and Pierson et al. (1991) observed that the direction of passive gaze can also affect response to tactile stimuli, reducing cutaneous reaction time in the fixated direction. Finally, Larmande and Cambier (1981) report that tactile extinction of the contralateral event on double simultaneous stimulation was reduced in right hemisphere patients when they were required to fixate toward the contralateral side. These data all suggest that the direction of gaze can affect attention in other modalities, in contrast with our null findings concerning passive fixation. There are many procedural differences between these prior studies and our own experiments, which might account for the discrepancy. However, Wolters and Schiano (1989) failed to replicate Reisberg, Scheiber, and Potemken's (1981) effect of fixation using their exact procedure. Thus, the precise circumstances under which passive fixation modulates selective listening or selection in other modalities remain unclear. However, our studies demonstrate that any effects of passive fixation on audition must be smaller than those produced by the direction of active endogenous visual attention toward visual events that must be processed to perform the ongoing task.

## 12.5 GENERAL DISCUSSION

We began with two fundamental questions: whether attentional mechanisms operate independently in distinct unimodal systems and how attention comes to be coordinated across the modalities despite their different input organizations. The results illustrate that endogenous attention does not operate independently for vision and audition. Three experiments found evidence for a spatial synergy between auditory and visual endogenous attention, such that it is difficult to attend to one side of the midline visually and the other auditorily. This opposite-side decrement was found for tasks requiring cross-modal integration (listening while lipreading in experiment 1) and for unrelated auditory and visual tasks (listening while RSVP monitoring in experiments 2 and 3), although the cost was larger in the integrative case. Experiment 3 found the opposite-side decrement in a conventional dual-task situation, when no distracting information was presented, suggesting that the spatial synergy may be a quite general limit on concurrent task performance. In contrast to the significant decrement found when endogenously attending to different locations, there was no observable decrement for passively fixating one location while attending auditorily to another.

The spatial synergy we have observed makes considerable functional sense from the perspective that attentional mechanisms serve to select relevant objects for the control of action (Allport 1987; Driver and Baylis 1989; Duncan 1984). Sights and sounds emanating from the same distal object are likely to come from approximately the same location. Spatial links between visual and auditory attention might therefore provide a rough solution to the problem raised by our second question: how attention is coordinated across modalities so that the same object is attended to visually and auditorily.

One extreme solution to the coordination problem would be to direct attention in a supramodal representation of the scene following cross-modal integration (Butter, Buchtel, and Santucci 1989) rather than within each modality. Can our data be taken as evidence for such a supramodal attentional system? We think there is currently no unequivocal evidence in favor of such a system. First, our data are as readily accommodated by the proposal of spatial links between otherwise distinct modality-specific systems. Second, experiment 1 found that while it was difficult to attend endogenously to different locations in vision and audition, it was nevertheless possible to some extent; a lip-read benefit was observed even in the Opposite-side condition. This is problematic for a purely supramodal account of spatial selectivity. Third, clinical evidence from attentional deficits following brain damage argues strongly for the existence of modality-specific attentional systems, since the severity of neglect or extinction in audition can be unrelated to the severity in vision (Barbieri and De Renzi 1989).

In contrast to these dissociations between modalities, cross-modal interactions can also arise in attentional deficits. For example, extinction on double simultaneous stimulation can be observed in unilateral parietal patients between vision and audition (Farah et al. 1989), if not between touch and vision (Inhoff, Rafal, and Posner 1992). These findings tempt one to postulate both modality-specific attentional mechanisms at lower levels of representation (responsible for the dissociations) and supramodal attentional mechanisms at higher levels (producing the cross-modal interactions). Posner (1990) proposes exactly this kind of hierarchical attentional model, with modality-specific systems feeding into a supramodal attentional system. The strength of such models is that they can accommodate both dependence and independence between modalities. However, for this very reason, they are difficult to falsify, unless couched in more precise neuroanatomical terms.

Although the case for a supramodal attentional system remains unproved, there is clear evidence that endogenous selection can take place after cross-modal integration in some cases. Driver (n.d.) examined this issue by exploiting an established audiovisual interaction; sounds tend to be mislocated toward the position of their apparent visual source (e.g., movie audiences typically mislocate the spoken soundtrack toward the actors appearing on the screen). This "ventriloquism" effect is particularly powerful for visual lip-read information and matching speech sounds (Witkin, Wapner, and Leventhal 1952). Driver presented his subjects with two concurrent messages spoken by the same person, as in our studies, but they were both played back from the same loudspeaker in mono. Subjects had to repeat one message, for which they were also given lip-read information on video, as in experiment 1. This visual information was either presented in the same location as the mono sound source or slightly displaced towards a dummy loudspeaker. Performance was improved in the displaced case. Driver's account is that the target sounds were mislocated toward the matching lips by means of the ventriloquism effect, while the distractor sounds were correctly located at the mono sound source because they did not match the lips and therefore were not subject to ventriloquism. This produced an illusion of auditory stereo when the lips were displaced from the mono sound source, which improved selective listening as for true auditory stereo. In other words, an illusion (mislocation of the target sounds by means of ventriloquism) actually strengthened veridical perception (report of the target words). The implication is that cross-modal matching must have taken place before endogenous attentional selection, because the improved performance with displaced lips requires that only the sounds that matched the lips were mislocated toward them, allowing enhanced segregation from the mismatching sounds.

On the face of it, these results appear to provide a counterexample to our finding that attending to different physical locations in distinct modalities carries a performance cost, since performance was enhanced in Driver's study when the visual lip-read information was slightly displaced away from the target (and distractor) sounds. Presumably, however, the target sights and sounds in Driver's study were coded as emanating from the same (or similar) location even in the displaced condition as a result of ventriloquism. In other words, the difficulty in attending to distinct locations may apply only for locations that are perceived as different following cross-modal integration, rather than applying for any locations that are sufficiently distinct physically to be discriminated within a modality.

We do not suggest that Driver's data establish a strong case for supramodal mechanisms of selection. They can be accommodated if selection proceeds within individual modalities, provided one allows cross-modal influences on the coding of location for each modality. However, the results clearly rule out an extreme modality-specific account, on which each sensory modality is an encapsulated module prior to the allocation of endogenous attention.

The spatial synergy we observed in our experiments could be used to examine the representation of space by different modalities. Each modality has a distinct spatial organization at receptor input. For example, there is no auditory equivalent to the retinotopic organization that provides the initial coordinate system for vision. This point raises many questions about the mappings that relate space in one modality to space in another to produce cross-modal spatial interactions and to allow the cross-modal coordination of attention. By systematically varying the relative locations of events in distinct modalities and examining any cost of attending to these locations simultaneously, we should be able to identify what counts as the same or different location across modalities at the processing stages where endogenous attention operates. In our experiments, stimuli were in either the same or opposite hemifields, so further studies are required to examine whether similar principles apply for distinct locations within a hemifield. Despite this uncertainty, our data cannot be accounted for in terms of differential hemisphere activation in the various conditions (Kinsbourne 1987). The activation produced by the requirement to fixate one side or the other should be identical for our Passive and Active conditions, yet differential results were observed. Equally, the visual events in the Same- and Opposite-side conditions should produce equivalent hemispheric activation since they were always at fixation, and yet differential results were again observed.

It remains for future research to establish the range of task and modality combinations for which the observed spatial synergy in active endogenous attention applies. The fact that we found this synergy for unrelated auditory and visual tasks suggests that it may be quite general. If so, the spatial synergy would place a major restriction on our ability to perform two tasks in different modalities simultaneously. It remains controversial whether previous studies of dual-task performance have succeeded in identifying general limits on performance or limits that are entirely specific to the pair of tasks in question (Allport 1980, 1992; Broadbent 1982; Shallice, McLeod, and Lewis 1985). The least controversial factors considered to improve dual-task performance include separation of input modality (Treisman and Davies 1973) and separation of response modality (McLeod 1977), leading to the widely held rule of thumb that dissimilar tasks are easier to combine than similar tasks. We appear to have identified one factor that violates this principle: similarity in the location of stimuli for tasks in different modalities helps rather than hinders task combination.

## NOTE

We thank Alan Allport for his encouragement and advice on these studies. The research was supported by a grant to the first author from the Medical Research Council (UK).

## REFERENCES

Allport, D. A. (1980). Attention and performance. In G. Claxton (Ed.), *Cognitive psychology: New directions*. London: Routledge and Kegan Paul.

Allport, D. A. (1987). Selection-for-action: Some behavioral and neurophysiological considerations of attention and action. In H. Heuer and A. F. Sanders (Eds.), *Perspectives on perception and action*, 395–419. Hillsdale, NJ: Erlbaum.

Allport, D. A. (1992). Selection and control: A critical review of 25 years. In S. Kornblum and D. E. Meyer (Eds.), *Attention and performance XIV: A silver jubilee*. Hillsdale, NJ: Erlbaum.

Barbierei, C., and De Renzi, E. (1989). Patterns of neglect dissociation. *Behavioural Neurology*, 2, 13–24.

Broadbent, D. E. (1958). *Perception and communication*. London: Pergamon.

Broadbent, D. E. (1982). Task combination and selective intake of information. *Acta Psychologica*, 50, 253–290.

Brown, G. D. A. (1984). A frequency count of 190,000 words in the London-Lund corpus of English conversation. *Behaviour Research Methods, Instrumentation and Computers*, 16, 502–532.

Buchtel, H. A., and Butter, C. M. (1988). Spatial attention shifts: Implications for the role of polysensory mechanisms. *Neuropsychologia*, 26, 499–509.

Butter, C. M., Buchtel, H. A., and Santucci, R. (1989). Spatial attentional shifts: Further evidence for the role of polysensory mechanism using visual and tactile stimuli. *Neuropsychologia*, 27, 1231–1240.

Cherry, E. C. (1953). Some experiments upon the recognition of speech, with one and two ears. *Journal of the Acoustical Society of America*, 25, 975–979.

Driver, J. (n.d.). Selective listening and lip-reading: Crossmodal integration can occur before attentional selection. In preparation.

Driver, J., and Baylis, G. C. (1989). Movement and visual attention: The spotlight metaphor breaks down. *Journal of Experimental Psychology: Human Perception and Performance*, 15, 448–456.

Duncan, J. (1984). Selective attention and the organization of visual information. *Journal of Experimental Psychology: General*, 113, 501–517.

Farah, M. J., Wong, A. B., Monheit, M. A., and Morrow, L. A. (1989). Parietal mechanisms of spatial attention: Modality-specific or supramodal? *Neuropsychologia*, 27, 461–470.

Gopher, D. (1973). Eye-movement patterns in selective listening tasks of focussed attention. *Perception and Psychophysics*, 14, 259–264.

Honoré, J., Bourdeaud'hui, M., and Sparrow, L. (1989). Reduction of cutaneous reaction time by directing eyes towards the source of stimulation. *Neuropsychologia*, 27, 367–371.

Inhoff, A. W., Rafal, R. D., and Posner, M. I. (1992). Bimodal extinction without crossmodal extinction. *Journal of Neurology, Neurosurgery and Psychiatry*, 55, 36–39.

Jack, C. E., and Thurlow, W. R. (1973). Effects of degree of visual association and angle of displacement on the "ventriloquism" effect. *Perceptual and Motor Skills*, 37, 967–979.

Jonides, J. (1981). Voluntary versus automatic control over the mind's eye's movement. In J. Long and A. Baddeley (Eds.), *Attention and performance IX*. Hillsdale, NJ: Erlbaum.

Kahneman, D., and Treisman, A. (1984). Changing views of attention and automaticity. In R. Parasuraman and D. R. Davies (Eds.), *Varieties of attention*. New York: Academic Press.

Kimura, D. (1961). Cerebral dominance and the perception of verbal stimuli. *Canadian Journal of Psychology*, 15, 166–171.

Kinsbourne, M. (1987). Mechanisms of unilateral neglect. In M. Jeannerod (Ed.), *Neurophysiological and neuropsychological aspects of spatial neglect*, 69–86. Amsterdam: North-Holland.

Klein, R. (1987). Covert cross-modality orienting of attention. Presented to the Psychonomic Society.

Larmande, P., and Cambier, J. (1981). Influence de l'état d'activation hemisphérique sur le phénomène d'extinction sensitive chez 10 patients atteints de lésions hemisphériques droites. *Revue Neurologique, 137,* 285–290.

Larmande, F., Elghori, D., Sintes, J., Bigot, T., and Autret, A. (1983). Test d'écoute dichotique verbal et non verbal chez le suject normal: influence de l'état d'activation hemispherique. *Revue Neurologique, 139,* 65–69.

McLeod, P. D. (1977). A dual-task response modality effect: Support for multiprocessor models of attention. *Quarterly Journal of Experimental Psychology, 29,* 651–667.

Morais, J., and Bertelson, P. (1975). Spatial position versus ear of entry as determinant of the auditory laterality effects: A stereophonic test. *Journal of Experimental Psychology: Human Perception and Performance, 1,* 253–262.

Muller, H. J., and Humphreys, G. W. (1991). Luminance-increment detection: Capacity-limited or not? *Journal of Experimental Psychology: Human Perception and Performance, 17,* 107–124.

Muller, H. J., and Rabbitt, P. M. A. (1989). Reflexive and voluntary orienting of visual attention: Time course of activation and resistance to interruption. *Journal of Experimental Psychology: Human Perception and Performance, 15,* 315–330.

Neumann, O., van der Heijden, A. H. C., and Allport, D. A. (1986). Visual selective attention: Introductory remarks. *Psychological Research, 48,* 185–188.

Pierson, J. M., Bradshaw, J. L., Meyer, T. F., Howard, M. J., and Bradshaw, J. A. (1991). Direction of gaze during vibrotactile choice reaction time tasks. *Neuropsychologia, 29,* 925–928.

Posner, M. I. (1980). Orienting of attention. *Quarterly Journal of Experimental Psychology, 32,* 3–25.

Posner, M. I. (1990). Hierarchical distributed networks in the neuropsychology of selective attention. In A. Caramazza (Ed.), *Cognitive neuropsychology and neurolinguistics: Advances in models of cognitive function and impairment,* 187–210. Hillsdale, NJ: Erlbaum.

Rafal, R. D., Henik, A., and Smith, J. (1992). Extrageniculate contribution to reflex visual orienting in normal humans: A temporal hemifield advantage. *Journal of Cognitive Neuroscience, 3,* 322–328.

Reisberg, D. (1978). Looking where you listen: Visual cues and auditory attention. *Acta Psychologica, 42,* 331–341.

Reisberg, D., Scheiber, R., and Potemken, L. (1981). Eye position and the control of auditory attention. *Journal of Experimental Psychology: Human Perception and Performance, 7,* 318–323.

Shallice, T., McLeod, P., and Lewis, K. (1985). Isolating cognitive modules with the dual task paradigm: Are speech perception and production separate processes? *Quarterly Journal of Experimental Psychology, 37A,* 507–532.

Spence, C. J., and Driver, J. (1994). Covert orienting in audition: Exogenous and endogenous mechanisms. *Journal of Experimental Psychology: Human Perception and Performance.* In press.

Thompson, G. C., and Masterton, R. B. (1978). Brain stem auditory pathways involved in reflexive head orientation to sound. *Journal of Neurophysiology, 41,* 1183–1202.

Tipper, S. P., Driver, J., and Weaver, B. (1991). Object-centred inhibition of return of visual attention. *Quarterly Journal of Experimental Psychology, 43A,* 289–298.

Treisman, A. M., and Davies, A. (1973). Divided attention to ear and eye. In S. Kornblum (Ed.), *Attention and performance IV.* London: Academic Press.

Treisman, A. M., and Gelade, G. (1980). A feature-integration theory of attention. *Cognitive Psychology, 12,* 97–136.

Tsal, Y., and Lavie, N. (1988). Attending to color and shape: The special role of location in visual processing. *Perception and Psychophysics, 44,* 15–21.

Whittington, D. A., Hepp-Reymond, M. C., and Flood, W. (1981). Eye and head movements to auditory targets. *Experimental Brain Research, 41,* 358–363.

Witkin, H. A., Wapner, S., and Leventhal, T. (1952). Sound localization with conflicting visual and auditory cues. *Journal of Experimental Psychology, 43,* 58–67.

Wolters, N. C. W., and Schiano, D. J. (1989). On listening where we look: the fragility of a phenomenon. *Perception and Psychophysics, 45,* 184–186.

# 13 Does Oculomotor Readiness Mediate Cognitive Control of Visual Attention? Revisited!

Raymond M. Klein and Amanda Pontefract

ABSTRACT   At Attention and Performance VIII, Klein proposed that endogenous covert orienting of attention might be accomplished by preparing to move the eyes to the to-be-attended location (Klein 1980). This "oculomotor readiness hypothesis" made two distinct predictions, each of which was tested in a dual-task situation. First, if the subject is attending to a location, eye movements to that location should be facilitated. Second, if the subject is preparing to move his or her eyes to a particular location, the detection of events presented there should be facilitated. Neither prediction was confirmed, and it was concluded that endogenous covert orienting is generated independently of the oculomotor system. The oculomotor readiness hypothesis has experienced something of a revival recently (cf. Rizzolatti et al. 1987; Shepard, Findlay, and Hockey 1986). This revival encouraged us to conduct two new tests of the predictions described above—tests not subject to alternative explanations that might apply to Klein's (1980) earlier experiments. The oculomotor readiness hypothesis was again disconfirmed. Our findings, together with the recent literature, suggest the following conclusions: (1) There is a tight linkage between attention and saccade execution; shifts of attention precede shifts in gaze; (2) attention is strongly activated by stimulus events that normally elicit eye movements even when they are suppressed; and (3) attention is not linked to endogenously generated saccadic programming when these programs are not executed.

## 13.1   INTRODUCTION

Visual orienting is most obviously accomplished when adjustments of gaze direction are used to select which regions of, or objects within, visual space are processed by the sensitive fovea and its associated neural machinery. In contrast to such overt adjustments of the sensory apparatus are covert or internal adjustments, which, in the absence of gaze changes, can be made to select specific objects or regions for preferential treatment. These two modes of visual orienting determine which aspects of the visual mosaic will have preferential access to limited-capacity visual routines or resources. Whether overt or covert, visual orienting can be controlled exogenously or endogenously. Exogenous control is exerted by stimulation outside the observer, as when sudden changes in peripheral vision, particularly abrupt onsets (Yantis and Jonides 1984; but see Folk, Remington, and Johnston 1992), attract oculomotor responses and/or visual attention. In contrast, endogenous control originates within the observer, and is characterized by a voluntary decision to shift attention (covert) or gaze (overt) to a region of, or object in,

|          | Covert | Overt |
|----------|--------|-------|
| Endogenous |      |       |
| Exogenous  |      |       |

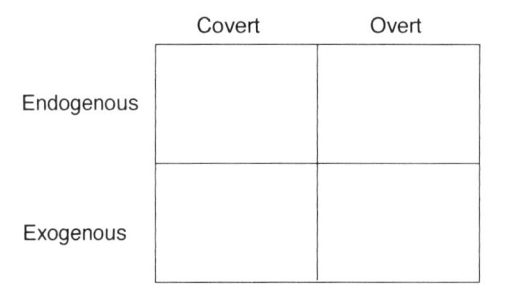

**Figure 13.1** Classification of visual orienting.

space. These two distinctions (Klein, Kingstone, and Pontefract 1992; Posner 1980) suggest the 2 × 2 classification scheme shown in figure 13.1.

Our research strategy has been aimed at understanding the individual cells of this matrix as well how they are related, with particular emphasis on endogenous control of covert orienting. The mental behaviors that fill this cell of the matrix might be described as prototypically conscious. This follows, first, from the purpose of covert orienting, which is to make a subset of the inputs reaching the visual system available to awareness directly (permitting detection and other nonreflexive responses) or to higher-level routines that may be controlled by, or may send their outputs to, systems mediating awareness; and second, from the source of endogenous control, which, being voluntary, is usually conscious awareness. Thus, endogenous covert orienting is, fundamentally, a consciously controlled gating mechanism for the contents of consciousness.

In this chapter we explore the possibility of a rather direct relationship between endogenous control of covert and overt orienting by asking whether the overt orienting system (in the form of oculomotor programming) plays a mediating role in covert endogenous orienting. Or, in other words, does oculomotor readiness mediate cognitive control of visual attention? The "revisited!" in our title refers to the fact that precisely this question was explored over a decade ago, in a paper published in *Attention and Performance VIII*. In that paper Klein (1980) proposed an explicit oculomotor readiness hypothesis (OMRH) suggesting that endogenous covert orienting of attention is accomplished by preparing to move the eyes to the to-be-attended location. That is, "When attention to a particular location is desired, the observer prepares to make an eye movement to that location; the oculomotor readiness, via as yet unknown feedforward pathways, has the effect of enhancing processing in or from sensory pathways dealing with information from the target location" (Klein 1980, p. 262).

Thus, in this view, the process of getting ready to move the eyes—oculomotor readiness—is the mechanism by which visual attention is endogenously oriented in advance of stimulation. Views of perception that, like this one, emphasize motor processes have several antecedents (Hebb 1949; Festinger et al. 1967; see Weimer 1977 for a review). Klein (1980) pointed out that there was a plausible neural substrate for such a mechanism (Mohler and

Wurtz 1976; Schiller and Koerner 1971; Schiller and Stryker 1972; Wurtz and Mohler 1974). Moreover, it was quite consistent with several findings in the area of eye movements and attention (Bryden 1961; Crovitz and Daves 1962; Rayner, McConkie, and Ehrlich 1978). In one such study (Bryden 1961), a horizontal array of digits was briefly presented centered at fixation, and subjects were instructed to move their eyes to one side or the other, at their discretion. Although the stimulus was turned off before the eye movement was executed, subjects reported more digits from the side they moved to. This finding and the others cited above are consistent with the OMRH, but because they involve attention shifts under exogenous as opposed to purely endogenous control and eye movements were actually executed, as opposed to merely prepared, they are flawed as tests of the view that covert endogenous orienting might be accomplished by oculomotor preparation. The simple, and aesthetically appealing, OMRH cried out for a more direct test.

The OMRH makes two distinct predictions, each of which was tested by Klein (1980) in a dual-task situation. First, if the subject is attending to a location, eye movements to that location should be facilitated. Second, if the subject is preparing to move his or her eyes to a particular location, the detection of events presented there should be facilitated. Since neither of these predictions was confirmed, it was concluded that endogenous covert orienting is generated independent of the oculomotor system.

At about the same time, Posner (1980) and Remington (1980) also reported results quite damaging to the OMRH. Posner demonstrated that attention could be moving in one direction while the eyes were moving in the opposite direction. Using endogenous control (central cues) to direct the saccadic system, Remington reported that detection accuracy at a to-be-fixated location did not begin to improve until the eyes actually reached the location. Together with the Klein (1980) findings, these results seemed to be quite devastating for the OMRH.

Although Klein (1980) concluded that "central adjustments other than oculomotor readiness must be assumed to explain how subjects allocate attention in vision" (p. 272), he was careful to point out that this conclusion did not necessarily apply to overt orienting or to exogenous control:

I am not claiming that eye movements are not related to attention. There is no question that shifts of visual attention are often, if not usually accomplished through shifts in eye position. The claim is that when shifts of attention are accomplished without eye movements, readiness to move the eyes plays no role in these shifts.... The onset of a [peripheral] stimulus may attract both the eye movement system and attention without any causal relation between the two systems being implicated.... It is possible that the actual execution of an eye movement is preceded by an attentional shift (see Nissen, Posner, and Snyder 1978) even if a readiness to move in the absence of execution is not.... [Such a] shift might operate on the iconic representation of the stimulus after it is turned off. Thus the linkage between the eye movement system and attention may be a reflexive one, not under cognitive control. Looking necessitates an attentional shift, whereas cognitive preparation to look does not. (P. 273)

In recent years, the oculomotor readiness hypothesis for endogenous covert orienting has experienced something of a revival. Rizzolatti, et al. (1987), in particular, have argued in favor of such a proposal, which they refer to as "premotor" theory. To quote them, "It would seem highly plausible ... that overt and covert orienting of attention are controlled by common mechanisms and that the absence of eye movements in case of covert orienting is a consequence of peripheral inhibition, which leaves unchanged the central programming" (p. 37). In their experiment subjects were endogenously cued to attend a peripheral location and costs were examined at uncued locations. Increased costs were found for otherwise equivalent locations when these were across the vertical or horizontal midline from the cued location. To explain this pattern, Rizzolatti et al. (1987) made three assumptions:

1. Attention must be directed to a location before an event can be detected there.

2. Programming the saccadic system to foveate a location carries attention to that location.

3. Saccadic programming changes that involve crossing the vertical or horizontal midline require more time than those that do not (presumably because selecting different muscle groups requires more time than changing the activation of already selected groups).

Assumptions 1 and 2 together imply that:

4. Invalid trials require a change in the eye movement program.

Together with assumption 3 this implies that:

5. Detection at invalid locations that are across the horizontal or vertical meridians from the cued location will be delayed relative to otherwise equivalent locations that do not cross a meridian.

The reasoning is elegant, but to be an explanation for the meridian effect, all three assumptions must be true. The first one, which follows from some of Posner's writing, is certainly not widely held. A much more commonly held view is that processing of all sorts is facilitated at attended locations but can proceed in any event when attention is directed elsewhere. The second assumption, of course, is the oculomotor readiness hypothesis. Direct tests of this hypothesis have not yielded positive results (Klein 1980). As for the third assumption, the evidence is mixed (Abrams and Jonides 1988).

The meridian effect may provide a poor basis from which to mount a resurrection of the OMRH, but it does, nevertheless, require an explanation. It appears that the meridian effect is not obtained when covert (Umiltà et al. 1991; Reuter-Lorenz and Fendrich 1992) or overt (Crawford and Muller 1992) orienting is controlled exogenously. With endogenous control of covert orienting (McCormick and Klein 1990; Reuter-Lorenz and Fendrich 1992; Rizzolatti, et al. 1987; Umiltà et al. 1991), a meridian effect has been consistently observed, and one study (Reuter-Lorenz and Fendrich 1992) has found a meridian effect with endogenous control of overt orienting. Given that Rizzolatti's explanation of the meridian effect depends critically on the selection of eye muscles to achieve a particular change in gaze direction, it appears odd to us that attentional or ocular shifts in response to abruptly presented visual targets do not produce meridian effects. Rizzolatti, Riggio, and Sheliga (chap. 9, this volume) explain this apparent anomaly by suggesting that reflexive control of the saccadic system may involve a holistic programming process in which the abrupt onset directly retrieves all the motor program parameters necessary to foveate it, whereas with endogenous control, a hierarchical retrieval process is used. Reuter-Lorenz and Fendrich (1992) suggest an alternative explanation for the meridian effect with endogenous control of overt and covert orienting that does not assume the OMRH or premotor theory. Their proposal, which we favor, is that endogenous shifts of attention or of the eye movement system require access to a cognitive representation of visual space and that the common meridian effect is due to anisotropies in this representational system rather than to hierarchical programming of the oculomotor system.

In contrast to Rizzolatti's explanation of the meridian effect, Shepherd, Findlay, and Hockey (1986) provide a more encouraging boost to the oculomotor readiness hypothesis. They used central arrow cues both as signals for saccadic eye movements and to provide information about the location of an upcoming target requiring a manual response. Unlike Remington, they found that an attention shift in the direction of the ensuing saccade precedes that saccade even when target probabilities indicate that attention should be directed toward the opposite location. (The discrepancy between the Remington and the Shephard, Findlay, Hockey results cannot be explained in terms of dependent variables because Subramaniam and Hoffman [1991] get the Shephard, Findlay, and Hockey result with the dependent variable used by Remington. That attention may shift before an endogenously generated saccade is consistent with the oculomotor readiness proposal, but as with the Bryden (1961) and Crovitz and Daves (1962) experiments, the Shepherd, Findlay, and Hockey finding relates attention shifts to actually executed saccades. It is possible that attention reaches the target location for a saccade-in-progress before the eyes do but that preparing to move the eyes has no effect on attention.

Although Klein's (1980) experiments provided negative evidence for the OMRH, we would be quite satisfied if some flaws in those experiments were elaborated and if positive evidence for the original proposal, which we still find aesthetically appealing, were reported. The experiments reported here start from the premise that it is possible to rescue the OMRH from the implications of Klein's original experiments by resorting to alternative explanations for his findings.

## 13.2 EXPERIMENT 1

Klein's (1980) first experiment tested the prediction that readiness to move the eyes to a particular location would produce covert orienting of attention to that location. Subjects were required to make an eye movement to a set location in response to an asterisk on 80 percent of the trials and a simple manual detection response to a simple luminance increment on 20 percent of the trials. Asterisks and luminance increments were equally likely to occur 4 degrees to the left or right of fixation such that, from the point of view of stimulus expectancy, there was no reason for attention to be biased in a particular direction. However, on 80 percent of the trials subjects had to move their eyes in a particular direction, so it was assumed that they would prepare this likely response. Results showed that detection latency was not facilitated when a luminance increment occurred at the prespecified eye movement location, which suggests that the presumed oculomotor readiness was not accompanied by an attentional shift to the eye movement location. An alternative explanation is that subjects were not actually preparing to make an eye movement, due to lack of incentive or the blocked manipulation of eye movement direction (Posner, Snyder, and Davidson 1980). The most serious problem with that experiment was that its design did not permit an independent assessment of whether eye movements were being prepared.

In experiment 1 we used trial-by-trial cueing of the saccadic response most likely to be required (primary task), with occasional luminance increment probes (secondary task) presented at one of the two possible target locations. The eye movement directional cues and imperative signals for saccadic responses were the auditorily presented words *left* and *right*. Because such auditory command signals do not reflexively elicit eye movement programming and because the auditory-visual discrimination is simpler than the visual-visual one used by Klein (1980), subjects were expected to have greater incentive to prepare the movements than in Klein's study, in which all the signals were visual. Moreover, it was possible to apply cost-benefit analysis to the eye movement data to determine if saccades are actually prepared. As in the 1980 study, the purpose was to determine whether detection of a luminance increment is facilitated in the region the eye movement system is prepared to fixate.

## Method

**Subjects** Sixteen subjects were tested in three to four sessions of approximately 1 hour each. Two other subjects were excluded because of low accuracy (less than 60 percent correct in any cell or less than 85 percent correct overall).

**Apparatus** The experiment was controlled by an MBD 11/23 computer, with visual stimuli displayed on the screen of a 12.5-by-10-cm Tektronix 604 oscilloscope. Auditory stimuli were presented by a DEC-Talk text-to-speech synthesizer. With head supported by a chin rest, each subject sat at a table in a dimly illuminated room facing the oscilloscope. The distance from the chin rest to the screen was 60 cm for three subjects and 44 cm for the remaining thirteen subjects. Horizontal position of the left eye was sampled at 500 Hz

(Eyetrac, model 210). Manual responses were made with a two-key response board positioned on the table within the subject's reach. Another switch, used for calibration and for initiation of each trial, was held in the subject's non-preferred hand and activated by the thumb.

**Stimuli** The fixation display, shown before each trial initiation, consisted of a horizontal row of three evenly spaced dots, with the middle dot placed in the center of the screen. The left and right dots were separated from the central (fixation) dot by 4 degrees (3 degrees for the three subjects at the longer distance). An auditory cue 500 ms after trial initiation, lasting approximately 300 ms, was spoken by a computer-generated male voice ("Perfect Paul"). This cue was the word *left*, *right*, or *ready*. Three types of trial were randomly intermixed: (1) catch trials, in which the display remained unchanged for 2,000 ms; (2) eye movement trials, in which approximately 1,000 ms after the onset of the cue a computer-generated female target voice ("Beautiful Betty") said "left" or "right";[1] and (3) detection trials, in which 1,000 ms after cue onset, the left or right dot increased in luminance by approximately a 0.4 log unit for 1,000 ms (this was accomplished by changing the refresh rate from one to four times per 10 ms). After the response period for the trial ended (1,000 ms), the subject received a feedback display for 1,000 ms, followed by an intertrial interval of approximately 1,000 ms, before the fixation display reappeared.

**Design and Procedure** In the first session subjects were exposed to the saccadic (with neutral, left, and right cues) and manual detection (neutral only) trials in separate practice blocks before the two tasks were intermixed in a combined practice block (36 trials with the same construction as the experimental blocks), which was repeated until a satisfactory level of accuracy was achieved. There were 144 trials in each experimental block (table 13.1). Most trials (96) consisted of the primary saccadic task, for which the male voice cue was 87 percent valid (that is, of the trials requiring an eye movement, the required direction as indicated by the female voice agreed with the cue [male

**Table 13.1** Number of Trials of Each Cue-Task-Target combination in Each Experiment

|  |  | Experiment 1, Cue | | | Experiment 2, Cue[a] | | |
|---|---|---|---|---|---|---|---|
|  |  | Ready | L | R | + | ← | → |
| Detection | L | 4 | 4 | 4 | 16 | 28 | 4 |
|  | R | 4 | 4 | 4 | 16 | 4 | 28 |
| Eye movement | L | 16 | 28 | 4 | 4 | 4 | 4 |
|  | R | 16 | 4 | 28 | 4 | 4 | 4 |
| Catch |  | 8 | 8 | 8 | 8 | 8 | 8 |

L = left field or direction; R = right field or direction.
a. For four subjects, the cue was verbal.

voice] 87 percent of the time). Trials requiring a manual response (24), for which the cues were uninformative, and catch trials (24) occurred less frequently. The remaining sessions began with a combined practice block followed by one or more experimental blocks. Subjects were tested until they provided at least five experimental blocks with a satisfactory level of accuracy.

Before every block of trials, horizontal eye position was calibrated, so that changes in eye position greater than 0.5 degrees could be detected and latencies determined.[2] The subjects initiated each trial by pushing the microswitch with the thumb of their nonpreferred hand once they had foveated the center dot of the display.

Subjects were instructed to prepare to make an eye movement toward the target dot indicated by the male voice without actually moving their eyes. They were informed that the most likely direction for their actual eye movement would be the same as the direction indicated by the male auditory cue. They were instructed that on "ready" trials (neutral condition), a saccade was likely to be made but that the two directions were equiprobable. The subjects were instructed that any time the male voice cue was followed by a female voice directing them to move their eyes (primary eye movement task), they were to do so as quickly and as accurately as possible. When, instead, the cue was followed by a luminance increment of the left or right dot, they were instructed to press the response key with the index finger of their preferred hand as quickly as possible without moving their eyes from fixation (secondary detection task). On catch trials, no imperative stimulus was presented, and subjects were instructed to refrain from making any ocular or manual responses until the display was turned off.

After each trial subjects received visual feedback on their performance. If a blink was detected, the subject saw BLINK? on the screen and received no further feedback. If the subject did not respond in the 1,000-ms interval following an imperative stimulus, the message TOO SLOW appeared on the screen. If the subject made an anticipatory response before the target occurred, or on a catch trial, the message TOO SOON was shown on the screen. The messages EYE ERROR or HAND ERROR were displayed if the subject made the wrong type of response. On eye movement trials, if the trial was completed correctly, the response time (RT) for the trial was displayed in the upper right-hand corner of the screen. The message ERROR was shown if they moved in the wrong direction. On catch trials and detection trials responded to correctly, the message OK was presented on the screen.

In presentations and analyses of the data, we will use the terminology neutral (N), valid (V), and invalid (I) to refer to the relationship between the cue and target location or movement direction. This terminology will be used when referring to the primary task, where the ratio of valid to invalid trials is seven-to-one, as well as to the secondary (probe) task, for which the cues are uninformative and this ratio is one-to-one (see table 13.1). Trials with blinks or with both manual and saccadic responses were excluded from the analyses.

## Results and Discussion

Mean RT as a function of cue condition and task is shown in figure 13.2. A detailed breakdown of the RT results and other dependent variables can be found in table 13.2. The purpose of the primary eye movement task was to encourage subjects to prepare an eye movement in the cued direction. An ANOVA revealed a highly significant effect of cue condition upon correct saccadic RT ($F(2,30) = 45.14, p < .001$).[3] Planned contrasts (LSD = 14.18) revealed significant benefits (V < N) and no costs (N = I). Thus, subjects did prepare to shift gaze direction in accordance with the cues.[4] This permitted more rapid saccades when the prepared response was called for, while preparing the incorrect response was no worse than the nonspecific preparation in the neutral condition. Subjects made an average of 3.24 percent directional errors on saccadic trials. An ANOVA revealed a significant effect of cue condition ($F(2,30) = 3.52, p < .05$), and planned contrasts (LSD = 2.17) revealed that only the overall cuing effect was significant (I > V). There was a significant interaction between cue condition and direction ($F(2,30) = 6.95, p < .005$), which was due to a particularly high error rate (6.33 percent) when a rightward movement was required after a "left" cue.

If OMRH is correct and preparation to make an eye movement to a given location draws attention covertly to that location, there should be a cuing effect for the detection trials. Although an ANOVA revealed a significant effect of cue condition upon manual detection RT ($F(2,30) = 5.87, p < .01$), planned contrasts (LSD = 11.06) revealed that this was due entirely to the neutral condition being faster than the valid and invalid conditions, which did not differ.[5] Apparently subjects are faster at the manual detection task

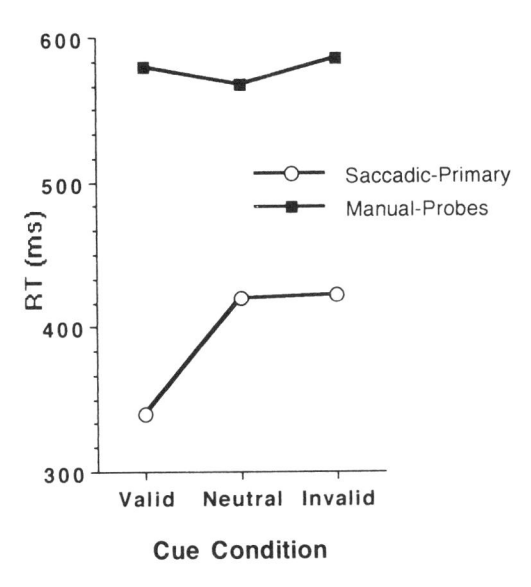

**Figure 13.2** Mean reaction time in experiment 1 as a function of cue condition and task. Open circles show data from the primary saccadic task; closed squares show data from the secondary (probe) detection task.

**Table 13.2** Performance Breakdown for Both Experiments

| | Cue Condition | | | | | |
| | V | | N | | I | |
| Target Direction | L | R | L | R | L | R |
|---|---|---|---|---|---|---|
| *Experiment 1* | | | | | | |
| (Primary) saccadic RT | 341.1 | | 419.8 | | 422.3 | |
| | 344.0 | 338.1 | 430.3 | 409.4 | 417.4 | 427.2 |
| % saccadic errors | 1.83 | | 3.24 | | 4.66 | |
| | 1.55 | 2.12 | 3.58 | 2.91 | 2.98 | 6.33 |
| (Secondary) detection RT | 579.8 | | 567.3 | | 585.5 | |
| | 576.2 | 583.5 | 567.6 | 567.1 | 598.1 | 572.9 |
| % detection omissions | 1.94 | | 2.33 | | 1.57 | |
| | 1.34 | 2.53 | 2.14 | 2.52 | 1.89 | 1.25 |
| *Experiment 2* | | | | | | |
| (Primary) detection RT | 385.6 | | 414.3 | | 428.8 | |
| | 385.0 | 386.3 | 412.9 | 415.8 | 426.3 | 431.3 |
| % detection omissions | 1.29 | | 1.79 | | 2.00 | |
| | 1.29 | 1.28 | 2.04 | 1.54 | 2.64 | 1.36 |
| (Secondary) saccadic RT | 563.5 | | 552.4 | | 549.2 | |
| | 567.3 | 559.8 | 554.8 | 550.1 | 547.9 | 550.4 |
| % saccadic errors | 7.67 | | 6.10 | | 3.98 | |
| | 8.40 | 6.93 | 4.69 | 7.51 | 4.29 | 3.68 |

when they are not preparing to move their eyes in a particular direction, but when they are preparing a saccade, it makes no difference whether the target is presented at the location specified in the prepared program. The overall miss rate on manual trials was 1.95 percent and did not differ across conditions (all Fs < 1).

On catch trials the mean percentage of eye movement responses was 4.44 following neutral cues and 4.53 following "left" and "right" (nonneutral) cues, and the mean percentage of manual responses (false alarms) was 1.6 following neutral cues and 4.1 following nonneutral cues. For neither type of error was the effect of cue condition significant.

This experiment provides no support for a hypothesis in which eye movement preparation to a given region is accompanied by an attentional shift to that region.

## 13.3 EXPERIMENT 2

Klein's (1980) second experiment tested the prediction that when attention was covertly shifted to a location under endogenous control, saccadic eye movements to that location would be facilitated. Arrow cues were used to direct the subject's attention for a highly likely luminance target, and the less likely appearance of an asterisk called for a compatible or incompatible eye movement (normal versus antisaccade). The direction of attention had no effect on saccadic latencies, so it was concluded that covert orienting was not accompanied by (or accomplished by) oculomotor preparation. However, it is possible that the appearance of a salient *visual* event such as an asterisk triggers the rapid and reflexive computation of a saccadic program to fixate the event. Such a program might "overwrite" a preprogrammed eye movement, thus destroying any evidence that a saccade had been prepared to produce the attentional shift.

In experiment 2, we eliminated this possibility by again using auditory imperative signals for the saccadic responses. Each trial began with an attentional cue indicating the location likely to contain a luminance increment requiring a manual response (primary task). On occasional trials (20 percent) an auditory probe stimulus indicated that the subject move his or her eyes to the left or to the right (secondary task). As in Klein (1980) the premise was to get subjects to attend to the cued location and then measure if eye movement latencies were quicker in the attended, rather than in the unattended, direction. The use of auditory and verbal signals to indicate which saccade was required was expected to overcome the objection that in Klein's study any saccade preparation (used to elicit orienting) might have been overwritten when a new saccade program was reflexively computed in response to the visually presented target.

### Method

Due to the similarities between the methods of experiments 1 and 2, only the differences will be described below.

**Subjects** The sixteen subjects, none of whom had participated in experiment 1, were tested in three or four experimental sessions lasting about 1 hour each. One other subject was excluded because of low accuracy.

**Apparatus** The distance from the chin rest to the screen was 60 cm for four subjects and 44 cm for the remaining twelve subjects.

**Stimuli** The first stimulus display was the same as for experiment 1.500 ms after trial initiation, an attentional cue was presented to inform the subject of the location that was likely to contain the detection target. For twelve subjects the cue was either an arrow pointing left or right or a plus sign, each measuring approximately 0.4 degree horizontally and centered at fixation. For the remaining four subjects, the cue was the auditory word *ready*, *left*, or *right* (spoken by "Perfect Paul"). The modality of the cue had no impact on the pattern of results and will not be further discussed. The imperative signals (female voice and luminance increments) were the same as in experiment 1.

**Design and Procedure** In the first session, subjects were exposed to the manual detection trials (with neutral, left, and right cues) and to the saccadic trials (neutral condition only) in separate practice blocks, following which the two tasks were intermixed in a combined practice block as in experiment 1.

There were 144 trials in each dual experimental block (see table 13.1): 96 detection trials, 24 eye movement trials, and 24 catch trials, distributed evenly for left, right, and neutral cues. The attentional cues were 87 percent valid on primary task trials requiring a detection response (the location of the luminance increment matched the direction indicated by the cue 87 percent of the time), whereas they conveyed no information about the direction of the eye movements required on occasional secondary task trials.

The attentional cue (left, right, or neutral) occurred 500 ms after the trial was initiated. The subjects were informed that the most likely location for the target brightening would be the same as the one indicated by the cue. The subject was explicitly instructed to prepare to detect a luminance increment of the target dot indicated by a left or right attentional cue during this warning interval and to do so without shifting gaze from the fixation point. On neutral trials (plus sign or "ready"), the subjects were instructed that a detection response was likely to be made but that the two target locations were equiprobable. The imperative signals were presented 1,000 ms after the cue onset. The subjects were asked to press the response key as quickly as possible without moving their eyes from fixation when the cue was followed by a luminance increment of the left or right dot (primary detection task). On some trials, when the cue was instead followed by a female voice saying "left" or "right," the subjects were instructed to move their eyes as quickly and as accurately as possible to the appropriate left or right dot (secondary eye movement task). On catch trials, no imperative stimulus was presented, and subjects were instructed to refrain from making any ocular or manual responses until the display was turned off.

Visual feedback was the same as in experiment 1 with the following exceptions: when detection trials were completed correctly, the RT for the trial was displayed in the upper-right-hand corner of the screen and on correct eye movement trials, the message OK was presented on the screen.

**Results and Discussion**

Mean reaction time as a function of cue condition and task is shown in figure 13.3. The purpose of the primary detection task was to give subjects incentive to direct their attention in the cued direction. An ANOVA revealed a highly significant effect of cue condition upon mean detection RT ($F(2,30) = 28.8$, $p < .001$). Planned contrasts (LSD = 11.8) revealed significant benefits (V < N) and costs (I > N), demonstrating that subjects were using the cues to direct their attention endogenously. The overall miss rate on detection trials was 1.7 percent, and there were no differences among conditions (all Fs < 1).

If OMRH is correct and covert endogenous shifts of visual attention are accomplished by preparing a saccadic program toward the attended location, then there should be a corresponding cuing effect for the saccadic trials. Although an ANOVA revealed a significant effect of cue condition ($F(2,30) = 3.99, p < .05$), the effect was in the opposite direction to that predicted by OMRH: saccades in the attended direction were significantly slower (LSD =

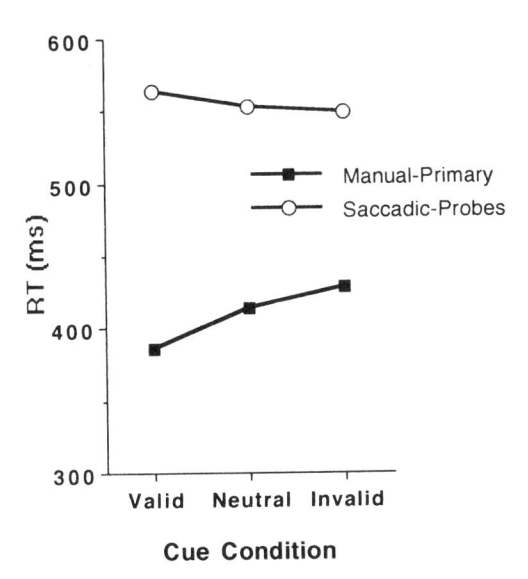

**Figure 13.3** Mean reaction time in experiment 2 as a function of cue condition and task. Closed squares show data from the primary detection task; open circles show data from the secondary (probe) saccadic task.

10.9) than in the unattended direction (or following a neutral cue). The mean rate of directional errors on saccade trials was 5.92 percent. An ANOVA revealed a significant effect of cue condition ($F(2,30) = 4.75, p < .025$), and planned contrasts (LSD = 2.6) revealed a higher error rate when eye movements were required in the attended direction (V > I), which demonstrates that the reverse cuing effect with saccades is not due to a speed-accuracy trade-off.

The interpretation of reverse cuing with saccadic responses that we favor is that in shifting attention, the subject engages in some degree of suppression of the natural tendency to foveate the cued location. Although it might be suggested that what we are seeing here is the effect of inhibition of the oculomotor program that was activated in order to shift attention—as in Rizzolatti et al.'s (1987) premotor theory—we think this view misreads Rizzolatti et al. and is inconsistent with the results of experiment 1. According to Rizzolatti et al. (1987), covert orienting is generated by activating an oculomotor program that is inhibited peripherally, thus preventing overt orienting while leaving the program unchanged. When the inhibition is removed in response to the voice command, the prepared saccade should be initiated faster than one in the opposite direction because the program is still activated. Moreover, in experiment 1, we demonstrated that when subjects are explicitly instructed to prepare an eye movement and yet must refrain from executing it until the imperative signal, it is the prepared movement that is faster, not the opposite one. Therefore, like the OMRH described here, premotor theory predicts that saccades in the attended direction should be faster than those in the unattended direction, and our failure to obtain this result disconfirms both theories.

On catch trials, the mean percentage of eye movement responses was 5.04 following neutral cues and 5.36 following "left" and "right" (nonneutral) cues, and the mean percentage of manual responses (false alarms) was 2.16 following neutral cues and 2.89 following nonneutral cues. For neither type of error was the effect of cue condition significant.

## 13.4 SUMMARY AND CONCLUSION

The oculomotor readiness hypothesis proposed by Klein (1980) claims that endogenous covert orienting of attention is accomplished by preparing to move the eyes to the to-be-attended location. Klein tested two predictions of this, each in a dual-task situation. First, if the subject is attending to a location, eye movements to that location should be facilitated. Second, if the subject is preparing to move his or her eyes to a particular location, the detection of events presented there should be facilitated. Neither prediction was confirmed. Revived interest in the oculomotor readiness hypothesis (cf. Rizzolatti et al. 1987; Shepard, Findlay, and Hockey 1986) encouraged us to conduct two new tests of these predictions; tests not subject to alternative explanations that might apply to Klein's earlier experiments.

The findings reported here continue to provide no support for the OMRH[6] as originally proposed by Klein (1980) and as subsequently endorsed by others (Rizzolatti et al. 1987; Rizzolatti, Riggio, and Sheliga, chap. 9, this volume). On the contrary, the findings provide strong support for the conclusion reached by Klein (1980) and others (Posner 1980; Remington 1980) that endogenous covert orienting is accomplished independent of eye movement programming.

Rafal et al. (1989) provide strong converging evidence for this conclusion. They used endogenous and exogenous cues to direct or prepare eye movements or generate attention shifts. On some trials, the eyes or attention were drawn back to fixation or the saccade preparation was cancelled, and a simple detection target was presented at the previously cued or uncued location. They found that an inhibitory effect (inhibition of return; cf. Posner and Cohen 1984; Maylor and Hockey 1985) accrues to locations that subjects had either planned to fixate or actually had just fixated and that these effects were independent of the nature of the cue. However, when the precues were used to direct attention and the subjects were instructed to keep their eyes fixed, the inhibitory effect was observed following peripheral cues that elicit exogenous orienting, but it was not observed following central cues that elicit endogenous orienting. The set of conditions that produces inhibition of return suggests that it is a consequence of prior saccadic programming. That inhibition of return does not accompany endogenous orienting suggests that such orienting is accomplished without any saccadic programming.

Together with our findings, the literature suggests the following conclusions:

1. There is a tight linkage between saccade execution and covert visual orienting: shifts of attention precede eye movements (Henderson, Pollatsek,

and Rayner 1989) whether the saccades are elicited endogenously (Shepard, Findlay, and Hockey 1986; Subramaniam and Hoffman, 1991) or exogenously (Posner 1980). In other words, overt orienting is preceded by covert orienting

2. Stimulus events that normally elicit eye movements may also attract attention even when the saccadic responses are suppressed. In other words, overt and covert orienting are exogenously activated by similar stimulus conditions.

3. Endogenous covert orienting of attention is not mediated by endogenously generated saccadic programming; in order words, the oculomotor readiness hypotheis (and Rizzolatti et al.'s premotor theory) may be aesthetically appealing, but it appears to be false.

## NOTES

The research reported in this chapter was supported by an NSERC of Canada operating grant to Raymond Klein and most of it was conducted by Amanda Pontefract in partial fulfillment of the requirements for the M. Sc. degree. Preliminary versions of the findings were reported briefly in Klein, Kingstone and Pontefract (1992).

1. DEC-Talk's initiation times for the verbal commands "left" and "right" had been measured by a separate calibration program, and appropriate measures were taken to cancel these delays in the experimental program. After most subjects had been run, we discovered that DEC-Talk's initiation times for the eye movement command signal ("Betty") in the experimental context proper were longer than in isolation (47 ms), and there was an additional delay (23 ms) when the cue ("Paul") had been the verbal instruction "left." Recorded saccadic RTs from the first twelve subjects were adjusted to remove these constant errors. For the last four subjects in each experiment, the timing errors were eliminated by increasing the cue/target stimulus onset asynchrony from 1,000 ms to 1,150 ms. Subsequent analyses revealed that this procedural change had no effect on the pattern of results.

2. Saccades were detected by an algorithm that sought four consecutive samples with a voltage change indicating a velocity of at least 50 degrees per second. For the first twelve subjects saccadic direction and latency were recorded; amplitudes were recorded only for the last four subjects in each experiment.

3. There was a significant interaction between cue condition and movement direction ($F(2,30) = 4.72, p < .05$) that was not present when the neutral condition was excluded from the analysis. The trend was for faster rightward movements in the neutral but not in the other cue conditions.

4. It might be argued that the RT advantage in the valid condition is due to the prior activation of a stimulus pathway or to stimulus expectancy rather than response preparation. The automatic pathway possibility can be ruled out on the basis of data from experiment 2. Four subjects in that experiment received the spoken cues "left", and "right" used here, but signaling the screen location where a visual target, requiring a manual response, was likely to appear. For those subjects the secondary task saccadic latencies (to the words *left* and *right* spoken in a different voice) were not facilitated when the cue and imperative signal matched (matching RT = 566; mismatching RT = 550); indeed, the pattern was the same as for the remaining twelve who received arrow cues. This shows that mere activation of the phonological/lexical pathway by the cue does not result in faster processing of a matching verbal command. The issue of stimulus versus response expectancy cannot be decided purely on the basis of our data. Undoubtedly, subjects might expect the more likely stimulus form, and this might speed its identification. In studies of visual orienting, however, when form and location cuing are combined in a single block of trials, the effects of form are smaller than those of

location (Lambert and Hockey 1986) and much smaller than those observed in this experiment. Moreover, when equiprobable stimuli are assigned to responses with different probabilities, RT is between 20 and 50 ms faster for the stimulus assigned to the more probable response (LaBerge, Legrand, and Hobbie 1969), which suggests that in our experiment response preparation accounts for at least some, and possibly all, of the cuing effect with the saccadic task.

5. There was a significant interaction between target location and cue condition. Detection targets in the left visual field were responded to more rapidly following a leftward cue (valid) than following a rightward cue (invalid), while the reverse was true for right field targets. This trend is not present in the saccadic latencies, which is one piece of evidence that it is not directly related to saccadic programming. An alternative way to describe this interaction is that detection latencies are influenced by oculomotor programming only following preparation to make rightward eye movements (598 > 583). Neither view of the interaction is consistent with OMRH, because it is difficult to conceive of any orienting system in which eye movement preparation is responsible for attentional shifts only toward location in the left visual field or only following rightward preparation. A simple correlation was computed between the eye movement and detection cuing effects following rightward preparation. This analysis revealed that the magnitude of the detection task cuing effect is not significantly correlated with the magnitude of the cuing shown by the eye movement system following rightward preparation ($R(16) = .133, p > .1$). Clearly the degree of rightward saccadic preparation is not related to the speed of processing the detection probes. We believe that this odd finding is spurious.

6. Is it possible to salvage the OMRH in spite of the rather direct negative results reported here? One might suggest that because of their low probability and relatively long response times, the secondary tasks used in each experiment were insensitive to the attentional (E1) and motor (E2) effects which, according to the OMRH, were elicited in these experiments. In response we would point out, as did Klein (1980), that in a variety of complex situations, "improbable secondary tasks have provided sensitive measures of attentional allocation ... (see Kerr 1973 for a review)" (p. 272). Nevertheless, this retort is indirect; a direct demonstration that the low probability secondary tasks we have used can be sensitive to attention and oculomotor preparation would be desirable. An alternative way to salvage the OMRH is to think in dynamic rather than static terms. Suppose that preparing an eye movement is the mechanism for directing attention but that once attention is shifted by this process, the oculomotor readiness need not be maintained. In this case, when attention has been directed to a location, one might not see faster saccades to that location unless one probes for this at the right time. Similarly, when subjects get ready to move their eyes to a location, one might see an effect upon detection efficiency only at the time the program is generated. There would be no point in maintaining the inappropriate attentional shift because all locations are equally likely to contain the target. Such a dynamic explanation is certainly ad hoc and in our view somewhat unlikely. Nevertheless, there is some precedence for a dynamic effect akin to this one—in the time course of involvement of limited capacity mechanisms in the generation of a nonspatial expectancy (McLean and Shulman 1978). It would be straightforward to evaluate the idea by parametric manipulation of the SOA between the cues for the primary tasks and the unlikely probe stimuli in both experiments.

## REFERENCES

Abrams, R. A., and Jonides, J. (1988). Programming saccadic eye movements. *Journal of Experimental Psychology: Human Perception and Performance, 14,* 428–443.

Bryden, M. P. (1961). The role of post-exposural eye movements in tachistoscopic perception. *Canadian Journal of Psychology, 15,* 220–225.

Crawford, T. J., and Muller, H. J. (1992). Spatial and temporal effects of spatial attention on human saccadic eye movements. *Vision Research, 32,* 293–304.

Crovitz, H. F., and Daves, W. (1962). Tendencies to eye movement and perceptual accuracy. *Journal of Experimental Psychology, 63*(5), 495–498.

Festinger, L., Burnham, C. A., Ono, H., and Bamber, D. (1967). Efference and the conscious experience of perception. *Journal of Experimental Psychology Monograph, 74*(4) (whole no. 636), 1–36.

Folk, C. L., Remington, R., and Johnston, J. C. (1992). Involuntary covert orienting is contingent on attentional control settings. *Journal of Experimental Psychology: Human Perception and Performance, 18,* 1030–1044.

Hebb, D. O. (1949). *The organization of behavior: A neuropsychological theory.* New York: Wiley.

Henderson, J. M., Pollatsek, A., and Rayner, K. (1989). Covert visual attention and extrafoveal information use during object identification. *Perception and Psychophysics, 45,* 196–208.

Kerr, B. (1973). Processing demands during mental operations. *Memory and Cognition, 1,* 401–412.

Klein, R. M. (1980). Does oculomotor readiness mediate cognitive control of visual attention? In R. Nickerson (Ed.), *Attention and performance VIII,* 259–276. Hillsdale, NJ: Erlbaum.

Klein, R. M., Kingstone, A., and Pontefract, A. (1992). Orienting of visual attention. In K. Rayner (Ed.), *Eye movements and visual cognition: Scene perception and reading,* 46–65. New York: Springer-Verlag.

LaBerge, D., Legrand, R., and Hobbie, R. K. (1969). Functional identification of perceptual and response biases in choice reaction time. *Journal of Experimental Psychology, 79,* 295–299.

Lambert, A., and Hockey, R. (1986). Selective attention and performance with a multidimensional visual display. *Journal of Experimental Psychology: Human Perception and Performance, 12,* 484–495.

Maylor, E. A., and Hockey, R. (1985). Inhibitory component of externally controlled covert orienting in visual space. *Journal of Experimental Psychology: Human Perception and Performance, 11,* 777–787.

McCormick, P. A., and Klein, R. (1990). The spatial distributon of attention during covert visual orienting. *Acta Psychologica. 75,* 225–242.

McLean, J. P., and Shulman, G. L. (1978). On the construction and maintenance of expectancies. *Quarterly Journal of Experimental Psychology, 30,* 441–434.

Mohler, C. W., and Wurtz, R. H. (1976). Organization of monkey superior colliculus: Intermediate layer cells discharge before eye movements. *Journal of Neurophysiology, 39,* 722–742.

Nissen, M. J., Posner, M. I., and Snyder, C. R. (1978). Relationship between attention shifts and saccadic eye movements. Paper presented at Psychonomics Society, San Antonio, TX., November.

Posner, M. I. (1980). Orienting of attention. *Quarterly Journal of Experimental Psychology, 32,* 3–25.

Posner, M. I., and Cohen, Y. (1984). Components of visual orienting. In H. Bouma and D. Bowhuis (Eds.), *Attention and Performance X,* 531–556. Hillsdale, NJ: Erlbaum.

Posner, M. I., Snyder, C. R., and Davidson, B. J. (1980). Attention and the detection of signals. *Journal of Experimental Psychology: General, 109*(2), 160–174.

Rafal, R. D., Calabresi, P. A., Brennan, C. W., and Sciolto, T. K. (1989). Saccade preparation inhibits reorienting to recently attended locations. *Journal of Experimental Psychology: Human Perception and Performance, 15,* 673–685.

Rayner, K., McConkie, G. W., and Erlich, S. (1978). Eye movements integrating information across fixations. *Journal of Experimental Psychology: Human Perception and Performance, 4,* 529–544.

Remington, R. W. (1980). Attention and saccadic eye movements. *Journal of Experimental Psychology: Human Perception and Performance, 6*(4), 726–744.

Reuter-Lorenz, P. A. and Fendrich, R. (1992). Oculomotor readiness and covert orienting: Differences between central and peripheral precues. *Perception and Psychophysics, 52*(3), 336–344.

Rizzolatti, G., Riggio, L., Dascola, I., and Umiltà, C. (1987). Reorienting attention across the horizontal and vertical meridians: Evidence in favor of a premotor theory of attention. *Neuropsychologia, 25*(1A), 31–40.

Schiller, P. H., and Koerner, E. (1971). Discharge characteristics of single units in superior colliculus of the alert rhesus monkey. *Journal of Neurophysiology, 34,* 920–936.

Schiller, P. H., and Stryker, M. (1972). Single unit recording and stimulation in superior colliculus of the alert rhesus monkey. *Journal of Neuropsychology, 35,* 915–924.

Shepherd, M., Findlay, J. M., and Hockey, R. J. (1986). The relationship between eye movements and spatial attention. *Quarterly Journal of Experimental Psychology, 38A,* 475–491.

Shepherd, M., and Muller, H. (1989). Movement versus focusing of attention. *Perception and Psychophysics, 42,* 146–154.

Shulman, G. L. (1984). An asymmetry in the control of eye movements and shifts of attention. *Acta Psychologica, 55,* 53–69.

Subramaniam, B., and Hoffman, J. E. (1991). Saccadic eye movement and visual selective attention. Paper presented at the Psychonomics Society, San Francisco, CA, November.

Umiltà, C., Riggio, L., Dascola, I., and Rizzolatti, G. (1991). Differential effects of peripheral cues on the reorienting of spatial attention. *European Journal of Cognitive Psychology, 3*(2), 247–267.

Weimer, W. (1977). A conceptual framework for cognitive psychology: Motor theories of the mind. In R. Shaw and J. Bransford (Eds.), *Perceiving, acting and knowing.* Hillsdale, NJ: Erlbaum.

Wurtz, R. H., and Mohler, C. W. (1974). Selection of visual targets for the initiation of saccadic eye movements. *Brain Research, 71,* 209–214.

Yantis, S., and Jonides, J. (1984). Abrupt visual onsets and selective attention: Evidence from visual search. *Journal of Experimental Psychology: Human Perception and Performance, 16,* 121–134.

# 14 Object-Based Attentional Mechanisms: Evidence from Patients with Unilateral Neglect

## Marlene Behrmann and Steven P. Tipper

ABSTRACT  There exists much debate concerning the status of the "neglected" information in patients who omit to report the contralateral information following unilateral brain damage. While some argue that this "neglected" information is processed deeply, others suggest that it is poorly perceived. In this chapter, we show that, under certain conditions, patients with left-sided neglect can process information appearing on the left better than information appearing on the right. Five patients with neglect performed a simple target detection paradigm in two conditions. In the *static* condition, the target appears on either the left or right side of a centrally presented object (barbell). In the *moving* condition, the patients watch the barbell undergoing a 180-degree rotation, and after the barbell is stationary, the target appears in the left or right "end state." Here, the side of space and the side of the object are decoupled: the right and left of the object fall into the left and right hemispace, respectively. In the static condition, performance was significantly worse for left- than for right-sided targets for all patients, while in the moving condition, three patients showed the reverse pattern. Relative to the static condition, in the moving condition, all patients showed significantly poorer performance on the right side and four showed significantly better detection on the left side. These findings suggest that attention cannot be accessing spatial representations solely; rather, the results are consistent with the view that attention is also directed to object-specific representations. We conclude that the attentional deficit in hemispatial neglect may affect processing at more than one level of representation.

## 14.1 INTRODUCTION

### Unilateral Neglect and Nonconscious Processing

Unilateral neglect refers to a rather common neurobehavioral disorder characterized by a failure to respond or orient to stimuli presented contralateral to the brain lesion. Neglect of the contralesional side, more commonly the left side following a right hemisphere lesion, is not confined to perceptual processing; patients may also show a decrease in exploration or in motor movement toward the contralateral side (Watson, Miller, and Heilman 1978) and may even neglect the contralesional side of an "imagined" internal representation in the absence of perceptual input (Bisiach and Luzzatti 1978; also see Bisiach and Vallar 1988, for a detailed overview of the disorder). Numerous interpretations of the deficit underlying neglect have been proposed, some of which have characterized neglect as arising from either a lateralized impairment of attention (Posner 1988; Riddoch and Humphreys 1987) or an impairment of spatial representation (Bisiach and Luzzatti 1979). Indeed, in more recent work, Bisiach (1993) has suggested that deficits of attention and deficits of representation are not alternative interpretations of neglect; rather, they are inextricably linked, with attention being superordinate to representation. Irrespective of the interpretation of the mechanisms giving rise to neglect, one outstanding question that has attracted much recent interest concerns the extent to which the "unreported" information from the left side is processed in patients with left-sided neglect. Like other neuropsychological phenomena such as amnesia, blindsight, and agnosia (Milner 1992; Schacter, McAndrews, and Moscovitch 1988), neglect appears to be a particularly suitable phenomenon in which to examine the dissociation between conscious and nonconscious processing of information.

Contrary to early views that the neglected stimulus is abolished or "erased" (Bender 1952; Friedland and Weinstein 1977), many recent studies have demonstrated that neglect patients possess tacit knowledge about information they do not report overtly. For example, examination of the reading errors made by patients with right hemisphere damage suggests that even when information on the left side of letter strings is misread (e.g., *harm* as *farm*), the neglected information is perceived since the paralexic substitutions are of approximately the same length as the target (Behrmann et al. 1990; Ellis, Flude, and Young 1987; Kinsbourne and Warrington, 1962). Further evidence for tacit knowledge of neglected information has been demonstrated by Marshall and Halligan (1988), who presented a neglect patient with two vertically arranged pictures of houses, one of which had flames on the left and one of which did not. Even though the patient judged the houses to be identical, she nevertheless was able to discriminate between them at an implicit level by consistently selecting the intact house as her preferred choice of home (but see Bisiach and Rusconi 1990). Experimental studies examining the dissociation between cognitive processing and conscious awareness of information have also demonstrated that left-sided information is being processed by the patients even if it is not consciously reported. Volpe, LeDoux, and Gazzaniga (1979), for example, presented pairs of stimuli (pictures or written words) to patients who extinguished or neglected the contralateral stimulus. Despite the fact that these patients were poor at naming the left stimulus, they performed remarkably well on a forced-choice same/different judgment task that did not require them to identify the stimulus explicitly.

The discrepancy between the patients' performance on tasks requiring explicit report and on more indirect tasks tapping implicit knowledge has been interpreted as evidence for the view that neglected information is processed implicitly but that this information fails to reach the patients' conscious awareness. This conclusion has been challenged by Farah, Monheit, and Wallace (1991), who have argued that the differences in performance yielded by direct and indirect methods do not necessarily reflect the impaired access to consciousness. Instead, they argued that information on the contralateral side is not fully processed by these patients. The minimal knowledge that is available, may be sufficient to support same/different judgments that can be performed on the basis of degraded visual information, but, it is not sufficient for object identification that requires detailed knowledge of the stimulus. Data addressing the pivotal claim made by Farah, Monheit, and Wallace (1991; see also Farah, chap. 2, this volume)—for example, that contralateral information is not fully processed—is available from a number of recent studies. Berti, et al. (1992), for example, replicated the Volpe, Le Doux, and Gazzaniga study using pairs of photographs of identical objects taken from the same or different viewpoints, pairs of different exemplars of the same object, and pairs of different objects. Despite the fact that their patient, E.M., could not name the left-sided stimuli, she was still able to make same-different judgments on the pairs of objects photographed from different viewpoints, as well as on the pairs of different exemplars of the same object. These results suggest that the patient's responses are not based solely on low-level, impoverished visual representations. Rather, these findings favor the view that the extinguished or neglected information is processed to a categorical level of representation but that this knowledge is either disconnected from consciousness or fails to reach the subject's awareness (Rizzolatti and Berti 1990). Finally, support for the view that neglected information is indeed processed to high levels of representation comes from priming studies in which the primes appear lateralized and the probes appear centrally. For example, in a study by McGlinchey-Berroth et al. (1993), neglect patients made lexical decisions to centrally located targets (e.g., "nose") following the presentation of lateralized picture primes to the left or right sides that were either related (e.g., *eye*) or unrelated to the target word (e.g., *anchor*). In these patients, lexical decision reaction time was facilitated equally by a related prime presented to the neglected left side as by a prime presented to the intact right side. This was so despite the fact that these same patients were unable to identify the left-sided pictures on a subsequent matching task. A similar finding of facilitation from so-called neglected stimuli on subsequent targets was reported by Berti and Rizzolatti (1992) in a task in which reaction time (RT) to categorize a picture (e.g., a chicken as an animal) was measured. Categorization performance was facilitated by the presence of the identical picture (a chicken) or by a picture of another member of the same category (e.g., a duck), which appeared to the left of the target even when the presence of the left-sided stimulus was not detected.

By showing that categorical and semantic information from the neglected stimulus is available to the patients, these studies provide compelling evidence in support of the view that neglected information is processed to deep levels of representation. Whether left-sided information is processed normally or as well as right-sided information, however, is still a topic of debate (Farah, Monheit, and Wallace 1991; Farah, chap. 2, this volume). Leaving this debate aside for a moment, one question that remains unanswered is whether there are any conditions under which left-sided information is reported better than right-sided information by patients with neglect. Several newly developed paradigms in cognitive psychology might be used to address this issue.

## Attention to Objects in Moving Displays

Recent studies in cognitive psychology have shown that when attention is allocated to a stationary object that then moves, attention is bound to the object and accompanies it to the new location. For example, Kahneman, Treisman, and Gibbs (1992, experiment 4) presented normal subjects with displays in which letters appeared in the center of each of two displayed geometric figures (e.g., a square and a triangle). When the letters disappeared, the two figures moved along separate trajectories and then stopped. Thereafter, a single letter reappeared in one of the two figures, and the subjects were cued for report. Letter naming was faster when the letter that appeared in the figure at report time was the same as (rather than different to) that which had appeared in the figure prior to moving. The facilitation from the co-occurrence of the letter and the geometric shape is explained in terms of a temporary perceptual memory or "object file" that binds together attributes of an attended object. This object file integrates visual information across time to represent a unitary moving object, linking the present state of an object to its preceding history (Kahneman and Treisman 1984; Treisman 1992).

Using a slightly different paradigm, Tipper, Driver, and Weaver (1991) have also shown that a previously attended object influences performance when the same object reappears, even when it reappears at a new location. In their study with normal subjects, attention was initially cued to one of two objects (black squares) appearing on either side of a central fixation point. After a short delay, the objects rotated around the fixation point, and when they became stationary once again, on two-thirds of the trials, after an unpredictable stimulus onset asynchrony (SOA), a probe (a small white square) appeared in one of the two objects. The probe appeared on either the object that had been cued initially or the uncued object, both of which now occupied new locations. Reaction time (key press) to detect the probe was measured. The subjects were significantly slower to respond to the probe in the cued than in the uncued object, even when the cued object no longer occupied the location at which the attentional cueing had originally occurred. These results show that attention (and its inhibitory counterpart) can move along with the object rather than remain tied to the spatial location to which attention was originally directed. The finding that inhibition of return (Posner and Cohen 1984) or dynamic inhibition can be associated with an object even when it moves through space has been replicated in a number of experiments (Tipper 1992; Tipper, Brehaut, and Driver 1990; Tipper et al. 1994).

## Attentional Allocation and Moving Stimuli in Neglect

Given that attention (and inhibition) can move dynamically with an object rather than remain tied to a spatial location, will we also see residual effects of previously distributed attention in patients with hemineglect when the stimulus moves to a different location? If attention can accompany an object, then we might expect that when a previously attended right-sided stimulus moves into the neglected left side, detection will be enhanced relative to a stimulus that remains stationary on the left side. Conversely, we might expect that when a previously attended (poorly attended in this case) left-sided stimulus moves into the intact ipsilesional right side of space, detection may be slowed relative to a stimulus that remained stationary on the right side all along.

To test these predictions, we presented an object consisting of two circles joined by a horizontal bar (a barbell) to patients with left neglect following a right hemisphere lesion. The subjects' task was to press a single response key when they detected the presence of the target, a small, white circle that appeared in the center of one of the two circles of the barbell. This simple detection task was performed in two conditions (see fig. 14.1).

In the static condition, the barbell appears on the computer screen and remains stationary; after some delay, the target appears in either the left or right circle. In the moving condition, the barbell appears on the computer screen, remains stationary, and after a short delay, the patients watch it undergoing a 180-degree rotation. After the barbell has reached its final destination, or end state, the target appears in either the left or right circle. The prediction is that in the static condition, because of the left-sided neglect, detection will be poorer for targets appearing in the left circle relative to those appearing in the right circle. More to the point is what happens when the barbell rotates, as in the moving condition. Here, the left side of the barbell moves into the

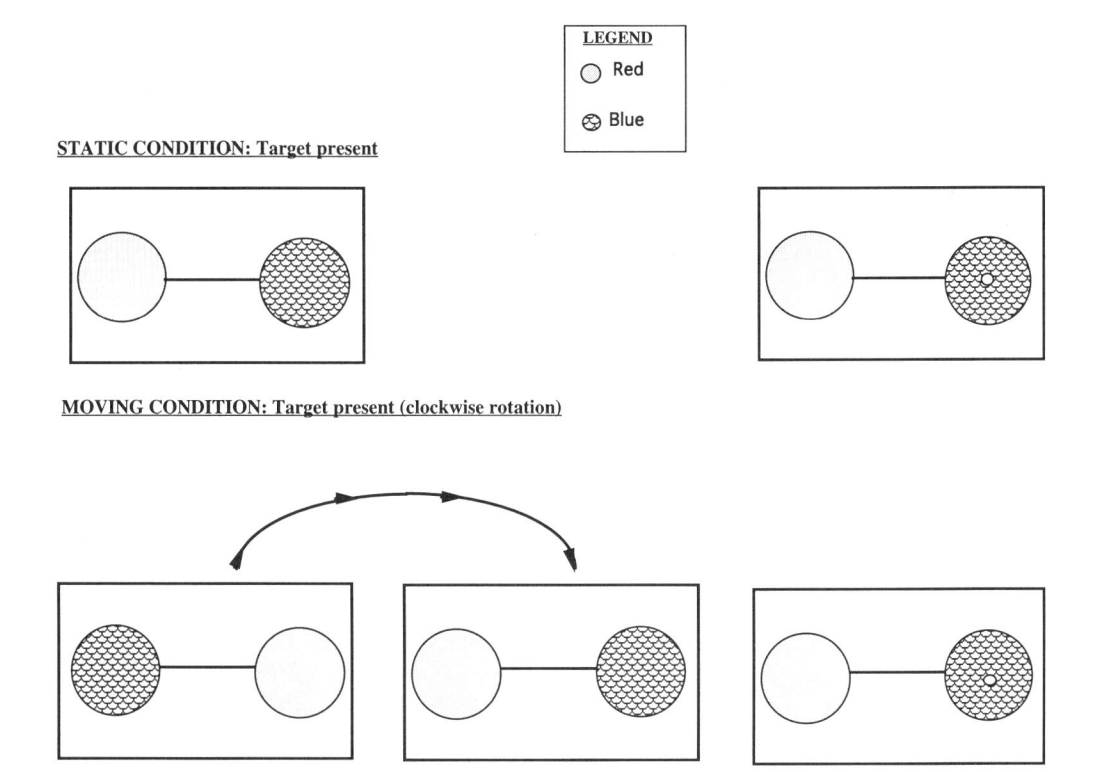

**Figure 14.1** Diagram depicting the barbell in the static and the moving condition.

opposite right side of space, and the right side of the barbell ends up on the left side of space. If attention is distributed only to the left and right sides of space rather than to the left and right of the barbell, then performance should be equal in the static and moving condition. If, however, attention is directed to the left and right sides of an object and attention moves with the object, then the results of the static condition should be reversed: detection should be faster for targets on the left side of space or left end state (the right side of the object ) compared to targets on the right side of space or right end state (the left side of the object).

A test of the costs and benefits associated with the stimulus rotation is to compare directly detection time for targets appearing on the left side of space in the moving and static conditions—that is, when they appear in the left hemispace on either the right of the object (moving condition) or the left of it (static baseline). Similarly, detection time for targets appearing on the right side of space is compared as a function of condition—that is, when they appear in the right hemispace on either the left of the object (moving condition) or the right of it (static baseline). One possible prediction is that if detection is both a function of the original distribution of attention to the object and the physical position in space in which the target appears, then an interaction between condition and side of target should be observed. Detection of left hemispace targets should be better when they appear in the right side of a moving barbell than when they appear in the left side of a stationary barbell. Furthermore, detection of right hemispace targets should be better when they appear in the right side of a stationary barbell than when they appear in the left side of a moving barbell.

## 14.2 METHOD

**Subjects** Five right-handed patients (three female, two male) with right hemisphere lesions documented by computerized tomography (CT) consented to participate in this experiment. All patients (Ps) suffered a right hemisphere infarct with the exception of patient 1 (P1), who had a middle cerebral artery (MCA) aneurysm. The mean age and education level of the patients were 72.8 years (S.D. 8.2) and 12 years (S.D. 2.7), respectively. Bedside testing revealed evidence of unilateral left-sided neglect for all patients. The testing included a line cancellation task (modified Albert's line cancellation task 1973), the Bells test (Gauthier, Dehaut, and Joanette 1989), and a line bisection task.

In the line cancellation task, twenty-one lines, each 3.3 cm in length, appeared on a page, one in the middle and ten scattered randomly on each of the left and right sides. The patients were instructed to mark or check all the lines, and the number of lines omitted per side was calculated. On the Bells test, five target bells in black silhouette appeared intermixed with 40 distractors in each of seven predefined vertical columns (three left, one center, three right), making a total of thirty-five bells and 280 distractors. The maximum number of omissions for the left, center, and right are 15, 5, and 15, respectively. The patients were required to circle the bells, and the number of omission errors was counted separately for the left, center, and right sides (see Gauthier, Dehaut, and Joanette 1989 for exact instructions). Finally, on the line bisection task, the patients were instructed to put a mark through the middle of the horizontal line. In total, the patients bisected four lines: two longer lines of 19.4 cm in length and two shorter lines of 15.2 cm in length. The mean percentage deviation is calculated, with a positive number reflecting rightward deviation and left-sided neglect.

Relevant case history details for the patients, including their scores on the line cancellation, Bells, and line bisection tests are shown in table 14.1.

Figure 14.2 below shows the performance of all five patients on a copying task in which the target was a daisy. The severity of neglect varies across the patients, with P1 showing a mild asymmetry between the number of petals on the left and right and the other patients omitting information on the left side to varying degrees. P4, a patient with severe neglect, initially drew the large daisy, neglecting the left-hand side. He then neglected the entire drawing and drew a second daisy to the right of the first one.

Thirteen elderly subjects (seven male, six female) with a mean age of 68.9 years (S.D. 8.1) and education level of 14.2 years (S.D. 3.1), recruited from the volunteer pool at the Rotman Research Institute, consented to serve as control subjects. All except one were right-handed. No control subject had any history of neurological disease, and none showed neglect on any of the bedside tests for neglect.

**Stimulus**  The stimulus was a barbell (see fig. 14.1), consisting of two circles, each 2.5 cm in diameter, drawn with a black perimeter. One of the circles was colored blue and the other red, and the side of the color was counterbalanced across subjects. The circles were joined by an 8-cm-long black horizontal line. The full horizontal extent of the barbell was 13 cm, and the visual angle subtended by the barbell was 12 degrees with the subject seated 40 cm from the screen. The target was a white circle, 0.75 cm in diameter.

**Table 14.1**  Case History Details of the Five Neglect Patients

| Patient | 1 | 2 | 3 | 4 | 5 |
| --- | --- | --- | --- | --- | --- |
| Initials | M.Z. | E.T. | F.R. | H.R. | R.G. |
| Age | 59 | 74 | 79 | 73 | 79 |
| Sex | F | F | M | M | F |
| Years of education | 16 | 12 | 13 | 10 | 9 |
| Months since onset | 4 | 5 | 37 | 61 | 60 |
| *Test results* | | | | | |
| Line cancellation omissions (left/right) | 0/0 | 0/0 | 10/2 | 0/0 | 0/2 |
| Bell's test—omissions (left/center/right) | 13/0/2 | 8/0/1 | 15/5/4 | 15/0/0 | 15/0/5 |
| Line bisection (%) | .1 | 3.1 | 62 | 44 | 12.1 |

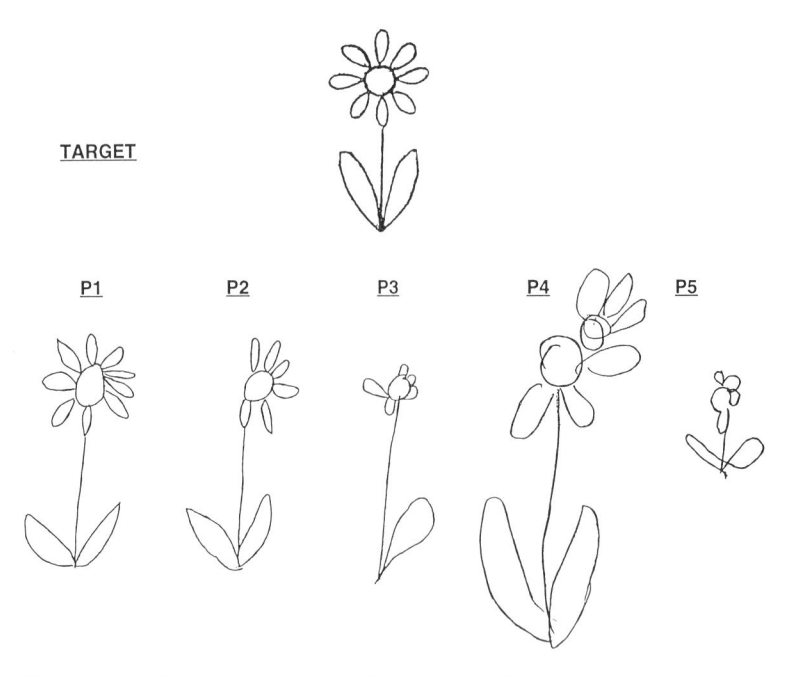

**Figure 14.2** Copying performance of a target daisy by the five neglect patients.

**Procedure** Stimulus presentation and response recording were controlled by an IBM PC-AT computer. The experimenter pressed a start key to initiate a trial. Immediately thereafter, the barbell appeared. In the static condition, the barbell remained static on the screen, and after 2.7 sec, on half the trials (N = 48), the white circular target appeared with equal probability in the center of either the left or the right circle of the barbell. In these target-present trials, the barbell and target stayed on the screen together until a response key was pressed or for an additional 3 sec if there was no response. In the remaining forty-eight target-absent trials, the barbell stayed on the screen alone for a further 3 sec before the trial was terminated. The subject was required to press a single key on a response box when a target was detected. If the subject failed to detect the target, a beep tone was sounded. All subjects used the index finger of their right hand for responding, except for the single left-handed control subject who used the index finger of the left hand. Reaction time (RT) and accuracy of target detection as a function of side were recorded. Subjects completed twenty-four practice trials prior to the experiment.

In the moving condition, the barbell remained static on the screen for 1 sec after which it began a 180-degree rotation (pivoting on the center of the bar) until it reached its final position, or end state. The rotation passed through sixteen intermediate positions, giving the impression of apparent motion. Each position was held for 106 ms, making rotation time 1.7 sec. The total time prior to the appearance of the target in the moving condition (2.7 sec) is equivalent to that of the static condition. On target-present trials (N = 48), immediately after the barbell reached its final end state, the target white circle appeared in either the left or right end state, and the barbell plus target remained on the screen until a response was made or for a further 3 sec. In the target-absent trials (N = 48), the barbell remained on the screen for 3 sec, and then the trial was terminated. The barbell rotated with equal frequency in a clockwise (CW) and an anticlockwise (ACW) direction. The procedure for responding was identical to that in the static condition and feedback (a tone) was provided on error trials. Reaction time and accuracy were obtained for target detection as a function of the direction of movement and of side of appearance of the target (end state). A block of twenty-four practice trials was completed prior to the moving condition.

Patients 1, 2, 4, and 5 had left visual field defects, and for them, the experimental displays were presented in their intact right field. For all other patients and control subjects, the barbell was centered on the middle of the screen. Order of condition was counterbalanced across the normal subjects, although, because of the odd number, the full replication was not completed. Patients 1–3 received the static condition before the moving condition, while patients 4 and 5 received the conditions in the reverse order.

## 14.3 RESULTS

Because of the heterogeneity of neuropsychological cases (see Caramazza and McCloskey 1988 for discussion of neuropsychological research with single subjects) and the possibility of markedly different patterns of neglect across the patients (Driver and Halligan 1991), the patients are treated as parallel single case studies. In contrast, the control data are analyzed as a group, and the means of the median reaction time are analyzed. Although for both patients and controls, analyses of variance are carried out on the RT data, because the error rate was particularly high for P5, statistical analyses were carried out only on her error data and not on her RT data. For all the analyses, the control data are presented before the patient data. The results from the static condition are presented first, followed by those of the moving condition, and finally, an analysis of the relative costs and benefits of the moving condition over the static condition is presented individually for each patient.

**Static Condition**

Figure 14.3 shows the RT and accuracy data (percentage errors) as a function of side of target for the control subjects and for each of the five patients in the static condition. The results for the control subjects are considered first. The control subjects were extremely accurate in their detection of the target, omitting to detect the target in only 1.3 percent of the trials. A one-way ANOVA performed on the mean of the subjects' median RT with side (left/right) as a within-subjects factor showed no significant side difference in RT in the static condition ($F(1,12) = 0.5, p > .10$). These results suggest no fundamental left-right asymmetries in detection ability in normal performance.

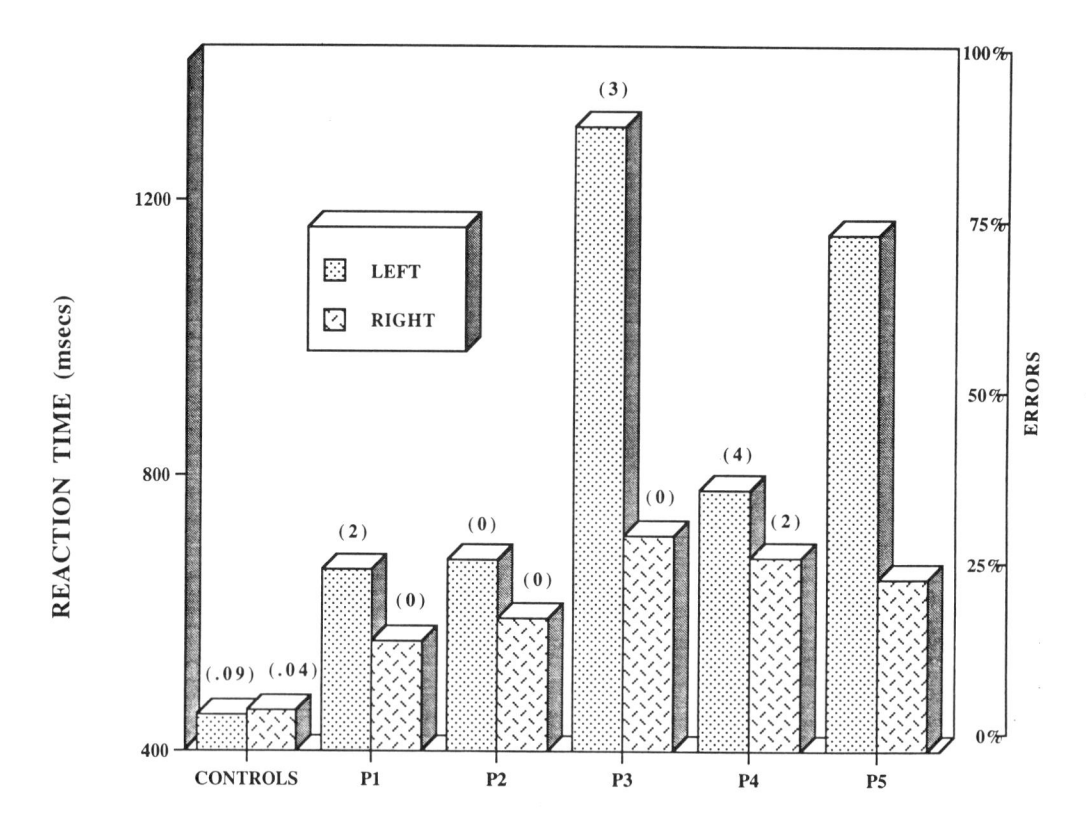

**Figure 14.3** Mean reaction time to detect the targets in the static condition as a function of side for control subjects and for patients. Error proportion for all except P5 are shown in brackets. The Y-axis of percentage errors on right side applies only to P5.

The patient data, however, revealed a markedly different pattern. ANOVAs were conducted for each patient separately. Because of the high variability of the RT data for P2 and P4, prior to the ANOVAs, their raw data were transformed. The inverse square root function was the optimal transformation to normalize the distribution.

The error rates for the first four patients were extremely low, ranging from 0 percent errors (P2) to 6 percent overall errors (P4). A one-way ANOVA with side (left/right) as a random factor showed that detection of left-sided targets was significantly poorer than detection of right-sided targets for all patients [P1 ($F(1,41) = 4.02, p < .05$); P2 ($F(1,41) = 9.5, p < .001$; P3 ($F(1,41) = 12.37, p < .001$; P4 ($F(1,41) = 4.8, p < .05$); P5 $x^2(1) = 12.0, p < .001$]. The inferior performance on the left compared to the right is consistent with the finding that these patients have left-sided neglect and that detection of information on the contralesional left side is poorer than detection of information on the ipsilesional right side.

## Moving Condition

Table 14.2 shows the mean of the median detection data for the normal subjects and the medians for patients as a function of direction of rotation of the barbell and end state in which the target appears. The statistical analysis of these data is presented below the table.

The control subjects made few errors, failing to detect the target on only 3 percent of the trials. For the control subjects, an ANOVA with direction of rotation (CW, ACW) and end state (left/right) as within-subject factors indicated no significant effect of direction of rotation on performance ($F(1,12 = 0.08, p > .5$), no influence of end state on target detection ($F(1,12) = 1.4$, $p > .10$), nor any interaction between direction and end state ($F(1,12) = 1.03$, $p > .10$). These findings suggest that, in normal performance, there are no inherent biases favoring direction of rotation or side of the target. The individual patient data, like those of the normal controls, reveal no significant effect of direction of rotation, nor an interaction between the direction of rotation and end state of the target. Although the data from P2 are suggestive of an interaction with faster detection on the clockwise right condition (536 ms) than the anticlockwise right condition (634 ms), the interaction does not approach significance. Having established that direction of rotation is not a relevant variable, the important result concerns that of the time taken to detect the target as a function of end state. Figure 14.4 shows the RT and accuracy (proportion errors) of target detection in the moving condition as a function of end state, collapsed across direction of rotation.

Although the error rates are still low for the most part, P3 and P4 failed to detect the target on the right end state on 29 percent and 27 percent of the trials, respectively. This is particularly interesting given that these patients have left-sided neglect and that the right side is their "good" side. In the analyses (correct RTs only) the results for P3, P4, and P5 indicated a significant difference in target detection as a function of end state, with better target detection in the left end state than in the right end state [P3 ($F(1,75) = 226.5, p < .0001$); P4 ($F(1,78) = 55.6, p < .001$); P5 $x^2(1) = 31.5, p < .001$]. P1 and P2 demonstrated no significant difference in their ability to detect targets in the right end state compared to the left end state [P1 ($F(1,91) =$

Table 14.2 Target Detection Data as a Function of Direction of Barbell Rotation and End State in the Moving Condition

|  | Clockwise Rotation | | Anticlockwise Rotation | |
| --- | --- | --- | --- | --- |
|  | Left | Right | Left | Right |
| Control subjects | 468 | 458 | 470 | 451 |
| P1 | 513 | 547 | 524 | 540 |
| P2 | 445 | 536 | 444 | 634 |
| P3 | 678 | 1660 | 670 | 1672 |
| P4 | 577 | 1439 | 564 | 1438 |
| P5 (%) | 11 | 69 | 17 | 65 |

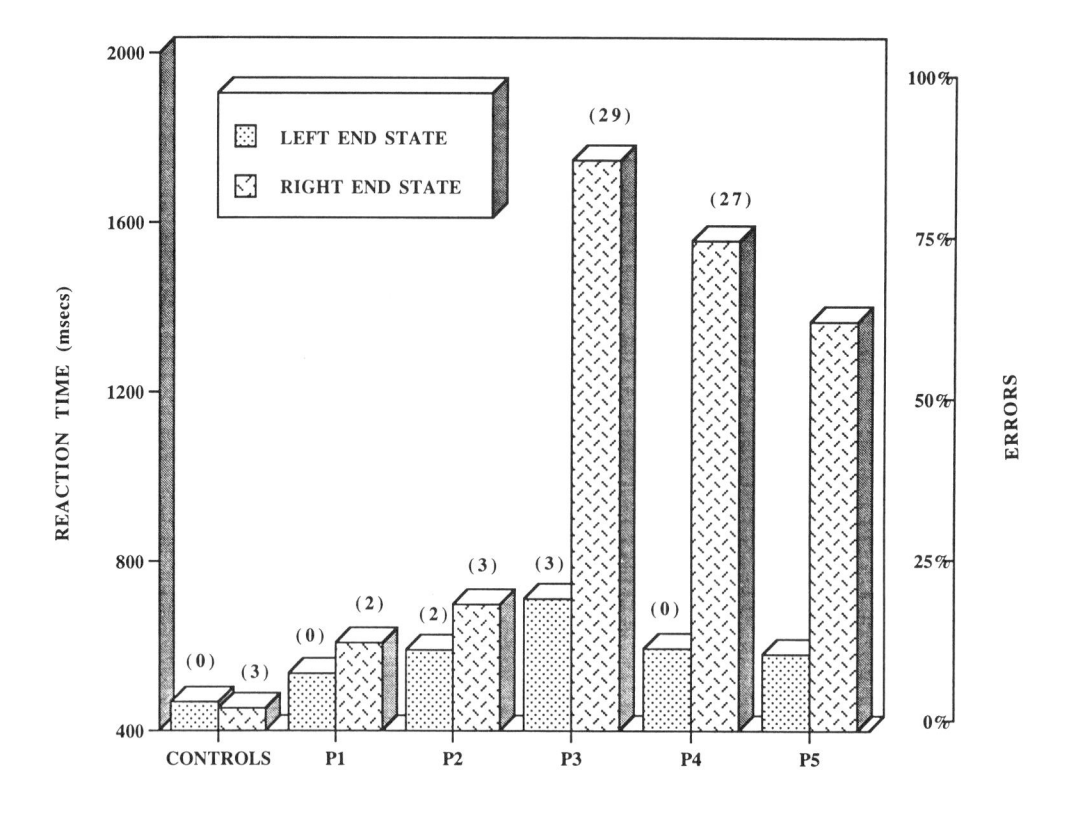

**Figure 14.4** Mean reaction time to detect the targets in the moving condition as a function of end state for control subjects and for patients. Error proportion for all except P5 are shown in brackets. The Y-axis of percentage errors on right side applies only to P5.

$1.99, p > .10$); P2 $F(1,88) = 3.83, p > .20$)], although for both cases, particularly for P2 (see table 14.2), the pattern of data is still in the right direction. The results of the moving condition suggest that, at least in the cases of P3, P4, and P5, it is possible to reverse the pattern found in the static condition. In the case of P1 and P2, even if the variable end state does not reach significance in the moving condition, the data suggest that the inferiority of the left side in the static condition has been neutralized. These findings demonstrate that under conditions of a rotating stimulus, it is possible to obtain better detection for targets appearing on the left side than for those appearing on the right side of space.

## Static versus Moving Condition

The data examined so far illustrate the results for the left- and right-sided targets in the static and the moving conditions separately. The final analysis evaluates the relative costs and benefits in the moving condition compared with the static condition, which serves as the baseline. For the control subjects, a two-way ANOVA with side of target (left/right) and condition (static/moving) as within-subjects variables showed no significant effects for side ($F(1,12) = 0.3, p > .5$) or condition ($F(1,12) = 0.04, p > .5$) on RT, or any interaction between these variables ($F(1,12) = 1.59, p > .2$). These results suggest no side asymmetries in normal performance, nor any difference in target detection for the static and moving conditions. Figure 14.5 shows the data for each patient separately as a function of side of appearance of the target in both the static and moving conditions.

The interaction between the side of target (left/right) and condition was significant for all patients [P1 ($F(1,137) = 4.02, p < .05$); P2 ($F(1,136) = 4.2, p < .05$); P3 ($F(1,118) = 96.1, p < .001$); P4 ($F(1,121) = 30.44, p < .001$); P5 $x^2_{(1)} = 22.4, p < .001$]. All planned comparisons between left and right targets as a function of condition (static/moving) were carried out using Tukey post hoc tests at .05 significance levels, and the significant comparisons are depicted with asterisks on figure 14.5. Post hoc testing reveals that all five patients were slower at detecting the target on the right side (right end state) in the moving condition compared to the static condition. Thus, there is a cost incurred or an inhibition of response when the target appears in the end of the barbell that rotated into the right side of space from the left side. Four of the five patients also showed significantly faster detection of targets appearing on the left side (left end state) in the moving condition relative to the static baseline condition (P1, P2, P3, and P5). Thus, there is also benefit associated with the detection of the target on the left side of space when it appears on the side of the barbell, which rotated in from the right side. P4 showed no significant facilitation in the detection of left-sided targets as a function of condition, although the pattern of data is in the correct direction. These findings suggest a benefit for the targets appearing on the left of space and a cost for the targets appearing on the right of space in the moving condition.

**Summary of Results**

Because there is some variability in the patients' performance, their individual patterns of performance are summarized here. P1 showed a significant left-right difference in the static condition but no significant left-right difference in the moving condition. He did, however, show the interaction between condition and side of target with facilitation to left-sided targets and inhibition to right-sided targets under stimulus rotation. P2 shows the identical results to P1. P3 and P5 both show significantly poorer detection on the left relative to the right in the static condition; this effect is reversed in the moving condition, with better detection on the left end state compared to the right. Both show significant inhibition to right-sided targets and significant facilitation to left-sided targets in the moving condition compared to the static condition. Finally, P4 detected left-sided targets significantly more slowly than right-sided targets in the static condition. He also showed the reverse pattern (left faster than right) in the moving condition and inhibition to right-sided targets in the interaction. He did not, however, show the

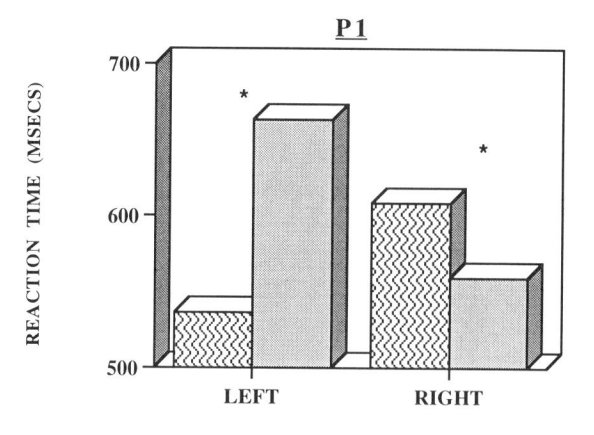

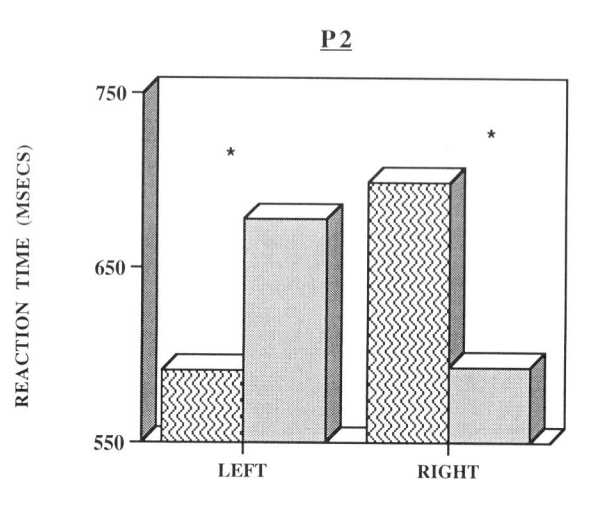

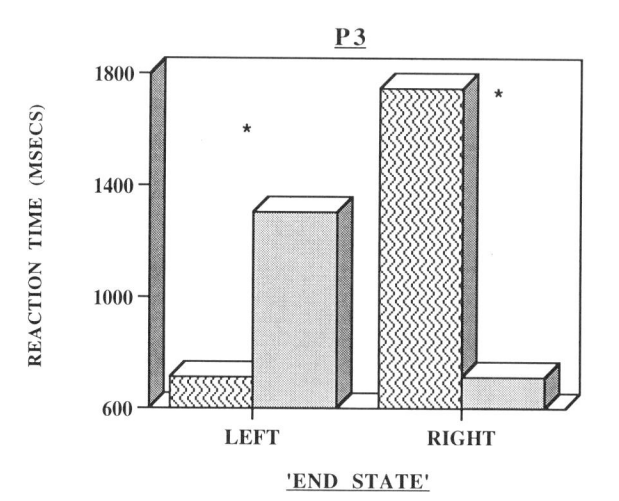

## P1

**REACTION TIME (MSECS)**

'END STATE' — LEFT, RIGHT

## P2

**REACTION TIME (MSECS)**

'END STATE' — LEFT, RIGHT

## P3

**REACTION TIME (MSECS)**

'END STATE' — LEFT, RIGHT

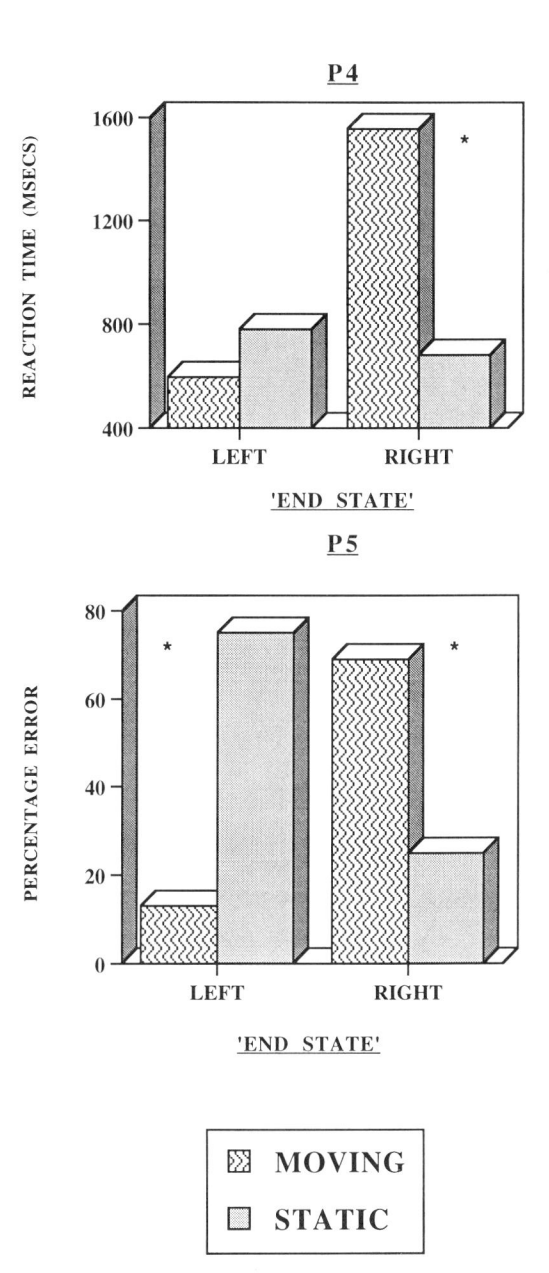

**Figure 14.5** Mean reaction time or errors to detect the targets as a function of end state and of condition for each patient plotted individually. Asterisks indicate a significant comparison on post hoc tests.

facilitation for the left-sided target in the moving condition over the static baseline data.

In sum, there are some individual differences in performance. What is common to all the patients, however, is the left-sided inferiority in the static condition and the poorer detection or inhibition of response time to a right-sided target when it appears on the end of the barbell that originated on the left side of space. Only three of the patients show the significant reverse pattern in the moving condition (P3, P4, and P5), and only four of the five patients (P1, P2, P3, P5) show the facilitation for targets on the left in the moving condition relative to the static condition.

## 14.4 DISCUSSION

The experiments conducted here examined the ability of patients with left unilateral neglect to detect a single target that appeared in the center of either of the right or left circles of a barbell. In the static condition, the left and the right of the barbell corresponded to the left and right of space, whereas in the moving condition, by rotating the barbell 180 degrees, the left and right of the barbell were decoupled from the left and right of space. The results revealed that target detection on the contralateral side of space was poorer than on the ipsilesional side. The major finding, however, was that under certain conditions, target detection on the contralateral left side may be better than on the ipsilesional right side. This latter result is at odds with most current interpretations of hemispatial neglect, which argue that the deficit in attention is related to the left and right sides of space.

One interpretation of visual neglect is that it reflects a deficit of attentional orienting systems. Most models of attentional orienting assume that attention has access to and operates in environment-based coordinates. The usual analogy adopted by these models is that of an attentional spotlight (Posner 1980) or "zoom lens" (Eriksen and Yeh 1985) that moves among different spatial loci. The processing of information within the attentional beam is facilitated relative to information outside the attended region. According to these models, in the case of unilateral neglect, attention is not directed equally to both sides of the environment-based representations. Consequently, stimuli on the one side of space (contralesional) are neglected. Clearly, the results reported here with better detection on the left than the right under some conditions cannot be accounted for by a model proposing that attention has access only to environment-based representations. Such a model would predict that stimuli on the left would always be neglected independent of object motion.

One possible interpretation of the left-sided enhancement is that the moving condition provides an attentional cue to the patients. Studies with patients with left neglect have shown that these patients orient early and automatically to the right side (D'Erme et al. 1992; Gainotti, D'Erme, and Bartolomeo 1991; Làdavas, Petronio, and Umiltà 1990; Riddoch and Humphreys 1987) and that they then have difficulty disengaging their attention from that side (Posner et al. 1984). In the barbell experiment, at the beginning of a trial, attention may be drawn to the right side of the barbell. In static displays, when a target is presented on the left, it is harder to detect because of the magnetic appeal of the right (Gainotti, D'Erme, and Bartolomeo 1991) or the problems disengaging from the right side of the object (Posner et al. 1984). When the barbell rotates 180 degrees, attention, which is engaged on the right side of the object, may be dragged along with the right side of the object. Hence, when the target is presented on the left, detection is faster because attention is oriented to that location. The rotating stimulus acts as an attentional cue, which the patients may exploit. The finding that neglect patients can take advantage of cues for volitionally deploying their attention has been demonstrated on several occasions. In a classic study using a simple target detection task with patients with neglect, single targets appeared on the left or right side, and RT to detect the target was measured (Posner et al. 1984). A cue that preceded the appearance of a target indicated the future location of the target (valid), indicated an alternative location (invalid), or conveyed no localizing information (neutral). Patients with neglect were significantly faster at detecting the presence of the left-sided target in the valid condition when the cue correctly indicated its location relative to the neutral condition, showing that these patients can take advantage of informative cues (Riddoch and Humphreys 1983). It is possible, therefore, that in our study, better performance to left-sided targets in the moving condition is a consequence of attentional cueing. Poorer performance to the right-sided targets and the magnitude of this effect (see fig. 14.5), however, cannot be accounted for by a view that assumes that attention is always drawn or biased to the right side of space. Such a view would not predict the inhibition to right-sided information in the moving condition; in fact, some studies have suggested that because of the strong rightward orientation, patients with neglect respond to information on the right-side of space even better than normal subjects (Kinsbourne 1987; Làdavas, Petronio, and Umiltà, 1990).

An alternative interpretation of these findings, and one we favor, can account for both the left-sided facilitation and the right-sided inhibition. This interpretation proposes that, in addition to accessing environment-based representations, attention also accesses object-based representations. It is this object-based attentional mechanism that gives rise to the counterintuitive pattern obtained in the experiments. The attentional deficit may affect both environment- and object-based representations in the following way. During visual processing of a scene, attention may be deployed in a spatial reference frame with left and right sides defined by the midline of the environment or scene (Feldman 1985; Hinton 1981). Within this spatial reference frame, information falling in the hemispace to the left of the midline will be neglected. This finding is not contentious, and the term *hemispatial neglect* is generally used to describe the performance of these patients. In addition to this spatial or environment reference frame, however, attention may also be deployed in a set of coordinates aligned with and intrinsic to the object itself in an object-centered (Marr 1982; Marr and Nishihara 1978) or a "perceptual-unit-centered" frame (Bisiach 1993). When attention is deployed in this frame, information appearing to the left of the midline of the object may be attended less well than information to the right of the object's midline.

When the barbell appears on the screen initially and remains static, attention is distributed to both the right and the left of space and the right and left of the object (barbell) itself. In the static condition, left and right are defined with respect to both the sides of the object (barbell) and the sides of space. These two variables are decoupled in the moving condition when the left of the barbell appears in the right side of space and the right of the barbell appears in the left side of space. When the compromised left side of the object moves into the intact right side of space, the poor attention is carried with it and so, notwithstanding the fact that the target is in the "good" side of space, detection is inhibited. When the well-attended right side of the object moves into the left side of space, detection is facilitated relative to the static condition. Thus, these data are consistent with the view that visual attention is not directed to spatial position alone but may also be directed to object tokens or representations (Kahneman, Treisman, and Gibbs 1992; Kanwisher and Driver 1992).

## Object-Based Attentional Mechanisms and Unilateral Neglect

Several lines of evidence supporting an object-based mechanism are available from studies with both normal subjects (Kahneman, Treisman, and Gibbs 1992; Tipper, Brehaut, and Driver 1990; Tipper, Driver, and Weaver 1991) and brain-damaged patients. Probably the most dramatic demonstration of the object-based effect in the neuropsychological literature to date comes from Driver and Halligan (1991), but additional affirmative evidence is provided by Caramazza and Hillis (1990a, 1990b) and by Young, Hellawell, and Welch (1992). Driver and Halligan (1991) tested their subject, P.P., on a same-different judgment task using vertically elongated nonsense shapes that were bottom heavy. When the two stimuli were different, the point of difference appeared with equal probability on the left and the right of the stimulus. The stimuli were presented in two conditions: either upright, in which the two stimuli were both vertically oriented (left of the stimulus coincided with the left from the viewer's perspective), or both tilted 45 degrees. In this latter condition, the viewer- and object-based frame are placed in opposition; the point of difference between the stimuli might fall on the left with respect to the object itself but on the right side of space from the viewer's perspective. P.P. was significantly poorer at detecting the difference when it appeared on the left than on the right of the object in the upright condition. More critical was the finding that P.P. still failed to detect the point of difference on a number of trials when it fell on the left of the object, even when the critical information was now on the right side of space. These data suggest that neglect occurs for information appearing on the left of the object independent of its spatial location.

Despite the affirmative evidence, other studies have suggested that neglect is based on environmental coordinates rather than on object-centered representations. For example, Farah et al. (1990) failed to find object-centered neglect in a study in which pictures of common objects were presented to patients with neglect. Within the boundaries of these pictures, letters were evenly distributed in each quadrant, and the patients were required to report the letters. The object frame of reference was decoupled by rotating the stimulus away from the viewer's midline. The findings suggested that neglect was determined by environmental or by viewer coordinates; letters to the left of the viewer's center were neglected independent of the orientation of the drawing. There was no effect of the object frame itself; letters to its left and right were reported equally well.

Recently, Behrmann and Moscovitch (1994) have attempted to elucidate the conditions under which object-centered effects are found. They conducted experiments similar to those of Farah et al. (1990) except that instead of reporting letters, subjects reported colors that appeared on the boundary or outline of the object. The requirement of naming the colors used to create the contours of the object ensured that attention was directed towards the object. In the Farah et al. study, it could be argued that the drawings are irrelevant to the task of identifying letters, and so were ignored. In addition to the drawings of familiar objects used by Farah et al., Behrmann and Moscovitch also had subjects report the colors from symmetrical and asymmetrical block capital letters. The result showed that object-centered neglect could be observed in this task but that it only appeared for the asymmetrical letters.

The interpretation proposed by Behrmann and Moscovitch is that a possible determinant of the object-based effect is whether the stimulus has an intrinsic handedness or an asymmetry in its representation. In these cases, it is necessary to mark the differences in the object in some way, to define the parts of the object relative to a midline axis and to maintain the absolute left and right of the object. In the case of asymmetrical letters, the left and right of the stimuli have different internal representations. For this type of object where the left and right sides must be marked and then attention directed separately to each side of the central axis, it is possible to see object-based neglect. In the case of the common objects, there is no canonical left-right; the tail of the cow might be on the left if the cow is facing right or on the right if the cow is facing left. It is not critical, therefore, to maintain the distinctive left and right of these objects. The argument applies equally to symmetrical letters of the alphabet, where there are no intrinsic left-right asymmetries that must be retained.

The observation that neglect arises in object-centered coordinates in the barbell experiment appears to be at odds with this view of intrinsic handedness since the barbells are essentially symmetrical. According to many theories of reference frames, however, it is precisely in this situation where an object frame serves its major purpose (Marr and Nishihara 1978; Plaut and Farah 1990). Since changes in the derived description of the visual image come about with movement of the object or the viewer, a representation idiosyncratic to a specific viewpoint is unstable. Coding the spatial structure of an object with respect to its own intrinsic frame therefore offers a more stable format in which to represent object structure. Thus, in situations in which the object moves, as in the case of the barbells, orientation-invariant object coordinates are essential for maintaining the canonical left and right of the object.

**Attentional Deficit in More Than One Frame of Reference**

All studies that have shown that attention (and neglect) may be tied to object-specific representations have also shown that attention (and neglect) is tied to spatial representations. For example, in P1 and P2, the neglect of the left side of space is so strong (see figure 14.4) that the benefit from the right side of the object is not powerful enough to overcome the fundamental neglect of the left side of space. In other words, the results suggest that both object-based and space-based attentional mechanisms may be operating. Whether these two forms of attentional mechanisms operate independently or interactively remains an open issue.

Findings suggesting independence of these mechanisms comes from the results by Tipper, Weaver, and Houghton (1994) in experiments using the paradigm in which the inhibition of return to both objects and space was evaluated. The results show that there is a cost in RT to detect a previously cued object both when it moves into a new location (object-based inhibition of return) and when it reappears in the original location in which it was cued (space-based inhibition of return). Similarly, Egly, Driver, and Rafal (1994), in a paradigm in which subjects have to shift their attention from one location to another or shift their attention from one object to another, showed that patients with right parietal lesions had more difficulties disengaging attention contralesionally than ipsilesionally (space) but also that they had difficulties switching attention between objects. However, the space and object cost effects did not interact.

It appears that attention may operate (possibly independently) at several levels of representation. Following brain damage, the attentional deficit or neglect may then be observed at more than one of these levels simultaneously (Caramazza and Hillis 1990b). How might this occur? It is generally acknowledged that during visual processing, the initial description of the visual image is represented relative to a spatiotopic frame of reference (Marr 1982; Marr and Nishihara 1982). This level of representation provides the most concrete perceptual description of the external world. It is also generally accepted that the object-based frame is derived from the initial, spatial coding by redescribing the spatiotopic input relative to a more abstract frame centered on object axes (Marr 1977; Marr and Nishihara 1978). Thus, in the course of processing a visual stimulus, there is a hierarchy of levels of representation, with each subsequent stage reflecting a progression of abstraction from the physical stimulus parameters to the canonical representation. Although these stages may be computed in parallel (Hinton 1981), there is still some advance lead for the spatiotopic frame, and it is from this that the object-based frame is derived.

It is reasonably straightforward to apply this hierarchical view to account for neglect in the following way. When attention is distributed during the initial registration of the stimulus, less attention is directed to the left than to the right of the visual image. Thus, within this concrete, spatiotopic representation, information appearing on the left is ignored relative to information appearing on the right. When the object is redescribed in the more abstract format, it is once again subject to inspection. At this stage, attention may be directed to the abstract image, with the left and right sides again receiving differential distributions of attention. The generally accepted theories of neglect that propose an underlying attentional disruption can then account for these findings fairly easily. For example, during the inspection of the derived object-centered representation, patients may be unable to disengage their attention from the intact right side (Posner et al. 1984; Posner 1988) and the "extinction-like" pattern may occur in object-centered coordinates (Làdavas, Petronio, and Umiltà 1990). Support for this conceptualization comes from findings from several studies that show that neglect may be observed for perceived stimuli as well as for the left side of abstract, internal mental representations (Bisiach 1993; Bisiach and Luzzatti 1978; Bisiach, Luzzatti, and Perani 1979).

The coexistence of neglect in multiple frames simultaneously suggests that more than one frame of reference is constructed on any particular task and that the attentional deficit may affect processing in more than one frame at any one time (Calvanio, Petrone, and Levine 1987; Caramazza and Hillis 1990a, 1990b). It is possible, however, that although multiple levels of representation are necessarily produced, neglect may not be observed on all frames of reference simultaneously. Rather, the task demands determine what frame of reference is controlling action, and attention, which is necessary to control selective action, may be directed to that particular frame (Tipper 1992). Evidence that attentional mechanisms can have selective access to particular forms of internal representation has recently been demonstrated by Tipper, Weaver, and Houghton (1994). Inhibition of distracting objects was selectively directed toward particular properties of the object. Thus, when locating targets, inhibition was directed to the spatial locus of the distractor. In contrast, when identifying targets, inhibition was selectively directed to the identity of the distractor. Similarly, in neglect, we predict that object-centered effects will be observed only when the behavioral goals of the experimental task require that attention is directed to object-centered representations. Tasks that require access to only environmental-based representations will not show object-centered effects even though objects are present in the display. These predictions, based on the idea that behavioral goals in an experimental task will determine what representations are accessed by attention (Allport 1987) and hence what frame of reference neglect will take, are yet to be tested.

**Concluding Remarks**

The purpose of this chapter has been to address the level of representation at which unilateral neglect arises. Until recently, the prevailing view was that, during visual processing, attention was distributed by a location or an environment-based mechanism. The experiments we conducted demonstrated that, in addition to this space-based mechanism, attention may also access object tokens or object-specific representations. It is this latter type of attention that mediates the paradoxical finding that targets may be detected better on the left than on the right under some circumstances in some patients with neglect. The view that neglect operates over spatial representations is well accepted. The findings from this study suggest that attention is not solely distributed in location- or spatial-based coordinates. Rather, the empirical results suggest that information may be coded in more than one map simultaneously and that, depending on the action required by the task, attention may select and operate at a particular level of representation. In the case of neglect, then, when attentional processing is disrupted through brain damage, the deficit may affect the left side of whatever representation is currently being selected and used.

## NOTES

This research was supported by grants from the Natural Sciences and Engineering Research Council to both M.B. and S.T. and by a Medical Research Council Scholarship to M.B. We thank Arloene Burak, Rhonda Feldman, and Bruce Weaver for their assistance with this research and Asher Koriat, Morris Moscovitch, Mike Mozer, and David Plaut for the many helpful discussions.

1. We discuss our results in terms of attention being initially directed to the right side of an object. It is possible, however, that the barbell displays are perceived as two separate objects: a blue circle to the left and a red circle to the right, for example. For the present purposes, it is not relevant whether the display is perceived as two separate objects or a single object. In either case, attention is associated with dynamic object-centered representations, and so this contrast is of little importance to the central issue of distinguishing between environment- and object-centered frames of reference in attention and neglect. Since the issue is of relevance to determining the specifics of the representations being accessed, we are conducting an experiment with neglect patients in which the two ends of the barbell are not connected and rotate independently.

## REFERENCES

Albert, M. L. (1973). A simple test of visual neglect. *Neurology, 23*, 658–664.

Allport, A. (1987) Selection for action: Some behavioural and neurophysiological considerations of attention and action. In H. Heuer and A. F. Sanders (Eds.), *Perspectives on perception and action*. Hillsdale, NJ: Erlbaum.

Behrmann, M., and Moscovitch, M. (1994). Object-centered neglect in patients with unilateral neglect: Effects of left-right coordinates of objects. *Jorunal of Cognitive Neuroscience, 6* (1), 1–16.

Behrmann, M., Moscovitch, M., Black, S. E., and Mozer, M. (1990). Perceptual and conceptual mechanisms in neglect: Two contrasting case studies. *Brain, 113* (4), 1163–1183.

Bender, M. B. (1952). *Disorders in perception*. Springfield: Charles C. Thomas.

Berti, A., Allport, A., Driver, J., Dienes, Z.; Oxbury, J., and Oxbury, S. (1992). Levels of processing for visual stimuli in an "extinguished" field. *Neuropsychologia, 30* (5), 403–415.

Berti, A., and Rizzolatti, G. (1992). Visual processing without awareness: Evidence from unilateral neglect. *Journal of Cognitive Neuroscience, 4* (4), 345–351.

Bisiach, E. (1992). Understanding consciousness: Clues from unilateral neglect and related disorders. In A. D. Milner and M. Rugg (Eds.), *The neuropsychology of consciousness*. London: Academic Press.

Bisiach, E. (1993). The Twentieth Bartlett Memorial Lecture: Mental representation in unilateral neglect and related disorders. *Quarterly Journal of Experimental Psychology, 46A* (3), 435–446.

Bisiach, E., and Luzzatti, C. (1978). Unilateral neglect of representational space. *Cortex, 14,* 129–133.

Bisiach, E., Luzzatti, C., and Perani, D. (1979). Unilateral neglect, representational schema and consciousness. *Brain, 102,* 609–618.

Bisiach, E., and Rusconi, M. L. (1990). Break-down of perceptual awareness in unilateral neglect. *Cortex, 26,* 643–649.

Bisiach, E., and Vallar, G. (1988). Hemineglect in humans. In F. Boller and J. Grafman (Eds.), *Handbook of neuropsychology,* vol. 1. Amsterdam: North Holland.

Calvanio, R., Petrone, P. N., and Levine, D. N. (1987). Left visual neglect is both environment-centered and body-centered. *Neurology, 3,* 1179–1183.

Caramazza, A., and Hillis, A. E. (1990a). Internal spatial representation of written words: Evidence from unilateral neglect. *Nature, 346,* 267–279.

Caramazza, A., and Hillis, A. E. (1990b). Levels of representation, co-ordinate frames, and unilateral neglect. *Cognitive Neuropsychology, 7,* 391–455.

Caramazza, A., and McCloskey, M. (1988). The case for single patient studies. *Cognitive Neuropsychology, 5* (5), 517–528.

D'Erme, P., Robertson, I., Bartolomeo, P., Daniele, A., and Gainotti, G. (1992). Early rightwards orienting of attention on simple reaction time performance in patients with left-sided neglect. *Neuropsychologia, 30* (1), 989–1000.

Driver, J., and Halligan, P. W. (1991). Can visual neglect operate in object-centered co-ordinates? An affirmative single-case study. *Cognitive Neuropsychology, 8,* 475–496.

Egly, R., Driver, J., and Rafal, R. D. (1994). Shifting visual attention between objects and locations: Evidence from normal and parietal-lesion subjects. *Journal of Experimental Psychology: General.* In press.

Ellis, A. W., Flude, B., and Young, A. W. (1987). "Neglect dyslexia" and the early visual processing of letters in words and nonwords. *Cognitive Neuropsychology, 4,* 439–464.

Eriksen, C. W., and Yeh, Y. (1985). Allocation of attention in the visual field. *Journal of Experimental Psychology: Human Perception and Performance, 11* (5), 583–597.

Farah, M. J., Brunn, J. L., Wong, A. B., Wallace, M. A., and Carpenter, P. A. (1990). Frames of reference for allocating attention to space: Evidence from the neglect syndrome. *Neuropsychologia, 28* (4), 335–347.

Farah, M. J., Monheit, M. A., and Wallace, M. A. (1991). Unconscious perception of "extinguished" visual stimuli: Reassessing the evidence. *Neuropsychologia, 29* (10), 949–959.

Feldman, J. A. (1985). Four frames suffice: A provisional model of vision and space. *Behaviour and Brain Sciences, 8,* 265–289.

Friedland, R. P., and Weinstein, E. (1977). Hemi-inattention and hemisphere specialization: introduction and historical review. In E. A. Weinstein and R. P. Friedland (Eds.), *Advances in neurology,* vol. 18. New York: Raven Press.

Gainotti, G., D'Erme, P., and Bartolomeo, P. (1991). Early orientation of attention toward the half space ipsilateral to the lesion in patients with unilateral brain damage. *Journal of Neurology, Neurosurgery and Psychiatry, 54*, 1082–1089.

Gauthier, L., Dehaut, F., and Joanette, Y. (1989). The Bells test: A quantitative and qualitative test for neglect. *International Journal of Clinical Neuropsychology, 11* (2), 49–54.

Hinton, G. (1981). A parallel computation that assigns canonical object-based frames of reference. Proceedings of the International Joint Conference on Artificial Intelligence, Vancouver, Canada.

Kahneman, D., and Treisman, A. (1984). Changing views of attention and automaticity. In R. Parasuraman, R. Davies and J. Beatty (Eds.), *Varieties of Attention*, 29–61. San Diego: Academic Press.

Kahneman, D., Treisman, A., and Gibbs, B. J. (1992). The reviewing of object files: Object specific integration of information. *Cognitive Psychology, 24*, 175–219.

Kanwisher, N., and Driver, J. (1992). Object, attributes, and visual attention: Which, what and where. *Current directions in Psychological Science, 1*, 26–31.

Kinsbourne, M., and Warrington, E. K. (1962). A variety of reading disability associated with right hemisphere lesions. *Journal of Neurology, Neurosurgery and Psychiatry, 25*, 339–344.

Kinsbourne, M. (1987). Mechanisms of unilateral neglect. In M. Jeannerod (Ed.), *Neuropsychological and physiological aspects of spatial neglect*, 69–86. New York: Elsevier.

Làdavas, E. (1987). Is the hemispatial deficit produced by right parietal lobe damage associated with retinal or gravitational co-ordinates? *Brain, 110*, 167–180.

Làdavas, E., Petronio, A., and Umiltà, C. (1990) The deployment of visual attention in the intact field of hemineglect patients. *Cortex, 26*, 307–317.

Marr, D. (1977). Analysis of occluding contour. *Proceedings of the Royal Society of London, Series B, 197*, 441–475.

Marr, D. (1982). *Vision*. San Francisco: W. H. Freeman.

Marr, D., and Nishihara, H. K. (1978). Representation and recognition of the spatial organization of three-dimensional shapes. *Proceedings of the Royal Society of London, Series B, 200*, 269–294.

Marshall, J., and Halligan, P. W. (1988). Blindsight and insight in visuo-spatial neglect. *Nature, 336*, 766–767.

McGlinchey-Berroth, R., Milberg, W. P., Verfaellie, M., Alexander, M., and Kilduff, P. T. (1993). Semantic processing in the neglected visual field: Evidence from a lexical decision task. *Cognitive Neuropsychology, 10* (1), 79–108.

Mesulam, M. M. (1981). A cortical network for directed attention and unilateral neglect. *Annals of Neurology, 10*, 309–325.

Milner, A. D. (1992). Disorders of perceptual awareness—a commentary. In A. D. Milner and M. D. Rugg (Eds.), *The neuropsychology of consciousness*. London: Academic Press.

Plaut, D., and Farah, M. J. (1990). Visual object representation: Interpreting neurophysiological data within a computational framework. *Journal of Cognitive Neuroscience, 2* (3), 320–343.

Posner, M. I. (1980). Orienting of attention. The VIIIth Sir Frederick Bartlett Lecture. *Quarterly Journal of Experimental Psychology, 32*, 3–25.

Posner, M. I. (1988). Structures and functions of selective attention. In T. Boll and B. Bryant (Eds.), *Clinical neuropsychology and brain function: Research, measurement and practice*, 173–202. Washington, DC: APA.

Posner, M. I., and Cohen, Y. A. (1984). Components of visual orienting. In H. Bouma and D. G. Bouwhuis (Eds.), *Attention and performance X*. Hillsdale, NJ: Erlbaum.

Posner, M. I., Walker, J. A., Friedrich, F. J., and Rafal, R. D. (1984). Effects of parietal injury on covert orienting of attention. *Journal of Neuroscience, 4*, 1863–1877.

Riddoch, M. J., and Humphreys, G. W. (1983). The effect of cueing on unilateral neglect. *Neuropsychologia, 21*, 589–599.

Riddoch, M. J., and Humphreys, G. W. (1987). Perceptual and action systems in unilateral visual neglect. In M. Jeannerod (Ed.), *Neuropsychological and physiological aspects of spatial neglect*, 151–181. New York: Elsevier.

Rizzolatti, G., and Berti, A. (1990). Neglect as a neural representation deficit. *Review of Neurology, 146*, 626–634.

Schacter, D., McAndrews, M. P., and Moscovitch, M. (1988). Access to consciousness: Dissociations between implicit and explicit knowledge in neuropsychological syndromes. In L. Weiskrantz (Ed.), *Thought without language*. Oxford: Oxford University Press.

Tipper, S. P. (1992). Selection for action: The role of inhibitory mechanisms. *Current Directions in Psychological Science, 1*, 105–109.

Tipper, S. P., Brehaut, J., and Driver, J. (1990). Selection of moving and static objects for the control of spatially-directed action. *Journal of Experimental Psychology: Human Perception and Performance, 16*, 492–504.

Tipper, S. P., Driver, J., and Weaver, B. (1991). Object-centered inhibition of return of visual attention. *Quarterly Journal of Experimental Psychology, 43* (4), 289–298.

Tipper, S. P., Weaver, B. and Houghton, G. (1994). Behavioural goals determine inhibitory mechanisms of selective attention. *Quarterly Journal of Experimental Psychology*. In press.

Tipper, S. P., Weaver, B., Jerreat, L. and Burak, A. (1994). Object- and environment-based inhibition of return of visual attention. *Journal of Experimental Psychology: Human Perception and Performance*. In press.

Treisman, A. (1992). Perceiving and re-perceiving objects. *American Psychologist, 47* (7), 862–875.

Volpe, B. T., LeDoux, J. E., and Gazzaniga, M. S. (1979). Information processing of visual stimuli in an "extinguished" field. *Nature, 282*, 722–724.

Watson, R. T., Miller, B. D., and Heilman, K. M. (1978). Nonsensory neglect. *Annals of Neurology, 3*, 505–508.

Young, A. W., Hellawell, D. J., and Welch, J. (1992). Neglect and visual recognition. *Brain, 115*, 51–71.

# 15 Awareness of Contralesional Information in Unilateral Neglect: Effects of Verbal Cueing, Tracing, and Vestibular Stimulation

Giuseppe Vallar, Maria Luisa Rusconi, and Edoardo Bisiach

ABSTRACT  The effects of verbal cueing on same/different judgments and identification of pairs of chimeric/nonchimeric animal figures were investigated in five right brain–damaged patients with left neglect. In the baseline condition, patients judged pairs differing in their left half as *same*, identifying them on the basis of the right half. *Direct* verbal cueing (i.e., the question as to whether, in pairs differing on the left side, one of the animals was more similar to the animal depicted in the left half) produced three kinds of response: (1) overt awareness and identification of the previously neglected left-sided information in three patients; (2) correct choice of the cued component of the pair (without perceptual awareness and identification) in one patient; and (3) paradoxical choice of the noncued component of the pair in another patient. *Indirect* verbal cueing (i.e., the question as to whether in pairs differing on the left side one of the animals was more similar to the animal depicted in the right half of the chimera) was less effective. These effects were temporary. Tracing the contour of the stimuli, though often very accurate, never led to the identification of information neglected in same/different judgments, while vestibular stimulation was effective in one patient. Its effects on the detection of a striking left-sided difference in a pair of drawings were also investigated in seven patients. The inability to detect the difference persisted after stimulation, in spite of a general improvement of neglect on cancellation tasks and, in two patients, in spite of the fact that tracing the left side of each drawing improved. These data suggest that in neglect patients covert processing of neglected information may take place up to the extraction of meaning. This information may be made temporarily available to perceptual awareness through verbal cueing. Our data also suggest that the improvement of neglect after vestibular stimulation may be highly task specific.

## 15.1 INTRODUCTION

A number of recent studies suggest that a basic feature of visuospatial neglect is the defective access of information, which has undergone a certain degree of nonconscious processing, to conscious awareness. Two sources of evidence support this view. First, right brain–damaged patients with left neglect may show entirely preserved sensory processing, as assessed by event-related evoked potentials, of visual and somatosensory stimuli they fail to detect (Vallar et al. 1991). Second, "neglected" left-sided information may, under specific circumstances, affect the patients' behavior. Patients with right parieto-occipital lesions can make accurate same/different judgments on pairs of stimuli simultaneously presented in the left and in the right visual half-field, respectively, although the left-sided stimulus is not identified and sometimes its presence is denied (Volpe, LeDoux, and Gazzaniga 1979). In right brain–damaged patients with contralateral neglect, stimuli presented in the left visual half-field may not be detected but may produce semantic priming effects (Berti and Rizzolatti 1992). Marshall and Halligan's (1988) patient P.S. judges the drawings of two houses to be identical, even though one has red flames on the left but, when requested to indicate which she would prefer to live in, consistently chose the nonburning house. This suggests that, at least in some neglect patients (see the related data of Bisiach and Rusconi 1990), overtly neglected left-sided information may undergo processing deep enough to allow the extraction of structural and even semantic features. Evidence to support the view that neglected information may affect the patient's performance has been also obtained from case E.B., studied by Bisiach, Meregalli, and Berti (1990). This patient made omission errors and pathological completion when reading aloud ten-letter words, but her performance improved significantly when the first five letters were replaced by a string of consonants, thus generating a nonpronounceable nonword.

The mode of assessing knowledge of left-sided information appears to be a crucial variable of neglect. Patients manifest neglect when overt report is required, but when knowledge of left-sided information is assessed by methods not requiring conscious report, evidence that processing has taken place may be found (Volpe, Ledoux and Gazzaniga 1979; Marshall and Halligan 1988; Bisiach and Rusconi 1990; Berti and Rizzolatti 1992).

Assuming that defective access to conscious experience is a basic feature of neglect, it can be predicted that cues concerning left-sided information may influence the choice between stimuli erroneously judged to be identical (Marshall and Halligan 1988; Bisiach and Rusconi 1990). In order to test this, we investigated the effect of verbal cues on the perception of chimeric stimuli, which have been shown to be a sensitive means for the detection of neglect (Kashiwagi et al. 1990; Young, Hellawell, and Welch 1992). The effects of manipulations that may induce patients to explore the neglected left space (tracing the contours of the stimuli: Bisiach and Rusconi 1990; vestibular stimulation: Rubens 1985) were also assessed.

## 15.2 PATIENTS

Ten right-handed patients with left sensory and/or motor deficits and visuospatial neglect on exploratory tasks requiring the crossing of targets (Albert 1973; Diller and Weinberg 1977; Bisiach, Luzzatti, and Perani 1979) were included in this study. Vascular lesions in the right hemisphere assessed by computerized tomography (CT) were present in all cases. No patient had any history of previous strokes, psychiatric disorders, or dementia, with the exception of patient F.G., in whom CT revealed a nonrecent vascular lesion in the left hemisphere. The demographic and neurological data of the patients and their performance in the crossing tasks are shown in table 15.1. Five patients (F.G., R.G., B.R., A.S., G.S.) participated in experiments 1 to 3 and seven patients (F.G., A.S., M.B., C.F., M.F., A.T., C.Z.) in experiment 4.

**Table 15.1** Demographic, Neurological, and Neuropsychological Features of Ten Right Brain–Damaged Patients

| Case | Age-Sex | Duration of Disease | Neurological Deficits | | | Lesion Site | Visual Neglect | | |
|---|---|---|---|---|---|---|---|---|---|
| | | | M | SS | V | | Circle | Letter | Line |
| F.G.*S | 69–F | 7 d | + | + | + | LN, ec ic, PVWM[a] | 8% | 33% | 0% |
| R.G.* | 57–M | 4 m | + | + | + | FTP | 23% | 86%[b] | 19% |
| B.R.* | 78–M | 15 d | – | – | + | PO | 54% | ne | ne |
| A.S.*S | 76–F | 12 m | – | – | + | FTP | 0% | 15% | 23% |
| G.S.* | 73–F | 3 m | + | – | – | FTP | 54% | 95%[b] | 71%[b] |
| M.B.S | 78–F | 1 m | + | + | + | LN, ic | ne | ne | 81%[b] |
| C.F.S | 80–F | 2 m | + | + | + | TPO | ne | ne | 52% |
| M.F.S | 69–F | 4 m | + | – | + | ic | 87%[b] | 89%[b] | ne |
| A.T.S | 69–M | 15 d | + | + | + | TPO | 85%[b] | 86%[b] | ne |
| C.Z.S | 76–F | 1 m | + | – | – | PO | ne | 6% | 0% |

Note: The neglect percentage scores refer to omissions in three cancellation tasks: circle = 13 targets; letter = 104 targets; line = 21 targets. Contralateral left neurological deficits (+/–: present/absent): M = motor, SS = somatosensory, V = visual. Lesion site: F: frontal, P: parietal, T: temporal, O: occipital, LN: lenticular nucleus, PVWM: periventricular white matter, e/i c: external/internal capsule. Patients participating in experiments 1–3 (*); in experiment 4 (S); in experiments 1–4 (*S). ne = not executed.
a. CT also showed a small, hypodense cortico-subcortical left anterior temporal lesion. The patient showed neither signs of dysphasia nor right sensory motor deficits.
b. The patient explored only the extreme right of the display.

### 15.3 EXPERIMENT 1: DIRECT VERBAL CUEING

**Materials and Methods**

**Stimuli** The stimuli were line drawings in black of twenty familiar animals The drawings were divided along the vertical midline into two halves, which were used to produce ten chimeras (fish-turtle, fly-rabbit, sheep-hen, cat-lion, crocodile-whale, shark-swan, giraffe-crane, deer-kangaroo, elephant-pig, horse-dog), composed according to the following criteria:

1. Chimeric animals were obtained by selecting the components of each chimera in such a way that the outer contours were continuous across the midline.

2. Stimuli symmetrical across the midline were obtained by using two half-animals as equal in length as possible on the horizontal axis.

3. In order to obtain stimuli that could be easily recognized, canonical (usually lateral) views of each animal were used, and each chimeric figure was made up by the two anterior halves of two animals, which typically include primary distinctive features. In one stimulus (a fly) a canonical upper view was used. The chimeric animals were not matched for real size.

Each chimeric figure was associated with a nonchimeric animal, identical to the right half of the chimera, producing ten "different" pairs. Each pair was printed on A4 cards. Two versions of each "different" pair were prepared, according to the upper/lower position of the chimeric animal in the card, thus making twenty pairs. To assess the reliability of the patients' responses, the test included ten "same" control pairs, which were generated associating two full nonchimeric drawings of the ten animals, the right half of which had been used to produce the chimeric figures; each "same" pair was presented twice, thus making twenty "same" stimuli. The twenty "different" pairs and the twenty "same" pairs were administered in a random fixed order. Examples of the stimuli are shown in figure 15.1.

**Procedure** The examiner held up each card in front of the patients, the center of the card lying in the midsagittal plane of the patients' trunk. Patients were free to move their head and eyes and were given an unlimited amount of time to provide their responses. The examiner, after a question was asked,

**Figure 15.1** Examples of chimeric (horse-dog/dog) and nonchimeric (crane/crane) pairs.

did not press patients for an answer in any of the steps. The test procedure consisted of the following steps for each stimulus pair:

Step 1: Patients were asked to judge whether the two animals of each pair were identical or different and to identify them, by naming.

Step 2: Step 2 was given immediately after Step 1 for each stimulus pair.

Step 2A. was "different pairs." If patients judged as same the two components of a "different" pair and identified them as the right half of the chimera (i.e., showed left neglect), the examiner asked whether one component of the pair was more similar to the animal depicted in the left half of the chimaera. For instance, if patients in step 1 judged as same and named as "two dogs" the two components of the "different" pair shown in figure 15.1, they were immediately asked to say whether one of the two "dogs" was more similar to a "horse" (the left half of the chimeric component of the pair). If patients correctly judged as different the two members of a "different" pair and identified both the left and the right halves of the chimera, no further questions were asked.

In the case of "same" pairs—step 2B—patients, after the same/different judgment and identification, were asked to say whether one component of the pair was more similar to the left half of the chimeric animal of the corresponding "different" pair. For instance, if patients correctly named and judged as same a pair showing "two dogs," they were required to say whether one of the two animals was more similar to a "horse."

## Results

**Step 1** Overall, patients showed a dramatic left neglect: they judged as same 98 percent of the "different" pairs, identifying each pair as the right half of the chimeric animal (table 15.2). In two trials, patient R.G. said that the

**Table 15.2** Judgments on Pairs

| | Experiment 1: Direct Cueing | | | | Experiment 2: Indirect Cueing | | | |
|---|---|---|---|---|---|---|---|---|
| | Step 1 | | Step 2A | | Step 1 | | Step 2A | |
| Case | S | D | Chi | Non-Chi | S | D | Chi | Non-Chi |
| F.G. | 20 | 0 | 20 | 0* | 20 | 0 | 19 | 1* |
| R.G. | 18 | 2 | 4 | 16** | 20 | 0 | 2[a] | 2[a] |
| B.R. | 20 | 0 | 20 | 0* | 20 | 0 | 8 | 12 |
| A.S. | 20 | 0 | 19 | 1* | 20 | 0 | 8 | 12 |
| G.S. | 20 | 0 | 15 | 5** | 20 | 0 | 7 | 13 |

Note: Step 1: same/different judgments on pairs "different" in their left half ($N = 20$). Step 2A: similarity judgments on the "different" pairs presented in step 1. The entries S/D (Same/Different) and Chi/Non-Chi (chimeric/nonchimeric) refer to the choice made by the patient.
* $p < 0.001$; ** $p < 0.05$.
a. In sixteen trials, the patient did not make any choice.

two animals differed slightly in their right-sided details but identified them as the right half of the chimera. When shown the shark(left)-swan(right)/swan "different" pair, patient R.G. said that the animals were "two swans," but that their beaks were slightly different. Similarly, he said that the horse(left)-dog(right)/dog pair showed "two dogs" but added that their ears were slightly different. (This confabulatory detection by neglect patients of right-sided differences in pairs of stimuli identical in their right side, but different in their left side, has been previously observed by Bisiach and Rusconi 1990.)

Virtually all "same" pairs (97 percent) were judged as identical and all animals were correctly named. Three patients (R.G., B.R., and G.S.) made each a single error on "same" pairs: they said that two members were the same animal, which was correctly identified, but made confabulatory comments, noting some minor differences in the right-sided contours of the drawings.

**Step 2** In the case of "different" pairs (step 2A) three patients (A.S., B.R., and F.G.) not only indicated the chimeric component of the pair as being more similar to the animal suggested by the examiner but also acknowledged its chimeric nature: they named the left half of the chimeric component by saying, for example, when shown the horse-dog/dog pair of figure 15.1, "Ah, yes, there is a horse here," and pointing to it. Patient G.S. indicated the chimeric component in 75 percent of the trials but never realized its chimeric nature. In most instances, patient R.G. showed a paradoxical choice of the nonchimeric component of the pair, contrary to the indication provided by the cue. When questioned about his options, he gave confabulatory responses, mentioning differences in the extreme right of the drawings. The animals of the "same" pairs (step 2B) were again judged as identical (neither was judged to be more similar to the suggested animal) in 90 percent of the trials. In the remaining 10 percent of the trials, patients said that although the two drawings showed the same animal, they might differ in the right-sided contours; none of them, however, was judged to be similar to the suggested animal.

In the three patients who showed overt knowledge of the left half of the chimera after cueing, the effect did not appear to be long lasting. Each chimeric pair was presented twice, since the chimeric component could be in either the upper or in the lower position in the card. However, although the verbal cue (step 2A) was effective in over 90 percent of the trials, patients judged as "same" all chimeric pairs in step 1 of the subsequent trials.

## 15.4 EXPERIMENT 2: NONDIRECT CUEING

### Materials and Methods

In this experiment, the effects of a less direct verbal cue were assessed. As in experiment 1, this cue hinted at a difference between the two components of the "different" pair but provided no specific information concerning the identity of the left half of the chimera.

The five patients were tested within twenty-four hours of the first study. The procedure differed from experiment 1 only in step 2. Patients who had judged as same and identified as the right half of the chimera pairs "different" in their left half were required to say whether one of the two animals of the pair was more similar to the right half of the chimaera (i.e., to the animal identified by the patient; (step 2A). For instance, patients who in step 1 judged as same the "different" pair shown in figure 15.1, identifying the two components as "two dogs," were then asked to decide whether one of the two components of the pair was more similar to a "dog" (the right half of the chimeric component of the pair). In the case of "same" pairs (step 2B), patients were required to say whether one of the two components of the pair was more similar to the animal shown in that pair. For instance, if patients judged a "same" pair, for example, figure 15.1 ("cranes"), as identical in step 1, in step 2B they were required to decide whether one of the components of the pair was more similar to a "crane."

**Results**

**Step 1**   As in experiment 1, the five patients showed an extremely severe neglect. They judged all "different" pairs as same (see table 15.2) and identified all "different" pairs according to their right halves. This confirms that the cueing effect found in the previous experiment was temporary. All "same" stimuli were judged as identical and correctly identified.

**Step 2**   In the case of "different" pairs (step 2A, table 15.2), three of the five patients (B.R., A.S., G.S.) did not display any significant preference, although some tendency to choose the nonchimeric component of the pair was present. Contrary to the previous experiment, patients never realized the chimeric nature of one of the components of the pair. Throughout the task while making their choice, the patients maintained that the two components of the pair were the same animal. Patients sometimes gave confabulatory responses, mentioning some small differences in the contours on the right side, to explain their choice. By contrast, patient F.G. selected the chimeric component of the pair in virtually all trials. She too showed confabulation, mentioning differences in the right side of the contours, and never realized the chimeric nature of the pairs. In sixteen of twenty trials, patient R.G. did not make any choice, stating that the two components of the pair were identical.

In the case of "same" stimuli (step 2B), in ninety-five of one hundred trials, patients said that the two components of the pair were identical and did not make any choice. In the remaining five trials, patients gave confabulatory responses, pointing out that small differences might be present in the right half of the animals but maintaining that the two components of the pair represented the same animal. A difference in the reactions of patients A.S., B.R., F.G., and G.S. to "different" versus "same" pairs should be noted. In the case of "different" pairs, these patients made their choice, even though this did not lead to an option for the nonchimeric component. By contrast, in virtually all nonchimeric trials, they maintained that the two components of the pair were identical and did not make any choice.

In order to assess whether the defective "same-different" judgment found in the previous studies was specific to pairs with a left-sided difference, namely, related to neglect, the ten "different" and the ten "same" pairs used in the previous experiments were printed mirror reversed. In the "different" pairs, the chimeric animal appeared five times in the lower and five in the upper position of the card. The twenty cards were presented in a random fixed order. The procedure was identical to that used in the first study. All five patients were given this task a few hours after the previous experiment. In step 1 all patients had an errorless performance with both "same" and "different" pairs.

## 15.5 EXPERIMENT 3: TRACING

**Materials and Methods**

Some neglect patients may be able to trace the left and right contours of drawings with their right forefinger without detecting previously neglected left-sided details (Bisiach and Rusconi 1990). In this experiment we explored the effects of this task on the identification of neglected left-sided information. The ten "different" pairs used in experiments 1 and 2 were utilized as stimuli. The chimeric component was printed in five pairs in the lower position of the card and in five in the upper. A transparency was superimposed on each stimulus card. Each pair was presented to the patients, who were required to judge whether the two components were identical or different and to identify the animals. If patients judged that the two components were identical, they were then required to trace the contours of the two drawings with their right hand, using a soft pen. After this task, patients were again required to judge whether the two animals, of which they had just traced the contours, were identical and to identify them. The test was given to patients F.G., R.G., B.R., and G.S., a few days after the previous experiments. Case A.S. no longer showed neglect in this task, being able to detect the chimeric nature of the stimuli.

**Results**

All four patients judged all the pairs to be identical and identified the animals on the basis of the right half of the pictures, both before and after tracing. All patients started tracing in the right half of the sheet.

For the purpose of quantitative analysis, the contour of each half-figure was subdivided into a number of component parts. For instance, the horse-dog chimera (fig. 15.1) included for the horse, head, mane, reins, saddle, chest, two legs, and stomach, and for the dog, leash, back, head, muzzle, chest, two paws, and stomach. Performance was scored as the percentage of left- and right-sided component parts of the contours of the chimeric and nonchimeric

**Figure 15.2** Tracings of chimeric stimuli (shown below the tracing), judged as identical to the nonchimeric component of the pair and identified as the right half of the chimera, both before and after tracing. *Patient B.R.*: shark-swan. *Patient F.G.*: deer-kangaroo. Notice the leftside omission below the horns of the deer.

figures, which were traced by each patient. Tracing performance was very accurate and often errorless (see an example in fig. 15.2). The average scores of the four patients were 84.75 percent (left half) and 95 percent (right half) for chimeric figures and 92.75 percent (left half) and 98.75 percent (right half) for nonchimeric figures. Patients F.G. and B.R. had remarkably good tracing performances, scoring over 90 percent in both halves of the figures.

While tracing the contours of the left half of the chimeras, patients B.R. and G.S. did not make any comment. Patient F.G. said to the examiner (M.L.R.), "What beautiful horns. Did you make them?" but maintained that the two animals of that pair (deer/kangaroo-kangaroo) were identical and were two kangaroos (see F.G.'s tracing of the chimeric stimulus in fig. 15.2). Patient R.G. commented on the chimeric drawings in three out of ten trials. While tracing the head of the kangaroo in the deer-left/kangaroo-right chimera, he said: "Here one could draw a deer." A similar comment ("Here one could draw a shark") was made while tracing the head of the swan in the shark-left/swan-right chimera. Finally, while tracing the head of the cat in the cat-left/lion-right chimera, he said, "This looks like a kitten." In spite of these comments, which suggest that the left half of the chimera had been identified in these trials, patient R.G. named the three chimeras on the basis of their right halves (kangaroo, swan, lion). In the three trials in which patient R.G. verbalized his knowledge of the left half of the chimera, tracing performance on the left side was defective. This pattern contrasts sharply with the behavior of patients F.G. and B.R., who in some trials made an errorless tracing performance but never gave any indication of having identified the left half of the chimera. Taken together, these observations suggest a dissociation between tracing and identification.

## 15.6 EXPERIMENT 4: DETECTION OF CONTRALESIONAL DIFFERENCES IN A NONCHIMERIC PAIR OF DRAWINGS: EFFECTS OF TRACING AND VESTIBULAR STIMULATION

**Materials and Methods**

This experiment was a partial replication and extension of an earlier study (Bisiach and Rusconi 1990). It was carried out on seven right brain–damaged patients selected on the basis of their inability to detect the difference between two drawings differing from one another on the left side.

Seven patients (F.G., A.S., M.B., C.F., M.F., A.T., C.Z.) entered this study (see table 15.1). Stimuli were the same as those used by Marshall and Halligan (1988): the black-and-white outlines of two identical houses, on the left side of one of which red flames were added. A single card was shown to each patient on each condition of the task, with the burning house directly below the nonburning one. Patients were asked to give a same/different judgment (S/D) at different steps in the following sequence: (1) S/D, (2) tracing of the nonburning and then of the burning house, (3) S/D, (4) vestibular stimulation, (5) S/D, (6) tracing as above, and (7) S/D. The procedure for tracing was the same as in experiment 3. Vestibular stimulation was produced by irrigating the external canal of the left ear with 20 cc of iced water for 1 min (see Vallar, et al. 1990 for a detailed description of the technique). One or more cancellation tasks (line: Albert 1973; letter: Diller and Weinberg 1977; circle: Bisiach, Luzzatti, and Perani 1979) were also given to patients before and after vestibular stimulation.

**Results**

Patients never managed to detect the difference between the two houses, which was, however, promptly indicated by all of them at the end of the experiment (after step 7) in a mirror-reversed version of the pair of drawings in which the flames lay on the right, ipsilesional, side.

Vestibular stimulation, therefore, though improving visual neglect on cancellation tasks in all patients (table 15.3), proved totally ineffective in the task under investigation. Tracing was also ineffective in all patients. Prior to vestibular stimulation, in step 2, patients M.B., M.F., and F.G. omitted the tracing of critical details. By contrast, the tracings of cases C.F., A.S. and C.Z. did

**Table 15.3** Influence of Vestibular Stimulation on Cancellation Tasks in the Seven Patients Participating in Experiment 4: Percentages of Omissions on Three Tasks before and after Stimulation

| Case | Line Before | Line After | Letter Before | Letter After | Circle Before | Circle After |
|---|---|---|---|---|---|---|
| M.B. | 81 | 71 | ne | ne | ne | ne |
| C.F. | 52 | 48 | ne | ne | ne | ne |
| M.F. | ne | ne | 89 | 83 | 87 | 62 |
| F.G. | 0 | 0 | 33 | 26 | 8 | 0 |
| A.S. | ne | ne | 86 | 76 | 46 | 23 |
| A.T. | ne | ne | 86 | 79 | 85 | 54 |
| C.Z. | 0 | 0 | 6 | 3 | ne | ne |

Note: ne = not executed.

extend to the critical details: patients A.S. and C.Z. drew the left-sided profile of the burning house without noticing that the tip of the pen went across the flames; patient C.F. even traced the left-sided profile of the flames but still denied any difference between the two houses. Tracing of the left-sided contour of the drawings improved after vestibular stimulation (step 4) in patients F.G. and C.Z., who in this step also traced the entire external profile of the flames; nevertheless, the difference between the two drawings was again totally disregarded.

## 15.7 DISCUSSION

The main result of this study is that a verbal, spatially neutral cue may affect same/different judgments or identification of left-sided portions of chimeras, previously totally neglected by the patient. These effects are not homogeneous across patients. Three different patterns of effect can be distinguished:

1. *Overt identification of previously neglected information.* A direct cue concerning the identity of the left-sided portion of the chimera may produce conscious awareness of the left half of the stimulus, as inferred by patients' correct naming and pointing. This pattern is present in patients F.G., B.R., and A.S.

2. *Choices suggesting processing of neglected information.* The direct verbal cue may prompt an appropriate choice in most trials but not conscious awareness of the identity of the left half of the stimulus, as witnessed by the absence of naming and pointing responses. This pattern was observed in patient G.S. with direct cueing. This option for the chimeric figure is similar to the preference for the nonburning house found by Marshall and Halligan (1988), when the question was which house the patient would prefer to live in. Bisiach and Rusconi (1990) also found significant preference effects, but their patients—in different experiments—did not always opt for the "best" component of their pairs, showing in some cases consistent preference for the burning house.

3. *Paradoxical responses*. By this we refer to the observation that cueing may also induce a preference opposite to the indication provided by the cue itself. This pattern was observed in two patients. In experiment 1, patient R.G. most frequently opted for the nonchimeric component of the pair when specifically cued toward the chimera. In experiment 2, patient F.G. preferred the chimeric component of the pair, when cued toward the nonchimeric one. Some of the response patterns co-occurred in the same patient. Patient F.G. showed an overt knowledge of the cued chimera in experiment 1 and made paradoxical choices in experiment 2.

The three response patterns provide different information about the processing undergone by the neglected material.

Pattern 1 (overt knowledge) may suggest that the neglected portion of the stimulus has been processed at a level deep enough to allow identification after direct cueing. Such processing is likely to have included covert access to semantic and lexical representations of the stimulus, since the verbal cue induced an overt identification of the left half of the chimera, as shown by patients' naming and pointing.

Also pattern 2 (choice of the chimeric stimulus without overt identification, after direct cueing) may reflect the covert identification of left-sided information. The choice, however, is compatible with a more shallow level of analysis, for example, visuospatial processing, which, as shown by the tracing experiment, is, at least to some extent, preserved. So, for example, patient G.S. might have opted for the chimeric component on the basis of the covert appreciation of left-sided differences in shape between the two components of the pair, so that the left and the right halves of the chimera are (covertly) judged as not fully compatible. This might, in turn, lead patients to infer that the chimeric component is likely to be more similar to the animal suggested by the examiner, without necessarily implying any covert identification of its left half. Evidence that neglected left-sided information may have been identified is, however, provided by the allochiria-type phenomenon observed in patient R.G., when he remarked that the animal depicted in the unidentified left side of the chimera could have been traced on its right side (experiment 3).

Pattern 3 (paradoxical responses) is more difficult to interpret. The observation of above-chance responses suggests that processing of left-sided information has taken place. As for pattern 2 (choice without overt identification), however, it cannot be unambiguously concluded that the left-sided part of the stimulus has been covertly identified. These paradoxical responses raise the possibility that patients may not only be oriented in the right direction by the cue (see patterns 1 and 2) or be unaffected by it. Some of them may also resist the cue, choosing the noncued component of the pair. This behavior might be interpreted in terms of avoidance (Denny-Brown and Chambers 1958).

We have suggested so far that some effects of cueing occur because covert processing of the neglected stimuli is substantially preserved and that such a processing is likely to involve the semantic level. An alternative explanation is that cueing may have prompted patients to explore actively the neglected side and therefore to identify the left half of the chimeras. That is, even if the verbal cue is spatially neutral, patients might have inferred that given the question asked by the examiner, the left part of the stimulus (neglected in their same/different judgments) carried some critical information. According to this view, patients prior to cueing may have not covertly processed left-sided information up to the semantic level. This interpretation, however, predicts that both the direct and the indirect cue may produce identification of the left half of the chimera, since they affect performance by prompting patients to explore the display further. By contrast, the selective effects of cueing (only the direct cue brings about identification of the previously neglected left half of the chimera) suggest an interaction between the cue and covertly processed information concerning the identity of the left part of the stimulus. Cues that specifically refer to the left half of the chimera are then more likely to produce overt identification. An interpretation in terms of exploration induced by the cue is also unable to account for the observation that patients may not only identify or choose the cued member of the pair (patterns 1 and 2) but may also opt for the noncued member (pattern 3).

The effects of verbal cues observed in experiments 1 and 2 may be contrasted with the results of experiment 3. Patients may trace with a good level of accuracy (in some trials with a flawless performance) the contours of the left half of chimeras, which nevertheless remain unidentified. A dissociation between tracing and identification is also suggested by experiment 4: the improvement in tracing in patient F.G. and C.Z. after vestibular stimulation did not entail the utilization of critical details for same/different judgments on the burning and nonburning houses. Preliminary evidence in a single patient suggests, however, that same/different judgments and identification may be improved by vestibular stimulation. Patient B.R. was shown fifteen cards (the ten "different" pairs used in experiments 1 to 3 and five "same" pairs, in random order) before and after vestibular stimulation. Before stimulation B.R. judged all ten "different" pairs as identical and identified them on the basis of their right halves. In the case of "same" pairs, performance was errorless throughout the study. After treatment the patient correctly judged as different nine of the ten "different" pairs, identified the left half of each chimera, and pointed to it. The effect persisted, albeit attenuated, after 60 min: seven pairs were correctly judged as different, and the left half of the chimera was identified. Twenty-four hours later, only three pairs were correctly judged as different. These results suggest that the effects of vestibular stimulation on visuospatial cognition may be highly selective.

Why do patients fail to identify stimuli when they are able to trace their contours accurately? The processing and identification of visual objects involve different levels of representation, which may be affected differentially in neglect patients. The minimal requirements for tracing the contours of drawings include a two-dimensional visuospatial representation, such as Marr's (1982) primal sketch. This level of representation may be relatively spared in neglect patients, accounting for the largely preserved tracing performance. In contrast, identification of visual objects requires a fuller processing, up to a

3-D model representation (Marr 1982). The observation that in some neglect patients verbal cues may induce a temporary perceptual awareness of left-sided information indicates that covert processes achieving identification of the stimulus have taken place. The overt identification of visual objects, however, may also require, in addition to a 3-D model representation, their localization, with reference to an egocentric representation of extrapersonal space. In neglect patients, this representation is pathologically displaced toward the ipsilesional right side (see Vallar et al. 1993). This rightward pathological displacement prevents perceptual awareness of left-sided information, which has undergone processing, including the appreciation of meaning. This may also account for the bizarre allochiria-type phenomenon observed in this study, whereby patients may say that one could draw on the right side of the card the left half of the stimulus, which they fail to identify. Finally, vestibular stimulation may temporarily improve the ability of neglect patients to identify the left half of chimeric stimuli by reducing the ipsilesional pathological displacement of the egocentric representation of extrapersonal space. This would allow the appropriate spatial localization and perceptual awareness of left-sided, neglected, information.

## NOTE

Research for this work was supported by grants from the Consiglio Nazionale delle Ricerche (G.V.) and the Ministero dell'Università e della Ricerca Scientifica e Tecnologica (G.V., E.B.).

## REFERENCES

Albert, M. L. (1973). A simple test of visual neglect. *Neurology, 23,* 658–664.

Berti, A., and Rizzolatti, G. (1992). Visual processing without awareness: Evidence from unilateral neglect. *Journal of Cognitive Neuroscience, 4,* 345–351.

Bisiach, E., Luzzatti, C., and Perani, D. (1979). Unilateral neglect, representational schema and consciousness. *Brain, 102,* 609–618.

Bisiach, E., Meregalli, S., and Berti, A. (1990). Mechanisms of production control and belief fixation in human visuospatial processing: Clinical evidence from unilateral neglect. In M. L. Commons, R. J. Herrnstein, S. M. Kosslyn, and D. B. Mumford (Eds.), *Quantitative analysis of behaviour: Computational and clinical approaches to pattern recognition and concept formation,* vol. 9, 3–21. Hillsdale, NJ: Lawrence Erlbaum.

Bisiach, E., and Rusconi, M. L. (1990). Break-down of perceptual awareness in unilateral neglect. *Cortex, 26,* 643–649.

Denny-Brown, D., and Chambers, R. A. (1958). The parietal lobe and behavior. *Research Publications: Association for Research in Nervous and Mental Disease, 36,* 35–117.

Diller, L., and Weinberg, J. (1977). Hemi-inattention in rehabilitation. The evolution of a rational remediation program. In E. A. Weinstein and R. P. Friedland (Eds.), *Hemi-inattention and hemisphere specialization,* Vol. 18: *Advances in neurology,* 62–82. New York: Raven Press.

Kashiwagi, A., Kashiwagi, T., Nishikawa, T., Tanabe, H., and Okuda, J-I. (1990). Hemispatial neglect in a patient with callosal infarction. *Brain, 113,* 1005–1023.

Marr, D. (1982). *Vision.* New York: Freeman.

Marshall, J. C., and Halligan, P. W. (1988). Blindsight and insight in visuo-spatial neglect. *Nature, 336,* 766–767.

Rubens, A. B. (1985). Caloric stimulation and unilateral visual neglect. *Neurology, 35,* 1019–1024.

Vallar, G., Sterzi, R., Bottini, G., Cappa, S., and Rusconi, M. L. (1990). Temporary remission of left hemianesthesia after vestibular stimulation. A sensory neglect phenomenon. *Cortex, 26,* 123–131.

Vallar, G., Sandroni, P., Rusconi, M. L., and Barbieri, S. (1991). Hemianopia, hemianesthesia and spatial neglect: A study with evoked potentials. *Neurology, 41,* 1918–1922.

Vallar, G., Bottini, G., Rusconi, M. L., and Sterzi, R (1993). Exploring somatosensory hemineglect by vestibular stimulation. *Brain, 116,* 71–86.

Volpe, B. T., Ledoux, J. E., and Gazzaniga, M. S. (1979). Information processing of visual stimuli in an "extinguished" field. *Nature, 282,* 722–724.

Young, A. W., Hellawell, D. J., and Welch, J. (1992). Neglect and visual recognition. *Brain, 115,* 51–71.

# V  Control Processes

# 16 Multiple Levels of Control Processes

Tim Shallice

ABSTRACT That a useful processing distinction can be made between the operation of the relatively permanent structural features of the cognitive system and processes briefly set up by subjects to attain a particular goal has been generally accepted since it was proposed by Atkinson and Shiffrin (1968). There has, however, been far less agreement on how control processes should be characterized. Early theorists saw them as the province of a single system or processing mode. Three later theories, those of Schneider, Newell, and Norman and Shallice, take more complex positions. These theories are reviewed in the light of two main sources of evidence: standard human experimental (in particular, dual-task performance) and neuropsychological (particularly studies of Parkinson's disease and frontal-lobe lesion patients).

## 16.1 CONTROLLED PROCESSING: THE THEORETICAL PROBLEM

The 1950s and 1960s saw the first concerted attempts to use the results of experimental psychology paradigms carried out on human subjects to make inferences about the organization of what would now be called the functional architecture. It rapidly became apparent that the behavior of human subjects in information-processing experiments depended not only on the structural organization of the cognitive system but also on the strategy employed to carry out such tasks. Thus, in Sperling's (1960) classic iconic memory experiments, when a matrix of letters is presented followed after a delay by a signal as to which row is to be reported, subjects claimed to be able to use at least two strategies: they either allocated attention as equally as possible to all rows or guessed which row would be relevant and concentrated on that. The former strategy tended to lead to better overall performance at very short matrix-signal delays, but the latter was preferable at longer delays.

The first systematic attempt to produce a theoretical framework that allowed for the codetermination of behavior by the subject's strategy and the operation of functional architecture was made by Atkinson and Shiffrin (1968) in their fundamental analysis of the organization of the human memory system. They put forward the distinction between memory structures, such as the sensory register, short-term memory, and long-term memory, on the one hand, and *control processes* on the other. The basic distinction between control processes and memory structures was introduced by the analogy of the relation between what a human programmer writes at a remote console and the computer hardware and built-in program that the written program controls.

Control processes were defined as those processes "that are not permanent features of memory, but are transient phenomena under *the control of the subject*" (p. 106) (italics added). Moreover with one exception—Sternberg's (1966) exhaustive serial scan, which was not generally invoked in their theoretical accounts—the examples given of control processes were reflections of subjective reports: *rehearsal* processes, *coding* processes, *attention*, and so on. Essentially, then, the term *control process* gained its empirical plausibility from reflection on strategies but with their use legitimized by being apparently stripped of their phenomenological content.

During the early 1970s, the idea of control processes was developed either explicitly or implicitly in two ways. The first was the idea that a separable system may be responsible for the operations related to control processes, represented by Baddeley and Hitch's (1974) central executive store and Laberge's (1975) attention center. The second was the development of a contrast between controlled processes and automatic ones (Posner and Snyder 1975). These trends were strengthened by the extensive empirical and theoretical work of Shiffrin and Schneider (1977) (see also Schneider and Shiffrin 1977). They produced experimental support for a larger set of criteria for distinguishing automatic and controlled processing than that produced by Posner and Snyder. The focus of their empirical investigations, search tasks, differed from that of Atkinson and Shiffrin (memory tasks) and Posner and Snyder (priming). They showed that situations in search tasks where the subject was employing automatic detection differed in a number of respects from those in which controlled search was used. Automatic detection was operationalized by subject's having to perform many trials using consistent mappings; targets on any trial are drawn from only a subset of the possible stimuli, and this subset is disjoint from that used for all the distractors. Controlled processing, by contrast, was assessed by using varied mappings: the above relation did not apply and a target on one trial can be one of the distractors on the next.

The behavior of subjects in these two types of situations differed in a number of respects: the slope of the function relating detection time with search set size (flat versus linearly increasing), the effect of reversing the positive and negative sets (severe versus little), the decrement in detecting a second target closely following a first one (none versus considerable), and the distracting effect of presenting a target in a to-be-ignored location (considerable versus little). Another criterion was added later: whether the search task could be combined with an unrelated but highly practiced task (little interference versus great) (Schneider and Fisk 1982, 1984; Fisk and Schneider 1983). In the earlier studies, the search task involved alphanumeric characters, and the positive set was either a prespecified subset of the same category (letter, digit) or members of the other of these categories. A somewhat different type of task situation was investigated in the later studies: detecting whether a presented word is a member of a particular semantic category. All, however, involved search tasks of one form or another.

To explain the contrasting patterns of performance they obtained, Shiffrin and Schneider argued that tasks where automatic detection is found and those where controlled search occurs differed in that the corresponding type of processing—automatic and controlled—is taking place. Automatic processing was held to have a number of types of properties and was defined in a stimulus-response fashion "as a sequence of nodes that nearly always becomes active in response to a particular input configuration where the input may be externally or internally generated" (p. 55). Critics have concentrated on this aspect of the theory because it represents a major advance (e.g., Broadbent 1982; Ryan 1983; Cheng 1985; but see for reply Schneider and Shiffrin 1985 and Shiffrin 1988). More relevant for this chapter is the nature of controlled processing. It was held to have the following properties: (1) to require attention and typically consist of a series of singly controlled unitary operations, (2) to be limited by short-term storage capacity, (3) to be easily adopted and modified, (4) to control the flow of information between STS and LTS, and (5) to show the rapid development of asymptotic performance.

Controlled search performance was fitted well by a self-terminating serial search model, so controlled processes were held to utilize "a temporary sequence of nodes under control of, and through attention by, the subject; the sequence is temporary in the sense that each activation ... requires anew the attention of the subject ... only one such sequence at a time may be controlled without interference" (p. 156). However, in essence the properties of accessible controlled search can be explained by two simple assumptions: that automatic processing is not operating and that the process used is flexible, subject controlled, and single-channel. The single-channel aspects of the data do not constrain the theory greatly (consider Broadbent 1983 and Pashler and Johnston 1989 for alternatives). In other respects, the account of controlled processing is hardly an advance on the one provided by Atkinson and Shiffrin.

## 16.2 ACCOUNTS OF CONTROLLED PROCESSING

The work of Atkinson and Shiffrin (1968) and of Shiffrin and Schneider (1977) made the concept of controlled processing almost indispensable for cognitive psychology. It acquired its support in three ways. It gained its plausibility negatively by contrast with the concept of automatic processing, positively but most strongly through the serial-channel operation of the subject in certain search tasks, and indirectly as a vehicle for an information-processing correlate of phenomological concepts like the strategy employed by the subject. Theoretically, however, Shriffin and Schneider's treatment of controlled processing was much weaker than that of automatic processing. A controlled response is normally held to involve an output of a controlled processing "box" to the response production "box" but the controlled processing box itself lacks input or innards except for the control of automatic attention responses (Shiffrin and Schneider 1977, fig. 11). Moreover, Shiffrin and Schneider echo Atkinson and Shiffrin in referring explicitly to controlled processing as "under [the] control of ... the subject" and "requiring the attention of the subject." Yet why, unlike automatic processing, it should be related to volition and have phenomenological correspondences is left unexplained.

Since 1980 a number of models have been developed that contain more articulated concepts that relate to that of control processes. I will consider three in this chapter. Two are selected because they have supported simulations. One, the connectionist model CAP of Schneider and his colleagues (Detweiler and Schneider 1991; Schneider and Detweiler 1987; Schneider and Oliver 1991), is the most faithful attempt to situate automatic and controlled processing within a model that combines connectionist and modular characteristics, unlike the earlier Schneider and Shiffrin model. A second, the symbolic model Soar (Newell 1990), while touching only tangentially on the automatic/controlled processing contrast, is included because it allows controlled processing to be situated within higher processes and so allows in principle for an implementation of the volitional/awareness aspects. The third model, that of Norman and myself (1980, 1986), has not been implemented. It is included because it provides a more complex division of control levels, which corresponds to the phenomenological ones between automatic, ideomotor, and willed actions.

The models differ in a number of ways, three of them critical. The first is whether the operation of basic-level cognitive processes involves a common system or processor, whatever the particular cognitive domain and that this system is a fundamentally serial processor that cannot be bypassed. This position, the traditional view in information-processing psychology, is assumed in Soar but not by the other two models. This results in a second key difference. For Soar, automatic processes represent ones that are happening within a single decision cycle of this processor. For the other two models, they represent processes capable of being carried in parallel to other processes. Third, the CAP model assumes only a single level of controlled processes, but on the other models, two different domains of controlled processing exist.

Two types of empirical studies will be discussed. First, a range of studies using normal experimental procedures will be reviewed. These involve a number of paradigms in which task switching occurs. Second, two types of neuropsychological studies are reviewed. The first set are concerned with dual-task performance in Parkinsonian patients. Together with the normal studies, the results of these investigations make it difficult to accept Soar's account of the domain. The second set of neuropsychological studies are of frontal lobe patients. They relate to the issue of the number of levels on which control processes operate.

**A Connectionist Approach: CAP**

The CAP model developed by Schneider and his colleagues has as its processing core a set of modules that are interconnected both vertically and horizontally in the sense of Fodor (1983).[1] Each module has two processing layers, input and output, and three types of control signal: the *gain*, which can act to attenuate the output of the module if higher systems consider it irrelevant, the *feedback*, also under the control of higher systems, which determines the strength of autoassociative feedback in the module, and, when high, the module latches on to the existing input, and when low, the module accepts new input; and the *activity* unit, which transmits to higher systems a signal that represents how active the module is.

For implementation purposes each module is treated as a three-layer back propagation net. Its input layer is considered to be the set of hidden units of the net; the units that feed them, the output units of the modules that provide input to the module currently being implemented, become the input units of the back propagation net. The three types of control signals are produced by or feed a final three-layer recurrent backpropagation network of the type analyzed by Elman (1990): the so-called sequential rule network. It takes as inputs two vectors, one derived from the activity outputs of the modules and another that represents the task and produces as outputs a vector representing a control operation and one representing its argument. A typical control operation is to compare outputs from different modules. It is hand-coded to work by modulating the gain and feedback inputs to particular modules.

This system represents a direct attempt to realize the Schneider-Shiffrin controlled processing approach in a framework that is both connectionist and modular (in the loose sense). The operation of the sequential rule network represents controlled processing and the autonomous operation of which the modules are capable the automatic processing. Thus, early in learning to use a gear lever in a car the explicit rules would correspond to the operation of the sequential rule network, which later in learning is no longer required because appropriate connections within the modular system have gained sufficiently strong weights to operate effectively autonomously.

The model has been applied to a number of different situations, such as working memory (Schneider and Detweiler 1987), dual-task performance (Detweiler and Schneider 1991), and electronic troubleshooting (Schneider and Oliver 1991). Actual simulations exist in at least the last three cases, although only a part of the total system appears to be implemented. Overall, the model represents a clear attempt to articulate automatic and controlled processing concepts in more detail. However, the claimed volitional aspects of control processes are not addressed.

### A Symbolic-Processing Approach to Control Processes: Soar

A very different approach to the automatic/controlled processing distinction is taken by Newell (1990) in his unified theory of cognition based on the general-purpose symbol-processing problem-solving program Soar. In Newell's meta-analysis of the organization of human action, automatic processing belongs to the neural circuit part of the so-called biological band, involving, it is claimed, time units of the order of 10 ms. Controlled processing belongs to the deliberate act part of the so-called cognitive band, with time units of the order of 100 ms. The concrete realization of his ideas depends on Soar, a model implemented in various forms (Laird, Newell, and Rosenbloom 1987; Rosenbloom et al. 1991). Soar is a problem-space architecture in that all the tasks it tackles are formulated in terms of problem spaces, and all of its basic functions are dependent on problem spaces. It can select a problem space or, within one, select a state or operator from those available, or apply the operator to obtain a new state.

At a more basic level, Soar is a production system model containing as subcomponents a production memory (a set of condition-action pairs) and a working memory (containing elements from the perceptual input and from the action part of productions). Soar productions have two special features by comparison with earlier production system models like Ops5 (McDermott and Forgy 1978). First, the only type of action a Soar production can take is to add elements to working memory; it cannot delete or amend them. Second, there is no automatic conflict resolution procedure. It frequently happens that multiple productions are fired by the current state of working memory. The system then operates in an entirely parallel way. All productions whose conditions are satisfied add new elements to working memory, and these elements, in turn, may lead to the firing of further productions until quiescence is reached. During this elaboration phase, however, many of the elements added to working memory, and in particular ones that may give rise to conflict, are preferences. At quiescence, a decision phase occurs, and the preferences are realized as concrete elements of working memory unless conflicting preferences have been set up. In this case, or if nothing is added to working memory, a so-called impasse has arisen, and Soar forms a new goal of resolving the impasse and a new problem space in which to do it. Once an impasse has been resolved, a process called chunking creates a new production, so that if conditions similar to those that existed prior to the impasse recur, the same "solution" elements can be added to working memory without an impasse occurring and having to be resolved.

The theory allows controlled and automatic processing to be studied within a model of cognition as a whole. Automatic processes become processes that require only a single decision cycle, so that once initiated they cannot be stopped. Controlled processing would require more than one decision cycle and would, in principle, be interruptable at the end of each decision cycle; hence, they are "voluntary." By this view, the automatic/voluntary contrast is well realized. Moreover, there are two qualitatively distinct types of controlled processing, depending on whether they involve impasses.

This model derives intellectually from the problem-solving area (see Newell and Simon 1972 for its major forebear). This might well seem an unrelated domain to the ones where control processes have typically been considered in the experimental literature. However, Newell extends the domain of the model to include so-called immediate behavior, where responses must be made to a stimulus within the order of a second (300 ms to 3 sec), and in which perceptual and motor behavior interface with cognition. The elements of working memory are held to include perceptual codes and high-level motor commands, and provided that the tasks modeled utilize individual symbolic or single stimuli and the responses are individual overlearned speeded responses like button presses or key strokes, the overall Soar model is held to provide an appropriate model of the domain. Since all Soar operations require a problem space, the minimal scheme for speeded responding utilizes the so-called base-level problem space. This involves perceptual encoding and motor decoding processes, which have not been implemented by the Soar group but are assumed to be relatively invariant in the situations under consideration. In addition, there are assumed to be a set of operations that occur in series: attend (focus on input), comprehend (analyze for significance), set task, and intend (determine and release action). All are reducible with practice, but comprehend and intend are held to have irreducible minima, of roughly 60 ms each.

Soar has been assessed empirically in a variety of domains (Newell 1990). Possibly the most impressive experimental correspondence is obtained in its mimicking of the protocol of cryptarithmetic solutions, a classic problem-solving paradigm within the production system literature (Newell and Simon 1972). It has also been applied in the skills area, where it mimics the power-law of learning (Snoddy 1926; Newell and Rosenbloom 1981)[2] and to a variety of information-processing tasks such as simple and choice reaction time (RT), item recognition, typing and sentence verification, with in my view, varying success (see for detailed assessments Norman 1990; Cooper and Shallice 1993).

**The Norman-Shallice Model**

An older model developed by Norman and Shallice (1980, 1986) (see also Norman 1986; Shallice 1982, 1988) contains three levels relevant to the automatic/controlled processing distinction. The lowest level consists of psychological processing structures, which correspond roughly to the modular sections of the Schneider et al. CAP model. How they operate is controlled by action or thought schemas, which are triggered from a trigger database and have a similar role to the productions in Soar except that they are subject to a mutual inhibitory conflict resolution process, contention scheduling, which allows only a very limited number to be selected at a time. Schemas can be hierarchically organized with activation passing to so-called component schemas from a source schema if it is selected.

In addition to the triggering of schemas in contention scheduling, the Norman and Shallice model, like Soar, has another domain of operation that comes into play in certain situations. The most characteristic situation is, again like Soar, one in which the routine operation of triggered schemas would be insufficient to produce an appropriate response; some form of novelty has to be confronted. However, other types of situation are also held to require qualitatively similar types of processes: those that involve error correction or troubleshooting, those that involve ill-learned or novel sequences of actions, those judged to be dangerous or technically difficult, and those that require the overcoming of a strong habitual response or temptation. Coping with such situations was held to require a separate system, the Supervisory System.[3] The output of this system would act as a separate source of activation in contention scheduling and so modulate its operation.

In its initial specification, the theory was applied to the attention literature and in particular to dual-task performance and action lapses. However, the main attempts to use the theory empirically have been in the neurological domain, particularly for the understanding of frontal lobe function (Shallice 1982, 1988; Shallice and Burgess 1991).

On the model, the term *automatic* has a number of different referents. It can refer to processes in which schema selection involves so little activation that the behavior that can be realized is parallel to other activities. Alternatively, and this corresponds more to the Schneider and Shiffrin sense, it can refer to processes controlled by their own single schema, triggered directly in a data-driven fashion. Complementarily, in an analogous fashion as for Soar, controlled processing would correspond to processes that require more than one schema to be selected in contention scheduling. However, because a highly overlearned schema can theoretically be selected while a second more powerfully activated schema is in operation, given that the two are not in structural competition and that the highly overlearned one exceeds its own threshold, activation selection can occur on a continuum of activation values. There would therefore be no clear line where processes having automatic characteristics are separated from those having controlled characteristics. This, however, fits with evidence that the automatic/controlled relation is a continuum, not a dichotomy (Logan 1988; MacLeod and Dunbar 1988). In addition, processes that are voluntary are ones that involve Supervisory System activation, so the link between a process being "controlled" and its being "voluntary" is also less clear than for Soar. Overall, although the model should deal with an overlapping domain of evidence to that of the Schneider and Shiffrin model, the sets of concepts do not correspond neatly.

## 16.3 THE THEORETICAL ACCOUNTS OF THE TRANSITION FROM CONTROLLED TO AUTOMATIC PROCESSING

It would seem natural to consider how the three models, as models of controlled processing, account for findings using the Schneider and Shiffrin paradigm. However, the ideas that Schneider and Shiffrin put forward on control processes were less incisive than those on automatic processes. This stems from the way that their search task is much better suited to examining the transition from controlled to automatic processing than the nature of controlled processing itself.

Controlled processing in the Schneider and Shiffrin search task occurs in the varied mapping conditions, which are closely related to the original Sternberg paradigm. It can, however, be argued that the variable-set findings are actually outside the domain of the theory. Starr et al. (1990) have shown that patients with specific phonological buffer difficulties have equivalent problems in the Sternberg paradigm to those they have in span tasks. The proper domain of explanation for the varied mapping findings would appear, therefore, to be short-term memory and not automatic/controlled processing. Any temporal parameters measured will reflect the specific properties of retrieval from phonological buffer storage as much as any general characteristics of controlled processing.

Turning to the fixed-set tasks, none of the three models gives an entirely satisfactory account of the empirical findings. The most detailed account of visual search is that provided for the CAP model. Detweiler and Schneider (1991) argue that when learning a particular skill, the model moves through five phases, from fully controlled to fully automatic processing. In learning of search tasks such as that used by Schneider and Fisk (1984), these correspond to five stages:

1. Controlled comparison from buffered memory (trials 1–4).
2. Context-maintained controlled comparisons (trials 5–20).[4]
3. Goal-state-maintained control comparison (trials 21–100).
4. Controlled assist of automatic processing (trials 101–200).
5. Automatic processing (trials 200 on).

This analysis is potentially an important advance derived from the model, but assessment of it is difficult at present. Consider dual-task performance. Automatic processing was claimed not to interfere with the operation of a co-occurring task when there is no structural competition (Schneider and Fisk 1982). Intuitively, it would appear that if two separate tasks are learned separately to the automatic processing phase, then it should be possible to combine them with little loss if they have no structural interference. In fact, Schneider and Fisk (1984) showed that even after 8 hours of practice on each of two such single tasks, subjects exhibited levels of performance that were near to those produced by novices when the two tasks were first combined. Detweiler and Schneider argue that the model would not make the predictions one would intuitively anticipate, but no simulations are provided. Instead, they argue that effective dual-task performance requires one of a number of compensatory strategies, but it seems unlikely that the generation of such strategies is within the domain of the model.

Soar has considerably more serious problems over the controlled-to-automatic transition. The only type of search task that is extensively treated within the Soar literature is the Sternberg paradigm, which gives rise, according to Shiffrin and Schneider, to veiled controlled processing. A theoretical account of how Soar predicts the classic Sternberg (1966) relationship is given by Newell (1990, p. 293). Essentially, he provides a form of exhaustive serial search explanation, a perspective that is currently out of favor (see Monsell 1978 for a critical experiment). On his account, there are no impasses involved in the production of a response, as the system remains in the base-level problem space. How, though, would the transition from controlled to automatic processing occur with consistent mappings? Since learning in Soar uses one mechanism only—chunking through its successfully resolving impasses—if impasses do not occur, learning does not occur. For Soar to provide an account of the transition, it would be necessary to assume that in the early stages of training, search is impasse driven. It is, then, most unclear why the transition from controlled to automatic processing for a fixed, small set of target items should take a hundred or more trials. It would appear that Soar in its present form gives no satisfactory account of the transition from controlled to automatic processing in search paradigms.

The Norman and Shallice model has not been applied to search tasks. Presumably it would give an account of the consistent mapping findings in terms of the formation of specific schemas for each member of the positive and negative sets. However, because there is no theoretical account of how changes occur in the system due to learning, the model is in an equivalent state to Soar in this respect except that its lack of theoretical claims means that it is spared Soar's specific difficulties.

Thus, none of the models gives an altogether satisfactory account of the original search findings and the transition from controlled to automatic processing. CAP gives the most satisfactory explanation because it contains concepts that provide a possible account of intermediate stages between purely controlled and purely automatic and because empirical correspondences have been at least provisionally produced. Soar has the most problems since a slow transition from controlled to automatic processing is very difficult for it to explain. However, if the argument presented is correct, search tasks at least of the Schneider and Shiffrin type do not provide a very satisfactory empirical paradigm for investigating control processes themselves.

## 16.4 APPROPRIATE PARADIGMS FOR INVESTIGATING CONTROLLED PROCESSING

The varied mapping procedure is not ideal for studying controlled processing because it essentially concerns search though a short-term memory buffer. Schema change, in the sense of the Norman and Shallice model, is not required. Dual-task situations where there are switching costs when moving from one task to the other seem potentially more informative.

The traditional situation of this type is the refractory period paradigm (Welford 1952). Recently, Pashler and Johnston (1989) have used the additive-factors methodology to investigate the locus of the delay that occurs to a second signal while the first is produced. A procedure that lengthens the perceptual processing stage produces underadditive results, which suggests that the interference lies later in the transmission of information from stimulus to response. By contrast, it is held that the speeding of the stimulus-to-response translation stage for second-response processing is additive with stimulus onset asynchrony (SOA), which is in accordance with a model in which the two tasks queue for access to a mechanism that determines response selection (Pashler 1993). This account fits particularly well with Soar, which is a single-channel theory as far as the problem space in which it is operating is concerned, and the problem space would be relevant for only the central cognitive components of the total RT.[5]

In another paper, Pashler (1990) compared a vocal-manual response combination with a manual-manual one. Bottleneck effects were somewhat less strong with the former combination, as models such as the first and third of those considered above, which are concerned with the control process/modular interface, would predict (see also McLeod 1977). A more surprising effect was that the manual-manual interference was much greater when the order of the two tasks was unknown. Pashler argues that this may well be due to the system's uncertainty in the manual-manual condition over separating the two response domains. This presumably forces the subject to undertake a more serial style of processing. This, in turn, however, implies that in the other condition, a more parallel style of processing is operating, as, say, McLeod (1977) would presuppose.

Knowledge-of-order is not the only higher-level variable that produces surprising effects on how control processes operate. A second such variable is the knowledge about a following task even when, in contrast to the refractory period situation, the second stimulus does not overlap the first in time. Umiltà et al. (1992) examined the situation in which a second unspeeded task using the same stimulus followed a speeded-choice RT task after a 2-sec interval (see also Nobel, Sanders, and Trumbo 1981). The primary task involved responding as to whether two vertically aligned letters were to the left or right of the fixation point. The unspeeded secondary task was to say whether the letters were same or different. Reactions to the primary task were 111 ms slower than if there was no secondary task. If, however, the unpaced secondary task involved a stimulus change with a response required to a new stimulus, an arrow, which appeared with a SOA of 1800 ms, then the primary task was slowed by only 17 ms.

To explain these phenomena, Umiltà et al. adopt Pashler's bottleneck thesis. In the critical condition, they hold that there is an additional processing stage concerning the decision about the group of responses to be produced first. One needs to consider, however, why this cannot be simply set up in advance. Consider what would happen if a light came on twice 2 sec apart with the instruction to press the left key on the first signal and the right key on the second and without the need to have both hands on the keys throughout. Would a simple RT also be slowed by the need to make a second one 2 sec later? The "decision" in the Umiltà et al. paradigm presumably must occur because the stimulus triggers both task schemas.

To obtain further information Umiltà et al. replaced the compatible choice RT as the primary task by an incompatible one. This naturally slowed responding, but the Umiltà cost was less if the stimulus-response (S-R) mapping was incompatible (48 ms) than if it was compatible (74 ms).[6] Umiltà et al. explained the underadditivity: "Incompatible S-R pairings render more time-consuming the process that takes place at the response selection stage. Consequently, the extra time that should have been spent waiting for the decision stage (i.e., the bottleneck) to become available, passes in part while the incompatible response is being selected, and is not entirely transferred to the response latency" (p. 34). This involves some alteration to Pashler's theory, where the bottleneck is in the response selection stage itself. Umiltà et al.'s position could, though, be interpreted as that whichever specific response is to be produced, it can be processed partially in parallel with determining which class of response is to be produced. This implies that top-down selection of the task schema is a process occurring in parallel with schema determination of the response. This fits better with the CAP and Norman and Shallice models than the purely serial Soar. Alternatively, one could argue that both the Umiltà et al. paradigm and the use of incompatible S-R pairings require a monitored processing style, possibly one associated with Supervisory System operation. They are therefore slower, but the combination is underadditive.

A third closely related paradigm derives from the work of Jersild (1927) and Spector and Biederman (1976). Two tasks alternate at a fairly rapid rate but without overlapping in time. When the tasks involve unambiguous cueing—the stimulus in one condition is not a possible stimulus for the other condition—both sets of authors found no switching cost when alternating tasks were compared with single-task conditions. In more recent investigations, however, it has been found that when the tasks are not unambiguously cued over the course of the experiment, very sizable switching costs occur (see the chapter by Allport et al. in this volume for an extensive discussion of this paradigm). For instance, Rogers and Monsell (1992) adapted this procedure so that the experimental and control conditions did not require separate blocks. Stimuli appeared in a completely predictable circuit of four positions—NW, NE, SE, SW, NW . . . —and all stimuli consisted of a pair of characters, with at most one a digit, at most one a letter, and at most one an irrelevant nonalphanumeric character like % or #. When the character pair appeared in one of the top two positions, the subject had to say whether the digit, which was always present, was odd or even. When the pair appeared in one of the two lower positions, the subject had to say whether the letter was a consonant or a vowel. Thus, task-switch trials were interleaved with task-stay trials. In this experiment, which did not involve unambiguous cueing, "switch costs" are large (100–500 ms), and greater if the stimulus block contains character pairs with both a digit and a letter.

How long does it take for the system to carry out task set reconfiguration, to use Rogers and Monsell's term? When a block of trials had a fixed intertrial (R-S) interval varying from 0.15 to 1.2 sec, the switch costs declined linearly from intertrial intervals of 0.15 to 0.45 sec, but for longer intervals, the cost remained constant at about 120 ms, much the same value as the cost in Umiltà et al.'s initial experiments. Rogers and Monsell suggest that task set reconfiguration has two components. One component, which can be carried out from top-down information alone, takes about half a second. However, the second component can be completed only when the stimulus actually arrives.

As in the Umiltà et al. paradigm, a task can be optimally performed only if it follows closely and without interruption a trial of the same task or if it is unambiguously (for that session) cued by the stimulus. In particular, a consistent ordering of the tasks is not sufficient for rapid effective selection. Whether the slowing is the reflection of the on-line selection time involved in the absence of eliciting stimuli or, more likely, a consequence of a strategic error-reducing process, as suggested for certain refractory period phenomena by Pashler (1990), is not clear.[7] Moreover, if the suggestions of Rogers and Monsell are correct, switching back to a new task cannot be completely carried out using top-down information alone. Stimulus-cued task selection and top-down task selection seem to have different properties.

Why task order should be an inefficient cue for task selection is unclear on the CAP model and particularly on Soar. In Soar, working memory consists of data elements that can be either the output of the perceptual systems or state outputs of previous productions. However, the speed and effectiveness of the selection of new operations are independent of whether the relevant working memory elements have arisen from perceptual or more central operations. If, then, operator selection through perceptual cueing has different properties than through central selecting (e.g., by order), then this seems difficult for Soar to explain. The CAP model is unclear on this point. It would, however, be straightforward to incorporate on the contention scheduling model because perceptual and top-down triggering are clearly differentiated.

Support for the idea that top-down task selection and stimulus-cued selection obey different principles comes from neuropsychology. In particular, in Parkinson's disease, simple RT is often grossly lengthened by comparison with normal controls, but in the same patients, choice RT is much less impaired and can even be normal (Bloxham, Mindell, and Frith 1984; Sheridan, Flowers, and Hurrell 1987; Goodrich, Henderson, and Kennard 1989; Pullman et al. 1990; see Henderson and Goodrich, n.d., for review and Dubois et al. 1991 for a somewhat different perspective and two failures to observe the simple RT versus choice RT contrast). Frith and Done (1986) argue that the selection problem these patients have with simple RT arises because that task requires a supplementary attention-demanding process. They provided additional evidence for this hypothesis by showing that in normal subjects a secondary oral reading task that did not produce structural interference with the RT task slowed simple RT much more than choice RT. Moreover, Goodrich, Henderson, and Kennard (1989) have combined the two procedures: dual tasks and the use of Parkinson's disease patients. Parkinson's patients show no difference in the degree of dual-task interference between simple and choice RT, unlike normal controls, who showed far more interference with simple RT.

Could this difficulty that Parkinson's patients have with the preparation presumably required for optimal performance in simple RT be a result of their inability to program response sequences in advance? Goodrich, Henderson, and Kennard (1989) reject this possibility because Parkinson's patients are able to anticipate targets accurately in a discrete response, coincidence timing task. However, the difficulty in initiating responses shown in RT tasks can occur in cognitive tasks with very different temporal parameters. Thus, in the Tower-of-London test, a test of short-term planning, it has been shown that medicated Parkinson's patients produced considerably longer initial thinking times —roughly double—than normal controls (Morris et al. 1988; Owen et al. 1992). Yet subsequent moves in the solution attempt are executed no slower than in normal controls, and some Parkinson's groups perform as well as controls on their rate of successful solutions. This fits with Frith and Done's

(1986) conclusion that control of action by an internal intention is impaired, but control of action by an external stimulus is intact.

As far as the three models of control processes are concerned, the dissociation between intact overall success rate and considerably lengthened initial thinking time, together with the relative intactness of choice RT, makes implausible an account within the framework of Soar that the deficit lies in a general inability to select operators. Instead, an explanation that would correspond closely to Frith and Done's position is available. Decreased activation in schema selection within contention scheduling would be assumed from the outputs of higher-level selected schemas, but intact triggering could occur from perceptual input.[8]

## 16.5 FRONTAL SYNDROMES INVOLVING DISORDERED ACTION ROUTINES

The idea that with the perceptual triggering of schema selection intact, the top-down activation of schemas may be selectively impaired relates closely to another well-known contrast in the neuropsychological literature. Goldberg (1985) (see also Roland, Larsen, and Shinhoj 1980; Eccles 1982) argued that structures in the medial frontal regions, in particular the supplementary motor area (SMA), are responsible for the predictive control of internally generated voluntary actions, while lateral premotor regions carry out closed-loop, perceptually driven actions. While the precise extent of the functions attributed by Goldberg to particular medial frontal regions such as the SMA is not entirely clear, it would be inappropriate to interpret the contrast too grandly. Thus, it is unreasonable to assume that an area as small as the SMA could organize, say, the prey-seeking behavior of a hungry animal, to use Rizzolatti's (1985) example. Moreover, because parkinsonism is held to be "the prototypical human disease process affecting the operation of the medial system" (Goldberg 1985, p. 582), Goldberg's position on that syndrome corresponds closely to Frith and Done's.

There is neuropsychological evidence that the role of cells in the SMA in the control of action is very different from that of premotor units in inferior area 6 (part of Goldberg's lateral system). Those in inferior area 6 cells discharge during specific motor acts like grasping, holding, and tearing, and they appear to distinguish specific types of hand grip (precision grip, finger prehension, whole hand prehension); the cells generally discharge during movements, and a visual stimulus that activates them must be of a size appropriate to the particular grip to which they relate (Rizzolatti et al. 1988). By contrast, the firing of cells on the medial surface ($6a\beta$) is not affected by the visual characteristics of an object except that they respond to graspable objects at a reachable distance and not to nongraspable ones (Rizzolatti et al. 1990). Moreover, the firing of many of these neurons is modulated prior to the movement, either congruently with the change occurring during movement (20/44 neurons) or noncongruently (24/44). Rizzolatti et al. (1990) claim that the mesial frontal areas control a variety of preparatory processes such as the inhibition of reflexlike movements toward interesting objects. (For related suggestions based on similar techniques, see Kurata and Wise 1988.)

Lesions to medial frontal regions also seem to be involved in a number of related syndromes. Most basic of these is the grasp reflex, when the patient tends to grasp the finger of the clinician when the palm is stroked and then the finger slowly withdrawn; this occurs despite specific instructions not to grasp the finger. De Renzi and Barbieri (1992) showed that this is found much more frequently following lesions to medial frontal cortex (17 of 24 patients) than following lesions to lateral frontal cortex (4 of 15 patients) or to other parts of the brain. As De Renzi and Barbieri (1992) argue, this syndrome can be understood easily in terms of damage to cells such as those in area 6aß that Rizzolatti et al. (1990) describe.

Somewhat more complex is utilization behavior (UB) (Lhermitte 1983), when an object placed in front of the patient triggers the action characteristically associated with the object. This can occur even when the patient is supposed to by carrying out other tasks, such as clinical neuropsychology tests (Shallice et al. 1989). Such incidental utilization behavior has also been observed by Brazzelli, Della Sala, and Spinnler (personal communication). It is clear that at least in such patients, the behavior is not secondary to a failure of the patients to understand what is required. From the anatomical perspective, the Goldberg thesis is only partly supported. Lhermitte, Pillon, and Serdaru (1986) found UB in 45 percent of their frontal patients as opposed to 7 percent of nonfrontal patients. However, although precise localization of the disorder within the frontal lobes is not (as yet) possible, Lhermitte (1983) suggested that UB resulted from lesions of the orbital surface of the inferior frontal lobes and possibly the caudate nucleus rather than the medial surface; the lesion site of the incidental utilization behavior patient studied by Shallice et al. (1989) fits with Lhermitte's position. Although strictly outside the anatomical suggestions of Goldberg, the idea that orbital and medial frontal lobe systems may have functions that collectively contrast with dorsolateral frontal ones is present in Fuster's (1989) thesis that "the control of interference is carried out by inhibitory counter-influences originating in orbital and perhaps also medial prefrontal cortex" (p. 165).

Before discussing explanations of utilization behavior, I will introduce another related condition: the action disorganization difficulty reported by Schwartz et al. (1991), which they term frontal apraxia.[9] Their patient, H.H., had sustained a lesion arising from a pericallosal artery aneurysm, which particularly affected the frontal lobes bilaterally. Schwartz et al. analyzed videos of H.H. while he was carrying out—on many occasions—two highly routine tasks: eating breakfast and brushing his teeth. They viewed H.H.'s behavior when eating breakfast in terms of a hierarchy of action events, A-1 to A-5 (table 16.1). A crux was defined as the A-1 action unit that accomplishes the goal of an A-2. An independent A-1 action is one that is not in the same A-2 level "bracketing" of the action stream as the crux of its A-2. Schwartz and her

**Table 16.1** Levels of Action Control Involved in the Activity of Eating an Institutional Breakfast

| | |
|---|---|
| (A5) | (Breakfast-eating) |
| (A4) | (Coffee-drinking); (Egg-eating)... |
| A3 | Coffee-preparing; (Coffee-consuming) |
| A2 | Coffee-grinds; Sugar-ing; Cream-ing |
| A1 | Sugar-shaking; Sugar-packet-opening; *Sugar-pouring* |

Note: Each level unpacks one activity on the level above. The nonbracketed elements are those considered in the empirical analysis of Schwartz et al. (1991). The italicized A1 is a crux.

colleagues showed that in the "coffee-making" task, not only did the number of errors decline over sessions ($s$) but so did the proportion of those that were independent ($y$), according to the function:

$$y = 0.7 - 0.4 \log s.$$

This means that initially a large number of errors were independents, indicating great disorganization in the overall action plan. In addition, errors that occurred on the crux were analyzed. These included place substitutions, such as transporting the cream (a coffee-related object) (say) to an anomalous destination ($N = 42$); object substitutions, such as adding oatmeal to the coffee ($N = 15$), and drinking anticipations, such as drinking the water without the coffee grinds ($N = 4$). These argument errors co-occur with action unit selection errors. A similar co-occurrence of these two types of error occurs in the action lapses produced by normal subjects (Reason 1984).

The capturing of behavior by perceptual triggers, as in the grasp reflex and utilization behavior, fits well with theories that differentiate perceptual triggers from top-down activation. However, if one considers normal performance in the breakfast-eating situation, it is clear that a number of different levels of control are operating simultaneously. This is much easier to represent in models with an explicit production system type of representation than in models such as CAP, where control is exerted through a single back propagation network.

On the other hand, the account given by Shallice et al. (1989) of utilization behavior was that it reflects the normal operation of contention scheduling in the absence of modulation by an additional system—the Supervisory System. This explanation was motivated by the parallel between such behaviors and the capture errors found in action lapses made by normal subjects, which Reason (1984) showed tend to occur when one is preoccupied with some other line of thought.[10] However, at least as plausible is the position taken by Schwartz et al. (1991) that they occur through weakened activation within the top-down control structure for the hierarchy of routine actions (contention scheduling). Argument errors, in particular, seem in principle easier to explain on the latter account.

Whatever the detailed nature of the mechanism that ensures the efficient control of a hierarchy of routine actions, which corresponds to contention scheduling on the Norman and Shallice theory, one aspect would presumably be that nonselected schemas (or their equivalent) are actively inhibited. Active inhibition seems likely to be a general design principle of the cognitive system. Houghton and Tipper (n.d.) have put forward a neural network model where corresponding to each representation there is both an excitatory and an inhibitory node, and when there is competition, the inhibitory nodes of the rejected candidates are activated. The model acounts well for inhibition of return and negative priming, and similar principles seem to apply when the competition is between objects toward which an action (like reaching) could be directed (Tipper, Lortie, and Baylis 1992).

To return to the task-switching paradigms, overcoming this active inhibitory process could well be at the root of the time cost entailed in the reconfiguration of mental set described by Rogers and Monsell (1992). In particular, they find that for intertrial intervals between 0.4 and 1.2 sec, the switch cost remains constant (at 120 ms in one paradigm), while declining steeply for intertrial intervals between 0.15 and 0.4 sec like a refractory period function. They assume that the residual switch cost can be removed only by acting on the presentation of the stimulus. This would correspond to schemas being in either a selected or an inhibited state, with full selection requiring the actual presentation of the stimulus.

## 16.6 BEYOND ROUTINE ACTION AND PREFRONTAL FUNCTIONS

Soar is the most developed of a number of artificial intelligence problem-solving programs that contain a key distinction between the tackling of routine and nonroutine tasks (Fahlman 1974; Sussman 1975). Thus, impasses are a key feature in the Soar architecture. They arise when the preference semantics of the system does not allow a decision to be produced from the preferences produced by the elaboration phase. It is only by resolving impasses that the system learns. The Norman and Shallice model was based on the related notion that concepts like novelty[11] can have a computational correspondence. It extended the idea of supraroutine processes by postulating a separate system—the Supervisory System—which modulates the operation of routine action selection (the domain of contention scheduling).

The major empirical evidence adduced that processes specialized for supraroutine operations might involve a separable system was the effect of prefrontal lesions (Shallice 1982, 1988). There are, however, two related major problems in assessing this line of evidence. First, the tasks that show selective effects of frontal lobe lesions tend to be derived from clinical practice and are not so easily analyzable empirically as more standard information-processing tasks; contrast, say, Wisconsin Card-Sorting (Milner 1963) with lexical decision. Second, computational models hardly exist of any task that is selectively affected by frontal lesions, and those that exist among them, Dehaene and Changeux (1991) of Wisconsin Card-Sorting and Cohen, Dunbar, and McClelland (1990) of Stroop (Cohen and Huston, chap. 18, this volume) have a single-layer control structure.

If, though, one accepts (1) an intuitive assessment of the key components of the task and (2) an intuitive characterization of the function that the component effects then, there is now evidence that a variety of suparoutine functions are affected by frontal lesions (table 16.2). It is proposed that the functions listed in table 16.2 require systems (collectively, the Supervisory System) separable from those responsible for routine action and thought control (collectively, contention scheduling). For instance, take preparation (long term) for a specific event or action, which corresponds to the setting up and realization of intentions. A system concerned with the on-line selection between routine actions using procedures that reflect well-learned relations between and priorities of the relevant actions would not seem able to implement the setting up and realizing of a particular intention specific to a particular occasion.

Tasks that appear to involve each of the postulated functions are impaired by frontal lobe lesions. However, although there are certain tasks such as Wisconsin Card-Sorting, which presumably requires dimensional relevance detection, in which good evidence exists that areas of the prefrontal lobes other than the medial structures discussed earlier are relevant for the effecting of the function (Milner 1963), in general this is merely an assumption. Most of the studies listed in table 16.2 are group studies contrasting the performance of groups of patients with lesions anterior of the central sulcus and groups of either posterior-lesioned patients or normal controls.[12] Thus, the neuropsychological evidence for the dissociability of contention scheduling functions and Supervisory System functions based on anatomical correspondences is far from solid.

Functional evidence does exist. Thus, deficits can occur on tasks of the type described in table 16.2 without, say, impairments on tasks that require contention scheduling alone (Owen et al. 1990; Shallice and Burgess 1991). However, without double dissociation evidence, the possibility of quantitative resource differences between tasks cannot be effectively ruled out, and such evidence would seem difficult to obtain between a suparoutine function and all contention scheduling ones. Thus, the claim of a qualitative distinction between contention scheduling functions and suparoutine (Supervisory System) ones remains still rather speculative. Even more so are ideas on the fractionation of Supervisory System functions and how the system might relate to consciousness (Shallice 1991; Shallice and Burgess 1991).

## 16.7 CONCLUSIONS

No theory of control processes can be considered as other than speculative. Of the three theories considered, Soar has the greatest problems, first from how automatic processes are ever achieved (in, say, search tasks), second from the way that it holds perceptual elements and the output states of productions to have similar control properties, and third because the suparoutine processes it has available are limited to impasses. Its difficulties are no doubt a reflection of its being capable of satisfactory implementation. However, in this

**Table 16.2** Postulated Nonroutine Functions Affected by Frontal Lobe Lesions

| Hypothetical function | Task | Evidence |
|---|---|---|
| Relevant dimension detection[a] | Attentional Set Shifting | Owen et al. 1991 |
| Anomaly detection | Deviant Stimulus ERP[b] | Knight 1984, 1991 |
| Error suspicious behaviour[c] | Reversed Maze Learning[d] | Karnath and Wallesch, n.d. |
| Relevant set/plan induction | Brixton Spatial Anticipation | Burgess and Shallice 1993[e] |
| Preparation (short term) for specific event/action | Delayed Response Paradigms[f] | Quintana and Fuster, 1989[g] Funahashi, Bruce, and Goldman-Rakic 1989 |
| Preparation (long term) for specific event/action[h] | Multiple Subgoal Scheduling | Shallice and Burgess 1991 |
| Planning for specific contingency | Tower-of-London[i] | Owen et al. 1990 |
| Inhibition of prepotent response | Stroop Sentence Completion | Perret 1974 Burgess and Shallice 1993[e] |
| Verified episodic memory utilization[j] | Recall | Delbecq-Derouesne, Beauvois, and Shallice 1990 Moscovitch 1989 |

a. Applies when dimension is nonsalient or habituated, that is, when contention scheduling will not be sufficient.
b. Relevant deficit characteristic is reduction of P3a (evoked response to "irrelevant" novel stimulus) with normal P3b (evoked response to target).
c. In the sense of Rizzo, Bagnara and Visciola (1987).
d. Deficit suggested by strong trend, in rate of:

$$\frac{\text{Self-correction of an error before reaching a dead end}}{\text{Visual feedback of an error in a dead end}}$$

e. See Shallice and Burgess (1993).
f. There are many other interpretation of delayed-response findings (e.g., Goldman-Rakic 1987).
g. See Fuster (1991).
h. Equivalent to intention generation and realization.
i. Deficit shown by significantly lengthened thinking times for moves after the first in the context of normal first move thinking times.
j. For relevant interpretation of confabulations in recall see Shallice (1988, pp. 377–379).

chapter it has been argued that any complete theory of control processes needs to account for phenomena at three different levels: the control process/processing subsystem (or network) interface, the hierarchical organization of the control of routine activities, and supraroutine processes.

## NOTES

1. A much simpler connectionist approach—that of Cohen, Dunbar, and McClelland (1990)—is discussed by Cohen (chap. 18, this volume). It takes the same position as the CAP model in contrast to the other models on the three critical differences discussed.

2. It actually gives an exponent for the power law that differs greatly from the correct one, but the general form of the curve is appropriate. Thus, in the simulation of Seibel's (1963) experiment on learning, a 1023-choice reaction time task, its exponent is $-0.80$, while for Seibel's subjects it was $-0.17$. Whether Soar could be altered in a principled way such that the qualitative fit was preserved and the quantitative parameters changed radically is unclear.

3. Later developments of the model (Shallice 1988) make an analogous contrast in the control of attention to that drawn by Posner and Peterson (1990) in anatomical terms between a posterior and an anterior attentional network, with the former being a visuospatial attentional control and the latter the Supervisory System.

4. The connections in the model have so-called fast weights (Hinton and Plaut 1987), as well as the standard slowly altering weights, so that recently occurring information can be effectively reused.

5. Pashler argued that his results are incompatible with the Norman and Shallice model. However, competition for schema selection cannot be identified with competition in response production. The relevant schema could well be that mediating the stimulus-response mapping.

6. In fact, the interaction was not quite significant, but the smaller incompatible slowing was replicated in a further experiment, when a value of 44 ms was obtained.

7. See, however, the paper by Allport, Styles, and Hsieh (chap. 17, this volume).

8. If perceptual triggering generally gives a stronger activation in schema selection than top-down activation, then the differential effect might arise merely from a general decrement in activating effect. To assess such a possibility would, however, require a computational model.

9. A complete listing of the disordered action routine syndromes of (medial) frontal origin should include the "alien hand" syndrome (Goldberg, Mayer, and Toglia 1981) and "akinetic mutism" (Damasio and Van Hoesen 1983). The region also includes the anterior cingulate often activated in positron emission tomography studies and called the site of the anterior antentional center (Posner and Peterson 1990). Posner and Rothbart (1992) hold it to be "related to awareness" (p. 98). Their evidence, though, seems as compatible with the more prosaic types of function discussed in this chapter.

10. A direct analogue of capture errors has been obtained by Della Malva et al. (1993) in a group study of frontal patients and involving higher-level processes: word and picture associations.

11. The use of the term *novel* in the theory has been interpreted by Karnath, Wallesch, and Zimmerman (1991) to apply to the first trial only on which a nonroutine task is posed to the subject. While it seems impossible to operationalize in a theory-independent way how many trials have to be carried out before routine processes are in effective operation, in most situations, more than one trial would be involved. A clear example is the number of trials in which a novelty response habituated in the event-related potential (ERP) paradigm of Knight (1984).

12. Such evidence exists in animal lesion studies (Petrides 1987), but it is unclear how the functions selectively impaired should be specified.

# REFERENCES

Atkinson, R. C., and Shiffrin, R. M. (1968). Human memory: A proposed system and its control processes. In K. W. Spence and J. T. Spence (Eds.), *The psychology of learning and motivation: Advances in research and theory*, vol. 2. New York: Academic Press.

Baddeley, A. D., and Hitch, G. (1974). Working memory. In *The psychology of learning and motivation*, vol. 8. New York: Academic Press.

Bloxham, C. A., Mindel, T. A., Frith, C. D. (1984). Initiation and execution of predictable and unpredictable movements in Parkinson's disease. *Brain, 107,* 371–384.

Broadbent, D. E. (1982). Task combination and selective intake of information. *Acta Psychologica, 50,* 253–290.

Cheng, P. W. (1985). Restructuring versus automaticity: Alternative accounts of skill acquisition. *Psychological Review, 92,* 414–423.

Cohen, J. D., Dunbar, K., and McClelland, J. L. (1990). On the control of automatic processes: A parallel distributed processing account of the Stroop effect. *Psychological Review, 97,* 332–361.

Cooper, R., and Shallice, T. (1993). Soar and the case for unified theories of cognition. Technical Report UCL-PSY-ADREM-TR7, Department of Psychology, University College, London.

Damasio, A. R., and Van Hoesen, G. W. (1983). Emotional disturbances associated with focal lesions of the frontal lobe. In K. Heilman and P. Satz (Eds.), *The neuropsychology of human emotion: Recent advances,* 85–110. New York: Guilford Press.

Dehaene, S., and Changeux, J-P. (1991). The Wisconsin Card Sorting test: Theoretical analysis and modelling in a neuronal network. *Cerebral Cortex, 1,* 62–79.

Delbecq-Derouesne, J., Beauvois, M-F., and Shallice, T. (1990). Preserved recall versus impaired recognition: A case study. *Brain, 113,* 1045–1074.

Della Malva, C. L., Stuss, D. T., D'Alton, J., and Willmer, J. (1993). Capture errors, and sequencing after frontal brain lesions *Neuropsychologia, 31,* 363–372.

De Renzi, E., and Barbieri, C. (1992). The incidence of the grasp reflex following hemispheric lesion and its relation to frontal damage. *Brain, 115,* 293–313.

Detweiler, M., and Schneider, W. (1991). Modelling the acquisition of dual task skills in a connectionist/control architecture. In D. Damos (Ed.), *Multiple-task performance: Selected Topics,* 69–99. London: Taylor & Francis.

Dubois, B., Boller, F., Pillon, B., and Agid, Y. (1991). Cognitive deficits in Parkinson's disease. In F. Boller and J. Grafman (Eds.), *Handbook of neuropsychology,* vol. 5, 195–240. Amsterdam: Elsevier.

Eccles, J. C. (1982). The initiation of voluntary movements by the supplementary motor area. *Archiv Fur Psychiatrie und Nervenkrankheiten, 231,* 423–441.

Elman, J. L. (1990). Finding structure in time. *Cognitive Science, 14,* 179–212.

Fahlman, S. E. (1974). A planning system for robot construction tasks. *Artificial Intelligence, 5,* 1–49.

Fisk, A. D., and Schneider, W. (1983). Category and word search: Generalising search principles to complex processes. *Journal of Experimental Psychology: Learning, Memory and Cognition, 2,* 177–195.

Fodor, J. A. (1983). *The modularity of mind.* Cambridge, MA: MIT Press.

Frith, C. D., and Done, J. S. (1986). Routes to action in reaction time tasks. *Psychological Research*, 48, 169–177.

Funahashi, S., Bruce, C. J., and Goldman-Rakic, P. S. (1989). Mnemonic coding of visual space in the monkey's dorsolateral prefrontal cortex. *Journal of Neurophysiology*, 61, 331–349.

Fuster, J. M. (1989). *The prefrontal cortex*. 2d ed. New York: Raven Press.

Fuster, J. M. (1991). Role of prefrontal cortex in delay tasks: Evidence from reversible lesion and unit recording in the monkey. In H. S. Levin, H. M. Eisenberg, and A. L. Benton (Eds.), *Frontal lobe function and dysfunction*, 59–71. New York: Oxford University Press.

Goldberg, G. (1985). Supplementary motor area structure and function: Review and hypotheses. *Behavioral and Brain Sciences*, 8, 567–616.

Goldberg, G., Mayer, N. H., and Toglia, J. U. (1981). Medial frontal cortex infarction and the alien hand sign. *Archives of Neurology*, 38, 683–686.

Goldman-Rakic, P. S. (1987). Circuitry of primate prefrontal cortex and regulation of behaviour by representational memory. In F. Plum (Ed.), *Handbook of physiology: The nervous system*, vol. 5, 373–417. Bethesda, MD: American Physiological Society.

Goodrich, S., Henderson, L., and Kennard, C. (1989). On the existence of an attention-demanding process peculiar to simple reaction time: Converging evidence from Parkinson's disease. *Cognitive Neuropsychology*, 6, 309–331.

Henderson, L., and Goodrich, S. (n.d.). Simple reaction time and predictive tracking in Parkinson's disease: Do they converge on a single fixed impairment of preparation? *Journal of Motor Behaviour*. In press.

Hinton, G. E., and Plaut D. C. (1987). Using fast weights to deblur old memories. In *Proceedings of the Ninth Annual Conference of the Cognitive Science Society*, 177–186. Seattle.

Houghton, G., and Tipper, S. P. (n.d.). A model of inhibitory mechanisms in selective attention. In D. Dagenbach and T. Carr (Eds.), *Inhibitory mechanisms in attention, memory and language*. New York: Academic Press. In press.

Jersild, A. T. (1927). Mental set and shift. *Archives of Psychology*, 89.

Karnath, H. O., and Wallesch, C. W. (n.d.). Inflexibility of mental planning: A characteristic disorder with prefrontal lobe lesions? *Neuropsychologia*. In press.

Karnath, H. O., Wallesch, C. W., and Zimmerman, P. (1991). Mental planning and anticipatory processes with acute and chronic frontal lobe lesions: A comparison of maze performance in routine and non-routine situations. *Neuropsychologia*, 29, 271–290.

Knight, R. T. (1984). Decreased response to novel stimuli after prefrontal lesions in man. *Electroencephalography and Clinical Neurophysiology*, 59, 9–20.

Knight, R. T. (1991). Evoked potential studies of attention capacity in human frontal lobe lesions. In H. S. Levin, H. M. Eisenberg, and A. L. Benton (Eds.), *Frontal lobe function and dysfunction*, 139–153. New York: Oxford University Press.

Kurata, K., and Wise, S. P. (1988). Premotor and supplementary motor cortex in rhesus monkeys: Neural activity during externally—and internally—instructed motor tasks. *Experimental Brain Research*, 69, 327–343.

Laberge, D. (1975). Acquisition of automatic processing in perceptual and associative learning. In P. M. A. Rabbitt and S. Dornic (Eds.), *Attention and performance*, vol. 5. New York: Academic Press.

Laird, J. E., Newell, A., and Rosenbloom, P. S. (1987). Soar: An architecture for general intelligence. *Artificial Intelligence*, 33, 1–64.

Lhermitte, F. (1983). "Utilization-behaviour" and its relation to lesions of the frontal lobes. *Brain, 106*, 237–255.

Lhermitte, F., Pillon, B., and Serdaru, M. (1986). Human autonomy and the frontal lobes I: Imitation and utilization behaviour: A neuropsychological study of 75 patients. *Archives of Neurology, 19*, 326–334.

Logan, G. D. (1988). Towards an instance theory of automatization. *Psychological Review, 95*, 492–522.

MacLeod, C. M., and Dunbar, K. (1988). Training and Stroop-like interference: Evidence for a continuum of automaticity. *Journal of Experimental Psychology: Human Perception and Performance, 2*, 371–379.

McDermott, J., and Forgy, C. (1978). Production system conflict resolution strategies. In D. A. Waterman and F. Hayes-Roth (Eds.), *Pattern-directed inference systems*. New York: Academic Press.

McLeod, P. D. (1977). Parallel processing and the psychological refractory period. *Acta Psychologica, 41*, 381–391.

Milner, B. (1963). Effects of different lesions on card-sorting. *Archives of Neurology, 9*, 90–100.

Monsell, S. (1978). Recency, immediate recognition memory and reaction time. *Cognitive Psychology, 10*, 465–501.

Morris, R. G., Downes, J. J., Evenden, J. L., Sahakian, B. J., Heald, A., and Robbins, T. W. (1988). Planning and spatial working memory in Parkinson's disease. *Journal of Neurology, Neurosurgery and Psychiatry, 51*, 757–766.

Moscovitch, M. (1989). Confabulation and the frontal system: Strategic versus associative retrieval in neuropsychological theories of memory. In H. L. Roediger and F. I. M. Craik (Eds.), *Varieties of memory and consciousness: Essays in honor of Endel Tulving*. Hillsdale, NJ: Erlbaum.

Newell, A. (1990). *Unified theories of cognition*. Cambridge, MA: Harvard University Press.

Newell, A., and Rosenbloom, P. (1981). Mechanisms of skill acquisition and the law of practice. In J. R. Anderson (Ed.), *Cognitive skills and their acquisition*. Hillsdale, NJ: Erlbaum.

Newell, A., and Simon, H. A. (1972). *Human problem solving*. Englewood Cliffs, NJ: Prentice-Hall.

Nobel, M. E., Sanders, A. F., and Trumbo, D. A. (1981). Concurrence cost in double stimulation tasks. *Acta Psychologica, 49*, 141–158.

Norman, D. A. (1986). Reflections on cognition and parallel distribution processing. In J. L. McClelland and D. E. Rumelhart (Eds.), *Parallel distributed processing: Explorations in the microstructure of cognition*, vol 2. Cambridge, MA: MIT Press.

Norman, D. A. (1991). Approaches to the study of intelligence. *Artificial Intelligence, 47*, 327–346.

Norman, D. A., and Shallice, T. (1980, 1986). Attention to action: Willed and automatic control of behaviour. Centre for Human Information Processing Technical Report No. 99. Reprinted in revised form in R. J. Davidson, G. E. Schwartz, and D. Shapiro (Eds.), *Consciousness and self-regulation*, vol. 4. New York: Plenum.

Owen, A. M., Downes, J. J., Sahakian, B. J., Polkey, C. E., and Robbins, T. W. (1990). Planning and spatial working memory following frontal lobe lesions in man. *Neuropsychologia, 28*, 1021–1034.

Owen, A. M., James, M., Leigh, P. N., Summers, B. A., Marsden, C. D., Quinn, N. P., Lange, K. W., and Robbins, T. W. (1992). Fronto-striatal cognitive deficits at different stages of Parkinson's disease. *Brain, 115*, 1727–1751.

Owen, A. M., Roberts, A. C., Polkey, C. E., Sahakian, B. J., and Robbins, T. W. (1991). Extradimensional versus intra-dimensional set shifting performance following frontal lobe excisions, temporal-lobe excisions or amygdala-hippocampectomy in man. *Neuropsychologia, 10*, 993–1006.

Pashler, H. (1990). Do response modality effects support multiprocessor models of divided attention in simple tasks? *Journal of Experiment Psychology: Human Perception and Performance, 16*, 826–842.

Pashler H. (1993). Dual-task interference and elementary mental mechanisms. In D. E. Meyer and S. Kornblum (Eds.), *Attention and performance XIV*. Cambridge, MA: MIT Press.

Pashler, H., and Johnston, J. C. (1989). Chronometric evidence for central postponement in temporally overlapping tasks. *Quarterly Journal of Experiment Psychology, 41a*, 19–45.

Perret, E. (1974). The left frontal lobe in man and suppression of habitual responses in verbal categorical behaviour. *Neuropsychologia, 12*, 323–330.

Petrides, M. (1987). Conditional learning and the primate frontal cortex. In E. Perecman (Ed.), *The frontal lobes revisited*, 91–109. New York: IRBN Press.

Posner, M. I., and Peterson, S. E. (1990). The attention system of the human brain. *Annual Review of Neuroscience, 13*, 25–42.

Posner, M. I., and Rothbart, M. K. (1992). Attentional mechanisms and conscious experience. In A. D. Milner and M. D. Rugg (Eds.), *The neuropsychology of consciousness*, 91–111. London: Academic Press.

Posner, M. I., and Snyder, C. R. R. (1975). Facilitation and inhibition in the processing of signals. In P. M. A. Rabbitt and S. Dornic (Eds.), *Attention and performance*, vol. 5. New York: Academic Press.

Pullman, S. L., Watts, R. L., Juncos, J. L., and Sanes, J. D. (1990). Movement amplitude choice reaction time performance in Parkinson's disease may be independent of dopaminergic status. *Journal of Neurology, Neurosurgery and Psychiatry, 53*, 279–283.

Reason, J. T. (1984). Lapses of attention. In R. Parasuraman, R. Davies, and J. Beatty (Eds.), *Varieties of attention*. Orlando, FL: Academic Press.

Rizzo, A., Bagnara, S., and Visciola, M. (1987). Human error detection processes. *International Journal of Man-Machine Studies, 27*, 555–570.

Rizzolatti, G. (1985). Free will and motor subroutines: Too much for a small area. *Behavioral and Brain Sciences, 8*, 597.

Rizzolatti, G., Camarda, R. M., Fogassi, L., Gentilucci, M., Luppino, G., and Matelli, M. (1988). Functional organisation of inferior area 6 in the macaque monkey. II Area F5 and the control of distal movements. *Experimental Brain Research, 71*, 491–507.

Rizzolatti, G., Gentilucci, M., Camerda, R. M., Gallese, V., Luppino, G., Matelli, M., and Fogassi, L. (1990). Neurons related to reaching-grasping arm movements in the rostral part of area 6 (area 6aß). *Experimental Brain Research, 82*, 337–350.

Rogers, R., and Monsell, S. (1992). Task-set reconfiguration during a predictable task switch. Paper presented to the Experimental Psychology Society meeting, Oxford, April.

Roland, P. E., Larsen, N. A., and Shinhoj, E. (1980). Supplementary motor area and other cortical areas in organization of voluntary movements in man. *Journal of Neurophysiology, 43*, 118–136.

Rosenbloom, P. S., Laird, J. E., Newell, A., and McCarl, R. (1991). A preliminary analysis of the Soar architecture as a basis for general intelligence. *Artificial Intelligence, 47*, 289–325.

Ryan, C. (1983). Reassessing the automaticity-control distinction: Item recognition as a paradigm case. *Psychological Review, 90*, 171–178.

Schneider, W., and Detweiler, M. (1987). A connectionist/control architecture for working memory. In G. H. Bower (Ed.), *The psychology of learning and motivation*, vol. 21, 54–119. New York: Academic Press.

Schneider, W., and Fisk, A. D. (1982). Concurrent automatic and controlled visual search: Can processing occur without resource cost? *Journal of Experimental Psychology: Learning, Memory and Cognition, 8,* 261–278.

Schneider, W., and Fisk, A. D. (1984). Automatic category search and its transfer. *Journal of Experimental Psychology: Learning, Memory and Cognition, 10,* 1–15.

Schneider, W., and Oliver, W. L. (1991). An instructible connectionist/control architecture: Using rule-based instruction to accomplish connectionist learning in a human time scale. In K. Van Lehn (Ed.), *Architectures for intelligence*. Hillsdale, NJ: Erlbaum.

Schneider, W., and Shiffrin, R. M. (1977). Controlled and automatic human information processing. I: Detection, search and attention. *Psychological Review, 84,* 1–66.

Schneider, W., and Shiffrin, R. M. (1985). Categorization (restructuring) and automatization: Two separable factors. *Psychological Review, 92,* 424–428.

Schwartz, M. F., Reed, E. S., Montgomery, M., Palmer, C., and Mayer, N. H. (1991). The quantitative description of action disorganisation after brain damage: A case study. *Cognitive Neuropsychology, 8,* 381–414.

Seibel, R. (1963). Discrimination reaction time for a 1023-alternative task. *Journal of Experimental Psychology, 66,* 215–266.

Shallice, T. (1982). Specific impairments of planning. *Philosophical Transactions of the Royal Society (London) B, 298,* 199–209.

Shallice, T. (1988). *From neuropsychology to mental structure*. Cambridge: Cambridge University Press.

Shallice, T. (1991). The revival of consciousness in cognitive science. In W. Kessen, A. Ortony, and F. I. M. Craik (Eds.), *Memories, thoughts and emotions: Essays in honor of George Mandler*. Hillsdale, NJ: Erlbaum.

Shallice, T., and Burgess, P. W. (1991). Higher-order cognitive impairments and frontal lobe lesions in man. In H. S. Levin, H. M. Eisenberg, and A. J. Benton (Eds.), *Frontal lobe function and dysfunction,* 125–138. New York: Oxford University Press.

Shallice, T., and Burgess, P. W. (1993). Supervisory control of thought and action. In A. D. Baddeley and L. Weiskrantz (Eds.), *Attention: Selection, awareness and control: A tribute to Donald Broadbent*. Oxford: Oxford University Press.

Shallice, T., Burgess, P. W., Schon, F., and Baxter, D. M. (1989). The origins of utilization behaviour. *Brain, 112,* 1587–1598.

Sheridan, M. R., Flowers, K. A., and Hurrell, J. (1987). Programming and execution of movement in Parkinson's disease. *Brain, 110,* 1247–1271.

Shiffrin, R. M. (1988). Attention. In R. C. Atkinson, R. J. Herrnstein, G. Lindzey, and R. D. Luce (Eds.), *Stevens' handbook of experimental psychology,* 2d ed., 739–811. New York: Wiley.

Shiffrin, R. M., and Schneider, W. (1977). Controlled and automatic human information processing II. Perceptual learning, automatic attending, and a general theory. *Psychological Review, 84,* 127–190.

Snoddy, G. S. (1926). Learning and stability. *Journal of Applied Psychology, 10,* 1–36.

Spector, A., and Biederman, I. (1976). Mental set and mental shift revisited. *American Journal of Psychology, 89,* 669–679.

Sperling, G. (1960). The information available in brief visual presentations. *Psychological Monographs, 74*, 498.

Starr, A., Barrett, G., Pratt, H., Michalewski, H. J., and Patterson, J. V. (1990). Electrophysiological measures of short-term memory. In G. Vallar and T. Shallice (Eds.), *Neuropsychological impairments of short-term memory*. Cambridge: Cambridge University Press.

Sternberg, S. (1966). High-speed scanning in human memory. *Science, 153*, 652–654.

Sussman, G. J. (1975). *A computational model of skill acquisition*. New York: American Elsevier.

Tipper, S. P., Lortie, C., and Baylis, G. C. (1992). Selective reaching: Evidence for action-centred attention. *Journal of Experimental Psychology: Human Perception and Performance, 18*, 891–905.

Umiltà, C., Nicoletti, R., Simion, F., Tagliabue, M. E., and Bagnara, S. (1992). The cost of a strategy. *European Journal of Cognitive Psychology, 4*, 21–40.

Welford, A. T. (1952). The "psychological refractory period" and the timing of high-speed performance—A review and a theory. *British Journal of Psychology, 43*, 2–19.

# 17 Shifting Intentional Set: Exploring the Dynamic Control of Tasks

Alan Allport, Elizabeth A. Styles, and Shulan Hsieh

ABSTRACT  We describe a series of seven exploratory experiments, designed to investigate the effects of shifting different components of task *set*, both in speeded response tasks and in monitoring rapidly presented word sequences. Subjects made preinstructed attention shifts between different stimulus dimensions, between different semantic categories or attributes, between different cognitive operations, and between different response modes. Under many task-shift conditions (but not all), we found large and systematic costs in the speed and/or accuracy of performance, compared to conditions in which the same set of cognitive and perceptual motor operations was performed repeatedly over successive stimuli.

Our intention was to make use of these behavioral costs to explore the time course of underlying, voluntary control processes, and—if possible—to identify separable and/or shared executive resources, responsible for different features of task control. For example, is the difficulty of shifting set affected by the difficulty of the individual tasks, or by the degree of "automaticity" or "control" required by one or both of them? Does the requirement to shift concurrently more than one task attribute increase the RT cost of shifting? Does a stimulus-cued shift of task show smaller (or even zero) RT costs? The answers to several of these questions are strikingly counterintuitive, and we report a number of behavioral phenomena not previously described.

As our exploration proceeded, however, it became increasingly clear that the RT costs of shifting or reorienting task *set* do not directly reflect the time needed to complete a hypothetical shift-of-set operation, prior to executing the shifted task. Instead, we demonstrate that the shift costs represent a form of proactive interference from features of the task set implemented in preceding tasks. This task set inertia persists over periods lasting very much longer than the RT costs themselves.

In semantic monitoring of word lists under rapid sequential visual presentation (RSVP) conditions, a voluntary shift of criterion causes a large and abrupt drop in target identification accuracy, which then progressively recovers, eventually to reach preshift levels of accuracy. However, we also found that the process of recovery from this shift cost, in RSVP monitoring, is not a function of the real-time delay of a target item after the shift cue. Neither the RT shift cost, therefore, nor the RSVP criterion shift cost in monitoring accuracy, directly reflect real-time control operations. These findings raise some fundamental questions for our understanding of voluntary executive control.

## 17.1  INTRODUCTION

Psychological experiments (with adult human subjects) typically depend on their subjects' ability to adopt "at will" now one task *set*, now another, according to the experimenter's instructions. Very often, experiments require the subject to maintain a given task set over many trials, in which the same cognitive operations are to be performed repeatedly. In everyday activity, on the contrary, subjects often shift rapidly, and repeatedly, from one intended set of cognitive operations to another, frequently without any immediate external cues. We are interested in the mechanisms of voluntary control responsible for implementing these intentional shifts of set. How is the cognitive system reconfigured, moment by moment, to enable now one task to be performed, now another? How long does it take? What factors affect this time course?

In this chapter we describe a series of exploratory experiments through which we attempted to address these questions. (We shall describe here seven experiments, using three somewhat contrasting experimental paradigms.) Since what we have to report is a record of a quite elementary exploration, far from completed, in an area in which there is relatively little existing data to go on, we think it best to recount our findings more or less in chronological sequence. As will become clear, certain assumptions that we made, and that seemed harmless enough at an earlier stage in our enquiry, turned out later to be seriously mistaken. Indeed, our whole preconception about what it was that we were investigating (a preconception we suspect, from numerous conversations, that others may easily share) turned out to be mistaken.

Research on dynamic shifting or orienting of visual attention from one spatial location to another has been studied extensively in recent years (Posner and Petersen 1990). In contrast, research on other (generally nonspatial) aspects of cognitive control has tended to focus on the efficiency with which a given task set can be *maintained*, either in the face of potentially conflicting stimuli, as in the many forms of "Strooplike" interference (MacLeod 1991), or under conditions of "divided attention" with multiple task set in concurrent, dual-task performance (Hirst 1986). Dynamic shifting of set has received much less attention.

One attractively simple experimental approach in this area was first devised by Jersild (1927), and his experiments were replicated some 50 years later by Spector and Biederman (1976). These authors presented their subjects with lists of items (e.g., two-digit numbers) and requested them to either perform the same task (e.g., adding 3's, or subtracting 3's) repeatedly through the list as fast as possible or, in an alternation or "task shift" condition alternately add 3 to and subtract 3 from successive items. The response to each item was spoken aloud. Comparing alternating with single-task lists, in these and similar pairs of tasks, Jersild found large time costs of task alternation over the list as a whole, amounting typically to many hundreds of milliseconds per item. (With certain task pairings, however, Jersild [1927] and Spector and Biederman [1976] found no alternation cost. We have explored this issue in experiments 3 and 4 below.)

In the first four experiments reported here, we used variations on Jersild's original method, measuring self-paced list completion times. Experiment 5, instead, used discrete reaction times, with experimenter-paced stimulus presentation, while experiments 6 and 7 explored a quite different paradigm in which subjects monitored rapidly presented word sequences, with either constant or shifting target criteria.

## 17.2 THE EXPERIMENTS

### Experiment 1: Shifting Task Set: Perceptual Versus Cognitive Task Variables

In this initial experiment we compared the time cost of regular task alternation (1) between two different cognitive operations (simple numerical judgments) with (2) the cost of alternating between two possible task-relevant stimulus dimensions, and (3) the cost of alternating on both judgment-type and stimulus dimension concurrently.

**Method** The stimuli for this experiment were groups of one to nine identical numerals arranged symmetrically inside an outline rectangle (fig. 17.1a). The numerals, like the group size, ranged in value from 1 to 9, excluding 5. The numeral value ($V$) of the digits was always different from the number of digits in the group ($G$)—$V$ and $G$ incongruent—and both $V$ and $G$ varied independently from one stimulus to the next. The two numerical judgments were to decide whether the relevant number was (1) odd or even (Odd) or (2) whether it was more or less than five (More). Subjects made their decisions with respect to either the numeral value ($V$) or the group size ($G$), as instructed. (As is well known, in naming tasks $V$ is consistently faster than, and interferes with, incongruent values of $G$. See experiment 3 for further commentary.) There were ten conditions in all: four nonalternating conditions (V/Odd, G/Odd, V/More, G/More), two conditions of judgment alternation, with the relevant stimulus dimension held constant (V/Odd ↔ V/More and G/Odd ↔ G/More), two of stimulus-dimension alternation (V/Odd ↔ G/Odd and V/More ↔ G/More), and finally two task alternation conditions in which both judgment and stimulus dimension were to be switched concurrently (V/Odd ↔ G/More and V/More ↔ G/Odd). The stimuli were presented in lists of seven items. To prevent preview, items appeared one at a time in a sliding window, under the subject's (self-paced) manual control. Subjects were requested to work down each list as fast as possible, giving their responses ("odd," "even," "more," "less") aloud. Task instructions were given prior to each list. When the subject said that she was ready, the first item was exposed. The order of conditions was randomized. One practice list was given for each of the ten conditions. Subjects then completed two further lists under each of the ten conditions. Any condition in which an error occurred was repeated later with a new stimulus list. There were twelve subjects, all students aged 18 to 24.

**Results** The mean list completion times are shown in figure 17.2. Baseline values are the means of the two relevant nonalternating conditions in each

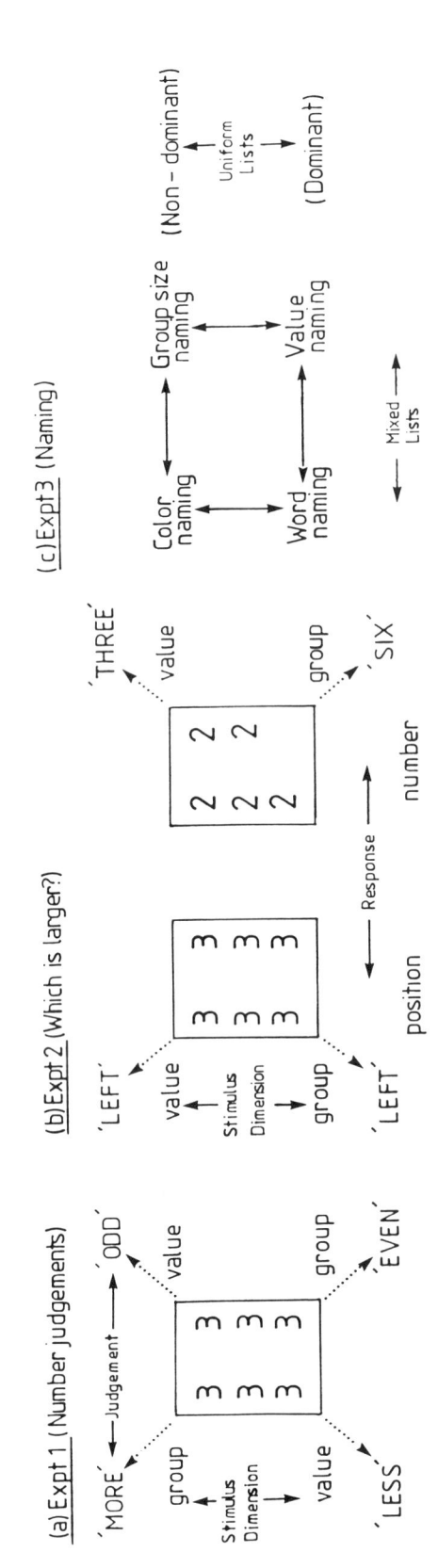

**Figure 17.1** The RT tasks and stimuli used in experiments 1–3.

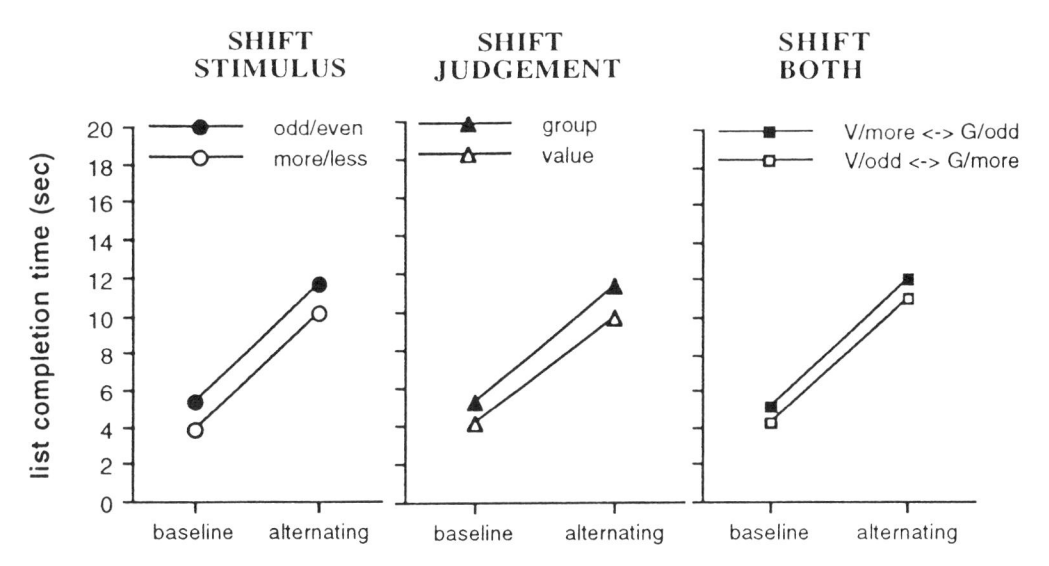

**Figure 17.2** List completion times in experiment 1. Stimuli were groups of numerals. Subjects attended to either the size of the group (G) or the symbolic value (V) of the numerals, and they judged either odd or even, or more or less than five. Left panel shows task alternation with respect to stimulus dimension (G or V) versus nonalternating baseline; center panel shows alternation of the two judgment tasks; right panel shows alternation on both task features concurrently.

case, representing the expected completion time for each alternation condition if there were no time cost involved in task alternation.

There were highly significant main effects of alternation and of task pairing within each of the three main conditions (all $p < 0.001$). These variables did not interact. Judgments of Odd/Even were consistently slower than More/Less, and judgments based on group size were slower than numeral value (both $p < 0.001$). However, there was no significant difference between the time cost of alternating stimulus dimension and judgment type, or between these conditions and the concurrent or double shift conditions. Errors were too infrequent to permit quantitative analysis. Discussion of these results is deferred until after experiments 2 and 3.

### Experiment 2: Shifting Task Set as a Function of Task (Decision) Difficulty

In experiment 1, manipulations of task difficulty—via attention to group size (G) versus value (V)—had small but highly consistent effects on list completion time, as did the two different judgment types, but these manipulations did not affect the time cost of task shifting. In experiment 2 we examined a different manipulation of task difficulty, this time holding constant the type of judgment to be made.

**Method** The task was to decide which of two integers was the greater, and task difficulty was manipulated by varying the numerical distance between them: the smaller the separation between the numbers to be compared, the harder (and slower) the decision (Besner and Coltheart 1979; Buckley and Gillman 1974; Moyer and Landauer 1967). Stimuli for the comparison task were composed of adjacent pairs of outline rectangles; each rectangle contained a group of from one to nine identical digits, similar to the stimuli in experiment 1 (see fig. 17.1b). Within each rectangle, $V$ and $G$ were always incongruent, and within each pair of rectangles, $V$ and $G$ of the right and left members of the pair also differed. In one set of stimuli ("Near" symbolic distance) $V$ on the left differed from $V$ on the right by one, two, or three units (mean difference of 2), and similarly for $G$. In the other set of stimuli ("Far" symbolic distance) the respective $V$ and $G$ values differed by three, four, or five units (mean difference of 4). The stimuli were presented in lists of seven pairs. As in experiment 1, they appeared one pair at a time in a sliding window. Subjects responded vocally to each stimulus pair, either by naming the larger of the two numbers being compared (Name) or by naming its position as right or left (Position). They compared either the two numeral values ($V$) or the two group sizes ($G$), as instructed. As in experiment 1, they were requested to work down a list of items as fast as possible without making any errors.

Using these materials and vocal responses, four basic tasks were defined: to respond with (1) the name of the larger digit value ($V_N$), (2) the name of the larger group ($G_N$), (3) the position of the larger digit value ($V_P$), and (4) the position of the larger group ($G_P$). Each of these tasks was performed as a uniform (nonalternating) task and in regular alternation throughout the list. In two of the alternation conditions (as in experiment 1), the subject was required to shift between the two stimulus dimensions ($V$ or $G$) for the numerical comparison, while holding the response dimension, $N$ or $P$, constant. In another two alternation conditions, subjects switched between the two response modes, $N$ or $P$, holding the task-relevant stimulus dimension constant. Subjects received one practice list for each of the four uniform tasks and for each of the alternation tasks. They then completed a total of four lists under each of the alternating and nonalternating conditions, in counterbalanced order. Lists in which an error occurred, or in which the subject stopped responding for more than 3 sec, were rerun (on new stimuli) at the end of the session. Twenty-four female subjects between ages 18 and 35 years were recruited from the Oxford University subject panel. Half the subjects were assigned randomly to the Far symbolic distance condition and the other half to the Near symbolic distance condition.

**Results** Correct list completion times are shown in figure 17.3. For each subject the times for the four nonalternating tasks were used, as in experiment 1, to calculate baseline values against which to compare any additional time costs of task alternation.

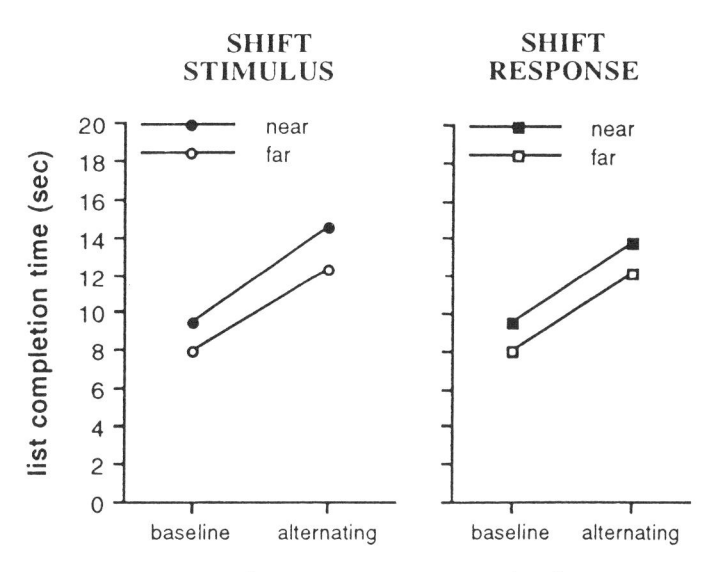

**Figure 17.3** List completion times in experiment 2 (number comparison task). Stimuli were pairs of numeral groups. Left panel: alternating task-relevant stimulus dimension (group size versus numeral value); right panel: alternating mode of response. Number comparisons were easy ("far") or difficult ("near").

Baseline and alternation times were compared in an analysis of variance with Near-Far symbolic distance as a between-subjects factor and baseline versus alternation conditions, and dimension of task shifting (stimulus, $S$, or response, $R$) as within-subjects factors. There was a significant main effect of decision difficulty (Near versus Far) ($F(1,22) = 4.36, p < .05$) and a highly significant effect of task alternation ($F(1,22) = 163.5, p < .0001$) but no significant interaction. That is, the time cost of task shifting was not significantly greater for difficult (Near) than for easy (Far) comparisons. In a further analysis, we confirmed that the two alternation conditions, $S$ and $R$, did not differ in magnitude of the shift cost ($F < 1.0$), and there was no interaction between these shift costs and Near/Far symbolic distance ($F < 1.0$).

## Experiment 3: Shifting Task Set within and between Different Stroop Task Domains

For this experiment, in addition to the Strooplike number stimuli ($V$ and $G$) used in experiment 1, we included also conventional color-word Stroop stimuli (Dyer 1973), composed of the words *red, blue, green, yellow,* and *brown,* printed equiprobably in one of the ink colors—red, blue, green, yellow, or brown—but with the constraint that the ink in which each word was written was incongruent with the color named by that word.

We wished to compare the costs of shifting task set, (1) when the stimulus ensemble remained constant from trial to trial, as in experiments 1 and 2, therefore providing no external cue to which task to perform ("uniform" lists), with the case (2) in which a change of stimulus type cued each shift of task, again in regular, preinstructed task alternation ("mixed" lists). For this purpose, we constructed three types of lists: (1) all color words, in incongruent ink colors; (2) all groups of numerals ($V$ and $G$ incongruent, as in experiment 1); and (3) "mixed" lists composed alternately of Stroop color words and of numeral groups. With the color word lists, subjects were required to read the words ($W$), or to name the color ($C$), or to alternate on successive stimuli between word naming and color naming. With the numeral group lists, they could name the numeral value ($V$), name the group size ($G$), or shift, on alternate stimuli, between $V$ and $G$. Finally, with the mixed stimulus lists (3), subjects were required to alternate between the two dominant naming tasks ($V$ and $W$) or between the two nondominant naming tasks ($G$ and $C$). Figure 17.1c summarizes these conditions.

As is well known, word naming is faster than color naming; moreover, incongruent color words interfere with naming the ink color, whereas an incongruent ink color generally has no effect on response time (RT) to name the word (Glaser and Glaser 1982). Similarly, RT to name group size is delayed by incongruent numeral values, but not vice versa (Fox, Shor, and Steinman 1971; MacLeod 1991). This pattern of results suggests that $C$ and $G$ correspond to weaker or nondominant mappings (Allport 1980a, 1980b; MacLeod and Dunbar 1988). Execution of these nondominant tasks, involving resistance to Stroop-like interference from the dominant task, is said to involve controlled processing (Shiffrin and Schneider 1977) or intervention of the supervisory attentional system (Norman and Shallice 1986). We were interested to establish, therefore, whether alternation between the two nondominant tasks ($C$ and $G$), in the mixed-list conditions, might entail greater shift costs compared to alternation between the two easy, or dominant, tasks ($W$ and $V$).

**Method** The stimuli were presented in lists of seven items, in the same way as in experiments 1 and 2. After minimal practice at each of the four basic naming tasks, subjects proceeded directly with the experiment. Instructions emphasized, as before, that the subject was to read each list aloud as fast as possible without making errors. Subjects performed each of the four nonalternating tasks once, followed immediately by each of the four alternating tasks, in counterbalanced order. This entire sequence (fixed for each subject) was then repeated eight times, with different stimulus lists, as eight successive runs, making a total of sixty-four lists per subject. Before each list, the subject received a new set of instructions, always different from the preceding list ("varied mapping" conditions). For the alternating tasks, the subject was also told with which of the two tasks to begin the list. If a subject stalled for more than 3 sec, or gave an incorrect response, that condition was repeated at the end of the run with a new list. Twelve female subjects were recruited from the Oxford University subject panel. Their ages ranged from 18 to 40 years.

**Results** Mean correct list completion times are shown in figure 17.4. The observed completion times in the four different alternation tasks were compared with the corresponding baseline values in a two-way analysis of variance, with task pair (four levels) and shift (two levels: alternation versus baseline) as repeated measures. Shift of set (alternation) was highly significant ($F(1,11) = 49.84, p < .0001$), as was task pair ($F(3,33) = 21.83, p < .0001$), and there was a significant interaction ($F(3,33) = 6.31, p < .002$). It is clear from figure 17.4 that this interaction occurs between the two alternation tasks with uniform stimulus lists, shown in panel a and the other two alternation tasks using mixed lists, shown in panel b. With uniform stimulus lists, alternating between tasks cost an increase in list completion time amounting, on average, to an additional 438 ms per item; with mixed lists the corresponding shift cost was 231 ms per item.

This pattern of results was tested in a further analysis, comparing uniform and mixed lists as two levels in the analysis. Uniform and mixed lists interacted strongly with alternation cost ($F(3,33) = 18.34, p < .0001$). However, partial comparisons showed no interaction between shift cost and list type within the two uniform-list conditions or, most important, within the two mixed-list conditions ($F < .5$). That is, alternating between the two nondominant (or Stroop) stimulus dimensions, C and G, showed the same time cost (mean 225 ms per item) as alternating between the two dominant (or non-Stroop) dimensions, W and V (mean 238 ms per item).

The analyses so far have been based on list reading times collapsed over the eight successive runs of the experiment. Reading times tended generally to decrease over successive runs, with the alternating tasks showing a slightly

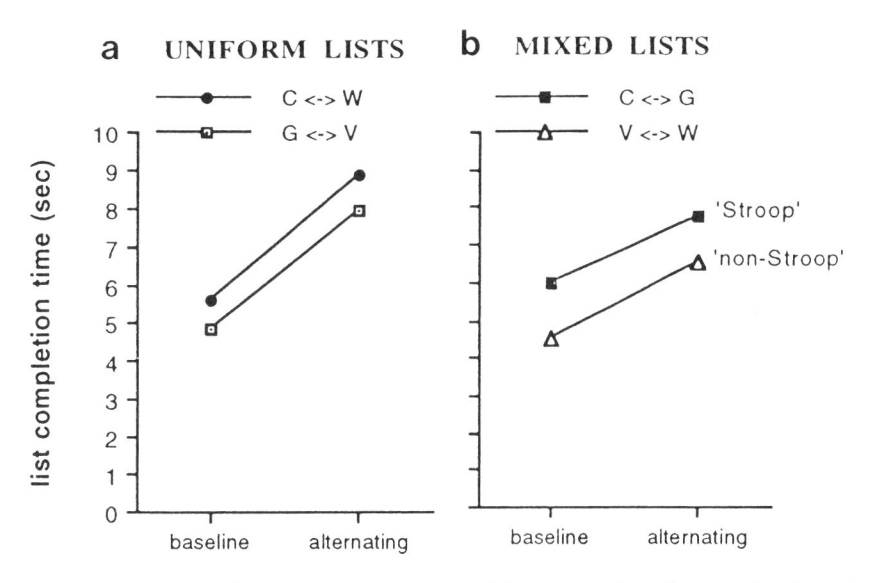

**Figure 17.4** List reading times in experiment 3. Subjects named words (W), ink colors (C), numeral values (V), or the number of numerals in a group (G), either as repeated tasks (baseline) or in pairwise alternation.

steeper reduction in reading times than the nonalternating conditions, at least over the first three or four runs. These effects were confirmed by the analyses as follows. In uniform lists there were significant effects of run ($F(7,77) = 15.62, p < .0001$), of alternation ($F(1,11) = 38.65, p < .001$), and of task pairing ($F(1,11) = 20.42, p < .001$). The cost of task alternation interacted with run ($F(7,77) = 7.68, p < .0001$), but task pairing did not ($F < 1.0$). Analysis of the mixed-list conditions showed the identical pattern. There was a highly significant effect of task pairing (Stroop versus non-Stroop tasks) ($F(1,11) = 39.50, p < .0001$), of alternation ($F(1,11) = 53.75, p < .0001$), and of run ($F(7,77) = 17.54, p < .0001$), and a highly significant interaction between alternation cost and run ($F(7.77) = 5.31, p < .0001$). However, there was no significant interaction between alternation cost and type of task (Stroop versus non-Stroop) ($F < 1.0$), and no significant three-way interaction.

Finally, both of these analyses were repeated once more, on the last four experimental runs alone. The pattern of results remains in all respects as before, except that the interaction between alternation cost and run now disappears ($F < 1.0$). That is, within the error limits of the data, after as few as four practice runs, the time cost of alternating in these tasks appears to have approximately stabilized, at least over the time scale tested.

**Discussion of Experiments 1–3**

Our main findings can be summarized as follows:

1. In all the conditions tested so far, we find large costs of shifting task set, in terms of list completion times, amounting to increases of several hundred milliseconds per item. Provided the shift of task was not also cued by a change of stimulus type, these effects amounted to increases of 50 percent or more in total time. While these time costs varied substantially from one experiment to another, we wish to emphasize the number of experimental variables that in fact did not affect the time costs of shifting task set; they are set out in findings 2–5.

2. We found no systematic differences between shifting cognitive operation (numerical judgments) and shifting task-relevant stimulus dimensions (experiment 1), or between shifting stimulus dimensions and response mode (experiment 2). Shifting task-relevant stimulus dimensions with color word versus number group stimuli similarly resulted in practically identical shift costs (experiment 3).

3. Concurrent shifts in task set on two different task features caused no greater shift cost than did shifts of a single task feature (experiment 1).

4. Variation in intrinsic task (or decision) difficulty, by manipulation of symbolic distance in numerical comparisons (experiment 2), although it had a consistent effect on performance speed overall, did not affect the cost of task alternation.

5. Shifting between two nondominant stimulus-response (S-R) mappings, that is, between two different Stroop tasks (C and G), resulted in identical time costs to those resulting from alternation between the two corresponding dominant, or non-Stroop mappings, V and W (experiment 3, mixed lists). A related finding can be seen, with uniform stimulus lists, in experiment 1 under the Shift Judgment condition, where Stroop and non-Stroop stimulus dimensions, G and V, respectively, are compared (figure 17.2, panel b).

Our intention in these experimental manipulations was to explore task variables that might be related to current ideas about "controlled" (or attentional or "supervisory mode") processing. Voluntary shifting of task set we took to be a prototypical function of executive or intentional control. According to a number of popular accounts, such control is postulated to be the responsibility of a unitary central executive or supervisory attentional system (Baddeley 1986; Johnson-Laird 1988; Norman and Shallice 1986; Posner 1982; Shiffrin 1988; Umiltà et al. 1992). An underlying theoretical distinction is made between a controlled system, which is essentially stimulus driven, and an autonomous control system, which does not depend on stimulus triggering (Shiffrin and Schneider 1977). While, in these accounts, the functional properties of the hypothetical, central control system remain largely unspecified, two essential features have been widely proposed. First, the central executive is of limited capacity; second, regarding this capacity limitation, it is a unitary system (e.g., Norman and Shallice 1986). (Thus, in Norman and Shallice's account, the same limited-capacity control system is needed, for example, for ill-learned or novel sequences of action (including, presumably, the alternating sequences studied here), for decision making, for evidently dangerous or difficult tasks, and for overcoming a strong habitual response, as in Stroop-like conflict situations.) It follows that, if the central executive is engaged in more than one of its many different control functions simultaneously, its limited control capacity must be shared out in some way among these different functions. While this rather abstract characterization may not be adequate to provide unambiguous predictions, it appeared to us, nevertheless, of some theoretical interest to investigate the efficiency of task shifting, under various conditions in which the concurrent load on the hypothetical central executive capacity was varied. Our provisional working assumptions were that the relative efficiency of executive control processes should be reflected, other things being equal, in the relative speed (i.e., we supposed, the relative time costs) of shifting task set, and that the efficiency of such control should depend, ex hypothesi, on the available capacity of the central executive.

Given these assumptions, we found at least three of these results quite surprising. We would expect shifts of two different task features to require more central executive capacity than a shift of only one task feature.[1] We would expect more difficult decisions, for which the subject could prepare (e.g., in the number comparison task, with blocked level of difficulty), to demand more central executive capacity, in anticipation as well as in execution. We would expect preparation for, as well as execution of, Stroop conflict tasks to require more central executive capacity (supervisory mode processing) than the corresponding dominant or non-Stroop tasks, and we would expect this increased load to affect all phases of the task. In none of these comparisons, however, did we find even a hint of differences in the efficiency with which subjects were able to shift set (as inferred from measures of shift cost). Evidently, either one or more of the working assumptions we have made, in our attempts to derive qualitative predictions from the hypothesis of a limited-capacity central executive, are incorrect, or the hypothesis itself is flawed.

One alternative interpretation of these results may be discounted: the suggestion that, in each case, the hypothetical central executive first controls the shift of task set, as one discrete processing stage, and then (and only then) allocates its capacity to the execution of the RT task itself (decision making). This interpretation has been put to us, in particular, in relation to the execution of the Stroop interference tasks. Consequently, the argument runs, task shifting and task difficulty will have additive time costs. There are several objections to this account. The first is that a shift of task set, in our alternation tasks, presumably consists of the disabling of, or disengagement from, readiness for task A and the preparation for task B. Hence, preparation for task B is an intrinsic component in the process of shifting task set. The more difficult (prone to conflict, etc.) is task B (perhaps also task A), the greater the control demands in its preparation, and hence in shifting set to that task. Indeed, accounts of central executive control generally assume that such control is exerted indirectly, through the anticipatory modulation of other, controlled processing systems. A second objection to the sequential stages interpretation is that it offers no account of the finding, in experiment 1, that shifts of two task features show the same time costs as shifts of one feature. If the central executive performs its different control operations strictly sequentially (as seems to be implied by this proposal), this should predict an increased time cost for two different kinds of task shift (stimulus dimension, judgment type) compared to just one. Alternatively, if these control operations can be performed concurrently, why is there no effect of the hypothetical shared/divided control capacity? (See note 1.) A third objection is derived from results of later experiments in this chapter, which appear to be incompatible with the idea that the observed time costs of shifting or alternating tasks reflect the time course of a stage like process, with a determinate duration, that is initiated and completed prior to execution of the next S-R task (experiments 4, 5, and 7). This third objection—to be elaborated later—is, we believe, conclusive.

In contrast to this conception of a unitary central executive, we may contrapose a hypothesis of distributed control. That is, we suggest that voluntary or intentional control of task set is realized through interactions among a variety of functionally specialized components, each responsible for specific features of executive control (Allport 1989, 1993). In this respect, at least, nonspatial attention would resemble spatial attention, which has been shown to depend on a number of both functionally and anatomically distinct subsystems (e.g., Desimone et al. 1990; Posner and Presti 1987; Rizzolatti,

Gentilucci, and Matelli 1985). We explore this idea further in the light of results from the following three experiments. (For further critical discussion of the idea of limited central capacity, see also Neumann 1987.)

To return, briefly, to the experimental results, there were two factors that did, nevertheless, have clear effects on the alternation costs:

6. Practice showed a reduction in alternation costs, at least over the first three or four runs (see experiment 3), although the effect appeared thereafter to have stabilized. Practice at the individual tasks, and practice at alternating, were obviously confounded. Practically every theory of task control that we can imagine would predict this result.

7. A change of stimulus type, which also cued a shift of task, reduced—but certainly did not eliminate—the cost of task alternating (experiment 3). This result contrasts with that reported by Jersild (1927) and by Spector and Biederman (1976), who found no cost of task shifting when subjects alternated between subtracting 3's from numeral pairs and giving verbal opposites to written words. In the next experiment we investigate some possible causes for this apparent contrast of results.

**Experiment 4: Consistent S-R Mapping and Its Reversal**

Summarizing their experiments, Spector and Biederman (1976) proposed that an alternation task that "requires different transforms to be performed on the stimuli will not suffer a sizable shift loss if these transforms are unambiguously cued by the stimuli," that is, "if the stimulus can serve as a retrieval cue for the operation to be performed on it" (p. 678). In considering the effectiveness with which a given stimulus may act as a retrieval cue for a given, preinstructed task, we presumably need to take into account not only relationships among the explicitly intended tasks, between which the subject currently has to shift set, but also the relationships of these tasks to other possible—and therefore potentially competing—S-R mappings that the stimuli afford, even though these do not form part of the subject's explicit or current instruction set. In Spector and Biederman's experiment, subjects performed just two tasks: subtracting 3's or naming opposites. While words and numerals obviously afford many other, similar, potential tasks, *within this set* of experimental tasks, each stimulus type provided affordance for only one of the two currently primed operations. In contrast, in experiment 3, our subjects performed four different tasks, two for each stimulus type. Although, in lists with mixed (alternating) stimulus type, each stimulus in principle cued just one of the two current tasks specified by the instructions for that list, previous lists (often the immediately preceding list) included instructions for a different S-R mapping using the same stimulus types.

In experiment 4 we therefore contrasted two principal conditions. In block 1, each subject received instructions about only two possible tasks, each task uniquely cued by a different stimulus type, and the subject then completed a series of alternating and nonalternating lists for these two tasks, where task alternation was cued by alternating (mixed) stimulus type. This condition, in block 1, thus resembled the conditions in Spector and Biederman's experiment. In subsequent blocks (blocks 2 and 3), each subject was introduced to a new pair of tasks but using the same stimulus types as in block 1, and they again completed a series of alternating and nonalternating lists (again with mixed lists). The first lists in each of blocks 2 and 3 thus resembled the conditions in experiment 3, where instructions for any list typically included different or conflicting S-R mappings from those in the preceding list(s). As each block proceeded, however, with the same pair of S-R tasks repeated over successive lists, the potentially competing, alternative set of S-R mappings from the preceding block became less and less recent. We supposed that, as the recency with which these alternative S-R mappings receded, so would their ability to interfere with preparation for the current task(s). Later trials in blocks 2 and 3, we reasoned, should therefore increasingly resemble the conditions studied by Spector and Biederman.

**Method** The procedure and stimulus materials were closely modeled on experiment 3, with the following exceptions. Subjects were assigned randomly to one of two groups according to the order in which they were to perform the tasks. At the start of the experiment, subjects allocated to order I were given the two tasks of reading aloud (1) color words and (2) numeral values, both as nonalternating (baseline) tasks with uniform lists and as an alternating task with mixed lists. No reference was made to the possibility of naming the ink color or the group size. As in experiment 3, minimal practice (one list each) was provided at these two tasks, sufficient only to establish that the subject understood what to do, before commencing the experiment.

The experiment was divided into three successive blocks. Each block consisted of eight complete runs, where a run is defined as three successive lists consisting of the three different tasks (two baseline, one alternation) specified for the subject at the start of the block. Half the subjects began each run with one of the two baseline tasks and half with the other. At the end of block 1, subjects assigned to order I were told that their tasks were now changed. They were now, in block 2, to name the ink color of the color words, and to count the number of numerals in each frame, both in the two repeated (baseline) tasks, with uniform lists, and in alternation, with mixed lists. As soon as the experimenter was satisfied that they understood these new instructions, the subjects immediately performed eight further runs with these three new tasks, as block 2 of the experiment. Finally, in block 3, the subjects in order I were required to go back to reading the lists according to their original instructions, as in block I.

Subjects allocated to order II performed an equivalent sequence of three blocks but in the inverse order (block 1, naming ink colors and counting numerals). Twenty-four female subjects were recruited from the Oxford University subject panel. Their ages ranged from 18 to 45 years. Twelve subjects were assigned to order I and the remaining twelve to order II. None of these subjects had participated in experiment 3.

**Results** The data are shown in figure 17.5, in terms of the mean reading times per item over successive runs. Several qualitative features of these results may be noted.

First, there is a large and consistent difference in reading time in favor of naming words ($W$) and numeral values ($V$) compared to naming colors ($C$) and group size ($G$). This is the asymmetrical Stroop effect, already noted in experiment 3. It is present in all three blocks and for both subject groups. Making the comparison between groups (order I versus order II), it amounts to an overall difference of 254 ms, 262 ms, and 165 ms in blocks 1, 2, and 3, respectively.

The second and striking feature of these results is that reading times in the alternation conditions show a very marked increment (alternation cost), relative to their corresponding baseline conditions, in the first run of each block (or, at the most, two runs). This effect is particularly marked in blocks 2 and 3 and appears essentially absent in block 1.

Third, after the first two or three runs in a block, the difference in reading times between alternating and nonalternating (baseline) conditions appears to settle down to a small but persistent alternation cost, in blocks 2 and 3, but to approximate zero alternation cost in block 1.

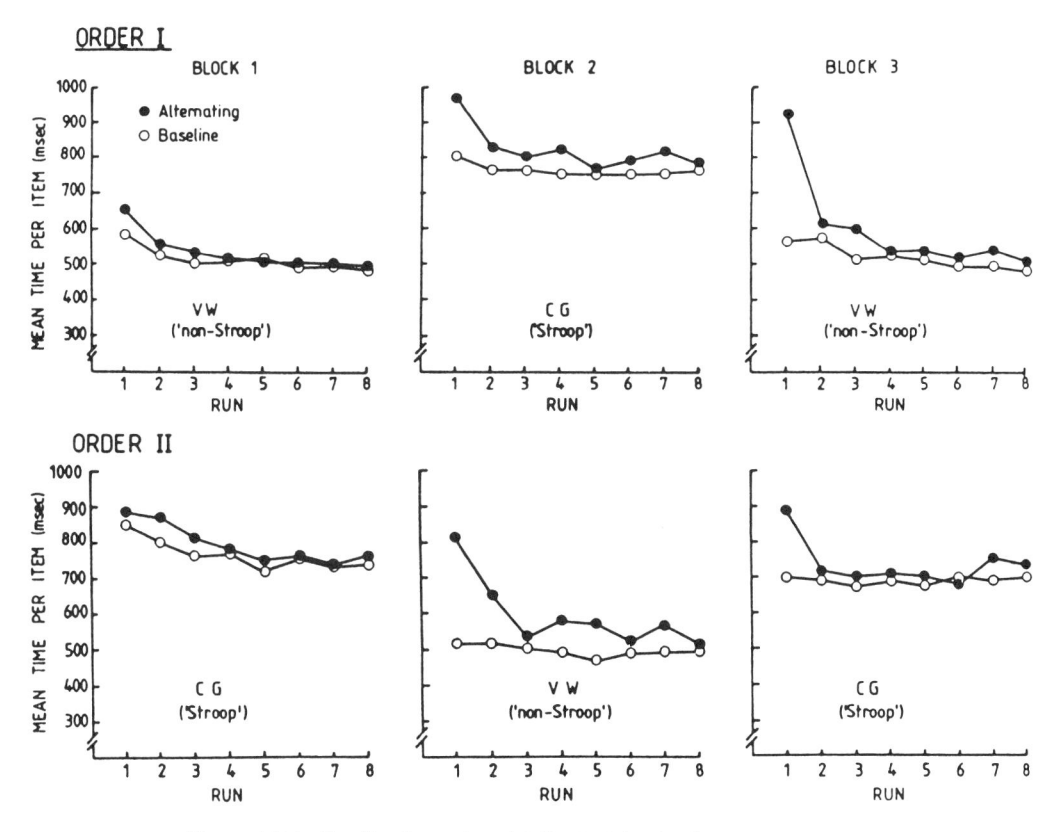

**Figure 17.5** Results of experiment 4. See text for details.

Analyses of variance confirmed all of these effects, separately for each block. First, in block 1 (over all eight runs), there were highly significant main effects of Run ($F(7,154) = 12.15, p < .0001$), of Alternation ($F(1,22) = 17.08, p < .001$), and of order (dominant versus nondominant Stroop tasks) ($F(1,22) = 13.81, p < .001$), but no interactions. However, repeating this analysis on the last five runs of block 1 only (excluding runs 1–3), only the Order (Stroop) effect remained ($F(1,22) = 14.21, p < .01$); no other factors were significant. In contrast, both blocks 2 and 3 showed highly significant effects of Run ($F(7,154) = 11.83$ and $15.88$) and of Alternation ($F(1,22) = 27.83$ and $28.31$, all $p < .0001$), but also a highly significant interaction between these ($F(7,154) = 6.49$ and $12.89$) in blocks 2 and 3 respectively (both $p < .0001$). Repeating these analyses for blocks 2 and 3 but excluding runs 1–3 showed the alternation cost still highly significant: ($F(1,22) = 26.40, p < .0001$ for block 2, $F(1,22) = 14.25, p < .001$ for block 3, and a significant Order (Stroop) effect, $F(1,22) = 17.90, p < .001$ and $F(1,22) = 8.65, p < .01$, respectively, but no effect of Run and no significant interactions.

**Discussion** The results are very clear-cut. On the first run of each of blocks 2 and 3, that is, following a reversal of the previously consistent S-R mappings, the observed shift cost averaged 250 ms per item. (This figure compares reasonably with the average shift cost of 304 ms, found on initial runs, with mixed lists, in experiment 3; in experiment 4, subjects were already more practiced at this general type of task by blocks 2 and 3 than at the beginning of experiment 3.) In contrast, in block 1 of this experiment—with identical stimulus lists but now with consistent S-R mappings within the experimental context—after the first two or three runs we found essentially zero alternation cost, as did Spector and Biederman (1976).

It is evident that the shift cost we observed in experiment 3, with mixed stimulus lists, reflects a kind of proactive interference (PI) from competing S-R mappings with the same stimuli, persisting from the instruction set on preceding trials. We might call this phenomenon task set inertia (TSI). As with some other forms of proactive interference (Loess and Waugh 1967), these interference costs diminished over the time scale of a minute or so (over the first one to three runs) in blocks 2 and 3. PI from other well-learned tasks outside the experimental context appears to have had little, if any, effect. For example, the subjects assigned to order II, who began with the two tasks of naming ink colors and of counting numerals in each group, had no doubt very frequently also read words aloud and named numerals—but not (yet) within this experiment. Whether the amount of TSI depends simply on the temporal recency of alternative (divergent) S-R mappings or whether there is some form of context-dependent TSI release across different experimental settings is a subject for future research.

The important implication of these results, however, is that the time costs of shifting task set that we observe in these experiments cannot be understood as the reflection of a discrete processing stage that must be completed before execution of the next S-R task can begin. Rather, like many other RT interference or conflict phenomena, they appear to represent the additional time needed for the system to settle to a unique response decision (or response retrieval) *after* the next imperative stimulus has arrived.

This hypothesis of TSI makes a very clear (and perhaps counterintuitive) prediction: if we delay the arrival of the next stimulus, even though the subject knows very well that a shift of task is required, essentially the same shift costs will be found. On the contrary, if the shift cost represents the time course of a stagelike, autonomous control process that precedes execution of the next S-R task, then increasing the intertrial interval by an amount greater than the maximum shift cost (i.e., greater than the duration of the postulated control operation) should simply eliminate the shift cost. In the next experiment, we set out to test these contrasted interpretations.

**Experiment 5:  Shifting Task Set over Varied Intertrial Intervals**

Self-paced list reading is obviously no longer appropriate if we wish to investigate the effect of increasing intertrial intervals. For this purpose we need to record discrete RTs under conditions of varied response-to-stimulus interval (RSI).

**Method**  In this experiment, as in experiment 3 (with uniform lists), we again used Stroop color word stimuli, in which color word and ink color were always incongruent. However, in experiment 5 we also included sequences of neutral stimuli: color words shown always in black for word reading and *xxxxx* shown in one of the five possible colors (red, blue, green, yellow, pink) for color naming. The principal purpose of including neutral stimuli was to provide a baseline against which to compare interference (Stroop) effects of the task-irrelevant stimulus dimensions, in the incongruent stimuli. We were also interested to see whether any alternation costs would be eliminated with neutral stimuli, where each stimulus type (word or colored *xs*) explicitly cued its corresponding naming task.

Stimuli were displayed one at a time on a VGA color monitor, and subjects responded orally by naming each stimulus (word or color, as instructed) as fast as possible, to trigger a voice key. An IBM PC recorded RTs to the nearest ms. RT trials occurred in successive pairs, five successive pairs forming one list. Closure of the voice key, triggered by the subject's response to the first stimulus of a pair, cleared the screen for a delay of 20, 550, or 1,100 ms RSI before onset of the second stimulus in the pair. RSI was held constant within a list and was blocked over eight successive lists; the order of different RSI conditions was counterbalanced across subjects. A fixed delay of 1.8 sec occurred between response to the second stimulus of a pair and presentation of the first stimulus of the following pair. The data of interest are RTs to the second stimulus of each pair (RT2).

As in experiment 3, prior to each list, subjects received instructions for the task conditions valid for that list. There were four nonalternating (baseline) conditions: two each of color naming and of word reading, separately with

Incongruent (Stroop) stimuli and with Neutral stimuli. And there were four alternating-task conditions: two in which the subject was instructed to name the ink color (C) of the first stimulus in each pair and to read the word (W) in response to the second, and two in the reverse sequence (W first, C second); both alternation tasks were performed separately with Incongruent and with Neutral stimuli. (In the latter case, the stimuli unequivocally cued the task to be performed on each trial; in the former there was no change of stimulus type to cue the shift of task.) These eight conditions, in randomized order, constituted a block of eight lists (a different condition on each successive list), three blocks at each RSI. There were twelve subjects from the Oxford University subject panel, aged between 24 and 40 years old. None had served in the previous experiments.

**Results** We describe first the results for RT2 with the Incongruent stimuli, where there was no change of stimulus type to cue the shift of task. Figure 17.6a shows the mean shift cost (mean of alternation minus baseline RT for each subject) over the three different delays (RSIs). Mean RTs and error rates for each condition are shown separately, for each value of RSI, in figure 17.6b.

Two very striking features of these results are immediately apparent. First, concerning the primary issue that the experiment was designed to address, the RT shift cost (observed at 20 ms RSI) is by no means eliminated by an RSI of 550 ms or even of 1,100 ms. Second, the RT cost of task alternation is confined to the word reading trials; color naming RTs show no shift cost. (This was evidently a feature of the results that was completely obscured by the measurement only of list completion times in the preceding experiments.) The error data follow a broadly similar pattern: a shift cost on word reading only and no reduction in this error cost, at least over the first 550 ms RSI.

Analysis of variance confirmed these findings as follows. There were highly significant main effects on RT of Task (C versus W) ($F(1,11) = 76.52$, $p < .0001$), of Alternation ($F(1,11) = 12.48, p < .005$), and of RS delay ($F(2,22) = 9.67, p < .001$), and a highly significant interaction of Alternation X Task ($F(1,11) = 59.06, p < .0001$). No other interaction terms were significant. In one-way ANOVAs performed on the shift costs against the three RS delays, however, the effect of delay was not significant. In the word reading task, the apparent reduction in shift cost between the 20- and 550-ms delay was not reliable.[2] In the color naming task, shift cost did not differ significantly from zero at any of the three RS delays. Analysis of the error data, similarly, showed a significant effect of Task (C versus W) ($F(1,11) = 12.42$, $p < .005$), and an interaction of Alternation X Task ($F(1,11) = 17.38$, $p < .001$). (The main effect of Alternation was not reliable: $F(1,11) = 3.2$, $p = 0.1$.) More important, there was no overall effect of RS delay ($F(2,22) = 1.40$), and there were no significant interactions with RS delay in the overall analysis. However, a one-way ANOVA on the word reading task alone, over the three RS intervals, found a marginally significant effect of RSI ($F(2,22) = 3.00, p = .07$). Newman-Keuls tests showed a significant ($p < .05$) reduction

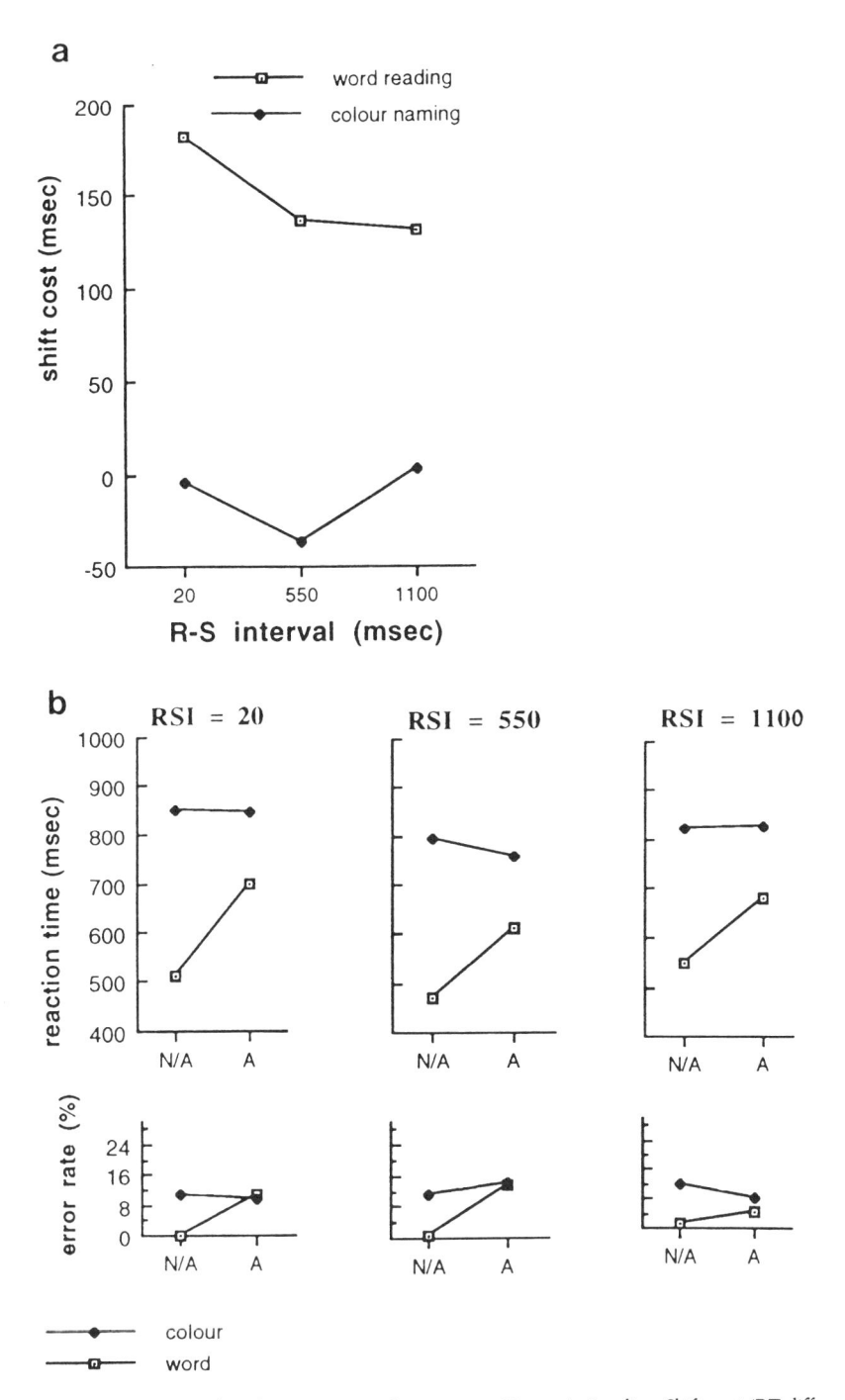

**Figure 17.6** Results of experiment 5: Incongruent (Stroop) stimuli. *a.* Shift cost (RT difference between alternating and nonalternating tasks) for word reading and for color naming, as a function of delay of the second task (RSI). *b.* Reaction times and errors.

in word reading errors between 550 and 1,100 ms RSI, though there was none (if anything, an increase) between 20 and 550 ms.

Turning to the Neutral stimuli, we found a small but consistent alternation cost for these conditions also, over both tasks ($F(1,11) = 22.62, p < .001$), but no significant interaction of Alternation X Task ($F(1,11) = 2.58, p = .137$). As with the Incongruent stimuli, however, this small shift cost was still not abolished at the longer RSIs (mean shift cost, for word reading, of 58, 41, and 46 ms at 20, 550, and 1,100 ms RSI, respectively; for color naming, 25, 29, and 21 ms, respectively). As expected, color naming was consistently slower than word reading ($F(1,11) = 97.58, p < .0001$). The errors, with neutral stimuli, showed the same general pattern as the RTs but were too few to permit statistical analysis. There was no reduction in errors between 20 and 550 ms RSI.

In these analyses, we find little, if any, indication of an autonomous control process—effecting disengagement from the task set for the preceding trial—over the 0.5- to 1-sec predictable preparation intervals following execution of the previous response. As a further test of autonomous disengagement from the previous task set, we also examined RT interference (Stroop interference) caused by the incongruent, task-irrelevant (but on the preceding trial task-relevant) stimulus dimension. These data—contrasting Incongruent with Neutral stimuli—are shown in figure 17.7a for nonalternating trials, and in figure 17.7b for the task-alternating conditions. Three features of these results are immediately noteworthy. First, as expected, in the nonalternating trials, there was a large, and strongly asymmetrical, Stroop interference effect on color

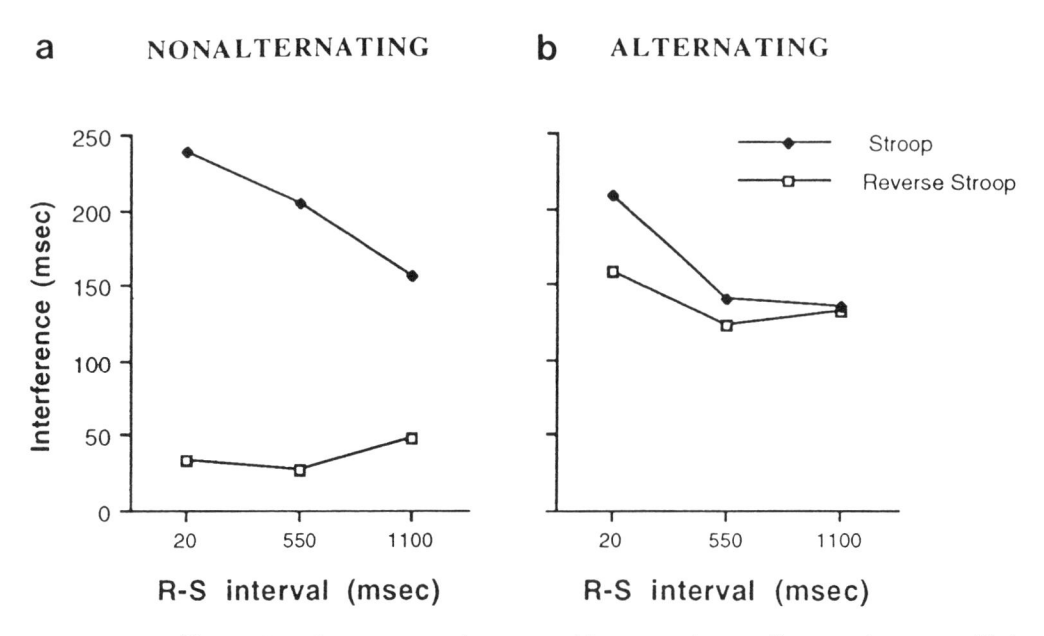

**Figure 17.7** Experiment 5. *a*. Asymmetrical Stroop interference effects on color naming (filled symbols) and word reading (open symbols), in nonalternating tasks. *b*. Symmetrical Stroop and Reverse Stroop interference effects, in alternating conditions.

naming, from the presence of incongruent color words ($F(1,11) = 124.82$, $p < .00001$). The reduction in Stroop interference over RSI was significant ($F(2,22) = 7.69, p < .003$). Second, and unusual, in these nonalternating conditions (interleaved with task-alternating conditions, however), there was also a small but consistent "reverse Stroop" effect on word reading RTs, ($F(1,11) = 6.24, p < .05$). The Stroop effect (on color naming), however, is clearly very much larger than the "reverse Stroop" effect ($F(1,11) = 52.96$, $p < .00001$). Third, and most dramatic, under task-alternating conditions, the interference effects of incongruent, task-irrelevant stimulus dimensions in color-naming and word reading (Stroop and Reverse Stroop effects, respectively) became practically symmetrical and equal—completely so at the longest RSI. While both these interference effects were highly significant ($F(1,11) = 39.30, p < .001$), differences between them were not reliable; the reduction in the Stroop effect from 20 to 550 ms RSI was just significant (Newman-Keuls test, $p < .05$).

**Discussion** The main purpose of this experiment was to test the hypothesis that the observed shift cost reflects the duration of an autonomous control operation (a voluntary shift of set) that can be (must be?) completed prior to execution of the next S-R task. Ex hypothesi, for fully predictable, preinstructed shifts of set from task A to task B, such a control operation could begin as soon as the response to task A has been completed. Accordingly, under conditions of predictable, extended RS interval (where RSI ≫ shift cost), no shift cost should be observed in RT to task B. The data unambiguously falsify this prediction. A large shift cost was still present at an RSI of 1,100 ms and indeed showed only a small (and nonsignificant) reduction from the shift cost at an RSI of 20 ms. The error data followed the same pattern.

Two further and completely unexpected features of these results also run counter to this hypothesis. First, if the observed shift cost reflects directly the duration of a stagelike control operation that precedes S-R task execution, it seems unaccountable that this operation should take some 150–200 ms in shifting to the (dominant) word reading task but apparently little or no time in shifting to the (nondominant) color naming task. Second, if the shift-of-set operation (including disengagement from the task set of the preceding trial) is completed before execution of task B (say, word reading), it is not clear why word reading RT should then be subject to interference from the incongruent ink color, since this effect is normally absent in nonalternating conditions (Glaser and Glaser 1982). Indeed, the data suggest that very little disengagement from the preceding color naming set has occurred during the available RSI.

All of these findings, on the contrary, appear compatible with the contrasting hypothesis, introduced in discussion of experiment 4, that the observed shift costs represent a form of proactive interference from the instruction set elicited by or for the preceding tasks (task set inertia). Active disengagement from the task set of preceding trials, it appears, must wait until triggered by the imperative stimulus for the following trial. We see little if any indication here of an autonomous (i.e., internally triggered) shift of set, prior to the next task stimulus. First, time delays of just 1–2 sec are typically quite insufficient for the dissipation of other, more familiar forms of PI (Loess and Waugh 1967). The small reduction in shift costs over delays of this order in this experiment accords with limited TSI dissipation over this time scale. Similarly, the approximately symmetrical Stroop and Reverse Stroop interference effects, found under conditions of alternation between word reading and color naming, accord with the assumption that features of the instruction set from the preceding trial remain active during execution of the following trial; hence, in the alternating task, incongruent color word stimuli evoke color naming and word reading responses with nearly equal strength, so causing nearly symmetrical conflict effects. In experiment 4 (blocks 2 and 3), interference from the conflicting task set, established in a preceding block of trials, evidently persisted over at least three lists of self-paced responses. In this experiment, two further features of the results indicate, similarly, the inertial effects of task set from previous list conditions (and not just from the immediately preceding trial): (1) the small, but highly significant, shift cost with neutral stimuli which, in principle, unambiguously cued the tasks to be performed (as in experiment 4), and (2) the reverse Stroop effect (of about 30 ms) found also in the nonalternating lists of trials.

The asymmetrical shift costs are a little more complicated. To make clear how the TSI model may account not only for these asymmetrical effects but also for the apparently invariant or symmetrical shift costs found in experiments 1–3 (when we compared alternation between relatively easy or more difficult pairs of tasks), we shall need to spell out three simple assumptions.

1. Any task feature representing a relatively nondominant (more difficult) S-R mapping will require a more strongly imposed set, with respect to that feature, than corresponding easy mappings, perhaps including active suppression of the competing, and potentially dominant, S-R mappings.

2. The more strongly imposed the S-R set is for a given task feature, the greater is the TSI, hence, the more proactive the interference it can exert on any subsequent task for which that task feature must be shifted.

3. The interference is task feature specific, however. That is, features that remain unchanged over a shift of set should have no effect on the amount of interference with a following (shifted) task, regardless of their control difficulty.

In experiments 1–3, we compared alternation between pairs of tasks that were both relatively easy or both relatively difficult. In those experiments, although, in a difficult task pair, each task was, of course, preceded by another difficult task, the feature responsible for the difficulty manipulation did not itself have to be shifted from trial to trial. Accordingly, in experiments 1–3, we should expect no greater interference (hence no greater shift costs) in the relatively difficult than in the easy tasks. The results are fully in accord with these predictions. In contrast, in experiment 5, subjects shifted between mutually incompatible, nondominant and dominant values of a specific task feature (the task-relevant stimulus dimension: C versus W). Accordingly, in experiment 5 we expect asymmetrical shift costs: TSI from the preceding nondominant set (C) exerting greater proactive interference on the dominant task (W).

This analysis emphasizes that, in understanding shift costs, it may not be appropriate to consider an S-R task *as a whole* as being more or less controlled; what is relevant is the degree or strength of control applied to individual features of each task. Only those features that must be changed with respect to the preceding (strongly imposed) instruction set should be subject to proactive interference, in the form of increased RTs (shift costs).

## Experiment 6: Shifting Attention in Semantic Space—Word-Monitoring Tasks

So far our experiments have used measures of response speed, either with self-paced list completion or with discrete RTs. We have argued that the shift costs observed with these methods reflect the persistence of conflicting features of the instruction set from preceding tasks (PI effects), rather than the time cost (i.e., the real-time duration) of a discrete control operation to shift task set. We do not know, as yet, how far these shift costs depend on, or are specific to, speeded responses. It seemed of interest, therefore, to explore the costs of task shifting using a different experimental paradigm, not dependent on speed of overt response. One such method that we have investigated requires the subject to make a preinstructed shift of criterion in the course of monitoring a word list, using rapid sequential visual presentation (RSVP).

**Method** Rapid sequences of from ten to thirty lowercase words were displayed one after another, at a constant rate, in the center of a computer monitor. There were three different semantic target criteria: (1) any member of the animal kingdom (Animal), (2) any object not a member of the animal kingdom (Not Animal), and (3) any physical object smaller, in its largest dimension, than a soccer football (Small Object). Any target word(s) detected were to be reported at leisure after the end of the list. Half the lists contained just one target word, and half contained two. The presentation rate was fast enough that not all targets could be reported.

Each word sequence was notionally subdivided into two immediately successive subsequences, following without interruption. In control (no shift) sequences, all words appeared in the same location; in shift sequences, words in the second subsequence appeared immediately above the previous location. Each trial began with two cue words, one above another, specifying the target type(s) (and locations) to be monitored for on that trial. One cue word, indicating the target category (T1) to be searched for first, appeared at the center of the screen, flanked by three asterisks on either side; immediately above it, another cue word specified the target category (T2) that might have to be searched for second. The subject could take as long as she wished to study the cue words. She then initiated the trial by pressing a key. Subjects were instructed to continue to monitor for T1 so long as the words appeared in the center location (between the asterisks). If or when the word sequence jumped to a location one line space above the center, they were instructed to cease monitoring for T1 and immediately to start monitoring for T2.

There were sixteen trials per block. On half the trials, there was an unpredictable shift of location of the RSVP word sequence, cueing a shift of criterion; on the remaining trials, there was no shift. (This was to prevent subjects from anticipating the spatial shift cue by disengaging from T1 search, particularly if they had already detected a T1 target; the data suggest that the manipulation was effective.) In each word sequence, the first subsequence contained one target word on 50 percent of trials; the second subsequence always contained one target word. In the first subsequence, targets occurred equiprobably between the third and tenth word; three words always followed the occurrence of a target in subsequence 1 before the onset of subsequence 2. For the second subsequence, the target was located randomly at either the first, third, seventh, or eleventh position from the onset of the subsequence. The list then continued for at least four words after the target. The dependent measure was the accuracy of target detection, as a function of position in the sequence. The words appeared for a duration of 150 ms each, followed after a 15-ms interval by the onset of the next word. Three types of criterion shift (Small Object to Animal, Not Animal to Animal, and Animal to Not Animal) occurred each in separate blocks, each of which also included 50 percent Non-Switch trials. These three types of block were each repeated six times, enabling twelve trials per target position per condition to be run, for each subject. Eighteen subjects from the Oxford University subject panel participated in this experiment.

Experiment 6 illustrates the RSVP criterion-shift method and its characteristic results. A particular question at issue in this experiment was whether a criterion shift that involved a reversal of semantic set inclusion (e.g., from Not-Animal to Animal) would show a larger (or smaller) shift cost than an orthogonal semantic shift (e.g., from Small Object to Animal).

**Results** A preliminary test was carried out on target identification in subsequence 2, in each condition, with and without a preceding T1. The presence of a T1 (followed by at least three intervening nontarget words) had no significant effect on T2 identification, in any of the conditions, regardless of whether the T1 target was correctly reported. Accordingly, T2 data for trials with and without a preceding target word were combined.

The results are illustrated in figure 17.8. They show a stable level of report accuracy for T1 (Animal) targets over the first half of the RSVP sequences, at around 80 percent correct, which is continued with little change, on No Shift trials, over the second half. The two criterion shift conditions, by contrast, show a very large drop in accuracy immediately following the shift cue, which then gradually recovers for targets occurring at later positions in the sequence.

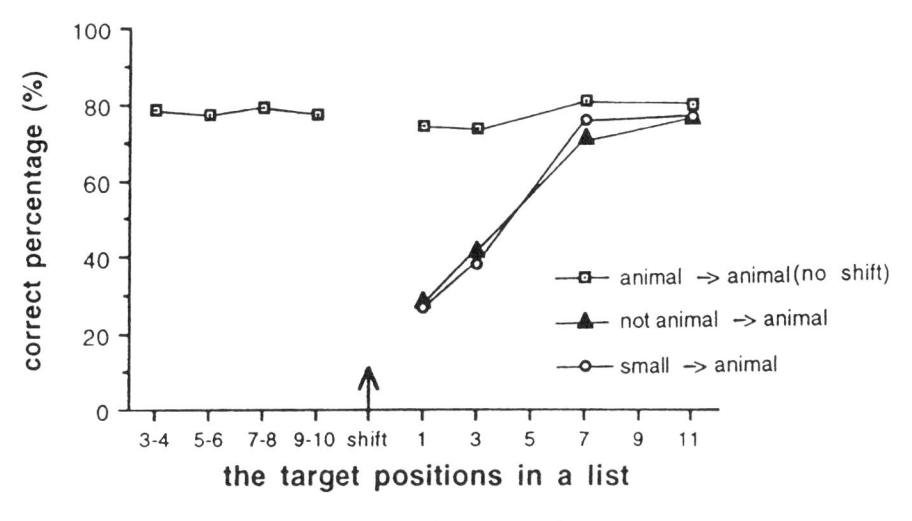

**Figure 17.8** Experiment 6. Accuracy of target identification in RSVP semantic monitoring tasks: no-shift control and two criterion-shift conditions.

No clear differences are apparent between the semantic reversal and orthogonal shift conditions.[3] Taking mean accuracy on Non-Switch trials (target positions 1, 3, 7, and 11) as a baseline, the differences from this baseline at each target position, on Switch trials, were subjected to a simple, two-way ANOVA. The effect of target position after the shift cue was highly significant ($F(3,51) = 61.91, p < .00001$). There was, however, no effect of shift type and no interaction ($F < 1.0$ in each case). Separate analyses of the Non-Switch trials showed no significant effect of target position.

**Discussion** The results provide considerable encouragement for the usefulness of the RSVP criterion shift paradigm. Large shift costs are obtained in target identification accuracy, showing a systematic course of recovery, without the need for speeded-response measures. Further discussion of these findings will be deferred until after experiment 7. For the present, the question that appeared to us most determinative for competing interpretations of these results was this: Does the systematic recovery of target identification accuracy, following a shift of criterion, depend primarily on the lapse of time following a shift cue? Or might it be paced in some way by the processing of successive (nontarget) items, independent of time delay? This is the issue that we addressed in the next (and concluding) experiment reported here. If time lapse is the critical variable, this would suggest that shift cost in the RSVP paradigm, and its gradual recovery, reflect substantially different causal processes from the shift costs found in the RT paradigm, where TSI effects showed little spontaneous recovery over delays of 1,100 ms. (For comparison, in experiment 6, a $T2$ target word occurring at position 7 after the shift cue, by which point $T2$ identification is nearly back to control level, disappears only 1,155 ms after the cue.)

**Experiment 7: RSVP Shift Cost—Time versus Items**

**Method** The procedure was identical to experiment 6 except for the following:

1. Word sequences were presented at two different rates: a fast rate, similar to that in experiment 6, and a slow rate, where stimulus onset asynchrony (SOA) from one word to the next was exactly twice the SOA at the fast rate. So that target identification at the slow rate should not approach 100 percent accuracy (in No-Switch conditions), which would have rendered comparison of shift costs in the two conditions problematic, for both fast and slow presentation rates, each word stimulus was followed immediately by a 30-ms pattern mask (*XCXCXCXCXC*); total duration of word plus mask was 150 ms in both conditions (word mask SOA, 120 ms). For the fast presentation rate, there was a 15-ms blank interval at mask offset, before onset of the next word stimulus, making word-word SOA 165 ms. For slow presentation, word-word SOA was 330 ms. Figure 17.9a illustrates these conditions.

2. To control for the possible cost of spatially reorienting attention to a new location, in experiment 7 we included additional blocks of Non-Switch trials in which, on 50 percent of trials, the word sequence jumped one line space below the center. Subjects were instructed to ignore this shift of location and to continue monitoring for T1 as before (Spatial shift control).

A target word occurred equiprobably at either the first, second, third, or fifth word after the shift cue. Two semantic target criteria were used: Small Objects and Large Objects. In Non-Switch blocks subjects searched for Small Objects throughout. In Switch blocks, T1 was Large Objects, T2 was Small Objects. A shift cue (spatial shift upwards) occurred on 50 percent of trials, in Switch blocks. Each subject served in four Switch blocks and four Non-Switch blocks, at each presentation rate, sixteen trials per block. The order was counterbalanced. There were eighteen subjects, recruited from the Oxford University subject panel. None had served in experiment 6.

**Results** As expected, target identification accuracy at the slow presentation rate was superior to that at the fast rate (T1 accuracy, on Non-Switch trials: 70% at fast, 85% at slow presentation rates). The shift cost at target position 1 was also somewhat smaller at the slow presentation rate ($-55\%$ fast, $-43\%$ slow). The most appropriate comparison of *recovery* from these shift costs, at the two presentation rates, is therefore to normalize shift cost (accuracy decrement below Non-Switch controls) at later target positions relative to the corresponding shift cost at target position one. This was done for each subject's data individually. The results are shown in this way in figure 17.9. Costs of a *spatial* shift alone (with no criterion shift) are shown similarly, for comparison.

The results are extremely clear. Recovery from shift cost as a function of time lapse (fig. 17.9b) shows completely different real-time recovery rates for fast and slow presentation (Interaction of time lapse × presentation rate,

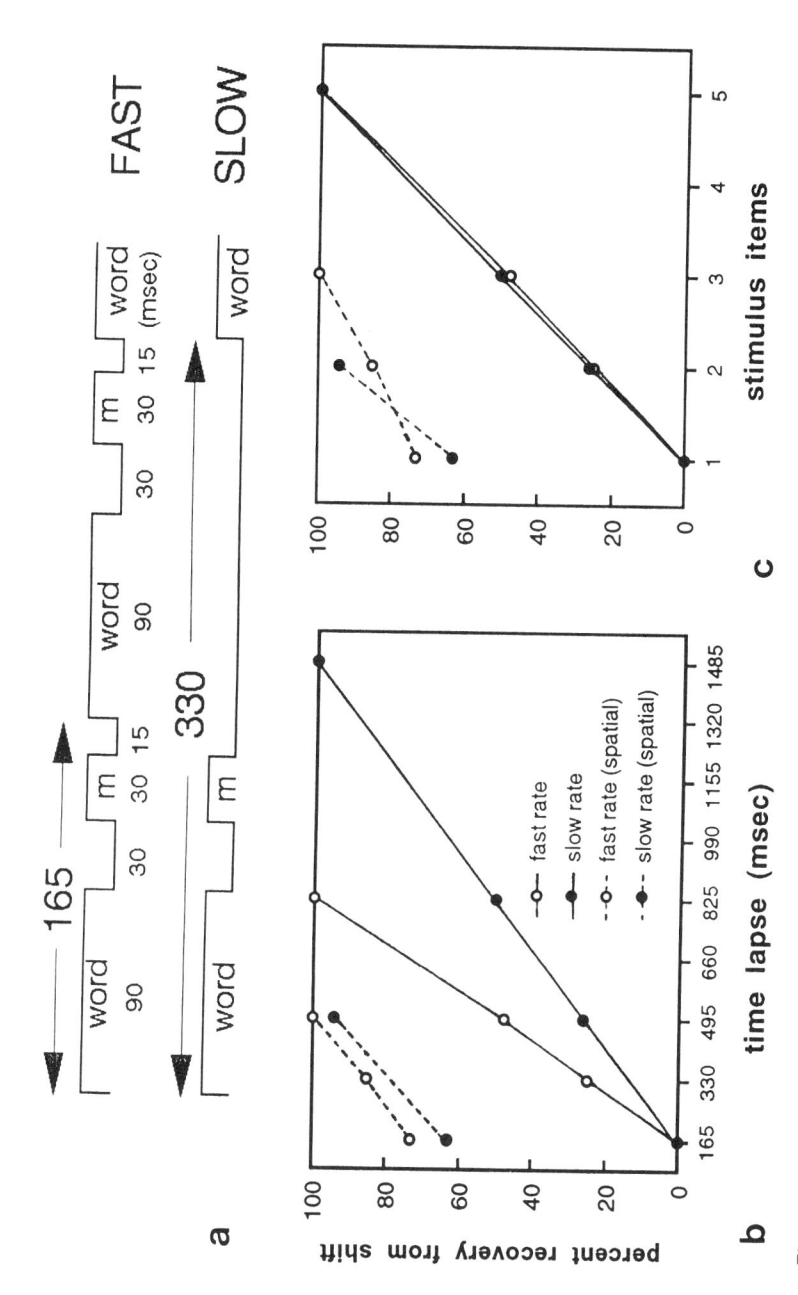

**Figure 17.9** Experiment 7. Recovery from shift cost in RSVP semantic monitoring, at slow and fast presentation rates. Panel *a* illustrates the two stimulus conditions (m = mask). The same data are shown as a function of (*b*) time since the shift cue (left panel), or (*c*) stimulus items since the cue (right panel). Dotted lines show spatial shift controls.

$F(2,34) = 4.83, p < .01$). In contrast, as a function of the number of stimulus items after the shift cue, the two sets of data are practically identical (fig. 17.9c). Main effect of stimulus items, $F(3,51) = 61.77, p < .00001$; no significant effect of presentation rate or of items × rate (Fs < 1.0). However counterintuitive it may seem, we are obliged to conclude that the shift cost observed in the RSVP criterion-shift paradigm does not represent a real-time–dependent shift process.

The spatial shift controls show much smaller costs, and generally faster recovery. The criterion shift costs cannot therefore be attributed to an artifact of spatial orienting. Interestingly, these spatial orienting costs appear to fit a simple time lapse function better than one paced by the succession of stimulus items, pointing out all the more sharply the quite different pattern of results for a (nonspatial) semantic criterion shift.

## 17.3 GENERAL DISCUSSION

Our explorations have encountered a variety of behavioral phenomena associated with preinstructed, intentional shifts of set that have not previously been described. We review here some of the more salient features of this natural history, together with some further predictions derived from our tentative explanation of these phenomena. First, we review some properties of the RT shift cost, that is, the RT difference between an alternated and nonalternated S-R task, as measured either by discrete RTs or over list completion times. (Whether these RT differences are labeled as task-shift costs or as task-repetition benefits, incidentally, appears to depend simply on whether repeated or nonrepeated tasks are considered the norm.)

In a pair of divergent S-R tasks, each cued potentially by the same stimuli, but in which A is the normally dominant (more strongly learned, more compatible) task and B is the nondominant one, the RT shift cost is greater in a shift from B to A (in returning to the dominant task) than from A to B. We have found this pattern in a wide variety of task pairs besides the one reported in experiment 5, including other Stroop-like task pairs (e.g., naming numerals, naming group size), as well as in shifting between a dominant first language and a weaker second language, in simple naming tasks (Meuter 1994). When both languages are equally strong, in balanced bilinguals, the shift cost is then symmetric. In the discussion of experiment 5 we put forward an explanation of this apparently paradoxical phenomenon in terms of proactive interference from the persisting task set implemented in the preceding task(s), an explanation that we applied also to the rest of the RT shift cost effects. This model, based on TSI, makes a number of clear predictions, some of which have been verified and some which are yet to be tested.

1. Suppose that four different S-R tasks are defined over the same stimulus set: two strong S-R mappings and two weak ones (e.g., naming numerals in four different languages: two equally strongly overlearned vocabularies, A and B, and two equally weak ones, C and D). The TSI model predicts that RT shift

cost should be greatest for shifts from either C or D to either A or B; intermediate, and symmetrical, between A and B and between C and D; and smallest for shifts from either A or B to either C or D.

2. In contrast, shifts to or from difficult tasks (requiring strong control) or to and from easy tasks (weakly controlled), but in which the particular difficult or easy task features do not themselves undergo a shifted S-R mapping, should not result in systematically different RT shift costs depending on the ease or difficulty of the preceding or following task. (This prediction is borne out repeatedly in the results of experiments 1–3.) In this respect, at least, it may be misleading to think of S-R tasks *as a whole* as being controlled or as requiring different degrees of control; control is not a global task function.

3. Predictable delays in stimulus presentation over a preinstructed, divergent shift of tasks should reduce RT shift cost only insofar as TSI from any preceding task(s) has dissipated. Experiment 5 confirmed this prediction over short delays; experiment 4 showed a progressive reduction in shift costs over successive repeated tasks, on a time-scale of 1 or 2 min.

Regarding the RSVP criterion shift cost, three further, interesting properties have been identified. First, following a cue to shift criterion, there is a very large reduction in monitoring accuracy, which thereafter shows a progressive, monotonic recovery. Second, at least under the conditions of experiment 6, the amplitude of the shift cost, and the course of recovery to asymptotic (nonshift) levels, was practically identical for a criterion shift that required a reversal of semantic set inclusion (i.e., where the nontargets for $T2$ were all potential targets under $T1$) and for an orthogonal shift (where only 50 percent of nontargets for $T2$ would have been valid targets under $T1$). Third, the course of recovery of RSVP shift cost (in another reversal shift) does not depend on the real-time interval from shift cue to target, unlike spatial orienting costs, but appears to be paced by the (typically incomplete, because repeatedly interrupted) processing of successive nontargets (potential targets). The more nontargets that have been monitored since the shift cue, the more efficient is detection, and subsequent report, of the following $T2$ target.

## 17.4 CONCLUSION

These are our principal findings. It is clear that neither in the case of RT shift cost nor in the case of the RSVP criterion shift cost have we been able to chart the time course of autonomous, real-time-dependent shifts of set, despite the fact that these were what we set out to study (and intentional shifts of set indubitably occurred). Perhaps other, quite different experimental paradigms will be more successful in this respect. For the present, however, we are somewhat at a loss to imagine what these behavioral indexes of intentional, dynamic task shifts might be. We have measured RT; we have measured accuracy. What other fundamental indicators are there of the efficiency of task-shifted performance? Could it be that the underlying and widely held assumption, formulated most influentially perhaps by Shiffrin and Schneider

(1977) and by Baddeley and Hitch (1974; Baddeley 1986), and from which these explorations began—the idea of a fundamental distinction between a controlled system (or systems) and a separate, autonomous controller (an executive system)—is misconceived? In these and related formulations, an essential feature of the controlled (or slave) system(s) is that they are exogenously triggered, or stimulus driven. In contradistinction, the postulated central executive, or supervisory attentional system, is not dependent on external triggering; its control operations are autonomous, initiated (in some way) from within. The problem is that the prototypical control operation of a shift of set (at least as exemplified in our experiments) appears here to depend on—to await triggering by—appropriate external stimuli.

These considerations prompt us to return also to the two working assumptions that we set out (in the discussion of experiments 1–3), in an attempt to derive testable predictions (*any* predictions!) from the hypothesis of a unitary, limited-capacity central executive. Fundamental to those assumptions was the idea that the observable shift costs in RT reflected the relative speed of an underlying shift-of-set operation, which, in turn, was an index of the relative efficiency of control processes, which in turn—*ex hypothesi*—should depend on central executive capacity. As we can now see, this inferential chain is broken at the first link. Nothing that we have succeeded in measuring reflects the relative speed (still less the real-time duration) of a shift of set. As we have seen, the stimulus-independent autonomy of such control operations must be seriously questioned. If the metaphor of a limited-capacity central executive can, in other respects, provide so little guidance—still less any testable predictions—for experiments of this kind, it may be time to look for a better metaphor.

## NOTES

1. This expectation assumes that one (or more) task feature(s) can be left unchanged while another one is being shifted. Our finding in experiment 1, on the contrary, might suggest that this assumption is incorrect. That is, maybe a shift of one task feature requires (re)establishing control over all features of the task. (We are indebted to S. Monsell for this suggestion.) If this were so, however, it becomes even more difficult to understand why variation in difficulty with respect to task features that are held constant over shifts of set (in experiments 1, 2, and 3) apparently has no effect on the resulting shift cost. We return to this issue in the discussion of experiment 5.

2. R. Rogers and S. Monsell, in Cambridge, have reported, independently, a replication of this experiment, with similar results (EPS meeting, Oxford, April 1992). In their data, however, the partial reduction in shift cost over a 0.5-sec RSI was statistically reliable. They interpret this as evidence for two components of the RT shift cost.

3. In other experiments we have found a reduced shift cost with orthogonal *T*1 and *T*2.

## REFERENCES

Allport, D. A. (1980a). Patterns and actions: Cognitive mechanisms are content-specific. In G. Claxton (Ed.), *Cognitive psychology: New directions*, 26–64. London: Routledge and Kegan Paul.

Allport, D. A. (1980b). Attention and performance. In G. Claxton (Ed.), *Cognitive psychology: New directions*, 112–153. London: Routledge and Kegan Paul.

Allport, [D.] A. (1989). Visual attention. In M. I. Posner (Ed.), *Foundations of cognitive science*, 631–682. Cambridge, MA: MIT Press.

Allport, [D.] A. (1993). Attention and control: Have we been asking the wrong questions? A critical review of 25 years. In D. E. Meyer and S. Kornblum (Eds.), *Attention and performance XIV: A silver jubilee*. Cambridge, MA: MIT Press.

Baddeley, A. (1986). *Working memory*. Oxford: Oxford University Press.

Baddeley A. D., and Hitch, G. (1974). Working memory. In G. A. Bower (Ed.), *Recent advances in learning and motivation*, vol. 8. New York: Academic Press.

Besner, D., and Coltheart, M. (1979). Ideographic and alphabetic processing in skilled reading of English. *Neuropsychologia*, 17, 469–472.

Buckley, P. B., and Gillman, C. B. (1974). Comparison of digits and dot patterns. *Journal of Experimental Psychology*, 103, 1131–1136.

Desimone, R., Wessinger, M., Thomas, L., and Schneider, W. (1990). Attentional control of visual perception: Cortical and subcortical mechanisms. *Cold Spring Harbor Symposia on Quantitative Biology*, 55, 963–971.

Dyer, F. N. (1973). The Stroop phenomenon and its use in the study of perceptual, cognitive and response processes. *Memory and Cognition*, 1, 106–120.

Fox, L. A., Schor, R. E., and Steinman, R. J. (1971). Semantic gradients and interference in naming color, spatial direction, and numerosity. *Journal of Experimental Psychology*, 91, 59–65.

Glaser, M. D., and Glaser, W. R. (1982). Time course analysis of the Stroop phenomenon. *Journal of Experimental Psychology: Human Perception and Performance*, 8, 875–894.

Hirst, W. (1986). The psychology of attention. In J. E. LeDoux and W. Hirst (Eds.), *Mind and brain: Dialogues in cognitive neuroscience*, 105–141. Cambridge: Cambridge University Press.

Jersild, A. T. (1927). Mental set and shift. *Archives of psychology*, whole no. 89.

Johnson-Laird, P. N. (1988). A computational analysis of consciousness. In A. J. Marcel and E. Bisiach (Eds.), *Consciousness in contemporary science*. Oxford: Oxford University Press.

Loess, H., and Waugh, N. C. (1967). Short-term memory and inter-trial interval. *Journal of Verbal Learning and Verbal Behavior*, 6, 455–460.

MacLeod, C. M. (1991). Half a century of research on the Stroop effect: An integrative review. *Psychological Bulletin*, 109, 163–203.

MacLeod, C. M., and Dunbar, K. (1988). Training and Stroop-like interference: Evidence for a continuum of automaticity. *Journal of Experimental Psychology: Learning, Memory and Cognition*, 14, 126–135.

Meuter, R. F. I. (1993). Language-switching in naming tasks. Unpublished Ph.D. thesis, University of Oxford.

Moyer, R. S., and Landauer, T. K. (1967). Time required for judgments of numerical inequality. *Nature*, 215, 1519–1520.

Neumann, O. (1987). Beyond capacity: A functional view of attention. In H. Heuer and A. F. Sanders (Eds.), *Perceptives on perception and action*, 361–394. Hillsdale, NJ: Erlbaum.

Norman, D. A., and Shallice, T. (1986). Attention to action: Willed and automatic control of behavior. In R. J. Davidson, G. E. Schwartz, and D. Shapiro (Eds.), *Consciousness and self-regulation*, vol. 4. New York: Plenum Press.

Posner, M. I. (1982). Cumulative development of attentional theory. *American Psychologist, 37,* 168–179.

Posner, M. I., and Petersen, S. E. (1990). The attention system of the human brain. *Annual Review of Neuroscience, 13,* 25–42.

Posner, M. I., and Presti, D. (1987). Selective attention and cognitive control. *Trends in Neuroscience, 10,* 12–17.

Rizzolatti, G., Gentilucci, M., and Matelli, M. (1985). Selective spatial attention: One center, one circuit, or many circuits? In M. I. Posner and O. S. M. Marin (Eds.), *Attention and performance XI,* 251–265. Hillsdale, NJ: Erlbaum.

Shiffrin, R. M. (1988). Attention. In R. C. Atkinson, R. J. Herrnstein, G. Lindzey, and R. D. Luce (Eds.), *Stevens' handbook of experimental psychology.* Vol. 2: *Learning and cognition,* 2d ed., 738–811. New York: Wiley.

Shiffrin, R. M., and Schneider, W. (1977). Controlled and automatic human information processing: II. Perceptual learning, automatic attending, and a general theory. *Psychological Review, 84,* 127–190.

Spector, A., and Biederman, I. (1976). Mental set and shift revisited. *American Journal of Psychology, 89,* 669–679.

Umiltà, C., Nicoletti, R., Simion, F., Tagliabue, M. E., and Bagnara, S. (1992). The cost of a strategy. *European Journal of Cognitive Psychology, 4,* 21–40.

# 18 Progress in the Use of Interactive Models for Understanding Attention and Performance

Jonathan D. Cohen and Therese A. Huston

## 18.1 INTRODUCTION

This chapter examines recent work using parallel distributed processing (PDP) models to simulate performance in attentional tasks that has led to new perspectives on the relationship between attention and performance. Phenomenologically, we are interested in two types of effects that can be associated with the operation of attentional mechanisms: the top-down effects of selective attention and the bottom-up effects of attentional capture. Traditionally, these have been treated as separate mechanisms. Here, we show how these can be understood in terms of a common set of mechanisms within the PDP framework.

## 18.2 SELECTIVE ATTENTION

Attention is most frequently thought of as the ability to process and respond to one source of information while ignoring others. William James (1890) captured this succinctly in what is perhaps his most often quoted passage: "Focalization, concentration, of consciousness are of its essence. It implies withdrawal from some things in order to deal effectively with others." To study this ability, psychologists have used a variety of tasks in which the subject must respond to one attribute of a stimulus while ignoring others. The first, and perhaps most commonly used, task of this type is the Stroop task (Stroop 1935; see MacLeod 1991 for a comprehensive review).

In the Stroop task, subjects are presented with color words (e.g., *red, green,* or *blue*) that appear in colored print and are asked either to read the words or name the color in which they appear. That is, they are asked to respond to one attribute of the stimulus (the word form or its actual color) and ignore the other. The irrelevant attribute can be either congruent with the relevant one (e.g., the word *red* printed in red), incongruent (e.g., the word *red* printed in green), or neutral (e.g., the word *red* in black ink in the word reading task, or a series of colored *X*'s in the color naming task). The basic finding in this task is that while subjects find it easy to ignore the color of a word they are reading, they are strongly influenced by the word itself when naming the color in which it appears. This is seen as interference (an increase in reaction

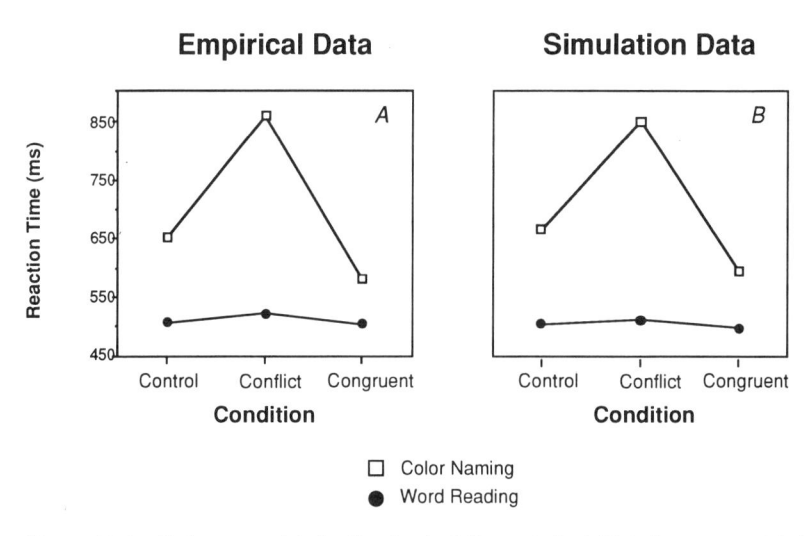

**Figure 18.1** Performance data for the standard Stroop task. A. Data from an empirical study (after Dunbar and MacLeod 1984). B. Results of the model's simulation of these data.

time) in the color naming task when the word conflicts with the color (e.g., the word *red* written in green ink) and facilitation when the word agrees with the color (e.g., *red* written in red ink). In contrast, the color of the stimulus has no influence on the reaction time for word reading (fig. 18.1). These findings indicate an asymmetry in the ability for selective attention: subjects are less able to control the processing of (i.e., ignore) word information than color information.

Recently, we proposed a PDP model of selective attention that can account for a number of the empirical findings from the Stroop task that previous theories were unable to account for (Cohen, Dunbar, and McClelland 1990). In the model, information about each attribute of a stimulus is processed along separate pathways that converge on a common set of response units. We train the model more on those attributes to which we assume subjects have had more practice generating the response called for in the task. Thus, in our model of the Stroop task (fig. 18.2), there are two processing pathways, one for color naming and one for word reading. This model is trained more on the word reading task than the color-naming task, corresponding to the assumption that people have had more experience generating a verbal response to written words than to colors they see. The effect of this training asymmetry is that the connection weights in the word-reading pathway become stronger than those in the color-naming pathway. As a result, when the network is presented with conflicting inputs to the two pathways (e.g., the word *red* and the color green), it responds preferentially (more quickly and more strongly) to the word input.

While this suggests a basis for the asymmetry in processing of words and colors, we know that subjects can correctly name the color of an incongruent stimulus. For the model to be able to do so, it must have some way of modulating the influence of information in the stronger word pathway. This

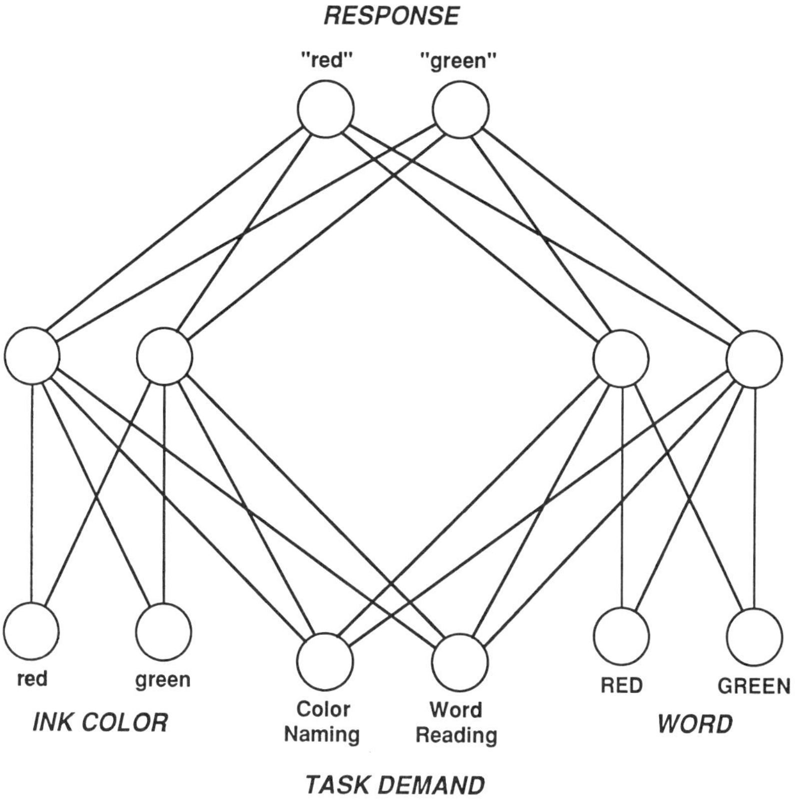

**Figure 18.2** Network architecture for the model of the Stroop task. Units at the bottom are input units, and units at the top are the output (response) units.

ability is provided by a set of task demand units, which represent the intended behavior (color naming versus word reading) and modulate processing in the two pathways. Connections from the task demand units to units in each of the processing pathways are such that when one of the task demand units is activated, it sensitizes units in the corresponding pathway, while desensitizing units in the competing one (see Cohen, Dunbar, and McClelland 1990 for a more detailed description). The result is that when the color task demand unit is activated and conflicting input units are activated in the color and word pathways, the signal in the color pathway is able to overcome the influence of the signal in the word pathway, even though the connection strengths in the word pathway are stronger than those in the color pathway. This modulatory influence of task demand information on processing in the two pathways is the mechanism for selective attention in our model.

This model captures all of the basic findings in the Stroop task. Processing words is faster than colors because the connections in the word pathway are stronger than those in the color pathway. The asymmetry of connection strengths also accounts for the facilitation and interference effects: word information influences color processing because the word connections are strong enough to allow information to be processed even in the absence of attention;

the connections in the color pathway are not strong enough—relative to those in the word pathway—to be able to do so. The model captures a number of other empirical phenomena associated with the Stroop task, including the effect of practice on interference effects, the relative nature of interference and facilitation effects (with respect to practice), response set effects, and the fact that colors fail to produce interference with word reading even when a conflicting color is presented before the word.

The most important observation about our model is that the mechanism for selective attention does not differ qualitatively from any other component of the model. Task demand information is represented, like any other, as a pattern of activation over a set of processing units, and attentional effects emerge entirely from the spread of activation from these units to others, over weighted connections. From this point of view, we can consider attention to be simply the influence of additional sources of information (in this case, a representation of the task to be performed) on the processing of information directly related to the stimuli. In the Stroop model, we implemented only one source of such information (a representation of the task to be performed); however, any number of other sources of information could come to bear on processing in a similar way (such as the relevance of particular stimuli or the location of stimuli). The work we report below provides some examples of this.

## 18.3 CAPTURE OF ATTENTION

The Stroop model focuses on the phenomenon of selective attention: the influence that subjects' intentions (e.g., their knowledge about the task) have on the processing of stimuli. However, the reverse can also occur: stimuli can influence attention, sometimes without the subject's knowledge or will. There is clear evidence of this in the psychological and neuropsychological literatures. For example, Posner (1980) has described results from a spatially cued simple reaction-time (RT) task that demonstrate such effects. In this task, subjects pressed a single button as soon as they saw a target that appeared to either the left or right of fixation. On 80 percent of trials, a cue (which was different from the target) preceded the target at the opposite location. Thus, subjects learned to predict the location of the target from the appearance of the cue on the opposite side. This was confirmed by a priming effect that was observed when a cue appeared 800 ms prior to the target at the opposite location. Interestingly, however, a priming effect was also observed when the cue appeared 100 ms prior to the target at the same location. In other words, at a very short stimulus onset asynchrony (SOA), there was a priming effect, even when the target appeared at the unexpected location. This finding strongly suggests that the stimulus itself was able to direct, or capture, attention, at least briefly.

The model that we used to account for the Stroop effect cannot account for this type of effect. This is because the connections in the model are unidirectional (or "feedforward"). In particular, activation can flow only from the task demand units to the intermediate units in each pathway, but not the reverse, so there is no way for stimulus information to influence attention. However, such effects can be accommodated if we include bidirectional connections. This is consistent with the GRAIN framework McClelland (1992) described. GRAIN stands for graded, random, activation-based, interactive, and nonlinear, a set of principles that constrain the more general PDP framework. The purpose of the GRAIN approach is to identify a limited set of principles that are sufficient to account for a wide variety of psychological phenomena and allow these to make contact with the biological mechanisms that underlie them. In particular, the principle of interactivity, implemented in the form of bidirectional connections between units, allows for capture-of-attention effects and provides a way of accounting for a number of neuropsychological phenomena in terms of these. Two examples of performance deficits associated with damage to the parietal lobes are illustrative of this approach.

**The Line Bisection Task**

Brunn and Farah (1991) examined the effects that familiar stimuli (words) can have on the allocation of attention in hemilateral neglect patients who have suffered right-sided parietal damage. Such patients tend to neglect stimuli appearing in the left half of space. To quantify this effect, Brunn and Farah asked such a patient to indicate the midpoint of a horizontal line. She marked the line well to the right of center, indicating neglect of its left end. Brunn and Farah next showed the patient a horizontal line beneath a string of letters (Fig. 18.3). When the string of letters formed a random sequence, the patient bisected the line as before. But when the string of letters formed a word, the patient bisected the line much closer to its true midpoint. This study strongly suggests that the word stimulus draws attention to the entire spatial region occupied by the word, thereby inducing the subject to notice the part of the line she otherwise tended to neglect.

On any account in which attention was a top-down process (as it is in our Stroop model), this finding must seem perplexing. If attention is a top-down process, why does the nature of the stimulus influence it? At the same time,

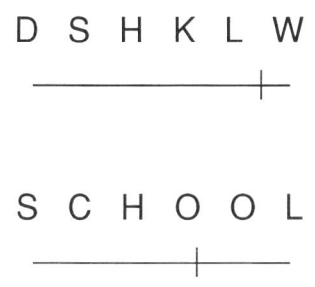

D  S  H  K  L  W
————————+—

S  C  H  O  O  L
————+————

**Figure 18.3**  Stimuli used in the Brunn and Farah experiment, with the kind of responses generated by their subject. (After Cohen, Servan-Schreiber, and McClelland 1992.)

the finding seems perplexing for any model in which perception is strictly bottom up (as in our Stroop model again), for if perception is bottom up, then surely the left-hand letters of the word suffer as much from neglect as the left-hand letters of a random string. Why, then, can their presence lead to a reorientation of perception?

We have recently offered a straightforward account for these findings in terms of interactivity between stimulus and attentional information (Cohen, Servan-Schreiber, and McClelland 1992). The idea is shown schematically in figure 18.4. Three modules are shown: one representing position-specific feature patterns (the letters in the string), one representing familiar objects (words), and one representing spatial location. We assume that in Brunn and Farah's neglect patient, the representation of spatial information on the left side was impaired; in the model, this would correspond to weaker or poorer activation of units representing left-sided locations in the spatial location module. When a random letter string is presented, this asymmetry leads to stronger activation of letters on the right, and since no familiar object is activated, performance is biased accordingly. But when a word is shown, the letters on the right, plus weak activations from the letters on the left, lead to the activation of a representation for the whole word in the familiar objects module. This feeds activation back to the position-specific feature level, strengthening the activations of the letters in the ordinarily neglected field. These strengthened feature level activations then lead to a strengthening in the activation of the location representations associated with the ordinarily neglected field. As a result, attention itself is allocated more evenly across the field.

Here, as in the Stroop model, we have not assumed that any explicit or qualitatively different mechanism is required for attentional processing. Rather, attentional effects emerge from the interaction between different sources of information as the system performs the task. A similar account can explain findings concerning the performance of both normal and parietally impaired

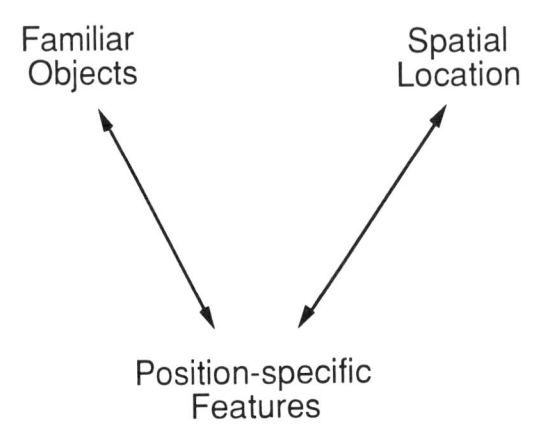

**Figure 18.4** Interactivity in perception, localization, identification, and attention. (Adapted from Cohen, Servan-Schreiber, and McClelland 1992.)

subjects in Posner's spatially cued RT task. Although we have not actually implemented the model of Brunn and Farah's task, we have implemented one for performance in Posner's RT task.

## The Spatially Cued Simple Reaction Time Task

In the typical version of this task (as opposed to the version described above), the cue usually appears at the same location as the target (valid trials), occasionally at the opposite location (invalid trials), and sometimes does not appear at all (neutral trials). The performance of subjects in these three conditions is shown in figure 18.5A. Figure 18.6 shows a model of this task that is analogous to the one for the Brunn and Farah task. Recently, we conducted simulations of performance in Posner's task using a modified version of the model in figure 18.6 (Cohen et al. 1993). The results of our simulation of normal performance are shown in figure 18.5B. As in the line bisection task, stimulus information can interact with location information to direct attention. Thus, when the cue appears at a particular location, it activates location units corresponding to that location. This, in turn, feeds activation back to stimulus units at that location. This reciprocity of activation between stimulus and corresponding location units facilitates processing of the target at that location. The facilitation effect that is observed in the valid versus neutral conditions is due to the fact that it takes longer for the target to establish this reciprocity when the cue has not preactivated the appropriate location units.

This model also possesses a set of inhibitory connections between units within the location module. Because of these inhibitory connections, units that represent different locations compete for activation. As a result, activation of units representing the cue location leads to inhibition of units representing other locations. If the target now appears at one of those other locations, it takes longer for the stimulus units to establish reciprocal activation with the

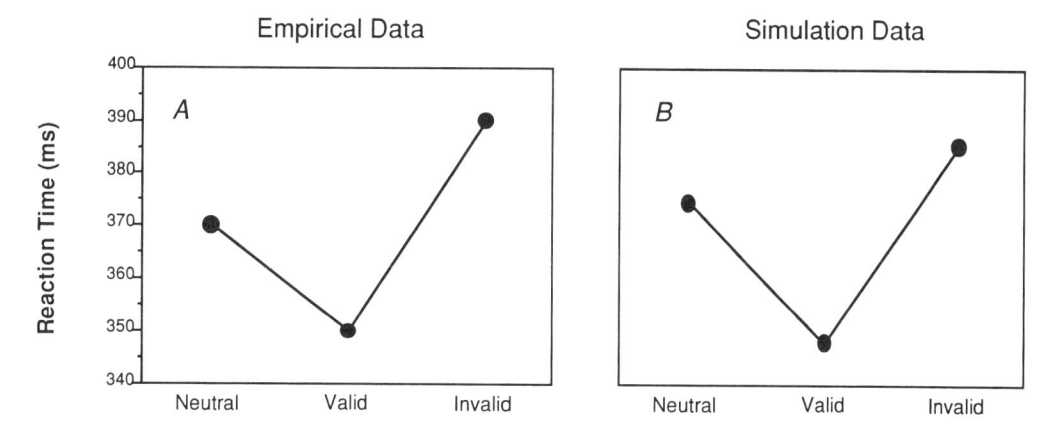

**Figure 18.5** A. Results from the performance of normal subjects in the spatially cued simple reaction time task (Posner et al. 1984). B. Simulated performance using the model of Cohen et al. (1993).

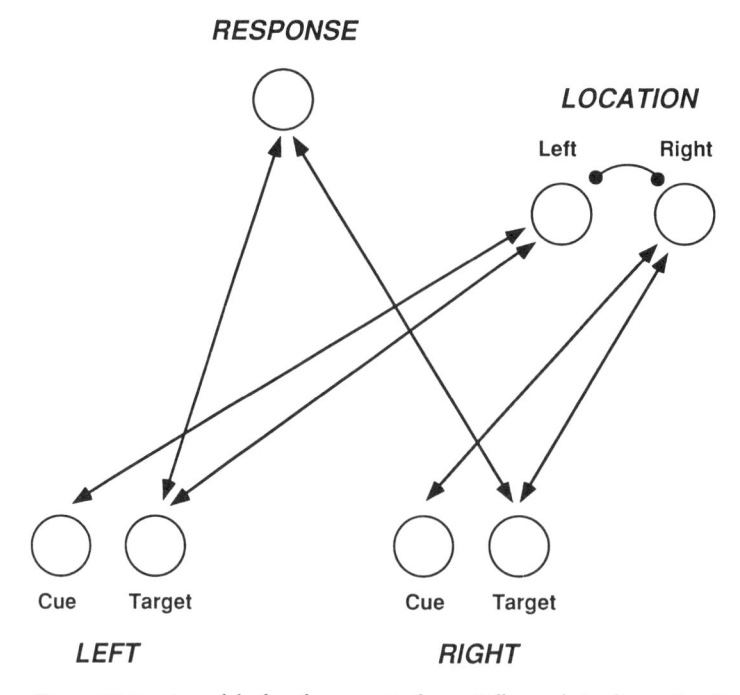

**Figure 18.6** A model of performance in the spatially cued simple reaction time task.

location units. This is the basis for the interference effect that the model, like human subjects, exhibits in the invalid versus neutral conditions of the task.

The model can also account for the performance deficits that parietally damaged subjects show in this task. The results of an empirical study of such subjects are shown in figure 18.7A. The primary finding is that patients show greatest impairment when the cue appears in the spared hemifield and the target in the damaged field. Posner and his colleagues have interpreted this pattern of effects in terms of a disturbance in the disengage function of attention, which they associate with parietal cortex (Posner et al. 1984). In other words, when—in the invalid condition—the cue appears in the spared hemifield, it then falls upon the damaged, contralateral parietal cortex to disengage attention from this location so that it can be shifted to the opposite, target location.

Our model suggests a somewhat different interpretation of the findings. We were able to reproduce the empirical results by damaging location units representing one half of space (fig. 18.7B). The observed effects arise as a consequence of the weakened ability of units on the damaged side to compete with units on the spared side. When the cue appears, it activates the location units on the intact side. These now have a dual advantage over units on the damaged side: they are intact and are preactivated. When the target appears on the opposite side, the stimulus units are unable to compete with the preactivated units on the spared side and therefore unable to establish reciprocal activation with the location units on that side. This greatly exacerbates the

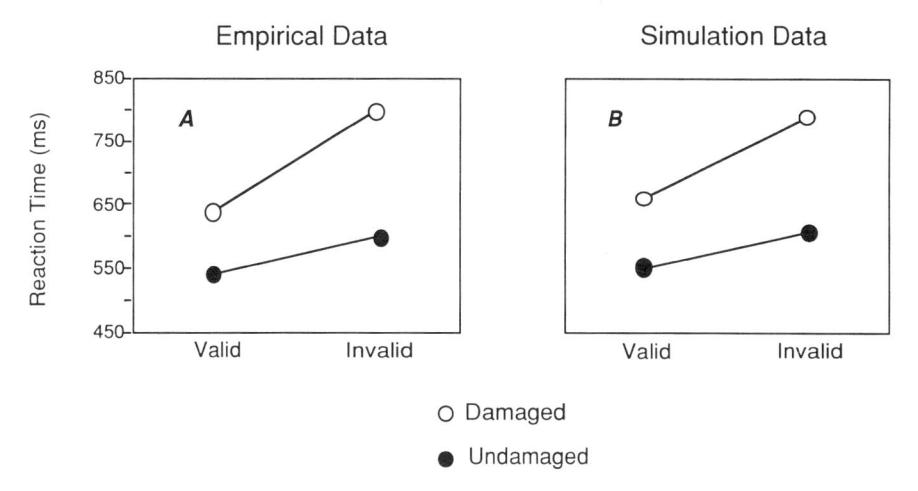

**Figure 18.7** Performance data for the spatially cued simple reaction time task. *A*. Data from an empirical study of patients with parietal damage (Posner et al. 1984). *B*. Results of the model's simulation of these data (Cohen et al. 1993).

interference effect that is normally observed. Thus, as with the other tasks we have discussed, attentional effects (and deficits) can be viewed entirely in terms of the interactions that occur between information in different parts of the system and, in this case, the competition that occurs between representations within a given module.

We have explored the use of interactive models of attentional effects to account for the findings from other tasks as well. For example, in Cohen, Servan-Schreiber, and McClelland (1992), we describe a GRAIN model that simulates detailed aspects of the time course of processing in the Eriksen response competition task (Eriksen and Eriksen 1974).

## 18.4 TOWARD A UNIFIED MODEL OF ATTENTIONAL EFFECTS

One important purpose of models is to unify the account of a variety of seemingly disparate phenomena in terms of a single theoretical explanation. Toward this end, it would be desirable if we could account for the top-down effects of selective attention, as are observed in the Stroop task, using the same kind of model that we have used to account for the bottom-up capture-of-attention effects observed in the Brunn and Farah and the Posner tasks. Beyond the unifying role of models, however, is the more valuable role that they can play in providing new insights. In the sections that follow, we describe our current efforts to develop a GRAIN model of the Stroop task. This work is still in progress, and the model we discuss below is not fully developed (for example, we have not yet addressed the learning phenomena accounted for by the original model). Nevertheless, adding interactivity to the model has already begun to provide new insights into the kind of interplay that can occur between processes and that may be involved in performance of the Stroop task.

## A GRAIN Model of the Stroop Task

**The Model** Figure 18.8 shows the model of the Stroop effect that we have been working with. Although the model is redrawn to correspond to the other interactive models discussed in this chapter, it has all of the same components as the original one: a set of task demand units (drawn in the upper right), a set of output units for the two responses, and a set of processing units for each dimension of the stimulus (color and word). The stimulus processing units in this model correspond to the intermediate units in the original model.[1] The activation function for each unit is also the same as the one used in the original model (the logistic of the time-averaged net input, with a time constant of 0.01). The activation of all units is computed synchronously in each processing cycle.

As in the original model, the weights in the word pathway are larger than those in the color pathway. However, unlike the original model, we did not train the GRAIN model to produce this difference. Our current efforts have focused largely on the dynamics of processing in interactive networks. While

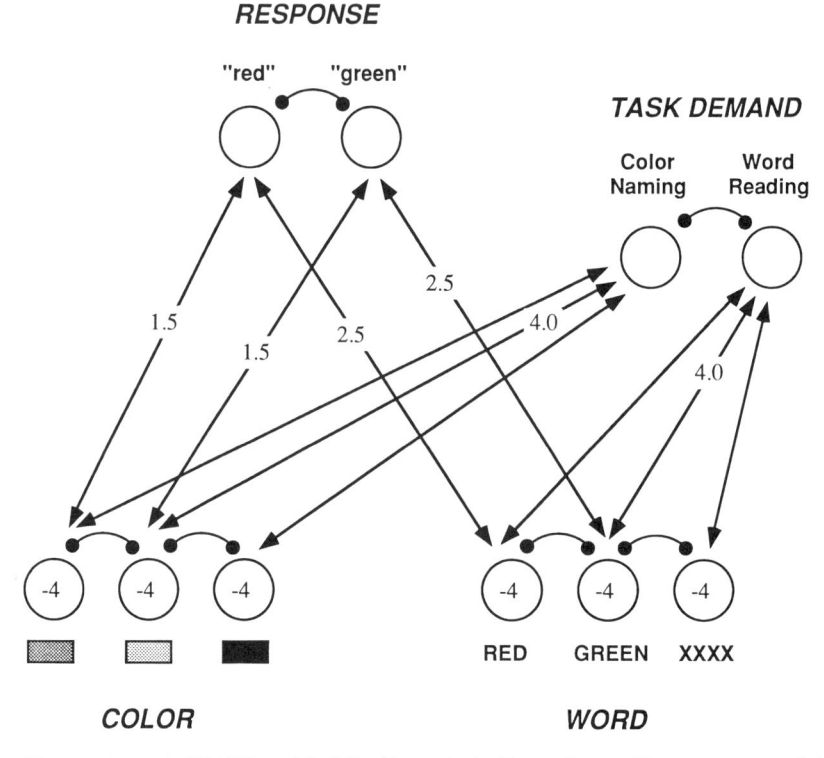

**Figure 18.8** A GRAIN model of the Stroop task. Connections with arrows are excitatory; connections with filled circles are inhibitory. (Every unit within each module is connected with an inhibitory weight to every other unit in that module.) All connection weights are bidirectionally symmetric. Numbers indicate values for excitatory weights. The value of all inhibitory weights is −2.0. The numbers within the stimulus processing units indicate the bias for these units; there was no bias on any of the other units.

training algorithms have been developed for such networks (Hinton 1989; Movellan and McClelland, n.d.; Peterson and Anderson 1987), we have not yet implemented one in this model. We have simply made the assumption that training the GRAIN network on words more than colors, as we did with the original model, would produce a similar asymmetry of weights. Figure 18.8 reports the weights and bias values assigned to the connections in the GRAIN network. The biases are identical to the ones used in the original model, and the excitatory weights between modules are identical to those that developed through training in the original model. In the GRAIN model, however, these are bidirectional. There are no inhibitory weights between modules; however, there are bidirectional inhibitory weights between units within each module. These were all assigned a fixed value of $-2$, which is approximately the average value of the inhibitory weights in the original model.

The bidirectionality of connections in the new model implements the principles of interactivity and competition, which are central to the GRAIN framework. The bidirectional excitatory connections between modules allow modules to interact in ways that were not possible in the original model (e.g., the response module can influence the stimulus processing modules, and these can influence the task demand module). The inhibitory connections between units within each module allow competition to occur among potential representations within them. As we will see, both the interactions between and the competition within modules can have important influences on processing.

Another difference between the GRAIN model and the original is that the GRAIN model does not have any supplementary mechanisms for implementing response competition. In the original model, response competition was implemented by adding a mechanism that tracked the difference between the cumulative activation of the two response units and generated a response when this difference exceeded a specified threshold. This is not necessary in the GRAIN model, since the bidirectional inhibitory connections between units within a module naturally cause them to compete. We simply assume that a response occurs when one of the units wins the competition, and exceeds a specified threshold of activation. A value of 0.6 was used for all of the simulations reported here.

Finally, in the GRAIN model, there are extra intermediate units in each processing pathway, which represent the irrelevant stimulus in the neutral condition of each task (e.g., XXXX in the color-naming task or the color black in the word-reading task). These correspond to the units added to the original model to simulate response set effects (Cohen, Dunbar, and McClelland 1990, simulation 6). They are important in the GRAIN model, given the added interactions that can occur between stimulus processing and attention.

**Simulation Procedures** Each simulation consisted of two stages. First, input was provided to the appropriate task demand unit, and the system was allowed to settle into a "ready state" for that task. As in the original model, this led to higher activation of the stimulus processing units in the task-relevant pathway (approximately 0.3) than in the competing pathway (0.05), making these more sensitive to subsequent input. Next, input was provided to the stimulus processing units corresponding to the stimulus for that trial. For example, in one of the conflict trials for the color-naming task, input would be provided to the red color unit and green word unit. The system was allowed to cycle until one of the response units exceeded the response threshold.

As in the original model, a small amount of noise (0.15) was added to the net input of each unit in each processing cycle. Simulation results correspond to the mean response times for 100 runs of the model in each condition. The response times have been converted to millisecond values by regressing the number of cycles in the six conditions of the standard task against empirical results (Dunbar and MacLeod 1984). The regression equation is reported in figure 18.9. As with the original model, the simulations account for only one component of the empirical RTs. We assume that the other component (represented by the intercept value of the regression, 298 ms) includes processes such as sensory encoding and motor execution, which the models were not intended to address.

**Simulation Results** The results of the GRAIN model's simulation of the standard Stroop task are shown in figure 18.9. This model, like its predecessor, demonstrates all of the primary phenomena associated with this task: word reading is faster than color naming, words can influence color naming but not the reverse, and interference is greater than facilitation. The fact that the new model can capture these effects with roughly the same parameters as the original model lends support to central features of our account: that the pattern of effects observed in Stroop-like tasks can be explained in terms of the differential strength of connections in competing pathways and their interac-

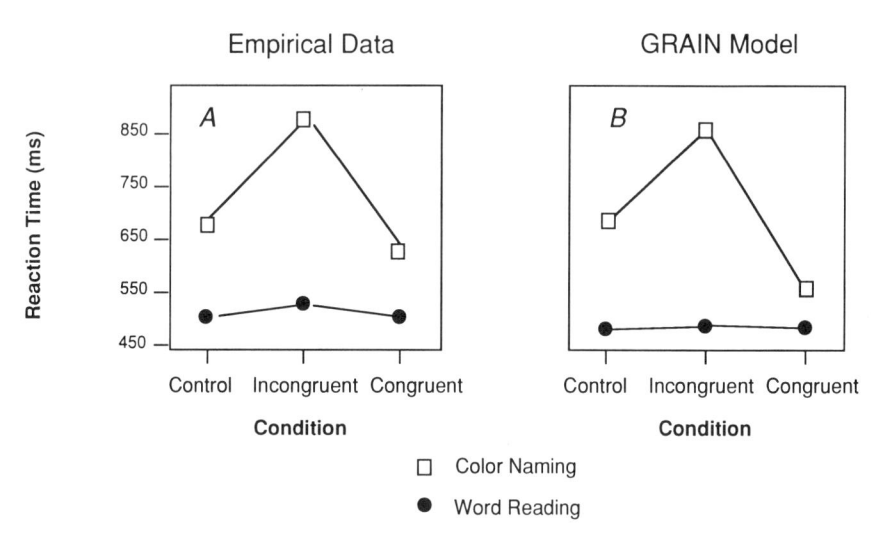

**Figure 18.9** Performance data for the standard Stroop task. *A*. The same empirical data as in figure 18.1. *B*. Results of the GRAIN model's simulation of these data. Simulation results are reported in millisecond equivalents, based on the following regression equation: $0.98 \times$ cycles $+ 298$.

tion with additional sources of information that serve to modulate processing in these pathways. However, the differences between the GRAIN and original model allow for differences in the way that processing actually occurs in each. These are made clear by a closer examination of the dynamics of processing in the GRAIN model.

**A Duck and a Stick**  When the GRAIN model is used to simulate the word-reading task, processing is straightforward. Activation of the word-reading task demand unit ensures that information in the word pathway will dominate processing. Because the connections are weaker in the color pathway, little activation flows along this pathway, even when input is provided to it in the congruent or incongruent conditions of the task. However, more interesting effects arise when the model is engaged in the color-naming task.

When, in the color-naming task, input is provided to a color unit, activation spreads to the corresponding output unit. However, because of the bidirectional connections between the output and stimulus units and because of the relatively strong weights in the word-reading pathway, activation spreads from the activated response unit back down to the corresponding word unit.[2] Activation of this unit both inhibits other word units and returns activation to the output unit. This reciprocity of activation within the word pathway indicates that, in effect, this pathway has been recruited into processing. This is possible, even in the absence of attention to the word pathway, because of the relatively stronger connections in that pathway. Information in the color pathway still determines the response, since it is primed by the task demand units and therefore has a large initial influence on processing. This determines how activation is fed back to the word processing units. However, with time, the word pathway begins to contribute to the response. It is as if attention enables a less powerful, less automatic process to direct a more automatic process in performing the task. The word pathway's contribution to processing in the color-naming task can be made evident by observing what happens when connections in this pathway are removed. For example, if the task is to name the color red and the connections between the red word unit and the red response unit are eliminated, then response times in the congruent and neutral conditions of this color-naming task are prolonged (894 ms and 770 ms, respectively), and the incongruent condition cannot be performed (activation of the red response unit never reaches threshold). In other words, activation of the word unit plays a critical role, even in the color-naming task.

By way of analogy, imagine a duck riding an elephant. They are at a crossroads, where a sign points in the direction they are to go. In one case (the word reading task), the elephant sees the sign. Here, the matter is simple: the elephant follows the sign, and it does not much matter what the duck says or does. Imagine, however, that the elephant is blindfolded (the color-naming task). In this case, the duck decides. If the elephant does not have any preference, then a lean or slight tap by the duck is sufficient to indicate the direction and get them on their way, though perhaps more slowly than had the elephant seen the sign for itself. If the elephant has a personal preference, or perhaps catches a brief glimpse of the sign, and it agrees with the duck, then again they are on their way. However, if the elephant wants to head in the opposite direction, then the duck has to insist more forcefully and may require some additional encouragement (fig. 18.10).

This examination of how the Stroop task is performed by the GRAIN model suggests how interactivity between stimulus and response modules may play an important role in processing, a possibility that has not traditionally been considered in accounts of the Stroop task. However, despite differences in the dynamics of processing between the two models, both account for the Stroop effect in the same basic terms: a difference in the strength of processing in the two competing pathways. This is further evidenced by the GRAIN model's ability to capture the same set of SOA effects as the original model.

**SOA Effects Revisited**  Glaser and Glaser (1982) conducted a series of studies in which they varied the relative onset of color and word information. Stimuli were made up of a white word superimposed on a colored background, so that the two components of the stimulus could be presented at different times. The results of one of their experiments are shown in figure 18.11A.

One of the most important results of these studies was the demonstration that presenting the color prior to the word did not have any effect on word reading. This establishes that a difference in the speed of processing colors and words cannot, on its own, account for the asymmetry of interference effects that are observed in the two tasks. Some other factor must be responsible. The GRAIN model, like the original, attributes these effects to differences in the strength of processing in the two competing pathways. Both models capture the fact that faster processing of words cannot be compensated for by

**Figure 18.10**  A duck with a stick and an attentive elephant.

presenting the color earlier (fig. 18.11, panels B and C). This is because color naming is weaker than word reading and therefore cannot influence it.

Although both models are able to capture this important finding, there are other features of Glaser and Glaser's (1982) data that are not accounted for by either model. For example, neither model accurately simulates performance in the color naming task at negative SOAs (irrelevant stimulus at the same time as or preceding the relevant one). As we have pointed out previously (Cohen, Dunbar, and McClelland 1990), this is most likely because both models lack any adaptive mechanisms (e.g., habituation or strategic processes) that could compensate for prior presentation of a distracting stimulus.

Another feature of the data that is not accounted for is the overall slowing of RT in the color naming task when the color and word are presented at the same time. This effect was observed in the neutral and congruent conditions, when there was no conflicting word information. This finding strongly suggests a capture-of-attention effect. That is, when the word is presented simultaneously with (or shortly after) the color, its appearance temporarily distracts the subject, drawing attention away from the color-naming task and slowing the response.

It is not surprising that the original model does not exhibit a capture-of-attention effect, since there is no mechanism by which the stimulus can influence attention. However, we might have expected the GRAIN model to do so, given the bottom-up connections between the stimulus processing and task demand units. That is, in principle, when a word unit receives activation, this can spread to the word task demand unit, which competes with the color task demand unit. Additional activation of the word unit would reduce activation of the color task demand unit, slowing processing of the color. This effect would tend to influence color naming more than word reading since, as we know from work with the original model, changes in the allocation of attention (activation of task demand units) have a greater influence on processing in weaker than stronger pathways. However, such effects are not observed in simulations using our current version of the GRAIN model. There is a small increase in response time at the 0 SOA in the neutral color-naming condition, but this is not due to an interaction between the neutral word stimulus and the word task demand units; severing the connections between these does not affect performance. Rather, this effect is most likely due to competition between the neutral and congruent word units (recall that the latter is recruited by the color naming process, even in the neutral and conflict conditions). In the current model, word input occurring during the color-naming task has virtually no influence on the activation of the task demand units. We will consider this limitation of the model in the general discussion that follows.

## 18.5 DISCUSSION

In describing a set of interactive models that address a variety of attentional effects, our goal has been to illustrate how the GRAIN framework can be used

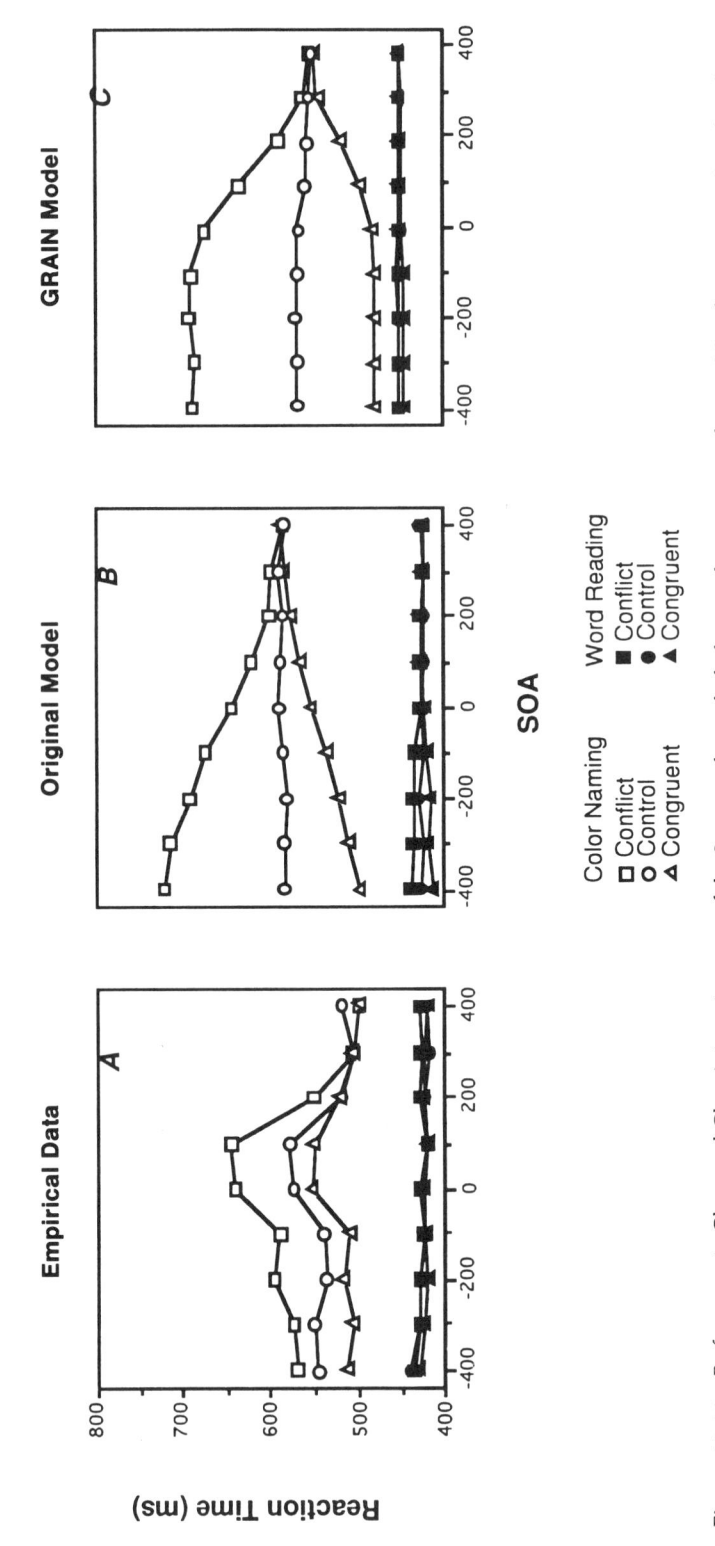

**Figure 18.11** Performance in Glaser and Glaser's (1982) version of the Stroop task, in which the stimulus onset asynchrony (SOA) between stimuli in the relevant and irrelevant dimension is varied. Negative SOAs indicate that the irrelevant stimulus appeared first; positive SOAs indicate that the relevant stimulus appeared first. *A.* Results from an empirical study by Glaser and Glaser (1982, experiment 1). *B, C.* Simulation results from, respectively, the original and GRAIN models. Processing times for the models are in ms equivalents, based on the regression equations for each model. (See Cohen, Dunbar, and McClelland 1990 for a discussion.)

to construct models that exhibit both top-down (e.g., the standard Stroop task) and bottom-up (e.g., the spatially cued RT) attentional effects. Our exploration of this framework is clearly in its early stages. It has not addressed learning phenomena, nor does it capture all of the attentional effects that appear to be relevant. We discuss these challenges now, offer some thoughts on how they might be addressed in future work, and consider how our approach relates to other efforts to understand attention.

**Learning**

Clearly, learning phenomena have played an important role in the development of theories of attention and automaticity. Our original model addressed a number of these, showing how the same basic learning mechanism can account for the power law of practice effects, the asymmetry of interference effects between highly and less-well-practiced tasks (or consistently versus variably mapped tasks), and the changes in interference effects that can occur with practice.

The interactive models that we have discussed do not address these phenomena. Connection weights in these models were all preassigned. One reason is that the recurrent connections in interactive networks require different or modified versions of the learning algorithms used in feed-forward networks. A number of algorithms have been developed that can be applied to GRAIN networks (Hinton 1989; Peterson and Anderson 1987; Movellan and McClelland, n.d.; Pineda 1987), and studies of the relationship of learning, automaticity, and attention are certainly an important direction in which to pursue work within the GRAIN framework.

**Interactivity and Attention**

The model of the spatially cued RT task simulates the bottom-up capture-of-attention effects observed in this task. These resulted from interactivity between the stimulus representation and the location (attentional) representations in this model. However, in its present form, the interactive (GRAIN) version of the Stroop model does not exhibit similar effects. It fails to demonstrate the increase in RT that is observed empirically when color and word are presented at the same time (Glaser and Glaser 1982, experiment 1). There are a number of reasons that this might be. One possibility is that we have not yet discovered the proper set of parameters. Word input occurring during the color naming task has no influence on the task demand units. It is possible that a different set of connection weights and biases would remedy this problem. However, a challenging set of constraints must be satisfied. For example, in order to produce the capture-of-attention effect, bottom-up activation of the word reading unit must have a greater influence inhibiting the color-naming unit than enabling the word-reading process. This is made clear by considering the congruent condition. In order for activation of the congruent word unit to slow RT, spread of activation to the word-reading unit must result in greater inhibition of the color-naming unit (which will slow the response) than it does in additional activation of the congruent word unit (which will speed the response).

We have begun to explore different values for the connection weights and biases in the model; however, these have largely been constrained by an attempt to keep the relative values consistent with those from the original model. A significantly different combination of connection weights, biases, and processing parameters may be able to capture the basic Stroop effect (which has endured most of the variations we have already explored), as well as the additional SOA effects observed in Glaser and Glaser's data.

Alternatively, these discrepancies may reflect principled shortcomings, such as the lack of additional mechanisms that are present in the natural system. One such limitation may have to do with the mechanism by which representations within a given module compete with one another. In the current model, this is implemented in the simplest possible way as a set of negatively weighted connections between competing units. One effect of this mechanism, in combination with a sigmoidal activation function, is that once a particular unit prevails, it becomes very difficult for others to have any further influence on processing. This is why, during color naming, activation of the word input unit has no influence on the task demand units. Once the color-naming task demand unit has been primed, it dominates the competition, making it very difficult to activate the word-reading unit.

One approach to this problem may be to assume that excitatory and inhibitory influences have different time courses. If inhibitory influences were more transient (that is, they had a more rapid onset but also decayed more rapidly), this might allow the appropriate task demand unit to be activated initially (during priming), while still allowing the competing unit to have an influence if it receives activation later on (if the inhibition it receives from the active unit has diminished by that time). Another possible explanation for the capture-of-attention effect may be spatial. In Glaser and Glaser's task, changes in one dimension occurred at a different spatial location than changes at the other. Our model of the Stroop effect, however, implicitly assumes that both stimuli are occurring at the same location (or that location does not matter). Our model of the spatially cued RT task, however, provides an account of how stimuli appearing at one location can slow processing of stimuli appearing at another location. A combination of these models might be able to account for the effects observed by Glaser and Glaser in terms of a bottom-up effect of the word stimulus on the spatial allocation of attention. We should note that this would be similar in a number of respects to a model that Phaf, Van der Heijden, and Hudson (1990) have described; however, our basic accounts of the Stroop effect differ.

**New Insights and Predictions**

The current model, notwithstanding its limitations, demonstrates that it is possible to account for top-down, selective attention effects such as those observed in the standard version of the Stroop task, using the same mechanisms that account for bottom-up, capture-of-attention effects such as those observed in the spatially cued RT task. However, the ability to provide a unified account is only one criterion on which a model should be judged. Perhaps more important, it should be able to provide new insights into the mechanisms that underlie performance. Recasting the Stroop model within the GRAIN framework has already begun to do this by suggesting interesting and unexpected ways in which processes can interact while the system performs the task.

The set of models we have described, taken together, also provide a consistent view of attentional effects. They attribute these directly to the impact that relevant sources of information (e.g., location information, task information, object information) have on the processing of stimuli. These attentional interactions are supported by mechanisms that are qualitatively identical to those that support the processing of the stimulus itself rather than by a qualitatively distinct attentional apparatus. While we have not specified all of the mechanisms that are responsible for generating these other sources of information, by adding interactivity to our models, we have begun to specify how they can be influenced by stimuli currently being processed.

Finally, a successful model should be able to make new predictions. Within the context of the Stroop effect, a long-standing challenge has been to predict if and how this effect can be reversed, that is, the circumstances under which colors can influence word reading. Our account of the Stroop task suggests that this should occur when the task demand representation for word reading has been reduced and the representation for color naming has been increased. In Cohen, Dunbar, and McClelland (1990, simulation 5), we demonstrated that, according to our model, even processes that satisfy all of the operational criteria for automaticity can still be subject to modulation by attention. Thus, decreasing the activation of the word-reading task demand unit not only slows this process but also makes it more susceptible to interference; this effect will be enhanced by providing activation to the color-naming unit. There are a number of ways that these conditions could be produced experimentally. One would be to vary the task from trial to trial (indicating the task by preceding each trial with a cue) and to produce a strong expectancy for color naming (by increasing the frequency of such trials). We would predict that with a sufficiently short delay between the task cue and the Stroop stimulus (that is, precluding a full shift in task demand representation prior to the stimulus), colors should influence word reading.[3]

**Relationship to Other Approaches**

It is important to note the relationship of our work to that of others who have considered similar questions. First, we should acknowledge the overall similarity of our GRAIN model of the Stroop effect to the approach taken by Phaf, van der Heijden, and Hudson (1990). They have described an interactive model of attentional effects that they have used to simulate processing in a variety of tasks. Both approaches share the same emphasis on the view that attentional effects reflect interactions between the different processes involved in a given task rather than the functioning of a dedicated, centralized attentional mechanism. However, there are important differences between their model of the Stroop task and our own. In their model, the asymmetry between word reading and color naming is implemented as a set of direct connections between words and verbal responses that bypasses the intermediate, feature-feature level of representation. The color naming process does involve this level, which makes it subject it to the competition that occurs at this level. This architectural asymmetry accounts for the asymmetry of speed and interference effects that are observed in the Stroop task.[4] This is closely related to translation theories, which also attribute the asymmetry of effects to an extra step involved in color naming (Glaser and Glaser 1989; Virzi and Egeth 1985). These accounts differ markedly from our own, in which the pathways involved in each task are architecturally identical, and asymmetric effects are attributed to differences in the strengths of connections in pathway rather than qualitative differences between them.

Judging from the results that have been produced by each to date, each approach appears to have its strengths and weaknesses. The Phaf, van der Heijden, and Hudson (1990) model produces the increase in RT at 0 SOA that is observed in the Glaser and Glaser data (1982) that our model is unable to capture. In this light, it would be valuable to understand precisely what produces this effect in Phaf, van der Heijden, and Hudson's model. On the other hand, our models do a better job of capturing the fact that presenting colors before words has little or no effect on word reading. That is, performance of Phaf, van der Heijden, and Hudson's model is closer to what would be predicted by a speed of processing model. In addition, our original model directly addresses the relationship between learning and automaticity and provides an account for the Stroop effect in these terms (that is, strength of processing). As we have pointed out, the GRAIN model provides the same basic account; however, in its current form, it does not include a learning component. This represents a direct challenge for both sets of interactive models (that is, the GRAIN and the Phaf, van der Heijden, and Hudson models), and constitutes an important direction for future research.

It is also worthwhile to consider how our approach stands in relationship to other accounts of attention and information processing. As we have pointed out previously (Cohen, Dunbar, and McClelland 1990), we view our theory of attention as closely related to the multiple resources view that has been expressed by a number of authors (Allport 1982; Hirst and Kalmar 1987; Navon and Gopher 1979; Wickens 1984). In both accounts, attentional effects are considered to rely on the interaction between the specific processes or resources demanded by the task rather than on a common, central attentional mechanism. We also consider our models to be closely related to the attenuation theory of attention (Treisman 1960) and to Kahneman and Treisman's (1984) notion of weak automaticity. In our models, as in these accounts, attention is modulatory. All processes are subject to its influence to varying degrees. In our models, this degree of influence depends on the strength of the connections in the corresponding pathway, which may be predetermined (in the case of innately "automatic" processes), or the result of learning. Of course, we consider it a strength of our models that they have begun to commit these ideas to a specific set of processing mechanisms, which permit both a detailed analysis of their functioning and quantitative comparisons with empirical data.

Finally, Kornblum, Hasbroucq, and Osman (1990) have recently proposed a dimensional overlap model of processing in stimulus-response compatibility tasks. Their theory provides a framework for analyzing and comparing performance according to the relationship among stimuli and between stimuli and their associated responses in different tasks. The dimensional overlap model is more general than any of the models we have proposed and can be applied to a wide variety of tasks. However, in its present form, it is a qualitative model that, as the authors point out, requires quantification. For example, it shares with our approach to the Stroop task the assumption that the relationship between a written word and its associated verbal response is stronger than between a color and its response (connection strengths correspond to dimensional overlap). It also assumes that stimuli automatically activate their associated responses, though this can be subject to attentional modulation. However, these factors have not yet been quantified in the dimensional overlap model. There is also an important difference from our approach. The dimensional overlap model postulates discrete, sequential processing stages, while processing in our models is continuous and interactive. These differences, as well as the specific ways in which dimensional overlap and attentional modulation are implemented, may have a significant influence on performance of the model. As we have seen with the GRAIN model of the Stroop effect, intuitions about how complex processing models will perform (e.g., that interactivity will produce capture-of-attention effects) are often misleading. Ultimately, it will be important to implement models of a variety of tasks fully within both frameworks, in order to compare the two approaches.

## 18.6 CONCLUSION

We have described a set of interactive models that address both bottom-up and top-down attentional effects. These models suggest the potential that the GRAIN framework holds for providing a unified account of such effects. The most important element of this account is that attentional effects are attributed to the interaction between different sources of information during task performance rather than to a unitary, dedicated attentional mechanism. More generally, the models we have described occupy an intermediate position between the extremes of discrete, stagelike models and undifferentiated connectionist models. They are made up of distinct but highly interconnected functional modules. They demonstrate that nonintuitive but nevertheless regular and identifiable behaviors can emerge from such systems, which may lead to new insights about psychological mechanisms. The GRAIN model of the Stroop task served as one example, showing how processes that would otherwise seem to be in competition may actually cooperate to perform the task and how a less automatic process may recruit a more automatic one in the service of the task.

Our current models are early representatives of the GRAIN framework and are still lacking in important ways. For example, they do not incorporate learning mechanisms. An important question is whether, by incorporating these, they will be able to account for the same set of phenomena that have been successfully addressed by noninteractive models. The models also currently fall short of accounting for all of the attentional phenomena that appear to be relevant. However, a consideration of these shortcoming has already suggested ways in which the models may be further developed. This inducement to reevaluate and generate new ideas, along with the kinds of new insights and unexpected results described above, indicate the importance of computational modeling. They are as important a benchmark for the success of a model as its ability to account for empirical data. They show that a model is not just a finished work but rather the expression of a medium that permits us to explore ideas in detail, discover their strengths and weaknesses, and ultimately produce new and better works.

**NOTES**

We thank Jay McClelland, Kevin Dunbar, and David Servan-Schreiber for their useful suggestions, and their contribution to the ideas discussed in this chapter and Sylvan Kornblum and Hans Phaf for their thoughtful reviews of the initial manuscript. This work was supported by an NIMH research grant (MH 47073, Project 2) to the first author and an NIMH training grant (MH 19102-03) awarded to the Department of Psychology, Carnegie Mellon University.

1. This model does not contain an explicit set of input units, as did the original model. These were not necessary because, in GRAIN, input to the network can be introduced by providing activation directly to (i.e., "soft-clamping") intermediate units, which is then integrated with the activation they receive along their connections to other units in the model. This is identical to the situation for the intermediate units in the original model.

2. The color and word processing units in this model should not be thought of as sensory units. Rather, they should be thought of as supporting the internal representation of information in each pathway. That is, the top-down activation of the word units should not be thought of as activating the sensory image of a word, but rather knowledge about that word, and its correspondence to a verbal response.

3. Phaf, van der Heijden, and Dunbar (1990) made a similar prediction, though they focused on an increase in the instructional set for colors, without referring to a corresponding decrease in that for words. This may be due to the different way in which the instructions for color naming and word reading are implemented in their model. See the following discussion and note 4.

4. Their method of presenting task instructions is also asymmetric. They present the instructions for color naming by activating the color units (analogous to our procedure); however, they present the instructions for word reading by activating the color word response units. The significance of this asymmetry is not entirely clear to us at present; however, it seems possible that this will also contribute to the asymmetry of effects that is observed.

# REFERENCES

Allport, D. A. (1982). Attention and performance. In G. I. Claxton (Ed.), *New directions in cognitive psychology*, 112–153. London: Routledge and Kegan Paul.

Brunn, J. L., and Farah, M. J. (1991). The relation between spatial attention and reading: Evidence from the neglect syndrome. *Cognitive Neuropsychology*, 8(1), 59–75.

Cohen, J. D., Dunbar, K., and McClelland, J. L. (1990). On the control of automatic processes: A parallel distributed processing account of the Stroop effect. *Psychological Review*, 97(3), 332–361.

Cohen, J. D., Romero, R. D., Servan-Schreiber, D., and Farah, M. J. (1993). Disengaging from the disengage function: The relation of macrostructure to microstructure in parietal attentional deficits. Technical Report PDP.CNS.93.2, Department of Psychology, Carnegie-Mellon University.

Cohen, J. D., Servan-Schreiber, D., and McClelland, J. L. (1992). A parallel distributed processing approach to automaticity: Principles and models. *American Journal of Psychology*, 105, 239–269.

Dunbar, K. N., and MacLeod, C. M. (1984). A horse race of a different color: Stroop interference patterns with transformed words. *Journal of Experimental Psychology: Human Perception and Performance*, 10, 622–639.

Eriksen, B. A., and Eriksen, C. W. (1974). Effects of noise letters upon the identification of target letter in a non-search task. *Perception and Psychophysics*, 16, 143–149.

Glaser, M. O., and Glaser, W. R. (1982). Time course analysis of the Stroop phenomenon. *Journal of Experimental Psychology: Human Perception and Performance*, 8(6), 875–894.

Glaser, W. R., and Glaser, M. O. (1989). Context effect in Stroop-like word and picture processing. *Journal of Experimental Psychology: General*, 118, 13–42.

Hinton, G. E. (1989). Deterministic Boltzmann learning performs steepest descent in weight-space. *Neural Computation* 1, 143–150.

Hirst, W., and Kalmar, D. (1987). Characterizing attentional resources. *Journal of Experimental Psychology: General*, 116(1), 68–81.

James, W. (1890). *Principles of psychology*. New York: Henry Holt and Co.

Kahneman, D., and Treisman, A. (1984). Changing views of attention and automaticity. In R. Parasuraman, R. Davies, and J. Beatty (Eds.), *Varieties of attention*, 29–60. New York: Academic Press.

Kornblum, S., Hasbroucq, T., and Osman A. (1990). Dimensional overlap: Cognitive basis for stimulus-response compatibility—A model and taxonomy. *Psychological Review* 97(2), 253–270.

MacLeod, C. M. (1991). Half a century of research on the Stroop effect: An integrative review. *Psychological Bulletin*, 109 (2), 163–203.

McClelland, J. L. (1992). Toward a theory of information processing in graded, random, interactive networks. In D. Meyer and S. Kornblum (Eds.), *Attention and performance XIV*, 655–688. Cambridge, MA: MIT Press.

Movellan J. R., and McClelland, J. L. (n.d.). Learning continuous probability distributions with symmetric diffusion networks. *Cognitive Science*. In press.

Mozer, M. C. (1991). *The perception of multiple objects*. Cambridge, MA: MIT Press.

Navon, D., and Gopher, D. (1979). On the economy of the human processing system. *Psychological Review*, 86, 214–255.

Peterson, C., and Anderson, J. R. (1987). A mean field theory learning algorithm for neural networks. *Complex Systems, 1*, 995–1019.

Phaf, R. H., van der Heijden, A. H. C., and Hudson, P. T. W. (1990). SLAM: A connectionist model for attention in visual selection tasks. *Cognitive Psychology 22*, 273–341.

Pineda, F. J. (1987). Generalization of back-propagation to recurrent neural networks. *Physical Review Letters, 59*, 2229–2232.

Posner, M. I. (1980). Orienting of attention. *Quarterly Journal of Experimental Psychology, 32*, 3–25.

Posner, M. I., Walker, J. A., Friedrich, F. J., and Rafal, R. D. (1984). Effects of parietal lobe injury on covert orienting of visual attention. *Journal of Neuroscience, 4*, 1863–1874.

Stroop, J. R. (1935). Studies of interference in serial verbal reactions. *Journal of Experimental Psychology, 18*, 643–662.

Treisman, A. M. (1960). Contextual cues in selective listening. *Quarterly Journal of Experimental Psychology, 12*, 242–248.

Virzi, R. A., and Egeth, H. E. (1985). Toward a translation model of Stroop interference. *Memory and Cognition, 13*, 304–319.

Wickens, D. D. (1984). Processing resources in attention. In R. Parasuraman and D. R. Davies (Eds.), *Varieties of attention*, 63–102. Orlando, FL: Academic Press.

# 19 Interhemispheric Control in the Normal Brain: Evidence from Redundant Bilateral Presentations

## Eran Zaidel and Janice Rayman

ABSTRACT   We studied the relationship between implicit hemispheric control and hemispheric specialization in the normal brain using brief redundant bilateral displays. The first experiment required lexical decision of from one to four copies of identical letter strings with no spatial cues. There was an accuracy gain from one to two copies in both visual hemifields (VFs) for words but only in the left visual hemifield (LVF) for nonwords. Bilateral presentations of one copy in each field showed an advantage over one copy in either VF alone for words but a loss for nonwords. The second experiment included spatial cues. Reaction times (RTs) showed a gain from one to two copies in both VFs for nonwords, but only in the LVF for words. Bilateral presentations followed a race model with the superior right visual hemifield (RVF) dominating responses.

The third experiment used lateralized hierarchic patterns and required identification of the local or global target. There was a global advantage and faster local decisions when the global target was consistent with the local target than when they were inconsistent (consistency effect). This pattern occurred in the LVF, in the RVF, and in bilateral presentations (BVF). There was also RVF specialization for local processing and LVF specialization for global processing. Bilateral presentations followed a race model with local decisions as fast as in the RVF and global decisions as fast as in the LVF. The fourth experiment attempted to replicate the third one. This time there was also a consistency effect in global decisions, though it was not as strong as in local decisions. Bilateral presentations showed either an advantage over both VFs or a race model with the superior RVF dominating the responses, depending on decision type (global or local), consistency of the global and local targets, and individual differences in hemispheric arousal. Multiple linear regression confirmed the hypothesis that the consistency effect in local decisions is interhemispheric and significantly correlated with the latency difference between local decisions in the RVF and global decisions in the LVF.

Together, the data show complex and dynamic forms of interhemispheric control, sensitive to task and individual differences and dependent on parallel and independent information processing in the two cerebral hemispheres.

## 19.1   INTRODUCTION: MODELS AND PREDICTIONS

There is compelling evidence, both clinical and normal, not only for the doctrine of complementary hemispheric specialization but also for the thesis of hemispheric independence (Zaidel, Clarke, and Suyenobu 1990). In this view, each of the two normal cerebral hemispheres has its own perceptual and cognitive machinery, each can process most environmental stimuli and control the behavior of the organism, and each can process information independently of, and simultaneously with, the other. Hemispheric independence requires mechanisms that control interhemispheric interaction. One such mechanism is hemispheric dominance, which is not the same as hemispheric specialization.

But other mechanisms exist, and one paradigm that allows us to observe some of them is redundant bilateral presentations (RBPs). What happens when identical copies of the same stimuli are presented to both hemispheres simultaneously? The purpose of this chapter is to review recent experiments in our laboratory that have incorporated RBPs in order to begin documenting the range and frequency of control modes observed in normal interhemispheric interaction, and in turn, note their relation to hemispheric specialization and to hemispheric independence. These control operations are unconscious, but they make possible a whole range of parallel operations that affect conscious outputs.

**Unilateral Presentations**

What happens when the same stimulus is projected simultaneously to both visual hemifields (VFs) of a normal subject? The results should depend, among other things, on the competence and specialization of the two cerebral hemispheres for this task, which are commonly studied in unilateral presentations. With unilateral presentations, we can think of three types of situations (Zaidel 1983; Zaidel, Clarke, and Suyenobu 1990):

1. Each hemisphere is competent for the task, although each may use a different information-processing strategy, and each will then process the information projected to it without recourse to interhemispheric exchange. Left visual hemifield (LVF) stimuli will be processed by the right hemisphere (RH), and RVF stimuli will be processed by the LH, direct access fashion (Direct Access model). In this case, we may find a VF × V interaction (V = independent stimulus variable) that cannot be attributed to callosal relay. Such an interaction will occur if V affects processing in each hemisphere (VF) differently. For example, the task may be lateralized lexical decision, and V may be the concreteness of the word stimuli. Then one may find a VF × Concreteness interaction where abstract words show an RVF advantage (RVFA) and concrete words do not, and where there is a concreteness advantage in the LVF but not in the RVF (Zaidel 1989).

2. One hemisphere, say the left, is exclusively specialized for the task. LVF stimuli will then be relayed from the RH to the LH through the corpus callosum prior to processing, with some attendant delay and stimulus degradation (Callosal Relay model). In this case, we should find no VF × V interaction, assuming that callosal transfer does not interact with V.

3. Each hemisphere contributes to the task, and performance reflects interhemispheric exchange (Interhemispheric Interaction model). But even here the nature of the separate hemispheric contributions and of the interhemispheric exchange may change depending on the hemisphere of input.

Different models may fit different lateralized tasks. We have developed various behavioral criteria for determining which model applies in a particular task (Zaidel 1983, 1986; Zaidel, Clarke, and Suyenobu 1990). Using such behavioral methods, we found that surprisingly many tasks are processed direct access fashion (for example, a lateralized lexical decision task with concrete noun targets and associated concrete primes), while others are callosal relay (for example, a dichotic listening test with stop consonant-vowel syllables). It is important to note that both the Direct Access and the Interhemispheric Interaction models make strong claims about access to callosally relayed information. Consider a direct access task. Although "early" transfer of "sensory copies" of lateralized information to the other hemisphere is possible, even likely, it appears that at the limit, either such information transfer is inhibited (sensory isolation) or that transfer occurs and the other hemisphere will process the information but its response will be inhibited (response inhibition) (Zaidel 1986). Similarly, interhemispheric interaction models posit that effective callosal exchange occurs only at certain strategic intermediate stages of information processing.

Callosal relay tasks may be regarded as tasks with a stable locus of control. Direct Access tasks, on the other hand, may be regarded as tasks in which locus of control is dynamic and depends on the hemifield of initial input. Elsewhere, we have shown that the pattern of control during a task can shift from Direct Access to Callosal Relay (exclusively specialized in either hemisphere) as a function of item difficulty, on a trial-by-trial basis (Zaidel et al. 1988; Rayman and Zaidel 1991). It is also plausible that, with experience, tasks that initially show a callosal relay pattern can shift to a direct access pattern. Indeed, it is likely that some individuals who have greater hemispheric competence may show a direct access pattern for tasks processed in a callosal relay fashion by other individuals with weaker hemispheric competence (Zaidel, Clarke, and Suyenobu 1990; Eviatar and Zaidel 1992).

## Unilateral versus Redundant Bilateral Presentations

Consider a lateralized task, specialized to the LH but showing a direct access pattern with purely unilateral presentations. Suppose some trials are unilateral, projected to one VF or the other, while some are bilateral, with identical copies projected simultaneously to both VFs. What patterns of bilateral relative to unilateral scores can we find? Suppose now unilateral trials show an RVFA—hence LH specialization. Figure 19.1 summarizes some possible outcomes of overall scores. The patterns in panels a and b reflect RH or LH dominance, respectively, in bilateral presentations. Pattern b represents a race model, but we shall see that it does not always prevail. Pattern c represents some average of the competencies in both hemispheres, as might occur with random assignment of control to one hemisphere at a time. Pattern d represents a bilateral advantage, presumably due to hemispheric cooperation. This pattern should be distinguished from a simple redundancy gain effect, which would reflect faster decisions due to parallel processing of multiple copies following visual callosal relay to one hemisphere. This possibility is depicted in pattern e, which may be regarded as a control condition for bilateral advantage, and where the improved score reflects merely the redundancy gain from

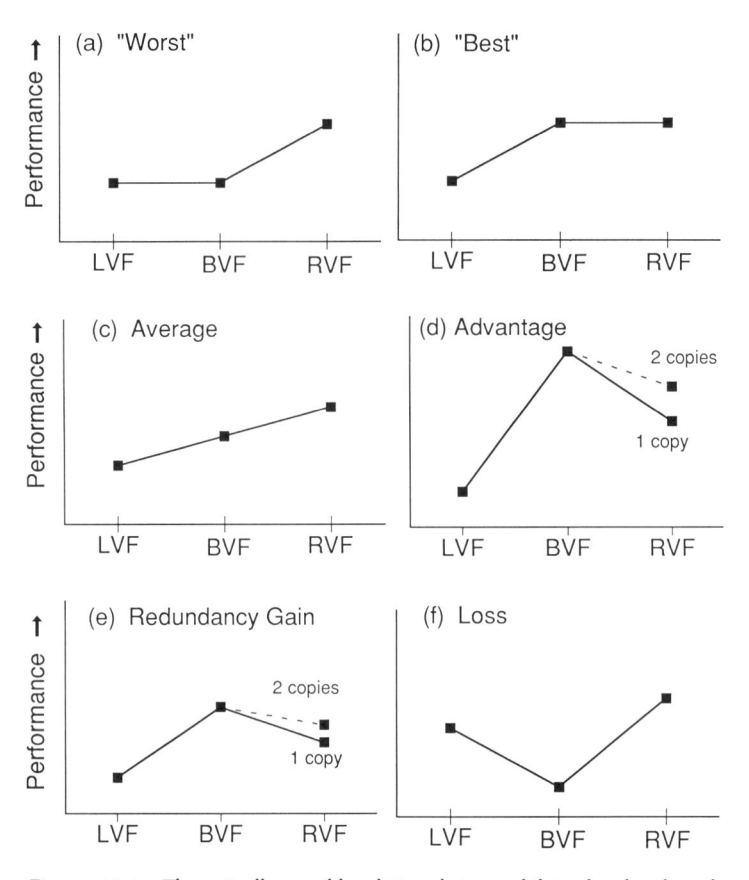

**Figure 19.1** Theoretically possible relations between bilateral and unilateral overall scores in experiments with LVF presentations, RVF presentations, and bilateral presentations with identical stimuli.

two stimulus copies, and thus the result of parallel processing, within the LH. A simplified way of contrasting patterns d and e is to say that in pattern d, two hemispheres are better than one, while in pattern e, two stimuli are better than one. If redundant bilateral presentations show merely the same advantage as redundant presentations in the superior VF, then the bilateral advantage may simply reflect effective cross-callosal transfer of one copy from the inferior to the superior hemisphere. However, this is unlikely given the VFA for one copy (pattern e). Of course, the failure of simple redundancy gain to occur with bilateral presentations in the normal brain when it does occur with unilateral presentations would reflect the effect of hemispheric control (unless visual callosal relay would degrade the stimulus enough to rob it of its potential contribution to the parallel process).

Patterns a, b, and c are consistent with direct access. But of these, only pattern b is plausibly consistent with callosal relay. Pattern d is consistent with direct access in the sense that there is independent competence in the RH, although it is logically possible that unilateral presentations are dominated by the LH, mask RH ability, and mimic callosal relay. If bilateral presentations exhibit an advantage due to interhemispheric cooperation, such cooperation could have occurred (but did not) with unilateral presentations as well, since early transfer of the sensory visual information probably makes the stimulus available to both hemispheres anyway. Thus, a bilateral advantage together with a direct access pattern in unilateral presentations suggest restricted interhemispheric exchange where the visual information reaches one VF and, effectively, only one hemisphere.

There are two ways RBPs may resemble or differ from unilateral presentations. First, the overall score in bilateral presentations may be higher or lower than unilateral scores or it may equal one of them. Second, the pattern of performance may resemble one VF rather than the other, suggesting that the strategy used in bilateral presentations is the same as that used by one hemisphere. More precisely, given a VF(L, R) × V interaction (V = independent stimulus variable), we may find a VF(L, R, B) × V interaction with VF(B, L) × V being significant and VF(B, R) × V being insignificant, or vice versa. In this case, bilateral performance parallels the RVF or the LVF, respectively. In general, we would expect bilateral overall score and bilateral pattern (strategy) to reflect the same mode of hemispheric control. Thus, pattern a in figure 19.1 predicts an RH strategy, pattern b predicts an LH strategy, and patterns c and d may not predict the strategy of either hemisphere alone. But it is logically possible for overall score and strategy in bilateral presentations to dissociate from each other. For example, pattern d could co-occur with an LVF strategy. In this case, presumably, hemispheric cooperation is facilitated by a strategy that is available to both hemispheres. This is a special case of Direct Access, where both strategies are available to the LH.

Further, pattern b cannot reflect a true race if bilateral presentations yield the same score as the RVF but exhibit the LVF strategy. Similarly, pattern a cannot reflect a true "worst" hemispheric control if bilateral presentations yield the LVF score but exhibit the same pattern of performance as the RVF. In the cases of both patterns a and b, a dissociation between overall score and strategy would signal complex interhemispheric interaction. Of course, even if bilateral overall score and bilateral strategy, as determined by some VF(L, R, B) × V interaction, reflect dominance by the same hemisphere, it is possible that some VF(L, R) × V', with a new independent variable, V', will yield a conflicting result in the future. Thus, any conclusion about hemispheric control must remain tentative.

Suppose some experiment exhibits a bilateral advantage that is greater than the redundancy gain exhibited by two copies in either VF alone. This would signal interhemispheric cooperation. It would then be of considerable interest to determine the level or stage of processing where the cooperation occurs. One approach is to vary stimulus parameters at different levels of processing and observe which variations affect the bilateral advantage. Presumably only variations at levels earlier than the locus of interhemispheric cooperation should have effects on the bilateral advantage. For example, if cooperation in some lexical task occurs at the level of orthographic analysis, then it may be affected by font or by case but not by semantic or phonological variables.

However, it should be noted that if processing stages are not strictly serial but overlap in a parallel or cascade fashion, then a stimulus variable that corresponds to a later stage may affect an earlier process (Measso and Zaidel 1990).

Another possible result of RBP is a decrease in performance under bilateral presentations (fig. 19.1f). This bilateral loss pattern is predicted to occur when the left and right hemispheres process stimuli in ways that are mutually incompatible.

Hellige and his associates conducted several experiments comparing unilateral to bilateral presentations by inferring hemispheric control from strategy rather than from overall score. One series of studies (reviewed in Hellige 1993) analyzed the error pattern in consonant-vowel-consonant (CVC) pseudoword identification. Although performance was more accurate in the RVF than in the LVF, the normalized error pattern in bilateral presentation paralleled that in the LVF. The authors interpret this as a possible bias for the brain to use a strategy that is available to both hemispheres. But since the overall error rate on bilateral trials was as low as or slightly lower than the overall error rate on RVF trials, this cannot be an example of RH dominance. They also believe that one hemisphere is more likely to dominate performance in bilateral presentations when both hemispheres are competent but when their strategies are mutually inconsistent. In another experiment, subjects compared cartoon faces. The task showed no VFA, but bilateral trials showed the RVF pattern of performance. Similarly, a letter comparison task revealed no VFA but showed LH dominance. In yet another task, subjects judged dots as being far from or near to a line or categorized them as being above or below the line. Bilateral decisions were faster than unilateral decisions, but the difference between the two tasks in the bilateral condition was the same as in the RVF. Hellige (1991) speculates that in the absence of hemispheric superiority, the LH dominates.

## 19.2 REDUNDANCY GAIN

The ability of target detection to benefit from multiple identical copies of the target (redundancy gain) is taken as evidence for parallel processing with unlimited resources (Egeth, Folk, and Mullin 1989). Further, an interaction of redundancy gain with a variable that acts at a particular locus in the information-processing sequence suggests that parallel processing, and therefore attentional selection, both occur at a stage as late as or later than that locus. In the following experiments we were interested in whether the two visual fields show different redundancy gain functions that reflect the processing styles and resources of the contralateral hemispheres, and whether there are discontinuities in the redundancy gain functions when there are copies on either side of the vertical meridian. If such a discontinuity is affected by some stimulus variable with a known information-processing locus, then the code shared between the hemispheres to permit redundancy gain is likely to be at least as late as that locus. Since sharing of earlier codes should always be possible but appears to be inhibited, the interaction would suggest that tasks or decisions at specific information-processing levels somehow make possible privileged access to interhemispheric codes at the same or subsequent stages.

A callosal relay task should yield parallel redundancy gain functions in the two visual hemifields, at least when all stimulus categories are about equally complex and cross the callosum with about equal delay, and assuming unlimited channel capacity so that several copies transfer across the corpus callosum as quickly as one copy. In the case of a callosal relay task that shows a redundancy gain in unilateral presentations, we may expect bilateral presentations with some copies in each VF to show weaker gains. This is because the copies flashed to the field ipsilateral to the specialized hemisphere need to be relayed across the corpus callosum, and this may effectively exclude them from the parallel race. Similarly, a bilateral gain function that exceeds the unilateral functions probably reflects interhemispheric cooperation and presupposes a direct access task.

The mechanism behind redundancy gain is still unclear. The independent parallel race model assumes a spatially parallel, self-terminating, unlimited capacity processor in which several inputs are processed in parallel and independently. Thus, the response latency is determined by the first input to finish processing, and this will occur sooner, on average, than the average processing time for a single input (Mullin and Egeth 1989). Assuming runners of equal ability and random fluctuations in their performance, on average the more runners there are in a race, the faster the winner will be even if all runners are generally equally fast. An alternative, coactivation account of redundancy gain was offered by Miller (1982). In the coactivation model, there is facilitation of postdetection processes by the redundant input prior to decision. Here, activation strength is summed across targets. When a critical amount of activation has accumulated, the subject responds, even if she or he does not know what any stimulus is at the moment. Mordkoff and Yantis (1991) proposed a hybrid interactive race model that incorporates elements of both of these accounts.

Egeth, Folk, and Mullin (1989) observed (1) a probable redundancy gain in a task that requires the identification of the orientation of line segments (horizontal, vertical), (2) a redundancy gain in a task that required the categorization of digits versus letters, and (3) a gain in a lexical decision task but not in a semantic categorization task. Banich and Karol (1992) asked subjects to decide if a central word rhymed with a single lateralized probe word or with either of two probe words presented to opposite VFs. Reaction times (RTs) to trials in which the two probes were identical were faster than to trials in which they were not identical but led to the same decision. This advantage disappeared when the identical words were presented in different fonts and cases, suggesting that the code for interhemispheric sharing is early perceptual rather than lexical.

It is customary to exclude alternative accounts of redundancy gain where the gain is not due to parallel processing but rather to spatial uncertainty about the location of the target, together with some fixed or random favored spatial position for a given subject. One way to exclude the account from spatial uncertainty is to show that the mean RT for the fastest position of the single-target trials and the mean of the randomly partitioned single-target trials distributions do not differ significantly (i.e., there is no fixed favored position), and that the means of the single target and redundant target trials for the fast and slow subjects do not interact. Another way to exclude spatial uncertainty is to cue one target position before each trial.

### Experiment 1: Lexical Decision, Two-Choice, No Cues

This experiment, by Zaidel and Rayman, presented from one to four identical copies of words or nonwords within the LVF, within the RVF, or divided between them. Our goals were to characterize the redundancy gain in each VF (i.e., the pattern of hemispheric independence) and for bilateral presentations (the pattern of hemispheric interaction and control, separately for words and for nonwords). An interaction of Wordness × Number of copies for bilateral presentations would suggest interhemispheric exchange in a code that carries lexical identity rather than "earlier" perceptual information.

**Methods**  This lexical decision task used a unimanual choice RT paradigm. Stimuli were letter strings four, five, and six letters long. Eighty-four were words, and eighty-four were orthographically regular nonwords. On each trial, one to four copies of a horizontal letter string appeared for 80 ms with the edge closest to fixation in any of eight possible positions equally spaced along a circle with a 1.5-degree radius surrounding the fixation cross. These positions corresponded to 3.75, 11.25, 18.75, 26.25, 33.75, 41.25, 48.75, and 56.25 min on a clock face. The letter strings subtended from 3 to 5 degrees of visual angle in length and 1.5 degrees in height. When there was more than one possible constellation of stimulus positions (e.g., there are four ways to present three stimulus copies within the LVF), each constellation appeared equally often in each VF. The inner edge of each string was 1.5 degrees from the fixation cross, which remained on the screen throughout the experiment. Unilateral trials contained one to four stimulus copies within one VF. Bilateral trials distributed one or more copies across the two VFs.

Forty-eight right-handed UCLA undergraduates participated in the experiment. Each subject participated in 24 practice trials followed by four blocks of 168 trials, with a rest period after the second test block. Each of the four test blocks contained a list of the same 168 stimuli (in a different random order), with each stimulus being presented in a different condition in each list. Response hand was counterbalanced within subjects by having subjects switch response hand when a new block was started.

**Results and Discussion**  Subjects' responses to items presented to the RVF (777 ms, 68.5 percent correct) were both faster and more accurate than those made to LVF items (801 ms, 64.0 percent correct). A significant Word advantage was also observed, with responses to words (747 ms, 69.1 percent correct) being both faster and more accurate than responses to nonwords

(831 ms, 63.4 percent correct). Visual Field interacted with Wordness for both accuracy and RT, producing no significant VF differences for nonwords but significant RVFAs for words. Latency data showed no further significant effects, and only accuracy data will be reported for this and the next experiment.

Figure 19.2a summarizes the accuracy data for words in each VF condition (LVF, RVF, BVF) as a function of number of copies of the word. There is a monotonic gain in the LVF, a gain only from one to two copies in the RVF, and no gain in bilateral presentations. The gain from one to two copies was significant in both the LVF ($p = .006$) and the RVF ($p = .006$). Restricting our attention to one and two copies in the two VFs, there is an RVFA and no interaction of VF × Number of copies. Most critical for our present concern, the bilateral condition with two copies, one in each VF, is significantly more accurate than one copy in either the RVF ($p = .043$) or the LVF ($p < .001$). This suggests a bilateral advantage due to hemispheric sharing. [Note that BVF (two copies), though significantly superior to LVF (two copies), is not significantly inferior to RVF (2 copies), and this could also be consistent with an (RH → LH) callosal transfer interpretation of the BVF advantage. However, if automatic RH → LH transfer occurred, then accuracy for LVF (one copy) should have been equal to accuracy for RVF (one copy), which it is not. Still, it is logically possible that transfer is effective for two copies but not for one copy.]

Figure 19.2b summarizes the accuracy data for nonwords. In both VFs, performance increases from one to two copies and declines with more copies. But the gain from one to two copies was significant only in the LVF. This would suggest parallel nonword processing in the LVF but not in the RVF even though the LVF is inferior. Restricting our attention to one and two copies in the two VFs, we find an RVFA and no interaction of VF × Number of copies. Turning to the critical comparison between bilateral (two copies)

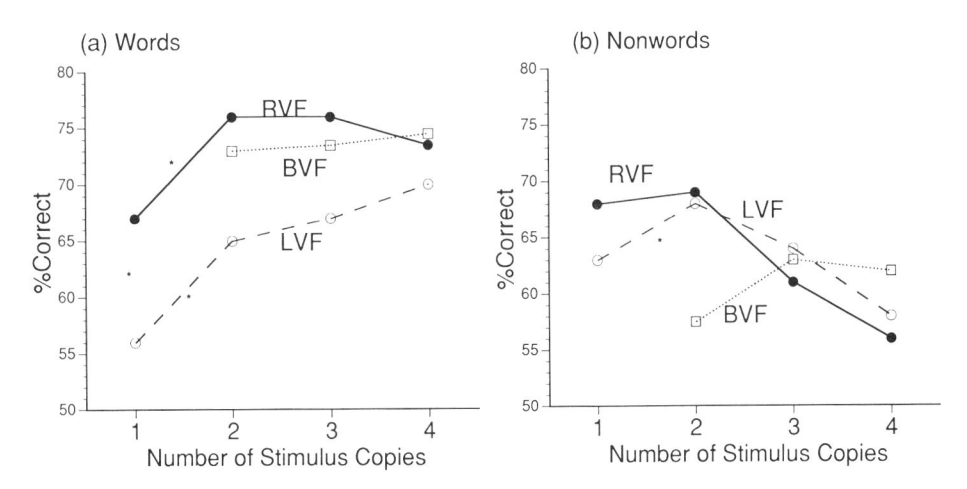

**Figure 19.2** Redundancy gain functions for unilateral (LVF, RVF) and bilateral (BVF) word targets in lexical decision with no cues and word/nonword unimanual forced-choice responses. *a*. Word detection. *b*. Nonword detection.

and unilateral (one copy) presentations, we find a bilateral loss relative to both the RVF ($p < .001$) and the LVF ($p = .022$). Indeed BVF (two copies) is significantly worse than either LVF (two copies) or RVF (two copies), arguing against a visual transfer interpretation of the bilateral loss.

Thus, words show a bilateral gain whereas nonwords show a bilateral loss (fig. 19.2) when both VFs show gains for either words or nonwords. This suggests that interhemispheric exchange is not early sensory but lexical. The reason for the loss is not clear. Perhaps it reflects incompatibility between nonword processing in the two hemispheres. It is noteworthy that no comparable loss is observed when go/no-go responses are used with nonword detection (see below), suggesting that the incompatibility is sensitive to small task differences.

An alternative view of the dissociation in bilateral advantage between words and nonwords is to argue that there are bias differences between the visual field conditions. In this view, there is no bias in the RVF, a nonword bias in the LVF, and a word bias in the BVF (fig. 19.3). Considering the bias-free measure of sensitivity, $d'$, we find that $d'$ in BVF is closer to $d'$ in RVF than in LVF and that sensitivity conforms to a race model, with LH dominance (see tables 19.1 and 19.2). However, this conclusion ignores the difference in bias between all three VF conditions, which suggests that BVF is unlike either VF. Further, accounting for word-nonword differences in terms of bias presupposes that they are the effects of a single process. Rather, we have repeatedly observed a dissociation between the interactions of word and nonword decisions and numerous lexical variables, arguing that these decisions reflect separate and parallel computations (Measso and Zaidel 1990; Zaidel 1989).

The data showed a position preference for both VFs, separately for words and nonwords, although subjects differed in their favorite position. This limits our ability to interpret the observed redundancy gain as evidence for parallel processing with unlimited resources.

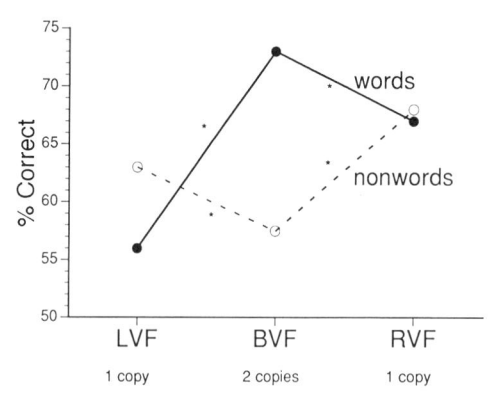

**Figure 19.3** Interaction of Wordness with Visual Field (LVF one copy, RVF one copy, BVF two copies) in the redundancy gain lexical decision experiment with no cues and forced-choice responses.

Table 19.1  Summary of Some Effect Involving LVF (one copy), RVF (one copy), and BVF (two copies).

| Experiment | Variable | Level | Dependent Variable | VF(L, R) | Bilateral Advantage | Interpretation |
|---|---|---|---|---|---|---|
| *Redundancy gain* | | | | | | |
| No cue/choice RT | Wordness | Nonwords | % corr | — | — | Loss |
| | | Words | % corr | R | + | Advantage |
| | | Words/nonwords | sensitivity | R | + | Average/best = RVF? |
| | | Words/nonwords | $\beta$ | — | + | Word bias |
| Cue/go/no go | Wordness | Nonwords | % corr | — | +(L) | Best = RVF |
| | | Words | % corr | R | +(L) | Best = RVF |
| | | Nonwords | sensitivity | — | — | Best = RVF |
| | | Words | sensitivity | R | — | Best = RVF/average? |
| | | Words | $\ln \beta$ | ~+ | — | Average? |
| | | Nonwords | $\ln \beta$ | — | — | ? |
| *Hierarchic perception* | | | | | | |
| Experiment 1 | Level | Local | RT | R? | +(L) | Best = RVF |
| | | Global | RT | L? | +(R) | Best = LVF |
| Experiment 2 | Level | Local | RT | R | +(L) | Best = RVF |
| | | Global | RT | — | + | Advantage |
| | Consistency | Consistent | RT | R | +(L)? | Best = RVF |
| | | Inconsistent | RT | — | +? | Advantage |
| | Arousal/Level | LHA Local | RT | R | +(L) | Best = RVF |
| | | LHA Global | RT | — | + | Advantage |
| | | RHA Local | RT | — | ~+(L) | ~Best = RVF |

Note: VF(L, R) = + denotes a significant difference between the LVF and the RVF; VF(L, R) = R denotes a RVF advantage; Bilateral advantage = + denotes a bilateral advantage relative to either VF; Bilateral advantage = +(L) denotes a bilateral advantage relative to the LVF; LHA = left hemisphere aroused.

Table 19.2 Summary of Some Effect Involving LVF (one copy), RVF (one copy), BVF (two copies), and Independent Variables (V).

| Experiment | Variable | Dependent Variable | VF(L, R) | VF(L, R) × V | VF(B, L, R) × V | VF(B, L) × V | VF(B, R) × V | Bilateral Advantage |
|---|---|---|---|---|---|---|---|---|
| Redundancy gain | | | | | | | | |
| No cue | Wordness | % correct | R | + | + | + | + | +/− |
| Cues | Wordness | % correct | R | − | − | − | ∼+ | Best(R) |
| Hierarchic perception | | | | | | | | |
| Experiment 1 | Level | RT | ∼R | + | + | +? | +? | Best(L, R) |
| | Consistency | RT | ∼R | − | − | | | |
| Experiment 2 | Level | RT | ∼R | − | + | + | + | +/Best |
| | Consistency | RT | ∼R | + | + | ∼+ | − | +/Best |
| | Arousal | RT | ∼R | − | − | + | − | |
| | Masculinity | RT | ∼R | + | + | + | − | Best(R) |

VF(L, R) = R denotes an advantage of RVF (1 copy) over LVF (1 copy), summing over both levels of V.

**Experiment 2: Lexical Decision, Go/No-Go, with Cues**

This experiment, by Zaidel and Rayman, was identical to experiment 1 with two exceptions. First, it used go/no-go responses alternately with words and nonwords as targets in order to increase redundancy gain effects (G. Grice, personal communication; T. Mordkoff, personal communication) and avoid compatibility effects (van der Heijden, Heij, and Boer 1983). Second, it used arrow cues to direct attention to a particular stimulus location in order to avoid effects due to spatial uncertainty. The arrow cues were presented extrafoveally and can be regarded as having a status intermediate between central (symbolic) and peripheral cues.

**Methods** Twenty-four different right-handed UCLA undergraduate students participated in this experiment. A bimanual, go/no-go paradigm was used, with half of the subjects responding to word targets and half to nonword targets. The stimuli were identical to the ones used in the previous (no cue) experiment, and they occurred in the same eight positions around the clockface but slightly farther away from fixation. Response times were recorded as the first of the two bimanual responses. Each subject received twenty-four practice trials and two test blocks of eighty-four trials each.

An arrow was used to cue one of the positions correctly where a stimulus was to appear. This was done in order to control for possible positional effects due to subjects moving their attention to certain positions and the increased consequent likelihood (with more stimuli) that a stimulus would appear in an attended position. The cueing arrow appeared 150 ms before the stimulus appeared and remained on the screen when the stimulus was present. The point of the arrow was 1.5 degrees from fixation, and the stimulus was 2 degrees from fixation at its closest edge. Finally, within each of the presentation conditions, the arrow pointed approximately equally often to each of the eight positions.

**Results and Discussion** Figure 19.4a summarizes the accuracy data for words in each visual field condition (LVF, RVF, BVF) as a function of the number of copies of the words in the word detection task. Although the VF × Number of copies interaction was not significant ($p = .249$), the three VF conditions showed different patterns. There was no effect for number of copies (i.e., no gain), in the RVF. There was a significant effect of number of copies in the LVF ($p = .04$), with a near-significant gain from one to two copies ($p = .054$) but no difference thereafter. There was no significant effect of number of copies in the bilateral condition, with insignificant gains from two to three and from three to four copies, but a significant gain from two to four copies ($p = .04$). There was a significant RVFA for 1 copy, but the VF(L, R) × Number of copies (1, 2) interaction was not significant. Most important for our concern, the bilateral condition with two copies—one in each VF—is significantly more accurate than one copy in the LVF ($p = .039$) but not significantly different from one copy in the RVF (figure 19.4a). This suggests a "race" with bilateral scores equal to the "best" condition, the RVF.

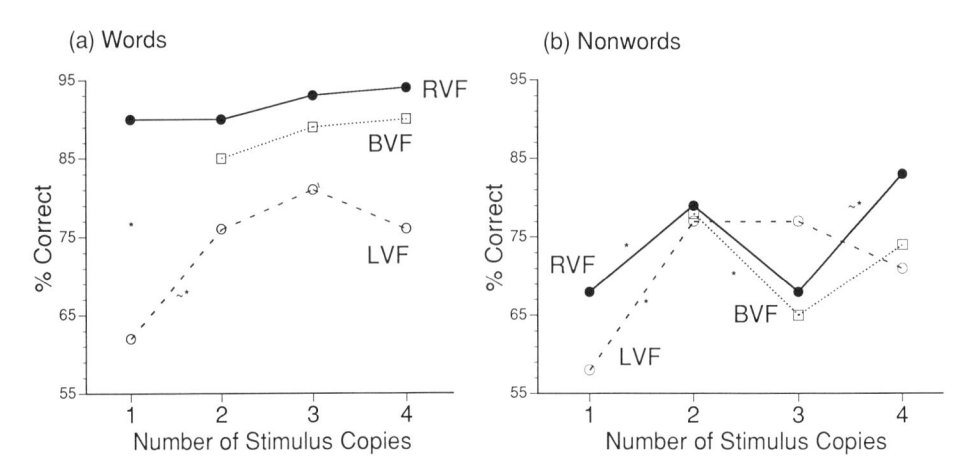

**Figure 19.4** Redundancy gain functions for targets in lexical decision with cues and unimanual go/no-go responses. *a*. Word targets. *b*. Nonword targets.

[Note that BVF (two copies) is not different from either RVF (two copies) or LVF (two copies) so that BVF performance could reflect either LH → RH or RH → LH transfer of one copy of the target. However, such automatic transfer would have erased the RVFA found for 1 copy.]

Figure 19.3b summarizes the accuracy for nonwords in the nonword detection task. This time there was a weak trend for a significant effect of number of copies in the RVF ($p = .096$), a significant effect in the LVF ($p = .049$), and a significant effect for bilateral presentations ($p = .04$). In the RVF there was a significant gain from one to two copies, a nonsignificant loss from two to three copies, and an almost significant gain from three to four copies ($p = .087$). In the LVF there was a significant gain from one to two copies and no differences thereafter. The bilateral condition showed a significant loss from two to three copies ($p = .038$) and an insignificant gain ($p = .107$) from three to four copies. The reason for the loss from two to three copies in the RVF and in the bilateral conditions remains unclear. The VF(L, R) × Number of copies (1, 2) interaction was not significant. Most important for us, the bilateral condition with two copies was significantly more accurate than the LVF with one copy ($p = .013$) and insignificantly more accurate than the RVF with one copy ($p = .144$) (fig. 19.5). This suggests again a "race" with Bilateral = "best" = RVF. Again, the accuracy for BVF (two copies) is not significantly different from that for RVF (two copies) or LVF (2 copies) (fig. 19.4b). This could be consistent with callosal transfer of the LVF copy to the LH or of the RVF copy to the RH in the BVF condition. But again that is unlikely in view of the failure of such transfer to occur for a single copy.

Again, it is possible to treat the word-nonword accuracy differences between the VF conditions as differences in bias. Then $d'$ in BVF approximates $d'$ in RVF and both are superior to $d'$ in LVF (see tables 19.1 and 19.2). Thus, in this case, sensitivity, like accuracy, would correspond to a race model showing LH dominance.

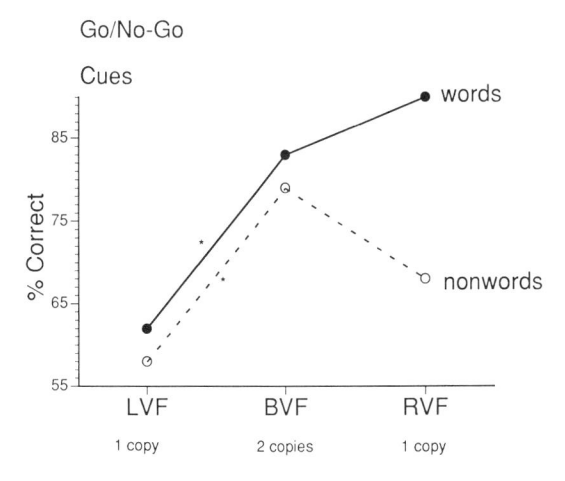

**Figure 19.5** Interaction of Wordness (LVF one copy, RVF one copy, BVF two copies) with Visual Field in the redundancy gain lexical decision experiment with cues and go/no-go responses. This graph combines data from the word detection task and from the nonword detection task.

## Conclusions

We found a different pattern of bilateral versus unilateral scores for words and for nonwords in experiment 1 and a different pattern in experiment 1 and experiment 2 for either words or nonwords. Experiment 1 revealed a bilateral advantage (though not necessarily gain due to parallel processing) for words and a bilateral loss for nonwords, whereas experiment 2 revealed a race for bilateral presentations of either words or nonwords. It is possible that spatial cueing changed the attentional demands and assignment of resources so as to erase the gain for words and the loss for nonwords. In any case, patterns of hemispheric control appear sensitive to task variables. An analysis of word/nonword responses in terms of sensitivity and bias would converge on a race model with LH dominance (fig. 19.1b) or an "average" model (fig. 19.1c). More generally, we have evidence for different parallel processing functions in the two normal hemispheres, extending the thesis of hemispheric independence to attentional processes. In particular, it is not the case that LVF presentations lead to automatic relay of stimuli from the RH to the LH prior to processing.

### 19.3 HIERARCHIC PERCEPTION

Does perception proceed bottom up, from detail to whole, or top-down, with the whole affecting the perception of its parts, or both? In 1977 Navon operationalized this question by constructing two large or global characters (H and S) made up of many copies of small or local characters (Hs or Ss) and requiring subjects to identify the global or the local element. The global and local characters could be either the same (consistent) or different (inconsistent), and subjects responded with two-choice manual button presses. Navon presented his stimuli peripherally and found that the global patterns were identified faster than the local patterns ("global advantage" or "global precedence") and that local identification was slowed by conflicting or inconsistent global information ("global interference" or "consistency effect"). No consistency effect was observed for global decisions when conflicting local information was present. Navon attributed the Consistency × Level interaction in latency to the faster processing of global patterns.

How can global and local perception be implemented computationally in the brain? One implementation solution is to have global and local perception carried out in different neural systems that operate in parallel. An attractive possibility is that global perception is assigned to one hemisphere and local perception to the other. Then both could co-occur, and their interaction would be mediated by interhemispheric exchange. Evidence that the LH is specialized for processing local (high relative spatial frequency) information whereas the RH is specialized for processing global (low relative spatial frequency) information comes from normal subjects (Sergent 1982), from patients with unilateral damage (Delis, Robertson, and Efron 1986), particularly in the temporal-parietal junction (Roberson, Lamb, and Knight 1988), and from split-brain patients (Delis, Kramer, and Kiefner 1988; Robertson, Lamb, and Zaidel 1993). In normals, some find a RVFA for the local level but no VFA for the global level (Martin 1979), while others find no significant VFA for either level (see van Kleek 1989 for a review). But hemispheric specialization should not be confused with hemispheric dominance; the LH may dominate, that is, exclusively control, local processing even though it also has competence for global processing and even though the RH has competence for local processing as well (D. W. Zaidel 1986, 1987).

Navon's account of global interference with local processing can be challenged. First, it is common to find local interference with global processing, although the effect is weaker than global interference with local processing (Kimchi and Merhav 1991). This interaction between the hierarchical level (global, local) and stimulus compatibility (consistent, inconsistent) is a ubiquitous result. But how to account for local interference in the face of the global advantage? Second, there is empirical evidence that the global advantage and global interference are independent processes. Thus, Lamb and Robertson (1989) manipulated the global advantage without changing the global interference, and Lamb and Robertson (1988) manipulated the global interference without changing the global advantage. Similarly, Lamb, Robertson, and Knight (1990) found that cerebro-vascular accident (CVA) patients with damage to the superior temporal gyrus showed normal patterns of global or local advantage (depending on manipulation of attentional processes) but no consistency effect. Finally, Lamb, Robertson, and Knight (1989) found that patients with unilateral temporoparietal lesions who show strong level deficits (global deficits with right hemisphere lesions, local deficits after left hemisphere lesions) do not show interference effects. Consequently, Robertson, and Lamb (1991) hypothesized that global interference is mediated by the posterior corpus callosum, the access to which was allegedly compromised in their patients.

**Experiment 1**

This experiment was originally designed to find out whether redundant bilateral presentations of identical lateralized hierarchical patterns yield the standard global advantage and consistency effect that are obtained with unilateral tachistoscopic presentations (Robertson, Lamb, and Zaidel 1993). In the context of this chapter, we are mainly interested in how the overall score and pattern of performance in bilateral presentations relate to those with unilateral presentations. Of particular interest is how the alleged interhemispheric consistency effect of unilateral presentations is affected by bilateral presentations.

**Methods**  Sixteen normal right-handed college students (mean age = 20) participated in this experiment. The stimuli consisted of large Hs and Ss made up of small Hs and Ss. The local elements were arranged to make the global form in a 5 × 4 imaginary grid measuring 3.6 cm vertically by 2.4 cm horizontally. Displays were presented on a Princeton Graphics SR-12 monitor and were white on a gray background. On unilateral trials the innermost edge of the pattern appeared randomly 2.7 degrees to the right or 2.7 degrees to the left of fixation. Each global pattern subtended 3.8 degrees of visual angle vertically. Subjects viewed the screen at a distance of 54 cm.

Each trial contained either unilateral or bilateral presentation of one of the four patterns. During instructions, it was emphasized that both patterns would be exactly the same on bilateral trials. One-third of the trials were bilateral, one-third unilateral RVF, and one-third unilateral LVF presentations. On each trial, a 300-ms auditory warning signal marked the beginning of the trial followed by a 500-ms fixation point in the middle of the screen. Hierarchical patterns then appeared for 100 ms, and the response followed. Subjects were instructed to fixate on the center point and not to move their eyes. In one block of trials, subjects judged whether the global form was an H or an S by pressing the appropriate key on a two-switch response box with the right hand, and in another block they made the same judgments about the local form. There were ninety-six trials per block with a short break in-between and thirty-six practice trials before each block.

**Results and Discussion**  The latency results (fig. 19.6) showed the usual global advantage ($F(1,14) = 37.25, p < .001$), consistency advantage ($F(1,14) = 36.78, p < .001$), and a significant Level (global, local) × Consistency (consistent, inconsistent) interaction ($F(1,14) = 19.03, p < .001$), showing a greater global advantage with inconsistent stimuli. But there was no Level × Consistency × VF interaction ($F < 1$), indicating that the consistency effect was the same in the bilateral condition and in each of the two VFs.

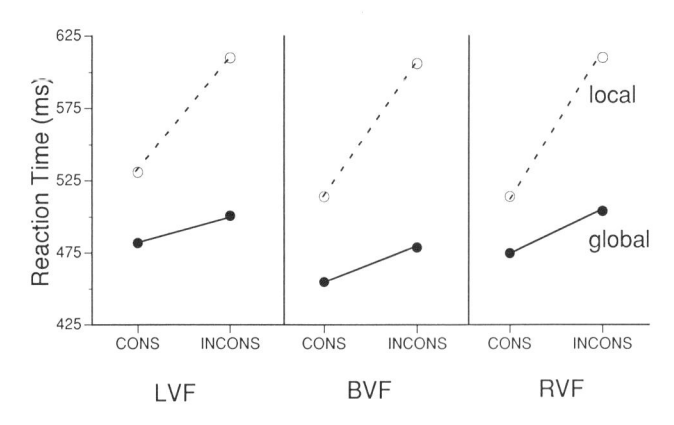

**Figure 19.6** Level × Consistency interaction for each VF condition in experiment 1: Hierarchic perception in normals (Robertson, Lamb, and Zaidel 1993).

There was an almost significant overall RVFA ($F(2,28) = 3.25, p < .055$) and a significant Level × VF interaction ($F(2,28) = 5.09, p < .02$). This Level × VF interaction remained significant for unilateral (LVF, RVF) trials ($F(1,15) = 7.46, p < .02$), with a 10-ms RVFA for local patterns and a 33-ms LVFA for global patterns. This pattern of processing dissociation between the two VFs suggests direct access, that is, independent target processing in the two hemispheres, with bilateral, though unequal, hemispheric competence for both global and local decisions.

Figure 19.6 shows that bilateral presentations parallel the RVF for local decisions but the LVF for global decisions. Indeed, when bilateral trials were compared to unilateral RVF trials, collapsed over consistency, there was a 16-ms bilateral advantage for global targets ($F(1,15) = 7.19, p < .02$), but no significant difference between bilateral and RVF presentations for local targets. Similarly, when bilateral trials were compared to LVF trials, collapsed over consistency, there was a 24-ms bilateral over LVF advantage for local targets ($F(1,15) = 5.91, p < .03$) but no significant difference between bilateral and LVF trials for global targets. Also, the variance was nearly equal when a stimulus was projected to the preferred hemisphere for the task whether accompanied by a second pattern in the opposite visual field or not. When it was projected to the nonpreferred hemisphere, variability increased.

It thus appears that bilateral presentations represent a race model of overall performance where each hemisphere dominates the responses for which it is specialized. As far as pattern (as opposed to level) of performance, the two VFs did not differ from each other or from bilateral presentations in the Level × Consistency interaction. It is particularly noteworthy that the consistency effect —the Level × Consistency interaction—was unchanged in the bilateral condition even though it is presumably mediated by callosal transfer. This is explained by the fact that callosal mediation of the facilitation/interference that make up the consistency effect in general, and global interference in particular, does not involve relatively early exchange of stimulus information between the two hemispheres but rather relatively late exchange of control signals.

## Experiment 2

This experiment, by Carusi and Zaidel, was designed to further explore individual differences in the contributions of interhemispheric relations to the consistency effect (Carusi 1992; Carusi and Zaidel, n.d.). Specifically, what role do hemispheric specialization for global and local processing and callosal connectivity play in the consistency effect? An interhemispheric model of the consistency effect could unfold as follows. Both hemispheres can process both local and global information, and both have access to all the information, even during lateralized presentation. But by some control process, the RH is biased to dominate global processing, while the LH is biased to dominate local processing. Global interference then reflects RH to LH communication, while local interference reflects LH to RH communication. The precise nature of the signals communicated cross-callosally remains unspecified.

The interhemispheric model then makes the following predictions: the consistency effect should be positively correlated with (1) the difference between latencies to global decisions in the LVF and local decisions in the RVF and (2) the degree of interhemispheric connectivity or sharing across individuals. We can sharpen prediction 2 by predicting that 2' global interference should correlate positively with the bilateral advantage for global decisions, and that 2" local interference should correlate positively with the bilateral advantage for local decisions. Here we index degree of callosal connectivity or hemispheric sharing by the bilateral advantage. The underlying rationale is that the corpus callosum can be regarded as a system of communication and control channels that interconnect different hemispheric cortical processing modules. Thus, we index the connectivity of the channels for global and local interference by the bilateral advantage for global and local decisions, respectively, that is, by the degree of hemispheric sharing for the stimuli that give rise to the consistency effect.

This constitutes a hypothesis that partly specifies the nature of the relevant interhemispheric communication. A subject who exhibits a bilateral advantage benefits from interhemispheric sharing and may also exhibit an enhanced facilitation in consistent trials. A subject who exhibits a bilateral disadvantage—lower scores in bilateral presentations than in either LVF or RVF presentations—may have enhanced connectivity in inhibitory interhemispheric pathways and may therefore also exhibit enhanced interference in the inconsistent condition. Both of these subjects should show an enhanced consistency effect relative to a subject whose bilateral scores are only as good as the best VF.

In this experiment, we posit that bilateral performance will exceed unilateral performance in either VF (hemisphere), and we predict that the bilateral advantage will increase the consistency effect beyond that observed in either VF (hemisphere). In other words, bilateral performance will differ from unilateral performance in both overall score and pattern of effects. But this bilateral-unilateral difference in effects could be the indirect result of difference in callosal connectivity or, alternatively, the direct result of changes in competence in the biased decisions/hemispheres.

But suppose the consistency effect in this task depends on some more general "off-line" index of hemispheric specialization rather than on hemispheric specialization indexed "on line" for global and local decisions. A candidate measure for such an off-line index is Levy et al.'s (1983) concept of hemispheric arousal. This is conceptualized as a stable individual difference where arousal asymmetry to one hemisphere will bias laterality effects in all tasks toward the aroused hemisphere in that individual. A common and simple putative measure of arousal asymmetry is the chimeric face task. Here, compound face photographs and their mirror images are shown in free vision with a smile on one side and a neutral expression on the other. Subjects choose the "happier" face and obtain a laterality score: the number of choices with the smile on the left side minus the number of choices with the smile on the right side. These laterality scores are then partitioned by a median split into LH-aroused (LHA) and RH-aroused (RHA) subjects.

The question is whether there is a relationship between arousal asymmetry and the consistency effect. For example, RHA subjects may make better global decisions in the RH and thus, by the interhemispheric model, show greater global interference. Alternatively, an RHA subject may show greater global interference by setting some control or bias parameter, independent of actual performance on global decisions in the LVF. Further, does arousal asymmetry predict the pattern of performance in bilateral relative to unilateral trials? For example, is an RHA subject more likely to exhibit bilateral scores equal to her or his LVF scores? Is a subject with no arousal asymmetry more likely to show a bilateral advantage?

Another potential variable for classifying subjects into groups with varying degrees of general or "generic" hemispheric specialization and of callosal connectivity is sex (Zaidel et al. in press). Indeed, sex can be treated as a continuous variable by considering level of "masculinity" or "femininity" within each gender, as measured by the Bem Sex Role Inventory (BSRI 1974).

**Methods** Twenty male and twenty female right-handed UCLA undergraduate students participated in this experiment. The stimuli and procedures were similar to those of experiment 1. The global Hs and Ss contained twelve local Hs or Ss. The global elements subtended 3.6 degrees by 2.3 degrees of visual angle, and the local elements subtended .64 degrees by .42 degrees at a viewing distance of 57.3 cm. Stimuli were presented on a Macintosh IIsi computer with a high-resolution RGB color monitor. The presentation sequence began with a 1-sec presentation of a central fixation black cross, measuring .5 degree by .5 degree, which remained on the screen through the rest of the block. There was a short delay, of only 1 sec, between the subject's response and the initiation of the next stimulus. This 1-sec pause was followed by a beep, a 600-ms pause, and a 105-ms presentation of a stimulus. Presentations consisted of either a single stimulus in the right or left visual field (unilateral conditions) or two identical stimuli, one in each visual field (bilateral condition). The innermost edge of each stimulus was positioned 2.7 degrees to the left or right of fixation. Subjects responded bimanually on the keyboard.

All subjects were also given the chimeric face test of arousal asymmetry prior to the hierarchic stimuli.

**Results and Discussion** An ANOVA with Sex (male, female) and Arousal (LHA, RHA) as between-subject variables, and with Level (global, local), VF (L, R, B) and Consistency (consistent, inconsistent) as within-subject variables, disclosed the classic global advantage, consistency effect (consistent better than inconsistent) and Level × Consistency interaction (greater consistency effect for local than global decision) (fig. 19.7). There was a main effect of VF representing an advantage of bilateral over unilateral stimuli; bilateral trials were significantly faster than both LVF and RVF trials. Further, there was a Level × VF interaction ($F(2,72) = 7.73, p < .01$). This interaction held when comparing bilateral to LVF presentations ($F(1,36) = 7.045, p < 05$). While there was a bilateral advantage relative to the LVF for both the global ($p < .01$) and local ($p < .01$) levels, there was a greater bilateral advantage at the global level (24 ms) than at the local level (11 ms). The Level × VF interaction also held when comparing bilateral to RVF presentations ($F(1,36) = 14.21, p < .01$). There was a 23-ms bilateral over RVF advantage for the global level ($p < .01$) but no significant advantage at the local level. But there was no Level × VF interaction when comparing RVF to LVF presentations (tables 19.1 and 19.2). This, then, is an example of a differential bilateral advantage as a function of decision type, greater for global than for local decisions.

There was also a Consistency × VF interaction ($F(2,72) = 4.665, p < .05$). This was due to a trend toward a stronger consistency effect with bilateral (68-ms advantage for consistent stimuli) than with LVF presentations (48-ms advantage) ($F(1,36) = 3.69, p < .06$). However, the Consistency × VF interaction disappeared when comparing bilateral to RVF presentations. The interaction was significant ($F(1,36) = 8.49, p < .01$) when comparing LVF to RVF presentations, the latter producing a 63-ms advantage with consistent stimuli (tables 19.1 and 19.2). In this case, then, the bilateral condition parallels the RVF rather than the LVF pattern.

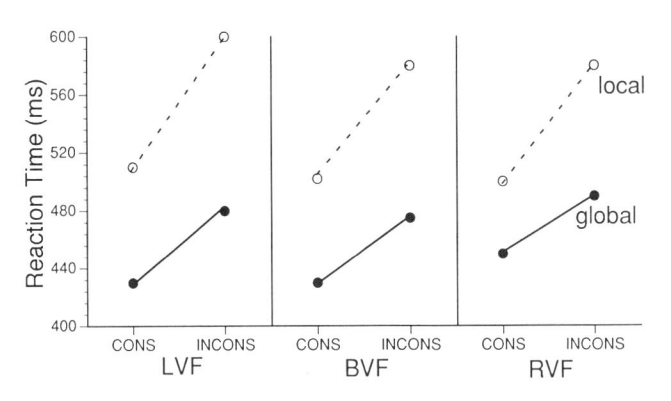

**Figure 19.7** Level × Consistency interaction for each VF condition in Experiment 2: Hierarchic perception in Normals (Carusi and Zaidel, n.d.).

***Arousal*** The only significant effect of arousal was an Arousal × Level × VF(L, R, B) interaction ($F(2,92) = 4.487, p < .05$). But when LVF and RVF scores were collapsed, there was no Arousal × VF (bilateral, unilateral) interaction at either the local or the global level. At the global level there was an Arousal × VF(L, B) interaction ($F(1,36) = 14.1, p < .01$), reflecting a greater bilateral advantage for right hemisphere aroused (RHA) than for LHA subjects (tables 19.1 and 19.2). It is noteworthy that arousal did not affect laterality in the predicted direction: the LHA group showed a 7-ms LVFA for global decisions, whereas the RHA group showed a 10-ms RVFA. Thus, the bilateral advantage is sensitive to individual differences that are not reflected in hemispheric differences. In particular, it is not simply the case that LHA subjects show a bilateral pattern that parallels the RVF (LH) pattern and that RHA subjects show a bilateral pattern that parallels the LVF (RH) pattern.

***Bem*** First, there was a significant Sex × Masculine level × Feminine level × Consistency interaction showing that both phenotypic gender and Bem scores affect the consistency effect. Second, an ANOVA including masculine and feminine scores regardless of phenotypic gender yielded a significant Masculine level × VF interaction ($F(2,72) = 3.2, p < .05$). Here there were significant Masculine level × VF(B, L) and Masculine level × VF(L, R) interactions but not a Masculine level × VF(B, R) interaction, suggesting that the bilateral condition parallels the RVF more than the LVF condition (tables 19.1 and 19.2). Thus, Bem scores rather than phenotypic gender affect the laterality effects and the bilateral advantage.

***Linear Regression*** In an attempt to assess the relative contributions of global and local decisions in the two VFs and of the bilateral advantage at the global or local levels to the consistency effect, we carried out a multiple stepwise regression (BMDP2R). The stepwise regression was carried out with the local consistency effect (Consistent/local − Inconsistent/local) (i.e., global interference) as a dependent variable and with the following independent variables: Global/LVF, Global/RVF, Local/LVF, Local/RVF, Precedence (i.e., global advantage) (Local − Global), Precedence/LVF, Precedence/RVF, Local/RVF − Global/LVF, Local/LVF − Global/RVF, Lateralization [(L − R)/(L + R)], Global Lateralization, Local Lateralization, Lateralized Precedence (Precedence/LVF − Precedence/RVF), Bilateral Advantage, Bilateral Global Advantage and Bilateral Local Advantage. The program selected two variables: Local/RVF − Global/LVF, with a multiple partial correlation of .5679, which accounted for 32.25 percent of the variance (fig. 19.8a), and Bilateral Local Advantage with an original correlation of .5292 (fig. 19.8b), and a step 2 multiple correlation of .6534 which accounts for 10.5 percent of the remaining variance. No further variables were selected. Together, then, the two variables account for 42.7 percent of the total variance.

This supports the interhemispheric model of global interference. Global intereference does depend, as predicted, on the speed advantage of global decisions in the LVF over local decisions in the RVF, but it also depends

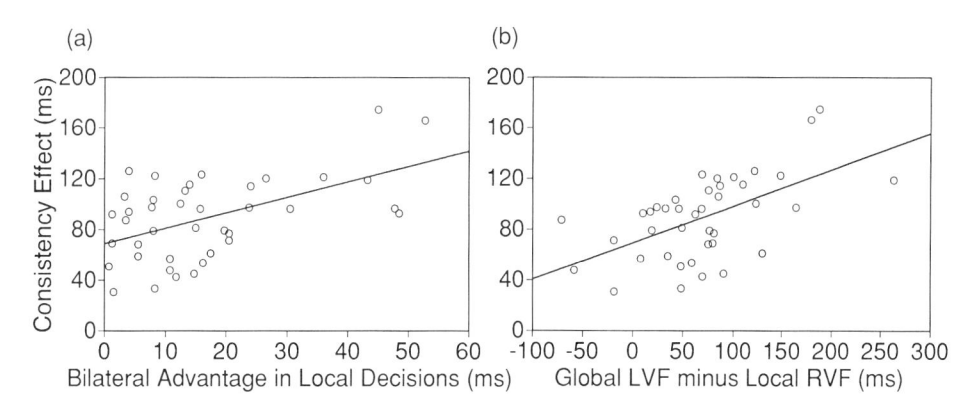

**Figure 19.8** *a*. Least-squares fit for the correlation between the local consistency effect (Consistent-Inconsistent targets in local decisions) and "specialized precedence" (Local/RVF minus Global/LVF) ($r(38) = .5679, p < .01$). Specialized precedence was the first variable accounting for the consistency effect using multiple linear regression. *b*. Least-squares fit for the correlation between the local consistency effect and the bilateral advantage (bilateral-unilateral targets) for local decisions ($r(38) = .5292, p < .01$). Bilateral advantage for local decisions was the second variable accounting for consistency effect, with a step 2 multiple correlation of .6543.

on the bilateral advantage for local decisions. Recall that there was a much smaller bilateral advantage for local than for global decisions and that bilateral local decisions were significantly faster than LVF but not RVF local decision. The significance of the contribution of this component (bilateral local advantage) to the global interference remains to be explained. But one could speculate that if the LH is biased to dominate local decisions, then a bilateral advantage for local decisions reflects RH-to-LH transfer of RH "contribution" to local decisions. (By the same token, the bilateral advantage for global decisions would have reflected LH-to-RH transfer of LH contribution to global decisions.) Then the contribution of the bilateral advantage for local decisions to global interference would reflect an asymmetric RH-to-LH cross-callosal effect.

A similar multiple stepwise regression with local interference (Consistent global − Inconsistent global) as the dependent variable selected global/LVF with a multiple correlation coefficient of $r = .4516$, which accounts for 20.4 percent of the variance. No further variables were selected. Thus, there is no support for an interhemispheric model of local interference, suggesting that the mechanisms responsible for the global and local interference effects are distinct.

### Conclusions

Although experiments 1 and 2 used very similar stimuli and procedures, they showed different bilateral patterns. Experiment 1 consistently showed a race pattern, where bilateral scores parallel the best unilateral scores, reflecting hemispheric control, whereas experiment 2 often showed a bilateral advantage, reflecting hemispheric sharing. But degree of sharing varied with decision type (greater for global) and was affected by individual differences in hemispheric arousal and in Bem masculinity score.

Moreover, if the interhemispheric account of the consistency effect is correct, then it illustrates how basic cognitive phenomena can have complex neuropsychological origins. In this case, the neuropsychological mechanism incorporates elements of control and of interhemispheric interaction. The control elements involve assigning control to the RH when making global decisions and to the LH when making local decisions, although both of these operations are available to each hemisphere and neither necessarily shows hemispheric specialization. The interhemispheric interaction elements involve the interference of global decisions in the RH with local decisions in the LH. The locus of global interference, its pathway, and its code remain to be discovered. But we already have some hints that the effect involves asymmetric RH-to-LH transfer.

## 19.4 CONCLUSION

The experiments reviewed above are relatively homogeneous. All employ linguistic stimuli, and most of them show an RVFA. And yet they show several patterns of hemispheric control, ranging from bilateral advantage to a race and a bilateral loss. Table 19.1 summarizes the relationship between the VFA and the bilateral advantage for most of the independent variables manipulated in the experiments. By far the most common pattern is a VFA (usually a RVFA) accompanied by a race, where bilateral = best, or a bilateral advantage. There can also occur a bilateral advantage or a race in the absence of a VFA. One case revealed a VFA and a bilateral loss.

Thus, the presence of a VFA is neither necessary nor sufficient for a bilateral race or for a bilateral advantage. In other words, either interhemispheric cooperation or hemispheric control can occur with or without hemispheric specialization. However, the presence of a VFA overwhelmingly predicts a bilateral race or a bilateral advantage. It is noteworthy that we did not observe a case with the worst hemisphere dominating bilateral performance, for example, an RVFA but LVF dominance. Perhaps such a pattern is less likely to be observed in the normal than in the disconnected brain because the corpus callosum makes possible a comparison of independent hemispheric performances at advanced stages of information processing, thus filtering out control by the weaker hemisphere. Still, the variety of patterns observed suggests a flexible and dynamic system of interhemispheric control, sensitive to task and stimulus variables.

Table 19.2 summarizes interactions between VF(L,R,B) and independent stimulus variables, and this allows us to compare processing strategies in unilateral and bilateral presentations. First, we see that the bilateral advantage is sensitive to lexical (wordness) and cognitive (hierarchical level, consistency) variables, suggesting hemispheric interaction at relatively late stages of processing. Second, the bilateral advantage is not proportional to hemispheric competence, particularly of the weaker hemisphere. Third, the bilateral advantage is also sensitive to individual differences, for example, in sex, Bem masculinity, and hemispheric arousal.

It is plausible that a bilateral advantage beyond redundancy gain should occur only for tasks that show evidence of hemispheric independence, that is, direct access tasks. Some processing dissociation VF(L, R) × Variable, indicating direct access, is available in the redundancy gain experiments and in the hierarchic perception experiment with Robertson and Lamb but not in the hierarchic perception experiment with Carusi. Thus, the processing dissociation criterion for Direct Access is likely very conservative and results in many false negatives. Table 19.2 shows that a bilateral advantage can occur for a variable that does not exhibit a direct access pattern. Thus, a direct access pattern is neither necessary nor sufficient for a bilateral advantage or a bilateral race.

We have, in effect, two tests of hemispheric control. One is the pattern exhibited by some independent variable V in a given VF, and it reflects hemispheric information-processing strategy. The other is the overall score, and it reflects hemispheric competence. In most cases, the bilateral pattern differs equally from both hemispheres; there is a V × VF(L, R, B) interaction that persists in the V × VF(L, B) and V × VF(R, B) interactions. Indeed, it is possible for this "pattern test" of dominance to fail (find no dominance) even though the overall scores show unilateral dominance, as in the case of Wordness × VF in the cued Redundancy Gain experiment. Similarly, it is possible for the "pattern test" to show RVF dominance when the scores show a bilateral advantage relative to both VFs, as in the case of Arousal × VF for global decisions in the second (Carusi) experiment on hierarchical perception. But the "pattern test" and the overall scores can converge on the same result, as in the case of Bem masculinity in experiment 2 on hierarchical perception, where both indicate RVF dominance. Of course, the "pattern test" is a relatively weak index of hemispheric strategy since the same pattern may reflect different strategies and since failure to find a VF × V interaction for some independent variable V does not preclude a VF × V' interaction with a new, yet-to-be discovered, variable V'.

It is important that in our data when the "pattern test" does suggest hemispheric dominance, this is almost always RVF dominance. It remains to be determined if this is a consequence of the pervasive RVFA reflecting the linguistic stimuli of our experiments. Although this did not occur here, it is also of interest to know whether the overall scores and the pattern test can diverge and show opposite hemispheric dominance. That would limit the coherence or the simplicity of the concept of hemispheric dominance in bilateral exchange.

Because the two normal cerebral hemispheres often process high-level information separately, differently, and simultaneously, they can serve as models of cognitive modules in general, and their interaction can serve as a model for intermodular communication. Much of such interaction is mediated by the neocortical commissures, and this makes available anatomical and physiological, in addition to behavioral, techniques for studying intermodular communication. Furthermore, the hemispheres illustrate how alternative computations compete for access to action and to consciousness. The mechanisms that mediate interhemispheric competition and cooperation are mechanisms of control, and they are complex. They are not limited to simple horse race models or to hemispheric dominance where one hemisphere gains privileged access to behavior as a function of stimulus and task parameters. Often behavior reflects interhemispheric interaction that differs from the behavior that would have been produced by either hemisphere alone, as well as from some average of their computations. The interaction is not always adaptive, and occasionally its net effect is inferior to either hemisphere alone, presumably because the two simultaneous computations are incompatible rather than complementary. And, of course, the interactions observed with redundant bilateral presentations are only a small subset of normal and possible interhemispheric relations. For example, the two hemispheres may benefit from some division of labor that is sequential rather than simultaneous.

Although the interactions we observed are unconscious, their net effect is to select a set of perceptions, actions, and awarenesses from a larger set that is potentially available. In that sense, interhemispheric interaction does not only construct consciousness but actually selects one from several, or at least two, available alternatives.

## NOTE

This work was supported by National Institute of Health grant NS 20187 and by a National Institute of Mental Health Research Scientist Award MH00179. We thank Elicia David for assistance and members of the "Z-lab," Morris Moscovitch, Michael Corballis, and an anonymous reviewer for comments on drafts of the chapter.

## REFERENCES

Banich, M. T., and Karol, D. L. (1992). The sum of the parts does not equal the whole: Evidence from bihemispheric processing. *Journal of Experimental Psychology: Human Perception and Performance*, 18, 763–784.

Bem, S. L. (1974). The measurement of psychological androgyny. *Journal of Counseling and Clinical Psychology*, 42, 155–162.

Carusi, D. A. (1992). The Global/local consistency effect between and within the hemispheres: Clues from individual differences. Honors undergraduate thesis, University of California at Los Angeles.

Carusi, D., and Zaidel, E. (n.d.). Interhemispheric determinants of the consistency effect in hierarchic perception. In preparation.

Delis, D. C., Kramer, J. H., and Kiefner, M. G. (1988). Visuospatial functioning before and after commissurotomy: Disconnection in hierarchical processing. *Archives of Neurology*, 45, 462–465.

Delis, D. C., Robertson, L. C., and Efron, R. (1986). Hemispheric specialization of memory for visual hierarchical stimuli. *Neuropsycologia*, 24, 205–214.

Egeth, H. E., Folk, C. F., and Mullin, P. A. (1989). Spatial parallelism in the processing of lines, letters, and lexicality. In B. E. Sheppa and S. Ballesteros (Eds.), *Object perception: Structure and process*, 19–52. Hillsdale, NJ: Erlbaum.

Eviatar, Z., and Zaidel, E. (1992). Letter matching in the hemispheres: Speed-accuracy tradeoffs. *Neuropsychologia, 30*, 699–710.

Hellige, J. B. (1991). Cerebral laterality and metacontrol. In F. Kitterle (Ed.), *Cerebral laterality: Theory and research*, 117–132. Hillsdale, NJ: Erlbaum.

Hellige, J. B. (1993). Unity of thought and action. *Current Directions in Psychological Science, 2*, 21–25.

Kimchi, R., and Merhav, I. (1991). Hemispheric processing of global form, local form, and texture. *Acta Psychologica, 6*, 133–147.

Lamb, M. R., and Robertson, L. C. (1988). The processing of hierarchical stimuli: Effects of retinal locus, locational uncertainty, and stimulus identity. *Perception and Psychophysics, 44*, 172–181.

Lamb, M. R., and Robertson, L. C. (1989). Do response time advantage and interference reflect the order of processing of global- and local-level information? *Perception & Psychophysics, 46*, 254–258.

Lamb, M. R., Robertson, L. C., and Knight, R. T. (1989). Attention and interference in the processing of global and local information: Effects of unilateral temporal-parietal junction lesions. *Neuropsychologia, 27*, 471–483.

Lamb, M. R., Robertson, L. C., and Knight, R. T. (1990). Component mechanisms underlying the processing of hierarchically organized patterns: Inferences from patients with unilateral cortical lesions. *Journal of Experimental Psychology: Learning, Memory and Cognition, 16*, 471–483.

Levy, J., Heller, W., Banich, M. T., and Burton, L. A. (1983). Are variations among right-handed individuals in perceptual asymmetries caused by characteristic arousal differences between hemispheres? *Journal of Experimental Psychology: Human Perception and Performance, 9*, 329–359.

Martin, M. (1979). Hemispheric specialization for global and local processing. *Neuropsychologia, 17*, 33–40.

McClelland, J. L. (1979). On the time relations of mental processes: An examination of systems of processes in cascade. *Psychological Review, 86*, 287–330.

Measso, G., and Zaidel, E. (1990). Effect of response programming on hemispheric differences in lexical decision. *Neuropsychologia, 28*, 635–646.

Miller, J. (1982). Divided attention: Evidence for coactivation with redundant signals. *Cognitive Psychology, 14*, 247–279.

Mordkoff, J. T., and Egeth, H. E. (1993). Response time and accuracy revisited: Converging support for the interactive race model. *Journal of Experimental Psychology: Human Perception and Performance, 19*, 981–991.

Mordkoff, J. T., and Yantis, S. (1991). An interactive race model of divided attention. *Journal of Experimental Psychology: Human Perception and Performance, 17*, 520–538.

Mullin, P. A., and Egeth, H. E. (1989). Capacity limitations in visual word processing. *Journal of Experimental Psychology: Human Perception and Performance, 15*, 111–123.

Navon, D. (1977). Forest before trees: The precedence of global features in visual perception. *Cognitive Psychology, 9*, 353–383.

Rayman, J., and Zaidel, E. (1991). Rhyming and the right hemisphere. *Brain and Language, 40*, 89–105.

Robertson, L. C., and Lamb, M. R. (1991). Neuropsychological contributions to theories of part/whole organization. *Cognitive Psychology, 23*, 299–330.

Robertson, L. C., Lamb, M. R., and Knight, R. T. (1988). Effects of lesions of temporal-parietal junction on perceptual and attentional processing in humans. *Journal of Neuroscience, 8*, 3757–3769.

Robertson, L. C., Lamb, M. R., and Zaidel, E. (1993). Interhemispheric relations in processing hierarchical patterns: Evidence from normal and commissurotomized subjects. *Neuropsychology, 7*, 325–342.

Sergent, J. (1982). The cerebral balance of power: Confrontation or cooperation? *Journal of Experimental Psychology: Human Perception and Performance, 8*, 253–272.

van der Heijden, A. H. C., La Heij, W., and Boer, J. P. A. (1983). Parallel processing of redundant targets in simple visual search tasks. *Acta Psychologica, 319*, 21–41.

Van Kleek, M. H. (1989). Hemispheric differences in global versus local processing of hierarchical visual stimuli by normal subjects: New data and a meta-analysis of previous studies. *Neuropsychologia, 27*, 1165–1178.

Zaidel, D. W. (1986). Memory for scenes in stroke patients. *Brain, 109*, 547–560.

Zaidel, D. W. (1987). Hemispheric asymmetry in memory for pictoral semantics in normal subjects. *Neuropsychologia, 25*, 487–495.

Zaidel, E. (1983). Disconnection syndrome as a model for laterality effects in the normal brain. In J. Hellige (Ed.), *Cerebral hemisphere asymmetry: Method, theory and application*, 95–151. New York: Praeger.

Zaidel, E. (1986). Callosal dynamics and right hemisphere language. In F. Lepore, M. Ptito, and H. H. Jasper (Eds.), *Two hemispheres—One brain? Functions of the corpus callosum*, 435–459. New York: Alan R. Liss.

Zaidel, E. (1989). Hemispheric independence and interaction in word recognition. In C. von Euler, I. Lundberg, and G. Lennerstrand (Eds.), *Brain and reading*, 77–97. Hampshire: Macmillan.

Zaidel, E., Aboitiz, F., Clarke, J., Kaiser, D., and Matteson, R. (n.d.). Sex differences in interhemispheric relations for language. In F. Kitterle (Ed.), *Hemispheric communication: Mechanisms and models*. Hillsdale, NJ: Erlbaum. In press.

Zaidel, E., Clarke, J., and Suyenobu, B. (1990). Hemispheric independence: A paradigm case for cognitive neuroscience. In A. B. Scheibel and A. F. Wechsler (Eds.), *Neurobiology of higher cognitive function*, 297–362. New York: Guilford Press.

Zaidel, E., White, H., Sakurai, E., and Banks, W. (1988). Hemispheric locus of lexical congruity effects: Neuropsychological reinterpretation of psycholinguistic results. In C. Chiarello (Ed.), *Right hemisphere contributions to lexical semantics*, 71–88. New York: Springer.

# VI  Semantic Memory

# 20 Of Cabbages and Things: Semantic Memory from a Neuropsychological Perspective—A Tutorial Review

Eleanor M. Saffran and Myrna F. Schwartz

ABSTRACT  We review research on impairments of object knowledge and discuss the implications of these impairments for theories of semantic memory. Two types of disorders are examined in detail: the gradual and general dissolution of semantic knowledge in patients with degenerative neurological disorders (*semantic dementia*) and disturbances in which knowledge of certain categories is disproportionately affected (living things; man-made objects). The evidence for category-specific semantic loss is discussed in relation to network models of semantic memory. We also consider neuropsychological evidence that bears on the relationship between object knowledge and object use.

## 20.1 INTRODUCTION

"The time has come," the Walrus said,
"To talk of many things:
Of shoes—and ships—and sealing wax—
Of cabbages—and kings—
And why the sea is boiling hot—
And whether pigs have wings."
—Lewis Carroll, "The Walrus and the Carpenter"

Although Lewis Carroll may not have been concerned with the representation of knowledge when he wrote these lines more than a century ago, the Walrus's query—whether pigs have wings—is precisely the kind of question that appears in semantic memory experiments. And, to anticipate a bit, the Walrus's seemingly tenuous hold on the properties of things typifies the impairments that are the subject of this review.

The impetus for such queries on the part of cognitive psychologists was a paper by Endel Tulving, published in 1972. Tulving distinguished between the sort of memory that psychologists had traditionally studied—episodic memory, or memory that has an autobiographical reference—and semantic memory—or general world knowledge, which does not. Although Tulving (1972) originally conceived of it as an information store necessary for the use of language, "a mental thesaurus, organized knowledge a person possesses about words and other verbal symbols, their meaning and referents, about relations among them, and about rules, formulas, and algorithms for the manipulation of these symbols, concepts and relations" (p. 386), semantic memory has since been construed as a more general knowledge base with a broader application. As Kintsch (1980) observed in a previous Attention and Performance tutorial on semantic memory, "Word meanings are an important part of this general knowledge store, but... attempts to equate semantic memory with word meanings only... are doomed to failure. Semantic memory is our whole-world knowledge—including what we know about robins. .., what to do in a restaurant, and the history of the Civil War" (p. 596).

Object concepts can be accessed from percepts as well as from words, and indeed this is the sole route of access in organisms that lack language, including adult humans with profound aphasic deficits and infants in the preverbal stage. Thus, the content of semantic memory is generally considered to include information about objects that is relevant to perceptual identification and action, as well as knowledge that underlies the use of words. In fact, the question of whether words and objects (or their visual depictions) are interpreted by a common knowledge base, as opposed to separate visual and verbal semantic systems, has been a central issue in the study of semantic memory (Snodgrass 1984; Glaser 1992).

In contrast to episodic memory experiments, which typically deal with factors that affect the veridicality and persistence of stored information, investigations of semantic memory have largely focused on the organization of semantic information (e.g., hierarchies versus property lists) and the form in which this information is represented (e.g., propositions versus images). The experimental literature is extensive though generally seen as inconclusive insofar as these central questions are concerned, and we will not attempt to review it here (for recent reviews see Chang 1986; Eysenck and Keane 1990). We focus, instead, on the growing literature on semantic memory loss and the implications of these disorders for the organization of this complex system.

## 20.2 IMPAIRMENTS OF SEMANTIC MEMORY

Although the inability to name objects, (anomia), may be the most common symptom of language breakdown in aphasia, this impairment need not reflect a loss of underlying conceptual knowledge. Often the patient claims to "know" the word in question and will frequently be able to produce it when given a phonological cue. In such cases, the impairment appears to reflect an inability to retrieve the phonological form of the word (Kay and Ellis 1987), an exaggerated form of the tip-of-the-tongue phenomenon that occurs in normal production. Aphasics may also fail to understand words, but these deficits often reflect impairments that impede access to semantics from words rather than the loss of semantic information.[1]

There are, however, disorders in which the inability to name objects does appear to reflect loss of the conceptual knowledge that underlies language production. The deficits in these patients extend to word comprehension and even to tasks that avoid verbal labels entirely (e.g., sorting pictures according to category). Such impairments can result from acute illnesses such as stroke or infection and may be selective for certain types of objects or aspects of meaning. We will discuss these category-specific disorders later in the chapter.

More commonly, semantic impairment is insidious in onset, reflecting a progressive, degenerative brain disease that selectively compromises semantic memory in its early stages but typically evolves into generalized cognitive impairment, or dementia. This disorder has recently been labeled *semantic dementia* (Snowden, Goulding, and Neary 1989).

## 20.3 SEMANTIC DEMENTIA

Semantic dementia is defined as an impairment of semantic memory, in the context of relative sparing of episodic memory and other cognitive functions. Difficulty in word finding (anomia) generally signals the onset of the disorder. Affected individuals are also impaired in word comprehension and demonstrate an impoverished fund of general knowledge.

Although patients with semantic deficits had been described by neurologists at the end of the last century (Poeck and Luzzatti 1988), the disorder did not attract the attention of psychologists until Elizabeth Warrington identified it, in the title of her 1975 paper, as a "selective impairment of semantic memory." Warrington described three patients who performed within the normal range on most measures of cognitive function but poorly on tasks that required knowledge of object and word meanings. Aside from difficulty in word finding and word comprehension, their language functions appeared to be intact. Warrington carried out a systematic investigation of object knowledge by means of an attribute verification task. She presented the patient with a picture of an object or the corresponding word and asked questions such as, "Is it an animal?" "Is it a bird?" "Is it foreign?" "Is it bigger than a cat?" The patients generally responded correctly to probes for superordinate category membership but performed poorly on the more specific attribute probes, on both the name and picture versions of the task. On a word definition task, all three were impaired in defining object terms, and two had difficulty defining abstract words as well. (Knowledge of abstract terms was remarkably spared in one of patients.) Superordinate terms were frequently given in lieu of more specific information (e.g., *geese*—"an animal but I've forgotten precisely"). All three patients exhibited a progressive decline in cognitive functions, such that two of them were untestable within 3 years.

Schwartz, Marin, and Saffran (1979) described a similar patient (W.L.P.) who was studied longitudinally. Severely anomic when first tested, W.L.P.'s stock of content words shrank over a 2-year period to the point where she relied on a single substantive ("shopping center") to fill noun and even some verb slots in her otherwise grammatical and fluent connected speech. Correlated with the loss of productive vocabulary was a comprehension disorder with features similar to those described in Warrington's (1975) patients. When first examined, W.L.P. failed to discriminate between targets and semantically related distractors in a picture-word matching-to-sample task; later, she began to choose indiscriminately between related and unrelated distractors. Similar deficits emerged in nonverbal tasks in which basic level categorization was tested with pictorial stimuli (pictures of cats, dogs, and birds with prototypical exemplars serving to identify the category). Some object-specific knowledge remained, however; given a picture of an object, she was able to indicate, through gestures, how it would be used. The preservation of object use was consistent with her behavior outside the laboratory, where misuse of objects was not noted until late in her clinical course. W.L.P. also performed well in language tasks that did not require an understanding of object names. She was able to use grammatical information to disambiguate homophones in writing words to dictation (e.g., *the road* versus *he rode*) and to identify noun referents in sentence contexts. Thus, though she otherwise failed to distinguish between horses and cows, she was able to do so when given a sentence (e.g., *The horse is kicking the cow*) along with an action picture. Given the same picture with a sentence in which the thematic roles were reversed (*The cow is kicking the horse*), she pointed to the horse when asked to indicate the cow and vice versa. Her performance was almost as good with passive sentences (*The cow is kicked by the horse*) as with the simpler active constructions.[2]

A systematic study of five similar cases has recently been carried out by Hodges et al. (1992). All of the patients showed a striking loss of vocabulary and demonstrated substantial impairment on tasks such as word-picture matching-to-sample, picture sorting, and generation of verbal definitions. All had great difficulty generating words given category labels, performing better when asked to produce words beginning with a particular letter. The picture sorting task, carried out at several different levels of specificity, revealed a consistent pattern of breakdown, with preservation of superordinate category knowledge (e.g., land animal versus sea creature versus bird) and loss of subordinate or attributional knowledge (e.g., British versus foreign animal; kitchen versus nonkitchen object). Three of the patients were also assessed on measures of semantic knowledge that were entirely nonverbal. All were impaired on an object/nonobject classification test in which the drawings of nonobjects consisted of parts of two different objects (e.g., a head of a mouse with a body of a lion; cf. Riddoch and Humphreys 1987). They also performed poorly on the Pyramids and Palm Trees Test (Howard and Patterson 1992), in which pictures are matched on the basis of conceptual associations (e.g., a pair of glasses to an eye or an ear). As in the cases described by Warrington (1975) and Schwartz, Marin, and Saffran (1979), abilities in other cognitive domains, as well as other language functions (with the exception of irregular word reading), were relatively preserved. Formal assessment of episodic memory was necessarily limited by the semantic impairment, but the investigators took the patients' ability to function in daily life, in keeping track of appointments and the like, to indicate that practical day-to-day memory was relatively preserved. Nonverbal memory, assessed by drawing and recognition memory tasks, was not materially affected. Anatomical data from neuroimaging studies (such as magnetic resonance imaging and positron emission tomography) consistently revealed damage to temporal lobe structures, bilaterally in some cases and in others restricted to the temporal lobe on the left.

A number of other case studies of patients with selective and progressive semantic memory disturbances have been reported (Holland et al. 1985;

Marin, Glenn, and Rafal 1983; Schwartz and Chawluk 1990). All show the same general pattern: word finding difficulty as the initial complaint; semantic loss demonstrable in verbal and nonverbal tasks, with relative preservation of other cognitive and linguistic capacities (though with some variability in this respect, which may reflect differences in the point at which the patients were studied or differences in the anatomical distribution of the pathological changes). In addition, though not studied formally, several authors comment on the preservation of object use, which is striking in view of the profound impairment of object knowledge otherwise demonstrated by these patients. The etiology has not been established with certainty, though Pick's disease, a degenerative disorder in which temporal and frontal lobes are predominantly affected, has been suspected in some cases (Marin, Glenn, and Rafal 1983; Schwartz and Chawluk 1990). It has also been suggested that these patients may have a variant of Alzheimer's disease in which the pathology is initially restricted to the temporal cortex, though it subsequently spreads to other areas, eventually resulting in a generalized loss of cognitive functions, or dementia (Poeck and Luzzatti 1988).

Semantic deficits have been identified in patients with a diagnosis of dementia of the Alzheimer's type (DAT), though these symptoms are generally seen in the context of more widespread cognitive impairment (see Nebes 1989 for a recent view). There are some DAT patients, however, who display significant naming difficulty early in their course. Chertkow and Bub (1990) investigated a group of ten DAT patients who met this description and found performance patterns very similar to those of the semantic dementia cases described above. The DAT patients were impaired on naming and and on word-picture matching, where they showed the pattern of performance observed in Schwartz, Marin, and Saffran's subject, W.L.P.: they failed to distinguish among semantically related items but remained sensitive to category membership. On an attribute probe task, they performed very much like Warrington's (1975) patients, seldom making errors on superordinate probes (e.g., *Is a saw a tool or clothing?*) but erring frequently on more detailed questions (e.g., *Is the tip made of metal or wood? Is it used on a piece of wood or on stone?*).

Thus, there is mounting evidence that semantic memory deficits can appear early in the course of degenerative brain disease, before other cognitive functions are seriously affected. Where brain imaging data have been available for such cases, temporal lobe structures have been implicated, particularly on the left. The evidence indicates that phonology and syntax are spared, in the face of even severe disruption of language processes dependent on word meaning. This finding is consistent with the modular view of the organization of these functions that is held by many cognitive scientists (Fodor 1983). The relative preservation of episodic memory[3] in patients who exhibit profound semantic loss is also consistent with the proposed distinction between episodic and semantic memory. It is worth noting in this context that semantic knowledge may be relatively preserved in patients who are severely amnesic (Kinsbourne and Wood 1975).

Thus, the fact that semantic memory can break down independently of other cognitive functions is quite compatible with widely held views of the architecture of the human cognitive system. Do the manifestations of semantic dementia also conform with descriptions of the semantic system that other lines of research have provided?

Experimental studies of semantic memory have focused on two issues: the manner in which semantic knowledge is organized and the format in which this information is represented. With respect to the first question, an early and influential view was that semantic memory has a hierarchical organization. Based on the finding that subjects were faster to verify specific attributes (e.g., *a canary is yellow*) than superordinate relationships (*a canary is an animal*) or general properties (*a canary eats*), Collins and Quillian (1969) proposed a network model in which concept nodes (e.g., canary, bird, animal) are arrayed hierarchically, with subordinates (canary) at the base of the hierarchy and broad superordinates (animal) at the apices. At each level, attributes are linked to their respective concept nodes (e.g., *yellow* to canary; *has wings* to bird; *eats* to animal). To determine that a yellow caged creature is an animal on this model, it is necessary to traverse the hierarchy from canary to bird to animal.[4] This implies that damage to structures at low levels of the hierarchy should impair access to information at higher levels. The pattern of knowledge loss in semantic dementia does not conform with this prediction. Specific attributes appear to be more vulnerable than subordinate information, and these patients are more likely to know that a canary is an animal than that it refers to something yellow.[5]

The second issue is the format in which information is represented in semantic memory and, related to it, the question of whether the system is unitary and homogeneous or differentiated in some way. The patients in the studies reviewed above were impaired irrespective of whether semantic knowledge was tested pictorially or verbally. There are indications, however, that some semantic dementia patients may be more impaired in one modality than the other (Warrington 1975; Chertkow and Bub 1990). There is also evidence that object use may be preserved in patients who perform poorly on all other tests of object knowledge (Schwartz, Marin, and Saffran 1979). These observations point to some degree of differentiation within the semantic system. The evidence to be discussed below argues compellingly for this view.

## 20.4 CATEGORY-SPECIFIC IMPAIRMENTS

Of the various ways in which brain damage fractionates cognitive functions, the category-specific semantic deficits must be counted among the most remarkable and, from a theoretical standpoint, the most provocative. Though deficits of this type had been reported earlier (Nielsen 1946), the groundbreaking studies in this area are again due to Elizabeth Warrington and her co-workers (Warrington and McCarthy 1983, 1987; Warrington and Shallice 1984). In a series of case studies, these investigators provided evidence for a double dissociation that, as a first approximation, respects the distinction between living things and nonliving objects: they described several patients who were more impaired on biological entities, such as animals, fruits, and vegetables, and two others who were more impaired on nonliving things, such as tools, furniture, and kitchen utensils. The double dissociation has since been confirmed in studies by other investigators.

**Loss of Knowledge of Living Things**

Of the two patterns that involve differential impairment on living and nonliving objects, loss of knowledge of living things relative to artifacts is the more frequently reported.[6] Warrington and Shallice (1984) described four such patients, all of whom had sustained bilateral damage to anterior and medial temporal lobe structures as a result of viral infection (herpes simplex encephalitis). We will discuss these cases in some detail, because the pattern and range of deficits are representative of the dozen or so cases that have been reported thus far.

In the herpes simplex cases, cognitive impairment is not limited to semantic memory loss. Damage to anterior and medial temporal lobe structures produces episodic memory deficits as well (that is, the patients are amnesic), and other functions may also be compromised depending on the exent of damage. The cases Warrington and Shallice (1984) studied vary in severity as well as extent of associated impairments. Two of their patients (K.B. and I.N.G.) were too impaired to be tested on expressive language tasks, such as picture naming; in these cases, category specificity was demonstrated in comprehension. The other patients (J.B.R. and S.B.Y.) were tested more extensively.

The Warrington and Shallice (1984) patients are the first four cases summarized in tables 20.1 and 20.2. J.B.R., the least impaired patient, was disproportionately impaired in identifying pictures of living things, whether by naming the object or by providing a verbal description that conveyed its core concept (table 20.2). S.B.Y., though virtually unable to name, was able to communicate knowledge of pictured objects by describing them (e.g., *towel*: "material used to dry people"). The difficulty with nonliving objects applied to words as well as pictures: both patients were better at defining names of objects than words denoting living things. Striking differences in the adequacy of their definitions to words in these two classes are evident in the examples below:

**Nonliving Objects**

*Briefcase*: "small case used by students to carry papers" (J.B.R.).

*Compass*: "tools for telling direction you are going" (J.B.R.).

*Wheelbarrow*: "object used by people to take material about" (S.B.Y.).

*Umbrella* "object used to protect you from water that comes" (S.B.Y.).

**Living Things**

*Daffodil*: "plant" (J.B.R.).

*Snail*: "an insect animal" (J.B.R.).

**Table 20.1** Background Information on Patients More Impaired on Living Things

| Patient | Reference | Etiology |
|---|---|---|
| J.B.R. | Warrington and Shallice (1984) | Herpes—bilateral temporal |
| S.B.Y. | Warrington and Shallice (1984) | Herpes—bilateral temporal |
| K.B. | Warrington and Shallice (1984) | Herpes—bilateral temporal |
| I.N.G. | Warrington and Shallice (1984) | Herpes—bilateral temporal |
| L.A. | Silveri and Gainotti (1988) | Herpes—bilateral frontotemporal, greater on left |
| M.S. | Newcombe, Young, and De Haan (1989) | Herpes |
| Michelangelo | Sartori and Job (1988) | Herpes—bilateral anterior temporal |
| R.M. | Pietrini et al. (1988) | Herpes—left anterior temporal insula, basal frontal |
| J.V. | Pietrini et al. (1988) | Herpes—left anterior temporal insula, basal frontal |
| N.V. | Basso, Capitani, and Laiacona (1988) | Progressive degenerative disorder, etiology unknown asymmetrical temporal lobe atrophy, greater on left |
| E.L.M. | Decter, Bub, and Chertkow (n.d.) | infarcts—right and left mediotemporal |
| S.B. | Sheridan and Humphreys (1993) | Herpes—left temporal |
| P.S. | Hillis and Caramazza (1991) | Subdural hematomas—bitemporal, left frontal |

*Wasp:* "bird that flies" (S.B.Y.).

*Duck:* "an animal" (S.B.Y.).

Both patients were also impaired in identifying food items (a mixed category containing fruits and vegetables, as well as manufactured food items) relative to artifacts. The three patients tested on word-picture matching to sample showed an advantage for nonliving objects on this task as well (table 20.2).

A finer grained examination of object categories was carried out in J.B.R., who was asked to provide definitions for words from twenty-six categories, including living (animals, insects, flowers, fruits, vegetables, body parts) and nonliving objects (e.g., clothing, furniture, kitchen utensils) as well as other categories representing other types of knowledge (e.g., sport, occupations, weather, science). He performed poorly on all categories of living objects except for body parts and relatively well on most categories of inanimate objects. There were some notable exceptions, however; J.B.R. had as much difficulty defining names of musical instruments and gemstones as he did with names of insects and flowers.

The pattern described by Warrington and Shallice has been replicated in at least nine other patients studied by other investigators (see table 20.2). In most cases, the causal agent was herpes simplex encephalitis, though the pattern has occasionally been found in association with other etiologies, such

Table 20.2  Patients More Impaired on Living Things: Summary of Performance (Percentage Correct)

| | J.B.R. | S.B.Y. | K.B. | I.N.G. | L.A. | M.S. | Michelangelo | R.M. | J.V. | N.V. | E.L.M. | S.B. | P.S. |
|---|---|---|---|---|---|---|---|---|---|---|---|---|---|
| *Pictures* | | | | | | | | | | | | | |
| Naming or Description | | | | | | | | | | | | | |
| Living | 6 | 0 | — | — | 20 | — | 33 | 29 | 20 | 8 | 48 | 37 | 12 |
| Nonliving | 90 | 75 | — | — | 79 | — | 75 | 77 | 47 | 38 | 88 | 94 | 81[a] |
| Foods | 20 | — | — | — | 58 | — | — | — | — | — | — | 0 | — |
| Body parts | — | — | — | — | 74 | — | — | — | — | — | — | — | — |
| *Words* | | | | | | | | | | | | | |
| Definitions | | | | | | | | | | | | | |
| Living | 8 | 0 | — | — | 30 | — | — | 57 | 63 | — | — | 48 | 84[b] |
| Nonliving | 79 | 52 | — | — | 90 | — | — | 97 | 90 | — | — | 90 | 100[b] |
| Foods | 30 | — | — | — | 58 | — | — | — | — | — | — | 22 | — |
| Naming to description | | | | | | | | | | | | | |
| Animals | — | — | — | — | — | 19 | — | 33 | 37 | — | — | 7 | — |
| Objects | — | — | — | — | — | 79 | — | 80 | 60 | — | — | 40 | — |
| Attribute judgments | | | | | | | | | | | | | |
| Size | | | | | | | | | | | | | |
| Animals | — | — | — | — | 70 | — | 100 | — | — | — | 93 | 90 | — |
| Objects | — | — | — | — | 95 | — | — | — | — | — | — | 90 | — |
| Foods | — | — | — | — | — | — | — | — | — | — | — | 40 | — |
| Color | | | | | | | | | | | | | |
| Animals | — | — | — | — | — | — | — | — | — | — | — | 15 | — |
| Objects | — | — | — | — | — | — | — | — | — | — | — | 45 | — |
| Foods | — | — | — | — | — | — | — | — | — | — | — | 10 | — |

**Table 20.2** (cont.)

| | J.B.R. | S.B.Y. | K.B. | I.N.G. | L.A. | M.S. | Michelangelo | R.M. | J.V. | N.V. | E.L.M. | S.B. | P.S. |
|---|---|---|---|---|---|---|---|---|---|---|---|---|---|
| *Category fluency* | | | | | | | | | | | | | |
| Living | — | — | — | — | 15[c] | 52[d] | — | — | — | — | — | — | — |
| Nonliving | — | — | — | — | 49[c] | 118[d] | — | — | — | — | — | — | — |
| *Word-to-picture matching* | | | | | | | | | | | | | |
| Living | 67 | — | 45 | 80 | 80 | — | — | 90 | 62 | 35 | 65 | — | — |
| Nonliving | 98 | — | 85 | 97 | 90 | — | — | 100 | 100 | 98 | 89 | — | — |
| Foods | 60 | — | 55 | 85 | 100 | — | — | — | — | — | — | — | — |
| Body parts | — | — | — | — | 100 | — | — | — | — | — | — | — | — |

a. Includes vegetables.
b. Tested 9 months after naming test.
c. Total number of words generated across all categories.
d. Percent of normal performance.

as closed head injury (P.S.), cerebrovascular disease (E.L.M.), and progressive degenerative disorder (N.V.). The locus of damage is consistent across patients: all sustained damage to the temporal lobes, especially to anterior, inferior, and medial structures; in most instances the damage is bilateral, but asymmetrical, with greater involvement of temporal tissue on the left. Inspection of these data indicates that while the ability to identify nonliving objects is not completely spared in these patients, they are significantly more impaired in naming or otherwise identifying pictures of living objects. The discrepancy between living and nonliving things is observed in other tasks as well: naming objects given verbal descriptions of them (M.S., R.M., J.V., S.B.); generating names of exemplars given a category label[7] (L.A. and M.S.); defining object terms (J.B.R., S.B.Y., L.A., R.M., J.V., S.B., P.S.); miming actions appropriate to names of foods and inanimate objects (J.B.R.); and, in most instances, in word-picture matching as well (J.B.R., K.B., I.N.G., J.V., N.V., E.L.M.; two patients, L.A. and R.M., performed well on this task). Although data are not available for all of the patients, a tendency to be impaired on foodstuffs appears to accompany the deficit on animals (J.B.R., L.A., S.B.).

In general, where a full range of tasks has been administered, superiority for nonliving objects has emerged whether knowledge is tested verbally (e.g., word definitions) or by means of tasks that entail cross-modality matches (e.g., naming, word-to-picture matching). Though there are some exceptions to this pattern, to be discussed later in this chapter, the category-specific disorder does not appear to be modality specific.

**Is Category Specificity an Artifact?**

Though hardly an everyday occurrence in the neurology clinic, the "living things" impairment cannot be dismissed as a curiosity. The deficit has now been observed by a number of investigators and bears a consistent relationship to a particular form of brain pathology. Nevertheless, there are some problems with these studies. Ideally, the demonstration of category differences should be based on item sets that sample representatively within categories and that are equated for difficulty across categories. This is not easy to do. Although living and nonliving stimulus sets have generally been matched for word frequency, there has been little attempt to control for other variables known to affect performance with such stimuli. This is of particular concern since living things tend to be ranked as more difficult on these dimensions: they are generally rated as lower in familiarity than nonliving objects and their visual forms as more complex (Snodgrass and Vanderwart 1980); they are also judged as having greater visual similarity to other objects within their respective categories (Humphreys, Riddoch, and Quinlan 1988). All three of these parameters affect naming performance in normal subjects. In two recent case studies, patients who were disproportionately impaired on living things when given uncontrolled lists showed no category specificity when tested with matched sets of materials (Funnell and Sheridan 1992;

Stewart, Parkin, and Hunkin 1992). The authors of both studies conclude that earlier demonstrations of category specificity, which were not based on closely matched lists, were artifactual.

This conclusion seems much too strong. Attempts to control for confounding variables were in fact made in previous investigations. In several studies, statistical methods were used to control for such effects, and the category differences remained significant in all of them (Basso, Capitani, and Laiacona 1991; Warrington and Shallice 1984; also see Farah, McMullen, and Myer 1991). In the study by Hillis and Caramazza (1991), the materials used to demonstrate selective impairment on living things in one patient (P.S.; table 20.2) produced the opposite pattern in a second patient (J.J.), that is, better performance on animals than on nonliving things. Although this finding does not exclude the possibility that one of these deficit patterns is artifactual, it argues compellingly that both could not be. Moreover, questions can be raised about the two studies that purport to show that the effect is an artifact. Funnell and Sheridan's (1992) patient showed no convincing evidence of category specificity to begin with, and Stewart, Parkin, and Hunkin's (1992) construal of the living/nonliving distinction differed from that of the earlier studies, where in virtually all instances "nonliving" was equated with "manmade." Along with tools and other man-made things, Stewart, Parkin, and Hunkin's stimuli included items such as *swamp, geyser, volcano,* and *waterfall*. Although a case can be made for better matching of stimulus materials,[8] there is no persuasive argument for dismissing the earlier demonstrations as artifactual.

## Evidence for a Double Dissociation: Artefacts Impaired Relative to Living Things

If disproportionate impairment on living things is attributable to effects of confounding variables, these same variables should reduce the likelihood of observing the opposite pattern, and we would not expect to find patients performing better on biological entities than on nonliving things. This pattern emerged, however, in patients studied by Warrington and McCarthy (1983, 1987) (table 20.3). Their first patient, V.E.R., had an extensive left hemisphere lesion that left her with a global aphasia, that is, profoundly impaired in both comprehension and production (Warrington and McCarthy 1983); the second, Y.O.T., was also severely aphasic (Warrington and McCarthy 1987). Though very impaired in matching words to both pictures and objects, both patients were selective in their response patterns, performing better on animal, food, and plant items than on nonliving objects (table 20.4). Y.O.T. also demonstrated superiority for animals versus artifacts in a purely visual task that involved matching different exemplars of the same types of objects (e.g., a vintage roadster with a late-model sedan). Though the authors did not attempt to match for frequency or other variables likely to affect performance on such tasks, the parameters that were problematic with respect to the opposite pattern (nonliving better than living) would be expected to work against

**Table 20.3** Background Information on Patients Impaired on Nonliving Things

| Patient | Reference | Etiology |
| --- | --- | --- |
| V.E.R. | Warrington and McCarthy (1983) | Left middle cerebral artery (LMCA) occlusion, extensive left frontoparietal global aphasic, 0 naming |
| Y.O.T. | Warrington and McCarthy (1987) | Left middle cerebral artery (LMCA) occlusion, extensive left frontoparietal global aphasic, 0 naming |
| C.W. | Sacchett and Humphreys (1992) | Infarct, large left frontoparietal, nonfluent, agrammatic |
| J.J. | Hillis and Caramazza (1991) | Infarct, left temporal lobe and basal ganglia |

the pattern demonstrated by these two patients; as noted, living things tend to be less familiar than nonliving objects and their perceptual forms more complex and subject to greater within-category similarity. The point is underscored by the following examples: V.E.R. did well on items like *daffodil* and *thistle* but failed to distinguish between such highly familiar objects as *briefcase* and *umbrella*.

Two additional cases of this type have recently been reported. Sacchett and Humphreys (1992) have described a patient (C.W.) with a similar performance pattern who was less severely aphasic than V.E.R. and Y.O.T. and was able to provide naming responses. As is evident from table 20.4, the discrepancy between C.W.'s ability to label living things and nonliving objects was as striking as the differences in the opposite direction that were found in the patients impaired on living things (table 20.2). Though somewhat less impaired on word-picture matching than Warrington and McCarthy's patients, C.W. showed the same pattern. Like their patients, she had a large left frontoparietal lesion. Another patient (J.J.) with a selective impairment on nonliving things has been reported by Hillis and Caramazza (1991). J.J.'s lesions were of cerebrovascular origin, like those of the other patients in this group, though the lesions were in a different location (left temporal lobe and basal ganglia).

The severity of their language deficits limited the testing that could be carried out with these patients. For example, word definitions could only be obtained from J.J., and not until a later point in his recovery than the naming data. However, Warrington and McCarthy (1987) were able to make use of a reading task to test semantic knowledge in Y.O.T. Due to a reading impairment that prevented direct print-to-sound mapping, Y.O.T. could match spoken to written words only on the basis of meaning. The cross-modal word matching task could therefore be used to examine the status of her semantic representations. Y.O.T.'s performance on an auditory-to-written word matching test again revealed superiority for words denoting living objects (Warrington and McCarthy 1987).

Table 20.4  Patients Impaired on Nonliving Things: Summary of Performance (Percentage Correct)

| Test | V.E.R. | Y.O.T. | C.W. | J.J. |
|---|---|---|---|---|
| *Picture Naming* | | | | |
| Living | — | — | 95 | 92 |
| Nonliving and body parts | — | — | 35 | 45 |
| *Word-to-picture matching* | | | | |
| Nonliving | 58 | 67 | 75 | — |
| Living | — | 86 | 100 | — |
| Food | 88 | 83 | — | — |
| Body parts | — | 22 | 88 | — |
| Large man-made | — | 78 | — | — |
| Manipulable objects | — | 58 | — | — |
| Famous people | — | 100 | — | — |
| Occupations | — | 100 | — | — |
| Buildings | — | 100 | — | — |
| Countries | — | 100 | — | — |
| Household objects | — | 50 | — | — |
| Clothing | — | 56 | — | — |
| Furniture | — | 39 | — | — |
| *Word-object matching* | | | | |
| Animals | 86 | — | — | — |
| Flowers | 96 | — | — | — |
| Objects | 63 | — | — | — |

Thus, there is evidence of a double dissociation in the domain of semantic memory: some patients are more impaired on biological entities than nonliving objects, while others are more impaired on nonliving objects than living things. The two patterns are associated with lesions in different anatomical structures and in most cases with different etiologies—the first with damage to temporal lobe structures, usually from viral infection, and the second with frontoparietal lesions of vascular origin. Neither set of data is problem-free, and it is unlikely that either would be persuasive on its own; together, they make a strong case for specificity in semantic loss. The implications of these patterns for semantic memory models warrant serious consideration.

**The Basis for Category-Specific Impairment**

If information about living and nonliving entities is represented differently in the brain, what could be the basis for this distinction? Living and nonliving may be natural categories for philosophers, but why should this distinction be respected in the organization of knowledge in the human mind/brain?

In fact, there were indications early on that the living/nonliving dissociation should be drawn somewhat differently. Warrington and Shallice (1984) found that J.B.R. was as impaired in defining terms from the categories of musical instruments, cloth, and precious stones as he was in defining names of living things. Basso, Capitani, and Laiacona's (1988) patient N.V. was also impaired on musical instruments relative to other objects. On the other hand, both patients performed quite well on body parts, which are constituents of living things. Anomalies were also reported in patients impaired on nonliving things. Warrington and McCarthy's (1987) Y.O.T. showed relatively preserved knowledge of large outdoor objects, such as vehicles and buildings, but performed poorly on body parts.

These observations led to the proposal that the category differences do not reflect categorical distinctions per se but stem, rather, from differences in the defining characteristics of objects. Warrington and Shallice (1984) point out that unlike most plants and animals, man-made objects

> have clearly defined functions. The evolutionary development of tool using has led to finer and finer functional differentiations of artifacts for an increasing range of purposes. Individual inanimate objects have specific functions and are designed for activities appropriate to their function. Consider, for instance, chalk, crayon and pencil; they are all used for drawing and writing, but they have subtly different functions.... Similarly, jar, jug and vase are identified in terms of their function, namely, to hold a particular type of object, but the sensory features of each can vary considerably. By contrast, functional attributes contribute minimally to the identification of living things (e.g., lion, tiger and leopard), whereas sensory attributes provide the definitive characteristics (e.g., plain, striped, or spotted). (P. 849)

Warrington and Shallice suggest that perceptual properties are weighted more heavily than functional attributes in the semantic descriptions of living things, while the balance shifts toward functional attributes in the descriptions of man-made objects. Warrington and McCarthy (1987) speculated further that there might even be finer-grained distinctions among representations for man-made objects that reflect the relative "importance of somatosensory information and information derived from actions. For small manipulable objects the information derived from fine distal arm movements is highly salient but clearly much less so for large man-made objects" (p. 1291).

In a recent study, Farah and McClelland (1991) obtained evidence that supports the distinction proposed by Warrington and Shallice (1984). Farah and McClelland asked normal subjects to count the number of visual and functional descriptors in the dictionary definitions of living and man-made objects. Though visual features predominated in both sets of definitions, visual descriptors were disproportionately represented (in a ratio of nearly 8:1) in the definitions of living things compared with artifacts (1.4:1). It appears that the distinction between semantic representations of living and nonliving objects can be restated as a difference between representations weighted more toward perceptual information on the one hand and more toward functional information on the other. Most living things belong to the former set (body parts with their very salient functional attributes being one exception), while most man-made objects belong to the latter (with gemstones and musical instruments among the exceptions). On this view, category-specific impairments emerge when perceptual or functional knowledge is disproportionately affected.

Performance patterns in several of the studies cited provide support for this interpretation of the dissociation pattern. For example, there is evidence that patients impaired on animals are especially impaired on tasks that probe knowledge of visual characteristics. Silveri and Gainotti (1988) asked their patient (L.A.) to identify animals on the basis of definitions based on visual features (e.g., "African wild animal with a long neck and long slender legs"; "an insect with broad, colored, ornate wings") or nonvisual (though not necessarily functional) attributes (e.g., "a wild animal whose tusks are used to obtain ivory"; "an animal that becomes dangerous when it sees red"). L.A. named 58 percent of the animals given nonvisual descriptions but only 9 nine of the animals that were defined visually. When asked to provide definitions of object terms, Sartori and Job's (1988) patient (Michelangelo) often cited perceptual features that were incorrect, more frequently in the case of living things (45 percent) than nonliving objects (18 percent). This patient also had difficulty discriminating drawings of real animals from composites constructed by combining heads and bodies of different animals (Riddoch and Humphreys 1987), though he performed normally on composites of man-made objects. Decter, Bub, and Chertkow's (in press) patient (E.L.M.) showed a similar performance pattern. In contrast, both patients performed relatively well on tasks that probed their knowledge of nonperceptual features of animals (e.g., relative ferocity, habitats, feeding habits), given their names. Sheridan and Humphrey's (1993) patient (S.B.) showed a different pattern, performing well on tasks that required knowledge of animal forms but poorly when tested on knowledge of color attributes. It may be significant that this patient was more impaired on food than on animals, color being a particularly salient characteristic of foodstuffs. One finding that appears inconsistent with the perceptual feature loss hypothesis is that all three of these patients were able to judge the relative sizes of animals, given their names. However, size lends itself to propositional representation more readily than color and shape do; in fact, while the relative sizes of the parts of an object are naturally and economically conveyed in a visual format, it is not so easy to represent the size of the whole object this way.

Also consistent with the loss of perceptual knowledge as the basis for the "living things" impairment is the co-occurrence of this impairment with disorders of face recognition (prosopagnosia). It is not unusual for prosopagnosic patients to have problems with other categories in which exemplars tend to be visually similar to each other. They may, for example, have difficulty distinguishing among makes of cars or in differentiating individual members of a flock of animals (Farah 1991). In some patients, the visual recognition deficits are more extensive but disproportionately involve living things.

Impairments of this type have been described in several recent reports. Farah et al. (1989) demonstrated category specificity in L.H., a prosopagnosic with bilateral temporo-occipital damage due to traumatic brain injury. They asked L.H. to answer questions pertaining to visual (e.g., "Is a canoe widest in the center?") and nonvisual characteristics (e.g., "Is peacock served in French restaurants?") of living and man-made objects. The patient was impaired, relative to normal controls, only on queries pertaining to visual characteristics of living things. In a subsequent study, Farah, McMullen, and Meyer (1991) tested L.H., as well as a second prosopagnosic patient, M.B., on naming of the 260 line drawings in the Snodgrass and Vanderwart (1980) corpus. The authors were careful to consider possible confounding variables (frequency, familiarity, visual complexity, and visual similarity) in their data analysis. Both patients showed a significant superiority for nonliving objects. Other prosopagnosic patients studied by Damasio and his colleagues (Damasio 1990) and De Haan, Young, and Newcombe (1992) have also shown an advantage for man-made objects. Although face recognition problems are not always accompanied by the semantic impairment (Farah, McMullen, and Meyer 1991), the fact that the two co-occur with some frequency is further grounds for linking the "living things" impairment to a breakdown in perceptual knowledge.

There is, then, a reasonable amount of support for the hypothesis that this impairment reflects the loss of perceptual features that figure significantly in the differentiation of one biological species from another. It seems equally plausible that deficits involving nonliving things reflect the loss of salient functional characteristics, though this hypothesis does not have as strong an empirical basis. Knowledge of functional attributes has not been assessed in patients with "nonliving things" deficits, nor is there any information on their ability to use objects.

## Implications for a Model of Semantic Memory

The perceptual/functional distinction proposed by Warrington and her colleagues offers a principled explanation for evidence that may at first have seemed rather surprising. While the notion that categories are assigned to distinct brain structures may be counterintuitive, the idea that the brain distinguishes between perceptual and functional information is not. We know that the nervous sytem segregates input systems from output systems and input systems from each other according to modality. Within sensory areas there is further differentiation; for example, various features of visual input (color, movement, etc.) are processed in discrete areas of cortex and can be disrupted independently (Kosslyn et al. 1990). It is not too much of an extrapolation to suggest that the neural substrates for object concepts differ as a function of the modality in which information was acquired (e.g., visual, auditory, linguistic), the type of knowledge represented (e.g., shape, color, function), and the manner in which it is used (e.g., visual recognition, language processing, action). Similar arguments have been made by cognitive psychologists who were not attempting to account for semantic memory impairments and may not even have been aware of these phenomena. For example, reacting against the notion of unitary conceptual representations, Kolers and Brison (1984) pointed out that recognition is "characteristically accomplished more readily in the modality of acquisition than in other modalities" and argued for consideration of the possibility that "knowledge is represented in means-specific ways" (p. 111). A similar view of semantic representations as reflecting the manner in which information is used has recently been proposed by Shanon (1988).

Jackendoff (1987) raises difficulties for any theory that assumes a single representational format for the encoding of object concepts. As he points out, certain distinctions (the difference between a duck, a goose and a swan, for example) rest largely on perceptual properties (here, the shape and length of the neck) that are not easily translated into feature lists. Similarly, the meanings of certain verbs (*run, jog,* and *lope,* for example) are difficult to differentiate without appealing to representations of motion. He suggests that shape and movement attributes are encoded in three-dimensional geometrical representations (Marr 1982), the latter in terms of the sequential motion of body parts. But the 3-D format does not encode other important distinctions: "A visual representation of the action of walking...requires by its very nature a walking *figure,* say a generalized human. But then, what is to make it clear that this is a representation of walking rather than of *human*? The requisite distinction is not available in the geometric representation" (p. 103). Jackendoff's solution is to posit two levels of conceptual structure, one geometric and the other algebraic (propositional) in format, the latter encoding core conceptual distinctions such as type/token and action/thing. "By linking the 3D figure in motion to an ACTION TYPE concept rather than to a THING TYPE concept," it is possible "to encode the fact that the motion of the figure rather than its shape is taken as the significant information in the 3D model" (p. 103). An important implication of Jackendoff's argument is that visual/imagistic (and other perceptual) formats do not suffice for the basic representation of object concepts. Considerations such as these seriously limit the conceptual capabilities of a putatively "visual" semantic system that, together with a "verbal" semantic system," is sometimes suggested as an account of modality-specific disorders observed in brain-damaged patients (e.g., Warrington 1975).

Reaction time studies provide some evidence for a processing distinction between perceptual and more abstract features of word meaning. Schreuder and Flores D'Arcais (1989) examined effects on lexical decision and word naming[9] of primes bearing either a perceptual (*ball*) or functional/categorical relationship (*banana*) to the target word (*cherry*). Perceptual and functional primes behaved differently in the two tasks: functional primes were more effective in lexical decision while perceptual primes were more effective in word naming. A possible account of these results rests on relative decision latencies in word naming versus lexical decision. Since it generally takes less time to name a word than to decide its lexical status, information that is accessed rapidly is more likely to affect word naming, while information that becomes available later is more likely to affect lexical decision. The finding that perceptual primes were more effective in the naming task suggested that perceptual attributes were accessed more rapidly than functional information. Schreuder and Flores D'Arcais tested this hypothesis by imposing deadlines to speed up lexical decision and by degrading target words to slow down naming. These manipulations reversed the effects of the original experiments: perceptual primes were now more facilitative in lexical decision and functional

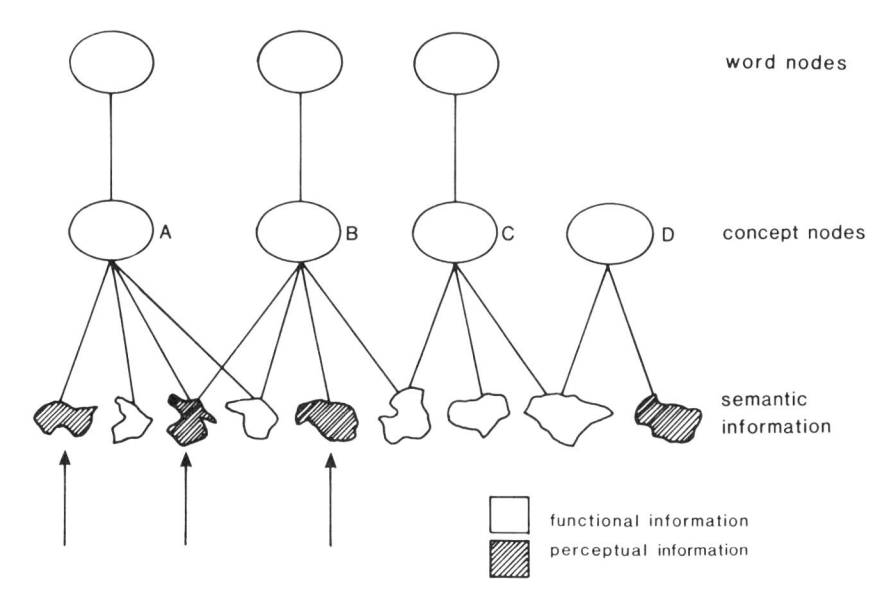

**Figure 20.1**  Three levels of representation in the mental lexicon (from Schreuder and Flores D'Arcais 1989).

primes more effective in word naming. The authors concluded that perceptual attributes are differentiated from functional information in semantic memory, as indicated in their model (fig. 20.1).

Allport (1985) outlined a model that introduces further distinctions among types of representations in semantic memory. This model (fig. 20.2) is a distributed network in which properties of an object are encoded in a number of different subsystems ("attribute domains"). Each object concept is represented as a pattern of activation over featural units in different attribute domains that have become "auto-associated," that is, interconnected so that partial activation will recreate the whole pattern. Allport assumes that

> the auto-associated patterns representing physical objects are *distributed across a very wide range of attribute domains*, encompassing every class of sensory and motor (action-related) attributes pertaining to the particular object-concept. The object concept of *telephone*, for example, must involve the convolution not only of many different complex properties of shape, surface texture, size and so forth that are codable in visual and tactile attribute domains, but also properties specific to auditory and to action-coding domains of representation, including manipulation and speech. (P. 52)

Individual units within the attribute domains participate in many different patterns representing different objects, and

> the same neural elements that are involved in coding the sensory attributes of a (possibly unknown) object presented to eye or hand or ear also make up the elements of the auto-associated activity-patterns that represent familiar object-concepts in "semantic memory." This model is ... in radical opposition to the view ... that "semantic memory" is represented in some abstract, modality-independent, "conceptual" domain remote from the mechanisms of perception and of motor organization. (P. 53)

**nonlinguistic attribute domains**

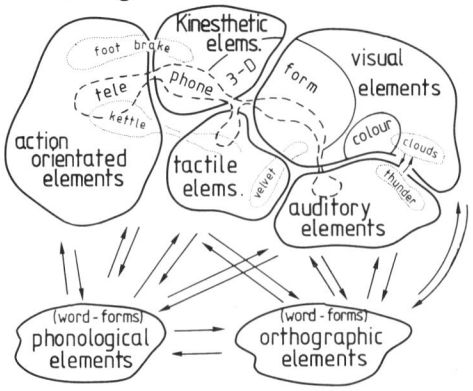

Figure 20.2 Schematic diagram to illustrate how object concepts might be represented as auto-associated activity patterns (dotted outlines) distributed across many different sensory and motor attribute domains. Spoken and written word forms are similarly represented as auto-associated patterns within their corresponding ("phonological"/"orthographic") attribute domains. Mappings between word forms and word meanings are embodied as distributed matrices of interconnections between attribute domains (from Allport 1985).

Somewhat similar proposals have been made by Shallice (1988) and Damasio (1990), among others.

The differentiated and distributed architecture of this model allows a number of neuropsychological phenomena to be understood as local disturbances within the network. Thus, a category-specific deficit for living things would involve the selective disruption of visual form elements (fig. 20.2). A disorder biased toward nonliving objects would involve selective damage to action-oriented elements as well as the loss of more abstract functional information represented propositionally.[10] The model also suggests the possibility of selective disruption of linkages between attribute domains, as distinct from local injury within a particular domain, as well as the possibility of damage to connections between specific attribute domains and input and output systems, including sensory and motor pathways as well as the verbal pathways diagrammed in figure 20.2 (Allport 1985). A disorder of this type has been described by McCarthy and Warrington (1988). Their patient (T.O.B.) was impaired on living relative to nonliving things in verbal tasks, as well as in word-picture matching but was able to provide rich descriptions of living things when provided with their pictures. Asked to define the word *dolphin*, for example, he said, "A fish or a bird," but given a picture of the animal he responded, "lives in water ... trained to jump up and come out.... In America during the war years they started to get this particular animal to go through to look into ships." This pattern could be accounted for on the model by the loss of associative links between lexical representations (referred to as word forms in fig. 20.2)[11] and critical elements in the visual attribute domain.

But while it appears possible to account for a wide range of breakdown patterns within a distributed network model of semantic memory, it could be argued that this reflects less on the adequacy of the model than it does on its lack of constraints. It is a virtue of the network model, however, that it can be made computationally explicit and tested by computer simulation.

Farah and McClelland (1991) have developed a computational model that incorporates many of the features of Allport's (1985) model, though fewer attribute domains are represented. The model is a parallel distributed processing network (e.g., McClelland and Rumelhart 1985) in which visual and functional information are differentiated and represented in different sets of units. To reflect their finding that dictionary definitions for object terms are weighted toward perceptual features, Farah and McClelland's network contains more visual than functional units in a ratio of 3:1. The network was trained, using an error-correcting procedure, to generate "correct" semantic representations (prespecified patterns of activation across units) when presented with either the corresponding picture or name pattern (prespecified patterns of activation across two distinct sets of input units, one "verbal" and one "visual") for each of ten living and ten nonliving things. The mean ratios of visual and functional units for the two types of objects differed in accordance with the findings of the dictionary definition study: 7.7:1 visual-to-functional for living objects and 1.4:1 for nonliving objects. After the network was trained to represent the prespecified patterns, it was "lesioned" by damaging a proportion of the memory units. While damage to visual units had a greater effect on naming living than nonliving things, reproducing the category-specific pattern, damage to functional units affected only naming of nonliving things. These results are not surprising, given the disproportionate weighting of these two types of units in the prespecified representations. A more interesting finding was that damage restricted to visual units affected the functional representations of living things. According to Farah and McClelland, this result mirrors the deficit patterns in the patients, which generally involve perceptual and functional attributes in different degrees rather than one class of features exclusively. Farah and McClelland account for this aspect of the model's performance in terms of a critical mass effect:

Given that most of the semantic features in the representations of living things are visual features, and they have been destroyed, then those few functional features associated with the representation might lack the critical mass to become activated.... The effect arises because the ability of any given unit to attain and hold its proper activation value depends on collateral connections with other units in the network. Although PDP systems are robust to small amounts of damage, if a large proportion of the units participating in a given representation are destroyed, the remaining units will not receive the necessary collateral inputs to achieve their activation values. (P. 347).

The model was also successful in simulating the pattern demonstrated by McCarthy and Warrington's (1988) patient T.O.B., who was impaired on living things only when knowledge was probed verbally. This pattern was produced by selectively damaging connections between the name units and the visual semantics units. An important result of the modeling study is that it was possible to produce category-specific semantic impairments by lesioning a system that lacks category-specific components. The architecture distinguishes only between functional and visual representations; category specificity emerges as a function of weighting these two types of attributes differently across categories, and in consequence of differential loss of the two types of representations.

Can we conclude, then, that category specificity is a reflection of differential weighting across attribute domains, or do categories, *qua* categories, have distinct representational structures? The deficits we have considered thus far apply to broad classes rather than narrowly defined categories; impairments that involve a single class of objects would be more difficult to explain on this model. Though circumscribed deficits involving fruits and vegetables (Hart, Berndt, and Caramazza 1985), colors (Goodglass et al. 1986), body parts (Dennis 1976), and proper names (Semenza and Zettin 1989) have been reported, these deficits appear to be restricted to naming. Thus, they are likely to reflect the manner in which conceptual representations articulate with lexical structures rather than damage to conceptual representations per se. A similar explanation can be given for a deficit pattern described by Hart and Gordon (1992), where the impairment was not limited to naming. In addition to difficulty naming animals, the patient showed a selective loss of perceptual attributes (e.g., color, size) for this class of objects but only when tested verbally. Other tasks involving animals were performed correctly, including probes of perceptual knowledge tested pictorially, probes of nonperceptual attributes tested verbally, and picture-name matches. Assuming that the lexicon has some degree of categorical organization,[12] this performance pattern could be explained by damage to linkages between the visual attribute domain and a particular set of (categorically organized) lexical structures.

**The Relationship between Object Knowledge and Object Use**

Semantic dementia patients may continue to use objects correctly at a point when their performance on other tests of object knowledge is significantly impaired. This dissociation poses a problem for the interactive network model outlined above (fig. 20.2). Though it is possible that "action-orientated" feature domains could be selectively preserved, significant damage to other attribute domains should result in perturbations even in structurally intact parts of the system. This principle of mass action is a key feature of the Farah and McClelland (1991) model and implicit in Allport's (1985) model as well.[13]

The same question can be addressed from a different vantage point: that of patients who are particularly impaired in the use of objects. What is the status of object concepts in ideational apraxia, a disorder defined by the misuse of objects and sequential disorganization in the performance of familiar tasks? While such disturbances are sometimes attributed to faulty access to conceptual-semantic representations (De Renzi and Lucchelli 1988; Ochipa, Rothi, and Heilman 1989; Ochipa, Rothi, and Heilman 1992), it is only recently that investigators have begun to examine these patients from the perspective of semantic memory loss, with the types of materials employed in the studies discussed elsewhere in this chapter.

Schwartz et al. (n.d.) studied a closed head injury patient who made frequent errors in the performance of basic living skills and who was unable to demonstrate the correct use of familiar objects seen and held. This patient was only mildly impaired on an attribute verification test with pictured targets (Chertkow and Bub 1990) and made more errors on animals than on tools and other artifacts. Moreover, he displayed excellent performance on a variety of picture matching and picture arrangement tests assessing functional knowledge. This patient's deficit appears not to reflect impaired conceptual knowledge of objects and actions but rather the use of that information to generate an appropriate plan of action.

A different pattern was observed in a case study by Ochipa, Rothi, and Heilman (1989). Their patient also made errors in everyday usage of objects and failed to demonstrate correct object use on direct testing but, unlike Schwartz et al.'s (n.d.) patient, was profoundly impaired on tests assessing function/use knowledge. In contrast, Ochipa, Rothi, and Heilman's patient had no difficulty naming the tools he could not use or in identifying them from their spoken names, though he could not point to tools when they were described by function.[14] This indicates that a deficit in functional semantics severe enough to disrupt object use does not necessarily affect naming and name recognition for the affected object. This finding complements the evidence of preserved object use in semantic dementia, and together these dissociations would suggest that verbal systems and action systems depend on different conceptual-semantic representations. But it would be premature to draw such a conclusion from the evidence at hand. First, Ochipa, Rothi, and Heilman's patient was left-handed, and his ideational apraxia resulted from a right hemisphere lesion. Since this disorder is usually associated with left hemisphere damage (e.g., De Renzi, Pieczulo, and Vignolo 1968), it is possible that the observed dissociation between verbal and action semantics was due to atypical brain organization. Second, we know too little about the action consequences of semantic memory loss, especially as that loss selectively or differentially implicates functional knowledge. Little formal testing of object use has been carried out in semantic dementia patients, and none at all in patients with category-specific impairments. We can, however, expect this to be an active area of investigation in the future.

**Unitary versus Multiple Formats**

We have interpreted the evidence from semantic breakdown as indicative of a differentiated system of semantic representation, which the models outlined by Allport (1985) and Farah and McClelland (1991) are illustrative of. Caramazza et al. (1990) have taken issue with proposals for multiple semantics, arguing that the putative subcomponents are no more than labels for the observed dissociations. They propose to accommodate the evidence for selective impairment within a unitary system that has the following properties: though "meaning is specified by semantic predicates represented in an amodal format," the representation is "internally structured," or "textured," or differentiated, in the sense that certain semantic features are more tightly linked than others, and different input systems have differential access to particular sets of features. Thus, for example,

> when the stimulus is an object there is a greater probability of successfully activating the semantic predicates corresponding to the perceptual properties that define an object than is the case when the stimulus is a word. Given that we may have more information about the semantic predicates of perceptual attributes when the stimulus is an object than when it is a word, and given the assumption of privileged relationships, there is a greater probability of activation of the semantic predicates of canonical actions when the stimulus is an object than when it is a word. (Pp. 184–185)

Given the assumptions of textured representation and privileged access, the major difference between this "organized unitary content hypothesis" (OUCH) and Allport's (1985) model, in particular, seems to be Caramazza et al.'s insistence on a uniform propositional format for semantic representation. We see this assumption as a misguided attempt at parsimony. Since the information entered into semantic memory is culled from different sources (e.g., visual, auditory, tactile, verbal), the unitary model requires a distinct translation process for each type of information. As Jackendoff (1987) observes, "suppose that in order to describe some phenomenon in a one-component theory one must introduce *ad hoc devices* that miss *generalizations* [italics added], whereas a two-component theory expresses these generalizations naturally.... In such a case, the two-component theory is clearly preferable" (p. 112). In this instance, the generalization—a reasonable one, we think—is that information in semantic memory bears the stamp of the channels through which it was acquired. We would argue that this generalization is preferable to ad hoc devices implicit in Caramazza et al.'s OUCH model and other unitary format approaches to semantic representation; these are the mechanisms required to translate information encoded visually, auditorally, kinesthetically, and verbally into a uniform propositional format.

The issue of format is linked to other assumptions about the architecture of semantic memory. If a semantic representation is construed as a network of units distributed across subsystems that are associated by virtue of repeated concurrence of activation, and connectivity in this network is assumed to be bidirectional, it is very likely that some of these units will be sensory in nature. Allport (1985) explicitly assumes that "the same neural elements that are involved in coding the sensory attributes of a (possibly unknown) object presented to eye or hand or ear also make up the elements of the auto-associated activity patterns that represent familiar object-concepts in semantic memory" (p. 53). And Damasio's (1990) neurologized version of a distributed model stipulates that some of the "feature fragments" that constitute object concepts "are inscribed in multiple early sensory and motor cortices." Such proposals are compatible with the assumptions of connectionist models and are potentially testable in patients with localized damage to sensory and motor systems.

## 20.5 SUMMARY

We have reviewed studies of disorders that involve the loss of object concepts. One set of disturbances, referred to under the label "semantic dementia," involves a progressive and general loss of object concepts, while other disorders, described as category specific, differentially affect knowledge either of biological entities or man-made things. Analysis of the deficit patterns suggests that category specificity reflects the selective loss of attributes that differentiate objects within these classes. Distinctions between animals such as lions and tigers, for example, primarily reflect differences in form and other perceptual characteristics. Since there tends to be little variation in the appearance of members of a particular species, form is also a reliable index of species identity. In contrast, artifacts are defined more by function than by form, which can vary considerably among exemplars of a given object (as, for example, in the case of sofas or radios). There is evidence, moreover, that patients who are selectively impaired on living things are especially deficient in their knowledge of the visual characteristics of these objects.

The category-specific deficits can be accounted for within the framework of a semantic memory model in which object knowledge is distributed across a number of different attribute domains that are linked bidirectionally so that activation of units in one part of the network is sufficient to reinstate the full object representation (fig. 20.2). An impairment that disproportionately affects a particular class of objects reflects selective damage to attribute domains that are particularly salient in the representation of that object. As activation in different parts of the network is mutually reinforcing, damage to a single attribute domain can affect the functioning of other parts of the distributed representation. Thus, knowledge of other properties of animals may be compromised by that damage to the part of the network that represents animal forms. Disorders that are not category specific, such as those observed in semantic dementia, presumably reflect more widespread damage across the differentiated system.

Whether this particular characterization proves useful or not, it should be evident that the breakdown patterns in patients with semantic impairments provide a unique database for probing the structure of semantic memory. At the very least, the neuropsychological data argue for a differentiated architecture that distinguishes between representations that draw heavily on sensory information and other aspects of conceptual representation. Theories of semantic memory will have to acknowledge such a distinction.

## NOTES

1. The point is that lexical impairment does not necessarily imply conceptual impairment, though the latter can certainly be found among patients with aphasia (Whitehouse, Caramazza, and Zurif 1978; Gainotti 1987).

2. A semantic dementia patient under study in our laboratory has shown perfect syntactic control of labeling performance with sentences as complex as object clefts (e.g., *It is the cow that the horse is kicking*) (Breedin and Saffran, n.d.).

3. The use of the word *relative* must be stressed here. Episodic memory is not normal when assessed by standard tests, but since depth of processing is likely to be affected by the semantic deficit, one would not expect it to be.

4. Evidence that conflicts with the hierarchical network model was obtained in subsequent studies with normal subjects (Smith, Shoben, and Rips 1984).

5. This knowledge is not totally secure, however. As Schwartz, Marin, and Saffran (1979) demonstrated with W.L.P., category constraints gradually erode as the disease progresses. The patient described by Marin, Glenn, and Rafal (1985) had already lost superordinate knowledge at the time she was tested. Though perceptually unimpaired, this patient sorted objects on the basis of single features (e.g., green crocodiles were placed with other green animals, such as parrots).

6. This should not be taken to reflect incidence in the brain-damaged population, which has seldom been examined with these distinctions in mind.

7. This task is generally referred to as word fluency in the clinical literature.

8. Controlling for familiarity differences can be problematic, since people are likely to rate things that they use as more familiar than objects encountered at a distance, on television, or in reading. Familiarity may therefore be confounded with manipulability.

9. Word naming refers to the task of reading a printed word aloud.

10. Allport uses the term *linguistic word-meanings*.

11. Most current models assume an intermediate level of representation between conceptual and word form specifications (e.g., Levelt 1989), as in fig. 20.1.

12. A discussion of the organization of the lexicon is beyond the scope of this chapter. However, the fact that semantic coordinates (such as animal names) tend to appear in similar syntactic environments and to serve as arguments for the same sorts of verbs suggests that lexical organization is likely to be influenced by semantic similarity.

13. However, there are reports of selective preservation of certain attributes (e.g., size, habitat, ferocity of animals) in patients with "living things" impairments that conflict with this assumption.

14. The ability of ideational apraxics to name the objects they are unable to use correctly has also been noted by Poeck and Lehmkulhl (1980) and De Renzi and Lucchelli (1989).

## REFERENCES

Allport, D. A. (1985). Distributed memory, modular subsystems and dysphasia. In S. K. Newman and R. Epstein (Eds.), *Current perspectives in dysphasia*, 207–244. Edinburgh: Churchill Livingstone.

Basso, A., Capitani, E., and Laiacona, M. (1988). Progressive language impairment without dementia: A case with isolated category specific semantic defect. *Journal of Neurology, Neurosurgery and Psychiatry*, 51, 1201–1207.

Breedin, S. D., and Saffran, E. M. (n.d.). Spared syntax in the face of semantic impairment. In preparation.

Caramazza, A., Hillis, A. E., Rapp, B. C., and Romani, C. (1990). The multiple semantics hypothesis: Multiple confusions? *Cognitive Neuropsychology*, 7, 161–189.

Chang, T. (1986). Semantic memory: Facts and models. *Psychological Bulletin*, 99, 199–220.

Chertkow, H., and Bub, D. (1990). Semantic memory loss in Alzheimer-type dementia. In M. F. Schwartz (Ed.), *Modular deficits in Alzheimer-type dementia*, 207–244. Cambridge, MA: MIT Press.

Collins, A. M., and Quillian, M. R. (1969). Retrieval time from semantic memory. *Journal of Verbal Learning and Verbal Behavior, 8*, 240–247.

Damasio, A. R. (1990). Category-related recognition defects as a clue to the neural substrates of knowledge. *Trends in the Neurosciences, 13*, 95–98.

Decter, M., Bub, D., and Chertkow, H. (N.d.). Multiple representations of object concepts: Evidence from category-specific agnosia. *Cognitive Neuropsychology*. Submitted.

De Haan, E. H. F., Young, A. W., and Newcombe, F. (1992). Neuropsychological impairment of face recognition units. *Quarterly Journal of Experimental Psychology, 44A*, 141–175.

Dennis, M. (1976). Dissociated naming and locating of body parts after left anterior temporal lobe resection: An experimental case study. *Brain and Language, 3*, 147–163.

De Renzi, E., Liotti, M., and Nichelli, P. (1987). Semantic amnesia with preservation of autobiographic memory. A case report. *Cortex, 23*, 575–597.

De Renzi, E., and Lucchelli, F. (1988). Ideational apraxia. *Brain, 111*, 1173–1185.

De Renzi, E., Pieczulo, A., and Vignolo, L. A. (1968). Ideational apraxia: A quantitative study. *Neuropsychologia, 6*, 41–52.

Eysenck, M. W., and Keane, M. T. (1990). *Cognitive psychology: A student's handbook*. London: Erlbaum.

Farah, M. J. (1991). Patterns of co-occurrence among the associative agnosias: Implications for visual object representation. *Cognitive Neuropsychology, 8*, 1–19.

Farah, M. J., Hammond, K. H., Mehta, Z., and Ratcliff, G. (1989). Category-specificity and modality-specificity in semantic memory. *Neuropsychologia, 27*, 193–200.

Farah, M. J., and McClelland, J. (1991). A computational model of semantic memory impairment: Modality specificity and emergent category specificity. *Journal of Experimental Psychology: General, 120*, 339–357.

Farah, M. J., McMullen, P. A., and Meyer, M. M. (1991). Can recognition of living things be selectively impaired? *Neuropsychologia, 29*, 185–193.

Fodor, J. A. (1983). *The modularity of mind*. Cambridge, MA: MIT Press.

Funnell, E., and Sheridan, J. (1992). Categories of knowledge? Unfamiliar aspects of living and nonliving things. *Cognitive Neuropsychology, 9*, 135–154.

Gainotti, G. (1987). The status of the semantic-lexical structures in anomia. *Aphasiology, 1*, 449–461.

Glaser, W. R. (1992). Picture naming. *Cognition, 42*, 61–106.

Goodglass, H., Wingfield, A., Hyde, M. R., and Theurkauf, J. C. (1986). Category-specific dissociations in naming and recognition by aphasic patients. *Cortex, 22*, 87–102.

Hart, J., Berndt, R. S., and Caramazza, A. (1985). Category-specific naming deficit following cerebral infarction. *Nature, 316*, 439–440.

Hart, J., and Gordon, B. (1992). Neural subsystems for object knowledge. *Nature, 359*, 60–64.

Hillis, A. E., and Caramazza, A. (1991). Category-specific naming and comprehension impairment: A double dissociation. *Brain, 114*, 2081–2094.

Hodges, J. R., Patterson, K., Oxbury, S., and Funnell, E. (1992). Semantic dementia: Progressive fluent aphasia with temporal lobe atrophy. *Brain, 115*, 1783–1806.

Holland, A. L., McBurney, D. H., Moossy, J., and Reinmuth, O. M. (1985). The dissolution of language in Pick's disease with neurofibrillary tangles: A case study. *Brain and Language, 24,* 36–58.

Howard, D., and Patterson, K. (1992). *Pyramids and palm trees: A test of semantic access from pictures and words.* Bury St. Edmunds: Thames Valley Test Company.

Huff, F. J., Corkin, S., and Growden, J. H. (1986). Semantic impairment and anomia in Alzheimer's disease. *Brain and Language, 28,* 235–249.

Humphreys, G. W., Riddoch, M. J., and Quinlan, P. T. (1988). Cascade processes in picture identification. *Cognitive Neuropsychology, 5,* 67–103.

Jackendoff, R. (1987). On beyond zebra: The relation of linguistic and visual information. *Cognition, 26,* 89–114.

Kay, J., and Ellis, A. E. (1987). A cognitive neuropsychological case study of anomia. *Brain, 110,* 613–629.

Kinsbourne, M., and Wood, F. (1975). Short-term memory processes and the amnesic syndrome. In D. Deutsch and J. A. Deutsch (Eds.), *Short-term memory,* 258–291. New York: Academic Press.

Kintsch, W. (1980). Semantic memory: A tutorial. In R. S. Nickerson (Ed.), *Attention and Performance VIII,* 595–620. Cambridge, MA: Bolt Beranek and Newman.

Kolers, P., and Brison, S. (1984). Commentary: On pictures, words, and their mental representation. *Journal of Verbal Learning and Verbal Behavior, 23,* 105–113.

Kosslyn, S. M., Flynn, R. A., Amsterdam, J. B., and Wang, G. (1990). Components of high-level vision: A cognitive neuroscience analysis and accounts of neurological syndromes. *Cognition, 34,* 203–277.

Levelt, W. (1989). *Speaking.* Cambridge, MA: MIT Press.

Marin, O. S. M., Glenn, C. G., and Rafal, R. D. (1983). Visual problem solving in the absence of lexical semantics: Evidence from dementia. *Brain and Cognition, 2,* 285–311.

Marr, D. (1982). *Vision.* San Francisco: Freeman.

McCarthy, R. A., and Warrington, E. K. (1988). Evidence for modality-specific meaning systems in the brain. *Nature, 334,* 428–430.

McClelland, J. L., and Rumelhart, D. E. (1985). Distributed memory and the representation of general and specific information. *Journal of Experimental Psychology: General, 114,* 159–188.

Nebes, R. D. (1989). Semantic memory in Alzheimer's disease. *Psychological Bulletin, 106,* 377–394.

Newcombe, F. Young, A. W., and De Haan, E. H. F. (1989). Prosopagnosia and object agnosia without covert recognition. *Neuropsychologia, 27,* 179–191.

Nielsen, J. M. (1946). *Agnosia, apraxia, aphasia: Their value in cerebral localisation.* New York: Hoeber.

Ochipa, C., Rothi, L. J. G., and Heilman, K. M. (1989). Ideational apraxia: A deficit in tool selection and use. *Annals of Neurology, 25,* 190–193.

Ochipa, C., Rothi, L. J. G., and Heilman, K. M. (1992). Conceptual apraxia in Alzheimer's disease. *Brain, 115,* 1061–1072.

Pietrini, V., Nertimpi, T., Vaglia, A., Revello, M. G., Pinna, V., and Ferro-Milone, F. (1988). Recovery from herpes simplex encephalitis: Selective impairment of specific semantic categories with neuroradiological correlation. *Journal of Neurology, Neurosurgery, and Psychiatry, 51,* 1284–1293.

Poeck, K., and Lehmkuhl G. (1980). Ideatory apraxia in a left handed patient with right-sided brain lesion. *Cortex, 16,* 273–284.

Poeck, K., and Luzzatti, C. (1988). Slowly progressive aphasia in three patients: The problem of accompanying neuropsychological deficit. *Brain, 111,* 151–168.

Riddoch, M. J., and Humphreys, G. W. (1987). A case of integrative visual agnosia. *Brain, 110,* 1431–1462.

Rosch, E., Mervis, C. B., Gray, W. D., Johnson, D. M., and Boyes-Bream, P. (1976). Basic objects in natural categories. *Cognitive Psychology, 8,* 382–439.

Sacchett, C., and Humphreys, G. W. (1992). Calling a squirrel a squirrel but a canoe a wigwam: A category-specific deficit for artifactual objects and body parts. *Cognitive Neuropsychology, 9,* 73–86.

Sartori, G., and Job, R. (1988). The oyster with four legs: A neuropsychological study on the interaction between vision and semantic information. *Cognitive Neuropsychology, 5,* 677–709.

Schreuder, R., and Flores D'Arcais, G. B. (1989). Psycholinguistic issues in the lexical representation of meaning. In W. Marslen-Wilson (Ed.), *Lexical representation and process,* 409–436. Cambridge, MA: MIT Press.

Schwartz, M. F., and Chawluk, J. B. (1990). Deterioration of language in progressive aphasia: A case study. In M. F. Schwartz (Ed.), *Modular deficits in Alzheimer-type dementia,* 245–296. Cambridge, MA: MIT Press.

Schwartz, M. F., Marin, O. S. M., and Saffran, E. M. (1979). Dissociation of language function in dementia: A case study. *Brain and Language, 7,* 277–306.

Schwartz, M. F., Montgomery, M. W., Fitzpatrick DeSalme, E. J., Ochipa, C., and Coslett, H. B. (N.d.). Analysis of a disorder of everyday action. Submitted.

Semenza, C., and Zettin, M. (1989). Evidence from aphasia for the role of proper names as pure referring expressions. *Nature, London, 342,* 678–679.

Shallice, T. (1988). *From neuropsychology to mental structure.* Cambridge: Cambridge University Press.

Shanon, B. (1988). Semantic representation of meaning: A critique. *Psychological Review, 104,* 70–83.

Sheridan, J., and Humphreys, G. W. (1993). A verbal-semantic category-specific recognition impairment. *Cognitive Neuropsychology, 10,* 143–184.

Silveri, M. C., and Gainotti, G. (1988). Interaction between vision and language in category-specific semantic impairment. *Cognitive Neuropsychology, 5,* 677–709.

Smith, E. E., Shoben, E. J., and Rips, L. J. (1974). Structure and process in semantic memory: A featural model for semantic decision. *Psychological Review, 81,* 214–241.

Snodgrass, J. G. (1984). Concepts and their surface representations. *Journal of Verbal Learning and Verbal Behavior, 23,* 3–22.

Snodgrass, J. G., and Vanderwart, M. (1980). A standardized set of 260 pictures: Norms for name agreement, image agreement, familiarity, and visual complexity. *Journal of Experimental Psychology: Human Learning and Memory, 6,* 174–215.

Snowden, J. S., Goulding, P. J., and Neary, D. (1989). Semantic dementia: A form of circumscribed cerebral atrophy. *Behavioural Neurology, 2,* 167–182.

Stewart, F., Parkin, A. J., and Hunkin, N. M. (1992). Naming impairments following recovery from herpes simplex encephalitis: Category specific? *Quarterly Journal of Experimental Psychology, 44A,* 261–284.

Tulving, E. (1972). *Episodic and semantic memory*. In E. Tulving, and W. Donaldson (Eds.), *Organization of memory*, 381–403. New York and London: Academic Press.

Warrington, E. K. (1975). The selective impairment of semantic memory. *Quarterly Journal of Experimental Psychology, 27,* 635–657.

Warrington, E. K., and McCarthy, R. A. (1983). Category-specific access dysphasia. *Brain, 106,* 859–878.

Warrington, E. K., and McCarthy, R. A. (1987). Categories of knowledge: Further fractionation and an attempted integration. *Brain, 100,* 1273–1296.

Warrington, E. K., and Shallice, T. (1984). Category-specific semantic impairments. *Brain, 107,* 829–853.

Whitehouse, P., Caramazza, A., and Zurif, E. (1978). Naming in aphasia: Interacting effects of form and function. *Brain and Language, 6,* 63–74.

# 21 Category Specificity and Informational Specificity in Neuropsychological Impairment of Semantic Memory

Giuseppe Sartori, Max Coltheart,
Michele Miozzo, and Remo Job

## 21.1 INTRODUCTION

The concept of semantic memory, developed by Quillian in his doctoral thesis (published as Quillian 1968), became the subject of much experimental and theoretical work. Five of the chapters in the book on the organization of memory by Tulving and Donaldson (1972) concerned semantic memory; notable among these was Tulving (1972), which dealt with, among another things, the question of what semantic memory is *not* (the answer Tulving offered was that it is not episodic memory). As for what semantic memory is, Tulving had this to say: "Semantic memory is the memory necessary for the use of language. It is a mental thesaurus, organized knowledge a person possesses about words and other verbal symbols, their meaning and referents, about relations among them, and about rules, formulas and algorithms for the manipulations of these symbols, concepts and relations."

Almost a decade after Tulving's chapter appeared, Kintsch (1980) reviewed that period's abundant experimental and theoretical work on semantic memory and reached the following conclusion: "So where are we after 10 years of semantic memory?... In terms of the issues that really have motivated this research, we have so far not received any clear answers. The impression is unavoidable that questions have been asked in the context of a research paradigm that was simply not rich enough to provide definitive answers. The data from the experiments described here do not provide enough constraints to enable us to decide the issues that everyone is interested in" (p. 603). Pointing out that almost all of this research used a single experimental task, he added: "I don't care about sentence verification data per se (and I don't suppose McCloskey and Glucksberg care either)—I want to know about semantic memory!" (p. 604).

This was Kintsch's first complaint about the literature on semantic memory. The solution he proposed for this problem was that a variety of tasks that draw upon semantic memory should be studied: "Sentence verification is not the only important task to be considered. One also needs to perform an action, to satisfy a request made by a sentence, or to find information to answer a question" (p. 614). A second recommendation he offered was that the study of semantic memory should involve a variety of investigational paradigms rather than solely laboratory studies of latencies and error rates with college student subjects: "The problem lies ... not in the generality of the theory but in the manner of evaluating it. It needs a much broader, richer data base. Not one experiment, nor a single experimental paradigm, but several converging experimental approaches might succeed where sentence verification alone failed" (p. 604). Finally, Kintsch raised objections to the definition of semantic memory that Tulving offered, which had been widely adopted:

> I shall argue that attempts to equate semantic memory with word meanings only, that is, with the "subjective lexicon", are misguided and doomed to failure. Semantic memory is our whole-world knowledge—including what we know about robins, $7 \times 4 = 28$, what to do in a restaurant, and the history of the Civil War, to cite some prominent examples.... In linguistics, semantics has become nice and clean by distinguishing between the concepts of lexicon and encyclopaedia. The former contains the defining properties of words, and it alone is important for the calculus of meaning elements that constitutes linguistic semantics. The encyclopaedia, on the other hand, is for the nondefinitional information about word meanings, including general word knowledge: it is a hopeless mess and not a proper subject for linguistic enquiry. The lexicon is relatively simple and all we need to know for the study of semantics. Semantic memory has become for the psychologist what the lexicon is for the linguist. Indeed, the term *subjective lexicon* is often used as a synonym for semantic or partial synonym for semantic memory, and more than one psychologist has deplored the fact that it is apparently not very well possible to keep the dreadful mess of "world knowledge" out of his neat subjective lexicon. (p. 609)

We quote at length here since we are entirely in agreement with Kintsch's conception of semantic memory as containing both lexical and encyclopedic information. Indeed, there seems to be general agreement about this, since Tulving (1983) himself subsequently adopted this view: "Semantic memory ... is involved ... with knowledge of the world" (p. 9) and "the fact that the engine of a train can whistle may also be entered into the semantic system" (p. 37).

In sum, then, Kintsch made three proposals that he believed would allow the study of semantic memory to advance. First, we should think of semantic memory as embodying a wide range of real-world knowledge, including knowledge about both defining and nondefining attributes of concepts; the representation of *budgerigar* in semantic memory should specify not only that it is a species of parakeet but also that it is often kept as a pet, and that its name is derived from a word in an Australian Aboriginal language. Second, a variety of different methodological paradigms should be applied to the study of semantic memory. Third, a variety of different tasks that draw upon information in semantic memory should be used within these paradigms: not only verifying sentences involving target words but also acting in response to these words, retrieving specific forms of information about them, and answering questions about them.

In the decade following the publication of this paper, the way ahead that Kintsch advocated was in fact pursued and did in fact enrich the study of semantic memory. The decade that has ensued since his paper was published has seen a large amount of research on semantic memory that has eschewed studies of sentence verification by college students and has taken the view that semantic memory is a loosely organized collection of knowledge that includes all kinds of real-world knowledge and has used such semantic-memory tasks as performing actions, satisfying requests, and finding information to answer a question. The research we are referring to here is the last ten years' program of cognitive-neuropsychological research on specific impairments of semantic memory after brain damage.

## 21.2 NEUROPSYCHOLOGICAL IMPAIRMENTS OF SEMANTIC MEMORY

The first study of this type of impairment was by Warrington (1975). She described three patients with progressive dementing illnesses who were impaired at providing definitions for spoken words (even though these patients could repeat these words) and at answering such questions as, "Is a cabbage bigger than a telephone book?" or "Is a cabbage an animal, a plant, or an inanimate object?" In one of these patients, there was evidence that the impairment of semantic memory was *selective*; that is, it was not equally evident for all types of information in semantic memory. This patient provided excellent definitions for abstract words ( such as *supplicate* or *arbiter*), while performing extremely poorly when attempting to define concrete words (such as *hay*, *needle*, or *acorn*). Several other studies of neuropsychological impairment of semantic memory by Warrington and her colleagues were published at about the same time as Kintsch's chapter (Coughlan and Warrington 1981; Warrington and McCarthy 1983; Warrington and Shallice 1984), and since then the topic has been intensively studied by a variety of investigators (e.g., Hart and Gordon 1992; Farah, McMullen, and Meyer 1991; Sartori, Job, and Coltheart 1993).

This work has led to various proposals about the functional organization of the semantic memory system. For example, Basso, Capitani, and Laiacona (1988), Silveri and Gainotti (1988), and Sartori, Job, and Coltheart (1993) have presented neuropsychological evidence for the existence of separate visual and conceptual subsystems of semantic memory—that is, for one subsystem that holds such information as that a canary is yellow and has legs, and a different subsystem that holds such information as that canaries are kept as pets and originally came from certain Atlantic islands. Hart and Gordon (1992), Warrington and McCarthy (1983), Sartori, Job, and Coltheart (1993), and several others have presented neuropsychological evidence for separate subsystems of semantic memory for animate and inanimate objects. Kintsch (1982, p. 603) wrote, "Just as a provocation, let me suggest that the sentence verification data of the last 10 years have told us precisely nothing about the structure of semantic memory." It is obvious that, in contrast, the neuropsychological data of the ten years since Kintsch wrote this have provided a wealth of ideas about the structure of semantic memory.

The data we report here are intended as a further contribution to the study of the structure of semantic memory as revealed by patterns of semantic breakdown after brain damage. The specific issues with which we are concerned are the principles by which semantic memory is organized. If there is an internal structure to semantic memory, is this based on semantic categories of items, or on the modality in which an item is presented (such as pictures versus words versus smells), or on type of semantic information (such as visual information versus conceptual information), or some or all of these? As we have indicated, a rich source of information about such matters is the cognitive neuropsychology of semantic disorders; hence we report studies of three patients with this type of disorder and consider what these can tell us about the structure of semantic memory.

## 21.3 SUBJECTS

The studies here reported have been conducted on three neurological patients on whom preliminary neuropsychological testing indicated possible disorders of semantic memory. In this clinical testing, patients were also worse at naming pictures of animals or vegetables than pictures of inanimate objects (table 21.1). Since this effect also appears in a task that requires semantic knowledge but not name production (the definition of concepts task; see the chapter appendix), these picture-naming deficits are not solely anomic in origin. The case histories and the basic neuropsychological findings of two of the patients, Bellini and Edea, presented here for the first time, are reported in the chapter appendix. The case history of the third patient, Michelangelo, is presented in full in Sartori and Job (1988).

## 21.4 STUDY 1: CATEGORY SPECIFICITY IN PICTURE NAMING

It has been shown by Stewart, Parkin, and Hunkin (1992) and by Funnell and Sheridan (1992) that apparent category-specific effects on picture naming can vanish when the different picture categories are matched on such variables as frequency, familiarity, and visual complexity, and indeed these authors have gone on to question whether there ever are genuine category-specific effects on picture naming. In order to determine, then, whether the three patients discussed in this chapter exhibit genuinely category-specific effects upon picture naming, a study that controls these potentially confounding variables was needed (the clinical data reported in table 21.1 were collected with pictures in which these variables were not controlled).

**Table 21.1** Naming of Pictures, from Snodgrass and Vandervart (1980)

|         | Vegetables ($N = 45$) | Animals ($N = 54$) | Objects ($N = 27$) |
|---------|------------------------|---------------------|---------------------|
| Bellini | 31%                    | 22%                 | 74%                 |
| Edea    | 42                     | 39                  | 78                  |

**Stimuli**

A set of forty animals and a set of fifty inanimate objects were selected, matching the two sets as far as possible on picture familiarity, name frequency, and visual complexity (for details, see Sartori, Miozzo, and Job 1993). The animals belonged to the following categories: birds, crustacea, fish, insects, mammals, molluscs, and reptiles. The inanimate objects belonged to the following categories: boats, transport, guns, structures, vehicles, and vessels. Statistical tests showed that the two lists did not differ on familiarity ($t(88) = -0.834$), complexity ($t(88) = 1.244$), or name frequency ($t(88) = 1.734$).

Ten control subjects showed no difference ($t(9) = -0.847$) in accuracy of naming the two sets, their scores being 97.75 percent (S.D. = 1.84) for the animals and 98.4 percent (S.D. = 1.83) for the inanimate objects. For name agreement, there was a difference between the two sets ($t(88) = 2.627$, $p = 0.01$), with inanimate objects eliciting more names per item than animals.

The visual similarity of items within the two sets was assessed by asking a group of twenty-two university students to judge the global visual similarity of all the items of each subset. A seven-point rating scale was used, with 1 indicating low similarity and 7 indicating high similarity. Items of a single subset were presented together on a page or were divided into two pages. To force subjects to use all the points of the scale, four foils with items from heterogeneous categories were included. The rated visual similarity for the two lists of animals (mean rating = 4.79) and inanimate objects (mean rating = 4.75) did not differ ($t(11) = 0.187$), while each of these lists differed significantly from the list of foils (mean rating = 2.10).

**Results**

The results of the three patients' naming performance are reported in table 21.2. The three patients previously showing a categorical effect on picture naming accuracy dissociate when tested with more stringent criteria. There are no longer category-specific effects evident in the naming performance of Bellini and Edea. However, Michelangelo still shows worse performance with animals than with inanimate objects (chi square $(1) = 12.80, p < .001$), indicating that genuine category-specific effects on picture naming can be found.

Semantic memory patients may differ from one another along different dimensions. Prominent among these is the categorical disorder just analyzed. Some patients (such as Michelangelo) show such category-specific effects, and

Table 21.2 Proportion Correct Naming of Pictures with Item Visual Similarity Controlled For

|  | Animals ($N = 40$) | Inanimate Objects ($N = 50$) |
| --- | --- | --- |
| Michelangelo | .40 | .76 |
| Bellini | .28 | .34 |
| Edea | .55 | .52 |

others (such as Bellini and Edea) do not. Indeed, double dissociations have been reported here; Warrington and McCarthy (1983, 1987) described patients whose picture-word matching was better with animals than with inanimate objects, and Sacchett and Humphreys (1992) describe a patient who named animals far better than inanimate objects even when the effects of frequency, familiarity, and complexity were taken into consideration, the opposite of the effect we report with Michelangelo.

Another important distinction is that between visual form knowledge and nonvisual knowledge, since it has been argued that the loss of knowledge may frequently he restricted to visual form knowledge (Silveri and Gainotti 1988; Hart and Gordon 1992). Since visual form knowledge is needed if pictures are to be recognized, it remains possible that our patients' difficulties with picture naming could be due to selective loss of visual form knowledge, with nonvisual knowledge relatively preserved.

Our second study therefore investigated the patients' knowledge concerning nonvisual properties of animals, such as habitat or edibility. This was done by asking the patients questions about animals that involved nonvisual characteristics and also by presenting the animals as pictures or as spoken words. Our view is that visual form knowledge is integral to the process of picture recognition. If we are correct that Michelangelo has a specific deficit of visual form knowledge and Bellini and Edea do not, then Michelangelo should perform less well when the stimulus is a picture than when it is a word, regardless of the type of semantic information that is being probed. Indeed, he should actually perform well when the stimulus is a spoken word and the semantic information required is nonvisual, and it should not matter, in this condition, whether the animal being probed is one whose picture he can name or one whose picture he cannot name. In contrast, Bellini and Edea, if they have a deficit of semantic memory that is not specific to visual form knowledge, should still perform poorly with nonvisual stimuli and testing of nonvisual knowledge and should be worse here for animals they cannot name than animals they can name.

## 21.5 STUDY 2: IS NONVISUAL KNOWLEDGE SEPARATE FROM VISUAL FORM KNOWLEDGE?

**Stimuli**

For each patient a set of forty animal pictures was selected; twenty of these were pictures that had been correctly named on previous testing occasions, and twenty were pictures that the patient had not been able to name. Therefore, the stimulus set differed somewhat from patient to patient.

**Task**

We wished to assess the patients' knowledge of nonvisual properties of these animals, and to do this we used a forced-choice task similar to that developed by Warrington (1975). For each item, either a two or three-alternative question was asked. These questions concerned one of six nonvisual semantic properties:

1. Superordinate category (Is X a bird, a mammal, or a member of another category?)
2. Usual habitat (Does X have an Italian or a foreign habitat?).
3. Type of food eaten (Is X carnivorous, herbivorous, or omnivorous?).
4. Ferocity (Is X ferocious or not?).
5. Domesticity (Is X domestic or not?).
6. Edibility (Is X edible or not?).

The task was administered twice to Michelangelo, on different sessions held 1 week apart. In one session, he was presented with the spoken names of the items, and in the other session he was presented with the picture of the items. Bellini and Edea were presented only with the verbal version of the test and with only five of the question types (their version of the test did not contain the question on edibility).

**Results**

For Michelangelo (table 21.3), performance with verbal presentation was good (mean correct, 88 percent), and there was no difference in accuracy for nameable and unnameable items when they were presented verbally, ($t(5) = 1, p = 0.363$). However, nameable items were responded to more accurately than unnameable items when these items were presented as pictures ($t(5) = 4.3, p = .007$), and the unnamed items yielded worse performance when presented as pictures than when presented as words ($t(5) = 3.606, p = .015$).

In contrast, both Bellini and Edea (table 21.4) were more accurate when answering questions about nameable items than unnameable items even when these were presented verbally (Bellini, $t(4) = 4.9, p = .008$; Edea, $t(4) = 3.3$, $p < .028$).

Table 21.3 Michelangelo's Proportions of Correct Responses to Questions about Nonvisual Properties of Animals

|  | Chance | Word | | Picture | |
| --- | --- | --- | --- | --- | --- |
|  |  | Named | Unnamed | Named | Unnamed |
| Superordinate | .33 | 1.00 | .85 | 1.00 | .85 |
| Habitat | .50 | .95 | .90 | .90 | .80 |
| Food | .33 | .80 | .75 | .95 | .60 |
| Ferocity | .50 | .85 | .95 | .95 | .80 |
| Domesticity | .50 | .95 | .90 | 1.00 | .85 |
| Edibility | .50 | .85 | .85 | .75 | .65 |
| Means |  | .90 | .87 | .93 | .76 |

**Table 21.4** Bellini's and Edea's Proportions of Correct Responses to Questions about Nonvisual Properties of Animals

|  | Chance | Bellini | | Edea | |
|---|---|---|---|---|---|
|  |  | Named | Unnamed | Named | Unnamed |
| Superordinate | .33 | .95 | .70 | .95 | .70 |
| Habitat | .50 | 1.00 | .70 | .90 | .80 |
| Food | .33 | .60 | .30 | .90 | .70 |
| Ferocity | .50 | .85 | .55 | .95 | .75 |
| Domesticity | .50 | .90 | .85 | .90 | .90 |
| Mean |  | .86 | .62 | .92 | .77 |

This pattern of results supports our interpretation of the deficits of these three patients. Bellini and Edea have a nonselective impairment of semantic memory, and Michelangelo has a specific deficit of the visual form knowledge component of semantic memory, a deficit that will impair performance when visual information is being probed ("Does an oyster have legs?") regardless of the modality of stimulus input (picture or spoken word), and that will also impair performance when the stimulus is a picture, regardless of the type of semantic information being probed (visual or nonvisual). This specific deficit is also a partial deficit; performance is better with pictures that can be named than with pictures that cannot be named, so visual form knowledge is relatively spared for some items and relatively impaired for others.

## 21.6 DISCUSSION

Bellini and Edea have a nonselective impairment of semantic memory. Their performance in tests of semantic memory does not depend on the semantic category of the stimulus (animal versus inanimate object) or on the type of semantic information being tapped (visual versus conceptual). In contrast, Michelangelo's impairment is doubly selective; his performance is influenced by both semantic category (worse with animals than inanimate objects) and type of information (worse with visual than with conceptual information). Sartori, Job, and Coltheart (1993) reported that Michelangelo was also worse with animals than inanimate objects in matching a part to an incomplete whole with picture stimuli, deciding whether a drawing was of a real or a nonexistent object or animal, answering such spoken questions as, "Does a motorbike have a steering wheel?" or "Does a rabbit have a curved beak?" and drawing to dictation. All of these tasks depend on the availability of specifically visual information, and so these results indicate that such information is less available to Michelangelo when the item is an animal than when it is an animate object. The results of study 2 show that whether visual information is available about an animal (as indexed by whether it can be named when its picture is presented) is not related to whether nonvisual information is available; hence, our inference that Michelangelo's disorder of semantic memory is doubly selective.

Another kind of doubly selective impairment of semantic memory was reported by McCarthy and Warrington (1988). With their patient, they manipulated both the type of input (picture versus spoken name) and the type of item (animal versus inanimate object). The patient's task was to say what he knew about each item. The patient's performance was poor only when the input was a spoken word and when it also referred to an animal. Performance was good with pictures of animals, and performance was good with spoken words as long as these referred to inanimate objects.

In both cases, one of the two dimensions of this double selectivity is animacy. We thank Jean Mandler for drawing our attention to a completely different but, we believe, highly relevant literature concerning animals versus inanimate objects as stimuli. This literature (Mandler, Bauer, and McDonough 1991; Mandler 1992; Mandler and McDonough 1993) provides evidence that conceptual categorization of things into the categories animal and inanimate object is a feature of the cognition of very young infants and that these categorizations are not based simply on the perception of elementary visual features. In a number of these experiments, a familiarization-dishabituation technique was used: 9-month-old infants are given a series of small toys to examine, one after the other, and the time spent in examination as a function of whether a toy is from the same category as previous toys is measured. A change of category from animal to inanimate object causes dishabituation; that is, the child inspects the new object for a longer period when it is from a new category than when it was from the same category as previous objects. This is not a simple perceptual effect, since a fish following a number of different kinds of dogs does not cause dishabituation, even though it is perceptually very different from all the dogs, and an airplane following a number of birds *does* cause dishabituation, despite the perceptual similarities between airplanes and birds. Thus, what seems important here is conceptual similarity rather than perceptual similarity. What might be the basis for this conceptualization? Mandler (1992) suggests that it has to do with movement possibilities, particularly with whether a thing can start to move by itself, to alter its direction of movement by itself, and to move to respond to an infant from a distance. Objects that possess these properties form a single class, the class of animals. Children do appear to distinguish inanimate objects from animals in relation to movement possibilities. For example, when the 1- to 2-year-old children in the Mandler, Bauer, and McDonough (1991) study picked up the toys and made them move, it was observed that some of them would make the animals hop while making the vehicles scoot along in a straight line (Mandler 1992).

If the conceptual distinction between animals and inanimate objects is so firmly established at so early an age, one is less surprised to find that this distinction is sufficiently fundamental to adult semantic memory that one sees double dissociation between the two categories in cases of neuropsychological impairment of semantic memory.

## 21.7 CONCLUSIONS

Many patients with impairments of semantic memory after brain damage have a nonselective impairment: they perform poorly on tests of semantic memory regardless of the semantic category of the stimulus, the type of semantic information that is being probed, or the modality of stimulus input (pictures versus words, for example). Patients Bellini and Edea belong to this category. In some patients, the impairment is selective, and three different forms of selectivity have been reported in the literature. In some patients, performance on semantic memory tasks varies as a function of the semantic category of the stimulus. Michelangelo is one example; for him, performance is worse when the stimulus item is an animal than when it is an inanimate object. In some patients, performance on semantic memory tasks varies as a function of the type of semantic information being probed, and Michelangelo is also an example of this. For him, performance is worse on tasks that require visual information than on tasks that require conceptual information. Finally, in some patients, performance on semantic memory tasks varies as a function of modality of stimulus input (Warrington and McCarthy 1988; but see Caramazza et al. 1990 and Rapp, Hillis, and Caramazza 1993, who query theoretical conclusions drawn from such results). Michelangelo is *not* an example of this pattern since he showed the same pattern of performance (worse with animals than inanimate objects) whether the input was a spoken word or a picture.

It is interesting to consider these neuropsychological data in relation to models of semantic memory developed on the basis of laboratory data gathered from normal subjects. An influential example is the original hierarchical model of Collins and Quillian (1969). Could models of this type account for the various forms of selective deficit of semantic memory described here? Since such models are nodular, category specificity poses no problem; there was an explicit node for "animal" in the original Collins and Quillian model, and if that node were deleted, all knowledge about animals would become inaccessible.

Consider, however, the entries for certain animals in the Collins and Quillian model (Collins and Quillian 1972, fig. 1): *canary* [can sing], [is yellow], *ostrich* [has long thin legs, is tall, cannot fly], *shark* [can bite], [is dangerous] and *salmon* [is pink], [is edible], [swims upstream to lay eggs]. Michelangelo (see, e.g., the task 8 results from Sartori and Job 1988), and patients like him, show preservation of some of these predicates and loss of others. They know that canaries sing, that ostriches cannot fly, that sharks can bite and are dangerous, and that salmon are edible and swim upstream to lay eggs. They do not know that canaries are yellow, that ostriches have long, thin legs and are tall, or that salmon are pink. This mixture of preserved and lost knowledge is inexplicable given models like that of Collins and Quillian; all of these predicates have the same status in the model, and there is nothing to explain why some are lost and some are not in patients like Michelangelo. Nor have such models anything to say about why performance on semantic memory tasks can depend on modality of input. Here are clear illustrations of the way in which the neuropsychological research has improved matters; no longer could anyone say of semantic memory, as Kintsch (1982) did, that "the data from the experiments ... do not provide enough constraints to enable us to decide the issues that everyone is interested in."

That is not to say that we now have a full understanding of semantic memory. If the situation 10 years ago was that we had theories but no constraints, the current situation is almost the reverse. Constraints we have in abundance; now we need theories. To conclude from the neuropsychological data on category specificity that semantic memory must be categorically organized, for example, is really just a redescription of the data, not a serious theory about the nature of semantic memory. But perhaps serious theories are now beginning to emerge. Cognitive neuropsychologists are collaborating with computational modelers to create computational models of semantic processing (Plaut and Shallice 1993)—even to create computational models that, when damaged, exhibit category-specific effects (Farah and McClelland 1991). Modeling of this sort can provide important new information about the functional organization of semantic memory. For example, Farah and McClelland's model is not categorically organized, so their work indicates that one cannot simply infer categorical organization of the underlying system from the observation of category-specific effects after damage.

Students of semantic memory live in exciting times, though perhaps we should heed a warning given us by Collins and Quillian (1972) themselves. Referring to research on semantic memory, they said, "All this is much like tramping around in a new world just discovered. Just about anywhere you go, you find something new, but there is always a good chance of disappearing in the quicksand."

## APPENDIX: CASE HISTORIES

### Bellini

Bellini is a 56-year-old man with 8 years of schooling. He was admitted to a neurological ward in 1985 where a diagnosis of herpes simplex encephalitis was made. He was readmitted in 1987 because of epileptic seizures. The computerized tomography (CT) scan showed a bitemporal necrosis. Neuropsychological investigation in 1985 indicated temporal and spatial disorientation, no aphasia, no dyslexia, and no dysgraphia. A severe anterograde amnesia was detected. A further investigation, conducted in 1992, confirmed the amnesia and the temporospatial disorientation. Disinhibited and stereotyped behavior, presumably caused by the frontal lesions, was evident. The basic neuropsychological findings follow:

| | |
|---|---|
| Raven PM47 | 29/36 |
| Wechsler Adult Intelligence Scale vocabulary standard score | 7 |
| Token test | 33/36 (cutoff = 26.5) |
| Definition of concepts | |
|   Objects | 10/10 |
|   Vegetables | 8/10 |
|   Animals | 5/10 |
| Verbal fluency (categories) | 9 (mean = 19) |
| Digit span | 4 |

| | |
|---|---|
| Paired associate learning | 4 (cutoff > 8.73) |
| Memory for text | |
|    Immediate recall | 6 (cutoff > 15.7) |
|    Delayed recall | 0 |
| Retrograde memory (memory for public events) | 29 (cutoff > 42) |
| Mini Mental State | 20/30 |
| Acalculia test | 80 (cutoff > 74) |

## Edea

Edea is a 57-year-old housewife with 5 years of schooling. In March 1991 she was admitted to the hospital for a cerebral hemorrhage caused by the rupture of an aneurysm of the left posterior communicating artery. The CT scan showed a hypodensity in the mesial sector of the left temporal lobe. A coronal reconstruction showed a lesion of the inferior left temporal gyrus. Basic neuropsychological findings were as follows:

| | |
|---|---|
| Raven PM47 | 31/36 |
| WAIS Vocabulary (scaled score) | 8 |
| Token test | 29/36 (cutoff = 27) |
| Verbal definition of concepts | |
|    Objects | 10/10 |
|    Vegetables | 8/10 |
|    Animals | 6/10 |
| Verbal fluency (categories) | 10 (mean = 19) |
| Digit span | 4 |
| Paired associate learning | 3 (cutoff > 9) |
| Memory for text | |
|    Immediate recall | 3 (cutoff > 16) |
|    Delayed recall | 0 |

## NOTE

We thank Steve Avons, Jean Mandler, Eleanor Saffran, and an anonymous reviewer for valuable criticisms of a draft of this chapter.

## REFERENCES

Basso, A., Capitani, E., and Laiacona, M. (1988). Progressive language impairment without dementia: A case with isolated category specific semantic deficit. *Journal of Neurology, Neurosurgery and Psychiatry, 51*, 1201–1207.

Caramazza, A., Hillis, A. E., Rapp, B., and Romani, C. (1990). Multiple semantics or multiple confusions? *Cognitive Neuropsychology, 7*, 161–168.

Collins, A. M., and Quillian, M. R. (1969). Retrieval time from semantic memory. *Journal of Verbal Learning and Verbal Behaviour, 8*, 240–247.

Collins, A. M., and Quillian, M. R. (1972). Experiments on semantic memory and language comprehension. In L. W. Gregg (Ed.), *Cognition in learning and memory*, 117–137. New York: Wiley.

Coughlan, A. K., and Warrington, E. K. (1981). The impairment of verbal semantic memory: A single case study. *Journal of Neurology, Neurosurgery and Psychiatry, 50*, 1110–1116.

Ellis, A. W., and Young, A. W. (1988). *Human cognitive neuropsychology*. London: Erlbaum.

Farah, M. J., and McClelland, J. L. (1991). A computational model of semantic memory impairment: Modality-specificity and emergent category-specificity. *Journal of Experimental Psychology: General, 120*, 339–357.

Farah, M. J., McMullen, P. A., and Meyer, M. M. (1991). Can recognition of living things be selectively impaired? *Neuropsychologia, 27*, 193–200.

Funnell, E., and Sheridan, J. (1992). Categories of knowledge? Unfamiliar aspects of living and nonliving things. *Cognitive Neuropsychology, 9*, 135–154.

Hart, J. H., Jr., and Gordon, B. (1992). Neural subsystems for object knowledge. *Nature, 359*, 60–64.

Kintsch, W. (1980). Semantic memory: A tutorial. In R. S. Nickerson (Ed.), *Attention and performance VIII*, 595–620. Hillsdale, NJ: Erlbaum.

Mandler, J. M. (1992). How to build a baby: II. Conceptual primitives. *Psychological Review, 99*, 587–604.

Mandler, J. M., Bauer, P. J., and McDonough, L. (1991). Separating the sheep from the goats: Differentiating global categories. *Cognitive Psychology, 23*, 263–298.

Mandler, J. M., and McDonough, L. (1993). Concept formation in infancy. *Cognitive Development*. In press.

McCarthy, R. A., and Warrington, E. K. (1988). Evidence for modality-specific meaning systems in the brain. *Nature, 334*, 428–430.

Plaut, D. C., and Shallice, T. (1993). Deep dyslexia: A case study in connectionist neuropsychology. *Cognitive Neuropsychology, 10*, 377–500.

Quillian, M. R. (1968). Semantic memory. In M. Minsky (Ed.), *Semantic information processing*, 227–270. Cambridge, MA: MIT Press.

Rapp, B., Hillis, A. E., and Caramazza, A. (1993). The role of representations in cognitive theory: More on multiple semantics and the agnosias. *Cognitive Neuropsychology, 10*, 235–249.

Sacchett, C., and Humphreys, G. W. (1992). Calling a squirrel a sguirrel but a canoe a wigwam: A category-specific deficit for artefactual objects and body parts. *Cognitive Neuropsychology, 9*, 73–86.

Sartori, G., and Job, R. (1988). The oyster with four legs: A neuropsychological study on the interaction of visual and semantic information. *Cognitive Neuropsychology, 5*, 103–132.

Sartori, G., Job, R., and Coltheart, M. (1993). The organization of object knowledge: Evidence from neuropsychology. In D. E. Meyer and S. Kornblum (Eds.), *Attention and performance XV*. Cambridge, MA: MIT Press.

Sartori, G., Miozzo, M., and Job, R. (1993). Category-specific naming impairments? Yes. *Quarterly Journal of Experimental Psychology, 46A*, 489–504.

Shallice, T. (1988). *From neuropsychology to mental structure*. Oxford: Oxford University Press.

Silveri, M. C., and Gainotti, G. (1988). Interactions between vision and language in category-specific language impairment. *Cognitive Neuropsychology, 5*, 677–710.

Snodgrass, J. G., and Vandervart, M. (1980). A standardised set of 260 pictures: Norms for name agreement, image agreement, familiarity, and visual complexity. *Journal of Experimental Psychology: Human Learning and Memory, 6*, 174–215.

Stewart, F., Parkin, A. J., and Hunkin, N. M. (1992). Naming impairments following recovery from herpes simplex encephalitis: Category-specific? *Quarterly Journal of Experimental Psychology, 44A*, 261–284.

Tulving, E. (1972). Episodic and semantic memory. In E. Tulving and W. Donaldson (Eds.), *Organization of memory*, 381–403. New York: Academic Press.

Tulving, E. (1983). *Elements of episodic memory*. New York: Oxford University Press.

Tulving, E., and Donaldson, W. (Eds.) (1972). *Organization of memory*. New York: Academic Press.

Warrington. E. K. (1975). The selective impairment of semantic memory. *Quarterly Journal of Experimental Psychology, 27*, 635–657.

Warrington, E. K., and McCarthy, R. A. (1983). Category-specific access dysphasia. *Brain, 106*, 859–876.

Warrington, E. K., and McCarthy, R. A. (1987). Categories of knowledge: Further fractionation and an attempted integration. *Brain, 110*, 1273–1290.

Warrington, E. K., and Shallice, T. (1984). Category-specific semantic impairment. *Brain, 107*, 829–853.

# 22 Semantic Processing of Ignored Stimuli: The Role of Attention in Memory

Shlomo Bentin

ABSTRACT  The possibility that words presented outside the focus of attention are semantically processed has implications for the automaticity and consciousness of word perception, as well as for selective attention and its role in semantic encoding. In a series of studies, we have investigated the role of attention in semantic processing and in encoding semantic information in memory. While subjects studied words presented to one ear for subsequent recognition, event-related potentials (ERPs) were modulated by semantic relations among words presented in the attended but not in the unattended channel. Subsequent explicit recognition was better for attended than for unattended words. However, the percentage of false alarms in recognition was equally elevated by lures semantically related to "old" attended and unattended words. This suggests that words unattended at study were nevertheless semantically processed, and that unattended semantic information is encoded in memory although it may not be available for explicit memory tests. A consequence of attending the stimulus at study may be that its trace in memory is labeled with a mark recognizable by the attention mechanism, so that explicit retrieval is facilitated. According to this conceptualization, a person becomes aware of information stored in memory if it is labeled by the attention mark. This mark, however, may be absent either because an item is not attended at study, or because the attention mark fades independently of the whole memory trace. When the mark is absent, an item cannot be retrieved explicitly but may, nevertheless, be accessed indirectly by implicit testing. Supporting this latter hypothesis, many ERP and performance studies have demonstrated independence between explicit and implicit forms of testing memory.

In everyday life, cognition and awareness are strongly interrelated. Although some psychological theories assume that humans are aware of only a small fraction of their mental activity, cognitive research deals mostly with explicit knowledge and its principles. Nonetheless, the existence of mental processes involving information of which humans are not aware can hardly be denied.

Two forms of cognition without awareness have been extensively investigated during the past two decades. One refers to the possibility that awareness and conscious identification are not necessary conditions for a stimulus to activate the semantic system and access semantic memory (Holander 1986). The second form of cognition without awareness has been described in memory. It has been demonstrated that stored information that is apparently forgotten and not consciously retrievable in direct tests of memory, such as recognition and recall, can influence performance as evidenced by the repetition effect in indirect tests of memory, such as stem or fragment completion (Richardson-Klavehn and Bjork 1988; Schacter 1987). However, implicit evidence for memory should not imply that a semantic memory system is accessed in the absence of conscious recollection. For example, several theorists have posited that repetition priming reflects the operation of a presemantic memory system dedicated to the representation and retrieval of form and structure but not of the meaning and associative properties of words and objects (Schacter 1990; Schacter et al. 1991; Tulving and Schacter 1990). Therefore, despite evidence for unconscious memory, access to semantic memory without awareness still needs to be proved.

Awareness is tightly related to attention. Although the overlap between these two concepts is not complete, we are usually aware of stimuli that we attend but may not be aware of unattended stimuli. In this chapter, I report the results of a study aimed at relating attention to perception and memory, and I address two main questions: whether unattended stimuli access semantic memory and what is the role of attention in memory.

Stimulus identification requires, almost by definition, access to semantic memory. Usually the perceiver is aware of this process and consciously attends to the meaning of the stimulus. However, the possibility of activating semantic attributes of stimuli without awareness has also been raised, and supporting evidence has been provided (Balota 1983; Fowler et al. 1981; Jacoby and Whitehouse 1989; Marcel 1980, 1983). Much of the supporting evidence comes from studies in which direct measures of awareness were dissociated from indirect measures of the consequences of semantic activation (for example, semantic priming of attended words by unattended words). These data have been questioned, however, because the measures of awareness used to obtain them were not sufficiently rigid, so the observed effects may have stemmed from stimuli of which the subjects were, in fact, aware (Holander 1986). Indeed, when more stringent measures of awareness are used, the dissociation between indirect measures of semantic activation and conscious identification of stimuli seems to disappear (Cheesman and Merikle 1984; Joordens and Merikle 1992; Hawley and Johnston 1991).

It is difficult to provide conclusive evidence in this debate, because even if semantic access without awareness does occur, the amount of perceptual input required for producing this phenomenon may be limited to a narrow range. A minimum amount of sensory information is probably necessary to initiate any perceptual phenomenon. Similarly, an identification threshold for accumulated information may govern when a stimulus is consciously identified. Whether semantic access can occur without awareness reverts, then, to the old psychophysical question of whether the detection and the identification thresholds coincide. Many studies have addressed this question by examining perception near either the low or the high limits of the interval between these thresholds. A weakness of the low limit approach is that negative results might occur simply because the amount of information provided to the system is below the absolute detection threshold. On the other hand, the weakness of the complementary high limit approach is that the system may receive too much information, so that some of the stimuli might be consciously identified, and they may account for any semantic activity observed. Yet a virtue of the latter approach is that conclusions from it may usually be based on positive results. Therefore, it is possible to compare the semantic activity induced by stimuli, among which at least part are not consciously identified and the semantic activity induced by stimuli all of which are above the threshold of conscious identification. If the performance in these two conditions is equal, we may conclude that all stimuli were similarly processed, independent of the difference in the level of awareness.

A possible way to manipulate a subject's awareness about a particular group of stimuli is to reduce the amount of attention that is available to these stimuli. This approach has been taken in several studies of semantic activation using divided and selective attention paradigms. A review of the obtained results reveals two predominant positions. One is that semantic processing and the allocation of attentional resources are independent (Deutsch and Deutsch 1963; Shiffrin 1985). This position is supported primarily by findings that unattended words may affect the processing of attended stimuli. These effects were found with visually presented stimuli (Bradshaw 1974; Dallas and Merikle 1976; Shaffer and LaBerge 1979; Underwood 1976) and with dichotic listening (Corteen and Wood 1972; Lewis 1970; Mackay 1973).

A second position is that the amount of semantic processing depends on the allocation of attention and, because the selection of the attended channel is based on "shallow" perceptual attributes such as spatial location, shape, or color, the meaning of unattended stimuli is processed very little, if at all (Broadbent 1971; Broadbent and Gathercole 1990; Johnston and Dark 1986; Kahneman and Treisman 1984; Treisman 1960, 1986). Proponents of the second position have pointed out that in all of the studies whose results suggest semantic processing without attention, the amount of semantic priming was larger when attention was divided between all the stimuli presented than when attention was focused by precueing the target (Dallas and Merikle 1976; Johnston and Wilson 1980; Kahneman, Treisman, and Burkell 1983). In addition, several studies have reported that when semantic processing of unattended words interferes with shadowing attended words, this interference decreases as the subject progresses through the stimulus list. This result suggests that the ability to focus attention improves with training and that when cross-channel interference does occur, attention is probably divided between the two channels (Ambler, Fisicaro, and Proctor 1976; Treisman, Squire, and Green 1974).

The manipulation of selective attention also has proved to be useful for studying unconscious memory. For example, Eich (1984) used a dichotic-listening paradigm in which subjects shadowed a passage presented to one ear while a list of words was simultaneously presented to the other ear. Among the unshadowed words were pairs composed of a nonhomographic homophone such as *deer* (compare with *dear*) and a disambiguating context word (such as *moose*) that biased the interpretation of the homophone toward its less frequent meaning. Two subsequent memory tests were administered. In a direct recognition test, subjects were virtually unable to distinguish "old" from "new" homophones, suggesting that unshadowed words were not attended during study. However, when they had to spell homophones, they revealed a bias toward producing the less common spelling for old but not for new homophones. Thus, the spelling test showed sensitivity to the old/new distinction, providing evidence of a memory about which the subjects were not consciously aware. This dissociation between recognition memory and spelling bias is important not only because it evidences unconscious memory but also because it suggests that unattended words may be processed semantically.

In most studies that have used the selective attention paradigm to investigate semantic processing without awareness, the amount of semantic processing of unattended words is estimated by assessing their effect on attended words. This assessment assumes that semantic relationships between unattended and attended words may influence the processing of attended words only if the semantic information carried by the unattended word has been processed. Therefore, semantic effects spreading from the unattended to the attended channel should denote semantic processing without awareness.

An obvious weakness of this paradigm for investigating semantic activity without awareness is the implicit assumption that subjects do not consciously identify the unattended words. However, even assuming perfect selection, the semantic relationship between the attended target and the unattended prime may reduce the identification threshold and make the unattended primes consciously available. The possibility that conscious identification of unattended words is facilitated by semantic activation from the attended words accentuates the need for an independent measure of awareness of the unattended words and restricts the ability to conclude, using this paradigm, that semantic processing without awareness is psychologically real.

The problem of the interchannels interaction can be solved by confining the analysis of semantic processing to the unattended channel. Although the need for an independent measure of awareness of unattended words is never eliminated, evidence for semantic priming of unattended targets by unattended primes may be a better index of semantic processing without awareness. Such evidence is possible to obtain by recording the electrophysiological activity of the brain and using event-related potential (ERP) measures of semantic priming.

ERPs reflect neural activity associated with stimulus processing. The ERP time-voltage waveform is composed of underlying components, each reflecting different aspects of sensory, cognitive, or motor function. A component is presumed to reflect activation of a neuronal ensemble. The locations and orientations of the neurons within the ensemble, and the time course of their activation, determine the distribution of voltage over the scalp. ERPs are usually recorded simultaneously from many scalp locations; the resulting spatial distribution helps to distinguish among different components. The amplitude and latency (from stimulus onset) of a component is governed by particular stimulus or task characteristics. Therefore, the strategy of much ERP research is to define the factors controlling the amplitude and latency of components and then to use these measures to make inferences about performance in new tasks (for reviews, see Hillyard and Picton 1989; Kutas 1991).

During the past decade, many studies have demonstrated that the ERP elicited by words contains a negative component whose peak occurs at about 400 ms after stimulus onset (N400). This component can be modulated by manipulating the semantic correspondence between a word and the context in which it is embedded (Kutas and Hillyard 1980; Bentin 1989; Kutas and Van Petten 1988). The N400 is also modulated by semantic priming in visual (Bentin, McCarthy, and Wood 1985) as well as auditory lexical decisions (Hollcomb and Neville 1990). Recent accounts of this component suggest that it could be related to a postlexical process of semantic integration (Rugg 1990) or to the process of accessing semantic memory (Bentin and McCarthy, n.d.). Most important for our purposes, semantic priming may modulate the amplitude of N400 even when subjects make no overt responses (Kutas and Hillyard 1984). Therefore, the modulation of N400 may evidence semantic priming between words when the targets as well as the context are not attended. In a series of experiments run in collaboration with Marta Kutas and Steve Hillyard, we used this advantage to examine the effect of selective attention and depth of processing on *on-line* manifestations of semantic priming and on the subsequent semantic activity induced in memory by attended and unattended words.

In a first experiment (Bentin, Kutas, and Hillyard 1993), words and nonwords were auditorily presented to either the left or the right ear. Semantic priming was manipulated by presenting designated target words either immediately following semantically related context words or unrelated context. In one condition, the subjects were instructed to detect and silently count nonwords that were interspersed among the words; in another condition, the subjects were instructed to memorize the words in anticipation of a subsequent recognition test. Although in both conditions all the stimuli were attended, we assumed that studying words from the memory list should induce a more extensive semantic elaboration than simply discriminating nonwords from words. The results showed that although semantic priming reduced the amplitude of N400 elicited by related targets relative to that elicited by unrelated targets in both tasks, the effect was significantly larger when words were studied for recognition than when subjects simply distinguished between nonwords and words (figure 22.1). This interaction between the task and the semantic priming effects on N400 can be accounted for by the levels-of-processing theory. Applied to semantic priming, this theory posits that the magnitude of the semantic priming effect correlates with the depth at which the prime is processed; priming was stronger when the primes were presented in tasks requiring deep processing than in tasks requiring shallow processing (Henik, Friedrich, and Kellogg 1983; Smith, Theodore, and Franklin 1983).

Hence, the results of our initial experiment indicated that N400 modulation is sensitive to the level at which the words eliciting it are processed. Consequently, if unattended words are processed only at a superficial level, semantic priming effects in the unattended channel should be very small. In addition, conforming to the levels-of-processing theory (Craik and Lockhart 1972), explicit memory for unattended words should be weak. In a subsequent study

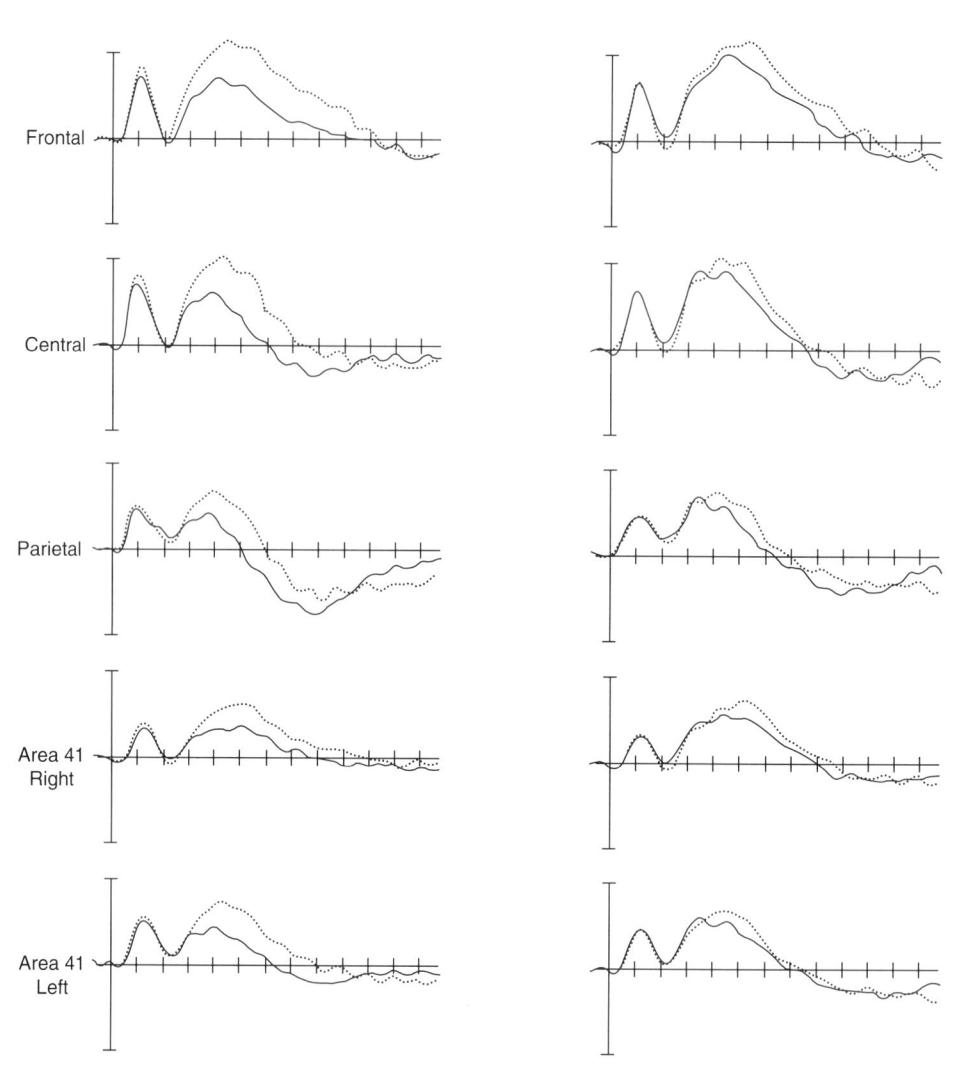

**Figure 22.1** Semantic priming effects on ERP (N400) in two tasks. In the "Memorize" task, subjects studied a list of words anticipating a memory test; in the "Count Nonwords" task, subjects kept a silent count of nonwords that were interspersed in a word list. Here and in the subsequent figures, the ERP polarity is negative up, and the calibration is $+/-5$ uV.

(Bentin, Kutas, and Hillyard, n.d.), we tested these hypotheses directly, using a dichotic listening task.

Our second study included several stages, two of which will be reported here in a greater detail. In a study stage, thirty-two right-handed native English-speaking subjects with normal hearing were instructed to memorize a list of 320 English words presented to one ear while ignoring a list of different 320 words that was simultaneously presented to the other ear. Although from the subjects' point of view all the words presented in the attended ear were equally relevant and all words presented in the unattended ear were equally irrelevant, from our point of view, each list contained a different set of 128 predesignated targets. Among these targets, 64 immediately followed a semantically related word (context) presented in the same ear and 64 followed an unrelated context word. An ERP index of semantic priming was obtained by comparing the amplitudes of N400 elicited by targets in the "related" and "unrelated" conditions. The effect of selective attention on semantic priming was assessed by comparing the target-relatedness effect for targets presented to the attended and unattended ears. If attended words are processed more deeply than unattended words, the N400 difference elicited by primed versus unprimed targets should be larger when the targets are attended than when they are not.

The words were produced by a native English speaker and digitally edited to eliminate irrelevant noises and silence periods and to minimize the differences among word durations. They have been reproduced by an IBM-AT compatible computer equipped with a D/A card (Data Translation Card 2821) and presented through headphones at a comfortable intensity. The durations of the words presented simultaneously to the two ears were identical for about 75 percent of the trials, and on no trial did the duration difference exceed 20 ms.

Across subjects, a complete counterbalanced design was constructed such that each target was attended by half of the subjects and unattended by the other half, appeared equally in the related and unrelated conditions, and was equally presented to the left and right ears. Stimuli were not repeated within subject. However, because both the attended and the unattended lists contained an equal number of related and unrelated targets, the influence of attention on the semantic priming effect could also be assessed within each subject.

Because the left and the right ear words were presented simultaneously, the ERP recorded on each trial represented the composite activity elicited by both words. Therefore, in order to assess the semantic priming effect in each channel separately, a target word in one channel could not be presented simultaneously with a target word in the other channel. In addition, a fixed pattern of alternating target words across channels was also not desirable. Such a pattern was avoided by supplementing the related word pairs in each of the lists with 64 filler words, randomly interspersed among the pairs. A target word in one channel was never paired with a target in the other channel; therefore, the ERP for the "unrelated" condition was elicited by two semantically unprimed

```
Trial           : . . n  n + 1  n + 2  n + 3  n + 4  n + 5  n + 6 . .
Right Channel: . . target filler prime target prime target filler . .
Left  Channel: . . prime target filler filler filler prime target . .
```

Example

```
Right Channel: . . table wall tiger lion daisy horse clock
Left  Channel: . . taxi cow grape paper glass milk chesse
```

Note: Half of the targets were semantically related to the immediately preceding primes and half were unrelated.

**Figure 22.2** Structure of the dichotically presented word lists.

words (an unrelated target in one ear and a word that was either filler or served as prime for a forthcoming target in the other ear), whereas for the "related" condition, the ERP was elicited by a combination of a semantically primed word in one ear and an unprimed word in the other ear (fig. 22.2).

The subjects were instructed to attend to one ear (right or left) and to memorize the words presented in that ear while ignoring words presented in the other ear. After instructions, 44 practice trials were presented. The 320 dichotic test trials followed in four blocks of 80 trials each. The word pairs were presented one every 1000 ms; the between-pair interval (ISI) varied with stimulus duration. Blocks were separated by 45-sec intervals of silence.

On the basis of our previous study (Bentin, Kutas, and Hillyard 1993), we anticipated that semantically primed words would elicit waveforms that are more positive than unprimed words during a relatively long epoch starting at about 300 ms and ending at about 900 ms from stimulus onset, reflecting primarily the modulation of N400 by semantic priming. The mean amplitude in each experimental condition was calculated during this epoch; these values were normalized according to McCarthy and Wood's (1985) procedure to allow comparisons across electrode sites. The normalized mean amplitudes were subjected to factorial analyses of variance (ANOVA) in order to determine the reliability of the differences. The degrees of freedom were adjusted, whenever necessary, according to the Geisser-Greenhouse procedure to compensate for inhomogeneous variances and covariances across treatment levels.

The pattern of the ERPs elicited by target words in the attended and unattended channels during the first 1000 ms from stimulus onset was similar: two main negative components were conspicuous. The first was a relatively sharp peak (N1) at a latency of about 100 ms. Following N1, there was a large and long sustained negative deflection. On the basis of its sensitivity to semantic priming, its scalp distribution, and its peak latency of 400–600 ms, we identified this potential as the N400. No other components were evident during this epoch. Across groups, the mean N400 amplitude (300–900 ms) elicited by unattended targets ($-1.84$ uV) was significantly more negative than that elicited by attended targets ($-1.32$ uV) [$F(1,30) = 15.31, MSe = 7.58, p < .001$), and the N400 elicited by unrelated targets ($-1.75$ uV) was significantly larger than that elicited by related targets ($-1.42$ uV) ($F(1,30) =$

8.24, $MSe = 5.40, p < .008$). However, the most interesting effect in this experiment was the significant Attention × Semantic relatedness interaction ($F(1,30) = 5.96, MSe = 4.91, p < .02$). Planned comparisons revealed that whereas the semantic priming effect in the attended channel was reliable ($p < .01$), the difference between the mean amplitude elicited by related and unrelated targets in the unattended channel did not reach significance. In addition, post hoc comparisons revealed that the N400 elicited by all targets in the unattended channel was as large as the N400 elicited by unrelated targets in the attended channel (fig. 22.3).

In summary, the results of this experiment showed that selective attention has a strong effect on the modulation by semantic priming. Despite a reliable ERP semantic priming effect among words presented to the attended ear, semantic relatedness between words presented to the unattended ear did not significantly modulate the N400 index of semantic priming. Similar effects of selective attention on semantic priming were found with visual presentation (McCarthy and Nobre 1993; Nobre 1992).

These results may suggest that semantic processing without attention is very limited and cast doubts on the view that extensive semantic processing is possible without awareness.

The absence of the N400 index of semantic priming for unattended words, however, is insufficient to determine that unattended words do not access semantic memory automatically, and possibly even without the subject's awareness. For example, because on each trial both an attended and an unattended word were presented, it was impossible to disentangle their separate contribution to the mere generation of N400 that probably indexes a process of accessing semantic memory. Perhaps N400 is generated by unattended as well as by attended words but not affected by semantic priming because its modulation (as opposed to mere generation) requires attention. Indeed previous studies suggested that N400 is sensitive primarily to expectancy or other nonautomatic aspects of processing words in context (Bentin 1987; Kutas, Lindamood, and Hillyard 1984). Moreover, the stimulus onset asynchrony (SOA) between prime and target words in this study (1000 ms) might have been too long for an automatic priming component to contribute. Therefore, these initial results were important primarily in providing evidence that the conscious processing of unattended words was limited relatively to attended words. Other measures, however, were needed to determine whether unattended words accessed semantic memory and to investigate the effect of selective attention at study on the subsequent availability of episodic and semantic traces of studied material. Such measures were obtained testing the subjects' recognition memory for studied words by an "old"/"new" discrimination task.

Semantically processed words are typically recalled and recognized better than superficially processed words (Craik and Lockhart 1972; Jacoby and Craik 1979; Lockhart, Craik, and Jacoby 1976). Therefore, if words presented to the unattended ear did not access semantic memory (as suggested by the N400

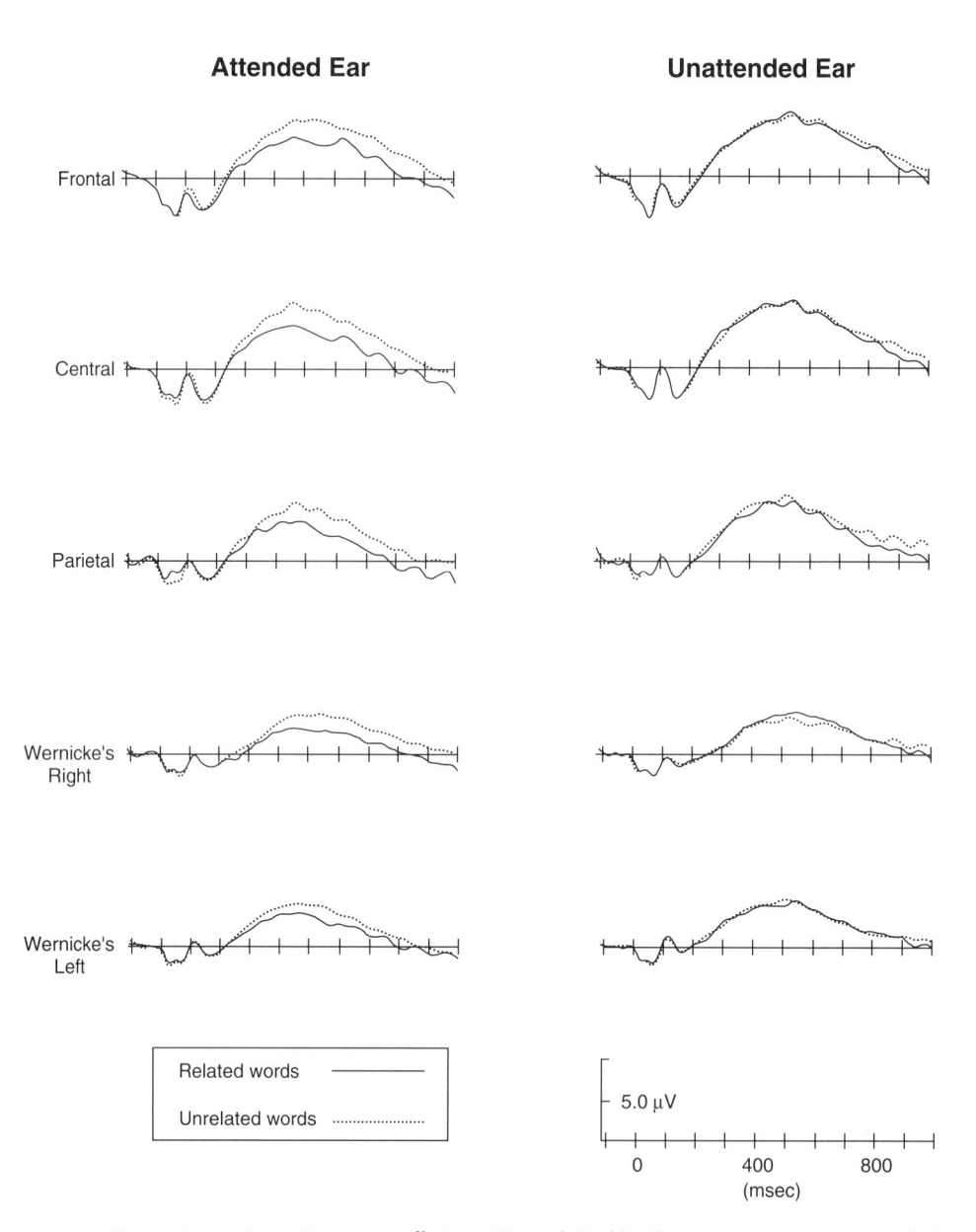

**Figure 22.3** Semantic priming effects on N400 elicited by the same targets in the attended and the unattended condition.

measure of semantic priming), we would expect the discrimination between "old" and "new" words to be better for those attended at study than for those unattended.

On the other hand, it has been shown that the level of word processing at study affects only direct measures of memory. For example, Graf and Mandler (1984) and Graf, Mandler, and Haden (1982) found that a levels-of-processing manipulation did not change the word repetition effect in fragment and stem completion tests. These results indicate that direct tests of memory might be insufficient for a complete assessment of memory for unattended words. Therefore, studies of explicit memory for attended and unattended words need to be complemented by measures that may be independent of conscious processing of words during study yet sensitive to any activity induced by these words within the semantic network. Such a measure was recently suggested by Jacoby and Whitehouse (1989), who found that the probability of false alarms in the recognition test is increased by semantic priming when the subject is not aware of the context word. Therefore, in this experiment, we also used the probability of false alarms to examine semantic activation using, however, a different manipulation.

The recognition test followed study after a short break. The stimulus list contained 210 test words, presented binaurally at a rate of one word every 2.5 sec. The subjects were instructed to press a right-hand button when they heard a word that they remembered as being presented at study regardless of the ear in which the word was presented and the left-hand button when they heard a new word. Speed and accuracy were equally emphasized.

Among the test words in the recognition list there were 100 "old" words and 110 "new" words. All the old words were presented as targets in the study list—50 in the attended channel and 50 targets in the unattended channel.[1] Because at study the lists were fully counterbalanced across subjects, the same 100 words were presented to all subjects, with each word having been attended by half of the subjects and unattended by the other half. Among the new words, 50 were "control" and 60 were "lures" aimed at increasing the percentage of false alarms. The lures were new words (ones not presented at study) semantically related to old unprimed targets. Half of the lures were related to old attended targets and half to old unattended targets. Semantic relationship to old words should increase the probability of false alarms only if the meanings of the old words are activated. Therefore, a lure effect for stimuli that were not attended at study might indicate that they nevertheless accessed their meanings and formed durable semantic traces. A dissociation between the direct (explicit recognition) and indirect (lure effect) measures of memory may suggest that unattended words activated semantic memory without awareness.

Words attended at study were recognized faster and more accurately than unattended words (fig. 22.4). ANOVA showed that the 16 percent decrease in the percentage of hit for old unattended words relative to old attended words was reliable ($F(1,30) = 100.20, MSe = 43.14, p < .0001$), as was the 67-ms increase in reaction time (RT) ($F(1,30) = 9.04, MSe = 7922.6, p < .006$).

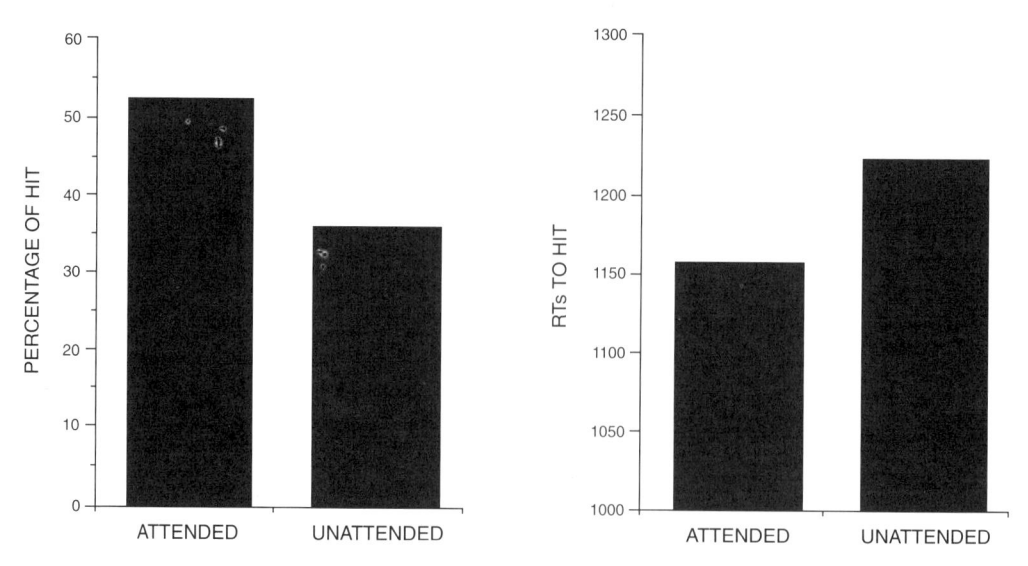

**Figure 22.4** Percentage and reaction times for "hit" responses to words in the attended and unattended study conditions.

The percentage of false alarms was higher for lures than for unrelated new words, and the RTs of these false alarms were faster for lures than for unrelated words (fig. 22.5). ANOVA showed that the effect of semantic relationship was reliable for the percentage of false alarms ($F(2,60) = 4.59, MSe = 53.7, p < .02$), as well as for the speed at which the false alarms were emitted ($F(2,60) = 3.68, MSe = 17986, p < .04$). Post hoc comparisons revealed that attention during study had no effect on the percentage of false alarms. The percentage of false alarms among lures that were related to targets in the attended channel did not differ from the percentage of false alarms among lures related to unattended targets ($HSD_{(p<.05)} = 4.40$ percent). The same pattern was found for RTs. The RTs of false alarms for the lures related to attended targets did not differ from the RTs for lures related to unattended targets ($HSD_{(p<.05)} = 80.6$ ms). As with hit responses, the attend-left and attend-right groups did not differ in the overall percentage of false alarms ($F(1,30) = 0.64$) or in the RTs to the false alarms ($F(1,30) = 0.42$).

The subjects' ability to discriminate between old target words and the different categories of new words, and the effect of selective attention on this ability, was assessed using the $d'$ measure of sensitivity. Six $d'$ measures were calculated for each subject: three reflecting the discrimination between old attended items and new items and three reflecting the discrimination between old unattended items and new items (table 22.1). Differences between these measures were assessed by two-way ANOVA with repeated measures. The factors were Attention at study (attended, unattended) and New word type (unrelated, related to initially attended words, related to initially unattended words).

ANOVA showed that old words attended at study were distinguished from new words significantly better ($d' = 0.6921$) than old words unattended

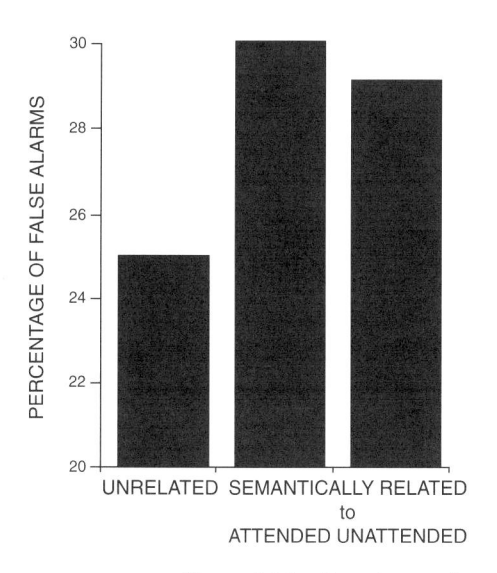

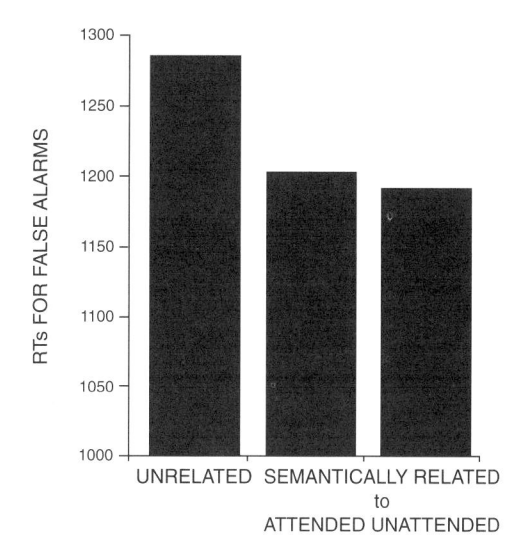

**Figure 22.5** Percentage and reaction times for false alarm responses elicited by unrelated new words and semantic lures that were related to targets presented in the attended and unattended study conditions.

**Table 22.1** $d'$ Values Reflecting Level of Discrimination of Words

| Old Words Type | New Words Type | | |
| --- | --- | --- | --- |
| | Unrelated | Related to Attended | Related to Unattended |
| Attended | 0.8151 | 0.6108 | 0.6540 |
| Unattended | 0.3221 | 0.1317 | 0.1999 |

at study ($d' = 0.2179$) ($F(1,31) = 67.28, MSe = 0.160, p < .0001$). In addition, the ability to distinguish between old and new words varied significantly across the different types of new words ($d' = 0.5686, 0.3712$, and $0.4252$ for unrelated, related to attended, and related to unattended old targets, respectively) ($F(2,62) = 5.37, MSe = 0.124, p < .01$). Most important, as demonstrated by the insignificant interaction between the two factors ($F(2,62) = 0.97, MSe = 0.008, p > .36$), the effect of new word type on $d'$ was similar for all old words, regardless of whether they were or were not attended at study. Post hoc comparisons (Tukey-A) revealed that the discrimination between old words and new words was significantly better if the new words were unrelated ($d' = 0.5686$) than if the new words were semantically related to attended old words ($d' = 0.3712$) or to unattended old words ($d' = 0.4252$). The latter two $d'$ measures were not significantly different from each other.

The most important result of the recognition memory test was that the increase in the false alarm probability caused by semantic relatedness between a new and a studied word was equal for words attended at study and unattended words. This equivalence suggests that the enhanced probability for false alarms for lures related to unattended old words cannot be accounted for by a proportion of these words that might have been, in fact, attended at study. Therefore, the lure effect suggests that unattended words may access the semantic system as well as attended words.

It is not clear, however, when this access occurs. Perhaps unattended words have accessed the semantic memory and activated semantic representations at study. The absence of attention-mediated semantic-priming effects and the significant effect of attention on explicit recognition suggest that such access must have been gained without on-line awareness and conscious identification. Alternatively, however, unattended words may have been stored by a perceptual memory system in a relatively superficially coded trace. These traces could have been reactivated and semantically elaborated by the conscious processing of the semantically related lures during the recognition test. The latter alternative may account for the semantic lure effect on the false alarm probability without assuming that semantic representations have been activated without awareness at study. The data cannot unequivocally distinguish between these two alternatives, but they suggest that the allocation of attention at study determines to a great extent the quality of the traces formed in memory and the manner by which these traces can subsequently be retrieved.

These studies suggest that selective attention significantly affects performance but does not prevent the encoding of unattended spoken words in memory and their semantic processing. The amplitude of the N400 potential, which is sensitive to controlled semantic processes and controlled access to semantic memory (Bentin and McCarthy, n.d.), was significantly reduced by semantic priming when the words were attended, but it was not affected when the same semantically related word pairs were presented to the unattended ear. In a subsequent recognition test, words attended at study were recognized considerably better than unattended words. These results suggest that if neither primes nor targets are attended, the attention-mediated semantic priming effect is severely compromised, and the memory trace established by unattended words is less accessible to conscious retrieval.

On the other hand, semantically induced false alarms in the recognition test occurred equally often for lures related to initially attended and unattended targets. This result suggests that although the memory traces established by unattended stimuli may have been less available to awareness, they could have been semantically elaborated as extensively as those established by attended stimuli.

On the basis of these results, I propose that when attended words are studied, their memory representations (traces) are marked and therefore become subsequently available to the attention mechanism. Conscious retrieval of these traces is also mediated by attention mechanisms. This process requires focusing attention on stored representations and actively searching for the attention marks that were initially attached to attended words during encoding. On the other hand, semantic memory traces can exist without an attention mark. This mark may be absent from a memory trace either because the item was not attended at study or because it faded independently of the whole trace. When the attention mark is absent, the item can no longer be consciously retrieved. However, absence of the attention mark does not prevent the trace from influencing performance. Therefore, indirect tests of memory that do not require awareness and conscious retrieval may provide evidence for the availability of a trace regardless of its being marked for attention or not.

Hence, according to this model and in agreement with processing accounts of the direct/indirect distinction of access to memory (Jacoby 1983; Masson 1989; Roediger 1990; Roediger and Blaxton 1987), the dissociation frequently found between direct and indirect tests of memory does not reflect different memory representations (such as episodic/semantic versus perceptual) but the different involvement of attention mechanisms in each test. Tests that require conscious introspection and awareness of the stored item use attention to search memory. This mechanism detects only traces that are labeled by the putative attention mark. Indirect tests of memory access the same traces automatically. Therefore, this form of access is indifferent to the existence or absence of the attention mark. Frequently, attention-labeled traces are accessed indirectly; in this case, awareness and conscious recollection may be elicited automatically and influence performance in implicit tests. This situation is more common in normal subjects than in amnesiacs, explaining why dissociations between the implicit and explicit evidence for savings are easier to find and more dramatic in the latter population.

The model implies that the content of the trace and the attention mark have an independent existence. One source of evidence of this independence is that unattended or explicitly forgotten stimuli may affect performance in indirect tests of memory. Thus, traces without the attention mark may be psychologically real.

## NOTES

The preparation of this chapter was supported by USA-Israel Binational Foundation Grant 90-105. I thank David Meyer and Danny Goffer for helpful comments on a previous version. Correspondence regarding this chapter should be addressed to Shlomo Bentin, Department of Psychology, Hebrew University, Jerusalem 91905, Israel.

1. Half of the targets (equally represented in each channel) were studied in the semantically related condition and half in the semantically unrelated condition. However, because post hoc comparisons showed no effect of this categorization, the results were collapsed across related and unrelated targets.

## REFERENCES

Ambler, B. A., Fisicaro, S. A., and Proctor, R. W. (1976). Temporal characteristics of primary-secondary message interference in a dichotic listening task. *Memory and Cognition, 4,* 709–716.

Balota, D. A. (1983). Automatic and semantic activation and episodic memory encoding. *Journal of Verbal Learning and Verbal Behavior, 22,* 88–104.

Bentin, S. (1987). Event-related potentials, semantic processes and expectancy factors in word recognition. *Brain and Language, 31,* 308–327.

Bentin S., (1989). Electrophysiology of word perception lexical organization and semantic priming: A tutorial review. *Language and Speech, 32,* 205–220.

Bentin, S., Kutas, M., and Hillyard, S. A. (1993). Electrophysiological evidence for task effects on semantic priming in auditory word processing. *Psychophysiology, 30,* 161–169.

Bentin, S., Kutas, M., and Hillyard, S. A. (n.d.). Semantic processing and memory for attended and unattended words in dichotic listening: Behavioral and electrophysiological evidence. *Journal of Experimental Psychology: Human Perception and Performance.* In press.

Bentin, S., and McCarthy, M. (1994). The effects of immediate stimulus repetition on reaction times and event-related potentials in tasks of different complexity. *Journal of Experimental Psychology: Learning, Memory and Cognition.* In press.

Bentin, S., McCarthy, G., and Wood, C. C. (1985). Event-related potentials, lexical decision, and semantic priming. *Journal of Electroencephalography and Clinical Neurophysiology, 60,* 343–355.

Bradshaw, J. L. (1974). Peripherally presented and unreported words may bias the perceived meaning of a centrally fixated homograph. *Journal of Experimental Psychology, 103,* 1200–1202.

Broadbent, D. E. (1971). *Decision and stress.* New York: Academic Press.

Broadbent, D. E., and Gathercole, E. S. (1990). The processing of nontarget words: Semantic or not? *Quarterly Journal of Experimental Psychology, 42A,* 3–37.

Cheesman, J., and Merikle, P. M. (1984). Priming with and without awareness. *Perception and Psychophysics, 36,* 387–395.

Corteen, R. S., and Wood, B. (1972). Autonomic responses to shock-associated words in unattended channel. *Journal of Experimental Psychology, 94,* 308–313.

Craik, F. I. M., and Lockhart, R. S. (1972). Depth of processing and the retention of words in episodic memory. *Journal of Verbal Learning and Verbal Behavior, 11,* 671–684.

Dallas, M., and Merikle, P. M. (1976). Semantic processing of non-attended visual information. *Canadian Journal of Psychology, 30,* 15–21.

Deutsch, J. A., and Deutsch, D. (1963). Attention: Some theoretical considerations. *Psychological Review, 70,* 80–90.

Eich, J. E. (1984). Memory for unattended events: Remembering with and without awareness. *Memory and Cognition, 12,* 105–111.

Fowler, C. A., Wolford, G., Slade, R., and Tassinary, L. (1981). Lexical access with and without awareness. *Journal of Experimental Psychology: General, 110,* 341–362.

Graf, P., and Mandler, G. (1984). Activation makes words more accessible, but not necessarily more retrievable. *Journal of Verbal Learning and Verbal Behavior, 23,* 553–568.

Graf, P., Mandler, G., and Haden, P. (1982). Simulating amnesic symptoms in normal subjects. *Science, 218,* 1243–1244.

Hawley, K. J., and Johnston, W. A. (1991). Long-term perceptual memory for briefly exposed words as a function of awareness. *Journal of Experimental Psychology: Human Perception and Performance, 17,* 807–815.

Henik, A., Friedrich, F. J., and Kellogg, W. A. (1983). The dependence of semantic relatedness effects upon prime processing. *Memory and Cognition, 11,* 366–373.

Hillyard, S. A., and Picton, T. W. (1987). Electrophysiology of cognition. In F. Plum (Ed.), *Handbook of physiology,* Vol. 5: *Higher functions of the brain,* 519–584. Washington, DC: American Physiological Society.

Holander, D. (1986). Semantic activation without conscious identification in dichotic listening, parafoveal vision, and visual masking: A survey and appraisal. *Behavioral and Brain Sciences, 9,* 1–66.

Hollcomb P. J., and Neville H. J. (1990). Auditory and visual semantic priming in lexical decision: A comparison using evoked potentials. *Language and Cognitive Processes, 5,* 281–312.

Jacoby, L. L. (1983). Perceptual enhancement: Persistent effects of an experience. *Memory and Cognition, 9,* 21–38.

Jacoby, L. L., and Craik, F. I. M. (1979). Effects of elaboration of processing at encoding and retrieval: Trace distinctiveness and recovery of initial context. In L. Cermak and F. I. M. Craik (Eds.), *Levels of processing in human memory,* 1–21. Hillsdale, NJ: Erlbaum.

Jacoby, L. L., and Whitehouse, K. (1989). An illusion of memory: False recognition influenced by unconscious perception. *Journal of Experimental Psychology: General, 118,* 126–135.

Johnston, A. W., and Dark, V. J. (1986). Selective attention. *Annual Reviews in Psychology, 17,* 3–75.

Johnston, A. W., and Wilson, J. (1980). Perceptual processing of nontargets in an attention task. *Memory and Cognition, 8,* 372–377.

Joordens, S., and Merikle, P. M. (1992). False recognition and perception without awareness. *Memory and Cognition, 20,* 151–159.

Kahneman, D., and Treisman, A. (1984). Changing views of attention and automaticity. In R. Parasuraman and D. R. Davis (Eds.), *Varieties of attention,* 29–61. New York: Academic Press.

Kahneman, D., Treisman, A., and Burkell, J. (1983). The cost of visual filtering. *Journal of Experimental Psychology: Human Perception and Performance, 9,* 510–522.

Kutas, M. (1991). Prophesies come true: What's new in event-related brain potential (ERP) research since 1984? In C. Barber and M. J. Taylor (Eds.), *Evoked Potentials Review,* No. 4, 73–91, IEPS Publications.

Kutas, M., and Hillyard, S. A. (1980). Reading senseless sentences: Brain potentials reflect semantic incongruity. *Science, 207,* 203–205.

Kutas, M., and Hillyard, S. A. (1984). Brain potentials during reading reflect word expectancy and semantic association. *Nature, 307,* 161–163.

Kutas, M., and Hillyard, S. A. (1989). An electrophysiological probe of incidental semantic association. *Journal of Cognitive Neuroscience, 1,* 38–49.

Kutas, M., Lindamood, T. E., and Hillyard, S. A. (1984). Word expectancy and event-related potentials during sentence processing. In S. Kornblum and J. Requin (Eds.), *Preparatory states and processes,* 217–234. London: LEA.

Kutas, M., and Van Petten, C. (1988). Event-related potential studies of language. In P. K. Ackles, J. R. Jennings, and M. G. H. Coles (Eds.), *Advances in psychophysiology,* 139–187. Greenwich, CT: JAI Press.

Lewis, J. L. (1970). Semantic processing of unattended messages using dichotic listening. *Journal of Experimental Psychology, 85,* 225–228.

Lockhart, R. S., Craik, F. I. M., and Jacoby, L. (1976). Depth of processing, recognition and recall. In J. Brown (Ed.), *Recall and recognition,* 456–468. New York: Wiley.

Mackay, D. G. (1973). Aspects of theory of comprehension, memory, and attention. *Quarterly Journal of Experimental Psychology, 25,* 22–40.

Marcel, A. J. (1980). Conscious and preconscious recognition of polysemous words: Locating the selective effects of prior verbal context. In R. S. Nickerson (Ed.), *Attention and performance VIII*, 435–457. Hillsdale, NJ: Erlbaum.

Marcel, A. J. (1983). Conscious and unconscious perception: Experiments on visual masking and word recognition. *Cognitive Psychology, 15*, 197–237.

Masson, M. E. J. (1989). Fluent reprocessing as an implicit expression of memory for experience. In S. Lewandowsky, J. Dunn, and K. Kirsner (Eds.), *Implicit memory: Theoretical issues*, 123–138. Hillsdale: NJ: Lawrence Erlbaum.

McCarthy, G., and Nobre, A. C. (1993). *Journal of Electroencephalography and Clinical Neurophysiology, 88*, 210–219.

McCarthy, G., and Wood, C. C. (1985). Scalp distributions of event-related potentials: An ambiguity associated with analysis of variance models. *Electroencephalography and Clinical Neurophysiology, 62*, 203–208.

Moscovitch, M. (1985). Memory from infancy to old age: Implications for theories of normal and pathological memory. *Annals of the New York Academy of Sciences, 444*, 78–96.

Moscovitch, M., and Bentin, S. (1993). On the fate of implicit memory when explicit memory is near to chance. *Journal of Experimental Psychology: Learning Memory and Cognition, 19*, 148–158.

Nobre, A. C. (1992). Linguistic processing in the human brain: Neurophysiological studies of neural organization and selective attention. Unpublished Ph.D. dissertation, Yale University.

Richardson-Klavehn, A., and Bjork, R. A. (1988). Measures of memory. *Annual Review of Psychology, 39*, 475–543.

Roediger, H. L. III (1990). Implicit memory: Retention without remembering. *American Psychologist, 45*, 1043–1056.

Roediger, H. L. III, and Blaxton, T. A. (1987). Retrieval modes produce dissociations in memory for surface information. In D. S. Gorfein and R. R. Hoffman (Eds.), *Memory and cognitive processes: The Ebbinghaus Centennial Conference*. Hillsdale, NJ: Erlbaum.

Rugg, M. D. (1990). Event-related brain potentials dissociate repetition effects of high and low-frequency words. *Memory and Cognition, 18*, 367–379.

Schacter, D. L. (1987). Implicit memory: History and current status. *Journal of Experimental Psychology: Learning Memory and Cognition, 13*, 501–518.

Schacter, D. L. (1990). Perceptual representation systems and implicit memory: Toward a resolution of the multiple systems debate. *Annals of the New York Academy of Science, 608*, 543–571.

Schacter, D. L., Cooper, L. A., Tharan, M., and Rubens, A. B. (1991). Preserved priming of novel objects in patients with memory disorders. *Journal of Cognitive Neurosciences, 3*, 117–130.

Shaffer, W. O., and LaBerge, D. (1979). Automatic semantic processing of unattended words. *Journal of Verbal Learning and Verbal Behavior, 18*, 413–426.

Shiffrin, R. M. (1985). Attention. In R. C. Atkinson, R. J. Hernstein, G. Lindsey, and R. D. Luce (Eds.), *Stevens' handbook of experimental psychology*. New York: Wiley.

Smith, M. C., Theodore, L., and Franklin, P. E. (1983). The relationship between contextual facilitation and depth of processing. *Journal of Experimental Psychology: Learning Memory and Cognition, 9*, 697–712.

Treisman, A. (1960). Contextual cues in selective listening. *Quarterly Journal of Experimental Psychology, 12*, 205–219.

Treisman, A. (1986). Features and objects in visual processing. *Scientific American, 255,* 106–115.

Treisman, A., Squire, R., and Green, J. (1974). Semantic processing in dichotic listening? A replication. *Memory and Cognition, 2,* 641–646.

Tulving, E., and Schacter, D. L. (1990). Priming and human memory systems. *Science, 247,* 301–306.

Underwood, G. (1976). Semantic interference from unattended printed words. *British Journal of Psychology, 67,* 327–338.

# 23 The Effect of Orthographic-Semantic Systematicity on the Acquisition of New Words

Jay G. Rueckl and Itiel E. Dror

ABSTRACT  According to connectionist models of word identification, semantic access occurs though an interactive associative mapping process. To test this account, subjects were asked to learn the definitions assigned to a set of pseudowords, and the systematicity of these assignments (i.e., the degree to which similarly spelled pseudowords were associated with semantically similar definitions) was varied. As predicted, the systematicity of the associations influenced both the rate of learning and performance on a subsequent tachistoscopic identification task.

## 23.1  INTRODUCTION

In alphabetic languages such as English, the mapping from orthography to phonology is far more regular than the mapping from orthography to semantics. That is, although there are some exceptions, most words that look alike also sound alike. In contrast, at least among morphologically simple words, similarly spelled words (e.g., *take, lake*) rarely have similar meanings. For users of the language, this difference is far from trivial. The structure of the phonological mapping means that one can learn to pronounce most written words, familiar or not, by learning the rules that relate spelling and sound. The structure of the semantic mapping, on the other hand, implies that word meaning must be learned on a case-by-case basis and that the meaning of an unfamiliar word must be inferred on the basis of something other than its spelling.

The properties of the two mappings are also important for psychologists interested in how each mapping is computed. The central issue in the study of the mapping from spelling to sound is whether phonological codes are assembled from prelexical orthographic codes or addressed by a lexical code (Carr and Pollatsek 1985; Humphreys and Evett 1985; Van Orden, Pennington, and Stone 1990). In contrast, the arbitrary nature of the mapping from spelling to meaning seems to preclude the possibility that semantic codes are assembled using rulelike procedures. Instead, it is generally held that semantic access also occurs solely through an addressing process.

The goal of this chapter is to elucidate some of the characteristics of the processes involved in accessing semantic information during reading. We will suggest that the process that maps from orthography to semantics is both associative and interactive; that is, it is the kind of process computed by connectionist networks. We begin by developing an account of this process based on the principles of the connectionist approach to cognitive modeling. We then report the results of an experiment testing several predictions derived from this account.

## 23.2 THE CONNECTIONIST APPROACH

A connectionist network consists of a set of simple, highly interconnected processing units that communicate by sending excitatory and inhibitory signals over weighted connections. At a molecular level, the behavior of a connectionist network is determined by two functions: an activation function, which determines the activation of each node as a function of the input it receives from other nodes and/or the environment, and a learning rule, which modifies the strength of each connection in order to encode knowledge acquired through experience. At a more global level, the behavior of a connectionist network exhibits a number of emergent properties, such as pattern recognition, pattern completion, automatic generalization, and graceful degradation, that make these networks attractive candidates for models of cognitive processes (Rumelhart and McClelland 1986).

Although connectionist models have been proposed for a variety of cognitive domains, one domain that has been of particular interest to the connectionist community is visual word identification. In the past few years, connectionist models of a number of processes involved in word identification have been developed (Farah and McClelland 1991; Golden 1986; Hinton and Shallice 1991; Masson 1991; Mozer 1987; Seidenberg and McClelland 1989; Van Orden, Pennington, and Stone 1990). These models, like their nonconnectionist counterparts (Forster 1979; Morton 1979), are founded on the assumption that the lexical processing system comprises a number of subsystems, each dedicated to a particular computation needed for reading words and naming them aloud. In the connectionist approach, this decomposition is accomplished by organizing the network into sets of nodes called modules.

Figure 23.1 illustrates a general connectionist framework for modeling the lexical system (Seidenberg and McClelland 1989). The basic premise of this framework is that reading a word entails the computation of at least three types of codes: orthographic, semantic, and phonological. Thus, the organization of the network includes three modules, each dedicated to the representation of one of these three codes. In addition, the network includes "hidden" nodes of two sorts: intermediate nodes, which allow a network to overcome significant limitations on the sort of transformations that can be performed (Hinton, McClelland, and Rumelhart 1986; Minsky and Papert 1969), and clean-up nodes, which facilitate the "settling" process that occurs within each module. When a word is seen, early visual processing is assumed to provide input to the orthographic module. Activation then flows throughout the network, such that over time, the network settles into a pattern of activity representing the orthographic, semantic, and phonological properties of the stimulus.

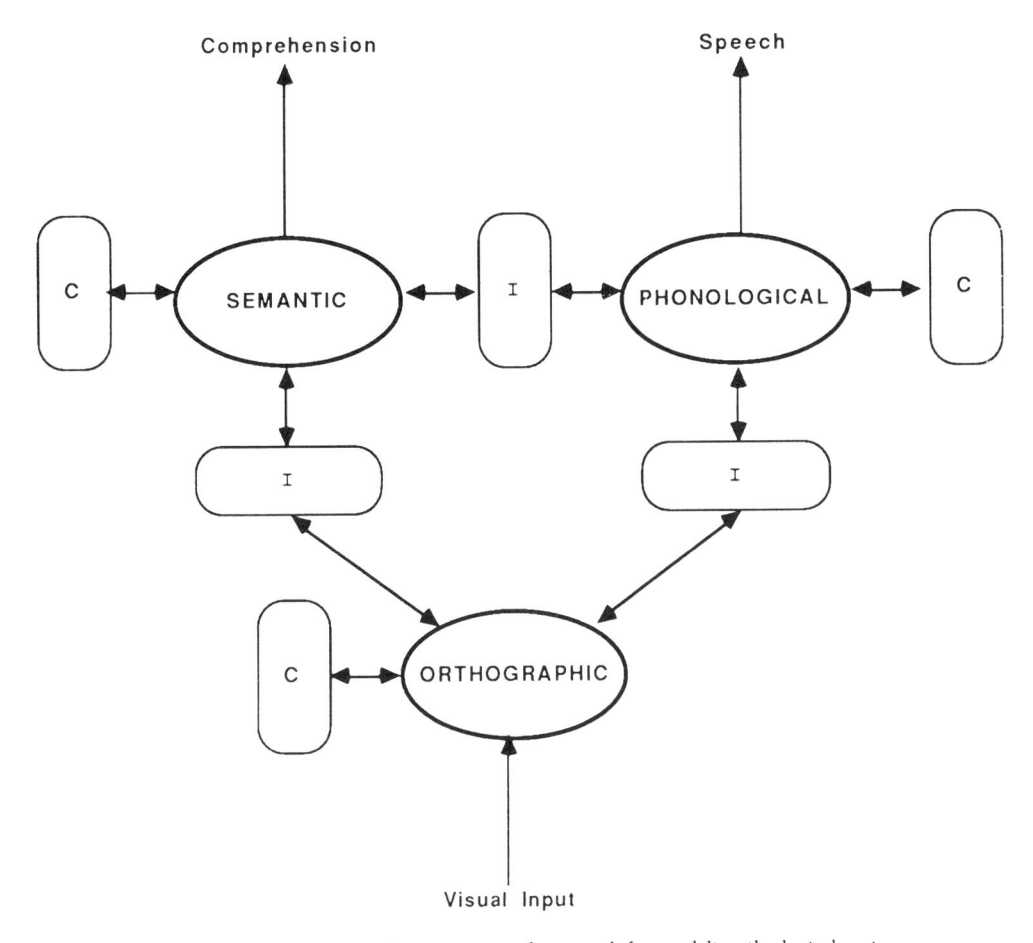

**Figure 23.1** A general connectionist framework for modeling the lexical system.

A number of points about the model should be noted. First, the various properties of a word are encoded by distributed representations—patterns of activity over a set of nodes. (See Dror, n.d., and Hinton, McClelland, and Rumelhart 1986 for discussions of distributed representation and its role in cognitive modeling.) These representations are chosen so that words that are similar in spelling, meaning, or pronunciation are represented by similar patterns of activity over the orthographic, semantic, or phonological modules, respectively. Second, processing is assumed to be interactive; the construction of a pattern of activity in one module influences, and is influenced by, the construction of patterns of activity in the modules to which it is connected. Third, the phonological code can be computed either directly, on the basis of orthographic information, or indirectly, by first constructing the semantic code; similarly, the semantic code can be computed either directly or via phonological mediation.[1] Fourth, although the model depicted in figure 23.1 includes only three representational modules, it is in the spirit of the model to assume that other modules might exist (say, for computing the syntactic or thematic properties of a word) and that the proposed modules may be decomposed further (for example, there may be a number of "semantic" modules, organized on the basis of content or modality; Farah and McClelland 1991).

## 23.3 THE ORTHOGRAPHIC-SEMANTIC PATHWAY

Although full-scale simulations of the entire network depicted in figure 23.1 have not yet been carried out, a number of studies investigating various components of the network have been reported. For example, both Seidenberg and McClelland (1989) and Sejnowski and Rosenberg (1987) constructed networks that modeled the pathway from the orthographic module to the semantic module. In a different vein, Mozer (1987) and McClelland (1985) developed networks modeling the interface between the visual and orthographic systems, and Golden (1986) investigated how the orthographic module might encode and use orthographic knowledge.

The focus of this chapter is on the pathway between the orthographic and semantic modules. A connectionist model of this pathway was developed by Hinton and Shallice (1991) and subsequently extended by Plaut and Shallice (1991).[2] The primary goal of Hinton and Shallice's work was to investigate whether damage to their network resulted in patterns of behavior similar to those found in the form of acquired dyslexia known as deep dyslexia. They trained their network to respond to an orthographic input pattern by producing the semantic pattern associated with that input. They then "lesioned" their network by removing subsets of the nodes or connections or by adding noise to the weights on the connections. They found that when the network failed to produce the correct response to a familiar input, the pattern of mistakes resembled the pattern observed in deep dyslexia. In particular, the network (like patients classified as deep dyslexics) made a variety of errors, including semantic errors (e.g., given the input for *cat*, responding with the semantic pattern for *dog*), visual errors (e.g., *cat* → *can*), and mixed visual and semantic errors (e.g., *cat* → *rat*).

To account for the joint occurrence of visual and semantic errors, and in particular for the occurrence of mixed visual and semantic errors, which occur at a rate higher than would be predicted on the basis of the independent probabilities of visual and semantic errors (Shallice and Coughlin 1980; Shallice and McGill 1978), traditional "box-and-arrow" models of the lexicon must assume two independent loci of damage: damage early in the system to produce visual errors and damage deeper in the system to produce semantic errors. In contrast, Hinton and Shallice found that in their network, a single locus of damage resulted in both visual and semantic errors. Indeed, although the relative frequencies varied, the same qualitative pattern of errors was observed regardless of where along the semantic pathway damage was inflicted.

To understand why this occurs, it is useful to think of the network as having two components. One component includes the feedforward connections linking the orthographic, intermediate, and semantic units, and the other includes the recurrent connections between the semantic and cleanup units.

The first component performs an associative mapping between patterns of activation in the orthographic module and patterns of activation in the semantic module. With enough training, the network can learn to map the orthographic pattern for each word to the exact semantic pattern representing the meaning of that word. However, due to the constraints of superimpositional memory storage, networks prefer to map similar input patterns to similar output patterns, and thus an arbitrary mapping, such as that from spelling to meaning, is relatively difficult to learn.

The difficulty of this task could be reduced if the feedforward component was provided with a margin of error, so that its input to the semantic module needed only to result in a pattern of activity that was roughly similar to the correct pattern. This is the role of the recurrent component; it serves to "clean up" the input to the semantic module by causing a pattern of activity similar to a word's definition to move toward that definition. Thus, due to the action of the recurrent component, patterns of activity corresponding to the meanings of familiar words act as "attractors," and the patterns of semantic activity drawn to each meaning define its "basin of attraction." Given these basins of attraction, the feedforward component can map an orthographic pattern anywhere within the correct basin, and the network will respond appropriately.

Because words with similar meanings are represented by similar semantic patterns, the basins of attraction for these words tended to be near one another. Interestingly, the attractor basins for similarly spelled words also tended to be near one another. This allowed the associative mapping function to map similarly spelled words to nearby points in semantic space, in accordance with the preference noted earlier; the attractor basins then pulled these initial semantic patterns away from one another and toward their respective target patterns (fig. 23.2). From this, it is easy to see why damage to the network produced the observed pattern of errors. Damage to the feedforward component distorts the associative mapping function. Damage to the recurrent component moves the boundaries of the basins of attraction. Either form of damage sometimes results in the initial semantic pattern's falling into a basin of attraction other than the correct one. Because words that are similar in either spelling or meaning are likely to have nearby basins of attraction, when the initial semantic pattern falls into the wrong basin, a visual, semantic, or mixed error often results.

## 23.4 THE ORTHOGRAPHIC-SEMANTIC PATHWAY IN NORMAL READING

In subsequent work, Plaut and Shallice (1991) extended the Hinton and Shallice model to cover a wider range of findings concerning deep dyslexia and demonstrated that, provided certain critical assumptions are met, the account holds across various architectures and learning and activation algorithms. Together, the Hinton and Shallice (1991) and Plaut and Shallice (1991) results provide strong support for a connectionist account of deep dyslexia. For this account to remain viable, it is important that it provide a compelling model of

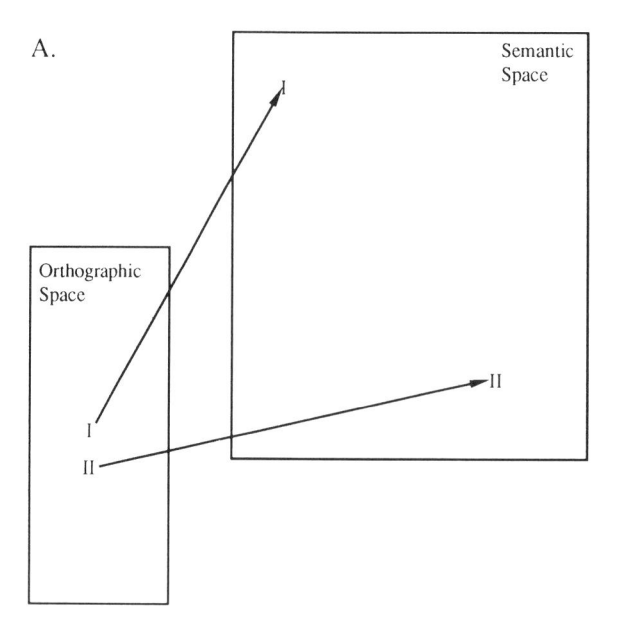

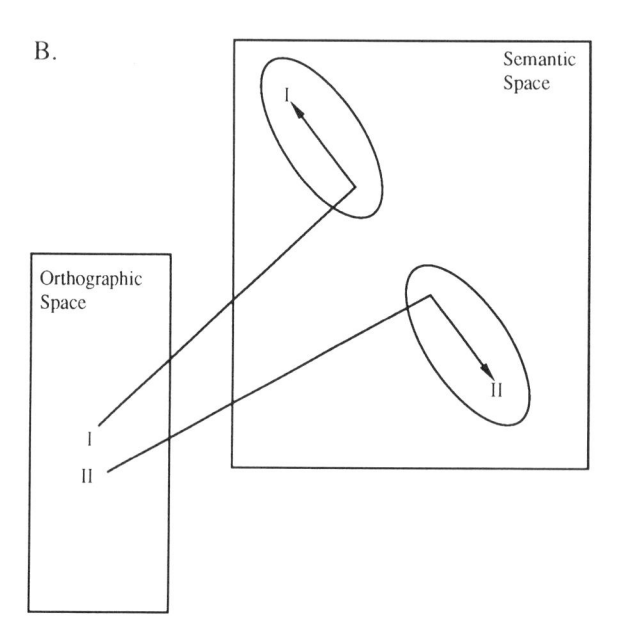

**Figure 23.2** *a*. Without recurrence, the feedforward component must map the orthographic representation of each word to the exact semantic pattern representing its meaning. This is a difficult task when, as illustrated here, similar inputs are mapped to dissimilar outputs. *b*. With recurrence, the network can construct basins of attraction that pull activity in the semantic module toward target patterns. Given appropriate attractors, the feedforward component can map similar words to nearby points in semantic space, even though their meanings are far apart. (Adapted from Hinton and Shallice 1991.)

the behavior of normal readers as well. Ideally, such an account would involve not only explaining previously reported findings but also generating new predictions that can be put to the test.

A good foundation for deriving new predictions is provided by the general principles describing the behavior of connectionist networks. One such principle was alluded to earlier: connectionist networks tend to map similar inputs to similar outputs. Hinton and Shallice (1991) demonstrated how this tendency results in the pattern of errors observed when damage is inflicted on their network. More generally, Rueckl, Kolodny, and McPeek (n.d.) examined how the behavior of connectionist networks varies as a function of the associative mapping it computes. They found that the systematicity of the mapping (the degree to which similar inputs are associated with similar outputs) is an important determinant of a network's behavior; systematic mappings are learned faster and to better levels of performance and are less susceptible to proactive and retroactive interference.

There are several ways in which the effects of systematicity on human behavior might be investigated. One approach is to examine how systematicity influences the processing of familiar items. For example, in English the mapping from spelling to sound is relatively systematic: similarly spelled words typically sound similar as well. However, there are also exceptions to this general rule (consider, for example, the contrast between *gave, cave*, and *wave* versus *have*). Thus, one might view the orthographic input space as consisting of a number of regions that vary in the systematicity of their mapping to phonology. As it turns out, a number of studies have found that the time needed to name a visually presented word varies with the systematicity of its region: words from systematic regions (the so-called regular consistent words) are named faster than words from less systematic regions, and among the latter, regularly pronounced words are named faster than exceptions (Baron and Strawson 1976; Glushko 1979; Seidenberg et al. 1984; see Seidenberg and McClelland 1989 for a connectionist interpretation of these findings).

An alternative to studying the effects of systematicity on the processing of familiar items is to look at its effects on the acquisition of new associations. Given the arbitrary nature of the mapping from spelling to meaning, this latter approach seems particularly appropriate for investigating the orthographic-semantic pathway. Thus, in the experiment reported below, subjects were asked to learn the meanings assigned to a set of pseudowords, and the systematicity of these sets of associations was varied. The connectionist account leads to at least two predictions about the effects of systematicity in this situation. First, just as connectionist networks learn systematic mappings more quickly than nonsystematic mappings (Rueckl, Kolodny, and McPeek, n.d.), so too should subjects learn systematic mappings more quickly. Second, in a perceptual identification task, pseudowords that are systematically related to their definitions should be more readily identified than pseudowords from a nonsystematic training set.

The logic underlying the first prediction is straightforward. The rationale for the latter prediction may be less intuitive. It is based on the assumption that word identification is an interactive process, so that semantic information influences the construction of orthographic codes, and vice versa. Given this, the systematicity of the new associations would be expected to influence the construction of both codes. In the feedforward direction, the input to the semantic module would depend in part on which semantic patterns had been associated with pseudowords that resemble the stimulus being processed. If the associations are systematic, these patterns would be similar to the correct response, and thus they would tend to facilitate the construction of the correct semantic code. Similarly, as the semantic code is constructed, the semantic module provides feedback to the orthographic module. In this case, the effect of this feedback depends on which pseudowords had been associated with semantic patterns similar to the current one. Given a systematic mapping, these pseudowords would be orthographically related, so that the feedback would be concentrated in one orthographic neighborhood. In contrast, if the mapping was not systematic, the relevant semantic patterns would be associated with orthographically dissimilar pseudowords, resulting in the partial activation of orthographic patterns unlike the correct one and slowing the construction of the orthographic code.[3]

Subjects in several recent studies (Dagenbach, Horst, and Carr 1990; Forster 1985; Rueckl and Olds 1993; Whittlesea and Cantwell 1987) have been asked to learn the definitions assigned to a set of pseudowords. Although the results of these studies indicate that only a few learning trials are needed for these associations to have an effect on identification, it appears that extensive training is required before the new associations are fully integrated with a reader's prior knowledge. For example, Dagenbach, Horst, and Carr (1990) found that new orthographic-semantic associations gave rise to normal semantic priming when training occurred extensively over a 5-week period but not when training took place within a single, 15-min session. Thus, following these researchers, our subjects were trained on a set of pseudoword-definition associations over a 5-week period. Cued recall tasks were used to track the course of learning over this period, and perceptual identification tasks were administered during the final 2 weeks in order to investigate the effects of systematicity on the identification of the pseudowords.

## 23.5 METHOD

### Subjects

Twenty-four Harvard University undergraduates served as subjects; each was paid $60 for participation.

### Design and Materials

The stimuli were thirty-six pseudowords and thirty-six definitions. The pseudowords consisted of six sublists of six items. Each sublist was formed by generating a word ending (*-urch, -rint, -arsh, -loon, -elly,* and *-eace*), and then finding six letters that could be affixed to that ending to form orthographically legal five-letter pseudowords The definitions also consisted of six sublists of six items; in this case, all items on a sublist belonged to the same semantic category. (The categories were animals, body parts, furniture, fruit, clothes, and kitchen utensils.) Both the pseudowords and the definitions were chosen to maximize within-group similarity and minimize between-group similarity.

The pairing of pseudowords and definitions varied across subjects. For subjects in the systematic condition, pseudowords and definitions were matched by sublist, so that all members of a particular pseudoword sublist were paired with definitions from the same semantic category (e.g., the pseudowords *durch, hurch,* and *kurch* were paired with the definitions *dog, cat,* and *bear*). In the nonsystematic condition, no two pseudowords from a given sublist were paired with members of the same category, and each semantic category included definitions paired with members of each of the pseudoword sublists. (For example, for some subjects *durch, hurch,* and *kurch* were paired with *dog, shirt,* and *table.*) Two such pairings were constructed for both the systematic and nonsystematic conditions.

### General Procedure

At the beginning of the study, each subject was given a list of pseudoword definition pairs and was told that he or she would perform a variety of tasks over a 5-week period measuring vocabulary acquisition. Each subject came into the laboratory once a week to perform the memory and identification tasks. In addition, each subject completed a sentence generation task at home three times each week. In this task, the thirty-six pseudowords were listed on a sheet of paper, and the subject was instructed to compose a sentence using each pseudoword correctly. After all thirty-six sentences had been written, the subject determined whether each pseudoword had been used correctly by consulting the list of pseudoword definition pairs. If a pseudoword had been used incorrectly, the subject crossed out the sentence he or she had written and replaced it with a sentence in which the pseudoword was used correctly.

### Memory Tasks

For the first 3 weeks, the laboratory session began with a 10-minute period during which the subject was to study the list of pseudoword definition pairs. Each subject then completed ten cued recall tasks. In each task, the subject was given a list of the pseudowords or definitions and was given $2\frac{1}{2}$ min to write down the item associated with each cue. Upon the completion of each list, the subject was given an answer key and told to note any mistakes and take the opportunity to attempt to learn the correct response. Both pseudowords and definitions were used as cues, and the pseudoword-cue and definition-cue tasks were alternated.

Memory tasks were also administered in the fourth and fifth weeks. In the fourth week, each subject completed five pseudoword-cue tasks like those completed during weeks 1–3. At the end of the last session, each subject completed a free-recall task by writing down as many of the pseudoword definition pairs as he or she could remember.

**Identification Tasks**

During the fourth and fifth weeks, each subject also performed several tachistoscopic identification tasks. The week 4 session began with a task designed to determine the presentation duration at which word identification accuracy was about 50 percent. Each subject was presented with a series of fifty five-letter words at durations varying from 33 to 100 ms in 17-ms intervals. Each word was preceded by a fixation point and followed by a pattern mask. For most subjects, the 33-ms duration resulted in an accuracy level closest to 50 percent. The one exception required a 50-ms duration to achieve this level of performance.

Later in the fourth session, each subject performed another tachistoscopic identification task, similar to the first except that the stimuli for this task included the pseudowords from the training set, eighteen unfamiliar pseudowords, and thirty-six five-letter words not presented during the first task. The stimulus duration for this task was the duration that resulted in an accuracy level closest to 50 percent in the previous task. In the fifth week, another identification task was administered: the pseudowords from the training set were again presented, along with a new set of words and unfamiliar pseudowords.

Because several prior studies (Forster 1985; Rueckl and Olds 1993; Whittlesea and Cantwell 1987) investigated the effect of new orthographic-semantic associations on repetition priming, a priming manipulation was also included in the present study. Thus, each subject performed a cued recall task immediately before the identification task. In the cued recall task, half of the pseudowords from the training set were presented sequentially on the computer monitor. The subject's task was to say aloud the definition associated with each pseudoword. Different subsets of the pseudowords were primed during the fourth and fifth weeks.

## 23.6 RESULTS

**Memory Tasks**

Figure 23.3 presents the results from the cued recall tasks in order of presentation. As is apparent in the figure, subjects in the systematic condition learned the associations more quickly, although by the end of the fourth week, recall was nearly perfect in both conditions.

As a simple statistical analysis of these results, the average score for each subject in each of the four weeks was computed. An analysis of variance revealed that although performance was on average better in the systematic condition, this difference was not statistically significant ($F(1,66) = 2.47, p <$

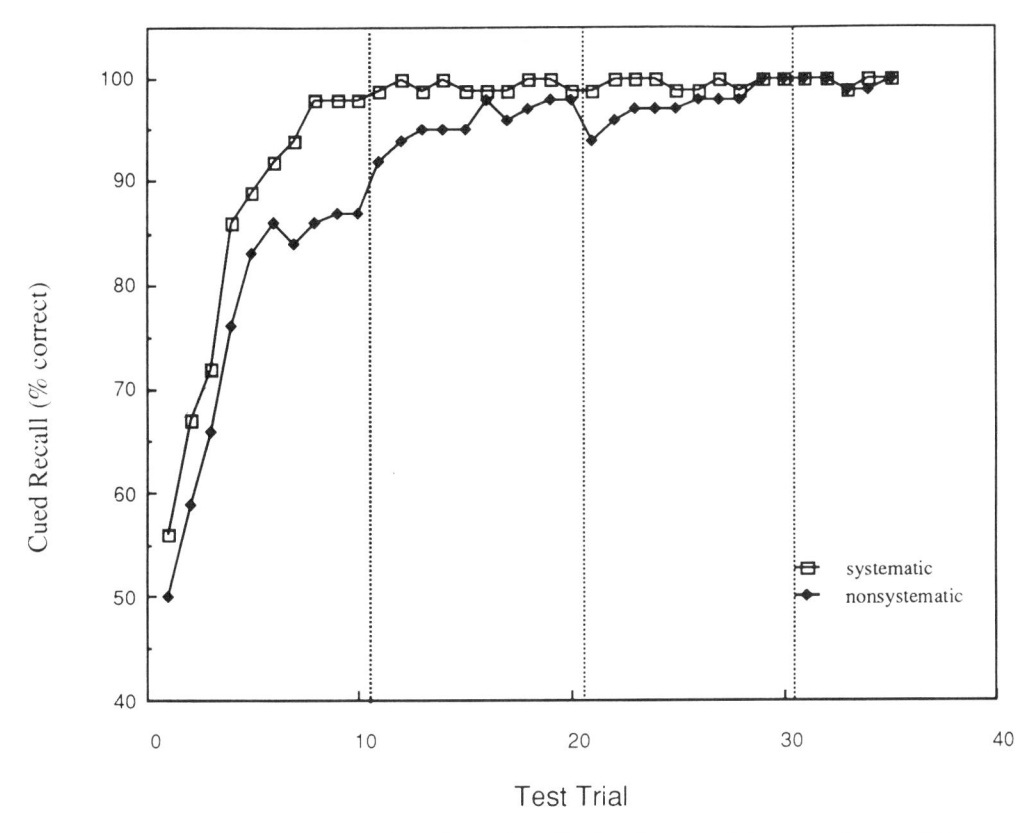

**Figure 23.3** Results from the cued recall tasks administered during weeks 1–4. Trials 1–10 were administered in the first week, 11–20 in the second week, 21–30 in the third week, and 31–35 in the fourth week.

.14). However, this might be expected, given the small number of subjects and the convergence of performance toward the end of the training period. A planned comparison indicated that in the first week, the systematic associations were more accurately recalled ($F(1,83) = 5.779, p < .02$). This difference was not significant in weeks 2–4, although it should be noted that recall was consistently worse in the nonsystematic condition and that this difference was particularly pronounced on the first few tasks performed each week.

Several additional measures also indicate that subjects in both groups had learned the associations quite well by the end of the study. First, in addition to the cued recall tasks reported above, in the fourth and fifth weeks cued recall tasks were also administered immediately before the identification tasks in order to study the effects of repetition priming. Performance on these tasks was at ceiling for both groups; in the fourth week, the proportion of correct responses was .99 for both groups, and in the fifth week, the analogous values were .99 and .98 for the systematic and nonsystematic conditions, respectively. Similarly, the proportion of associations remembered in the free-recall task at the end of the fifth week was .96 in the systematic condition and .95 in the nonsystematic condition.

## Identification Tasks

Table 23.1 presents the proportion of correct responses in the identification tasks administered during weeks 4 and 5. In general, pseudowords in the systematic condition were identified more accurately than pseudowords in the nonsystematic condition, but this effect interacted with repetition priming ($F(1,22) = 5.746, p < .05$). When unprimed, the advantage for pseudowords in the systematic condition was .15 in week 4 ($t(22) = 1.886, p < .05$, one-tailed) and .10 in week 5, ($t(22) = 1.244, p < .15$). However, for stimuli that had been primed, the effect of systematicity was .04 in week 4 and .02 in week 5 (neither difference approached significance).

Several other aspects of the results should be noted. First, priming had quite different effects in the systematic and nonsystematic conditions. In the nonsystematic condition, pseudowords that had been primed were more accurately identified in both week 4 ($t(11) = 2.064, p < .05$) and week 5 ($t(11) = 2.236, p < .05$). In contrast (and rather surprisingly), in the systematic condition primed pseudowords showed no advantage whatsoever. There are several possible explanations for this. Conceivably, the differential effect of priming in the two conditions may be directly related to differences in the systematicity of the orthographic-semantic associations, although why this might be is not readily apparent. Alternatively, the lack of a priming effect in the systematic condition may simply be due to a ceiling effect. Given all the factors that limit performance and create variability in a tachistoscopic identification task, it may well be that in practice, the ceiling on performance is something less than 100 percent accuracy. If performance in the unprimed condition was near the true ceiling, any benefits of priming would go undetected.

An additional point about the results is that the differences between the systematic and nonsystematic conditions appear to be smaller in week 5 than in week 4. Although this trend is small and not statistically significant, a reduced effect of systematicity with continued training would certainly be expected. The reason is that as the familiarity of a given stimulus increases, knowledge of other stimuli has less effect on its processing. This same principle accounts for the widely observed finding that the effects of factors such as orthographic and phonological regularity are far greater for low-frequency words than for high-frequency words (Seidenberg and McClelland 1989).

**Table 23.1** Proportion of Correct Responses in the Identification Tasks

|  | Primed | Unprimed |
|---|---|---|
| Week 4 | | |
| Systematic | .80 | .84 |
| Nonsystematic | .76 | .69 |
| Week 5 | | |
| Systematic | .81 | .81 |
| Nonsystematic | .79 | .71 |

Finally, it is worth noting that the stimuli in the identification task also included medium-frequency five-letter words and novel, orthographically legal pseudowords. On average, the subjects identified 75 percent of the words and 15 percent of the pseudowords. Thus, the pseudowords in the training set were identified about as accurately as medium-frequency words.

## 23.7 GENERAL DISCUSSION

When pseudowords are assigned definitions, assignments that systematically relate spelling and meaning are easier to learn than arbitrary assignments, and, once learned, systematic assignments make the pseudowords relatively easy to identify. These results are consistent with a connectionist account of the role of the semantic pathway in word identification. According to this account, systematic associations are easier to learn because similar associations produce less interference (and more positive transfer) when they are superimposed on the same set of weights. Systematic associations facilitate identification because similar associations provide congruent information that allows activity in the orthographic and semantic modules to settle more quickly.

Although the results were predicted by the connectionist model, it should be noted that some of these findings may be open to alternative explanations. For example, if the subjects in the systematic condition noticed the relationship between word ending and category membership and made explicit use of this information during the recall task, the effect of systematicity on learning rate might be explained without recourse to superimpositional memory. Although the best counter to this argument would be to show that systematicity influences learning rate even when it is not explicitly noticed, it might also be noted that the connectionist account of the learning results draws on the same principles used to explain both learning in other linguistic domains (Rumelhart and McClelland 1986; Seidenberg and McClelland 1989) and learning in tasks where subjects do not become explicitly aware of the underlying structure inherent in the to-be-learned material (Cleeremans and McClelland 1991).

The effect of systematicity on tachistoscopic identification seems more difficult to explain by other means. One alternative that depends on neither interactive processing nor distributed representation assumes that on trials where a stimulus is not completely identified, semantic information is used to generate a response. Clearly this sort of account could explain the finding that pseudowords are easier to identify when they are associated with meanings than when they are not. However, in order to explain the effect of systematicity on identification, the semantic activation account must also assume that orthographic-semantic associations are stronger in the systematic condition, which begs the question of why these associations are stronger in the first place. In contrast, an important strength of the connectionist model is that it provides a unified account of the processes by which new orthographic-semantic associations are acquired, stored, and used in the course of identification.

## Previous Studies Involving New Orthographic-Semantic Associations

Several other recent studies have investigated the effects of associating pseudowords with meanings. Whittlesea and Cantwell (1987) found greater repetition priming for pseudowords when the priming task involved associating each pseudoword with a meaning than when the pseudowords were initially presented in a nonsemantic task. Forster (1985) found masked repetition priming for unfamiliar, obsolete words but only when these words had been assigned meanings earlier in the experimental session. Finally, Rueckl and Olds (1993) found that associating pseudowords with meanings resulted in a qualitative change in the effects of repetition priming. In their study, repetition priming increased with additional repetitions of the pseudowords when the priming task involved associating each pseudoword with a meaning but not when the priming task was simply to name each pseudoword aloud.[4]

In contrast to our account, Whittlesea and Cantwell (1987) have suggested that these findings need not be taken to indicate that newly learned orthographic-semantic associations influence identification directly. Instead, they proposed that the organization of the memory trace that results from processing an item depends on how that item is processed. In their view, if a pseudoword is treated as a "meaning-bearing unit," the resulting memory trace will be relatively well integrated and thus will contribute more to the subsequent identification of that stimulus.

Whittlesea and Cantwell's integration hypothesis is consistent with the results of the earlier studies, where the effects of the training task were manifested by a perceptual advantage for pseudowords that had been processed semantically over pseudowords that had been processed nonsemantically. However, in this study, pseudowords in both the systematic and nonsystematic conditions were treated as meaning-bearing units. Thus, it is not clear how the effect of systematicity on identification might be accounted for by the integration hypothesis. Instead, this finding suggests that the newly acquired orthographic-semantic associations play a direct and significant role in the identification process.

## Orthographic-Semantic Associations and the Implicit-Explicit Distinction

Memory for a recent event can be demonstrated either explicitly, as conscious recollection, or implicitly, as a change in test performance without conscious recollection (Schacter 1987). Implicit and explicit memory can be dissociated in a variety of ways; they are differentially affected by the manipulation of variables such as modality of presentation and depth of processing, and perhaps most striking, amnesiacs often demonstrate normal implicit memory in conjunction with the complete absence of explicit memory (Richardson-Klavehn and Bjork 1988; Roediger and Blaxton 1987; Schacter 1987). There are two leading accounts of the relation between implicit and explicit memory. According to the multiple-systems account (Schacter 1990; Tulving and Schacter 1990), dissociations between implicit and explicit memory occur because perceptual memory systems underlie implicit memory and conceptual systems underlie explicit memory. In contrast, the main tenet of the transfer-appropriate processing account (Roediger and Blaxton 1987) is that memory tasks are composed of a number of component processes, and dissociations between implicit and explicit tasks reflect the operation of different cognitive processes during these tasks.

The results of our experiment indicate that orthographic-semantic systematicity had similar effects on implicit and explicit memory (as measured by the cued recall and tachistoscopic identification tasks, respectively). These results provide constraints for both the multiple-systems and transfer-appropriate processing accounts. Because orthographic-semantic associations do not obviously belong to either the perceptual or conceptual system, it appears that the systems account needs to make more finely grained distinctions about which systems are involved in identification and recall. In contrast, although the processing account can readily accommodate the notion of orthographic-semantic associations, it is not clear from this account why performance should be influenced by the systematicity of those associations. This theory needs a more detailed account of how memories for recent events influence ongoing processing.

In this light, it is worth noting that the connectionist model instantiates many of the principles of both the multiple-systems and transfer-appropriate processing accounts, but at a finer level of detail. Like a systems account, the connectionist model provides a description of the structure of the system involved in lexical processing. Like a processing account, the connectionist model describes both how the lexical system operates and how the memory for a prior event influences these processes. This suggests that perhaps the multiple-systems and transfer-appropriate processing accounts are better viewed not as competitors but instead as complementary theories, each of which captures some important general principles.

## Conclusion

The behavior of a connectionist network is determined by the knowledge encoded by the weights on its connections. Because information about many associations is superimposed on the same set of weights, a network's response to an input depends not just on its experiences with that input but also on its experiences with other, similar inputs. Seidenberg and McClelland (1989) demonstrated how this fundamental property of connectionist networks accounts for a wide variety of phenomena related to how people compute the mapping from orthography to phonology. In this chapter, we have reported evidence of superimpositional memory effects in the computation of the mapping from orthography to semantics. Given the many differences between these domains, we find the potential for a unified account of these computations quite appealing.

## NOTES

Correspondence may be sent to Jay G. Rueckl, Department of Psychology, University of Connecticut, Storrs, CT 06269 USA. This work was supported in part by a grant from the Maria E. McMaster Fund. We thanks Maggie Keane, Shlomo Bentin, Nachson Meiran, and an anonymous reviewer for comments on an earlier draft, and Craig Stark and I-Han Chou for their assistance in carrying out this project.

1. There is considerable debate about the degree to which access to semantic information depends on phonological mediation (Henderson 1982; Humphreys and Evett 1985; Patterson and Coltheart 1986; van Orden 1991). We side with those who claim that meaning can be accessed directly on the basis of orthography. However, because the mapping from phonology to semantics is as arbitrary as the mapping from orthography to semantics, even if the assumption of direct access were to be disproved, much of the essence of the account we develop here would remain viable.

2. Hinton and Shallice (1991) did not include a phonological module in their network. Their assumption was that it would play only a secondary role in the phenomena of interest. In subsequent work, Plaut and Shallice (1991) added a phonological module to the Hinton and Shallice network and found no theoretically interesting changes in the behavior of the net as a result.

3. This is essentially a distributed version of the "friends and enemies" account of context effects in letter perception described by McClelland and Rumelhart (1981).

4. Typically, pseudoword priming increases with additional repetitions regardless of the training task (Solomon and Postman, 1952; Salasoo, Shiffrin, and Feustel 1985; Whitlow and Cebollero 1989). What appears to a critical difference is that in the Rueckl and Olds (1993) study, there was a great deal of orthographic similarity among the pseudowords.

## REFERENCES

Baron, J., and Strawson, C. (1976). Use of orthographic and word specific knowledge in reading words aloud. *Journal of Experimental Psychology: Human Perception and Performance, 2*, 386–393.

Carr, T. H., and Pollatsek, A. (1985). Recognizing printed words: A look at current models. In D. Besner, T. G. Waller, and G. E. MacKinnon (Eds.), *Reading research: Advances in theory and practice*, vol. 5, 2–82. Orlando, FL: Academic Press.

Cleeremans, A., and McClelland, J. L. (1991). Learning the structure of event sequences. *Journal of Experimental Psychology: General, 120*, 235–253.

Dagenbach, D., Horst, S., and Carr, T. H. (1990). Adding new information to semantic memory: How much learning is enough to produce automatic priming? *Journal of Experimental Psychology: Learning, Memory, and Cognition, 16*, 581–591.

Dror, I. E. (n.d.). Cognitive computations, modeling, and representations. *Journal of Pragmatics and Cognition*. In press.

Farah, M. J., and McClelland, J. L. (1991). A computational model of semantic memory impairment: Modality-specificity and emergent category-specificity. *Journal of Experimental Psychology: General, 120*, 339–357.

Forster, K. I. (1979). Levels of processing and the structure of the language processor. In R. J. Wales and E. Walker (Eds.), *New approaches to language mechanisms*. Amsterdam: North-Holland.

Forster, K. I. (1985). Lexical acquisition and the modular lexicon. *Language and Cognitive Processes, 1*, 87–108.

Glushko, R. J. (1979). The organization and activation of orthographic knowledge in reading aloud. *Journal of Experimental Psychology: Human Perception and Performance, 5,* 674–691.

Golden, R. M. (1986). A developmental neural model of visual word perception. *Cognitive Science, 10,* 241–276.

Henderson, L. (1982). *Orthography and word recognition in reading.* New York: Academic Press.

Hinton, G. E., McClelland, J. L., and Rumelhart, D. E. (1986). Distributed representations. In D. E. Rumelhart and J. L. McClelland (Eds.), *Parallel distributed processing: Explorations in the microstructure of cognition.* Vol. 1: *Foundations,* 77–109. Cambridge, MA: MIT Press.

Hinton, G., and Shallice, T. (1991). Lesioning an attractor network: Investigations of acquired dyslexia. *Psychological Review, 98,* 74–95.

Humphreys, G. W., and Evett, L. J. (1985). Are there independent lexical and nonlexical routes in word processing? An evaluation of the dual-route model of reading. *Behavioral and Brain Sciences, 8,* 689–740.

Masson, M. (1991). A distributed memory model of context effects in word identification. In D. Besner and G. Humphreys (Eds.), *Basic processes in reading: Visual word recognition.* Hillsdale, NJ: Erlbaum.

McClelland, J. L. (1985). Putting knowledge in its place: A scheme for programming parallel processing structures on the fly. *Cognitive Science, 9,* 113–146.

McClelland, J. L., and Rumelhart, D. E. (1981). An interactive activation model of context effects in letter perception: Part 1. *Psychological Review, 88,* 375–407.

Minsky, M., and Papert, S. (1969). *Perceptrons.* Cambridge, MA: MIT Press.

Morton, J. (1979). Facilitation in word recognition: Experiments causing a change in the logogen model. In P. A. Kolers, M. E. Wrostal, and H. Bouma (Eds.), *Processing visible language I,* 259–268. New York: Plenum Press.

Mozer, M. C. (1987). Early parallel processing in reading: A connectionist approach. In M. Coltheart (Ed.), *Attention and Performance XII,* 83–104. Hillsdale, NJ: Erlbaum.

Patterson, K., and Coltheart, V. (1987). Phonological processes in reading: A tutorial review. In M. Coltheart (Ed.), *Attention and performance XII,* 421–447. Hillsdale, NJ: Erlbaum.

Plaut, D., and Shallice, T. (1991). Deep dyslexia: A case study of connectionist neuropsychology. Technical Report CRG-TR-91-3, Connectionist Research Group, Department of Computer Science, University of Toronto.

Richardson-Klavehn, A., and Bjork, R. A. (1988). Measures of memory. *Annual Review of Psychology, 39,* 475–543.

Roediger, H. L. III, and Blaxton, T. A. (1987). Retrieval modes produce dissociations in memory for surface information. In D. S. Gorfein and R. R. Hoffman (Eds.), *Memory and cognitive processes: The Ebbinghaus Centennial Conference,* 349–379. Hillsdale, NJ: Erlbaum.

Rueckl, J. G. (1990). Similarity effects in word and pseudoword repetition priming. *Journal of Experimental Psychology: Learning, Memory, and Cognition, 16,* 374–391.

Rueckl, J. G., Kolodny, J., and McPeek, R. M. (n.d.). Systematicity and structure in associative mapping functions. In preparation.

Rueckl, J. G., and Olds, E. M. (1993). When pseudowords acquire meaning: The effect of semantic associations on pseudoword repetition priming. *Journal of Experimental Psychology: Learning, Memory, and Cognition, 19,* 515–527.

Rumelhart, D. E., and McClelland, J. L. (1986), *Parallel distributed processing: Explorations in the microstructure of cognition.* Vol. 1: *Foundations.* Cambridge, MA: MIT Press.

Salasoo, A., Shiffrin, R., and Feustel, T. (1985). Building permanent memory codes: Codification and repetition effects in word identification. *Journal of Experimental Psychology: General, 114,* 50–77.

Schacter, D. L. (1987). Implicit memory: History and current status. *Journal of Experimental Psychology: Learning, Memory, and Cognition, 13,* 501–518.

Schacter, D. L. (1990). Perceptual representation systems and implicit memory: Toward a resolution of the multiple memory systems debate. *Annals of the New York Academy of Sciences.*

Seidenberg, M. S., and McClelland, J. L. (1989). A distributed, developmental model of visual word recognition. *Psychological Review, 96,* 523–568.

Seidenberg, M. S., Waters, G. S., Sanders, M., and Tanenhaus, M. K. (1984). When does irregular spelling or pronunciation influence word recognition? *Journal of Verbal Learning and Verbal Behavior, 23,* 383–404.

Sejnowski, T. J. and Rosenberg, C. (1987). Parallel networks that learn to pronounce English text. *Complex Systems, 1,* 145–168.

Shallice, T., and Coughlin, A. K. (1980). Modality specific word comprehension deficits in deep dyslexia. *Journal of Neurology, Neuroscience and Psychiatry, 43,* 866–872.

Shallice, T., and McGill, J. (1978). The origins of mixed errors. In J. Requin (Ed.), *Attention and performance VII,* 193–208. Hillsdale, NJ: Erlbaum.

Solomon, R., and Postman, L. (1952). Frequency of usage as a determinant of recognition thresholds for words. *Journal of Experimental Psychology, 43,* 195–201.

Tulving, E., and Schacter, D. L. (1990). Priming and human memory systems. *Science, 247,* 301–306.

Van Orden, G. C. (1991). Phonological mediation is fundamental to reading. In D. Besner and G. Humphreys (Eds.), *Basic processes in reading,* 77–103. Hillsdale, NJ: Erlbaum.

Van Orden, G. C., Pennington, B. F., and Stone, G. O. (1990). Word identification in reading and the promise of subsymbolic psycholinguistics. *Psychological Review, 97,* 488–522.

Whitlow, J. W., and Cebollero, A. (1989). The nature of word frequency effects in perceptual identification. *Journal of Experimental Psychology: Learning, Memory, and Cognition, 15,* 643–656.

Whittlesea, B. W., and Cantwell, A. (1987). Enduring influence of the purpose of experiences: encoding-retrieval interactions in word and pseudoword identification. *Memory and Cognition, 15,* 465–472.

# 24 Semantic Effects on Syntactic Ambiguity Resolution: Evidence for a Constraint-Based Resolution Process

Patrizia Tabossi, Michael J. Spivey-Knowlton, Ken McRae, and Michael K. Tanenhaus

ABSTRACT  Resolution of syntactic ambiguity was used to explore differences between modular and constraint-based approaches to language comprehension. Typicality, as measured by semantic fit of a noun to a verb's thematic roles, was determined in a norming study in which subjects rated how commonly the noun plays a specific role in an event described by the verb. The influence of typicality on the resolution of the main clause/reduced relative clause ambiguity was tested using a self-paced reading task. The experiment was designed so that both regressions and analyses of variance could be used to examine the effect of semantic fit. Analyses of variance revealed relatively late effects of semantic fit on the disambiguation process. However, regression analyses, which are more sensitive to continuous variables, showed an earlier influence of semantic fit. It was concluded that, although the results can be accommodated by certain modular accounts, they are more naturally accounted for by constraint-based models of ambiguity resolution.

## 24.1 INTRODUCTION

Ambiguity is present at all levels at which one can analyze a linguistic utterance, from how the speech stream is to be segmented to how a speaker's intentions are to be interpreted. It is especially pervasive when viewed from the perspective of a system that attempts to analyze linguistic input incrementally. Given a system that interprets incrementally, both spoken and written language contain a great deal of local ambiguity; that is, the input is often temporarily ambiguous between two or more alternatives.

Ambiguity resolution is of general interest for several reasons. For researchers interested in how natural language is processed, ambiguity is a powerful tool that can be used to explore how different types of information are coordinated during language comprehension. It also presents a theoretical challenge because models of language processing must incorporate mechanisms that resolve ambiguity as a natural by-product of language understanding. Finally, ambiguity resolution has featured prominently in ongoing debates about the architecture of the language processing system and cognitive architectures in general.

Two competing conceptions of cognitive architecture are being studied in detail. In modular architectures, there are a set of encapsulated processors, each of which computes an output based on input from a restricted domain (Fodor 1983; Forster 1979). A consequence of a strictly modular architecture is that mutually relevant constraints will often be separated into different processing modules. In constraint-based systems, however, processing is based on different types of information/knowledge and the architecture is organized to allow the system to make use of constraints from different domains (McClelland 1987; Rumelhart and McClelland 1986).

Ambiguity resolution is typically handled differently in modular and constraint-based systems. There are two natural ways of handling ambiguity within a modular system. One approach is to have a module compute multiple outputs, which are then filtered by subsequent modules (Forster 1979). The alternative is to incorporate decision principles within a module so that it computes a single output without appealing to extramodular information. In contrast, a constraint-based system will make use of the available constraints that are relevant to resolving the ambiguity. Alternatives will be more or less active, depending on their likelihood given the ambiguous input and their degree of support from other constraints.

Although the modular and constraint-based approaches to ambiguity resolution differ conceptually, empirically distinguishing between them has proved difficult. Differences between the approaches often hinge on subtle predictions about how and when constraints are used during the resolution process. This will become clear as we consider the two best-known and most commonly investigated types of ambiguity within natural language: lexical and syntactic ambiguity.

## 24.2 LEXICAL AMBIGUITY

The following example, taken from Johnson-Laird (1983), illustrates two important characteristics of lexical ambiguity:

The plane banked just before landing, but then the pilot lost control. The strip on the field runs for only the barest of yards and the plane just twisted out of the turn before shooting into the ground.

First, that this passage is not particularly difficult to understand in spite of the fact that all of its content words are ambiguous suggests that ambiguity is unlikely to invoke special resource-demanding processing mechanisms but rather is handled as a by-product of normal comprehension. Second, there are a number of ways in which a word can be ambiguous. The word *plane*, for example, has several noun meanings, and it can also be used as a verb. The word *twisted* could be an adjective and is also morphologically ambiguous between the past tense and participial forms of the verb *to twist*.

Several studies in the late 1970s and early 1980s found that multiple senses of ambiguous words were temporarily activated, even when preceding context was biased in favor of one of the readings (Swinney 1979; Tanenhaus, Leiman, and Seidenberg 1979). These results were widely interpreted as among the strongest support for modular filtering models in which a lexical module made available all of the alternative senses of a word, without taking into account contextual constraints (Fodor 1983; Prather and Swinney 1988;

Tanenhaus, Carlson, and Seidenberg 1985). However, these multiple-access results can also be naturally modeled within a constraint satisfaction framework (Cottrell 1988; Kawamoto 1988).

Constraint-based models make the additional prediction that extremely strong contextual constraints will have rapid effects on ambiguity resolution and that effects of context will interact with the relative frequency of the alternative senses. Recent evidence has provided some support for these predictions (but cf. Onifer and Swinney 1981; Lucas 1987). When a word is presented without context (Burgess and Simpson 1985) or in a neutral sentential context (Simpson and Krueger 1991), activation of the dominant meaning is faster, stronger, and longer lasting than activation of the subordinate meaning. In context, the dominant meaning is initially activated regardless of the strength of the context (Onifer and Swinney 1981; Rayner and Frazier 1989; Tabossi, Colombo, and Job 1987). In contrast, several studies suggest that the subordinate meaning may not be significantly activated when a strongly constraining context biases the dominant meaning (Rayner and Frazier 1989; Tabossi 1988).

The nature of some of these constraints was explored by Tabossi (1988). She found that only the dominant meaning was activated when context made salient a prominent feature of that meaning. These results could perhaps be accommodated within modular approaches by assuming that, with featural contexts, filtering occurs so rapidly that it is difficult to observe the output of the lexical module before it has been filtered (but cf. Tabossi and Zardon, n.d.). Nonetheless, these findings are most naturally modeled within a constraint-based framework.

## 24.3 SYNTACTIC AMBIGUITY

Syntactic ambiguity occurs when a sequence of words can be structured in alternative ways that are consistent with the syntax of the language. For example, each of the fragments in (1) is ambiguous:

(1) a. John told the woman that Bill was dating
    b. The man told the story

In 1a, "that Bill was dating" could either be a relative clause (as in "John told the woman that Bill was dating a lie") or a sentence complement (as in "John told the woman that Bill was dating a liar"). In 1b, "The man told the story" could either be a main clause (as in "The man told the story to his kids") or a relative clause (as in "The man told the story was shocked").

These examples also illustrate that syntactic ambiguity is often dependent upon lexical ambiguity. The ambiguity in 1a arises, in part, because *that* can be a complementizer or a relative pronoun. The main clause/reduced relative ambiguity in 1b hinges on a morphological ambiguity of the surface form *told*, which could be either a simple past tense or a past participle. Ambiguity does not arise with verbs whose past tense and participial forms differ (e.g., *chose*, *chosen*).

The most influential modular accounts of syntactic ambiguity resolution have assumed that an autonomous syntactic processor computes a single structure for the local input (Frazier 1987). For example, in the garden path model developed by Frazier and Rayner (1982), the syntactic processor "attaches" each word or phrase into the constituent structure that it is building. The model incorporates a simplicity-based decision principle. When the input is locally ambiguous, the simplest attachment is chosen, where simplicity is defined in terms of the number of nodes that must be added to the constituent structure. Constraints that might be relevant to resolving the local ambiguity are ignored by the module responsible for making initial attachments. These constraints include semantic and syntactic information associated with specific lexical items, plausibility, and information from the discourse context. Information that is not used in making these attachments is then used to evaluate and, if necessary, revise the initial structure.

Constraint-based approaches treat syntactic ambiguity resolution similarly to lexical ambiguity resolution (McClelland, St. John, and Taraban 1989; Taraban and McClelland 1990). The available alternatives are continuously evaluated with respect to other relevant constraints. As in lexical ambiguity, constraint-based models predict an interaction between strength of context and availability of alternatives. Furthermore, availability of alternatives will depend on the temporal relationship between the contextual cues and the ambiguity, that is, whether the relevant cues precede or follow the point of ambiguity (MacDonald, n.d.). In addition, even relatively subtle constraints may affect the speed with which alternative analyses are computed and an ambiguity is resolved, particularly when a highly active alternative turns out to be inconsistent with subsequent input. The current work explores this hypothesis, making use of the main clause–reduced relative clause ambiguity originally introduced by Bever (1970).

**Reduced Relative Clauses**

Consider the example presented in:

(2)   The reporter interviewed by the editor proved unfit for the job.

The fragment "the reporter interviewed" is temporarily ambiguous between the beginning of a main clause and a relative clause. The ambiguity arises because English typically uses the "verb + -ed" form for both the past tense and participle. Thus, *interviewed* is morphologically ambiguous. When it is a past tense verb, *the reporter interviewed* is the beginning of a main clause. The noun phrase, *the reporter*, is the logical subject of the verb, and it is interpreted as the agent of the interviewing event, that is, the person who is doing the interviewing. If *interviewed* is a participial, *the reporter interviewed* begins a reduced relative clause. *The reporter* is the logical object of the verb, and it is interpreted as the patient or theme of the interviewing event—the person who is being interviewed. The main verb phrase, *proved unfit for the job*, resolves the ambiguity in favor of a relative clause.

Numerous empirical studies have demonstrated that readers have a clear bias to interpret a noun phrase verb + *-ed* sequence as the beginning of a past tense main clause, resulting in longer reading latencies when information inconsistent with this interpretation is encountered (Ferreira and Clifton 1986; Rayner, Carlson, and Frazier 1983). This preference could be explained in terms of syntactic simplicity: the constituent structure of a relative clause contains more nodes than that of a main clause. Alternatively, it could be due to the relative frequency of the main clause and relative clause structures. In English, a noun phrase followed by a verb + *-ed* form is far more likely to begin a main clause than a relative clause. In addition, there may be strong pragmatic and discourse constraints on when a reduced relative clause can be used felicitously (Crain and Steedman 1985). Whether the main clause preference is reduced or eliminated when the discourse establishes the appropriate constraints is an unresolved issue that is currently the focus of extensive research (Britt et al. 1992; Ferreira and Clifton 1986; Spivey-Knowlton, Trueswell, and Tanenhaus 1993; Trueswell and Tanenhaus 1991, 1992).

**Effects of Semantic Fit**

In a main clause–relative clause ambiguity, the semantic or thematic role of the noun phrase that precedes the ambiguous verb differs depending on how the ambiguity is resolved. For a main clause, the noun phrase is the agent, whereas it is the patient for a relative clause. Several studies have investigated whether the semantic fit between the initial noun and these potential thematic roles influences the resolution process.

Rayner, Carlson, and Frazier (1983) conducted an eye movement study with sentences such as those that follow:

(3)  a. The florist sent the flowers was very pleased.
     b. The performer sent the flowers was very pleased.

Florists are more likely to send flowers than are performers, whereas performers are more likely to receive flowers than are florists. If real-world knowledge about typical events and participants influences syntactic analysis, then readers should have less difficulty when encountering the disambiguating region "was very pleased" in 3b than in 3a. Rayner, Carlson, and Frazier found faster total reading latencies to more plausible sentences, but first-pass reading latencies at the disambiguating region were not affected by plausibility. This result is clearly consistent with a serial modular model in which plausibility information influences syntactic reanalysis but not initial syntactic decisions. However, the results are also consistent with constraint-based models. In Rayner, Carlson, and Frazier's stimuli, plausibility differences often depended on the noun phrase that *followed* the ambiguous verb. For example, it is not clear that "florists" and "performers" differ in the likelihood that they send or receive things. Thus, the sentences may have been equally plausible at the verb. Florists and performers do, however, differ in the likelihood that they would be sending or receiving flowers. Thus, the plausibility information may not have been available until relatively late in the sentence (at "flowers").

Ferreira and Clifton (1986) more directly manipulated thematic fit to the ambiguous verb by contrasting animate and inanimate noun phrases, as in 4a and 4b (unreduced relative clauses served as unambiguous controls):

(4) a. The evidence examined by the judge turned out to be unreliable.
    b. The witness examined by the judge turned out to be unreliable.

Animate nouns are typically plausible agents, whereas inanimate nouns are typically implausible, if not incongruous, agents for many active verbs. If information about thematic fit is used in evaluating alternatives during parsing, then ambiguity resolution should occur more rapidly with inanimate nouns.

Ferreira and Clifton (1986) found longer reading times to the verb when the noun phrase was inanimate, suggesting that animacy information was available when the ambiguous verb was encountered. However, animacy *did not* interact with ambiguity resolution. Both first- and second-pass reading times were longer for the ambiguous sentences, regardless of animacy. These results appear to provide strong evidence that thematic information is not used to constrain initial parsing. In addition, unlike Rayner, Carlson, and Frazier, (1983), Ferreira and Clifton found no evidence that thematic fit influenced even late effects on ambiguity resolution. However, in the Ferreira and Clifton materials, the word that followed the ambiguous verb typically provided strong probabilistic evidence in favor of a relative clause reading. This might suggest that semantic information is used in ambiguity resolution—perhaps as part of a controlled process—only when disambiguating syntactic information is delayed.

Ferreira and Clifton's (1986) results provide the strongest type of evidence that can be marshaled in favor of a modular architecture, in that they found that a clearly available constraint did not affect a computation in another module. However, there are several problems with the materials and presentation mode that Ferreira and Clifton used (Trueswell, Tanenhaus, and Garnsey, n.d.; Tanenhaus, Carlson, and Trueswell 1989). More recent studies have found results that are more consistent with constraint-based approaches. Several studies have demonstrated that thematic constraints are effective in ambiguity resolution but only under conditions that enhance availability of the participial form of the verb. These studies have used both self-paced reading and eye-tracking methodologies. In eye movement recording studies in which the short, high-frequency preposition *by* followed the verb, animacy interacted with ambiguity in both first- and second-pass fixation durations (Trueswell, Tanenhaus, and Garnsey, n.d.). Clear ambiguity effects were found for sentences with animate nouns, indicated by longer reading times to sentences with reduced relatives compared to unreduced relatives. However, no ambiguity effects were found for sentences with inanimate nouns (Burgess 1991; Burgess and Tanenhaus, n.d.; Trueswell, Tanenhaus, and Garnsey, n.d.).

In the self-paced reading studies, rapid interactions with animacy obtained only when the reader could view the preposition along with the verb (Burgess 1991; Burgess and Tanenhaus, n.d.). Allowing the reader to see the preposition at the same time as the verb is important because it typically provides strong probabilistic evidence in favor of a reduced relative interpretation. However, it does not unequivocally disambiguate the sentence as a reduced relative. For example, the preposition *by* may indicate location, as in "The prowler stalked by the house...," so that *stalked* is the main verb of the sentence. When Burgess used a one-word presentation window, thus separating the verb and preposition, the pattern of results was similar to that found by Ferreira and Clifton (1986). Reading times were longer at the verb for reduced relative clauses with inanimate nouns compared to the unreduced controls. In addition, animacy did not interact with ambiguity at the *by* phrase. However, with a two-word window, with the verb and *by* presented simultaneously, the same pattern obtained as in the eye-tracking studies. Reading times to the verb + *by* and the determiner plus noun (det + noun) regions were longer for the ambiguous sentences when the initial noun was animate but not when it was inanimate.

There is a simple reason that the two-word window with self-paced reading leads to results that are similar to those of eye tracking, whereas the one-word window does not. In normal reading, readers typically do not fixate on short function words, which indicates that they encode these words parafoveally in the previous fixation. For example, in a sentence such as "The evidence examined by the lawyer...," a reader normally reads *by* when fixating on the verb *examined*. Similarly, readers typically do not fixate on the following determiner *the*. Thus, with two-word presentation, the sentences are grouped into units that approximate those of normal reading.

Why then, does access to the participial form depend so heavily on the readers seeing the *by* along with the verb? One possibility is that the past tense form is far more frequent then the participial form. In addition, the relative frequency of the two forms may vary depending on the preceding syntactic environment. It has recently been demonstrated that co-occurrence patterns clearly affect structural availability for at least some syntactic category ambiguities (Juliano, Trueswell, and Tanenhaus 1992; Tanenhaus and Juliano 1992). Thus, the participial form may be only weakly activated when the verb alone is read, especially when it occurs prior to the main verb of the sentence.

The pattern of results described—an interaction between the effects of semantic fit and availability of syntactic alternatives—is clearly consistent with predictions of constraint-based models. However, there are ways of accommodating the results within a modular architecture. For example, one could argue that animacy is a special category of semantic feature that is directly incorporated into the syntax. Animacy is morphologically marked in many languages, suggesting that it may have special grammatical properties. In fact, features like animacy were incorporated into the syntax in early forms of transformational grammar (e.g., as "selectional restrictions" in the Aspects framework; Chomsky 1965).

MacDonald (n.d.) and Pearlmutter and MacDonald (1992) have identified another prediction made by constraint-based models. Even relatively subtle constraints that are biased against a preferred alternative should facilitate the resolution process when further inconsistent information is encountered. Pearlmutter and MacDonald, in fact, observed just this pattern using both inanimate nouns and animate nouns that were more plausible themes than agents. However, the effects that they observed were often delayed by several words and were sometimes only marginally reliable. In addition, the clearest effects occurred when inanimate nouns were used.

Pearlmutter and MacDonald (1992) also presented cogent arguments for combining regression techniques with standard analysis of variance designs. In an analysis of variance design, variables are treated as discrete. However, most variables that are manipulated in sentence processing studies, including semantic fit, are actually continuous. Constraint-based models predict graded effects of semantic fit, with resolution occurring most rapidly for the most constraining items. If items with differing degrees of constraint are grouped together within a category in an analysis of variance, then differences will be treated as within-category noise, with an accompanying tendency to mask effects. One possible solution to this problem might be to norm materials carefully in order to select items so that all items within a category embody similar constraints. However, there may be too few items available for this to be a practical research strategy. Furthermore, choosing only extreme items does not allow one to explore whether the effects are, in fact, continuous.

There is another reason for making use of regression analyses in conjunction with analyses of variance. As MacDonald (n.d.) points out, many of the syntactic "cues" for disambiguation provide probabilistic, rather than definitive, evidence in support of a particular structure. For example, *by* in a sequence such as, "The evidence examined by...," provides strong evidence in favor of a reduced relative clause because it is likely to begin an agentive prepositional phrase. However, *by* could also be a manner preposition ("by night") or a locative preposition ("by the door"), each consistent with a main clause. On a constraint-based view, the interpretation of *by* will be influenced by the strength of the evidence supporting a main clause and a relative clause, including the semantic fit of the noun as agent. As a result, the point of disambiguation might shift downstream for sentences beginning with noun phrases that are good agents, compared to those beginning with poor agents. Under these circumstances, elevated reading times immediately after a disambiguating word or phrase may reflect the beginning of the resolution process for some sentences but the end for others. This might result in a main effect in an analysis of variance at a particular region of the sentence. However, if items were, in fact, acting differently, contrasting patterns of correlations might be revealed in regression analyses. Consider a few possibilities. First, for sentences with good agents, the reduction effect might correlate negatively with goodness of agent of the initial noun because of delayed resolution for the best agents. That is, at the verb + *by* region, because agenthood of the best agents is strong, there may be no competition from the reduced relative clause interpretation, resulting in fast reading times. In contrast, for items with poor agents, the reduction effect might correlate positively with goodness of agent of the initial noun because the poorest agents would show less initial bias toward a main clause, with resulting competition between a main clause and a reduced relative clause. Alternatively, the initial difficulty in the resolution for poor agent sentences might be influenced by the goodness of patient of the initial noun, whereas for sentences with good agents this variable would not influence reading times until later. Under any of these circumstances, regressions could provide information to clarify the results obtained from analyses of variance. In fact, Pearlmutter and MacDonald (1992) report revealing patterns of correlations based on post hoc ratings in regions of their sentences in which the statistical patterns found with analyses of variance were equivocal.

The study reported here had two primary goals. The first goal was to replicate and extend Pearlmutter and MacDonald's (1992) work by determining whether a relatively subtle semantic constraint would interact with syntactic ambiguity resolution. We used relative clauses and varied semantic fit between the initial noun phrase and the verb. A norming study was conducted to develop two groups of stimuli, one for which the noun was rated as a common agent in an event described by the verb but an atypical patient (e.g., a reporter often interviews people but is not usually interviewed), and the other for which the noun was rated as an atypical agent but a common patient (e.g., a candidate is often interviewed by someone but seldom interviews others). A self-paced reading study was then conducted to determine whether semantic fit would interact with ambiguity resolution. Both regression analyses and analyses of variance were used. Stimuli were selected so that typicality of the nouns as the agent and the patient varied even for the typical and atypical agents. Under these conditions, we might expect to observe effects in regression analyses before the effects would emerge in the analyses of variance. The second goal was to use corpus-based analyses to correlate different measures of frequency with semantic fit. Constraint-based models predict that ambiguity resolution will be fastest for those verbs that are most likely to be used as participles in relative clauses.

## 24.4 METHOD

### Subjects

Thirty-two University of Rochester undergraduate and graduate students were paid to participate. All were native English speakers and had normal or corrected to normal vision.

## Materials

Thirty-six verbs were paired with two nouns. The verbs were split into three subsets: for thirty-two verbs, one noun was a typical agent of the verb but an atypical patient, and the other noun was an atypical agent but a typical patient; for twenty-four of these thirty-two verbs, both the good agent/poor patient and poor agent/good patient nouns were animate; for eight verbs, the poor agent/good patient was inanimate; for the remaining four verbs, agenthood and patienthood of both nouns were relatively balanced. Agenthood and patienthood were determined in an independent norming study in which twenty-four subjects were asked questions of the following form:

How common is it for a reporter to interview someone? *or*

How common is it for a reporter to be interviewed by someone?

Subjects indicated typicality of an event on a 1–7 scale, where 1 corresponded to very uncommon and 7 to very common. Agenthood and patienthood ratings were as follows: thirty-two biased items, good agent (agenthood: mean = 6.4, range = 5.4–7.0; patienthood: mean = 2.1, range = 1.3–3.2), good patient (agenthood: mean = 1.6, range = 1.0–3.1; patienthood: mean = 6.2, range = 4.3–6.9); four unbiased items, agent (agenthood: mean = 5.9, range = 5.4–6.3; patienthood: mean = 3.8, range = 3.3–4.2), patient (agenthood: mean = 3.5, range = 2.8–4.3; patienthood: mean = 5.1, range = 3.4–6.0).

Two sentences (reduced and unreduced versions) were constructed from each noun-verb combination. The noun was used in an initial noun phrase, and the verb was used as a past participle in a relative clause that modified the initial noun. For example, according to the norms, a reporter is a typical interviewer but is rarely interviewed; in contrast, a candidate is typically interviewed but rarely interviews people. Therefore, for the verb *interview*, the four sentences were:

The reporter [who was] interviewed by the editor proved unfit for the job.

The candidate [who was] interviewed by the editor proved unfit for office.

The complete set of thirty-six sentence pairs appears in the appendix to this chapter. When constructing the pairs, we attempted to make all sentences plausible, including nouns that were rated as poor patients of the verb. Plausibility is important; if a number of experimental items are not plausible, subjects may tend to reject plausibility as a cue, decreasing the probability of detecting its effect on comprehension. To increase meaningfulness of the items, each target sentence was followed by a filler sentence that continued the narrative.

Four lists were constructed so that no subject saw any verb or critical noun phrase more than once. Each list contained all of the verbs—half with good agents and half with good patients. Half of the sentences contained a reduced relative clause, and half retained an overt relative clause marker (*who was* or *that was*). Therefore, across the four lists, each noun-verb combination appeared with and without an overt relative clause marker. Forty-four two-sentence filler items were constructed and interleaved throughout the target sentences such that no two targets were adjacent, and each block of trials began with a filler. Therefore, 36 of 160 sentences (23 percent) contained a sentence-initial relative clause. Ten additional practice items were also constructed.

## Procedure

A session began with the ten practice items. By pressing a button, subjects saw sentences presented two words at a time in a moving window format (Just, Carpenter, and Woolley 1982). For example, the following sentence was presented in the regions separated by slashes:

The reporter / who was / interviewed by / the editor / proved unfit / for the / job.

Following practice, subjects read forty of eighty sentence pairs. After a brief break, the remaining forty were presented. For each list, order of the two blocks was counterbalanced. The critical regions of all target sentences fit on one line of the cathode ray tube display. Approximately one-third of the eighty trials were followed by yes-no comprehension questions. Subjects were instructed to read at a comfortable pace that best approximated their natural reading style. The experimental session lasted approximately 30 minutes. Sentences were presented on, and button pressing latency was measured by, an IBM-AT clone containing a Digitry timing board.

## Design

Analyses of variance and regression analyses were conducted on the thirty-two biased verbs to determine availability and use of semantic fit information. For the analyses of variance, there were two factors, each with two levels: semantic fit (good agent/poor patient versus poor agent/good patient) and reduction (unreduced versus reduced). Both factors were within subjects and within items. Analyses were conducted on reading latencies for the three critical two-word regions separately: verb + $by$; det + noun; and the main verb region.

Regression analyses were conducted to explore whether people's knowledge of event-entity typicality can predict the ease with which a reduced relative clause is comprehended. That is, we tested to see if ratings of goodness of agent and patient for noun-verb combinations could be used to predict reduction effects in the three regions. Regression analyses were conducted separately for the thirty-two good agents, thirty-two good patients, and twenty-four animate good patients (in order to ensure that effects were not being carried by the eight inanimate items). Separate analyses were used because we hypothesized that the good agent/poor patient items might act differently from the poor agent/good patient items; that is, we hypothesized separate regression lines for the two groups of stimuli. Because different subjects contributed to the reduced and unreduced means of each item and because there were only six subjects per mean, each subject's reading times were converted to standard scores based on his or her mean reading latency. Item means for the regression analyses were computed from these standard scores. The dependent variable was reading latency for the reduced version of each sentence. Reading latency for the unreduced version was forced into the regression equation as the first independent variable. This procedure was used in order to factor out effects due to variables such as string length and word frequency, as the same words appeared in the critical regions of the reduced and unreduced versions. Three independent variables were tested in separate regressions: agenthood rating, patienthood rating, and the difference between them.

## 24.5 RESULTS AND DISCUSSION

This section describes the results of the corpus-based verb-form availability analysis and presents results of the analyses of variance and regression analyses for the three scoring regions (table 24.1 and fig. 24.1).

For the unreduced versions of the sentences (the open circles and triangles in fig. 24.1), semantic fit appears to have influenced reading times throughout the final three regions. In the verb + *by* and noun phrase regions, the reduction effect (the difference in reading times between reduced and unreduced sentences) is similar in magnitude for the good agent/poor patient and the poor agent/good patient sentences. However, in the disambiguating region containing the verb phrase (*proved unfit*), the reduction effect is clearly larger for the good agent/poor patient sentences. This might suggest that semantic fit has only delayed effects. However, the fact that the pattern of effects is clearly different for sentences with good agents/poor patients versus those with poor agents/good patients suggests that semantic constraint might have had a more immediate influence. Finally, it can be seen from table 24.2 that the twenty-four animate items exhibit roughly the same pattern.

**Table 24.1** Reading Times (in ms) for Critical Regions and the Effect of Relative Clause Reduction in the Different Thematic Contexts

|  | Verb + *by* | Det + Noun | Main Verb |
|---|---|---|---|
| *Good agents* | | | |
| Reduced | 550 | 619 | 656 |
| Unreduced | 526 | 600 | 580 |
| Reduction effect | 24 | 19 | 76 |
| *Good patients* | | | |
| Reduced | 544 | 584 | 579 |
| Unreduced | 504 | 553 | 557 |
| Reduction effect | 40 | 31 | 22 |

Note: When the noun is a typical agent for the verb, the reduction effect greatly increases at the last recorded sentence region. When the noun is a typical patient for the verb, however, the reduction effect gradually decreases.

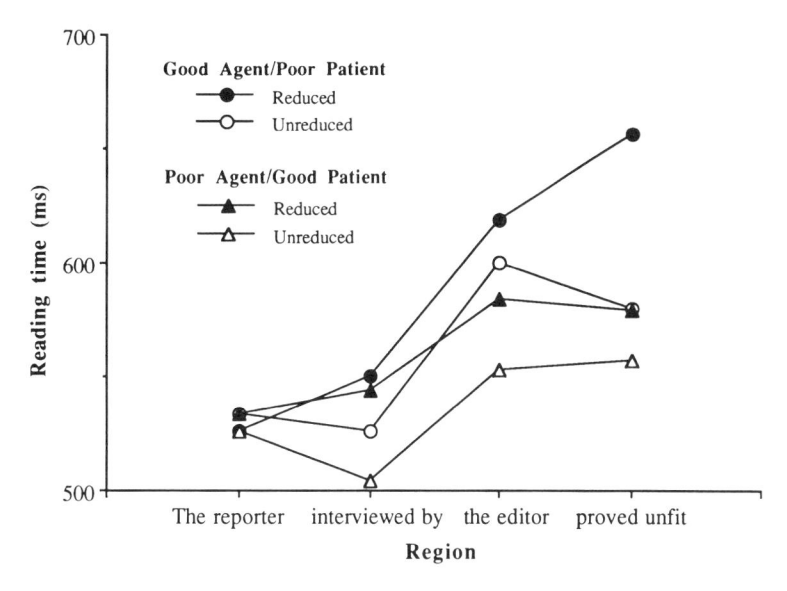

**Figure 24.1** Reading times for each sentence region in the four sentence types. When the noun is a typical agent for the verb (circles), the processing difficulty associated with relative clause reduction becomes quite large by the last recorded region. In contrast, when the noun is a typical patient for the verb (triangles), this processing difficulty has diminished by that region.

### Verb-Form Availability

Verb-specific biases were quantitatively analyzed using a sample of approximately 25,000 sentences taken from the Kucera and Francis (1967) corpus. Structures in which the -ed forms of the thirty-two verbs appeared were enumerated. Due to the small number of occurrences of many of the verbs (only seventeen of thirty-two occurred greater than nine times in its -ed form), it was not appropriate to use availability of the participial form as a predictor of reading latencies. Interesting trends emerged, however, when data were considered for the thirty-two verbs as a whole. In 772 sentences in which the -ed forms of the verbs were present, it occurred as part of a simple main clause in 37 percent of the sentences, a relative clause in 9 percent, a reduced relative in 6 percent, and a reduced relative that occurred prior to the main verb of the sentence 2 percent of the time. Furthermore, although 83 of 772 sentences (11 percent) contained a sentence-initial main clause noun-verb sequence, only 7 sentences (less than 1 percent) contained a sentence-initial reduced relative; thus, the critical structure used in the experimental stimuli occurred extremely rarely in this corpus.

### Analyses of Variance

**Verb Plus *by*** In the reading times for the verb + *by* region, a nonsignificant main effect of semantic fit was found (14-ms effect) ($F(1,28) = 1.19$, $MS_e = 5438, p > .2$ by subjects; $F(1,31) = 1.37, MS_e = 6670, p > .2$ by

**Table 24.2** Reading Times (in ms) for the Twenty-four Animate Items for Critical Regions and the Effect of Relative Clause Reduction

|  | Verb + by | Det + Noun | Main Verb |
|---|---|---|---|
| *Good agents* | | | |
| Reduced | 552 | 618 | 635 |
| Unreduced | 531 | 597 | 562 |
| Reduction effect | 21 | 21 | 73 |
| *Good patients* | | | |
| Reduced | 538 | 609 | 588 |
| Unreduced | 499 | 562 | 570 |
| Reduction effect | 39 | 47 | 18 |

Note: When the noun is a typical agent for the verb, the reduction effect greatly increases at the last recorded sentence region. For typical patient sentences, however, the reduction effect decreases.

items). There was a reliable difference between reduced and unreduced versions of the sentences (32-ms effect) $F(1,28) = 7.65, MS_e = 4201, p < .02$ by subjects; $F(1,31) = 3.89, MS_e = 8824, p < .06$ by items). As would be expected given no effect of semantic fit in this region, it did not interact with reduction: $F < 1$ in both analyses. Planned comparisons revealed that the reduction effect was marginally significant in the verb + by region when the initial noun was a poor agent/good patient ($F(1,56) = 5.97, MS_e = 4285, p < .02$ by subjects; $F(1,62) = 3.50, MS_e = 6946, p < .07$ by items), but not when it was a good agent/poor patient ($F(1,56) = 2.15, MS_e = 4285, p > .1$ by subjects; $F(1,62) = 1.56, MS_e = 6946, p > .2$ by items).

**Determiner Plus Noun** In the det + noun region, semantic fit affected subjects' interpretation. Stronger availability of semantic fit information was indicated by a 40-ms main effect that approached significance ($F(1,28) = 5.19, MS_e = 10256, p < .05$ by subjects; $F(1,31) = 1.40, MS_e = 29539, p > .2$ by items). A nonsignificant reduction effect was found (25-ms effect) ($F(1,28) = 0.64, MS_e = 31416, p > .4$ by subjects; $F(1,31) = 1.09, MS_e = 20798, p > .3$ by items). The interaction between semantic fit and reduction was nonsignificant ($F < 1$ in both analyses). For good agents/poor patients, planned comparisons showed no reduction effect ($F < 1$ in both analyses). Also, for poor agents/good patients, the effect of reduction was nonsignificant ($F < 1$ by subjects; $F(1,62) = 1.40, p > .2$ by items).

**Main Verb** By the main verb region, reading difficulty for a reduced relative clause had been nearly eliminated for sentences containing poor agents/good patients but continued to be robust for ones containing good agents/poor patients. Overall, reading latencies were faster for sentences with a poor agent/good patient initial noun phrase (50-ms effect) ($F(1,28) = 4.27, MS_e = 18478, p < .05$ by subjects; $F(1,31) = 4.75, MS_e = 19156, p < .05$ by items). As in the verb + by region, sentences containing a relative pronoun (*who was*) were read marginally faster in this region (48-ms effect) ($F(1,28) = 6.63$, $MS_e = 11500, p < .02$ by subjects; $F(1,31) = 3.33, MS_e = 25957, p < .08$ by items). The interaction between semantic fit and reduction was nonsignificant ($F(1,28) = 1.79, MS_e = 13408, p > .1$ by subjects; $F(1,31) = 2.56, MS_e = 12958, p > .1$ by items). However, planned comparisons revealed that subjects had not resolved the ambiguity caused by the absence of the relative clause marker when the initial noun was a good agent/poor patient ($F(1,56) = 7.42, MS_e = 12454, p < .01$ by subjects; $F(1,62) = 5.94, MS_e = 19457; p < .02$ by items). In contrast, the reduction effect for poor agent/good patient initial noun phrases was not reliable ($F < 1$ in both analyses).

**Summary** The ANOVAs provided little evidence that semantic fit influenced ambiguity resolution until relatively late in the sentence. It was only at the main verb that planned comparisons indicated that subjects had used their knowledge of events and their likely participants to resolve the ambiguity. However, two aspects of the data are left unexplained if it is assumed that semantic fit had only delayed effects. First, the pattern of reduction effects differs for good agent versus poor agent sentences. The largest reduction effects for the good agent sentences occurred late, at the main verb region, whereas the largest reduction effects for the poor agent sentences occurred earlier, at the determiner plus noun. A second rather striking aspect of the data was the large increase in within-category variance at the noun phrase and main verb regions. This variance indicates the possible existence of substantial between-item differences with respect to the extent to which semantic fit between the verb and the initial noun influenced subjects' ability to resolve the ambiguity. The different numerical trends in the reduction effects and the increase in within-category variance suggest that semantic fit was influencing ambiguity resolution earlier than the main verb region. Both the time course differences and the increase in within-category variance are consistent with a continuous constraint-based resolution process. Also, regression analysis can be used to provide relevant evidence. Therefore, we conducted regression analyses in which event-entity typicality ratings were used to predict reading times in each of the three regions. The results are described in the following section.

### Regression Analyses

**Verb Plus *by* Region** Regression analyses revealed one suggestive result in this region. Within the twenty-four animate sentences with typical patients (poor agent/good patient), the agenthood ratings for these items marginally predicted the reduction effect ($r = .39, R^2 = .15, p < .07$). That is, for the poor agent/good patient sentences, reading time in the reduced relative clause sentences increased with the agenthood rating of the initial noun phrase.

**Determiner Plus Noun Region** For sentences containing initial noun phrases rated as common agents of the verb, agenthood rating predicted size of the reduction effect ($r = .54, R^2 = .29, p < .003$). The positive correlation indicates that reduction effect varied directly with an entity's agenthood rating; that is, difficulty in resolving the main clause/reduced relative clause ambiguity increased with agenthood of the initial noun phrase because correct resolution of the sentence required treating it as a patient. Also, for sentences containing initial noun phrases rated as good patients, the difference between the agenthood and patienthood ratings predicted the reduction effect ($r = .37$, $R^2 = .14, p < .05$). Predictive ability was carried by patienthood ratings ($r = -.33, R^2 = .11, p < .07$ as compared to $R^2 = .03$ for agenthood). The same pattern was found when the twenty-four animate good patients were analyzed separately. Although the predictive ability of the difference between agenthood and patienthood ratings was marginal ($r = .36, R^2 = .13, p < .1$), patienthood ratings significantly predicted the reduction effect ($r = -.48$, $R^2 = .23, p < .03$). The negative correlation between patienthood and reduction effect indicates that the more commonly an entity participates as a patient in an event described by a verb, the more easily a reader interpreted it as the patient of a reduced relative clause.

**Main Verb Region**  In regression analyses, for sentences containing initial noun phrases rated as good agents/poor patients, agenthood rating predicted the reduction effect ($r = .40, R^2 = .16, p < .03$). Again, a positive correlation indicates that difficulty in resolving the main clause/reduced relative ambiguity, which depended on treating the initial noun phrase as the patient of the verb, increased with agenthood. Furthermore, the difference between agenthood and patienthood ratings predicted the reduction effect for good patient items ($r = .43, R^2 = .18, p < .04$). The positive correlation indicated that the larger the absolute difference was between the two ratings (the better that a noun was a patient, in relation to its agenthood), the smaller the reduction effect was. The difference scores were negative because patienthood ratings were higher than ratings of agenthood.

**Summary**  The regression analyses revealed evidence for the use of semantic fit information throughout the ambiguity resolution process. There was suggestive evidence of an influence of semantic fit even at the verb + *by* region. In addition, we had observed that regression analyses might reveal interesting trends at the det + noun and the main verb, due to large within-category variation at these regions. Consistent with this hypothesis, it was found that people's knowledge of agenthood/patienthood consistently modulated the reduction effect; regression analyses, that is, showed that the resolution process was clearly influenced by item-specific differences in the noun phrase region.

Although the pattern of results for the poor agent/good patient sentences is clear, the pattern for the good agents/poor patients may seem somewhat puzzling at first. In particular, the reduction effects were relatively small for these items until the main verb, although the reduction effect was correlated with goodness of agent. Recall that we suggested earlier that *by* provides only probabilistic support for a relative clause. From a constraint-based perspective, the strength of the evidence provided by the disambiguating information is modulated by the semantic fit of the first noun phrase. In order to provide a preliminary test of this hypothesis, we conducted a completion study in which subjects were presented with the initial fragment, up to and including *by*, of each of the test and filler sentences. Their task was simply to extend the fragment into a complete sentence. Sentence fragments with initial poor agents/good patients were completed as relative clauses 97 percent of the time as compared to 63 percent for fragments with good agents/poor patients. This difference was significant both by subjects ($F(1,16) = 19.348, p < .0001$), and items ($F(1,31) = 113.781, p < .0001$). This analysis shows that offline, subjects found the fragments up to and including *by* less ambiguous for the poor agent/good patient sentences. This suggests that on some occasions subjects retained a main clause interpretation well past *by*, resulting in a delayed garden path effect, as evidenced by an increased ambiguity effect at the main verb region of the good agent/poor patient sentences.

## 24.6  GENERAL DISCUSSION

### Semantic Fit

Typicality had clear effects on ambiguity resolution. When the noun that preceded a morphologically ambiguous verb was a typical agent of the verb but an atypical patient, ambiguity resolution was delayed compared to sentences in which the noun was an atypical agent and a typical patient. In analyses of variance, differential effects of semantic fit did not emerge until the disambiguating main verb region of the sentence. However, the combined results of the regression analyses and the sentence completion norms showed that typicality had continuous effects on the resolution process. Regression analyses showed that agenthood influenced ambiguity resolution in the det + noun region. For sentences with good agents, reading difficulty increased with agenthood rating of the initial noun. Furthermore, for good patient sentences, reading difficulty decreased as patienthood rating increased. There was also a suggestion that typicality had immediate effects; at the verb + *by* region, agenthood for the atypical agent nouns marginally predicted reading difficulty.

It might be argued that because the regression analyses averaged across subjects, thus treating them as a fixed effect, the results may not generalize to the population. This seems unlikely because the event-entity typicality ratings and reading times were collected from distinct sets of subjects. Moreover, different subjects contributed to means for reduced and unreduced versions of each item; that is, it was essentially a between-subjects design with respect to the regression analyses. There is an additional concern about using both analyses of variance and regression analyses; because both used the same data set, the probability of finding spurious effects was increased. Given these concerns, the results reported here should be taken as suggestive rather than definitive. Nonetheless, they indicate that further research of this type is likely to be enlightening; specifically, studies designed primarily to facilitate regression analyses may be particularly valuable.

The effects of typicality presented here are not as strong as the animacy effects reported by Burgess (1991) in self-paced reading and by Trueswell, Tanenhaus, and Garnsey (n.d.) in eye tracking. There are two accounts for why animacy and typicality might differ. One possibility is that there is a small set of semantic features that are used in initially evaluating the fit between a noun and an argument position. These "thematic features," such as animacy, would roughly correspond to the notion of "selectional restrictions" that was incorporated into earlier versions of transformational grammar (Chomsky 1965). According to this view, typicality information is used later in processing than animacy because they correspond to different informational types. This idea is being explored by Caplan, Hildebrandt, and Waters (n.d.). Dowty (1991) describes characteristics of good agents that are plausible candidates for these features, although he endorses a view of thematic roles as prototypes.

It seems more plausible to us that the thematic role for an argument position for a particular verb can be viewed as a semantic space in which goodness of fit for an argument position is defined in terms of featural overlap with the center of the space or prototype (Rosch and Mervis 1975). For example, for a verb such as *devour*, the agent space might center on animate entities that are known to eat voraciously, such as lions and lumberjacks. The patient space would center on things that are eaten in quantity or favorite meals of the typical agents. Therefore, the agent and patient spaces would have little overlap because entities that devour things tend to differ greatly from things that are devoured. In contrast, for the verb *fight*, fighters tend to be very similar to entities that are fought. Therefore, the agent and patient semantic spaces would highly overlap. A related consideration is the size of the agent and patient spaces; some verbs may have more restricted spaces than others. For example, it is reasonable to assume that the agent space for *talk* is much smaller than for *breathe*.

When accounting for the influence of semantic fit or thematic role typicality on the resolution of the main clause/reduced relative ambiguity, there are (at least) three important factors associated with the initial noun: (1) the fit between the initial noun and the typical agent of the verb, (2) the fit between the initial noun and the typical patient of the verb, and (3) the proximity in semantic space of the typical agent and typical patient spaces. Inanimate initial nouns can show strong effects because they can be chosen so that they are distant from the space defining the typical agent of a verb and near the center of the space defining the typical patient (Burgess 1991; Burgess and Tanenhaus, n.d.). For example, a lawn is never an agent in a raking event, but it is the prototypical patient of raking. The effects reported above were weaker than in the animacy studies because twenty-four of thirty-two sentences used animate initial nouns. Animate nouns tend to share properties with typical agents of verbs. For example, although reporters are typical interviewers and candidates are typically interviewed, it is possible for a reporter to be interviewed and for a candidate to interview someone. Unlike the gardening sense of *rake*, where typical agents share no properties with typical patients, typical interviewers and interviewees tend to share a number of properties. Returning to the semantic distance metaphor, typical agents and patients are much more distant for a verb like *rake*, which prefers animate agents and inanimate patients, than for a verb like *interview*, which prefers animate agents and patients. We are exploring further implications of conceptualizing thematic roles in this manner.

The results reported here complement those reported by Pearlmutter and MacDonald (1992). Taken together, these studies demonstrate interactions between subtle semantic constraints and subsequent ambiguity resolution. This pattern of results clearly supports predictions made by constraint-based models. However, it does not provide definitive evidence against two-stage models, particularly if the revision stage is viewed as an interactive constraint-satisfaction process. A two-stage model can point to delayed effects as evidence that there is an initial stage in structure building that is unaffected by semantic constraint. This account becomes less plausible as the temporal window of the first stage shrinks and as an increasing range of relevant contextual variables are shown to influence ambiguity resolution rapidly (Spivey-Knowlton, Trueswell, and Tanenhaus 1993). More research that directly manipulates strength of constraint and availability is clearly necessary before the issue can be completely resolved. In particular, it will be necessary to show that even subtle constraints will have immediate effects under conditions in which the less preferred alternative is more likely.

## Availability

We had hoped to explore the interaction of typicality with availability by using corpus-based measures to compare verbs that are typically used in reduced relative clauses with those that are not. This was not feasible because the corpus that we used contained too few examples of most of the verbs. The corpus analysis did suggest that reduced relative clauses rarely occur immediately after the first noun phrase in a sentence. Given recent evidence that accessibility of alternatives for a categorical ambiguity is strongly affected by co-occurrence information (Tanenhaus and Juliano 1992), it seems unlikely that the simple frequency with which a verb is used as a participial will by itself have clear effects on the availability of the participial in a sentence-initial reduced relative clause. Thus, it will be important to find alternative ways of manipulating availability with this structure, perhaps by combining typicality with some form of referential manipulation.

## Matching Variables with Analyses

The pattern of results with the analyses of variance and regression analyses clearly highlights the importance of incorporating measures that are suited to continuous variables in studies of syntactic processing. In the analyses of variance, there was little evidence for the effects of typicality on ambiguity resolution until the last region of the sentence, and even then, interactions between goodness of fit and ambiguity did not approach significance. In contrast, the regression analyses presented a much clearer picture. These analyses indicated that typicality affected ambiguity resolution at the noun phrase following the verb + *by* region. Subtle effects like these are likely to be masked in analysis of variance designs in which continuous variables are treated as if they were discrete, with a resulting loss of power. It should be noted that the design that we chose was in fact a compromise because standard practice in the area is to use analysis of variance designs. However, to exploit the power of regression analyses fully, it will be important to use designs in which the relevant variables are treated as continuous, that is, one that includes a uniform and wide-ranging distribution of the independent variable. This suggests a research strategy in which analysis of variance designs may be most useful in establishing the basic validity of a variable; once this is done, statistical techniques better suited to continuous variables will be required to obtain a clearer picture.

## Conclusions

We have presented evidence that subtle differences in semantic fit, as measured by typicality norms, have clear effects on ambiguity resolution when regression analyses are used. The results do not provide definitive evidence against two-stage models of syntactic ambiguity resolution; however, they clearly confirm predictions made by models that treat syntactic ambiguity resolution as a continuous constraint-based process.

## APPENDIX

Following are the target items along with the agenthood (A) and patienthood (P) ratings of the event-entity pair, the percentage of reduced relative completions in the sentence completion norms (RRC), and the unreduced and reduced reading times in the verb + *by* (V + *by*), determiner + noun (D + N), and main verb (MV) regions.

### Inanimate Patients

1. a. The researcher studied by the historian was known for discovering the tuberculosis vaccine. He also had a reputation as an alcoholic and a womanizer.
      A: 6.8  P: 2.4  RRC: 44  V + *by*: 458, 585  D + N: 764, 782  MV: 586, 1402
   b. The topic studied by the student was broader than the teacher wanted. Trying to write a 5-page paper on the history of modern science is not a feasible objective.
      A: 1.1  P: 6.2  RRC: 100  V + *by*: 429, 707  D + N: 439, 436  MV: 605, 556
2. a. The savage devoured by the leopard was weaker than the others. He let out a blood curdling scream as his rib cage was crushed.
      A: 6.3  P: 1.3  RRC: 56  V + *by*: 717, 678  D + N: 671, 499  MV: 558, 547
   b. The dinner devoured by the lumberjack was bigger than everyone else's. It didn't have a chance to cool down because he ate it so quickly.
      A: 1.1  P: 6.8  RRC: 100  V + *by*: 561, 505  D + N: 680, 529  MV: 568, 467

3. a. The groupie admired by her brother was leaving for Chicago that day. She would have died if she were to miss the Grateful Dead.
   A: 6.4  P: 2.2  RRC: 86  V + by: 444, 573  D + N: 818, 404  MV: 555, 585
   b. The necklace admired by the customer was priced too high for her. It had once been owned by Elizabeth Taylor.
   A: 1.1  P: 5.1  RRC: 100  V + by: 696, 544  D + N: 517, 488  MV: 673, 518

4. a. The manager sent by his boss was unhappy to be delivering the message. So on the way, he stopped at a bar and killed some time.
   A: 5.4  P: 2.7  RRC: 100  V + by: 474, 387  D + N: 448, 395  MV: 669, 546
   b. The application sent by the graduate was poorly prepared. It had been written in pencil and didn't contain the correct information.
   A: 1.3  P: 5.7  RRC: 100  V + by: 584, 469  D + N: 684, 465  MV: 700, 483

5. a. The guard watched by the prisoners was getting very nervous. Due to budget cuts, he found himself alone on the nightshift.
   A: 6.9  P: 2.6  RRC: 40  V + by: 427, 464  D + N: 476, 518  MV: 560, 638
   b. The movie watched by the neighbors was getting great reviews. It had Robin Williams and Jeff Bridges as the main characters.
   A: 1.0  P: 6.8  RRC: 100  V + by: 409, 485  D + N: 450, 444  MV: 445, 639

6. a. The scientist examined by the doctors was seventy years old. His cancer seemed to be going into remission.
   A: 6.4  P: 2.4  RRC: 75  V + by: 433, 584  D + N: 494, 560  MV: 478, 659
   b. The fossil examined by the scientist was seventy thousand years old. No one was sure what species of fish it was from.
   A: 1.1  P: 6.2  RRC: 100  V + by: 467, 742  D + N: 450, 622  MV: 410, 670

7. a. The tourist visited by the sheriff was suspected of murder. He had no idea how he had gotten involved in this.
   A: 6.8  P: 1.7  RRC: 57  V + by: 459, 499  D + N: 473, 688  MV: 561, 808
   b. The museum visited by the tourists was founded in the 18th century. It had been built by the Czars to house great Russian paintings.
   A: 1.0  P: 6.8  RRC: 100  V + by: 359, 495  D + N: 369, 642  MV: 335, 533

8. a. The archeologist found by the police was locked in a pharaoh's tomb. No one knew how Indiana Jones had been trapped there.
   A: 6.2  P: 1.4  RRC: 56  V + by: 534, 513  D + N: 440, 544  MV: 523, 501
   b. The treasure found by the pirates was locked inside a golden chest. The diamonds had been hidden there for 110 years.
   A: 1.1  P: 4.3  RRC: 100  V + by: 500, 558  D + N: 450, 488  MV: 456, 402

## Animate Patients

9. a. The priest worshipped by his followers was ignorant of their strife. He often turned away the homeless when they sought shelter in his church.
   A: 6.6  P: 3.2  RRC: 56  V + by: 525, 652  D + N: 584, 895  MV: 463, 744
   b. The goddess worshipped by her followers was ignorant of their strife. She often wished they would just go away and leave her alone.
   A: 2.0  P: 6.5  RRC: 100  V + by: 456, 571  D + N: 542, 626  MV: 432, 497

10. a. The professor taught by the specialists was better skilled than the others. Her exceptional training had allowed her to get a job at Stanford.
    A: 6.9  P: 2.8  RRC: 44  V + by: 476, 476  D + N: 519, 719  MV: 560, 490
    b. The trainee taught by the specialists was better skilled than the others. He moved to a management position much more quickly than normal.
    A: 1.5  P: 6.2  RRC: 100  V + by: 581, 484  D + N: 722, 834  MV: 844, 537

11. a. The policeman captured by the CIA was frightened for his life. He had accidentally murdered an agent in New Orleans.
A: 6.3  P: 2.2  RRC: 71  V + by: 483, 463  D + N: 522, 559  MV: 522, 532
    b. The fugitive captured by the CIA was frightened for his life. He had accidentally murdered an agent in New Orleans.
A: 1.7  P: 5.4  RRC: 100  V + by: 480, 563  D + N: 506, 1087  MV: 471, 602

12. a. The postman carried by the paramedics was having trouble breathing. He suffered from asthma, but this attack was worse than usual.
A: 6.9  P: 1.9  RRC: 56  V + by: 455, 439  D + N: 787, 625  MV: 458, 837
    b. The newborn carried by the paramedics was having trouble breathing. It looked as though something was stuck in her throat.
A: 1.2  P: 6.8  RRC: 100  V + by: 592, 557  D + N: 743, 1040  MV: 605, 588

13. a. The prosecutor accused by the court pleaded guilty of falsifying evidence. He said he regretted his actions, but the judge was still harsh.
A: 5.8  P: 1.7  RRC: 71  V + by: 499, 572  D + N: 457, 551  MV: 544, 629
    b. The defendant accused by the court pleaded guilty of falsifying evidence. He said he regretted his actions, but the judge was still harsh.
A: 3.1  P: 6.5  RRC: 88  V + by: 419, 612  D + N: 472, 737  MV: 708, 906

14. a. The warden released by the inmates insisted that the terms be met. He didn't want the other hostages to come to any harm.
A: 6.2  P: 1.8  RRC: 67  V + by: 503, 504  D + N: 591, 670  MV: 545, 758
    b. The inmate released by the warden insisted that he was never guilty. Regardless, his reputation in the community had been ruined.
A: 1.6  P: 5.2  RRC: 100  V + by: 453, 497  D + N: 484, 557  MV: 533, 834

15. a. The waiter served by his trainee was displeased with her attitude. He complained to the manager about her lack of enthusiasm.
A: 7.0  P: 1.7  RRC: 43  V + by: 450, 612  D + N: 792, 940  MV: 667, 1208
    b. The customer served by the waitress was displeased with her attitude. He complained to the manager about her lack of enthusiasm.
A: 1.7  P: 6.7  RRC: 86  V + by: 460, 520  D + N: 510, 475  MV: 523, 592

16. a. The teacher dismissed by the principal was happy to leave the school. She had been an outcast there since the day she arrived.
A: 6.0  P: 2.3  RRC: 67  V + by: 634, 566  D + N: 525, 499  MV: 502, 431
    b. The pupil dismissed by the teacher was happy to get out early. It was a sunny day and he wanted to play baseball.
A: 1.8  P: 5.7  RRC: 100  V + by: 474, 475  D + N: 593, 459  MV: 416, 408

17. a. The prowler stalked by the police was about to be caught. They had him surrounded at a small hotel just outside of town.
A: 5.9  P: 1.5  RRC: 22  V + by: 809, 448  D + N: 698, 545  MV: 536, 456
    b. The prey stalked by the lion was about to be caught. The antelope's leg was injured and it had little chance of getting away.
A: 1.6  P: 6.9  RRC: 100  V + by: 480, 535  D + N: 514, 462  MV: 476, 554

18. a. The rapist tortured by the townspeople was played by Dennis Hopper. The character died a horrible death in the middle of the village square.
A: 6.6  P: 2.9  RRC: 50  V + by: 506, 567  D + N: 493, 560  MV: 530, 572
    b. The victim tortured by the townspeople was played by Dennis Hopper. The character died a horrible death in the middle of the village square.
A: 1.1  P: 5.8  RRC: 88  V + by: 494, 592  D + N: 556, 845  MV: 676, 651

19. a. The reporter interviewed by the editor proved unfit for the job. Although his resume looked promising, the editor found him to be immature and egotistical.
A: 6.8  P: 2.3  RRC: 71  V + by: 453, 531  D + N: 712, 439  MV: 621, 690

b. The candidate interviewed by the editor proved unfit for office. Although the interview went well, many of his promises turned out to be lies.
A: 2.4  P: 6.7  RRC: 100  V + by: 587, 572  D + N: 742, 592  MV: 953, 821

20. a. The employer fired by the owner was jobless for several months. He had worked no other jobs, and now found himself without a recommendation.
A: 6.7  P: 2.3  RRC: 60  V + by: 556, 481  D + N: 520, 463  MV: 654, 569

b. The employee fired by the owner was jobless for several months. He had worked no other jobs, and now found himself without a recommendation.
A: 2.5  P: 6.2  RRC: 88  V + by: 512, 547  D + N: 517, 466  MV: 767, 590

21. a. The cop arrested by the detective was guilty of taking bribes. He was let off because no one would testify against him.
A: 6.5  P: 2.6  RRC: 67  V + by: 542, 487  D + N: 731, 548  MV: 908, 628

b. The crook arrested by the detective was guilty of grand larceny. They had been following him for months and finally had the evidence to convict him.
A: 1.3  P: 6.6  RRC: 100  V + by: 483, 468  D + N: 588, 426  MV: 477, 453

22. a. The boss hired by the corporation was perfect for the job. In addition to his great resume, he was a damn nice guy.
A: 6.6  P: 1.9  RRC: 67  V + by: 531, 506  D + N: 432, 520  MV: 448, 605

b. The applicant hired by the corporation was perfect for the job. In addition to his great resume, he was a damn nice guy.
A: 1.1  P: 6.6  RRC: 89  V + by: 417, 552  D + N: 705, 623  MV: 524, 462

23. a. The auditor investigated by the authorities was indicted for accepting bribes. He had been accepting them for years and finally slipped up.
A: 6.3  P: 2.6  RRC: 71  V + by: 470, 1001  D + N: 563, 598  MV: 620, 569

b. The criminal investigated by the authorities was indicted for murder. Although Manson hadn't committed the murders himself, he was still held directly responsible.
A: 2.1  P: 5.7  RRC: 100  V + by: 569, 613  D + N: 641, 612  MV: 688, 625

24. a. The coach instructed by her mentor had made similar career decisions. They both ended up at Ivy League schools.
A: 6.2  P: 2.5  RRC: 56  V + by: 491, 470  D + N: 401, 591  MV: 679, 919

b. The novice instructed by her mentor had made several judgment errors. She was still learning to cope with the fast pace of the game.
A: 2.2  P: 6.7  RRC: 88  V + by: 742, 567  D + N: 912, 841  MV: 498, 670

25. a. The butcher slaughtered by the Mafia was getting too bold for their liking. He refused to pay his protection money and had threatened to go to the police.
A: 6.4  P: 1.4  RRC: 56  V + by: 505, 552  D + N: 847, 549  MV: 631, 586

b. The cow slaughtered by the farmer was getting too old to give milk. She had been a good cow and he felt bad doing it.
A: 1.2  P: 6.4  RRC: 100  V + by: 476, 449  D + N: 424, 404  MV: 704, 467

26. a. The lion chased by his mate tried to lose her in the bushes. They often played this game during the mating season.
A: 6.1  P: 1.8  RRC: 86  V + by: 665, 466  D + N: 403, 464  MV: 548, 493

b. The mouse chased by the cat tried to lose him in the bushes. He would have gotten away if he had been just a little faster.
A: 1.9  P: 5.8  RRC: 100  V + by: 457, 575  D + N: 458, 514  MV: 472, 795

27. a. The knight rescued by the soldier was forever indebted to him. He vowed to protect him and his family in return.
A: 5.8  P: 1.8  RRC: 88  V + by: 567, 512  D + N: 610, 573  MV: 698, 508

b. The hostage rescued by the soldier was forever indebted to him. He felt that he could never fully repay him for what he had done.
A: 2.9  P: 6.6  RRC: 100  V + by: 400, 471  D + N: 437, 470  MV: 434, 469

28. a. The monster frightened by the flames moved away as quickly as it could. He ran back to Frankenstein's castle where he felt safe.
    A: 6.8  P: 1.7  RRC: 67  V + by: 519, 470  D + N: 462, 457  MV: 508, 483
   b. The baby frightened by the flames moved away as quickly as it could. Her mother picked her up and tried to calm her down.
    A: 1.7  P: 6.6  RRC: 100  V + by: 487, 474  D + N: 481, 488  MV: 545, 505

29. a. The Indian hunted by the sheriff ran deep into the hills. He left no noticeable tracks so the sheriff gave up.
    A: 5.5  P: 2.0  RRC: 44  V + by: 433, 512  D + N: 599, 543  MV: 425, 535
   b. The rabbit hunted by the sheriff ran deep into the hills. It left no noticeable tracks so the sheriff gave up.
    A: 2.1  P: 5.1  RRC: 100  V + by: 485, 530  D + N: 540, 593  MV: 424, 586

30. a. The hunter shot by his buddy was only thirty years old. He left his wife and child penniless.
    A: 6.8  P: 2.8  RRC: 44  V + by: 476, 510  D + N: 713, 827  MV: 377, 554
   b. The deer shot by the hunter was only used as a trophy. He was the biggest buck killed that year.
    A: 1.0  P: 6.3  RRC: 100  V + by: 454, 421  D + N: 398, 464  MV: 378, 471

31. a. The judge convicted by the jury was sentenced to five years in prison. He expected to be out on parole in three years.
    A: 6.3  P: 1.7  RRC: 56  V + by: 619, 630  D + N: 850, 572  MV: 563, 924
   b. The criminal convicted by the jury was sentenced to five years in prison. He expected to be out on parole in three years.
    A: 1.2  P: 6.0  RRC: 100  V + by: 486, 549  D + N: 522, 549  MV: 666, 569

32. a. The inspector interrogated by the FBI was found guilty of drug trafficking. He had been obtaining cocaine from a narcotics officer.
    A: 6.4  P: 1.8  RRC: 44  V + by: 571, 819  D + N: 522, 1076  MV: 470, 515
   b. The suspect interrogated by the FBI was found guilty of drug trafficking. He had been obtaining cocaine from a narcotics officer.
    A: 1.4  P: 6.7  RRC: 100  V + by: 524, 726  D + N: 476, 456  MV: 470, 468

## Weakly Biased Items

33. a. The judge selected by the committee acted in a tasteless manner. She scoffed at the credentials of her competitors.
    A: 5.4  P: 4.1  RRC: 63  V + by: 462, 604  D + N: 459, 742  MV: 528, 488
   b. The contestant selected by the judges acted in a tasteless manner. She scoffed at the credentials of her competitors.
    A: 3.8  P: 5.2  RRC: 88  V + by: 487, 596  D + N: 460, 499  MV: 469, 520

34. a. The accountant audited by the government had all her assets frozen. She had cheated on her taxes for a number of years.
    A: 5.8  P: 4.2  RRC: 50  V + by: 544, 735  D + N: 1509, 973  MV: 470, 691
   b. The corporation audited by the government had all its assets frozen. Its owner had cheated on the corporation's taxes for a number of years.
    A: 4.3  P: 5.5  RRC: 100  V + by: 798, 477  D + N: 534, 445  MV: 494, 408

35. a. The kid startled by the cockroach jumped up and screamed. He had never seen one that large before.
    A: 6.3  P: 3.2  RRC: 100  V + by: 502, 520  D + N: 878, 516  MV: 607, 576
   b. The librarian startled by the cockroach jumped up and screamed. He had never seen one that large before.
    A: 3.2  P: 6.0  RRC: 80  V + by: 556, 392  D + N: 521, 567  MV: 513, 796

36. a. The donkey kicked by the farmer deserved to be punished. It had been so stubborn all day that the farmer couldn't get anything done.
    A: 5.9  P: 3.5  RRC: 50  V + by: 481, 413  D + N: 448, 411  MV: 684, 708
   b. The dog kicked by the farmer deserved to be punished. It had been scaring the cows when he was trying to milk them.
    A: 2.8  P: 3.4  RRC: 100  V + by: 630, 462  D + N: 526, 576  MV: 610, 438

## NOTE

This research was supported by Fondi Ministeriali 40 percent and 60 percent to the first author, and National Science Foundation Graduate Student Research Fellowship to the second author, an National Science and Engineering Research Council (NSERC) Postdoctoral Fellowship to the third author, and National Institute of Health (NIH) grant HD27206 to the fourth author. We thank Jay McClelland for suggesting the completion analyses.

## REFERENCES

Bever, T. G. (1970). The cognitive basis for linguistic structure. In J. R. Hayes (Ed.), *Cognitive development of language*. New York: Wiley.

Britt, M. A., Perfetti, C. A., Garrod, S., and Rayner, K. (1992). Parsing and discourse: Context effects and their limits. *Journal of Memory and Language*, 31, 293–314.

Burgess, C. (1991). Interaction of semantic, syntactic, and visual factors in syntactic ambiguity resolution. Unpublished Ph.D. diss. University of Rochester, Rochester, NY.

Burgess, C., and Simpson, G. B. (1985). Activation and solution processes in the recognition of ambiguous words. *Journal of Experimental Psychology: Human Perception and Performance*, 11, 28–39.

Burgess, C., and Tanenhaus, M. K. (n.d.). Semantic, syntactic, and visual factors in syntactic ambiguity resolution. In preparation.

Caplan, D., Hildebrandt, N., and Waters, G. S. (n.d.). Effects of verb selectional restrictions on the construction of syntactic form. In press.

Chomsky, N. (1965). *Aspects of the theory of syntax*. Cambridge, MA: MIT Press.

Cottrell, G. W. (1988). A model of lexical access of ambiguous words. In S. L. Small, G. W. Cottrell, and M. K. Tanenhaus (Eds.), *Lexical ambiguity resolution: Perspectives from psycholinguistics, neuropsychology, and artificial intelligence*, 179–194. San Mateo, CA: Morgan Kaufmann.

Crain, S., and Steedman, M. (1985). On not being led up the garden path: The use of context by psychological syntax processor. In D. Dowty, L. Kartunnen, and A. Zwicky (Eds.), *Natural language parsing: Psychological, computational, and theoretical perspectives*, 320–358. Cambridge: Cambridge University Press.

Dowty, D. (1991). Thematic proto-roles and argument selection. *Language*, 3, 547–619.

Ferreira, F., and Clifton, C. (1986). The independence of syntactic processing. *Journal of Memory and Language*, 25, 348–368.

Fodor, J. A. (1983). *The modularity of mind*. Cambridge, MA: Harvard University Press.

Forster, K. I. (1979). Levels of processing and the structure of the language processor. In W. E. Cooper and E. C. T. Walker (Eds.), *Sentence processing: Psycholinguistic studies presented to Merrill Garrett*, 27–85. Hillsdale, NJ: Erlbaum.

Frazier, L. (1987). Theories of syntactic processing. In J. Garfield (Ed.), *Modularity in knowledge representation and natural language processing*, 291–307. Cambridge, MA: MIT Press.

Frazier, L., and Rayner, K. (1982). Making and correcting errors during sentence comprehension: Eye movements in the analysis of structurally ambiguous sentences. *Cognitive Psychology*, 14, 178–210.

Johnson-Laird, P. N. (1983). *Mental models*. Cambridge, MA: Harvard University Press.

Juliano, C., Trueswell, J. C., and Tanenhaus, M. K. (1992). What can we learn from "that"? Paper presented at the 33d Annual Meeting of the Psychonomic Society, St. Louis, MO, November.

Just, M., Carpenter, P., and Woolley, J. (1982). Paradigms and processes in reading comprehension. *Journal of Experimental Psychology: General*, 111, 228–238.

Kawamoto, A. (1988). Distributed representations of ambiguous words and their resolution in a connectionist network. In S. L. Small, G. W. Cottrell, and M. K. Tanenhaus (Eds.), *Lexical ambiguity resolution: Perspectives from psycholinguistics, neuropsychology, and artificial intelligence*, 194–228. San Mateo, CA: Morgan Kaufmann.

Kucera, H., and Francis, W. N. (1967). *Computational analysis of present-day American English*. Providence, RI: Brown University Press.

Lucas, M. M. (1987). Frequency effects on the processing of ambiguous words in sentence contexts. *Language and Speech*, 30, 25–46.

MacDonald, M. C. (n.d.). Probabilistic constraints and syntactic ambiguity resolution. In press.

McClelland, J. L. (1987). The case for interactionism in language processing. In M. Coltheart (Ed.), *Attention and performance, XII: The psychology of reading*, 3–36. London: Erlbaum.

McClelland, J. L., St. John, M., and Taraban, R. (1989). Sentence comprehension: A parallel distributed approach. *Language and Cognitive Processes*, 4 (Special Issue), 287–335.

Onifer, W., and Swinney, D. A (1981). Accessing lexical ambiguity during sentence comprehension: Effects of frequency of meaning and contextual bias. *Memory and Cognition*, 9, 225–236.

Pearlmutter, N., and MacDonald, M. C. (1992). Plausibility and syntactic ambiguity resolution. In *Proceedings of the Fourteenth Annual Conference of the Cognitive Science Society*, 498–503. Hillsdale, NJ: Erlbaum.

Prather, P. A., and Swinney, D. A. (1988). Lexical processing and ambiguity resolution: An autonomous process in an interactive box. In S. L. Small, G. W. Cottrell, and M. K. Tanenhaus (Eds.), *Lexical ambiguity resolution: Perspectives from psycholinguistics, neuropsychology, and artificial intelligence*, 289–310. San Mateo, CA: Morgan Kaufmann.

Rayner, K., Carlson, M., and Frazier, L. (1983). The interaction of syntax and semantics during sentence processing. *Journal of Verbal Learning and Verbal Behavior*, 22, 358–374.

Rayner, K., and Frazier, L. (1989). Selection mechanisms in reading lexically ambiguous words. *Journal of Experimental Psychology: Learning, Memory, and Cognition*, 15, 779–790.

Rosch, E., and Mervis, C. B. (1975). Family resemblances: Studies in the internal structure of categories. *Cognitive Psychology*, 7, 573–605.

Rumelhart, D. E., and McClelland, J. L. (1986). *Parallel distributed processing: Explorations in the microstructure of cognition*, vol. 1. Cambridge MA: MIT Press.

Simpson, G. B., and Krueger, M. A. (1991). Selective access of homograph meanings in sentence context. *Journal of Memory and Language*, 30, 627–643.

Spivey-Knowlton, M. J., Trueswell, J. C., and Tanenhaus, M. K. (1993). Context and syntactic ambiguity resolution: Discourse and semantic influences in parsing reduced relative clauses. *Canadian Journal of Psychology* (Special Issue).

Swinney, D. A. (1979). The resolution of indeterminacy during language comprehension: Perspectives on modularity in lexical, structural, and pragmatic processing. In G. B. Simpson (Ed.), *Understanding word and sentence* 367–385. Amsterdam: North-Holland.

Tabossi, P. (1988). Accessing lexical ambiguity in different types of sentential context. *Journal of Memory and Language, 27,* 324–340.

Tabossi, P., Colombo, L., and Job, R. (1987). Accessing lexical ambiguity: Effects of context and dominance. *Psychological Research, 49,* 161–167.

Tabossi, P. and Zardon, F. (n.d.). Processing ambiguous words in context. *Journal of Memory and Language.* In press.

Tanenhaus, M. K., Carlson, G., and Seidenberg, M. S. (1985). Do listeners compute linguistic representations? In D. Dowty, L. Kartunnen, and A. Zwicky (Eds.), *Natural language parsing: Psychological, computational, and theoretical perspectives,* 359–407. Cambridge: Cambridge University Press.

Tanenhaus, M. K., Carlson, G., and Trueswell, J. C. (1989). The role of thematic structures in interpretation and parsing. *Language and Cognitive Processes, 4* (Special Issue), 211–23...

Tanenhaus, M. K., and Juliano, C. (1992). There's a lot to say about "that": The use of co-occurrence information in parsing and interpretation. Paper presented at the Fifth Annual CUNY Sentence Processing Conference, Rochester, NY, March.

Tanenhaus, M. K., Leiman, J. M., and Seidenberg, M. S. (1979). Evidence for multiple stages in the processing of ambiguous words in syntactic contexts. *Journal of Verbal Learning and Verbal Behavior, 18,* 427–440.

Taraban, R., and McClelland, J. L. (1990). A theory of parsing is a theory of comprehension. In D. Balota, I. Flores d'Arcais, and K. Rayner (Eds.), *Comprehension processes in reading,* 231–263. Hillsdale, NJ: Erlbaum.

Trueswell, J. C., and Tanenhaus, M. K. (1991). Tense, temporal context and syntactic ambiguity resolution. *Language and Cognitive Processes, 6,* 303–338.

Trueswell, J. C., and Tanenhaus, M. K. (1992). Consulting temporal context in sentence comprehension: Evidence from the monitoring of eye movements in reading. In *Proceedings of the Fourteenth Annual Meeting of the Cognitive Science Society.* Hillsdale, NJ: Erlbaum.

Trueswell, J. C., Tanenhaus, M. K., and Garnsey, S. M. (n.d.). Semantic influences on parsing: Use of thematic role information in syntactic disambiguation. In press.

# VII Explicit and Implicit Memory

# 25 Memory without Conscious Recollection: A Tutorial Review from a Neuropsychological Perspective

Morris Moscovitch, Yonatan Goshen-Gottstein, and Ellen Vriezen

ABSTRACT  Four different types of implicit tests of memory are identified: (1) item-specific perceptual tests; (2) item-specific conceptual tests; (3) procedural, sensorimotor tests; and (4) procedural, ordered/rule-based tests. They all show the quality that memory is tested indirectly by changes in performance with experience without requiring that the subject refer directly or explicitly to the past in performing the tests. The review is concerned primarily with the first type of test, but it deals with each of the others as well. The effects of a variety of variables on performance are noted, as are the various deficits caused by damage to different neural structures. A number of theories of performance on perceptual item-specific tests are evaluated. We prefer a component of processing theory that states that performance on memory tests depends on the operation of potentially independent, but typically interactive, components that are assembled for use in a given task. Correspondences and dissociations between one memory test and another are determined by the extent to which the components involved in the test overlap or differ. In this proposal, we attempt to identify the components mediating performance on the various implicit tests at both a functional and structural level. Performance on different explicit tests also involves various components with the proviso that one component, associated with the functions of the hippocampus and related structures, is implicated in each test. Based on this assumption, and on Fodor's ideas concerning modules and central systems, a neuropsychological model of memory is proposed that accounts for the relationship between consciousness and memory on implicit and explicit tests.

## 25.1  INTRODUCTION

The relation between consciousness and memory was considered important by theorists as diverse in their interests as James and Freud, Ebbinghaus, Korsakoff, and Ribot, who were writing during what Rozin (1976) called the golden age of memory research at the end of the nineteenth century. The advent and success of behaviorism at the beginning of the twentieth century effectively banished the study of both memory and consciousness from experimental psychology, though both continued to play a critical role in psychodynamic theory and psychotherapy. It was only as cognitive psychology and neuropsychology replaced behavioral learning theory as the dominant doctrines for experimental psychology that it again became legitimate to study memory. Once released from the constricting and fundamentally flawed doctrines of learning theory, work on memory began to flourish. It was only a matter of time before the relation of consciousness to memory would once again occupy the interests of experimental psychologists.

The current interest in consciousness on memory derived from the mounting, converging evidence from studies of normal and amnesic people of striking dissociations in performance between tests of memory that require conscious recollection, such as recognition and recall, and on those that assess memory merely by noting if behavior is altered by experience (Milner 1966; Moscovitch 1982a). Memory tests that depend on conscious recollection have come to be known as *direct* or *explicit tests* (Graf and Schacter 1985; Richardson-Klavehn and Bjork 1988) because reference to a past episode is explicit in both the instructions and the subject's own reflections in performing the test. In contrast, *implicit tests* make no direct reference to the past but rather assess memory simply by noting changes in performance with experience or practice. The subject may not be aware of a relation between the study and test conditions or even that memory is being tested. In short, implicit tests are tests of nonconscious memory, or, more appropriately, they are tests of memory without conscious awareness of the past (see Moscovitch 1984 for other criteria that distinguish implicit from explicit tests of memory). To give a concrete example, memory for words or pictures may be tested implicitly by seeing whether identification latency is superior for studied than for nonstudied items. This contrasts with an explicit test, such as recognition, in which the subject must directly indicate those items he or she remembers studying. An ordinary life analogue of an implicit test might be the more rapid typing of a word one had typed earlier, the more rapid solution to an item in a crossword puzzle that one had previously solved, or the humming of a tune that one had heard earlier, without remembering the initial occurrence of any of these events.

This chapter will address two questions: What distinguishes performance on implicit tests of memory from that on explicit tests and, also, what distinguishes performance on one implicit test from that on another? Why is conscious awareness of the target as a memory associated with performance on explicit but not implicit tests?

The literature concerned with distinctions between explicit and implicit tests of memory has grown too large to allow this review to be anything more than selective (for detailed reviews see Richardson-Klavehn and Bjork 1988; Schacter 1987a; Moscovitch, Vriezen, and Goshen-Gottstein 1993; Roediger and McDermott 1993). Although the review will cover studies of normal and brain-damaged people, the focus will be on the neuropsychological literature, both because it is more manageable and because issues concerning neurological mechanisms and memory are addressed most clearly there. In that literature, the terms *declarative* and *nondeclarative* or *procedural memory* are often used interchangeably with the terms *explicit* and *implicit* (Squire 1992), but we prefer the latter terms because they carry fewer theoretical overtones.

We will begin by providing a classification of implicit tests of memory. Then we will concentrate on only one type, perceptual item-specific implicit tests, both because more is known about this test than any other and because it is in relation to this test that issues and theories on consciousness and memory are most clearly explicated. After indicating the characteristics of this test, we will consider briefly some of the theories that have been proposed to account for distinctions between performance on implicit and explicit tests with particular emphasis on how the theories deal with the issue of consciousness. Next we will present a neuropsychological model of memory that we think not only can accommodate the relevant data but also make predictions about the memory performance of various neurological populations. The model also offers an explanation as to why conscious awareness accompanies performance on some tests but not on others. We end by considering very briefly some of the other different types of implicit tests mentioned in the initial classification.

## 25.2 CLASSIFICATION OF IMPLICIT TESTS OF MEMORY

Implicit tests can be divided into two major categories: item specific and procedural. Item-specific tests are those that assess memory for a particular item, such as a certain word, face, or object. Memory for the item typically is inferred from changes in the efficiency or accuracy with which the item is processed when it is repeated or in the probability and efficiency that it is reproduced or elicited by appropriate cues. The change in item-specific processing efficiency is known as the repetition priming effect because the initial presentation of the item is assumed to prime it so that it is more readily accessible for later processing. Procedural tests, on the other hand, are not concerned with acquisition and retention of a particular item but rather with learning a general cognitive or sensorimotor skill, as is involved in tracking moving objects, reading peculiar scripts, or solving puzzles. Here, too, memory is inferred from changes in performance with practice (table 25.1).

Each of these two major categories can be divided into two further subtypes. Item-specific tests can be either perceptual or conceptual, the subtype being determined by the demand characteristics of the test and by the attributes of the cues to which responses are generated. On perceptual tests, the study material is reinstated in whole or in part, and perceptual identification of the target or some aspect of it is required. Conceptual tests, on the other hand, do not provide any perceptual information about the target. Instead, the target is generated in response to a semantic or conceptual cue. Performance on perceptual tests is affected by sensory variables, whereas that on conceptual tests is affected more by semantic variables.

Procedural tests can be either sensorimotor or ordered/rule-based. Implicit sensorimotor tests measure changes in some sensory, perceptual, or motor skill with mere repetition or practice, as is the case on pursuit-rotor or mirror-tracing tests. Ordered or rule-based implicit tests, such as solving puzzles like the Tower of Hanoi, involve the acquisition or application of sequential patterns or rules. In contrast to sensorimotor tests that are driven by external cues, ordered or rule-based tests involve a measure of internal organization based on strategic processes such as monitoring, planning, and developing and testing hypotheses.

**Table 25.1** Classification of Implicit and Explicit Tests

| Type of Test | Characterization | Some Variables and Factors That Influence Performance | Typical Tests Used to Assess Memory | Probable Neural Substrate |
|---|---|---|---|---|
| **Implicit** | | | | |
| *Item Specific* | | | | |
| Perceptual | Identification or classification of particular stimuli based on sensory cues | Perceptual (e.g., modality, representational format), retention interval | Identification of fragmented words or pictures (e.g., fragment completion or perceptual identification) | Perceptual input modules (representational systems) in posterior neocortex |
| Conceptual | Generation, production, or classification of targets in response to conceptual or semantic cues | Semantic (e.g., levels of processing), number of trials, proactive interference, (attention?) | Exemplar generation to category cues | Interpretative central systems in lateral temporal, parietal, and possibly frontal lobes |
| *Procedural* | | | | |
| Sensorimotor | Acquisition and improvement of motor or sensory skills | Number of trials, feedback | Pursuit rotor, mirror drawing, general skill component of reading transformed script, classical conditioning | Basal ganglia, cerebellum |
| Ordered/Rule-based | Learning to solve problems based on rules or organized response contingencies | Number of trials, feedback, hierarchical organization, monitoring | Tower of Hanoi, (serial reaction time test?) | Dorsolateral and midlateral frontal lobes |
| **Explicit** | | | | |
| Associative | Conscious recollection of episodes in which the cue is sufficient for retrieval | Semantic (e.g., levels of processing), retention interval, stimulus duration and repetition, interference, attention | Simple recognition or cued recall | Hippocampus and related limbic structures in medial temporal lobes and diencephalon |
| Strategic | Conscious recollection of episodes in which extra-cue strategic factors are critical | Organizational variables (e.g., clustering), attention, cognitive resources | Free recall, particularly of categorized lists, memory for temporal order, conditional associative learning | Dorsolateral and ventromedial frontal lobes and cingulate cortex |

Admittedly, the proposed classification is rather crude and will need to be refined as more is learned about the tests currently in use and as new ones are developed. Although classifiable as primarily one type or another, few tests are so pure that they comprise only one element. The classificatory scheme suggests ideal prototypes against which impure tests can be compared and thus provides a framework for task analysis. That the classification captures important distinctions among the various tests is indicated by its good correspondence to memory deficits associated with damage to different structures. Thus, although the classification is based on operational, psychological criteria, it maps well onto the neural substrates that mediate performance on the various types of tests.

It is important not to confuse the operational definition of each test with the processes that are involved in performing it. A test that is ostensibly perceptual may be influenced by conceptual processes, and vice versa. Ultimately the success of the classification will be judged by the consistency between the operational definition and the underlying process, but for the time being, it is necessary to keep the two separate.

This issue takes on special force in determining the phenomenological status of implicit memory tests. A test may honor all the relevant operational criteria to make it implicit, but if recollective processes are involved in performing it, its inclusion as an implicit test is meaningless. If it is to be a true test of memory without conscious awareness, an implicit test, must, by definition, also satisfy a processing criterion: that retrieval of the relevant information did not involve conscious recollection. To deal with this problem, a number of different methods have been developed to help decide whether conscious recollection is a critical factor on implicit tests. Discussions of the problem and a critical assessment of some of the methods can be found in Jacoby (chap. 26, this volume; 1991), Mayes (1992) Roediger and McDermott (1993), and Schacter, Bowers, and Booker (1989). Although it is necessary to remain vigilant, there is little evidence to indicate that performance on implicit tests is sufficiently contaminated by conscious recollection to invalidate them (Roediger and McDermott 1993). Besides, the most powerful techniques have not been applied widely enough to provide information about many variables. Consequently, unless there is evidence to the contrary, we will accept at face value the results reported in the literature. Considering that our review focuses on neurological patients whose conscious recollection is severely compromised, we are on safe ground in taking this position.

## 25.3 PERCEPTUAL ITEM-SPECIFIC TESTS

A variety of perceptual tests have been used to assess memory without awareness. What they all have in common is that they measure the individual's ability to supply or identify an item primarily on the basis of perceptual information. Typically, the item is degraded so that features, such as letters, or parts thereof, are either eliminated or blurred, and accuracy of identification is the dependent measure. For example, one of the most commonly used tests is stem completion in which the first letters of a word are presented (e.g., *Str-*) and the subject is required to complete the stem with the first word that comes to mind. Priming effects are obtained when percent completion of studied words is above the baseline guessing rate and exceeds that of nonstudied words. Fragment completion is similar, except that a word fragment is presented (e.g., __t__i__g, for *string*) instead of the stem. Another test is word identification in which the test item is visually degraded by presenting it at very brief exposures, by masking it, or by deleting parts of it. Here, too, memory of studied items is inferred if they can be identified better than nonstudied items.

Sometimes the test items are presented in their full, nondegraded form, and latency to identify them is the dependent measure. This is the case in lexical decision tasks, in which subjects are asked to determine whether letter strings form legitimate words, or in naming tasks, in which subjects are asked to read aloud words in normal or transformed script. Shorter response latencies to studied than nonstudied items are taken as evidence of retention.

All of the tests mentioned so far are visual (for a list of tests, see Roediger and McDermott 1993). Auditory analogues of some of these tests, such as stem completion and perceptual identification, also have been used with neurologically intact people (Bassilli, Smith, and MacLeod 1989; Jackson and Morton 1984) but very seldom with brain-damaged patients (but see Schacter 1992; Johnson, Kim, and Risse 1985). When they are used, the results are consistent with those on visual tests.

**Words**

Most of the literature on implicit tests, like the literature on explicit tests, is concerned with memory for visually presented words. Amnesic patients consistently show normal priming when the studied items are single words, even though their memory for the same words is severely impaired when it is tested explicitly. This pattern of results is observed when the implicit test is stem completion (Diamond and Rozin 1984; Graf, Squire, and Mandler 1984; Squire, Shimamura, and Graf 1987; Warrington and Weiskrantz 1968, 1970), perceptual identification (Warrington and Weiskrantz 1974; Cermak, Chandler, and Wolbarst 1985; Cermak et al. 1991), word fragment completion (Tulving, Hayman, and MacDonald 1991), and lexical decision (Glass and Butters 1985; Gordon 1988; Moscovitch 1982b, 1985; Smith and Oscar-Berman 1990; Verfaellie et al. 1991). Latency to read words in a normal (Moscovitch, Winocur, and McLachlan 1986; Musen and Squire 1991) or geometrically transformed script is also reduced with repetition in amnesic patients (Cohen and Squire 1980; Squire, Cohen, and Zouzoumis 1984; Moscovitch, Winocur, and McLachlan 1986; Nichelli et al. 1988; Verfaellie, Bauer, and Bowers 1991) though sometimes not to the same extent as in normal people (Cohen and Squire 1980; Martone et al. 1984), who presumably can benefit from their explicit memory of the items. Using the galvanic skin response as implicit memory measure, Rees-Nishio (1984; cited in Moscovitch 1985) found that in amnesics, as in normal people, amplitude of the response to studied words was higher than to nonstudied words, especially when the words were emotional. Explicit recognition of the same words was at chance for the amnesic patients. Similar results have recently been reported by Verfaellie, Bauer, and Bowers (1991) and by Diamond (cited in Mayes 1992, p. 252).

Priming can be measured not only in terms of facilitated performance due to ease of processing but also in terms of biasing of judgment that is the result of an attribution process based on increased perceptual fluency. Witherspoon and Allen (1985) have found that when presentation of degraded words was repeated, normal subjects tended to judge the duration of the second presentation to be longer than that of words that were seen only once. It seems likely that subjects misattributed the ease of processing on the second presentation to length of presentation rather than to familiarity. Amnesic patients of mixed etiology have also been shown to display this effect, in a magnitude that equals that of normal people (Paller et al. 1991).

## Objects and Faces

A similar pattern of results is obtained when pictures, rather than words, are the stimuli. Perceptual identification of degraded line drawings of familiar objects improves in amnesic patients if they previously had seen the intact drawing, even though their explicit memory for the drawing is severely impaired (Milner, Corkin, and Teuber 1968; Warrington and Weiskrantz 1968, 1970). The amnesic patients' improvement on perceptual identification did not always match that of normal, control subjects (Mayes, Meudell, and Neary 1978; Mortensen 1980; Squire, Wetzel, and Slater 1978; Wetzel and Squire 1982), suggesting that normal subjects may have used their explicit memory of the items to improve their performance.

More recently, perceptual repetition priming of visual objects has been obtained in amnesic patients using a speeded naming task. Mitchell and Brown (1988) showed that picture-naming latencies in normal subjects were reduced if they had identified the picture at study. Using this task with amnesic patients, Cave and Squire (1992) found normal repetition effects.

Priming of familiar faces by amnesic patients has been reported by Paller et al. (1992) who adapted Roberts's (1988) technique of presenting pictures of pairs of faces that were of the same person or of two different persons. Subjects were asked to judge whether the faces were the same or different. The pairs comprised either of two views of one famous person or views of two different famous persons. Decision times in amnesic patients, as in normal controls, were shorter when the faces were repeated than when they were viewed on the first presentation.

## Characteristics of Implicit Tests of Memory

Unlike explicit tests, which are sensitive to semantic manipulations, performance on perceptual implicit tests is affected much more by perceptual variables (Kirsner and Dunn 1985).

**Modality Specificity**   Repetition priming effects on perceptual implicit tests are far greater when study and test materials are presented in the same modality than in different modalities. Cross-modal repetition reduces the priming effect considerably both when the test is visual (Roediger and McDermott 1993; Moscovitch, Vriezen, and Goshen-Gottstein 1993) and when the test is auditory (Schacter 1992; Schacter and Church 1992). The modalities tested have been exclusively auditory and visual, with most of the tests being conducted in the visual modality, though some auditory tests have been reported (Jackson and Morton 1984; Schacter 1992; Bassili, Smith, and MacLeod 1989). Though small by comparison to unimodal priming, cross-modal priming is nonetheless significant in many studies on normal people (Kirsner, Dunn, and Standen 1989; Roediger et al. 1992), leading some investigators to argue that abstract, semantic processes can contribute to performance on perceptual implicit tests. Because theoretical conceptions about the nature of the processes mediating priming hinge on this issue, it is important to determine whether the cross-modal effects are associated with recollective processes that can contaminate performance on implicit tests or whether cross-modal priming is a natural concomitant of the implicit test itself. Although more studies are needed, the evidence favors the former interpretation. When the influence of recollective processes is greatly diminished, as in a patient with pure alexia (Schacter et al. 1990), even the small cross-modal priming effect is eliminated. Graf, Shimamura, and Squire (1985), however, found normal cross-modal priming in amnesic patients. A similar conclusion is reached by Jacoby (personal communication) based on a study in which he applied his process dissociation procedure (Jacoby 1991; chap. 26, this volume) to a test of fragment completion. He found that cross-modal priming was associated exclusively with conscious, controlled processes in memory and not with automatic memory processes that were truly implicit.

**Format Specificity**   Even when stimuli are presented in the same modality at study and test, priming is diminished considerably if they are presented in different formats, such as words on one occasion and pictures on the next (Weldon 1991; Weldon and Roediger 1987; for review, see Kirsner and Dunn 1985; Roediger and McDermott 1993), or the voices and names of people at study and their faces at test (Young, chap. 6, this volume; Jones 1993). Changing the language between study and test will also reduce repetition effects for written words (Kirsner and Dunn 1985). These greatly diminished cross-format priming effects on implicit tests are all the more striking when one considers that they are either weak or absent on explicit tests, or, if present, they may act in the opposite direction, as is the case even when word recognition for names of pictures is better if pictures, rather than words, were presented at study (Paivio 1986; Madigan 1983). As with cross-modality effects, some small, but consistent, cross-format effects are found, but these, too, may be attributable to the slight contaminating effects of conscious recollection on implicit tests. As yet, this conjecture has not been put to any rigorous test using the more powerful methods that have recently been developed.

**Item Specificity**  By comparison to the effects of cross-format priming, repetition priming effects are attenuated slightly, if at all, if the format is kept constant but only the physical features of the item vary between study and test. In normal people, repetition priming effects of line drawings of objects are maintained across transformations of size, reflection, and foreshortening, if critical features are visible (Biederman and Cooper 1991; E. E. Cooper, Biederman, and Hummel 1992; L. Cooper et al. Moore 1992; Jolicoeur 1985; Jolicoeur and Milliken 1989). Similar effects have been observed in amnesic patients (Cave and Squire 1992) and in memory-impaired patients with Alzheimer's disease (Gabrieli et al. 1990). These same changes lead to poorer performance on explicit tests in normal people (Kolers, Duchnicky, and Sundstroem 1985; Jolicoeur, and Milliken 1989; L. Cooper et al. 1992). Repetition priming effects for faces also survive changes in viewpoint, though the effect is somewhat greater than when viewpoint is kept constant (Ellis et al. 1987; Young, chap. 6, this volume). For words, changes in font, size, spacing, and script have little effect on repetition priming for words on tests of lexical decision, naming, and perceptual identification (Carr, Brown, and Charalombous 1989). Although alteration in surface features between study and test has little effect on repetition priming, it can be reduced considerably by changing exemplars from one presentation to another, say, from one kind of clown to another that looks quite different (Bartram 1974; Clarke and Morton 1983; Jacoby, Woloshyn, and Kelley 1989; E. E. Cooper, Biederman, and Hummel 1992).

Based on these studies, the following rule of thumb seems to apply. Repetition priming effects can tolerate changes in surface features so long as the structurally invariant properties of the item are similar at study and at test. In other words, repetition priming is dependent on maintaining a common structural description of the item across repetitions. Repetition priming is item specific not with respect to a generic item but with regard to the particular item that is presented.

Possible exceptions to this rule of thumb are reported in the literature, but they may be peculiar to word stem and fragment completion (Roediger 1990; Tulving and Schacter 1990) tests for words and to identification of degraded pictures (Snodgrass 1989; Snodgrass and Feenan 1990; Srinivas 1993). A possible reason is that because the stimuli are degraded or fragmented along arbitrary lines, the gestalt of the target is broken, and more specific, precise information is needed to recover it from memory. Changes in surface features are less critical when items are presented intact at both study and test, as they are on tests of naming and lexical decision. In addition, as was the case for modality and format specificity, it is possible that conscious recollection may contribute to hyperspecificity in normal people. This suggestion is supported by Kinoshita and Wayland's 1993 finding that the effects of surface features on repetition priming that are observed in normal people are eliminated in amnesic patients.

**Insensitivity to Semantic Manipulations**  Manipulations of semantic variables at study, such as the level to which an item is processed, is known to have profound effects on performance on explicit tests of memory (Craik and Lockhart 1972). The semantically deeper the level is, the better is the memory. By contrast, it is now well established that these variables have little influence on perceptual, item-specific implicit tests of memory in normal people (Roediger 1990; Roediger and McDermott 1993; Schacter 1987b) and in amnesic patients (Graf, Shimamura, and Squire 1985). As before, a relatively slight, but consistent, level of processing effect can be noted on many implicit tests, but here, too, the evidence suggests that it is due to contamination by conscious recollective processes. The level of processing effect is not observed in amnesic patients (Graf, Shimamura, and Squire 1985), and it is eliminated in normal people who are truly unaware of the relation between study and test items on the stem completion test (Bowers and Schacter 1990; but see Howard, Fry, and Brune 1991).

These studies indicate that a class of implicit tests is truly item specific and perceptual, not only in terms of operational definition but also with regard to the processes and representations involved in performing the tests. Semantic representations and processes seem not to be implicated. As we shall see, the neural mechanisms mediating these effects are also involved in perception and are distinct from those mediating performance on explicit tests and other types of implicit tests. To appreciate fully the nature of perceptual repetition priming effects, it is necessary to examine two other properties that are not directly linked to the issue of whether the processes involved are perceptual or semantic.

**Duration**  Initial reports indicated that repetition priming effects on tests of word stem completion were short-lived, lasting no more than a couple of hours in both normal and amnesic people (Rozin 1976; Diamond and Rozin 1984; Squire, Shimamura, and Graf 1987). The same was assumed to be true of other implicit tests, such as perceptual identification and lexical decision.

It quickly became apparent, however, that the longevity of repetition priming effects depends on the test and the material involved. If the word stems used have one or two, as opposed to many, possible completions, then the repetition priming effect can be extended by hours and even days (Graf, Shimamura, and Squire 1985; Warrington and Weiskrantz 1978). Similarly, when fragment completion tests that have only one possible solution are used as the implicit test, repetition priming effects were first reported to be undiminished even after a week (Tulving, Schacter, and Stark 1982) and can last as long as a year in normal people (Sloman et al. 1988) and in at least in one amnesic patient with closed head injury (Tulving, Hayman, and MacDonald 1991). Exactly why limiting the number of solutions should prolong repetition priming effects is not known, but one possibility is that priming is related to the extent that a fragment uniquely specifies the memory representation that it activates.

Long-lasting perceptual repetition priming effects have also been found on other tests using verbal and nonverbal material. On lexical decision tasks, repetition priming effects have been reported at lags of at least 3 days in normal people (Scarborough, Gerard, and Cortese 1979) and at least twenty-nine items in amnesics (Moscovitch 1985). In speeded reading of geometrically transformed script, effects have been reported over intervals lasting hours (Martone et al. 1984), days (Cohen and Squire 1980), and weeks (Moscovitch, Winocur, and McLachlan 1986) in amnesic people and over a year in normal subjects (Kolers 1976). On picture naming tasks, repetition priming effects were found that lasted at least a week in amnesics (Cave and Squire 1992) and more than 6 weeks in normal people (Mitchell and Brown 1988). Galvanic skin response (GSR) to exposure of previously seen words also lasted a week in normal and amnesic people (Rees-Nishio 1984, reported in Moscovitch 1985; Verfaellie et al. 1991). Similarly long-lasting repetition priming effects have been observed on tests of perceptual identification of words (Jacoby and Dallas 1981) and meaningless patterns (Musen and Treisman 1990). Together, these results suggest that some relatively long-lasting neural changes must underlie the observed perceptual repetition priming effects (see also Milner, Corkin, and Teuber 1968; Warrington and Weiskrantz 1968, 1970).

Having emphasized the longevity of repetition priming effects, it is important not to leave the impression that repetition priming effects do not decay with time and that they necessarily last longer than memory assessed by explicit tests. Studies of normal subjects have shown that repetition priming effects show a reduction during the first few seconds or minutes after the initial presentation of the item and then asymptote for relatively long intervals that range from hours to years, depending on the test (Sloman et al. 1988; Moscovitch and Bentin 1993 and references therein; Roediger and McDermott 1993). Performance on explicit tests, such as recognition, do not show as precipitous a decline in the first few minutes but have a more pronounced decay rate over the next few hours or days. What is important to keep in mind, however, is that recognition also rarely falls to chance, even when the retention interval is longer than a year (Kolers 1976; see Moscovitch and Bentin 1993 for other references).

The likelihood that long-term retention on perceptual, item-specific implicit tests is mediated by processes associated with conscious recollection is remote given that similar retention functions are observed in amnesic patients as in normal people. The reverse is considered more likely: that implicit memory processes contribute, surreptitiously, to performance on what is ostensibly an explicit test of recognition. As yet, it has not been possible to determine empirically whether this is correct, though our reading of the circumstantial evidence does not favor this interpretation, primarily because performance on recognition can be reduced to chance in amnesic patients whose performance on implicit tests for the very same items is normal (Hirst 1989; Moscovitch and Bentin 1993).

**Novelty: Unfamiliar Words** Early reports on repetition priming effects for novel stimulus material indicated that they were difficult or impossible to obtain for nonsense words (Moscovitch 1982b, 1985; Rozin 1976; Diamond and Rozin 1984; Schacter 1985) and for unfamiliar faces, at least if they were exposed only once at study (Bentin and Moscovitch 1988; but see Paller et al. 1992). When positive results were reported on tests of perceptual identification (Cermak, Chandler, and Walbarst 1985, 1988; Gabrieli and Keane 1988) or lexical decision (Gordon 1988; Smith and Oscar-Berman 1990; Verfaellie, Bauer, and Bowers 1991) in normal and amnesic people, the effects were not always consistent (Moscovitch 1985; Scarborough, Cortese, and Scarborough 1977).

As with duration, as better techniques were developed, it became apparent that the absence of a nonword priming effect is attributable more to the nature of the task than to some intrinsic property of nonconscious memory. Consider the instruction to complete a stem with the first item that comes to mind. The possibility of producing a correct nonword ending is virtually nil if the person has no explicit memory for the studied items. A word, rather than a nonword, is the most likely response. As support for this argument, Bowers and Schacter (1990, 1992) and Haist, Musen, and Squire (1991) showed that when the possibility of using explicit memory is reduced in normal people, through deception and by embedding very few target items in a very large set of lures, then their performance comes to resemble that of amnesics.

When lexical search is not a prominent feature of the task, as it is in stem completion, then repetition priming effects for nonwords are reported in both normal and amnesic patents, although the effects are not always consistent. Borrowing a technique from Moscovitch, Winocur, and Mahachlan (1986), Musen and Squire (1991) measured the time subjects took to read a list of nonwords. Reading times improved for lists of repeated but not of newly presented nonwords. This item-specific repetition effect was substantial—as great in amnesic patients as in normal control subjects—and was independent of their explicit recognition of the items. This finding has now been replicated in normal young people and in a population of old people (Light and Lavoie 1993).

**Novelty: Unfamiliar Objects, Faces, and Melodies** Evidence for perceptual repetition priming effects is stronger, and more consistent, when nonverbal stimuli are used. To our knowledge, there is only one study on implicit tests of novel, item-specific auditory information in amnesic patients. Johnson, Kim, and Risse (1985) demonstrated that a group of Korsakoff patients showed a normally enhanced preference for Korean tunes that they had recently heard. In contrast, their explicit memory for these tunes was severely impaired.

In the vast majority of studies, visual stimuli are used. In two similar studies, Gabrieli et al. (1990) and Musen and Squire (1992) showed that normal people and amnesic patients, including H.M., could retain a simple, meaningless visual pattern they had studied and reproduce it when given a matrix of dots to connect either spontaneously or in response to a subsequent brief exposure of the stimulus. Performance on this implicit test was independent of their explicit recognition of the pattern.

In an implicit test using novel faces, Johnson, Kim, and Risse (1985) found that preference ratings for faces varied according to whether the "story" presented with each face was positive or negative, even though their explicit memory for the stories and the faces was severely impaired. Paller et al. (1992) also reported normal priming in amnesic patients in a same-different face-matching task. Reaction times were faster to faces that had been seen once previously than to faces that were viewed for the first time.

The most extensive studies on perceptual, item-specific tests of memory for novel objects have been conducted by Schacter et al. (1990, 1991). In their studies, subjects are asked to examine novel, potentially three-dimensional line drawings that can represent objects that are structurally possible (can exist in the real world) whereas others are structurally impossible (like some figures by the artist Escher). When the drawings are exposed very briefly at test, the accuracy of determining whether the drawings are possible is higher for previously studied drawings of possible objects, and the effect is independent of the subjects' explicit recognition of the drawings. No repetition priming effect was observed for impossible objects in either normal or amnesic people.

Overall, there is converging evidence from studies of normal and amnesic people that perceptual repetition priming effects can be obtained for different types of novel items on various implicit tests.

**Forming New Associations: Associative Repetition Priming** Previous attempts to find associative repetition priming effects yielded inconclusive results. McKoon and Ratcliff (1979, 1986) reported finding associative repetition priming effects in a sequential, lexical decision task in normal people, but many investigators failed to replicate their findings (see reviews in Lewandowsky, Kirsner, and Bainbridge 1989; Moscovitch, Vriezen, and Goshen-Gottstein 1993). Graf and Schacter (1985) reported that word stem completion is greater when the stem presented at test is paired with a word with which it was associated at study than with a new word. Moreover, the effect was modality specific, consistent with the idea that it was mediated by input modules. Unfortunately, this associative priming effect was not found reliably in severely amnesic patients (Cermak, Bleich, and Blackford 1988; Mayes and Gooding 1989; Schacter and Graf 1986; Shimamura and Squire 1989) or in normal people who were truly unaware of the relation between study and test pairs (Bowers and Schacter 1990, 1992; but see Howard, Fry, and Brune 1991). Although some amnesic patients demonstrated the effect, the overall impression from these studies is that associative priming in stem completion has an explicit memory component.

Speeded reading may be a better implicit test of memory than stem completion because its rapid pace may not allow the intrusion of explicit retrieval strategies. Using speeded reading, Moscovitch, Winocur, and McLachlan (1986) had subjects study pairs of randomly associated words and at test had the subjects read lists of studied pairs, new pairs, or old words in new pairings.

All items were slightly visually degraded at test to slow reading speed and allow the priming effect to emerge. They found that reading speed was fastest for the studied pairs when the results from amnesic patients and normal people were combined, indicating that repetition priming effects can be found for newly formed associations. They obtained a similar but even stronger effect using sentences in which words could be interchanged to produce, at test, sentences that contained old words in new combinations (recombined sentences). Reading speed was fastest for the old, intact sentences than for recombined sentences. Musen and Squire (1993), however, could not obtain associative repetition priming in the word-pair experiment unless multiple learning trials were provided. It should be noted that their scoring and testing procedure differed somewhat from Moscovitch, Winocur, and McLachlan's and that they never attempted to replicate the sentence study that produced the stronger effect (but see Musen, Shimamura, and Squire 1990 for a comparable study on sentences with comparable results). In a subsequent experiment using perceptual identification as the measure, Musen and Squire did find a weak associative priming effect but only when the results from amnesic and normal control subjects were combined. Since then, however, Light and Lavoie (1993), using a similar but more sensitive procedure, have reported a strong associative repetition priming effect in normal young and old people.

The partial successes of the previous studies and the indication that priming of new associations is perceptual prompted Goshen-Gottstein and Moscovitch (1992) to design a new procedure for obtaining reliable associative repetition priming effects. As before, subjects studied simultaneously presented written pairs of randomly associated words. At test, old pairs, new pairs, and recombined pairs were again presented simultaneously, and subjects had to indicate whether both members of the pair were words. On negative trials, at least one member of the pair was a pronounceable but meaningless letter string.

This modified lexical decision task produced reliable associative repetition priming effects in normal people (table 25.2). Reaction times were about 50 ms faster for old than for recombined pairs, and the latter were about 70 ms faster than for new pairs. Changing modalities between study and test, from auditory to visual, eliminated the repetition priming effect, indicating that it was domain specific, resembling priming for single items in this regard. Most important, using this procedure, we have now obtained reliable repetition effects in amnesic patients with confirmed bilateral, medial temporal lobe lesions and in patients with right temporal lobectomy that included large hippocampal excisions.

**Table 25.2** Reaction Times (in ms) to Lexical Decision for High- and Low-Frequency Pair Types

|  | Intact | Recombined | Control |
| --- | --- | --- | --- |
| High frequency | 899 | 922 | 977 |
| Low frequency | 975 | 1053 | 1149 |

**Speed of Acquisition** Numerous studies have shown that perceptual repetition priming effects can be obtained after a single, brief exposure to the stimulus, and in many, but not all, cases the effect often is not augmented by increasing exposure duration and by multiple presentations. Sometimes the exposure duration can be as short as 100 ms (Hirshman and Mulligan 1991), or so brief that the subject is not even aware that a stimulus has been presented. Even such brief exposures are sufficient to produce small but long-lasting, perceptual repetition priming effects (for recent evidence and references, see Challis and Sidhu 1993; Hirshman and Mulligan 1991; Moscovitch and Bentin 1993; Roediger and McDermott 1993).

### Summary

The foregoing review indicates that repetition priming effects that index performance on perceptual item-specific implicit tests are modality specific, format specific, and item specific. Also, studies on amnesic patients and on normal people indicate that conscious recollection has little or no effect on performance. In short, in a deep sense, the tests are true to their name: perceptual, item specific, and implicit. In addition, perceptual repetition priming effects are long-lasting; they can be obtained for novel and preexisting items and for newly formed associations; and the memories that mediate their effects can be formed rapidly in only one trial. The relevance of these findings to theories of repetition priming will be examined in the next section.

## 25.4 THEORIES OF PERFORMANCE ON PERCEPTUAL ITEM-SPECIFIC IMPLICIT TESTS OF MEMORY

A number of different types of theories have been proposed to account for perceptual repetition priming effects and their dissociation from performance on explicit tests of memory. We will sketch some of the main ones, noting their strengths and deficiencies, and propose a conceptual framework based on components consisting of modules and central systems.

### Activation/Elaboration

When perceptual repetition priming effects were first reported in normal and in amnesic people, they were interpreted as arising from the temporary activation of preexisting, abstract representation in semantic memory (Graf, Mandler, and Haden 1982; Graf and Mandler 1984; Morton 1969; Mandler 1980; Rozin 1976; Diamond and Rozin 1984). On the other hand, the formation, retention, and recovery of long-term memories that support performance on explicit tests depend on elaboration that involves processing the stimulus information meaningfully, forming associations to it, generating images, and so on. Very soon, evidence that repetition priming was modality specific forced the abandonment of the notion that the activated representations were abstract in favor of the idea that they were modality specific (Jackson and Morton 1984). The more recent finding that repetition priming is long-lived and can be obtained for novel material and associations effectively disconfirms the two remaining postulates of the theory: namely, that the activation is temporary and that only preexisting representations can be primed. As Roediger and McDermott (1993) rightly note, these setbacks have induced proponents of the theory to modify it so that it has come to resemble transfer-appropriate-processing theories (Graf, chap. 27, this volume).

**Transfer-Appropriate-Processing Theories**

The transfer-appropriate-processing approach states that the degree of transfer between study and test depends on the overlap between the processes instituted on both occasions (Morris, Bransford and Franks 1977; Bransford et al. 1989; Kolers 1973; Kolers and Roediger 1984). The less the overlap is, the greater is the likelihood of finding dissociations. The dissociations and independence between implicit and explicit tests of memory arise because implicit tests are primarily mediated by data-driven perceptual processes and explicit tests are driven by conceptual processes (Blaxton 1989; Roediger 1990; Roediger, Weldon, and Challis 1989). The idea that performance on implicit tests is data driven is consistent with the finding that perceptual priming effects are sensitive to manipulations of physical features but are relatively unaffected by semantic variables. Using this interpretation, proponents of the transfer-appropriate-processing approach have also accounted for dissociations among various implicit tests of memory, so long as one is conceptual and the other perceptual (Blaxton 1989; Roediger 1990). Independence between two purportedly data-driven tests might cause difficulties for this approach (Hayman and Tulving 1989; Witherspoon and Moscovitch 1989), but there is always the recourse that finer distinctions among the processes can be made.

Despite its success (Roediger and McDermott 1993), a major deficiency with this approach is that it does not capture fully the difference between conscious recollection and memory without awareness at either the phenomenological or the empirical level. The division into conceptual and data-driven processes is not adequate for this purpose. If most explicit tests of memory are conceptually driven, then no dissociations should be found in amnesics or normal people between explicit and implicit tests that are conceptually driven; yet there is evidence from both populations that contradicts this prediction (Gardner et al. 1973; Tulving, Hayman, and MacDonald 1991; Graf, Shimamura, and Squire 1985; Roediger 1990; but see Blaxton 1992). In addition, by concentrating on processes to the exclusion of structure, the approach effectively forfeits the opportunity to relate its data and theory to neurology. Except for the rare study (Blaxton 1992), the neuropsychological field has been relinquished to the system theorists.

## Memory Systems Theories

At first only two memory systems were postulated—one for dealing with explicit tests and one for implicit tests—though the organization and characteristics of the systems varied from theory to theory (Schacter 1987a; Squire 1992). As more was learned about memory without awareness and as dissociations were found among implicit tests, in both normal people (Witherspoon and Moscovitch 1989) and neurological patients (Butters, Heindel, and Salmon 1990; Heindel et al. 1989), proponents of the memory systems approach began to fractionate implicit memory into various subsystems (Butters, Heindel, and Salmon 1990; Heindel et al. 1989; Keane et al. 1991; Squire 1992; Tulving and Schacter 1990; Schacter 1992). This trend is considered disturbing by critics of memory systems theories because they fear that systems theorists have abandoned strict criteria for proposing memory systems (Sherry and Schacter 1987) for the more expedient option of postulating a system every time new dissociations are discovered.

We think that systems theorists would concede that the main deficiency of their approach is that it has difficulty in dealing with dissociations within its major divisions, but it is premature to accuse them of being unprincipled. The subsystems are still linked to the processes they are presumed to mediate and to the neural substrates whose damage leads to deficits that implicate only the affected subsystem.

Using these guidelines, systems theorists have made impressive advances in identifying at both a functional and a neurological level a collection of subsystems that mediate performance on perceptual-item-specific implicit tests of memory. This collection, called a perceptual representation system (PRS) by Schacter and Tulving (Schacter 1990a, 1992; Tulving and Schacter 1990), consists of separate, domain-specific processing units that are involved in deriving and storing a structural, presemantic representation of stimulus input. The output from these systems can activate nonconscious procedural systems, which can influence behavior without awareness, or the output can be delivered to a conscious awareness system (CAS) (Schacter 1989), which would lead to the phenomenological awareness of the perceived material. Reactivation of the stored, domain-specific structural representations results in perceptual repetition priming effects and accounts nicely for the perceptual, nonsemantic aspects of those effects. Performance on other implicit tests, such as conceptual or sensorimotor, is believed to be mediated by other systems (Butters, Heindel, and Salmon 1990; Heindel et al. 1989). As for performance on explicit tests, systems theorists consider that it is mediated by yet another system that processes rich, multimodal, contextual information and is centered on the hippocampus and related structures in the medial temporal lobe and diencephalon (Squire 1992). As with perceptual representation systems, rich memory traces become available to consciousness by interacting with the CAS (Schacter 1989).

In many ways, the new version of the systems theorists, consisting of many subdivisions within a larger system, is similar to the components of processing theory that Moscovitch and Umiltà developed at about the same time (Moscovitch 1989, 1992a, 1992b; Moscovitch and Umiltà 1990, 1991; Witherspoon and Moscovitch 1989). There are, however, some important differences, which we will note after presenting the theory.

**Components of Processing Theory**

The central idea is that memory is not unitary but depends on the operation of potentially independent, but typically interactive, components that are assembled for use in a given task. Dissociations in performance on different tests of memory are determined by the extent to which they recruit different components, leaving open the possibility that some components may be more critical than others.

The components approach, therefore, accepts as its initial assumption what systems theorists were led to conclude after their simple models failed: that each system is divisible into separate components. Insofar as components have certain processes associated with them, they can incorporate many of the data gathered by proponents of the transfer-appropriate-processing theorists. Like systems theory, the components approach does not hold that components are isolable, free-floating units. The function the component serves in behavior is determined not only by its internal organization but probably also by a network of connections to other components, which together form a functional unit or system. A single component can belong to a number of different systems. The unit of analysis is not the large-scale system but the smaller components and their interactions with each other. The components approach, therefore, provides a middle ground between systems and processing theories of memory.

The particular version of a component of processing approach to memory that Moscovitch and Umiltà advocate is based on Fodor's (1983) proposal that modules and central systems are the constituents of mind (and brain). Although Moscovitch and Umiltà took exception with some of Fodor's ideas and modified them accordingly, they retained what they believed were his core assumptions and suggested how his criterion of modularity can be translated at a neuropsychological level (for details, see Moscovitch and Umiltà 1990, 1991).

Modules are computational devices that have propositional content and satisfy all of the following three criteria: domain specificity, informational encapsulation or cognitive impenetrability, and shallow output. Domain specificity entails that the type of information modules accept for processing is restricted or circumscribed. Informational encapsulation implies that modules are resistant to the effects of higher-order knowledge on processing and are cognitively impenetrable to probes of their content or operation. Only the module's shallow output is available for conscious inspection. Shallow output is output that has no meaning beyond the value assigned to it by the module; interlevel representations that led to the shallow output are not available for conscious inspection.

Thus, a module, no matter how complex its inner workings, is essentially a "stupid," closed computational device that delivers its shallow output to interpretative central systems where meaning and relevance are assigned and where strategies and plans can be devised to guide thought and action. None of the criteria of modularity applies to central systems (but see Moscovitch and Umiltà 1990 for some provisos). Unlike modules, central systems integrate information from superficially dissimilar domains and are open to top-down influences. The output of central systems is deep or meaningful, and the interlevel representations that give rise to the final output may be available to consciousness. These characteristics of modules and central systems will become critical in our analysis of the relationship between consciousness and memory.

## Registration: The Rapid Formation of Records by Neocortical Structures

According to the components' approach, performance on item-specific, implicit tests of memory is mediated by the very structures involved in picking up and interpreting incoming stimulus information: the perceptual input modules and semantic central systems. The perceptual input modules pick up and transform stimulus events into structural, presemantic representations. The shallow output of these modules is delivered to central system structures for early semantic interpretation. In processing this information, the input modules and interpretative central systems are modified, thereby leaving, respectively, a perceptual and semantic record (Kirsner and Dunn 1985) of their activity. The altered neuronal circuitry (which may involve strengthening old synapses and creating new connections) that underlies the records preserves information about the stimulating event and enables subsequently related events to be processed more quickly. Reactivation of perceptual and semantic records is the basis for perceptual and conceptual repetition priming effects, respectively. The formation of long-term records is called registration, a term I (Moscovitch 1992) proposed so as to distinguish this process from consolidation, which involves the formation of long-term, episodic memories that are involved in conscious recollection.

As is apparent, perceptual input modules are similar to the system theorists' perceptual representation systems. Both share the characteristic of being domain specific and of representing presemantic, structural information. As such, both account for evidence that perceptual repetition priming effects are modality and format specific. Being caused by reactivation of perceptual records, the repetition priming effect must preserve the form of representation characteristic of the module or PRS that is being altered. For that reason as well, semantic variables have little influence on perceptual repetition priming effects since the perceptual record is not semantic. Because perceptual input modules and PRS are necessary for the structural identification of objects, sounds, words, and so forth, they must by necessity be modifiable by experience to represent the myriad of items we encounter in our lives. This quality is manifested in the rapid registration of novel information which accounts for repetition priming effects for unfamiliar items.

The idea that perceptual records retain information of the activity of modules is consistent with one of the main assumptions of transfer-appropriate-processing theory and provides a bridge between structurally based, representational theories and processing theories of repetition priming. To account for dissociations within a particular domain, such as between two types of repetition priming tests for words (Witherspoon and Moscovitch 1989), it is necessary to postulate that, in addition to the record of the item, the processes involved in gaining access to it must differ across tasks. These processes or procedures must also be modified with experience independent of the item and reactivated as needed (McAndrews and Moscovitch 1990; Schwartz and Hashtroudi 1991; Moscovitch 1992a, p. 265).

### Anatomical Localization of Perceptual Input Modules and PRS

Evidence from patients with agnosia, dyslexia, and dementia indicates that modules and PRS are not mere hypothetical constructs but are localizable to structures in the posterior neocortex, in what Luria (1966) called secondary zone structures. Thus, damage to those structures leads to modular deficits: visual word form deficits (word form dyslexia) are associated with left extrastriate, occipital cortex lesions (Warrington and Shallice 1980); phonological or auditory word form deficits (pure word deafness) with left, superior posterior temporal lesions (Kohn and Friedman 1986; Saffran and Marin 1977); face recognition deficits (prosopagnosia) with right or bilateral lingual and fusiform cortex lesions (Sergent, MacDonald, and Zuck, chap. 8, this volume; Young, chap. 6, this volume) and object recognition deficits (visual object agnosia) with temperoparietal lesions, possibly bilaterally (Warrington and Taylor 1978; see McCarthy and Warrington 1990 for review). Recent positron emission tomography (PET) studies conducted on normal people and using subtraction techniques have corroborated the evidence from lesion studies that the aforementioned regions are critical for performance on the perceptual tasks believed to be mediated by the various modules (Peterson et al. 1989).

Additional evidence, however, is needed to confirm that the structures in the posterior neocortex support perceptual repetition priming effects. These effects should be present in patients whose input modules are sufficiently intact to pick up information and absent, or greatly reduced, in patients with damage to those modules. Though incomplete, the evidence is generally consistent with this prediction.

One source of evidence comes from a variety of different patient groups who show normal perceptual repetition priming effects despite poor performance on explicit tests of memory, other types of implicit tests, or both. Thus, perceptual repetition priming effects are well preserved in amnesic patients with damage to the hippocampus and surrounding cortex in the medial temporal lobes, as well as to related limbic structures in the diencephalon (Moscovitch, Vriezen, and Goshen-Gottstein 1993; Shimamura 1986; Squire 1992).

Similarly, patients with Alzheimer's disease whose pathology spares the sensory or parasensory areas of the posterior neocortex perform well on most perceptual, item-specific tests of memory but poorly on conceptual tests and on explicit tests (Keane et al. 1991; Moscovitch, Vriezen, and Goshen-Gottstein 1993). Patients with Parkinson's or Huntington's disease, which affect the basal ganglia and, indirectly, the frontal cortex (Butters, Heindel, and Salmon 1990; Heindel et al. 1989) and patients with frontal lesions (Shimamura, personal communication) are not impaired on perceptual, item-specific tests, though their performance on procedural tests of memory is often compromised (Butters, Heindel, and Salmon 1990; Heindel et al. 1989; Shallice 1982).

A valuable potential source of evidence are functional neuroimaging studies of repetition priming effects in normal people. As yet, only one PET study using the subtractive technique (Peterson et al. 1989) has been published showing that repetition priming effects in word stem completion are associated with reduced activation in the extrastriate cortex in a region corresponding to the visual word form system (Squire et al. 1991). Of concern, however, is that the target area is in the right hemisphere, rather than left, where the visual word form system had been identified in both lesion and PET studies (Peterson et al. 1990; Warrington and Shallice 1980). Squire et al. (1991) argue that the homologous region on the right side stores information about sensory features of words. This suggestion is consistent with evidence from tachistoscopic visual half-field studies (Marsolek, Kosslyn, and Squire 1992) and dichotic listening studies (Schacter 1992) that repetition priming effects that are sensitive to changes in surface features are associated only with left field/right hemisphere presentation. These right hemisphere modules that are sensory sensitive are the mates of corresponding left hemisphere visual word form and phonological word form modules that code information about format-invariant graphemic and phonological features of words, respectively. The evidence for corresponding, but different, left and right modules is in line with studies of left and right hemisphere reading (Moscovitch 1976, 1981; Rabinowicz and Moscovitch 1984; Coslett and Saffran 1989; Patterson, Vargha-Khadem, and Polkey 1989; Zaidel and Peters 1981; Coltheart 1980) and speech perception (Schacter 1992; Zaidel 1985). Nonetheless, because there has been some difficulty in replicating the PET (Raichle, personal communication) and visual half-field studies (Tulving, personal communication), the results must be treated with caution until further work confirms them.

**Perception without Awareness Leads to Memory without Awareness**

The most interesting evidence in favor of the modularity hypothesis of repetition priming comes from agnosic patients whose modules or PRS are sufficiently intact to process information but who are not consciously aware of the information they processed (Moscovitch and Umiltà 1990, 1991; Schacter, McAndrews, and Moscovitch 1988). In other words, these are patients who show evidence of preserved perception on implicit, but not explicit, tests of knowledge. If the mere pick-up of information by the module is sufficient to modify it and leave a perceptual record of the stimulating event, then normal repetition priming effects should be evident in patients who have implicit, perceptual knowledge but not in patients whose implicit, as well as explicit, knowledge is absent.

These hypotheses have been fully confirmed in prosopagnosic patients who show evidence of face perception without awareness (De Haan, Young, and Newcombe 1987; Bauer 1984; Tranel, Damasio, and Damasio 1985) and whose damage presumably spares the lingual and fusiform cortex (Sergent, MacDonald, and Zuck, chap. 8, this volume; Young, chap. 6, this volume). Such patients have strong priming effects for familiar and unfamiliar faces (Greve and Bauer 1990; De Haan, Bauer, and Greve 1992; Sergent, MacDonald, and Zuck, chap. 8, this volume; Young, chap. 6, this volume). On the other hand, prosopagnosic patients who cannot distinguish between familiar and unfamiliar faces even on implicit tests of knowledge (Young, this volume) also do not show repetition priming effects for faces (De Haan, Young, and Newcombe 1987; Sergent, MacDonald, and Zuck, chap. 8, this volume).

With regard to the visual word form module, Schacter et al. (1990) reported normal repetition priming effects in a dyslexic, letter-by-letter reader who has a viable visual word form system. Although she could not read explicitly words that were presented briefly, her identification of tachistoscopically presented words improved dramatically if she had been previously exposed to them. Repetition priming in this patient is observed only if presentation at study is visual rather than auditory, consistent with the idea that modules or PRS are domain specific. No repetition priming studies have yet been reported in patients, such as surface dyslexics, whose word form module is damaged but who can read using another route.

These findings on different types of agnosic patients are consistent with evidence of substantial and long-lasting perceptual repetition effects in studies of normal people in which the stimulus is so degraded that the subject is often not aware of it and his or her explicit recognition of it is at chance (Kunst-Wilson and Zajonc 1980; Merikle and Reingold 1991; Seamon, Brody, and Kauff 1983; for a summary of studies see Moscovitch and Bentin 1993). Similarly, reducing awareness by engaging attention with a demanding concurrent task at study has relatively little influence on perceptual, item-specific implicit tests of memory but a marked influence on explicit tests (Eich 1984; Jacoby, Woloshyn, and Kelley 1989; Parkin, Reid, and Russo 1990). Most impressive of all are a number of reports that repetition priming can be observed for items that are picked up even while the individual is anesthetized (Kilstrohm et al. 1990; Kilstrohm and Conture 1992; Bonke, Fitch, and Millar 1990).

These demonstrations in normal people use repetition priming as evidence for perception without awareness. It is informative and important that independent evidence of perception without awareness be provided in studies of normal people as it was in studies of brain-damaged patients.

## 25.5 WHY REPETITION PRIMING EFFECTS ARE NOT ASSOCIATED WITH CONSCIOUS RECOLLECTION OF THE TARGET EVENT

Having reviewed the empirical and theoretical literature on implicit tests of memory, we can now turn to the central question regarding the relationship between consciousness and memory: Why should the "memory" that is registered by input modules or PRS not be made conscious? Why can't perceptual records retain their properties yet still give rise to memory with conscious awareness when they are reactivated? There seems to be nothing inherently contradictory about this, yet it does not occur. Not unexpectedly, the answers to these questions are influenced by the theories that the authors hold.

### Processing Theories

As Roediger and McDermott (1993) admit, "The transfer appropriate processing approach has virtually nothing to say about the important issue of consciousness in intentional and incidental retrieval" (p. 118). This statement may be too strong, but insofar as it has something to say about consciousness, it concerns the processes that can be used to distinguish conscious from nonconscious retrieval of memories. (See, for example, Jacoby, chap. 26, this volume; Graf, chap. 27, this volume.) Processing theorists have made important contributions for devising techniques that provide markers of consciousness but have shied away from the question of why conscious awareness accompanies some memories but not others.

### Systems and Content Theories

According to some systems theorists, like Schacter (1989, 1990b) whose views we partially share (Moscovitch 1989; Schacter, McAndrews, and Moscovitch 1988), there is a system for consciousness, the CAS, just as there are systems for perception. For any mental event to become conscious, it must first gain access to the CAS. Thus, when a record in a PRS or input module is reactivated, it produces an output that is consciously experienced as a percept, not a memory, when it contacts the CAS. To explain why it is not experienced as a memory, Schacter provides an explanation in terms of the content of the record. Because "access of an activated representation to CAS does not provide any *contextual information* [our italics] about the occurrence of a recent event, [it] therefore does not provide a basis for explicit remembering" (p. 367). In other words, explicit remembering involves not just consciousness but some added content: the context in which the target item that gave rise to the percept occurred. Yet Schacter's own work on source amnesia or forgetting contradicts this statement: normal people and amnesic patients can have explicit memory for the target without memory for the context (Schacter, Harbluk, and McLachlan 1984; Schacter 1987b). Moreover, it is not inconceivable that one will find that performance on implicit tests might be influenced by context (Oliphant 1983; MacLeod 1989; Masson and Freedman 1990; Goshen-Gottstein and Moscovitch 1992; Graf, chap. 27, this volume; Lewandowsky, Kirsner, and Bainbridge 1989). Consciousness, not context, is the critical element of explicit remembering.

Other systems theorists, like Tulving (1985), on the other hand, hold that different kinds of consciousness are inherent properties of specific memory systems. Autonoetic (knowing with the self in it) consciousness is "correlated with episodic memory. It is necessary for the remembering of personally experienced events.... It is autonoetic consciousness that confers the phenomenal flavour to the remembering of past events, the flavour that distinguishes remembering from other kinds of awareness such as those characterizing perceiving, thinking, imagining or dreaming" (p. 3). According to Tulving, the system mediating performance on perceptual item-specific implicit tests is characterized by anoetic consciousness. Tulving's proposals are inconsistent with the idea that all systems or modules feed into a common consciousness system. Because Schacter believes they do, he is forced to say that the memories must be distinguished on the basis of content, of some properties other than consciousness, but we have seen that this is not always the case in principle or in fact. Tulving's proposal, though appealing on some grounds, lacks any principled rationale for assigning different types of consciousness to different systems. Tulving answers the question with which this section began by definition. Anoetic consciousness is an attribute of repetition priming as much as "autonoetic consciousness is a *necessary correlate* of episodic memory.... There is no such thing as 'remembering without awareness.' Organisms can [perceive] behave and learn without (autonoetic) awareness, but they cannot *remember* without awareness" (p. 5). But why? What is it about these systems that makes them that way?

**Component Theory**

According to component theory, the answer lies in combining aspects of Tulving's and Schacter's explanations. Rather than being dichotomous, their explanations can become complementary. As Schacter asserts, processes that are confined to perceptual modules do not give rise to conscious experience. Some interaction with other functional systems or components is necessary for phenomenal awareness to occur. Yet whether that interaction gives rise to a sense of familiarity, a recollection of the past, or a thought or percept without a sense of familiarity is not simply a function of contacting or failing to contact the CAS but of the properties of the perceptual modules themselves. By virtue of their being modular, perceptual representation systems cannot by their nature give rise to a sense of familiarity. That perceptual repetition priming effects are not accompanied by memory with awareness follows from the fact that they are mediated by input modules.

Being shallow, the output of perceptual input modules, is presemantic and ahistorical in the sense that it conveys no information on how the output was derived. All that can be made conscious on the basis of this output is information at the level at which the module processes it and commensurate with the domain-specific representation that the module forms. Typically, it is information about the structural features of the processed stimulus. What perceptual input modules make available to consciousness is a percept stripped of meaning and history, though the percept may be contextually bound at the perceptual level (Goshen-Gottstein and Moscovitch 1992) and may be delivered more quickly and fluently with repetition. But it is still a percept and not a memory, not even an impoverished one. Even if we supposed that the modules retained but did not deliver some historical information about the perceptual record's antecedents, the criterion of informational encapsulation indicates that we cannot penetrate the module to gain conscious access to that information. Finally, because the pickup of domain-specific information is obligatory, conscious awareness need not accompany this process or the formation of perceptual records.

Jacoby (1983) has argued that perceptual fluency associated with more rapid identification of repeated, as opposed to new, stimuli can give rise to a feeling that the target stimulus had been encountered previously (Johnson, Dark, and Jacoby 1985). As Jacoby and his colleagues have indicated, this sense of familiarity is an attribution based on perceptual judgments; it is not an attribute of the information that the shallow output conveys. What the subject experiences is that perception proceeded fluently and from that he or she infers that the stimulus so perceived may have been familiar (but see Brooks and Watkins 1989; Watkins and Gibson 1988, who even dispute that perceptual fluency can be the basis for recognition based on familiarity).

## 25.6 WHY CONSCIOUS AWARENESS ACCOMPANIES PERFORMANCE ON EXPLICIT TESTS OF MEMORY: A THEORY OF CONSCIOUS RECOLLECTION AND HIPPOCAMPAL FUNCTION

We can now address the converse question: Why does some of the information we retain carry with it a subjective awareness of pastness when it is recovered? What confers a conscience sense of familiarity to our memories that is immediate and not inferential?

One suggestion is that the formation and retrieval of semantically rich, contextual associations leads to conscious remembering when they contact the CAS (Mayes 1992; Schacter 1989). As we noted earlier, not all conscious recollection is accompanied by memory for context (Schacter, Harbluk, and MaLachlan 1984), and there is suggestive evidence that contextual information can improve performance on implicit tests without an accompanying sense of familiarity (Graf, chap. 27, this volume). The "contextual" hypothesis deals with the content of that which we are consciously aware of as a memory rather than with the conscious awareness itself.

We side with Tulving's (1985) proposal that conscious awareness, autonoetic consciousness, is a property of explicit remembering. To understand what this means and how it comes about, we offer a theory based on a component process model of hippocampal function (for more details, see Moscovitch 1992a, 1992b, 1994).

The central idea is that the hippocampal component, which consists of the hippocampus and related structures in the medial temporal lobe and diencephalon, acts as an associative, episodic memory module that mandatorily picks up information that is consciously apprehended. To the extent that an event does not receive full conscious awareness, it is not picked up by the hippocampal component. Using reciprocal pathways that connect parts of the hippocampal complex to the cortex, the hippocampal component binds or integrates into a memory trace the neural elements that mediate the information that constituted the conscious experience. That includes the collection of records or engrams of the modules and central systems whose output formed the content of the conscious experience as well as whatever component processes made the experience conscious. In this way, "consciousness" is bound by the hippocampal component to other aspects of the event and becomes an intrinsic property of the memory trace. The process-involved in the formation of episodic memory traces is known as consolidation. The memory trace is then encoded as a file entry or index within the hippocampal component.[1]

At a neurophysiological level, one can think of collections of neurons or cell assemblies whose firing pattern determines the different properties of the event we experience—its color, form, texture, spatial relations, and so on. Insofar as conscious awareness is a quality of our experience, there also must be neural correlates of it that interact with these cell assemblies or are part of them. It is this network of cell assemblies, which includes the neural correlates for consciousness, that are bound together.

To recollect an event consciously, the memory trace must be reactivated. This occurs when an external or internally generated cue automatically interacts with the memory trace, a process called ecphory (Semon 1921; cited in Schacter, Eich, and Tulving 1978). If the event was experienced recently, the hippocampus may still be needed to keep the elements of the trace bound together and so it participates, indirectly, in the ecphoric process. For remote events, the hippocampus is not involved.

In previous papers, it was stated that the product of the ecphoric process is delivered to consciousness (Moscovitch 1989, 1992a, 1992b). This language suggests that there is a system, such as Schacter's (1989) CAS, that confers consciousness on information that gains access to it. If "consciousness," however, is an intrinsic property of the memory trace, it may be more appropriate to say that the product of the ecphoric process becomes conscious, as if ecphory enabled that which was dormant to become active. In either case, the important point is that "consciousness" is recovered along with other elements of the memory trace: *consciousness in, consciousness out*.

It is the recovery of a trace imbued with consciousness that makes it feel familiar and immediately recognizable as something that had been previously experienced. This *recovered consciousness* is the signal that distinguishes a memory from thoughts and perceptions and is at the core of conscious recollection. With respect to remembering, and perhaps with respect to no other function, "consciousness" is an inherent property of the very thing we apprehend (see also Bentin, chap. 22, this volume).

We have tried to convey the central idea of a theory that accounts for the relationship between consciousness and memory. Elsewhere, we have discussed more fully other aspects of this theory and its implications, as well as considered the role of other components that contribute to successful remembering (Moscovitch 1992a, 1992b, 1994). Because our subject is implicit memory, we end with a brief review of other implicit tests of memory (for extended reviews, see Moscovitch, Vriezen, and Goshen-Gottstein 1993; Roediger and McDermott 1993).

## 25.7 CONCEPTUAL, ITEM-SPECIFIC TESTS OF MEMORY

Conceptual tests are distinguished from perceptual ones in that a semantic, rather than a perceptual, cue is provided to help elicit the target. For example, after studying a set of words that are drawn from different superordinate categories, subjects may then be given a category name and asked to supply the first exemplars that come to mind. Conceptual repetition priming effects are obtained if the exemplars generated are influenced by exposure to them at study.

Using techniques of this sort, it has been shown that conceptual repetition priming effects, unlike perceptual ones, are neither modality nor format specific but rather are influenced by levels of processing manipulations and by number of repetitions (Roediger and McDermott 1993). They are also quite susceptible to interference (Mayes, Pickering, and Fairbairn 1987; Winocur and Moscovitch 1994; Winocur and Weiskrantz 1976) whereas perceptual repetition priming effects are relatively resistant to interference (Graf and Schacter 1987).

The variables influencing performance on conceptual implicit tests are similar to those that affect explicit tests, suggesting a deep link between them that has yet to be explored empirically or theoretically. Nonetheless, performance on conceptual implicit tests is dissociable from performance on explicit tests in both normal people and amnesic patients (Roediger and McDermott 1993; Tulving, Hayman, and MacDonald 1991). Amnesic patients with medial temporal/hippocampal or diencephalic damage can perform well on various conceptual implicit tests while failing utterly on comparable explicit tests (for references, see Moscovitch, Vriezen, and Goshen-Gottstein 1993).

These results are consistent with the view that performance on conceptual implicit tests is mediated by central system, semantic structures that interpret the shallow output of perceptual modules and store a semantic record of their activity or representations (Moscovitch 1992a, 1992b; Tulving and Schacter 1990). As predicted by this interpretation, conceptual repetition priming effects are eliminated by damage to association cortex, particularly the temporal lobes, caused by degeneration, as in Alzheimer's disease (Martin 1992; Salmon et al. 1988), or by surgical excision (Blaxton 1992). Perceptual repetition priming effects, however, are preserved (Keane et al. 1991).

According to our theory, only those memory traces that have consciousness bound to them can support explicit remembering. Though central system structures that retain semantic records are open to conscious influences, there is no indication that the record itself contains more than semantic information. As a result, reactivating it cannot lead to conscious recollection. The same principle applies in considering performance on procedural, implicit tests.

## 25.8 PROCEDURAL TESTS

Procedural tests assess learning and retention of sensorimotor skills, procedures, and rules. Of the various types of tests, procedural ones are the most heterogeneous, consisting of a large variety of subtypes whose components are often difficult to specify. The tests range from mastering a sensorimotor skill (e.g., pursuit rotor or mirror drawing) to acquiring general perceptual skills (reading geometrically transformed texts) to learning and applying the rules or contingencies necessary to solve intellectual puzzles such as the Tower of Hanoi. Even classical or operant conditioning is considered by some to be a subtype of implicit procedural tests of memory (Squire 1992).

Some of the literature and many of the issues involving different types of procedural tests of memory are covered in the section on implicit learning in this volume. One of the primary questions addressed by the authors is whether learning is truly implicit, that is, whether subjects are aware of the knowledge they have acquired (Berry, chap. 30, this volume; Perruchet, chap. 32, this volume). A related question is whether conscious awareness is necessary at acquisition or retrieval. Taken together, the chapters in the section on learning (this volume, part VIII) offer a balanced review of a literature that is still grappling with these questions. There is an important distinction, however, that the authors did not consider in trying to determine whether procedural knowledge is implicit or explicit. The distinction concerns the relation of procedural knowledge to memory. The question of whether the knowledge subjects have of certain contingencies or rules is explicit or implicit is logically, but not necessarily empirically, orthogonal to the question of whether they can consciously recollect acquiring that knowledge. Thus, for example, it is possible that amnesic patients can acquire knowledge of serial sequences (Nissen, Willingham, and Hartman 1989) or the rules of artificial grammars (Knowlton, Ramus, and Squire 1992) and even know what those sequences or rules are explicitly, at least according to criteria that some authors wish to apply. Yet the same patients may lack explicit memory for how they came to acquire that knowledge, much as we lack explicit memory for our own semantic or procedural knowledge. In short, it is important to distinguish between implicit and explicit knowledge of procedures and implicit and explicit memory for them. What is striking in reviewing the neuropsychological literature is that there is double dissociation between them: a failure by some subjects, such as patients with basal ganglia damage, to acquire procedural knowledge with intact memory for the acquisition episodes (Butters, Heindel, and Salmen

1990) and the reverse effect in other types of subjects such as amnesic patients and patients with Alzheimer's disease.

In the brief review that follows, we will deal almost exclusively with the neuropsychological literature on two subtypes of procedural implicit tests: those that involve (1) sensorimotor learning and (2) learning rules and organized, response sequences. (For more detailed reviews, see Moscovitch, Vriezen, and Goshen-Gottstein 1993; Butters, Heindel, and Salmon 1990 and part VII, this volume).

**Sensorimotor**

Moscovitch (1992a, 1992b) has speculated that sensorimotor implicit tests are the procedural counterpart to perceptual item-specific tests. Improved performance on them, sometimes called habit formation (Mishkin and Appenzeler 1987), depends on the modification of neural structures associated with both sensory and motor functions that are involved in executing the task. Put another way, improved performance depends on the registration of sensorimotor records.

At the neuropsychological level, this hypothesis predicts that deficits on sensorimotor implicit tests should be associated only with damage to sensorimotor structures, such as the basal ganglia, that are involved in executing the tasks. To the extent that these structures are not involved in item-specific tests, there should be evidence of double dissociation between them and sensorimotor tests. Also, since sensorimotor tests are implicit tests of memory, performance on them should be independent of explicit tests and be preserved in amnesic patients.

By and large, the neuropsychological literature is consistent with these predictions. Deficits on sensorimotor tests such as pursuit-rotor, prism-adaptation, and sensory-adaptation level effects in a weight judgment task have been noted in patients with Parkinson's or Huntington's disease. These are neurodegenerative disorders that affect the basal ganglia, structures that are part of the extrapyramidal motor system (Benzig and Squire 1989; Heindel, Salmon, and Butters 1990; Canavan et al. 1990). Similar deficits are noted in these patients in acquiring general perceptual skills, such as are involved in reading geometrically transformed script and identifying degraded pictures (Bondi and Kaszniak 1991; Martone et al. 1984; but see Moscovitch, Vriezen, and Goshen-Gottstein 1993 for exceptions and for a discussion of the association between performance on procedural tests and degree of motor impairment and dementia). Importantly, performance on perceptual item-specific tests is spared in these patients as is memory on those explicit tests that do not have a strategic, retrieval component (Butters, Heindel, and Salmon 1990; Moscovitch 1989, 1992a, 1992b).

By contrast, and as predicted, sensorimotor learning on a wide variety of tests is spared in amnesic patients with damage to the medial temporal/ hippocampal region and to diencephalic structures (Butters, Heindel, and

Salmon 1990; Corkin 1965; Milnes 1966; Moscovitch, Vriezen, and Goshen-Gottstein 1993; Squire 1992) and in patients with Alzheimer's disease whose pathology affects neocortical structure much more severely than the basal ganglia (Bondi and Kaszniak 1990; Butters, Heindel, and Salmon 1990; Moscovitch, Vriezen, and Goshen-Gottstein 1992).

**Ordered/Rule Based**

Improved performance on implicit tests that require mastering rules or organized sequences demands planning, hypothesis formation and testing, organization, and monitoring of response sequences in addition to mere repetition. Performance on tests in which such strategic, organizational factors play an important role is expected to be adversely affected by frontal lesions or frontal dysfunction that accompanies some neurological disorders. This seems also to be the case for rule-based implicit memory tests, but there is still too little evidence to assert this with confidence.

The most extensively studied test is the Tower of Hanoi, in its various versions. In this task, subjects must move a set of discs graded in size, one at a time, from the first of three posts to the third, such that a larger disc never comes to rest on a smaller one. Improved performance depends on acquiring a cursive rule. Patients with focal frontal lesions are impaired in learning even simple versions of this test (Shallice 1982; Owen et al. 1990), as are patients with frontal dysfunction associated with basal ganglia disorders (Saint-Cyr, Taylor, and Lang 1988). Amnesic patients can master at least simple versions of the task (Cohen et al. 1985; Saint-Cyr, Taylor, and Lang 1988), unless, like Korsakoff amnesics, they also have noticeable frontal impairment (Joyce and Robbins 1991; Butters et al. 1985).

Performance on other rule-based tests, such as learning mathematical rules (Kinsbourne and Wood 1975; Nichelli et al. 1988; Charness, Milberg, and Alexander 1988; Milberg et al. 1988), is preserved in amnesia and may even be normal in Korsakoff amnesics with frontal dysfunction if the rules did not have to be derived and their application provided little opportunity to diverge from the goal-directed path.

Similarly, amnesic patients, including Korsakoff amnesics, can learn artificial grammars (Knowlton, Ramus, and Squire 1992) and a repeating ten-trial sequence of lights in a serial reaction time test (Nissen, Willingham, and Hartman 1989; but see the critique in Perruchet, chap. 32, this volume). It has yet to be determined, however, whether patients with frontal lesions or more severe frontal dysfunction can learn these tasks.

What is critical in testing the "frontal-lobe hypothesis" is whether organizational factors are necessary in learning tasks that are ostensibly rule based and sequential but can be mastered by simpler means. For example, Cohen, Ivry, and Keele (1990) have noted that the sequence in Nissen, Willingham, and Hartman's (1989) serial reaction time test can be learned as a simple chain of responses (nonorganizational) or as a nested hierarchy of responses with subgroups at different levels (organizational). Patients with frontal deficits should be impaired only on the latter test. It is significant in this regard that old people, in whom frontal dysfunction is not uncommon (Moscovitch and Winocur 1992a,b), are only impaired at learning based on hierarchy formation (Jackson and Jackson 1992).

## NOTES

Preparation of this chapter was supported by an Ontario Mental Health Foundation Research Associateship and by the Natural Sciences and Engineering Research Council of Canada, Grant A 8347, to Morris Moscovitch and the Medical Research Council of Canada Fellowship to Ellen Vriezen. We thank Marlene Behrmann, Kim Kirsner, Tim Shallice, and Andy Young for their helpful comments. Correspondence: Morris Moscovitch, Psychology, Erindale College, University of Toronto, Mississauga, Ontario, Canada, L5L IC6. E-mail: MOMOS@credit.erin.utoronto.ca or fax: 905-569-4326.

1. Alternatively, the hippocampus may be necessary initially and temporarily only for keeping elements of the trace bound together, but the trace itself may be accessed directly. After a while, the hippocampus is no longer necessary.

## REFERENCES

Bartram, D. (1974). The role of visual and semantic codes in object naming. *Cognitive Psychology, 10,* 325–356.

Bassilli, J. N., Smith, M. C., and MacLeod, C. M. (1989). Auditory and visual word stem completion: Separating data-driven and conceptually-driven processes. *Quarterly Journal of Experimental Psychology, 41A,* 439–453.

Bauer, R. M. (1984). Automatic recognition of names and faces in prosopagnosia: A neuropsychological application of the guilty knowledge test. *Neuropsychologia, 22,* 457–469.

Bentin, S., and Moscovitch, M. (1988). The time course of repetition effects for words and unfamiliar faces. *Journal of Experimental Psychology: General, 117,* 148–160.

Benzig, W. C., and Squire, L. R. (1989). Preserved learning and memory in amnesia: Intact adaptation-level effects and learning of stereoscopic depth. *Behavioral Neuroscience, 103,* 538–547.

Biederman, I., and Cooper, E. E. (1991). Evidence for complete translational and reflectional invariance in visual object priming. *Perception, 20,* 585–593.

Blaxton, T. A. (1989). Investigating dissociations among memory measures: Support for a transfer appropriate processing framework. *Journal of Experimental Psychology: Learning, Memory and Cognition, 15,* 657–668.

Blaxton, T. A. (1992). Dissociations among memory measures in both normal and memory impaired subjects: Evidence for a processing account of memory. *Memory and Cognition, 20,* 549–562.

Bondi, M. W., and Kaszniak, A. W. (1991). Implicit and explicit memory in Alzheimer's disease and Parkinson's disease. *Journal of Clinical and Experimental Neuropsychology, 13,* 339–358.

Bonke, B., Fitch, W., and Millar, K. (Eds.) (1990). *Memory and awareness in anaesthesia.* Amsterdam: Swets and Zeitlinger.

Bowers, J. S., and Schacter, D. L. (1990). Implicit memory and awareness. *Journal of Experimental Psychology: Learning, Memory, and Cognition, 16,* 404–416.

Bowers, J. S., and Schacter, D. L. (1992). Priming of novel information in amnesia: Issues and data. In P. Graf and M. E. J. Masson (Eds.), *Implicit memory: New directions in cognition, development, and neuropsychology*. New York: Academic Press.

Bransford, J. D., Franks, J. J., Morris, C. D., and Stein, B. S. (1979). Some general constraints on learning and memory research. In L. S. Cermak and F. I. M. Craik (Eds.), *Levels of processing in human memory*. Hillsdale, NJ: Erlbaum.

Brooks, J. O., and Watkins, M. J. (1989). Recognition memory and the mere exposure effect. *Journal of Experimental Psychology: Learning, Memory and Cognition, 15*, 968–976.

Butters, N., Heindel, W. C., and Salmon, D. P. (1990). Dissociation of implicit memory in dementia: Neurological implications. *Bulletin of the Psychonomic Society, 28*, 359–366.

Butters, N. Wolfe, J., Martone, M., Granholme, E., and Cermak, L. S. (1985). Memory disorders associated with Huntington's disease: Verbal recall, verbal recognition and procedural memory. *Neuropsychologia, 23*, 729–743.

Canavan, A. G. M., Passingham, R. E., Marsden, C. D., Quinn, N., Wyke, M., and Polkey, C. E. (1990). Prism adaptation and other tasks involving spatial abilities in patients with Parkinson's disease, patients with frontal lobe lesions and patients with unilateral temporal lobectomies. *Neuropsychologia, 28*, 969–984.

Carr, T. H., Brown, J. S., and Charalambous, A. (1989). Repetition and reading: Perceptual encoding mechanisms are very abstract but not very interactive. *Journal of Experimental Psychology: Learning, Memory, and Cognition, 15*, 763–779.

Cave, C. B., and Squire, L. R. (1992). Intact and long-lasting repetition priming in amnesia. *Journal of Experimental Psychology: Learning, Memory and Cognition, 18*, 509–520.

Cermak, L. S., Blackford, S. P., O'Connor, M., and Bleich, R. P. (1988). The implicit memory ability of a patient with amnesia due to encephalitis. *Brain and Cognition, 7*, 312–323.

Cermak, L.S., Bleich, R. P., and Blackford, M. (1988). Deficits in the implicit retention of new associations by alcoholic Korsakoff patients. *Brain and Cognition 7*, 145–156.

Cermak, L. S., Chandler, K., and Wolbarst, L. R. (1985). The perceptual priming phenomenon in amnesia. *Neuropsychologia, 23*, 615–622.

Cermak, L. S., Verfaellie, M., Milberg, W., Letourneau, L. and Blackford, S. (1991). A further analysis of perceptual identification priming in alcoholic Korsakoff patients. *Neuropsychologia, 29*, 725–736.

Challis, B. H., and Sidhu, R. (1993). Massed repetition has a dissociative effect on implicit and explicit measures of memory. *Journal of Experimental Psychology: Learning, Memory and Cognition, 19*, 115–127.

Charness, N., Milberg, W., and Alexander, M. P. (1988). Teaching an amnesic a complex cognitive skill. *Brain and Cognition, 8*, 253–272.

Clarke, R., and Morton, J. (1983). Cross-modality facilitation in tachistoscopic word recognition. *Quarterly Journal of Experimental Psychology, 35A*, 79–96.

Cohen, A., Ivry, R. I., and Keele, S. W. (1990). Attention and structure in sequence learning. *Journal of Experimental Psychology: Learning, Memory and Cognition, 16*, 17–30.

Cohen, N. J., Eichenbaum, H., Deacedo, B. S., and Corkin, S. (1985). Different memory systems underlying acquisition of procedural and declarative knowledge. *Annals of the New York Academy of Sciences, 444*, 54–71.

Cohen, N. J., and Squire, L. R. (1980). Preserved learning and retention of pattern analysing skill in amnesia: Dissociation of "knowing how" and "knowing that." *Science, 210*, 207–209.

Coltheart, M. (1980). Deep dyslexia: A right hemispheric hypothesis. In M. Coltheart, K. Patterson, and J. C. Marshall (Eds.), *Deep dyslexia*. London: Routledge and Kegan Paul.

Cooper, E. E., Biederman, I., and Hummel, J. E. (1992). Metric invariance in object recognition. A review and further evidence. *Canadian Journal of Psychology, 46,* 191–214.

Cooper, L. A., Schacter, D. L., Ballesteros, S., and Moore, C. (1992). Priming and recognition of transformed three dimensional objects: Effects of size and reflectance. *Journal of Experimental Psychology: Learning, Memory and Cognition, 18,* 43–57.

Corkin, S. (1965). Acquisition of motor skill after bilateral medial temporal-lobe excision. *Neuropsychologia, 6,* 255–265.

Coslett, B., and Saffran, E. M. (1989). Evidence of preserved reading in pure alexia. *Brain, 112,* 327–359.

Craik, F. I. M., and Lockhart, R. S. (1972). Levels of processing: A framework for memory research. *Journal of Verbal Learning and Verbal Behavior, 11,* 671–684.

De Haan, E. H. F., Bauer, R. N., and Greve, K. W. (1992). Behavioral and physiological evidence for covert face recognition in a prosopragnosic patient. *Cortex, 28,* 77–96.

De Hann, E. H. F., Young, A., and Newcombe, F. (1987). Face recognition without awareness. *Cognitive Neuropsychology, 4,* 385–415.

Diamond, R., and Rozin, P. (1984). Activation of existing memories in anterograde amnesia. *Journal of Abnormal Psychology, 93,* 98–105.

Eich, E. (1984). Memory for unattended events: Remembering with and without awareness. *Memory and Cognition, 12,* 105–111.

Ellis, A. W., Young, A. W., Flude, B. M., and Hay, D. C. (1987). Repetition priming of face recognition. *Quarterly Journal of Experimental Psychology, 39A,* 193–210.

Fodor, J. (1983). *The modularity of mind.* Cambridge, MA: MIT Press.

Gabrieli, J. D. E., and Keane, M. M. (1988). Priming in the patient H.M.: New findings and a theory of intact and impaired priming in patients with memory disorders. *Society for Neuroscience Abstracts, 14,* 1290.

Gabrieli, J. D. E., Milberg, W., Keane, M. M., and Corkin, S. (1990). Intact priming of patients despite impaired memory. *Neuropsychologia, 28,* 417–428.

Gardner, H., Boller, F., Moreines, J., and Butters, N. (1973). Retrieving information from Korsakoff patients: Effects of categorical cues and reference to the task. *Cortex, 9,* 165–175.

Glass, A. L., and Butters, N. (1985). The effects of associations and expectations on lexical decision making in normals, alcoholics, and alcoholic Korsakoff patients. *Brain and Cognition, 4,* 465–476.

Gordon, B. (1988). Preserved learning of novel information in amnesia: Evidence for multiple memory systems. *Brain and Cognition 7,* 257–282.

Goshen-Gottstein, Y., and Moscovitch, M. (1992). Repetition priming effects for pre-existing and novel associations between words. Paper presented at the Psychonomic Society, St. Louis, MO.

Graf, P., and Mandler, G. (1984). Activation makes words more accessible, but not necessarily more retrievable. *Journal of Verbal Learning and Verbal Behavior, 23,* 553–568.

Graf, P., Mandler, G., and Haden, P. E. (1982). Simulating amnesic symptoms in normal subjects. *Science, 218,* 1243–1244.

Graf, P., and Schacter, D. L. (1985). Implicit and explicit memory for new associations in normal and amnesic patients. *Journal of Experimental Psychology: Learning, Memory and Cognition, 11,* 501–518.

Graf, P., and Schacter, D. L. (1987). Selective effects of interference on implicit and explicit memory for new associations. *Journal of Experimental Psychology: Learning, Memory and Cognition, 13*, 45–53.

Graf, P., Shimamura, A. P., and Squire, L. R. (1985). Priming across modalities and priming across category levels: Extending the domain of preserved functioning in amnesia. *Journal of Experimental Psychology: Learning, Memory and Cognition, 11*, 385–395.

Graf, P., Squire, L. R., and Mandler, G. (1984). The information that amnesic patients do not forget. *Journal of Experimental Psychology: Learning, Memory and Cognition, 10*, 164–178.

Greve, K. W., and Bauer, R. M. (1990). Implicit learning of new faces in prosopagnosia: An application of the mere-exposure paradigm. *Neuropsychologia, 28*, 1035–1042.

Haist, F., Musen, G., and Squire, L. R. (1991). Intact priming of words and nonwords in amnesia. *Psychobiology, 19*, 275–285.

Hayman, C. A. G., and Tulving, E. (1989). Contingent dissociation between recognition and fragment completion: The method of triangulation. *Journal of Experimental Psychology: Learning, Memory and Cognition, 15*, 228–240.

Heindel, W. C., Salmon, D. P., and Butters, N. (1991). The biasing of weight judgments in Alzheimer's and Huntington's disease: A priming or programming phenomenon? *Journal of Clinical and Experimental Neuropsychology, 13*, 189–203.

Heindel, W. C., Salmon, D. P., Shults, C. W., Walicke, P. A., and Butters, N. (1989). Neuropsychological evidence for multiple implicit memory systems: A comparison of Alzheimer's, Huntington's, and Parkinson's disease patients. *Journal of Neuroscience, 9*, 582–587.

Hirshman, E., and Mulligan, N. (1991). Perceptual interference improves explicit memory but does not enhance data-driven processing. *Journal of Experimental Psychology: Learning, Memory and Cognition, 17*, 507–513.

Hirshman, E., Snodgrass, J. G., Mindes, J., and Feenan, K. (1990). Conceptual priming in fragment completion. *Journal of Experimental Psychology: Learning, Memory and Cognition, 16*, 634–647.

Hirst, W. (1989). On consciousness, recall, recognition, and the architecture of memory. In S. Lewandowsky, J. C. Dunn, and K. Kirsner (Eds.), *Implicit memory: Theoretical issues*. Hillsdale, NJ: Erlbaum.

Howard, D. V., Fry, A. F., and Brune, C. M. (1991). Aging and memory for new associations: direct versus indirect measures. *Journal of Experimental Psychology: Learning, Memory and Cognition, 17*, 779–792.

Jackson, G. M., and Jackson, S. (1992). *Sequence structure and sequential learning: The evidence from aging reconsidered*. University of Oregan Institute of Cognitive and Decision Sciences, Technical Report 92-9.

Jackson, A., and Morton, J. (1984). Facilitation of auditory word recognition. *Memory and Cognition, 12*, 568–574.

Jacoby, L. L. (1983). Perceptual enhancement: Persistent effects of an experience. *Journal of Experimental Psychology: Learning, Memory and Cognition, 9*, 21–38.

Jacoby, L. L. (1991). A process dissociation framework: Separating automatic and intentional uses of memory. *Journal of Memory and Language, 30*, 513–541.

Jacoby, L. L., and Dallas, M. (1981). On the relationship between autobiographical memory and perceptual learning. *Journal of Experimental Psychology: General, 110*, 306–340.

Jacoby, L. L., Woloshyn, V., and Kelley, C. M. (1989). Becoming famous without being recognized: Unconscious influences of memory produced by dividing attention. *Journal of Experimental Psychology: General, 118*, 115–125.

Johnson, H. I. L., Kim, J. K., and Risse, G. (1985). Do alcoholic Korsakoff's syndrome patients acquire affective reactions? *Journal of Experimental Psychology: Learning, Memory and Cognition, 11,* 22–36.

Johnson, W. A., Dark, W. J., and Jacoby, L. L. (1985). Perceptual fluency and recognition judgments. *Journal of Experimental Psychology: Learning, Memory and Cognition, 11,* 3–11.

Jolicoeur, P. (1985). The time to name disoriented natural objects. *Memory and Cognition, 13,* 289–303.

Jolicoeur, P., and Milliken, B. (1989). Identification of disorientated objects: Effects of context of prior presentation. *Journal of Experimental Psychology: Learning, Memory and Cognition, 15,* 200–210.

Jones, D. (1993). Recognizing people by voice. Paper presented at the Eleventh European Workshop on Cognitive Neuropsychology, Bressanone, Italy.

Joyce, E. M., and Robbins, T. W. (1991). Frontal lobe function in Korsakoff and non-Korsakoff alcoholics: Planning and spatial working memory. *Neuropsychologia, 29,* 709–723.

Keane, M. M., Gabrieli, J. D. E., Fennema, A. C., Growdon, J. H., and Corkin, S. (1991). Evidence for a dissociation between perceptual and conceptual priming in Alzheimer's disease. *Behavioral Neuroscience, 105,* 326–342.

Kilstrohm, J. F., and Conture, L. J. (1992). Awareness and information processing in general anaesthesia. *Journal of Psychopharmacology, 6,* 410–417.

Kihlstrom, J. F., Schacter, D. L., Cork, R. C., Hurt, C. A., and Behr, S. E. (1990). Implicit memory following surgical anaesthesia. *Psychological Science, 1,* 303–306.

Kinoshita, S. and Wayland, S. V. (1993). Effect of surface features on word fragment completion in amnesic subjects. *American Journal of Psychology, 106,* 67–80.

Kinsbourne, M., and Wood, F. (1975). Short-term memory processes and the amnesic syndrome. In D. Deutsch and J. A. Deutsch (Eds.), *Short-term memory,* 258–291. New York: Academic Press.

Kirsner, K., and Dunn, D. (1985). The perceptual record: A common factor in repetition priming and attribute retention. In M. I. Posner and O. S. M. Marin (Eds.), *Attention and performance XI,* 547–566. Hillsdale, NJ: Erlbaum.

Kirsner, K., Dunn, J. C., and Standen, P. (1989). Domain-specific resources in word recognition. In S. Lewandowsky, J. C. Dunn, and K. Kirsner (Eds.), *Implicit memory: Theoretical issues,* 99–122. Hillsdale, NJ: Erlbaum.

Knowlton, B. J., Ramus, S. J., and Squire, L. R. (1992). Intact artificial grammar learning in amnesia: Dissociation of classification learning and explicit memory for specific instances. *Psychological Science, 3,* 172–179.

Kohn, S. E., and Friedman, R. B. (1986). Word-meaning deafness: A phonological-semantic dissociation. *Cognitive Neuropsychology, 3,* 291–308.

Kolers, P. (1973). Remembering operations. *Memory and Cognition, 1,* 347–355.

Kolers, P. (1976). Reading a year later. *Journal of Experimental Psychology: Human Learning and Memory, 2,* 554–556.

Kolers, P., Duchnicky, R. L., and Sundstroem, G. (1985). Size in the visual processing of faces and words. *Journal of Experimental Psychology: Human Perception and Performance, 11,* 726–751.

Kolers, P., and Roediger, H. L. (1984). Procedures of mind. *Journal of Verbal Learning and Verbal Behavior, 23,* 425–429.

Kunst-Wilson, W. R., and Zajonc, R. B. (1980). Affective discrimination of stimuli that cannot be recognized. *Science, 207,* 557–558.

Lewandowsky, S., Kirsner, K., and Bainbridge, V. (1989). Context effects in implicit memory: A sense-specific account. In S. Lewandowsky, J. C. Dunn, and K. Kirsner (Eds.), *Implicit memory: Theoretical issues*. Hillsdale, NJ: Erlbaum.

Light, L. L., and Lavoie, D. (1993). Direct and indirect measures of memory in old age. In M. E. J. Masson, and P. Graf (Eds.), *Implicit Memory: New directions in cognition, development and neuropsychology*. Hillsdale, NJ: Erlbaum.

Luria, A. R. (1966). *Higher cortical functions in man*. New York: Basic Books.

MacLeod, C. M. (1989). Word context during initial exposure influences degree of priming in word fragment completion. *Journal of Experimental Psychology: Learning, Memory and Cognition, 15*, 398–406.

Madigan, S. (1983). Picture memory. In J. C. Yuille (Ed.), *Imagery, memory and cognition: Essays in honor of Allan Paivio*. Hillsdale, NJ: Erlbaum.

Mandler, G. (1980). Recognizing: The judgment of previous occurrence. *Psychological Review, 87*, 252–271.

Marsolek, C. J., Kosslyn, S. M., and Squire, L. R. (1992). Form specific visual priming in the right cerebral hemisphere. *Journal of Experimental Psychology: Learning, Memory and Cognition, 18*, 492–508.

Martin, A. (1992). Degraded knowledge representations in patients with Alzheimer's disease: Implications for models of semantic and repetition priming. In L. R. Squire and N. Butters (Eds.), *Neuropsychology of memory*. New York: Guilford Press.

Martone, M., Butters, N., Payne, M., Becker, J., and Sax, D. S. (1984). Dissociations between skill learning and verbal recognition in amnesia and dementia. *Archives of Neurology, 41*, 965–970.

Masson, M. E. J., and Freedman, L. (1990). Fluent identification of repeated words. *Journal of Experimental Psychology: Learning, Memory and Cognition, 16*, 355–373.

Mayes, A. R. (1992). Automatic memory processes in amnesia: How are they mediated? In A. D. Milner and M. D. Rugg (Eds.), *The neuropsychology of consciousness*. New York: Academic Press.

Mayes, A. R., and Gooding, P. (1989). Enhancement of word completion priming in amnesics by cueing with previously novel associates. *Neuropsychologia 27*, 1057–1072.

Mayes, A. R., Meudell, P. R. and Neary, D. (1978). Must amnesia be caused by either encoding or retrieval disorders? In M. M. Gruneberg, P. E. Moris, and R. N. Sykes (Eds.), *Practical aspects of memory*. London: Academic Press.

Mayes, A. R., Meudell, P. R., and Pickering, A. D. (1985). Is organic amnesia caused by a selective deficit in remembering contextual information? *Cortex, 21*, 313–324.

Mayes, A. R., Pickering, A. D., and Fairbairn, A. (1987). Amnesic sensitivity to proactive interference: Its relationship to priming and the causes of amnesia. *Neuropsychologia, 25*, 211–220.

McAndrews, M. P., and Moscovitch, M. (1990). Transfer effects in implicit tests of memory. *Journal of Experimental Psychology: Learning, Memory, and Cognition, 16*, 772–788.

McCarthy, R., and Warrington, E. (1990). *Cognitive neuropsychology: A clinical introduction*. New York: Academic Press.

McKoon, G., and Ratcliff, R. (1979). Priming in episodic and semantic memory. *Journal of Verbal Learning and Verbal Behavior, 18*, 463–480.

McKoon, G., and Ratcliff, R. (1986). Automatic activation of episodic information in a semantic memory task. *Journal of Experimental Psychology: Learning, Memory and Cognition, 12*, 108–115.

Merikle, P. M., and Reingold, E. M. (1991). Comparing direct (explicit) and indirect (implicit) measures to study unconscious memory. *Journal of Experimental Psychology: Learning, Memory, and Cognition, 17*, 224–232.

Milberg, W., Alexander, M. P., Charness, N., McGlinchey-Berroth, R., and Barrett, A. (1988). Learning of a complex arithmetic skill in amnesia: Evidence for a dissociation between compilation and production. *Brain and Cognition, 8*, 91–104.

Milner, B. (1966). Amnesia following operation on the temporal lobe. In C. W. M. Whitty and O. L. Zangwill (Eds.), *Amnesia*. London: Butterworth.

Milner, B., Corkin, S., and Teuber, H.-L. (1968). Further analysis of the hippocampal amnesic syndrome: 14-year follow-up study of H. M. *Neuropsychologia, 6*, 215–234.

Mishkin, M., and Appenzeler, T. (1987). The anatomy of memory. *Scientific American, 256*, 80–89.

Mitchell, D. B., and Brown, A. S. (1988). Persistent repetition priming in picture naming and its dissociation from recognition memory. *Journal of Experimental Psychology: Learning, Memory and Cognition, 14*, 213–222.

Morris, C. D., Bransford, J. P., and Franks, J. J. (1977). Levels of processing versus transfer appropriate processing. *Journal of Verbal Learning and Verbal Behavior, 16*, 519–533.

Mortensen, E. L. (1980). The effects of partial information in amnesic and normal subjects. *Scandinavian Journal of Psychology, 21*, 75–82.

Morton, J. (1969). Interaction of information in word recognition. *Psychological Review, 76*, 165–178.

Moscovitch, M. (1976). On the representation of language in the right hemisphere of right-handed people. *Brain and Language 3*, 43–71.

Moscovitch, M. (1981). Right-hemisphere language. *Disorders of Language, 1*, 41–61.

Moscovitch, M. (1982a). Multiple dissociations of function in amnesia. In L. S. Cermak (Ed.), *Human memory and amnesia*. Hillsdale, NJ: Erlbaum.

Moscovitch, M. (1982b). A neuropsychological approach to perception and memory in normal and pathological aging. In F. I. M. Craik and S. Trehub (Eds.), *Aging and cognitive processes*. New York: Plenum Press.

Moscovitch, M. (1984). The sufficient conditions for demonstrating preserved memory in amnesia: A task analysis. In N. Butters and L. R. Squire (Eds.), *The neuropsychology of memory*. New York: Guilford Press.

Moscovitch, M. (1985). Memory from infancy to old age: Implications for theories of normal and pathological memory. *Annals of the New York Academy of Sciences, 444*, 78–96.

Moscovitch, M. (1989). Confabulation and the frontal systems: Strategic versus associative retrieval in neuropsychological theories of memory. In H. L. Roediger III and F. I. M. Craik (Eds.), *Varieties of memory and consciousness: Essays in honor of Endel Tulving*, 133–160. Hillsdale, NJ: Erlbaum.

Moscovitch, M. (1992a). Memory and working-with-memory: A component process model based on modules and central systems. *Journal of Cognitive Neuroscience, 4*, 257–267.

Moscovitch, M. (1992b). A neuropsychological model of memory and consciousness. In L. R. Squire and N. Butters (Eds.), *The neuropsychology of memory*, 2d ed. New York: Guilford Press.

Moscovitch, M. (1994). Models of memory and consciousness. In M. S. Gazzaniga (Ed.), *The cognitive neurosciences*. Cambridge, MA: MIT Press.

Moscovitch, M., and Bentin, S. (1993). The fate of repetition effects when recognition is at or near chance. *Journal of Experimental Psychology: Learning, Memory and Cognition, 19*, 148–158.

Moscovitch, M., and Umiltà, C. (1990). Modularity and neuropsychology: Implications for the organization of attention and memory in normal and brain-damaged people. In M. E. Schwartz (Ed.), *Modular processes in dementia.* Cambridge, MA: MIT Press.

Moscovitch, M., and Umiltà, C. (1991). *Conscious and nonconscious aspects of memory: A neuropsychological framework of modules and central systems.* In R. G. Lister and H. J. Weingartner (Eds.), *Perspectives on cognitive neuroscience.* Oxford: Oxford University Press.

Moscovitch, M., Vriezen, E., and Goshen-Gottstein, Y. (1993). Implicit tests of memory in patients with focal lesions and degenerative brain disorders. In H. Spinnler and F. Boller (Eds.), *Handbook of neuropsychology,* vol. 8. Amsterdam: Elsevier.

Moscovitch, M., and Winocur, G. (1992a). The neuropsychology of memory and aging. In T. A. Salthouse and F. I. M. Craik (Eds.), *The handbook of aging and cognition.* Hillsdale, NJ.: Erlbaum.

Moscovitch, M., and Winocur, G. (1992b). Frontal lobes and memory. In L. R. Squire (Ed.), *Encyclopedia of learning and memory: Neuropsychology.* New York: Macmillan.

Moscovitch, M., Winocur, G., and McLachlan, D. (1986). Memory as assessed by recognition and reading time in normal and memory impaired people with Alzheimer's disease and other neurological disorders. *Journal of Experimental Psychology: General, 115,* 331–347.

Musen, G., Shimamura, A. P., and Squire, L. R. (1990). Intact text-specific reading skill in amnesia. *Journal of Experimental Psychology: Learning, Memory, and Cognition, 16,* 1068–1076.

Musen, G., and Squire, L. R. (1991). Normal acquisition of novel verbal information in amnesia. *Journal of Experimental Psychology: Learning, Memory and Cognition, 17,* 1095–1104.

Musen, G., and Squire, L. R. (1992). Nonverbal priming in amnesia. *Memory and Cognition, 20,* 441–448.

Musen, G., and Squire, L. R. (1993). On the implicit learning of novel associations by amnesic patients and normal subjects. *Neuropsychology, 7,* 119–135.

Musen, G., and Triesman, A. (1990). Implicit and explicit memory for visual patterns. *Journal of Experimental Psychology: Learning, Memory and Cognition, 16,* 127–137.

Nichelli, P., Bahmanian-Behbahani, G., Gentilini, M., and Vecchi, A. (1988). Preserved memory abilities in thalamic amnesia. *Brain, 111,* 1337–1353.

Nissen, M. J., Willingham, D., and Hartman, M. (1989). Explicit and implicit remembering: When is learning preserved in amnesia? *Neuropsychologia, 27,* 341–352.

Oliphant, G. W. (1983). Repetition and recency effects in word recognition. *Australian Journal of Psychology, 35,* 393–403.

Owen, A. M., Downes, J. J., Sahakian, B. J., Polkey, C. E., and Robbins, T. W. (1990). Planning and spatial working memory following frontal lobe lesions in man. *Neuropsychologia, 28,* 1021–1034.

Paivio, A. (1986). *Mental representations: A dual coding approach.* New York: Oxford University Press.

Paller, K. A., Mayes, A. R., McDermott, M., Pickering, A. D., and Meudell, P. R. (1991). Indirect measures of memory in a memory duration judgment task are normal in amnesic patients. *Neuropsychologia, 29,* 1007–1018.

Paller, K. A., Mayes, A. R., Thompson, K. M., Young, A. W., Roberts, J., and Meudell, P. R. (1992). Priming of face matching in amnesia. *Brain and Cognition, 18,* 46–59.

Parkin, A. J., Reid, T., and Russo, R. (1990). On the differential nature of implicit and explicit memory. *Memory and Cognition, 18,* 307–314.

Patterson, K., Vargha-Khadem, F., and Polkey, C. E. (1989). Reading with one hemisphere. *Brain, 112*, 39–63.

Peterson, S. E., Fox, P. T., Posner, M. I., Mintun, M. A., and Raichle, M. E. (1989). Positron emission tomographic studies of the processing of single words. *Journal of Cognitive Neuroscience, 1*, 153–170.

Peterson, S. E., Fox, P. T., Synder, A. Z., and Raichle, M. E. (1990). Activation of extrastriate and frontal cortical areas by visual words and word-like stimuli. *Science, 249*, 1041–1044.

Rabinowicz, B., and Moscovitch, M. (1984). Right hemisphere literacy: A critique of some recent approaches. *Cognitive Neuropsychology, 1*, 343–350.

Rees-Nishio, M. (1984). Memory, emotion, and skin conductance responses in young and elderly normal and memory-impaired people. Unpublished Ph.D. dissertation. University of Toronto, Toronto, Ontario.

Richardson-Klavehn, A., and Bjork, R. A. (1988). Measures of memory. *Annual Review of Psychology, 39*, 475–543.

Roberts, J. (1988). A new method for testing implicit memory in normal and amnesic patients. Msc. thesis, University of Lancaster.

Roediger, H. L. (1990). Implicit memory: Retention without remembering. *American Psychologist, 45*, 1043–1056.

Roediger, H. L., and McDermott, K. B. (1993). Implicit memory in normal human subjects. In H. Spinnler and F. Boller (Eds.), *Handbook of neuropsychology*, vol. 8. Amsterdam: Elsevier.

Roediger, H. L., Weldon, M. S., and Challis, B. H. (1989). Explaining dissociations between implicit and explicit measures of retention: A processing account. In H. L. Roediger and F. I. M. Craik (Eds.), *Varieties of memory and consciousness: Essays in honour of Endel Tulving*. Hillsdale, NJ: Erlbaum.

Roediger, H. L., Weldon, M. S., Stadler, M. A., and Riegler, G. H. (1992). Direct comparison of word stems and word fragments in implicit and explicit retention tests. *Journal of Experimental Psychology: Learning, Memory and Cognition, 18*, 1251–1269.

Rozin, P. (1976). The psychobiological approach to human memory. In M. R. Rosenzweig and E. L. Bennet (Eds.), *Neural mechanisms of learning and memory*. Cambridge, MA: MIT Press.

Saffran, E. M., and Marin, O. S. M. (1977). Reading without phonology: Evidence from aphasia. *Quarterly Journal of Experimental Psychology, 29*, 515–525.

Saint-Cyr, J. A., Taylor, A. E., and Lang, A. E. (1988). Procedural learning and neostriatal dysfunction in man. *Brain, 111*, 941–959.

Salmon, D. P., Shimamura, A. P., Butters, N., and Smith, S. (1988). Lexical and semantic priming deficits in patients with Alzheimer's disease. *Journal of Clinical Experimental Neuropsychology, 10*, 477–494.

Scarborough, D. L., Cortese, C., and Scarborough, H. S. (1977). Frequency and repetition effects in lexical memory. *Journal of Experimental Psychology: Human Perception and Performance, 3*, 1–17.

Scarborough, D. L., Gerard, L., and Cortese, C. (1979). Accessing lexical memory: The transfer of word repetition effects across task and modality. *Memory and Cognition, 7*, 3–12.

Schacter, D. L. (1987a). Implicit memory: History and current status. *Journal of Experimental Psychology; Learning, Memory, and Cognition, 13*, 501–518.

Schacter, D. L. (1987b). Memory, amnesia, and frontal lobe dysfunction. *Psychobiology, 15*, 21–36.

Schacter, D. L. (1989). On the relation between memory and consciousness: Dissociable interactions and conscious experience. In H. L. Roediger and F. I. M. Craik (Eds.), *Varieties of memory and consciousness: Essays in honor of Endel Tulving*. Hillsdale, NJ: Erlbaum.

Schacter, D. L. (1990a). Perceptual representation systems and implicit memory: Toward a resolution of the multiple memory systems debate. *Annals of the New York Academy of Sciences, 608*, 543–571.

Schacter, D. L. (1990b). Toward a cognitive neuropsychology of awareness: Implicit knowledge and anosagnosia. *Journal of Clinical and Experimental Neuropsychology, 12*, 155–178.

Schacter, D. L. (1992). Priming and multiple memory systems: Perceptual mechanisms of implicit memory. *Journal of Cognitive Neuroscience, 4*, 244–256.

Schacter, D. L., Bowers, J., and Booker, J. (1989). Intention, awareness and implicit memory: The retrieval intentionality criterion. In S. Lewandowsky, J. C. Bunn, and K. Kirsner (Eds.), *Implicit memory: Theoretical issues*. Hillsdale, NJ: Erlbaum.

Schacter, D. L., and Church, B. (1992). Auditory priming: Implicit and explicit memory for words and voices. *Journal of Experimental Psychology: Learning, Memory and Cognition, 18*, 915–936.

Schacter, D. L., Cooper, L. A., and Delaney, S. M. (1990). Implicit memory for unfamiliar objects depends on access to structural descriptions. *Journal of Experimental Psychology: General, 119*, 5–24.

Schacter, D. L., Cooper, L. A., Tharan, M., and Rubens, A. B. (1991). Preserved priming of novel objects in patients with memory disorders. *Journal of Cognitive Neuroscience, 3*, 118–131.

Schacter, D. L., Eich, J. E., and Tulving, E. (1978). Richard Semon's theory of memory. *Journal of Verbal Learning and Verbal Behavior, 17*, 721–743.

Schacter, D. L., and Graf, P. (1986). Preserved learning in amnesic patients: Perspectives on research from direct priming. *Journal of Clinical Experimental Neuropsychology, 8*, 727–743.

Schacter, D. L., Harbluk, J. L., and McLachlan, D. R. (1984). Retrieval without recollection: An experimental analysis of source amnesia. *Journal of Verbal Learning and Verbal Behavior, 23*, 593–611.

Schacter, D. L., McAndrews, M. P., and Moscovitch, M. (1988). Access to consciousness: Dissociations between implicit and explicit knowledge in neuropsychological syndromes. In L. Weiskrantz (Ed.), *Thought without language*. Oxford: Oxford University Press.

Schacter, D. L., Rapcsak, S. Z., Rubens, A. B., Tharan, M., and Laguna, J. M. (1990). Priming effects in a letter-by-letter reader depend on access to the word form system. *Neuropsychologia, 28*, 1079–1094.

Schwartz, B. L., and Hashtroudi, S. (1991). Priming is independent of skill learning. *Journal of Experimental Psychology: Learning, Memory and Cognition, 17*, 1177–1188.

Seamon, J. G., Brody, N., and Kauff, D. M. (1983). Affective discrimination of stimuli that are not recognized: II. Effect of delay between study and test. *Bulletin of the Psychonomic Society, 21*, 187–189.

Shallice, T. (1982). Specific impairments of planning. *Philosophical Transactions of the Royal Society of London, B298*, 199–209.

Sherry, D. F., and Schacter, D. L. (1987). The evolution of multiple memory systems. *Psychological Review, 94*, 439–454.

Shimamura, A. P. (1986). Priming effects in amnesia: Evidence for a dissociable memory function. *Quarterly Journal of Experimental Psychology, 38A*, 619–644.

Shimamura, A. P., and Squire, L. R. (1989). Impaired priming of new associations in amnesia. *Journal of Experimental Psychology: Learning, Memory and Cognition, 15*, 721–728.

Sloman, S. A., Hayman, C. A. G., Ohta, N., Law, J., and Tulving, E. (1988). Forgetting in primed fragment completion. *Journal of Experimental Psychology: Learning, Memory and Cognition, 14,* 223–239.

Smith, M. E., and Oscar-Berman, M. (1990). Repetition printing of words and pseudowords in divided attention and in amnesia. *Journal of Experimental Psychology: Learning, Memory and Cognition, 16,* 1033–1042.

Snodgrass, J. G. (1989). Sources of learning in the picture fragment completion task. In S. Lewandowsky, J. C. Dunn, and K. Kirsner (Eds.), *Implicit memory: Theoretical issues.* Hillsdale, NJ: Erlbaum.

Snodgrass, J. G., and Feenan, K. (1990). Priming effects in picture fragment completion: Support for the perceptual closure hypothesis. *Journal of Experimental Psychology: General, 119,* 276–296.

Squire, L. R. (1992). Memory and the hippocampus: A synthesis from findings with rats, monkeys and humans. *Psychological Review, 99,* 195–231.

Squire, L. R., Cohen, N. J., and Zouzounis, J. A. (1984). Preserved memory in retrograde amnesia: Sparing of a recently acquired skill. *Neuropsychologia, 22,* 145–152.

Squire, L. R., Ojemann, J., Miezin, F., Petersen, S., Videen, T., and Raichle, M. (1991). Activation of the hippocampus in normal humans: A functional anatomical study of memory. *Proceedings of the National Academy of Sciences, 89,* 1837–1841.

Squire, L. R., Shimamura, A. P., and Graf, P. (1987). Strength and duration of priming effects in normal subjects and amnesic patients. *Neuropsychologia, 25,* 195–210.

Squire, L. R., Wetzel, C. D., and Slater, P. C. (1978). Anterograde amnesia following ECT: An analysis of the beneficial effect of partial information. *Neuropsychologia, 16,* 339–347.

Srinivas, K. (1993). Perceptual specificity in nonverbal priming. *Journal of Experimental Psychology: Learning, Memory and Cognition, 19,* 582–602.

Tranel, E., and Damasio, A. R. (1985). Knowledge without awareness: An automatic index of facial recognition by prosopagnosics. *Science, 228,* 1453–1454.

Tulving, E. (1985). Memory and consciousness. *Canadian Psychology, 25,* 1–12.

Tulving, E., Hayman, C. A. G., and MacDonald, C. (1991). Long-lasting perceptual priming and semantic learning in amnesia: A case experiment. *Journal of Experimental Psychology: Learning, Memory and Cognition, 17,* 595–617.

Tulving, E., and and Schacter, D. L. (1990). Priming and human memory systems. *Science, 247,* 301–306.

Tulving, E., Schacter, D. L., and Stark, H. A. (1982). Priming effects in word-fragment completion are independent of recognition memory. *Journal of Experimental Psychology: Learning, Memory, and Cognition, 8,* 336–342.

Verfaellie, M., Bauer, R. M., and Bowers, D. (1991). Autonomic and behavioral evidence of "implicit" memory in amnesia. *Brain and Cognition, 15,* 10–25.

Verfaellie, M., Cermak, L. S., Letourneau, L., and Zuffante, P. (1991). Repetition effects in a lexical decision task: The role of episodic memory in alcoholic Korsakoff patients. *Neuropsychologia, 29,* 641–657.

Warrington, E. K., and Shallice, T. (1980). Word-form dyslexia. *Brain, 103,* 99–112.

Warrington, E. K., and Taylor, H. M. (1978). Two categorical stages of object recognition. *Perception, 7,* 695–705.

Warrington, E. K., and Weiskrantz, L. (1968). New method of testing long-term retention with special reference to amnesic patients. *Nature, 217,* 972–974.

Warrington, E. K., and Weiskrantz, L. (1970). The amnesic syndrome: Consolidation or retrieval? *Nature, 228*, 628–630.

Warrington, E. K., and Weiskrantz, L. (1974). The effect of prior learning on subsequent retention in amnesic patients. *Neuropsychologia, 12*, 419–428.

Warrington, E. K., and Weiskrantz, L. (1978). Further analysis of the prior learning effect in amnesic patients. *Neuropsychologia, 10*, 169–177.

Watkins, M. J., and Gibson, J. M. (1988). On the relation between perceptual priming and recognition memory. *Journal of Experimental Psychology: Learning, Memory and Cognition, 14*, 477–483.

Weldon, M. S. (1991). Mechanisms underlying priming on perceptual tasks. *Journal of Experimental Psychology: Learning, Memory and Cognition, 17*, 526–541.

Weldon, M. S., and Roediger, H. L. (1987). Altering retrieval demands reverses the picture superiority effect. *Memory and Cognition, 15*, 269–280.

Wetzel, C. D., and Squire, L. R. (1982). Cued recall in anterograde amnesia. *Brain and Language, 15*, 70–81.

Winocur, G., and Moscovitch, M. (1994). Negative transfer (A–B, A–C learning) in patients with unilateral temporal-lobe as frontal-lobe lesions: A case of heightened interference on conceptual, implicit tests of memory? *Brain and Cognition*. In press.

Winocur, G., and Weiskrantz, L. (1976). An investigation of paired-associate learning in amnesic patients. *Neuropsychologia, 14*, 97–110.

Witherspoon, D., and Allen, L. G. (1985). The effects of prior presentation on temporal judgments in a perceptual identification task. *Memory and Cognition, 13*, 101–111.

Witherspoon, D., and Moscovitch, M. (1989). Independence of the repetition effects between word fragment completion and perceptual identification. *Journal of Experimental Psychology: Learning, Memory, and Cognition, 15*, 22–30.

Zaidel, E. (1985). Language in the right hemisphere. In D. F. Benson and E. Zaidel (Eds.), *The dual brain: Hemispheric specialization in humans*, 205–231. New York: Guilford Press.

Zaidel, E., and Peters, A. M. (1981). Phonologic encoding and ideographic reading by the disconnected right hemisphere: Two case studies. *Brain and Language, 14*, 205–234.

# 26 Measuring Recollection: Strategic versus Automatic Influences of Associative Context

Larry L. Jacoby

ABSTRACT There has been much recent interest in the finding of dissociations between performance on indirect and direct tests of memory. Indirect tests (e.g., word-stem completion) are said to primarily reflect automatic or unconscious uses of memory, whereas direct tests (e.g., cued recall) primarily reflect strategic or consciously controlled uses of memory. Rather than identifying processes with tasks, as is done by use of the contrast between indirect and direct tests, I (e.g., Jacoby 1991) have used a "process-dissociation procedure" to separate the within-task contributions of consciously controlled and automatic uses of memory. I describe advantages of the process-dissociation procedure over standard direct tests as a means of measuring recollection. Because of its failure to distinguish between automatic and strategic uses of memory, reliance on standard, direct tests is shown to produce serious errors in conclusions that are drawn. I propose a distinction between strategic and automatic influences of associative context, and report two new experiments to show the utility of that distinction. As will be discussed, the strategic/automatic distinction is important for answering questions about the effectiveness of providing environmental support to aid the performance of memory-impaired individuals.

## 26.1 INTRODUCTION

How should one measure an amnesiac's ability to recollect memory for a prior event? An obvious means of measuring recollection would be to question the person directly about memory for the event; for example, a test of cued recall might be used. However, there are problems for measuring recollection in that way. To illustrate, consider difficulties for interpreting an amnesiac's performance on a test of recall cued by presentation of word stems. Suppose that amnesiacs were presented with a long list of words that they were told to remember, and then memory was tested by providing word stems that were to be used as cues for recall of the words presented earlier (e.g., mot___ as a cue for recall of *motel*). To measure memory, the probability of completing stems with old words is compared with the base rate probability of completing those stems. A measure of base rate is gained by presenting stems that can be completed only with words not presented earlier.

Experiments using these sorts of procedures have shown that amnesiacs' recall performance is sometimes nearly as good as that of subjects with normal functioning memory (Graf, Squire, and Mandler 1984; Warrington and Weiskrantz 1974). Consequently, it might be concluded that given word stems as cues, amnesiacs preserve an almost normal ability to recollect memory for a prior experience (Warrington and Weiskrantz 1974). However, amnesiacs might achieve their high level of cued recall performance by a means other than recollection. They may complete word stems with the first word that comes to mind without being aware that their completions are the words that they were instructed to recall. Indeed, amnesiacs' cued recall performance sometimes does not differ greatly from what would be observed if they were given an indirect test of memory.

For an indirect test, people are not asked to report on memory for an event as they would be for a direct test, such as a test of recognition memory or recall. Rather, they engage in some task that can indirectly reflect memory for the occurrence of that event. Word stem and fragment completion tasks are among the most popular indirect tests of memory (Warrington and Weiskrantz 1974; Tulving, Schacter, and Stark 1982; Graf and Mandler 1984). Dissociations between performance on direct and indirect tests supply examples of effects of the past in the absence of remembering (Richardson-Klavehn and Bjork 1988; Hintzman 1990). Some of the most striking examples of dissociations come from the performance of patients suffering a neurological deficit. Korsakoff amnesiacs, for example, show near-normal effects of memory in their performance of a stem completion task, although their performance on direct tests of memory is severely impaired (for reviews, see Ostergaard and Jernigan, n.d.; Shimamura 1986; Moscovitch, chap. 25, this volume).

The problem for gaining an accurate measure of recollection (a strategic, consciously controlled use of memory) is that performance of a direct test may be contaminated by automatic influences of the sort reflected by performance on indirect tests of memory. Automatic influences of memory increase the probability of correct guessing. This informed guessing inflates estimates of recollection and may be largely responsible for accurate memory reports produced by amnesiacs (Gabrieli et al. 1990). Guessing could be discouraged by instructions, but it is unlikely that it could be fully eliminated. Rather than attempting to eliminate guessing, it would be better to measure its effects.

How should one correct for informed guessing on a direct test so as to gain an accurate measure of recollection? One answer to that question is to measure recollection as the difference between performance on a direct test and that on an indirect test of memory. For example, stem-completion performance might be subtracted from recall cued with word stems to gain a measure of recollection. However, that solution is unlikely to be satisfactory. Performance on indirect tests is sometimes contaminated by strategic uses of memory and so cannot be treated as a pure measure of automatic influences of memory (Richardson-Klavehn and Bjork 1988). Another problem for measuring recollection and automatic influences with different tasks is that processes may be qualitatively different across tasks. The issue here is something like the commonplace belief that people express what they "truly believe" when drunk. It is possible that what people believe when drunk is qualitatively different from what they believe when sober. Similarly, the automatic influences revealed by an indirect test may be different from those that are in play on a direct test of memory.

Rather than identify processes with tasks, as is done by use of the contrast between indirect and direct tests, I have used a "process-dissociation procedure" to separate the within-task contributions of consciously controlled and automatic uses of memory (Jacoby, 1991). Elsewhere we (e.g., Jacoby and Kelley 1991; Jacoby et al. 1992) have written much about the advantages of the process-dissociation procedure over indirect tests as a means of investigating automatic influences of memory. Here, I change focus by describing the advantages of the process-dissociation procedure over the use of direct tests as a means of measuring recollection.

Reliance on direct tests of memory to measure recollection fails to separate strategic and automatic influences of memory and, consequently, can lead to erroneous conclusions. Failure to distinguish between automatic and strategic influences might account for the disarray in the literature concerning the effects of some variables on performance of direct tests. I present evidence to illustrate problems for interpreting performance on direct tests of memory. After describing advantages of the process-dissociation procedure, I propose a distinction between strategic and automatic influences of associative context and report new experiments to show the utility of that distinction.

## 26.2 MEASURING RECOLLECTION

The problem of correcting measures of recollection for guessing is as important for measuring normal memory as for measuring the memory performance of amnesiacs. It is classic test theory that motivates the common practice of correcting for guessing by subtracting the probability of false recall from the probability of correct recall or, for measuring recognition memory performance, subtracting false alarms from hits (see Kintsch 1970 for a discussion of high-threshold models). Similar to classic test theory, we assume that guessing is independent of true remembering (recollection). Unlike classic test theory, we assume that memory influences guessing. That is, guessing is informed by automatic influences of memory.

### When Recollection is Zero

The first case that I consider is one in which the process-dissociation procedure shows recollection to be zero, and the absence of recollection could not be detected by use of either classic test theory or signal detection theory. After describing an example to show the use of those standard means of correcting for guessing, I describe the process-dissociation procedure.

In an experiment done by Jacoby, Toth, and Yonelinas (experiment 1b, 1993), people studied a set of words under conditions of full or divided attention and were later given the first three letters of the words as cues for recall. Subjects in a full-attention condition were told to read the words aloud and remember them for a later test of memory. Subjects in a divided-attention condition read aloud the same list of words while simultaneously engaging in a listening task. For the listening task, a long series of numbers was presented, and subjects were to indicate when they heard a sequence of three odd numbers in a row (e.g., 3 9 7). Subjects were told that the task of reading words aloud was designed to interfere with performance on the listening task; no mention was made of the fact that subjects' memory for the read words would later be tested. By confounding attention condition with the deletion of instructions to remember, we hoped to eliminate the possibility of later recollection in the divided-attention condition so as to mimic results one would expect to be produced by amnesia (Craik 1982).

For an inclusion test (later contrasted with an exclusion test), a list of word stems was presented, and subjects were instructed to use each stem as a cue for recall of an earlier-presented word that could be used to complete the stem. If their attempt at recall was unsuccessful, they were to complete the stem with the first word that came to mind. That inclusion test is the same as a standard test of cued recall with instructions to guess when recollection fails. Within the test list were some stems that could be completed only with a new word. Completion of those stems served as a measure of base rate or "false recall." A standard means of correcting cued recall performance for guessing is to subtract the probability of false recall from that of correct recall (Weldon, Roediger, and Challis 1989).

Results showed that cued recall performance in the divided-attention condition was poorer than that in the full-attention condition (.62 versus .46). However, in the divided-attention condition, the probability of completing a stem with an old word was well above base rate (.46 versus .35). Should it be concluded that dividing attention did not fully eliminate the possibility of later recollection, or does the above-base-rate level of performance in the divided-attention condition only reflect guessing informed by automatic influences of memory? Neither classic test theory nor signal detection theory (Swets, Tanner, and Birdsall 1961) helps to answer that question because neither distinguishes between recollection and automatic influences of memory.

The process-dissociation procedure can be used to show that dividing attention during study reduced later recollection to zero and left only automatic influences of memory. An important difference between recollection and automatic influences of memory is that recollection affords a level of strategic, conscious control over responding that is not afforded by automatic influences. Suppose that for an exclusion test, subjects were instructed to complete stems with words that were not presented earlier. For that test, recollection would serve to exclude earlier-presented words as completions for word stems, an effect opposite to that for the inclusion test. To the extent that subjects recollected earlier-presented words, they should be more likely to complete stems with those old words when trying to (inclusion test) than when trying not to (exclusion test) respond with old words. That is, recollection can be measured as the difference between performance in the inclusion and exclusion test conditions, a measure of control. In contrast to recollection, automatic influences of memory are assumed not to support such selective responding. Automatic influences of memory act to increase the probability of completing stems with old words regardless of whether an exclusion or an inclusion test is given.

Subjects in the experiment described were given an exclusion test as well as an inclusion test. For the exclusion test, they were instructed to use the stems as cues for recall of words presented earlier but not to give a recalled word as a completion for a stem. That is, for the exclusion test, subjects were told to complete stems with words that were not presented earlier. Results from the inclusion and exclusion test conditions are shown in the left half of table 26.1. Looking at results for the exclusion test, subjects in the divided-attention condition were less able to use recollection to exclude old words than were subjects in the full-attention condition. Indeed, after divided attention, the probability of completing a stem with an old word for the exclusion test was identical to that for the inclusion test. That identity in performance provides evidence that dividing attention during the study presentation of words reduced later recollection to zero. It can be concluded that responding with an old word did not result from a strategic, consciously controlled use of memory, because such responding was as likely when subjects were trying not to as when they were trying to respond with an old word. After divided attention to study, all that remained were automatic influences of memory.

Performance in the divided-attention condition provides clear evidence of automatic influences. Although the probability of responding with an old word was equal for the inclusion and exclusion tests, that probability was above the base rate gained from stems that could only be completed with new words (.46 versus .35). When recollection can be shown to be zero, subtracting base rate or false recall from correct recall gives a measure of automatic influences.

How can automatic influences be measured when recollection is greater than zero, as in the full-attention condition? Translating the above arguments into a set of simple equations that describe performance in the inclusion and exclusion test conditions provides a means of estimating the separate contributions of automatic and strategic processes. Stated formally, the probability of responding with a studied word in the inclusion test condition is the probability of recollection ($R$) plus the probability of the word's automatically coming to mind when there is a failure of recollection, $A(1-R)$:

$$\text{Inclusion} = R + A(1-R). \tag{1}$$

**Table 26.1** Probabilities of Responding with an Old Word and Estimates of Recollection ($R$) and Automatic Influences ($A$)

| Attention | Probabilities Test | | Estimates | |
| --- | --- | --- | --- | --- |
| | Inclusion | Exclusion | R | A |
| Full | .61 | .36 | .25 | .47 |
| Divided | .46 | .46 | 0 | .46 |

Note: Base rate = .35.

For the exclusion test, a studied word will be produced only when a word automatically comes to mind and there is a failure to recollect that it was on the list, or more formally:

$$\text{Exclusion} = A(1 - R). \tag{2}$$

In the inclusion test, automatic and intentional influences act in concert. Performance in that condition clearly overestimates recollection and does not provide unambiguous evidence even for its existence. The exclusion test places recollection and automatic influences in opposition. If the probability of completing stems with studied words in that condition is higher than base rate, then one can be sure that automatic influences exist. However, if the probability of recollection is above zero, performance in the exclusion condition underestimates the magnitude of automatic influences.

The probability of recollection ($R$) can be estimated as the probability of responding with a studied word in the inclusion condition minus the probability of responding with a studied word in the exclusion condition:

$$R = \text{Inclusion} - \text{exclusion}. \tag{3}$$

Once an estimate of conscious recollection has been obtained, unconscious or automatic influences can be estimated by simple algebra:

$$A = \text{Exclusion}/(1 - R). \tag{4}$$

We call this the process-dissociation procedure because what we are looking for are factors that produce dissociations in their effects on the estimates of the different types of processes. Equations 1–4 can be applied to the data in table 26.1 to separate recollection and automatic influences. Doing so (right half of table 26.1) shows that dividing attention produced a process dissociation. Although dividing attention reduced the probability of recollection to zero, the estimated contribution of automatic influences was near identical for the full- and divided-attention conditions.

It is important to be able to find such process dissociations. One of the strongest assumptions underlying the procedure is that automatic and strategic uses of memory are independent. If this assumption is valid, we should be able to identify factors that have large influences on one process but leave the other process unchanged. The strategy is analogous to that used by proponents of signal detection theory to justify the assumed independence of discriminability and bias. For signal detection theory, if discriminability and bias are independent, it should be possible to vary bias and leave $d'$ (the estimate of discriminability) unchanged (Snodgrass and Corwin 1988) or vice versa. For our approach, the process dissociation produced by dividing attention during study provides support for the assumption of independence of recollection and automatic influences. Jacoby, Toth, and Yonelinas (1993) further describe the assumptions underlying the process-dissociation procedure and review data that provide support for those assumptions. Process dissociations such as those produced by dividing attention during study have been found in several other experiments.

Even when giving a correct memory response, amnesiacs often deny having the subjective experience of remembering and claim to be only guessing (Moscovitch, Winocur, and McLachlan 1986). For amnesiacs, the probability of recollection is likely very low and, so the probability of completing a stem with an old word should be nearly the same in inclusion and exclusion test conditions. Results consistent with that prediction have been obtained recently (Cermak et al. 1992). The process-dissociation procedure holds an important advantage over other means of measuring memory in that it allows one to separate recollection, an ability that is largely lost by amnesiacs, and, when attention is divided, from automatic or unconscious influences, a use of memory that is preserved by amnesiacs and when attention is divided.

**Offsetting Effects of Recollection and Automatic Influences**

The above example shows that reliance on standard means of correcting for guessing can overestimate recollection. The next case I consider shows an even more serious error in conclusions that can result from reliance on such standard procedures. A manipulation can have effects on strategic uses of memory that are fully offset by its opposite effects on automatic uses of memory. Given such offsetting effects, reliance on standard procedures for measuring memory leads to the mistaken conclusion that the manipulation had no effect.

Among the effects most intensely investigated using direct tests of memory is the finding that words generated in response to a question are later better remembered than are words that were simply read (Slamecka and Graf 1978; Jacoby 1978; for a review, see Hintzman 1990). Jacoby, Toth, and Yonelinas (experiment 3, 1993) examined this generation effect in recall cued with word stems. In their experiment, words were presented as anagrams to be solved or in their normal form to be read, and then word stems were presented as cues for recall. The test of cued recall took the same form as the inclusion test described in the preceding section. A generation effect would be shown by recall of words presented as anagrams being superior to that of words that were read. The results failed to show an effect of that sort. Instead, the probability of correctly recalling words that had been presented as anagrams was identical to that of recalling words that had been read.

If we had relied on cued recall performance, we would have concluded that the read/generate manipulation had no effect. However, by use of the process-dissociation procedure, we were able to show that the manipulation produced opposite and perfectly offsetting effects on recollection and automatic influences of memory. The experiment made use of both an exclusion and an inclusion test condition, just as did the experiment described in the preceding section. Although the read/generate manipulation had no effect on performance when an inclusion test was given, there was a large effect on performance when an exclusion test was given (left half of table 26.2). For the

**Table 26.2** Probabilities of Responding with an Old Word and Estimates of Recollection (R) and Automatic Influences (A)

| Study | Probabilities Test | | Estimates | |
|---|---|---|---|---|
| | Inclusion | Exclusion | R | A |
| Read | .82 | .49 | .33 | .73 |
| Anagram | .82 | .25 | .57 | .59 |

Note: Base rate = .56.

exclusion test, subjects were much more successful at avoiding responding with an old word when the word had earlier been produced as a solution for an anagram rather than simply read.

Equations 1–4 can be used to separate the contributions of recollection and automatic influences. Doing so allows one to see the differential effects of the read/anagram manipulation (right half of table 26.2). By use of the process-dissociation procedure, one sees that generating a word as a solution for an anagram produced an advantage in recollection that was perfectly offset by a disadvantage in automatic influences of memory.

The pattern of results found using the process-dissociation procedure parallels dissociations found between performance on indirect and on direct tests of memory. For example, Jacoby (1983) showed that words generated as an antonym of a presented word were later better recognized as old but were less likely to be perceptually identified as compared to words that were read earlier. Jacoby interpreted those results as showing that perceptual identification primarily relies on prior data-driven processing, whereas recognition memory primarily relies on prior conceptually driven processing. Roediger (1990) has extended that argument to account for a variety of dissociations between performance on indirect and direct tests.

Results of the above experiment show that a dissociation of the form found between tasks can also be found between processes within a task. The read/generate effect found for automatic influences in stem-completion performance is the same as found using indirect tests and the effect in recollection is the same as found using direct tests. Consequently, one might conclude that automaticity reflects data- or stimulus-driven processing (Posner and Snyder 1975) and that only recollection is enhanced by prior conceptually driven processing of the sort required to solve anagrams. However, it is important to note that for automatic processes in recognition memory, the read/generate effect is the opposite of that found for automatic processes in stem completion (Jacoby 1991). Because of differences in cues provided for retrieval and differences in task demands, automatic influences on stem-completion performance are more reliant on perceptual characteristics than are automatic influences on recognition-memory performance. I have used differences of that sort to argue for the task dependency of automaticity. Jacoby, Ste-Marie, and Toth (1993) provide a discussion of the relativity of automaticity that draws on theorizing done by Neumann (1984).

Some might object that our inclusion test condition is not a standard test of cued recall but, rather, a mix of a direct and an indirect test because we encouraged guessing. Further, it might be argued that had we instructed subjects to report only words that they were certain were old, we would have found an advantage in cued recall of anagram over read words in the experiment just described and, perhaps, found that cued recall performance was near zero in the divided-attention condition in the experiment described earlier. However, instructing subjects not to guess does not reliably eliminate guessing. So long as guessing is not fully eliminated, automatic influences of memory on guessing do contaminate standard measures of recollection. By encouraging guessing and using the process-dissociation procedure, we gain a measure of automatic influences of memory on guessing and, so, also better measure recollection.

## Comparison of Assumptions Underlying Different Measures of Recollection

The standard practice of subtracting false recall from correct recall so as to remove the effects of guessing (Weldon, Roediger, and Challis 1989) derives from classic test theory and is based on assumptions that are likely seldom examined. The assumptions underlying that procedure are that guessing is uncorrelated with true recollection and that memory influences only recollection. The assumed independence of recollection and of guessing is used to separate their effects.

It is assumed that correct recall can be accomplished either by recollecting an old item ($R_o$) or by producing the old item as a guess ($G$) when recollection fails ($1 - R_o$):

Correct recall $= R_o + G(1 - R_o)$. (5)

In contrast, false recall of the same item, if it were not presented, would require that the item be given as a guess ($G$) and not be recollected as being new ($1 - R_n$):

False recall $= G(1 - R_n)$. (6)

Subtracting false recalls (equation 6) from correct recalls (equation 5) to measure recollection, as is standard, rests on the assumption that $R_o$ equals $R_n$. That is, it is assumed that the probability of recollecting that an item was presented ($R_o$) is the same as the probability of recollecting that an item was not presented ($R_n$). That assumption is probably seldom valid and is particularly problematic when assessing the effects of study manipulations. For example, consider the use of that assumption in the context of examining the effects of the read/generate manipulation.

An advantage of generated words in correct recall would be described as reflecting a higher probability of recollecting that an item was old ($R_o$) for generated as compared to read words. The problem comes when one corrects for guessing by subtracting false recalls (base rate) from correct recalls.

Reliance on stems that can be completed only with new words to measure false recall forces one to use the same base rate to "correct" recall of read words and recall of anagrams. Doing so requires the contradictory assumptions that $R_n$ for new words is equal to $R_o$ for anagrams and $R_o$ for read words but that $R_o$ is different for the two classes of words. What is needed is separate measures of false recall for read and anagram words.

The exclusion condition used in the process-dissociation procedure provides separate measures of false recall for different classes of studied words. The equations for the process-dissociation procedure (equations 1 and 2) are identical to equations 5 and 6, except for the change from two parameters ($R_o$ and $R_n$) to one parameter ($R$) to represent recollection. For the process-dissociation procedure, we assume that the recollection used for inclusion is the same as that used for exclusion. Although the validity of that assumption might sometimes be arguable, it is much more tenable than the standard assumption that $R_o$ equals $R_n$. Our use of the exclusion test condition allowed us to see that recollection was different for anagram and read words. That difference would not have been revealed had we relied on a test of cued recall (the inclusion test condition) and corrected for guessing by subtracting base rate from correct recall of anagram and read words.

Another difference between the process-dissociation approach and classic test theory is that unlike classic test theory, we assume that memory influences guessing. Without separating the different influences of memory, the memory preserved by amnesiacs and after divided attention might be mistaken for recollection rather than correctly being seen as an automatic influence of memory. Also, a failure to distinguish between different influences of memory can lead to the false conclusion that a factor had no effect when, in actuality, there were two offsetting effects.

## 26.3 STRATEGIC AND AUTOMATIC INFLUENCES OF ASSOCIATIVE CONTEXT

The effectiveness of a recall cue depends on the relation between the cue and the study encoding of the item that is to be recalled. For example, presentation of an associate of a studied word as a cue for its recall is much more effective if the associate and the to-be-remembered word were studied together (Tulving and Thomson 1973). Such "encoding-specificity effects" might be interpreted as showing the importance for recollection of the compatibility of the retrieval cue and the study encoding of the target word. However, encoding-specificity effects might also originate from automatic influences of memory. In line with that possibility, Shimamura and Squire (1984) found that amnesiacs show "associative priming" effects. They presented word pairs, such as *table-chair*, to amnesiacs and control subjects. After presentation, subjects were shown the first word of each pair and were asked to say the first word that came to mind. The likelihood of subjects' responding with the second member of the pair was found to be almost three times above baseline level for amnesiacs as well as for control subjects (For a review of similar results from other experiments, see Moscovitch, chap. 25, this volume; Shimamura 1986.)

How should recall cued with associates be corrected for guessing? The problem is the same as described for recall cued with word stems. The standard procedure of subtracting a baseline level obtained using new items from correct recall does not take automatic influences into account and, consequently, can overestimate the probability of recollection. Further, manipulations of the compatibility of retrieval cues and study encoding likely affect both recollection and automatic influences of memory. To measure effects on recollection accurately, one needs to separate effects on recollection from those on automatic influences.

## Experiment 1: Placing Strategic and Automatic Influences in Opposition

A first experiment was done to demonstrate that associative context affects both recollection and automatic influences of memory. In phase 1 of that experiment, associatively related words were presented in pairs (e.g., *talk-chat*; *eat-drink*) or were repaired and presented as pairs of unrelated words (e.g., *turtle-cider*; *apple-shell*). Subjects judged whether words in each pair were related or unrelated. Subjects in one condition devoted full attention to making those judgments, whereas subjects in a second condition engaged in a listening task while simultaneously judging whether words were related. For an exclusion test, the first member of each studied pair was presented as a cue along with the initial letter of the associatively related target word (e.g., *eat-d*). Subjects were instructed to produce a word that was associatively related to the cue and began with the presented letter but had not been presented earlier (acceptable responses would be *dine* or *devour*, for example).

Recollection that a word was presented earlier allowed subjects to avoid giving that word as a response. Automatic influences, in contrast, would have the opposite effect by acting to increase the probability of responding with an old word. Only when words were presented in related pairs did the cues provided at test reinstate the associative context of studied words. Consequently, words presented in related pairs were expected to produce both better recollection and larger automatic influences of memory as compared to words presented in unrelated pairs. Based on results of the sort described earlier, dividing attention during the study presentation of pairs was expected to reduce later recollection but leave automatic influences of memory unchanged. Because of the effect on recollection, the probability of mistakenly responding with an old word was expected to be higher in the divided- than in the full-attention condition. The obtained pattern of results was such as to allow one to be certain that associative context affected both automatic and strategic influences of memory.

**Subjects** Subjects were volunteers from a first-year introductory psychology course at McMaster University who participated in the experiment for course credit. Eighteen subjects were randomly assigned to each of two experimental conditions created by a manipulation of full versus divided attention at study.

**Materials and Design**   A pool of 220 related word pairs was selected from *The Connecticut Free Associational Norms* (Bousfield et al. 1961), *The University of South Florida Associative Meaning Norms* (McEvoy et al., n.d.), and the *Norms of Word Association* (Postman and Keppel 1970). The associated words were chosen from a range of association frequencies, with the majority being from the medium range. The highest-frequency associates were not selected, and an additional criterion was that there must be at least one other associate beginning with the same letter as the selected associate (e.g., *burial—coffin, casket, ceremony, crypt*). From the selected pairs, three sets of forty pairs each were formed, and those sets were used to represent the three presentation conditions: presented in related pair, presented in unrelated pair, and new at test. Unrelated pairs were formed by repairing words in related pairs. Each set was balanced with regard to the probability of the selected associates being given as a response when new. Across formats, the sets were rotated through experimental conditions. Remaining pairs were used as fillers for the study list or for the test list.

The study list contained 120 pairs, with the first 20 pairs and the last 20 pairs in the list serving as fillers. Of those fillers, half were related and the other half were unrelated pairs. The order of items in the study list was random, with the restriction that not more than 3 pairs of the same condition could appear in a row. The test list contained 200 pairs, 80 of them fillers. The first 40 pairs in the test list were fillers (20 pairs of which had been presented during study). The fillers at the beginning of the list were used to allow subjects to become acquainted with the task before data were collected. The remaining 40 fillers were words from new pairs and were spread through the list so as to make the number of cues that would only allow responding with a new word equal to the number of cues that would allow responding with an old word.

**Procedure**   In the study phase, the word pairs were presented on a monitor for 2 sec each with a 1/2-sec delay, during which the screen was blank, between the presentation of pairs. For each pair, subjects pressed one key to indicate that the pair of words was related or another key to indicate that they were unrelated. Subjects in the divided-attention condition engaged in a listening task while simultaneously judging whether words were related. The listening task was one previously used by Craik (1982). Subjects monitored a tape-recorded list of digits to detect target sequences of three odd numbers in a row (e.g., 9  3  7). Digits were recorded at a 1.5-sec rate. Subjects signaled their detection of a target sequence by saying "now."

For the test, the first word from each pair was presented followed by two spaces and then the first letter of its selected associate. The cue remained on the screen until the subject gave a response or until 15 sec elapsed; then the next test item was presented. Subjects were told that they were to produce a word that was associatively related to the cue and began with the provided first letter but had not been presented earlier. They were told that if they were able to recall a previously presented, related word, even if the word had not been paired with the cue word, they were not to use that old word as a response.

The significance level for all tests was set at $p < .05$.

**Results** The probability of mistakenly responding with an old word is shown in table 26.3 for words presented in related and unrelated pairs along with the baseline probability of responding with those words when they were new. Analysis of those probabilities revealed a significant interaction between prior presentation and full versus divided attention ($F(2,68) = 11.62$, $MS_e = .005$).

Results from the full-attention condition provide evidence that reinstating associative context improved recollection. After full attention to judging pairs, words presented in related pairs were given as a response less frequently than were new words and were also less likely to be mistakenly given as a response than were words presented in unrelated pairs. That pattern of results shows that recollection of words presented in related pairs was often sufficiently good to allow subjects to exclude those words as permissible responses. In contrast, results from the divided-attention condition provide evidence of automatic influences of memory. After divided attention, old words from related pairs were more likely to be given as a response than were new words. This increased probability must have resulted from an automatic influence of memory, because an intentional use of memory (recollection) would have produced an opposite effect. Weak evidence of an effect of associative context on automatic influences is provided by the finding that after divided attention, words from related pairs were slightly more likely to be mistakenly given as a response than were words from unrelated pairs.

### Experiment 2: Separating Strategic and Automatic Influences

The results of experiment 1 provide evidence that reinstating associative context affects both recollection and automatic influences of memory. However, the design of that experiment was not sufficient to allow one to separate effects of associative context fully on the two types of processes. To accomplish that goal, experiment 2 made use of the process-dissociation procedure.

Table 26.3 Probabilities of Responding with an "Old" Word on an Exclusion Test

| Attention | Pair Type | | New |
| --- | --- | --- | --- |
| | Related | Unrelated | |
| Full | .21 | .30 | .29 |
| Divided | .36 | .33 | .27 |

Note: New pairs provide a measure of base rate.

**Materials and Procedure** The materials and procedure for experiment 2 were the same as those for experiment 1, except an inclusion test condition was added. Inclusion and exclusion test items were randomly intermixed, with the color of test items (green or red) signaling their type. For green test items, subjects were instructed to use the presented cue word and first letter to recall an earlier-presented word that was associatively related to the cue word and began with the provided first letter. If subjects were unable to recall a suitable old word, they were told to respond with the first word that came to mind that fit the restrictions. For red stems, in contrast, subjects were instructed not to respond with old words. The instructions for that exclusion test were the same as for experiment 1.

The procedure of randomly intermixing inclusion and exclusion test items was used to equate the interval between prior presentation of an item and type of test. The addition of the inclusion test condition reduced by half the number of words representing each combination of experimental conditions as compared to experiment 1. The only other difference between the two experiments is that pairs were presented for 1.5 sec in phase 1 for subjects to judge whether words were related in experiment 2 but for 2 sec in experiment 1.

**Results** The baseline probability of producing the selected associates when new did not differ significantly across type of test (inclusion versus exclusion) or attention condition (full versus divided attention), and averaged .29. For words presented in related or unrelated pairs, an analysis of the probability of responding with an old word revealed a significant interaction among type of pair (related versus unrelated), type of test, and attention condition ($F(1,34) = 16.57, MS_e = .008$). The results in the left half of table 26.4 show that effects for the exclusion test were similar to those of experiment 1 in that dividing attention increased the probability of subjects' mistakenly responding with words from related pairs. For the inclusion test condition, in contrast, dividing attention decreased the probability of subjects' correctly responding with words from related pairs. That pattern of results is what would be expected if dividing attention reduced the probability of recollection.

Table 26.4 Probabilities of Responding with an Old Word and Estimates of Recollection (R) and Automatic Influences (A)

| Pair Type | Probabilities Test | | Estimates | |
|---|---|---|---|---|
| Attention | Inclusion | Exclusion | R | A |
| Related | | | | |
| Full | .60 | .24 | .36 | .37 |
| Divided | .48 | .36 | .12 | .40 |
| Unrelated | | | | |
| Full | .37 | .30 | .07 | .32 |
| Divided | .37 | .29 | .08 | .31 |

Note: Base rate = .29.

So as to better examine differential effects of dividing attention and associative context, the equations presented earlier were used to estimate the separate contributions of automatic and strategic uses of memory (right half of table 26.4). The estimates of recollection reveal that words from related pairs were more likely to be recollected than were words from unrelated pairs. Dividing attention reduced recollection of words from related pairs but did not affect recollection of words from unrelated pairs, perhaps because recollection of words from unrelated pairs was near zero even in the full-attention condition. Thus, the results provided strong evidence that dividing attention reduced recollection, whereas reinstating associative context improved recollection.

An analysis of the estimated automatic influences showed that dividing attention did not produce a significant main effect or a significant interaction with type of pair. This result agrees with those from earlier experiments in showing that although dividing attention radically reduces later recollection, automatic influences of memory are left unchanged. More interesting, reinstating associative context increased automatic influences of memory. Estimated automatic influences for words presented in related pairs were larger than for words presented in unrelated pairs ($F(1,34) = 10.99, MS_e = .008$). The estimated automatic influence for words presented in unrelated pairs was not significantly larger than baseline. That is, the results provided no evidence that presenting words in unrelated pairs had the automatic influence of increasing the likelihood of those words being given as a response. Data-driven processing required to read the words earlier was not enough to produce such automatic influences of memory. Rather, to produce automatic influences, it was necessary that words be presented in related pairs so that the associative relation dealt with during study was the same as that used at test.

**Effects of Providing Environmental Support**

The estimates of recollection gained by use of the process-dissociation procedure differ from estimates that would result if false recall (baseline) was subtracted from correct recall, as is standard. For the full-attention condition, the standard measure of recollection underestimates recollection of words from related pairs (.60 − .29 = .31 versus .36), whereas for the divided-attention condition, the standard measure overestimates recollection (.48 − .29 = .19 versus .12). In part, this difference results because the standard measure rests on the contradictory assumptions that the probability of recollecting that an item was not earlier presented ($R_n$) is the same for the full- and divided-attention conditions and equal to the probability of recollecting that an item is old ($R_o$), which is assumed to differ for the two attention conditions. In contrast, the process-dissociation procedure provides different baselines (measures of exclusion) for the full- and divided-attention conditions and takes effects of automatic influences of memory on guessing into account.

The results of the experiments provide clear evidence for the utility of a distinction between strategic and automatic influences of associative context.

Reinstating associative context has the separate effects of improving recollection and increasing the probability that an old item will be given as a guess. The two effects work in concert to improve performance on direct tests of memory such as a test of cued recall. Because they work in concert for those tests, it is impossible to separate the two effects of associative context or even to see that there are separate effects. Much of the disarray in results from experiments using direct tests might be produced by the two effects of associative context being mistakenly treated as if they originate from a single source. The contradictory results from experiments examining the memory effects of providing environmental support serve as an example.

Craik (1983, 1986) proposed an environmental support hypothesis to account for variation across situations in the severity of the memory deficit suffered by the elderly. The primary assumptions of that hypothesis are that age-related deficits are at least partially due to deficiencies in self-initiated processing and information present in the environment (environmental support) can have effects that compensate for deficient self-initiated processing. A prediction of the environmental support hypothesis is that age differences in performance on direct tests of memory should decrease as environmental support is increased. Craik and Jennings (1992) reviewed the relevant literature and concluded that the results of some experiments agree with the environmental support hypothesis, whereas results of other studies conflict with that hypothesis by showing that age differences are constant across different levels of environmental support or even larger when greater enviromental support is provided. That is, all possible patterns of results have been obtained.

Such mixed results are easily explained if providing environmental support has separate effects on recollection and automatic influences of memory. The aged may suffer a deficit in self-initiated processing and, consequently, show smaller effects of enviromental support (e.g., associative context) on recollection. Indeed, reinstating associative context may affect only automatic uses of memory for the aged but both automatic and strategic uses of memory for younger subjects. The overall effect of providing environmental support would then depend on whether automatic or strategic uses of memory were given the heavier weight by the particular test situation. To examine this possibility, effects on strategic and automatic uses of memory must be separated, as is done by the process-dissociation procedure.

## 26.4 CONCLUSIONS

Findings of dissociations between performance on direct and indirect tests of memory have been cause for a great deal of excitement and have resulted in renewed interest in automatic or unconscious influences of memory. A widely recognized problem for interpreting performance on indirect tests comes from the possibility that performance on indirect tests is contaminated by intentional uses of memory. Much less attention has been given to the possibility that performance on direct tests of memory is contaminated by automatic influences of memory.

Rather than identify processes with tasks, I have used the process-dissociation procedure to separate the contributions of strategic and automatic influences within a task. The results reported here weigh on theorizing about automatic influences of memory. For example, the experiments examining the effects of associative context on automatic influences could have been described as showing the advantage of the process-dissociation procedure over the use of indirect tests as a means of measuring effects of conceptually driven processing. Elsewhere (Jacoby et al. 1992; Toth, Reingold, and Jacoby, n.d.) we provide discussions of that sort and argue that the process-dissociation procedure holds important advantages over indirect tests as a means of investigating automatic influences of memory. Jacoby, Toth, and Yonelinas (1993) discuss the relation between the "direct retrieval" assumptions that underlie the equations presented here and the "generate/recognize" assumptions (Jacoby and Hollingshead 1990) that are often used to describe cued recall performance. They argue that the invariance in automatic influences across manipulations of attention cannot be predicted by a generate/recognize model of cued recall performance.

The process-dissociation procedure can be applied in a wide range of situations. Debner and Jacoby (n.d.) have extended the procedure to separate conscious and unconscious effects of perception. The arguments for "seeing" are the same as for recollection in the case of separating conscious and unconscious influences of memory. Supposed demonstrations of unconscious perception that have relied on indirect tests have been dismissed by critics (Holender 1986) on the grounds that performance on the indirect test may have been contaminated by the effects of conscious perception. Here, too, we turn the tables by showing that performance on direct tests, which is usually taken at face value as measuring conscious perception, is sometimes badly contaminated by the effects of unconscious perception.

The implications of the distinction between strategic and automatic uses of memory are, in some ways, even more important for direct than for indirect tests of memory. It is performance on direct tests of memory such as tests of cued recall that has been the traditional focus of investigations of memory. The measures of memory gained using those standard, direct tests do not distinguish between recollection and automatic influences of memory. The results described here show that by failing to distinguish between those two effects of memory, one risks serious errors in conclusions that are drawn.

**REFERENCES**

Bousfield, W. A., Cohen, B. H., Whitmarsh, G. A., and Kincaid, W. D. (1961). *The Connecticut Free Associational Norms*. Technical Report 35. Storrs, CT: University of Connecticut. November.

Cermak, L. S., Verfaellie, M., Sweeney, M., and Jacoby, L. L. (1992). Fluency versus conscious recollection in the word completion performance of amnesic patients. *Brain and Cognition, 20*, 367–377.

Craik, F. I. M. (1982). Selective changes in encoding as a function of reduced processing capacity. In F. Klix, J. Hoffman, and E. van der Meer (Eds.), *Cognitive research in psychology*, 152–161. Berlin: Deutscher Verlag der Wissenschaffen.

Craik, F. I. M. (1983). On the transfer of information from temporary to permanent memory. *Philosophical Transactions of the Royal Society, B302*, 341–359.

Craik, F. I. M. (1986). A functional account of age differences in memory. In F. Klix and H. Hapendorf (Eds.), *Human memory and cognitive capabilities, mechanisms and performances*, 409–422. Amsterdam: North-Holland.

Craik, F. I. M., and Jennings, J. M. (1992). Human memory. In F. I. M. Craik and T. A. Salthouse (Eds.), *The handbook of aging and cognition* 51–110. Hillsdale, NJ: Erlbaum.

Debner, J., and Jacoby, L. L. (n.d.). Unconscious perception: Attention, awareness, and control. *Journal of Experimental Psychology: Learning, Memory, and Cognition*. In press.

Gabrieli, J. D. E., Milberg, W., Keane, M. W., and Corkin, S. (1990). Intact priming of patterns despite impaired memory. *Neuropsychologia, 28*, 417–428.

Graf, P., and Mandler, G. (1984). Activation makes words more accessible, but not necessarily more retrievable. *Journal of Verbal Learning and Verbal Behavior, 23*, 553–568.

Graf, P., Squire, L. R., and Mandler, G. (1984). The information that amnesic patients do not forget. *Journal of Experimental Psychology: Learning, Memory, and Cognition, 10*, 164–178.

Hintzman, D. L. (1990). Human learning and memory: Connections and dissociations. *Annual Review of Psychology, 41*, 109–139.

Holender, D. (1986). Semantic activation without conscious identification in dichotic listening, parafoveal vision, and visual masking: A survey and appraisal. *Behavioral and Brain Sciences, 9*, 1–23.

Jacoby, L. L. (1978). On interpreting the effects of repetition: Solving a problem versus remembering a solution. *Journal of Verbal Learning and Verbal Behavior, 17*, 649–667.

Jacoby, L. L. (1983). Remembering the data: Analyzing interactive processes in reading. *Journal of Verbal Learning and Verbal Behavior, 22*, 485–508.

Jacoby, L. L. (1991). A process dissociation framework: Separating automatic from intentional uses of memory. *Journal of Memory and Language, 30*, 513–541.

Jacoby, L. L., and Hollingshead, A. (1990). Toward a generate/recognize model of performance on direct and indirect tests of memory. *Journal of Memory and Language, 29*, 433–454.

Jacoby, L. L., and Kelley, C. M. (1991). Unconscious influences of memory: Dissociations and automaticity. In D. Milner and M. Rugg (Eds.), *The neuropsychology of consciousness*, 201–233. London: Academic Press.

Jacoby, L. L., Ste-Marie, D., and Toth, J. P. (1993). Redefining automaticity: Unconscious influences, awareness and control. In A. D. Baddeley and L. Weiskrantz (Eds.), *Attention, selection, awareness and control: A tribute to Donald Broadbent*, 261–282. London: Oxford University Press.

Jacoby, L. L., Toth, J. P., Lindsay, D. S., and Debner, J. A. (1992). Lectures for a layperson: Methods for revealing unconscious processes. In R. Bornstein and T. Pittman (Eds.), *Perception without awareness*, 81–120. NY: Guilford Press.

Jacoby, L. L., Toth, J. P., and Yonelinas, A. P. (1993). Separating conscious and unsciocous influences of memory: Measuring recollection. *Journal of Experimental Psychology: General, 122*, 139–154.

Kintsch, W. (1970). *Learning, memory, and conceptual processes*. New York: Wiley.

McEvoy, C. M., Oth, J. E., Walling, J. R., Wheeler, J. W., and Nelson, D. (n.d.). The University of South Florida Associative Meaning Norms. Tampa, FL: University of South Florida. Unpublished.

Moscovitch, M., Winocur, G., and McLachlan, D. (1986). Memory as assessed by recognition and reading time in normal and memory-impaired people with Alzheimer's disease and other neurological disorders. *Journal of Experimental Psychology: General, 115,* 331–347.

Neumann, O. (1984). Automatic processing: A review of recent findings and a plea for an old theory. In W. Prinz and A. F. Sanders (Eds.), *Cognition and motor processes,* 255–293. Berlin: Springer-Verlag.

Ostergaard, A. L., and Jernigan, T. L. (n.d.). Are word priming and explicit memory mediated by different brain structures? In P. Graf and M. Masson (Eds.), *Implicit memory: New directions in cognition, development and neuropsychology.* Hillsdale, NJ: Erlbaum. In press.

Posner, M. I., and Snyder, C. R. R. (1975). Attention and cognitive control. In R. L. Solso (Ed.), *Information processing in cognition: The Loyola Symposium,* 55–85. Hillsdale, NJ: Erlbaum.

Postman, L. J., and Keppel, G. (1970). *Norms of word association.* New York: Academic Press.

Richardson-Klavehn, A., and Bjork, R. A. (1988). Measures of memory. *Annual Review of Psychology, 39,* 475–543.

Roediger, H. L. (1990). Implicit memory: Retention without remembering. *American Psychologist, 45,* 1043–1056.

Shimamura, A. P. (1986). Priming effects in amnesia: Evidence for a dissociable memory function. *Quarterly Journal of Experimental Psychology, 38A,* 619–644.

Shimamura, A. P., and Squire, L. R. (1984). Paired-associate learning and priming effects in amnesia: A neuropsychological study. *Journal of Experimental Psychology: General, 113,* 556–570.

Slamecka, N. J., and Graf, P. (1978). The generation effect: Delineation of a phenomenon. *Journal of Experimental Psychology: Human Learning and Memory, 4,* 592–604.

Snodgrass, J. G., and Corwin, J. (1988). Pragmatics of measuring recognition memory: Applications to dementia and amnesia. *Journal of Experimental Psychology: General, 117,* 34–50.

Swets, J. A., Tanner, W. P., and Birdsall, T. G. (1961). Decision processes in perception. *Psychological Review, 68,* 301–340.

Toth, J. P., Reingold, E. M., and Jacoby, L. L. (n.d.). Towards a redefinition of implicit memory: Process dissociations following elaborative processing and self-generation. *Journal of Experimental Psychology: Learning, Memory, and Cognition.* In press.

Tulving, E., Schacter, D. L., and Stark, H. A. (1982). Priming effects in word-fragment completion are independent of recognition memory. *Journal of Experimental Psychology: Learning, Memory, and Cognition, 8,* 336–342.

Tulving, E., and Thomson, D. M. (1973). Encoding specificity and retrieval processes in episodic memory. *Psychological Review, 80,* 352–373.

Warrington, E. K., and Weiskrantz, L. (1974). The effect of prior learning on subsequent retention in amnesic patients. *Neuropsychologia, 12,* 419–428.

Weldon, M. S., Roediger, H. L., and Challis, B. H. (1989). The properties of retrieval cues constrain the picture superiority effect. *Memory and Cognition, 1,* 95–105.

# 27 Explicit and Implicit Memory: A Decade of Research

Peter Graf

## 27.1 INTRODUCTION

Explicit and implicit memory have been subjected to systematic investigations for little more than a decade, but several hundred articles have already appeared in the cognitive psychology literature alone. Substantial additional contributions have come from neuropsychology, from life span developmental psychology, and more recently from personality psychology, clinical psychology, marketing research, and other areas. This chapter is not a comprehensive review of this research; instead, the goal is to outline an explanatory framework that we have used to gain insight into the basic findings emerging from research on implicit and explicit memory. The framework focuses on the relationship between conscious perception and episodic recollection, and I report several new experiments that investigated this relationship.

## 27.2 THE DOMAINS OF IMPLICIT AND EXPLICIT MEMORY

An up-to-date popularity chart for psychology jargon would include the words *implicit* and *explicit*. Today, these words are used in conjunction with *learning, memory, knowledge,* and others, but it is not likely that they mark the same distinction in each case. In the domain of memory, Dan Schacter and I (Graf and Schacter 1985) first used *implicit* and *explicit* to specify different modes or kinds of memory, or two phenomenologically different ways of recollecting specific events and experiences.

The idea that we use memory in phenomenologically different ways had been proposed before. A particularly relevant example comes from William James and Herman Ebbinghaus, respectively. To James, memory proper was "the knowledge of an event, or fact, of which meantime we have not been thinking, with the additional consciousness that we have thought or experienced it before" (James 1890, p. 648). Memory proper was the focus of most of the research that followed in the Ebbinghaus tradition. However, based on findings with the savings method, Ebbinghaus himself had a more general view of memory, according to which "the vanished mental states [created by prior episodes could] give indubitable proof of their continuing existence even if they themselves do not return to consciousness at all, or at least not exactly at the given time" (Ebbinghaus 1964, 2).

The critical difference between the modes of memory highlighted by the quotations from James and Ebbinghaus is the state of consciousness that accompanies successful recollection of an episode. By contrast, the labels *implicit* and *explicit* denote different ways of engaging memory; they specify the mental attitudes that are used to initiate and guide recollection of episodes. When Dan Schacter and I first used the terms (Graf and Schacter 1985), we stated that explicit memory concerns performance that is initiated and guided by a conscious plan or by an intention to recollect specific prior episodes, whereas implicit memory concerns test performance influences due to specific prior episodes that occur in the absence of a conscious intention to recollect them. It seems important to make a distinction between mental states that initiate and guide recollection versus those that might accompany recollection. One critical reason is the fact that amnesic patients and healthy control subjects can show comparable levels of priming on a word completion test, for example, and yet only the control subjects may be aware of the relationship between the study list and what they wrote on the test. Similar dissociations between what is recollected on implicit memory tests and awareness of its relationship with a prior study list have been found with various experimental manipulations in groups of normal subjects (Gardiner and Parkin 1990; Gardiner and Java 1991).

The phrases *implicit* and *explicit memory* define a dichotomy between mental states, but this dichotomy probably turns into a continuum when test performance is used as an index for a particular mode of recollecting prior episodes. I assume that any memory test (a situation defined by cues, instructions, setting, etc.) can be located along this continuum and that some tests, such as free and cued recall, fall closer to the explicit end, whereas other tests, such as word completion and free association, are closer to the implicit end. Thus, when referring to subjects' performance in a particular experimental condition, I use *explicit memory* when I am confident that recollection of specific prior episodes was initiated and guided primarily by a conscious intention, and I attribute to *implicit memory* test effects that occur primarily in the absence of a conscious intention to recollect specific prior episodes.

## 27.3 BASIC FINDINGS

A decade of research has produced an abundance of data and yielded many insights into the domains of implicit and explicit memory (Graf and Masson 1993). One of the best-known and most thought-provoking observations has come from experiments with amnesic patients who, despite their severely impaired performance on explicit memory tests, can show entirely normal performance on implicit memory tests (for a recent review, see Moscovitch, Vriezen, and Goshen-Gottstein 1993; Shimamura 1993). Developmental studies have revealed that whereas explicit memory test performance increases throughout childhood and then declines in late adulthood, implicit memory test performance becomes functional earlier in life and remains stable across the adult life span (for recent reviews see Parkin 1993; Naito and Komatsu 1993; Mitchell 1993). By far the largest collection of findings, however, has come from studies with healthy young adults, and it shows that a variety of materials, study tasks, and test manipulations have different effects on performance of implicit and explicit memory tests (for recent reviews see Graf and Masson 1993). The combined findings from these investigations permit several generalizations about the domain of implicit and explicit memory. This section focuses on three such generalizations—the automaticity, specificity, and longevity of priming—and it illustrates each with a specific experiment. The next section offers a theoretical account for them.

One of the best-established findings in the memory literature, following on the heels of Craik and Lockhart's (1972) levels of processing framework, is that memory test performance is better after tasks that require subjects to study words by attending to their semantic than their nonsemantic aspects. Limits to this finding were discovered by some of the first experiments on implicit and explicit memory (Graf and Mandler 1984; Graf, Mandler, and Haden 1982; Jacoby and Dallas 1981). To illustrate, Graf and Mandler (1984) presented subjects with words, such as *chapel, files,* and *parcel,* in study conditions that required making decisions about either their meaning or their appearance. After a short delay, we assessed memory for the words either with a cued recall test or with a stem completion test. We gave exactly the same cues—the initial three letters of the words (e.g., *cha___, fil___*)—for both tests and used only the instructions to induce and specify the mental sets appropriate for cued recall versus stem completion testing, respectively. The results showed a typical level of processing effect on cued recall, with higher performance after the semantic (41 percent) than the nonsemantic (8 percent) study task; more important, priming effects on the word stem completion test were similar across these conditions (23 percent and 20 percent after the semantic and nonsemantic task, respectively). This pattern of performance suggests that priming is an automatic consequence of studying familiar words, whereas explicit memory test performance varies with the specific requirements of each study task. A similar claim about automaticity seems justified by the finding that implicit but not explicit memory is spared in patients with anterograde amnesia and by the finding that implicit but not explicit memory remains stable across the life span (Graf 1990).

A second basic fact about implicit and explicit memory is illustrated by the finding that priming effects are typically larger for words that are studied and tested in the same sensory modality (e.g., visual) than for words presented in different sensory modalities (e.g., auditory for study and visual for testing) (Roediger and Blaxton 1987; Kirsner and Dunn 1985). By contrast, explicit memory test performance shows no effect or only a minimal effect due to similar study and test manipulations. Such findings emphasize that priming, but not explicit memory, is specific to the materials that are presented at study and test. A more compelling illustration of the specificity of priming effects comes from a recent experiment with Laureen Miki (Graf and Miki 1990). We

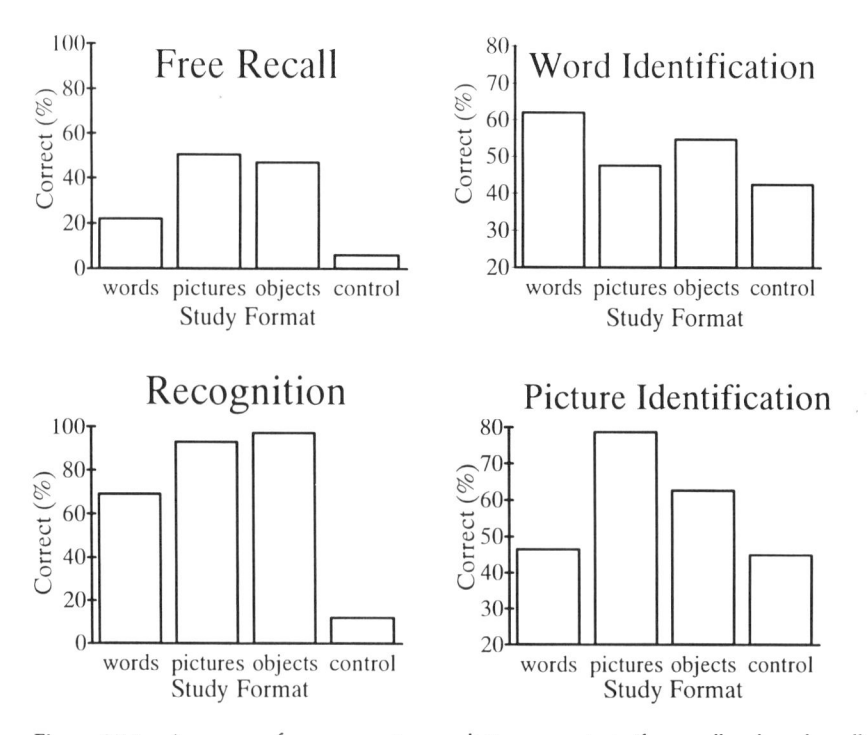

**Figure 27.1** Average performance on two explicit memory tests (free recall and cued recall) and two implicit memory tests (word identification and picture identification), following study of common objects, pictures of objects, or the printed names of objects. On the explicit tests, performance is higher for pictures and objects than for printed words. On the implicit tests, performance is highest when materials were presented in the same format at study and test.

presented subjects with common objects (e.g., a pen, a key, glasses), photographs of these objects, or the printed names of the objects and then assessed implicit memory with a word identification test or a picture identification test and explicit memory with a free recall test or a word recognition test. The results are shown in figure 27.1. Consistent with extant findings, both free recall and word recognition test performance were higher for the objects and pictures than for the words. More critical are the findings from the implicit memory tests. On the word identification test, we found more priming for items studied as words than for those studied as pictures or objects; by contrast, on the picture identification test, priming was higher for items studied as pictures than for those studied as words or objects. In short, we found large priming effects when the same materials were presented for study and test and reduced effects or no priming in the other conditions. Roediger and his colleagues have provided numerous compelling demonstrations of the same kind (Roediger and Srinivas 1993). Moreover, they showed that even on the same test, priming effects are larger when the exact same versus different fragments of pictures are displayed at study and test. In view of such findings, the specificity of priming effects is often regarded as a key feature that distinguishes explicit from implicit memory test performance (Moscovitch, Goshen-Gott, and Vriezen, chap. 25, this volume; Roediger and Srinivas 1993).

A third generalization about priming has come from experiments that measured retention after various delays (Graf and Mandler 1984; Flude 1991; Kolers 1976; Sloman and Hayman 1988). Tulving, Schacter, and Stark (1982), who conducted one of the first experiments of this kind, assessed memory for words with a recognition and a fragment completion test, either a few minutes after study or after a 1-week delay. Recognition test performance showed a substantial decline over the retention interval, but the amount of priming did not significantly decrease.[1] More recently, Sloman and Hayman (1988) have shown that priming effects can persist for more than a year. What is astonishing about such long-lasting effects is that they occur with materials, such as familiar words, that are likely to be encountered on many other occasions between study and testing.

We have learned much more than the foregoing generalization from a decade of research on implicit and explicit memory. The main reason for featuring the automaticity, specificity, and longevity of priming is that these are solidly established in the literature and thus must be accommodated by any comprehensive theoretical account. In the next section, these findings are used to highlight various aspects of the interpretive framework that has guided our efforts to learn and understand more about the nature of implicit and explicit memory.

## 27.4 AN INTERPRETIVE FRAMEWORK

The basis of our interpretive framework for implicit and explicit memory test performance is Mandler's dual process recognition model (Mandler 1980, 1988; Graf and Mandler 1984; Graf and Ryan 1990). We view memory in terms of the processing that is engaged by different study and test activities (Kolers 1976; Kolers and Ostry 1974) and postulate a large population of processing units with different subsets dedicated to the analysis of sensory, perceptual, semantic, and other aspects of stimuli. In order to represent an event in memory, a subset of these processing units must become interconnected. We assume that any subset of units that is activated or engaged simultaneously—that participates in the construction of the same conscious percept—becomes interconnected, and if already connected, becomes more strongly associated. We further assume that once connected, a set of units has the tendency to become completely reactivated when a critical portion of its members are subsequently reengaged.

We distinguish between two memory organizing processes, integration and elaboration (Mandler 1980, 1988), which forge or modify different connections among processing units. Integration focuses on connections among the units that define an individual item, such as a word, an object, or a sentence; these kinds of connections are formed or strengthened when the subject either perceives coherence among separate stimulus components (e.g., under the guidance of preexisting representations or gestalt laws like proximity or common fate) or conceives a structure for processing target features as a single entity (Graf and Schacter 1989). Elaboration involves connections between or among individual items, and they are formed or strengthened when a target is considered in relation to the experimental situation (e.g., other targets, situational cues, relevant prior knowledge).

The nature of processing—whether it is integrative or elaborative—is always relative to, and decided by, the target item that is being processed. If the target (the unit of processing) is a word, then reading it and relating it to other words in a sentence constitutes elaborative processing of that word; but if the target is the sentence as a single whole, then the processing of any of its words is integrative when a word is read and interpreted as part of the larger whole. Differentiating between integrative and elaborative processing is complicated because it is often difficult to define what is meant by a "target item," which is like one of Miller's (1956) chunks: a unit of processing whose extension depends on several factors, such as a subject's knowledge of the materials and the requirements of each particular processing task.

We assume that priming effects reflect primarily the increased integration produced by study trial processing, whereas explicit memory test performance reflects primarily study trial elaborative processing. This assumption is consistent with an intuitive analysis of the basic requirements of implicit and explicit memory tests. Implicit memory tests require subjects to name items in response to category labels, to complete words in response to word stems or fragments, or to identify briefly presented words; in all cases, performance requires perceiving or conceiving a structure that organizes or integrates the cueing information and thereby specifies a target or target set. Study trial integration facilitates this type of processing because once connected, a representation (an organized set of processing units) has the tendency to become completely reintegrated even when only some of its components are subsequently reprocessed. By contrast, explicit memory tests require subjects either to recollect previously studied items in response to cues (cued recall test), in the absence of specific cues (free recall test), or to decide what targets had appeared in a previously studied list (recognition test). In all cases, performance requires accessing information that associates a target with a specific prior episode or situation. We assume that elaboration during the study trial facilitates explicit remembering because it involves encoding targets in a distinct relation to the experimental situation, thereby establishing the associations that link each target with a specific learning episode.

By this framework, we can explain a broad range of findings from the extant literature on implicit and explicit memory. Consider first the finding that priming effects with familiar word targets appear to be mediated by automatic processes. The framework explains that priming effects occur "automatically" because preexisting representations are engaged for processing familiar items (because perception is interactive and always involves both top-down and bottom-up contributions). Because the items are familiar, even a small amount of bottom-up processing is sufficient to reactivate (and thus further integrate) their preexisting long-term memory representations completely, and this is equally likely to occur with semantic and nonsemantic study tasks, thereby producing comparable priming effects. By contrast, explicit memory test performance varies across conditions because semantic tasks involve more extensive encoding of targets in a distinctive relation to the experimental situation than do nonsemantic tasks, thereby establishing the associations that connect the targets with a specific study episode.

The framework uses the simultaneity assumption—the notion that a subset of processing units that is activated at the same time becomes integrated or unitized—to explain the specificity and longevity of priming effects. The specificity of priming occurs because under most circumstances, we typically construct different percepts for spoken and written words, for words and pictures, and for words from different languages. By the view that an item's memory representation encompasses various kinds of processing units (e.g., sensory, perceptual, lexical) and that different percepts involve different subsets of these units, it follows that for words presented in the same modality at study and test, there is more specific overlap in the "sensory" units engaged for perception on each occasion, and thus more priming may occur because these units provide the most direct means by which to recruit and benefit from the increased integration achieved at the time of study. Similarly, the degree of study and test overlap in specific sensory and perceptual processing units explains Graf and Miki's (1990) finding of larger priming effects on a picture identification test for items studied as pictures than for those studied as words, and vice versa for priming effects on a word identification test. The finding of reduced but significant priming across modalities (e.g., spoken versus written words) or item formats (e.g., pictures versus written words) is explained in terms of overlapping processing units beyond those required for the sensory and perceptual analysis of a stimulus (Kirsner and Dunn 1985).

The longevity of priming effects is also explained by the framework's core assumption that any subset of processing units that is activated simultaneously becomes interconnected. By this assumption, any processing unit that is activated by a particular experimental situation (e.g., by a smell in the room, the impression made by the laboratory, the cognitive, affective, and motivational state induced by the experiment) becomes part and parcel of an item's unitized representation. This contextualization of item representations provides a basis for long-lasting priming effects. We assume that at least part of this specific context is reestablished when the subject returns for testing after a delay (because, for example, testing occurs in the same laboratory, by the same experimenter, with the subject in a similar cognitive, affective, and motivational state), and the cues provided by this context serve to "bias" or select the specific integrated item representations established at study. Thus, repetition priming can occur despite the fact that the same items may have been encountered on many other occasions between study and test.

The contextual influences observed on implicit and explicit memory test performance are mediated by different processes. Implicit effects occur because the experimental situation shapes or biases a subject's perception and cognition in subtle ways that are not usually under conscious control. By contrast, explicit effects occur only when the subject becomes aware, at study and at test, of a distinctive relation between the to-be-remembered (TBR) items and the context in which each occurs. For this reason, it is possible that a subtle stimulus, like a perfume, affects implicit memory but is not consciously perceived and thus has no effect on explicit memory. Other aspects of the experiment, like my knowledge of the fact that I am studying a word list on Friday the 13th, may not influence the manner in which I perceive or conceive the list (and thus having no effect on implicit memory test performance), but it may serve as a useful cue for explicit recollection of that specific list.

## 27.5 PRIMING AND THE CONSTRUCTION OF CONSCIOUS PERCEPTS

The explanation we offer for the automaticity, specificity, and longevity of priming effects is based on several assumptions about memory, about how events are represented and how representations are mapped onto performance of implicit and explicit memory tests. The most critical is the simultaneity assumption: the notion that any processing units that participate in the construction of the same conscious percept become part of an item's memory representation. By this assumption, it follows that memory test performance will be affected by any factors that influence the construction of conscious percepts at study and at test. In this section, we focus on experiments that manipulated conscious perception in three different ways: by means of unusual stimuli, by task instructions, and by task contexts. The overall goal is to highlight that memory test performance is a product of conscious perception and that perception is determined by a range of different factors.

**Stimulus Familiarity**

One factor that influences how we perceive a TBR item is its novelty, and thus, item novelty is expected to affect the size of repetition priming effects. We assume that this occurs because both study and test trial processing of TBR items is interactive and always involves both bottom-up and top-down contributions. For familiar items (e.g., common words), which have preexisting long-term memory representations, only a small portion of their sensory features needs to be processed to activate their existing representations and thereby construct a novel unified percept, whereas for unfamiliar new items, which have no preexisting memory representation, more extensive processing of sensory features is required to construct a unified percept. By the simultaneity assumption of our framework, we expect that the memory representations established for unfamiliar, novel items encompass more sensory-feature specific processing units than the representations established for familiar items, and thus, a change in the sensory features of the items presented for study and test should have a larger effect for unfamiliar new items than for familiar old items.

To my knowledge, this expectation has not yet been examined directly. As a more indirect test, however, the framework also predicts an influence on perception and thus priming when only the appearance of TBR targets is novel. When the targets are familiar words, perception is likely to require extensive processing of features related to their appearance only when they are displayed in a highly unusual, novel format. This is because with an average of almost two decades of practice at reading printed and handwritten text from diverse displays, the typical college student subject has accumulated a large repertoire of well-practiced ways or procedures for identifying words, and thus, only extreme manipulations are likely to necessitate a detailed feature analysis of TBR words. Consequently, by the simultaneity assumption of our framework, we predict that a change in sensory features of the items presented for study and test will have a large effect only when they are presented in a highly unusual format and will have no effect or only a minimal effect when they are displayed in more familiar formats.

This expectation is consistent with findings in the literature. In several experiments, familiar words have been presented for study and test in either highly unusual display formats or more familiar formats, and the findings showed format-specific effects only in the former case. For example, Kolers (1976) found long-lasting format-specific priming effects with materials presented in unfamiliar spatially transformed displays. Jacoby and Hayman (1987) found display format-specific priming effects with words tested in a normal-sized lowercase typeface, when subjects studied the words either in the same lowercase format or in a large (10 times larger than normal) and unusual font. By contrast, many studies have found no change in priming effects when the display format of words was changed in more familiar ways between study and test, for example, from handwriting to typewriting (Carr, Brown, and Charalambous 1989; Clarke and Morton 1983; Levy and Kirsner 1989). Our framework provides insight into this pattern of priming effects by focusing on how we perceive common words displayed in familiar versus highly unfamiliar formats.

**Study Task**

Familiar items are encodable in several different ways, but study tasks can be used to manipulate how we perceive them. To use a concrete example, consider a list of words that are handwritten by different individuals. We can ask subjects to sort these words in terms of their meaning (e.g., to group together words that are semantically related) or by writing style. These two tasks are likely to induce subjects to construct different percepts for the TBR words, with the latter emphasizing details about similarities and differences in appearance. Consequently, on a subsequent test of implicit memory, we would expect that priming is more affected by a change in the appearance of words between study and testing in conditions that focus on writing style than in conditions that focus on meaning.

We examined this prediction in a recent experiment in which familiar words were displayed in two unfamiliar type fonts called pudgy and shadow (for example of fonts, see Graf and Ryan 1990). The words were displayed either in the same font at study and test or in different fonts. At study, subjects were asked either to make a decision about the meaning of each word or to rate the words for their readability. We assumed that in order to make decisions about word meanings, their sensory and perceptual encoding can be guided primarily by preexisting memory representations, whereas making decisions about readability requires more extensive analysis of sensory features (the construction of a detailed and different kind of perceptual representations). On a subsequent word identification test, we found more priming for words displayed in the same font at study and test (18.8%) than for words displayed in different fonts (11.2%) but only in the readability rating condition. There was no display format effect on priming in the semantic condition (18.8% and 17.9% for the same and different font conditions, respectively). These findings, together with results from the experiments in the foregoing section, emphasize that there are limits to the format specificity of priming effects and that these limits are critically dependent on factors that influence how subjects perceive TBR targets at study and test.

**Test Context**

A more global factor that influences the construction of conscious percepts, and thus the pattern of priming effects, is the context in which TBR items are studied and tested. To illustrate the influence of context on perception, consider how we encode homophones (e.g., *dear, deer*) that appear in different sentences. The context in which a TBR item is presented for study and test affects how we perceive it and, in turn, influences whether (or how much) priming will occur. We have conducted two lines of research to investigate this expectation. The first shows that a change in context can eliminate repetition priming effects, and the second reveals a reduction in priming with a shift in context between study and test.

The initial motivation for the first investigations was to develop a test involving the use of familiar, complete words and yielding an accuracy measure of priming as opposed to a speed measure. For this purpose, we presented subjects with word pairs, such as those shown in table 27.1, and asked them to select the one word that occurs less commonly in the language. Initial

**Table 27.1** Examples of Word Pairs Used for the Relative Frequency Decision Task

| Low | 1 versus 10 |
| | *Fabricate—generosity* |
| Medium | 3.5 versus 35 |
| | *Molecule—genius* |
| High | 10 versus 100 |
| | *Yearly—opinion* |

Notes: Each pair had two words that differed by 1 log unit in language frequency. Subjects' task was to select the less common word from each pair.
Numbers indicate the frequency of the left and right word according to the norms of Kucera and Francis (1967).

experiments showed that if two words differ by 1 log unit in language frequency (according to Kucera and Francis 1967), subjects can select the less common word correctly with about 80 percent accuracy. Subjects' ability to make such relative frequency decisions can be explained by several of the existing models. By our framework, more common words have a more strongly integrated preexisting representation in memory, and we assume that the speed with which these representations can be reactivated or recruited gives rise to the feeling of familiarity that is used to make the relative frequency decisions (Ryan and Graf 1992).

In the critical experiments, subjects studied the lower-frequency words from the test pairs prior to receiving the relative word frequency decisions test. We assume that studying the lower-frequency words enables the construction of yet another integrated representation, thereby making the integrated representations for lower-frequency words more similar in strength to those for the nonstudied higher-frequency word. Thus, we expected that priming should result in a reduction in subjects' ability to make accurate relative frequency decision. But the results, shown in figure 27.2, do not support this expectation. They do show that subjects can make accurate frequency decisions on pairs with words that were not presented for study, but there was no evidence of priming, and subjects were equally accurate on the pairs containing the words from the study list. We conducted several experiments in which we manipulated study tasks, test instructions, and the materials; none showed any evidence of priming on the relative frequency decision test (Ryan and Graf 1992).

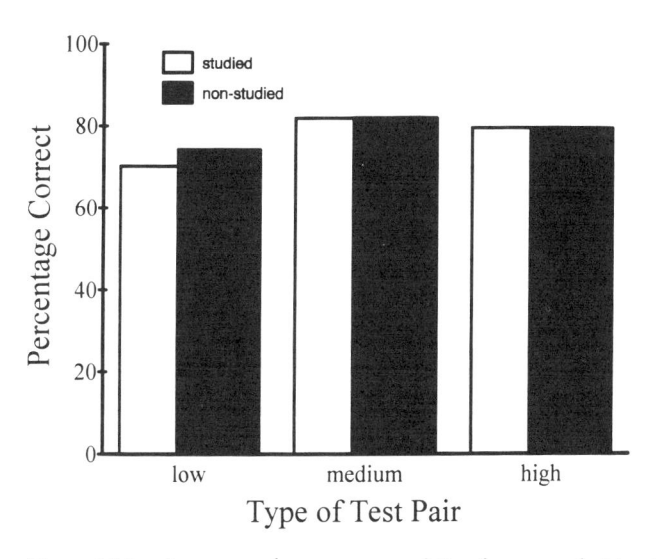

**Figure 27.2** Average performance on a relative frequency decision task. Subjects were presented pairs with words that differed by 1 log unit in terms of language frequency and were required to select the lower-frequency word from each pair. The means show no difference on frequency decisions between pairs with two nonstudied words and pairs in which the less common word had been included in a previously studied list.

These findings seem surprising at first glance, but they are consistent with any framework that allows context to influence how we perceive the TBR words at the time of study and test. In our experiments, the words were presented for study one at a time, but they were presented in the context of another word at test. More important, our test required subjects to make decisions about the frequency of words in the language, thereby triggering strong perceptual habits—a set of language processing constraints—that have minimal overlap with those that were active at the time of study. Mandler (chap. 1, this volume) has discussed how a similar factor, which he calls the restricting effects of awareness, can prevent access even to recently established memory representations. We believe that on our test, the language habits triggered by the test context (instructions, other words) constrained how subjects perceived the words in such a way that the test percepts had minimal overlap with those created at study, thus yielding no evidence of priming.

Additional evidence that the context or setting in which TBR items are studied and tested influences priming comes from another set of experiments (Graf 1988), in which TBR words were studied in one of two settings: the gallery of the University of British Columbia's (UBC) main swimming pool or a games arcade at the UBC undergraduate student center. Testing occurred either in the same setting as study or in the other setting. Implicit memory was assessed with a category production test or a word completion test, whereas explicit memory was assessed with a category-cued recall test and a letter-cued recall test. The swimming pool and the games arcade, which are located in adjacent buildings on the campus, differ in several respects, including visual and spatial cues, smell, temperature, noise, and crowd levels. We assume that these cues cannot be easily ignored and that they have a strong influence on how subjects perceive TBR words at study and testing. Consequently, we predicted that a change in setting between study and test would reduce priming.

The results are shown in table 27.2. They underline two findings: priming effects were larger when study and test were in the same versus different

Table 27.2  Memory Test Performance by Setting

|  | Study-Test Setting | |
|---|---|---|
|  | Same | Different |
| Explicit test | | |
| Category-cued recall | 62 | 62 |
| Letter-cued recall | 46 | 43 |
| Implicit tests | | |
| Category production | 33 | 22 |
| Word-stem completion | 24 | 14 |

Note: The settings were the gallery of a large swimming pool and a games arcade in an undergraudate student center. The tabled values show average priming on the implicit memory tests.

setting, and this manipulation had no effect on either explicit memory test. The latter finding conflicts with the results from studies like Godden and Baddeley (1975), but it is consistent with a report by Smith (1979), who showed that setting effects disappear when test instructions direct subjects to think themselves back into the original learning environment. All explicit tests require thinking back; the appropriate mental set is induced by the instructions to recollect information from a specific prior episode. In contrast, in the absence of an instruction defined episode—directed mental set, implicit memory test performance is guided only by the cues from the test form, the instructions, and the setting and thus is highly likely to be influenced by a change in the setting between study and test.

**Conclusions**

The core assumption of the framework that guides our research is that the sensory, perceptual, and conceptual stimulus analyzing procedures that are engaged simultaneously—that are recruited for the construction of the same percept—are integrated and become part of a TBR item's memory representation. Familiar items, such as common words, already have preexisting memory representations, but they are further integrated as a result of appearing as targets in an experiment. By virtue of the cues and instructions that they provide, implicit memory tests require subjects to perceive or construct a coherent percept for an item, and for this reason, we postulate that priming effects reflect primarily the increased integration resulting from study trial processing. Consistent with the notion of transfer-appropriate processing (Morris, Bransford, and Franks 1977), we postulate that priming effects will be larger when study and test trial processing give rise to similar percepts than when different percepts are constructed.

The main purpose of the new research reported in this chapter was to focus on factors that are known to affect perception of TBR items and to investigate their influence on the size of priming effects. We know from previous research that what we perceive can be affected by the novelty of items, by what we are required to do with them (task demands), and by the context in which they occur, and our findings show that all of these factors influence priming in the expected manner. The experiments that we reported do not exhaust the factors that are known to influence perception, but they serve to illustrate the broad range of factors that will have to be considered by a comprehensive account of implicit and explicit memory.

**NOTES**

Preparation of this chapter was funded by a research grant from the Natural Sciences and Engineering Research Council of Canada.

1. Graf and Mandler (1984) examined word completion test performance with stems or word beginnings (e.g., Mot___) that permitted at least ten different completions, and they found

priming effects that decayed to chance level within 2 hours. They explained the difference between the long-lasting priming effects reported by Tulving, Schacter, and Stark (1982) (whose word fragment cues permitted only a single completion each) and their findings in terms of the cues that are provided on the priming test.

# REFERENCES

Carr, T. H., Brown, J. S., and Charalambous, A. (1989). Repetition and reading: Perceptual encoding mechanisms are very abstract but not very interactive. *Journal of Experimental Psychology: Learning, Memory, and Cognition, 15*, 763–778.

Clarke, R., and Morton, J. (1983). Cross modality facilitation in tachistoscopic word recognition. *Quarterly Journal of Experimental Psychology, 35A*, 79–96.

Craik, F. I. M., and Lockhart, R. S. (1972). Levels of processing: A framework for memory research. *Journal of Verbal Learning and Verbal Behavior, 11*, 671–684.

Ebbinghaus, H. E. (1964). *Memory: A contribution to experimental psychology*. New York: Dover (originally published in 1985; translated in 1913).

Flude, B. (1991). Long-term repetition priming of faces. Paper presented at the International Conference on Memory, University of Lancaster, July.

Gardiner, J. M., and Java, R. I. (1991). Forgetting in recognition memory with and without recollective experience. *Memory and Cognition, 19*, 617–623.

Gardiner, J. M., and Parkin, A. J. (1990). Attention and recollective experience in recognition memory. *Memory and Cognition, 18*, 579–583.

Godden, D. R., and Baddeley, A. D. (1975). Context-dependent memory in two natural environments: On land and under water. *British Journal of Psychology, 66*, 325–331.

Graf, P. (1988). Implicit and explicit memory in same and different environments. Paper presented at the Psychonomics Society, Chicago, November.

Graf, P. (1990). Life span changes in implicit and explicit memory. *Bulletin of the Psychonomic Society, 28*, 353–358.

Graf, P., and Mandler, G. (1984). Activation makes words more accessible but not necessarily more retrievable. *Journal of Verbal Learning and Verbal Behavior, 23*, 553–568.

Graf, P., Mandler, G., and Haden, P. E. (1982). Simulating amnesic symptoms in normal subjects. *Science, 218*, 1243–1244.

Graf, P., and Masson, M. E. J. (1993). *Implicit memory: New directions in cognition, development, and neuropsychology*. Hillsdale, NJ: Erlbaum.

Graf, P., and Miki, L. (1990). Modality specific processing in implicit and explicit memory. Paper presented at the annual convention of the Canadian Psychological Association, Ottawa, June.

Graf, P., and Ryan, L. (1990). Transfer-appropriate processing for implicit and explicit memory. *Journal of Experimental Psychology: Learning, Memory, and Cognition, 16*, 978–992.

Graf, P., and Schacter, D. L. (1985). Implicit and explicit memory for new associations in normal and amnesic subjects. *Journal of Experimental Psychology: Learning, Memory, and Cognition, 11*, 501–518.

Graf, P., and Schacter, D. L. (1989). Unitization and grouping mediate dissociations in memory for new associations. *Journal of Experimental Psychology: Learning, Memory, and Cognition, 15*, 930–940.

Jacoby, L. L., and Dallas, M. (1981). On the relationship between autobiographical memory and perceptual learning. *Journal of Experimental Psychology: General, 110*, 306–340.

Jacoby, L. L., and Hayman, C. G. (1987). Specific visual transfer in word identification. *Journal of Experimental Psychology: Learning, Memory, and Cognition, 13*, 456–463.

James, W. (1890). *Principles of psychology*. New York: Holt.

Kirsner, K., and Dunn, J. C. (1985). The perceptual record: A common factor in repetition priming and attribute retention. In M. I. Posner and O. S. M. Marin (Eds.), *Mechanisms of attention: Attention and performance XI*, 547–565. Hillsdale, NJ: Erlbaum.

Kolers, P. (1985). Memorial consequences of automatized encoding. *Journal of Experimental Psychology: Human Learning and Memory, 1*, 689–701.

Kolers, P. A. (1976). Reading a year later. *Journal of Experimental Psychology: Human Learning and Memory, 2*, 554–565.

Kolers, P., and Ostry, D. J. (1974). Time course of loss of information regarding pattern analyzing operations. *Journal of Verbal Learning and Verbal Behavior, 13*, 599–612.

Kucera, M., and Francis, W. (1967). *Computational analysis of present-day American English*. Providence, RI: Brown University Press.

Levy, B. A., and Kirsner, K. (1989). Reprocessing text: Indirect measures of word and message level processes. *Journal of Experimental Psychology: Learning, Memory, and Cognition, 15*, 407–417.

Mandler, G. (1980). Recognizing: The judgment of previous occurrence. *Psychological Review, 87*, 252–271.

Mandler, G. (1988). Memory: Conscious and unconscious. In P. R. Solomon, G. R. Goethals, C. M. Kelley, and B. R. Stephens (Eds.), *Memory: Interdisciplinary approaches*, 84–106. New York: Springer-Verlag.

Miller, G. A. (1956). The magical number seven, plus or minus two: Some limits on our capacity for processing information. *Psychological Review, 63*, 81–97.

Mitchell, D. B. (1993). Implicit and explicit memory for pictures: Multiple views across the life span. In P. Graf and M. E. J. Masson (Eds.), *Implicit memory: New directions in cognition, development and neuropsychology*, 171–190. Hillsdale, NJ: Erlbaum.

Morris, C. D., Bransford, J. D., and Franks, J. J. (1977). Levels of processing versus transfer appropriate processing. *Journal of Verbal Leaving and Verbal Behavior, 16*, 519–533.

Moscovitch, M., Vriezen, E., and Goshen-Gottstein, J. (1993). Implicit tests of memory in patients with focal lesions or degenerative brain disorders. In F. Boller and J. Grafman (Eds.), *Handbook of neuropsychology*, vol. 8. Amsterdam: Elsevier.

Naito, M., and Komatsu, S. (1993). Processes involved in childhood development of implicit memory. In P. Graf and M. E. J. Masson (Eds.), *Implicit memory: New directions in cognition, development and neuropsychology*, 231–260. Hillsdale, NJ: Erlbaum.

Parkin, A. (1993). Implicit memory across the life span. In P. Graf and M. E. J. Masson (Eds.), *Implicit memory: New directions in cognition, development and neuropsychology*, 191–206. Hillsdale, NJ: Erlbaum.

Roediger, H. L., and Blaxton, T. A. (1987). Effects of varying modality, surface features, and retention interval on priming in word fragment completion. *Memory and Cognition, 15*, 379–388.

Roediger, H. L., and Srinivas, K. (1993). Specificity of operations in perceptual priming. In P. Graf and M. E. J. Masson (Eds.), *Implicit memory: New directions in cognition, development and neuropsychology*, 17–48. Hillsdale, NJ: Erlbaum.

Ryan, L., and Graf, P. (1992). Decisions about relative word frequency are not influenced by priming. Paper presented at the American Psychological Society meeting, San Diego, June.

Shimamura, A. P. (1993). Neuropsychological analyses of implicit memory: History, methodology, and theoretical interpretations. In P. Graf and M. E. J. Masson (Eds.), *Implicit memory: New directions in cognition, development and neuropsychology*, 265–285. Hillsdale, NJ: Erlbaum.

Sloman, S. A., and Hayman, C. G. (1988). Forgetting in primed fragment completion. *Journal of Experimental Psychology: Learning, Memory, and Cognition, 14*, 223–239.

Smith, S. M. (1979). Remembering in and out of context. *Journal of Experimental Psychology: Human Learning and Memory, 5*, 460–471.

Tulving, E., Schacter, D. L., and Stark, H. A. (1982). Priming effects in word-fragment completion are independent of recognition memory. *Journal of Experimental Psychology: Learning, Memory, and Cognition, 8*, 336–342.

# 28 Acquiring General Knowledge from Specific Episodes of Experience

Thomas H. Carr, Dale Dagenbach, Debra VanWieren, Laura A. Carlson Radvansky, AnnJanette R. Alejano, and Joseph S. Brown

ABSTRACT  Three lines of research are described on the acquisition of new semantic knowledge. The first demonstrates that massive amounts of practice are required to learn new associations sufficiently well to produce automatic priming in lexical decision, where "automatic" is defined as priming at short prime-target stimulus onset asynchronies (SOAs) in the absence of specific expectations about prime-target relatedness. The second line of research presents evidence for a special attentional mechanism that aids in retrieving semantic codes early in learning, while they are relatively weak and hence especially susceptible to interference from older, stronger codes. This retrieval mechanism appears to work on the center-surround principle, facilitating sought-for codes and inhibiting related but unwanted codes. The third line of research investigates the stimulus properties, in particular visual surface form, that act as cues for retrieving semantic codes. Using transfer-of-repetition effects as a diagnostic, retrieval processes appear to be quite abstract and transferable when familiar words are organized into a coherent text and presented in a familiar typography. However, surface-form specificity of repetition effects appears when words are encountered individually or in random lists rather than in coherent texts, and when typography is unfamiliar rather than familiar. The possibility is raised that specificity may also appear, even when typography is familiar, when semantic codes are new and weakly established.

## 28.1  INTRODUCTION

Current thinking has it that "semantic," "conceptual," or "generic" knowledge arises in some way from the accumulated impact of individual episodes of experience. Even the strongest nativist positions include empiricist principles. The particular content of perceptual, taxonomic, and grammatical categories must be given by experience, even if the forms or defining characteristics of the categories are not.

This widespread belief in the empirical, episodic orgins of at least some of our semantic knowledge raises many issues that cognitive scientists are actively debating. Among the most basic is this one: exactly what constitutes "semantic" or "generic" knowledge? Is there an enduring level of memorial representation that stores directly retrievable abstractions on a long-term basis? Students of semantic memory have long thought so, including such otherwise diverse figures as Plato and Aristotle, Kant, Wittgenstein, Bruner, Rosch, Posner, Collins, Morton, and Anderson. During the past decade, however, a very different view has gained considerable credence. Perhaps abstract, conceptual properties and relations are *not* permanently stored in long-term memory. Perhaps they get computed "on the fly," to borrow McClelland's (1985) term, as they are needed, from a memorial storehouse that consists entirely of concrete episodes of past experience. Jacoby and Brooks held a conference on this possibility, about ten years ago, called "The Primacy of the Specific." This conference brought together people who were wondering just how abstract stored human knowledge really is—and they were beginning to think, "not very." Since then, several versions of such an idea have been well received in the cognitive scientific community.

## 28.2 WHAT IS AT STAKE?

No one denies that people store episodic memories of their experiences, though there is considerable uncertainty about what details are stored in what form and how accessible different details are to subsequent implicit and explicit retrieval. By the same token, no one denies that people have conceptual abilities. People generalize from one experience to another, even though the two experiences are not identical; they organize exemplars into categories and categories into higher-order schemas; and this conceptual organization exerts significant impact on the real-time progress and final outcomes of cognitive performance.

Thus, the debate is not about the functional reality of the two forms of knowledge, semantic and episodic. Instead, it is about the relation between them and the nature of the mechanisms that produce them. From a strongly abstractionist point of view, directly retrievable concepts and schemas are a part of the enduring, long-term knowledge base—"generic knowledge" is stored in "semantic memory." This semantic memory can operate independently of episodic or autobiographical memory. However, its contents do need to be developed out of the contents of episodic memory through some process of consolidation, perhaps analogous to prototype formation in which successive episodic representations are overlaid and their central tendencies extracted (Posner and Keele 1968; Rosch and Mervis 1975). In contrast, from a strongly episodic point of view, only specific episodes of experience are stored on a long-term basis. Concepts and schemas are generated by retrieval processes. Again, the genesis of a concept can be thought of as prototype formation, but the prototypes are constructed on demand rather than stored permanently (Hintzman 1986). In this type of theory, there is literally no such thing as semantic memory, though there is certainly semantic or generic knowledge (at least temporarily, while it is being used). In between these extremes, one can take hybridized positions in which concepts and episodes are both stored and interact with one another in various ways during retrieval and deployment to produce the observable properties of task performances (Brooks 1987; Brooks and Vokey 1991; Brown and Carr 1993; Carr and Brown 1990; Carr, Brown, and Charalambous 1989; Jacoby and Brooks 1984; Kahneman and Miller 1986; Oden 1987; Medin and Smith 1984; Salasoo, Feustel, and Shiffrin 1985).

Despite the differences among these points of view, they share the notion that concepts arise in one way or another from episodes. Each of the positions along the abstractionist-episodic continuum offers a different theoretical characterization of the transition from episodic to semantic, but such a transition must occur in some fashion if one is to take an empiricist approach to the origins of knowledge.

## 28.3 THREE EMPIRICAL QUESTIONS ABOUT THE EPISODIC-TO-SEMANTIC TRANSITION

Relatively little is known about the empirical properties of this transition—its time course, conditions that facilitate or impede it, or what impact adding the ability to use a new semantic fact might have on old facts or their organization (regardless of whether that organization represents the structural properties of an enduring memory store or arises from the operating characteristics of a construction process). Therefore, studying the empirical properties of the episodic-to-semantic transition is useful. Such study illuminates an important but poorly understood aspect of adult cognition—how new semantic knowledge is added to an already established knowledge base—and in the process it may help to distinguish between abstractionist and episodic accounts of human cognition.

In this context, our research during the past few years has addressed three questions about the acquisition of new semantic knowledge:

1. How much accumulation of episodic experience must occur, and under what conditions, to support a transition from "episodic" to "semantic" as the basis for cognitive performance? To answer this question, we must choose criteria for deciding that performance is supported by episodic versus semantic knowledge, and we must monitor performance over a period of practice or accumulation of the underlying information.

2. Are new facts or new associations retrieved and deployed in the same way as older, better-learned knowledge? Suppose the episodic-to-semantic transition is gradual, requiring a long period of time or a large number of encounters with a new fact before the transition is fully achieved. Under these conditions new knowledge is likely to be weaker and harder to activate than old knowledge, creating special problems for retrieval. Perhaps a special attentional mechanism helps to retrieve or construct semantic knowledge early in its genesis, a mechanism that is no longer needed once semantic knowledge becomes strong and well established. To answer this question, we must find a way to measure the retrieval process and the consequences of its efficiency, success, and failure.

3. On what basis are individual episodes recognized as repeated or related? The information-processing system must achieve such recognition if accumulation of episodes into semantic knowledge is to occur at all—whether by consolidation in a memory store or by computation on the fly. To answer this

question, we must identify stimulus properties whose variation reduces the magnitude of the benefit to performance that usually occurs when a stimulus is repeated. These will include the properties that the system uses to recognize repetitions.

In this chapter, we briefly summarize past research on the first question and then describe new research on the second and third questions. In each case we propose a tentative answer that looks promising.

## 28.4 QUESTION 1: THE EPISODIC-TO-SEMANTIC TRANSITION APPEARS TO BE SLOW AND LABORIOUS

Dagenbach, Horst, and Carr (1991) studied consolidation of new information into semantic knowledge, using the emergence of automatic semantic priming with practice as a diagnostic for consolidation. First we examine the choice of diagnostic and then the results.

### Criteria for Tracing the Transition

How can one decide whether performance is based on "episodic" or "semantic" knowledge? A number of dimensions of difference might be considered—some definitional and others more theoretically or empirically motivated.

**Number of Exposures** By definition an episodic memory is unique to a particular episode of experience, whereas a semantic memory is true or applicable across many different contexts of occurrence and therefore is likely to be encountered or used many different times (Ashcraft 1989; Tulving 1972). Hence, a fundamental criterion for laboratory study involves manipulating number of exposures. The quintessential episodic memory is based on a single exposure or, more loosely, some very small amount of study. The quintessential semantic memory is based on an inestimably large number of exposures or amount of study, as with well-known words and the most common associative and taxonomic relations between them—for example, *dog-cat, car-truck, bread-butter*. Comparing associations studied or used once to associations studied or used many, many times, then, is basic to the investigation of episodic and semantic memory.

**Speed and Automaticity** In every current theory of skill acquisition, speed and automaticity in the retrieval and deployment of knowledge are intimately related to number of exposures (Logan 1988; Neumann 1984). Hence, as a natural consequence of number of exposures, the quintessential semantic memory is overlearned and easy to retrieve or construct. Its utilization is likely to be fast and automatic, whereas utilization of an episodic memory is likely to be slower and more effortful. Therefore, automatic activation and spread of activation, creating automatic priming, are widely regarded as signature properties of well-established semantic knowledge (Anderson 1983;

Cheesman and Merikle 1985; Collins and Loftus 1975; Fischler 1977; Marcel 1983; McNamara 1992; Neely 1977, 1991; Posner and Snyder 1975). Obviously the language of spreading activation is more closely aligned with abstractionist than with episodic generation theories of semantic knowledge, but automatic priming can be implemented in either type of system; see, e.g., Ratcliff and McKoon (1988).

**Source Memory versus Source Amnesia**  Again by definition, an episodic memory is closely associated with the context in which it was acquired, whereas a semantic memory applies to so many contexts that such associations have either been lost completely or have ceased to play a role in the memory's retrieval and deployment. Hence, the quintessential episodic memory contains or is accompanied by information about context of encounter whenever it is retrieved, but the quintessential semantic memory is not. This makes source amnesia a phenomenon of interest in episodic memory but something to be expected and to be taken for granted in semantic memory. By this reasoning, dense amnesiacs are a logical population in which to study semantic memory in a fairly pure form. Because they show no explicit evidence of remembering context of encounter and hence no explicit evidence of episodic memory, one might make an initial assumption that cognitive performance is based entirely on semantic knowledge—that is, on knowledge that is context free. An example of this approach is Tulving, Hayman, and Macdonald's (1991) recent investigation of associative and perceptual learning in K.C., an unusually dense amnesiac with left-hemispheric brain damage from a closed head injury. Other examples can be found in the work of Schacter (e.g., 1987) and Shimamura and Squire (e.g., 1991).

**Context-Dependent Retrieval**  A corollary of the source memory criterion concerns context-dependent retrieval. Regardless of whether source information is explicitly remembered, reinstatement of the context of encounter is always important to retrieval efficiency for an episodic memory, even under conditions of implicit remembering. This need not be so for semantic memory, where, almost by definition, a generic fact should be approximately equally accessible across a wide range of contexts. Potts, St. John, and Kirson (1989) provide an excellent example of the application of this principle in a study of learning new information as a function of whether subjects believed it to be fact or fiction.

**Large and Persistent Effects of a Single Exposure**  A fifth criterion has been used very effectively by Jacoby and Brooks (1984; Jacoby 1983) to argue against strongly abstractionist accounts of perceptual recognition and concept formation. One might think of this as the "Webers Law" criterion. If a single encounter with an already very familiar stimulus produces a large impact on a subsequent performance, especially a delayed performance, episodic memory must be involved. Were only an abstract, overlearned semantic memory supporting performance, how could just one more encounter among so many make such a noticeable impact? Applications of this criterion include Jacoby's (1983) demonstration that having read a word on a study list increases its likelihood of being correctly identified up to a week later in a tachistoscopic report task (but not a year later—see Salasoo et al. 1985) and studies of the "frequency attenuation effect" by Scarborough, Cortese, and Scarborough (1977), Forster and Davis (1984), and Rajaram and Neely (1992). Ordinarily, high-frequency words are processed more rapidly than low-frequency words in paradigmatic semantic memory tasks such as lexical decision or speeded pronunciation. However, a single recent presentation of a low-frequency word can reduce this difference or even eliminate it altogether.

## Research Results on the Emergence of Automatic Priming with Practice

Each of these five criteria has something to recommend it, and eventually one ought to combine them all in studying the episodic-to-semantic transition. In our own work to date, we have focused on the first two. Comparisons across differing numbers of exposures are quite basic to the definition of episodic versus semantic memory, and the growth of automaticity is thought to be associated with number of exposures in a very fundamental way. Therefore, building on the work of several previous investigators, Dagenbach, Horst, and Carr (1991) measured the amount of practice with new information that was needed for the information to produce priming at a short, 200-ms prime-target stimulus onset asynchrony (SOA). Such priming would indicate automatic activation and deployment of the newly learned information according to common conventions. Two types of new information were investigated: arbitrary associations between two already known words and meanings of new words learned by association to already known synonyms.

Previous investigations of arbitrary associations had failed to find good evidence of automatic priming after small amounts of practice. For example, Neely (1977) showed that instructions to expect a member of a particular well-known taxonomic category (building parts) as the target in a lexical decision task whenever the prime was the name of another well-known taxonomic category (body parts) supported long-SOA strategic priming but not short-SOA automatic priming. McKoon and Ratcliff (1986) reported automatic priming from arbitrary associations between previously unrelated words —such as *dog-truck* or *car-butter*—when the associations were actually studied rather than merely described. However, Durgunoglu and Neely (1987) showed that this outcome was obtained only under conditions in which biases in the decision process could explain the effect without appeal to a modification in the semantic encoding structures or construction processes themselves. In these experiments, the arbitrary associations were encountered only a time or two during a study phase prior to collecting priming data.

Dagenbach, Horst, and Carr (1991) simply increased the amount of learning activity. In one experiment, college students learned pairs of previously unrelated word in an hour-long study-test procedure that produced nearly perfect recall of the target given the prime as a cue. Afterward, subjects encountered these pairs in a primed lexical decision task. Familiar associations such as *doctor-nurse* produced facilitation, but the new associations did not. In another experiment, subjects studied word pairs in the study-test procedure and then took the materials home and constructed sentences that related the two words together in sensible ways, carrying out this activity over a 5-week period along with periodic study-test sessions. Though these new associations yielded a hint of facilitation in a subsequent lexical decision task, the effect was much smaller than priming from familiar associations, and it was not statistically significant. Apparently, then, although arbitrary associations can support strategic priming after very little study, it is quite difficult to integrate them sufficiently into the knowledge base of semantic processing to support automatic priming.

One possible explanation for this result is that proactive interference from relations already captured in semantic knowledge inhibits either the formation or deployment of new associations that are inconsistent with the existing organization. This suggests that adding new but consistent structures to semantic memory might be easier than arbitrarily modifying old ones. That is, while adding an association such as *car-butter* violates the already existing pattern of associative and semantic relations and hence might be expected to meet with substantial organizational inertia or resistance to change, adding an associative such as *canine-dog* (assuming the learner does not already know *canine*) simply extends existing patterns in consistent ways and might be expected to be easier to accomplish. Therefore, Dagenbach, Horst, and Carr (1991) conducted two more experiments analogous to those already described but with pairs consisting of a rare, unknown word and a familiar synonym as the studied materials. The first experiment, using one session of the study-test procedure, produced results similar to those obtained with arbitrary associations: no significant priming from the new words to their familiar synonyms presented as targets. However, the second experiment, using the extended 5-week learning protocol, found significant priming between the newly learned vocabulary words and the synonyms. This priming equaled the facilitation obtained between two related words that were both already well known.

These experiments suggest that fully integrating new information into semantic memory is a difficult, time-consuming process and that it is easier to add a new item than to modify the associations between preexisting items. The difficulty in modifying semantic memory that we have observed is consistent with Tulving, Hayman, and Macdonald's (1991) case study. The amnesiac K.C. was able to add new facts to semantic memory but only after very extensive study (and, of course, K.C. could demonstrate this learning only implicitly). Tulving and colleagues concluded that the faster deployment of new facts observed in other experiments, like those of Neely (1977) or McKoon and Ratcliff (1986), resulted from retrieval of episodic memories rather than from rapid establishment of semantic knowledge.

## 28.5 QUESTION 2: A CENTER-SURROUND ATTENTIONAL MECHANISM SUPPORTS THE RETRIEVAL OF NEW KNOWLEDGE

Our second question concerns intentional rather than automatic deployment of new learning. A common view in cognitive science is that activation within an encoding mechanism such as semantic memory is necessary but not sufficient for a code to become available for intentional higher-order processing and control of action. To gain such availability, the code must be transferred from the encoding mechanism to working memory. In other words, it must be attended and retrieved (Anderson 1983; Baddeley 1986; Duncan and Humphreys 1989; Posner, Snyder, and Davidson 1980).

It is possible that attending to a new semantic code poses problems that do not arise very often with older, better-learned knowledge. As already discussed, most accounts of semantic memory assume that activation of a concept causes activation to spread to related concepts, increasing their activation and hence their accessibility to perceptual input or memory search. Such activation is often thought to be proportional to the strength of the codes involved and the pathways between them. This raises the question of how a newly learned, weakly established code in a semantic network can be singled out and successfully retrieved given a spreading activation process that can increase the activation of other codes that are stronger and potentially more easily activatable. Similar difficulties arise in retrieval-based systems that store instances as feature vectors or as modifications to weights connecting feature nodes in a connectionist network, especially if the vector or network system has pattern completion capabilities. Our research suggests there may be an attentional mechanism specially designed for trying to retrieve very weakly or very slowly activated semantic codes when they are suffering intense competition from related codes.

### Evidence from Masked Priming

So far, the evidence for such a special attentional mechanism comes from demonstrations of inhibitory semantic priming when an attempt to retrieve a weakly activated semantic code fails. Such inhibitory priming was first observed in a lexical decision task using heavily masked primes (Dagenbach, Carr, and Wilhelmson 1989). During a preliminary threshold setting session, college students made judgments about the meaning of each of a series of masked primes by choosing which of two alternatives was semantically related to each prime. In an immediately succeeding lexical decision task with similarly masked primes, these subjects showed inhibition in responding to related targets. This inhibition contrasted with facilitation for related targets shown by subjects who had made nonsemantic threshold setting judgments, even though the stimulus presentation parameters were identical. None of the words in the primed lexical decision task had been encountered during threshold setting, so these effects had to arise from a general strategic change in how meanings were being activated and deployed. We speculated that the semantic threshold setting procedure might induce a general strategy for processing the masked primes in which attention is directed to codes in semantic memory in order to try to retrieve them, affecting those codes in a way that produces inhibition when the retrieval attempt ultimately fails because of the masking. We call this idea the "semantic retrieval failure" hypothesis.

**Evidence from Vocabulary Learning**

If this speculation were correct, one might expect to observe inhibitory semantic priming under conditions other than masked priming in which an attempt to retrieve a semantic code fails. Therefore, Dagenbach, Carr, and Barnhardt (1990) taught college students new vocabulary words to a criterion that permitted recall of some but not all of the meanings when the new words were presented as recall cues. The new words were then used as primes in a lexical decision task, and subjects were instructed to try to bring each prime's meaning to mind before the target appeared. To allow enough time for the retrieval attempt, the prime target SOA was 2000 ms. According to the semantic retrieval failure hypothesis, semantic inhibition should arise from primes whose meanings had been stored but could not be successfully retrieved. Identification of primes for which this might be true was done by two memory tests after the priming task. The first required subjects to try to recall the definitions of the studied words. The second presented each vocabulary word along with four definitions: the correct one, another studied one, and two distractors. Successful recognition performance was taken to indicate that the new word's meaning was stored, and priming data were analyzed only for lexical decision trials on which the prime was a recognized word. This analysis was conditionalized on performance in the recall test. If the word's meaning was not recalled, we assumed that retrieval had probably failed during the primed lexical decision task as well. The outcome predicted by the semantic retrieval hypothesis was observed in this conditionalized analysis. Primes whose meanings could be recognized but not recalled produced inhibitory semantic priming. Primes whose meanings were both recognized and successfully recalled produced either no significant effect or facilitation, depending on the experiment.

**The Center-Surround Retrieval Hypothesis**

In response to these findings (and some others; see Carr and Dagenbach 1990), we proposed that the attentional retrieval mechanism produces the observed semantic inhibition according to a center-surround principle. The mechanism is used under certain conditions of very low or very slow code activation that arise when stimulus input is severely limited, as in masked priming or when a stored code's asymptotic strength or activatibility is severely limited by low levels of learning. Under these conditions, similar or related codes may be activated nearly as much as the sought-for code, due to noise, spread of activation, and the greater inherent activatibility of better-learned codes. When activation in the sought-for code is in danger of being hidden by activation in other related codes, activation in the sought-for code is enhanced and activation in related codes is dampened by the center-surround retrieval mechanism. If successful, this process enables the sought-for code to be discriminated and its information entered into working memory. Presumably the need for the center-surround mechanism decreases with increasing activatibility of the sought-for code. When there is no masking and the stimulus word is well learned, data-driven activation should be fast and accurate enough that the sought-for code will be retrieved with very little engagement of the inhibitory surround or without it altogether.

This center-surround retrieval hypothesis continues a history of proposals dating back at least to Pillsbury (1908) in which attention has been thought to increase the activation of codes toward which it is directed while at the same time decreasing the activation of codes to be ignored. The most direct precursor is Wally and Weiden's (1973) speculation that attention to semantic memory works on the center-surround principle. We think we have discovered a specific set of conditions under which this speculation is correct.

**A New Training Study**

This is where our work stood until a few months ago, when we decided to follow the advice Doug Hintzman gave at the 1990 Attention and Performance meeting in Ann Arbor: to revive verbal learning. Taking up the tradition begun by Ebbinghaus, we have been trying to install artificial semantic memories in our subjects, category by category, exemplar by exemplar, and association by association. If the attentional retrieval mechanism we think we have discovered is a general feature of the cognitive apparatus, then we should be able to observe its deployment under the carefully regulated conditions of artificial category learning, where we have complete control over the contents and amount of practice of the knowledge being established. The idea was to teach subjects to classify a set of new stimuli they had not seen before into categories they did not previously know. After the initial set of stimuli was well learned, new exemplars would be introduced, so that each of the artificial categories would consist of old, well learned members and new, weakly learned members. At this point, subjects would engage in a primed categorization task in which the targets to be classified would be the old, well-learned category members. Each prime would be either an old member or one of the new, weakly learned members. Old members should produce facilitatory priming, but new members should produce inhibition, at least if they could be caught early enough in learning that their "meanings"—the category-level codes needed for correct classification—were difficult to activate and susceptible to competition from the better-learned members stored in a noisy representational system.

In accord with this plan, college students engaged in a multisession experiment in which they practiced classifying unfamiliar visual shapes (fig. 28.1). In

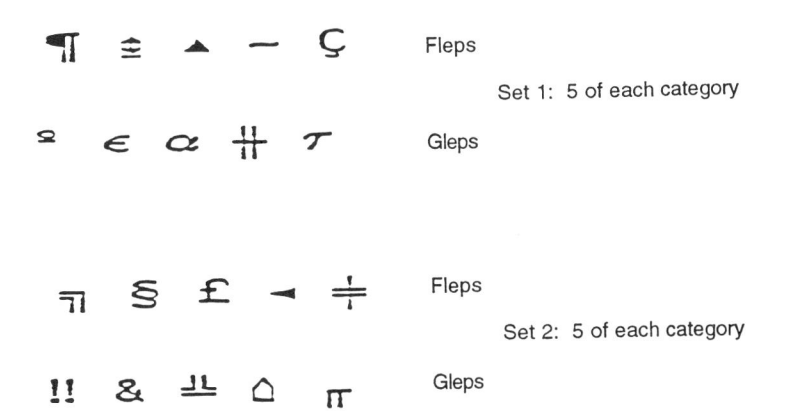

**Figure 28.1** Shapes used as stimuli in the artificial category learning experiment. Sets 1 and 2 demonstrate one random assignment of shapes to the two categories, fleps and gleps. In this assignment, Set 1 comprised the stimuli for sessions 1–7 and therefore were the old, well-learned category members in session 8 when new members were added. Set 2 comprised the new members studied briefly at the beginning of session 8 and included as primes in that session's primed categorization task. Several different random assignments of shapes to sets and to categories within sets were used in the experiment.

this way the experiment tried to extend the evidence for the center-surround attentional mechanism from word recognition to shape recognition, as a further test of its generality. Session 1 started with 5 min of studying ten shapes that had been assigned at random to two categories: "fleps" and "gleps." Because of the random assignment, category membership was unrelated to perceptual features of the shapes and therefore could not be predicted from the perceptual features. This is much like the standard situation with words in alphabetic writing systems, including English, and with objects in some taxonomic categories, but unlike the standard situation with objects in most base-level categories (Carr et al. 1982; Rosch and Mervis 1975). (Work remains to be done to determine whether learning retrieval processes are the same when perceptual and conceptual features are correlated. Rueckl, this volume, has begun to investigate this question.)

The initial study period was followed by ten blocks of forced-choice categorization trials. Each of the ten shapes appeared ten times in each block. On each trial, a single shape was presented, and the subject pressed either the flep button or the glep button as rapidly and accurately as possible, receiving corrective feedback if the response was wrong. Session 2 consisted of ten more blocks of categorization trials. Mean categorization times showed a reasonably standard learning curve (fig. 28.2), though session 2's performance may have been a bit more variable from block to block than would be expected in advance. At the end of session 2, subjects had seen each flep and glep 200 times and were quite skilled at discriminating between them.

Session 3 added priming to the categorization task, in order to discover whether well-learned exemplars in these artificial categories would prime one another as do the members of naturally learned, real-world categories. Each of

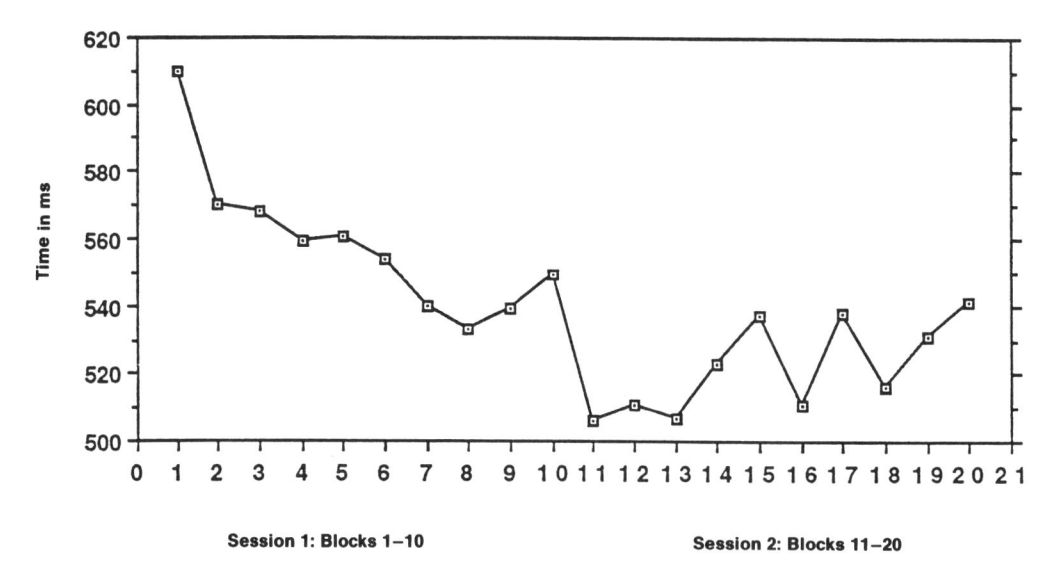

**Figure 28.2** Mean categorization times in each block of sessions 1 and 2.

four blocks contained 120 related trials on which the prime and the target were both from the same category, 40 neutral trials on which the prime was a cross, and 28 unrelated trials in which the prime and the target were from opposite categories. Not all of the possible prime-target pairings were presented. Instead, an attempt was made to train specific associations within each category by selecting a subset of the possible pairings and presenting each one several times. As a result, the related trials consisted of fifteen repetitions of each of eight different particular pairings, four in each category. The prime-target SOA was 200 ms. Thus, we were looking at short SOA priming in order to diagnose the firm establishment of new categorical knowledge, but the proportion of related trials was higher than would ordinarily be used in a test for completely automatic priming because of our desire to train several specific within-category associations during the session.

Mean categorization times showed a clear priming effect (fig. 28.3A). Overall, related trials were 38 ms faster than neutral trials, which were, in turn, 42 ms faster than unrelated trials, for a total facilitatory priming effect of 80 ms. There was no interaction between relatedness and block; priming was present in the first block and changed little in magnitude as the session progressed. First-block related trials were 43 ms faster than neutral trials, and neutral trials were 34 ms faster than unrelated trials, for a total facilitatory effect of 77 ms. These differences were all statistically significant.

In addition to the 120 related trials, each of the four blocks contained one example each of three more kinds of trials in which prime and target were from the same category. Two tested for mediated priming: one for two-step and one for multistep mediation (McNamara and Altarriba 1988; Ratcliff and McKoon 1988). If the related trials included pairs A-B, B-C, C-D, and D-E, a two-step mediated trial might measure priming between A and C, whereas a multistep mediated trial might measure priming between A and D or A and E.

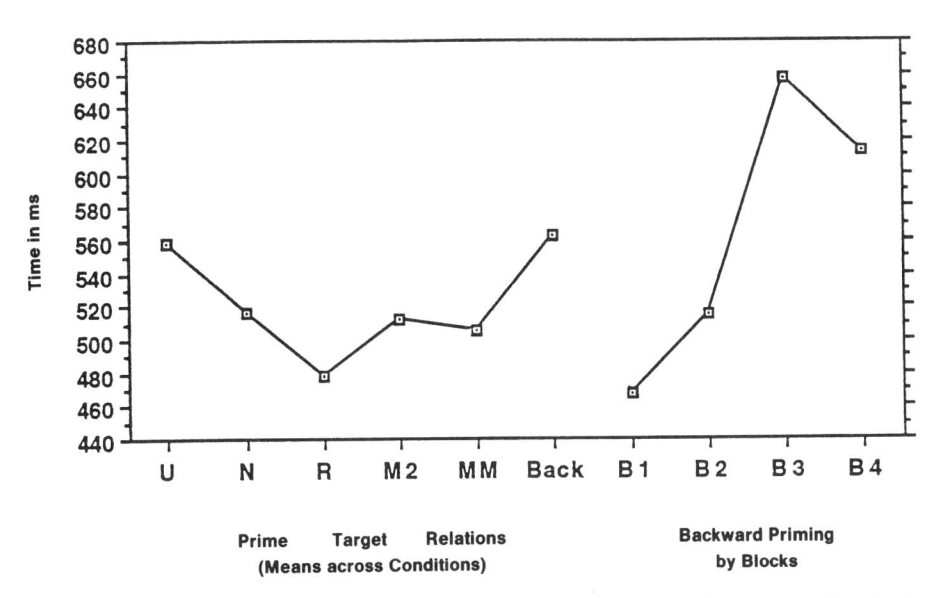

**Figure 28.3** Mean primed categorization times in session 3. A. Times in the Unrelated, Neutral, and Related conditions testing for priming from prime-target pairings that were repeated fifteen times each during the session. B. Times for three kinds of related pairings that appeared four times each during the session, once in each block. Two of these were "mediated" trials, in which the prime and target were not directly directly associated via the repeated pairings. M2 represents mean time for two-step mediated trials, and MM represents mean time for multistep mediated trials. The remaining trial type were backward-association trials in which the prime and target reversed roles from prime-target pairings that were repeated. *Back* represents the mean time averaged across all four backward trials. B1, B2, B3, and B4 represent mean times for each successive block, showing the increase in backward-trial categorization time as practice at primed categorization progressed.

The third kind tested for priming from backward associations. If the related trials included the pairs above, then the backward trial might measure priming from B to A, or from D to C.

The mediated and backward associations behaved differently from the directly trained one-step associations (fig. 28.3B). Overall, neither the two-step nor the multistep primes differed significantly from the neutral condition, producing 4 and 11 ms of facilitation, respectively. The backward primes actually hurt performance, though not significantly, producing a mean categorization time that was 5 ms slower than the unrelated condition. However, this overall effect is misleading (fig. 28.3C) because performance in the backward association condition changed dramatically over blocks: 467 ms in the first block, 515 in the second, 657 in the third, and 613 in the fourth. Thus, it appears that early on, backward associations were just as effective at facilitating categorization as the forward associations that were being directly trained, but as experience in the priming task increased, the prospective influence of the directly trained associations remained important, while the backward associations, which reversed the direction of training, became increasingly difficult to traverse. Koriat (1982), using well-known words as stimuli in primed lexical decision, also found that the relative dominance of forward and backward associations can change in favor of the forward associations as experience in a priming task increases. However, in Koriat's experiment, the impact of backward associations was initially facilitatory and fell to zero, while the impact of forward assocations was initially zero and grew to significant facilitation.

Following session 3, four more sessions of primed categorization confirmed that the artificial category structures we taught our subjects were functioning roughly like the already familiar category knowledge standardly tapped in experiments on semantic memory. These sessions also served to further strengthen the artificial structures. Table 28.1 shows the mean categorization times for each of these sessions, along with the prime target SOA and the proportion of related trials, which varied from session to session.

This brings us to session 8, in which subjects were exposed to new category members, and we tested for the operation of the special attention mechanism in retrieving them. The session began with a 5 sec presentation of a group of five new fleps and a 5 sec presentation of a group of five new gleps. Again, assignment of shapes to categories was random and could not be predicted from perceptual features. These brief study periods were intended to produce weak, perhaps incomplete learning of the new category members, which were then included, along with old members, as primes in four blocks of primed categorization. The targets were always old members. Across the four blocks, each of the new primes was paired with four old members of the same category and four old members of the opposite category. Prime target SOA was 2000 ms. Subjects were instructed to try to bring each prime's category to mind before the target appeared. This combination of long SOA and instructions to deal actively with the prime's meaning recreated the conditions in which inhibitory priming had been observed for recognized but unrecalled new vocabulary words. We expected (a) that old, well-learned, and hence easily retrievable category members would produce facilitation when used as primes; (b) that at least some of the newly learned exemplars would produce inhibition; and (c) that the inhibition would arise from the weaker

Table 28.1  Mean Target Categorization Times, Sessions 4–7

|  | Session 4 | Session 5 | Session 6 | Session 7 |
|---|---|---|---|---|
| Prime-target SOA | 2000 ms | 200 ms | 200 ms | 2000 ms |
| Proportion related | 124/192 | 124/192 | 84/248 | 124/192 |
| Categorization times |  |  |  |  |
| Unrelated | 570 ms | 557 ms | 534 ms | 555 ms |
| Neutral | 551 | 516 | 520 | 537 |
| Related | 522 | 475 | 510 | 508 |
| Two-step | 543 | 495 | 503 | 548 |
| Multistep | 577 | 547 | 511 | 526 |
| Backward | 589 | 496 | 496 | 520 |
| Basic priming effect (unrelated-related) | 48 | 82 | 24 | 47 |

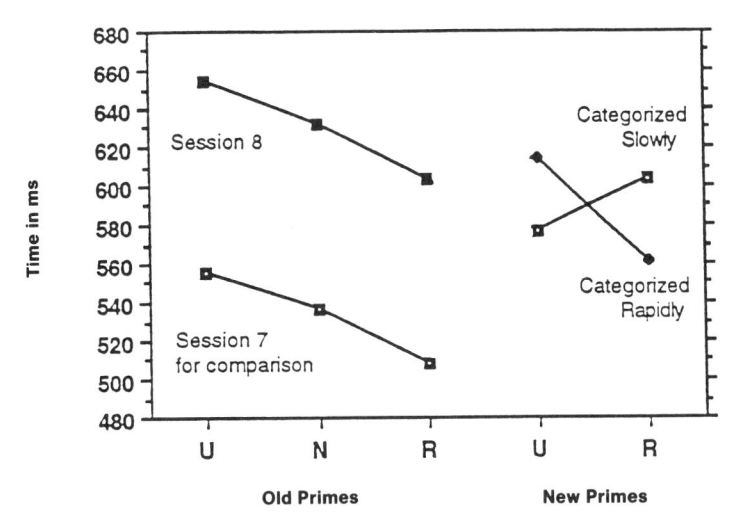

**Figure 28.4** Mean primed categorization times in session 8. The upper line in A shows times for Unrelated, Neutral, and Related trials on which both the primes and the targets were old, well-learned category members. The lower line, included for comparison purposes, shows times for Unrelated, Neutral, and Related trials from the immediately preceding session 7, prior to the introduction of new, weakly-learned category members. Panel B show times for Unrelated and Related trials on which the primes were the new members, as a function of whether each prime was categorized rapidly or slowly in the test block of unprimed categorization trials.

new members for which intentional retrieval of category membership was most likely to fail.

The first data for session 8 come from targets primed by old, well-learned category members (fig. 28.4A). The priming effects were similar to those in previous sessions: related trials were 28 ms faster than neutral trials, which were 22 ms faster than unrelated trials, for a total facilitatory priming effect of 50 ms. However, the absolute categorization times for these old, now very well-learned category members were quite slow. Mean categorization time in the neutral condition was 632 ms, which was 95 ms slower than the neutral condition of the immediately preceding session 7 in which only old members were encountered. In fact, one has to go all the way back to the first block of categorization training in session 1 to find times that are even close to these. There, mean categorization time was 610 ms.

Slower categorization of practiced exemplars upon introduction of new exemplars is not an unprecedented phenomenon. Schneider and Fisk (1984) trained college students on a category-level visual search task in which the targets were a small set of well-known words from a single taxonomic category and distractors were words from other categories. After target detection performance reached asymptote, several well-known but unpracticed target exemplars were introduced in a transfer session. Detection time for the unpracticed exemplars was slower than detection time for the practiced exemplars in this transfer session, and in turn detection time for the practiced exemplars was slower than it had been at the end of the training session.

Although a proper explanation of such slowing awaits future work, it is well known that weakening of old associations can accompany mastery of new associations in connectionist network learning models (Ratcliff 1990). In our case of human rather than model learning, adding five new members to each category clearly slowed categorization time substantially for the old members. However, it did not eliminate semantic priming from one old member to another.

The more important data for present purposes come from targets primed by the new members. Our hypothesis was that the center-surround attentional mechanism would come into play in dealing with new members for which semantic activation was especially weak or slow. To enable us to identify those members, subjects performed a test block of unprimed categorization trials on the ten new fleps and gleps after each of the four blocks of primed categorization trials. Feedback on accuracy was provided during these categorization test blocks, so each test increased the degree of learning of the new members. Therefore, in order to examine new members early in learning, we focused on the first of the four blocks. The idea was to analyze the amount of priming from new members in the first block of primed categorization as a function of speed in the first categorization test block. New members that were correctly identified in the first test block were divided by a median split into those that were categorized rapidly ($m = 900$ ms) and those that were categorized slowly ($m = 1250$ ms). We assumed that the rapid ones had already become reasonably well learned and were less likely to engage the center-surround attentional mechanism, whereas the slow ones were poorly learned and hence were good candidates to require the mechanism's help in order for categorization to succeed. (Note that although there was a substantial difference in categorization time between the two groups of new members, even the rapid ones were categorized much more slowly than the old members that had been practiced for the preceding seven sessions.) The primed categorization trials were then divided into those whose newly learned prime was categorized rapidly in the test block and those whose newly learned prime was categorized slowly. Priming was calculated separately for the two groups of trials.

These data produced a crossover interaction much like the effects observed in our previous study of vocabulary acquisition (fig. 28.4B). Following rapidly categorized new primes, which we are assuming were relatively easy to retrieve, target categorization time was 614 ms when the prime was unrelated and 561 ms when the prime was related, for a facilitatory priming effect of 53 ms. Following slowly categorized new primes, which we are assuming were quite difficult to retrieve, target categorization time was 576 ms when the prime was unrelated and 604 ms when the prime was related—an inhibitory priming effect of 28 ms.

Thus, the data from trials with new category members as primes were clearly consistent with the center-surround hypothesis. However, they did present a puzzle. Whereas learning new members slowed categorization times for old members, this overall slowing was much more apparent when old members were primed by other old members than when they were primed by the new members. Averaged across all trials on which the prime was a correctly categorized new member, mean target categorization time was 589 ms —still slower than in previous sessions of primed categorization but 43 ms faster than target categorization time in the neutral condition and 41 ms faster than target categorization time averaged across all trials on which the prime was an old member rather than a new one. While this result seems difficult to explain, a possibility is that the difference in target processing speed was caused by a difference in the alerting properties of the old and new primes. Kraut and Smothergill (1978) showed that familiar stimuli are less effective as preparatory warning signals than unfamiliar stimuli, and certainly the old and new primes differed substantially in familiarity. Therefore, it does not seem likely that this overall difference between old and new primes compromises the interpretability of the pattern of facilitation and inhibition produced by the new primes.

To summarize the experiment, we believe it was a strong test of our hypothesis about a special attentional mechanism for retrieving poorly learned and hence weakly activated semantic knowledge. Rather than relying on retrieval failure versus retrieval success to tell us where to look for evidence of the mechanism's operation, we applied a finer-grained diagnostic—something more like retrieval efficiency. The results indicate that when retrieval efficiency for a new category member presented as a prime was very low, the center-surround mechanism was deployed to aid in retrieving the weakly or slowly activated code. As a consequence, related items, including the upcoming target when it was a member of the same category, were temporarily inhibited, making them less accessible to perceptual input and attentional retrieval operations. This inhibition showed itself in the slower categorization times for related targets.

## 28.6 QUESTION 3: SURFACE FORM AND MEANING AS CUES FOR RECOGNIZING REPETITION AND ACCUMULATING REPETITION BENEFITS

We have been operating on the assumption that learning in semantic memory relies on accumulating information from multiple experiences. If this is to happen, perceivers must recognize that a current stimulus is a repetition of a previous one. Recognition need not be conscious or intentional, but it must be accomplished; otherwise the notion of accumulation loses its meaning. How is this done? When people are reading and come across a rare word, it is the visual properties of the word that serve as the first retrieval cues provided by the external stimulus. These cues begin the process of contacting memories left from any previous encounters. Hence, similarity of visual surface form is potentially crucial to successful accumulation. Theories that posit accumulation through enduring abstract representations must consider the role of such cues, if each representation does its own accumulating by recognizing and encoding all incoming instances of the concept it represents. Morton's (1969, 1979) logogens are supposed to do this, as must any encoding mechanism based on prototypes stored in long-term memory. Strongly episodic theories of perceptual recognition, such as described by Jacoby and Brooks (1984) or Jacoby and Hayman (1987), also depend on visual surface form cues, except that the cues retrieve a range of similar instance memories rather than activating a single prototype. Finally, superimpositional memory systems that make episodic assumptions about storage of instances might also be sensitive to visual surface form similarity, depending on which stimulus features or properties are encoded in the feature vectors that represent a given series of instances (Hintzman 1986). The potential importance of visual cues to successful accumulation raises the question of how similar the typographies or surface forms of repeated stimuli must be in order for the information processing system to count them as repetitions of one another.

### Research Suggesting Abstract Encoding

A large body of recent research addresses this question, using variation in repetition benefits to identify the determinants of transfer between a past processing experience and current processing demands. The majority of the research in which basic reading tasks have been used, such as lexical decision, speeded pronunciation, or proofreading, suggests that the encoding mechanisms involved in reading might be very abstract with respect to variations of surface form. As an example, Carr, Brown, and Charalambous (1989) had college students read paragraphs aloud twice, measuring reading time. The second or target presentation of the paragraph was either typed or handwritten, and the first was either in the same surface form or the opposite. Repetition benefit was just as large when surface forms mismatched as when they matched, as shown by the equivalence of second reading times between the two conditions. This indicates that encoding mechanisms could generalize or abstract across the surface form differences between typing and handwriting in bringing past experience to bear on current performance. Scarborough, Cortese, and Scarborough (1977) obtained similar results in speeded pronunciation of single words and in lexical decision, though they altered surface form by changing letter case within a type font rather than by switching between typing and handwriting. Again, repetition benefit was just as large when surface forms mismatched as when they matched.

### Limits on Abstraction: Effects of Unfamiliar Typography

A number of studies have shown that such complete abstraction depends on perceivers' being reasonably familiar with the typographies being used in the experiments. Kolers (1973, 1975) observed significant reductions of repetition benefit when surface form was switched between a familiar type font and a highly distorted one that fell well outside the boundaries of common reading experience. Kolers's subjects read passages twice. The first reading was either typed normally, or it was distorted by turning the type upside down and backward. The second reading also occurred in either normal or inverted type, creating a factorial combination of the two surface forms. Kolers's finding was that with these stimulus materials, repetition benefit decreased when surface form mismatched between presentations. An unemphasized curiosity in Kolers's results concerns the magnitude of the reduction of repetition benefit due to surface form change, which was less when the target presentation was typed normally than when it was inverted. Thus, the degree of abstraction versus surface form specificity of repetition benefits appeared to depend on the familiarity of the type font of the second, target reading—the encounter with the passage that would enjoy the benefits of repetition if such repetition was recognized by the information processing system.

Recent research by Brown (Brown and Carr 1993; see also Carr and Brown 1990) has confirmed and extended the pattern apparent in Kolers's results, showing that similar asymmetries in abstraction across surface form can be found with much less unusual typographies. College students performed two blocks of either speeded pronunciation or lexical decision on familiar words and unfamiliar but pronounceable pseudowords. Half the words and pseudowords were typed, and half were handwritten. The second block contained words and pseudowords from the first block plus new ones. When the second-block target stimulus was typed, repetition benefits were independent of the surface form in which the stimulus had appeared in the first block and were just as big for pseudowords as for words. However, when the second-block target stimulus was handwritten, repetition benefit was smaller when surface form mismatched, and the cross-form transfer that did occur was restricted to words. This pattern characterized both speeded pronunciation and lexical decision.

Brown's and Kolers's results suggest that when the typography being processed is familiar, and very typical of typographies commonly encountered, abstraction is maximized, and its magnitude does not depend very much on familiarity at phonological or semantic levels of processing. When typography is less familiar, as with handwriting in Brown's experiment or inverted type in Kolers's, transfer may be limited to more similar surface forms, and, according to Brown's results, it becomes dependent on whatever familiarity might exist at higher levels of processing.

**Role of Higher Levels of Lexical Representation and Text Processing**

Apparently, then, accumulating and integrating related experiences can be difficult if well-learned phonological and semantic structures are lacking, at least when typography is unfamiliar. For beginning readers, all typographies are relatively unfamiliar, and well-learned phonological and semantic structures are often lacking. As readers gain experience, phonological and semantic unfamiliarity become less common, but in the case of new vocabulary acquisition, higher-level structures are lacking by definition. Thus, the apparent dependence of surface form abstraction on higher-level familiarity carries implications for reading development and for new learning in semantic memory even after reading is quite skilled.

Might there be factors other than knowledge of typography that mediate the dependence of abstraction on higher-level familiarity? Our recent work suggests that the degree of abstraction across surface form is influenced by whether the reading task involves single words or text. The argument begins with a study in which surface form was not manipulated. Carlson, Alejano, and Carr (1991) reported that the level of linguistic analysis at which repetition benefits accrue changes as a function of whether attention is devoted to higher-level text processing or is restricted to lexical processing. When attention is devoted to text processing, repetition benefits attach to higher, propositional, syntactic, and thematic levels. This was shown by the fact that instructions to understand and remember the message a text is conveying render repetition benefits sensitive to a word-scrambling manipulation that disrupts those levels. In contrast, when instructions focus readers on accurately identifying and remembering the individual words of which a text is composed, rather than the message the text is conveying, repetition benefits lose their sensitivity to text scrambling and appear instead to accrue at the level of the individual words. The fact that sensitivity to text scrambling seems to be the more common outcome in the literature suggests that attention to the text is hard to prevent, at least among highly literate adults (for reviews and examples, see Carlson, Alejano, and Carr 1991; Levy and Burns 1990). Healy has called this the "draw of the text." Thus, when text is being read, repetition benefits commonly depend on higher-order, text-level processes, and as a result they may be less sensitive to surface form than repetition benefits in reading of single words.

**Using Transfer between Words and Pictures to Test the Impact of Text Processing on Surface Form Abstraction**

A test of this idea has recently been conducted by Alejano. In order to change surface form as much as possible without altering other levels of linguistic analysis, Alejano examined repetition effects created by rebus texts, in which pictures are substituted for content words. Rebuses are commonly used as teaching devices in the early elementary grades. Because young children can name and understand pictures before they can name and understand printed words, teachers hope that the rebus will increase the range of texts a child can read and hence increase the child's enjoyment and motivation during the beginning stages of reading development. However, little is known about the information processing involved in rebus reading, despite its use in teaching. Potter et al. (1986) have found that rebus texts take longer to read aloud than regular texts, which is consistent with the common finding in studies of single-stimulus processing that pictures take longer to name than words (Potter and Faulconer 1975; Carr et al. 1982). However, pictures substituted for content words when text is read under rapid serial visual presentation conditions produce little, if any, loss of comprehension (Potter et al. 1986). This is consistent with the finding in single-stimulus processing that pictures can be categorized or understood just as fast as words (Theios and Amrhein 1989) or even faster (Potter and Faulconer 1975; Smith and Magee 1980). Furthermore, contextual priming effects in reading text aloud are about the same for substituted pictures as for the content words they replace in the text (Kroll 1990). This finding converges on the possibility that at the semantic level and above, processing of rebus texts is quite similar to processing of regular, all-word texts.

What might one expect of repetition effects created by rebus texts? Single-stimulus processing studies show that repetition priming can occur between pictures and words. However, the magnitude of cross-modal repetition benefit is less than when prime and target are of the same type, meaning that a degree of surface form specificity attaches to repetition priming with single pictures and words (Lupker 1985; Huttonlocher and Kubicek 1983; Monsell 1985). Therefore, a comparison of rebus-text and text-text priming seemed a good vehicle for testing the notion that shared surface form may be less important to repetition benefit with text than with single words.

College students read a series of eighteen three-sentence paragraphs, some of them rebuses. Each paragraph contained forty-two words, twenty-three of which were content words. In the rebus paragraphs, eight of the nouns were replaced with pictures of their referents. On average, this was 19 percent of the total number of words and 35 percent of the content words. The series contained six sets of three paragraphs, with each set representing one cell of the overall design. In each set, the third paragraph was the target, and it was always a regular text. The first two paragraphs were either both regular texts or both rebuses and consisted of either two new texts, one repetition of the target and one new text, or two repetitions of the target. The sets that were entirely regular texts, which we call the "within" sets, provided a baseline estimate of the benefits of exact repetition. The "between" sets estimated benefits when surface form similiarity was as low as it can be made within the visual domain for the words that had been replaced by pictures.

Reading times for the regular texts that served as targets are shown by the lower line in figure 28.5. The critical comparison involved the two-repetition "within" condition and the two-repetition "between" condition; there was no difference. Rebus texts produced just as much repetition benefit in reading regular texts as did the regular texts themselves.

One might wonder how compelling a demonstration this is, since only eight words were replaced with pictures in each text. Before drawing any firm conclusions about scope of abstraction, it is necessary to show that this paradigm can detect the difference between picture-word and word-word repetition benefits that is commonly observed in single-stimulus processing. To do this, a second experiment was conducted that was the same in every way, except the words of the paragraphs were randomly scrambled to destroy grammaticality and textual coherence. The stimuli were now lists of random

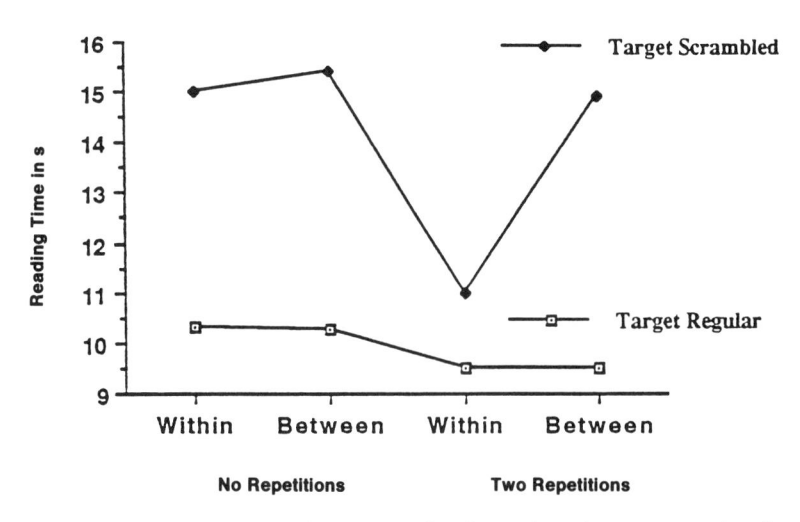

**Figure 28.5** Mean target reading times in the rebus and regular text repeated reading experiment. The lower line shows times for regular text targets. The upper line shows times for scrambled text targets (random word lists).

words rather than paragraphs, with some of the lists containing a few pictures. Reading times from this experiment are shown by the upper line in figure 28.5. When higher-order linguistic organization was removed from the stimuli, creating word and rebus lists rather than texts, repetition benefits from the word and rebus stimuli were no longer equal.

Alejano's results support the idea that abstraction across changes in surface form is greater when text is being read than when single words are being read. Surely the increased scope of transfer results from the higher levels of semantic, syntactic, and thematic processing that are engaged by text. We do not yet know whether it arises directly in the processing at one or more of these higher levels, which are sufficiently abstract to be insensitive to surface form, or indirectly in feedback from higher levels back down to lexical and orthographic processing.

To summarize our research to date on the third question, we have pursued what we believe to be an important issue for learning in semantic memory: how are repetitions recognized so that accumulation of episodic experiences can occur? In the belief that visual stimulus properties might provide crucial retrieval cues to guide such accumulation, we have tried to identify factors that influence the scope of transfer of repetition benefits across variation in visual surface form. We find that one factor is the familiarity of the surface form of the word currently being processed, and another is whether the current word is part of a text and hence is participating in higher levels of semantic, syntactic, and thematic processing. We suspect that a third factor will turn out to be the already accumulated semantic familiarity of the word itself, with surface form specificity being more pronounced early in lexical learning but giving way to greater abstraction as codes in semantic memory become better established. This is only a suspicion, however, and it awaits future work to be confirmed or disproved.

## 28.7 CONCLUSION

We have summarized progress in three lines of research on the acquisition of new semantic knowledge. The first demonstrates that strengthening new associative structures enough to support automatic priming in tasks such as lexical decision is slow and laborious. Different kinds of structures differ in the amount of practice they require to become automatically activatable. New associations that extend existing patterns of relationships in consistent ways are relatively easier to automate than new associations that violate or cut across existing patterns, but neither kind of modification is achieved without considerable effort.

The second line of research explores the properties of an attentional mechanism that aids in retrieving semantic codes early in learning when they are weak, slow to activate, and susceptible to competition from older, stronger codes. This mechanism appears to operate on the center-surround principle so common in the nervous system, increasing the activation of a sought-for code while inhibiting similar or related codes that are unwanted.

Several questions come immediately to mind concerning the center-surround attentional mechanism. One is what triggers its deployment. A likely possibility, it seems to us, is the rate at which differential activation develops among the codes in the region of semantic space containing the code for the stimulus. If several codes in this region become activated and one does not begin to grow at a substantially faster rate than any of the others, then it is a good bet that retrieval will be difficult and may fail. This intuition suggests that if one could tap early enough into the activation process, perhaps by using short prime-target SOAs, one would find semantic facilitation from a newly learned word—initially many related codes will be activated. The inhibition observed at SOAs of 2000 ms in the experiments we have done to date would emerge in reaction to this initial state of multiple activation and overly slow differentiation. Another question concerns the time course of the center-surround mechanism's deployment. When does inhibition begin to emerge, how long does it take to reach maximal levels, and how long is it maintained? Again, manipulation of prime-target SOA seems to be called for. Finally, it is natural to wonder what relation, if any, the inhibition process we have observed bears to the inhibition documented by Neill (1977; Neill and Valdes 1992) and Tipper (Tipper and Cranston 1985; Tipper and Driver 1988) in the Stroop task and other situations requiring selection of one code to control action in the face of competition from another code that is logically irrelevant but strongly activated because of its strength and automaticity (Cohen, Dunbar, and McClelland 1990; MacLeod 1991). Detailed consideration of such "negative priming" is beyond the space limits of this discussion. However, Houghton and Tipper (n.d.) have crafted a computational model of the various negative priming phenomena that we believe might also be able to encompass our own results. Accommodation of both of these inhibitory processes by the same computational model is a theoretical exercise worth pursuing.

The third line of research investigates the stimulus properties that are used to recognize repetitions so that the accumulation of experience required for consolidation of new semantic knowledge can take place. We have shown that similarity of visual surface form is an important cue when the typography is relatively unfamiliar or atypical, and perhaps also when higher-order phonological and semantic representations are lacking. This leads to the speculation that surface form similarity might be important to retrieval early in the acquisition of new semantic knowledge, when higher-order representations are very weak, perhaps even when the writing system in which new words are encountered is already well learned. Future research might pursue this issue, including the possibility that larger differences in surface form between repetitions might decrease rate of learning and, as a result, increase the need for the center-surround mechanism if retrieval of a new meaning is to succeed. We have also shown that surface form specificity may be smaller when reading text than when reading isolated words. Future research might pursue this possibility as well, since it implies that retrieval processes may operate differently during text processing than during isolated word recognition.

## NOTE

Some of the research described in this chapter was supported by National Science Foundation Grant BNS 85-19735 to Michigan State University. We thank Morris Moscovitch, Jay Reuckl, and an anonymous reviewer for helpful comments and criticisms. Address correspondence to Thomas H. Carr, Department of Psychology, Michigan State University, East Lansing, MI 48824-1117, USA.

## REFERENCES

Anderson, J. R. (1983). *The architecture of cognition.* Cambridge, MA: Harvard University Press.

Ashcraft, M. H. (1989). *Human memory and cognition.* New York: Harper Collins.

Baddeley, A. D. (1986). *Working memory.* Oxford: Clarendon Press.

Brooks, L. R. (1987). Decentralized control of categorization: The role of prior processing episodes. In U. Neisser (Ed.), *Concepts and conceptual development: Ecological and intellectual factors in categorization,* 141–174. Cambridge: Cambridge University Press.

Brooks, L. R., and Vokey, J. R. (1991). Abstract analogies and abstracted grammars: Comments on Reber (1989) and Mathews et al. (1989). *Journal of Experimental Psychology: General, 120,* 316–323.

Brown, J. S., and Carr, T. H. (1993). Limits on perceptual abstraction in reading: Asymmetric transfer between surface forms differing in typicality. *Journal of Experimental Psychology: Learning, Memory, and Cognition, 19,* 1277–1296.

Carlson, L. A., Alejano, A. R., and Carr, T. H. (1991). The level-of-focal-attention hyothesis in oral reading: Influence of strategies on the context specificity of lexical repetition effects. *Journal of Experimental Psychology: Learning, Memory, and Cognition, 17,* 924–931.

Carr, T. H., and Brown, J. S. (1990). Perceptual abstraction and interactivity in repeated oral reading: Where do things stand? *Journal of Experimental Psychology: Learning, Memory, and Cognition, 16,* 731–738.

Carr, T. H., Brown, J. S., and Charalambous, A. (1989). Repetition and reading: Perceptual encoding mechanisms are very abstract but not very interactive. *Journal of Experimental Psychology*: Learning, Memory, and Cognition, 15, 763–778.

Carr, T. H., and Dagenbach, D. (1990). Repetition priming and semantic priming from masked words: Evidence for a center-surround retrieval mechanism in perceptual recognition. *Journal of Experimental Psychology: Learning, Memory, and Cognition, 16*, 341–350.

Carr, T. H., McCauley, C., Sperber, R. D., and Parmelee, C. M. (1982). Words, pictures, and priming: On semantic activation and the automaticity of information processing. *Journal of Experimental Psychology: Human Perception and Performance, 8*, 757–777.

Cheesman, J., and Merikle, P. (1985). Word recognition and consciousness. In D. Besner, T. Waller, and G. MacKinnon (Eds.), *Reading research: Advances in theory and practice*, vol. 5. Orlando FL: Academic Press.

Cohen, J. D., Dunbar, K., and McClelland, J. L. (1990). On the control of automatic processes: A parallel distributed processing account of the Stroop effect. *Psychological Review, 97*, 332–361.

Collins, A. M., and Loftus, E. F. (1975). A spreading activation theory of semantic processing. *Psychological Review, 82*, 407–428.

Dagenbach, D., Carr, T. H., and Barnhardt, T. M. (1990). Inhibitory semantic priming of lexical decisions due to failure to retrieve weakly activated codes. *Journal of Experimental Psychology: Learning, Memory, and Cognition, 16*, 328–340.

Dagenbach, D., Carr, T. H., and Wilhelmsen, A. (1989). Task-induced strategies and near-threshold priming: Conscious effects on unconscious perception. *Journal of Memory and Language, 28*, 412–443.

Dagenbach, D., Horst, S., and Carr, T. H. (1991). Priming studies of learning in semantic memory. *Journal of Experimental Psychology: Learning, Memory, and Cognition, 16*, 581–591.

Duncan, J., and Humphreys, G. W. (1989). Visual search and stimulus similarity. *Psychological Review, 96*, 433–458.

Durgonoglu, A., and Neely, J. H. (1987). On obtaining episodic priming in a lexical decision task following paired-associate learning. *Journal of Experimental Psychology: Learning, Memory, and Cognition, 13*, 206–222.

Fischler, I. (1977). Associative facilitation without expectation in a lexical decision task. *Journal of Experimental Psychology: Human Perception and Performance, 3*, 18–26.

Forster, K., and Davis, C. (1984). Repetition priming and frequency attenuation in lexical access. *Journal of Experimental Psychology: Learning, Memory, and Cognition, 10*, 680–698.

Hintzman, D. (1986). "Schema abstraction" in a multiple-trace memory model. *Psychological Review, 93*, 411–428.

Hintzman, D. (1990). Twenty-five years of learning and memory: Was the cognitive revolution a mistake? Paper presented at Attention and Performance XIV, Ann Arbor, Michigan, July.

Houghton, G., and Tipper, S. P. (n.d.). A model of inhibitory mechanisms in selective attention. In D. Dagenbach, and T. H. Carr (Eds.), *Inhibitory processes in attention, memory, and language*. San Diego: Academic Press. In press.

Huttonlocher, J., and Kubicek, L. F. (1983). The source of relatedness effects on naming latency. *Journal of Experimental Psychology: Learning, Memory, and Cognition, 9*, 486–496.

Jacoby, L. L. (1983). Perceptual enhancement: Persistent effects of an experience. *Journal of Experimental Psychology: Learning, Memory, and Cognition, 9*, 21–38.

Jacoby, L. L., and Brooks, L. R. (1984). Nonanalytic cognition: Memory, perception, and concept learning. In G. H. Bower (Ed.), *The psychology of learning and motivation: Advances in research and theory*, vol. 18, 1–47. New York: Academic Press.

Jacoby, L. L., and Hayman, C. A. G. (1987). Specific visual transfer in word identification. *Journal of Experimental Psychology: Learning, Memory, and Cognition, 13*, 456–463.

Kahneman, D., and Miller, D. T. (1986). Norm theory: Comparing reality to its alternatives. *Psychological Review, 93*, 136–153.

Kolers, P. A. (1973). Remembering operations. *Memory and Cognition, 3*, 347–355.

Kolers, P. A. (1975). Specificity of operations in sentence recognition. *Cognitive Psychology, 1*, 289–306.

Koriat, A. (1982). Semantic facilitation in lexical decision as a function of prime-target association. *Memory and Cognition, 9*, 587–598.

Kraut, A. G., and Smothergill, D. W. (1978). A two-factor theory of stimulus-repetition effects. *Journal of Experimental Psychology: Human Perception and Performance, 4*, 191–198.

Kroll, J. F. (1990). Recognizing words and pictures in sentence contexts: A test of lexical modularity. *Journal of Experimental Psychology: Learning, Memory, and Cognition, 16*, 747–759.

Levy, B. A., and Burns, K. I. (1990). Reprocessing text: Contributions from conceptually driven processes. *Canadian Journal of Psychology, 44*, 465–482.

Logan, G. D. (1988). Toward an instance theory of automatization. *Psychological Review, 95*, 492–527.

Lupker, S. J. (1985). Relatedness effects in word and picture naming: Parallels, differences, and structural implications. In A. W. Ellis (Ed.), *Progress in the psychology of language*, vol. 1, 109–142. Hillsdale, NJ: Lawrence Erlbaum.

Marcel, A. J. (1983). Conscious and unconscious perception: Experiments on visual masking and word recognition. *Cognitive Psychology, 15*, 197–237.

McClelland, J. L. (1985). Putting knowledge in its place: A scheme for programming parallel processing structures on the fly. *Cognitive Science, 9*, 113–146.

McKoon, G., and Ratcliff, R. (1986). Automatic activation of episodic and semantic memory. *Journal of Experimental Psychology: Learning, Memory, and Cognition, 12*, 108–115.

MacLeod, C. M. (1991). Half a century of research on the Stroop effect: An integrative review. *Psychological Bulletin, 109*, 163–209.

McNamara, T. P. (1992). Priming and constraints it places on theories of memory and retrieval. *Psychological Review, 99*, 650–662.

McNamara, T. P., and Altarriba, J. (1988). Depth of spreading activation revisited: Semantic mediated priming occurs in lexical decisions. *Journal of Memory and Language, 27*, 545–559.

Medin, D. L., and Smith, E. E. (1984). Concepts and categories. *Annual Review of Psychology, 35*, 113–138.

Monsell, S. (1985). Repetition and the lexicon. In A. W. Ellis (Ed.), *Progress in the psychology of language*, vol. 2, 147–195. Hillsdale, NJ: Erlbaum.

Morton, J. (1969). Interaction of information in word recognition. *Psychological Review, 76*, 165–178.

Morton, J. (1979). Facilitation in word recognition: Experiments causing change in the logogen model. In P. A. Kolers, M. E. Wrolstad, and H. Bouma (Eds.), *Processing visible language 1*, 259–268. New York: Plenum.

Neely, J. H. (1977). Semantic priming and retrieval from lexical memory: Role of inhibitionless spreading activation and limited-capacity attention. *Journal of Experimental Psychology: General, 106*, 226–254.

Neely, J. H. (1991). Semantic priming effects in visual word recognition: A selective review of current findings and theories. In D. Besner and G. I. Humphreys (Eds.), *Basic processes in reading: Visual word recognition,* 264–336. Hillsdale, NJ: Erlbaum.

Neill, W. T. (1977). Inhibition and facilitation processes in selective attention. *Journal of Experimental Psychology: Human Perception and Performance, 3*, 444–450.

Neill, W. T., and Valdes, L. A. (1992). Persistence of negative priming: Steady state or decay? *Journal of Experimental Psychology: Learning, Memory, and Cognition, 18*, 565–576.

Neumann, O. (1984). Automatic processing: A review of recent findings and a plea for an old theory. In W. Prinz and A. F. Sanders (Eds.), *Cognition and motor processes* 255–293. Berlin: Springer-Verlag.

Oden, G. C. (1987). Concepts, knowledge, and thought. *Annual Review of Psychology, 38*, 203–227.

Pillsbury, W. B. (1908). *Attention.* New York: Macmillan.

Posner, M. I., and Keele, S. W. (1968). On the genesis of abstract ideas. *Journal of Experimental Psychology, 77*, 353–363.

Posner, M. I., and Snyder, C. R. R. (1975). Attention and cognitive control. In R. L. Solso (Ed.), *Information processing and cognition: The Loyola Symposium,* 55–85. Hillsdale, NJ: Lawrence Erlbaum.

Posner, M. I., Snyder, C. R. R., and Davidson, B. J. (1980). Attention and the detection of signals. *Journal of Experimental Psychology: General, 109*, 160–174.

Potter, M. C., and Faulconer, B. (1975). Time to understand pictures and words. *Nature, 253*, 437–438.

Potter, M. C., Kroll, J. F., Yachzel, B., Carpenter, E., and Sherman, J. (1986). Pictures in sentences: Understanding without words. *Journal of Experimental Psychology: General, 115*, 281–294.

Potts, G. R., St. John, M. F., and Kirson, D. (1989). Incorporating new information into existing world knowledge. *Cognitive Psychology, 21*, 303–333.

Rajaram, S., and Neely, J. H. (1992). Dissociative masked repetition priming and word frequency effects in lexical decision and episodic recognition tasks. *Journal of Memory and Language, 31*, 152–182.

Ratcliff, R. (1990). Connectionist models of recognition memory: Constraints imposed by learning and forgetting functions. *Psychological Review, 97*, 285–308.

Ratcliff, R., and McKoon, G. (1988). A retrieval theory of priming in memory. *Psychological Review, 95*, 385–408.

Rosch, E., and Mervis, C. (1975). Family resemblances: Studies in the internal structure of categories. *Cognitive Psychology, 7*, 573–605.

Salasoo, A., Feustel, T. C., and Shiffrin, R. M. (1985). Building permanent memory codes: Codification and repetition effects in word identification. *Journal of Experimental Psychology: General, 114*, 50–77.

Scarborough, D. L., Cortese, C., and Scarborough, H. (1977). Frequency and repetition effects in lexical memory. *Journal of Experimental Psychology: Human Perception and Performance, 3*, 1–17.

Schacter, D. L. (1987). Implicit expressions of memory in organic amnesia: Learning of new facts and associations. *Human Neurobiology, 6*, 107–118.

Schneider, W., and Fisk, A. D. (1984). Automatic category search and its transfer. *Journal of Experimental Psychology: Learning, Memory, and Cognition, 10,* 1–15.

Shimamura, A. P., and Squire, L. R. (1991). The relationship between fact and source memory: Findings from amnesic patients and normal subjects. *Psychobiology, 19,* 1–10.

Smith, M. C., and Magee, L. (1980). Tracing the time course of picture-word processing. *Journal of Experimental Psychology: General, 109,* 373–392.

Theios, J., and Amrhein, P. C. (1989). Theoretical analysis of the cognitive processing of lexical and pictorial stimuli: Reading, naming, and visual and conceptual comparisons. *Psychological Review, 96,* 5–24.

Tipper, S. P., and Cranston, M. (1985). Selective attention and priming: Inhibitory and facilitatory effects of ignored primes. *Quarterly Journal of Experimental Psychology, 37A,* 591–611.

Tipper, S. P., and Driver, J. (1988). Negative priming between pictures and words: Evidence for semantic analysis of ignored primes. *Memory and Cognition, 16,* 64–70.

Tulving, E. (1972). Episodic and semantic memory. In E. Tulving and W. Donaldson (Eds.), *Organization of memory,* 381–403. New York: Academic Press.

Tulving, E., Hayman, C. A. G., and Macdonald, C. A. (1991). Long-lasting perceptual priming and semantic learning in amnesia: A case experiment. *Journal of Experimental Psychology: Learning, Memory, and Cognition, 17,* 595–617.

Wally, R. E., and Weiden, T. D. (1973). Lateral inhibition and cognitive masking: A neuropsychological theory of attention. *Psychological Review, 80,* 458–466.

# 29 A Connectionist View on Dissociations

R. Hans Phaf, Nico M. Mul, and Gezinus Wolters

ABSTRACT  This chapter develops a view on dissociations between conscious and unconscious processes within a connectionist framework that has previously been used to simulate memory processes (Phaf 1991). It consists of three sections. In the first, several accounts for these dissociations are discussed, focusing on the mechanisms underlying the dissociations between explicit and implicit memory tasks and the relationship between attention and consciousness. It is argued that dissociation effects can best be described by a multimodular memory system (consisting of many interrelated subsystems) in which activation and elaboration learning processes (Mandler 1979, 1980) occur. In the second, an empirical study is reported in which effects of an attentional manipulation were determined in explicit and implicit memory tests. The results suggest that attention and consciousness cannot be completely equated. A simulation of these effects by a connectionist model based on the account discussed in the introduction is presented. The third section is a rather speculative discourse on the additional processes needed to extend the attentional capabilities to include some functional aspects of consciousness. Simulations are carried out with an extended version of the model presented in the second section, incorporating a working memory ability in the form of a rehearsal loop (Baddeley 1986, 1992a, 1992b; Baddeley and Hitch 1974). This model not only performs short-term memory functions but also is capable of recursive and combinatory processing of activated memory representations. It shows some symbol manipulation abilities and may form a first step toward modeling processes essential in constructing conscious experience.

## 29.1 INTRODUCTION

Two global classes of theories have been proposed to explain differential effects of testing memory with either conscious (explicit, direct) or unconscious (implicit, indirect) measures. One class assumes neuroanatomically separate memory systems, whereas the other postulates different memory processes within a unitary, presumably distributed, memory system (Richardson-Klavehn and Bjork 1988). The multiple systems explanation accounts for dissociative phenomena but does not specify how the memory tasks are performed and how the systems cooperate to form an integrated memory function. The multiprocess position, on the other hand, fails to account for the observation that different neural systems may sometimes be involved in different memory tasks. The multiprocess position, however, has the advantage of suggesting a specification of the processes involved in implicit and explicit memory tasks.

At least two different multiprocess accounts have been put forward. One account is based on the idea that memory performance critically depends on the similarity between information encoded during study and information addressed during testing (Blaxton 1989; Jacoby 1983; Neill et al. 1990; Roediger and Blaxton 1987). Dissociations occur whenever tests are compared that differ in the degree to which information addressed during testing matches information stored during study.

The other type of multiprocess account distinguishes between two different learning processes: activation and elaboration learning. In this view, the two learning processes strengthen different components of a single, unitary memory representation that are differentially addressed by explicit and implicit memory tests (Graf and Mandler 1984; Mandler 1979, 1980; Phaf 1991). Activation learning is supposed to be an automatic consequence of stimulus processing, leading to the strengthening of preexisting mental representations. An implicit memory test requires the partial or complete reinstatement of a stimulus representation by using the relations that make up the representation. Performance in such a test is enhanced when a prior stimulus presentation has strengthened the preexisting internal relations. Explicit memory tests require access to a stimulus representation by retrieval routes that make use of newly formed links between the representation and information specific for the episode. This kind of test depends on the formation of new relationships, which presumably requires an elaboration learning process resulting from active attentional processing.

None of the accounts (multiple memory systems, study-test compatibility, or activation-elaboration learning) seems to be completely sufficient to explain all dissociation results. They represent extreme positions that do not logically exclude one another and may have to be combined in a more complete account (see Hintzman 1990 for a similar argument). Such a combinatorial account is suggested here; it merges the activation-elaboration view with assumptions about the structural characteristics of a memory system. Much evidence suggests that memory is composed of a multitude of interconnected subsystems or modules. If this structural characteristic is combined with activation-elaboration learning, all accounts seem to be satisfied. Differences in the memory pathways created during study and addressed during test will account, for example, for dissociations caused by modality shifts (Bassili, Smith, and MacLeod 1989; Jacoby and Dallas 1981; Schacter and Graf 1989). The activation-elaboration processes can account for dissociation effects caused by attentional manipulations (Eich 1984; Parkin and Russo 1990; Smith and Oscar-Berman 1990) and for the result that material presented under general anesthesia raises implicit but not explicit performance (Jelicic et al. 1992; Kihlstrom et al. 1990; Roorda-Hrdlicková et al. 1990). Although this model is constructed from a number of modules (which all independently have the ability to learn by activation or by elaboration), it does not support a multiple memory systems view, because memory representations are distributed over the modules.

The incorporation of the activation-elaboration hypothesis not only explains attention-related dissociations; it also seems to provide a critical process for the distinction between conscious and unconscious information processing. According to Mandler (1989), "The simultaneity of objects and events in consciousness makes possible the formation of new associations" (p. 88). Although many theorists in the past have labeled this process attention, Mandler (1989) prefers to distinguish the selective aspects of attention from the construction function of consciousness. For too long "attention has served as a synonym or hiding place for consciousness" (Mandler 1989, p. 87). In his view, attention is restricted to the spatiotemporal orientation by which specific targets become objects for further processing. Posner and Rothbart (1992), presenting both neuropsychological and experimental evidence, also argue that orienting can be dissociated from consciousness (e.g., in studies of blindsight). They even suggest different neurological subsystems for these processes. We believe, however, that also for this dissociation there might be a multiprocess alternative (with different distributions of processing sites) for the multiple systems account given by Posner and Rothbart. In this chapter, we will attempt to develop such a multiprocess account for the dissociation of conscious and unconscious processes, extending our connectionist work on modeling in the more restricted domain of implicit and explicit memory tasks.

Recent developments in connectionism (Cohen, Dunbar, and McClelland 1990; Phaf, van der Heijden, and Hudson 1990) have provided a view on attention that is somewhat different from older views. The older views tend to be based on a computer metaphor for the human system, with a limited-capacity central processor determining the interaction between input and long-term memory. In a connectionist view, selection need not be localized but can be distributed along the processing route. Moreover, it is characterized by a specific type of process and not by the contents the process is working on. It can be seen as the integration of previously unrelated parallel activity from independent sources into the activation of a coherent but distributed representation. The multiple constraint satisfaction (convergence) processes that are ubiquitous in network models form a suitable mechanism for this. The Phaf, van der Heijden, and Hudson (1990) model performs this relaxation function in an explicitly modular fashion with different aspects of the information being made coherent in different modules. Such a view of attention would allow for a cascade of selections based on relaxations in different modules starting at very low subcortical levels to very high levels, where selection may be guided by abstract representational cues.

The question, then, is what kind of mechanism makes possible the function that, according to Mandler (1989), creates the conscious contents out of unconscious activations. Here we will follow Mandler and examine what mechanism may be required to add conscious processing to the general attentional selection capabilities of a network model. We will suggest that for conscious experience to arise, an explicit construction process is required that is based on the same mechanism responsible for sequential recursive reasoning and for temporarily joining arbitrary representations in working memory. Such a mechanism could be the articulatory rehearsal loop concept of Baddeley (1986; Baddeley and Hitch 1974), which is as readily implemented in the connectionist language as activation-elaboration learning. Baddeley (1986) grants this short-term storage system only the status of a "slave" system. In the present model, however, a more central role is assigned to it because it is postulated that the combination of a rehearsal system with a network not only represents a short- and a long-term memory system but also provides a means for flexible processing of activated memory representations. We will tentatively explore here the opportunities for simulating processes involved in consciousness in such a recursive network system.

## 29.2 ATTENTION AND CONSCIOUS AND UNCONSCIOUS MEMORY TASKS

The discussion of activation-elaboration learning could suggest, desspite the original formulation by Mandler (1979), a dichotomous view of the two processes: one corresponding to unconscious automatic processing and the other with orienting and high-level processing tasks (resulting in conscious experience). It would, thus, conform to the identity position, "which postulates that conscious states are to be seen as merely another state of a preconscious structure" (Mandler 1985, p. 57). A continuous view, however, allows for different degrees of attentional processing and makes it less likely that consciousness should be equated with amounts of attention. In such a view, even influences of elaboration learning on unconscious memory tasks would not be excluded. An experimental demonstration of any attentional effect on implicit memory performance would support a continuous view and may indicate that consciousness is related but not identical to attention.

To examine the effect of divided (visual) attention on performance in both implicit and explicit tasks, we conducted an experiment in which words were learned incidentally. In the study phase, subjects had to name one of two words presented on a computer screen. The words were presented to the left and to the right of a fixation point. Visual attention was manipulated by cuing one of the two words by an arrow pointing to the attended word. The subjects had to name the cued word as quickly as possible and to ignore the other. At the onset of the response by the subject, both words disappeared from the screen. Memory was assessed with a word completion task, a threshold identification task, or a free recall task.

### Experimental Method and Results

**Procedure** Sixty subjects were shown word pairs on a computer screen. All stimulus words were selected from the normative study (Phaf and Wolters, n.d.) with spontaneous completion frequencies of Dutch word stems. After 2 sec of presenting a fixation dot, it was replaced by two words: one to the left and one to the right of it. After 200 ms, one of the words was cued by an arrow. The location cue was positioned horizontally at the outside of the word and pointed toward the center. At the onset of the response by the subject, both words disappeared from the screen. (The experimental procedure is treated in more detail in Phaf 1991.)

The subjects were told that the influence of the uncued word on the speed of naming the cued word was being investigated. After presentation of all word pairs, three groups of twenty subjects received a word completion task, a threshold identification task, or a free recall task. In the first two implicit tests, subjects were told that they were participating in another reaction time (RT) experiment. Subjects in the first group completed three-letter word stems. Word stems from the cued words (cues), the noncued words (nocues), and nonpresented control words (distractors) were presented in a random order. The RT was defined as the time between the onset of the stimulus and the start of the verbal response.

Subjects in the second group identified words that were presented under threshold conditions. The threshold was determined for each subject (to allow correct identification at about $p = 0.50$) on the day before the actual experiment (with words not used in the experiment) by varying brightness and duration of presentation and was held constant throughout the rest of the experiment.

The subjects in the third group had to recall as many words as possible from all words presented. Between presentation and testing, a rehearsal-preventing task was given for 2 min, after which the subjects were unexpectedly asked to write down as many nocues as they could recall (for 2 min), and only then to try to recall as many cues as possible (for 2 more min).

**Memory Performance**  Cues were clearly remembered better in all three tests (table 29.1) than nocues ($F(1,54) = 87.1, p < 0.001$). There was no significant interaction between type of test and type of word (cues versus nocues) ($F(2,54) = 1.11$, n.s.). An ANOVA including only word completion and threshold identification with cues, nocues, and distractors as a within-subjects factor, revealed significant differences between the two tests ($F(1,36) = 68.66, p < 0.001$) and between the three kinds of words ($F(2,72) = 73.11, p < 0.001$). Also a significant interaction was found between type of test and type of words ($F(2,72) = 3.86, p < 0.05$). A post hoc test (Newman-Keuls at a 0.05 significance level) showed that with the exception of the word completion noncued/distractor comparison (which was marginally significant), all other comparisons of this interaction were statistically significant.

**Reaction Times**  RTs required for producing a response could, of course, be obtained only in the two implicit tasks. Table 29.2 shows the mean RTs (taken over correct responses only) for the three kinds of words in the implicit

**Table 29.1** Proportions Correct in the Three Memory Tests

|  | Cues | Nocues | Distractors |
| --- | --- | --- | --- |
| Threshold identification | 0.64 | 0.45 | 0.33 |
| Word completion | 0.22 | 0.08 | 0.03 |
| Free recall | 0.16 | 0.01 | — |

Table 29.2 Mean Reaction Times (in ms) for Threshold Identification and Word Completion

|                          | Cues | Nocues | Distractors |
|--------------------------|------|--------|-------------|
| Threshold identification | 843  | 851    | 980         |
| Word completion          | 1048 | 1128   | 1159        |

memory tests. An analysis of variance with only threshold identification again showed a significant effect of the type of words ($F(2,36) = 7.40, p < 0.01$) with cues being produced faster than nocues and nocues faster than distractors. A Newman-Keuls post hoc test ($p < 0.05$) showed that only the difference between the RTs for the distractors and the RTs for the other two kinds of words was significant. When threshold identification and word completion were analyzed together, the difference between the two kinds of tests was again significant ($F(1,36) = 14.88, p < 0.001$), with faster responses for threshold identification than for word completion. Now the effect of the type of words was only marginally significant ($F(2,72) = 2.49$, p = 0.09). The interaction between type of (implicit) test and type of word was not significant ($F(2,72) = 0.40$, n.s.).

**Discussion** Three aspects of these results are relevant to the discussion of the influence of attention on implicit performance. First, in the threshold identification task, and, albeit marginally significant, also in the word completion task, there is implicit memory performance for uncued words, whereas these words cannot be recalled explicitly. Second, there are clear differences in performance in implicit tasks between the cued and the uncued words. Manipulating attention clearly resulted in performance differences in both implicit memory tests. Third, we have not found a dissociation between implicit and explicit tasks in this experiment, showing that attention can have a similar effect in both types of task.

Evidence for attentional processing having effects on implicit performance that are similar (though perhaps somewhat smaller) to those on explicit performance was also presented by Anooshian (1989). Small effects of an attentional manipulation (spaced versus massed processing) on word completion have been obtained by us (only in matching modality conditions; see experiment 8, Phaf 1991). Also, level of incidental processing, which may be related to attention, showed, in contrast to the results of Graf and Mandler (1984), a small but significant effect on word completion and category exemplar generation in one of our experiments (experiment 9, Phaf 1991).

## Modeling Attentional Effects on Learning

Here and elsewhere (e.g., Phaf 1991) we have argued that not only different learning processes but also some form of study-test compatibility plays a role in implicit-explicit memory dissociations. This can be implemented optimally in a modular framework with representations distributed over modules, where every module represents different components. In each module, elaboration and activation learning processes occur. We will briefly discuss such a model based on the competitive learning module presented in Murre, Phaf, and Wolters (1992; see also Phaf 1991). The model described is a simple multi-module system, and we will explore its potential for simulating the experimental results presented earlier.

We cannot recapitulate and justify here all properties of the competitive learning procedure we have chosen, but we will discuss some important features of the building block learning module. Every CALM (Categorizing And Learning Module; see Murre, Phaf, and Wolters 1992) performs an attentional relaxation on its incoming activations by means of a competition process. Activations are transferred between modules by connections between the Representation-nodes (R-nodes). All intermodular connections, which may be bidirectional but are not symmetric, are between R-nodes of different modules. Only these connections change due to learning. Within modules, connections are fixed and are chosen in such a way as to implement winner-take-all competition between R-nodes. Though this leads to local representations on a modular scale, on a global scale representations can still be considered to be distributed. Excitatory and inhibitory processes have been explicitly separated by distinguishing nodes giving off only excitatory connections (R-nodes) and nodes giving off only inhibitory connections (Veto or V-nodes). Each R-node activates only one V-node, which strongly inhibits all other R-nodes, as well as all other V-nodes, thus ensuring competition in the module.

Generally a competitive learning scheme will tend to reduce the amount of competition with every subsequent presentation of the same activation pattern. The amount of competition, which thus serves as a measure of novelty, can be determined by comparing the total activation in the R-node layer to the total activation in the V-node layer. When there is relatively much R-node activation, this signals much competition. This comparison has been implemented in network terms by assuming an Arousal-node (A-node), which receives excitation from all R-nodes and inhibition from all V-nodes. The A-node connects to a further External-node (E-node). If there is no competition in the module (e.g., when an already represented pattern is given and only one R-node is active), the A- and E-nodes will not be activated, and there will only be base rate learning. This instantiates activation learning. If there is much competition, the A- and E-nodes will be highly activated, which induces elaboration learning. This consists of an increase in learning rate (proportional to the E-node activation) and a random exploratory process, which helps to resolve the competition in the module. The amplitude of the random activations to the R-nodes is again proportional to the E-node activation. The basic function of this modular learning procedure is to make categorizations of arbitrary module input without supervision.

Two preliminary remarks should be made about our implementation of the activation-elaboration hypothesis by Mandler (1979, 1980). First, the dichotomy suggested by the two terms is instantiated in the model as a continuum. Activation and elaboration learning are the poles of this continuum, representing maximal emphasis either on strengthening of existing representational connections or on formation of new representational connection patterns. Second, elaboration learning (the formation of new representations) has not been implemented as the formation of completely new connections but as the formation of a differentiated pattern of connection weights in connections that formerly had equal, nonzero, connection weights. In competitive learning, winner-take-all networks such undifferentiated connection schemes correspond to the absence of a winner (a representation), so that only with the evolution of weight differences new representations may develop.

**Outline of the Model**

The model presented here consists of a number of modules similar to the module described in the previous section. Its modular architecture can be derived from the functional requirements for simulating the experiment. To simulate the three tasks, at least three kinds of input representations have to be available to the model: word beginnings, word endings, and environmental contexts. This requires three input modules. Since the model is not intended to simulate low-level word recognition, there is no provision for encoding single letters or the ordering of word parts. Since the only output representations are complete words, only one output module is needed. Figure 29.1 shows the simple network used for the simulation. The core of the network is formed by two CALM modules (labeled "words" and "contexts"). In the word and context CALMs, each node represents a potential pattern (words or contexts) presented to those modules through the input modules. The two CALMs consist of twenty-five word representation nodes and seven context representation nodes, respectively (the numbers of nodes are chosen rather arbitrarily). These CALMs are linked by bidirectional connections between all R-nodes of both modules. The activation of a pair of nodes, one in each of the two word-part input modules, signals the presentation of a complete word. After learning has taken place, pairs of input nodes become associated to a single node in the CALM representing the full word. The third input module represents seven arbitrary contexts. Input modules are fully connected to their corresponding CALM modules by unidirectional learning connections. Before learning, all variable connections have the same initial value, which was taken at half the maximum value of these weights.

Retrieval of a word can take place in this model by presenting either a context or a word part as a cue. The output is, however, the same for both routes: complete words are produced as output. The output module has been specifically designed for producing sequential responses. The output module is coupled to the word-CALM (fig. 29.1). An active output node in the output module represents the response production of a particular word. The output

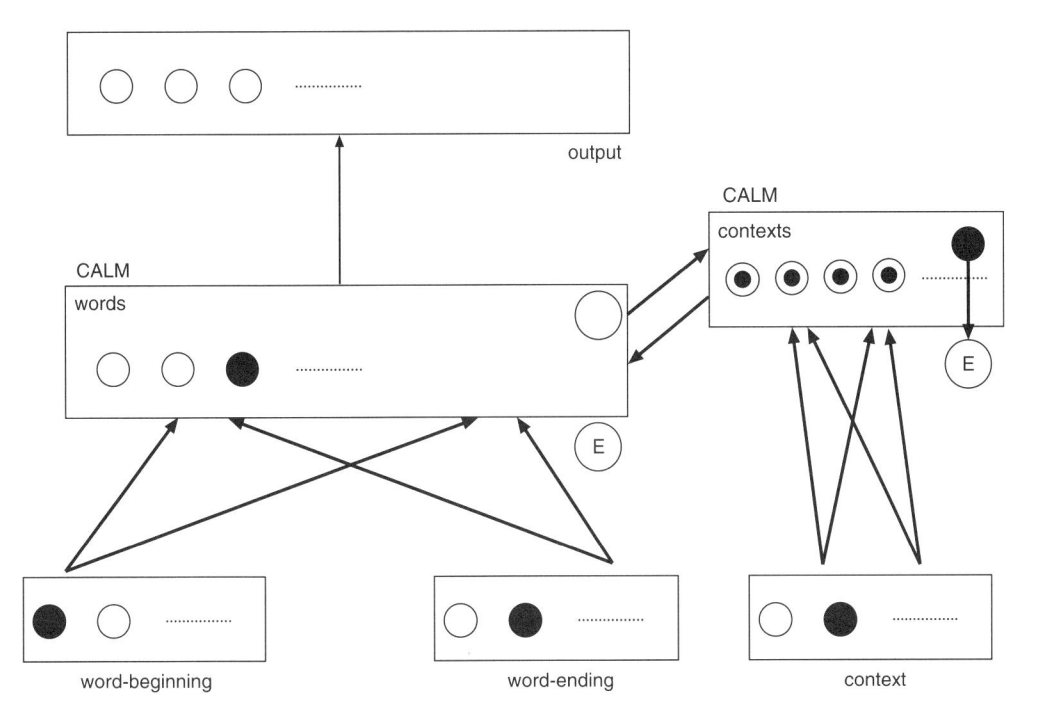

**Figure 29.1** The full ELAN-1 model with schematic wiring pattern. Between CALM and input modules, full unidirectional connectivity exists between input- and R-nodes. Between CALM modules, there is full bidirectional connectivity for the R-nodes. The output module is connected by one-to-one connections from the R-nodes of the CALM module to the output nodes. Black or partly black nodes show possible activation states. The activation of a word in a context is shown.

nodes are directly activated by the nodes in the word-CALM through one-to-one nonlearning connections from the representation nodes to the output nodes. An output node can get activated only after one word-node in the CALM has won the competition and all other activations in the CALM module have decayed sufficiently. The output module thus enables the selection of a single node with a probability that is a function of the activity of the corresponding word-CALM R-node.

The output module (for more detail, see Phaf 1991) selects the winning node for output after the resolution of competition in the word-CALM. After having done so, the CALM module is subsequently inhibited by a strong activation coming from the output module. The input that is still present will then start the next (stochastic) activation-selection cycle, which may produce either the same word as before or a different one. All of these "control processes" have been implemented in terms of nodes and connections and therefore do not violate the connectionist formalism. The word-CALM–output module combination functions as a kind of parallel serial converter that allows for sequential response production. Such a converter is, of course, required for producing sequences of responses, as is the case in free recall.

## Simulations with the Model

Simulations with the model proceed in three stages: (1) old preexperimental representations are formed, (2) a subset of these words is presented in a new study context, and (3) memory for the words is tested either implicitly or explicitly.

The first stage of the simulations corresponds to preexperimental learning. It simulates the knowledge a subject possesses before taking part in an experiment (e.g., a subject has to be able to recognize a word). Therefore, before the simulation of the actual memory experiments can begin, artificial subjects (ASs) have to be created by exposing the "empty" network to a basic lexicon of twenty words presented in a number of different environments or contexts. All word beginnings and word endings were used twice in the basic lexicon. Because the model behaves stochastically, and more so with new stimuli, presentation of the same stimuli to the same initial network does not lead to the same connection weight changes. Each presentation of a series of words in contexts leads to a different network, of which twelve were created in the present simulations (Phaf 1991).

In the second stage of the simulations, a subset of all words was presented to all ASs with a new, not previously used, experimental context. The experimental word list consists of ten words, all with different word beginnings and endings.

In the third stage, implicit and explicit memory tests were simulated. In the simulation of a word completion task, only a word beginning is presented as input. No context cue is presented, which may be compared to the absence of an explicit reference to the study context in implicit tasks. The active word beginning node causes the activation of the nodes of all words with the same beginning. Words presented earlier in the experimental context will be connected somewhat more strongly with the stimulus and will thus have a slightly better chance of being generated as a response than words not presented in the experimental context. In the simulation of a free recall task, the experimental context is given as input. This can be compared to giving a subject the instruction to recall all words learned previously in a specific spatiotemporal context. Here, a sequence of words is produced by resetting the word-CALM module after a word has won the competition and has been produced as a "response." The context input node, which is still active after resetting, subsequently triggers further memory search.

Both the free recall and the word completion tests are applied before and after the learning of the experimental list for each AS. In this way, the experimental performance of the simulated subjects can be compared to their base rate performance (i.e., without second-stage learning). Because after the prelearning tests the ASs were restored in their pretest state, the experimental presentations that followed were not confounded by the prelearning test. Also word completion and free recall testing can be performed without one test confounding the other. With both word completion and free recall, learning (mainly activation learning) continues during testing. The model, therefore, also shows learning during retrieval.

To simulate the effects of both attention (cued words) and the lack of attention (noncued words) on implicit and explicit memory tasks, a suitable implementation of attentional selection has to be found. We followed Phaf, van der Heijden, and Hudson (1990) by assuming that selection takes place by the resolution of competition between mutually inhibiting stimuli caused by additional activation of the stimulus that is task relevant. The nocue, however, also activates its representation. To simulate this, the cued word merely has a higher activation than the noncued word. It wins the competition and is subject to more learning. The Hebbian type of learning rule used in the model allows for some learning of the nocue as well. It should be noted that we have not simulated the causes for the selection. To do so, we would have needed to extend the model with representations for positions and for cues on these positions (Phaf, van der Heijden, and Hudson 1990).

A further extension of the simulation procedure is required for fully simulating the experiment. To perform threshold identification with the model, a number of exploratory simulations were performed to investigate whether it is possible to find presentation durations (in number of iterations) and input activation values that would reliably produce about 50 percent correct identifications of the words. Just as in the experiment, such a threshold (activation) value was determined for each AS.

For the experimental list, ten words from the basic word pool (consisting of twenty words) were used as targets. Five words were selected as cued words. The remaining five words were used as uncued words. None of these words had a word part in common. The five cued and the five noncued words were arranged in pairs. Position of a word was not represented in the model, so in this respect the simulation was simpler than the actual experiment.

In the experimental learning stage, all twelve ASs were presented with the list of word pairs. We will not go into the details of the simulation (specific activation values, number of iterations, and so forth). The details are important, of course, but they are irrelevant here and have been presented elsewhere (see Phaf 1991). Both before and after experimental presentation, all ASs were tested for the experimental words with the implicit and the explicit memory tests. Results from testing prior to the experimental presentation stage are used as an estimation of distractor performance.

## Simulation Results

Memory performance for both preexperimental (distractor) and postexperimental testing (cues and nocues) for the three kinds of tests are shown in table 29.3. Qualitatively, the correspondence with the experimental results (see table 29.1) was reasonably good. Moreover, attempts to get better quantitative fits would do no more than disguise the fact that such a simple model must necessarily have shortcomings relative to the actual system performing

**Table 29.3** Proportions Correct in the Simulation of Three Memory Tests

|  | Cues | Nocues | Distractors |
|---|---|---|---|
| Threshold identification | 0.67 | 0.52 | 0.39 |
| Word completion | 0.65 | 0.47 | 0.51 |
| Free recall | 0.28 | 0.02 | 0.0 |

these tasks. Nevertheless, we conclude that our theoretical starting point produces results that are compatible with the main features of experimental data.

The three kinds of words showed clear differences ($F(2,22) = 17.94, p < 0.001$), with generally higher performance on the cues than on the nocues and the nocues higher than the distractors. The interaction between type of test and type of word was not significant ($F(4,44) = 1.58$, n.s.), so the simulation revealed no dissociation between the tests. As in the experiment, free recall for the nocues was very low. In the threshold identification task, the nocues reveal a facilitation in performance relative to the distractors. In the word completion task, distractor performance was high compared to the experimental data. It may be noted, however, that words used in the experiment were selected on having a low spontaneous completion frequency.

The RTs (the interval in number of iterations between onset of the word or word stem and the convergence in the output module) were also determined for both implicit tasks. The direction of the differences between cues, nocues, and distractors is similar to the experimental results. However, the differences were much smaller than in the experiment (an ANOVA revealed no significant differences except for type of task, $F(1,11) = 16.16, p < 0.01$). Moreover, threshold identification took longer than word completion in the model. So, for the present, the model does not seem very well suited for simulating RTs.

## 29.3 ATTENTION AND CONSCIOUSNESS IN NETWORKS

The previous simulation provides a nice illustration of a connectionist conceptualization of attention. Different stimuli (as well as instructions, expectations, etc.) first cause a spread of activation through the network along all possible representational components that are related to the stimuli. The ensemble of activations does not form a unitary representation but contains different degrees of evidence for representational components that may be incompatible. At the same time as the spread commences, a relaxation process is started in the network by which mutually exclusive components compete and inhibit each other, whereas compatible parts support and amplify one another. Eventually, the relaxation process leads to a convergence into a coherent set of activated components. Although no clear line can be drawn between attended and preattentive processing in the network, the distributed set of activations after convergence corresponds to what is being attended to. Because spread and relaxation proceed simultaneously, the top of the hierarchy of representational components may show less evidence of competition and unattended processing. The gradual selection in this view results in an apparent emphasis on selectivity for the early components in the hierarchy.

In general, a broader but less coherent range of components will be activated before convergence than after this attentional process has been completed. This process shows resemblance to the view of Marcel (1983) that unconscious perceptual mechanisms extract meaning from stimulus input by parsing it in all alternative manners that are possible given the available representations. The conscious percept would then arise through a process of recovery where the unconscious units are synthesized into environmental objects and events. According to Marcel (1983), it is obtained by a constructive act of fitting a perceptual hypothesis to its sensory source. Such a formulation appears to stem from the more classical information-processing approach, though it has some connectionist elements, such as the distributed and hierarchical structure of the systems involved in automatically processing sensory inputs. A more radical view, attributed to connectionism by Kihlstrom (1987), is to assert that "at this point of relaxation the information represented by a steady state becomes accessible to phenomenal awareness" (p. 1446). Delays in the relaxation process due to ambiguities in the stimulus pattern may lead to seemingly serial processing accompanied by shifts in the contents of consciousness. According to Kihlstrom (1987) "The clear implication of the PDP framework is that unconscious processing is fast and parallel, while conscious processing is slow and sequential" (p. 1446). Moreover, "PDP models seem to consider almost all information processing, including the higher mental functions involved in language, memory, and thought, to be unconscious" (p. 1446).

The key question in the positions of both Marcel and Kihlstrom is for the relation between attention and consciousness: is attention necessary and sufficient for consciousness, or is it merely necessary? The Kihlstrom view on connectionism comes very close to an identity position, whereas Marcel stresses a constructive process following the relaxation process for combining different activated representations (which may be temporarily distinct and from different sources) into a conscious percept. This position has been forcefully reiterated by Mandler (1985, 1989).

The idea that representations when selected by relaxation may exceed some threshold and become conscious seems at first sight to fit the connectionist approach best (see Kihlstrom 1987), but a constructionist view distinguishing between a parallel relaxation and a sequential construction process may also be implemented quite easily in a connectionist scheme. In the following section, we will develop such a scheme in which network relaxation is assumed to be a sufficient process for attentional selectivity but in which consciousness requires an additional constructive network process using the results of ongoing relaxations.

## The Construction Process and a Working Memory Architecture

What are the functional requirements for the construction process? First, it should be able to contain a number of different activated representations (records of sensory analysis and perceptual hypotheses, Marcel 1983; preconscious structures, Mandler 1985) derived from either previous sensory stimulations or previous constructions, in order to construct or synthesize a conscious phenomenal experience. A literal version of the representation with a conscious record of all its components is probably not kept, but there is some abstract version that is capable of evoking relevant parts of the representation. Such abstract representations probably correspond to externally meaningful objects and actions (e.g., words, visual images of objects) and may, therefore, be called symbolic representations. Second, subsequent relaxation processes can be guided from the present contents of the construction process, so that a sequential chain of manipulations of abstract representations can be created. Because the representations are abstract, the actions that would actually change the environment need not be performed. It will be hypothesized that the construction process is derived from the internalization of systems that actually manipulate the environment. Third, the most important prerequisite is, probably, that a conscious content can be related to almost everything else the system is capable of representing. Temporary couplings of representations, which have not been explicitly connected in the system, are constructed here. Both the abstract representations and the cues necessary for using them in new relaxations (the symbols and the rules working on them) must be available in the construction.

From these requirements, it will be clear that the construction process, in our view, stands for a specific version of working memory implementing both short-term memory and symbol manipulation capabilities. The association between consciousness and some form of short-term memory (also primary memory or working memory) is, of course, a very common one. In the classical information-processing approach, consciousness has been identified with the workings of a separate short-term store (Atkinson and Shiffrin 1968).

The concept of working memory implicitly present in most current connectionist views seems to be psychologically naive. If the topic is mentioned at all in a particular connectionist model, it is usually seen as the ensemble of activations in the network. The slowly changing weights of the connections between the nodes represent long-term memory, whereas the decaying activations of the nodes represent short-term retention (Grossberg 1988). Careful experimentation (Baddeley 1986, 1992a, 1992b) has shown that this point of view is insufficient. Baddeley (1986) proposed a working memory ("the system that is necessary for concurrent storage and manipulation of information," Baddeley, 1992b, p. 556) in which two "slave" systems can be distinguished: a phonological loop and a visuospatial sketch pad. Much more is known about the phonological loop than about the sketch pad, but it is clear that they differ in at least one important respect from the activation view on working memory: both are associated with a particular modality. The representations held in these slave systems are not the fuzzy, subsymbolic, distributed representations, characteristic of many network models, but symbolic representations of words and visual objects.

Another aspect that is not covered by the activation view is the apparent sequentiality of the phonological loop (and possibly also of the visuospatial sketch pad). It maintains memory traces by subvocal rehearsal. Because it is a speech-based system, it may register material presented in other modalities by subvocal naming. Translated in the connectionist language, this would imply that the attentional function of the network transforms and integrates subsymbolic input into a symbolic (e.g., verbal) format, which, in turn, is maintained and manipulated in the rehearsal loop. The sequentiality of the loop is related to the fact that an articulatory output system is involved that can produce only symbolic chunks (such as words), one after another. Whether a similar sequential output system can be found for the visuospatial sketch pad is not yet clear. The sketch pad may even be separable into spatial and visual components with different output systems associated with them. An interesting candidate for one such output system may be the eye movement system, which allows for serial scanning of the visual field.

It is attractive to speculate about the origins of such a sequential feedback system. The simplest way of maintaining the activations of a representation is by keeping the object that causes the activations present in the sensory input. If, however, an internal sequential feedback loop is available, maintaining (and manipulating) representations is no longer limited by the presence or absence of physical objects, so that a more flexible and wider range of representations can be held active in working memory. The resulting (limited) span of symbolic chunks is just what an activation view on working memory will find difficult to explain. The number of verbal chunks in the span will depend on both the decay rate of the activations and the time it takes to produce the chunks. In sum, it is hypothesized here that working memory arises through the internalization of sequential feedback processes. In the human system, probably, only the visuospatial and the auditory-articulatory systems have undergone such internalization, whereas other input systems only have access to it by a transformation (such as naming) into one of the two systems.

There is some neuropsychological evidence supporting the working memory architecture we have outlined. Notably, these studies point to the same general areas for working memory as where Posner and Rothbart (1992) localize the production of consciousness. The prefrontal cortex (or the anterior attention network according to Posner and Rothbart 1992) has been found in microelectrode studies on monkeys to contain neurons that are active only when a specific target object is concealed in a delayed-response task, thus signaling a short-term memory for the representation of this target (Goldman-Rakic, Funahashi, and Bruce 1990). Lesions in this area lead to a disruption of performance in delayed-response tasks and an inability to remember concealed objects over short periods. The idea that working memory should be associated with particular output systems is supported by the fact that the prefrontal cortex has close connections to premotor areas in the cortex and to areas that exert oculomotor control. It was suggested that working memory should also be involved in sequential behavior. This function of the prefrontal cortex is strongly endorsed by the observation that patients with damage to the prefrontal cortex are specifically impaired on memory for temporal order information (Milner, Petrides, and Smith 1985).

## A Sequentially Recurrent Network Model

In this section we will extend the model presented earlier to fit the working memory architecture. Network models that look somewhat similar to this architecture have previously been developed under the name of simple recurrent networks (SRN, Elman 1990; Jordan 1986). Both types of SRN rely on (nonlearning) feedback from either the output layer (Jordan 1986) or the middle (so-called hidden) layer to the input layer. They are usually embedded in a backpropagation framework (Rumelhart, Hinton, and Williams 1986), which means that long-term memory storage takes place in a supervised fashion (both the input and the prospected output patterns are presented in an initial training phase). Furthermore, such networks mostly have three layers (input, hidden, and output) of nodes with feedforward connections between all nodes of subsequent layers. The origins of the SRNs lie in the difficulty backpropagation has in handling not only feedforward but also feedback connections.

The SRNs form a first approximation to fully recurrent networks by having fixed connections that copy the activations from a particular layer (either output layer, Jordan 1986; or hidden layer, Elman 1990) to a new region, or module, in the input layer. The main application of SRNs is to encode sequences of input-output relations in long-term memory and to reproduce the sequences when a particular input pattern from the sequence is presented. This application is demonstrated by both Jordan (1986) and Elman (1990) in a number of rather abstract tasks where serial order plays a role, such as learning the sequential XOR function. These SRNs are able to discover underlying structure from being presented with examples from the structure. Elman (1990), for instance, shows that an SRN can distill lexical class by merely presenting sentences. Another interesting example of this generalization is the SRN by Cottrell and Tsung (1989), which learns to add multidigit numbers in a columnar fashion. Despite having learned additions of up to only three-digit numbers, the network generalized well to longer additions. From these simulations, it can be concluded that if the SRN has an output system containing both symbols and a small set of simple operations, infinitely long sequences of operations can, in principle, be performed. This is also possible in SRNs with subsymbolic feedback. Servan-Schreiber, Cleeremans, and McClelland (1991; Cleeremans, Servan-Schreiber, and McClelland 1989), for instance, demonstrate that a finite state Reber grammar can be learned by an Elman SRN with three hidden units after training with 60,000 randomly generated strings from the grammar. They also show that the network has a limited ability to deal with embedded sentences.

Feedback in the SRNs is neither explicitly symbolic nor explicitly sequential, as we have required for the construction process. Feedback does not originate from the actions of some output system but from simultaneously copying all activations from either the hidden or the output layer. All subsymbolic information from that layer is fed back in parallel. In our model, the transformation from subsymbolic and parallel to symbolic and sequential is made by the output module. Activation of a node in the output module signals the production of a full word (a symbolic representation). In a similar way, activations in an output module may represent other symbols and operations (e.g., digits and operations, such as add, carry, or stop).

In the recurrent model we suggest, which is an extended version of the model described earlier, sequentiality is accomplished by feeding back the representations of the output module that become available successively. Because the CALM framework allows for learning with bidirectional connections more easily than backpropagation and the feedback has been made explicitly sequential, we will call the extended model a sequentially recurrent network (SeRN) instead of a simple recurrent network.

A requirement not met by the SRNs is that a number of different representations can be kept activated simultaneously, so that they can be coupled temporarily without having been bound together permanently in the network. They show powerful long-term memory sequential storage capabilities after extensive training but are lacking the flexible and temporary binding characteristics of the working memory domain. Although the Jordan SRN retains some activations from output patterns before the previous cycle, these activations do not fully represent these output patterns because they are mixed and interfered with by subsequent feedback. The subsymbolic character of the feedback in this SRN makes it very difficult to keep more than one symbolic chunk activated temporarily. In fact, the span of SRNs relative to nonrecurrent networks generally can be said to be increased by only one output pattern, which is very low compared to a human span of up to seven chunks. If symbol manipulation abilities are to be obtained that not only depend on following strict sequences laid down in long-term memory, a longer span will be required.

In the SeRN model, a longer span is realized because it feeds back single localized activations (which stand for symbolic chunks) to different nodes in an input module that are not connected and therefore will not interfere with one another. An important condition is that activations resulting from the feedback should be smaller than the actual input activations resulting from external stimuli, so that real input can override the rehearsal. The model should learn primarily on the basis of such external input and should not function completely independently of its environment, as would be the case if the rehearsed activations were too strong.

To show the possibilities of the SeRN model, two tasks were simulated: (1) a simulation of the serial position effects in recall, and (2) learning and reproducing a sequence and its inverse. Effects of rehearsal on learning a list of words can be seen clearly in the serial position curve. Generally the idea is that the primacy effect would reflect the extra rehearsal that the first items of the list receive, whereas the recency effect would be a consequence of the words that are still active in the short-term memory span. Although in some conditions this account may be too simple (e.g., different forms of rehearsal may be distinguished, Craik and Watkins 1973; and recency effects may also occur in long-term memory tasks, Baddeley and Hitch 1977), an important role of rehearsal in primacy and recency effects cannot be denied.

**Simulation of Serial Position Effects**

Results obtained with the model for simulating the effects of list learning on implicit and explicit memory tests have also been analyzed on the occurrence of serial position effects. In simulations of a free-recall task, no primacy effect was found, but a long-term recency effect was clearly observable (Phaf 1991). Further analysis revealed that both the absence of a primacy effect and the presence of a recency effect were caused by retroactive interference from new words on prior words in the list. Such interference is quite customary in network learning (Ratcliff 1990). The amount of interference may actually be considerably smaller than is often the case in backpropagation networks. It is expected that in the extended SeRN model, the interference will be counteracted by the rehearsal of previous words in the presentation intervals. A primacy effect will appear as a consequence of the greater chance of rehearsing the first items during the presentation of the remainder of the list. A recency effect will occur in an immediate recall task, because the more recent items will still be active in the memory span when retrieval starts. This recency effect will vanish, however, in a delayed recall task because, as rehearsal is prevented, the activation of the last presented item will decay.

The extended model that will be used to simulate primacy and recency effects is shown in figure 29.2. It has all the features discussed in the previous section. Symbolic output is produced by an output module that has only one single active output node when convergence in the corresponding CALM module has been completed. This single node activation is fed back into a rehearsal input module via fixed one-to-one connections with a low weight (0.1). Similar to the other input modules, this module consists of two layers of nodes. In contrast to the other input modules, however, inhibition within the second layer of nodes in the input module has been omitted, so several nodes may remain active simultaneously. To increase this (temporary) storage function, the spontaneous decay of the activations of these nodes has been reduced. The nodes have fixed one-to-one connections (0.5) to an additional CALM module. The representation nodes in this module are connected (all-to-all) to the R-nodes in the word-CALM. The new CALM module channels one of the active items (by weighted stochastic selection) into the process of preparing new output.

Compared to the old model, the word input has been simplified. Word beginnings and endings are no longer separated, but one input module is used for presenting complete words. To make sure that actual inputs can override

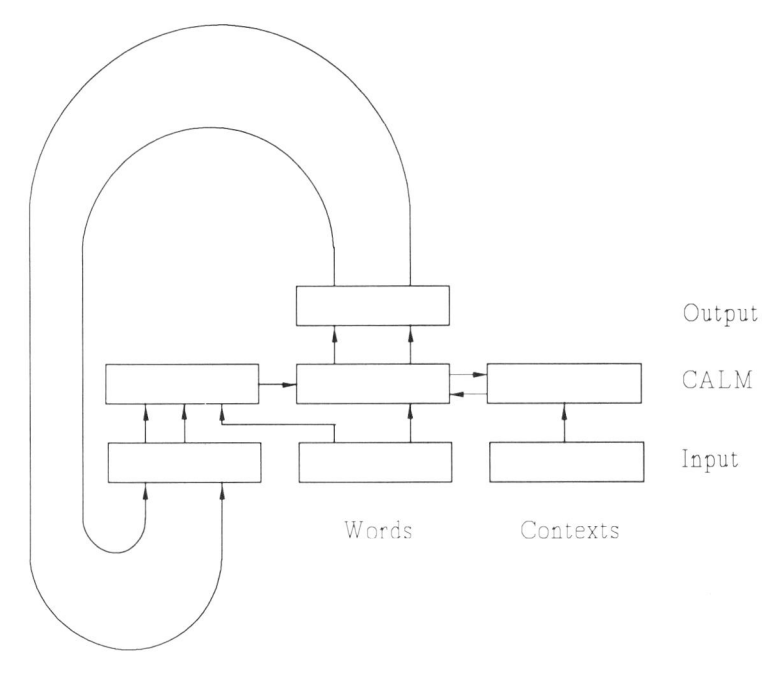

**Figure 29.2** Schematic representation of the extended model with a rehearsal loop between the output module and a new input module. The input module is linked to a new CALM module by fixed one-to-one connections. The connections from the new CALM to the word-CALM are learning and code sequential relations.

virtual (rehearsed) inputs, additional all-to-all learning connections (with initial weight 0.1) from the word input to the new CALM have been included. The interval between rehearsals in the model is based on the time it takes to produce output and subsequently to inhibit all the output and CALM activation. Rehearsal in this model is thus self-paced, depending on the ease of finding suitable output.

The simulation procedure (Mul 1993) was largely comparable to the procedure followed in the model discussed previously. Again, three stages can be distinguished: a preexperimental learning stage, an experimental learning stage, and a testing stage. The stages differed only in the nature and duration of the input patterns, but no explicit change was made in the processing mode of the network. This contrasts with backpropagation, where a network is in either a training or a testing mode. Since this recurrent network learns without supervision, it establishes representations only through the presentation of input. As a result, the learning procedure resembles the experimental protocol much more closely than is customary in most network simulations.

To create a basic word pool, the model was first presented with twenty different words under six of the available seven contexts. A single artificial subject (AS) was created. Subsequently, an experimental list consisting of ten words was presented under the seventh experimental context. In the delayed recall condition, all activations were initialized before providing the experimental context as a cue. With immediate recall, there was no initialization

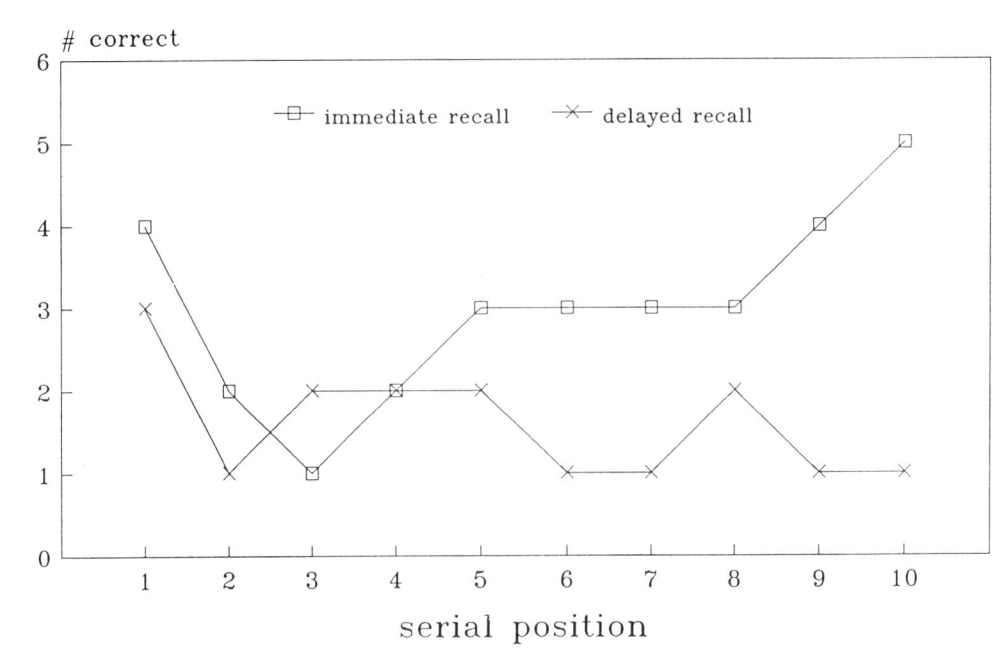

**Figure 29.3** Serial position curves obtained with the model for immediate and delayed free recall.

between list and cue. The experimental simulation was repeated five times. The results are shown in figure 29.3.

The simulations reveal a small primacy effect in both the delayed and immediate recall conditions. A recency effect that appears to extend from the fifth to the tenth position is observed only in the immediate recall condition. The long-term recency effect in previous simulations has disappeared. Presumably, the model has developed a short-term memory span that extends over a number of words. The number of rehearsals of words during experimental list learning was counted. The pattern of rehearsals supports the idea that a long-term recency effect was compensated for by rehearsals and that the primacy effect arises through a large number of rehearsals for the first items. These items were rehearsed very frequently during the successive presentations of list items (more than twice as often as the last words). The level of rehearsal declined steadily until about the seventh word, after which it remained constant. The serial position curve thus shows evidence of rehearsal and short-term memory effects. In the model, primacy and recency arise in a relatively complicated interaction between short- and long-term memory abilities.

**Sequence Learning**

It is essential to our line of reasoning that the SeRN is not only able to hold a number of patterns active in its working memory but can also encode sequential rule schemes in long-term memory that can be called upon from working memory. We therefore want to show that, despite the extension with a working memory span, it retains some of the capacities of the original SRNs.

In the following simulation, we decided to investigate the encoding of a rather "pathological" set of sequences. From the available set of twenty items, seven sequences of five items were constructed. One of these sequences was unique; it did not share a word with any of the other sequences. Of the remaining six sequences, three were the exact reverse of three others in the set. Therefore, every element in these sequences, except the first one, suffers from the ambiguity that it is part of two sequences. The gross architecture of the network (but see Mul 1993 for some minor differences) was similar to the previous network, but a learning connection from the word input to the additional CALM module was absent. Inhibition within this CALM module was also set to zero, so that the module would contribute further to the working memory abilities of the network.

Training of the network started with presentation of the sequences (eighty times) without any preexperimental training of single words. Each sequence was accompanied by its own unique context. Presentation of the next element of a sequence was conditional upon the output production of the previous element. Presentation was thus self-paced, and there was no fixed presentation duration. Initializations occurred only between, not within, sequences.

Every sequence was tested by presenting its corresponding context. The unique sequence was always reproduced correctly. The nonunique sequences, however, showed a systematic confusion. The sequences were all reproduced correctly up to the fifth element. This element was replaced by the second and was again followed by the third. A confusion of the sequence and its reverse in working memory is the cause for this phenomenon. With initial training of the sequences, stronger interitem associations will be formed between early members of the sequence than between later members. The reason is that later on, more items are active in working memory, which are all competing for connection weights (from the additional CALM to the word-CALM) to the next word. When, during testing, the fourth item is produced, the prior items will still be active in working memory. The active third and fourth items are more likely to produce the second than the fifth. This simulation provides a further indication of the capacity of the rehearsal loop to encode different sequential schemes in long-term memory. Moreover, it shows that in principle, the capacity to hold different items simultaneously in working memory may result in sequential manipulations that have not been explicitly learned.

## Consciousness in Networks

We have not fully explained what consciousness is. What we have done is to argue that consciousness cannot be equated with selective attention. In our opinion, consciousness (or, better, conscious information processing) requires additional processes carried out on information that is selectively attended. We have also argued that these processes may arise quite naturally in a connectionist framework by internalizing interactions with the environment.

We have suggested that the additional processing should show the following characteristics: a capacity of temporarily holding selectively attended (symbolic) information and a capacity of performing constructive processes allowing the temporal binding and manipulation of information that is not explicitly connected in long-term memory.

These characteristics are provided by the concept of a working memory whose primary function is rehearsal in which a number of abstract codes is maintained over variable intervals. The rehearsal process can be seen as an internalization of input-output relations and the manipulation of symbolic codes of objects in the environment that formerly occurred only in direct interaction with that environment. Abstract verbal codes (words) are very well suited for this purpose, although abstract visual codes and possibly other types of abstract codes may be used as well. Verbal codes can be addressed from different input sources, and, in turn, they refer to a wealth of other memory codes. The abstract verbal codes themselves are relatively context free (i.e., symbolic) although their meanings (i.e., their associations to other information) may often be context dependent (Barsalou 1987).

The information that is temporarily held should be capable of contacting (in a sequential chain of operations) almost any other information available in memory. When, for instance, one is driving a car, sensory information may selectively activate a (subvocal) code for "I am driving my car." This code may successively activate codes for episodic memories of driving lessons, codes for a scheme how to drive a car, codes for traffic rules, or codes for models of how combustion engines can drive the wheels.

The opportunity for the constructive process to have access to a large diversity of episodes, schemes, and models laid down in memory may serve two purposes. First, the development of conscious experience may be based on the possibility of relating actual experiences subsequently to a wealth of former person-environment interactions. Second, it seems necessary in all situations where both specific retrieval from long-term memory and the application of general rules on specific stimulus information are required. An example of such a situation is performing mental calculations on problems never encountered before. This requires holding the original stimulus information, retrieving solutions to elementary calculations (e.g., adding or multiplying single digits), and performing calculation rules (e.g., carrying a result to the next decimal position). Another example is Pinker's (1991) account on forming the past tense in English. According to Pinker, irregular past tenses are retrieved directly from memory, whereas regular past tenses are constructed by applying a rule.

As yet, the problem remains how to implement the application of rule schemes to every possible appropriate symbol. The rules that can be learned are generally not context free. Though it is not entirely clear how good the human system is in applying context-free rules (Elman 1991), some flexibility is certainly required. One way to achieve such flexibility is suggested by Cottrell and Tsung (1989). In their simulations, simple context-free operations form part of the output produced by the SRN. Unfortunately, however, no connectionist process is known that could maintain the context freedom of the operations after internalization of the feedback loop.

We have tried to show that all the processes suggested as necessary requirements for conscious information processing can be implemented in a connectionist model. We are not claiming to have built a connectionist model for consciousness, but we do think that the connectionist formalism (with some of its recurrent extensions) provides a useful language for making theorizing about the subject somewhat more concrete. The particular model we propose has a modular structure, with modules being richly, but not completely, interconnected. The modular structure extends in both the vertical and the horizontal directions. Each module is specialized in processing and storing specific types and aspects of information (there are different input modules for different modalities, and "higher" modules represent more general codes of inputs by combining specific codes represented in lower-level modules). It should be noted that such a multimodular architecture seems well suited to explain several dissociation effects, such as dissociations between attention and consciousness, for instance, in blindsight (Posner and Rothbart 1992). Due to the modular structure, only some of the modules will be connected directly with the output module feeding the rehearsal loop. Activations in other modules either must be transformed to a relevant format or, in certain cases, may not be able to reach the rehearsal loop at all. In these latter modules, selective attention convergence may take place (and activated codes are thus attended), but the activations cannot reach the recursive loop and therefore are not subject to the construction process involved in conscious experience. Similar dissociations may arise in the domain of emotions as a consequence of the dual pathway model of LeDoux (1986). He distinguishes a direct and an indirect pathway for affective processing, which may be put in opposition under specific experimental conditions (Raccuglia and Phaf 1993).

Three modes of recursive processing can occur in the SeRN model. The first two modes correspond to the maintenance and elaborative rehearsal modes. If input is rehearsed again and no (new) input is presented, there is almost no competition, and mainly activation learning will take place. The items will be rehearsed literally, with only some strengthening of existing representations. Elaborative rehearsal, however, will occur when the same items are rehearsed in addition to processing new input. In that case, more competition will arise, and more modules will show elaboration learning, so that representations may be extended and new associations are formed. In the third mode of recursive processing, an item is no longer continuously rehearsed, but chains of different items are produced in the rehearsal loop. This can be based on either addressing stored sequences or generating new productions as a consequence of elaboration in the network (which also increases exploratory behavior in our model).

This distinction can again be applied to conscious and unconscious memory measures. Productions in an unconscious memory task are always conscious, and so the name *unconscious memory task* may not be fully appropriate. What remains unconscious, however, is the explicit connection to the presentation episode. Conscious or explicit (or direct) memory tasks require an explicit reference to this episode. The instructions and the task context trigger some recursive processing, which retrieves the episode's context and uses it as a cue for further retrieval. Thus, for explicit performance, an active construction is necessary at retrieval. In an implicit test, such a recursive retrieval in principle does not take place, and the retrieval of representations is based only on cues provided directly in the task. Facilitation of this retrieval is found due to the strengthening of these representations at presentation. For explicit retrieval, elaboration learning is always required at presentation, because the old items must have been associated to a new context.

The SeRN is no more than a start in exploring the possibilities for symbol manipulation in networks. Many extensions to the connectionist formalism will be needed before we even come close to simulating all processes involved in consciousness. For the moment, we must content ourselves with showing the potential of a network model for accommodating some of the dissociations related to the concept of consciousness.

## NOTE

The first (R.H.P.) and second (N.M.M.) authors have been supported by the Dutch Organization for Scientific Research (NWO). We wish to acknowledge the assistance of Raymond van Beekum and Veronica Roorda-Hrdlicková in performing the experiment.

## REFERENCES

Anooshian, L. J. (1989). Effects of attentive encoding on analytic and nonanalytic processing in implicit and explicit retrieval tasks. *Bulletin of the Psychonomic Society*, 27, 5–8.

Atkinson, R. C., and Shiffrin, R. M. (1968). Human memory: A proposed system and its control processes. In K. W. Spence and T. J. Spence (Eds.), *The psychology of learning and motivation: Advances in research and theory*, vol. 2, 89–195. New York: Academic Press.

Baddeley, A. D. (1986). *Working memory*. Oxford: Clarendon Press.

Baddeley, A. D. (1992a). Is working memory working? The fifteenth Bartlett lecture. *Quarterly Journal of Experimental Psychology*, 44A, 1–31.

Baddeley, A. D. (1992b). Working memory. *Science*, 255, 556–559.

Baddeley, A. D., and Hitch, G. J. (1974). Working memory. In G. H. Bower (Ed.), *Recent advances in learning and motivation*, vol. 8, 47–90. Academic Press: New York.

Baddeley, A. D., and Hitch, G. J. (1977). Recency re-examined. In S. Dornic (Ed.), *Attention and performance VI*, 647–667. Hillsdale, NJ: Erlbaum.

Barsalou, L. W. (1987). The instability of graded structure: Implications for the nature of concepts. In U. Neisser (Ed.), *Concepts and conceptual development: Ecological factors in categorization*. Cambridge: Cambridge University Press.

Bassili, J. N., Smith, M. C., and MacLeod, C. M. (1989). Auditory and visual word-stem completion: Separating data-driven and conceptually driven processes. *Quarterly Journal of Experimental Psychology*, 41A, 439–453.

Blaxton, T. A. (1989). Investigating dissociations among memory measures: Support for a transfer-appropriate processing framework. *Journal of Experimental Psychology: Learning, Memory, and Cognition, 15,* 657–668.

Cleeremans, A., Servan-Schreiber, D., and McClelland, J. L. (1989). Finite state automata and simple recurrent networks. *Neural Computation, 1,* 372–381.

Cohen, J. D., Dunbar, K., and McClelland, J. L. (1990). On the control of automatic processes: A parallel distributed processing model of the Stroop effect. *Psychological Review, 97,* 332–361.

Cottrell, G. W., and Tsung, F. S. (1989). Learning simple arithmetic procedures. In *Proceedings of the Eleventh Annual Conference of the Cognitive Science Society,* 58–65. Hillsdale, NJ: Erlbaum.

Craik, F. I. M., and Watkins, M. J. (1973). The role of rehearsal in short-term memory. *Journal of Verbal Learning and Verbal Behavior, 12,* 599–607.

Eich, E. (1984). Memory for unattended events: Remembering with and without awareness. *Memory and Cognition, 12,* 105–111.

Elman, J. L. (1990). Finding structure in time. *Cognitive Science, 14,* 179–211.

Elman, J. L. (1991). Distributed representations, simple recurrent networks, and grammatical structure. *Machine Learning, 7,* 195–225.

Goldman-Rakic, P. S., Funahashi, S., and Bruce, G. J. (1990). Neocortical memory circuits. *Cold Spring Harbor Symposium on Quantitative Biology, 55,* 1025–1038.

Graf, P., and Mandler, G. (1984). Activation makes words more accessible but not more necessarily more retrievable. *Journal of Verbal Learning and Verbal Behavior, 23,* 553–568.

Grossberg, S. (1988). Nonlinear neural networks: Principles, mechanisms, and architectures. *Neural Networks, 1,* 17–61.

Hintzman, D. L. (1990). Human learning and memory: Connections and dissociations. *Annual Review of Psychology, 41,* 109–139.

Jacoby, L. L. (1983). Remembering the data: Analyzing interactive processes in reading. *Journal of Verbal Learning and Verbal Behavior, 22,* 458–508.

Jacoby, L. L., and Dallas, M. (1981). On the relationship between autobiographical memory and perceptual learning. *Journal of Experimental Psychology: General, 110,* 306–340.

Jelicic, M., Bonke, B., Wolters, G., and Phaf, R. H. (1992). Implicit memory for words presented during anaesthesia. *European Journal of Cognitive Psychology, 4,* 71–80.

Jordan, M. (1986). *Serial order: A parallel distributed processing approach.* Technical Report 8604, Institute for Cognitive Science, University of California, San Diego.

Kihlstrom, J. F. (1987). The cognitive unconscious. *Science, 237,* 1445–1452.

Kihlstrom, J. F., Schacter, D. L., Cork, R. C., Hurt, C. A., and Behr, S. E. (1990). Implicit and explicit memory following surgical anaesthesia. *Psychological Science, 1,* 303–306.

LeDoux, J. E. (1986). Sensory systems and emotion: A model of affective processing. *Integrative Psychiatry, 4,* 237–248.

Mandler, G. (1979). Organization and repetition: Organizational principles with special reference to rote learning. In L.-G. Nilsson (Ed.), *Perspectives on memory research,* 293–327. Hillsdale, NJ: Erlbaum.

Mandler, G. (1980). Recognizing: The judgement of previous occurrence. *Psychological Review, 87,* 252–271.

Mandler, G. (1985). *Cognitive psychology: An essay in cognitive science.* Hillsdale, NJ: Erlbaum.

Mandler, G. (1989). Memory: Conscious and unconscious. In P. R. Solomon, G. R. Goethals, C. M. Kelley, and B. R. Stephens (Eds.), *Memory: Interdisciplinary approaches*, 84–106. New York: Springer-Verlag.

Marcel, A. J. (1983). Conscious and unconscious perception: An approach to the relations between phenomenal experience and perceptual processes. *Cognitive Psychology, 15*, 238–300.

Milner, B. M., Petrides, M., and Smith, M. L. (1985). Frontal lobes and the temporal organization of memory. *Human Neurobiology, 4*, 137–142.

Mul, N. M. (1993). *Short-term memory effects by simple recurrency*. Internal report, Leiden University.

Murre, J. M. J., Phaf, R. H., and Wolters, G. (1992). CALM: A categorizing and learning module. *Neural Networks, 5*, 55–82.

Neill, W. T., Beck, J. L., Bottalico, K. S., and Molloy, R. D. (1990). Effects of intentional versus incidental learning on explicit and implicit tests of memory. *Journal of Experimental Psychology: Learning, Memory, and Cognition, 3*, 457–463.

Parkin, A. J., and Russo, R. (1990). Implicit and explicit memory and the automatic/effortful distinction. *European Journal of Cognitive Psychology, 2*, 41–80.

Phaf, R. H. (1991). *Learning in natural and connectionist systems*. Ph.D. diss., Leiden University. The Netherlands; also in press with Kluwer Academic Publishers.

Phaf, R. H., Van der Heijden, A. H. C., and Hudson, P. T. W. (1990). SLAM: A connectionist model for attention in visual selection tasks. *Cognitive Psychology, 22*, 273–341.

Phaf, R. H., and Wolters, G. (n.d.). *Spontane aanvulfrequenties voor 168 twee- en drieletterige woordstammen* (Spontaneous completion frequencies for 168 two- and three-letter word stems). In preparation.

Pinker, S. (1991). Rules of language. *Science, 253*, 530–535.

Posner, M. I., and Rothbart, M. J. (1992). Attentional mechanisms and conscious experience. In A. D. Milner and M. D. Rugg (Eds.), *The neuropsychology of consciousness*, 91–112. London: Academic Press.

Raccuglia, R. A., and Phaf, R. H. (1993). Asymmetric affective evaluation of words and faces. Internal report, University of Amsterdam.

Ratcliff, R. (1990). Connectionist models of recognition memory: Constraints imposed by learning and forgetting functions. *Psychological Review, 97*, 285–308.

Richardson-Klavehn, A., and Bjork, R. A. (1988). Measures of memory. *Annual Review of Psychology, 39*, 475–543.

Roediger, H. L. III, and Blaxton, T. A. (1987). Effects of varying modality, surface features, and retention interval on priming in word fragment completion. *Memory and Cognition, 15*, 379–388.

Roorda-Hrdlicková, V., Wolters, G., Bonke, B., and Phaf, R. H. (1990). Unconscious perception during general anaesthesia demonstrated by an implicit memory task. In B. Bonke, W. Fitch, and K. Millar (Eds.), *Memory and awareness in anaesthesia*, 150–155. Amsterdam: Swets and Zeitlinger.

Rumelhart, D. E., Hinton, G. E., and Williams, R. J. (1986). Learning internal representations by error propagation. In D. E. Rumelhart, J. L. McClelland, and the PDP Research Group (Eds.), *Parallel distributed processing. Explorations in the microstructure of cognition*, Vol. 1: Foundations 318–362. Cambridge MA: MIT Press.

Schacter, D. L., and Graf, P. (1989). Modality specificity of implicit memory for new associations. *Journal of Experimental Psychology: Learning, Memory, and Cognition, 15,* 3–12.

Servan-Schreiber, D., Cleeremans, A., and McClelland, J. L. (1991). Graded state machines: The representation of temporal contingencies in simple recurrent networks. *Machine Learning, 7,* 161–193.

Smith, M. E., and Oscar-Berman, M. (1990). Repetition priming of words and pseudowords in divided attention and in amnesia. *Journal of Experimental Psychology: Learning, Memory, and Cognition, 16,* 1033–1042.

# VII  Explicit and Implicit Learning

# 30 Implicit Learning: Twenty-Five Years on. A Tutorial

Dianne C. Berry

ABSTRACT  In recent years, a considerable debate has arisen over the extent to which cognitive tasks can be learned nonconsciously or implicitly. On one side of the debate, many studies have demonstrated a discrepancy between measured performance and explicit verbalizable knowledge (e.g., Reber 1989; Berry and Broadbent 1984, 1988; Willingham, Nissen, and Bullemer 1989). On the other side of the debate, however, a number of researchers have claimed that these discrepancies can be accounted for without resorting to the notion of implicit learning (e.g., Dulany, Carlson, and Dewey 1984; Perruchet and Pacteau 1990; Perruchet and Amorin 1992). Instead, they argue that the lack of explicit knowledge may be attributed to factors such as inadequate testing methods. This chapter reviews many of the studies that have contributed to the debate. In particular, it focuses on the three research paradigms that have generated the most research—artificial grammar learning, control of complex systems, and sequence learning. It concludes that although early claims about implicit learning need to be modified somewhat in the light of more recent evidence, we should not dismiss the concept altogether.

## 30.1  INTRODUCTION

It is twenty-five years since Arthur Reber published his paper, "Implicit Learning of Artificial Grammars." Since then, implicit learning has been investigated in a number of other experimental paradigms, including probability learning (Reber and Millward 1968, 1971), control of complex systems (Berry and Broadbent 1984, 1987, 1988; Stanley et al. 1989), serial reaction time (Nissen and Bullemer 1987; Hartman, Knopman, and Nissen 1989; Lewicki, Czyzewska, and Hoffman 1987), learning of conditional responses (Shanks, Green, and Kolodny, chap. 23, this volume), acquisition of invariant characteristics (McGeorge and Burton 1990), perceptual learning (Kolers and Roediger 1984), learning of perceptual categories (Jacoby and Brooks 1984), and second language acquisition (Ellis 1993). In recent years, however, a considerable debate has arisen over the extent to which cognitive tasks can, in fact, be learned nonconsciously or implicitly. A number of researchers have argued that the reported discrepancies between measured performance and explicit verbalizable knowledge can be accounted for without resorting to the notion of implicit learning.

This chapter reviews many of the studies that have contributed to this debate. Given the extent of work in this area, it is necessarily selective. It focuses on the three research paradigms that have generated the most research on implicit learning: artificial grammar learning, control of complex systems, and sequence learning. Before describing particular studies, however, it is necessary to clarify the use of the terms *implicit* and *explicit*, because some confusion has arisen in the literature. On the one hand, the implicit-explicit distinction has been used to refer to knowledge that has been acquired by a person. In general, explicit knowledge is said to be accessible to consciousness and can be communicated or demonstrated on demand, whereas implicit knowledge is said to be less accessible to consciousness and cannot easily be communicated or demonstrated on demand. On the other hand, the implicit-explicit distinction has been applied in a different way to methods of acquiring knowledge. Learning itself may be explicit, when deliberate strategies such as generating and testing hypotheses are used. It may also be implicit, when people learn to exploit the structure of an environment, without the use of conscious analytic strategies. Many researchers have failed to distinguish between these two uses of *implicit* and *explicit*. There has also been a tendency in the literature to focus on the implicit-explicit knowledge (rather than learning) distinction and to equate implicitly acquired knowledge with unconscious knowledge. In contrast, I argue here that it is necessary to separate methods of acquiring knowledge from the acquired knowledge itself and that less emphasis should be placed on the unconscious nature of implicitly acquired knowledge.

Finally, the implicit-explicit distinction has also been used in the context of memory tasks. Implicit, rather than explicit, memory is shown on tasks that do not require deliberate recollection of a past event, although the event influences performance. Research relating to implicit memory will not be discussed in this chapter. (Interested readers are referred to reviews by Schacter 1987; Lewandowski, Dunn, and Kirsner 1989; Roediger 1990; and Berry and Dienes 1991.)

## 30.2 EARLY STUDIES

### Artificial Grammar Learning

Reber's (1967) study is generally recognized as being the starting point for current work on artificial grammar learning. He showed that people become increasingly sensitive to the constraints of a synthetic grammar simply from exposure to exemplary strings. In the first part of his experiment, subjects were shown a series of letter strings that were generated by a finite state grammar. They were not told about the existence of the grammar and were told simply to memorize the letter strings. A control group of subjects were given random strings to learn. In the second phase of the experiment, subjects were told about the existence of the grammar and were given an unexpected classification task. They were given a new set of strings (half of them grammatical and half ungrammatical) and had to classify them as being grammatical or not. Reber found that subjects given grammatical strings to memorize in phase 1 showed superior memory performance to those given random strings.

More important, subjects given grammatical strings performed significantly above chance on the unexpected classification task, although they were unable to explain how they made their decisions or what the rules of the grammar might be.

This basic finding has been replicated and extended in a number of follow-on studies (Reber 1976; Reber and Lewis 1977; Reber and Allen 1978). Reber (1976), for example, compared the original neutral memorization procedure (the subjects simply memorized the letter strings and were then given the unexpected classification task) with one in which subjects were told during the memory phase that the strings conformed to certain grammatical rules. They were told that it might help them to memorize the strings better if they tried to work out the rules. Reber found that this explicit search instruction, as he called it, had a negative effect on performance on all aspects of the experiment. Subjects receiving the search instruction took longer to memorize the exemplars, were poorer at determining well-formedness of strings, and showed evidence of having induced rules that were not representative of the grammar. Reber concluded that explicit processing of complex materials had a decided disadvantage in relation to implicit processing. However, not all subsequent studies (Dulany, Carlson, and Dewey 1984) have replicated the negative effect of the explicit search instruction. Hence, it is probably safest to conclude that implicitly trained subjects do at least as well on subsequent attempts to discriminate between grammatical and ungrammatical strings as subjects who attempt to work out the rules explicitly. This conclusion is supported by a recent study by Mathews et al. (1989), who employed a more extreme manipulation of implicit versus explicit processing. In their "implicit" match task, subjects held single exemplars in memory only long enough to select the same item from a subsequent set of five items. They did not know that the items were generated by a grammar. They also had no opportunity or incentive for explicit abstraction of similarities among items. Yet their performance on a subsequent classification task was as good as that of subjects who carried out an explicit edit task in the learning phase, which involved the continuous generation and testing of rules for letter order.

**Control of Complex Systems**

The earliest studies looking at the implicit-explicit distinction in relation to the control of complex systems were carried out by Broadbent (1977) and Broadbent and Aston (1978). In the initial study, people took on the role of controller of a city transport system. Their task was to control the number of passengers using the buses and the number of empty car parking spaces by varying the time interval between buses and the car parking fee. The experiment was set up so that subjects were given starting values for all four variables and were asked to reach specified target values of bus load and number of parking spaces.

Broadbent found that although people improved in their ability to make the right decisions, they did not improve in their ability to answer questions about the relationships within the system on a posttask questionnaire. There was also no correlation between ability to control the system and scores on the questionnaire. He concluded that ability to control the system bore little connection to the ability to answer verbal questions about it. Broadbent and Aston (1978) noted a similar dissociation. They found that teams of managers making decisions on a model of the British economy improved in decision-making performance with practice. Yet individuals making up the team did not improve on multiple choice questions about the principles governing the economic model.

These early findings were extended and refined in two further studies (Berry and Broadbent 1984; Broadbent, FitzGerald, and Broadbent 1986). Berry and Broadbent devised two new tasks, sugar production and person interaction tasks, and examined the effects of task experience, verbal instruction, and concurrent verbalization. In the sugar production task, subjects took on the role of manager of a simple sugar production factory and were required to reach and maintain specified levels of sugar output by varying the number of workers employed. In the person interaction task, subjects were required to interact with a "computer person." The communication was based on a fixed set of adjectives describing various degrees of intimacy of personal interaction. Subjects were told to shift the behavior of the person to the very friendly level and to attempt to maintain it at that level. The tasks were mathematically identical. The equation relating sugar output to work force was the same as that relating the computer person's responses to those of the subject. The nature of the equation was such that there was not a unique output associated with any one input. In the case of sugar production, for example, the resulting sugar output depended on the previous sugar output, as well as the new work force figure. Following experience with the task, subjects were required to complete written questionnaires that asked about the relationships within the system. Typically, they were given a series of input and output values and were asked to predict the next output value (e.g., sugar output) given a new input value (e.g., work force).

The results were very similar for both tasks. In both cases, practice significantly improved ability to control these tasks, but had no effect on ability to answer posttask written questions. Subjects who had received sixty trials of practice were on target on an average of 80 percent of the final five trials. Despite this relatively high level of performance, their posttask questionnaire scores were no higher than those of subjects who had received either thirty trials of practice or no experience of the task at all. In contrast, detailed verbal instruction on how to reach and maintain the target value significantly improved ability to answer questions but had no effect on control performance. As well as these differential effects, there was also no evidence for a positive association between task performance and question answering. Individuals who were better at controlling the task were significantly worse at answering the questions. Berry and Broadbent concluded that these tasks might be performed in some implicit manner under certain conditions.

Broadbent, FitzGerald, and Broadbent (1986) came to a similar conclusion using the city transport system. They found that subjects improved in ability to control the tasks with practice but that there was not a corresponding increase in the number of correct answers to verbal questions about the system. They also found that verbal explanation had no effect on task performance (although the verbal explanation simply consisted of presenting the written questionnaire with the correct answers filled in) and that there was no correlation between control performance and question answering. In a second experiment, these authors used a simplified version of Broadbent and Aston's economic model. Again, they found evidence of performance improving with practice and question answering not doing so, and also of question answering improving under various treatments but performance not doing so.

One criticism of the Berry and Broadbent and Broadbent, FitzGerald, and Broadbent studies is that the questions used in the posttask questionnaires may not have been appropriate to the particular ideas of the people learning to control the systems. The subjects might have had knowledge that was relevant to controlling the tasks but was not tested by the questions. Berry (1991), however, used a number of question types and still found evidence for a dissociation. For example, the original questionnaire presented people with a series of input and output values and asked them to predict the new state of the output variable given a new input value. Berry (1991) also worded questions such that subjects were again given a series of input and output values but were asked which input value would be needed to bring the output value to target. Although this is more in line with what is required while controlling the task, performance was not better on these "estimated input questions."

Furthermore, Stanley et al. (1989) asked people to practice at either the sugar production or person interaction task and then to explain verbally to somebody else how to control it. Although in this case people could choose their own form of words, their own performance improved before they could tell somebody else how to succeed. Individual learning curves associated with the tasks showed sudden improvements in performance that were not accompanied by a similar increase in verbalizable knowledge. Stanley et al. suggested that there is a considerable difference between the amount of time it takes to acquire verbalizable knowledge and knowledge used to perform the control tasks. Subjects tend to become quite skilled in controlling the tasks long before there is much gain in verbalizable knowledge.

**Sequence Learning**

Early studies in this area focused on two main tasks: the serial reaction time (RT) task initiated by Nissen and Bullemer (1987) and the matrix scanning task initiated by Lewicki and colleagues (Lewicki, Czyzewska, and Hoffman 1987). (Studies using Kushner, Cleeremans, and Reber's 1991 explicit sequence prediction task are reviewed in chap. 32 by Perruchet and chap. 31 by Cleeremans, this volume.)

Nissen and Bullemer (1987) used a serial RT task in which a light appeared at one of four locations (arranged horizontally) on a video monitor (see also Shanks, Green, and Kolodny, chap. 33, this volume). Subjects were required to press the one key, out of four keys, that was directly below the position of the light. The sequence of lights was either determined randomly or appeared in a repeating ten-trial sequence. The results showed a rapid decrease in RT with training in the repeating sequence condition but not in the random condition. Furthermore, when subjects in the repeating condition were switched to a random sequence, RT increased substantially. The majority of subjects in the repeating sequence condition reported noticing the sequence, and some were able to describe parts of it spatially. This contrasts with the performance of a group of amnesic patients, who showed a similar pattern of performance to the normal subjects but were totally unaware of the existence of the repeating pattern.

In a follow-up study, Willingham, Nissen, and Bullemer (1989) attempted to determine whether there were normal subjects who demonstrated procedural learning of the sequence in the absence of explicit verbalizable knowledge of it. They identified two subgroups of subjects: unaware subjects, who either claimed they had not noticed that there was a pattern or failed to specify more than three positions of the sequence correctly, and aware subjects, who claimed to have noticed a pattern and could reproduce the sequence. Both groups showed substantial procedural learning of the sequence. In particular, the response times of the unaware group decreased by nearly 100 ms. Furthermore, their performance on a subsequent generate task was at the same level as that of control subjects who had not been exposed to the repeating sequence. The generate task involved displaying the repeating sequence but required subjects to predict the next stimulus position, rather than responding to the present stimulus position. (Hartman, Knopman, and Nissen 1989 reported similar findings with a verbal analogue of the serial RT task.)

Lewicki, Czyzewska, and Hoffman (1987) used a matrix scanning task, in which subjects had to indicate, by pressing a button, which of four quadrants on a monitor contained a target digit. The task was structured in blocks of seven trials. During the first six trials of each block, only the target appeared on the screen (hence, the search task was simple). On the seventh trial, the target was embedded in a field of thirty-five distractors, making search much more difficult. The experiment was set up so that four of the six "simple" trials (first, third, fourth, and sixth) predicted the location of the target on the seventh ("complex") trial. On the complex trials, twenty-four possible target locations were used, each associated with a unique sequence of simple trials. (Hence, the task was based on twenty-four rules, where a rule consisted of a series of six locations, two of them irrelevant.) In order to learn the relations between the simple and complex trials, subjects had to learn not only specific and relatively long sequences of target locations but also which particular trials should be attended to and which ignored.

After extensive training, Lewicki, Czyzewska, and Hoffman changed the relations between the simple and complex trials so that the target location on the complex trial was in the quadrant diagonally opposite its original location. The results showed that prior to this change, performance was improving slowly but steadily. When the change was made, however, large negative transfer effects were observed. Upon questioning, subjects were unable to report anything related to the underlying rules and denied awareness of their existence. These basic findings were replicated by Stadler (1989), who went on to investigate the issue of knowledge accessibility in more detail. Again, subjects showed substantial learning of the task with practice, but there was no evidence for any awareness of the underlying rules.

Lewicki, Hill, and Bizot (1988) reported similar findings to Lewicki, Czyzewska, and Hoffman (1987) using a modified version of the search task. In the 1988 version, the sequential structure of the material was manipulated to generate sequences of five elements according to a set of simple rules. Each rule defined where the next stimulus could appear as a function of the locations at which the two previous stimuli had appeared. The first two elements of each sequence were unpredictable, and the last three were determined by their predecessors. Lewicki, Hill, and Bizot (1988) reported a progressively widening difference between the number of fast and accurate responses, elicited by predictable and unpredictable trials, emerging with practice. They also found a sharp increase in response latencies when they altered the sequential structure of the stimuli. Again, when asked after the task, subjects failed to report having noticed any pattern in the sequence of exposures, and none even suspected that the sequential structure of the material had been manipulated.

The studies initiated by Nissen and colleagues and Lewicki and colleagues suggest that subjects can acquire knowledge about the sequential structure of stimuli without intending to do so and in such a way that the acquired knowledge is difficult to articulate.

## 30.3 CONDITIONS AND MODES OF LEARNING

Following these preliminary studies, it became apparent that rather than simply demonstrating (or in some cases denying) dissociations between performance and verbalizable knowledge, a more interesting approach is to look at the conditions that give rise to such dissociations. Some progress has been made in this direction, mostly in relation to artificial grammar learning and the control tasks. As far as artificial grammar learning is concerned, Reber et al. (1980) followed up Reber's (1976) study showing the negative effect of the explicit search instruction. Reber et al. found that the explicit search instruction interacted with what they termed structural salience, that is, the degree to which the critical patterns of letter ordering were obvious to subjects. They found that when the stimuli were presented in a structured display so that the rules for letter ordering were more obvious or salient, then the search instruction had a positive effect on grammar learning.

Salience has also been found to be a crucial factor in relation to the computer control tasks. In the case of the sugar production and person interaction tasks used by Berry and Broadbent (1984) and Stanley et al. (1989), the underlying relationship was relatively nonobvious. Berry and Broadbent (1988) reasoned that if the underlying relationship was made more obvious or salient, performance and verbalizable knowledge might be positively associated. We devised a pair of person interaction tasks to test out this suggestion. In both cases, each control action by the person produced an output from the system that depended only on that input and simply added a constant to it. In the salient case, the output appeared immediately; in the nonsalient case, it appeared only after the next input (that is, there was a lag). The results showed that in the case of the salient task, post-task questionnaire scores were high and positively associated with control performance, whereas in the case of the nonsalient version, post-task questionnaire scores were low and uncorrelated with control performance. Like Reber, we also found that salience interacted with the provision of an explicit search instruction. Telling people to search for the underlying rule had a detrimental effect on controlling the nonsalient person but a beneficial effect on controlling the salient person.

Further evidence for a distinction between implicit and explicit learning modes was provided by Hayes and Broadbent (1988) and Berry (1991). In the latter case it was found that the experience of watching another person interacting with the salient person control task had a beneficial effect on subsequent control performance with the same task, whereas experience of watching another person interacting with the nonsalient person control task had no beneficial effect on subsequent control performance.

On the basis of the 1988 results, Berry and Broadbent postulated two different possible modes of learning in complex situations where people have to acquire knowledge about the relationships between a number of variables without necessarily knowing in advance what the key variables are. We suggested that one mode is an implicit or unselective one in which a person observes the variables unselectively and stores the contingencies between them. The contingencies could be represented as a set of procedures or as some form of lookup table. In either case, a particular set of circumstances would give rise to a particular response. An alternative mode of learning was described as an explicit or selective one in which a few key variables are selected and only the contingencies between these key variables are stored. Provided that the correct variables are selected, this can be a fast and effective method of learning. It is also likely to result in knowledge that can be made explicit because of the relatively small number of relationships involved. However, if the task contains many variables and the wrong variables are selected, learning with this mode will do badly compared with the implicit one.

Hayes and Broadbent argued that the difference between the two modes of learning is an architectural one: each reflects the operation of different processes within the cognitive system. In line with this, they suggested that S-mode (or selective learning) involves the use of abstract working memory (Broadbent 1984), whereas U-mode (or unselective learning) does not. Instead, it involves the unselective and passive aggregation of information about the co-occurrence of environmental events and features. They also suggested that S-mode learning might interfere with U-mode learning when both are active simultaneously. More recent studies, however, have not supported this suggestion. In fact, Mathews et al. (1989) have demonstrated that explicit and implicit modes can interact positively when they occur simultaneously.

One difficulty with the Berry and Broadbent and Hayes and Broadbent conceptualizations centers around the notion of salience. Berry and Broadbent (1988) defined salience as the probability that if a person learns by the selective rather than the unselective mode, the key variables in the task will be chosen. We suggested a number of ways in which this probability could be increased, such as by reducing the number of irrelevant variables in a situation, by making the key events act in accordance with general knowledge from outside the task, or by making them happen at the same time rather than widely separated in time. Despite this, there is no independent means of defining salience in relation to particular tasks. The two person tasks devised by Berry and Broadbent (1988), for example, differ in many ways, most notably in terms of task difficulty. It could be differences on this, or some other factor, that lead to the pattern of results observed.

Even if the problem of salience could be overcome, I think that it is fair to say that we now see the notion of there being just two modes of learning as being a little extreme. Instead, we believe that it is more useful to think in terms of a number of different learning modes that fall along more of a continuum. These different learning modes, or styles, differ in the extent to which actions (or decisions) are driven by conscious beliefs. It also seems unlikely that each mode operates in isolation. Rather, performance in complex learning situations is likely to involve a subtle combination of implicit and explicit processes. Similarly, knowledge gained is likely to involve both implicit and explicit aspects rather than relying solely on one or the other. The particular balance will depend on such factors as the experimental instructions and the salience (however this is defined) of the crucial variables (Berry and Broadbent 1987).

## 30.4 CHALLENGES AND QUALIFICATIONS

The early studies on implicit learning aroused considerable interest but also a certain amount of skepticism. As far as artificial grammar learning is concerned, there have been two main areas of debate. The first concerns whether learning should be characterized as an unconscious abstraction process that gives rise to abstract knowledge. An alternative suggestion (Brooks and Vokey 1991; Vokey and Brooks 1992) is that during the string classification task, new items are classified as being valid or invalid depending on their similarity to items retrieved from memory (those seen during the original learning phase).

The second line of debate concerns the accessibility of implicitly acquired knowledge. Reber originally claimed that knowledge acquired during artificial grammar learning was completely unavailable to consciousness. More recently

(Reber 1989), he has modified his position to suggest that "knowledge acquired from implicit learning processes is knowledge that, in some raw fashion, is always ahead of the capability of its possessor to explicate it." However, other researchers (Perruchet and Pacteau 1990) believe that such modifications are insufficient and argue that there is no evidence that knowledge acquired during artificial grammar learning is implicit in nature. A similar debate has arisen in relation to the computer control and sequence learning tasks. In these fields also, original claims have been modified in the light of more recent evidence.

**Abstraction or Similarity-Based Processing?**

Studies attempting to provide evidence for implicit abstraction rather than for similarity-based processing have focused on the issue of transfer. An early study by Reber (1969) required subjects to memorize two sets of grammatical letter strings, one after the other. For some subjects, the letter strings in the second set were made up of the same letters as those in the first set, but the underlying rules were modified. For other subjects, the rules were the same, but the actual letters changed. Reber found that changing the rules had a disruptive effect on subjects' performance, but changing the letter set had no detrimental effect. More recently, Mathews et al. (1989) have also shown that subjects are fairly resilient to changes of letter set. Their experiment was run over a 4-week period. They found that subjects who each week received a new letter set based on the same underlying grammatical structure performed as well as subjects who worked with the same letter set throughout the experiment.

At first glance, it is difficult for similarity-based models to account for transfer across different letter sets. According to such accounts, classification performance should decline as a function of distance from training items. However, as Brooks and Vokey (1991) have pointed out, similarity-based models can account for transfer across different letter sets if it is assumed that transfer to "changed letter set" strings is due to abstract similarity between test strings and specific training stimuli. For example, a string such as *MXVVVM* could be seen as similar to *BDCCCB* in that both start and end with the same letter and have a repeated letter triplet next to the end. Hence, transfer to a different letter set could be due to reliance on abstract (relational) analogies to individual items, rather than to reliance on knowledge of the structure of the grammar abstracted across many training items.

Mathews et al. (n.d.) have recently attempted to distinguish between similarity and abstractionist theories. They suggest that the critical feature that distinguishes abstraction from similarity-based models is the selective weighting of relevant versus irrelevant features. According to abstractionist theories, it should be possible to find exceptions to the typical distance from training item effects reported by Brooks and Vokey (1991) and Vokey and Brooks (1992). That is, it should be possible to find transfer tasks in which many features of the stimuli are altered without loss in classification accuracy. Mathews et al. presented evidence in favor of abstractionist models from five artificial grammar learning experiments showing that implicit learning induces selective responding to category-relevant cues. Similarity to training item effects was found when changed features of training items were relevant (valid) cues for classification but not when irrelevant cues were changed to produce transfer items. Thus, the results could not be completely accounted for by the notion of similarity-based processing.

## The Accessibility of Implicitly Acquired Knowledge

Reber's original claim that knowledge acquired during artificial grammar learning is completely unconscious was based on subjects' post-task introspections. Subjects were able to classify new strings as being grammatical or not with a greater than chance accuracy but were not able to describe how they did this or on what basis they were making their decisions. However, it soon became apparent that Reber's original claim was, at the least, an oversimplification. Studies in his own laboratory (Reber and Lewis 1977; Reber and Allen 1978) showed that subjects could report some of what they knew. For example, Reber and Allen reported that "specific aspects of letter strings were often cited as important in decision making.... First and last letters, bigrams, the occasional trigams and recursions were mentioned" (p. 202). Unfortunately, Reber and Allen did not analyze subjects' verbal reports in such as way as to be able to predict performance levels.

More recent investigators have adopted more systematic approaches to assess whether subjects' verbalizable knowledge can account for their classification performance. Mathews et al. (1989), for example, used the teach-back technique, in which subjects were asked to provide instructions for an unseen partner. The experiment was set up so that subjects first briefly studied a set of exemplars and then classified for 600 trials with feedback. After each ten-trial block, subjects were asked to provide instructions for an unseen partner on how to classify the strings. The transcribed instructions were subsequently given to yoked control subjects, who were then tested on the same classification task. Mathews et al. found that although the yoked control subjects performed significantly above chance and improved across blocks in the same manner as the original experimental subjects, their performance remained behind that of the experimental subjects, at roughly half their level of accuracy. However, as Dienes, Broadbent, and Berry (1991) have pointed out, there are some problems with using yoked subjects to assess the validity of the rules stated by experimental subjects. If the instructions contain exemplars, or parts of exemplars, implicit learning on the yoked subjects' part may lead to an overestimation of the explicit rule content of the instructions. Conversely, application errors by the yoked subjects may lead to an underestimation of the validity of the instructions.

Dienes, Broadbent, and Berry (1991) employed a more direct method of assessing the validity of rules elicited in free recall. In this study, subjects were exposed to grammatical strings for 10 min and then made 100 classification decisions. They were then asked to describe as fully as possible the rules or strategy they used to classify. Dienes, Broadbent, and Berry used the elicited rules to simulate classification performance. It was found that simulated performance (53 percent) was considerably less than that of actual classification performance (63 percent). Hence, as with the Mathews et al. study, not all of subjects' classification knowledge could be elicited with free recall.

Other investigators have argued that free-recall measures are insufficiently sensitive and have applied a variety of forced-choice measures in order to assess classification knowledge. Dulany, Carlson, and Dewey (1984), for example, asked subjects during the classification task to underline that part of a string that "made it right" if it was grammatical or that part that violated the rules if it was classified as ungrammatical. They then analyzed the extent to which the rules implied by subjects' underlinings could be used to classify strings as valid or invalid. They found that the induced rules were sufficient to account for the full set of classification decisions made and argued that knowledge of the grammar must therefore be held consciously. However, the interpretation of this study has been challenged by Reber and colleagues (and will be returned to below).

Another line of attack has come from Perruchet and Pacteau (1990). They have argued that exposure to grammatical strings results in little more than knowledge of particular pairs of letters or bigrams that occur in the grammar. Their claim is based on two main findings. First, subjects exposed to pairs of letters rather than whole strings in phase 1 of the experiment performed just as well on the subsequent classification task as did subjects who were presented with the whole strings (provided that strings beginning with an illegal first letter were excluded from the analysis). Second, in a separate experiment, subjects were exposed to complete exemplars and were asked to rate isolated bigrams for their legitimacy. It was found that they were able to do so with above-chance accuracy and that their ratings could predict observed classification performance without error. Although it is clear that subjects undoubtedly did acquire appreciable bigram knowledge in this study, other studies show that subjects do learn more than just bigrams (see, for example, Mathews 1990).

Finally, Dienes, Broadbent, and Berry (1991) employed a new knowledge test (the sequential letter dependency, or SLD, test) in which subjects were asked which letters could occur after different stems varying in length from zero letters upward. The SLD test differs from Perruchet and Pacteau's bigram rating task in that it allows an assessment of subjects' knowledge of positional dependence of bigrams. Perruchet and Pacteau (experiment 2) showed that subjects can use such knowledge of positional dependence in making classification decisions. Hence, it is important to see whether this information can be elicited out of context of particular exemplars. These authors found a positive correlation between classification performance and ability to answer the SLD test (whereas they found no correlation between classification performance and free report). More important, there was a close match between classification performance and predicted performance that was based on answers to the

SLD test. Hence, the results of this study were in line with those of Perruchet and Pacteau. They also extend Perruchet and Pacteau's results in showing that subjects' knowledge of positional dependence of bigrams could be elicited out of context of particular exemplars.

The various findings together seem to make clear that there is no evidence to support Reber's original claim that knowledge acquired during artificial grammar learning is completely unconscious. If accessibility is judged in terms of performance on free-recall tests, then there is evidence to support Reber's more recent view that knowledge acquired from implicit learning processes is knowledge that is always ahead of the capability of its possessor to explicate it. The difficulty arises when interpreting the findings of the forced-choice tests. If forced-choice tests are viewed as measuring explicit knowledge, then even Reber's modified position seems questionable. However, the interpretation of the results of forced-choice tests is still a matter of considerable debate and will be returned to after looking at evidence for the accessibility of implicitly acquired knowledge in relation to the computer control and sequence learning tasks.

**Accessibility of Control Task Knowledge**

The debate over the accessibility of implicitly acquired knowledge has been less extensive in relation to the computer control tasks, but there have been a number of new findings that require some of the earlier claims to be modified. First, Stanley et al. (1989) have shown that dissociations between task performance and associated verbalizable knowledge are not as complete as was at first thought. Stanley et al. asked subjects to practice at either the sugar production or personal interaction task and then to describe to somebody else how to control it. They found that although there was a marked dissociation between performance and verbalizable knowledge at moderate levels of practice, highly experienced subjects (570 trials) were able to give verbal statements that helped novices to perform more successfully. Stanley et al. suggested that people draw on two separate but interacting knowledge structures to perform these tasks, one based on memory for past experiences (close analogies) and the other based on one's current mental model of the task. Implicit sets of competing rules that control response selection are derived from both sources of knowledge. They suggested that dissociations between task performance and verbalizing occur because memory-based processing tends to have more control over response selection because of its greater specificity, whereas a mental model tends to be the preferred mode for verbal reporting because of its greater accessibility.

McGeorge and Burton (1989) also used a teach-back method (getting subjects to provide instructions for the next subject) to elicit verbalizable knowledge after performance on the sugar production task. Rather than presenting the elicited instructions to subsequent subjects, however, they used them to develop computer simulations of subjects' control performance. Comparisons were then made between simulated performance and observed performance.

Using this method, McGeorge and Burton found that about one-third of their subjects reported heuristics that resulted in simulated performances that were either equivalent to or better than observed performance. Hence, after ninety trials of practice, some subjects were able to produce accurate verbal statements. McGeorge and Burton suggested that this may reflect the initial stages of development of a mental model.

Marescaux, Luc, and Karnas (1989), again using the sugar production task, demonstrated that subjects know more about situations that they have personally experienced. Their experiment was set up so that subjects interacted with the sugar production task for two sets of thirty trials and then answered a number of posttask questions. The questions, matched closely to the task, required subjects to estimate how many workers would be needed to reach target in different situations, and they were presented on the computer so that subjects saw just what they might have seen on the full task. The questions varied along two basic dimensions: (1) the target sugar output was either the same as or different from that experienced while controlling the task, and (2) the mini-history given to subjects at the start of each question was taken from either their own immediately preceding interaction or a hypothetical interaction. The results showed superior questionnaire performance when subjects had to reach the same target as they had experienced while interacting with the task and when the minihistories were taken from their own past experience. The key factor seemed to be that subjects were tested on specific situations that they themselves had experienced while interacting with the task. They did not seem to have learned anything that could be used in other novel situations.

Finally, Sanderson (1989) reported associations between performance and verbalizable knowledge under certain conditions, using Broadbent, FitzGerald, and Broadbent's (1986) city transport task. She suggested that the combination of high levels of practice with a larger solution space (in this case, produced by requiring decimal precision as opposed to integer values) is particularly important in bringing positive associations out. She also stressed the weakness of assessing verbalizable knowledge solely by means of posttask questionnaire (as in other studies). Instead, she advocated use of a mental models analysis technique in which subjects' question answers are compared with those that would be produced by a number of different mental models. She suggested that such a mental models analysis makes it clear that verbal knowledge can show a distinct change before it is reflected in raw questionnaire score.

Taken together, the studies by Stanley et al., McGeorge and Burton, Marescaux et al., and Sanderson suggest that the dissociation between task performance and associated verbalizable knowledge may not be as complete as was at first thought. People appear to develop some explicit knowledge as a result of task experience. The evidence seems to indicate, however, that increases in explicit knowledge occur after improvements in task performance and that this knowledge may be largely limited to knowledge of specific personally experienced situations.

## Knowledge of Sequential Structure

A number of investigators (Perruchet, Gallego, and Savy 1990; Perruchet and Amorin 1992; Shanks, Green, and Kolodny, chap. 33, this volume) have recently argued against the evidence for the acquisition of implicit knowledge in sequence learning tasks. They have suggested that improvements in performance on such tasks can be accounted for without resorting to the notion of nonconscious processing.

As far as the studies initiated by Nissen and Bullemer are concerned, Perruchet and Amorin (1992) have identified a number of problems with the generate task. In this task, the stimulus is displayed until the subject makes the correct prediction for the next trial, although in some experiments (Cohen, Ivry, and Keele 1990) it is displayed at its correct location after the subject's response, whether correct or not. Perruchet and Amorin put forward two specific criticisms: that the instructions given to subjects before the generate task did not mention that subjects should reproduce prior sequences and that there were problems with the correction procedure. Perruchet and Amorin therefore modified the generate task in two ways: they changed the instructions to emphasize the relation between study and test phase and did not provide feedback on response accuracy. Using this modified test, they found that subjects could acquire conscious knowledge of substantial portions of the repeating sequence after only two 100-trial blocks of training. In a second experiment, in addition to the generate task, Perruchet and Amorin assessed knowledge using a recognition procedure of the 4-trial chunks composing the repeating sequence. As in their artificial grammar learning studies, they found that subjects could recognize chunks that did follow the constraints of the training stimuli. (See also Shanks, Green, and Kolodny, chap. 33, this volume.)

Perruchet, Gallego, and Savy's (1990) criticisms have focused on the Lewicki, Hill, and Bizot (1988) study. They have argued that the latter findings can be accounted for without suggesting that subjects acquire tacit knowledge of the composition rules and that subjects partition the sequence into logical blocks of five trials. Rather, they suggested that the results could be explained by the relative frequency of a few simple sequences of target locations. Perruchet, Gallego, and Savy focused on the nature of the "movement" of the target from one location to the next rather than on the location of targets per se (which Lewicki, Hill, and Bizot were careful to equalize for each quadrant). They suggested that frequent and infrequent movements were not equally distributed over the predictable and unpredictable trials. In particular, infrequent movements occurred mainly in unpredictable trials, hence giving rise to longer RTs. They used a similar argument to account for the increase in RTs when the sequential structure was changed in the latter part of the experiment.

Perruchet, Gallego, and Savy carried out an extended replication of the Lewicki, Hill, and Bizot experiment and found that their alternative explanation accounted for many finely grained features of subjects' performance. They confirmed that differences in RT on the first two and last three trials of each logical block of five trials could be attributed to the relative frequency of particular target transitions throughout the experiment. Subjects reacted more slowly to infrequent events, which as a consequence of the composition rules tended to be located in the first two trials of each block. Perruchet, Gallego, and Savy suggested that one of the main pieces of knowledge underlying performance was that the target tended to move through all its possible locations before returning to a previously occupied one. Importantly, this knowledge was available to subjects, as assessed by a subsequent explicit prediction test.

Taken together, the studies by Perruchet and colleagues, and Shanks, Green, and Kolodny suggest that evidence for implicit learning of sequential structure may not be as convincing as was at first thought. In some cases, subjects have more explicit knowledge available than had previously been believed. In other cases, the results could be accounted for without resorting to the notion of implicit learning at all.

## 30.5 AN ATTEMPTED SYNTHESIS

Putting the various findings together, it seems clear that knowledge arising from artificial grammar learning or from interacting with the control or sequence learning tasks cannot be fully elicited by free recall (particularly in the early stages of learning). These findings could be taken as evidence that learning on such tasks gives rise to a relatively specific knowledge base that cannot be tapped by free report. However, as other researchers (Brewer 1974; Brody 1989) have argued, free recall is a relatively insensitive and incomplete measure. Poor performance on free-recall tests may simply reflect the problem of having to retrieve large amounts of low-confidence knowledge rather than reflecting a deeper incompatibility between the mechanisms employed in free recall and the type of knowledge stored.

This possibility has led some investigators to employ forced-choice tests in order to assess acquired knowledge. Whereas free report gives subjects the option of not responding, forced-choice measures do not. Indeed, the results of experiments using a variety of such tests show that grammar learning knowledge, and to some extent control task knowledge (Berry and Broadbent 1987) and knowledge of sequential structure (Perruchet and Amorin 1992), can be elicited using forced-choice measures. The problem comes, however, when interpreting the results of such tests. Dulany, Carlson, and Dewey (1984) and Perruchet and Pacteau (1990) use these tests to measure explicit knowledge but, as Dienes, Broadbent, and Berry (1991) have recently pointed out, there are problems with this approach. In particular, it is far from clear whether forced-choice tests should be considered as measuring explicit or implicit knowledge.

The problem of the interpretation of forced-choice tests stems from another problem in this area: the failure of authors (including ourselves) to define what they mean by terms like *implicit* or *unconscious*. In terms of the artificial grammar learning debate, both Reber and Dulany use the term *conscious* in different ways. Broadbent has made this point in a recent theoretical paper (Broadbent 1992). Reber believes that Dulany's underlining task and Perruchet's bigrams task are tests of implicit or unconscious knowledge. He suggests, for example, that subjects' underlinings could be the result of vague guesses that could be made on the basis of implicit knowledge. In contrast, Dulany, Carlson, and Dewey (1984) seem to believe that data can be called unconscious only if they can never reveal themselves by any event that the person can report. According to them, if people can correctly underline key letters, an act of which they are conscious, then that knowledge cannot be unconscious. The trouble is that neither side gives a good account of what they mean by unconscious or implicit, and neither presents adequate criteria for deciding if a test is of implicit or explicit knowledge. Dulany, Carlson, and Dewey and Perruchet and Pacteau have used their results as evidence that there should be no distinction between implicit and explicit. Yet is this the most profitable way forward?

It is interesting to note that not all learning tasks are associated with impoverished free report. Indeed, Mathews et al. (1988) reported a series of experiments, using the Bouthilet concept discovery task, in which classification knowledge was adequately elicited by free report. Similarly, not all learning tasks are associated with relatively passive learning conditions. Explicit, or conscious, hypothesis testing is a necessary ingredient in many learning situations. Even within the area of grammar learning, Mathews et al. (1989) found that learning a biconditional grammar (but not a finite state grammar) was impaired by incidental rather than intentional learning conditions. Hence, there may well be other grounds for distinguishing between implicit and explicit knowledge, and between implicit and explicit learning, rather than relying solely on the thorny question of consciousness.

Considerations such as these have recently led Berry and Dienes (1991, 1993) to put forward the following working characterization of implicit learning, in that we believe it to be associated with the following features:

1. Shows transfer specificity: relative inaccessibility of knowledge with free recall (Dienes, Broadbent, and Berry 1991; Stanley et al. 1989), limited accessibility of knowledge with forced-choice tests (Dulany, Carlson, and Dewey 1984; Berry and Broadbent, 1987), and limited transfer to related tasks (Berry and Broadbent 1988; Willingham, Nissen, and Bullemer 1989).

2. Tends to be associated with incidental learning conditions rather than with deliberate hypothesis testing (Reber 1976; Berry and Broadbent 1988).

3. Gives rise to a phenomenal sense of intuition (Reber 1967; Berry and Broadbent 1984).

4. Remains relatively robust in the face of time (Allen and Reber 1980), psychological disorders (Abrams and Reber 1989), and secondary tasks (Cohen, Ivry, and Keele 1990).

These four features are important because they are associated with certain conditions of learning. Any argument against an implicit-explicit distinction on the grounds that subjects can underline key features in strings, or can rate bigrams, is therefore begging the question of why certain learning conditions are associated with these features. Why, for example, are some learning tasks associated with passive learning conditions whereas others are not? Why does learning in some situations give rise to knowledge that is highly context bound and difficult to express or demonstrate, whereas in other situations it gives rise to knowledge that can be characterized as being context free, symbolic and manipulable? As Berry and Broadbent suggested in 1988, and Reber in 1989, we still need to identify the key factors that give rise to the different types of learning and the different types of knowledge.

## 30.6 THE FUTURE OF IMPLICIT LEARNING

So what does the future look like for implicit learning? Will it continue to be a flourishing research area for the next twenty-five years, or will interest gradually fade away as more and more counterevidence is put forward? At this stage, it is difficult to predict its ultimate fate, but recent advances in three areas—computational modeling, neuropsychology, and some even more recent experimental studies—suggest that interest will continue for some time to come.

### Computational Modeling

A possible limitation of the human experimental studies is that they have tended to ignore the question of knowledge representation. They have also tended to focus on what subjects do not know or have not learned rather than what they have learned. A possible benefit of computational modeling studies is that they can tell us more about what people have learned and can indicate what sorts of mechanisms could produce the patterns of results obtained in the experiments.

Some interesting advances have been made in this area, particularly in relation to artificial grammar learning. A number of recent studies are described below. Computational models of performance on the control tasks can be found in Dienes (1990) and Dienes and Fahey (n.d.). Modeling of Kushner, Cleeremans, and Reber's (1991) sequence prediction task is described by Cleeremans (chap. 31, this volume).

As far as artificial grammar learning is concerned, Dienes (1992) attempted to model grammar learning using a range of connectionist and exemplar models. The data used to evaluate the models was taken from Dienes, Broadbent, and Berry (1991) and Dulany, Carlson, and Dewey (1984). Dienes found that the only model to pass all of the set criteria was a connectionist simultaneous delta rule model. He argued that this class of model can be regarded as abstracting a set of representative but incomplete rules of the grammar. Cleeremans and McClelland (1991) have also recently applied a connectionist model to the learning of finite state grammars. They used the recursive network model of Elman (1990), incorporating hidden units, to model sequential learning of a noisy finite state grammar in an RT paradigm. They found that with an augmented version of the model, the match to subject data was good; the model could account for 81 percent of variance in subject data.

Other approaches to modeling artificial grammar learning include the THIYOS classifier system of Druhan and Mathews (1989) and the competitive chunking model of Servan-Schreiber and Anderson (1990). Classifier systems are a generic learning mechanism, discussed in detail by Holland et al. (1986). They involve a large number of rules, or classifiers, that post messages on a message list. Different classifiers can be given different priorities by tuning their strengths. Druhan and Mathews (1989) embodied the rules given in the instructions of Mathews et al.'s "original" subjects (see above) in classifiers of equal strengths. When there was no tuning, THIYOS (using these classifiers) classified as well as the yoked subjects but not as well as the original subjects themselves. When the rules were maximally tuned, THIYOS classified better than the yoked subjects and about as well as the original ones. Druhan and Mathews concluded that the original subjects could verbalize the rules they were using; what they did not verbalize was the relative priority given to the different rules (their strengths).

A particularly influential approach to modeling artificial grammar learning is the competitive chunking model of Servan-Shreiber and Anderson (1990), which models perception and memory as a process of successive chunk formation. As well as their content, chunks have an associated strength parameter that reflects how frequently and recently they have been used. According to this approach, a letter string is first analyzed into its elementary chunks. Different higher-level chunks then compete to represent the stimulus until it has been parsed to its highest level. Servan-Shreiber and Anderson successfully applied their competitive chunking model to subjects' memorization and classification performance. On the basis of their results, they suggested that the content of the chunks may be available to consciousness but that the strength and support (given by average strength of its subchunks) may well not be. Hence, as with the THIYOS model, there is some content available to consciousness. The implicit knowledge seems to be in the pattern of strengths determining what content is made available to consciousness.

**Neuropsychological Studies**

The second reason for feeling optimistic about the future of implicit learning comes from neuropsychological studies. Recently there has been a large number of studies of neuropsychological patients that support the notion of a distinction between implicit and explicit processing (see Schacter, McAndrews, and Moscovitch 1988 and Milner and Rugg 1992 for reviews). Studies have demonstrated that patients with various lesions and deficits frequently show implicit knowledge of stimuli that they cannot explicitly perceive, identify, or process semantically. This pattern of normal or near-normal performance on implicit tests, compared with severely impaired performance on explicit tests, has been observed in patients suffering from blindsight (Weiskrantz 1986, 1990), alexia (Shallice and Saffran 1986; Coslett and Saffran

1989), prosopagnosia (Young and DeHaan 1988, 1990), neglect (Marshall and Halligan 1988; Bisiach 1992), amnesia (Graf, Squire, and Mandler 1984; Squire and Frambach 1990; Knowlton, Ramus, and Squire 1992), aphasia (Milberg and Blumstein 1981; Tyler 1992), and agnosia (Margolin, Friedrich, and Carbon 1983; Humphreys et al. 1992).

In the case of amnesia, recent experiments have tested patients on Berry and Broadbent's sugar production task (Squire and Frambach 1990), Reber's artificial grammar learning task (Knowlton, Ramus, and Squire 1992), and Nissen and Bullemer's serial RT task (Nissen and Bullemer 1987; Willingham, Nissen, and Hartman 1989). In the former case, Squire and Frambach examined whether amnesiac patients could learn to control, and answer questions about, the sugar production task at the same level as normal subjects. Their experiment was set up so that patients and control subjects interacted with the task for ninety trials and then completed a sixteen-item questionnaire. The questionnaire was divided into three sections: simple factual questions, general strategy questions, and specific strategy questions (similar to those used by Berry and Broadbent 1984).

Squire and Frambach found that the amnesiacs performed just as well as the control subjects in an initial training session. However, in a second session (approximately 27 days later), they performed significantly worse than the controls. By this stage of practice, Squire and Frambach suggested, the normal control subjects were starting to build up explicit knowledge that could be used to improve performance still further. The amnesiacs, in contrast, were not able to do this. Questionnaire results showed that control subjects scored significantly better on the factual questions, and to some extent on the general strategy questions, but at the same level as the amnesiac patients on the specific strategy questions. Hence, the results are in line with the earlier suggestion that dissociations between performance and verbalizable knowledge, while still evident, are not complete.

Knowlton, Ramus, and Squire (1992) have also recently found support for implicit learning of artificial grammars. They investigated whether ability to classify on the basis of rules can be learned independent of memory for specific instances used to teach the rules. They suggested that if ability to make classification decisions depends on the use of imperfectly formed rules or direct comparisons with stored exemplars, the amnesiac patients should perform more poorly. In their experiment, patients and control subjects studied a set of grammatical letter strings, followed by the usual classification test. In a second session, approximately 45 days after the first, they studied grammatical exemplars from another grammar and then carried out a yes-no recognition task. Finally, in a third session, approximately 30 days after the recognition test, patients and control subjects were given a set of study strings taken from the original grammar and were then given a second classification test but were told to base their classification decision on explicit comparisons with original exemplars.

The authors found that the amnesic patients performed as well as the normal control subjects on the initial classification task. However, they performed more poorly than the controls in the yes-no recognition test and in the final classification test, where they had to base decisions on explicit comparisons with original exemplars. They suggested that the finding that amnesiac patients perform as well as normal subjects on the initial classification task suggests that implicitly acquired information is adequate for grammatical classification.

Finally, Nissen and Bullemer (1987) tested amnesiac patients on their serial RT task. They found that the amnesiacs performed at the same level as a group of age-matched controls. That is, they showed the same improvement in RT with the repeating sequence and the same slowing upon transfer to the random sequence. Importantly, none of the amnesiacs reported that they had noticed the repeating pattern, whereas many of the normal controls did. These results were replicated by Willingham, Nissen, and Bullemer (1989), who also tested performance on the repeating sequence 1 week later. Neither group demonstrated forgetting across the 1-week delay.

Not all syndromes have been investigated as thoroughly as amnesia as far as implicit learning is concerned. In fact, the amount of evidence bearing on implicit-explicit dissociations varies considerably from syndrome to syndrome. It ranges from isolated, almost anecdotal findings to systematic, well-replicated studies. However, as Schacter, McAndrews, and Moscovitch (1988) noted, there is an impressive generality to the available findings. Similar patterns of results have been observed across different patient groups, experimental tasks, types of information, and perceptual-cognitive processes.

Considering all of the syndromes together, it seems uncertain whether the observed implicit-explicit dissociations can be accounted for by a single common mechanism (Schacter, McAndrews, and Moscovitch 1988). Our level of understanding is not sufficiently advanced to make such a claim. However, in the current context, evidence from neuropsychological studies does add considerable weight to the importance of implicit processing.

## Experimental Studies

Although many of the recent experiments have been aimed at countering early claims about implicit learning and knowledge, a number of new studies have produced findings that shed positive light on the distinctions between implicit and explicit modes of learning and implicit and explicit types of knowledge. These studies not only provide interesting results but also suggest directions for future research. In terms of sequence learning, a number of recent studies have suggested that implicitly acquired knowledge of sequential structure may have distinct properties of storage and retrieval; For example, using a dual-task procedure, Cohen, Ivry, and Keele (1990) provided evidence for a double dissociation between performance on the RT and generation task. Similarly, Howard, Mutter, and Howard (1992) showed that subjects who initially observed the sequence subsequently responded just as fast as subjects who responded to the sequence from the beginning. However, observation rather than responding led to superior generation performance, indicating a further dissociation between generation and RT.

In terms of the control tasks, Dienes and Fahey (n.d.) have recently conducted one of the few studies that has directly addressed the question of knowledge representation. They asked whether implicit learning of the control tasks is mediated by a lookup table consisting of implicit memory of previously successful trials on the task. Their experiments were similar to those of Marescaux, Luc, and Karnas, in that subjects interacted with Berry and Broadbent's (1984) sugar production task and were then presented with a series of old and new situations (e.g., "If you had just employed 400 workers and if the sugar production was then 8000 tons, what should you do next to bring the sugar production to target?"). However, Dienes and Fahey added an interesting extra question in that they asked subjects whether they could explicitly recognize the situations.

Like Marescaux, Luc, and Karnas, Dienes and Fahey found that subjects performed best on old situations in which they had previously been successful and that subjects were consistent in their responding to a situation for which they were previously correct. This consistency was greater than a chance baseline, and there was also some evidence that consistency for correct situations was greater than that for incorrect situations. An important finding was that there was no relation between correct responses on the old correct situations and subjects' ability to recognize them as old. This suggests that any lookup table would not be based on explicit memory.

Finally, in terms of artificial grammar learning, Chan (1992) has adapted Reber's paradigm in two interesting ways. In his first set of studies, he used nonverbal symbols rather than letters as the elements in the grammar, and in his second set of experiments, he used semantic meaningful stimuli (database commands) as the elements in the grammar. With these two adaptations, Chan replicated Reber's basic finding that learning can occur in the absence of conscious intention to learn and that acquired knowledge cannot be fully elicited by free report. He also found that much knowledge could be elicited using a bigrams test and a modification of Dienes's SLD test.

Chan went on to perform a number of experimental manipulations and carried out some very finely grained analyses of the data. Contrary to Perruchet and Pacteau (1990), he provided converging evidence for a dissociation between classification and bigrams knowledge. Most interesting, by carrying out an analysis of confidence ratings, he showed that subjects were sensitive to the accuracy of their responses on the bigrams test, but this was not so for the classification test.

Following on from this analysis of confidence ratings, Chan has put forward a confidence accuracy slope (CAS) theory that incorporates a computational index, the CAS value. The CAS value is the slope of the standardized regression line on subjects' self-reported confidence rating and the accuracy of performance on a test. More simply, it can be thought of as the correlation between subjective confidence and objective accuracy. Chan suggests that the index can be used as a criterion for deciding whether performance is implicit or explicit. Implicit processes usually produce a CAS value of zero, and explicit processes usually produce a CAS value of greater than zero. One reason that this measure is interesting is that it can be used to distinguish between different types of performance that might be viewed as being the same on the basis of other measures. For example, Chan has shown that different forms of training (e.g., bigrams versus whole exemplars) can give rise to equal levels of classification knowledge but to different relationships between confidence and accuracy.

Chan's CAS theory is intriguing and warrants further investigation. It is interesting to note that Chan found a difference between making the right decision and having the further knowledge that the decision is correct, just as Dienes and Fahey found a difference between having the right knowledge to act correctly in a specific situation and having the further knowledge that one has seen that situation before. Future experiments should extend Chan's research to see whether similar effects are found using other measures of confidence/feeling of knowing, and whether similar patterns of correlations are observed using paradigms other than artificial grammar learning. Given the considerable problems of interpreting measures of knowledge, it is important to know whether the correlation between confidence and accuracy is a reliable measure of degree of explicitness.

## 30.7 CONCLUSION

What can we conclude about implicit learning after twenty-five years of research? Reber himself concluded in 1989 that "a considerable portion of memorial content is unconscious and, even more important, a goodly amount of knowledge acquisition takes place in the absence of intent to learn." In line with Reber, this chapter has also advocated that it is necessary to separate methods of acquiring knowledge from the acquired knowledge itself and has described a number of studies that support the notion of distinguishing between different modes, or styles, of learning. However, contrary to Reber, it has advocated that less emphasis should be placed on the unconscious nature of implicitly acquired knowledge. Many of the studies reviewed here indicate that implicitly acquired knowledge is more available to consciousness than was originally thought. This is not to suggest that there are no grounds for distinguishing between different types of knowledge. Rather, given the problems of assessing implicitly acquired knowledge and interpreting the results of the different knowledge measures, a more profitable approach might be to see whether such knowledge can be distinguished on other grounds. For example, does it have different properties of storage and retrieval (Dienes, Broadbent, and Berry 1991; Dienes and Fahey, n.d.), and does it give rise to different correlations between performance and confidence (Chan 1992)? At present, it is difficult, and probably unnecessary, to make a firm conclusion about what proportion of implicitly acquired knowledge will ultimately prove to be unconscious. One thing that is certain, however, is that there are sufficient remaining questions to keep researchers busy for another twenty-five years.

My personal view is that 1992 should be viewed as a silver anniversary rather than as a funeral. While earlier accounts of implicit learning and knowledge may need to be modified in the light of current evidence, there is no reason to dismiss the concepts altogether.

## NOTE

I am very grateful to Donald Broadbent, Axel Cleeremans, Pierre Perruchet, and Morris Moscovitch for their helpful comments on an earlier draft of this chapter.

## REFERENCES

Abrams, M., and Reber, A. S. (1989). Implicit learning in special populations. *Journal of Psycholinguistic Research, 17*, 425–439.

Allen, R., and Reber, A. S. (1980). Very long term memory for tacit knowledge. *Cognition, 8*, 175–185.

Berry, D. C. (1991). The role of action in implicit learning. *Quarterly Journal of Experimental Psychology, 43*, 881–906.

Berry, D. C., and Broadbent, D. E. (1984). On the relationship between task performance and associated verbalisable knowledge. *Quarterly Journal of Experimental Psychology, 36*, 209–231.

Berry, D. C., and Broadbent, D. E. (1987). The combination of explicit and implicit learning processes. *Psychological Research, 49*, 7–15.

Berry, D. C., and Broadbent, D. E. (1988). Interactive tasks and the implicit-explicit distinction. *British Journal of Psychology, 79*, 251–272.

Berry, D. C., and Dienes, Z. (1991). The relationship between implicit memory and implicit learning. *British Journal of Psychology, 82*, 359–373.

Berry, D. C., and Dienes, Z. (1993). *Implicit learning: Theoretical and empirical issues.* London: Lawrence Erlbaum Associates.

Bisiach, E. (1992). Understanding consciousness: Clues from unilateral neglect and related disorders. In A. Milner and M. Rugg (Eds.), *The neuropsychology of consciousness*, 113–138. London: Academic Press.

Brewer, W. F. (1974). There is no convincing evidence for operant or classical conditioning in adult humans. In W. B. Weimer and D. S. Palermo (Eds.), *Cognition and symbolic processes.* Hillsdale, NJ: Erlbaum.

Broadbent, D. E. (1977). Levels, hierarchies and the locus of control. *Quarterly Journal of Experimental Psychology, 29*, 181–201.

Broadbent, D. E. (1984). The Maltese cross: A new simplistic model for memory. *Behavioral and Brain Sciences, 7*, 55–94.

Broadbent, D. E. (1992). Recall, recognition and implicit knowledge. In W. Kessen, A. Ortony, F. I. M. Craik (Eds.), *Essays in honour of George Mandler*, 125–134. Hillsdale, NJ: Erlbaum.

Broadbent, D. E., and Aston, B. (1978). Human control of a simulated economic system. *Ergonomics, 21*, 1035–1043.

Broadbent, D. E., FitzGerald, P., and Broadbent, M. H. P. (1986). Implicit and explicit knowledge in the control of complex systems. *British Journal of Psychology, 77*, 33–50.

Brody, N. (1989). Unconscious learning of rules: Comment on Reber's analysis of implicit learning. *Journal of Experimental Psychology: General, 118,* 236–238.

Brooks, L., and Vokey, J. (1991). Abstract analogies and abstracted grammars: Comment on Reber (1989) and Mathews et al (1989). *Journal of Experimental Psychology: General, 120,* 316–20.

Chan, C. (1992). Implicit cognitive processes: Theoretical issues and applications in computer system design. D.Phil. thesis, University of Oxford.

Cleeremans, A., and McClelland, J. (1991). Learning the structure of event sequences. *Journal of Experimental Psychology: General, 120,* 235–253.

Cohen, A., Ivry, R., and Keele, S. (1990). Attention and structure in sequence learning. *Journal of Experimental Psychology: Learning, Memory and Cognition, 16,* 17–30.

Coslett, H., and Saffran, E. (1989). Evidence for preserved reading in pure alexia. *Brain, 112,* 327–59.

Dienes, Z. (1990). Implicit concept formation. Unpublished D.Phil. thesis, University of Oxford.

Dienes, Z. (1992). Connectionist and memory array models of artificial grammar learning. *Cognitive Science, 16,* 41–79.

Dienes, Z., Broadbent, D. E., and Berry, D. C. (1991). Implicit and explicit knowledge bases in artificial grammar learning. *Journal of Experimental Psychology: Learning, Memory and Cognition, 17,* 875–887.

Dienes, Z., and Fahey, R. (n.d.). The role of implicit memory in controlling a dynamic system. In preparation.

Druhan, B., and Mathews, R. (1989). THIYOS: A classifier system model of implicit knowledge of artificial grammars. In *Proceedings of the Eleventh Annual Conference of the Cognitive Science Society.* Hillsdale, NJ: Erlbaum.

Dulany, D. E., Carlson, R., and Dewey, G. (1984). A case of syntactical learning and judgment: How concrete and how abstract? *Journal of Experimental Psychology: General, 113,* 541–555.

Ellis, N. (1993). Rules and instances in foreign language learning: Interactions of explicit and implicit knowledge. *European Journal of Cognitive Psychology, 5,* 289–318.

Elman, J. (1990). Finding structure in time. *Cognitive Science, 14,* 179–211.

Graf, P., Mandler, G., and Squire, L. (1984). The information that amnesic patients do not forget. *Journal of Experimental Psychology: Learning, Memory and Cognition, 10,* 164–78.

Hartman, M., Knopman, D., and Nissen, M. J. (1989). Implicit learning of new verbal associations. *Journal of Experimental Psychology: Learning, Memory and Cognition, 15,* 1070–1082.

Hayes, N., and Broadbent, D. E. (1988). Two modes of learning for interactive tasks. *Cognition, 28,* 249–276.

Holland, J. H., Holyoak, K. J., Nisbett, R. E., and Thagard, P. R. (1986). *Induction: Processes of inference, learning and discovery.* Cambridge, MA: MIT Press.

Howard, J., Mutter, S., and Howard, D. (1992). Serial pattern learning in event observation. *Journal of Experimental Psychology; Learning, Memory and Cognition, 18,* 1029–1039.

Humphreys, G., Troscianko, T., Riddoch, J., Boucart, M., Donnelly, N., and Hardy, G. (1992). Covert processes in different visual recognition systems. In A. Milner and M. Rugg (Eds.), *The neuropsychology of consciousness.* London: Academic Press.

Jacoby, L. L., and Brooks, L. R. (1984). Nonanalytic cognition: Memory, perception, and concept learning. In G. H. Bower (Ed.), *The psychology of learning and motivation: Advances in research and theory,* vol. 18, 1–47. New York: Academic Press.

Kolers, P. A., and Roediger, H. L. (1984). Procedures of mind. *Journal Verbal Learning and Verbal Behaviour, 23*, 425–449.

Knowlton, B., Ramus, S., and Squire, L. (1992). Intact artificial grammar learning in amnesia: Dissociations of classification learning and explicit memory for specific instances. *Psychological Science, 3*, 172–179.

Kushner, M., Cleeremans, A., and Reber, A. (1991). Implicit detection of event interdependencies and a PDP model of the process. In *Proceedings of the Thirteenth Annual Conference of the Cognitive Science Society*, 215–220. Hillsdale, NJ: Erlbaum.

Lewandowski, S., Dunn, J., and Kirsner, K. (1989). *Implicit memory: Theoretical issues*. Hillsdale, NJ: Erlbaum.

Lewicki, P., Czyzewska, M., and Hoffman, H. (1987). Unconscious acquisition of complex procedural knowledge. *Journal of Experimental Psychology: Learning, Memory and Cognition, 13*, 523–530.

Lewicki, P., Hill, T., and Bizot, E. (1988). Acquisition of procedural knowledge about a pattern of stimuli that cannot be articulated. *Cognitive Psychology, 20*, 24–37.

Marescaux, P., Luc, F., and Karnas, G. (1989). Modes d'apprentissage sélectif et nonsélectif et connaissances acquises au control d'un procès. *Cahiers de psychologie cognitive, 9*. 239–264.

Margolin, D., Friedrich, F., and Carbon, N. (1983). Visual agnosia and optic aphasia: A continuum of visual semantic dissociation. *Neurology, 33*, 242.

Marshall, J., and Halligan, P. (1988). Blindsight and insight in visuo-spatial neglect. *Nature, 336*, 766–767.

Mathews, R. (1990). Abstractiveness of implicit grammar knowledge: Comments on Perruchet and Pacteau's analysis of synthetic grammar learning. *Journal of Experimental Psychology: General, 119*, 412–416.

Mathews, R., Buss, R., Chinn, R., and Stanley, W. (1988). The role of explicit and implicit learning processes in concept discovery. *Quarterly Journal of Experimental Psychology, 40*, 135–165.

Mathews, R., Buss, R., Stanley, W., Blanchard-Fields, F., Cho, J., and Druhan, B. (1989). Role of implicit and explicit processes in learning from examples: A synergistic effect. *Journal of Experimental Psychology: Learning, Memory and Cognition, 15*, 1083–1100.

Mathews, R., Roussel, L., Blanchard-Fields, F., and Norris, L. (n.d.). Implicit induction of abstract knowledge: The nonconscious Sherlock Holmes in us all. In preparation.

McGeorge, P., and Burton, M. (1989). The effects of concurrent verbalisation on performance in a dynamic systems task. *British Journal of Psychology, 80*, 455–465.

McGeorge, P., and Burton, M. (1990). Semantic processing in an incidental learning task. *Quarterly Journal of Experimental Psychology, 42*, 597–610.

Milberg, W., and Blumstein, S. (1981). Lexical decision and aphasia: Evidence for semantic processing. *Brain and Language, 14*, 371–385.

Milner, A. D., and Rugg, M. D. (1992). *The Neuropsychology of Consciousness*. London: Academic Press.

Nissen, M. J., and Bullemer, P. (1987). Attentional requirements of learning: Evidence from performance measures. *Cognitive Psychology, 19*, 1–32.

Perruchet, P., and Amorin, M. (1992). Conscious knowledge and changes in performance in sequence learning: Evidence against dissociation. *Journal of Experimental Psychology: Learning, Memory and Cognition, 18*, 785–800.

Perruchet, P., Gallego, J., and Savy, I. (1990). A critical reappraisal of the evidence for unconscious abstraction of deterministic rules in complex experimental situations. *Cognitive Psychology, 22*, 493–516.

Perruchet, P., and Pacteau, C. (1990). Synthetic grammar learning: Implicit rule abstraction or explicit fragmentary knowledge? *Journal of Experimental Psychology: General, 119*, 264–275.

Reber, A. S. (1967). Implicit learning of artificial grammars. *Journal of Verbal Learning and Verbal Behaviour, 5*, 855–863.

Reber, A. S. (1969). Transfer of syntactic structures in synthetic languages. *Journal of Experimental Psychology, 81*, 115–119.

Reber, A. S. (1976). Implicit learning of synthetic languages: The role of instructional set. *Journal of Experimental Psychology: Human Learning and Memory, 2*, 88–94.

Reber, A. S. (1989). Implicit learning and tacit knowledge. *Journal of Experimental Psychology: General, 118*, 219–235.

Reber, A. S., and Allen, R. (1978). Analogy and abstraction strategies in synthetic grammar learning: A functionalist interpretation. *Cognition, 6*, 189–221.

Reber, A. S., Kassin, S., Lewis, S., and Cantor, G. (1980). On the relationship between implicit and explicit modes in the learning of a complex rule structure. *Journal of Experimental Psychology: Human Learning and Memory, 6*, 492–502.

Reber, A. S., and Lewis, S. (1977). Toward a theory of implicit learning: The analysis of the form and structure of a body of tacit knowledge. *Cognition, 5*, 331–361.

Reber, A. S., and Millward, R. (1968). Event observation in probability learning. *Journal of Experimental Psychology, 77*, 317–327.

Reber, A. S., and Millward, R. (1971). Event tracking in probability learning. *American Journal of Psychology, 84*, 85–99.

Roediger, H. L. III (1990). Implicit memory. *American Psychologist, 45*, 1043–1056.

Sanderson, P. (1989). Verbalizable knowledge and skilled task performance: Associations, dissociations and mental models. *Journal of Experimental Psychology: Learning, Memory and Cognition, 15*, 729–747.

Schacter, D. L. (1987). Implicit memory: History and current status. *Journal of Experimental Psychology: Learning, Memory and Cognition, 13*, 501–518.

Schacter, D. L., McAndrews, P., and Moscovitch, M. (1988). Access to consciousness: Dissociations between implicit and explicit knowledge in neuropsychological syndromes. In L. Weiskrantz (Ed.), *Thought and language*. New York: Oxford University Press.

Servan-Schreiber, E., and Anderson, J. R. (1990). Learning artificial grammars with competitive chunking. *Journal of Experimental Psychology: Learning, Memory and Cognition, 16*, 592–608.

Shallice, T., and Saffran, E. (1986). Lexical processing in the absence of explicit word identification: Evidence from a letter by letter reader. *Cognitive Neuropsychology, 3*, 429–458.

Squire, L., and Frambach, M. (1990). Cognitive skill learning in amnesia. *Psychobiology, 18*, 109–117.

Stadler, M. (1989). On learning complex procedural knowledge. *Journal of Experimental Psychology: Learning, Memory and Cognition 15*, 1061–1069.

Stanley, W. B., Mathews, R., Buss, R., and Kotler-Cope, S. (1989). Insight without awareness: On the interaction of verbalisation, instruction and practice on a simulated process control task. *Quarterly Journal of Experimental Psychology, 41*, 553–577.

Tyler, L. (1992). The distinction between implicit and explicit language functions: Evidence from aphasia. In A. Milner and M. Rugg (Eds.), *The neuropsychology of consciousness*. London: Academic Press.

Vokey, J., and Brooks, L. (1992). The salience of item knowledge in learning artificial grammars. *Journal of Experimental Psychology: Learning, Memory and Cognition, 18*, 328–344.

Weiskrantz, L. (1986). *Blindsight: A case study and implications*. Oxford: Oxford University Press.

Weiskrantz, L. (1990). Outlooks for blindsight: Explicit methodologies for implicit processes. *Proceedings of Royal Society, B239*, 247–278.

Willingham, D., Nissen, M., and Bullemer, P. (1989). On the development of complex procedural knowledge. *Journal of Experimental Psychology: Learning, Memory and Cognition, 15*, 1047–1060.

Young, A., and DeHaan, E. (1988). Boundaries of covert recognition in prosopagnosia. *Cognitive Neuropsychology, 5*, 317–336.

Young, A., and DeHaan, E. (1992). Face recognition and awareness after brain injury. In A. Milner and M. Rugg (Eds.), *The neuropsychology of consciousness*. London: Academic Press.

# 31 The Representation of Structure in Sequence Prediction Tasks

## Axel Cleeremans

ABSTRACT   Is knowledge acquired implicitly abstract or based on memory for exemplars? This question is at the heart of a current, but long-standing, controversy in the field of implicit learning (see Reber 1989 for a review). For some authors, implicit knowledge is best characterized as rulelike. For others, however, knowledge acquired implicitly is little more than knowledge about memorized exemplars or, at best, knowledge about elementary features of the material, such as the frequency of particular events. In this chapter, I argue that the debate may be ill-posed, and that the two positions are not necessarily incompatible. Using simulation studies, I show that abstract knowledge about the stimulus material may emerge through the operation of elementary, associationist learning mechanisms of the kind that operate in connectionist networks. I focus on a sequence learning task first proposed by Kushner, Cleeremans, and Reber (1991), during which subjects are exposed to random fixed-length sequences and are asked to predict the location at which the last element of each sequence will appear. Unknown to them, the location of the last element is determined based on the relationship between specific previous elements. This situation is thus quite complex, because the relevant information is relational, and because it is embedded in a large number of irrelevant contexts. Kushner, Cleeremans, and Reber (1991) showed that human subjects are able to learn this material despite limited ability to verbalize their knowledge. In this chapter, I first present simulation studies in which connectionist networks are trained to predict the last event of the sequences in the same conditions as subjects were. I focus on issues of representation and transfer. What knowledge do the networks acquire about the temporal extent of the material? What is the form of this knowledge? The results highlight limitations of two well-known models of sequential processing, that is, the SRN model (Cleeremans and McClelland 1991) and Jordan's recurrent network (Jordan 1986), and indicate that a simple decay-based, buffer network may be sufficient to account for human performance. Next, I explore how well the model can transfer to various test situations, in which new sequences may include either relevant or irrelevant sequence elements that have never been presented during training. I discuss the results in light of the abstraction and memory for instances debate. Based on these and other results, I suggest that the kind of representations developed by connectionist models are intermediate between abstract representations and exemplar-based representations, and that these two extreme forms of representation are points on a continuum.

## 31.1   INTRODUCTION

What do people learn when they do not know what they are learning? This is the kind of question researchers working on implicit learning would like to ask subjects directly. Unfortunately for them, in many learning tasks subjects appear incapable of reporting what they have learned despite detectable improvements in performance. However, we do not have to rely exclusively on introspection to start thinking about the nature of knowledge acquired during practice at a task. Many implicit learning experiments of the past few decades have indeed been designed to circumvent or to overcome subjects' relative unawareness of their own knowledge. This is typically achieved by a variety of familiar designs and techniques, including necessarily weak methods, such as verbal protocols and directed interviews (Lewicki, Hill, and Bizot 1988), or more accurate—but indirect—methods, such as transfer (Reber 1989) or recognition tests (Perruchet and Amorim 1992), or several variants of a generation task (Nissen and Bullemer 1987; Perruchet and Amorim 1992) that follow acquisition. Several robust results have emerged from this impressive array of experimental situations, although many of them are still somewhat contentious. Perhaps the simplest way to provide an overview of the main points in a nutshell is to take Reber's (1989) definition of implicit learning. He endows implicit learning with three main characteristics: "(a) Implicit learning produces a tacit knowledge base that is abstract and representative of the structure of the environment; (b) such knowledge is optimally acquired independently of conscious effort to learn; and (c) it can be used implicitly to solve problems and make accurate decisions about novel stimulus circumstances" (219).

To reword this definition, implicit learning is thought of as an essentially unintentional process by which a system acquires information about the structure of the stimulus environment in such a way that the resulting knowledge is general enough to be be used with new instances but is also hard to express. A classic example of implicit learning is language acquisition and use. Although formal instruction certainly helps to learn language, it is not necessary to support adequate performance or productivity. Further, typical language users have little access to the rules of their language and acquire basic skills in an essentially unintentional way. Laboratory situations are necessarily much simpler than that faced by language learners but share with this domain a number of basic characteristics, among which are the facts that the rules that underlie stimulus generation are unknown to subjects and that subjects typically learn in an incidental way. These features stand in sharp contrast with the kind of learning that is observed in problem-solving or categorization tasks, for instance, where subjects typically use hypothesis testing and goal-directed strategies, thereby accumulating knowledge that is fully accessible to consciousness. The idea that learning can proceed in an implicit way has been under attack since its inception, however. In particular, the notion that implicit learning produces knowledge that is abstract and unavailable to consciousness is the object of ongoing controversies. A number of experiments now appear to have demonstrated that some knowledge acquired implicitly is in fact available to consciousness when elicited properly (Dulany, Carlson, and Dewey 1985; Perruchet and Amorim 1992) and that knowledge acquired implicitly need not necessarily be cast as abstract (Vokey and Brooks 1992). But many problems of interpretation remain. Which criteria should be used to decide how conscious or how abstract a particular bit of knowledge is? Addressing issues such as these in a purely empirical way is likely not to be very productive, for essentially three different reasons (Cleeremans 1993).

First, concepts such as "unconscious" or "abstract" are notoriously hard to define and may in fact be just points on a continuum rather than one of the two branches of a binary alternative. That consciousness has degrees is confirmed by day-to-day introspection. Similarly, abstractness also appears to be a matter of degree, in that there are many ways to represent structures that fall between storage of unanalyzed instances and rulelike general descriptions. In the discussion, I provide several examples of how connectionist networks may develop internal representations that exhibit various degrees of internal organization.

Second, systems based on abstraction and systems based on memory for instances may often be functionally equivalent (see Dienes 1992 for a discussion of this point).

Third, even if the concepts of abstraction and of consciousness were binary, it may be very hard to design discriminating experiments that allow one to distinguish between the effects of explicit knowledge and strategies on the one hand and the effects of implicit knowledge on the other hand. The basic empirical problem is that performance in any given task almost certainly involves both explicit code-breaking strategies and the more passive learning and observation processes referred to as implicit learning. This simple fact makes it very hard to develop decisive arguments in favor of either position. For instance, if one recognizes that subjects engaged in an implicit learning task are nevertheless aware of what they are doing, then it is not surprising to find that they end up knowing something about the task and the material. It is not surprising either to find that this knowledge sometimes correlates very well with performance. Should this be taken as evidence that knowledge acquired implicitly is in fact conscious? The answer depends on what theoretical stance one prefers but seems quite hard to settle in a purely empirical way.

I do not mean to suggest that no advances have been made in our understanding of these issues or that it is impossible to do so. On the contrary, the past decade has been rich in novel empirical approaches to both issues, and considerable progress has been made on both counts. However, the complications that arise from both the fact that the concepts at hand are hard to define and potential experimental confounds also seem to warrant exploration of other approaches. As for other research (Cleeremans and McClelland 1991), I think that a good strategy to start addressing such hard questions consists of proposing plausible mechanisms that may account for performance and of finding out what the properties of these mechanisms are and how they relate to human performance. This modeling approach, when combined with experimentation, has already proved very useful in understanding performance in other sequence learning situations (Cleeremans 1993) as well as in grammar learning tasks (Dienes 1992; Servan-Schreiber and Anderson 1990).

In this chapter, I examine how such an approach may be useful in addressing the following issue: Does implicit learning result in abstract knowledge of the stimulus regularities? Consider, for instance, the well-known case of artificial grammar learning (see Reber 1989 for a review). Typically, subjects are first exposed to a series of strings of letters generated from a finite state grammar and asked to memorize them. Next, they are unexpectedly presented with another set of strings, which includes old strings as well as new grammatical and ungrammatical strings, and asked to classify each string as grammatical or not. As a large number of studies have repeatedly demonstrated (Reber 1989), subjects perform well above chance on this discrimination task, despite limited ability to report on the criteria they used for making classification judgments. For some authors (Reber 1967, 1989), the fact that subjects can classify new strings is an indication that the knowledge they acquired during training is abstract, that is, rulelike. For others, however, performance can be accounted for by assuming that subjects classify based on similarity with stored exemplars (Brooks 1978; Hintzmann 1986; Medin and Schaffer 1978; Perruchet and Pacteau 1990; Vokey and Brooks 1992.) In the latter theoretical context, implicit abstraction thus boils down to mere sensitivity to elementary features of the material, such as the frequency of particular events. The goal of this chapter is not to resolve this debate but simply to shed a somewhat different light on it. The main argument that I will develop is that the opposition that is often made between abstract, rulelike knowledge and association-based knowledge tends to fade away when one considers the way in which some connectionist models represent knowledge. Of course, this argument is well known, and indeed it has been extensively discussed in the context of memory and language acquisition theories, but the point is well worth restating here because of the emerging controversy that centers around the existence of implicit abstraction.

In the rest of this chapter, I describe an experimental situation used by Kushner, Cleeremans, and Reber (1991), as well as two extensions of it designed to test for transfer. In this task, subjects are exposed to random sequences of five elements and are asked to predict the location at which the sixth element of each sequence will appear. Unknown to them, the location of the sixth element is determined based on the relationship between elements 2 and 4.

I introduce a computational model of performance in this task, in the form of a simple backpropagation network (Rumelhart, Hinton, and Williams 1986) that keeps a record of previous events in the form of a decaying trace of successive sequence elements. The model accounts quite well for the data and generates new predictions about performance in transfer situations designed to test for abstract knowledge. In the course of developing this model, I also examine the performance of several other models that have been proposed recently to account for implicit sequence learning. This comparison gives me the opportunity to discuss in depth how the different models represent time and to highlight interesting shortcomings of each. In particular, I show that neither of two otherwise successful models (the SRN model, Cleeremans and McClelland 1991, Cleeremans 1993; Jordan's network, Jordan 1986) can learn material from this task. Finally, I examine the notion that subjects who learn implicitly develop abstract knowledge of the stimulus material by exploring how well the model is able to transfer to new material.

## 31.2 EXPLICIT SEQUENCE LEARNING

Most sequence learning situations that have been explored so far in the context of implicit learning research are choice reaction tasks (Lewicki, Hill, and Bizot 1988; Cleeremans 1993). In these tasks, subjects are asked to respond as if in a classic choice reaction time (RT) task, but, unknown to them, the material has temporal structure in that successive events depend on each other in a probabilistic way. Over training, subjects' distribution of RTs typically reflects a progressively better encoding of the sequential contingencies, despite a relative lack of corresponding improvements in their ability to report on these contingencies. However, sequence learning in general is not limited to choice reaction paradigms. For instance, another kind of situation that requires temporal context to be integrated consists of asking subjects to make explicit predictions about the successor of observed sequences. At first sight, it may appear that these situations are not likely to involve implicit learning processes, but this need not be so. Indeed, there is ample evidence that implicit learning processes play an important role even in situations where explicit decisions are required. The classic Reber task (Reber 1989) is a perfect example of such situations: although subjects are required to make overt decisions about the grammaticality of letter strings, the knowledge they use in doing so appears to have been acquired implicitly, through mere exposure to the training material. By the same token, it is also likely that explicit prediction tasks involve additional, more explicit processes, because they place different demands on subjects. Specifically, in both the Reber task and in explicit sequence learning situations such as the one described here, subjects are undoubtedly aware of the fact that the only information available to them to perform successfully is contained in the stimulus material, and they are thus much more likely to engage in active hypothesis-testing strategies than in the case of sequential choice reaction tasks.

### An Explicit Prediction Task

Recently, Kushner and Reber (personal communication, December 1990; see also Kushner, Cleeremans, and Reber 1991) started exploring a situation analogous to the original Reber task but in the context of sequence learning. Their subjects were exposed to a series of five events presented successively on a computer screen and were asked to predict the location of the sixth stimulus. There were three possible locations at which the stimulus might appear, organized as the vertices of an inverted triangle. The first five stimuli appeared at random locations. The location of the sixth stimulus, in contrast, was determined based on the spatial relationship between the second and fourth stimuli. If they had appeared at the same screen location, then the sixth stimulus appeared at location A. If they had been in a clockwise relationship, the sixth stimulus appeared at location B. The sixth stimulus appeared at location C if the second and fourth stimuli had been in a counterclockwise relationship. The first, third, and fifth stimuli were thus always irrelevant.

What makes this design attractive is its complexity. First, there are more irrelevant events than useful ones. Second, the rule that defines the location of the sixth stimulus is complex because it involves a relationship between two events rather than the two particular events themselves (that is, each crucial event is useless in and of itself). This results in each component of the rule being instantiated by different pairs of events, each of which may, in turn, be embedded in a large number of different irrelevant contexts.

The experiment Kushner and Reber conducted was divided into three phases. In a first phase, subjects were asked to make 2,430 predictions, as already described. In a second phase, the rule was surreptitiously modified by shifting the location of the sixth stimulus by one position for each component of the rule. For instance, sixth events that had appeared at location A in the first phase of the experiment now appeared at location B, and so on. Finally, in the third phase, the rule was again modified. This time, the location of the sixth event was determined at random. Thus, the material of the second phase tested for transfer, whereas the material of the third phase may be used to assess how much performance improvement depends on knowledge of the rule. Subjects were asked to make 972 predictions in each of the second and third phases.

The results are illustrated in figure 31.1. Subjects became increasingly better at making accurate predictions over the first ten sessions of training and ended up reaching about 45 percent correct responses in the tenth session. This is significantly above chance level (33 percent) and indicates that subjects had acquired knowledge about the relevant regularities in the material. The second

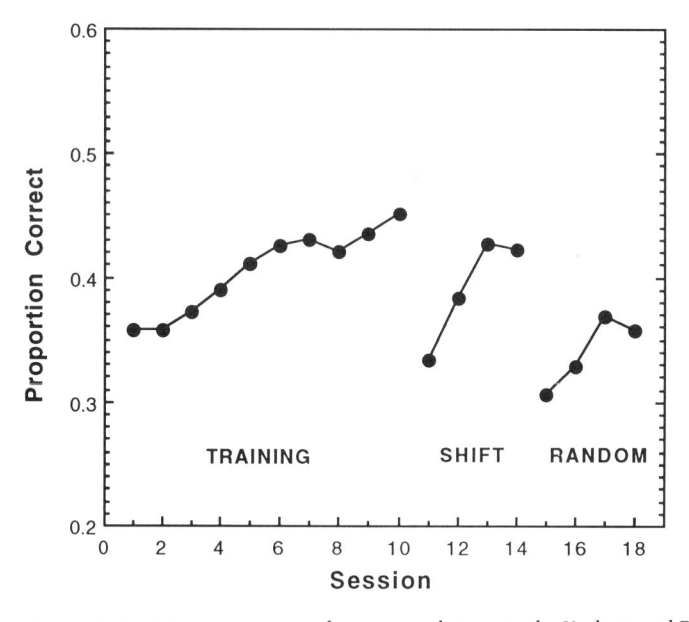

**Figure 31.1** Mean proportion of correct predictions in the Kushner and Reber task, over the eighteen sessions of training, and for the three phases of the experiment.

phase began with a dramatic drop in performance (to chance level), but there was again evidence of learning over the next three sessions, suggesting that subjects were able to transfer relatively easily from one stimulus-response set to another. By contrast, performance in the third, random, phase was low and failed to be significantly over chance level.

Despite this clear sensitivity to the complex regularities embedded in the material, none of the subjects exhibited knowledge of the sequential structure when asked after the task. In particular, subjects were unable to specify which covariations were crucial in the sequence of five stimuli, not even in a general form such as, "When the $n$th stimulus was in box X, the correct answer was usually Y." No subject reported awareness of the rule shifts between the three phases of the experiment. Subjects' poor knowledge of the constraints embedded in the material was also confirmed by their performance on a ranking task, in which they were asked to rate each of the five stimuli in terms of their relevance in predicting the location of the sixth stimulus. The results failed to reveal sensitivity to the crucial events. On a scale of 1 (very important) to 5 (not important), the crucial events received average ranks of 3.5 (second event) and 2.67 (fourth event), whereas the first, third, and fifth events were ranked 3.33, 3.67, and 1.83, respectively. However, there was some evidence that particularly salient sequences that were reported by subjects also elicited very good predictions. For instance, sequences in which the first five stimuli had appeared at the same location always entailed the same particular location for the sixth trial (e.g., the sequences *AAAAA*, *BBBBB*, and *CCCCC* all predict *A* as their successor). Subjects could correctly predict the successor of these sequences in about 61 percent of the cases of phase 1, considerably better than average.

Other data (Reber, personal communication, December 1990) from an identical experiment but in which subjects received considerably more training also indicated that at least one subject did become fully aware of the contingencies and was able to report them to the experimenter. These results clearly indicate that, at least in some specific cases like this, subjects may rely on explicit knowledge to determine their response. Note, however, that performance cannot be solely accounted for by knowledge of the salient sequences. Indeed, the average prediction score during phase 1 dropped by only .0046 percentage point when the three possible "repeating" and six possible "single alternating" (e.g., *ABABA*) sequences were eliminated from the analysis. Having ruled out raw memory of salient sequences as a potential account of the data, what kind of mechanisms may drive performance in this task? This is the object of the next section.

## Simulations

A natural starting point for modeling performance in this task is the simple recurrent network (SRN) model developed by Cleeremans and McClelland (1991) to account for performance in sequential choice reaction tasks.

**SRN Simulations** Figure 31.2 shows an SRN. In this backpropagation network (see also Elman 1990), the hidden units receive activation not only from the input units but also from a pool of context units that hold a copy of the activation of the hidden units at the previous time step. This recurrence gives it the means of representing temporal information, as previous states are allowed to modulate processing of the current event. The task of this network consists of predicting each element of a sequence. On each time step, processing consists of three phases. First, the current element of the sequence is presented on the input units, along with a copy of the previous activation of the hidden units, copied onto the context units. Typically (but not necessarily), elements of the sequence are represented locally on the input units, so that there is one unit that codes for each possible sequence element. Second, activation is propagated through the network, which ends up producing a response representing the next sequence element on its output units (again using local representations). Third, the network's response is compared to the actual successor of the sequence as generated by the rules, and the error is then backpropagated to modify the weights. On the next time step, the successor of the sequence is presented as the next input to the network, the activation of the hidden units is copied to the context units, and the network again has to predict the successor.

How could the SRN model be applied to Kushner and Reber's experimental situation? And is it appropriate to do so? The answer to the latter question resides in the mechanisms that underlie the SRN's performance. At a general level, the central processing features of the SRN model are that it elaborates representations of sequential material and its responses consist of predictions about subsequent events. In the choice reaction tasks explored by Cleeremans and McClelland (1991), these predictions were assumed to result in preparation for the next event (no explicit response was required from subjects), but it seems reasonable to imagine that the same mechanisms may apply in cases where overt predictions are required. That is, although it is quite likely that

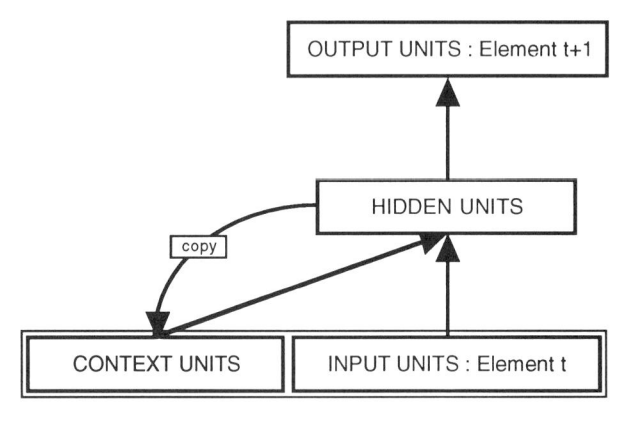

**Figure 31.2** A simple recurrent network (SRN). The recurrent connections marked "copy" are not modifiable and implement a simple one-to-one copy operation. In both the input and output pools, sequence elements are represented by activating one of three units.

other, more explicit mechanisms play a role in situations like Kushner and Reber's, the results also make it clear that most of subjects' predictions are based on implicit knowledge. How, then, may the SRN model be applied to this situation? I used the same architecture as described by Cleeremans and McClelland (1991), but with the following three modifications.

First, it is obvious that short-term priming effects of the kind reported in Cleeremans and McClelland (1991) play no role whatsoever in this situation. The corresponding mechanisms in the SRN model (dual weights on the connections and running average activations on the output units) were therefore prevented from operating by setting all the relevant parameters to zero.

Second, since no predictions are required from subjects during presentation of the first five trials of a series, learning was turned off for those trials. The network was therefore merely storing successive events during presentation of the first four trials. When the fifth trial was presented as input to the network, however, learning was turned on, and the network was trained to activate the unit corresponding to the location of the sixth event on its output layer.

Third, since trials (blocks of five events) were totally independent from each other, the context units were reset to zero at the beginning of each trial. Thus, the temporal context could influence processing within a block of five events, but it was prevented from carrying over to the next block.

Ten SRNs with fifteen hidden units each and a learning rate of 0.8 were trained on material identical to Kushner and Reber's and for the same number of exposures. The three possible sequence elements were represented by a single unit each in both the input pool and the output pool, as illustrated in figure 31.2. Each network used a different set of initial random weights. On each of the eighteen sessions of training (ten during phase 1 and four each during phases 2 and 3), each network was exposed to 243 random sequences of five events. A prediction response was considered correct if the activation of the unit corresponding to the actual sixth event was higher than the activation of the two other units. Figure 31.3 compares the human data with the average proportion of correct prediction responses produced by the networks during each of the eighteen sessions of training.

Perhaps surprisingly, the model fails completely to learn the regularity,[1] its proportion of correct predictions hovering around chance (33 percent) during the entire simulation. One may wonder about the effects of using such a high value for the learning rate (epsilon = 0.8), but additional simulations revealed that the network also failed with considerably lower learning rates (e.g., epsilon = 0.01) or when trained for many additional trials. The reasons for this failure are in fact familiar. As Servan-Schreiber, Cleeremans, and McClelland (1991) pointed out, representing temporal context in the SRN model requires the material to be prediction relevant at each step. That is, each element of the sequence needs to contain some information about which successor will occur. This is because context representation develops based on such event-to-event associations. However, none of the sequence elements of the material used in this experiment is prediction relevant when considered

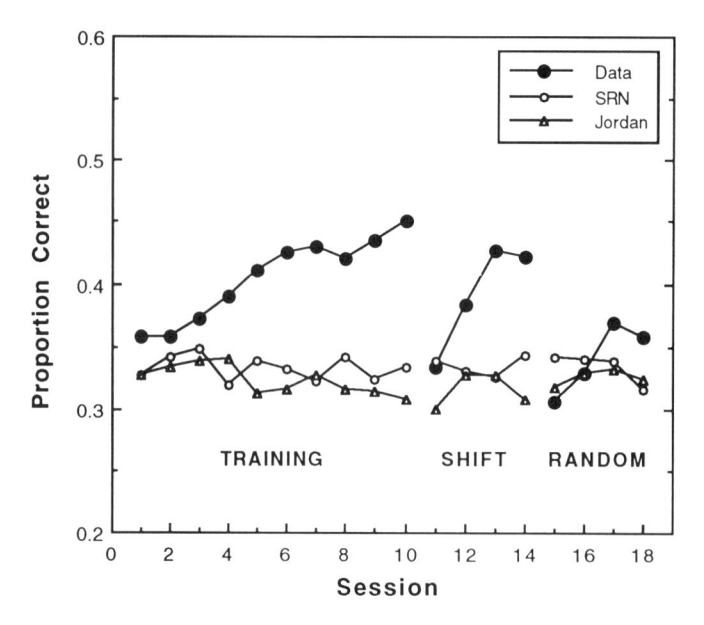

**Figure 31.3** Mean proportion of correct predictions in the Kushner and Reber task, over the eighteen sessions of training, and for the three phases of the experiment. Filled circles: human data; open circles: SRN model; open triangles: Jordan model.

independently, since each sequence was generated randomly. As a result, no representation of the context can start to develop, because the material does not contain any pairwise, event-to-event associations and because the associations that do exist span too many irrelevant elements to be encoded naturally by the network. Further training tends only to make this situation worse, because the concomitant changes to the connections weights will tend to homogenize the network's internal representations even more.[2]

What alternative model may be successful in mastering this task's material? An obvious candidate is the network proposed in 1986 by Jordan, because it was applied successfully to choice reaction sequence learning situations by Cleeremans (1993) and by Jennings and Keele (1990).

**Jordan Network Simulations** Figure 31.4 represents the architecture of a simplified Jordan (1986) network (Jordan's original network also contains additional input units, called plan units, and has recurrent connections from the output units to the input units. When the task is prediction, this amounts to having recurrence on the input units because the previous output is identical with the next input).

In a Jordan network, temporal context is maintained by having an explicit trace of the sequence represented over the input units. This temporal trace arises as the result of time-averaging the current activation of each input unit with its own previous value. How much averaging takes place is defined by a single parameter, $\mu$, according to the following equation:

Activation $(t)$ = activation $(t)$ + $\mu^*$ activation $(t-1)$.

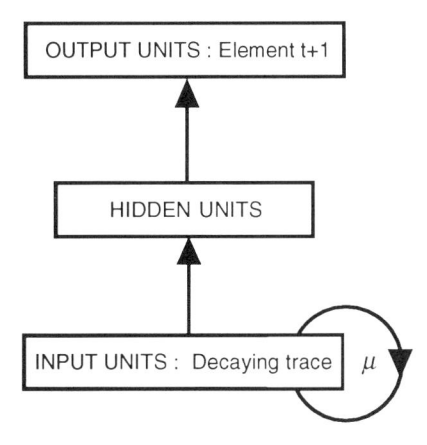

```
        ┌─────────────────────────────────────┐
        │ OUTPUT UNITS : Element t+1          │
        └─────────────────────────────────────┘
                         ▲
                         │
        ┌─────────────────────────────────────┐
        │           HIDDEN UNITS              │
        └─────────────────────────────────────┘
                         ▲
                         │
        ┌──────────────────────────────┐
        │ INPUT UNITS : Decaying trace │  μ
        └──────────────────────────────┘
```

**Figure 31.4** A simplified Jordan network. The recurrent connections on the input units are not modifiable and implement a simple one-to-one "copy and decay" operation.

How long the trace of a particular past event is maintained depends on both the magnitude of $\mu$ and the structure of the material. Training Jordan networks to predict successive elements otherwise proceeds in the same way as for the SRN model. On each time step, the network is presented with element $t$ of the sequence. The pattern of activation corresponding to element $t$ is time averaged with the pattern of activation that already exists over the input units, and the resulting vector is then clamped back onto these units. The network is then trained to produce element $t + 1$ on its output layer. Some investigators have explored how this kind of network (augmented with Jordan's original "plan" units) may be used to disambiguate subsequences in a prediction task similar to Cleeremans and McClelland's. For instance, Jennings and Keele (1990) have used a Jordan network to model the effects of attention in a sequence learning task similar to that used by Cleeremans and McClelland's (1991). When several identical subsequences may be followed by different successors, the network's prediction performance may be improved by disambiguating each subsequence with different patterns of activation on the plan units.

Because Jordan networks do not have to elaborate their own representations of the sequence, the question of the prediction relevance of successive elements is much less of an issue. Indeed, the time-averaged traces present on the input layer incorporate information about remote past events regardless of whether the more recent events are relevant for predicting the next one. More specifically, it would appear that the ability of Jordan networks to maintain information about the temporal context depends only on the width and on the resolution of the temporal window. As described earlier, the width of the temporal window depends on the magnitude of the $\mu$ parameter. The resolution depends on both the complexity of the sequence and the ability of the network to make fine discriminations between levels of activation in the input layer.

Ten Jordan networks were trained in conditions identical to those used for the SRN simulations described in the previous section and with the same parameters and performance criteria. All the networks used a $\mu$ of 0.5. The average proportion of correct responses produced by the networks is illustrated along with the corresponding human data in figure 31.3.

Again, the model fails to learn the regularities: the average proportion of correct predictions remains at chance level in all three phases of the experiment. Additional simulations with different parameters yielded similar results: neither changes in the learning rate nor in the value of $m$ resulted in the network's mastering the material. A careful analysis of the network's performance revealed that the network's inability to learn the material appears to stem from interference by the irrelevant elements that occur on positions 1, 3, and 5 of each sequence. Since the Jordan network's representation of the temporal context depends on a decaying trace of each element presented, a single unit in the input pool is used to represent the same event at different time steps. If repetitions are allowed, the time averaging will necessarily result in a loss of information, as the traces corresponding to the repeated elements are blended together to determine the activation of the corresponding input unit. With a $\mu$ of 1.0, for instance, the network would have no means of discriminating between identical events that occurred at different time steps. In effect, $\mu$ determines the relative weight given to recent versus older events. In cases where events may be repeated, it is easy to see that the network will sometimes have to make very fine discriminations between input activations. The problem comes from the fact that sequences that differ in either their second or first element are often indistinguishable from each other. So, for instance, the sequences *AAAAA*, *ABAAA*, and *BAAAA* are represented by the following input patterns (table 31.1) after all five elements have been presented to the network.

The first and third sequences predict the same successor (*A*), whereas the second one predicts a different one (*B*). Yet its representation is almost identical to those of the other two sequences. This discriminability problem is repeated at many different places all over the space and makes it impossible for the network to learn the material. Using a different value of $\mu$ does not help solve this problem. This analysis is confirmed by the fact that if irrelevant events are not presented to the network (by setting the corresponding input pattern to 0.0), the network has no trouble learning the material.

The failure of both the SRN and the Jordan network to learn the material prompted me to reevaluate the task in terms of its contrasting characteristics

**Table 31.1** Final Representation of Three Sequences over the Input Units of a Jordan Network

|  | A | B | C |
|---|---|---|---|
| *AAAAA* | 1.94 | 0.00 | 0.00 |
| *ABAAA* | 1.88 | 0.12 | 0.00 |
| *BAAAA* | 1.81 | 0.06 | 0.00 |

with the choice RT tasks that they were successful models of. After analysis, there are two main relevant differences between choice reaction tasks and Kushner and Reber's explicit prediction task. First, it appears likely that subjects involved in the latter task will engage in an explicit effort to remember as much as they can from the sequence of five events that they observe during each trial. Indeed, subjects are certainly aware of the fact that the information they need to make correct predictions has to be present in the sequence for the task to make sense. A second difference is that the stimulus material used in Kushner and Reber's experiment is presented in chunks of five elements, and the instructions make it clear that sequences are independent of each other. Both aspects of this situation stand in sharp contrast with the characteristics of the choice reaction tasks that the SRN and the Jordan network are such good models of. Indeed, in these tasks, encoding the temporal context is not even necessary to comply with task instructions and to attain satisfactory performance levels. These differences would seem to make it plausible that subjects maintain detailed information about a fixed number of time steps.

Another way to think of this task is that the temporal dimension is not really relevant. In other words, this task is more akin to standard categorization tasks than to the choice reaction tasks explored elsewhere (Cleeremans 1993). Indeed, one may think of subjects as being asked to classify the sequences in three groups based on some features that are to be discovered. The fact that the elements are presented sequentially rather than simultaneously only makes it harder for subjects to encode the relevant regularities. It is likely that a simultaneous version of this task (using strings of letters, for instance) would be easier than the sequential version, because subjects would have more opportunity to detect common features among different sequences.

One class of connectionist models that does not suffer from either interference from subsequent events (as the Jordan network) or from the lack of trial-to-trial contingencies (as the SRN) is instantiated by buffer networks. Although such networks are somewhat implausible in the context of choice reaction tasks and are computationally very limited, the features of Kushner and Reber's task make them good candidates here.

**Buffer Network Simulations** A well-known and comparatively ancient way to represent time in connectionist networks is instantiated by architectures that use a spatial metaphor to represent successive events (Cottrell, Munro, and Zipser 1987; Elman and Zipser 1988; Hanson and Kegl 1987). Figure 31.5 illustrates one such model in which five identical pools of input units are used to represent the possible sequence elements that may occur on each of five time steps. On each time step, the contents of each pool are copied (and possibly decayed) to the previous one (in time: e.g.; $t-5 = t-4$, etc.), and a new element is presented on the pool corresponding to time $t$, the current time step. The contents of the pool corresponding to the most remote time step are lost. As Elman (1990) suggested, buffer networks represent time by means of making the effects of events occurring at different time steps explicit, as opposed to models such as the SRN or Jordan's network, in

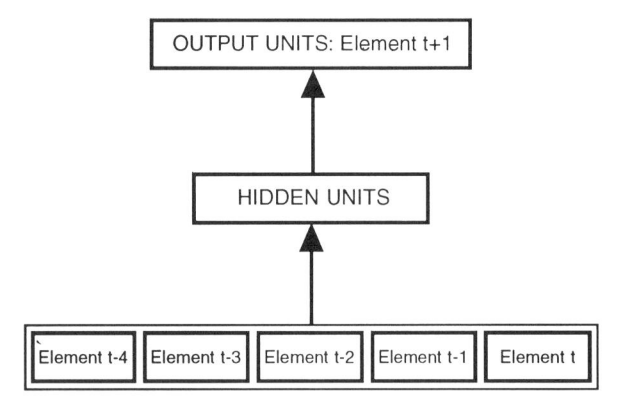

**Figure 31.5** A buffer network with a temporal window of five time steps. Each pool of input units is used to represent the occurrence of a sequence element at a specific time step.

which previous history modulates processing of subsequent events by virtue of the fact that these networks have a dynamic memory of their own past. In Elman (1990), buffer networks were dismissed as interesting computational objects based on the fact that they have a number of important limitations. In addition to the wasteful duplication of input units that the buffer architecture entails, the most important limitation of these models is that events that fall outside the temporal window available to the network are irretrievably lost for further processing. Thus, one is faced with two equally awkward possibilities: to determine the size of the window based on the longest (and potentially infinite) interval between the time when relevant information is presented and the time when it is needed to make a prediction response; or settle for a necessarily arbitrary size and forfeit the network's ability to process sequences longer than the chosen length. Either possibility is computationally undesirable, and both seem psychologically implausible (particularly in the light of language processing facts). Despite these important shortcomings, buffer networks are worth considering here as an instantiation of another elementary way to represent time. The fact that they keep separate traces of individual events may also prove to be crucial in helping them master Kushner and Reber's material.

How well would a network of this kind learn the material? To find out, I trained ten buffer networks with five pools of three input units each (a temporal window of five time steps) for the same number of trials as subjects in the experiment. As for human subjects, the network was only required to predict the next event when presented with the last event of each series of five. As a simplification, traces were not decayed; that is, the decay rate was 0.0. This effectively eliminates any representation of the temporal dimension from the architecture: the network is identical with a simple three-layer backpropagation network. As before, a learning rate of 0.8 was used. The results are illustrated in figure 31.6.

The results indicate that the network is not only able to learn the contingency between events 2 and 4 during training but that it is also able to

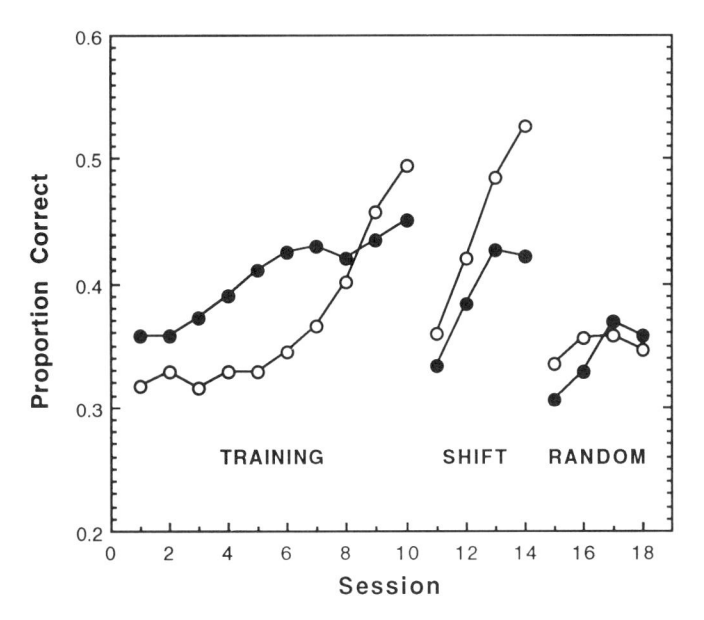

**Figure 31.6** Mean proportion of correct predictions in the Kushner and Reber task, over the eighteen sessions of training, and for the three phases of the experiment. Filled symbols represent human data; open symbols represent simulated data (buffer model).

transfer successfully to the shifted material. That these improvements depend specifically on learning of the contingency is demonstrated by the fact that performance on random material remains at chance level. Several interesting differences with the human data are also present.

First, the network tends to learn slowly at the beginning of training and faster at the end, whereas human subjects improve their performance at a more constant rate. This trend was present over a number of additional simulations with different learning rates and may be an indication that subjects also rely on memory for specific instances during early training. There is evidence that subjects quickly learn to respond correctly to sequences that are particularly salient, such as sequences that consist only of one repeated element or that contain simple alternations between two elements. By construction, all sequences of this kind have the same successor, and it is therefore very likely that subjects rely on knowledge of these sequences to respond during early training. The network model has no means of capturing this effect, since it is not sensitive to psychological salience and treats all sequences as equivalent.

Second, the network's performance on the shifted material presented during the second phase of the experiment is somewhat better than that of human subjects. Why is it so easy for the network to transfer to the shifted material? The answer lies in an examination of how the model stores and processes knowledge about sequences. In the case of this particular task, the connections between the input units and the hidden units implement a mapping between sets of sequences of events and distinct internal representations. Optimally, each set of sequences that results in the same prediction about the sixth event should be associated to a unique code on the hidden units. More likely, there are a number of distinct clusters of internal representations, with each cluster grouping those internal representations that result in the same response (see Servan-Schreiber, Cleeremans, and McClelland 1991) for several detailed examples of this kind of organization). The connections between the hidden units and the output units, in turn, map these clusters of internal representations onto the responses. The rule shift introduced in the experiment is, in effect, a change in this latter mapping. Indeed, it does not result in any change in which events are important or in the number of possible responses. As a result, all the network really needs to do to produce the shifted responses is to adjust the connections from the hidden units to the output units. Weight adjustments are typically much faster in the last layer of connections than in the others because the error signals are themselves much larger. This analysis is supported by the fact that the slope of the curve corresponding to the shifted material is steeper than that corresponding to the training material for both the simulation and human subjects.

Finally, the very last point of the "shifted" curve for the human subjects may just be atypical.

**Discussion**

The simulation results described in this section highlight interesting shortcomings of both the SRN and the Jordan network. Both models were unable to learn material from the explicit prediction task proposed by Reber and Kushner (Kushner, Cleeremans, and Reber 1991), but for different reasons. In the case of the SRN, the problem stems from the fact that representing temporal context requires sequence elements to be prediction relevant at every step, a property that is not exhibited by Kushner and Reber's material. In the case of the Jordan network, the problem resulted from interference from repeated events and from the ensuing loss of discriminability among sequences requiring different prediction responses. I argued that buffer networks, which do not suffer from the above limitations, may well be an adequate model of this particular task, even if they lack generality as plausible models of temporal processing and suffer from other kinds of computational limitations. This analysis is based on the observation that Kushner and Reber's task places different demands on subjects than do the choice reaction tasks explored in Cleeremans (1993). In particular, the task is more akin to a standard classification task made harder by the fact that the material has temporal extent. The observation that the network succeeds even without any representation of the fact that the material has temporal extent reinforces the notion that the task is rather different from the choice reaction tasks explored elsewhere (Cleeremans 1993). Using nonzero values for the decay rate results essentially in slower learning and has effects that are similar to changes in the learning rate.

Despite the fact that buffer networks appear to be good models of human performance in Kushner and Reber's task, other data suggest that other processes not implemented by the model may play an important role. Specifically, it would appear that subjects also rely on memory for particularly salient sequences. The basic model has no way of representing the influence of such salient items and can only capture the emerging gradual sensitivity to the regularities present in the material. That the task involves both implicit, gradual processes, as well as more explicit processes such as memory for specific items, strategic readjustments, or active hypothesis testing, is not surprising. On the contrary, it appears likely that most experimental tasks used to explore implicit learning (or, for that matter, most real-life learning situations as well) involve both kinds of processes. This obviously contributes to the difficulty of assessing which processes are responsible for particular aspects of performance in any given situation. One strategy that appears useful in overcoming these essentially methodological difficulties consists of minimizing the role that either source of knowledge may play in performance. Sequential choice reaction tasks are very successful in this respect. Another approach consists of exploring what minimal mechanisms may be applied to model human performance and to search for plausible accounts of the unexplained variance. The buffer networks described in this section come close to implementing the minimal mechanisms needed to sustain performance in this task, although it is likely than even simpler architectures may be successful.

As a final comment on the data, it is interesting to elaborate on the fact that subjects in this task were found to be able to readjust their performance to the shifted material very quickly. This may be taken as an indication that subjects have developed abstract representations of the material, but as Perruchet (chap. 32, this volume) rightly points out, successful transfer to the shifted material in Kushner and Reber's experiment is more akin to "reversal" than to abstract transfer. In the next section, I examine experimental and simulation data that constitute more direct tests of transfer based on abstraction.

## 31.3  TRANSFER

The task proposed by Kushner and Reber is interesting because the simplicity of its design interacts usefully with the complexity of the material. These features make it possible to design straightforward transfer situations during which subjects are presented with material that was not presented during training and to start addressing difficult questions related to knowledge representation. What kind of knowledge of the sequences do subjects end up with after training? It is likely that subjects develop both a knowledge base about specific salient sequences and more gradual knowledge about the regularities embedded in the material. The buffer network proposed as a model of performance captures this latter aspect of subjects' knowledge. What kind of internal representations does the network develop during training? An analysis of the pattern of connection weights between input units and hidden units revealed that the network progressively learns to ignore information presented on the pools corresponding to time steps 1, 3, and 5, on which only irrelevant sequence elements may occur; all the corresponding connection weights were very close to 0.0 after training. By contrast, the weights on connections between the pools corresponding to elements 2 and 4 were large. In the network's layer of hidden units, specific units were used to encode the different possible combinations of elements 2 and 4 that may occur. Thus, the network has clearly learned to distinguish between relevant and irrelevant sequence elements. Does this mean the network possesses abstract knowledge of the material? One strategy in answering this question consists of first asking another one: what kind of data would constitute evidence for rulelike abstraction in this task, that is, abstraction that may not be accounted for by similarity to stored exemplars? An interesting suggestion (Perruchet, chap. 32, this volume) is to test subjects on new components or new instances of the generation rules used during training. Abstraction would be demonstrated if subjects were able to predict successfully the location of the successor of the sequence for new transitions between the locations at which events 2 and 4 appeared. As a reminder, the rule used to generate the material consisted of three components:

1. If events 2 and 4 appeared at the same location, the location of the sixth event was box A.

2. If events 2 and 4 were in a clockwise relationship, event 6 appeared in box B.

3. If events 2 and 4 were in counter clockwise relationship, then event 6 appeared in box C.

Each component of the rule was instantiated by three different contingencies between events 2 and 4, and each of these three specific pairs of events was embedded in the irrelevant context set by the other elements of the sequences. There is a variety of ways of testing for generalization with this material. For instance, one could train subjects on two instances of each component of the rule (say, *A* and *A* in positions 2 and 4 and *B* and *B*), and find out whether they generalize to material generated based on the third instance (*C* and *C*). Another similar, but maybe less stringent, test would be to compare performance on test sequences of equal similarity to the training sequences but that vary in the location of the changes. For instance, the sequences *ABCBB* (which predicts *A*) and *CAACB* (which predicts *B*) both differ equally from *CBABB* (which predicts *A*). Assume subjects are trained on the latter sequence and are then subsequently presented with the other two, which were never presented during training. The new sequence *ABCBB* predicts the same sixth event as the old *CBABB* because they differ only in their irrelevant elements (the crucial second and fourth elements are the same in both sequences). By contrast, the new *CAACB* differs from the old *CBABB* in the second and fourth elements, and so predicts a different sixth event. Different results would be expected in this situation depending on whether performance is based on abstract knowledge or on memory for exemplars. If performance is based on memory for exemplars, then subjects should predict the successor equally well in each case (regardless of the actual performance level), since the new sequences of the example are equally similar to the old one. By contrast, if subjects abstracted that only the second and fourth events determine the successor (as well as which successor occurs in each case), then performance should be better on new sequences that share these events with the old ones than on those that do not.

**Transfer to Sequences with New Relevant Elements**

Perruchet (chap. 32, this volume) conducted an interesting and straightforward experiment inspired from the design of the original task. His subjects were trained on only 162 sequences out of the possible 243 used in Kushner and Reber's original design. The sequences that were eliminated contained specific combinations of elements 2 and 4 drawn from each component of the generation rule. Recall that each of the three components (same, clockwise, and counterclockwise) was instantiated by three different pairs of elements 2 and 4. Perruchet removed one instance of each component from the training material and presented them to subjects during a transfer phase. For instance, sequences containing the pairs A and A, B and B, and C and C as events 2 and 4, respectively, all instantiate the "same" component of the generation rules and predict the same sixth event. During training, subjects saw only sequences containing A and A and B and B as their second and fourth events and were subsequently tested on sequences containing C and C. If subjects acquire abstract representations that characterize the relationship between elements 2 and 4 in terms of their spatial relationships ("same," etc.), then they should be able to transfer successfully to new instances of each component of the rule (i.e. respond to sequences containing C and C in the same way as to sequences containing A and A or B and B). By contrast, if performance is based on memory of stored instances, then a different response pattern is expected. For instance, when presented with sequences containing C and C as events 2 and 4, subjects may respond based on memory for sequences containing A and C, B and C, C and A, or C and B as events 2 and 4. All these other sequences predict different sixth events from that predicted by sequences containing A and A or B and B.

Subjects were trained for nine sessions of 162 trials each and tested during a single session consisting of two presentations of the remaining 81 sequences. After training, subjects could predict the location of the sixth stimulus in about 41 percent of the cases, a performance level roughly similar to that observed by Kushner and Reber. By contrast, performance dropped to about 20 percent on the transfer material. An analysis of subjects' prediction preferences during transfer revealed that they responded based on similarity with the training material rather than based on abstract knowledge of the generation rules. Indeed, the proportion of correct transfer responses assessed to reflect an abstract encoding of the rules (e.g., choosing the same successor for sequences containing C and C as for sequences containing A and A or B and B as events 2 and 4) averaged only .227.

To find out how buffer networks would perform on this task, I conducted several simulations of Perruchet's experiment using the buffer network architecture described above. For each simulation, ten buffer networks were trained and their performance averaged for further analysis. I adjusted the learning rate until performance after training was roughly equivalent to that of subjects in Perruchet's experiment (41 percent of correct predictions). A learning rate of 0.6 yielded good fits with the data, resulting in an average proportion of correct responses of 39 percent. Over transfer, the average proportion of correct responses dropped to 19 percent. Next, I computed the networks' response preferences as described above and found that the proportion of responses reflecting an encoding of the generation rules averaged .198—a value close to the .227 observed by Perruchet. Higher learning rates resulted in most networks' learning the task perfectly. For those networks, the proportion of prediction responses reflecting an encoding of the generation rules fell to 0.0. Buffer networks produce response patterns that reflect those of subjects. In both cases, there are clear indications that predictions are based on similarity with stored exemplars rather than on abstract knowledge of the generation rules.

**Transfer to Sequences with New Irrelevant Contexts**

If the results described in the previous section appear to rule out performance based on abstract knowledge, there may be other conditions in which transfer would be successful. Consider, for instance, what would happen if the transfer material differs from the training material only in the irrelevant elements of the sequences. One could train subjects on sequences that contain all the possible combinations of events 2 and 4 but embedded in only some of the possible random contexts. Transfer would then consist of presenting subjects with sequences containing new random contexts. Table 31.2 shows one possible design for such an experiment, in which only two-thirds of all possible random contexts are used during training. A buffer network exhibits perfect

Table 31.2 The Twenty-seven Possible Random Contexts in Which Relevant Sequence Elements May Be Embedded

| Serial Position | 1 | 3 | 5 | 1 | 3 | 5 | 1 | 3 | 5 |
|---|---|---|---|---|---|---|---|---|---|
| | A | A | A | B | A | A | *C* | A | A |
| | A | A | B | B | A | B | *C* | A | B |
| | A | A | C | B | A | C | *C* | A | C |
| | A | B | A | B | B | A | *C* | B | A |
| | A | B | B | B | B | B | *C* | B | B |
| | A | B | C | B | B | C | *C* | B | C |
| | A | C | A | B | C | A | *C* | *C* | *A* |
| | A | C | B | B | C | B | *C* | *C* | *B* |
| | A | C | C | B | C | C | *C* | *C* | *C* |

Note: Italicized items are presented only during transfer; the other items are presented only during training.

transfer to the new material because during training, it learns to ignore information coming from pools of input units representing irrelevant elements. If subjects were to perform as well as the model on this kind of transfer material, it would be a good indication that they learned to differentiate relevant events from irrelevant ones. Whether one wants to take this ability as an indication of abstraction is a matter of language, but it certainly is an indication that the model's performance is based on knowledge that is a step away from rote memory of specific exemplars, in that it was able to extract the relevant structural properties of the material and to respond based on this information.

## 31.4 GENERAL DISCUSSION

I have proposed a computational model of performance in explicit prediction tasks such as the one first proposed by Kushner and Reber (Kushner, Cleeremans, and Reber 1991). The model turns out to be surprisingly simple, since it is an instance of a simple three-layer backpropagation network with no recurrence. The simulation work suggests that prediction performance is largely based on the gradual accumulation of information about the structure of the material. This gradual sensitivity comes about by the fact that the model learns to discriminate between relevant and irrelevant elements of the input. The data also suggest that other processes, such as memory for salient sequences and strategic readjustments, play a nonnegligible role in this task. This reflects the fact that subjects placed in any experimental situation will attempt to use whatever explicit strategies and knowledge are available, even in cases where this is detrimental to performance (Reber 1976). Thus, these additional, explicit processes are particularly inefficient when the stimulus material is as complex and ill defined as in this experiment. This is confirmed by the fact that subjects typically report discontinuing the use of such hypothesis-testing strategies soon after training has begun. In other words, these strategies do play a role in performance but are rather ancillary in nature. The core mechanism that drives prediction performance in the task I have explored here is the gradual learning of associations between sequences and their successors.

What alternative accounts of the data may be plausible? One possibility may be that subjects merely memorize sequences during training. This is not as implausible as it may first appear, because memorizing only thirty sequences would yield the observed improvements in performance over training. This figure is not at all unlikely given the fact that subjects are exposed to 2430 trials over training and also that some sequences are particularly easy to remember and to recode. There are several problems with such an account, however. First, such a memorization strategy is one that subjects would conduct in a very explicit way. Therefore, one may expect them to report on their using this strategy during the interviews and even to be able to report some of the sequences themselves. However, no subject did so, except for a few of the most salient sequences. One may still argue that subjects may have a memory of specific sequences without being able to report on them, however.

A reanalysis of the data in which performance is assessed on a sequence-per-sequence basis should be useful in determining whether this is the case.

Second, this hypothesis cannot account adequately for transfer to the shifted material. There is a marked difference between the slope of the curve corresponding to the last four sessions of training and that of the curve corresponding to the four transfer sessions. One may argue that this difference comes from the fact that subjects benefit so much from general familiarity with the task that they are able to learn a lot faster during transfer than during training. However, one would expect the effects of such familiarization to be gradual, which is not consistent with the actual data. The simulation work reported here suggests that the difference comes specifically from the fact that only responses have to be readjusted when switching to the shifted material.

Third, knowledge based on "raw" memory would fail to transfer differently to stimuli with new relevant events than to stimuli with new irrelevant events. Although this is a matter for further experimentation, the simulation work described in this chapter predicts that transfer is good only when the irrelevant events have been changed. Such a contrast between relevant and irrelevant events cannot be accommodated by a theory that assumes subjects are storing information uniformly for all sequences and for all their elements. These theoretical difficulties may be alleviated by assuming that what gets memorized are fragments, or chunks of the sequences. But how are these chunks acquired? The basic problem with memory-based theories is that they tend to be purely descriptive and fail to give insight into the processes at play. Process theories based on chunking, such as Servan-Schreiber and Anderson's (1990), on the other hand, are probably indistinguishable from other strength-based mechanisms such as those instantiated by the networks explored here. In short, theories that assume that every instance is memorized appear implausible and unable to account for the data, and theories that assume some form of chunking may very well be equivalent to those explored here.

Knowledge acquired implicitly is often characterized as abstract. What is generally meant by *abstraction* is that the knowledge is not about specific exemplars or based on processes that operate on the common relevant features of these exemplars but that it is rulelike. This strong position is almost certainly wrong. There is abundant evidence that what subjects acquire is fragmentary knowledge about local constraints, and little evidence at all for the idea that the acquired knowledge is abstract in the sense defined above. Two kinds of arguments have been used to support the abstractness position. One is that subjects show evidence of possessing knowledge that is clearly more abstract than mere memory for exemplars; the other is that they transfer to material that does not share surface features with the material used during training. To address the second argument first, the main evidence that supports it consists of the artificial grammar studies in which subjects were trained on a grammar using one letter set and then subsequently tested on material generated from the same grammar but using a different letter set (Reber 1969; Mathews et al. 1989). Transfer performance was quite good, thus suggesting that subjects have acquired representations of the training strings that are independent of the surface features of these strings, that is, abstract representations. Recent evidence by Brooks and Vokey (1991), however, suggests that transfer performance may be based on a process that the authors called abstract analogy, by which subjects perceive the abstract relationships between corresponding strings (e.g., the letters of both *MXVVVM* and *BDCCCB* enter in similar relationships with each other). They provide evidence for this process through a clever design that manipulates grammatical status and similarity independently. That is, some new nongrammatical strings may be more similar to old grammatical strings than new grammatical strings.

The first argument—that subjects exhibit knowledge that goes beyond mere sensitivity to stored exemplars—is still the object of debate. In some cases, it appears that performance may be accounted for by assuming that subjects base classification performance on similarity with stored exemplars; in others, this explanation does not hold. For instance, subjects correctly classify new nongrammatical strings even though they may be very similar to old grammatical strings (McAndrews and Moscovitch 1985). Thus, both similarity to old instances and reliance on higher-level abstract representations seem to play a role in discrimination performance, and the available empirical evidence does not make it easy to distinguish between the effects of either variable. Further, task instructions and the training environment may also contribute to induce subjects to adopt different strategies with regard to the processing of specific exemplars. For instance, McAndrews and Moscovitch (1985) suggest that the training procedure later reported in Vokey and Brooks (1992), in which relatively few strings were presented many times, may have induced subjects to rely more on memory for specific items than typical in artificial grammar learning experiments.

Evidence for abstraction would come from studies that indicate clearly that subjects generalize based on the abstract rules defining the structure of the material. At least one experiment (Perruchet, chap. 32, this volume) indicates unambiguously that subjects tend to generalize based on similarity with old exemplars. However, one may argue with what is meant by *abstraction*. According to the *Online American Heritage Dictionary*, to abstract is the "act or process of separating the inherent qualities or properties of something from the actual physical object or concept to which they belong." By that definition, the simple buffer networks that were found to account for performance in Kushner and Reber's task do acquire abstract representations of the stimulus material because they have isolated which features of the input are relevant and which are not. Subjects in the experiment conducted by Perruchet (chap. 32, this volume) may similarly exhibit knowledge of which events are relevant for the prediction task. It remains to be seen how well human subjects transfer to material that incorporates new random contexts. But rather than speculate, I would like to examine whether connectionist models may be able to achieve successful transfer in these situations and what it means for such models to develop abstract representations.

When one looks inside an SRN trained on material from a finite state grammar, it becomes apparent that the representations of the network may, under some conditions, be very close to the abstract representation of the grammar: each state is encoded by a different cluster of similar patterns of activity over the hidden units of the network (see Servan-Schreiber, Cleeremans, and McClelland 1991 for many examples). Is this kind of representation abstract? In some ways it is, because the network has clearly developed representations that encode relevant underlying dimensions of the training material (as opposed to, say, representations that are literal copies of specific training items). But in other ways, it is not abstract, because performance is still very much dependent on surface features of the material. That is, if one were to switch to a different letter set (represented by using new input units), for instance, the network would fail completely to predict the successor, even if this new material had been generated from the same grammar. This, of course, is not surprising, since there is no way for the network to induce that different letters play similar roles in each grammar. Additional mechanisms that allow the network to evaluate and use the abstract similarity between the strings generated from either grammar would be necessary to allow it to generalize in this way.

This is not to say that connectionist networks cannot, in principle, exhibit sensitivity to the abstract dimensions of the stimulus material. On the contrary, there is abundant evidence that they do. For instance, Hinton (1986) showed that a backpropagation network trained to produce the patient of an agent-relationship pair given as input (for instance, Maria is the wife of Roberto) developed internal representations that captured relevant abstract dimensions of the domain (here, family trees), such as nationality or age. The crucial point is that the input representation contained no information whatsoever about these abstract dimensions: each person or relationship was represented by activating a single input unit. Further, the model generalized to new instances of specific input-output pairings that had never been presented during training (albeit in only a limited number of test cases). Thus, in Hinton's words, "The structure that must be discovered in order to generalize correctly is not present in the pairwise correlations between input units and output units" (9). Examples from work on recurrent connectionist architectures such as the SRN also support this notion. For instance, an SRN trained on only some of the strings that may possibly be generated from a finite state grammar will generalize to the infinite set of all possible instances (Servan-Schreiber, Cleeremans, and McClelland 1991). Connectionist networks of this kind are clearly more than simple associators that only encode input-output correspondences based on a set of stored training examples. Indeed, as McClelland and Rumelhart (1985) suggest, depending on factors such as the number of hidden units or the structure of the training set, such networks may develop internal representations that are best characterized as storage of exemplars (i.e., many microassociations) or as an encoding of the shared properties of many instances (i.e., a few general associations). Thus, there appears to be a representational continuum that extends from the specific to the general, and the opposition that is often made between abstract (implicit) knowledge and fragmentary (explicit) knowledge that is at the heart of so many debates about implicit learning performance begins to fade when one considers the way in which connectionist models represent and use information.

To conclude, there is no clear evidence that knowledge acquired in implicit learning situations is abstract. But this does not necessarily entail that human performance is based only on knowledge about stored exemplars. By suggesting that abstract representations can emerge from elementary learning mechanisms based on the processing of exemplars, the simulation work described in this chapter suggests a third possibility that borrows features from the two extreme positions described above. In more ways than one, architectures such as the SRN or other connectionist models force us to reconsider traditional perspectives on cognition.

## NOTES

Preparation of this chapter was supported by the National Fund for Scientific Research (Belgium), where the author is a research associate. I thank Arthur Reber and Pierre Perruchet for stimulating discussions and access to their data, and Alain Content and two anonymous reviewers for many useful comments on an earlier version of this chapter. Some sections of this chapter have been adapted from Cleeremans (1993).

1. The successful SRN simulations reported in Kushner, Cleeremans, and Reber (1991) are erroneous. A bug in the stimulus generation program resulted in material that is learnable by the network, but different from the actual material used in the Kushner and Reber experiments.

2. It may seem surprising to expect that the network would learn under the training conditions used here. However, the network also fails to learn when trained to predict each successive event of the sequence, not merely the previous one. This is precisely because of the reasons discussed in the text. Further, other simulations show that for some problems, intermittent training (where the network is only trained to predict some elements of a sequence) results in better learning than when the network is trained to predict each successive element.

## REFERENCES

Brooks, L. R. (1978). Nonanalytic concept formation and memory for instances. In E. Rosch and B. B. Lloyd (Eds.), *Cognition and categorization*. New York: Wiley.

Brooks, L. R., and Vokey, J.R. (1991). Abstract analogies and abstracted grammars: Comments on Reber (1989) and on Mathews et al. (1989). *Journal of Experimental Psychology: General, 120*, 316–323.

Cleeremans (1993). *Mechanisms of implicit learning: Connectionist models of sequence processing*. Cambridge: MIT Press.

Cleeremans, A., and McClelland, J. L. (1991). Learning the structure of event sequences. *Journal of Experimental Psychology: General, 120*, 235–253.

Cottrell, G. W., Munro, P. W., and Zipser, D. (1987). Image compression by back-propagation: A demonstration of extensional programming. In N. E. Sharkey (Ed.), *Advances in cognitive science*, vol. 2. Chichester: Ellis Horwood.

Dienes, Z. (1992). Connectionist and memory array models of artificial grammar learning. *Cognitive Science, 16*, 41–79.

Dulany, D. E., Carlson, R. A., and Dewey, G. I. (1985). On consciousness in syntactical learning and judgment: A reply to Reber, Allen and Regan. *Journal of Experimental Psychology: General, 114*, 25–32.

Elman, J. L. (1990). Finding structure in time. *Cognitive Science, 14*, 179–211.

Elman, J. L., and Zipser, D. (1988). Discovering the hidden structure of speech. *Journal of the Acoustical Society of America, 83*, 1615–1626.

Hanson, S., and Kegl, J. (1987). PARSNIP: A connectionist network that learns natural language from exposure to natural language sentences. In *Proceedings of the Ninth Annual Conference of the Cognitive Science Society*. Hillsdale, NJ: Erlbaum.

Hinton, G. E. (1986). Learning distributed representations of concepts. In *Proceedings of the Eighth Annual Conference of the Cognitive Science Society*. Hillsdale, NJ: Erlbaum.

Hintzmann, D. L. (1986). "Schema Abstraction" in a multiple-trace memory model. *Psychological Review, 93*, 411–428.

Jennings, P. J., and Keele, S. W. (1990). A computational model of attentional requirements in sequence learning. In *Proceedings of the Twelfth Annual Conference of the Cognitive Science Society*. Hillsdale, NJ: Erlbaum.

Jordan, M. I. (1986). Attractor dynamics and parallelism in a connectionist sequential machine. In *Proceedings of the Eighth Annual Conference of the Cognitive Science Society*. Hillsdale, NJ: Erlbaum.

Kushner, M., Cleeremans, A., and Reber, A. S. (1991). Implicit detection of event interdependencies and a PDP model of the process. In *Proceedings of the Thirteenth Annual Conference of the Cognitive Science Society*. Hillsdale, NJ: Erlbaum.

Lewicki, P., Hill, T., and E. Bizot, E. (1988). Acquisition of procedural knowledge about a pattern of stimuli that cannot be articulated. *Cognitive Psychology, 20*, 24–37.

McAndrews, M. P., and Moscovitch, M. (1985). Rule-based and exemplar-based classification in artificial grammar learning. *Memory and Cognition, 13*, 469–475.

McClelland, J. L., and Rumelhart, D. E. (1985). Distributed memory and the representation of general and specific information. *Journal of Experimental Psychology: General, 114*, 159–188.

Mathews, R. C., Buss, R. R., Stanley, W. B., Blanchard-Fields, F. Cho, J.-R., and Druhan, B. (1989). The role of implicit and explicit learning processes in learning from examples: A synergistic effect. *Journal of Experimental Psychology: Learning, Memory, and Cognition, 15*, 1083–1100.

Medin, D. L., and Schaffer, M. M. (1978). Context theory of classification learning. *Psychological Review, 85*, 207–238.

Nissen, M. J., and Bullemer, P. (1987). Attentional requirements of learning: Evidence from performance measures. *Cognitive Psychology, 19*, 1–32.

Perruchet, P., and Amorim, M-A. (1992). Conscious knowledge and changes in performance in sequence learning: Evidence against dissociation. *Journal of Experimental Psychology: Learning, Memory, and Cognition, 18*, 785–800.

Perruchet, P., and Pacteau, C. (1990). Synthetic grammar learning: Implicit rule abstraction or explicit fragmentary knowledge? *Journal of Experimental Psychology: General, 119*, 264–275.

Reber, A. S. (1967). Implicit learning of artificial grammars. *Journal of Verbal Learning and Verbal Behavior, 6*, 855–863.

Reber, A. S. (1969). Transfer of syntactic structure in synthetic languages. *Journal of Experimental Psychology, 81*, 115–119.

Reber, A. S. (1976). Implicit learning of synthetic languages: The role of the instructional set. *Journal of Experimental Psychology: Human Learning and Memory, 2*, 88–94.

Reber, A. S. (1989). Implicit learning and tacit knowledge. *Journal of Experimental Psychology: General, 118,* 219–235.

Rumelhart, D. E., Hinton, G., and Williams, R. J. (1986). Learning internal representations by error propagation. In D. E. Rumelhart and J. L. McClelland (Eds.), *Parallel distributed processing, explorations in the microstructure of cognition,* Vol. 1: *Foundations.* Cambridge, MA: MIT Press.

Servan-Schreiber, D., Cleeremans, A., and McClelland, J. L. (1991). Graded state machines: The representation of temporal contingencies in simple recurrent networks. *Machine Learning, 7,* 161–193.

Servan-Schreiber, E., and Anderson, J. R. (1990). Learning artificial grammars with competitive chunking. *Journal of Experimental Psychology: Learning, Memory and Cognition, 16,* 592–608.

Vokey, J. R., and Brooks, L. R. (1992). Salience of item knowledge in learning artificial grammars. *Journal of Experimental Psychology: Learning, Memory, and Cognition, 18,* 328–344.

# 32 Learning from Complex Rule-Governed Environments: On the Proper Functions of Nonconscious and Conscious Processes

Pierre Perruchet

ABSTRACT Improvement in performance of people faced with a complex rule-governed situation can occur without the emergence of any conscious knowledge of the rules. This chapter illustrates with a new example, and subsequently generalizes, the proposal that this phenomenon does not testify to the unconscious abstraction of the rules underlying the situation, as held by the prevalent, abstractionist interpretation. Indeed, performance improvement can be accounted for by a memory-based framework positing that subjects only learn specific fragments of the material, which constitute the basic functional unit of knowledge in most learning conditions. More important, findings lend weight to this framework when the experimental design contrasts its predictions with those derived from the abstractionist standpoint.

This theoretical shift has major consequences for the alleged implicitness of the processes engaged in this mode of learning. In particular, specific knowledge accounting for performance improvement appears to be usually available to conscious reflection upon explicit request in normal subjects. However, there is evidence that this knowledge can be used automatically to satisfy the demands of a subsequent task involving the same or similar material. Possible implications of these data on the role of nonconscious and conscious processes in adaptive behavior are discussed.

## 32.1 INTRODUCTION

Research on human learning has traditionally focused on simple experimental settings, such as classical conditioning and paired associate learning. Although some studies on concept or category learning have involved more complex situations, the level of complexity is generally adjusted so that subjects can break at least some of the rules structuring the material within one or a few experimental study sessions. These paradigms parallel the learning conditions in some real-world situations, such as scholastic ones, but there is no doubt that they provide a poor analogue of most natural settings. Indeed, the natural environment is structured by rules, whether physical, linguistic, social, or other, a majority of them so complex that they remain beyond the scope of common understanding. In addition, subjects in experimental situations of concept or category learning are typically asked for intentional rule searching, whereas laypeople rarely engage in active analysis of their natural environment in order to penetrate its deep structure.

Experimental paradigms involved in artificial grammar learning (Reber 1989), pattern sequence learning (Shanks, chap. 33, this volume), and learning in interactive situations (Berry, chap. 30, this volume) are devised to better fit natural conditions of adaptation. In these so-called implicit learning paradigms, subjects are faced with situations governed by complex, arbitrary rules, without being prompted for an explicit analysis of the task. In these conditions, performance improves, although subjects remain unable to articulate the rules governing the situations. This empirical outcome, first evidenced in the pioneering work of Arthur Reber (1967), has been unambiguously confirmed by all subsequent studies.

Demonstrating the ability of human subjects to improve their performance in a complex environment even though the structure of this environment is unavailable to the subjects' conscious awareness constitutes in itself a genuine contribution, and the novelty and implications of it are largely unnoticed. For example, the ability of people to learn from situations structured by complex arbitrary rules provides powerful support for the empiricist standpoint in the longstanding metatheoretical debate on the role of innate processes on behavior.

However, the major interest of disposing of laboratory analogues to complex learning in natural environments is that they offer an opportunity to explore the nature of the psychological processes involved in this form of adaptive behavior. The earlier interpretation (Reber 1967) accounts for improved performance by positing that human subjects unconsciously abstract rules embodied in the complex situations at hand and implicitly use this abstract knowledge to cope with subsequent situations. This interpretation is still advocated (Reber 1989; Lewicki, Hill, and Czyzewska 1992), and may even be prevalent, at least among investigators engaged primarily in related areas of research (e.g., Roediger 1990; Schacter 1987).

This interpretation has been the object of controversy, initiated by the papers of Brooks (1978) and Dulany, Carlson, and Dewey (1984) and extensively developed since then. At the heart of the debate are the two main components of the conventional position, centered on the abstract and the unconscious nature of the knowledge base acquired during learning.

It is important to make clear the relationships between the criticisms addressing the abstractionist stance and those addressing the claim about unconsciousness. From a logical standpoint, the availability in consciousness of the knowledge base underlying improved performance is independent of the nature of this knowledge. However, the two aspects cannot be handled separately in any empirical inquiry for an obvious reason: assessing whether the knowledge base responsible for improved performance is conscious or nonconscious requires this base to be clearly identified. Everyone presumably agrees that demonstrating subjects' unconsciousness of the abstract rules underlying the situation should be irrelevant if the change in performance is in fact attributable to quite a different form of knowledge. The argument developed in this chapter is that the main drawback of the conventional position is related primarily to the role this position confers to abstract knowledge in adaptive behavior, and only as a way of consequence, to its claims about unconsciousness or implicitness.

The shift away from an abstractionist stance has historical antecedents in research areas involving simpler learning paradigms. One example can be found in research on classical and instrumental conditioning in animals and humans. Rats' sensitivity to contingency relationships between stimuli in a conditioned suppression paradigm was originally demonstrated in the oft-cited paper by Rescorla (1968). The fact that a variety of animal species, including humans, are sensitive to contingency relationships in classical and instrumental conditioning paradigms has been abundantly confirmed since then (Wasserman 1990). The original interpretations naturally posited that this sensitivity to contingency testified to a genuine ability to abstract the covariations embedded in the conditioning situation. However, most current explanatory models of conditioning no longer assume that animals actually engage in contingency abstraction processes. As first demonstrated by Rescorla and Wagner (1972) and expanded on amply later, empirical results may be conveniently accounted for by simple associative processes (for recent reviews, see Papini and Bitterman 1990; Shanks 1991).

Categorization learning research was the theater for a similar conceptual shift. By and large, this field of research has been characterized by an upsurge in models postulating that the specific properties of items belonging to the same category are condensed into a small amount of abstract information (e.g., prototypes, occurrence frequency of independent features, or feature covariation). People were assumed to rely on this condensed form of representation when they had to make category assignments of new items in a subsequent test phase.

Since the seminal papers by Brooks (1978) and Medin and Shaffer (1978), such models have been challenged by models in which no abstraction takes place. The study exemplars are stored in memory with their specific properties, and subsequent categorization judgments of new items are made on the basis of their degree of similarity with the stored exemplars. These exemplar-similarity models have been tentatively applied to situations in which categories are ill defined (Perruchet, Pacteau, and Gallego 1993) or defined by logical rules (Nosofsky 1991). In all cases, stored exemplars were found to form a major, or at least substantial, component of the category representation, even when the classification rule was simple and made explicit for the subjects (Allen and Brooks 1991). Similar examples can be found in the problem-solving literature reviewed by Medin and Ross (1990).

This brief incursion into areas of research involving relatively simple experimental settings reveals a strikingly similar evolution in thought. The very patterns of performance that seemed at one time to be clear support for the engagement of abstractive processes have been subsequently reinterpreted within far more parsimonious frameworks, which no longer assume rule abstraction.

Recent work on implicit learning suggests that the evidence put forward for rule abstraction in more complex experimental settings is ready for a similar reappraisal. For the purposes of illustration, this chapter first presents a reinterpretation of a recent study on predictive behavior carried out in Reber's laboratory (Kushner, Cleeremans, and Reber 1991) in which subjects had to learn a rule that, according to the authors, was "far more complex than anything that has been studied to date." Then I will tentatively demonstrate that all the alleged evidence for abstraction amassed in the prior literature on implicit learning is inconclusive, because an alternative model accounts for the empirical data as well as, or better than, the mechanisms involved in the abstractionist framework. The model used here is similar to Brooks's (Brooks 1978; Vokey and Brooks 1992), insofar as it relies essentially on memory for specific events. However, it departs from Brooks's model regarding the notion of specific events, in a way that considerably extends the model's field of application.

This fundamental theoretical shift has major consequences with regard to the issue of implicitness, which will be discussed next. To anticipate, redirecting the postexperimental tests of awareness from an abstract form of knowledge to the memory of specific events leads us to find in the subjects' knowledge available to conscious awareness a sufficient basis to account for performance improvement in implicit learning situations. However, this does not imply that everything occurring in these situations relies on a conscious form of processing. I will argue that the involvement of nonconscious processes in the use of the memory for specific past events ought to be acknowledged.

## 32.2  AN ILLUSTRATIVE EXAMPLE

### The Kushner, Cleeremans, and Reber Study

In the Kushner, Cleeremans, and Reber (1991) experiment, subjects viewed a computer screen on which a square stimulus could appear in three possible numbered locations, arranged to form the vertices of an invisible triangle. An event was defined as the appearance of the stimulus in a given location. A trial consisted of six successive events. The first five stimuli were displayed in rapid succession. After the fifth event had occurred, subjects were asked to predict where the sixth event would appear and had to enter their prediction by typing 1, 2, or 3 on a numeric keypad. Then the sixth stimulus appeared in its correct location. The location of the sixth event was determined on the basis of the relation between the locations at which the second and fourth stimuli had appeared. If these stimuli appeared at the same location, the sixth stimulus appeared in location 1. If they had been in a clockwise relation, the sixth stimulus appeared in location 2, and if they had been in a counterclockwise relation, the sixth stimulus appeared in location 3.

Discovering this set of rules from the displayed sequences involves very sophisticated operations: (1) picking up relevant events from the irrelevant context (the first, third, and fifth events in each trial were always irrelevant) and (2) abstracting a rule based on the relationships between the location of the relevant stimulus (considered in isolation, the location of stimulus on the second or on the fourth event had no predictive value). Despite this considerable difficulty, subjects did learn. Prediction accuracy, which started near chance level (33 percent correct responses), improved over the ten sessions of training and reached about 45 percent correct responses at the end.

From session 11 to session 14, the previous rules were modified by shifting the location of the sixth stimulus by one step: the sequences that previously ended in location 1 now ended in location 2, and so on. Subjects' prediction accuracy dropped back to chance level on session 11 and then improved again over the next sessions. In the four subsequent and final sessions, the location of the sixth stimulus was determined at random; as expected, subjects' performance remained around chance level.

Extensive postexperimental interviews revealed that in some specific cases, subjects had become aware of some of the regularities embedded in the material (for instance, the fact that sequences in which the five stimuli occurred in the same location always ended in location 1). However, these very fragmentary pieces of knowledge were clearly insufficient to account for performance. By and large, subjects were unable to report the correct rules and, in particular, the nature of the crucial events. When they were asked to rate each of the five stimuli in terms of their relevance to the prediction task on a five-point scale, the mean ratings were respectively 3.33, 3.5, 3.67, 2.67, and 1.83. At first glance, these results provide a compelling argument for the authors' conclusion: "Clearly, subjects have become sensitive to contingencies about which they are unable to report."

**A Memory-based Reinterpretation**

Suppose now that subjects memorize parts of the specific sequences of events, without abstracting any rules, and make predictions on the basis of their memory for earlier sequences. Each sequence was displayed once per session, so that the gradual improvement in performance across the first ten sessions would naturally be expected to occur under this assumption. The drop in prediction accuracy when rules are shifted in session 11 may also be readily explained, insofar as changing rules also change specific sequences. The fast subsequent improvement from sessions 11 to 14 may be accounted for by the familiarity subjects acquired with the material at this stage of the experiments, which is known to facilitate coding and hence memorization of new sequences. Finally, the drop in performance when the sixth event occurred randomly during the final phase of the experiment is also compatible with a pure memory account for trivial reasons.

In Kushner, Cleeremans, and Reber's experiment, the exhaustive set of possible sequences (243 [$3^5$]) was displayed during the training phase. This procedure makes abstractionist and memory interpretations impossible to disentangle, because abstracting rules and memorizing their product lead to the same outcome. In the experiment reported here, only two of the three possible instantiations of each rule were displayed during training, and the remaining possibilities were shown in a subsequent transfer phase. The particular sequences presented in each phase were chosen in order to pit the predictions of the two models against each other.

Table 32.1 shows that the rule "Same position, then issue A" was instantiated by 1-1 and 2-2 in the study phase. When 3-3 was displayed in the transfer phase, subjects who abstracted the rule were expected to predict A. However, subjects who memorized part of the sequences were expected to predict B or C, because the transfer sequence had one additional element in common with the study sequences ending with B or C than with the study sequences ending with A. Indeed, the former always included one stimulus in location 3, whereas the latter never did. The other predictions specified in table 32.1 were generated by applying similar reasoning.

## Method

**Subjects**  The subjects were six females, fourth-year university students majoring in psychology. They were paid 80 FF (around $14) and received a bonus of 0.10 FF (around 1.7 cents) per correct prediction.

**Material**  The stimuli were white disks, 10 mm in diameter. They appeared within one of the three empty circles permanently displayed on the screen and numbered 1, 2, and 3. The circles were located at the vertices of an invisible equilateral triangle (10 cm per side).

**Table 32.1**  Summary Design of the Study and Transfer Phases of the Experiment

a. Study Phase (Sessions 1–9)
Observed Sequences

| Second Event | Fourth Event | Sixth Event | Rule |
| --- | --- | --- | --- |
| 1 | 1 | A | Same position |
| 2 | 2 | A | |
| 1 | 3 | B | Clockwise |
| 3 | 2 | B | |
| 2 | 3 | C | Counterclockwise |
| 3 | 1 | C | |

b. Transfer Phase (Session 10)

| Observed Sequences | | Model Predictions for the Sixth Event | |
| --- | --- | --- | --- |
| Second Event | Fourth Event | Rule Abstraction | Memory Based |
| 3 | 3 | A | B or C |
| 2 | 1 | B | A or C |
| 1 | 2 | C | A or B |

Note: This table shows the observed (a) and predicted (b) locations of the sixth event as a function of the preceding events. This location is symbolized by letters rather than digits because allocation of the physical positions to each of the three rules was counterbalanced across subjects.

There were 162 (6 × 27) different sequences in the study phase. Indeed, only 6 out of the 9 ($3^2$) different possible combinations of events 2 and 4 were shown (see table 32.1), and each of these combinations was presented in 27 ($3^3$) different contexts, made up by the exhaustive combination of events 1, 3, and 5. In the transfer phase, there were 81 (3 × 27) different sequences, corresponding to combinations not displayed previously.

**Procedure** Subjects were recruited to participate in ten experimental sessions with the following constraints: no more than two immediately successive sessions, no more than four sessions a day, and no more than a 48-hour. interval between any two sessions. All subjects completed the experiment within 5 days. As in Kushner, Cleeremans, and Reber, the study was presented as being about predictive behavior.

The 162 different study sequences were shown on each of the first nine sessions. For the first five stimuli of each trial, duration of both stimulus and interstimulus was set to 250 ms each. After subjects had pressed 1, 2, or 3 on the keyboard to enter their predictions, the stimulus was displayed in its correct location for 2000 ms. This location was counterbalanced across subjects, so that each subject had one of the 6 (3!) possible assignments of issues to the sequences. The next trial began 500 ms later. After trials 54 and 108, subjects were prompted on the screen to take a break; they had to press any key on the keyboard to continue with the experiment. The number of correct predictions was displayed on the screen at the end of each session.

Session 10 also consisted of 162 trials, with the 81 different transfer sequences presented twice. Subjects were kept unaware of the change in sequences; however, they were informed that they would no longer see the stimulus appearing in its correct location after entering their prediction. (Correctness of prediction in this session depended on the choice of a theoretical model, so it seemed preferable not to provide information at this stage.)

Order of trials was randomized without any constraints, both between sessions and between subjects, for study as well as for the transfer sessions.

Subjects were interviewed at the end of the experiment. They were questioned about their general strategy, their hypotheses about the structure of the task, and their ability to recall specific sequences. This interview was intended to replicate the Kushner, Cleeremans, and Reber procedure and not to provide a sensitive test of memory for the study sequences (which would have required the running of a recognition test before the transfer session). Subjects were debriefed about the objective of the study only after all of them had completed the entire experiment.

### Results and Discussion

Figure 32.1 shows the proportion of correct predictions on the nine training sessions. Mean performance gradually improved from random level to a proportion of .415 correct (which significantly differs from .33, $t = 2.71, p =$

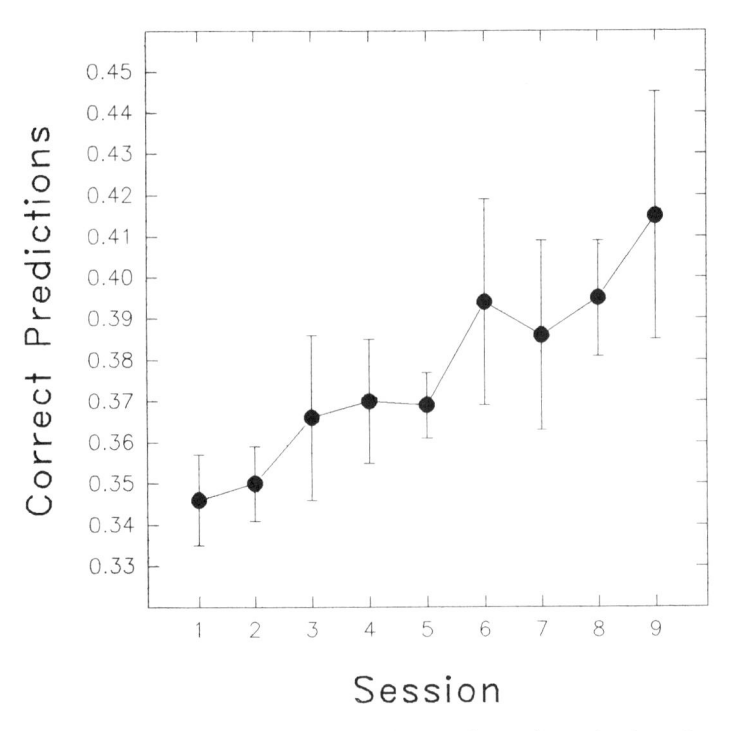

**Figure 32.1** Proportion of correct predictions during the study phase. Error bars represent standard errors of the mean.

.042, $df = 5$) on the ninth session. Standard error also tended to increase over sessions, indicating that subjects did not learn at the same rate. The mean individual proportion of correct predictions on the whole study phase ranged from .340 to .407.

Results on the transfer session are shown in table 32.2. The data fitted nicely with the predictions of the memory model. Statistical analyses confirm that issues B and C, considered together, were predicted more often than chance after the sequences instantiating the rule "same position" ($t = 6.78$, $p = .001, df = 5$), and issues A and B were predicted more often than chance for the rule "counterclockwise" ($t = 3.99, p = .010, df = 5$). Although results also fit with the predictions of the memory model for the rule "clockwise," the difference from chance failed to reach significance ($t = 1.89, p = .116$, $df = 5$).[1]

Although performances exhibited the same general trend for all the subjects, individual patterns of responding were unequally differentiated. An individual degree of differentiation was computed as the overall proportion of predictions fitting with the memory model during the transfer phase. Interestingly, this score correlated strongly with the rate of correct predictions made during the first nine sessions (Pearson $r$: .804, $p = .027$). This result lends weight to the idea that predictions performed during the training and transfer phases tap the same knowledge base.

**Table 32.2** Mean Proportion of Predictions Falling into A, B, and C, as a Function of the Preceding Events during the Transfer Phase

| Observed Sequences | | Predictions for the Sixth Event | | |
|---|---|---|---|---|
| Second Event | Fourth Event | A | B | C |
| 3 | 3 | .204 | .376 | .420 |
| 2 | 1 | .494 | .213 | .293 |
| 1 | 2 | .426 | .309 | .265 |

Overall, these findings provide compelling evidence in favor of the memory model. One possible counterargument starts from considering that the present situation differs from Kushner, Cleeremans, and Reber's insofar as subjects were deprived of part of the information during training in the former but not in the latter situation. It may be that the whole set of possible exemplars is needed to abstract generative rules. This hypothesis has two damaging properties. The first is its unfalsifiability. The only way to test whether rules have been abstracted is to observe the ability of subjects to deal with new situations in transfer tasks. Presenting the whole set of exemplars generated by the rules during training makes the rule abstraction and pure memory models impossible to disentangle. Second, hypothesizing that subjects need all the possible instantiations of a rule to abstract this rule deprives the process of abstraction of its primary functional value: allowing adaptation to new situations.

One final experimental result pertains to the postexperimental interviews. They revealed extremely poor explicit knowledge about the task. Most subjects actively searched for regularities in the first few sequences, but gave up after their repeated failures to find an even partially successful rule. That is exactly what Kushner, Cleeremans, and Reber also reported about their study. However, it should be clear now that my conclusion is exactly the opposite from theirs. Whereas they inferred from the fact that performance improves without subjects being able to verbalize the rules that these rules were unconsciously abstracted, the conclusion of my experiment is that subjects did not abstract any rule at all, consciously or unconsciously (see Cleeremans, chap 31, this volume, for other arguments stemming from connectionist simulations of the same task).

## 32.3 GENERALIZING THE REFUTATION OF THE ABSTRACTIONIST MODEL

This section aims to show that virtually all the alleged evidence for abstraction may be accounted for by simple memory for the displayed items or, more generally, for a fragmentary part of them, and when predictions from abstractionist and memory-based models are pitted against each other, the results unambiguously stand in favor of the latter.

## The Memory-based Model as an Alternative Framework

**The Case of No or Inadequate Transfer Procedure**  The fact that performance of subjects repeatedly exposed to a structured situation improves across trials or sessions is obviously congruent with the hypothesis that subjects acquire a structural representation of this situation. Thus, the mere occurrence of learning is commonly cited in support, although rarely in isolation, for the abstractionist position. It is clear that a memory-based model makes exactly the same predictions, for trivial reasons. Making abstractionist and memory based models distinguishable implies in all cases the assessing of learning through a transfer procedure in which subjects are exposed to a new situation.

The Kushner, Cleeremans, and Reber (1991) study illustrates a case in which transfer consists in changing or suppressing the rules underlying the study material. This procedure has been used in a few studies on artificial grammar learning (e.g., Reber 1969) and, on a larger scale, on sequential pattern learning (e.g., Lewicki, Hill, and Bizot 1988). In all of these studies, this procedure results in a sharp drop in subjects' performance, which is taken as evidence for implicit rule knowledge. It is worth noting that a pure memory account again predicts the same outcome. This occurs because changing the rules also changes the product of the rules that subjects, supposedly, memorize. The decrease in performance when rules are changed must not be confused with a genuine transfer effect, which involves the reverse: (relative) stability of performance when the same rules apply to different material. All the studies reviewed below involved genuine transfer paradigm.[2]

**Transfer to New Material with Similar Surface Features**  In most studies including a transfer procedure, the surface features of the stimuli are left unchanged between study and test. In artificial grammar learning, for example, transfer items are typically new strings made up of the same letters as the study strings. Subjects have been shown to perform above chance in assessing the grammaticality of these items.

At first glance, only an abstractive mechanism is able to account for this result, given that the test items were not previously displayed. However, the experimental data may still be accommodated within a memory-based model. One possibility has been put forward by Brooks (1978), who reasons that subjects perform the grammaticality task by assessing the degree of similarity of new test items with the stored representation of a specific study item. Grammaticality and similarity to specific items, Brooks argues, are confounded in typical procedures, so that judging from similarity leads to mimicking performances obtained by applying grammatical rules to the new material. Subsequent studies (McAndrews and Moscovitch 1985; Vokey and Brooks 1992) demonstrated that when the test material was devised to make grammaticality and specific similarity independent, a substantial part of the variance in grammaticality judgments was indeed accounted for by the similarity of test items with a specific study exemplar. However, another part of the variance was linked to the genuine grammaticality of test items. These results led Vokey and Brooks (1992) to conclude in favor of a dual model, reserving a place for abstractive processes in addition to memory-based mechanisms.

My colleagues and I explored a somewhat different way of accounting for transfer data (Perruchet, Gallego, and Pacteau 1992; Perruchet and Pacteau 1990). Our framework is close to Brook's in that grammaticality judgments also rely on memory for specific events, but the events of interest no longer match what are the logical units from the experimenter's standpoint. The level of analysis is shifted from whole exemplars to small chunks of letters such as bigrams or trigrams. These chunks typically vary in frequency across the set of items. In keeping with the ubiquitous laws of memory, the strength of the memory trace is thought to be sensitive to this frequency of occurrence. The sensitivity to frequency information provided by our model is crucial, because it can be shown that the frequency of occurrence of chunks conveys part of the structural information about items. Hence, the simple and automatic effect of occurrence frequency of chunks on performance mimics the effects of knowing and applying the abstract rules underlying the material.

This change in the size of the basic units of knowledge has dramatic consequences on the explanatory power of memory-based accounts of artificial grammar learning. I have shown elsewhere (Perruchet, n.d.) that taking trigrams as the basic unit of knowledge explains within a memory-based framework the variance in performance that Vokey and Brooks (1992) failed to account for with a memory-based model that posited the primacy of item knowledge (and that they consequently attributed to genuine abstraction processes). In addition to converging results from other laboratories (Dienes, Broadbent, and Berry 1991; Servan-Schreiber and Anderson 1990), these data lead to the conclusion that transfer on items built from the same letter set as the study items does not provide evidence for abstraction in the area of artificial grammar.

Studies in sequence pattern learning (Cleeremans and McClelland 1991) and control process situations (Marescaux, Dejean, and Karnas 1990) exhibit remarkable convergences with the conclusion drawn from artificial grammars.

**Transfer to New Material with Dissimilar Surface Features** The rationale for changing the surface features of the material between the study and transfer phases is straightforward. This procedure makes irrelevant an account for transfer in terms of components common to study and test material. Hence, the occurrence of positive transfer should ensure that performance is mediated by the knowledge of abstract rules. However, the experimental literature consistently shows that transfer on superficially different, although structurally similar, material is, at best, an uncommon phenomenon.

Studies in the grammar learning area (Brooks and Vokey 1991; Mathews et al. 1989; Reber 1969; Whittlesea and Dorken 1993) support this assertion, despite the optimistic claims of most of their authors. In these studies, the letters making up the items were changed in a consistent way between the study and the test phases, with the structure of the grammar left unchanged.

The proportion of correct responses in the changed letter set condition was typically found to be around .55, a proportion higher than the .50 correct proportion corresponding to random responding.

Unfortunately, none of these studies included a genuine control group receiving no prior training with structured strings, which is needed to assess the occurrence reliably, and the magnitude of transfer effects observed in the experimental group (see Perruchet, n.d., for a more detailed criticism). Even if further studies with adequate control showed some transfer effects, it remains to be proved that these effects stem from implicit processes. One possibility is that subjects engage in a controlled search for abstract rules during the study phase, even though there was no explicit request. In line with this hypothesis, Whittlesea and Dorken (1993) report that any trend for transfer to a new letter set disappears when the study strings are presented as distractors devised to prevent rehearsal in what is disguised as a number learning experiment. Another possibility stems from the fact that subjects at the beginning of the test phase are typically informed that the strings they saw during study were generated by a complex set of rules and that they have to assess the well-formedness of new items with regard to these rules. These instructions inevitably shift subjects to a rule discovery mental set. Thus, abstractive operations on the recalled representation of study items may be performed at this time.

The findings are still more clear-cut in other subareas of research. Total failure to obtain transfer to new material with dissimilar surface features is the rule in studies on serial reaction time tasks (Stadler 1989; Willingham, Nissen, and Bullemer 1989), as well as in studies on control process tasks (Berry and Broadbent 1988; Squire and Frambach, 1990).

## Contrasting Predictions from Abstractionist and Memory-based Models

The literature reviewed up to now offers no straightforward evidence that a genuine abstraction process mediates performance in implicit learning paradigms, insofar as a memory-based interpretation conveniently accounts for the same data. However, both models have the status of alternative accounts. A memory-based model may be preferred for its economy or some other extraneous features, but the validity of an abstract standpoint remains intact. The search for a stronger test implies devising procedures aimed at contrasting the predictions of the two models. The experiment presented at the beginning of this chapter illustrates such a procedure. Recall that findings unambiguously supported the memory-based model.

Following the same strategy, my colleagues and I (Perruchet, Gallego, and Savy 1990) conducted further analyses of the sequence learning situation initially explored by Lewicki, Hill, and Bizot (1988). We pointed out that an interpretation positing that subjects were sensitive to the frequency of occurrences of small components of the study sequence accounted for the rough performance pattern as well as Lewicki, Hill, and Bizot's interpretation that subjects abstracted the generative rules of the sequence. However, we also derived from the two models a set of contrasted predictions pertaining to specific features in the fine-grained pattern of subjects' performance (Perruchet, Gallego, and Savy 1990, table 1). The empirical data exhibited a strikingly good fit with our predictions, while the predictions derived from the abstractionist framework were clearly disconfirmed. This result was due again to the acknowledgment of the primacy of small chunks of trials over the "logical" unit of the task.

To recapitulate, a memory-based model taking small fragments of stimulus material as basic units of knowledge not only provides an economical alternative account to the abstractionist model; the empirical data clearly lend support to the former when predictions based on the two models are experimentally contrasted.

## Does a Model Based on Memory for Small Units Really Exclude Abstraction?

The preceding analysis shows to what extent the explanatory power of memory-based models is enhanced when psychological units are conceived of as fragments of physical or logical units. The formation of these subunits may be described in terms of abstraction from larger units. Similarly, the effect of the occurrence frequency of these small units may be described as the abstraction of the most relevant information from the whole initial data.

Abstraction as a descriptive concept, however, must not be confused with abstraction as a psychological process. For the sake of illustration, consider the status of the fragments of letters such as bigrams or trigrams in artificial grammars. These chunks may be described as abstracted from a string of letters. Similarly, strings of letters are abstracted from the list of strings, and letters are abstracted from chunks. This nested listing may be lengthened at both ends. Any event may be considered as abstracted from its context. This makes it clear that the descriptive definition of abstraction is psychologically irrelevant.

The term *abstraction* refers in this chapter to analytical operations performed to extract componential information from a primitive entity. Considering chunks as abstracted from strings in this psychologically relevant way is tantamount to confounding the experimenter's units with the subject's units. In fact, a number of arguments support the idea that in the standard conditions of training used in artificial grammar paradigms, subjects primarily encode fragments of items such as bigrams or trigrams (for arguments, see Perruchet and Pacteau 1991; Perruchet, n.d.). The resulting primacy of fragments over the whole exemplars in subjects' representations is beneficial to subsequent grammaticality judgments, but no special processing linked to the grammatical structure of the study items needs to be assumed. Chunking would occur also with random sets of letters, because it depends on fundamental and ubiquitous properties of the perceptual system.

The same line of reasoning applies to frequency effects. As argued by Mathews (1991), forgetting infrequent units can abstract knowledge. When forgetting infrequent units occurs on structured material, its consequences on grammaticality judgments parallel the effects of rule-based processing. However, the psychological process at hand is forgetting, not abstraction.

These remarks lead to the tentative characterization of the memory-based model put forward here as a model that involves only the perceptual and memory processes that are engaged and exert observable consequences upon performance in all situations, whether they are structured or random. Claiming that implicit learning in rule-governed environments is based on memory-based processes means that no processes are engaged other than those recruited in, for instance, list learning or other "pure memory" paradigms. The fact that engaging these simple and ubiquitous processes in rule-governed situations generates performances that generally parallel those expected from subjects fully informed of the rules leads to an emphasis on their powerful adaptive value but has no implications with regard to the intrinsic sophistication of these processes.

**Summary**

Thus, the entire body of data collected in the implicit learning area can be encompassed within a memory-based framework positing the primacy of small functional units of knowledge. More important, the results lend support to this framework when the experimental design contrasts its predictions with those derived from the abstractionist standpoint. These findings suggest that the simple and ubiquitous processes recruited in any memory paradigm are a far more general and efficient way of coping with structured environments than was previously acknowledged, thus extending the conclusion reached in other areas of research dealing with simpler pattern stimuli to very complex situations.

## 32.4 IMPLICATIONS FOR THE IMPLICITNESS OF PROCESSING

Such a radical change in our conception about how humans learn from rule-governed environments has major consequences for the issue of implicitness. Reber (1989, p. 219) defines implicit learning by three criteria: "(a) Implicit learning produces a *tacit knowledge base* that is abstract and representative of the structure of the environment; (b) such knowledge is *optimally acquired independently of conscious effort* to learn; and (c) it can be *used implicitly* to solve problems and make accurate decisions about novel stimulus circumstances" (emphasis added). Although there is no evidence for Reber's requirement for an abstract knowledge base, these criteria can still serve to define implicitness, although the knowledge base subtending performance improvement is conceived of as a pool of specific events rather than a set of abstract rules.

## Is the Knowledge Base Unavailable to Conscious Reflection?

Studies in the abstractionist framework naturally focus on knowledge of the rules underlying the situation and, unsurprisingly, fail to reveal any conscious knowledge of these rules. Studies aimed at investigating memory for specific items or fragments of items provide a totally different picture.

Subjects typically exhibit a large amount of specific knowledge when tests are devised to tap this feature. Convincing demonstrations that the pieces of knowledge available to consciousness are sufficient to account for performance improvement have been made in the artificial grammar learning area (Dienes, broadbent, and Berry 1991; Druhan and Mathews 1989; Dulany, Carlson, and Dewey 1984; Perruchet and Pacteau 1990), as well as in process control situations (Marescaux and Karnas 1991; Sanderson 1989).

In the sequence learning area, the early evidence for unconsciousness was also dismissed when the level of inquiry was shifted from the knowledge of rules to the knowledge of specific sequences. For instance, Perruchet, Gallego, and Savy (1990) showed that the demonstration provided by Lewicki, Hill, and Bizot (1988) falls short when the measure of consciousness no longer bears on the abstract two-order dependency rules generating the sequences but rather on short segments of the sequences (Cleeremans, 1993 Cleeremans and McClelland 1991).

In some respects, the same analysis can be made on the Nissen and Bullemer (1987) experiments and on studies patterned after the same paradigm. In these studies, the sequences are not the product of abstract generative rules but nevertheless embed some kind of regularity. Indeed, a single, arbitrary sequence is repeated throughout the training session. Several authors (Cohen, Ivry, and Keele 1990; Nissen, Willingham, and Hartman 1989; Willingham, Nissen, and Bullemer 1989) claimed that in order to gain place reaction times improve with repetition of this sequence without subjects acquiring conscious knowledge of the sequence (or at least before they do so). Most of this evidence is again grounded on a confounding between the logical units of the task: namely, the whole repeated sequence and the psychologically relevant units. For instance, in the studies above cited postexperimental interviews were devised to assess if subjects realized that they saw the repetition of the same sequence, which is generally ten trials long. In a still more recent experiment, Willingham, Greeley, and Bardone (1993) assessed explicit knowledge of their sixteen-trial sequences through a recognition test in which they present the old sixteen-trial sequence mixed with new sixteen-trial sequences. The problem is that subjects can learn part of the sequence before noticing that the same sequence is continuously repeated or before being able to recognize the whole repeated sequence. Amorim and I (Perruchet and Amorim 1992) showed that when subjects were instructed to generate a sequence that looked like the one they had encountered in the training phase or were asked to recognize small fragments of this sequence, reliable explicit knowledge of salient fragments was revealed after an amount of practice that was hardly sufficient to improve mean motor performance. Importantly, the trials within the sequence on which reaction times were the lowest were the ending elements of the best-recalled or best-recognized chunks of trials.

Overall, shifting the object of inquiry from the abstract rules or from the logical units of the task to fragmentary specific knowledge leads to the conclusion that the knowledge base underlying performance improvement in implicit learning paradigms is normally available to consciousness.[3]

**Is the Knowledge Base Optimally Acquired without Conscious Effort to Learn?**

Obviously, Reber's criterion refers tacitly here to conscious effort to learn the rules. In a memory-based framework, the lack of a positive effect of this strategy would call for a straightforward interpretation: rules are useless for performance improvement. But empirical data reveal not only a lack of positive effect but a detrimental effect of rule-searching instructions. One explanation may be that omitting instructions for rule searching facilitates memory for specific study items. This would occur because the search for rules diverts subjects from paying full attention to the specific items. The instructions used by default, which typically call for rote memory of items,[4] are well suited to promote acquisition of specific knowledge and hence should be associated with better performance.

Is the (specific) knowledge base optimally acquired without conscious effort to learn exemplars? The evidence about the beneficial effect of rote memory instructions on performance is in line with a negative response. However, focusing on the role of conscious effort to learn may be misguided. The actual causal factor is more probably the nature of the processing that such a strategy elicits. Attempting to memorize the items would be efficient because this strategy leads to the allocation of attentional processing to the relevant features of the material. But any orienting task eliciting similar processing would be efficient as well, even if subjects are not conscious that they are learning. These kinds of ideas are reminiscent of the framework that evolved in the memory area during the past two decades around the notions of encoding specificity or transfer-appropriate processing. Whittlesea and Dorken (1993) have cogently argued for applying this framework to the artificial grammar learning area. In support of their so-called episodic processing account, they show through several experiments that performance in transfer tasks is altered in consonance with transfer-appropriate processing principles by manipulating the specific demands of the study task.

**Is the Knowledge Base Used Implicitly?**

In the abstractionist point of view, the implicit use of knowledge is a straightforward consequence of its alleged unconscious status. In the context of a memory-based framework, the availability in consciousness of fragmentary specific knowledge makes it possible for subjects to use this knowledge deliberately to cope with the test situation. This hypothesis has been advocated by Dulany, Carlson, and Dewey (1984) and endorsed by Perruchet and Pacteau (1990) in the artificial grammar area. In the standard procedure, subjects make their well-formedness assessment of test strings while they are fully informed of the rule-governed nature of the situation and without time pressure. These conditions make it likely that subjects engage in deliberate use of all the information they can explicitly retrieve about the study strings. However, what happens if such deliberate control processing is impeded, or at least not explicitly prompted by, the procedure?

In an early study on artificial grammar learning, Reber (1967) observed that subjects instructed to learn the letter strings by rote performed better when the strings were generated by the grammar than when strings were generated randomly, although they were never informed about the nature of the strings. Similarly, in sequential pattern learning paradigms, subjects are never instructed about the structure of the sequence. In addition, they have to respond as fast as possible to successive targets. These conditions make it unlikely that they engage in deliberate strategies of responding based on the explicit representation of the sequence, at least during the early stage of training. Introspective subjects' reports support this assertion. Nevertheless, reaction times are sensitive to the structure of the sequence after remarkably little practice. Moreover, the improvement in performance still occurs when subjects perform the task under attentional distraction (Cohen, Ivry, and Keele 1990; Nissen and Bullemer 1987; Perruchet and Amorim 1992).

These data suggest that performance improvement is at least partially independent of the deliberate use of retrievable information. However, this independence remains debatable, given that postexperimental tests consistently show that the knowledge base underlying performance improvement is available to normal subjects' awareness upon explicit request.

Studies conducted with patients who have no conscious access to the knowledge base as a result of neurological impairements provide a unique opportunity to assess the role of conscious knowledge on performance improvement. Knowlton, Ramus, and Squire (1992) submitted amnesic patients with various etiologies to a standard artificial grammar learning paradigm. They reported that patients performed as well as normal subjects on the grammaticality task, although they were impaired on a recognition test of letter strings. Likewise, several pattern sequence learning studies conducted with individuals with Korsakoff's syndrome reported that reaction times improved with training (Nissen and Bullemer 1987), even with a 1-week interval between study and test (Nissen, Willingham, and Hartman 1989), although patients lacked the corresponding explicit knowledge. Normal improvement in performance despite a severe impairment of explicit representations has also been found in patients with amnesia resulting from Alzheimer's disease (Knopman and Nissen 1987). Overall, these findings clearly run counter to the idea that changes in performance are necessarily mediated by the aware knowledge of the components of the situation in which these changes are observed. At least some of these changes could originate from the automatic use of memory (to borrow Jacoby's terms, e.g., Jacoby, chap. 26, this volume).

Of course, performance usually can also be influenced by conscious, deliberate use of memory. Some insight about the dual influence of automatic and intentional processes on performance is provided in the Knowlton, Ramus, and Squire (1992) study. This study reported no difference in grammaticality judgments between amnesic patients and control subjects, but this result was observed only when judgments were performed on the basis of subjective feelings. A difference emerged when subjects were encouraged to use their conscious memory of study strings. Performance of normal subjects, who presumably have conscious knowledge of some fragments of the study strings, benefited from this change in instructions, demonstrating that intentional use of memory can assist grammaticality judgments (see also Willingham, Nissen, and Bullemer 1989 for similar evidence in sequence learning). By contrast, performance of amnesic patients, who presumably have inadequate conscious knowledge of the study material, tended to deteriorate in the same conditions. Although it would be premature to propose a complete interpretation of these results, they suggest that automatic and conscious uses of memory interact in complex ways, according to laws that warrant further empirical and theoretical research.

This research should benefit from increased proximity with research in memory. The rejection of the abstractionist model of learning leads to drawing a close parallelism between the operations involved when subjects are faced with a rule-governed environment and with a set of unrelated items, as in typical memory paradigms. Studies on implicit memory as assessed by repetition priming tests (Moscovitch, chap. 25, this volume; Roediger 1990; Schacter 1987) teach us a fundamental principle: that a specific past event can exert an influence on subsequent performance without this event being explicitly remembered. In this domain, the joint influence of deliberate and automatic processes has generated an abundant literature. For instance, several theories posit that recognition partly relies on subjective familiarity with the test items, with familiarity being construed as the automatic consequence of the earlier processing of the same material (e.g., Mandler 1990). Conversely, the possible influence of explicit retrieval on performance in nominally implicit tests of memory also has be acknowledged (e.g., Schacter 1987). There is now a large consensus around the idea that there are no process-pure memory tasks (Jacoby 1991). Presumably, similar developments in the context of learning in complex situations are warranted.

**Summary**

Experimental data provide striking evidence that an amount of specific knowledge sufficient to account for performance improvement is available to conscious reflection upon explicit request, at least when normal subjects are submitted to standard experimental conditions. This knowledge is closely dependent on the operations engaged in by the subjects to satisfy the demands of the study task. However, these results do not entail that performance is causally determined by the intentional use of this knowledge. Introspective evidence in normal subjects suggests, and studies on neurologically impaired patients confirm, that changes in performance can occur without the involvement of concious, intentional processes, as in typical implicit memory tests.

## 32.5 THE FUNCTIONS OF NONCONSCIOUS AND CONSCIOUS PROCESSES

On the basis of the empirical evidence put forward so far, this section is devoted to more speculative developments on the function of nonconscious and conscious processing. I argue that the new perspective leads us to differentiate more clearly the role of nonconscious processes from the role of conscious processes than was the case in the conventional, abstractionist framework.

### Conceiving Nonconscious Processes in the Model of Conscious Processes

Anyone attempting to learn from a new structured stimulus pattern invariably engages in a deliberate controlled strategy that searches for deep regularities in order to store in memory a small number of ready-to-use abstract laws and apply them when required by the situation. When researchers observed that subjects' performance improved in complex situations even though these operations were not intentionally engaged and available to retrospective awareness, they naturally hypothesized that the same operations were performed by an autonomous, unconscious processor. The only acknowledged differences between the two modes of processing pertain to their power (with nonconscious processing viewed as more powerful than conscious processing) and their rapidity (with nonconscious processing viewed as faster than conscious processing). As claimed by proponents of this view, "Our conscious thinking needs to rely on notes (with flowcharts or lists of if-then statements) or computers to do the *same job* that our nonconsciously operating processing algorithms can do instantly and without external help" (Lewicki, Hill, and Czyzewska 1992, 798; emphasis added).

Postulating unconscious activity in direct analogy with human conscious processing is by no means specific to this area of research. This view is standard in domains such as cognitive ethology, linguistics, psychoanalysis, formal models in artificial intelligence, and the information-processing approach in cognitive psychology.

### A Crucial Difference

This standard view has been challenged in several ways. Searle (1990) has forcefully argued that this view anthropomorphizes the nonconscious processes in the brain. Dulany (1991) remarks that even Freud was concerned about this aspect, as shown by the following quotation: "The psychoanalytic assumption of unconscious mental activity appears to us, on the one hand, as a further expansion of the primitive animism which caused us to see copies of our own consciousness all around us" (Freud [1915] 1957, 171).

The framework outlined in this chapter leads to hypothesizing qualitative, and not only quantitative, differences between nonconscious and conscious processing. The evidence reviewed suggests that nonconscious processes are operative in the use of specific knowledge, while conscious processes can deal with both specific and abstract knowledge.

Reintroducing abstraction here may seem paradoxical, insofar as the general stance of this chapter runs counter to an abstractionist standpoint. The paradox, however, is only apparent. The memory-based model of learning put forward here is intended to be relevant only in usual paradigms of implicit learning, that is, when subjects are not prompted for intentional rule searching or, more generally, for abstract processing of the study material. Obviously other forms of knowledge can be acquired under other conditions. For instance, Turner and Fischler (1993) and Wittlesea and Dorken (1993) show that subjects can learn abstract rules of the grammar underlying strings of letters when they are instructed to search for rules, or when they are given incidental instructions orienting toward the structure of the material (see also Shanks and St. John in press, for additional evidence for abstraction in other areas of experimental research). At a more general level, the very existence of sciences such as logics, linguistics, and physics also testifies to the human ability to abstract the structure of complex environments. The point of this chapter is not that learning from complex situations never involves abstractive operations but that these operations require explicit thinking for them to be performed.

These claims about the specific properties of nonconscious and conscious processing are intrinsically speculative. Indeed, demonstrating that the unconscious is unable to perform some operations goes beyond any experimental inquiry; it can be shown only that the reverse proposal—the unconscious is endowed with such abilities—has no empirical support.

**Is the Unconscious Smart or Dumb?**

In the target paper of a set of contributions introduced under this title (Loftus and Klinger 1992) in the *American Psychologist*, Greenwald (1992) argued for an unconcious that would be far less sophisticated than commonly thought. This chapter unambiguously supports this standpoint.

The Greenwald claim, however, could be misguiding, insofar as the lack of sophistication is usually associated with the lack of power. Therefore, it is worth emphasizing that the analysis in this chapter leads to conceive the unconscious as both "dumb" and considerably powerful. Indeed, by and large, the reappraisal presented in this chapter consists in changing the nature of the adaptive operations performed without conscious awareness, without questioning their end product. These operations have limited sophistication insofar as they consist essentially in benefiting from the earlier processing of similar specific events. But they are performed with considerable efficiency, presumably due to a massively parallel mode of processing. In fact, they almost perfectly simulate the action of a sophisticated processor.

## 32.6 ABOUT EVOLUTION THEORY

Nonconscious processes are conceived in this chapter as oriented toward the exploitation in parallel of a large database of specific pieces of knowledge to satisfy immediate demands. Conversely, abstract operations are linked with conscious and controlled thought. This conception corresponds to a profound change in perspective with regard to the conventional position (e.g. Reber 1989), in which abstract knowledge is acquired and used by an unconscious, autonomous processor.

Recently Reber (1992) framed his position within a functionalist perspective, anchored within evolutionary biology. He forcefully argues that implicit systems ought to be conceived of as fundamental in adaptation, given that consciousness is a late arriver in ontogenetic and phylogenetic development. In keeping with this claim, he puts forward a set of observations leading support to the "primacy of the implicit" (Reber 1990). I entirely agree with this perspective.

Reber's line of reasoning, however, provides no support for his view concerning the nature of implicit processes. His contention—that viewing abstraction as a primitive and fundamental adaptive process is consonant with the basic tenets of evolutionary biology—in fact uses the claim that implicit learning generates abstract knowledge as one of its premises. Introducing evolution theory here provides no additional support for this premise. If it is replaced, as I think it must be, by "implicit learning engages memory-based processes only," then the conclusion that memory-based processes are primitive and fundamental adaptive processes follows as well.

It may be argued further that the position advocated in this chapter is closer to evolution theory principles than usual on at least two key points. The first pertains to the unrealistic view that species low in the phylogenetic scale are endowed with sophisticated processing systems. A memory-based model of implicit learning rests on far simpler (although equally powerful) processes, which are easier to account for by elementary neurophysiological mechanisms.

The second point may be more important. Reber's framework gives no place to consciousness in the learning process. Consciousness is construed as a simple epiphenomenon, when its intervention is not perceived as detrimental to efficient learning (Reber 1989). This conception is undermined by a serious flaw. As Dulany (1991) noted, "We may wonder why consciousness evolved at all if it is the poor thing it is often said to be" (p. 101). The recency of the emergence of consciousness in phylogenetic history must not overshadow the fact that this emergence has apparently been accompanied by a major improvement in adaptive abilities. The framework outlined here accounts for this feature by construing consciousness as a prerequisite for analytic reasoning and genuine abstraction.

## NOTES

Preparation of this chapter was supported by the Centre National de la Recherche Scientifique and the Université René Descartes, Paris, France. I thank D. Berry, J. Gallego, J. Lautrey, and one anonymous reviewer for their helpful comments on an early version of the chapter.

1. For the three rules, *t*-tests compared the observed proportion of responses falling into one of the two issues predicted by the memory model with .66. For two of these rules (clockwise and counterclockwise relations), the probability of selecting one or another of these issues substantially differed. This trend was not anticipated by any of the competing models of the task, and its interpretation is not clear.

2. For alleged evidence of abstraction that relies on another, somewhat complex procedure, and its reinterpretation within a nonabstractionist framework, see Perruchet, Gallego, and Pacteau (1992).

3. For the sake of brevity, I pass over in silence the problems surrounding the nature of the tests devised to assess awareness, and especially the problems related to the sensitivity of these tests. Priority is given in this chapter to *what* to measure, rather than to *how* to measure. For an analysis including other aspects, see the overview by Shanks and St. John (N.d.).

4. In artificial grammar learning, instructions asking for rote learning are termed implicit, and instructions asking for rule searching are termed explicit. These labels are appropriate to the abstractionist standpoint. However, they have to be reversed to be consonant with a memory-based framework. If performance improvement is due to the memory for specific events, instructions stressing rote learning would be more correctly called explicit, and conversely, rule-searching instructions become implicit in nature.

## REFERENCES

Allen, S. W., and Brooks, L. R. (1991). Specializing in the operation of an explicit rule. *Journal of Experimental Psychology: General, 120,* 3–19.

Berry, D. C., and Broadbent, D. E. (1988). Interactive tasks and the implicit-explicit distinction. *British Journal of Psychology, 79,* 251–272.

Brooks, L. R. (1978). Nonanalytic concept formation and memory for instances. In E. Rosch and B. B. Lloyd (Eds.), *Cognition and categorization,* 169–215. Hillsdale, NJ: Erlbaum.

Brooks, L. R., and Vokey, J. R. (1991). Abstract analogies and abstracted grammars: A comment on Reber, and Mathews et al. *Journal of Experimental Psychology: General, 120,* 316–323.

Cleeremans, A. (1993). *Mechanisms of implicit learning: A connectionist model of sequence processing.* Cambridge, MA: MIT Press.

Cleeremans, A., and McClelland, J. L. (1991). Learning the structure of event sequences. *Journal of Experimental Psychology: General, 120,* 235–253.

Cohen, A., Ivry, R. I., and Keele, S. W. (1990). Attention and structure in sequence learning. *Journal of Experimental Psychology: Learning, Memory, and Cognition, 16,* 17–30.

Dienes, Z., Broadbent, D., and Berry, D. (1991). Implicit and explicit knowledge bases in artificial grammar learning. *Journal of Experimental Psychology: Learning, Memory, and Cognition, 17,* 875–887.

Druhan, B. B., and Mathews, R. C. (1989). THIYOS: A classifier system model of implicit knowledge of artificial grammars. Paper presented at the annual meeting of the Cognitive Science Society, Ann Arbor, MI.

Dulany, D. E. (1991). Conscious representation and thought systems. In R. S. Wyer and T. K. Srull (Eds.), *Advances in social cognition*, vol. 4, 97–120. Hillsdale, NJ: Erlbaum.

Dulany, D. E., Carlson, A., and Dewey, G. I. (1984). A case of syntactical learning and judgment: How conscious and how abstract? *Journal of Experimental Psychology: General, 113*, 541–555.

Freud, S. [1915] (1957). The unconscious. In J. Strachey (Ed. and Trans.), *The standard edition of the complete psychological works of Sigmund Freud*, vol. 14, 159–215. London: Hogarth Press.

Green, R. E. A., and Shanks, D. R. (1993). On the existence of independent learning systems: An examination of some evidence. *Memory and Cognition, 21*, 304–317.

Greenwald, A. G. (1992). New look 3: Unconscious cognition reclaimed. *American Psychologist, 47*, 766–779.

Jacoby, L. L. (1991). A process dissociation framework: Separating automatic from intentional uses of memory. *Journal of Memory and Language, 30*, 513–541.

Knopman, D. S., and Nissen, M. J. (1987). Implicit learning in patients with probable Alzheimer's disease. *Neurology, 37*, 784–788.

Knowlton, B. J., Ramus, S. J., and Squire, L. R. (1992). Intact artificial grammar learning in amnesia: Dissociation of classification learning and explicit memory for specific instances. *Psychological Science, 3*, 172–179.

Kushner, M., Cleeremans, A., and Reber A. (1991). Implicit detection of event interdependencies, and a PDP model of the process. In *Proceedings of the Thirteenth Annual Conference of the Cognitive Science Society, Chicago*.

Lewicki, P., Hill, T. and Bizot, E. (1988). Acquisition of procedural knowledge about a pattern of stimuli that cannot be articulated. *Cognitive Psychology, 20*, 24–37.

Lewicki, P., Hill, T., and Czyzewska, M. (1992). Nonconscious acquisition of information. *American Psychologist, 47*, 796–801.

Loftus, E. F., and Klinger, M. R. (1992). Is the unconscious smart or dumb? *American Psychologist, 47*, 761–765.

Mandler, G. (1990). Your face looks familiar but I can't remember your name: A review of dual process theory. In W. E. Hockley and S. Lewandowsky (Eds.), *Relating theory and data: Essays on human memory in honor of Bennet B. Murdock*. Hillsdale, NJ: Erlbaum.

Marescaux, P-J., Dejean, K., and Karnas, G. (1990). *Acquisition of specific or general knowledge at the control of a dynamic simulated system: An evaluation through a static situations questionnaire and a transfer control task*. Report 2PR2GK of the KAUDYTE project (ESPRIT BRA 3219).

Marescaux, P-J., and Karnas, G. (1991). *The implicit versus explicit knowledge distinction revisited: When finding associations between verbalizable knowledge and some performance criteria*. Report 4PR3GK of the KAUDYTE project (ESPRIT BRA 3219).

Mathews, R. C. (1991). The forgetting algorithm: How fragmentary knowledge of exemplars can abstract knowledge. *Journal of Experimental Psychology: General, 120*, 117–119.

Mathews, R. C., Buss, R. R., Stanley, W. B., Blanchard-Fields, F., Cho, J.-R., and Druhan, B. (1989). Role of implicit and explicit processes in learning from examples: A synergistic effect. *Journal of Experimental Psychology: Learning, Memory, and Cognition, 15*, 1083–1100.

McAndrews, M. P., and Moscovitch, M. (1985). Rule-based and exemplar-based classification in artificial grammar learning. *Memory and Cognition, 13*, 469–475.

Medin, D. L., and Ross, B. H. (1990). The specific character of abstract thought: Categorization, problem solving, and induction. In R. J. Sternberg (Ed.), *The psychology of human intelligence*, vol. 5, 189–223. Hillsdale, NJ: Erlbaum.

Medin, D. L., and Shaffer, M. M. (1978). A context theory of classification learning. *Psychological Review, 85*, 207–238.

Nissen, M. J., and Bullemer, P. (1987). Attentional requirements of learning: Evidence from performance measures. *Cognitive Psychology, 19*, 1–32.

Nissen, M. J., Willingham, D., and Hartman, M. (1989). Explicit and implicit remembering: When is learning preserved in amnesia? *Neuropsychologia, 27*, 341–352.

Nosofsky, R. M. (1991). Typicality in logically defined categories: Exemplar-similarity versus rule instantiation. *Memory and Cognition, 19*, 131–150.

Papini, M. R., and Bitterman, M. E. (1990). The role of contingency in classical conditioning. *Psychological Review, 97*, 396–403.

Perruchet, P. (n.d.). On defining the knowledge units of a synthetic language: Comment on Vokey and Brooks (1992). *Journal of Experimental Psychology: Learning, Memory, and Cognition*. In press.

Perruchet, P., and Amorim, M. A. (1992). Conscious knowledge and changes in performance in sequence learning: Evidence against dissociation. *Journal of Experimental Psychology: Learning, Memory, and Cognition, 18*, 785–800.

Perruchet, P., Gallego, J., and Pacteau, C. (1992). A reinterpretation of some earlier evidence for abstractiveness of implicitly acquired knowledge. *Quarterly Journal of Experimental Psychology, 44A*, 193–210.

Perruchet, P., Gallego, J., and Savy, I. (1990). A critical reappraisal of the evidence for unconscious abstraction of deterministic rules in complex experimental situations. *Cognitive Psychology, 22*, 493–516.

Perruchet, P., and Pacteau, C. (1990). Synthetic grammar learning: Implicit rule abstraction or explicit fragmentary knowledge? *Journal of Experimental Psychology: General, 119*, 264–275.

Perruchet, P., and Pacteau, C. (1991). The implicit acquisition of abstract knowledge about artificial grammar: Some methodological and conceptual issues. *Journal of Experimental Psychology: General, 120*, 112–116.

Perruchet, P., Pacteau, C., and Gallego, J. (1993). Abstraction of covariation in category learning: A critical note on K. Richardson's studies. *British Journal of Psychology, 84*, 289–295.

Reber, A. S. (1967). Implicit learning of artificial grammars. *Journal of Verbal Learning and Verbal Behavior, 6*, 855–863.

Reber, A. S. (1969). Transfer of syntactic structure in synthetic languages. *Journal of Experimental Psychology, 81*, 115–119.

Reber, A. S. (1989). Implicit learning and tacit knowledge. *Journal of Experimental Psychology: General, 118*, 219–235.

Reber, A. S. (1990). On the primacy of the implicit: A comment on Perruchet and Pacteau. *Journal of Experimental Psychology: General, 119*, 340–342.

Reber, A. S. (1992). The cognitive unconscious: An evolutionary perspective. *Consciousness and Cognition, 1*, 93–133.

Rescorla, R. A. (1968). Probability of shock in the presence and absence of CS in fear conditioning. *Journal of Comparative and Physiological Psychology, 66*, 1–5.

Rescorla, R. A., and Wagner, A. R. (1972). A theory of Pavlovian conditioning: Variations in the effectiveness of reinforcement and non-reinforcement. In A. H. Black and W. F. Prokasy (Eds.), *Classical conditioning II: Current theory and research*, 64–99. New York: Appleton-Century-Crofts.

Roediger, H. L., III (1990). Implicit memory: A commentary. *Bulletin of Psychonomic Society, 28*, 373–380.

Sanderson, P. M. (1989). Verbalizable knowledge and skilled task performance: Association, dissociation, and mental models. *Journal of Experimental Psychology: Learning, Memory, and Cognition, 15*, 729–747.

Schacter, D. L. (1987). Implicit memory: History and current status. *Journal of Experimental Psychology: Learning, Memory, and Cognition, 13*, 501–518.

Searle, J. R. (1990). Consciousness, explanatory inversion, and cognitive science. *Behavioral and Brain Sciences, 13*, 585–642.

Servan-Schreiber, D., and Anderson, J. R. (1990). Learning artificial grammars with competitive chunking. *Journal of Experimental Psychology: Learning, Memory, and Cognition, 16*, 592–608.

Shanks, D. R. (1991). Instrumental actions and the acquisition of causal beliefs. Report 9102. University of California, Department of Cognitive Science.

Shanks, D. R., and St. John, M. F. (n.d.). Characteristics of dissociable human learning systems. *Behavioral and Brain Sciences*. In press.

Squire, L. R., and Frambach, M. (1990). Cognitive skill learning in amnesia. *Psychobiology, 18*, 109–117.

Stadler, M. A. (1989). On learning complex procedural knowledge. *Journal of Experimental Psychology: Learning, Memory, and Cognition, 15*, 1061–1069.

Turner, C. W., and Fischler, I. S. (1993). Speeded tests of implicit knowledge. *Journal of Experimental Psychology: Learning, Memory, and Cognition, 19*, 1165–1177.

Vokey, J. R., and Brooks, L. R. (1992). Salience of item knowledge in learning artificial grammar. *Journal of Experimental Psychology: Learning, Memory and Cognition, 18*, 328–344.

Wasserman, E. A. (1990). Detecting response-outcome relations: Toward an understanding of the causal texture of the environment. In G. H. Bower (Ed.), *The psychology of learning and motivation*, vol. 26, 27–82. New York: Academic Press.

Whittlesea, B., and Dorken, M. D. (1993). Incidentally, things in general are incidentally determined: An episodic-processing account of implicit learning. *Journal of Experimental Psychology: General, 22*, 227–248.

Willingham, D. B., Greeley, T., and Bardone, W. (1993). Dissociation in a serial response time task using a recognition measure: Comment on Perruchet and Amorim (1992). *Journal of Experimental Psychology: Learning, Memory and Cognition, 19*, 1424–1430.

Willingham, D. B., Nissen, M. J., and Bullemer, P. (1989). On the development of procedural knowledge. *Journal of Experimental Psychology: Learning, Memory and Cognition, 15*, 1047–1060.

# 33 A Critical Examination of the Evidence for Unconscious (Implicit) Learning

David R. Shanks, Robin E. A. Green, and Jonathan A. Kolodny

## 33.1 INTRODUCTION

In this chapter we address a deceptively simple question—concerning the role of awareness in cognitive processes—that has challenged researchers for several decades: can learning occur without awareness? Such learning has been termed "implicit" (Reber 1989). Although our interest in this topic is principally empirical, there is no doubt that implicit learning is important for theoretical reasons too. As a casual examination of recent developments in learning theory reveals (Hayes and Broadbent 1988; Mathews et al. 1989; Reber 1989), considerable attention is being paid to possible mechanisms that might mediate implicit learning. Furthermore, the extraordinary amount of recent evidence concerning implicit retrieval (Schacter 1987) makes it important to establish the relationship between these two closely related unconscious processes.[1] In the course of our exploration of implicit learning, we will discuss what we believe its relationship is to implicit retrieval.

The question of whether learning can occur without awareness seems at first glance to be a straightforward one, but two problems have repeatedly arisen in examinations of unaware learning. First, the concept of awareness is a notoriously problematic one (see Holender 1986 and accompanying commentaries). We need to be quite clear what empirical observations would make us want to describe a person as "aware" or "unaware." We hope that it will become clear in our discussion exactly how this problem might be addressed.

Second, it is very important that the question of the relationship between awareness and learning be kept separate from questions concerning the nature of the knowledge that the learning process gives rise to. If learning consists of the encoding of some information that can influence future behavior, then we are interested in whether this encoding process can occur without the information being represented in consciousness *at the time that the encoding takes place*. Whether implicit learning—if it exists—gives rise to a particular type of knowledge is a quite separate matter. Some authors (Reber 1989) have characterized implicit learning in terms of both the state of awareness at encoding and the nature of the acquired knowledge, but we are interested solely in the first of these two dimensions.

Most recent attempts to examine whether implicit learning is feasible have asked whether people can learn about *relationships* between stimuli without being aware of those relationships. The main part of our chapter considers experiments that have investigated that question. Before discussing the results of such studies, however, we will briefly consider evidence from experiments adopting a rather more direct approach.

## 33.2 IMPLICIT LEARNING WITH SUBLIMINAL STIMULI

One situation in which implicit learning would, on the face of it, be fairly straightforward to establish is one in which a subject is entirely unaware that the critical stimulus in the learning phase is present at all yet still shows evidence of learning something about that stimulus. Schacter (1987) reviews a variety of studies that appear to demonstrate learning under these circumstances. Such effects, if genuine, provide evidence for implicit learning because unawareness of the occurrence of a stimulus presumably entails that any learning about relationships between that stimulus and other stimuli is in turn unconscious.

The *mere exposure effect* is one simple learning phenomenon that lends itself rather straightforwardly to this sort of test of implicit learning. The phenomenon refers to the well-established fact that repeated unreinforced exposure to almost any stimulus will lead to an increase in a person's liking of that stimulus (see Bornstein 1989 for an extensive review). Although the basis of this effect is unclear, we can nevertheless ask whether this sort of learning will occur when the exposures are below the subject's threshold of awareness.

Bornstein, Leone, and Galley (1987) exposed subjects to masked 4-ms presentations of faces or geometrical figures. On an immediate test, subjects showed a significant tendency to prefer the preexposed stimuli over novel ones, indicating that some learning had occurred. Confirmation that the stimuli really had been subliminal came from an independent forced-choice present/absent discrimination task in which performance was at chance. This test illustrates what is generally meant (Holender 1986; Merikle and Reingold 1990) by "awareness" of the occurrence of a stimulus: subjects are assumed to be unaware of a stimulus if, under appropriate task instructions, they cannot indicate by their overt behavior that they have detected or identified the stimulus.

These mere exposure effect results provide us with at least one apparent example of unconscious learning that merits replication and further study. At present we do not know whether this effect would show any long-term persistence and still be present in a preference test presented minutes or hours after the preexposure phase. Furthermore, a replication is needed because subjects did in fact detect more stimuli than not in the forced-choice test. In each of three experiments, detection was better (though not significantly) than the chance level of 50 percent.

Bornstein, Leone, and Galley's findings are consistent with the widespread belief among the public that subliminal messages in visual images and audiotapes can condition attitudes or preferences or otherwise influence behavior. However, recent investigations suggest that the concern is misplaced. Controlled experiments attempting to see whether subliminal messages can influence subsequent behavior have yielded exclusively negative results (Greenwald et al. 1991; Vokey and Read 1985). The difference compared to Bornstein, Leone, and Galley's study is that in these other investigations, retention is tested more than a few seconds after the study phase, suggesting that the results Bornstein, Leone, and Galley reported may have depended on some short-term perceptual enhancement effect, which we may be reluctant to call learning.

Another way to examine implicit learning with subliminal stimuli is to see if learning is possible under general anesthesia. If the anesthetic has been adequately administered and renders the patient entirely unconscious, then spared learning must in turn be unconscious. Several studies have indeed obtained small but reliable amounts of learning, but regrettably these are matched by a comparable number of negative results. A typical positive result was reported by Jelicic et al. (1992). They gave anesthetized patients repeated auditory presentations of two words (e.g., *yellow, green*) from a semantic category. Later, when the anesthetic had worn off, subjects were asked to generate members of those categories, and Jelicic et al. found that they were more likely to produce the preexposed words than were control patients who had not been read the words. Thus, some degree of learning seems possible.

Against this are the many clear-cut failures to obtain evidence of learning. For instance, Ghoneim, Block, and Fowles (1992) were unable to obtain Pavlovian conditioning in anesthetized patients, using experimental procedures that did reveal conditioning in nonanesthetized subjects. Andrade (1994) discusses over twenty published reports of such failures but is unable to find any clear factors that determine whether learning will or will not occur. It remains an open possibility that many positive results have been due to inadequately administered anesthetic that left the patient at least partially conscious.

In sum, experiments in which subjects are presented with stimuli of which they are likely to be unaware yield some evidence of unconscious learning, but this is offset by a substantial body of negative evidence. Caution suggests that unaware learning has not yet been categorically established under these conditions.

## 33.3 CRITERIA FOR ESTABLISHING IMPLICIT LEARNING WITH SUPRALIMINAL STIMULI

In the rest of this chapter we focus on situations in which the stimuli are above the threshold for detection and identification. In such situations, subjects may be unaware of the relationships between the stimuli even though they are aware of the stimuli themselves.

Figure 33.1 illustrates the bare essentials of an implicit learning situation in which the stimuli are above the threshold for detection; we will argue that essentially all implicit learning experiments can be conceptually reduced to the

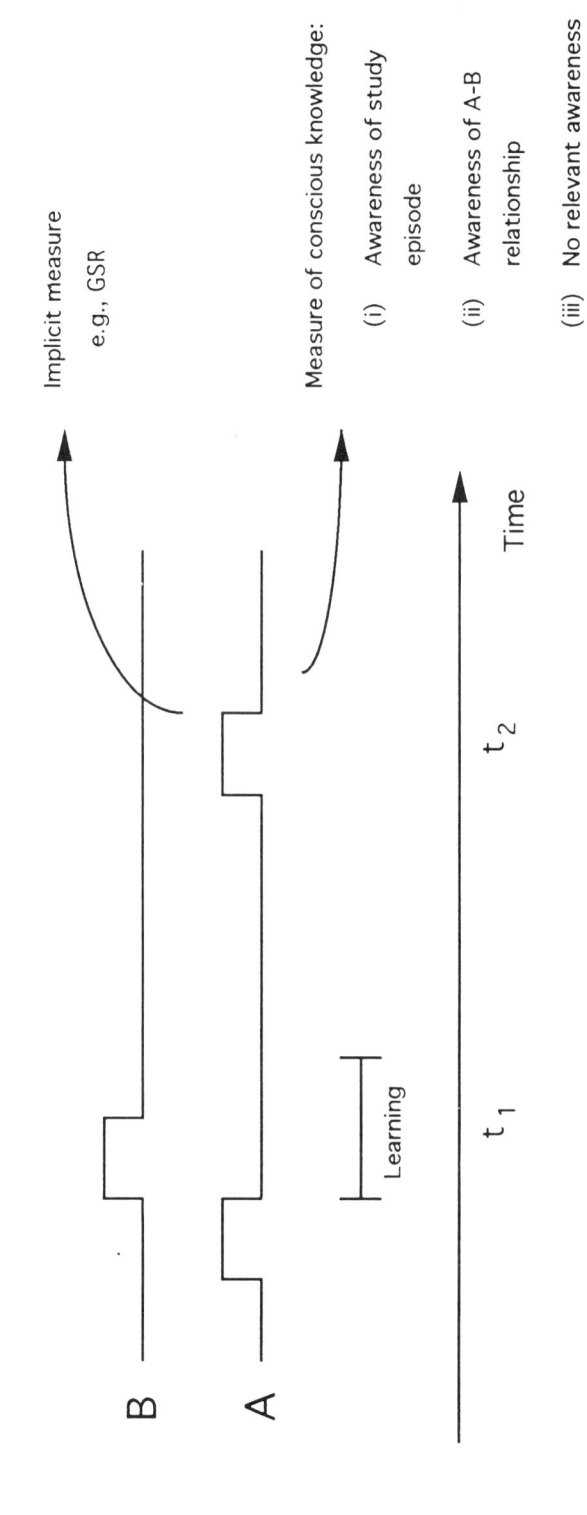

**Figure 33.1** Schematic illustration of events in experiments that investigate the role of awareness in the learning of predictive relationships. Subjects witness a predictive relationship between stimuli $A$ and $B$, with learning presumed to occur during the interval marked $t_1$. At some later time ($t_2$) stimulus $A$ is presented again. Performance on an implicit test at $t_2$ is taken as an index of learning at $t_1$, while a concurrent measure of awareness at $t_2$ is used to infer the content of the subject's awareness at $t_1$. This latter test will reveal one of three possible states of awareness.

arrangement shown in that figure. The figure illustrates an associative learning episode in which subjects have the opportunity to learn that two events, A and B, stand in a predictive relationship. Event A might be a tone conditioned stimulus (CS) and event B a shock unconditioned stimulus (US), and the measure of learning might be a galvanic skin response (GSR) at time $t_2$ when the CS is presented again. We are interested in whether subjects can learn the predictive relationship in the absence of concurrent awareness of that relationship. We assume for the sake of simplicity that there is just one learning trial.

Learning itself presumably takes place during and/or after presentation of event B, and we wish to ascertain the subject's state of awareness during this learning episode. Unfortunately, there are likely to be profound technical difficulties involved in assessing awareness of a predictive relationship at just the moment ($t_1$) that learning itself occurs. Apart from anything else, asking the subject at time $t_1$ whether he or she is aware of the relationship between stimuli A and B is likely to direct his or her attention to that relationship. Hence, we will usually have to settle for assessing it at some later time. At this time ($t_2$ in figure 33.1), suppose we present event A and both measure the GSR and also ask the subject whether he or she has any particular conscious expectancy of event B. If we obtain a GSR but no evidence of an expectancy of event B (or any other evidence of awareness of the A → B relationship), then we have obtained the crucial finding that lies at the heart of all attempts to demonstrate implicit learning with supraliminal stimuli. For if the subject has no conscious expectancy of event B at $t_2$, we have some basis for inferring that he or she was not aware of the A-B relationship at $t_1$.

While this might seem like a very strong inference, we believe that such inferences will inevitably have to be accepted if implicit learning is to be established. It is very difficult to assess awareness concurrently with learning, and so we are forced to rely on some later test. Of course, we also make a backward inference concerning learning itself: if performance at time $t_2$ is no better than we would expect by chance, we are likely to infer that learning did not occur at $t_1$. Conversely, if performance is better at $t_2$ than we would expect by chance, then we conclude that learning did occur.

It follows from our analysis that except when the stimuli are presented subliminally, evidence for implicit learning relies on how far one can justify backward inferences concerning awareness. Such inferences will be strengthened, for instance, if the test ($t_2$) occurs shortly after the study trial ($t_1$) so that we can rule out significant amounts of forgetting, if it is as similar as possible to the study trial, and if we can be sure that it is a sensitive test. This last requirement encourages us to treat the results of verbal free recall tests with a good deal of caution, since such tests are known to be relatively insensitive. Clearly, tests of unconscious or implicit learning become stronger the better they support the relevant backward inference.

**The Relationship between Implicit Learning and Implicit Retrieval**

The basic design shown in figure 33.1 makes it clear that there is an intimate relationship between implicit learning and implicit retrieval: demonstrations of implicit learning are a proper subset of the larger set of demonstrations of implicit retrieval.

Implicit retrieval is defined as the ability of information from some prior episode to be retrieved and hence to influence current processing but in the absence of conscious retrieval *of that prior episode* (Schacter 1987). Thus, implicit retrieval requires the absence of a conscious reexperience of the study episode.[2] Now, lack of awareness of a contingency at $t_2$ presumably means the absence of any episodic memory traces in which that contingency is embedded, and hence any piece of evidence that allows us to infer implicit learning must also be an example of implicit retrieval: this is case (iii) shown in figure 33.1.

However, the converse does not hold: an example of implicit retrieval does not necessarily represent evidence of implicit learning. Suppose that a subject gives a GSR when presented with a tone stimulus. There are three possible scenarios, shown in figure 33.1:

1. The subject remembers the study episode. In this case, the GSR response does not count as an example of implicit retrieval according to Schacter's (1987) definition.

2. The subject does not remember the study episode but is aware—that is, has semantic knowledge—that this tone predicts shock (cf. source amnesia). In this case, we would not infer that learning itself had been unconscious, since the subject at $t_2$ is aware that A predicts B[3].

3. The subject neither remembers the study episode nor has semantic knowledge of the relationship. In this case, we have evidence that is relevant to implicit learning, since lack of awareness of the relationship at retrieval licenses the inference that learning too took place without awareness.

Thus, we can spell out the principal conditions that are necessary to allow us to infer implicit learning from implicit retrieval: (1) the subject must be unaware of the relevant relationship that occurred in the study episode, and (2) the backward inference from $t_2$ to $t_1$ must be acceptable. In summary, an implicit learning experiment just *is* an implicit retrieval experiment, but with the added components of meeting these two further conditions. For researchers in the field of implicit retrieval, a long delay between $t_1$ and $t_2$ would be irrelevant if a dissociation is still obtained at $t_2$, but for investigators interested in implicit learning, such a delay would make the backward inference to the subject's state of awareness at time $t_1$ unsupportable. Similarly, all that is of interest in implicit retrieval is whether the subject is unaware of the relevant study episode as in cases (ii) and (iii). But it is only case (iii) that is relevant to the question of unconscious learning; the subject must also be unaware of the relationship that occurred in that episode.

We now go on to discuss experiments, including some new ones of our own, from three areas of research: conditioning, instrumental learning, and sequence learning in reaction time studies. Together with the subliminal learning studies already discussed, these experimental tasks account for almost all of the relevant empirical data on implicit learning. It is impossible to cover these areas in exhaustive detail, but we hope to illustrate some of the main issues that have arisen in this research. The one area we do not discuss concerns the learning of artificial grammars (Reber 1989), but recent results have suggested that the evidence for implicit learning in that domain is rather weak (Dienes, Broadbent, and Berry 1991; Shanks and St. John 1992).

## 33.4 AWARENESS AND CONDITIONING

### Pavlovian Conditioning

In 1974 Brewer published a classic article in which he examined a very large number of Pavlovian and instrumental learning studies that had looked at the relationship between conditioning and awareness. Brewer concluded that neither form of learning could occur in the absence of awareness of the reinforcement contingency. The years since that review have seen many further experiments attempting to improve on the earlier techniques; we will not attempt to provide an extensive analysis here (Boakes 1989) but instead will describe two recent Pavlovian learning experiments that yielded typical results.

Lovibond (1992) gave subjects repeated presentations of two stimuli (slides depicting flowers or mushrooms), one of which was paired with a shock US while the other was nonreinforced. If we designate the CS paired with shock as A and the one not paired with shock as B, then learning would be manifest in the development of conditioned responding to A but not to B. The measure of learning was the subject's GSR during presentation of the stimuli. Awareness of the relationship between the stimuli and shock was measured in two ways. First, during the learning phase subjects continually adjusted a pointer to indicate their moment-by-moment expectation of shock, and second, at the end of the experiment, they were given a structured interview designed to assess their awareness. Note that asking for a rating of shock expectancy does not specifically direct attention to the A-B relationship.

It should be apparent how the design conforms to the basic procedure depicted in figure 33.1, except that there are four learning trials. In Lovibond's experiments, each of trials 2–4 in fact represents a new learning trial, an assessment of whether learning occurred on the preceding trial(s), and an assessment of the subject's awareness on the preceding trial(s).

In each of the experiments, some subjects gave no indication on either of the tests of awareness that they associated A with shock to a greater extent than B. Critically, these subjects also gave no hint of more conditioned responding to A than to B. For subjects who were aware of the conditioning contingencies, GSRs were stronger to A than to B. Thus, on these results, we would have to conclude that learning about a CS-shock relationship does not occur in the absence of awareness of that relationship.

Since there is a high probability of the development of awareness in a simple conditioning experiment, a common approach is to try to mask the

CS-US relationship so that the subject fails to become aware of it, and see whether conditioning can still be obtained. Many studies using this general masking procedure have been performed, of which the following one by Marinkovic, Schell, and Dawson (1989), is representative. These authors used two odors as the CSs, one of which was followed by shock (CS+), the other of which was not (CS−). Two other odors were also used in the experiment. The relationship between CS+ and the shock US was masked by giving subjects a primary odor memory task. On each trial, one of the two additional odors was presented as a memory item for 8 sec, followed by three further odors in succession. Subjects had to indicate which was the same as the memory item. One of the three test items was either CS+ (with shock being administered at the offset of the odor) or CS−.

Marinkovic, Schell, and Dawson assessed subjects' awareness by asking them to indicate continuously through a trial what their expectancy was of shock. For this, subjects used a dial varying from 0 (no shock expected) to 7 (shock definitely expected). Subjects whose expectation of shock was no greater during CS+ than during CS− can be regarded as unaware of the conditioning contingency, and for these subjects, there was no evidence of conditioned changes in skin conductance. On the other hand, conditioning did emerge in subjects who expected the shock more during CS+ than CS−. Finally, even in subjects who did show differential conditioning, this only emerged after the onset of awareness.

For a variety of reasons that need not detain us, some reseachers have questioned whether GSRs condition in the same way as other responses, such as the eyeblink or salivary reflexes. Thus, it is worth noting that correspondences between awareness and conditioning seem to occur with other response systems as well (e.g., for eyelid conditioning, Baer and Fuhrer 1982). Also, claims that the relationship between learning and awareness is different for phobic and nonphobic stimuli have not been supported by recent examinations (Davey 1992).

The conclusion from these studies is clear and confirms Brewer's (1974) earlier analysis: Pavlovian conditioning, which is often cited as a fundamental form of learning, does not appear to occur in the absence of awareness of the reinforcement contingency.

**Evaluative Conditioning**

Evaluative conditioning, like the mere exposure effect, refers to a form of learning that manifests itself in changes in affective responding to a stimulus. Specifically, it refers to the transfer of affect from a US to a CS. Some authors have suggested that—unlike standard Pavlovian conditioning—this form of learning can proceed in the absence of awareness of the CS-US relationship. We briefly review some of the relevant evidence.

Baeyens, Eelen, and Van den Bergh (1990) presented subjects with ten repetitions of a CS-US pair in which the CS slide had previously been evaluated by the subject as affectively neutral and the US slide as either liked, neutral, or disliked. Evaluative conditioning was observed in that on a postconditioning test of affect, the CS slides became affectively positive (liked) if they had been paired with a liked US, negative (disliked) if they had been paired with a disliked US, and remained neutral if they had been paired with another neutral stimulus. As a test of awareness, at the end of the learning phase, the researchers showed the subjects each of the CS pictures and asked them to identify which picture had been the relevant US. If subjects failed to respond correctly, they were then asked whether the US had been liked, neutral, or disliked. They were classed as "unaware" of the CS-US relationship if they failed on both of these questions. Evidence that evaluative conditioning occurred without awareness emerged in the observation that evaluative conditioning was the same for CS-US pairs regardless of whether the subject was aware or not of the relationship.

Of course, the test of awareness may have been an insensitive one. Baeyens, Eelen, and Van den Bergh (1990) tried, therefore, to use a more sensitive concurrent measure of awareness. One group of subjects was required to indicate during the 4-sec interval between the onset of the CS and US slides whether they expected a liked, neutral, or disliked US stimulus on that trial. Subjects were classified as "unaware" if they failed to respond correctly on the final three pairings of each stimulus combination. Unfortunately, results from this group undermine the notion of unaware learning. Subjects could accurately report most of the pairings, and for those few they could not report, there was no significant evaluative conditioning. Further, in another study, Baeyens et al. (1992) found that while the magnitude of evaluative conditioning increased in groups of subjects given increasing numbers of CS-US pairings, awareness as measured by a postconditioning test did too. In sum, studies of evaluative conditioning have failed to prove that it can occur implicitly.

Although not usually classified as studies of evaluative conditioning, Lewicki's (1986; Lewicki, Hill, and Sasaki 1989) experiments on the learning of nonsalient contingencies can be readily conceived as such. Lewicki presented subjects with photographs of people, accompanied by personality descriptions such as "kind" or "capable." In fact, for some subjects, all "kind" people had long hair, and all "capable" people had short hair, while for other subjects, the opposite was the case. Lewicki reported that on test trials in which subjects had to affirm or disconfirm statements classifying new people as either "kind" or "capable," they responded "yes" more often when the description preserved the study phase correlation than when it broke the correlation.

Lewicki's subjects were apparently unaware of the relationship between hair length and personality description. If we take the personality description as being an evaluative response conditioned to the cue of hair length, then the results would again appear to suggest unconscious evaluative learning. However, these results have proved hard to replicate (Dulany and Poldrack 1991), and so we must at this stage reserve judgment on whether this form of learning really can occur unconsciously.

## 33.5 AWARENESS IN INSTRUMENTAL LEARNING TASKS

In contrast to the conditioning studies described above, instrumental tasks establish some contingency between an action the subject performs and an associated outcome. Learning is measured as an increase across trials in the propensity to perform the action. Naturally, the question we may again ask is whether such learning can occur without awareness. As with his review of Pavlovian learning studies, Brewer (1974) concluded that the answer to this question is "no." But some recent experiments have suggested that implicit instrumental learning is possible. We consider results separately from tasks in which the instrumental contingency is simple or more complex.

**Simple Instrumental Learning Tasks**

Svartdal (e.g., 1991) has reported experiments in which subjects are led to believe that there is a relationship between a reinforcer and one aspect of responding, when in fact the critical variable is some other aspect of responding. For example, Svartdal (1991) presented subjects with brief trains of between four and seventeen auditory clicks. Subjects immediately had to press a response button the same number of times and were instructed that feedback would be presented when the number of presses matched the number of clicks. In fact, though, feedback was contingent on the rate of responding: for some subjects, feedback was given when the interresponse times (IRTs) were lower than in a baseline phase, and for others it was given when IRTs were higher.

Svartdal (1991) obtained evidence of learning in that IRTs adjusted appropriately to the reinforcement contingencies. But subjects seemed to be unaware that it was rate of responding that was important. A structured questionnaire revealed no evidence of awareness of the contingency between response rate and feedback in subjects whose response rate had adjusted appropriately.

Such demonstrations appear superficially to be quite compelling, especially because the contingency to be learned is such a simple one. However, it is very difficult to rule out the possibility that subjects in experiments such as these acquire "incorrect" hypotheses about the reinforcement contingency that happen to produce response profiles correlated with those generated by the correct hypothesis. For example, suppose that subjects learn that resting their hand in a certain position increases reinforcement rate. This could be a true experienced contingency if that hand position is conducive to a fast or slow response rate. Such an "incorrect" hypothesis would generate behavior that is very similar to what would be produced by the correct hypothesis, yet a subject who reported hand position as the crucial variable would be regarded by the experimenter as "unaware" of the reinforcement contingency. In sum, even ignoring possible insensitivity in the test of verbal awareness, results such as Svartdal's cannot be taken as conclusive evidence of unaware learning. Subjects may learn a rather different contingency from that explicitly programmed by the experimenter.

In contrast to such apparent dissociations between learning and awareness, Shanks and Dickinson (1991) have argued that there are a number of variables that seem to have rather similar effects on performance assessments of learning and on awareness. In two studies, subjects performed a simple operant learning task in which pressing a key on a computer keyboard was related, by a schedule of reinforcement, to a triangle flashing on the screen. Subjects were exposed to a reinforcement contingency in which they scored points whenever the triangle flashed but lost points for each response, so that they were encouraged to adapt their response rate to the reinforcement schedule. Learning was demonstrated by changes in subjects' rates of responding. As a measure of awareness, subjects were asked to report on a scale from 0 to 100 what they thought the relationship was between the response and the reinforcer.

Shanks and Dickinson (1991) found that response rate was sensitive to both the degree of contiguity between the response and reinforcer and the degree of contingency between them. At the same time, subjects' judgments were equally sensitive to these factors. Furthermore, certain judgmental illusions also manifested themselves in performance measures. For instance, a frequently seen phenomenon is that subjects judge an action and an outcome to be related when in fact they are not. Shanks and Dickinson found that this effect appears in performance measures like response rate as well as in verbal judgments. Of course, the appearance of a bias in two behavioral measures strongly suggests that they are mediated by a common underlying process.

These experiments represent the first step of a research strategy that is rather different from that adopted in most other studies of implicit learning. The notion that learning and awareness proceed in tandem is corroborated to the extent that they are affected in similar ways by various manipulations. Shanks and Dickinson's results indicate that, at least for two important factors, this is exactly the case.

**Complex Instrumental Control Tasks**

Several experiments have investigated the relationship between learning and awareness in more complex instrumental learning tasks in which the subject has to learn to control a complex system. Again, the basic idea is as shown in figure 33.1, with some learning episode followed by an assessment of awareness. In most of these tasks, awareness at time $t_2$ is not measured by presenting any relevant cues but simply by verbally questioning the subject.

Berry and Broadbent (1984) reported an experiment in which there was an apparent dissociation between learning and awareness. One of the tasks they used required subjects to interact with a computer "person." On each trial, the subject entered an attitude (e.g., *polite*) to the computer, which then responded with its attitude (e.g., *unfriendly*). The subject's task was to try to get the computer to be *friendly*. If we designate the twelve possible attitudes—going from *very unfriendly* to *loving*—with the numbers 1–12, then the computer's attitude on each trial was a simple numerical function of the subject's input on that trial and the computer's previous attitude. Inclusion of the computer's attitude on the previous trial in this function makes the relationship quite a difficult one to learn.

Berry and Broadbent (1984, experiment 1) found, not surprisingly, that performance improved with practice: significantly more trials on target occurred during a second block of thirty trials than during the first block. However, scores on a structured questionnaire designed to assess the subjects' reportable knowledge of the task were no better after the second block than after the first one. Hence, here we have apparent evidence that learning to perform a task can occur without any change in awareness of the underlying structure of the task. Similar results have been obtained by Stanley et al. (1989) (but see Sanderson 1989 for evidence of correspondences rather than dissociations between performance and reports).

Further, in another experiment Berry and Broadbent (1984) found the converse effect: reportable knowledge improving without corresponding improvements in task performance. One group simply completed two sets of trials, while between the two sets another group received detailed verbal instructions about the nature of the input-output relationship. These instructions essentially represented a verbal description of the equation governing the computer's attitude. When questioned at the end of the experiment, subjects who had received instructions outscored those who had not, yet the groups were indistinguishable in terms of their number of trials on target. Thus, a change in awareness (or at least a change in reportable knowledge of the task) was not accompanied by a change in task performance.

What are we to make of such dissociations? One possibility is that it is not only possible for learning to proceed without awareness, but in addition the system responsible for implicit learning is quite independent of another (explicit) system in which learning is accompanied by awareness. Such a systems account would then be able to explain why we can obtain double dissociations of the sort reported by Berry and Broadbent: learning to perform the control task involves the implicit system and proceeds without awareness, while a change in awareness involves the explicit system and can proceed without any benefit in task performance.

While such results are certainly consistent with the notion that learning to perform a task can involve a system that is independent of the one that underlies awareness, we feel that an alternative account is equally feasible. The basic problem is that we do not know that the sort of knowledge subjects in Berry and Broadbent's experiments acquire when learning to perform the task is at all the same as the knowledge they require to score well on the test of reportable knowledge. Suppose, for the sake of argument, that good task performance simply depends on learning an unrelated set of stimulus-response (S-R) pairs. It is, then, not hard to imagine that although practice provides the subjects with more and more knowledge of this sort, they might be hard pressed to use such knowledge when faced with questions about possible structural rules underlying the task. At the same time, giving the subjects detailed instructions about the task may improve their knowledge of the rules, and hence their questionnaire scores, but might not transfer to better performance on the task since that requires S-R knowledge. But, of course, the subjects' inability to describe the rules underlying the task does not imply that the S-R learning occurred without awareness: if they were asked to report *that* knowledge, perhaps subjects would be able to do so. In sum, there are ways of interpreting such data that do not appeal to implicit learning.

A second (and perennial) problem concerns the sensitivity of the test of awareness. Can we be certain that the questionnaire procedure exhausts the subject's knowledge of the task? Rather than relying solely on such a questionnaire, one alternative strategy is to ask each subject to instruct a yoked partner how to perform the task. If the partner could then perform the task as well as the original subject, we would conclude that the original subject was in fact able to articulate all his or her task knowledge. Such procedures have shown that subjects can articulate most, though probably not all, of their task knowledge (Stanley et al. 1989).

In order to address some of these problems, Hayes and Broadbent (1988) conducted some further experiments that appear to provide rather stronger support for the notion of a separate implicit learning system, since they are not compromised by possible insensitivity in the assessment of awareness. Hayes and Broadbent began by postulating that not only is implicit learning possible but also that it is under the control of a system separate from that involved in conscious (explicit) learning. On such an account, the explicit system would consciously test hypotheses, while the implicit one would slowly and unconsciously accumulate information about a potentially large number of predictive events in the environment. Hayes and Broadbent assumed further that the explicit system would be highly dependent on a limited-capacity working memory system, while the implicit system would be independent of any such limited-capacity memory system.

A rather straightforward prediction emerges from this plausible model of the cognitive system. Since the explicit learning mechanism relies on working memory, there should be situations in which learning is profoundly affected by loading the working memory system with a secondary task such as generating random numbers. At the same time, since the implicit system is not dependent on working memory, other (implicit) learning tasks should be unaffected by such a secondary task. Indeed, Hayes and Broadbent went so far as to suggest that implicit learning might even be facilitated by a secondary task if it prevented the explicit system from exerting an interfering influence on the implicit system. The importance of the Hayes and Broadbent (1988) study is that, in accordance with their model, they appeared to have found two learning tasks that differed in only a minor way but for which one was affected by a secondary task and the other was not.

In their experiments Hayes and Broadbent contrasted performance in two new versions of the computer "person" task described earlier. In one (No-Lag) condition, the computer's attitude ($O_t$) on each trial was a function of the subject's attitude ($I_t$):

$$O_t = I_t - 2 + r, \qquad (1)$$

where $r$ is a random number ($-1$, 0, or 1) and the attitudes have the twelve numerical values mentioned previously. In the other (Lag) condition, $I_t$ was replaced by $I_{t-1}$, so that the computer's attitude was determined by the subject's attitude on the preceding trial:

$$O_t = I_{t-1} - 2 + r. \qquad (2)$$

Performance was measured in terms of the number of trials in which the subject's input was one that could (given the random element) have produced a *friendly* response from the computer person. While learning occurred in both groups, Hayes and Broadbent found that subjects could give highly accurate verbal reports about the No-Lag task, indicating that their learning had been accompanied by awareness, whereas the verbal reports of subjects in the Lag version were very poor. This result encourages the view that learning in the No-Lag task can be readily achieved by the explicit system but that the Lag task requires the implicit system. Thus we might predict that a concurrent secondary task would have an effect on learning in the No-Lag but not the Lag condition.

To test this, Hayes and Broadbent (1988) gave subjects a block of learning trials using either equation 1 (No-Lag group) or equation 2 (Lag group). After thirty trials in the No-Lag condition and fifty in the Lag condition, performance was approximately equated, and at this point Hayes and Broadbent changed the rules by replacing the $-2$ in the equations with $+2$. They then presented a further thirty (No-Lag group) or fifty (Lag group) relearning trials. Under single-task conditions (Hayes and Broadbent 1988, experiment 1), performance in the Lag condition was affected more detrimentally than performance in the No-Lag condition by this rule change. In contrast, when subjects were required to perform a concurrent secondary task (generating random letters or digits; experiments 2 and 3), a change in the rule interfered more with performance in the No-Lag than in the Lag task, exactly the opposite of the result obtained when there was no secondary task.

The results conform to Hayes and Broadbent's theory—and hence to their conception of separate implicit and explicit learning systems—if we simply assume that the secondary task occupied the conscious working memory system and therefore interfered with the explicit system, while removal of the working memory system had no effect on the implicit system.

**Experiment 1**

Because dissociations such as this are typically very difficult to explain in terms of a single system, we attempted to replicate Hayes and Broadbent's results. We used exactly the same procedure as they did. In the dual-task groups, subjects had to generate random digits throughout the experiment at the rate of one every 1.75 sec. All subjects were required to achieve a learning criterion of five correct responses in the ten trials immediately prior to the equation change. Under single-task conditions, there were twelve subjects in the Lag group and fifteen in the No-Lag group who met this criterion, while under dual-task conditions there were twenty subjects in each group.

Figure 33.2 shows the relevant data, which are the mean numbers of correct responses in each condition in the final ten trials of the learning and relearning stages. In the single-task groups (left panel), the introduction of the equation change had similar adverse effects on performance in the No-Lag and Lag groups, and an analysis of variance comparing performance in the two groups before versus after the equation change failed to find any evidence of a Group × Stage interaction ($F < 1$). Thus, we were unable to replicate Hayes and Broadbent's (1988, experiment 1) finding that performance was more detrimentally affected in the Lag condition. Under dual-task conditions (figure 33.2, right panel) the situation was the same: performance was approximately equally affected in the two groups. There was not the slightest hint that performance in the Lag group was less affected by the equation change, and hence we failed to replicate Hayes and Broadbent's (1988, experiments 2 and 3) dual-task results. The interaction was again nonsignificant ($F < 1$). What we did find was that the Lag task was rather harder than the No-Lag task: nonsignificantly so under single-task conditions ($F(1,25) = 1.29, p > 0.2$) but significantly so under dual-task conditions ($F(1,38) = 6.07, p < 0.05$).

Hayes and Broadbent's dissociation posed a genuine problem for theories of learning relying on a single learning mechanism and also provided indirect support for the idea that learning can proceed without awareness in the implicit system. Obviously, the fact that we were unable to replicate their results undermines those conclusions.

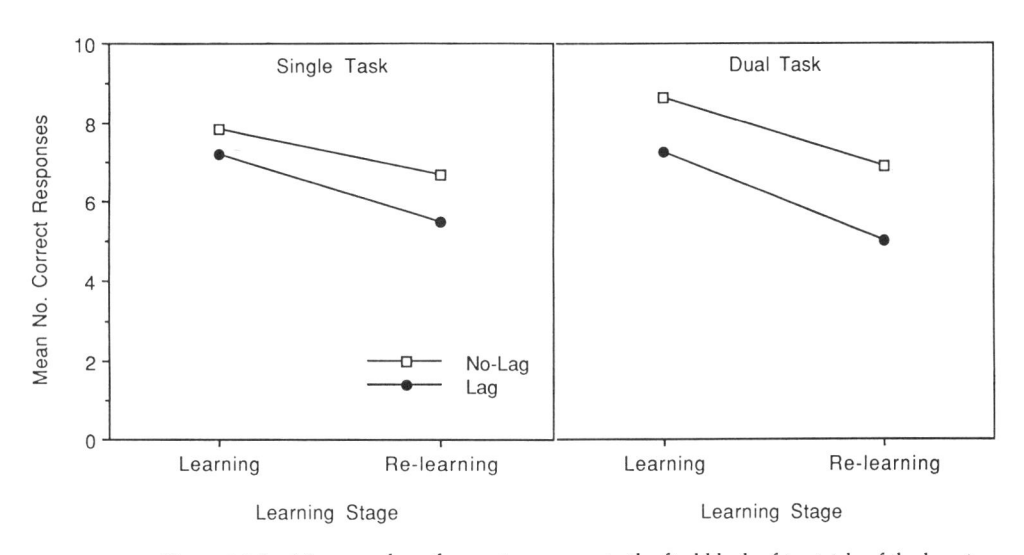

**Figure 33.2** Mean number of correct responses in the final block of ten trials of the learning and relearning stages in the No-Lag and Lag groups of experiment 1. Left panel: single-task conditions. Right panel: dual-task conditions.

## 33.6 AWARENESS IN SERIAL REACTION TIME TASKS

Lewicki, Czyzewska, and Hoffman (1987) and Nissen and Bullemer (1987) introduced an ingenious and simple technique, the serial reaction time (RT) task, for attempting to demonstrate implicit learning. We will concentrate on Nissen and Bullemer's version, in which a stimulus is presented in one of four locations (A–D) on each trial, and the subject simply has to press as fast as possible the button corresponding to that location. The subject is given instructions appropriate for a typical choice RT task, but in fact there is a sequence underlying the selection of the stimulus on each trial. In most of the experiments we discuss, the ten-trial stimulus sequence *DBCACBDCBA* was repeated many times over. The question is, Can subjects learn the sequence without being aware of that sequence?

There is little doubt that RTs decrease significantly in this task, indicating that sequence learning can occur. The crucial result, with respect to the question of implicit learning, comes from experiments (e.g., Willingham, Nissen, and Bullemer 1989, experiment 1) that have found that subjects who subsequently reported no awareness of the existence of a sequence nonetheless speeded up during the RT trials. With respect to figure 33.1, the subject is presented with a series of learning trials in which there are predictive relationships between stimuli. These are accompanied by both a concurrent assessment of learning (RT) and a later assessment of awareness (verbal report).

While such results suggest the possibility of implicit learning, there are a number of significant problems with these experiments. The first is that the demonstration of sequence learning has typically involved one of the following two comparisons: a comparison (Willingham, Nissen, and Bullemer 1989) between a group exposed to the sequence versus one for whom the stimulus on each trial is chosen at random, with the constraint that stimuli never repeat on consecutive trials; or a within-subjects comparison (Nissen and Bullemer 1987) between performance at the end of a long period of exposure to the sequence versus performance on a subsequent block of trials where the stimuli are chosen at random, again with the constraint that stimuli never repeat on consecutive trials. The problem with both of these comparisons is that performance can differ between the sequence and random trials without the subject having any knowledge, implicit or otherwise, of the sequential dependencies that are present.

As a moment's reflection reveals, faster responses on the *DBCACBDCBA* sequence compared to a random sequence might simply be due to response biases developing during exposure to the sequence. The stimuli are not equally frequent (*B* and *C* occur three times *D* and *A* twice) in the ten-trial sequence. Thus, in the sequence but not the random conditions, the subject is to some degree able to predict which stimuli are most probable, a factor that—as has been extensively demonstrated (see Broadbent 1971)—allows fast responses to develop. Some evidence for this differential speedup is apparent (at least with respect to stimulus *C*) in Perruchet and Amorim's (1992) data.

**Experiment 2**

Clearly, the appropriate comparison is with a group of subjects who receive a "pseudorandom" series constrained to have the same number of each of stimuli A, B, C, and D per ten trials as appear in the sequence proper and in which stimuli never repeat on consecutive trials. In experiment 2, we compared two such conditions. One group of subjects ($N = 43$) was presented with the normal sequence, another ($N = 23$) with our pseudorandom series, and a third ($N = 12$) with a truly random sequence in which again there was the constraint that stimuli never repeated on consecutive trials. The stimuli were asterisks arranged in a horizontal row, and the general procedure followed that of Willingham, Nissen, and Bullemer (1989).

After 400 RT trials, subjects in the sequence group were classified on the basis of a structured interview as having no knowledge of the sequence ($N = 12$), some knowledge ($N = 19$), or full knowledge ($N = 12$). Our prediction was that if the no-knowledge subjects had indeed learned something about the sequential dependencies, they should have speeded up more than the pseudorandom subjects.

The top panel of figure 33.3 shows the RT difference between the first and fourth block of 100 trials for each group. To simplify the presentation, we have omitted the some-knowledge subjects, whose performance, as expected, fell between that of the full-knowledge and no-knowledge groups. In all but the random group, the RT difference was significantly greater than zero. The full-knowledge group speeded up more than any of the others ($t > 4.90$, $p < 0.001$ in each case); the difference between the full-knowledge and pseudorandom groups confirms that the full-knowledge subjects had indeed learned something about the sequence.

However, there was no significant difference between the no-knowledge and pseudorandom groups ($t < 1$), though both speeded up more ($t > 3.23$, $p < 0.01$ in each case) than subjects exposed to the truly random series. Thus, we suggest that most, if not all, of the supposedly implicit learning in the no-knowledge group is simply due to the development of response biases reflecting knowledge of the frequencies of the different stimuli. Hence, the subjects' apparent inability to articulate information about the sequence counts for little; it is not knowledge of the sequence that leads to response speedup.

In addition to problems created by use of an inappropriate control group, a further problem is that (even ignoring the above considerations) we cannot rely just on the subjects' reports as assessments of their state of awareness some seconds or even minutes previously. The backward inference (figure 33.1) may simply not be valid. Willingham, Nissen, and Bullemer (1989) attempted to avoid this problem by using a very ingenious modification of the RT task, previously introduced by Nissen and Bullemer (1987). After the RT phase of the experiment, Willingham, Nissen, and Bullemer instructed subjects to try to predict on each trial where the stimulus would appear next, with no requirement for rapid responses. Subjects simply chose response keys on each trial until they picked the correct one, at which point they would then try to

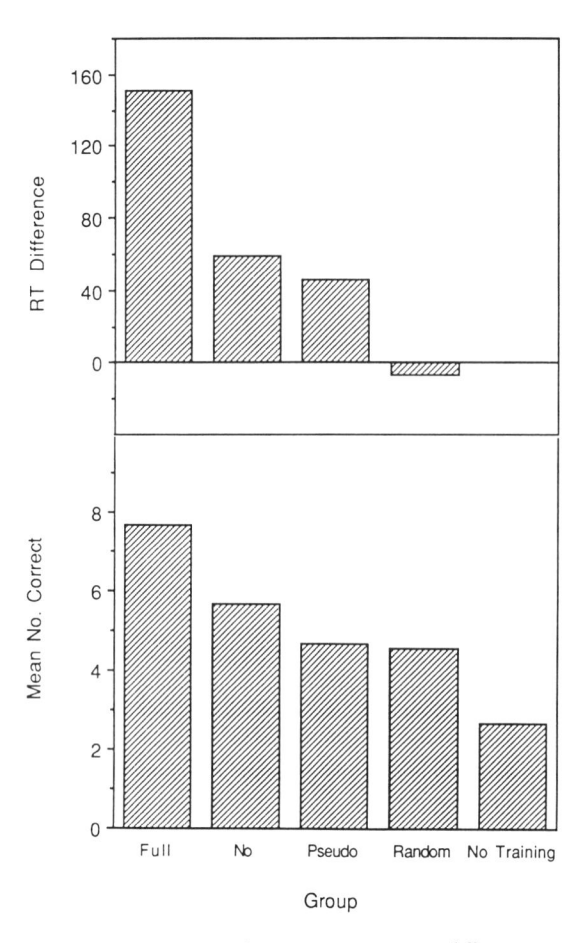

**Figure 33.3** Top panel: Mean reaction time differences (msec) between the first and fourth block of 100 trials in experiment 2. Bottom panel: Mean number of correct responses in the first 10 trials of the prediction task. Full = subjects assessed prior to the prediction phase as being fully aware of the sequence, No = subjects with no verbalizable sequence knowledge, Pseudo = pseudorandom sequence, Random = real random sequence, No Training = subjects who performed only the prediction task.

predict the next stimulus, and so on. Across many blocks of this prediction task, the subject again had the opportunity to learn the sequence.

Since this task requires the subject to act on a conscious expectancy concerning which stimulus will appear next, Willingham, Nissen, and Bullemer argued that it constitutes a test of awareness of elements of the sequence. At the same time, since it involves presentation of the same cues that were present in the learning phase, backward inferences about the subject's prior state of awareness are much more readily defended.

Willingham, Nissen, and Bullemer (1989, experiment 1) discovered that subjects whom they had classified as unaware on the basis of their verbal reports not only had speeded up in the preceding RT phase but also showed no evidence of awareness as assessed by the prediction task. Such a result appears to provide quite compelling evidence of implicit learning, even if the learning only relates to frequency information. It suggests that sequence learning was implicit in that it allowed RTs to decrease but could not be used in a task requiring conscious retrieval. But again there are some difficulties. Willingham, Nissen, and Bullemer compared the performance of their unaware, no-knowledge subjects in the prediction task with that of a "no-training" group who had not received the RT phase at all. The bottom panel of figure 33.3 shows the performance of our subjects when they were asked to perform the prediction task. The no-training subjects ($N = 12$) had not, of course, performed the RT task. Data are from the first ten prediction trials, in which performance cannot be attributed to new sequence learning.

The comparison between the no-knowledge and no-training groups in Willingham, Nissen, and Bullemer's experiment was the critical evidence that the sequence learning in the no-knowledge subjects was implicit. In fact, there was a small but clear trend (Willingham, Nissen, and Bullemer 1989, fig. 3) in their study for the no-knowledge subjects to outperform the no-training subjects, but this was not significant. We obtained a rather clearer result: our no-knowledge subjects performed much better (mean 5.7 correct) than the no-training control subjects (mean 2.7) at the outset of the prediction phase ($t(22) = 4.83, p < 0.001$), indicating that at least some of the knowledge they had acquired in the RT phase, but were unable to report verbally, was available for transfer to the prediction task.

Despite this failure to replicate Willingham, Nissen, and Bullemer's results, some further data of ours are at least suggestive of an implicit learning effect. Rather than comparing the prediction performance of the no-knowledge subjects to that of the no-training group, a better comparison is with the group who had received a truly random series in the RT phase. These subjects, unlike the no-knowledge subjects, had not had the opportunity to learn about either the sequence or the relative frequencies of the stimuli in the sequence but had had equal exposure to the task. Thus, if learning in the no-knowledge group is entirely conscious, they should outperform the truly random group in the prediction task. Figure 33.3 shows that there was only a slight trend for this to occur: performance in the truly random group was not markedly different ($t(22) = 1.74, 0.1 > p > 0.05$) from that in the no-knowledge group. Furthermore, the pseudorandom and real random groups, who differed considerably in the RT phase, did not differ at all in terms of prediction accuracy ($t < 1$). (Interpretation of the failure to obtain reliable differences between the random group and either the no-knowledge or the pseudorandom groups is problematic since the expected mean number of correct responses in the random group should have been no more than 3.3 out of 10.) Thus, we do have some weak evidence that the stimulus-frequency learning that allowed the no-knowledge and pseudorandom subjects to speed up more in the RT task than the truly random subjects was not available for transfer to the prediction task.

Our general caution with respect to the data from sequential RT studies is confirmed by an analysis of several other studies (Hartman, Knopman, and Nissen 1989; Perruchet, Gallego, and Savy 1990; Stadler 1989) that have used the prediction task, where examination of the results reveals small but generally consistent evidence of transfer effects. Table 33.1 shows the results of five studies that have examined prediction performance in subjects supposedly unaware (according to their verbal reports) of the presence of a sequence. In all cases, subjects showed significant learning in the RT task. The question is, Do they show any evidence of awareness on the prediction task? We have already mentioned that there was a clear but nonsignificant trend in the Willingham, Nissen, and Bullemer study. As the table shows, in all but one of the other studies (Stadler 1989) there is also evidence of a small amount of transfer, indicating that the subjects probably were aware of some sequential information.

Of course, one could argue that the small amount of savings seen in the prediction task (which in these experiments tends to be about 5 percent) does not match the large RT speedup, and so there is still evidence of a dissociation: some learning must have been implicit. But without measures of the amount of information that is transmitted when a subject shows an RT speed up of $X$ ms and the amount of information the subject is transmitting when their prediction performance improves by $Y$ percent, it is very hard to assess such objections.

## 33.7 CONCLUSIONS

Several strategies have been used to assess, more or less directly, the content of a subject's awareness during a learning episode. Our evaluation of the results that have emerged is similar to Holender's (1986) conclusion concerning unconscious semantic activation. While there are some interesting pieces of evidence, a cautious approach would suggest that unaware learning has not yet been satisfactorily established. We certainly feel that some of the techniques that have been developed in the past few years, such as the prediction task used in conjunction with sequential RT experiments, provide us with powerful tools for future research and that continued use of such techniques offers the possibility of perhaps establishing beyond doubt the existence of implicit learning. However, we would also argue that theories built around the

**Table 33.1** Results of Prediction Tests in Five Experiments Demonstrating Significant Sequence Learning in the Absence of Verbally Reportable Awareness

| | |
|---|---|
| Hartman, Knopman, and Nissen (1989, experiment 2) | + |
| Hartman, Knopman, and Nissen (1989, experiment 3) | + |
| Perruchet, Gallego, and Savy (1990) | + + |
| Stadler (1989) | 0 |
| Willingham, Nissen, and Bullemer (1989, experiment 1) | + |

Note: In each experiment, sequence learning was indexed by decreases in RTs relative to control groups. In these studies, subjects were classified by their verbal reports as unaware but were also tested using the prediction procedure. 0 indicates no significant transfer to the prediction task, + indicates a trend toward transfer, and + + indicates significant transfer.

notion of implicit learning (Hayes and Broadbent 1988; Reber 1989) stand at present on rather weak foundations. As yet, the two necessary conditions for establishing unconscious learning that we described in section 2 have not been met.

We end by returning to the relationship between implicit learning and implicit retrieval. Given the doubts that exist concerning unconscious learning, and the close relationship that exists between the evidence that constitutes implicit retrieval and the evidence that implies implicit learning, it is natural to ask what our analysis says about implicit memory or retrieval. It might appear that our conclusions cast doubt on demonstrations of implicit retrieval, but in fact this phenomenon has now been established beyond question (Schacter 1987), if by "implicit retrieval" we mean the ability of some information to be retrieved in the absence of conscious memory of the relevant study episode. The best examples come from neurological patients suffering from anterograde amnesia, who can benefit enormously from training despite having extremely poor episodic memory for the training experience (see Moscovitch, chap. 25, this volume).

What has not been well established (but see Young, chap. 6, this volume), however, is the ability of information to be retrieved from memory *in the absence of awareness of that information per se*, which is quite a different matter. It is this that is the real parallel to implicit learning. With respect to figure 33.1, a typical example of implicit memory involves demonstrating above-chance performance on an implicit measure such as GSR, in the absence of explicit memory for the $A-B$ learning episode. The figure shows that there are two ways in which this might come about. One is that the subject is aware of the A–B relationship but not of the study episode; the other is that the subject is unaware of both the episode and the content of that episode (the $A-B$ relationship). The first of these is case (ii) in the figure; the second is case (iii). But just as there is little evidence of implicit learning involving case (iii), so there is little evidence of implicit retrieval involving case (iii). Instead, demonstrations of implicit retrieval typically leave open the possibility that subjects are aware of the content of the study episode.

An example will serve to illustrate the point. In a prototypical experiment, Weiskrantz and Warrington (1979) demonstrated Pavlovian conditioning in two amnesiacs who simultaneously had extremely poor episodic memory of the training procedure: they were effectively unaware of the prior learning episode. But what would have happened if they had been presented with the CS and asked what expectation they had concerning its consequences? It is quite possible that, like normals, these amnesiacs would have shown a strong association between conditioning and awareness of the reinforcement contingency. If that were indeed the case, then there is nothing in the data to disprove the hypothesis that awareness and performance go hand in hand: conditioned responses are accompanied by awareness of the relevant contingency.

The key observation, expressed most clearly by Humphreys, Bain, and Pike (1989), is that successful performance on implicit and explicit tasks requires different sorts of information. Explicit tests require the ability to isolate an episodically unique memory; in contrast, implicit tests require nothing more than generic knowledge that is free from any specific episode. Thus, an implicit task can be performed in the absence of awareness of the relevant learning episode, but this is in general the only sense in which implicit memory tasks dissociate learning from awareness. Just as there is little evidence that knowledge can be acquired unconsciously, so there is little evidence that an implicit test can be performed in the absence of awareness of the generic information that supports successful performance on that test.

## NOTES

This chapter benefited considerably from discussions with Axel Cleeremans, Tony Dickinson, Tony Marcel, Pierre Perruchet, Arthur Reber, and Mark St. John, to whom we express our thanks. The research was supported by the UK Medical Research Council.

1. We use the expression *implicit retrieval* rather than the more common term *implicit memory* to emphasize that we are specifically considering what happens during the retrieval process.

2. Note that although the term *episode* has been taken to refer to either target information or the associated context (Mayes 1988), we are referring to the conjunction of these. Episodic memory is absent if the subject is unable to retrieve either.

3. This ignores the possibility that the subject could have been unaware of the $A-B$ relationship at $t_1$ but aware of it at $t_2$ as a result of observing his or her own behavior. Observation of a GSR in response to the tone might lead the subject to believe that the tone must therefore predict shock. Similarly, a blindsight patient may in some circumstances "know" the location of a stimulus as a result of observing his or her own response to the stimulus.

## REFERENCES

Andrade, J. (1994). Learning during anaesthesia: A review. *British Journal of Psychology*. In press.

Baer, P. E., and Fuhrer, M. J. (1982). Cognitive factors in the concurrent differential conditioning of eyelid and skin conductance responses. *Memory and Cognition*, 10, 135–140.

Baeyens, F., Eelen, P., Crombez, G., and Van den Bergh, O. (1992). Human evaluative conditioning: Acquisition trials, presentation schedule, evaluative style and contingency awareness. *Behaviour Research and Therapy*, 30, 133–142.

Baeyens, F., Eelen, P., and Van den Bergh, O. (1990). Contingency awareness in evaluative conditioning: A case for unaware affective-evaluative learning. *Cognition and Emotion*, 4, 3–18.

Berry, D. C., and Broadbent, D. E. (1984). On the relationship between task performance and associated verbalizable knowledge. *Quarterly Journal of Experimental Psychology*, 36A, 209–231.

Boakes, R. A. (1989). How one might find evidence for conditioning in adult humans. In T. Archer and L. -G. Nilsson (Eds.), *Aversion, avoidance and anxiety: Perspectives on learning and memory*, 381–402. Hillsdale, NJ: Erlbaum.

Bornstein, R. F. (1989). Exposure and affect: Overview and meta-analysis of research, 1968–1987. *Psychological Bulletin*, 106, 265–289.

Bornstein, R. F., Leone, D. R., and Galley, D. J. (1987). The generalizability of subliminal mere exposure effects: Influence of stimuli perceived without awareness on social behavior. *Journal of Personality and Social Psychology*, 53, 1070–1079.

Brewer, W. F. (1974). There is no convincing evidence for operant or classical conditioning in adult humans. In W. B. Weimer and D. S. Palermo (Eds.), *Cognition and the symbolic processes*, 1–42. Hillsdale, NJ: Erlbaum.

Broadbent, D. E. (1971). *Decision and stress*. London: Academic Press.

Davey, G. C. L. (1992). An expectancy model of laboratory preparedness effects. *Journal of Experimental Psychology: General, 121*, 24–40.

Dienes, Z., Broadbent, D. E., and Berry, D. (1991). Implicit and explicit knowledge bases in artificial grammar learning. *Journal of Experimental Psychology: Learning, Memory, and Cognition, 17*, 875–887.

Dulany, D. E., and Poldrack, R. A. (1991). Learned covariation: Conscious or unconscious representation? Paper presented at the Annual Meeting of the Psychonomic Society, San Francisco.

Ghoneim, M. M., Block, R. I., and Fowles, D. C. (1992). No evidence of classical conditioning of electrodermal responses during anesthesia. *Anesthesiology, 76*, 682–688.

Greenwald, A. G., Spangenberg, E. R., Pratkanis, A. R., and Eskenazi, J. (1991). Double blind tests of subliminal self-help audiotapes. *Psychological Science, 2*, 119–122.

Hartman, M., Knopman, D. S., and Nissen, M. J. (1989). Implicit learning of new verbal associations. *Journal of Experimental Psychology: Learning, Memory, and Cognition, 15*, 1070–1082.

Hayes, N. A., and Broadbent, D. E. (1988). Two modes of learning for interactive tasks. *Cognition, 28*, 249–276.

Holender, D. (1986). Semantic activation without conscious identification in dichotic listening, parafoveal vision, and visual masking: A survey and appraisal. *Behavioral and Brain Sciences, 9*, 1–66.

Humphreys, M. S., Bain, J. D., and Pike, R. (1989). Different ways to cue a coherent memory system: A theory for episodic, semantic, and procedural tasks. *Psychological Review, 96*, 208–233.

Jelicic, M., Bonke, B., Wolters, G., and Phaf, R. H. (1992). Implicit memory for words presented during anaesthesia. *European Journal of Cognitive Psychology, 4*, 71–80.

Lewicki, P. (1986). Processing information about covariations that cannot be articulated. *Journal of Experimental Psychology: Learning, Memory, and Cognition, 12*, 135–146.

Lewicki, P., Czyzewska, M., and Hoffman, H. (1987). Unconscious acquisition of complex procedural knowledge. *Journal of Experimental Psychology: Learning Memory and Cognition, 13*, 523–530.

Lewicki, P., Hill, T., and Sasaki, I. (1989). Self-perpetuating development of encoding biases. *Journal of Experimental Psychology: General, 118*, 323–337.

Lovibond, P. F. (1992). Tonic and phasic electrodermal measures of human aversive conditioning with long duration stimuli. *Psychophysiology, 29*, 621–632.

Marinkovic, K., Schell, A. M., and Dawson, M. E. (1989). Awareness of the CS-UCS contingency and classical conditioning of skin conductance responses with olfactory CSs. *Biological Psychology, 29*, 39–60.

Mathews, R. C., Buss, R. R., Stanley, W. B., Blanchard-Fields, F., Cho, J. R., and Druhan, B. (1989). Role of implicit and explicit processes in learning from examples: A synergistic effect. *Journal of Experimental Psychology: Learning, Memory, and Cognition, 15*, 1083–1100.

Mayes, A. R. (1988). *Human organic memory disorders*. Cambridge: Cambridge University Press.

Merikle, P. M., and Reingold, E. M. (1990). Recognition and lexical decision without detection: Unconscious perception? *Journal of Experimental Psychology: Human Perception and Performance, 16,* 574–583.

Nissen, M. J., and Bullemer, P. (1987). Attentional requirements of learning: Evidence for nonrecognized items. *Cognitive Psychology, 19,* 1–32.

Perruchet, P., and Amorim, M.-A. (1992). Conscious knowledge and changes in performance in sequence learning: Evidence against dissociation. *Journal of Experimental Psychology: Learning, Memory, and Cognition, 18,* 785–800.

Perruchet, P., Gallego, J., and Savy, I. (1990). A critical reappraisal of the evidence for unconscious abstraction of deterministic rules in complex experimental situations. *Cognitive Psychology, 22,* 493–516.

Reber, A. S. (1989). Implicit learning and tacit knowledge. *Journal of Experimental Psychology: General, 118,* 219–235.

Sanderson, P. M. (1989). Verbalizable knowledge and skilled task performance: Association, dissociation, and mental models. *Journal of Experimental Psychology: Learning, Memory, and Cognition, 15,* 729–747.

Schacter, D. L. (1987). Implicit memory: History and current status. *Journal of Experimental Psychology: Learning, Memory, and Cognition, 13,* 501–518.

Shanks, D. R., and Dickinson, A. (1991). Instrumental judgment and performance under variations in action-outcome contingency and contiguity. *Memory and Cognition, 19,* 353–360.

Shanks, D. R., and St. John, M. F. (1992). *Characteristics of dissociable human learning systems.* Technical Report No. 9203, Department of Cognitive Science, University of California, San Diego, La Jolla, CA.

Stadler, M. A. (1989). On learning complex procedural knowledge. *Journal of Experimental Psychology: Learning, Memory, and Cognition, 15,* 1061–1069.

Stanley, W. B., Mathews, R. C., Buss, R. R., and Kotler-Cope, S. (1989). Insight without awareness: On the interaction of verbalization, instruction and practice in a simulated process control task. *Quarterly Journal of Experimental Psychology, 41A,* 553–577.

Svartdal, F. (1991). Operant modulation of low-level attributes of rule-governed behavior by nonverbal contingencies. *Learning and Motivation, 22,* 406–420.

Vokey, J. R., and Read, J. D. (1985). Subliminal messages: Between the devil and the media. *American Psychologist, 40,* 1231–1239.

Weiskrantz, L., and Warrington, E. K. (1979). Conditioning in amnesic patients. *Neuropsychologia, 17,* 187–194.

Willingham, D. B., Nissen, M. J., and Bullemer, P. (1989). On the development of procedural knowledge. *Journal of Experimental Psychology: Learning, Memory, and Cognition, 15,* 1047–1060.

# 34 Implicit Learning in Neural Networks: The Importance of Starting Small

Jeffrey L. Elman

## 34.1 INTRODUCTION

The ability to learn complex domains has been a hallmark of human cognition, and so it is not surprising that learning has been a central focus in both the experimental and theoretical literature. Nor is it surprising, given the wide range of capacities demonstrated across various domains, that there have been hypothesized a variety of learning mechanisms. Thus, we find that procedural learning is contrasted with declarative learning (Anderson 1983), stochastic learning (Estes 1957) is contrasted with language (presumably rule-based) learning (Miller and Chomsky 1963), and deductive reasoning is contrasted with inductive problem solving (Hunt 1966).

More recently, it has been suggested that an important dichotomy exists between learning that is explicit and learning that is implicit (Berry and Broadbent 1984; Broadbent 1977; Cleeremans 1993; Cleeremans and McClelland 1991; Lewicki, Czyzewska, and Hoffman 1987; Lewicki, Hill, and Bizot 1988; Reber 1965, 1967, 1969, 1989; Reber and Allen 1978). The distinction is generally understood as hinging on whether learning is carried out as a conscious process. Explicit learning is typically assumed to require conscious, attentive effort; implicit learning is carried out nonconsciously and may be less affected by attentional variables.

This distinction has an intuitive appeal, but it is not entirely clear that there exist clear operational definitions. Nonetheless, there are compelling reasons to try to understand the phenomena described as involving implicit learning. There are certainly situations in which explicit learning in the style of scientific reasoning occurs (Dunbar and Klahr 1989; Lea and Simon 1979). But much of what people learn is not accompanied by explicit instruction and does not appear to be learned by conscious deliberation. Nor are people always able later to articulate the contents of their knowledge. Language learning seems like a paradigm example in which implicit learning occurs, but there are many other instances of skill acquisition that bear the hallmark of implicit learning.

While various models exist for explicit learning, until recently there have been no computationally detailed models for implicit learning. Indeed, the only such model (to my knowledge) is that provided by Cleeremans (1993; Cleeremans and McClelland 1991). The model is based on the simple recurrent network architecture (SRN) introduced by Elman (1990, 1991). The network model, it turns out, exhibits many of the specific characteristics shown by humans in implicit learning. In the work to date, the model has been shown to be capable of providing a good fit to the data and has also provided a mechanistic explanation of the data. The model is conceptually simple, but its behavior is complex and frequently not obvious. In particular, it is often not clear which conditions are conducive to learning and which impede learning.

I have two goals in writing this chapter: To try to characterize the principles of learning in simple recurrent networks, on the conjecture that these systems may tell us something about the nature of implicit or nonconscious learning in humans; and to try to make sense of some of these results by relating characteristics of implicit learning to developmental phenomena. It turns out that viewed in isolation, network learning has certain undesirable properties; if it is also true that this sort of learning underlies nonconscious learning in humans, it would seem to be very maladaptive. Similarly, it can be argued that characteristics of development in humans are are maladaptive. Infancy and childhood are times of great vulnerability and severely restrict the range of activities of the adult caretakers. It is difficult to see why evolutionary pressures should not therefore have led to a much shorter period of immaturity in our species. Instead, we observe that development is greatly prolonged in humans, in comparison with other species.

But if learning is viewed as being carried out in the context of maturational changes, then we discover that there exist important synergies between learning and development. Developmental limitations (such as restricted working memory), which themselves might be thought to be maladaptive for a species, may turn out to be highly beneficial for learning. So although both learning and development may have characteristics that would appear to be deleterious when looked at in isolation, operating together—as, after all, they do in children—they result in successful outcomes. This make sense when one considers that both learning and development are the outcome of evolutionary change. Evolution selects for the fitness of whole individuals, not traits in isolation.

This chapter begins by reporting the results of several simulations with artificial neural networks. The goal of these simulations was to train the networks to process complex sentences in order to test their ability to learn and to represent part/whole relationships and embedded clauses. The networks were able to learn the task only when they were handicapped by being forced to begin with severe memory limitations. These have the effect of restricting the range of data they were exposed to during initial learning—thus, the "importance of starting small."

However, this result (the need to start small) contrasts with other findings in the connectionist literature. It is known, for instance, that there are problems that can best be learned when the entire data set is made available to a network (Harris 1991). If a network is given only a subset of the data, it often fails to learn the correct generalization and remains stuck in a local error minimum. This result is thus just the opposite of the starting small finding; instead, it seems sometimes to be necessary to "start big."

This apparent paradox leads to the second part of the chapter, where I attempt to understand the deeper principles that underlie learning in connectionist systems. These principles explain why it is that sometimes it is necessary to start small and at other times start big. More basically, we see that these principles of learning interact with characteristics of human development in a beneficial manner.

## 34.2 THE IMPORTANCE OF STARTING SMALL

One of the most visible domains in which humans learn is language. It is also one of the most theoretically problematic domains for understanding learning, in part because of what has been called the projection problem: if the task of the language learner is to figure out the underlying regularities—that is, the grammar—that are responsible for the language he or she hears, then the data available to the learner may not be sufficient to determine the correct grammar uniquely.

This problem of the apparent insufficiency of the data has been discussed in many contexts (Baker 1979; Bowerman 1987; Pinker 1989; Wexler and Cullicover 1980), but one of the simplest demonstrations comes from Gold's (1967) work. Gold shows that if a language learner is presented with positive-only data, only regular languages can be learned (regular languages are languages that can be generated by finite state automata). The rub is that, on the one hand, natural languages appear to belong to a more powerful class than this (Chomsky 1957), and on the other, there is no good evidence that children receive or use negative data during learning (Brown and Hanlon 1970; Hirsh-Pasek, Treiman, and Schneiderman 1984; Braine 1971).

Gold advances several suggestions in order to account for the fact that, despite his findings, children do learn language. Although children do not appear to receive explicit negative evidence, they may receive indirect negative evidence. Or possibly, some of what children know is innate; thus, they need not infer the grammar solely on the basis of positive data.[1] Almost certainly both of these possibilities are true to some extent. That is, the child is not an unconstrained learning mechanism in the sense of being able to learn any possible languages. Rather, innate predispositions narrow the range of what can be learned. Of course, it is very much an open (and controversial) question exactly what form that innate knowledge takes. A number of investigators have also proposed that although direct negative evidence may not be available, there are subtler forms of negative evidence. For example, the non-occurrence of an expected form constitutes an indirect sort of negative evidence. Just how far this sort of evidence can be used has been challenged (Pinker 1989). Thus, although innateness and indirect evidence plausibly participate in the solution of the learnability problem, their contribution is not known and remains controversial.

I suggest that there may be a third factor in helping to account for the apparent ability of learners to go beyond the data. This factor hinges on the simple fact that first language learners (children) are themselves undergoing significant developmental changes during precisely the time that they learn language. Indeed, language learning after these developmental changes have completed seems to be far less successful. This is often attributed to the passing of a "critical period" for language learning, but this is no more than a restatement of facts. What I would like to consider here is the question of what it is about the so-called critical period that might facilitate learning language.

Interestingly, almost all learnability work ignores the fact that learning and development co-occur. It is typically assumed that both the learning device and training input are static. One might wonder what the consequences are of having either the learning device (network or child) or the input data not be constant during learning. Plunkett and Marchman (1990) have shown that while the basic influences of type/token frequency and phonological predictability are similar to the condition of non incremental learning, better overall learning is achieved when the training corpus for a connectionist model is allowed to grow slowly in size. We might also ask what the consequences are when the learning mechanism itself is changing.

In this section, I report the effect of staged input on learning in a connectionist model. The network fails to learn the task when the entire data set is presented all at once but succeeds when the data are presented incrementally. I then show how similar effects can be obtained by the more realistic assumption that the input is held constant but the learning mechanism itself undergoes developmental changes. Finally, I examine the network to see what the mechanism is that allows this to happen and suggest what conditions are necessary for incremental learning to be useful.

**Simulations**

This work was originally motivated by an interest in studying ways in which connectionist networks might use distributed representations to encode complex, hierarchically organized information. By this I mean just the sort of relationships that typically occur in language. For example, in the sentence *The girls whom the teacher has picked for the play which will be produced next month practice every afternoon*, several events are described. Some are backgrounded or subordinate to the main event. This has grammatical consequences. Thus, the main verb (*practice*) is in the plural because it agrees with *the girls* (not *the teacher*, or *the play*). And although *picked* is a transitive verb, which often takes a direct object following it, no noun appears after the verb because the direct object (*the girls*) has already been mentioned.

These sorts of facts (and specifically, the recursive nature of embedded relative clauses) led many linguists to conclude that natural language could not be modeled by a finite state grammar (Chomsky 1957), and that statistical inference as a learning mechanism for language was untenable (Miller and Chomsky 1963). These conclusions about the representational and learnability requirements of natural language seem to pose real problems for connectionist networks, which typically rely heavily (though not necessarily exclusively) on statistical inference and which are more similar to finite state machines than other sorts of computational devices (e.g., pushdown automata; but see Pollack 1990).

My first approach was to try construct a semirealistic artificial language with some of the crucial properties cited by Chomsky and his colleagues as being problematic for finite state automata and statistical learning and to train a neural network to process sentences from this language. The network was a simple recurrent network (Elman 1990, 1991; Jordan 1986; Servan-Schreiber, Cleereman, and McClelland 1988). The salient property of this architecture is that it is a kind of dynamic system that allows inputs to be processed in sequence and in which the internal states are fed back at every time step to provide an additional input. The network must learn to develop internal states (the hidden unit activation patterns) that encode temporal information in ways which enable the network to produce the correct outputs. The network architecture that was used is shown in figure 34.1.

The input corpus consisted of sentences generated by a grammar that had certain critical properties: (1) there was number agreement between subject nouns and their verbs; (2) verbs differ with regard to argument expectations

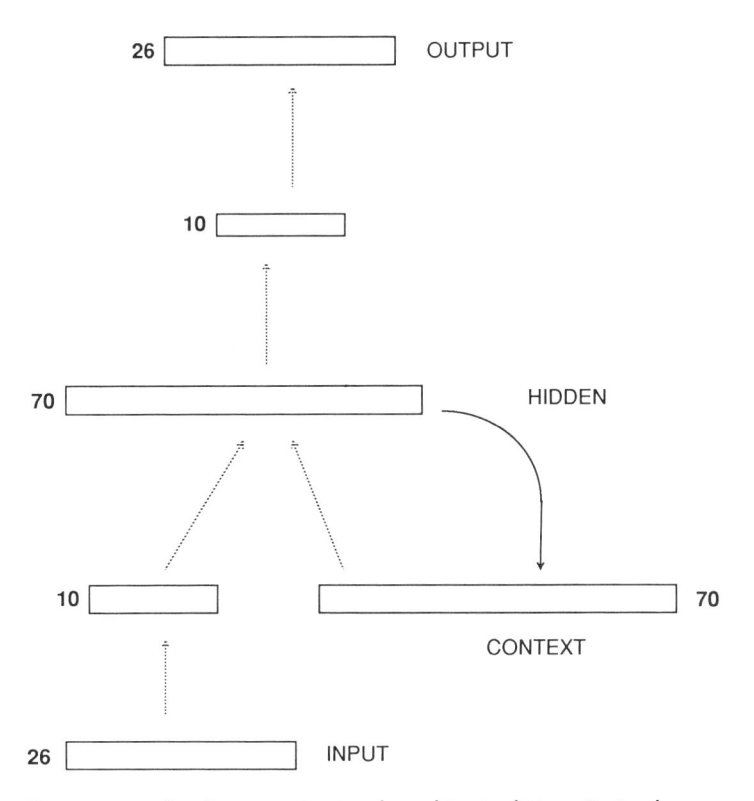

**Figure 34.1** Simple recurrent network used in simulations. Rectangles represent groups of units; numbers indicate how many units are in each group. Dotted lines represent fully distributed connections that are modifiable through learning; the solid line from Hidden to Context units represents one-to-one links, each connection fixed at 1.0. Context units have linear activation functions. All other units have sigmoidal activation functions.

(some required direct objects, others optionally permitted objects; others precluded direct objects); (3) sentences could contain multiple embeddings in the form of relative clauses (in which the head could be either the subject or object of the subordinate clause). The existence of these relative clauses considerably complicated the set of agreement and verb argument facts. Some sample sentences follow:

boys who chase dogs see girls.

girl who boys who feed cats walk.

cats chase dogs.

mary feeds john.

dogs see boys who cats who mary feeds chase.

Each word was encoded as a vector of 0's in which a single bit was randomly set to 1. Thus, the form of the input contained no information about the nature of the input (e.g., grammatical category, meaning, number). In this sense, of course, this makes the representational problem a great deal more difficult for the network than it is for the child. In natural languages, for example, morphologically related items typically share formal resemblance. This relationship is not always transparent, however, so it was of interest to see how much could be inferred based on distributional properties alone.

The network was trained to take one word at a time and predict what the next word would be. Because the predictions depend on the grammatical structure (which may involve multiple embeddings), this forces the network to develop internal representations that encode the relevant grammatical information. (See Elman 1991 for details of this language.)

The results of the first trials were quite disappointing. The network failed to master the task, even for the training data. Performance was not uniformly bad. Indeed, in some sentences, the network would correctly coordinate the number of the main clause subject, mentioned early in a sentence, with the number of the main clause verb, mentioned after many embedded relative clauses. But it would then fail to get the agreement correct on some of the relative clause subjects and verbs, even when these were close together. For example, it might predict *The boys who the girl chase see the dog*, getting the number agreement of *boys* and *see* right, but failing on the more proximal— and presumably, easier—*girl chases*. This failure, of course, is exactly what might have been predicted by Chomsky, Miller, and Gold.

**Incremental Input**

In an attempt to understand where the breakdown was occurring and just how complex a language the network might be able to learn, I next devised a regimen in which the training input was organized into corpora of increasing complexity, and the network was trained first with the simplest input. There were five phases in all. In the first phase, 10,000 sentences consisting solely of simple sentences were presented. The network was trained on five exposures ("epochs") to this database. At the conclusion of this phase, the training data were discarded and the network was exposed to a new set of sentences. In this second phase, 10,000 new sentences were generated; 7,500 of these were simple, and 2,500 were complex. As before, the network was trained for five epochs, after which performance was also quite high, even on the complex sentences. In phase 3, the mixture was 5,000 new simple/5,000 new complex sentences, for five epochs. In phase 4, the mixture was 2,500 simple/7,500 complex. And in phase 5, the network was trained on 10,000 complex sentences.

Since the prediction task, given this grammar, is nondeterministic, the best measure of performance is not the extent to which the literal prediction is correct (measured thus, an error of 0.0 would require that the network memorize the training data) but rather the degree to which the network's predictions match the conditional probability distributions of the training data. Performance using this metric was very good at the conclusion of all phases of training, including the final phase. Final performance yielded an error of 0.177, with network output measured against the empirically derived likelihood estimates. (Alternatively, one can measure the cosine of the angle between these two vectors. Mean cosine at the end of training was 0.852; perfect performance would have been 1.00.) Furthermore, the network's high performance generalized to a variety of novel sentences that systematically test the capacity to predict grammatically correct forms across a range of different structures.

This result contrasts strikingly with the earlier failure of the network to learn when the full corpus was presented at the outset.[2] Put simply, the network was unable to learn the complex grammar when trained from the outset with the full "adult" language. However, when the training data were selected such that simple sentences were presented first, the network succeeded not only in mastering these, but then going on to master the complex sentences as well.

In one sense, this is a pleasing result, because the behavior of the network partially resembles that of children. Children do not begin by mastering the adult language in all its complexity. Rather, they begin with the simplest of structures and build incrementally until they achieve the adult language.

There is an important disanalogy, however, between the way in which the network was trained and the way children learn language. In this simulation, the network was placed in an environment that was carefully constructed so that it encountered only the simple sentences at the beginning. As learning and performance progressed, the environment was gradually enriched by the inclusion of more and more complex sentences. But this is not a good model for the situation in which children learn language. Although there is evidence that adults modify their language to some extent when interacting with children, it is not clear that these modifications affect the grammatical structure of the adult speech. Unlike the network, children hear exemplars of all aspects of the adult language from the beginning.

If it is not true that the child's environment changes radically (as in this first simulation), what is true is that the child changes during the period he or she is learning language. A more realistic network model would have a constant learning environment, but some aspect of the network itself would undergo change during learning.

**Incremental Memory**

One developmental change that is plausibly relevant to learning is the gradual increase in memory and attention span that is characteristic of children. In the network, the analogue of memory is supplied by the access the network has (via the recurrent connections) to its own prior internal states. The network can be given a more limited memory by depriving it of access, periodically, to this feedback. The network would thus have only a limited temporal window within which patterns could be processed.

A second simulation was therefore carried out with the goal of seeing what the effect would be, not of staging the input, but of beginning with a limited memory and gradually increasing memory span. The rationale was that this scenario more closely resembled the conditions under which children learn language.

In this simulation, the network was trained from the outset with the full adult language (the target corpus that had previously been shown to be unlearnable when it was presented from the beginning). However, the network itself was modified such that during the first phase, the recurrent feedback was eliminated after every third or fourth word (randomly).[3] In the second phase, the network continued with another set of sentences drawn from the adult language (the first set was discarded so the network would not be able to memorize it); more important, the memory window was increased to four to five words. In the third phase, the memory window was increased to five or six words; in the fourth phase, to six or seven words; and in the fifth phase, the feedback was not interfered with at all.

It turned out that the first phase had to be extended to much longer than in the previous simulation in order to achieve a comparable level of performance (twelve epochs rather than five; for purposes of comparison, performance was measured only on the simple sentences although the network was trained on complex sentences as well). However, once this initially prolonged stage of learning was over, learning proceeded quickly through the remaining stages (five epochs per stage). At the end, performance on both the training data, and also on a wide range of novel data, was as good as in the prior simulation. If the learning mechanism itself was allowed to undergo "maturational changes" (in this case, increasing its memory capacity) during learning, the outcome was just as good as if the environment itself had been gradually complicated.

Before discussing some of the implications of this finding, it is important to try to understand exactly what the basic mechanism is that results in the apparently paradoxical finding that learning can be improved under conditions of limited capacity. One would like to know, for example, whether this outcome is always to be expected or might be obtained in only special circumstances.

We begin by looking at the way the network eventually solved the problem of representing complex sentences. The network has available to it, in the form of its hidden unit patterns, a high-dimensional space for internal representations. In such networks these internal representations can play a key role in the solution to a problem. Among other things, the internal representations permit the network to escape the tyranny of a form-based interpretation of the world. Sometimes the form of an input is not a reliable indicator of how it should be treated; put another way, appearances can deceive. In such cases, the network uses its hidden units to construct a functionally) based representational scheme. Thus, the similarity structure of the internal representations can be a more reliable indicator of "meaning" than the similarity structure of the bare inputs.

In this simulation, the network utilized the various dimensions of the internal state to represent a number of different factors relevant to the task: individual lexical item; grammatical category (noun, verb, relative pronoun, etc.), number (singular versus plural), grammatical role (subject versus object), level of embedding (main clause, subordinate, etc.), and verb argument type (transitive, intransitive, optional). Principal component analysis (Gonzalez and Wintz 1977) can be used to identify the specific dimensions associated with each factor. The internal representations of specific sentences can then be visualized as movements through this state space (one looks at selected dimensions or planes, chosen to illustrate the factor of interest). Example trajectories for several sentences are shown in figure 34.2.

One might think of such plots as the network equivalent of graphs of electroencephalographic activity recorded from human subjects while they process various types of sentences. Figure 34.2a, for example, shows how the singular/plural distinction of the main clause subject is encoded and preserved during an embedded relative clause. Figure 34.2b shows how differences in verb-argument structure are encoded (in this grammar, *chases* requires a direct object, *sees* optionally permits one, and *walks* is intransitive). Figure 34.2c demonstrates the way in which the network represents embedded relative clauses.

One can also visualize the representational space more globally by having the network process a large number of sentences, and recording the positions in state space for each word; and then displaying the overall positions. This is done in figure 34.3a. Three dimensions (of the seventy total) are shown; the $x$ and $y$ coordinates together encode depth of embedding and the $z$ coordinate encodes number (Elman 1991).

At the outset of learning, none of these dimensions has been assigned to these functions. If one passes the same sentences through a network prior to training, the internal representations have no discernible structure. These internal representations are the important outcome of learning; they are also the necessary basis for good performance.

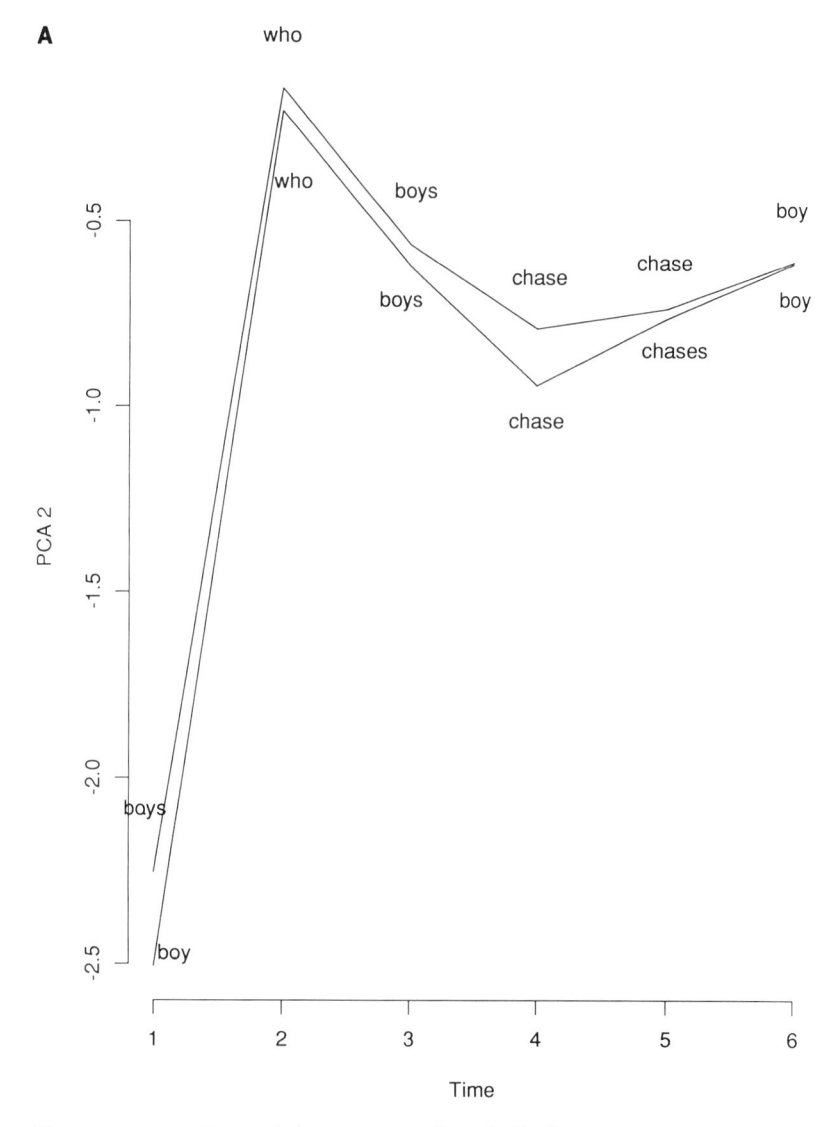

**Figure 34.2** *a.* Graph of the movement through Hidden unit activation state space as a trained network processes the sentences boys who boys chase chase boy and boy who boys chase chases boy. The horizontal axis represents time (successive words); the vertical axis represents movement along the second principle component. *b.* Graph of the movement through state space (in the plane of principle components 1 and 3) as the network processes the sentences boy chases boy, boy sees boy, and boy walks. (The final word in each sentence is bracketed with ]S.) *c.* Graph of the movement through state space (in the plane of principle components 1 and 11) as the network processes the sentence boy chases boy who chases boy who chases boy. (The final noun is bracked with ]S.)

**B**

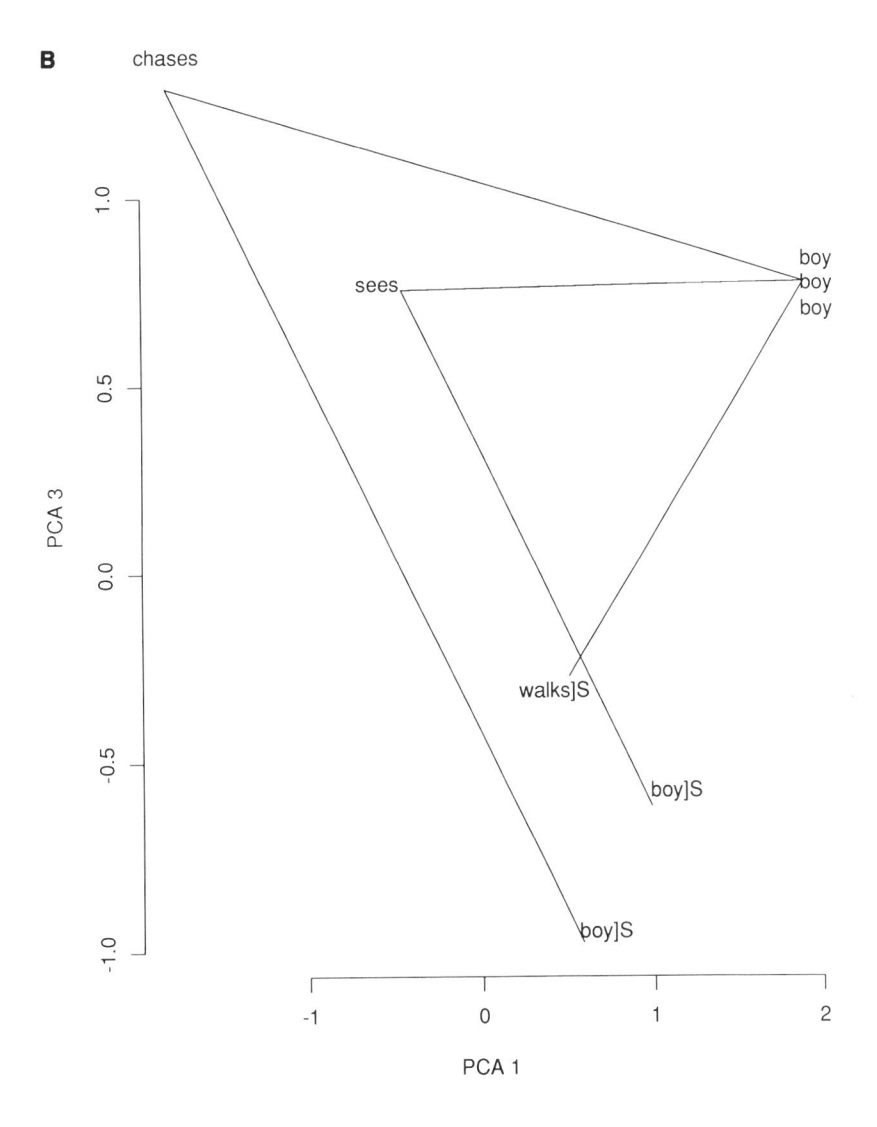

[Figure: PCA state-space plot with PCA 1 on x-axis and PCA 3 on y-axis, showing labeled points: chases, sees, boy, boy, boy, walks]S, boy]S, boy]S]

The state-space graph shown in figure 34.3a was produced under conditions of incremental training, which is crucial for successful learning. What does the state-space look like under conditions of failure, such as when we train a fully mature network on the adult corpus from the beginning? Figure 34.3b shows such a plot. Unlike figure 34.3a, part b reveals a less clearly organized use of the state space. There is far greater variability, and words have noisier internal representations. We do not see the kind of sharp distinctions associated with the encoding of number, verb argument type, and embedding as we do when the network has succeeded in mastering the language. Why might this be?

When the network is confronted from the beginning with the entire adult corpus, the problem is this. There are actually a relatively small number of sources of variance (number, grammatical category, verb-argument type, and level of embedding). However, these sources of variance interact in complex

**c**

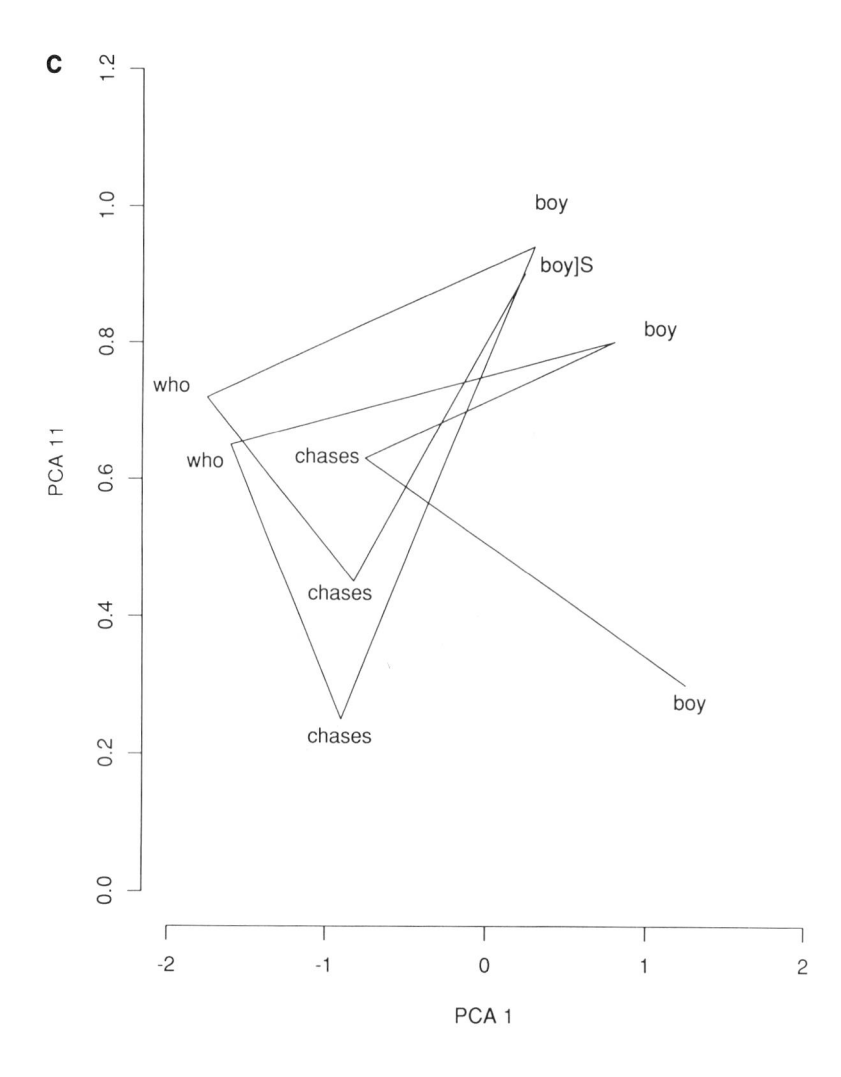

[Figure: PCA plot with axes PCA 1 (x-axis, -2 to 2) and PCA 11 (y-axis, 0.0 to 1.2), showing labeled points: boy, boy]S, boy, who, who, chases, chases, chases, boy, connected by lines.]

ways. Some of the interactions involve fairly long distance dependencies. For example, in the sentence *The girl who the dogs that I chased down the block frightened, ran away*, the evidence that the verb *frightened* is transitive is a bit obscure, because the direct object (*the girl*) not only does not occur after the verb (the normal position for a direct object in simple English sentences) but occurs ten words earlier, and there are several other nouns and verbs in between. The simple recurrent network does not have perfect memory. All things being equal, information decays exponentially. What happens is that the network finds a solution to the task that works enough of the time to yield reasonable performance. However, the solution is imperfect and results in a set of internal representations that do not reflect the true underlying sources of variance. The resulting failure when using the full data set is consistent with the claims of Chomsky (1957), Miller and Chomsky (1963), and Gold (1967).

But when learning proceeds in an incremental fashion, either because the environment has been altered or because the network itself is initially resource limited, the result is that the network sees only a subset of the data. When the

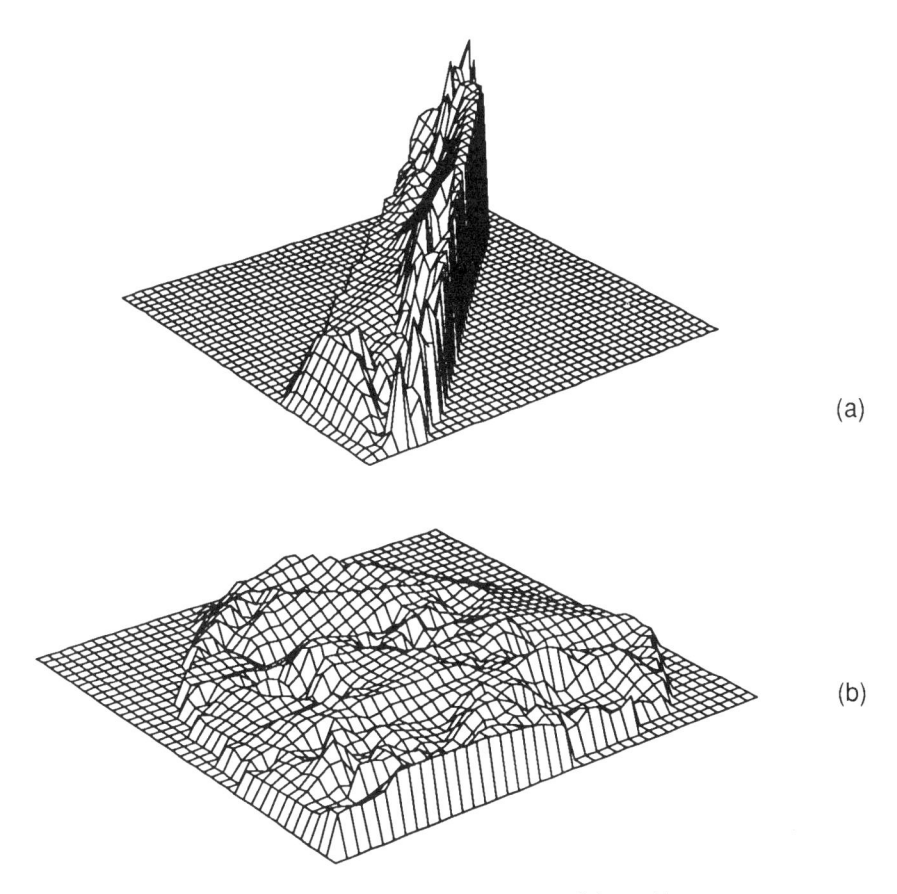

**Figure 34.3** *a.* Plot of the locations in three dimensions of the Hidden unit activation state space that are occupied as a successfully trained network processes several thousand test sentences. *b.* Plot of the state space locations that are occupied when an unsuccessfully trained network attempts to process several thousand test sentences.

input is staged, the data are just the simple sentences. When the network is given a limited temporal window, the data are the full adult language, but the effective data are only those sentences, and portions of sentences, that fall within the window. These are the simple sentences. (Now we see why the initial phase of learning takes a bit longer in this condition; the network also has to wade through a great deal of input, which is essentially noise.)

This subset of data, the simple sentences, contains three of the four sources of variance (grammatical category, number, and verb argument type), and there are no long-distance dependencies. As a result, the network is able to develop internal representations that encode these sources of variance. When learning advances (either because of new input or because improvements in the network's memory capacity give it a larger temporal window), all additional changes are constrained by this early commitment to the basic grammatical factors.

The effect of early learning, thus, is to constrain the solution space to a much smaller region. The solution space is initially very large and contains many false solutions (in network parlance, local minima). Whether it is really the case that the data truly underdetermine the solution, it does seem to be true that the chances of stumbling on the correct solution are small. However, by selectively focusing on the simpler set of facts, the network appears to learn the basic distinctions—noun/verb/relative pronoun, singular/plural and so forth—that form the necessary basis for learning the more difficult set of facts that arise with complex sentences.

Seen in this light, the early limitations on memory capacity assume a more positive character. It is natural to believe that the more powerful a network is, the greater is its ability to learn a complex domain. However, this appears not always to be the case. If the domain is of sufficient complexity and if there are abundant false solutions, then the opportunities for failure are great. What is required is some way to constrain the solution space artificially to just that region containing the true solution. The initial memory limitations fill this role; they act as a filter on the input, and focus learning on just the subset of facts that lay the foundation for future success.

## 34.3 HOW NETWORKS LEARN

We turn now to an intriguing problem. Answering that problem will require that we seek a deeper understanding of the principles that constrain learning in networks of the sort we have studied here and ways in which network learning may differ from more classical learning systems. The problem is this. We have just seen that there are conditions where a network appears to do better at learning a problem when it begins with a restricted subset of the data. This is the starting small result. However, we also know that there are conditions in which starting small can be absolutely fatal; restricting the training data will lead the network to learn the wrong generalization.

A simple example of this is the exclusive-OR function (XOR), a Boolean function of two inputs. When the inputs are identical, the function maps to false (or 0); when the inputs are different, the function maps to true (or 1):

| Input | Output |
|-------|--------|
| 1 0   | 1      |
| 0 1   | 1      |
| 0 0   | 0      |
| 1 1   | 0      |

This function cannot be learned by two-layer networks with sigmoidal activation functions but require at least one additional intermediate layer. Even then, the function is not always learned successfully. It is particularly important that the network see all the patterns from the outset. If the fourth pattern (for example) is withheld until late in training, the network will typically fail to learn XOR. Instead, it will learn logical OR, since this is compatible with the first three patterns. Worse, having learned OR, the network will be unable to modify its weights in a way that accommodates the final pattern.

Harris (1991) has shown that similar results hold for the parity function (of which XOR is a reduced case). In general, experience with neural networks suggests that these systems not only thrive on training data but may require large data sets in order to learn a difficult function.

These results appear to be at sharp variance with the results presented earlier in this chapter. However, both effects arise as a consequence of fundamental properties of learning in connectionist models.[4] I would therefore now like to consider what some of these properties might be, how they might differ from other approaches to learning, and what relevance they might have to understanding the interaction between learning and development in humans.

There are four properties I will focus on here, although a number of others are relevant and have been discussed elsewhere (Bates and Elman 1993; McClelland, n.d.). The properties I consider here are (1) the statistical basis for learning and the problem of small sample size (2) the representation of experience (3) constraints on new hypotheses and (4) how the ability to learn changes over time. Each property imposes a small constraint on learning, but together the four characteristics sharply limit the power of networks. As we shall see, the effect of embedding learning in a system that develops over time (i.e., starts small) is to compensate for these limitations exactly.

## Property 1: Statistics as the Basis for Learning—The Problem of Sample Size

In most neural network learning algorithms, the driving force for inference is statistics. The nature of statistical inference is a complex topic, and the importance of statistics for learning in neural networks has engendered a certain amount of controversy.

To a large extent, conclusions about the inadequacy of statistically based learning arise from claims advanced in connection with language learning. In a well-known paper, Miller and Chomsky (1963) argued that certain properties of natural language make statistically based learning infeasible. The problem is exemplified in sentences such as *The people who say they want to rent your house next summer while you are away in Europe are from California*. Note that there exists a dependency between the number (plural) of *people* early in the sentence and the number (plural) of the second occurrence of the verb *are*, seventeen words later. Let us suppose that a learner is confronted with the task of determining the conditions under which *are*, rather than *is*, should be used. Miller and Chomsky argued that if the learner is able to use only co-occurrence statistics, then an inordinate number of sentences will have to be sampled. This is because if the dependency is viewed as a matter of statistical co-occurrence rather than as a structural fact relating to subject-verb agreement in sentences (which may contain embedded relative clauses), the learner will have to have previously sampled all the possible sentences that contain *people* and *are* separated by all possible seventeen-word combinations. This number is astronomical (it actually outstrips the number of seconds in an individual's lifetime by many orders of magnitude). Miller and Chomsky concluded that statistically based learning is therefore inadequate to account for language acquisition.

The weakness with Miller and Chomsky's argument is that it fails to distinguish between the use of statistics as the driving force for learning and statistics as the outcome of learning. If the learning mechanism is merely compiling a lookup table of co-occurrence facts (i.e., statistics as output), the approach is indeed doomed for the reasons they give. But this is not what neural networks do. Neural networks are function approximators, not compilers of lookup tables. The goal of learning is to discover the function that underlies the training data. The learning algorithm is statistically driven and is highly sensitive to the statistics of the training data. The outcome of learning, however, is rather closer to what Miller and Chomsky would have called a rule system (although the network's version of rules differs considerably from what Miller and Chomsky had in mind) than it is to a lookup table of statistics. Practically, this means that networks are able to extrapolate beyond their training data in ways that obviate the need (for example) to see all possible combinations of words in sentences. In other words, networks generalize.

There is a problem associated with statistical-based learning, however, and it is relevant here. This is the problem that arises when statistics are computed over small sample sizes. In general, the smaller the sample size, ($N$) is, the riskier it is that the sample statistics provide a good estimate of the population statistics. With small $N$, there may be a large number of reasonable generalizations compatible with the data at hand; as $N$ grows, new data will typically exclude some of these generalizations. (In principle, there is always an infinite number of generalizations compatible with any data set of any given size; but in practice, the effect of additional data is to constrain the number "reasonable" generalizations more highly)

The case of XOR cited earlier is one example of this. Or consider the following data in which patterns are classified into one of two categories (0 or 1):

| Pattern | Classification |
|---|---|
| 1 0 1 1 0 1 | 1 |
| 0 0 0 0 0 0 | 1 |
| 0 0 1 1 0 0 | 1 |
| 0 1 0 1 1 0 | 0 |
| 1 1 1 0 1 1 | 0 |
| 0 0 0 1 1 1 | 0 |

Let us assume that a network is trained on these data. We then present it with a novel pattern,

0 1 1 1 0 1.

The question is, will this be classified as a member of class 0 or class 1?

The answer depends on which generalization the network has extracted from the training data. There are multiple possibilities consistent with the limited observations. The network might have discovered that the first three patterns (in class 1) are symmetrical about the center (the last three bits are the mirror image of the first three), in which case the network will assign the test pattern to class 0 (because it is nonsymmetrical). Alternatively, the network might have discovered that all members of class 1 have even parity, and so it will classify the test pattern as class 1 (because it has even parity). Or the network might have extracted the generalization that all members of class 0 have a 1 in the fifth bit position, while class 1 patterns have a 0 in that position. In this case the test item belongs in class 1. (And, of course, because the outcome is the same as symmetry, we cannot know with this test item whether the network is making the classification on the basis of symmetry or contents of fifth bit position; further probes would be needed.) Thus, the effect of limited data is to impose minimal constraints on the nature of the generalizations possible. Increasing the data set may restrict the range of generalizations that the network can extract.

Why should this be a problem for neural networks? Certainly at early stages of learning, there may be a limited amount of training data, but why should the problem not disappear with continued exposure to new data? To understand why the problem persists, we need to consider the remaining three properties of learning.

**Property 2: The Representation of Experience**

Given the importance of data to all models of learning, a very basic question arises about lifetime of the data and about the form in which prior training examples are stored. This question is rarely addressed in any explicit way; in many models of learning (Dunbar and Klahr 1989; Lea and Simon 1979; Osherson, Stob, and Weinstein 1986) it seems to be assumed that the data accumulate and are available in a more or less veridical form for as long as they may be needed. Whenever a current hypothesis is rejected or found to be lacking, a new hypothesis (or modification) must be generated, based on the old data plus whatever new information prompts the revision. So it would seem that the data must be preserved for as long as they are needed and must be maintained in a more or less unprocessed form. Exemplar-based models make this assumption quite explicitly (Estes 1986; Medin and Schaffer 1978; Nosofsky, n.d.) and claim that experiences are stored as individually retrievable exemplars.

Connectionist models of the sort described here make very different assumptions regarding the lifetime and representational form of training examples. When a network is presented with a training pattern, the learning algorithm results in small changes in the connection strengths (weights) between nodes. These weights implement the function the network has learned up to that point. Once a given pattern has been processed and the network has been updated, the data disappear. Their effect is immediate and results in a modification of the knowledge state of the network. Data persist only implicitly by virtue of the effect they have on what the network knows. The data themselves are lost and are not available to the learning algorithm for later reprocessing (for example, in a way that might allow the learning mechanism to generate alternative hypotheses). This leads us to the next property of learning, which has to do with constraints on the generation of new hypotheses.

**Property 3: Constraints on New Hypotheses—The Continuity of Search**

Consider the space of all possible hypotheses that a system might entertain. In traditional learning models, these hypotheses usually take the form of symbolic propositions or rule sets. The space of possible hypotheses for such a system consists of all rules that conform to the grammar of the system. In connectionist models, on the other hand, hypotheses are implemented as values of the weights on connections between nodes.

Now consider the trajectory, over time, of the search in the two spaces. In the traditional system, this trajectory need not be continuous. That is, successive hypotheses need not be particularly similar to one another. When one hypothesis is discarded, the succeeding hypothesis may differ wildly from it. In part, this follows as a consequence of having some faithful and enduring record of the prior evidence (see property 2). The evidence may be rearranged in novel ways that are unconstrained by the temporal history of learning.

In neural networks employing gradient descent, the picture is quite different. The search through hypothesis space is necessarily continuous. To make this somewhat clearer and to introduce some concepts that will be useful in later discussion, imagine the simple network shown at the top of figure 34.4. The network has only one input and two nodes (one hidden and one output); there are two weights (one from the input and one from hidden to output). Below the network is shown a hypothetical graph of the error that might be produced (for some hypothetical data set, not specified here) as we systematically vary values of the two weights. The different values of the two weights are shown along the $x$ and $y$ axes, and the error that would be produced by the network at the different possible weight values is shown along the $z$ axis. (By error, I mean the discrepancy between what the network would output in response to the training data, compared with the correct output for those data.) If we knew this error surface in advance, of course, we could set the network to the combination of weights that produces the lowest error (marked as point $d$ in the figure). Not knowing what this surface looks like, we might determine it empirically by systematically sweeping through all possible combinations of weights and testing the network at each point. This is, of course, quite tedious (particularly given networks with a larger number of weights). What gradient descent learning algorithms provide are techniques

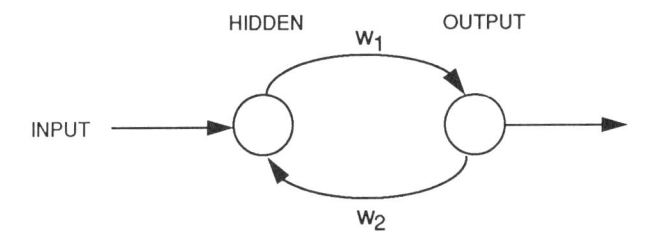

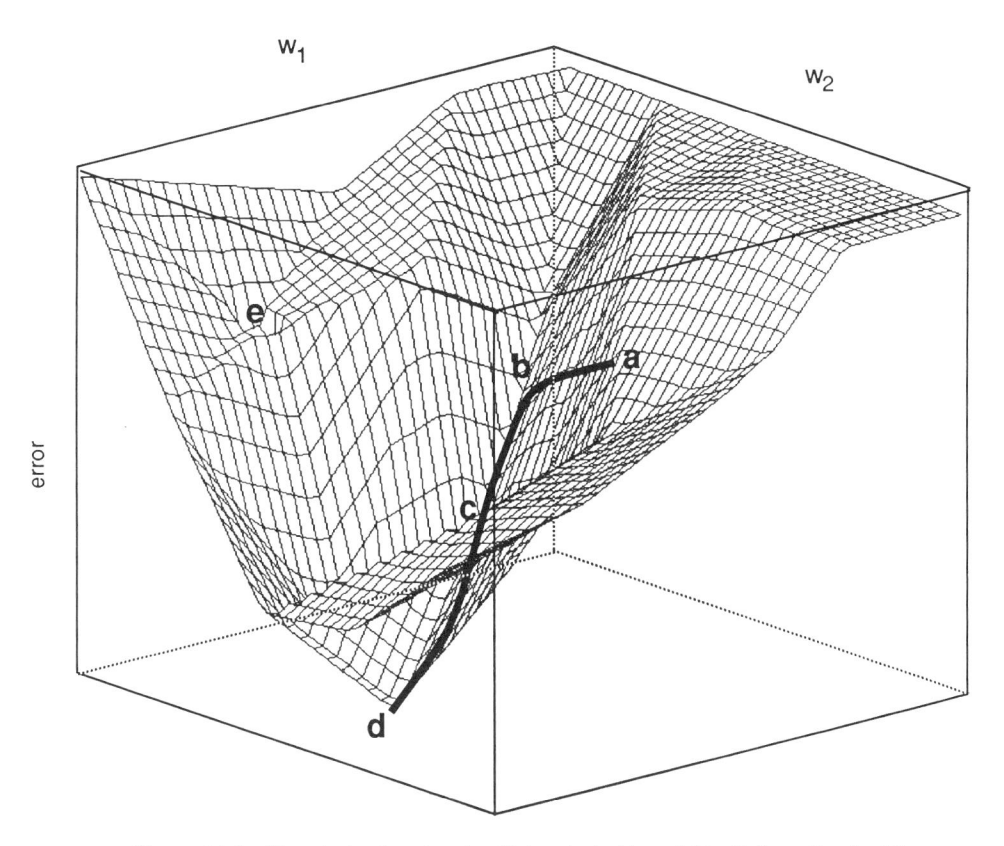

**Figure 34.4** Top: A simple network with two trainable weights. Bottom: Graph of the error surface that might be produced (for some hypothetical data set) as we systematically vary values of the two weights. $x$ and $y$ coordinates measure values of the two weights; $z$ measures the error associated with all possible combinations of weights (low error is down).

for exploring the error surface in an efficient manner, which should allow us to determine the combination of weights yielding the minimum error.

We begin with weights that are chosen randomly, often from a uniform distributed between +/− 1.0 so that we begin near the centroid (the importance of this will become apparent later). A possible starting point is shown in figure 34.4 as point a. As data are processed, the learning algorithm lets us make small adjustments in current weights in a way that leads to lower error (i.e., we follow the error gradient). Our goal is to proceed in this manner until we find the global error minimum (point d). Whether or not we succeed or get trapped in a local minimum (point e; any small change in weights will increase the error, although the current error is nonzero) depends on a number of factors, including how big are the steps through the weight space we allow ourselves, as well as what the shape of the error surface looks like (because the error surface is a joint function of the network architecture and the problem at hand).

We will return to some of these issues shortly, but for present purposes we note that the nature of the network's hypothesis testing has a qualitatively different character from that in traditional systems. These latter approaches to learning permit a succession of radically different hypothesis to be entertained. The network, on the other hand, begins with some randomly chosen hypothesis (the initial weight settings) and is allowed to make small, incremental changes in those settings. If we plot the trajectory of weight settings explored by gradient descent, we might see something that looks like the curve in figure 34.4. New hypotheses are required to be similar to old hypotheses—but note that any two very similar hypotheses may differ dramatically in the output they produce (compare the error at points b and c). Thus, similar hypotheses may give rise to very different behaviors. But the important point here is that the gradient descent approach to learning imposes a constraint that prevents the network from generating wildly different hypotheses from one moment to the next. Learning occurs through smooth and small changes in hypotheses. Unfortunately, if the network falls into a local minimum, as at point e, this constraint may prevent it from escaping, dooming it forever to believe a hypothesis that is only partially correct.[5]

We turn now to a final property, which once again constrains the nature of learning in networks.

## Property 4: How the Ability to Learn Changes over Time—Early Flexibility versus Late Rigidity

The networks described here use backpropagation of error as a learning algorithm. This algorithm permits us to modify the weights in a network in response to the errors produced on training data. In most general terms, the algorithm can be understood as a way to do credit/blame assignment. Somewhat more specifically, the change involves the following weight adjustment equation:

$\Delta w_{ij} = \eta \delta_i a_j.$

This equation says that the weight change between any two units $i$ and $j$ (where $i$ indexes the receiver unit and $j$ the sender unit) is the product of three terms. The first term, $\eta$, is a scaling constant and is referred to as the learning rate; it is typically a small value so that learning occurs in small increments. (Consider what might happen in figure 34.4 if we begin at point a and make a very large weight change; we might oscillate forever between points a and e, missing the terrain in between.) The last term, $a_j$ is the activation of the sender and implements the credit/blame aspect of the algorithm. The middle term, $\delta_i$, is the one I wish to focus on here. It is calculated as

$$\delta_i = error\ f'(net),$$

where *error* (in the case of an output unit) simply represents the discrepancy between the target output of the unit and the actual output, and $f'(net)$ is the derivative of the receiver unit's activation function, given its current *net* input. The activation function used in most networks is sigmoidal, typically

$$f(a) = \frac{1}{1 - e^{-net}}.$$

This activation function has several important properties: (1) all input is "squashed" so that the unit's resulting activation lies between 0.0 and 1.0; (2) net input of 0 results in an activation of 0.5, which is in the middle of the unit's activation range; positive inputs result in activations greater than 0.5 and negative inputs yield activations less than 0.5; and (3) the activation function is monotonic but nonlinear. The range of greatest sensitivity is around 0.0 input; the node's response saturates at large magnitude inputs (positive or negative).

This activation function has several interesting consequences as far as learning is concerned. Recall that it is customary to initialize networks to small random values around 0.0, lying near the centroid of the weight space (e.g., the region near the center of the space in figure 34.4). This means that at the outset of learning, the net input to a node will typically be close to 0 (because the small negative and positive weights act as multipliers on the inputs, and since they are randomly determined with mean of 0.0, they tend to cancel each other out). Since net inputs close to 0.0 lie in the range of a unit's greatest sensitivity, *t* at the outset of learning, nodes are activated in the region where they are most sensitive.

Second, the derivative (or slope) of the activation function is greatest in the mid-range. Near both extremes, the slope diminishes asymptotically toward 0.0. Recalling now that the actual weight change is a product of three terms, with one containing the slope of the activation function (for the given input), we see that weight changes will tend to decrease as a unit's activation saturates. This is true regardless of the unit's actual error. (A large error multiplied times a vanishingly small slope will still be a small number.)

Since at early stages of learning the input to units tends to be in the mid-range, the consequence of all of this is that not only are units most sensitive to input during the onset of learning, but they are almost most easily modified. As learning progresses, the weights to a network tend to grow, and the net input increases. This brings the units' activation into a range where they are less sensitive to small differences in input and leads to a behavior that tends to be more categorical. The earlier malleability also gives way to an increasing rigidity, such that the network is able to respond more effectively to mistakes early during learning and less so as learning progresses. Note that this "ossification" is not the result of an independent process of maturation but rather the direct result of learning itself. The more the system knows (whether right or wrong), the harder it is to learn something new.

We have considered four properties of learning in connectionist networks. We have seen that each of these properties in some way constrains or limits the ability of networks to learn. Summarizing the main conclusions:

1. Networks rely on the representativeness of their data sets. With small sample size, a network may not discover the generalization that characterizes the larger population. This problem will be most serious at the early stages of learning since the sample size is necessarily smaller then.

2. Networks are also most sensitive during the early period of learning. As learning progresses, networks are less likely to be able to modify their weights. Taken together with the first observation, the network is most inclined to use information at a point in learning (the early stage) when that information may be least reliable.

3. Gradient descent learning makes it difficult for a network to make dramatic changes in its hypotheses. Once a network is committed to an erroneous generalization, it may be unable to escape this local minimum. Taken together with the second observation, the problem gets worse as earning proceeds.

The picture that emerges is of a system that is highly constrained and in which the outcome of learning may be far from optimal. Indeed, it seems like a recipe for disaster. The approach differs markedly with other models of learning, in which—at least in principle, given deterministic inputs—"a 100% success rate can ... be achieved on the basis of information available to the learner" (Estes 1986). Networks can fail to learn a task for any of the reasons described above. They are far from perfect learners.

If this were all that one could say, the story would not be terribly interesting. But in fact, there are several strategies that may ameliorate these limitations. One can "arrange" to have better initial data, or one can "arrange" to have worse initial data. Oddly, both work.

The incremental learning strategy employed in the simulations described here is an example of how a system can learn a complex domain by having better initial data. The language problem is hard for the network to learn because crucial primitive notions (such as lexical category, and subject/verb agreement) are obscured by the complex grammatical structures. This makes it difficult to learn the primitive representations. But it's a catch-22 problem:

the network is also unable to learn about the complex grammatical structures because it lacks the primitive representations necessary to encode them. These difficulties are compounded by the network's early commitment to erroneous hypotheses and its tendency to "ossify" over time. Incremental learning solves the problem by presenting the network with just the right data (those that permitted the network to learn the basic representational categories) at just the right time (early on, when the network's plasticity is the greatest). A key aspect to the solution, as far as its possible relevance to the human case, is that there is a natural mechanism available for doing the filtering. By starting with an immature and impoverished working memory that allows the system to process only simple sentences, the network constructs a scaffolding for later learning.[6] As time progresses, the gradual improvement in memory capacity selects more and more complex sentences for processing.

Interestingly, exactly the opposite strategy can be employed: arrange to have worse initial data. This can happen if the data are noisier at the outset of learning than later on. The network's learning capacity is greatest at early stages, but this is also the time when its training data are most limited, and so the network runs the risk of committing itself to the wrong generalization. If the initial data are corrupted by noise, on the other hand, the increased variability may retard learning and keep the network in a state of flux until it has enough data to make reasonable approximations at the true generalization.

Note that both effects may be achieved through the same mechanism: a developmental schedule in which initial capacity is reduced relative to the mature state.

This leads us to what is perhaps not an intuitively obvious perspective on development in biological systems and, in particular, on the value of early limitations. It is tempting to view early stages of development in a negative light. Infancy is sometimes seen as a period that must be somehow gotten through. And certainly there are negative consequences to having sensorimotor, perceptual, and cognitive systems that are not fully developed. Any individual who cannot perceive threats or flee in the face of danger must be at an adaptive disadvantage. So it is surprising that evolutionary forces have not selected for individuals who are born fully functional. To be sure, there is great variation across species in the maturity of the newborn and the newborn of some species are very mature. But perhaps counterintuitively, the more complex the species, the greater is the tendency for long periods of infancy. Humans are an extreme example, in which a significant fraction of an individual's lifetime is spent in childhood.

One common explanation why prolonged infancy might not be selected out in humans is that, although maladaptive in itself, infancy is a compromise between two other traits—increased brain size and upright posture—that separately have significant adaptive value but are at odds with each other. For example, there is a positive advantage to upright posture, in that it frees two of the limbs for manipulative purposes. For biomechanical reasons, however, upright posture tends to force a narrowing of the pelvis, which in females also leads to a constriction in the birth canal. But this is at cross-purposes with the larger cranium associated with higher primates. There are two partial solutions to the problem. Females tend to have a slightly wider pelvic girdle than males, and this partially accommodates the larger brain cases that must pass through the birth canal. But also the cranium in the infant is reduced in size relative to the adult cranium. The price paid—a longer period of immaturity—may have negative consequences, but these are outweighed by the positive advantages conferred by the ability to walk upright and to have a larger adult brain.

This is a plausible story and not at all inconsistent with the current findings. What the current work suggests is another reason why early immaturity may be adaptive. Furthermore, this reason is more directly positive, as opposed to simply a lesser price for a greater benefit. Although I have focused here on limitations on learning, the kind of learning mechanism afforded by a neural network is actually quite powerful, and there are good reasons that such a mechanism might be favored by evolution. But it is not a perfect system. It is subject to various limitations. In addition, the environment in which humans function is itself highly complex, and some of the domains (e.g., language) may have a large number of "false solutions" (those that fit the examples but do not lead to correct generalizations).

With this perspective, the limited capacity of infants assumes a positive value. Limited capacity acts like a protective veil, shielding the infant from stimuli that may either be irrelevant or require prior learning to be interpreted. Limited capacity reduces the search space, so that the young learner may be able to entertain a small number of hypotheses about the world. And the noisiness of the immature nervous system may encourage generalizations based on larger sample size.

The idea that limitations on processing capacity may play a positive role in learning has been suggested by others. Based on findings from the language acquisition literature, Newport (1988, 1990) has proposed what she calls the "less is more" hypothesis, which is very similar in spirit to the "starting small" results obtained here. Newport suggests that the critical period is a critical by virtue of maturational limitations that help in the learning process, which is precisely the outcome observed here.[7] Turkewitz and Kenny (1982) have argued that developmental limitations may not only be adaptive for an individual's current state (e.g., the immature motor system of a newborn animal prevents it from wandering away from its mother) but may also assist in neurogenesis and provide a basis for later perceptual development. For example, consider the problem of size constancy. This would seem to be a major prerequisite to an infant's maintaining order in a world in which the projected size of an object may change dramatically with its distance from the infant. Turkewitz and Kenny suggest that the problem of learning size constancy is probably made much easier by the fact that initially the infant's depth of field is restricted to objects that are very close. The means that the problem of size constancy effectively does not arise at this stage. During this period, therefore, the infant is able to learn the relative size of objects in the absence of size constancy. This knowledge might then make it possible to learn about size constancy itself. (Consistent with this hypothesis is the observation that when size constancy comes in, around 4 to 6 months, it develops first for objects that are close; McKenzie, Tootell, and Day 1980; but see also Slater 1990)

The results reported here reinforce this perspective on development. There has been a tendency to view infancy and childhood in terms that are either negative (e.g., periods that can best be understood by reference to the adult skills or capabilities that are lacking) or positive (periods in which special skills are present, e.g., the "critical period" hypothesis of language learning). It may be more insightful to recognize that the developmental timetable has evolved jointly with other traits. To understand either development or learning, it is important to study their interaction. In isolation, we see that both learning and prolonged development have characteristics that appear to be undesirable. Working together, they result in a highly adaptive combination.

## NOTES

I am grateful to Elizabeth Bates, Cathy Harris, Mark Johnson, Annette Karmiloff-Smith, Virginia Marchman, Jay McClelland, and Domenico Parisi for many stimulating discussions about the issues discussed in this chapter. I thank Annette Karmiloff-Smith, Carlo Umiltà, and two anonymous reviewers for reading and providing helpful suggestions on an earlier version of this chapter. The work was supported by a contract from Army Avionics (Ft. Monmouth) and by a grant from the John D. and Catherine T. MacArthur Foundation.

1. Gold mentions a third possibility: if the text is ordered, then positive-only presentation is sufficient to learn even the most complex set of languages he considers. The details of this proposal are not well developed, however.

2. Both this result and the earlier failure were replicated several times with different starting conditions, a variety of different architectures, and various settings of the learning parameters (learning rate, momentum, bounds on beginning random weight initialization). The failure may not be inevitable, but it is certainly robust.

3. This was done by setting the context units to values of 0.5.

4. To be precise, it should be made clear that the properties to be discussed here are associated with a specific approach to learning (gradient descent) and a specific class of connectionist networks (those involving distributed representations over populations of units with continuously valued nonlinear activation functions). A variety of other architectures and learning algorithms have been studied in the literature. The principles proposed here do not necessarily extend to those approaches.

5. Is this true of people? Perhaps. Or as Annette Karmiloff-Smith has pointed out to me, it may be that in the case of humans, consciousness and self-monitoring function to prevent us from getting stuck in "local minima." When we realize we are getting nowhere, we consciously restart our search.

6. Note the distinction here between working memory and long-term memory. Long-term memory is modeled in the network as the set of weights that are learned. Short-term or working memory is represented through the activation of the context units. In the network—as also seems to be true of children—long-term memory is not particularly deficient. It is the limitation in the working memory (context-units) that responsible for the effects obtained here.

7. An important but unresolved question that must be asked if the critical period is to be associated with limitations in working memory—as is suggested here—is why it should be that 4-year-old and 9-year-old children should both be capable of learning a second language in a native-like fashion (unlike much older children and adults), even though the memory and attentional resources of the 9-year-old are significantly greater than the 4-year-old's.

## REFERENCES

Anderson, J. R. (1983). *The architecture of cognition*. Cambridge: Harvard University Press.

Baker, C. L. (1979). Syntactic theory and the projection problem. *Linguistic Inquiry, 10*, 533–581.

Bates, E. A., and Elman, J. L. (1993). Connectionism and the study of change. In Mark Johnson (Ed.), *Brain development and cognition: A reader*, 623–642. Oxford: Oxford University Press.

Berry, D. C., and Broadbent, D. E. (1984). On the relationship between task performance and associated verbalizable knowledge. *Quarterly Journal of Experimental Psychology, 36*, 209–231.

Bowerman, M. (1987). The "no negative evidence" problem: How do children avoid constructing an overly general grammar? In J. A. Hawkins (Ed.), *Explaining language universals*. Oxford: Basil Blackwell.

Braine, M. D. S. (1971). On two types of models of the internalization of grammars. In D. I. Slobin (Ed.), *The ontogenesis of grammar: A theoretical perspective*. New York: Academic Press.

Broadbent, D. E., (1977). Levels, hierarchies, and the locus of control. *Journal of Experimental Psychology: General, 29*, 181–201.

Brown, R., and Hanlon, C. (1970). Derivational complexity and order of acquisition in child speech. In J. R. Hayes (Ed.), *Cognition and the development of language*. New York: Wiley.

Chomsky, N. (1957). *Syntactic structures*. The Hague: Mouton.

Cleeremans, A. (1993). *Mechanisms of implicit learning: A parallel distributed processing model of sequence acquisition*. Cambridge, MA: MIT Press.

Cleeremans, A., and McClelland, J. L. (1991). Learning structure of event sequences. *Journal of Experimental Psychology: General*.

Dunbar, K., and Klahr, D. (1989). Developmental differences in scientific discovery processes. In D. Klahr and K. Kotovsky (Eds.), *The 21st Carnegie-Mellon Symposium on Cognition: Complex information processing: The impact of Herbert A. Simon*. Hillsdale, NJ: Erlbaum.

Elman, J. L. (1990). Finding structure in time. *Cognitive Science, 14*:179–211.

Elman, J. L. (1991). Distributed representations, simple recurrent networks, and grammatical structure. *Machine Learning, 7*, 195–225.

Estes, W. K. (1957). Toward a statistical theory of learning. *Psychological Review, 57*, 94–107.

Estes, W. K. (1986). Array models for category learning. *Cognitive Psychology, 18*, 500–549.

Gold, E. M. (1967). Language identification in the limit. *Information and Control, 16*, 447–474.

Gonzalez, R. C., and Wintz, P. (1977). *Digital image processing*. Reading, MA: Addison-Wesley.

Harris, C. (1991). Parallel distributed processing models and metaphors for language and development. Ph.D. dissertation, University of California, San Diego.

Hirsh-Pasek, K., Treiman, R., and Schneiderman, M. (1984). Brown and Hanlon revisited: Mothers' sensitivity to ungrammatical forms. *Journal of Child Language, 11*, 81–88.

Hunt, E. B. (1966). *Concept learning: An information processing problem*. New York: John Wiley.

Jordan M. I. (1986). *Serial order: A parallel distributed processing approach*. Institute for Cognitive Science Report 8604. University of California, San Diego.

Lea, G., and Simon, H. A. (1979). Problem solving and rule induction. In H. A. Simon (Ed.), *Models of thought*. New Haven, CT: Yale University Press.

Lewicki, P. Czyzewska, M., and Hoffman, H. (1987). Unconscious acquisition of complex procedural knowledge. *Journal of Experimental Psychology: Learning, Memory and Cognition, 13*, 523–530.

Lewicki, P., Hill, T., and Bizot, E. (1988). Acquisition of procedural knowledge about a pattern of stimuli that cannot be articulated. *Cognitive Psychology, 20*, 24–37.

McClelland, J. L. (n.d.) Parallel distributed processing: Implications for cognition and development. In R. Morris (Ed.), *Parallel distributed processing: Implications for psychology and neurobiology*. Oxford: Oxford University Press. In press.

McKenzie, B. E., Tootell, H. E., and Day, R. H. (1980). Development of visual size constancy during the first year of human infancy. *Developmental Psychology, 16*, 163–174.

Medin, D. L., and Schaffer, M. M. (1978). Context theory of classification learning. *Psychological Review, 85*, 207–238.

Miller, G. A., and Chomsky, N. (1963). Finitary models of language users. In R. D. Luce, R. R. Bush, and E. Galanter (Eds.), *Handbook of mathematical psychology*, vol. 2. New York: Wiley.

Newport, E. L. (1988). Constraints on learning and their role in language acquisition: Studies of the acquisition of American Sign Language. *Language Sciences, 10*, 147–172.

Newport, E. L. (1990). Maturational constraints on language learning. *Cognitive Science, 14*, 11–28.

Nosofsky, R. M. (n.d.). Exemplars, prototypes, and similarity rules. In A. Healy, S. Kosslyn, and R. Shiffrin (Eds.), *From learning theory to connectionist theory: Essays in honor of William K. Estes*, vol. 1. Hillsdale, NJ: Erlbaum. In press.

Osherson, D. N., Stob, M., and Weinstein, S. (1986). *Systems that learn: An introduction to learning theory for cognitive and computer scientists*. Cambridge, MA: MIT Press.

Pinker, S. (1989). *Learnability and cognition*. Cambridge, MA: MIT Press.

Plunkett, K., and Marchman, V. (1990). *From rote learning to system building*. Center for Research in Language, TR 9020. University of California, San Diego.

Pollack, J. B. (1990). Language acquisition via strange automata In *Proceedings of the Twelfth Annual Conference of the Cognitive Science Society*, 678–685. Hillsdale, NJ: Erlbaum.

Reber, A. S. (1965). Implicit learning of artificial grammars. Unpublished master's thesis, Brown University.

Reber, A. S. (1967). Implicit learning of artificial grammars. *Journal of Verbal Learning and Verbal Behavior, 6*, 855–863.

Reber, A. S. (1969). Transfer of syntactic structure in synthetic languages. *Journal of Experimental Psychology, 81*, 115–119.

Reber, A. S. (1989). Implicit learning and tacit knowledge. *Journal of Experimental Psychology: General, 118*, 219–235.

Reber, A. S., and Allen, R. (1978). Analogy and abstraction strategies in synthetic grammar learning: A functionalist interpretation. *Cognition, 6*, 189–221.

Rumelhart, D. E., Hinton, G. E., and Williams, R. J. (1986). Learning internal representations by error propagation. In D. E. Rumelhart and J. L. McClelland (Eds.), *Parallel distributed processing: Explorations in the microstructure of cognition*, vol. 1, 318–362. Cambridge, MA: MIT Press.

Servan-Schreiber, D., Cleeremans, A., and McClelland, J. L. (1986). *Encoding sequential structure in simple recurrent networks.* CMU Technical Report CMU-CS-88-183. Computer Science Department, Carnegie-Mellon University.

Slater, A. (1990). Size constancy and complex visual processing at birth. Poster presented at the IVth European Conference on Developmental Psychology, University of Stirling.

Turkewitz, G., and Kenny, P. A. (1982). Limitations on input as a basis for neural organization and perceptual development: A preliminary theoretical statement. *Developmental Psychobiology,* 15(4), 257–368.

Wexler, K., and Cullicover, P. (1980). *Formal principles of language acquisition.* Cambridge, MA: MIT Press.

# 35 Recognition, Categorization, and Perceptual Learning (or, How Learning to Classify Things Together Helps One to Tell Them Apart)

I. P. L. McLaren, H. J. Leevers, and N. J. Mackintosh

ABSTRACT  Whether animals are or are not conscious as they learn or process information is, we suspect, probably an idle question. But some light might be shed on the role of awareness in human learning by studying cases where people appear to behave in a manner indistinguishable from animal subjects, and their behavior accords with simple associative learning theory. At least some such cases can be loosely described as involving unreflective, incidental learning. In this chapter, we examine the role of perceptual learning in experiments on recognition and categorization by people and pigeons that satisfy some of these criteria.

First, we demonstrate an effect of perceptual learning in a recognition experiment involving stimuli drawn from categories not definable in terms of a prototype. In a running recognition task, subjects are asked to make one response to a stimulus on its first presentation, another on its second. One would expect that the discrimination would be less difficult if the stimuli had never been seen before than if the same set was repeated from one session to the next, but pigeons find this latter task substantially easier, suggesting that a perceptual learning effect can override the proactive interference that must occur when one is asked to judge the *relative* novelty of a stimulus. A similar experiment with people reveals a similar effect, together with more detailed information on the buildup and release from proactive interference.

We then show that perceptual learning will also occur during the course of categorization: asked to categorize a series of stimuli generated by allowing variations from two prototypical patterns, people (and perhaps pigeons) subsequently learn to discriminate faster between two *novel* exemplars drawn from a single category than between two control stimuli drawn from a category that the subject has not previously experienced. Our preferred explanation of this result (appealing to the differential latent inhibition of common and unique elements) is well supported by other animal studies. We close with some speculative comments on the role of perceptual learning in face recognition.

## 35.1  INTRODUCTION

As animal learning theorists, our perspective on some of the questions at issue in this book may differ from that of other contributors. Although some ethologists, most notably Donald Griffin (1976), have argued that it is time to drop the ban imposed by J. B. Watson on talk of animal consciousness, we remain moderately skeptical. As far as we can see, there is little to be gained by wondering whether rats or pigeons are learning consciously or unconsciously when they associate a conditioned stimulus (CS) with the delivery of a reinforcer or attribute its occurrence to their performance of some arbitrary action. What evidence would allow one to decide between these alternatives? We cannot ask inarticulate animals whether they were aware of the contingencies between stimuli, responses, and reinforcers that the experimenter has been manipulating. We can only observe the behavioral changes produced by those contingencies. This suggests to us that the behavior of an animal in a conditioning experiment can be regarded as a paradigm instance of implicit learning. But this is not because we *know* that such learning is unconscious. The virtue of this suggestion is that it maps onto a second criterion for drawing a distinction between implicit and explicit learning: whereas explicit learning involves deliberate use of strategies and other complex, cognitive processes, implicit learning and memory can be understood in terms of the simple associative learning theories developed to account for the results of conditioning experiments with animals (see McLaren, Green, and Mackintosh 1993 for a development of this argument).

The strategy we pursue in this chapter is to ask to what extent the behavior of more articulate subjects (students at Cambridge University) resembles that of pigeons and is thus potentially explicable by the same simple associative theory. There will, of course, be numerous situations in which no similarities are discernible. Students will solve mathematical problems rather better than pigeons, and pigeons will find their way home rather better than students. Even studies of supposedly simple Pavlovian and operant conditioning have revealed significant differences between the behavior of people and other animals (Davey 1983; Bentall and Lowe 1987), largely, we suspect, because the relatively simple procedures and slow pace of such experiments give too much opportunity for human subjects to bring complex preconceptions and strategies to bear on the problem that they imagine the experimenter has set them. The experimental situations we have chosen for study require subjects to respond rapidly to rapidly repeated stimuli, usually of a rather arbitrary and meaningless nature, such as computer-generated random checkerboard patterns. We believe that such situations have a better chance of revealing some of the standard operating characteristics of human information processing.

The more particular issue with which our experiments are concerned is the relationship between the familiarity and the discriminability of a stimulus. Under what circumstances will familiarization with a set of stimuli enhance their discriminability, and what is the explanation of such effects? That enhanced discriminability is often a consequence of familiarization is widely assumed or recognized; it is usually referred to as perceptual learning and has even been documented by some experimental studies. William James, having given examples of "the well-known virtuosity displayed by the professional buyers and testers of various kinds of goods," thought the fact that practice improves sensory discrimination "so familiar that few, if any, psychologists have even recognized it as needing explanation" (James 1890, pp. 509–510).

But require explanation it surely does, for although one can point to experimental demonstrations of perceptual learning effects in both animal and human experiments (Gibson 1969; Hall 1992), it is equally easy to point to other results seemingly the reverse of perceptual learning. One of the more ubiquitous findings in the conditioning literature is the phenomenon of latent inhibition: prior exposure to a stimulus significantly retards subsequent conditioning to that stimulus (Lubow 1989; Hall 1992). At the very least, then, we need to understand how familiarization can have such apparently opposed effects. In fact, we believe that the paradox is more apparent than real: exposure to a stimulus or set of stimuli can simultaneously reduce the speed with which those stimuli enter into new associations with other events and enhance their discriminability from one another. In experiments on latent inhibition, we are seeing only the former process in operation; in studies of perceptual learning, however, the latter effect may outweigh the former.

One reason, then, for choosing the phenomenon of perceptual learning for our studies is that it is not well understood. A second is that it undoubtedly occurs in both humans and other animals. And a third is that some perceptual learning effects in people seem to be instances of just the sort of unreflective, incidental learning that is most likely to reveal parallels with the behavior of animals in conditioning experiments. We report here the results of two sets of experiments. In the first, subjects are engaged in a continuous recognition task; in the second they are required to categorize a set of stimuli. But the question at issue in both cases is whether familiarization with a particular set of stimuli enhances their discriminability, and, if so, how such an effect is to be explained.

## 35.2 EXPERIMENTS ON RECOGNITION MEMORY

Pigeons and people were tested on a running recognition task. The general procedure was to require subjects to make one response the first time a particular stimulus was presented and a different response on its second presentation. For the pigeons, the stimuli were colored pictures of natural scenes or objects; for the people, they were black and white line drawings of various objects, or rather more meaningless black and white checkerboard patterns. We shall argue, however, that our results and theorizing are relevant to other cases, for example, to the recognition of words, pictures, faces, and other meaningful material. The literature on face recognition suggests that we are better at recognizing faces from our own ethnic and racial group than faces from other groups (Valentine and Bruce 1986), and equally that we are better at recognizing a new picture of a familiar face (someone we know) than a new picture of an unfamiliar face (Bruce 1982). Will familiarity improve recognition memory for less meaningful material, and in subjects such as pigeons?

In this experimental task, it is not only the phenomenon of latent inhibition that might be thought to act in opposition to a perceptual learning effect. Proactive interference might also do so. The task requires subjects to decide of each of a series of stimuli whether they have seen it before. If the experiment employs a large set of novel stimuli, each of which is presented only twice, any sense of familiarity, however slight, can serve as a cue to respond "old." Familiarizing subjects with some of the stimuli means using a restricted set of stimuli, all of which will eventually have occurred before. But this will mean that such a sense of familiarity does not allow one to discriminate between "old" and "new." Will not this make the task harder—by turning it into a relative recency discrimination?

Certainly those who have undertaken recognition memory experiments with animals have tacitly, and sometimes explicitly, assumed this. In a large number of procedures that can be regarded as variants of the running recognition experiment with animal subjects, it has generally been assumed that the larger the total set of stimuli used, and therefore the less frequently any individual stimulus occurs, the easier the task will be (Mishkin and Delacour 1975; Sands and Wright 1980). There is, of course, good theoretical and empirical reason to expect this. In delayed matching to sample, for example, animals are required to choose, from between two alternatives, that which is the same as, or matches, the sample stimulus shown at the outset of that trial. The smaller the total set of stimuli used, the greater is the probability that the incorrect alternative was recently correct, and experiments with both monkeys and pigeons have shown that performance deteriorates the more recently this has happened (Grant 1975). We are witnessing, it is assumed, a form of proactive interference. Subjects are being asked to make a relative recency judgment: which of these two stimuli did I see most recently? By contrast, with an indefinitely large set of stimuli (usually called trial-unique delayed matching), they are asked to make an absolute novelty-familiarity judgment: which of these two stimuli has ever occurred before in this situation?

When we ran the experiment with pigeons, we were surprised to find that the relative recency discrimination was substantially easier (Todd and Mackintosh 1990). The procedure we employed was similar to that of a continuous recognition experiment with human subjects. In each of two sessions each day, twenty stimuli (pictures of natural scenes) were presented, each occurring twice in a session The pigeons' task was to discriminate between first and second presentations of each stimulus, being rewarded for a response to a first presentation but not for a response to a second presentation. In one of the two daily sessions a new set of twenty pictures was used each day; this is the absolute novelty/familiarity discrimination. In the second session, the same set of twenty pictures was repeated every day; after the first day, therefore, all the pictures might be supposed to be familiar, and the task becomes a relative recency discrimination. It was substantially easier than the absolute novelty/familiarity discrimination. Figure 35.1 shows the results from one of the two experiments reported by Todd and Mackintosh, in a form similar to that used in some human experiments: accuracy of performance as a function of lag between first and second presentations of the stimulus. It is clear that under the conditions of this experiment, pigeons were substantially more accurate with the repeated set of stimuli than with the novel set and that this difference increased as the delay between first and second presentations of each stimulus increased. The effect of familiarization with the stimuli outweighed any proactive interference effect.

One possible reason is that the relative recency judgment was not particularly difficult—requiring discrimination between a stimulus presented a few

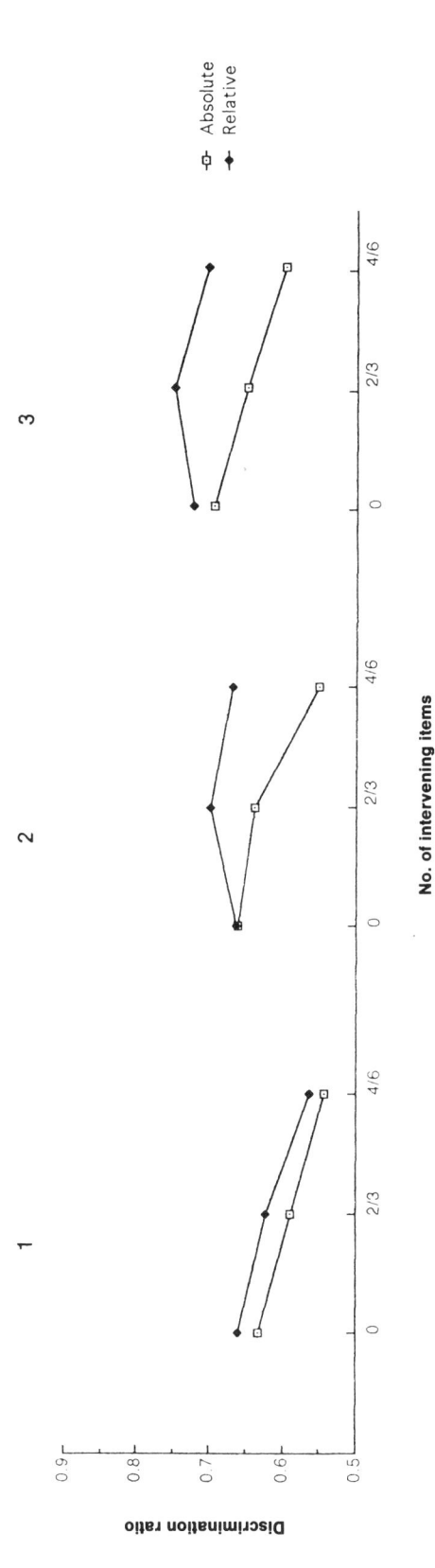

**Figure 35.1** Performance on absolute and relative recency discriminations for pigeons across 3 days. The ordinate gives the number of pecks to the first presentation of a stimulus divided by the total number of pecks to that stimulus on first and second presentations. The abscissa gives the number of items intervening between first and second presentations of a stimulus (e.g., 2/3 means 2 or 3 items).

seconds, or at most a few minutes, ago and one that had not been seen since the preceding day's session. Had there been several sessions a day with the repeated set of stimuli, the results might have been different. Evidence for proactive interference effects in animal experiments on recognition memory comes from studies of delayed matching to sample where the interval between the presentation of target and of interfering event is relatively short.

Proactive interference does not provide the only possible reason for expecting that recognition memory for familiar stimuli might not always surpass that for unfamiliar stimuli. There is a second possible reason, suggested by the word frequency effect commonly cited in the verbal learning literature (Shepard 1967). The typical finding is that there is an advantage for low-frequency over higher-frequency words. The implication is that the low-frequency (and hence less familiar) words are more easily discriminated in terms of whatever attribute serves as the basis for the recognition process. The full story is somewhat more complex than this, however, as Schulman (1976) indicated. When very rare (extremely low frequency of fewer than 1 per million) words are used, then within this range it is the more familiar, higher-frequency items that are better recognized. Zechmeister, Curt, and Sebastian (1978) were able to integrate these results by showing that recognition memory is poor for very rare words, better for standard low-frequency words, and then poor again for high-frequency items. Thus, there is evidence for a curvilinear relationship between word frequency and recognition memory.

One explanation for the improvement in recognition performance with increasing frequency for the rare words could be that this is another manifestation of perceptual learning. The decline in recognition memory with increasing word frequency thereafter could be due to a combination of at least two factors. One is that any further perceptual learning on a word above a certain frequency threshold is likely to be negligible. The word has been encountered sufficiently often that perceptual learning will be near asymptote. Some other factor(s) must then be responsible for poorer recognition memory on these stimuli. There is no shortage of possible explanations for this (e.g., see Zechmeister, Curt, and Sebastian 1978; Underwood and Freund 1970), which we will not consider any further here, except to label the phenomenon as high-frequency fall off. The clear implication of these results, however, is that familiarity may benefit recognition memory only up to a point. Extrapolating this finding to stimuli other than words, we would expect that the strongest perceptual learning effect in the context of a recognition memory experiment will be found with novel stimuli.

We were able to manipulate frequency and proactive interference in two experiments run with students that were analogous to the pigeon experiments of Todd and Mackintosh; the major procedural difference was that now the experiments were compressed into two days, with several sessions (more properly, blocks of trials) within each day. In the first experiment, the subjects' instructions were to withhold a response to the first presentation of a stimulus in each block of trials and to press a key on its second presentation. In order to mark off the trial blocks from one another, as well as to test the generality of any results obtained, in alternate blocks two quite different sets of stimuli were used, checkerboards and line drawings (see fig. 35.2 for examples of these stimuli). Use of line drawings enabled us to control the frequency of the word corresponding to the pictorial image explicitly. All the drawings were easily nameable and had been used in psycholinguistic experiments by Wheeldon (1989). Some of the words corresponding to the drawings were high frequency (more than 50 per million), some low (between 1 and 5), and this factor was orthogonal to the repeated versus novel factor. Obviously the frequency manipulation does not apply to the checkerboard stimuli.

We will not report the findings of this experiment (run by Sophie Rimmington) in any detail because there are difficulties of interpretation due to the use of a single response key. Although there was the predicted (significant) advantage for the repeated stimuli, especially on the second day, it is possible to argue that subjects adjusted their response biases to the familiar stimuli and simply became readier to press the key to them. There were indications of this in some of the error data, since there tended to be more false alarms to the repeated stimuli. Given this, there must be some doubt about the nature of the repetition effect, especially for the pictorial stimuli, where reaction time was the main dependent measure. The results for the checkerboard stimuli seem

**Figure 35.2** Examples of stimuli used in the recognition memory experiment with people. The bottle is a high-frequency item, the acorn a low-frequency stimulus. The checkerboards are randomly generated.

more secure. Also of interest were the results of the frequency manipulation for the line drawings. There was suggestive evidence that the low-frequency items were more rapidly recognized than the high-frequency items, implying that high-frequency falloff can coexist with a perceptual learning effect in this type of experiment.

The design of the second of the two experiments, run with the assistance of Lindsay Matthews, is shown in table 35.1. In each block of thirty-two trials, sixteen different stimuli were each presented; half of these stimuli were entirely novel to each block of trials and the other half was repeated from one block to the next. The checkerboards were unsurprisingly harder to identify and remember than the line drawings and were shown for up to 3.33 sec per trial, while the line drawings were shown for only 1.66 sec. In either case, however, the subject's response immediately terminated the stimulus and produced a 1-sec feedback signal, either "correct" or "error" (plus a beep), followed immediately by the next trial. At the end of each thirty-two-trial block, the subjects were shown their score in that block (percentage correct and reaction time on correct trials) and then allowed to start the next block of trials in their own time.

On each of the two days of the experiment, there were six blocks of trials, three with the checkerboard stimuli alternating with three with the line drawings, half of the subjects starting with the checkerboards and the other half with the drawings. In the first pair of blocks, of course, all stimuli were equally novel; thereafter, the question at issue was whether performance would improve faster with the restricted set of repeated stimuli or with the novel stimuli. To the extent that increased familiarization with the repeated stimuli improves performance, this perceptual learning effect should increase steadily over the course of the experiment; any deleterious effect of proactive interference, however, might have a rather different time course. The problem of deciding whether a repeated stimulus is familiar because previously seen in this block of trials, or in an earlier block, should increase during the course of each day's trials but decrease from the end of day 1 to the beginning of day 2. If both perceptual learning and proactive interference effects occur, therefore, we might expect to see little or no difference between repeated and novel stimuli on day 1 (as both effects increase and cancel each other out); but the release from proactive interference at the beginning of day 2, combined with the ever increasing familiarization effect, should lead to a clear difference emerging on day 2, especially on early blocks.

Table 35.1  Design of the Experiment on Recognition Memory

| Stimulus | Day 1 (Three Blocks) | Day 2 (Three Blocks) |
| --- | --- | --- |
| Pictures | Repeated/novel × high/low frequency | Repeated/novel × high/low frequency |
| Checkerboards | Repeated/novel | Repeated/novel |

Note: The three blocks per day for each stimulus type were run in alternation, with order counterbalanced across subjects.

The subjects were nineteen undergraduates from Cambridge plus one older man. The experiment was run on an Apple Macintosh Plus computer, and the stimuli displayed on the center of the screen measured approximately 2 cm square. The task was explained to each subject, and four practice trials with each type of stimulus were given. Subjects were required to press one key ("x") on the first presentation of a stimulus in each block and a second key (".") for the second presentation. They were told to respond as rapidly as possible consistent with accuracy but assured that they had longer to respond to the checkerboards. There was a total of fifty-six line drawings available, eight of which were randomly assigned to each subject as their repeated set (a different set for each subject—four high frequency, four low), while the remaining forty-eight served as a novel pool for that subject (twenty-four high, twenty-four low). Similarly, the computer generated a random fifty-six different checkerboard patterns for each subject, of which eight were chosen as a repeated set while the remainder served as a novel set. The data recorded were both percentage correct responses and reaction time on correct trials only. The data for the first three trials and the last trial of any block were excluded; the former were always the first presentation of a stimulus in that block, the latter necessarily a second presentation. On all other trials, there was an equal probability that the stimulus was being presented for the first or second time. Both percentage correct and reaction time data gave similar results, but since accuracy was nearly at ceiling on the line drawings, while this was not the case for the checkerboard stimuli, we report the percentage correct data for the checkerboards and the reaction times for the line drawings. The results are shown in figure 35.3 for the line drawing reaction time data and in figure 35.4 for the percent correct data for the checkerboards.

From figure 35.3 it is clear that subjects showed a significant increase in speed of responding to the line drawings from day 1 to day 2 but that this increase was more marked for the repeated than for the novel stimuli ($F1,19 = 8.93, p < 0.01$ for the interaction between days and stimulus set).

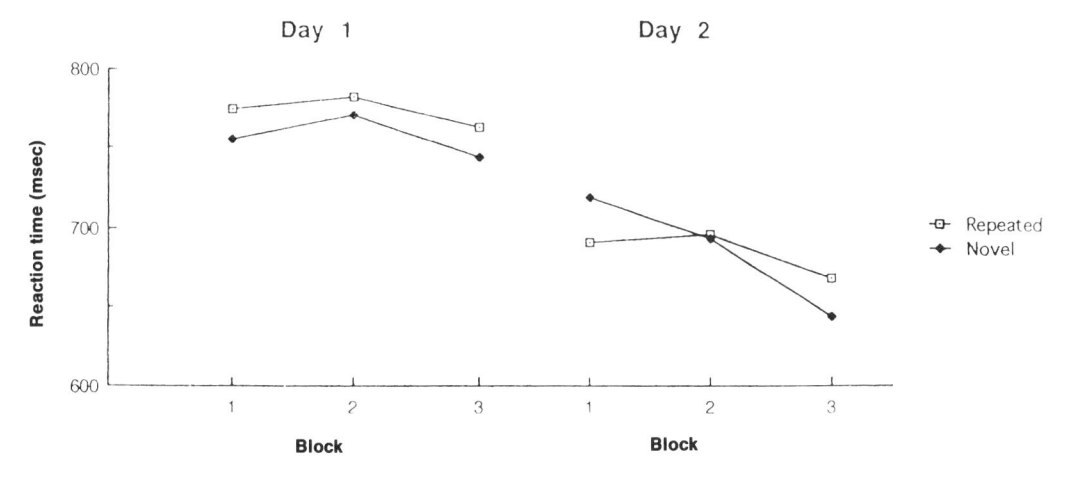

**Figure 35.3** Reaction time data for the line drawings over the three blocks of each day.

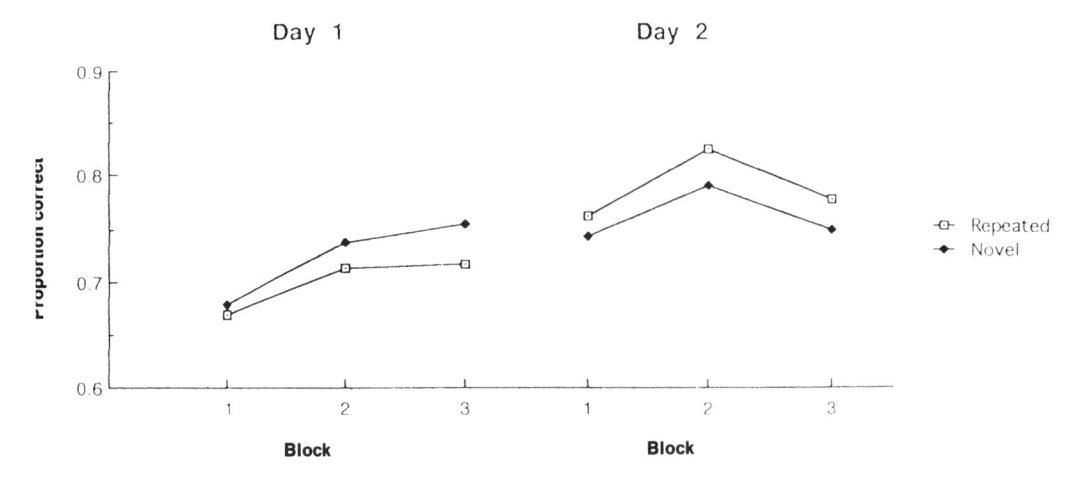

**Figure 35.4** Proportion correct data for the checkerboards over the three blocks of each day.

Although there was also a significant interaction between repeated versus novel stimuli and blocks ($F_{5,95} = 2.54, p < 0.05$), simple effects analysis of each block revealed a significant difference between stimuli only on the first block of day 2 ($p < 0.01$). Figure 35.4 shows a similar improvement in accuracy of performance on the checkerboards from day 1 to day 2 but again that this improvement was greater for repeated than novel stimuli ($F_{1,19} = 5.59$, $p < 0.05$ for the interaction), and a simple effects analysis revealed a significant difference between repeated and novel stimuli on day 2 ($p < 0.01$). With both classes of stimuli, then, subjects showed rather worse performance with repeated stimuli on day 1 but superior performance either at the beginning or over the whole of day 2. This pattern of results (exactly the same as that found in the earlier version of this experiment run by Sophie Rimmington) is consistent with the analysis that we have outlined. Discriminating between first and second presentations of a stimulus within a given block of trials is initially easier if the stimuli have not already appeared in an earlier block that day, but eventually some other factor overrides this proactive interference effect. By day 2 the benefits of familiarization with a restricted set of stimuli repeated from one block to the next may outweigh the disadvantage of having to make a relative recency judgment, rather than merely deciding whether a particular stimulus has ever occurred in this situation before. There is also some suggestion that the benefits of familiarization were greater or longer lasting with the less familiar checkerboard stimuli than with the line drawings. This is consistent with our expectations and with the effects of word frequency on performance with the pictures. If repetition improves performance by a perceptual learning effect that somehow increases the discriminability of the repeated set of stimuli, this is an effect most likely to occur with the wholly novel stimuli (the pictures seen by the pigeons or the checkerboards seen by the students). Sufficiently familiar stimuli will gain little additional advantage from repetition, and, seemingly in support of this, in both human experiments, subjects were slower to report that a high-frequency picture had already occurred once in that block than to report that a low-frequency picture had already appeared. There was, however, no sign of the repetition by frequency interaction needed to support this analysis. The beneficial effect of experience with a restricted set of repeated stimuli is not therefore necessarily the same as an effect of overall frequency of occurrence.

## 35.3  THEORIES OF PERCEPTUAL LEARNING

Cambridge undergraduates, then, will behave rather like pigeons in certain experiments on recognition memory, but this observation hardly elucidates the nature of the processes responsible for their behavior. Why should it eventually prove easier to discriminate first from second presentations of a restricted set of repeated stimuli than of a comparable set of novel stimuli? We have described the results as an instance of perceptual learning, but this does not take us very much further. Although the phenomena of perceptual learning are themselves familiar enough, they are hardly well understood. And the design of these experiments was not such as to elucidate the nature of the processes underlying any perceptual learning effect. In this particular case indeed (unlike many other instances of perceptual learning), there was a clear and explicit payoff for discriminating between the stimuli to which subjects were being exposed. In order to decide that this was a first presentation of a particular stimulus, subjects had to discriminate this stimulus from all others they had seen that day. In order to decide that it was a second presentation, they had to match it to the stored representation of that stimulus seen earlier and to discriminate it from the stored representations of all other stimuli seen earlier in the session. Under these circumstances, therefore, one could appeal to one of the mechanisms of perceptual learning suggested by Eleanor Gibson (1969): that during exposure to a set of stimuli, subjects learn to attend to their differentiating features and to ignore their common features. We regard this as an extremely plausible account of at least some instances of perceptual learning. The problem has always been to see why subjects should learn to do this in many other cases, for one of the puzzles of perceptual learning is that mere exposure to a set of stimuli is often sufficient to enhance their discriminability. In some of Gibson's own experiments (Gibson 1969) there was no payoff for discriminating between the test stimuli during the course of initial exposure to them, and in some cases subjects were given tasks that implied that the critical stimuli were incidental to their main goal in this preexposure phase of the experiment. It is, of course, difficult to assess how human subjects interpret an experimenter's instructions, but experiments with animal subjects have unequivocally shown that simple exposure to stimuli in the absence of any differential reinforcement is quite sufficient to enhance their discriminability. Gibson and Walk (1956) found that rats, exposed to circles and triangles hanging from the walls of their home cage, subsequently learned to discriminate more rapidly between these stimuli than control animals that had never seen them before. We have shown that thirsty rats who, over a period of ten days or so, on alternate days drink two equally palatable, flavored liquids will subsequently discriminate between them much better than controls, when one of the flavors, but not the other, is made aversive by pairing its consumption with an injection of lithium chloride (Mackintosh, Kaye, and Bennett 1991).

A second apparent puzzle about perceptual learning effects is how they may be reconciled with the phenomenon of latent inhibition, where prior exposure to a simple stimulus can retard the rate at which it is associated with any new consequence. We argued above that this paradox is more apparent than real. We can pursue this argument further, for it is possible to show that the processes responsible for latent inhibition effects actually provide one major mechanism of perceptual learning. To see how this could be so, we need to ask why it might be difficult to discriminate between two or more stimuli in the first place. The traditional learning theorist's answer is that there is generalization between them and the reason for this generalization is that the stimuli share common elements. Thus, two confusable stimuli, $A$ and $B$, should be conceptualized as each consisting of a set of unique elements, $a$ and $b$, and also a set of shared elements, $x$ (so that $A = a + x$ and $B = b + x$), and the extent of generalization between them will depend on the proportion of common $x$ elements to unique $a$ and $b$ elements. Consider, then, the subject required to discriminate between $A$ and $B$, that is, to associate $A$ with one consequence and $B$ with another. Such discrimination learning will be slow to the extent that the outcome of each trial is associated with the common $x$ elements and rapid to the extent that those outcomes are associated with the unique $a$ and $b$ elements. Gibson's analysis implied that subjects would learn to attend to the unique $a$ and $b$ elements and to ignore the common $x$ elements during the course of exposure to $A$ and $B$. We have already seen reason to question the plausibility of this analysis in situations where there is no differential reinforcement for discriminating $A$ from $B$ during the exposure phase of the experiment. But the process of latent inhibition will produce exactly the same outcome in the absence of any differential reinforcement. Exposure to a simple stimulus or element causes latent inhibition, that is, a retardation in the association of that stimulus or element with any new consequence; but fifty trials of exposure to $A$ and fifty to $B$ will result in fifty trials of exposure to the unique $a$ and $b$ elements and a hundred trials of exposure to the common $x$ elements. In other words, exposure to two or more stimuli will result in *differential* latent inhibition of their common and unique elements, thus enhancing their discriminability.

## 35.4 PERCEPTUAL LEARNING DURING CATEGORIZATION

We have obtained direct evidence for such a process in our experiments on flavor aversion conditioning in rats (Mackintosh, Kaye, and Bennett 1991). Rather than describe those experiments, however, we illustrate the application of this principle to a case of greater relevance to our general argument: that of subjects learning to classify or partition a series of stimuli into different categories and at the same time learning to identify particular instances of each category. According to many theories, including the venerable account of perceptual learning originally proposed by William James and subsequently known as the acquired distinctiveness and equivalence of cues, learning to classify a number of distinguishable stimuli into a single category should make it harder to classify them apart—to discriminate between them when one is called upon to do so. Any associative theory is likely to predict this sort of effect: if two stimuli have been associated with a common consequence (the same category membership), this should increase generalization between them, that is, make it difficult to learn to discriminate between them. In general terms, the theory we have advanced (McLaren, Kaye, and Mackintosh 1989) is an associative theory and will also expect to see effects of acquired equivalence and distinctiveness. But other processes identified by our theory, notably the differential latent inhibition of common and unique elements, will act in opposition to any acquired equivalence effect and allow us to predict that learning to categorize a set of stimuli will increase the discriminability of members of the same category. We spell out this explanation below. Common experience suggests that this is the likely outcome. We are, for example, exceptionally skilled at categorizing a wide variety of stimulus configurations as faces or, say, as white female faces. But we are equally adept at identifying one particular face as Jane or Mary, that is, at discriminating among white female faces. Is this generally true? Does experience with a category enhance or detract from our ability to distinguish its members from one another?

Our next experiment with human subjects attempts to answer this question. For each subject, two prototype patterns were created: random checkerboards of the same type as used in the experiments on recognition memory; and, as in those experiments, the stimuli were presented on an Apple Macintosh Plus computer, running Microsoft Basic. They were 2 cm square, and subjects sat approximately 50 cm from the screen. From the two prototypes, a series of exemplars were constructed by changing at random a certain proportion of the elements of each prototype from black to white or viceversa. Since this was done on-line during the experiment, it was necessary to devise a more efficient technique than the alteration of individual elements. The technique employed involved changing whole horizontal lines of elements by replacing that line with another randomly generated one. This was done stochastically, with the probability of a line being replaced being .39, so that on average 6.25 lines were changed. This could be done very rapidly and resulted in considerable distortion of the base stimulus. We thus have two sets of variable exemplars of two different categories, and in the first phase of the experiment, the subject's task was simply to sort these exemplars into their two categories; stimuli were shown one at a time, and the subject's task was to press one key for one category and another for the other. Immediate feedback was given, and all subjects were trained for a minimum of fifty trials, with the added requirement that their final six responses should all be correct. Thirty-two subjects successfully completed this phase of the experiment and proceeded to the next phase, in which they were required to learn several discriminations: between two new (hitherto unseen) exemplars of one of their two categories, between the two prototypes of the two categories experienced in the first phase, and between control stimulus pairs. The control stimuli were, in fact, the experimental stimuli for another subject.

In the categorization phase of the experiment, subjects were told that once they pressed the space bar, a constant stream of stimuli would appear on screen, and their task was to sort these stimuli into two categories. They were to do this by pressing one of two keys ("x" or ".") and would receive immediate feedback as to the correctness of the response. If they did not respond within a few seconds (4.25 sec) they would be timed out. The subjects were warned that the task would be quite difficult initially, because the stimuli would vary considerably, and some would be quite ambiguous. Nevertheless, the stimuli belonging to a given category would tend to share features in common, though the variability would be such that no particular feature would be a reliable index of category membership. For this reason, they were encouraged to scan the stimulus before making a decision; speed of response was relatively unimportant, and the need for accuracy was emphasized. Once the subject initiated the experiment, trials were continuous. Stimuli were presented singly, with 1 sec allowed for feedback and a 1-sec pause before the next stimulus came on screen, during which a fixation stimulus was displayed (a "+"). No summary feedback was presented when the session terminated.

Five minutes after they had completed the categorization phase, subjects progressed to the discrimination phase of the experiment. For each subject the "preexposed" stimuli were the two base patterns from that subject's categorization phase and two new exemplars (from one category) that were generated so as to be very similar both to one another and to the prototype for their category. This was achieved by making the probability of altering a line only one-sixteenth, so that only one line was expected to change. Checks were run to ensure that the resulting exemplars were not in fact the same distortion of the prototype or the prototype itself. The effect of all this was to produce one pair of stimuli that were moderately similar (the two base stimuli) and one pair that were very similar but discriminable. Control, non-preexposed stimuli were taken from another subject so that all stimuli were used in the same way in both the preexposed and non-preexposed conditions, but for different subjects. The stimuli were presented 0.5 cm either side of a central fixation point.

Subjects were told to inspect the stimuli carefully and then make a choice of one of them. Immediate feedback was given: "correct" displayed in the center of the screen or "error" and a beep if the wrong stimulus was chosen. It was emphasized to the subjects that the designation of one member of a stimulus pair as correct was arbitrary, consistent within the experiment, and that members of a given pair would always be presented together but with either member equally often to the left or right of the other. Their task was to learn which member of a pair was the positive stimulus. A block of sixteen trials commenced when the subject pressed the space bar. A warning fixation stimulus ("+" for 1 sec) was followed by a pair of stimuli; these remained on either until the subject responded by pressing the "x" or "." key, with the "x" key indicating choice of the left-hand pattern, or until a time-out at 4.25 sec.

Appropriate feedback was then displayed for 1 sec, and the next trial commenced. Summary feedback on the number of errors and the mean correct reaction time was given at the end of each block. Each pair of stimuli was presented four times in each block—twice in each spatial relation (left/right). The chief dependent measure was number correct, with reaction time of subsidiary interest. In summary, the experiment was a two-way factorial within-subjects design with pre-exposure and stimulus type as the two factors.

Two methods of analysis were used to assess performance on the categorization phase of this experiment. One was the total number of trials taken to reach the criterion of six correct classifications in a row, bearing in mind that subjects had to complete fifty trials or more. The overall mean for the number of trials to acquisition was 69.9, with a standard error of 4.0. Another measure of how well subjects categorized the stimuli is given by the percentage of correct categorizations over the total number of trials attempted by a given subject. The last six correct trials were excluded from this analysis, so that a null hypothesis of 50 percent correct could be assumed to apply. Overall the mean percentage correct was 60.3, with a standard error of 2.0. Each subject's percentage correct was converted into a Z score based on a mean chance expectation of 50 percent. Fourteen of the subjects were significantly better than chance on this measure ($p_1 < .05$). The mean Z score was 1.56, with a standard error of .31. Though eighteen subjects failed to reach significance on this measure, all showed substantial improvement over trials, and the overall impression given by these results is of rapid acquisition of the ability to differentiate between stimuli in the two categories.

Turning to the discrimination phase of the experiment, the results for the error measure will be reported first, though note that the first presentation of a stimulus pair is not counted in the results, because the response must be a guess. The mean percentages of correct responses in each of the four conditions are shown in figure 35.5. They indicate that preexposure resulted in faster acquisition of both the exemplar and the prototype discrimination and that the prototypes were somewhat easier to discriminate than the exemplars. Analysis of variance revealed a significant effect of preexposure ($F(1,31) = 5.71, p < .025$); the only other $F > 1$ was for stimulus type ($F(1,31) = 1.87$, $p =$ n.s.), with the prototypes having the higher percentage correct. Preexposure facilitated acquisition of the discrimination roughly equally for both stimulus types as assessed by planned comparisons ($F(1,31) = 3.51, p_1 < .05$ for the exemplars, and $F(1,31) = 2.86, p_1 < .05$ for the prototypes). There were no other effects ($F < 1$). There were no significant effects on reaction time. Group means were: preexposed prototypes = 1654, preexposed exemplars = 1631, non-preexposed prototypes = 1588, non-preexposed exemplars = 1724 (ms). These results are consistent with the prototype stimuli being more discriminable than the exemplars and perhaps weaken the case for a preexposure effect on the prototypes.

Given the finding that preexposure had much the same effect on both prototypes and exemplars, we can take as a measure of the preexposure effect the summed proportion correct for the two stimulus types on the preexposed

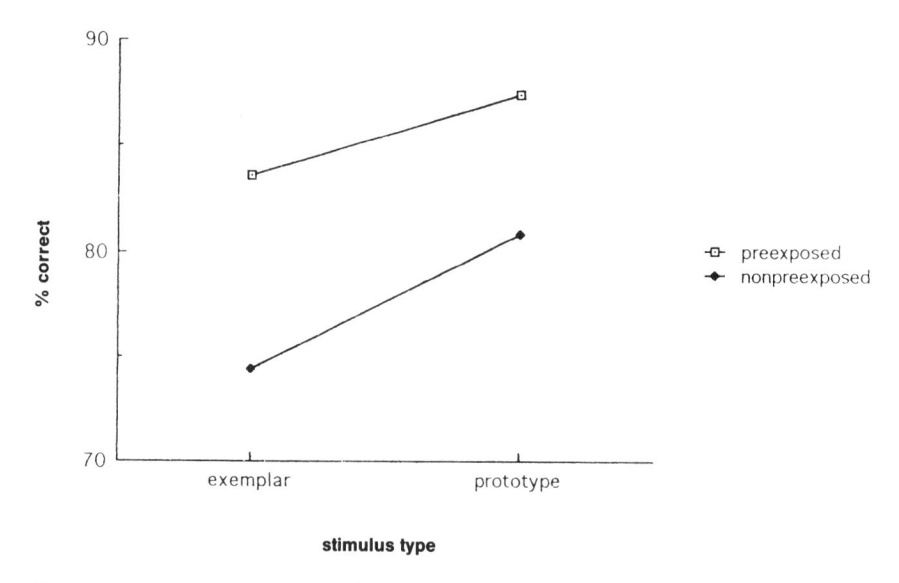

**Figure 35.5** Percentage correct for the discrimination learning phase of experiment on categorization.

discrimination minus the equivalent from the non-preexposed discrimination. This measure was computed for each subject and correlated with the Z score and the number of trials to criterion measures derived from the categorization data. Our account suggests that it should be the amount of preexposure that determines the extent of perceptual learning, not necessarily how good at categorization the subject has become (McLaren, Kaye, and Mackintosh 1989). In the limit, simple exposure to the stimuli, without learning to categorize at all, should produce similar perceptual learning. It follows that the preexposure effect should correlate with number of trials rather than percentage correct, since all subjects were trained to the same criterion. Note that this prediction is contrary to the direction of the effect that might be expected if variation in performance on the two measures is due to some subjects being slow/bored and others quick/interested, which should produce a negative correlation between perceptual learning and the number of trials to criterion. Using the Kendal rank correlation coefficient, the correlation between preexposure effect and Z is $-.08$, between Z and number of trials .04, and between number of trials and preexposure effect .19 (Spearman equivalent is .27). Partialing out the effects of the Z variable, the correlation remains at .19 ($p_1 < .1$). These results are probably as strong as one can expect given that all subjects received a minimum of fifty preexposure trials.

Learning to categorize two sets of exemplars thus improves one's ability to discriminate between new exemplars belonging to one category. We have some very preliminary evidence of a similar effect in pigeons. For the pigeons, the stimuli were again pictures, this time of other birds. The categorization task required half the pigeons to learn to discriminate pictures of owls from pictures of hawks (by rewarding responses to one set of pictures but not responses to the other) and the other half to discriminate pictures of thrushes from pictures of finches. Several hundred pictures of each type of bird were available—some in flight, some stationary, some close up, some far away, some of a single bird, some of several birds. With the restriction that these different types of pictures were sampled with the same frequency for each kind of bird, the program elected a different picture at random for each trial of this category discrimination phase of the experiment. Once each pigeon had successfully completed this phase, they were all required to learn four new discriminations, between two particular pictures of each kind of bird—two owls, two hawks, two thrushes, and two finches—with responses to one (arbitrarily chosen) picture of each bird being rewarded and responses to the other nonreinforced. Each pigeon was thus required to learn one discrimination between two pictures from its initially rewarded category, one between two pictures from its initially unrewarded category, and two discriminations between pictures that were taken from categories that it had not experienced (controls). If acquired equivalence were the only effect operating, the pigeons should have been slow to learn the first two discriminations and quick to learn the others. In fact, they were equally slow to learn the control discriminations and the discrimination between pictures taken from their rewarded category but substantially faster to discriminate between two pictures from their unrewarded category. We interpret this pattern of results to mean that there was a perceptual learning effect with pigeons as there was with the human subjects—an advantage for the stimuli drawn from the familiar category—but that in the case of the previously rewarded category, this was counteracted by a strong acquired equivalence effect. It is, indeed, well established in animal experiments that prior association of two stimuli with the same reinforcer makes their subsequent discrimination harder (Honey and Hall 1989); presumably if two stimuli are associated with a less salient outcome (the absence of a reinforcer), the acquired equivalence effect is too weak to cancel the perceptual learning effect.

The results of these two experiments demonstrate that learning to categorize two sets of stimuli that can be characterized as deviations from a prototype may increase the discriminability of the two prototypes and of two novel exemplars drawn from one of the categories. Our argument is that the mechanism for perceptual learning given in this chapter, the differential latent inhibition of common and unique elements, enables efficient categorization and identification to occur. Experience of a category that is meaningfully described in terms of a prototype will result in the latent inhibition of those features typical of the category, that is, the features defining the prototype. At the same time, these features will become associated with class membership, making categorization of examplars straightforward. Any given exemplar will, of course, tend to possess two sets of features—those shared with the prototype and those not. The former will now enable categorization but will not readily enter into new associations. The latter will tend to be unique to each exemplar and will be salient (not have suffered latent inhibition) and hence will be ready to form new associations that can support identification. Thus, learning to categorize stimuli through experience with the appropriate stimulus set should also render exemplars of that set more discriminable from one another, making their individual identification easier.

The same point can be illustrated by considering the results of a slightly different experimental design. Attneave (1957) gave subjects the task of inspecting, and then reproducing, an abstract pattern that later served as a prototype from which a set of exemplars could be generated by random modifications. The subjects' second task was to identify individual exemplars; this they did more successfully if they had been preexposed to (and been required to reproduce) the prototype than if they had not. In this case, there is no difficulty in seeing that the preexposure phase would have resulted in the latent inhibition of the prototype's features, and thus of the features common to all exemplars, thus increasing the relative salience of their unique identifying features.

Once again, we have some preliminary data from a pigeon experiment that confirms this finding. Birds were required to learn a discrimination between two randomly generated black and white checkerboard patterns. From one of these two (prototype) patterns, two exemplars were then generated by randomly changing some of the elements, and the birds were now required to discriminate between these two ("familiar") exemplars and also between two wholly novel checkerboards (matched for difficulty with the two familiar exemplars). All four birds that have so far completed the experiment learned to discriminate between the two familiar exemplars faster than between the two novel stimuli. Familiarization with the prototype ensured latent inhibition of the elements the two familiar exemplars shared in common; only their unique elements were novel and therefore salient.

## 35.5 CONCLUSIONS

The notion of latent inhibition, which is familiar enough to students of animal learning and conditioning, may be relatively novel to cognitive psychologists. We hope that the experiments we have described in the preceding section will persuade the latter to take the concept more seriously. We believe that differential latent inhibition of common and unique elements provides a simple but powerful explanation of a variety of perceptual learning effects. We are not so foolish as to suggest that it is the only mechanism (see McLaren, Kaye, and Mackintosh 1989 for an outline of at least two others), but it certainly seems sufficient to account for the effects observed in these studies of categorization. As we have noted, it will always allow for the development of efficient identification of individual exemplars at the same time as subjects are learning to sort them into larger categories.

How do other theories fare when confronted by these sorts of results? A straightforward associative analysis (without any mechanism for latent inhibition) will predict increased generalization between exemplars associated with common category membership. In McClelland and Rumelhart's (1985) model of categorization, indeed, a further problem will arise: exposure to a series of exemplars based on a prototype will result in more input to the elements representing prototypical features (features common to the exemplars) than to the elements unique to each exemplar. A stronger input here translates into greater salience, thus ensuring that the features common to two new exemplars will enter into new associations more readily than the features unique to each. Much the same problem arises from an application of the type of attentional analysis favored by Gibson (1969). In order to categorize exemplars together, attention must be directed toward the features they share in common, not to the features that differentiate one exemplar from another: once again the wrong outcome is predicted. One might perhaps wish to argue that the attentional or coding stage had learned to be maximally sensitive to the prototype and that this involves something analogous to adaptation, so that the system is now more sensitive to fluctuations around the prototype as a kind of zero point. The fact remains that the latent inhibition of common elements achieves exactly the same outcome, so that there is no need to appeal to a coding stage.

We argued at the outset of this chapter that our data and theoretical analysis might be relevant to a wider range of phenomena and ideas. Consider, for example, the notion of schema abstraction. The concept of a schema has a distinguished history stemming from Bartlett (1932). Woodworth (1938) and Hebb (1949) used the term to denote, at least in part, the central tendency of a class of stimuli. Woodworth considered that stimuli might be represented as a "schema, with correction." The idea was that stimuli would be coded in terms of "good figures" plus any minor deviations from the schema for that figure; an example would be a somewhat distorted square. Hebb emphasized the importance of acquiring the schema of a class of objects if they were to be successfully differentiated from one another. He gives the example of Chinese who all look alike to the occidental eye unfamiliar with their particular physiognomy. Experience with individual Chinese enables extraction of some modal form for this stimulus class, schema abstraction, and individuals may then be coded in terms of their deviations from it. This removes much of the representational similarity between the stimuli, accentuating their differences in a way that allows improved recognition and identification.

We suggest that the account of perceptual learning and categorization advanced here provides the mechanism that allows such schema abstraction to occur. That account states that improvements in discriminability of instances of a category are brought about by the latent inhibition of the common elements defining the modal stimulus in that category, which leaves the elements unique to any one stimulus in a position of enhanced salience relative to the common ones that would otherwise promote generalization. There are many findings in the area of face recognition entirely consistent with this position. Consider, for example, the advantage in recognition tasks enjoyed by caricatures of faces, found by Rhodes, Brennan, and Carey (1987); this is predicted on the assumption that exaggerated differences from the average result in maximal salience of the elements unique to that stimulus. Consider also the finding that faces belonging to other ethnic groups (e.g., Chinese) do not behave in the same way as faces belonging to one's own group in recognition tasks (Valentine and Bruce 1986). Finally, our account resolves the apparent conflict between the effects of typicality and of distinctiveness (Bruce 1988). Faces rated as typical are more readily classified as faces than are faces rated as less typical. But at the same time, faces rated as distinctive are more readily recognized as having been seen before in a running recognition experiment. Typical faces presumably share more features in common with a face prototype than do distinctive faces. Typical faces, therefore, have more features already associated with the label "face," but by the same token fewer unique features that retain their salience ready for association with one particular outcome. On the other hand, more distinctive faces have fewer features in common with the prototype, hence less associative strength to category membership, but a higher proportion of unique features that are salient and available for learning.

Neuropsychologists are wont to point to the dissociations observed between impairments of face recognition and impairments of other visual discriminations as evidence of distinct mechanisms subserving different functions. Such dissociations no doubt provide evidence of a difference in localization of function but not necessarily of any difference in operating characteristics. Pigeons and Cambridge undergraduates use rather different brain structures to solve the recognition and categorization problems we set them. But the evidence of our experiments encourages us to suppose that the standard operating characteristics of both systems share at least some features in common.

## REFERENCES

Attneave, F. (1957). Transfer of experience with a class-schema to identification-learning of patterns and shapes. *Journal of Experimental Psychology*, 54, 81–88.

Bartlett, F. C. (1932). *Remembering: A study in experimental and social psycholoqy*. London: Cambridge University Press.

Bentall, R. P., and Lowe, C. F. (1987). The role of verbal behavior in human learning: III. Instructional effects in children. *Journal of the Experimental Analysis of Behavior*, 41, 177–190.

Bruce, V. (1982). Changing faces: Visual and nonvisual coding processes in face recognition. *British Journal of Psycholoqy*, 73, 105–116.

Bruce, V. (1988). *Recognizing faces*. Hillside, NJ: Erlbaum.

Davey, G. C. L. (1983). An associative view of human classical conditioning. In G. C. L. Davey (Ed.), *Animal models of human behavior: Conceptual evolutionary, and neurobiological perspectives*, 95–114. Chichester: John Wiley.

Gibson, E. J. (1969). *Principles of perceptual learning and development*. New York: Appleton-Century-Crofts.

Gibson, E. J., and Walk, R. D. (1956). The effect of prolonged exposure to visually presented patterns on learning to discriminate them. *Journal of Comparative and Physiological Psycholoqy*, 49, 239–242.

Grant, D. S. (1975). Proactive interference in pigeon short-term memory. *Journal of Experimental Psycholoqy: Animal Behavior Processes*, 1, 207–220.

Griffin, D. R. (1976). *The question of animal awareness*. New York: Rockefeller University Press.

Hall, G. (1992). *Perceptual and associative learning*. Oxford: Oxford University Press.

Hebb, D. O. (1949). *The organisation of behaviour*. New York: Wiley.

Honey, R. C., and Hall, G. (1989). The acquired equivalence and distinctiveness of cues. *Journal of Experimental Psycholoqy: Animal Behaviour Processes, 15*, 338–346.

James, W. (1890). *Principles of psychology*. New York: Holt.

Lubow, R. E. (1989). *Latent inhibition and conditional attention theory*. Cambridge: Cambridge University Press.

McClelland, J. L., and Rumelhart, D. E. (1985). Distributed memory and the representation of general and specific information. *Journal of Experimental Psycholoqy: General, 114*, 159–188.

Mackintosh, N. J., Kaye, H., and Bennett, C. H. (1991). Perceptual learning in flavor aversion conditioning. *Quarterly Journal of Experimental Psychology, 43(B)*, 297–322.

McLaren, I. P. L., Green, R. E. A., and Mackintosh, N. J. (1993). In N. Ellis (Ed.), *Implicit and explicit learning of languages*. New York: Academic Press.

McLaren, I. P. L., Kaye, H., and Mackintosh, N. J. (1989). An associative theory of the representation of stimuli: Applications to perceptual learning and latent inhibition. In R. G. M. Morris (Ed.), *Parallel distributed processing—Implications for psychology and neurobiology*. Oxford: Oxford University Press.

Mishkin, M., and Delacour, J. (1975). An analysis of short term visual memory in the monkey. *Journal of Experimental Psychology: Animal Behavior Processes, 1*, 326–334.

Rhodes, G., Brennan, S., and Carey, S. (1987). Recognition and ratings of caricatures: Implications for mental representations of faces. *Cognitive Psychology, 19*, 473–497.

Sands, S. F., and Wright, A. A. (1980). Serial probe recognition performance by a rhesus monkey and a human with 10- and 20-item lists. *Journal of Experimental Psychology: Animal Behavior Process, 4*, 386–396.

Schulman, A. I. (1976). Memory for rare words previously rated for familiarity. *Journal of Experimental Psychology: Human Learning and Memory, 2*, 301–307.

Shepard, R. N. (1967). Recognition memory for words, sentences, and pictures. *Journal of Verbal Learning and Verbal Behavior, 6*, 156–163.

Todd, I. A., and Mackintosh, N. J. (1990) Evidence for perceptual learning in recognition of pictures by pigeons. *Quarterly Journal of Experimental Psychology, 42(B)*, 385–400.

Underwood, B. J., and Freund, J. S. (1970). Relative frequency judgments and verbal discrimination learning. *Journal of Experimental Psychology, 83*, 343–351.

Valentine, T., and Bruce, V. (1986). Recognising familiar faces: The role of distinctiveness and familiarity. *Canadian Journal of Psychology, 40*, 300–305.

Wheeldon, L. (1989). Priming of spoken word production. Unpublished Ph.D. dissertation, University of Cambridge.

Woodworth, R. S. (1938). *Experimental psychology*. New York: Holt.

Zechmeister, E. B., Curt, E., and Sebastian, J. A. (1978). Errors in a recognition memory task are a U-shaped function of word frequency. *Bulletin of the Psychonomic Society, 11*, 371–373.

# Author Index

Names are listed in the form in which they appear in the references.

Abeles, M., 82, 85, 94, 95
Aboitiz, F., 496
Abrams, M., 771
Abrams, R. A., 268, 270, 271, 272, 273, 274, 275, 276, 280, 282, 283, 284, 285, 286, 287, 336
Acuna, C., 236
Adrian, E. D., 93
Aersten, A., 94, 95
Aertsem, A. M. H. J., 85, 88
Aglioti, S., 42, 249
Ahissar, E., 94, 95
Aiple, F., 85
Albert, M., 207, 218
Albert, M. L., 356, 371, 378, 386
Albright, T. D., 78
Alejano, A. R., 716
Alexander, G. E., 307
Alexander, M., 60, 353
Alexander, M. P., 169, 648
Allen, L. G., 625
Allen, R., 757, 765, 771, 861
Allen, S. W., 813
Allport, A., 60, 65, 238, 353
Allport, D. A., 312, 326, 328, 428, 432, 472, 525, 526, 528, 529, 530
Alpern, M., 124
Altarriba, J., 709
Ambler, B. A., 553
Ammons, H., 4
Amorim, M.-A., 784, 825, 827, 852
Amorin, M., 755, 769, 770
Amrhein, P. C., 717
Amsterdam, J. B., 523
Andersen, R. A., 233, 234
Anderson, D. N., 169
Anderson, J. R., 469, 700, 704, 772, 785, 798, 804, 806, 821, 861

Andrade, J., 839
Angelergues, R., 161
Anooshian, L. J., 730
Anton, G., 168
Appenzeler, T., 647
Arbib, M. A., 235
Artola, A., 92, 96, 99
Artola, F., 92, 99
Arzi, M., 88
Asanuma, C., 233
Ascher, P., 96
Aseron, R., 16
Ashcraft, M. H., 700
Aslin, R. N., 304
Atkeson, C. G., 287
Atkinson, J., 292, 296, 297, 302
Atkinson, R. C., 15, 395, 397, 738
Attneave, F., 906
Autret, A., 325
Averbach, E., 124

Bacharach, V. R., 244
Baddeley, A. D., 396, 693, 704, 725, 727, 738, 742
Baddely, A., 431, 450
Baer, P. E., 844
Baeyens, F., 844, 845
Bagnara, S., 405, 413, 431
Baguler, T., 155, 156
Baguley, T., 204
Bahmanian-Behbahani, G., 624, 648
Bailey, P., 233
Bain, J. D., 857
Baker, C. L., 863
Ballard, P. B., 4
Ballesteros, S., 179, 181, 196, 627
Balota, D. A., 27, 552
Balthazard, C., 19

Bamber, D., 334
Banich, M. T., 483, 496
Banks, W., 479
Barash, S., 233
Barbierei, D. E., 326
Barbieri, C., 252, 409
Barbieri, S., 377, 386
Bargh, J. A., x, 10
Barlow, H. B., 79, 80
Barner, P. J., 22
Barnhardt, T. M., 705
Baro, J. H., 113, 118
Baron, J., 577
Barrett, A., 648
Barrett, G., 402
Barsalou, L. W., 5, 746
Bartlett, F. C., 907
Bartolomeo, P., 366, 367
Bartram, D., 627
Basar, E., 93
Basar-Eroglu, C., 93
Bashinski, H. S., 244
Bashore, T. R., 146
Bassilli, J. N., 624, 626, 726
Basso, A., 514, 518, 520
Bates, E. A., 975
Bauer, R., 85, 88, 95
Bauer, R. M., x, 46, 49, 50, 51, 52, 53, 162, 163, 169, 624, 625, 629, 630, 640
Baylis, G. C., 80, 252, 312, 326, 411
Beauvois, M.-F., 413
Beck, J. L., 726
Becker, J., 4, 5, 624, 629, 647
Becker, W., 245
Behr, S. E., 640, 726
Behrens, M. M., 166
Behrmann, M., 65, 168, 352, 369
Belmore, S. M., 17, 18
Bem, D. J., 15
Bender, D. B., 78, 80
Bender, M. B., 110, 352
Bennett, C. H., 900
Benson, D. F., 169, 218, 224
Benson, P. J., 154, 187, 236
Bentall, R. P., 170, 890
Bentin, S., 555, 557, 558, 559, 564, 629, 630, 633, 640
Benton, A. L., 153, 154, 155
Benton, A. R., 205
Benzig, W. C., 647
Bergman, H., 94
Bergmann, I. I., 94, 95
Berlucchi, G., 244, 246, 249, 250
Berndt, R. S., 528

Berry, D., 843
Berry, D. C., 10, 755, 756, 758, 759, 762, 763, 765, 766, 770, 771, 772, 774, 776, 777, 822, 847, 848, 861
Bertelson, P., 318
Berti, A., 60, 65, 165, 168, 238, 353, 378
Besner, D., 426
Bettucci, D., 236
Biederman, I., 179, 180, 181, 196
Biedermann, I., 422, 433, 436
Biedermann, J., 95
Bienenstock, E., 92
Bierderman, I., 406, 627
Bigot, T., 325
Birdsall, T. G., 664
Biscaldi, M., 250
Bisiach, E., 61, 66, 165, 168, 237, 351, 352, 367, 371, 378, 382, 384, 386, 387, 774
Bitterman, M. E., 813
Bizot, E., 761, 769, 784, 787, 820, 822, 825, 861
Bizzi, E., 267, 268, 269, 270, 282, 283
Bjork, E. L., 26
Bjork, R. A., 26, 551, 584, 620, 662, 725
Black, S. E., 65, 168, 352
Blackford, M., 631
Blackford, S., 624
Blakemore, C., 90, 91
Blanchard-Fields, F., 804, 821, 837, 849
Blankenship, S. E., 8
Blaxton, T. A., 565, 584, 585, 634, 645, 683, 726
Bleich, R. P., 631
Block, R. I., 839
Bloxham, C. A., 407
Boakes, R. A., 843
Bodis-Wollner, I., 110
Boer, J. P. A., 489
Bogen, J. E., 168
Boller, F., 634
Bolton, J. P. R., 93
Bondi, M. W., 647, 648
Bonke, B., 640, 726, 839
Booker, J., 623
Borges, M. A., 17
Bornstein, R. F., 163, 838
Bottalico, K. S., 726
Bottini, G., 390
Boucart, M., 163, 774
Bouma, D., 252
Bourdeaud'hui, M., 325
Bousfield, W. A., 672
Bouyer, J. J., 93, 100
Bower, G. H., 16

Bowerman, M., 863
Bowers, D., 624, 625, 629, 630
Bowers, J., 623
Bowers, J. S., 628, 630, 631
Bowers, K. S., 19
Boynton, R. E., 245
Bracewell, R. M., 233
Bradshaw, J. A., 325
Bradshaw, J. L., 325, 553
Braine, M. D. S., 863
Braitenberg, V., 82
Brandt, J. P., 218, 224
Bransford, J. D., 634, 693
Bransford, J. P., 634
Breedin, S. D., 531
Bregestovski, P., 96
Brehaut, J., 354, 368
Breitmeyer, B. G., 111, 124, 125
Brennan, C., 43, 44, 45
Brennan, C. W., 244, 297, 304
Brennan, S., 187, 907
Brennen, T., 155, 156, 204
Brenner, C., 11
Brewer, W. F., 770, 844, 846
Briand, K., 157, 184
Bridgeman, B., 143, 272, 276, 284, 285
Bright, J., 155, 156, 204
Brison, S., 523
Britten, K. H., 82
Broadbent, D., 821, 825
Broadbent, D. E., 10, 240, 311, 328, 397, 553, 757, 758, 759, 762, 765, 766, 768, 770, 771, 772, 777, 822, 837, 843, 847, 848, 849, 850, 851, 852, 857, 861
Broadbent, M. P. H., 758, 759, 768
Brocher, S., 92, 99
Brodmann, K., 233
Brody, N., 640, 644, 770
Bronson, G. W., 292
Brooks, J. O., 643
Brooks, K., 13, 23
Brooks, L. R., 698, 701, 714, 755, 784, 786, 805, 812, 813, 814, 820, 821
Brosch, M., 85, 88, 95
Brown, A. S., 24, 27, 625, 629
Brown, G. D. A., 315
Brown, J. S., 627, 689, 698, 715
Brown, R., 863
Bruce, C., 78
Bruce, C. J., 233, 234, 413
Bruce, G. J., 739
Bruce, V., 50, 51, 153, 154, 155, 156, 157, 158, 159, 160, 162, 163, 164, 171, 172, 179, 181, 182, 183, 184, 185, 186, 187, 188, 189, 196, 197, 203, 204, 223, 891, 908
Brunas, J., 183, 197
Brunas-Wagstaff, J., 160, 184, 197
Brune, C. M., 628, 631
Bruner, J. S., ix
Brunn, J. L., 65, 369, 457
Brust, J. C., 166
Bruyer, R., 47, 161, 162
Bry, I., 306
Bryden, M. P., 209, 335, 337
Bub, D., 511, 512, 514, 529
Buchtel, H. A., 295, 313, 326
Buckley, P. B., 426
Bullemer, P., 755, 759, 760, 771, 774, 775, 784, 822, 825, 827, 828, 852, 853, 854, 855, 856
Bullier, J., 88
Burgess, P. W., 402, 409, 410, 412, 413
Burke, J. A., 119
Burke, W., 119
Burkell, J., 553
Burnham, C. A., 334
Burns, K. I., 716
Burr, D. C., 95
Burton, A. M., 50, 51, 154, 158, 159, 162, 163, 164, 171, 172, 179, 182, 185, 186, 187, 188, 196, 197
Burton, L. A., 496
Burton, M., 188, 189, 197, 755, 767
Buser, P., 93
Buss, R., 757, 763, 764, 765, 771
Buss, R. R., 804, 821, 837, 848, 849
Butter, C. M., 313, 326
Butters, N., 624, 629, 634, 635, 639, 645, 646, 647, 648

Calabresi, P. A., 244, 297, 304
Callaway, E. M., 90, 91
Calvanio, R., 371
Camarda, R., 233, 234, 235, 236, 239, 247, 248
Camarda, R. M., 408
Cambier, J., 325
Camerda, R. M., 409
Campbell, D. T., 20, 25
Campbell, R., 155
Campion, J., 44
Canavan, A. G. M., 647
Candido, C. L., 170
Cantor, G., 10, 761
Cantwell, A., 578, 580, 584
Capgras, J., 169
Capitani, E., 514, 518, 520

Caramazza, A., 359, 368, 370, 371, 514, 518, 528, 529, 531
Carbon, N., 774
Carey, D. P., 236
Carey, S., 187, 907
Carlson, A., 825, 827
Carlson, L. A., 716
Carlson, R., 755, 757, 766, 770, 771
Carlson, R. A., 784
Carlton, L. G., 271
Carpenter, E., 716, 717
Carpenter, P. A., 369
Carr, T., 161
Carr, T. H., 161, 571, 578, 627, 689, 698, 700, 702, 703, 704, 705, 706, 707, 715, 716
Carson, R. E., 205
Carusi, D., 495, 497
Carusi, D. A., 495
Cave, C. B., 625, 627, 629
Cave, K. R., 163
Cebollero, A., 586
Cermak, L. S., 624, 629, 630, 631, 648, 667
Challis, B. H., 5, 16, 634, 664, 669
Challis, X., 633
Chambers, D., 268, 279
Chambers, R. A., 388
Chan, C., 776, 777
Chandler, K., 624, 630
Chang, T., 508
Changeux, J.-P., 411
Charalambous, A., 627, 689, 698, 714
Charness, N., 648
Chawluk, J. B., 511
Cheesman, J., 23, 145, 146, 552, 701
Chelazzi, L., 249
Cheng, P. W., 397
Cherry, E. C., 240, 311
Chertkow, H., 511, 512, 514, 529
Chiarello, C., 61
Chinn, R., 771
Chitty, A. J., 80
Cho, J.-R., 804, 821, 837, 849
Choate, L. S., 296, 297
Chomsky, N., 861, 863, 864, 872, 875
Chorover, S. L., 125
Christen, L., 168
Christman, S., 111
Chugani, H. T., 307
Church, B., 626
Clark, M. C., 16
Clarke, J., 477, 478, 479, 496
Clarke, R., 627, 689
Cleeremans, A., 583, 740, 759, 772, 783, 784, 785, 786, 787, 789, 790, 791, 792, 793, 795, 798, 803, 807, 821, 825, 861, 865
Cleland, B. G., 118
Clohessy, A. B., 296
Cohen, A., 43, 44, 45, 624, 629, 648, 769, 771, 775, 825, 827
Cohen, B. H., 672
Cohen, G. H., 245
Cohen, J. D., 411, 414, 454, 455, 457, 458, 459, 461, 463, 467, 468, 471, 472, 719, 727
Cohen, N. J., x, 624, 635
Cohen, Y., 240, 244, 295, 296
Coles, M. G. H., 146
Colheart, M., 639
Collingridge, G. L., 96
Collins, A. M., 512, 701
Collins, J., 111
Collins, L., 212
Coltheart, M., 109, 111, 118, 426
Coltheart, V., 586
con Noorden, G. K., 91
Conel, J. L., 306
Connor, L. T., 27
Conture, L. J., 640
Cooper, E. E., 179, 180, 181, 196, 627
Cooper, G. F., 90
Cooper, L. A., 179, 181, 196, 552, 626, 627, 631
Cooper, L. N., 92
Cooper, R., 401
Cope, P., 213
Corbetta, M., 239
Coren, S., 279
Coriell, S., 124
Cork, R. C., 640, 726
Corkin, S., 625, 648, 662
Corking, S., 627, 630
Corteen, R. S., 553
Cortese, C., 179, 629, 630, 702, 714
Corwin, J., 666
Coslett, B., 639
Coslett, H., 773
Coslett, H. B., 12, 67, 528, 529
Coss, R. G., 78
Cotard, J., 169
Cottee, L. J., 119
Cottrell, G. W., 740, 746, 795
Coughlin, A. K., 574
Cowell, E. S., 155
Cowey, A., 42, 43, 45, 154, 237
Craik, F. I. M., 6, 555, 559, 628, 664, 672, 676, 683, 742

Crammond, D. J., 268, 282
Cranston, M., 719
Craw, I., 154, 159, 171, 179, 182, 186, 197
Crawford, T. J., 251, 336
Crick, F., 22, 27, 38, 84, 99, 101, 256
Critchley, E. M. R., 171, 204
Critchley, M., 235, 237
Crombez, G., 845
Crovitz, H. F., 250, 335, 337
Crowder, R. G., 16
Cullicover, P., 863
Cummings, J. L., 168
Cunningham, C. J., 213
Curro-Dossi, R., 89
Curt, E., 894
Cutting, J., 169
Czarkowska, J., 85
Czyzewska, M., 755, 759, 760, 761, 812, 829, 852

D'Alton, J., 414
Dagenbach, D., 578, 700, 702, 703, 704, 705
Dallas, M., 15, 553, 629, 683, 726
Damasio, A., 46
Damasio, A. R., x, 38, 63, 84, 161, 204, 205, 218, 223, 224, 414, 523, 526, 530, 640
Damasio, H., 204, 205, 218, 223, 224
Daniele, A., 366
Dannenbring, G. L., 157, 184
Dark, V. J., 238, 241, 553
Dark, W. J., 643
Dascola, I., 242, 243, 244, 249, 250, 251, 252, 307, 333, 336, 345, 346
Daves, W., 250, 335, 337
Davey, G. C. L., 844, 890, 907
Davidson, B. J., 242, 338, 704
Davidson, D. L. W., 236
Davies, A., 328
Davies, G. M., 187
Davis, C., 702
Dawson, M. E., 844
Day, R. H., 885
Deacedo, B. S., 648
Debner, J. A., 663, 677
Debray, O., 93, 100
Decter, M., 514
Dedet, L., 93, 100
De Falco, F. A., 67
De Haan, E. H. F., 47, 48, 49, 51, 52, 155, 157, 161, 162, 163, 164, 166, 167, 168, 185, 204, 206, 514, 523, 640, 774
Dehaene, S., 411
Dehaut, F., 356, 357
Deiber, M.-P., 213

Dejean, K., 821
Delacour, J., 892
Delany, S. M., 179, 181, 626, 631
Delbecq-Derouesne, J., 413
Delis, D. C., 492
Della Malva, C. L., 414
DeLong, M. R., 307
Dench, N., 185, 186, 188, 189, 197
Denies, Z., 238
Dennis, M., 528
Denny-Brown, D., 388
De Renzi, E., 155, 163, 237, 252, 326, 409, 528, 529, 532
D'Erme, P., 165, 366, 367
de Schonen, S., 306
Desimone, R., 78, 80, 154, 241, 432
Detweiler, M., 398, 399
Deutsch, D., 553
Dewey, G., 755, 757, 766, 770, 771
Dewey, G. I., 784
Dewey, G. L., 825, 827
DeYoe, E. A., 109, 292
Diamond, R., 624, 628, 630, 633
Dickinson, A., 847
Dienes, Z., 60, 65, 353, 756, 759, 765, 766, 770, 771, 772, 777, 785, 821, 825, 843
Diller, L., 378, 386
di Pellegrino, G., 234, 235
Di Stefano, M., 244
Dixon, N. F., 11
Dobmeyer, S., 239
Donchin, E., 146
Done, J. S., 407
Donnelly, N., 163, 774
Dorfman, J., 19, 24, 27
Dorken, M. D., 821, 822, 826, 830
Douglas, R. M., 295
Downes, J. J., 407, 412, 413, 648
Downing, C. J., 244
Driver, J., 60, 65, 238, 312, 326, 353, 354, 359, 368, 370, 719
Dror, I. E., 573
Druhan, B., 773, 804, 821, 837, 849
Druhan, B. B., 825
Duchnicky, R. L., 627, 634
Duckman, R. H., 245
Duhamel, J., 235
Dulaney, D. E., 755, 757, 766, 770, 771, 845
Dulany, D. E., 784, 825, 827, 830, 831
Dumais, S. T., 144
Dunbar, K., 402, 411, 414, 428, 454, 455, 463, 467, 468, 471, 472, 719, 727, 861, 877
Dunbar, K. N., 454, 464

Duncan, J., 312, 326, 704
Dunkelberger, G. R., 119
Dunn, D., 625, 626, 637
Dunn, J., 756
Dunn, J. C., 626, 683, 687
Durgonoglu, A., 702
Dyer, F. N., 427
Dziurawiec, S., 154

Eagle, M., 22
Easter, S. S., 270
Ebata, S., 166, 167, 172
Ebbinghaus, H. E., 682
Eccles, J. C., 408
Echallier, J. F., 252
Eckhorn, R., 85, 88, 95
Edelman, S., 92
Edelmann, G. M., 82, 83, 85
Eelen, P., 845
Efron, R., 492
Egeth, H. E., 472, 482, 483
Egly, R., 252, 370
Ehrlich, S., 250
Eich, E., 640, 726
Eich, J. E., 553, 644
Eichenbaum, H., 648
Elghori, D., 325
Ellis, A. E., 508
Ellis, A. W., 50, 51, 154, 155, 160, 163, 171, 182, 183, 184, 186, 187, 197, 203, 204, 224, 352, 627
Ellis, H., 154
Ellis, H. D., 153, 155, 158, 163, 169, 171, 187
Ellis, N., 755
Elman, J., 772
Elman, J. L., 399, 740, 746, 790, 795, 796, 862, 865, 866, 869, 975
Elster, J., 13
Engel, A. K., 86, 87, 88, 91, 100
Engstler-Schooler, T. Y., 13
Enoch, M. D., 170
Erdelyi, M., 4, 5, 6, 26
Erdelyi, M. H., x, 5, 18
Eriksen, B. A., 146, 461
Eriksen, C. W., ix, 127, 145, 146, 366, 461
Erikson, C., 111
Erlich, S., 335
Eskenazi, J., 839
Essick, G., 233
Essick, G. K., 234
Estes, W. K., 861, 882, 977
Etcoff, N. L., 163
Evans, A., 212

Evenden, J. L., 407
Evett, L. J., 571, 586
Eviatar, Z., 479
Eysenck, M. W., 508

Fadiga, L., 234, 235
Faglioni, P., 163, 252
Fahey, R., 772, 777
Fahle, M., 92
Fahleman, S. E., 411
Fairbaim, A., 645
Farah, M. J., 40, 51, 53, 54, 56, 58, 63, 64, 65, 66, 313, 326, 352, 353, 369, 457, 459, 520, 522, 526, 528, 529, 572, 574
Faria, R. B., 244, 252
Faulconer, B., 717
Feenan, K., 627
Fehrer, E., 123, 125
Feldman, A., 268, 282
Feldman, J. A., 367
Felleman, D. J., 80, 232
Fendrich, R., 44, 244, 249, 251, 336, 337
Ferro-Milone, F., 514
Ferster, D., 94, 96
Festinger, L., 245, 334
Fetz, E. E., 93, 94, 95, 98, 100
Feuerstein, N., 11
Feustel, T., 586
Feustel, T. C., 698, 707
Feyereisen, P., 47, 161, 162
Fidell, L. S., 127
Findlay, J. M., 242, 245, 250, 279, 307, 333, 337, 346, 347
Fischler, I., 702
Fisher, C., 11, 22
Fisicaro, S. A., 553
Fisk, A. D., 396, 403, 711
Fisk, J. D., 256
Fiss, H., 11
Fitch, W., 640
FitzGerald, P., 758, 759, 768
Fitzpatrick DeSalme, E. J., 528, 529
Flanders, M., 268, 269, 271
Flood, W., 312
Flores, D'Arcais, G. B., 524, 525
Flowers, K. A., 407
Flude, B., 184, 186, 195, 352, 685
Flude, B. M., 155, 183, 187, 204, 224, 627
Flynn, R. A., 523
Fodor, J., 171, 636
Fodor, J. A., 398, 511
Fogassi, L., 233, 234, 235, 408
Fogassi, M., 236

Folk, C. F., 482, 483
Folk, C. L., 333
Ford, M. R., 93
Forgy, C., 400
Forster, K., 702
Forster, K. I., 572, 578, 580, 584
Foulkes, D., x
Fowler, C. A., 552
Fowlers, D. C., 839
Fox, L. A., 428
Fox, P. T., 208, 213, 215, 217, 218, 223, 238, 638, 639
Frackowiak, R. S. J., 213
Fragassi, N. A., 67
Frambach, M., 774, 822
Francis, W., 690, 691
Frank, J. S., 269, 282
Franklin, P. E., 555
Franks, J. J., 634, 693
Freedman, L., 642
Freeman, B., 90
Freeman, R., 163
Freeman, R. D., 89, 94
Freeman, W. J., 93
Freidland, R. P., 352
Freidman, R. B., 638
Freidrich, F. J., 297, 307, 366, 367, 371, 459, 460, 461, 555
Freud, S., 13, 22, 27, 830
Freund, J. S., 894
Friedrich, F., 774
Friston, K. J., 213
Frith, C. D., 407
Frost, D., 41
Frost, D. O., 91
Fry, A. F., 628, 631
Fuhrer, M. J., 844
Fulgosi, A., 8
Funahashi, S., 413, 739
Funnell, E., 510, 517–518
Fuster, J. M., 409, 413

Gabrieli, J. D. E., 627, 630, 662
Gainotti, G., 165, 366, 367, 514, 522, 531
Galambos, R., 93
Galanter, E., ix
Gallego, J., 769, 813, 821, 822, 823, 825, 832, 855, 856
Gallen, C., 93
Gallese, V., 234, 235, 247, 248, 409
Galley, D. J., 838
Ganz, L., 124, 125
Gardiner, J. M., 682

Gardner, H., 634
Gardy, C. L., 205
Garvey, J., 119
Gassaniga, M. S., 58, 59, 60, 62
Gathercole, E. S., 553
Gauthier, L., 356, 357
Gawryszewski, L., 244, 252
Gazzaniga, M. S., 38, 44, 63, 238, 352, 377, 378
Gelade, G., 311
Gentilini, M., 252, 624, 648
Gentilucci, M., 233, 234, 235, 236, 238, 252, 408, 409, 433
Georgopoulos, A., 236
Georgopoulos, A. P., 78, 236, 269, 270, 282
Gerard, L., 629
Gerstein, G. L., 85, 88
Geschwind, N., 66, 163
Ghez, C., 270
Ghoneim, M. M., 839
Ghose, G. M., 89, 94
Gibbs, B. J., 354, 368
Gibling, F., 155
Gibson, E. J., 890, 899
Gibson, J. M., 643
Gilbert, C., 85
Gillespie, G. L., 5, 27
Gillman, C. B., 426
Giszter, S., 267
Glaser, M. D., 428, 441
Glaser, M. O., 466, 467, 468, 469, 472
Glaser, W. R., 428, 441, 466, 467, 468, 469, 472
Glass, A. L., 624
Glenn, C. G., 511, 532
Glovinski, Y., 119
Glushko, R. J., 577
Gnadt, J. W., 233, 234
Gochin, P. M., 85
Godden, D. R., 693
Gold, E. M., 863, 872
Goldberg, F., 11
Goldberg, G., 408, 414
Goldberg, M. E., 233, 234, 246, 247
Golden, R. M., 572, 574
Goldman-Rakic, P. S., 233, 413, 739
Gonzalez, R. C., 869
Goodale, M. A., 236, 237, 256, 285
Goodglass, H., 528
Gooding, P., 631
Goodman, G. S., 309
Goodrich, S., 407
Gopher, D., 325, 472

Gordon, B., 257, 528, 624, 630
Goshen-Gottstein, Y., 620, 626, 632, 638, 639, 642, 643, 645, 647, 648
Gottstein, J., 682
Goulding, P. J., 509
Graesser, A. C., 16, 17
Graf, P., 11, 27, 561, 620, 624, 626, 628, 631, 633, 634, 645, 661, 662, 667, 682, 685, 687, 689, 691, 693, 726, 730, 774
Granholme, E., 648
Grant, D. S., 892
Gratton, G., 146
Gray, C. M., 40, 85, 86, 87, 94, 96, 100
Graziano, M. S. A., 234
Green, J., 553
Green, R. E. A., 890
Greenwald, A. G., 145, 830, 839
Greitschus, F., 93
Greve, K. W., 49, 53, 162, 163, 640
Griffin, D. R., 889
Gross, C. G., 78, 80, 85, 154, 234
Grossberg, S., 82, 83, 738
Grossi, D., 67, 163
Growden, J. H., 0
Grupp, L. A., 247, 248
Grusser, O.-J., 124, 235
Guilford, J. P., 8
Guitton, H. A., 295
Guthrie, P. B., 96

Hacaen, H., 161
Haden, P., 561
Haden, P. E., 633, 683
Haist, F., 630
Haith, M. M., 309
Hall, G., 890, 891, 905
Hallett, P. E., 293
Halligan, P., 774
Halligan, P. W., 61, 62, 238, 352, 359, 368, 378, 386, 387
Hamilton, K., 119
Hammond, K. H., 522
Hampson, S., 93
Hamsher, K. D. S., 205
Hancock, P. J. B., 92
Hanley, J. R., 155
Hanlon, C., 863
Hanna, E., 188, 189, 197
Hanson, S., 795
Harbluk, J. L., 641, 643
Harding, G. F. A., 163
Hardy, G., 774
Harman, C., 304, 306, 308
Harris, C., 862, 875

Hart, J., 528
Hartje, W., 58
Hartman, M., 646, 648, 755, 760, 825, 827, 855, 856
Hasbroucq, T., 473
Hashtroudi, S., 15, 638
Hasson, R., 93
Hawkins, B., 269, 282
Hawkins, H. L., 244
Hawley, K. J., 552
Haxbey, J. V., 205
Hay, D. C., 0, 154, 155, 160, 168, 171, 182, 183, 187, 204
Hayes, N., 762
Hayes, N. A., 837, 849, 850, 851, 857
Hayman, C. A. G., 624, 628, 629, 634, 645, 701, 703, 714
Hayman, C. G., 685, 689
Hazan, C., 309
Heald, A., 407
Healey, P., 188, 189, 197
Hebb, D. O., 82, 83, 334, 907
Hecaen, H., 207, 218
Heeley, D. W., 236
Heilman, K. M., 351, 528, 529
Heindel, W. C., 635, 639, 646, 647, 648
Heit, G., 284, 285
Held, R., 41
Helfand, R., 27
Helfer, M. S. A., 124
Hellawell, D., 47, 52, 157, 162, 169, 185
Hellawell, D. J., 165, 168, 169, 368, 378
Heller, W., 496
Hellige, J. B., 207, 208, 218, 482
Henderson, J. M., 307, 336
Henderson, L., 407, 586
Henik, A., 313, 555
Hepp-Reymond, M. C., 312
Herbet, A., 96
Herman, E., 282, 284
Hermann, D. J., 15
Herscovitch, P., 205, 212
Heuer, F., 268, 279
Heywood, C. A., 154
Hietanen, J. K., 154, 187
Hikosaka, O., 246, 247
Hill, D. C., 197
Hill, T., 761, 769, 784, 787, 812, 820, 822, 825, 829, 845, 861
Hillis, A. E., 368, 370, 371, 514, 518, 529
Hillyard, S. A., 93, 244, 554, 555, 557, 558, 559
Hinton, G., 55, 367, 370, 572, 574, 575, 576, 577, 786

Hinton, G. E., 27, 55, 414, 463, 469, 573, 586, 740, 806
Hintzman, D., 698, 714
Hintzman, D. L., 662, 667, 726, 786
Hirsh-Pasek, K., 863
Hirshman, E., 633
Hirst, W., 422, 472, 629
Hitch, G., 396, 450
Hitch, G. J., 725, 727, 742
Hobbie, R. K., 348
Hobson, J. A., 22, 25, 27
Hockey, R., 242, 244, 336, 348
Hockey, R. J., 250, 307, 333, 337, 346, 347
Hodges, J. R., 510
Hoffman, H., 755, 759, 760, 761, 852
Hoffman, J. E., 337, 347
Hoffman, S. A., 27
Hogan, N., 270
Hogeboom, M. M., 146
Hoke, M., 93
Holander, D., 551
Holender, D., 145, 677, 837, 838, 856
Holland, A. L., 510
Holland, B., 22
Hollcomb, P. J., 555
Hollerbach, J. M., 287
Hollingshead, A., 677
Holopigian, K., 119
Honda, H., 276, 278, 282, 284, 285
Honey, R. C., 905
Honore, J., 325
Hood, B., 296, 297, 302, 308
Horst, S., 578, 700, 702, 703
Horwitz, B., 205
Houghton, G., 354, 370, 411, 719
Howard, D., 510, 775
Howard, D. V., 628, 631
Howard, J., 775
Howard, M. J., 325
Hubel, D., 276
Hubel, D. H., 91
Hudson, P. T. W., 470, 471, 472, 474, 727, 735
Hughes, H. C., 113, 118, 244
Hummel, J. E., 627
Humphreys, G., 774
Humphreys, G. W., 163, 244, 312, 351, 366, 367, 510, 514, 517, 519, 522, 571, 586, 704
Humphreys, M. S., 857
Hunkin, N. M., 518
Hunt, E. B., 861
Hurrell, J., 407
Hurt, C. A., 640, 726

Hurtig, R., 161
Huttonlocher, J., 717
Hyde, M. R., 528
Hyvarinen, J., 233, 234, 235

Imhof, H.-G., 168
Inhoff, A. W., 325
Innocenti, G. M., 90, 91, 95
Irion, A. I., 4
Ivry, R., 769, 771, 775
Ivry, R. I., 648, 825, 827

Jack, C. E., 320
Jackendoff, R., 524, 530
Jackson, A., 624, 626, 634
Jackson, G. M., 649
Jackson, S., 649
Jacoby, L., 559
Jacoby, L. L., 15, 552, 559, 561, 565, 626, 627, 629, 640, 643, 661, 663, 666, 667, 668, 677, 683, 689, 698, 701, 702, 714, 726, 755, 828
Jagadeesh, B., 94, 96
Jahnsen, H., 256
Jakobson, L. S., 236
James, M., 154, 407, 413
James, W., 242, 453, 681, 890
Java, R. I., 682
Jeannerod, M., 235, 252
Jelicic, M., 726, 839
Jennings, J. M., 676
Jennings, P. J., 792, 793
Jernigan, T. L., 662
Jerreat, L., 371
Jersild, A. T., 406, 422, 433
Joanette, Y., 356, 357
Joannides, A. A., 93
Job, R., 514, 522
Johnson, H. I. L., 624, 630, 631
Johnson, M. H., 154, 291, 292, 293, 304, 305, 309
Johnson, W. A., 643
Johnson-Laird, P. N., 431
Johnston, A. W., 553
Johnston, J. C., 333
Johnston, R. A., 50, 51, 158, 162, 163, 164, 171, 172, 185, 187, 196
Johnston, R. M., 154, 163, 171
Johnston, R. S., 236
Johnston, W. A., 238, 241, 552
Jolicoeur, P., 627
Jones, D., 626
Jonides, J., 242, 313, 333, 336
Joordens, S., 552

Jordan, M., 740
Jordan, M. I., 783, 786, 792, 865
Jordan, T. R., 236
Jordan, W., 85, 88, 95
Joyce, E. M., 648
Judge, S. J., 248
Juncos, J. L., 407
Jurgens, R., 245

Kahneman, D., 27, 124, 125, 240, 311, 354, 368, 472, 553, 698
Kaiser, D., 496
Kalaska, J. F., 268, 282
Kalmar, D., 472
Kanaka, K., 94
Kaney, S., 170
Kanwisher, N., 368
Kaplan, C. A., 8, 27
Karanath, H. O., 58
Karnas, G., 0, 821, 825
Karnath, H. O., 413, 414
Karni, A., 92
Karol, D. L., 483
Kashiwagi, A., 378
Kashiwagi, T., 378
Kassin, S., 761
Kassin, S. M., 10
Kaszniak, A. W., 647, 648
Katz, L. C., 90, 91
Kauff, D. M., 640, 644
Kay, J., 67, 155, 224, 508
Kay, M. C., 154, 155
Kaye, H., 900, 901, 904, 906
Keane, M. M., 627, 630, 635, 639, 645
Keane, M. T., 508
Keane, M. W., 662
Keele, S., 769, 771, 775
Keele, S. W., 271, 648, 698, 792, 793, 825, 827
Kegl, J., 795
Kehl, S. J., 96
Keifner, M. G., 492
Kelley, C. M., 627, 640, 663
Kellogg, W. A., 555
Kennard, C., 213, 407
Kenny, P. A., 884
Keppel, G., 672
Kerr, B., 348
Kerr, L., 119
Kettner, R. E., 269, 270, 282
Kihlstrom, J. F., x, 16, 640, 726, 737
Kilduff, P. T., 60, 353
Kim, J. K., 624, 630, 631

Kimchi, R., 492
Kimura, D., 318
Kimura, M., 85
Kincaid, W. D., 672
Kingstone, A., 257, 307, 334, 347
Kinsbourne, M., 39, 63, 66, 71, 252, 257, 328, 352, 367, 511, 648
Kintsch, W., 5, 508, 663
Kirch, M., 143, 272, 284
Kirsner, K., 244, 625, 626, 637, 683, 687, 689, 756
Kirson, D., 701
Klahr, D., 861, 877
Klein, G. S., 11
Klein, R., 250, 257, 313, 336
Klein, R. M., 307, 333, 334, 335, 336, 337, 338, 342, 343, 346, 347, 348
Klein, S. B., 16
Kleinbard, J., 18
Klinger, M. R., 830
Knight, R. T., 413, 414, 492
Knopman, D., 755, 760
Knopman, D. S., 827, 855, 856
Knowlton, B., 774
Knowlton, B. J., 646, 648, 827, 828
Koch, C., 38, 84, 99, 101
Koch, R., 123, 127, 143
Koener, F., 236
Koerner, E., 335
Koerner, F., 45
Kohn, S. E., 638
Kohonen, T., 183
Kolers, P., 523, 627, 629, 634
Kolers, P. A., 685, 689, 714, 755
Kolodny, J., 577
Komatsu, S., 683
Komilis, E., 252
Komoda, M. K., 245
Konig, P., 86–87, 88, 89, 91, 95, 100
Koopmans, H. J., 14
Koriat, A., 11, 710
Kornblum, S., 268, 270, 271, 273, 274, 275, 276, 280, 282, 283, 284, 285, 286, 287, 473
Kory, R., 119
Kosslyn, S. M., 523, 639
Kostner, D., 27
Kotler-Cope, S., 848
Kramer, J. H., 492
Krantz, J., 43, 44, 45
Kraut, A. G., 713
Kreiter, A. K., 85, 86, 87, 94, 98
Kroll, J. F., 716, 717

Kruger, J., 85
Kruse, W., 85, 88, 95
Kubicek, L. F., 717
Kubota, K., 94
Kucera, M., 690, 691
Kumarasinghe, R., 119
Kunst-Wilson, W. R., 163, 640
Kuperstein, M., 268, 269
Kurata, K., 409
Kushner, M., 759, 772, 783, 786, 787, 798, 803, 807, 814, 820
Kutas, M., 554, 555, 557, 558, 559
Kyriacou, C., 119

LaBerge, D., 241, 348, 396, 553
Ladavas, E., 252, 366, 367, 370
Lado, F., 93
Laguna, J. M., 626, 631
La Heij, W., 146, 489
Laiacona, M., 514, 518, 520
Laird, J. E., 399
Lamain, W., 146
Lamb, M. R., 492, 493
Lambert, A., 348
Lambert, A. J., 242
Lammertsma, A. A., 213
Landauer, T. K., 426
Landgraf, J. Z., 268, 272, 275, 283, 285, 287
Landis, T., 66, 155, 168, 235
Lang, A. E., 648
Lange, K. W., 407, 413
Lange, L., 142, 143
Langton, S., 197
Larmande, F., 325
Larmande, P., 325
Larsen, N. A., 408
Laterre, C., 47, 161, 162
Latto, R., 44, 237
Lavie, N., 311
Lavner, Y., 94
Lavoie, D., 630, 632
Law, J., 628, 629
Lazarus, R. S., 145
Lea, G., 861, 877
Lean, D. S., 5, 27
LeBarge, D., 144
LeDoux, J. E., 58, 59, 60, 62, 238, 352, 377, 378, 747
Legrand, R., 348
Lehmkugle, S., 113, 118
Lehmkuhl, G., 532
Lehtio, P., 183
Leigh, P. N., 407, 413

Leinonen, L., 233, 234
Lennie, P., 109, 110
Leonard, C. M., 80
Leone, D. R., 838
Lesgold, A. M., 16
Letourneau, L., 624, 629
Levelt, W., 532
Leventhal, T., 327
Levesque, M., 208, 211
Levick, W. R., 118
Levin, H. S., 154, 155
Levine, D. N., 371
Levy, B. A., 689, 716
Levy, J., 496
Lewandowsky, S., 631, 642, 756
Lewicki, P., 755, 759, 760, 761, 769, 784, 787, 812, 820, 822, 825, 829, 845, 852, 861
Lewis, J. L., 553
Lewis, K., 328
Lewis, S., 10, 284, 285, 757, 761, 765
Lewis, S. W., 169
Lhermitte, F., 409
Light, L. L., 630, 632
Lindamood, T. E., 559
Lindsay, D. S., 663, 677
Linnankoski, I., 233, 234
Linszen, D. H., 171
Livingstone, M., 276
Livingstone, M. S., 85
Llinas, R., 93, 256
Lockhart, R. S., 555, 559, 683
Loess, H., 436, 442, 628
Loftus, E. F., 701, 830
Loftus, J., 16
Logan, G. D., 144, 402, 700
Lorenzo, M., 119
Lortie, C., 252, 411
Lovibond, P. F., 843
Lowe, C. F., 890
Lowel, S., 91
Lubow, R. E., 890
Lucchelli, F., 155, 528, 532
Luck, S. J., 244
Lueck, C. J., 213
Luhmann, H. J., 90–91
Lupker, S. J., 700
Luppino, G., 233, 234, 235, 236, 408, 409
Luria, A. R., 638
Lutzemberger, L., 42
Luzzatti, C., 351, 352, 371, 378, 386, 509, 510
Lynch, J. C., 236

MacDonald, B., 154, 204, 205, 208, 211, 215, 221
MacDonald, C., 624, 628, 634, 645
Macdonald, C. A., 701, 703
Mack, A., 268, 279, 282, 284
Mackay, D. G., 553
Mackintosh, N. J., 890, 892, 900, 901, 904, 906
Macko, K. A., 80
MacLeod, C. M., 402, 422, 428, 453, 454, 464, 642, 719, 726
Madigan, S., 5, 17, 626
Madler, C., 93
Magee, L., 717
Makeig, S., 93
Malone, D. R., 154, 155
Mandler, G., ix, 5, 11, 14, 15, 16, 17, 18, 20, 21, 23, 25, 26, 27, 171, 561, 624, 633, 661, 662, 683, 685, 693, 725, 726, 727, 728, 730, 731, 737, 738, 774, 828
Marcel, A. J., ix, x, 11, 12, 13, 17, 21, 64, 552, 701, 737, 738
Marchman, V., 864
Marescaux, P.-J., 821, 825
Marescaux, P., 768
Margolin, D., 774
Marham, J., 212
Marin, O. S. M., 509, 510, 511, 512, 532, 638
Marinkovic, K., 844
Marr, D., 180, 367, 369, 370, 389, 390, 524
Marrett, S., 212
Marsden, C. D., 407, 413, 647
Marshall, J., 41, 42, 352, 774
Marshall, J. C., 61, 62, 238, 378, 386, 387
Marsolek, C. J., 639
Martin, A., 645
Martin, L. L., 10
Martin, M., 492
Martin, P. R., 119
Martin, W. R. W., 212
Martinez-Millan, L., 90–91
Martone, M., 624, 629, 647, 648
Marzi, C. A., 42, 244, 249, 250
Masson, M., 572
Masson, M. E., 642
Masson, M. E. J., 565, 682, 683
Masterton, R. B., 312
Matelli, M., 233, 234, 235, 236, 238, 252, 408, 433
Mathews, R., 757, 763, 764, 765, 766, 771, 773
Mathews, R. C., 804, 821, 824, 825, 837, 848, 849

Matterson, R., 496
Maury, L.-F.-A., 13
Mayer, M. L., 96
Mayer, N. H., 414
Mayes, A. R., 160, 623, 625, 630, 631, 643, 645, 858
Maylor, E. A., 244, 295, 296, 336
Mayron, C., 119
Mays, L. E., 269, 270, 283
Mayzner, M. S., 124
Mazziotta, J. C., 307
McAndrews, M. P., 38, 39, 69, 164, 352, 638, 639, 641, 805, 820
McAndrews, P., 773
McBurney, D. H., 510
McCarl, R., 399
McCarthy, G., 558, 559
McCarthy, M., 555, 564
McCarthy, R. A., 205, 206, 207, 224, 512, 518, 519, 521, 526, 527
McCauley, C., 161, 707
McCleary, R. A., 145
McClelland, J., 520, 526, 528, 529, 772
McClelland, J. L., 24, 411, 414, 454, 455, 457, 458, 461, 463, 467, 468, 469, 471, 472, 527, 572, 573, 574, 577, 582, 583, 585, 586, 698, 719, 727, 740, 783, 785, 786, 789, 790, 791, 793, 806, 821, 825, 861, 865, 875, 906
McCloskey, D., 125
McCloskey, M., 359
McClurkin, J. W., 246
McConkie, G. W., 250, 335
McCormick, P. A., 336
McDermott, J., 400
McDermott, K. B., 268, 620, 623, 624, 626, 629, 633, 634, 635
McDermott, M., 625
McEvoy, C. M., 672
McGeorge, P., 755, 767
McGill, J., ix, 574
McGinnies, E., 145
McGlinchey-Berroth, R., 60, 353, 648
McGown, C. M., 283
McKenzie, B. E., 885
McKoon, G., 631, 701, 702, 703, 709
McLachlan, D., 624, 629, 630, 631, 666
McLachlan, D. R., 641, 643
McLaren, I. P. L., 890, 901, 904, 906
McLennan, H., 96
McLeod, P., 328
McLeod, P. D., 328, 405
McMullen, P. A., 518, 523
McNamara, T. P., 701, 709

McNeil, J. E., 163
McPeek, R. M., 577
McWeeney, K. H., 155, 160
McWeeny, H. H., 204
Meadows, J. C., 161, 163
Measso, G., 482, 486
Medin, D. L., 698, 786, 813, 877
Mehta, Z., 522
Meregalli, S., 378
Merhav, I., 492
Merikle, P., 23, 701
Merikle, P. M., 145, 146, 552, 553, 640, 838
Mervis, C., 698, 707
Meudell, P. R., 160, 625, 630, 631
Meuter, R. F. I., 448
Meyer, D. E., 19, 25, 268, 270, 271, 273, 274, 275, 276, 280, 282, 283, 284, 285, 286, 287
Meyer, T. F., 325
Michalewski, H. J., 402
Michalski, A., 85
Miezin, F., 639
Miezin, F. M., 239
Mikami, A., 94
Miki, L., 687
Milberg, W., 624, 627, 630, 648, 662
Milberg, W. P., 60, 353
Miliken, B., 627
Millar, K., 640
Miller, B. D., 351
Miller, D. L., 861, 864, 872, 875
Miller, D. T., 698
Miller, E. K., 85
Miller, G. A., ix, 686
Miller, J., 483
Millward, R., 755
Milner, A. D., 236, 237, 352, 773
Milner, B., x, 411, 412, 620, 625, 648
Milner, B. M., 740
Milner, P. M., 84
Milosavljevic, M., 119
Mindel, T. A., 407
Mine, S., 236
Minsky, M., 572
Mintun, M., 213
Mintun, M. A., 212, 213, 638, 639
Mishkin, M., 80, 96, 205, 232, 235, 237, 647, 892
Mistlin, A. J., 80
Mitchell, D. B., 625, 629, 683
Mitchison, G., 22, 27
Mizuno, Y., 166, 167, 172
Mogilner, A., 93

Mohler, C. W., 246, 247, 334–335, 335
Molloy, R. D., 726
Monheit, M. A., 40, 58, 63, 65, 66, 313, 326, 352, 353
Monsell, S., 179, 403, 406, 411, 717
Montaron, M. F., 93
Montaron, M. P., 93
Monteleone, D., 165
Montgomery, M., 409, 410
Montgomery, M. W., 528, 529
Moore, C., 179, 181, 196, 627
Moossy, J., 510
Morais, J., 318
Moran, J., 78, 80, 241
Morasso, P., 269, 282, 287
Mordkoff, J. T., 483, 489
Moreines, J., 634
Morris, C. D., 634, 693
Morris, H. H., 154, 155
Morris, L. R., 146
Morris, R. G., 407
Morrow, L. A., 313, 326
Mortara, F., 236
Mortensen, E. L., 625
Morton, J., 154, 180, 183, 572, 624, 626, 627, 633, 634, 689, 714
Moscovitch, M., xii, 38, 39, 65, 69, 164, 168, 352, 369, 413, 620, 624, 626, 629, 630, 631, 632, 633, 634, 635, 636, 637, 638, 639, 640, 641, 642, 643, 644, 645, 647, 648, 649, 666, 682, 773, 805, 820
Moss, A., 154, 155
Mouloua, M., 244
Mountcastle, V. B., 82, 83, 236
Moushon, M. A., 82
Movellan, J. R., 463, 469
Moyer, R. S., 426
Mozer, M., 65, 168, 352
Mozer, M. C., 65, 574
Mukhametov, L. M., 256
Mul, N. M., 743
Mulder, G., 146
Mulder, L. J. M., 146
Muller, H. J., 242, 244, 251, 312, 313, 336
Mulligan, N., 633
Mullin, P. A., 482, 483
Munk, M., 85, 88, 95
Munk, M. H. J., 88
Munro, P. W., 795
Munroe, P., 92
Munsterberg, H., 143
Murata, A., 236
Murre, J. M. J., 731

Murthy, V. N., 93, 94, 95, 98, 100
Musen, G., 624, 629, 630, 632
Mussa-Ivaldi, F. A., 267, 270
Musunoki, M., 236
Mutani, R., 236
Mutter, S., 775

Nagle, M., 284, 285
Naito, M., 683
Nakamura, K., 94
Nakamura, Y., 12
Navon, D., 472
Neary, D., 509
Nebes, R. D., 511
Neely, J. H., 27, 701, 702, 703
Neill, W. T., 719, 726
Neipel, M., 143, 144
Neisser, U., 145
Nelson, D., 672
Nelson, J. I., 10, 88
Nemire, K., 276
Nertimpi, T., 514
Neuenschwander, S., 85, 93, 94
Neumann, O., 123, 126, 127, 143, 144, 311, 433, 668, 700
Neville, H. J., 555
Newcombe, F., 47, 48, 49, 51, 52, 154, 155, 161, 162, 163, 164, 166, 167, 168, 204, 206, 514, 523, 640
Newell, A., 398, 399, 400, 401, 403
Newport, E. L., 884
Newsome, W. T., 80, 82
Nichelli, P., 163, 624, 648
Nicoletti, R., 405, 431
Nielson, J. M., 512
Niepel, M., 123, 127, 143
Nishihara, H. K., 180, 367, 369, 370
Nishikawa, T., 378
Nissen, M., 755, 760, 771, 774, 775
Nissen, M. J., 335, 646, 648, 755, 759, 760, 774, 775, 784, 822, 825, 827, 828, 852, 853, 854, 855, 856
Nobel, M. E., 405
Nobre, A. C., 559
Norman, D. A., 398, 401, 431
Nosofsky, R. M., 813, 877
Nowak, L., 96
Nunn, M. B., 128
Nyman, G., 233, 234

Oakson, G., 89
Ochipa, C., 528, 529
Oden, G. C., 698
Ogawa, M., 166, 167, 172
O'Hara, R., 5, 17
O'Hara, W. P., 146
Ohlsson, S., 13, 23
Ohta, N., 628, 629
Ohta, S., 154, 204, 205, 208, 215, 221
Oja, E., 183
Ojemann, J., 639
Okuda, J.-I., 378
Olds, E. M., 578, 580, 584, 586
Oliphant, G. W., 642
Oliver, W. L., 398, 399
Ono, H., 334
Oram, M. W., 154, 187
O'Reilley, R. C., 40, 53, 54, 56, 64, 65
Orsini, A., 67
Oscar-Berman, M., 624, 630, 726
Osherson, D. N., 877
Osman, A., 473
Ostergaard, A. L., 662
Oth, J. E., 672
O'Toole, A. J., 197
Overson, C., 11
Owen, A. M., 407, 412, 413, 648
Oxbury, J., 60, 65, 238, 353
Oxbury, S., 60, 65, 238, 353, 510

Pacteau, C., 0, 10, 786, 813, 821, 823, 825, 827, 832
Paillard, J., 271
Paiusco, E., 304, 306, 308
Paivio, A., 6, 18, 626
Paller, K. A., 160, 625, 630, 631
Pallos, I., 128
Palm, G., 82, 83
Palmer, C., 409, 410
Pandya, D. N., 233, 242, 244
Pantev, C., 93
Papagno, C., 165, 168
Papert, S., 572
Papini, M. R., 813
Pare, D., 89
Pare, E. B., 80
Parker, K., 19
Parkin, A., 683
Parkin, A. J., 518, 640, 682, 726
Parmelee, C., 161
Parmelee, C. M., 161, 707
Parry, F. M., 154, 155
Pashler, H., 404, 407
Passingham, R. E., 647
Patterson, J. V., 402
Patterson, K., 510, 586, 639

Patterson, K. E., 5, 67
Paul, I. H., 11, 22
Pavesi, G., 238, 252
Payne, D. G., 4, 5, 6, 16, 24, 26, 27
Payne, M., 624, 629, 647
Pearlstone, Z., 14, 16
Pearson, D. E., 188, 189
Pedotti, A., 235
Pelisson, D., 285
Pennington, B. F., 571, 572
Pentland, A., 197
Perani, D., 165, 168, 371, 378, 386
Perenin, M.-T., 286
Perkel, D. H., 88
Perlmutter, J. S., 213
Perret, E., 413
Perrett, D. I., 80, 154, 236
Perrett, D. I. P., 187
Perruchet, P., 10, 755, 764, 766, 769, 770, 776, 784, 786, 813, 821, 822, 823, 825, 827, 832, 852, 855, 856
Peruchet, P., 755, 769, 770
Peters, A. M., 639
Peters, T. M., 212
Petersen, S., 639
Petersen, S. E., 215, 217, 218, 223, 238, 239, 422
Peterson, C., 469
Peterson, M. A., 179, 181
Peterson, S. E., 291, 414, 638, 639
Petrides, M., 414, 740
Petrone, P. N., 371
Petronio, A., 252, 366, 367, 370
Phaf, R. H., 470, 471, 472, 474, 725, 726, 727, 728, 730, 731, 733, 734, 735, 742, 747, 839
Phelps, M. E., 307
Phillips, L. J., 245
Phillips, W. A., 92
Pickering, A. D., 625, 645
Picton, T. W., 554
Pieczulo, A., 529
Pierce, L., 245
Pierrard, E., 47, 161, 162
Pierson, J. M., 325
Pietrini, V., 514
Pigarev, I. N., 233, 234
Pike, R., 857
Pillon, B., 409
Pillsbury, W. B., 706
Pine, F., 11
Pineda, F. J., 469
Pinheiro, W. M., 244, 252

Pinker, S., 244, 746, 863
Pinna, V., 514
Pisa, M., 247, 248
Plaut, D., 369, 574, 575, 586
Plaut, D. C., 55, 69, 414
Plunkett, K., 864
Poeck, K., 509, 510, 532
Poggio, T., 92
Poldrack, R. A., 845
Polit, A., 268, 269, 282, 283
Polkey, C. E., 412, 413, 639, 647, 648
Pollack, J. B., 864
Pollatsek, A., 61, 307, 336, 571
Poncet, M., 162, 164, 204, 205, 206, 223
Pontefract, A., 257, 307, 334, 347
Poppel, E., 41, 93
Posner, M. I., ix, 7, 19, 61, 161, 162, 215, 217, 218, 223, 238, 239, 240, 242, 244, 291, 295, 296, 297, 304, 305, 306, 307, 308, 309, 311, 312, 325, 326, 334, 335, 338, 346, 347, 351, 354, 366, 367, 371, 396, 414, 422, 431, 432, 456, 459, 460, 461, 638, 639, 668, 698, 701, 704, 727, 739, 747
Possamai, C. A., 244
Postman, L., 586
Postman, L. J., 672
Potemken, L., 325
Potter, M. C., 716, 717
Potts, G. R., 701
Prablanc, C., 252, 285
Pratkanis, A. R., 839
Pratt, H., 402
Presti, D., 432
Pribram, K., ix
Price, D. J., 91
Prinz, W., 123, 126
Prochiantz, A., 96
Proctor, R. W., 128, 553
Proffitt, D. R., 285
Pullman, S. L., 407

Quigley, H. A., 119
Quillian, M. R., 512
Quinlan, P. T., 517
Quinn, J. T., Jr., 269, 282
Quinn, N., 647
Quinn, N. P., 407, 413

Raab, E., 123, 125
Raaijmakers, J. G. W., 27
Rabbitt, P. M. A., 242, 313
Rabinowicz, B., 639

Rabinowitz, J. C., 5, 18
Raccuglia, R. A., 747
Raether, A., 85, 86, 94
Rafal, R., 43, 44, 45
Rafal, R. D., 244, 296, 297, 304, 307, 313, 325, 366, 367, 370, 371, 459, 460, 461, 511, 532
Raichle, M., 639
Raichle, M. E., 208, 212, 213, 215, 217, 218, 223, 638, 639
Rajaram, S., 702
Ramus, S., 774
Ramus, S. J., 646, 648, 827, 828
Rapcsak, S. Z., 626, 631
Rapoport, S. I., 205
Rapp, B. C., 529
Rappold, V. A., 15
Ratcliff, G., 522
Ratcliff, R., 631, 701, 702, 703, 709, 712, 742
Raushercker, J., 90
Rayman, J., 479
Rayner, K., 250, 307, 335, 336
Read, J. D., 839
Reason, J. T., 410
Reber, A., 759, 772
Reber, A. S., 10, 755, 756, 757, 761, 764, 765, 771, 783, 784, 785, 786, 787, 798, 803, 804, 807, 811, 812, 820, 824, 827, 831, 837, 843, 861
Reber, M. I., x
Reboul-Lachaux, J., 169
Rectem, D., 47, 161, 162
Reed, E. S., 409, 410
Rees-Nishio, M., 624, 629
Regard, M., 66, 155
Regehr, G., 19
Reichle, M. E., 238
Reid, I., 169
Reid, T., 640
Reingold, E. M., 145, 640, 838
Reinman, E. M., 213
Reinmuth, O. M., 510
Reisberg, D., 17, 312, 325
Reitboeck, H. J., 85, 88, 95
Remington, R., 245, 333
Remington, R. W., 335, 336
Rescorla, R. A., 813
Reuter-Lorenz, P. A., 244, 249, 251, 336, 337
Revello, M. G., 514
Rhodes, G., 187, 907
Ribary, U., 93
Richardson-Klavehn, A., 551, 584, 620, 662, 725
Richmond, B. J., 248

Riddoch, J., 774
Riddoch, M. J., 163, 351, 366, 367, 510, 517, 522
Riegler, G. H., 626
Riggio, L., 242, 243, 244, 249, 250, 251, 252, 307, 333, 336, 345, 346
Rips, L. J., 532
Risse, G., 624, 630, 631
Rizzo, A., 413
Rizzo, M., 161
Rizzolatti, G., 233, 234, 235, 236, 238, 239, 242, 243, 244, 246, 247, 248, 249, 250, 251, 252, 256, 257, 307, 333, 336, 345, 346, 353, 378, 408, 409, 433
Robbins, T. W., 407, 412, 413, 648
Robert, W., 22
Roberts, A. D., 187
Roberts, J., 160, 625, 630, 631
Roberts, T., 155
Robertson, I., 366
Robertson, L. C., 492–493
Robinson, D. L., 246
Robinson, J. A., 188, 189
Rocha-Miranda, E. C., 78, 80
Roediger, H. L., 5, 6, 16, 27, 268, 565, 584, 585, 620, 623, 624, 626, 627, 628, 629, 633, 634, 635, 641, 664, 668, 669, 683, 684, 726, 755, 756, 812, 828
Rogers, R., 406, 411
Roland, P. E., 408
Roll, R., 271
Rolls, E. T., 78, 80, 94
Romani, C., 529
Romero, R. D., 459
Romney, D. M., 170
Roorda-Hrdlickova, V., 726
Rosch, E., 698, 707
Rosen, B., 93
Rosenberg, C., 574
Rosenbloom, P., 401
Rosenbloom, P. S., 399
Ross, B. H., 813
Rothbart, M. J., 727, 739, 747
Rothbart, M. K., 296, 304, 305, 306, 308, 309, 414
Rothi, L. J. G., 528, 529
Rougeul, A., 93, 100
Rozin, P., x, 619, 624, 628, 630, 633
Rubens, A. B., 378, 552, 626, 631
Rueckl, J. G., 577, 578, 580, 584, 586
Rugg, M. D., 555, 773
Rumelhart, D. E., 24, 527, 572, 573, 583, 586, 740, 786, 806, 906
Rusconi, L. L., 61, 66

Rusconi, M. L., 165, 352, 377, 378, 382, 384, 386, 387, 390
Rushton, J. P., 22
Russo, R., 640, 726
Ryan, C., 397
Ryan, L., 685, 689, 691

Sacchett, C., 519
Saffran, E., 67, 773
Saffran, E. M., 12, 67, 509, 510, 512, 531, 532, 638, 639
Sagi, D., 92
Sahakian, B. J., 407, 412, 413, 648
Saint-Cyr, J. A., 648
Sakamoto, M., 247
Sakata, H., 236
Sakitt, B., 268, 282
Sakurai, E., 479
Salasoo, A., 586, 698, 707
Salin, P. A., 88
Salmon, D. P., 635, 639, 645, 646, 647, 648
Salzman, C. O., 82
Sanders, A. F., 405
Sanders, M., 577
Sanders, M. D., 41, 42
Sanderson, K. J., 118
Sanderson, P., 768
Sanderson, P. M., 825, 848
Sandroni, P., 377, 386
Sands, S. F., 892
Sanes, J. D., 407
Santucci, R., 313, 326
Sartori, G., 514, 522
Sasaki, I., 845
Saul, J. S. M., 154, 155
Savy, I., 769, 822, 823, 825, 855, 856
Sawyers, B. K., 16
Sax, D. S., 624, 629, 647
Scandolara, C., 233, 234
Scarborough, D. L., 179, 629, 630, 702, 714
Scarborough, H., 702, 714
Scarborough, H. L., 179
Scarborough, H. S., 630
Schacter, D., 352
Schacter, D. L., 38, 39, 69, 164, 179, 181, 196, 551, 552, 584, 585, 620, 623, 624, 626, 627, 628, 630, 631, 635, 639, 640, 641, 643, 644, 645, 662, 681, 682, 685, 694, 701, 726, 756, 773, 812, 828, 837, 838, 842, 857
Schaffer, M. M., 786, 877
Schapiro, M. B., 205
Scheiber, R., 325
Scheich, H., 82

Schein, S. J., 78, 80
Schell, A. M., 844
Schiano, D. J., 325
Schillen, T. B., 89, 95
Schiller, P. H., 45, 124, 125, 236, 291, 293, 335
Schmidt, R. A., 269, 282, 283
Schneider, W., 83, 144, 240, 241, 396, 397, 398, 399, 403, 428, 431, 432, 449, 711
Schneiderman, M., 863
Schooler, J. W., 13, 23
Schor, R. E., 428
Schreuder, R., 524, 525
Schulman, A. I., 894
Schuster, H. G., 89, 95
Schvaneveldt, R. W., 19
Schwartz, A. B., 269, 270, 282
Schwartz, B., 17
Schwartz, B. L., 638
Schwartz, H., 12
Schwartz, M. F., 409, 410, 509, 510, 511, 512, 528, 529, 532
Sciolto, T. K., 244, 297, 304
Seamon, J. G., 640, 644
Searle, J. R., 829
Sebastian, J. A., 894
Segraves, M. A., 233
Seibel, R., 414
Seidenberg, M. S., 572, 574, 577, 582, 583, 585
Seiple, W., 119
Sejnowski, T. J., 55, 574
Seltzer, B., 233
Semenza, C., 155, 528
Sepe, O., 67
Serdaru, M., 409
Sergent, J., 154, 162, 164, 168, 204, 205, 206, 208, 211, 215, 217, 219, 220, 221, 222, 223, 225, 492
Seron, X., 47, 161, 162
Serrat, A., 66
Servan-Schreiber, D., 457, 458, 459, 461, 740, 791, 821, 865
Servan-Schreiber, E., 772, 785, 798, 804, 806
Shaffer, M. M., 813
Shaffer, W. O., 553
Shallice, T., ix, 66, 67, 69, 328, 398, 401, 402, 411, 412, 413, 414, 431, 512, 513, 514, 518, 520, 521, 526, 572, 574, 575, 576, 577, 586, 638, 639, 648, 773
Shanks, D. R., 813, 830, 832, 843, 847
Shannon, B., 524
Shebliske, W. L., 285
Sheer, D. E., 93, 100

Shephard, M., 307
Shepherd, J. W., 187
Shepherd, M., 244, 250, 251, 333, 337, 346, 347
Shepherd, R. N., 894
Sheridan, J., 514, 517, 518, 522
Sheridan, M. R., 407
Sherman, J., 716, 717
Shiffrin, R., 586
Shiffrin, R. M., 27, 144, 240, 241, 395, 396, 397, 428, 431, 449, 553, 698, 707, 738
Shimamura, A. P., 624, 626, 628, 631, 632, 634, 639, 645, 648, 662, 670, 671, 682, 701
Shinhoj, E., 408
Shoben, E. J., 532
Shulman, F. L., 239
Shults, C. W., 635, 639
Sidhu, X., 633
Siegel, R. M., 233, 234
Sieroff, E., 61
Signoret, J.-L., 154, 204, 205, 206, 217, 219, 220, 222, 223, 225
Silveri, M. C., 165, 514, 522
Simion, F., 304, 306, 308, 405, 431
Simon, H. A., 400, 401, 861, 877
Singer, W., 40, 82, 83, 85, 86, 87, 90–91, 92, 94, 96, 98, 99, 100
Singh, K. D., 93
Sintes, J., 325
Skarda, C. A., 93
Slade, R., 552
Slamecka, N. J., 667
Slater, A., 885
Slater, P. C., 625
Sloman, S. A., 628, 629, 685
Smid, H. G. O. M., 126, 146
Smith, E. E., 532, 698
Smith, J., 43, 44, 45, 313
Smith, J. E. K., 270, 271, 273, 274, 280, 282
Smith, L. S., 92
Smith, M. C., 555, 717, 726
Smith, M. E., 624, 630, 726
Smith, M. L., 740
Smith, S., 645
Smith, S. M., 8, 17, 24, 693
Smith, Y. M., 44
Smothergill, D. W., 713
Sno, H. N., 171
Snoddy, G. S., 401
Snodgrass, J. G., 508, 517, 523, 627, 666
Snowden, J. S., 509
Snyder, C. R., 335, 338

Snyder, C. R. F., 242
Snyder, C. R. R., ix, 161, 162, 396, 668, 701, 704
Soechting, J. F., 268, 269, 271
Solomon, R., 586
Spangenberg, E. R., 839
Sparks, D. L., 269, 270, 283
Sparrow, L., 325
Spector, A., 406, 422, 433, 436
Spence, C. J., 312
Spence, D. P., 22
Spencer, M. B. H., 242
Sperber, R., 161
Sperber, R. D., 161, 707
Sperling, A., 143, 272, 284
Sperling, G., 395
Sprague, J. M., 246
Spreen, O., 205
Spydell, J. D., 93
Squire, L., 52, 774
Squire, L. R., x, 27, 620, 624, 625, 626, 627, 628, 629, 630, 631, 632, 634, 635, 638, 639, 646, 647, 648, 661, 670, 701, 822, 827, 828
Squire, R., 553
Srinivas, K., 627, 684
St. John, M. F., 701, 830, 832, 843
Stadler, M., 761
Stadler, M. A., 626, 822, 855, 856
Standen, P., 626
Stanley, W., 757, 763, 764, 765, 771
Stanley, W. B., 755, 759, 762, 767, 804, 821, 837, 848, 849
Stark, H. A., 628, 662, 685, 694
Starr, A., 402
Ste-Marie, D., 668
Stein, B. E., 257
Stein, B. S., 634
Stein, J. B., 5
Steriade, M., 89
Sterinman, R. J., 428
Sternberg, S., 396, 406
Sterzi, R., 390
Stewart, F., 518
Stigler, R., 124
Stob, M., 877
Stoerig, P., 42, 43, 45
Stone, G. O., 571, 572
Strawson, C., 577
Strick, P. L., 307
Stroop, J. R., 146, 453
Strycker, M., 335
Stryker, M. P., 91
Strypstein, E., 161, 162

Stuss, D. T., 169, 414
Stypstein, E., 47
Subramaniam, B., 337, 347
Summers, B. A., 407, 413
Sundstroem, G., 627, 634
Sussman, G. J., 411
Suyenobu, B., 477, 478, 479
Svartdal, F., 846
Sweeney, M., 667
Swets, J. A., 664

Tagliabue, M. E., 405, 431
Taira, M., 236
Talairach, J., 213
Talmachoff, P. J., 93
Tamecki, R., 85
Tanabe, H., 378
Tanaka, K., 85
Tanaka, Y., 166, 167, 172
Tanenhaus, M. K., 577
Tanner, W. P., 664
Tappe, Th., 123, 127, 143, 144
Tassinari, C., 42
Tassinari, G., 244, 249, 250
Tassinary, L., 552
Taylor, A. E., 648
Taylor, H. M., 638
Taylor, T. L., 125
Terazzi, E., 236
Tesser, A., 10
Teuber, H.-L., 625
Tharan, M., 179, 181, 552, 626, 631
Theios, J., 717
Theodore, L., 555
Theurkauf, J. C., 528
Thomas, L., 432
Thomaz, T. G., 244, 252
Thompson, G. C., 312
Thompson, K. M., 160, 625, 630, 631
Thomson, D. M., 168, 670
Thorpe, L. A., 5
Thurlow, W. R., 320
Tipper, S. P., 252, 312, 354, 368, 370, 371, 411, 719
Titchener, E. B., 242, 247
Todd, I. A., 892
Toglia, J. U., 414
Toni, I., 234
Tootell, H. E., 885
Toth, J. P., 663, 666, 668, 677
Tournoux, P., 213
Tovee, M. J., 94
Toyama, K., 85
Tradardi, V., 256

Tranel, D., 46, 161, 204, 205, 218, 223, 224
Tranel, E., x, 640
Treiman, R., 863
Treisman, A., 27, 240, 311, 354, 368, 472, 553, 629
Treisman, A. M., 240, 311, 328, 472
Tresselt, M. E., 124
Trethowan, W. H., 170
Trevarten, C., 109, 110
Troscianko, T., 163, 774
Trumbo, D. A., 405
Tsal, Y., 311
Ts'o, D., 85
Tsung, F. S., 740, 746
Tulving, E., 6, 16, 507, 552, 585, 624, 627, 628, 629, 634, 635, 642, 643, 644, 645, 662, 670, 685, 694, 700, 701, 703
Turk, M., 197
Turkewitz, G., 884
Tyler, L., 774

Uleman, J. S., x, 10
Umiltà, C., xii, 242, 243, 244, 249, 250, 251, 252, 304, 306, 307, 308, 333, 336, 345, 346, 366, 367, 370, 405, 431, 636, 637
Underwood, B. J., 894
Underwood, G., 146, 553
Ungerleider, L. G., 78, 80, 205, 232, 235, 237
Usui, S., 247

Vaadia, E., 94, 95
Vaglia, A., 514
Valdes, L. A., 719
Valentine, T., 154, 157, 159, 160, 182, 183, 185, 891, 908
Valenza, E., 304, 306, 308
Vallar, G., 165, 168, 237, 351, 377, 386, 390
Van Allen, M. W., 205
Van den Bergh, O., 844, 845
van der Heijden, A. H. C., 146, 311, 470, 471, 472, 474, 489, 727, 735
Vanderwart, M., 517, 523
Van Essen, D. C., 80, 109, 110, 232, 292
Van Hoessen, G. W., 414
Van Kleek, M. H., 492
Van Lancker, D., 171
Van Orden, G. C., 571, 572, 586
Van Petten, C., 555
Varela, F. J., 85, 93, 94
Vargha-Khadem, F., 639
Varney, N., 205
Vaughan, J., 296, 297
Vecchi, A., 624, 648
Vecera, S. P., 40, 53, 54, 56, 64, 65

Vela, E., 17, 24
Velay, J.-L., 271
Velmans, M., x
Verfaellie, M., 60, 353, 624, 625, 629, 630, 667
Vevera, S., 296
Videen, T., 639
Vighetto, A., 286
Vignolo, L. A., 529
Villardi, K., 268, 279
Villemure, J.-G., 163, 168
Virzi, R. A., 472
Visciola, M., 413
Vokey, J., 763, 764
Vokey, J. R., 698, 784, 786, 805, 814, 820, 821, 839
Volpe, B. T., 58, 59, 60, 62, 238, 352, 377, 378
Von Bonin, G., 233
von der Malsburg, C., 82, 83
Vriezen, E., 620, 626, 638, 639, 645, 647, 648, 682

Waessle, H., 109, 110
Wagner, A. R., 813
Wagner, P., 89, 95
Walicke, P. A., 635, 639
Walk, R. D., 899
Walker, J. A., 297, 307, 459, 460, 461
Wallace, M. A., 40, 53, 58, 63, 65, 66, 352, 353, 369
Wallas, G., 7, 27
Wallesch, C. W., 413, 414
Walling, J. R., 672
Wally, R. E., 706
Wang, G., 523
Wapner, S., 327
Warren, C., 180, 183
Warrington, E. K., 27, 66, 154, 163, 205, 206, 224, 352, 509, 510, 511, 512, 518, 519, 521, 524, 526, 527, 624, 625, 628, 638, 639, 661, 662, 857
Wasserman, E. A., 813
Waters, G. S., 577
Watkins, M. J., 643, 742
Watson, R. T., 351
Watts, A. W., 24
Watts, R. L., 407
Waugh, N. C., 436, 442
Weaver, B., 312, 354, 368, 370, 371
Weiden, T. D., 706
Weimer, W., 334
Weinberg, J., 378, 386
Weinstein, E., 352

Weinstein, S., 877
Weintraub, D. J., 127
Weiskrantz, L., x, 12, 27, 41, 42, 624, 625, 628, 661, 662, 773, 857
Weisstein, N., 124
Welch, J., 165, 168, 169, 368, 378
Weldon, M. S., 626, 634, 664, 669
Welford, A. T., 404
Werner, H., 124
Wescourt, K. T., 15
Wessinger, C. M., 44
Wessinger, M., 432
Westbrook, G. L., 96
Wetzel, C. D., 625
Wexler, K., 863
Wheeldon, L., 895
Wheeles, L., Jr., 245
White, H., 479
Whitehouse, K., 552, 561, 565
Whitehouse, P., 531
Whitlow, J. W., 586
Whitmarsh, G. A., 672
Whittington, D. A., 312
Whittlesea, B., 821, 822, 826, 830
Whittlesea, B. W., 578, 580, 584
Wickens, D. D., 472
Wiesel, T. N., 85, 91
Wilhelmsen, A., 704
Williams, R. J., 740, 786
Willingham, D., 646, 648, 755, 760, 771, 774, 775, 825, 827
Willingham, D. B., 822, 825, 828, 852, 853, 854, 855, 856
Willmer, J, 414
Wilson, J., 553
Wingfield, A., 528
Winocur, G., 624, 629, 630, 631, 645, 649, 666
Winzenz, D., 16
Wise, S. P., 409
Witherspoon, D., 625, 634, 635, 636, 638
Witkin, H. A., 327
Wlaker, J. A., 366, 367, 371
Wolbarst, L. R., 624, 630
Wolfe, J., 648
Wolford, G., 552
Woloshyn, V., 627, 640
Wolters, G., 726, 728, 731, 839
Wolters, N. C. W., 325
Wong, A. B., 313, 326, 369
Wood, B., 553
Wood, C. C., 555, 558
Wood, F., 511, 648
Woodward, D. P., 244

Woodworth, R. S., 19, 271, 907
Worden, P. E., 17
Wright, A. A., 892
Wright, C. E., 270, 271, 273, 274, 280, 282
Wright, S., 169
Wundt, W., 142
Wurtz, R., 246, 247
Wurtz, R. H., 246, 247, 248, 334–335
Wyke, M., 647

Yachzel, B., 716, 717
Yamane, S., 94
Yaniv, I., 19, 25
Yantis, S., 242, 333, 483
Yarney, A. D., 180, 183
Yeh, Y., 366
Yonelinas, A. P., 663, 666, 667, 677
Yoshida, M., 166, 167, 172
Young, A., 47, 48, 49, 51, 52, 154, 155, 158, 159, 162, 163, 164, 181, 182, 184, 185, 640, 774
Young, A. M., 187
Young, A. W., 47, 50, 51, 52, 154, 155, 158, 160, 162, 163, 164, 169, 171, 182, 183, 184, 186, 187, 197, 203, 204, 206, 223, 352, 368, 378, 514, 523, 625, 627, 630, 631
Young, M. P., 94
Young, R. A., 245

Zaidel, D. W., 492
Zaidel, E., 477, 478, 479, 482, 486, 492, 493, 495, 496, 497, 639
Zajonc, R. B., 163, 640
Zechmeister, E. B., 894
Zeki, S., 213
Zelaznik, H., 269, 282
Zettin, M., 155, 528
Zimba, L. D., 244
Zimmerman, P., 414
Zipser, D., 795
Zouzounis, J. A., 624, 635
Zuck, E., 208, 211
Zuffante, P., 624, 629

# Subject Index

Abstraction, 785–786, 804, 813, 819–824
Abstractionist model, 819–824
Acoustic system, 82
Activation, 14–16, 26
  explicit, 15
  implicit, 15
  processes, 15
  state-of-the-world (SOW), 15
Activation/elaboration, 633–634
Activation/integration, 14–16
  increased familiarity, 15
  perceptual fluency, 15
Activation learning, 375, 726, 727, 732, 733
Affective processing, 747
Agnosia, 638–640
Aimed limb movements, 281–286
  equilibrium-point model, 282
  eye movement mechanisms, 283–284
  feedback, 283
  glissade, 284
  impulse-variability model, 282
  motor system, 284–286
  optic ataxia, 286
  perceptual system, 284–286
  visual-spatial information, 282–286
Alexia, pure, 37, 38, 66–70
  disconnection account, 66
  visual impairment hypothesis, 66
  word form hypothesis, 66
Alzheimer's disease, 511, 627, 639, 645
Ambiguity, 589–591, 595–605. *See also* Ambiguity resolution; Syntactic ambiguity
  lexical, 590
    constraint-based models, 591
    modular filtering models, 590–591
  syntactic, 591–597
    constraint-based models, 592
    main clause/reduced relative clause, 592–593
    modular models, 592
    semantic fit, effects of, 593–597
Ambiguity resolution, 589–590. *See* Ambiguity
  cognitive architecture, 589–590
  constraint-based systems, 590
  language comprehension, 589–590
Amnesia, 774
Anomia, 508, 511
Anosognosia, 168, 171
ANOVA, 214, 219, 299, 300, 318, 323, 324, 600–602
Antisaccades, 252
Aphasia, 508, 518–519
Arousal, 496, 498
Arousal node, 731
Artifact explanation, 44
Artificial grammar learning, 755, 756–757, 772, 773, 785, 811, 820, 825, 827
Artificial neural networks, 874. *See* Neural networks
Artificial subject (AS), 734–735
Assemblies, 82–86
  coding, 82, 84
  connections, 83–84
  covariance of responses, 85
  excitatory input, 85
  inhibitory input, 85
  segregated, 88
  temporal, 84
Associative context, 670–676
  associative priming, 670
  automatic influences on, 670–676
  cued recall, 671
  divided-attention condition, 673–675
  full-attention condition, 673–675
  process-dissociation procedure, 673–675
  strategic influences on, 670–676
Associative repetition priming, 631–633, 670. *See* Priming; Repetition priming

Atkinson and Shiffrin model, 396–397
Attention, 99–101, 232, 250–255, 311–313, 314–328, 337–347, 351, 354, 453–473, 551–565, 726–727, 728–736. *See also* Attentional effects; Attentional mechanisms; Endogenous attention; Semantic processing; Spatial attention; Visual attention
 auditory, 311–313
 covert, 312
 cross-modal integration, 211–213
 cueing paradigm, 312, 313
 divided, 728–736
 endogenous, 312
 exogenous, 312
 object-based, 367, 368–370, 551–561
 parallel distributed processing (PDP) model, 454–456
 premotor theory of, 250–255, 337–347
 selective, 232, 311–313, 453–456
 spatial, 238–256
 visual, 311–313
Attentional effects, 457–461, 461–473. *See also* Attention
 bottom-up capture-of-attention, 461
 GRAIN model, 461, 467, 469
 interactive models, 467
 Stroop model, 461, 469
 top-down effects, 461
Attentional mechanisms, 99–101, 325–328, 453. *See also* Attention
 auditory and visual tasks, 326
 bottom-up capture-of-attention, 453
 cross-modal integration, 326
 spatial synergy, 326
 top-down effects of selective attention, 453
 unimodal systems, 325
Attentional tasks, 453–473
Attention shifting, 421. See Task set, semantic space
Attribute domains, 525–526
Attribution, 525–526
Auditory attention, 311–313
Automatic memory, 664–667, 668–669, 670–676, 677. *See also* Memory
Automatic processing, 123, 396–404. *See also* Controlled processing
 CAP model, 404
 in memory, 396–397
 Norman and Shallice model, 404
 Schneider and Shiffrin model, 402
 Soar model, 403
 Sternberg paradigm, 402

Automatic vs. deliberate use of memory, 824–829
Automaticity, 144, 683, 686, 700–702
 attention, 144
 awareness criterion, 144
 processing, 144
Autonoetic consciousness, 642, 643
Autonomous processes, 421. *See also* Task set
Awareness, 37, 38, 62, 142, 377, 551–552, 846–851
 in instrumental learning tasks, 846–851
 in serial reaction time tasks, 852–856
 visual, 37

Backpropagation, 399, 740, 741, 743, 790, 803, 880–882
Basal ganglia, 237
Binding, 79–82, 81
 by convergence hypothesis, 80
 dynamic, 82
 motor, 79–82
 problem, 79–82
 sensory, 79–82
 temporal, 82
Biographic memory, 205, 223. *See also* Memory
 familiarity decision, 206
Blindsight, 37, 41–46, 70–71
 extrastriate cortical mediation, 71
 mechanisms of, 44–46
 perception, 43
 preserved visual function, 41
 spectral sensitivity functions, 42
Brain, 477–500
 hemispheric control, 477–500
 hemispheric specialization, 477–500
Brain systems, 26, 38–41, 727, 745–748
Bruce-Young model, 185, 204
Buffer network, 795–798, 802

Callosal relay, 480
Capgras delusion, 169
CAP model, 398–399. *See also* Controlled processing
 control signal, 398
 processing layers, 398
 sequential rule network, 399
 three-layer backpropagation, 399
Cartoons, computer-drawn, 187–189
Categorization, 891, 900–906
 discrimination, 902, 903–905
 distinctiveness, 901

equivalence, 901
exemplars, 902, 903, 905, 906
prototypes, 903, 905
Categorizing and learning module (CALM), 731, 732–733, 742, 745
Category exemplar generation, 730
Category-specific deficits, 513–519
Category specificity, 517–518
Center-surround mechanism, 704–713. *See also* Knowledge
  associations, 709–710
  forced-choice categorization trials, 707–708
  inhibition, 713
  learning, intentional, 704
  priming, 704–705, 711
  unpracticed target exemplars, 712
  vocabulary learning, 705
Central executive, 633, 637
Central systems, 633, 637
Cerebral activation, 204
Cerebral blood flow, 238
Cerebral cortex, 205, 207, 226, 232–238, 739
  frontal, 232–238
  parietal, 232–238
  prefrontal, 232–238
  premotor, 232–238
Cerebral hemispheres, 477–484
  dominance, 477–484
  independence, 477–484
  redundant bilateral presentations (RBPs), 478
  specialization, 477–484
  unilateral presentations, 478–479
  unilateral versus redundant bilateral presentations, 479–482
Classifier systems, 773
Codes, mapping, 571
Cognitive control, 333–347
Cognitive neuropsychiatry, 169–170
Coherent states, 97–99
  sensory-motor cortex, 98
  simultaneous discharges, 98
  tuned connections, 98
Cohesion, 97–99
Collicular neurons, 248
Color naming, 427–430, 434–436, 453–456
Competitive chunking model, 773
Competitive learning, 731
Completion test, 631, 639, 662, 684
  word fragment, 662
  word stem, 631, 639, 684

Complex systems, control of, 755–759
  person interaction task, 758
  sugar production task, 758
  verbal instruction, 758
Computational modeling, 772–773, 786, 803
  backpropagation network, 803
  salient sequences, 803
  strategic readjustments, 803
Computerized tomography (CT), 378
Conceptual, item-specific tests, 645–646. *See also* Implicit memory
Conditioning, 843–845. *See also* Awareness
  evaluative, 844–845
  Pavlovian, 843–844
Confidence accuracy slope model, 776–777
Connectionism, 572–574, 585, 727, 732, 736, 737, 745, 747, 862, 864–873
  automatic, 572
  orthographic, 572
  phonological, 572, 573
  semantic, 572
  weighted, 572
Connectionist models, 574, 577, 772, 864–873
Connections, associative, 171
Conscious awareness, 38, 146. *See also* Awareness
Conscious awareness system (CAS), 38
Conscious information processing, 726
Consciousness, 20–21, 26, 38–41, 727, 745–748, 769, 770
  brain systems, 38–40
  discrimination, 133
  neural information processing, 40
  preconscious representation, 26
  recognition, 159–161
  recovered, 644
Conscious perception, 685, 688–693
Consolidation, 644
Constraint-based models, 590, 591, 592, 597–605
Construction process, 738–740, 741
Contention scheduling, 410–411
Context-CALM, 732–733
Continuous flow, 146
Continuous processing, 123
Contralesional, 386–387
  same/different judgment, 386
  tracing, effects of, 386–387
  vestibular stimulation, effects of, 386–387
Controlled processing, 395–397, 404–408, 409–414
  Atkinson and Shiffrin model, 396–397

Controlled processing (cont.)
  automatic detection and processing, 396–397
  bottleneck effects, 404–405
  CAP model, 398–399
  neuropsychological studies, 408–412
  Norman and Shallice model, 401–402
  paradigms of, 404–408, 405
  Parkinson's disease, 407
  Posner and Snyder model, 396–397
  Shiffrin and Schneider model, 396–397
  Soar model, 399–401
Control of tasks, 395–414, 767–768
Convergence, 82, 736–737
Cooperation, hemispheric, 481
Cortical development, 232–238, 637–638
Cotard delusion, 169
Covert orienting, 242
Covert recognition, 161–164. See also Recognition
Cross-modal integration, 326
Cued-recall test, 578–583, 662, 667, 670, 671, 682–686, 692
Cueing, 382–384, 389

Deep dyslexia, 575
Delayed matching to sample, 892
Delusions, 169
Dementia. See Semantic dementia
DICE (dissociated interactions and conscious experience), 38, 69
Dichotic listening task, 557
Differences, detection of, 386–387, 700–701
Direct access model, 478–479
Direct memory, 555–561, 620, 624, 627, 643–644, 662–663, 667, 676–677. See also Memory; Recollection
Direct parameter specification, 123, 127, 134, 137, 142–144, 146
  apperception, 142, 143
  complete reactions, 142
  dissociations, 143
  foreshortened reactions, 142
  implicit learning, 143
  implicit memory, 143
  S-R mappings, 143
Discrimination, 890, 892, 898, 899–900, 902, 903–905
  without awareness, 123, 145–146
Dissociated awareness, 70–72
Dissociation, 62–66, 143, 725–727, 747
  covert face recognition model, 64
  integration account, 63
  perceptual, 62–66
  privileged role account, 63
  quality of representation account, 63
  semantic priming, 64
  spatial, 143
  temporal, 143
Distance effect, 282–286
Distinctiveness, acquired, 901
Distributed organization, 573
Distributed representation, 573
Divided visual-field study, 211–212. See Hemispheric interaction and control
Dreams, 13, 21–22
  activation-synthesis hypothesis, 22
  biological function, 22
  hypermnesic content, 13
  memories, 13
Dual pathway model, 747
Dual process recognition, 685
Dual task performance, 323–324, 335
Duration, 628–629. See also Implicit memory

Ecphory, 644
Elaboration, 7, 14–16, 26, 685–686, 726, 727, 732, 747
  learning, 726, 727, 732
Elaborative processing, 685–686
Elaborative rehearsal, 747
Endogenous attention. See Attention
  spatial links in vision and audition, 213, 225
Episodic memory, 181, 507, 508. See Memory
Equilibrium point model, 282
Equivalence, acquired, 901
Error analyses, 141–142
Event-related potential (EPR), 377, 554–555
Evolution theory, 831–832
Excitatory connections, 159
Exclusion test, 664, 667, 670, 674
Exclusive-OR function (XOR), 874–877
Exemplar models, 772, 813, 820
Exemplars, 712, 783, 805, 813, 902, 903, 905, 906–907
Explicit knowledge, 756
Explicit memory, 620, 624, 627, 628, 631, 634, 643–644, 681–688, 725, 726, 728, 734, 748. See also Memory
External node, 731
Extinction, 55–66
Eye movement, 213–225, 244, 252, 270–271, 272–275, 276–281, 291–308, 337–342, 346, 594, 595
  control of, 291–308

detection accuracy, 335
endogenous control, 335
Meridian effect, 336, 337
smooth-pursuit, 271
Eye tracking, 594, 595

Face recognition, 153–154, 155, 189, 196, 204, 210–211, 891, 907–908. *See also* Faces
  exposure duration, effect of, 191
  expressions, processing of, 155
  format, effect of, 190, 193
  impairments in, 168
  lipreading, 155
  matching, 155
  Pearson-Robinson algorithm, 189
  representations, structural encoding of, 204
  semantic information, access, 205
Faces, 155, 186–187, 197, 203–209, 215, 221–223. *See also* Face recognition; Recognition
  appearance, structural encoding, 203
  covert recognition, 161–164
  distinctiveness, 186–187
  familiarity decision, 210, 215
  gender categorization, 210, 215
  identification, 182–184
  learning, 187
  neurofunctional organization, 221–223
  processing, 155, 225
  recognition, 46–48, 49, 50–55, 71
  semantic information, access to, 204
Facilitation, 713
Familiarity, 171, 206, 215, 683, 686, 888–889
  priming (*see* Priming)
  in prosopagnosic patients, 206
Familiarization, 890, 891, 896, 898, 906
Feedback, sequential, 739
Feedforward connections, 82
Fehrer-Raab metacontrast paradigm, 123, 125–127, 128, 142
  masking, 125
Forced choice measures, 766
Format specificity, 626, 633
Foveation, 312
Fragment completion, 624
Frame of reference, 367, 368–371
Free recall task, 728, 729–730
Frontal apraxia,
Frontal eye fields, 293, 306
Frontal lobes, 638, 639, 648
Functional knowledge, 697–720

Galvanic skin response, 841
Generalization, 900, 906
Geons, 180
Glissade, 284
Global effect, 279–281
Go/no-go, with cues, 484–490
GRAIN model, 457, 461, 462–473. *See also* Attention; Attentional effects; Stroop task
  asymmetry of weights, 463
  bidirectionality of connections, 463
  simulation, 463–466
  SOA effects, 466–467
Grammatical strings, 766
Grasp reflex, 410
Grouping criteria, 92
  biphasic modification rule, 92
  connections, 92

Hebbian learning rule, 735
Hemispatial neglect, 35–56, 366–371, 382–384. *See also* Neglect
  attentional deficit, 370–371
  attentional mechanisms, object-based, 367, 368–370
  counterintuitive pattern, 367
  facilitation, left-sided, 367
  frame of reference, 367, 368–371
  information, processing, 366
Hemispheric interaction and control, 479–482, 484–491
  redundant bilateral displays, 479–482, 484–491
Hippocampus, 632, 643–644
Hypermnesia, 3, 4–7, 5, 16–19, 25–26
  categorical, 18
  depth of processing, 6
  focal, 18
  imagery hypothesis, 5, 6
  memory, long-term, 5
  multidimensional, 18
  recall, 16
  reminiscence, 17

Identification, 11
Identification of pairs, 379–384
Imagery, 5–6
Immediate recall, 5
Imperative stimulus display, 129, 132
Implicit-explicit distinction, 756, 757, 771
Implicit learning, 755, 756, 762, 783–786, 811–814, 824, 837–843, 856–858, 861–863, 889–891. *See also* Rule learning

Implicit learning (cont.)
  abstract knowledge in adaptive behavior, 812
  generation task, 784
  knowledge-based model, 812
  paradigms, 811
  recognition tests, 784
  retrieval, 841–843
  simple recurrent network, 862
  subliminal stimuli, with, 838–839
  supraliminal stimuli, with, 839–841
  transfer, 784
  verbal protocols, 784
Implicit memory, 620, 621–623, 624, 628–633, 634, 681–688, 689, 692, 725, 728, 729, 732, 756. *See also* Indirect memory; Memory; Priming; Procedural tests; Repetition priming
  conceptual test, 621–623, 634, 635, 645–646
  item-specific, 621–623, 628–640
  ordered/rule-based, 621–623, 648–649
  perceptual test, 623–633, 633–640, 643
  procedural, 621–623, 646–649
Implicitness, 824–829. *See also* Implicit learning; Rule learning
  knowledge-based, 824–828
Implicit reading, 71
Implicit retrieval, 837, 841–843, 856–858. *See* Implicit learning
Inclusion test, 664, 667, 674
Incubation, 3, 7–9, 19–20, 25–26
  activation processes, 19, 20
  problem solving, 7, 19, 20
Indirect memory, 555–561, 620, 628–633, 662–663, 667, 676–677, 725. *See also* Implicit memory; Memory; Recollection
  fragment completion task, 662
  tests of, 620, 628–633, 662–663, 667, 676–677
  word stem completion task, 662
Induced motion. *See* Motion, induced
Infancy, 291–308, 883–885
Information processing, 366, 726
Inhibition, 367
Inhibitory connection, 731
Input domain, 158
Input module, 732, 743
Integration, 320, 685–686, 691
Intention, 10
Intentional set, 421. *See* Task set
Interactive activation and completion model (IAC), 158, 184–187
  Bruce-Young model, 185
  faces, 186–187

person identity nodes, 185
  priming, 184–185
Interactive processing. *See* Processing
Interference, 742
Irrelevant stimulus, 129
Item-specific memory, 621–623, 633–640, 643, 646–649
Item-specific tests, perceptual, 623–640. *See also* Implicit memory
  associative repetition priming, 631–633
  neocortical structures, 637–638
  novelty, 630–631
  objects and faces, 625
  parallel distributed processing (PDP) model, 454–456
  perception without awareness, 639–640
  perceptual input modules, 638–639
  processing theory, components of, 636–637
  registration, 637–638
  semantic manipulations, insensitivity, 628
  theories of, 633–640
  words, 624–625

Jordan network, 792–795, 798
  activation, 793
  choice reaction tasks, 795, 799
  explicit prediction task, 795
Judgments, 11

Knowledge, 697–720, 765–768, 823–824
  accessibility, 765–768
  automaticity of, 700–701
  conceptual, 697–698
  episodic, 699–719
  explicit, 756
  generic, 697–698
  implicit, 756
  priming, 702
  retrieval, 701
  semantic, 697–719
  unit, 823–824

Language, 589–590, 597–605, 863–873
  comprehension, 589–590, 597–605
  learning, 863–873
Latent inhibition, 890–891, 900, 901, 906–907
Lateral geniculate nucleus, 109
Learning, 863–873. *See also* Activation learning; Artificial grammar learning; Implicit learning; Perceptual learning; Rule learning; Unconscious learning
  connectionist model, 864

distributed representations, 864
hidden unit activation state space, 872–873
incremental, 866–868
Left ventral posterior cortex, 207
Lexical acquisition, 571–586. *See also*
    Hemispheric interaction and control
Lexical ambiguity, 590–591
Lexical tasks, 484–491, 627, 631, 632
Limbic system, 638
Lingual and fusiform gyri, 204, 206, 207
Lipreading, 155, 213–224
Long-term memory, 738, 741, 746. *See also*
    Memory

Magnetic resonance imaging (MRI), 212
Manipulation, sequential, 749–741
Mapping, 232–238, 255–256, 571–572,
    575. *See also* Pragmatic maps
from orthography to phonology, 571
from orthography to semantic, 571
phonological, structure of, 571
semantic, structure of, 571
Mauthner cells, 77
Medial temporal lobes, 635, 638, 644
Memory, 24–25, 206, 507–509, 512, 523–
    528, 537–547, 555–561, 585, 620, 624,
    627, 628–634, 635–636, 641–644, 661–
    663, 664–677, 681–688, 689, 692, 725,
    726, 728, 729, 732, 734, 738, 741, 746,
    748, 756. *See also* Automatic memory;
    Explicit memory; Implicit memory;
    Recollection; Semantic memory
access to, 555–561
automatic, 662, 664–667, 824–829
biographic, 205, 223
conceptual systems, 585
deliberate, 824–829
explicit, 584–585, 620, 624, 627, 628, 631,
    634, 643–644, 681–688, 725, 726, 728,
    734, 748
implicit, 206, 584–585, 620, 621–623, 624,
    628–633, 634, 681–688, 689, 692, 725,
    728, 729, 732, 756
indirect, 662
long-term, 738, 741, 746
organization of, 24–25
perceptual systems, 585
semantic, 507, 512, 523–528, 537–547
short-term, 738, 742
strategic, 663, 665
systems theory, 635–636, 641–643
working, 738–740, 745, 746
Memory-based model, 819–824, 830
vs. the abstractionist model, 819–824

transfer, 820–822
Memory tasks, 396–397, 728–736
conscious, 728–736
detection and, 396–397
free recall, 728, 729–730, 734, 736
threshold identification, 728, 729–730
unconscious, 728–736
word completion, 728, 730, 736
Meridian effect, 242, 244–245, 251
Metacontrast, 124–125, 145
apparent motion, 124
contour formation, 124
inhibition, 124
metaphotic contrast, 124
paradigm, 145
saccadic suppression, 124
Mind popping, 9–13, 20–25
activation, 23, 25
awareness, 24
networks, operation of, 9
subthreshold studies, 9
suprathreshold studies, 9
unconscious material, 24
verbalization, 23
Modality, 626, 632, 683
effects, 683
specificity, 626, 632
Modeling priming effects, 156–159. *See*
    Priming
repetition, 156–159
semantic, 156–159
Models, exemplar. *See* Exemplar models
Modes of learning, 761–763
Modular-based models, 590–592, 593–595,
    597–605
Modularity, 731, 732
Modules, 626, 632, 633, 636–638, 726, 731
Motion, induced, 267–286
eye movements, 270–271
limb movements, 267–286
perceptual manipulation, 267
submovement, 270–271, 272–275, 276–
    278, 279–281
visual-spatial information, 267, 268–270,
    272–275, 276–278, 279–281
Motor programs, 78
Motor response, 123
Multiple memory systems, 725, 726

Name input units (NIUs), 158
Neglect, 55–66, 165, 171, 354, 356–366. *See
    also* Hemispatial neglect; Unilateral
    neglect; Visuospatial neglect
attention, 354

Neglect (cont.)
  attentional allocation, 354–356
  target detection paradigm, 356–366
  unilateral, 55–56, 165, 167, 351–355, 356–372, 377–390
  visuospatial, 377–378
Neglected information, 387–390. *See also* Neglect
Neocortex, 77–79, 96, 638, 639
Neural information processing, 38, 40
Neural networks, 50, 54–55, 864, 874–882. *See also* Connectionism
  artificial, 84
  incremental learning strategy, 882
  learning in, 874–882
  multilayered feedforward, 79
  organization of, 225
  time, changes over, 880–882
Neuroimaging, 204, 208–209, 214–220, 238
Neuronal adaptation, 99–101
Neuronal responses, 96
Neuronal systems, 77
Neurons, 77, 78, 79, 81
  direction-specific, 77
  effector, 77
  firing rate, 79
  motor command, 78
Neuropsychological studies, 408, 412, 773–775
  contention scheduling, 410–411
  disordered action routines, 408–412
  frontal syndromes, 408–412
  grasp reflex, 410
  inhibition of return, 411
  negative priming, 411
  supplementary motor area, 408–412
  utilization behavior, 409–410
Nonconscious and conscious processes, 829–831
Nonelaboration, 7–9
Nonintentional control, 12
Nonintentional processing, 11
Nonsemantic processing, 11
Nonwords, 484–490
Norman and Shallice model, 401–402
Novelty, 630–631
Numeral naming, 423–425, 434–436

Object-based attention, 351–372
Oculomotor, maps, 245
Oculomotor control, 250, 291–308
Oculomotor readiness hypothesis (OMRH), 250, 337–347
  auditory-visual discrimination, 337–342
  cueing, 340, 345
  endogenous orienting, 346
  exogenous orienting, 346
  eye movement, 337–342, 346
  fixation, 346
  inhibitory effect, 346
  orienting, covert, 337–342, 342
  saccades, 337–342, 345, 346
  visual feedback, 340, 344
  visual-visual discrimination, 337–342
Optic axons, 119
Optic chiasma, 109, 110
Optic nerve, 119
Optic tract, 109
Optic tract lesions, 110
Orienting, 241–252, 337–347
Orthographic representation, 571–586
Orthographic-semantic pathway, 574–578
  associative mapping function, 575
  connectionist model, 574
  cued recall, 578–583
  feedforward connections, 574–575
  in normal reading, 575–578
  pseudoword-definition associations, 578–583
  recurrent connections, 574–575
Oscillations, 93–94, 96–97
Oscillatory activity, 95–97
Output module, 732–733, 743
Overt recognition, 161

Parahippocampal gyrus, 206, 207
Parallel distributed processing (PDP) models, 453–473
Parallel pathways, 109–111
Parietal cortex, 306–307, 460
Parietal lobe damage, 457–461
  attentional, 458
  hemilateral neglect, 457
  Posner's RT task, 459
  top-down process, 457
Parietofrontal circuits, 232–238
  organization, 232–238
  perceptual deficits, 237
Parieto-occipital lesions, 377
Parkinson's disease, 407
Parsing, 589. *See also* Ambiguity resolution; Language, comprehension
Parvocellular system, 109
Patterning, temporal, 81
Pavlovian conditioning, 890
Perception, 10, 37, 58, 60–61, 62, 79, 491–498

architectures, 79
awareness of, 32, 37, 62
bilateral, 58, 495
hemispheric, 492, 495
hierarchic, 491–498
manipulation, 272–275
systems, 170, 625, 639–640
unilateral, 493–494
unconscious, 58
visual, 37
Perceptual dissociations, 62–66
Perceptual learning, 521, 889–891, 899, 900–908
during categorization, 900–906
Performance, 99–101, 453–473
Performance deficits
attentional effects, 457–461
parietal lobe damage, 457–461
Person identity nodes (PINs), 158
Phonological loop, 739
Phonological mapping, 571
Pituitary adenoma, 118
Positron emission tomography (PET), 204, 208–209, 214–220, 238
activation data, 215
behavioral data, 214–215
divided visual field study, 219
Posner and Snyder model, 396–397
Pragmatic maps, 232–238, 255–256. See also Mapping
Prediction task, explicit, 787–792
Preexisting representations, 688
Preexperimental learning, 735, 743
Prefrontal cortex, 739
Premotor theory of attention, 239–256, 337–347. See also Attention; Oculomotor readiness hypothesis
criticisms of, 250–252
supporting, evidence for, 252–255
Primacy effect, 742
Primary visual cortex, 44
Prime-target pairs, 131
Priming, 11, 52, 123, 154, 156–158, 159–161, 162, 184, 456, 552, 555–561, 625, 627, 631–633, 682–693, 702–703, 791. See also Implicit memory; Indirect memory; Repetition priming
automatic, 161, 683, 686, 702–703, 719
effects, retention of, 684
explicit memory, 160
and familiarity, 683, 686, 688–689
format-specific, 689–690
longevity of, 683, 687

semantic, 64, 160, 162, 170, 184, 555–561
specificity of, 683, 687
Principal components analysis (PCA), 197
Privileged role, brain-consciousness relation, 45
Proactive interference, 436, 443, 891–894, 896
Problem solving, 13, 19
Procedural tests, 646–649. See also Implicit memory
ordered/rule-based, 648–649
sensorimotor, 647–648
Process-dissociation procedures, 663, 664–667, 670, 673–675, 677
Processing, 79–82, 551–561
proper name, 223–224
Processing theory, components of, 636–637, 643
Prosopagnosia, 37, 46–55, 71, 161–164, 170, 204, 206, 522–523. See also Faces
Pseudoword identification, 578–584
free-recall task, 581
identification tasks, 582
integration hypothesis, 584
memory tasks, 579
priming manipulation, 580
systematicity, 583
tachistoscopic identification tasks, 580
Pseudowords, 577–583, 715

Rapid sequential visual presentation (RSVP), 443–448
Reaction time (RT), 112, 125, 127–146, 190, 297–299, 404–408, 432, 459–461
Reading, implicit, 66–70, 67
explanations of, 69
perception, awareness, 68
picture-word matching, 67
word frequency, 67
Recall, 4
Recognition, 153, 154, 155, 164, 168, 169, 187, 891–899. See also Episodic memory; Explicit memory; Memory
automatic components, 171
cognitive, 169
conscious, 154, 164
covert face, 46–47, 71
dissociation with, 46
errors, 168
facial, 187
memory, 153, 891–899
Recollection, measurement of, 663–670. See also Episodic memory; Explicit memory; Memory

Recollection, measurement of (cont.)
  absence of recollection, 663–667
  automatic influences, 667–669
  recollection, 667–669
Recovered consciousness, 644
Recurrent networks, 740–742, 744, 747, 789–792, 798, 862, 864–865
Redundancy gain, 482–484. *See also* Cerebral hemispheres
Regional cerebral blood flow (rCBF), 204, 208–209
Registration, 637–638
Regression analysis, 596, 599–600, 603–605
Rehearsal, 728, 739, 741, 744, 745, 746
Relaxation, 736–737, 738
Reminiscence, 3, 4, 5
Repetition priming, 170, 179, 182, 195–197, 621, 626, 627–632, 633–640, 641–643, 687–688. *See also* Implicit memory; Priming
  component theory, 642–643
  delay, effects of, 184
  episodic influences on, 183
  face recognition, 182–184
  identity priming, 179
  recognition, 180, 195
  resemblance, effects of, 183
  theories of, 633–640, 641–642
Representations, 82, 83, 351, 798, 799, 801–807
  abstract, 783, 801, 805, 806–807
  exemplar-based, 783, 805
  internal, 798, 799
  node, 731, 732–733, 742
  object-specific, 351
  spatial, 351
Response synchronization, 86–88, 88–90, 95, 99–101. *See also* Synchronization
  coding, assembly, 89
  congruence, 138
  reciprocal connections, 89
  stimulus-induced, 95
  temporal correlation, 95
Response time (RT) analyses, 139–141
Retinal ganglion cells, 118
Retino-geniculo-striate pathway, 109
Retinotectal pathway, 109
Retrieval, 701, 704–713, 837, 841–853, 856–858
  implicit, 837, 841–853, 856–858
  mechanism, 701, 704–713, 841–843
Retroactive interference, 742
Rule learning, 811, 814–819, 824–829, 830
  memory model, 819

rule abstraction, 814–819
rule memorization, 815–816
set of rules, 814
transfer phase, 818

Saccades, 245, 253, 254, 276–278, 291–292, 295–297, 302–303, 307–308, 337–342, 345, 346
Salience, structural, 761–763
Same/different judgment, 379–384
Scanning and analysis, 212
Schema abstraction, 907
Schneider and Shiffrin model, 396–397, 402
Search instruction, explicit, 757
Search tasks, 396–397
Segregation, spatial, 86
Selective attention paradigms, 553–554
Semantic codes, retrieval, 713–718
  abstract encoding, 714
  lexical representation, 715–716
  pseudowords, 715
  stimulus properties, 713–718
  superimpositional memory systems, 714
  surface form abstraction, 716–718
  text processing, 715–716, 716–718
Semantic deficits, 512–523
  aphasia, 518–519
  loss of knowledge, 513–517, 521
  prosopagnosia, 522–523
Semantic dementia, 507, 509–512, 528–530. *See also* Semantic memory
  Alzheimer's disease, 511
  anomia, 511
  ideational apraxia, 528
  object knowledge, 528–529
  Pick's disease, 511
  task impairment, 509–511
  temporal lobe structures, 511
Semantic fit, 593–597, 605–607. *See also* Ambiguity resolution
  continuous variables, 596
  disambiguating syntactic information, 594
  eye-tracking, 594–595
  interactive processes, 607
  main clause/reduced relative clause, 597
  modular model, 593–595
  regression analysis, 596, 605
  self-paced reading tasks, 595
  sentence completion norms, 605
Semantic information, 159, 223
Semantic information units (SIUs), 158
Semantic judgments, 11
Semantic knowledge, 704–713
Semantic maps, 238

Semantic memory, 507–509, 512, 523–528, 537–547. *See also* Memory
   hierarchical organization, 512
   models of, 523–528
   neuropsychological impairments in, 508, 512–523, 539–540
   subordinate knowledge, 512
   superordinate knowledge, 512
Semantic priming, 60, 61, 64, 162, 170, 184, 378, 556–561. *See also* Priming; Semantic memory; Semantic processing
Semantic processing, 551–561. *See also* Attention; Semantic memory
   activation, 552
   access, 552
   attention, 552, 564
   awareness, 551, 552
   cognition, 551
   dichotic listening task, 557
   interchannels interaction, 554
   memory representations, 552, 564, 565
   perception, 552
   priming, 553, 555–561
   recognition memory, 559, 561–564
   selective attention paradigms, 553
   unconscious memory, 553
   word processing, 561
Semantic representation, 571–586
Sensorimotor transformation, 267–286
Sensory activity, 77, 78
Sequence learning, 756, 759–761, 769–770, 787–799, 811, 821
   explicit, 787
   generate task, 760, 769
   matrix scanning task, 759
   serial reaction time task, 759
Sequential feedback, 789–790
Sequentially recurrent networks. *See* Simple recurrent networks
Serial position, 739, 742
Serial reaction time (RT) task, 852–856
Set, 421. *See* Task set
Shadowing, 213–224, 323, 325
Shift cost, 423–430, 433, 441–442
Shifting attention, 421. *See* Task set
Shifting tasks, 421. *See* Task set
Shift of set, 422–433, 437–443
Signal detection method, 146
Signal transmission, 97
Similarity-based processing, 764–765
Simple recurrent networks (SRN), 740–742, 744, 747, 789–792, 798, 862, 864–865
   backpropagation network, 790
   choice reaction tasks, sequential, 789

   learning, sequential, 790
   priming effects, 791
   sequence learning situations, 792
   simulations, 790
Skin conductance response (SCR), 46
Soar model, 399–401
Space, 232–238
   coding, 232–238
   in frontal lobe, 233–234
   in parietal lobe, 233–234
Spared primary visual cortex, 45
Spatial attention, 238–256. *See also* Attention
Spatial information, 272–281
   distortion, effect of, 272–275
   eye movements, 276–281
   global effect, 279–281
   location, 272–275
   manipulation, perceptual, 276–281
   movement analysis, 273, 277, 280
   saccades, 276–278
   smooth-pursuit eye movements, 276–281
   submovement, 272–275, 276–281
Spreading activation, 20
Stem completion, 631, 639
Stimulus identification, 137
Stimulus onset asynchrony, 125, 354, 404, 456
Stimulus-response (S-R) mapping, 142
Strategic memory, 663, 665, 667, 670–676, 677
Stroop task, 427–430, 453–456, 461, 469
Structural encoding, 207
Study-test compatibility, 726, 730
Subcortical visual system, 45
Submovements, 270–281
Substantia nigra, 247, 293
Subsymbolic representation, 740, 741
Subvocal rehearsal, 739
Sugar production task, 758
Superior colliculus, 246–249
Symbolic manipulation, 740–741
Symbolic representation, 740–741
Synaptic plasticity, 96–97
Synchronization, 84, 85, 86–91, 95, 99–101. *See also* Response synchronization
   activity, 86
   burst-and-pause sequence, 86
   connections, 90–91
   interareal, 88
   long-distance, 86
   long-range response, 93
   oscillatory patterns, 93
   responses to, 85, 86, 93, 100

Synergy, spatial, 311–328
  active conditions, 328
  audiovisual interactions, 327
  differential hemisphere activation, 328
  opposite-side, 328
  passive, 328
  same-side, 328
  supramodal representation, 326
Syntactic ambiguity, 595–605. *See also* Ambiguity; Ambiguity resolution
  determiner plus noun, 602, 603
  main verb, 602, 604
  regression analysis, 600–601, 603–605
  semantic fit, 599
  sentence pairs, 598–600
  verb plus *by*, 601–602, 603
  verb-form availability analysis, 600–601
  verb-noun pairs, 598–600

Target detection paradigm, 356–366. *See also* Neglect
  left visual field defects, 359
  line bisection task, 357
  line cancellation task, 356
  moving condition, 361–363
  static condition, 359–360, 362–363
Task demands, 686–687, 688
Task selection, 407
Task set, 421–450
  cognitive operation, 430
  controlled processing, 431
  perceptual versus cognitive variables, 423–425
  semantic space, 443–446
  shift cost, 423–430, 433, 441–442
  shift of set, 422–424, 423–433, 437–443
  speeded response, 422–424
  stimulus-response (S-R) mapping, 431, 432, 433–437
  Stroop task, 427, 433, 437, 440
Task set inertia (TSI), 422–424, 436, 437, 443–446, 448. *See also* Proactive interference
Temporal
  binding, 746
  coding, 82–84
  hemiretina, 116–117
  integration, 111, 113
Test-retest, 4
Threshold identification task, 728, 729–730, 735, 736
Top-down and bottom-up processing, 457, 686, 688
Tracing, 377–390, 384–386

Transfer, 799–803, 820–822
  appropriate processing, 634, 638, 693
  to new material with dissimilar surface features, 821
  to new material with similar surface features, 820–821
  to sequences with new irrelevant contexts, 802–803
  to sequences with new relevant elements, 801–802
Transient ganglion cells, 118
Two-choice, no cues, 484–489

Unconscious information processing, 726
Unconscious learning, 837–843, 856–858. *See also* Implicit learning; Learning
Unilateral neglect, 165, 167, 351–355, 356–372, 377–390. *See also* Hemispatial neglect; Neglect
  contralesional, 351
  deficits, 352
  degraded visual information, 353
  hemispatial neglect, 351
  impairment, 351–352

Varied intertrial intervals, 437–443
Verbal cueing, 377–390, 379–382
Vestibular stimulation, 377–390
Veto node, 731
Visible persistence, 110
Vision, 37, 38, 80, 109, 110, 118, 153, 165
  alexia, pure, 38
  awareness, 37
  blindsight, 37
  pathways, 109, 110, 118
  persistence, 109
  prosopagnosia, 37
  recognition, 165
  similarity, 153
Visual attention, 291–308, 333–347. *See also* Attention
  covert adjustments, 333
  endogenous control, 333, 334
  exogenous control, 333
  eye movements, 335
  oculomotor readiness hypothesis (OMRH), 334, 335
  overt adjustments, 333
  peripheral, 333
Visual cortex, 87, 217
Visual fields, 484. *See also* Hemispheric interaction and control
Visual orienting, 291–306
  covert, 295–306

endogenous, 291–292, 304–306
exogenous, 291–292, 304–306
overt, 292–295
saccade, 291–292, 295–297
Visual-spatial information, for induced motion, 268–270
equilibrium-point model, 269–270
location specification, 268–269
mass-spring model, 269–270
movement planning, 268–270
neural network models, 269
saccadic eye movements, 269
Visuospatial neglect, 377–378. *See also* Neglect
Visuospatial sketch pad, 739
Volitional control, 306–308

Winner-take-all competition, 731
Word-CALM, 732–733, 742, 743, 745
Word completion, 692, 728, 729–730, 736
Word comprehension, 509
Word frequency, 894–896
Word identification, 571–586
Word monitoring, 443–446
Word perception, 551–561
Word reading task, 454–456
Word recognition, 732
Word sequences, 422–424
Word stem completion task, 684
Working memory, 738–740, 745, 746